Network Analysis and Synthesis

(A Simplified Approach)

Ramana Pilla

Associate Professor
Department of Electrical and Electronics Engineering
GMR Institute of Technology, Rajam, AP

Universities Press

NETWORK ANALYSIS AND SYNTHESIS (A Simplified Approach)

Universities Press (India) Private Limited

Registered Office
3-6-747/1/A & 3-6-754/1. Himayatnagar, Hyderabad 500 029, Telangana, India
e-mail: info@universitiespress.com; *www.universitiespress.com*

Distributed by
Orient Blackswan Private Limited

Registered Office
3-6-752, Himayatnagar, Hyderabad 500 029 (Telangana), India

Other Offices
Bengaluru, Bhopal, Chennai, Guwahati, Hyderabad, Jaipur,
Kolkata, Lucknow, Mumbai, New Delhi, Noida, Patna, Vijayawada

First published 2019

ISBN: 978-93-86235-66-4

Typest in Minion Pro 10/12 by
Bookcraft Publishing Services (I) Pvt Ltd, Chennai

Printed at
Rajiv Book Binding House, Delhi

Published by
Universities Press (India) Private Limited
3-6-747/1/A & 3-6-754/1, Himayatnagar,
Hyderabad 500 029, Telangana, India

Dedication

I dedicate this book to my family, my teachers and my students

Ramana Pilla

Preface

This book is designed specially for undergraduate students of the following branches of engineering—Electrical and Electronics, Electronics and Communication, Electronics and Instrumentation, and Instrumentation and Control. It covers the syllabi of the core subjects—Electrical Circuits, Network Theory, Circuit Theory, Network Analysis, and Networks and Synthesis. This textbook covers all the above subjects in detail in a simple manner and at the same time improves problem solving skills among students.

This book has evolved from the lecture material prepared by the author to teach the course 'Network analysis and synthesis'. The book is laid out in a systematic, lucid and user-friendly manner. It consists of fifteen chapters, each containing solved examples, review questions, multiple choice questions and practice problems to test the reader's understanding of the subject.

The various chapters in the book are organised as follows:

Chapter 1 deals with basic network elements, energy sources, Kirchhoff's laws and network reduction techniques for network analysis. **Chapter 2** describes various wave forms including sinusoidal and other periodic wave forms for the evaluation of RMS value, average value, form factor and peak factor. It also focusses on the representation of phasors in the complex plane. **Chapter 3** deals with the analysis of single phase circuits with various circuit elements. Their series and parallel combinations have been described when connected to sinusoidal excitations. **Chapter 4** describes the fundamentals of magnetic circuits, various magnetic properties, coupled circuits and ideal transformers. **Chapter 5** describes the resonance phenomenon in both series and parallel circuits. It also focusses on circle diagrams.

Chapter 6 illustrates 3-phase balanced and unbalanced circuits, and methods to measure active and reactive powers. **Chapter 7** is devoted to various network theorems required for simplified analysis of electrical problems. **Chapter 8** discusses the applications of concepts of network topology in network analysis. **Chapter 9** deals with the classical method of solving differential equations and transient analysis of *RL*, *RC* and *RLC* circuits. **Chapter 10** introduces a new method of circuit analysis—Laplace transform method. Starting from the fundamental concept of the Laplace transform, its applications in various complicated circuit problems have been discussed in detail in this chapter.

Chapter 11 deals with the concept of two-port networks, which have numerous applications in fields such as transmission lines, filters and attenuators, and so on. **Chapter 12** deals with the relations between various voltages and currents in circuits. These have been discussed in terms of network functions and responses. **Chapter 13** deals with Fourier series and Fourier transforms. **Chapter 14** is devoted to passive filters and attenuators. **Chapter 15** introduces a new concept - network synthesis - which aims at determining a suitable electrical network given some operating characteristics.

In addition, each chapter consists of a set of multiple choice questions, review questions and additional solved problems.

The author welcomes suggestions from the users of this book—both teachers and students.

Ramana Pilla

Acknowledgements

I wish to express my wholehearted thanks to all those who helped directly or indirectly in turning this book into reality. I would like to express my gratitude to our beloved Chairman Dr G M Rao, Chief Executive Officer Col. V Rajendra Prasad, GMRVF, Principal Dr C L V R S V Prasad, Vice Principal Dr J Raja Murugadoss, GMR Institute of Technology (GMRIT), for providing me with a conducive work atmosphere and complete support for writing this book.

I am grateful to Dr K Alice Mary, Professor, Gudlavalleru College of Engineering, Dr M Surya Kalavathi, Professor, JNTUH and Dr K B Madhu Sahu, Principal, Aditya Institute of Technology and Management for their valuable suggestions and help in the preparation and presentation of the content.

I express my sincere thanks to my colleagues (both teaching and non-teaching) and students of the EEE department of GMRIT, who have directly or indirectly helped me to bring out this book in its present form.

My sincere thanks to Dr Gita S Dattatri and Mr Kallol Das, Universities Press (India) Pvt Ltd, for providing excellent editorial suggestions.

I am deeply indebted to my family for their encouragement, support and cooperation at every step in the process of of bringing out this book.

Finally, I would like to appreciate the role of all the reviewers for their valuable inputs and constructive comments, to strengthen this book in all aspects: Prof. K Ramalingeswara Prasad (Department of EEE, Lakkireddy Bali Reddy College of Engineering, Andhra Pradesh), Prof. M S Naruka (Department of EEE, IEC College of Engineering and Technology, Uttar Pradesh), Prof. S V D Anil Kumar (Department of EEE, St. Ann's College of Engineering and Technology, Andhra Pradesh), Prof. P Upendra Kumar (Department of EEE, GMR Institute of Technology, Andhra Pradesh), Prof. G V Narayana (Department of EEE, Guntur Engineering College, Andhra Pradesh), Prof. G T Chandra Sekhar (Department of EEE, Sri Sivani College of Engineering, Andhra Pradesh), Prof. H D Mehta (Department of Electrical Engineering, Government Engineering College, Gujarat) and Prof. N Samba Sivarao (Department of EEE, NRI Institute of Technology, Andhra Pradesh).

Ramana Pilla

Contents

1 Introduction to Electrical Circuits

Learning Outcomes

After reading this chapter, the reader will able to

- ➢ Outline the basic terminology used in electrical circuits
- ➢ Illustrate Ohm's and Kirchhoff's laws
- ➢ Describe resistance, inductance and capacitance parameters
- ➢ Illustrate various energy sources
- ➢ Analyse series, parallel and series–parallel circuits
- ➢ Apply different network reduction techniques
- ➢ Analyse circuits using mesh, super mesh, node and super node concepts

1.1 INTRODUCTION

When humans discovered the secret of energy conversion, they harvested all possible energy sources available in the world and utilised the energy for production. Electrical energy is the most convenient form of energy for generation and transportation through thousands of kilometers with the least possible loss. Hence, it has become the most popular form of energy throughout the world and without it, the present social infrastructure would not exist. It finds innumerable uses in domestic, industrial, agricultural and even in transportation sectors.

Electrical engineers are therefore interested in transmitting energy from one point to another. This can be achieved by the interconnection of the electrical devices. Such interconnections are known as *electric circuits* and the components are called *circuit elements.*

The closed path followed by direct current (DC) is called a DC circuit. A DC circuit essentially consists of a DC source, the conductors used to carry current and the load. The source supplies electrical energy to the load which converts it into heat or other forms of energy. In a DC circuit, loads may be connected in series, parallel or series–parallel.

1.2 DEFINITIONS

Charge Charge is the characteristic property of an elementary particle of matter, such as a proton, neutron or electron. Protons possess positive charge, electrons possess negative charge and neutrons posses neutral charge. The unit of charge is coulomb.

Current It is defined as the time rate change of charge passing through a cross-sectional area of a conductor.

A steady current can be expressed as $I = \dfrac{Q}{T}$

where Q = charge and T = time. The time varying current can be expressed as $i = \dfrac{dq}{dt}$. The unit of current is ampere.

Voltage or **absolute potential** It is defined as the amount of work to be done to move a unit positive test charge from infinity to a point in the field.

Potential difference It is defined as the amount of work to be done to move a unit positive test charge from one place to another.

A steady voltage can be expressed as $V = \dfrac{W}{Q}$

where Q = charge, W = work done.

The time varying voltage can be expressed as $v = \dfrac{dw}{dq}$. The unit of voltage is volt.

Energy It is defined as the capacity to do work. It can also be defined as the stored work. Energy may exist in many forms such as electrical, mechanical, chemical, thermal, and so on. The unit of energy is joule.

Power The rate at which electric energy is converted to other forms of energy, equal to the product of current and voltage drop.

Average power is given by $P = \dfrac{W}{t} = VI$

Instantaneous power is given by $P = \dfrac{dw}{dt} = vi$. The unit of power is watt.

1.3 CLASSIFICATION OF NETWORK ELEMENTS

Network elements are the mathematical models of two terminal electric devices which can be characterised by its voltage and current relationship at the terminals. These network elements can be classified as follows.

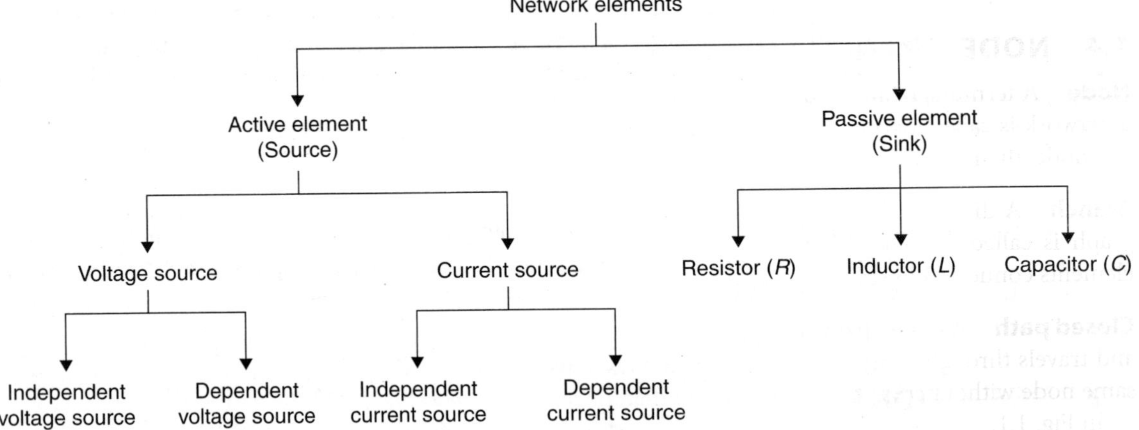

Another method of classification is given below.

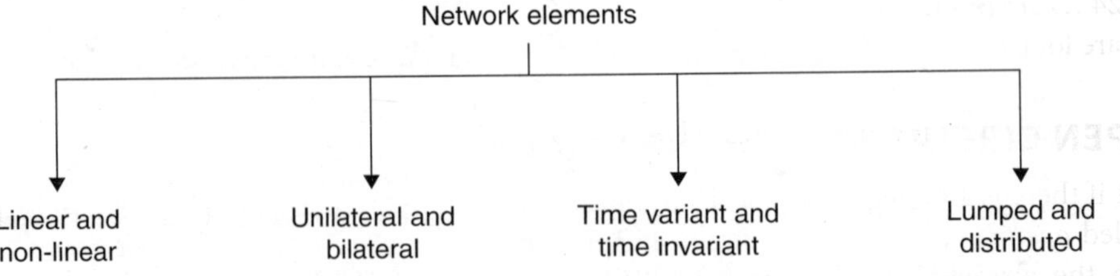

(i) ***Active and passive elements*** The elements which can deliver energy are called *active elements.* Active elements are the sources of energy. For example, voltage source and current source.

The elements which consume energy either by absorbing or storing are called *passive elements.* For example, resistor, inductor and capacitor.

(ii) ***Unilateral and bilateral elements*** A unilateral element offers low resistance (impedance) to the flow of current in one direction and high resistance (impedance) to the flow of current in the opposite direction. That is, an unilateral element will have different voltage–current relationship for the two possible directions of current. For example, vacuum diodes and semiconductor devices.

Bilateral elements offer the same resistance (impedance) to the flow of current in either direction. That is, a bilateral element will have the same voltage current relationship for the two possible directions of current. For example, resistor, inductor and capacitor.

(iii) ***Linear and non-linear elements*** A circuit element is said to be linear if it satisfies the relationship between voltage and current (Ohm's law) as follows.

$$V = R.i,\ V_L = L\frac{di}{dt},\ V_C = \frac{1}{C}\int i.dt$$

For example, resistor, inductor and capacitor.

If an element does not satisfy the above relations, then it is called a non-linear element. For example, diode, thermistor, and so on.

(iv) ***Lumped and distributed elements*** The elements that are physically separable are called lumped elements. For example, resistor, inductor and capacitor.

The elements which are physically inseparable are called distributed elements. For example, a transmission line which has distributed resistance, inductance and capacitance along its length.

(v) ***Time variant and time invariant elements*** If the parameters of the network elements do not vary with time, they are called time invariant elements, otherwise they are called time variant elements.

Generally, we consider networks whose elements are linear, time invariant and lumped.

1.4 NODE, BRANCH AND CLOSED PATH

Node A terminal of any branch of a network or an interconnection common to two or more branches of a network is called a node. If more than two elements meet at a node, then it is called the *principal node.*

Branch A direct path joining two nodes of a network or graph is called branch. A branch may have one or more elements connected in series.

Closed path A closed path is a path which starts at a node and travels through some part of the circuit and arrives the same node without crossing the node more than once.

In Fig. 1.1,

- 1, 2, 3 and 4 are nodes,
- 12, 23, 24 … are branches, and
- X, Y, Z are loops.

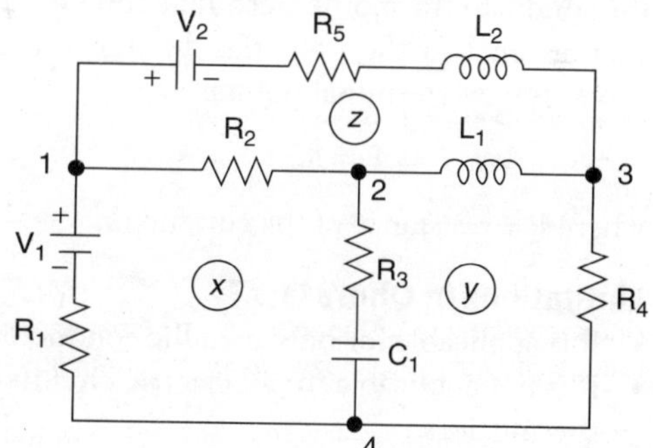

Fig. 1.1 Circuit diagram which shows nodes, branches and closed paths

1.5 OPEN CIRCUIT AND SHORT CIRCUIT

In a circuit if there is an open path or path of infinite resistance (impedance) between two nodes then that path is called *open circuit.* The open circuit is denoted as O.C. (Fig. 1.2). Since the current can flow in a closed path, the current in the open circuit will be zero.

While applying KVL to a closed path, the open circuit can be included as an element of infinite resistance in the path, because a voltage exists between the two open nodes of a circuit. In a circuit if there is a closed path or path of zero resistance (impedance) between two nodes, then that path is called *short circuit.* The

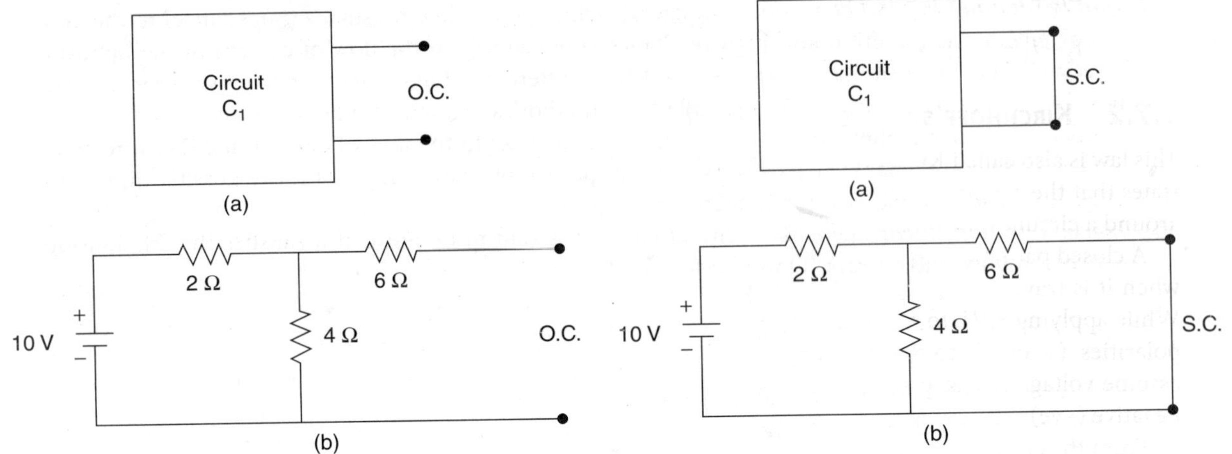

Fig. 1.2 Examples of open circuit

Fig. 1.3 Examples of short circuit

short circuit is denoted as S.C. (Fig. 1.3). Since the impedance of the short circuit is zero, the voltage across the short circuit is zero.

In a circuit, if there are elements parallel to a short circuit then they will not carry any current, because the current will prefer the path of least impedance and so the entire current will flow through the short circuit. Hence the elements parallel to a short circuit need not be considered for analysis.

1.6 OHM'S LAW

It states that, at constant temperature, in an electrical circuit, the current passing through a conductor, from one terminal point on the conductor to another terminal point on the conductor, is directly proportional to the potential difference (voltage drop or voltage) across the two terminal points.

$$V \propto I \Rightarrow V = RI \tag{1.1}$$

Fig. 1.4 Resistor across a DC source

where R = resistance of the conductor.

Limitations of Ohm's law

- It is applicable for only metallic conductors such as copper, silver, nichrome, and so on.
- It is not applicable for all electric circuits such as vacuum tubes, semiconductor devices, transistors and thermistors.

1.7 KIRCHHOFF'S LAWS

1.7.1 Kirchhoff's Current Law (KCL)

This law is also called Kirchhoff's junction rule or Kirchhoff's point rule. It states that the algebraic sum of the currents meeting at a node or junction is equal to zero. Alternatively, the sum of the currents entering at a node is equal to the sum of the currents leaving that node.

From the circuit (Fig. 1.5),

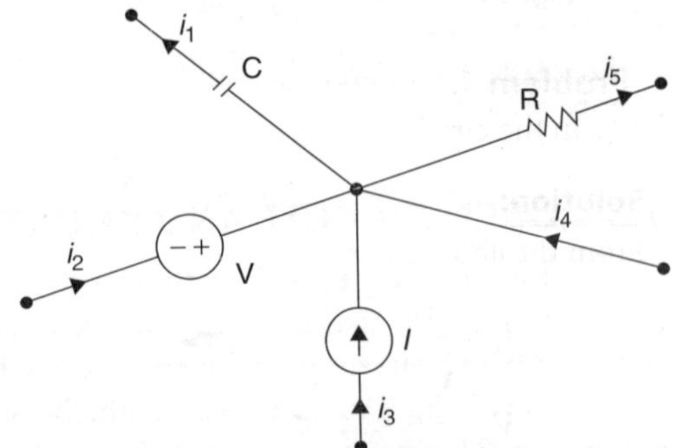

Fig. 1.5 Application of KCL

$$-i_1 + i_2 + i_3 + i_4 - i_5 = 0$$

$$i_2 + i_3 + i_4 = i_1 + i_5 \quad (1.2)$$

1.7.2 Kirchhoff's Voltage Law (KVL)

This law is also called Kirchhoff's loop rule. It is a consequence of the principle of conservation of energy. It states that the algebraic sum of the potential differences around a circuit must be zero.

A closed path may have voltage rises and voltage falls when it is traversed or traced in a particular direction. While applying KVL to a closed path we have to assign polarities (+ or –) to voltage falls and rises. Let us assume voltage rise as positive (+ve) and voltage fall as negative (–ve).

From the circuit (Fig. 1.6),

$$V_s - V_1 - V_2 - V_3 = 0$$

$$\Rightarrow \quad V_s = V_1 + V_2 + V_3 \quad (1.3)$$

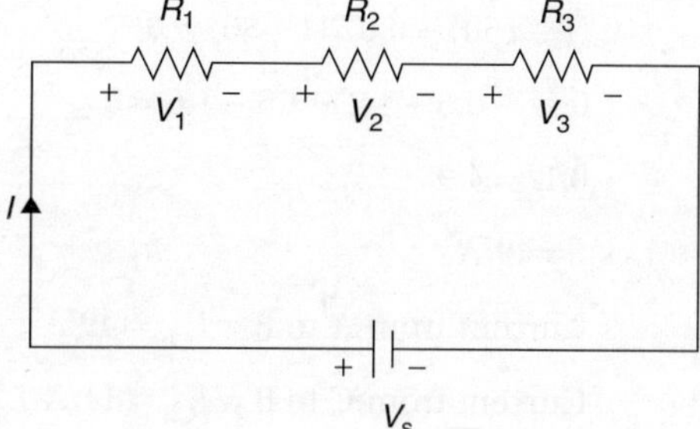

Fig. 1.6 Three resistances are connected in series

1.7.3 Determination of Sign

A rise in potential can be considered as positive whereas a fall in potential can be taken as negative. The reverse is also applicable and both conventions will give the same result.

- If we move from the positive terminal of a battery or source to the negative terminal, there is a fall in potential and so the emf should be assigned a negative sign [Fig. 1.7(a)]. However, if we move from the negative terminal of a battery or source to the positive terminal, there is a rise in potential and so the emf should be assigned a positive sign [Fig. 1.7(b)].
- When a current is flowing through a resistor (or inductor or capacitor), there is a voltage drop across it. If we move through the resistor in the same direction as the current, there is a fall in potential and the sign of this voltage drop is taken as negative [Fig. 1.8(a)]. When we move in a direction opposite to the current flow, there is a rise in potential and hence the sign of voltage drop is taken as positive [Fig. 1.8(b)].

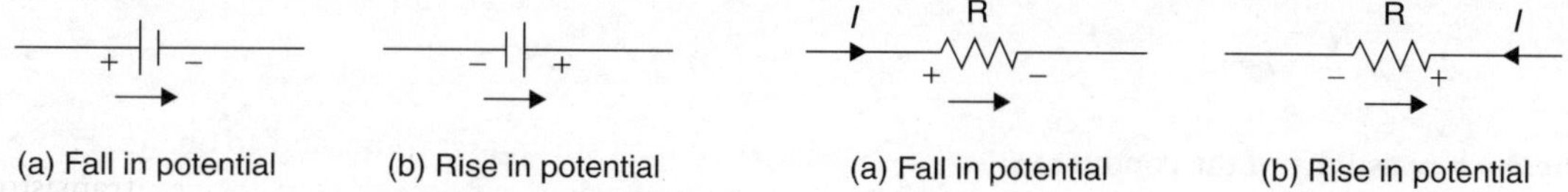

(a) Fall in potential (b) Rise in potential

Fig. 1.7 Sign convention in source or battery

(a) Fall in potential (b) Rise in potential

Fig. 1.8 Sign convention in resistor

Problem 1.1 Obtain the potential difference V_{AB} in the circuit using Kirchhoff's laws.

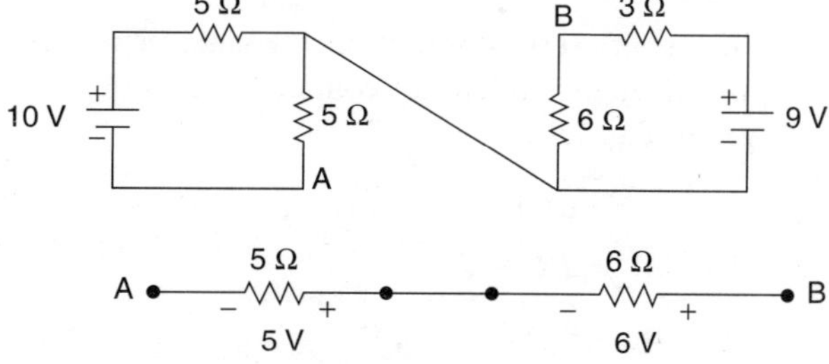

Solution:

From the above circuit,

$$I_1 = \frac{10}{5+5} = 1\text{ A};\ I_2 = \frac{9}{6+3} = 1\text{ A}$$

$$V_{AB} = 5 + 6 = 11\text{ V}$$

Problem 1.2 Find the current in all the branches of the network.

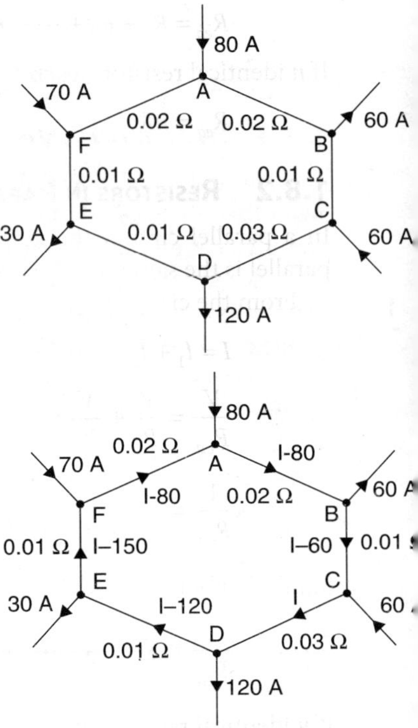

Solution:

Let us assume that the current flowing through branch AB is I amperes. Then the current distribution through the entire circuit is as shown below.

Applying KVL to loop ABCDEFA

$$0.02I + 0.01\,(I - 60) + 0.03I + 0.01\,(I - 120) + 0.01\,(I - 150) + 0.02\,(I - 80) = 0$$

$$\Rightarrow \quad 0.1I - 0.6 - 1.2 - 1.5 - 1.6 = 0$$

$$\Rightarrow \quad 0.1I = 4.9$$

$$\Rightarrow \quad I = 49 \text{ A}$$

Current from A to B $= I_{AB} = 49$ A

Current from C to B $= I_{CB} = 11$ A

Current from C to D $= I_{CD} = 49$ A

Current from E to D $= I_{ED} = 71$ A

Current from F to E $= I_{FE} = 101$ A

Current from A to F $= I_{AF} = 31$ A

1.8 RESISTANCE PARAMETER

It is the property of the circuit element by which it opposes the flow of current. The resistance of the conductor is directly proportional to the length of the conductor and inversely proportional to the area of the cross-section.

That is, $R \propto l, \quad R \propto \dfrac{1}{a}, \quad R \propto \dfrac{l}{a}$

$$\therefore \quad R = \rho . \frac{l}{a} \tag{1.4}$$

where ρ = resistivity of the conductor.

The unit for resistance is ohm and the circuit symbol is •—R—•

1.8.1 Resistors in Series

In the case of a series connection, the same current will flow through all the elements which are connected in series. From the circuit diagram (Fig. 1.9),

$$V = V_1 + V_2$$

$$IR_{eq} = IR_1 + IR_2$$

$$R_{eq} = R_1 + R_2 \tag{1.5}$$

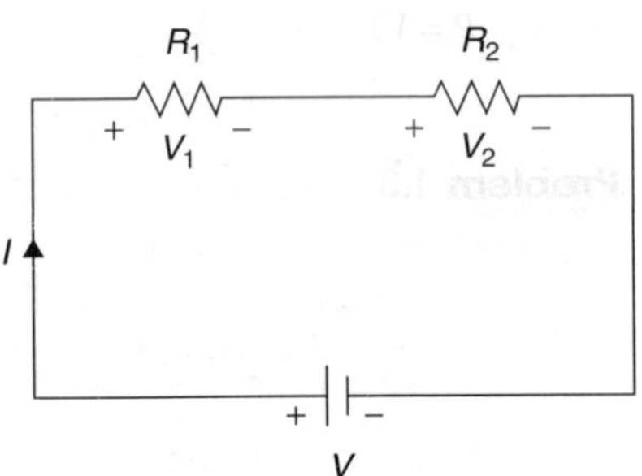

Fig. 1.9 Resistances are connected in series

Similarly n resistors, each with resistances of $R_1, R_2 \ldots R_n$ respectively, are connected in series, then

$$R_{eq} = R_1 + R_2 + \cdots + R_n \tag{1.6}$$

If n identical resistors, each with a resistance of R are connected in series, then

$$R_{eq} = nR \tag{1.7}$$

1.8.2 Resistors in Parallel

In a parallel circuit, the voltage across each branch connected in parallel is the same.

From the circuit (Fig. 1.10),

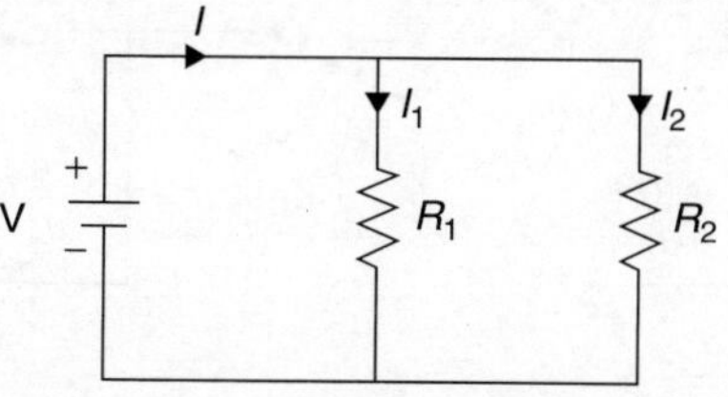

Fig. 1.10 Resistances are connected in parallel

$$I = I_1 + I_2$$

$$\frac{V}{R_{eq}} = \frac{V}{R_1} + \frac{V}{R_2}$$

$$\frac{1}{R_{eq}} = \frac{1}{R_1} + \frac{1}{R_2} \tag{1.8}$$

Similarly if n resistors, with resistances of $R_1, R_2 \ldots R_n$ respectively, are connected in parallel, then

$$\frac{1}{R_{eq}} = \frac{1}{R_1} + \frac{1}{R_2} + \cdots + \frac{1}{R_n} \tag{1.9}$$

If n identical resistors, each with a resistance of R are connected in parallel, then

$$R_{eq} = \frac{R}{n} \tag{1.10}$$

1.8.3 Power Dissipation in a Resistor

From Ohm's law

$$V = IR \Rightarrow I = \frac{V}{R}$$

Power in a resistance is given by

$$P = VI = V \times \frac{V}{R} = \frac{V^2}{R}$$

or $$P = VI = IR \times I = I^2 R$$

$$P = VI = \frac{V^2}{R} = I^2 R \tag{1.11}$$

Problem 1.3 Find the equivalent resistance between the terminals XY.

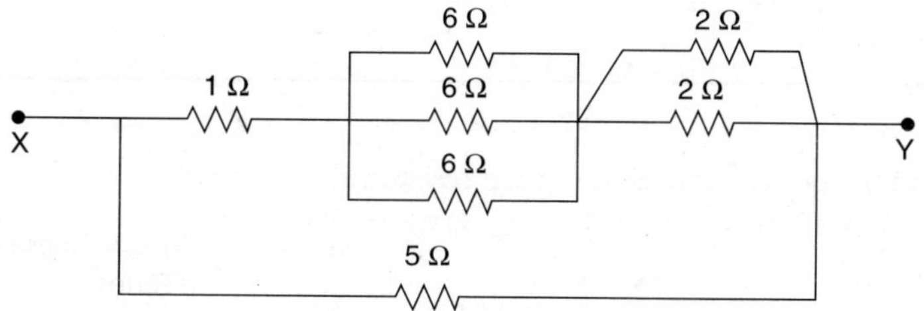

Solution:

Given that

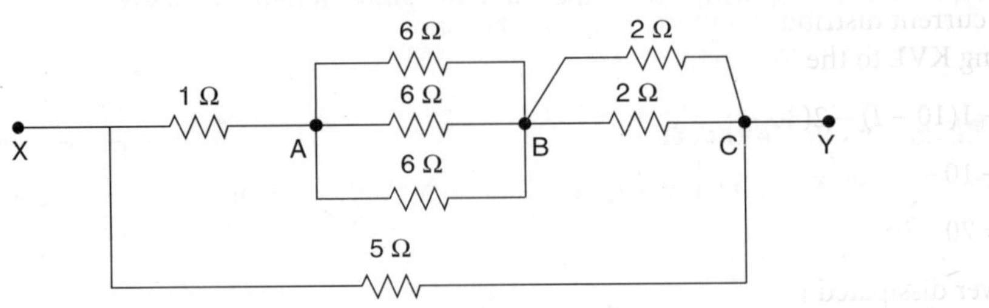

$$R_{AB} = \frac{6}{3} = 2\,\Omega$$

$$R_{BC} = \frac{2 \times 2}{2+2} = 1\,\Omega$$

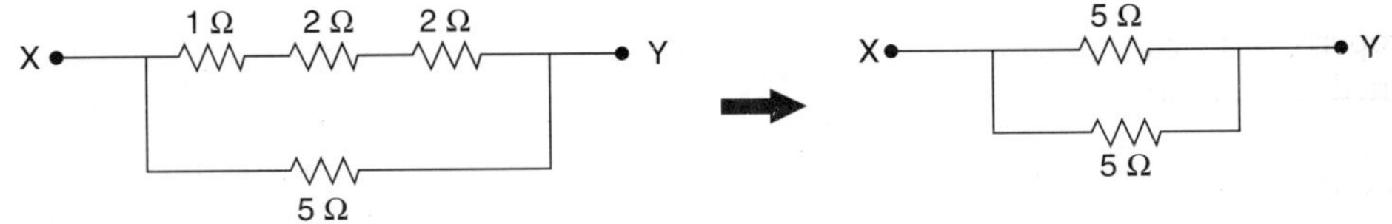

$$R_{XY} = \frac{5 \times 5}{5+5} = 2.5\,\Omega$$

Problem 1.4 Find the equivalent resistance of the circuit between the terminals A and B.

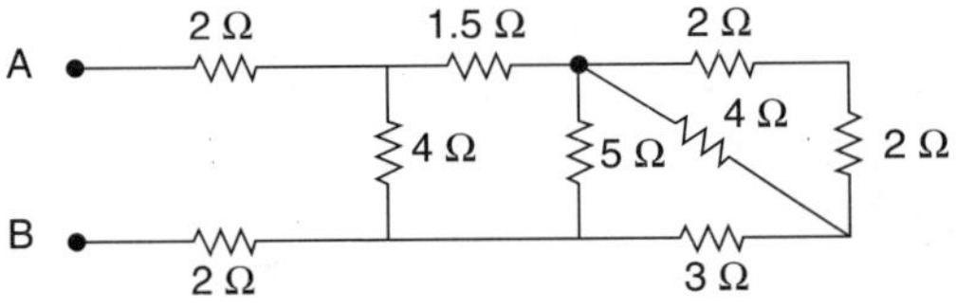

Solution:

The above circuit can be reduced to

$\therefore \quad R_{AB} = 2 + 2 + 2 = 6\,\Omega$

Problem 1.5 Find the power dissipated in each resistor in the circuit.

Solution:

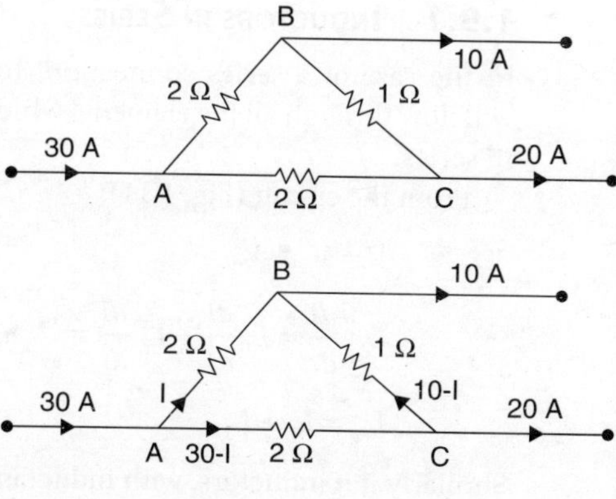

Let us assume, the current flowing through the branch AB is I. Then, the current distribution in the resistors is as shown below.

Applying KVL to the loop ABC

$$2I - 1(10 - I) - 2(30 - I) = 0$$

$$2I - 10 + I - 60 + 2I = 0$$

$$5I = 70 \quad \Rightarrow \quad I = 14 \text{ A}$$

Power dissipated in 2 Ω resistor (AB) = $14^2 \times 2 = 392$ W

Power dissipated in 2 Ω resistor (AC) = $(30 - I)^2 \times 2 = 512$ W

Power dissipated in 1 Ω resistor (BC) = $(10 - I)^2 \times 1 = 16$ W

1.9 INDUCTANCE PARAMETER

It is the property of a circuit element by which it opposes the change in flux or current. The inductance of a coil is defined as the ratio of flux linkage to the current flowing through the coil.

That is, Inductance $L = \dfrac{N\Phi}{i}$ (1.12)

where N = number of turns, Φ = flux in weber and I = current in ampere.

The unit of inductance is henry and circuit symbol is L

From the Eq. 1.12,

$$Li = N\Phi$$

$$\Rightarrow \quad L\frac{di}{dt} = N\frac{d\Phi}{dt}$$

$$\Rightarrow \quad L\frac{di}{dt} = v$$

The v–i relationship in the case of pure inductor is

$$v = L\frac{di}{dt} \quad \Rightarrow \quad i = \frac{1}{L}\int v\,dt \tag{1.13}$$

The power in an inductor is given by

$$P = v \times i = Li\frac{di}{dt}$$

From the above discussion we can conclude that:

- The induced voltage across an inductor is zero, if the current through it is constant. That means an inductor acts as a short circuit to DC.
- A small change in the current within zero time through an inductor gives an infinite voltage across the inductor, which is physically impossible. In a fixed inductor the current cannot change abruptly.
- The inductor can store a finite amount of energy, even if the voltage across inductor is zero.

1.9.1 Inductors in Series

In the case of a series connection, the same current will flow through all the elements which are connected in series.

From the circuit (Fig. 1.11),

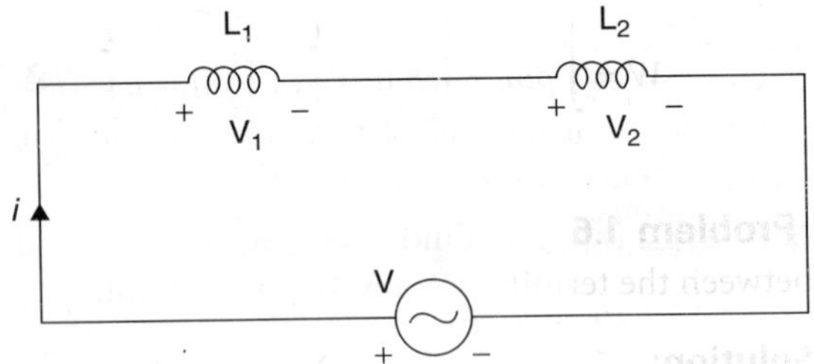

Fig. 1.11 Inductances are connected in series

$$V = V_1 + V_2$$

$$L_{eq}\frac{di}{dt} = L_1\frac{di}{dt} + L_2\frac{di}{dt} = (L_1 + L_2)\frac{di}{dt}$$

$$L_{eq} = L_1 + L_2 \tag{1.14}$$

Similarly if n inductors, with inductances of $L_1,\ L_2 \ldots L_n$ respectively, are connected in series, then

$$L_{eq} = L_1 + L_2 + \cdots + L_n \tag{1.15}$$

If n identical inductors, with an inductance of L are connected in series then

$$L_{eq} = nL \tag{1.16}$$

1.9.2 Inductors in Parallel

In a parallel circuit, the voltage across each branch connected in parallel is the same.

From the circuit (Fig. 1.12),

Fig. 1.12 Inductances are connected in parallel

$$i = i_1 + i_2$$

$$\Rightarrow \quad \frac{di}{dt} = \frac{di_1}{dt} + \frac{di_2}{dt}$$

$$\Rightarrow \quad \frac{V}{L_{eq}} = \frac{V}{L_1} + \frac{V}{L_2}$$

$$\Rightarrow \quad \frac{1}{L_{eq}} = \frac{1}{L_1} + \frac{1}{L_2} \tag{1.17}$$

Similarly n inductors, with inductances of $L_1,\ L_2 \ldots L_n$ respectively, are connected in parallel, then

$$\frac{1}{L_{eq}} = \frac{1}{L_1} + \frac{1}{L_2} + \cdots + \frac{1}{L_n} \tag{1.18}$$

If n identical inductors, each with an inductance of L are connected in parallel then,

$$L_{eq} = \frac{L}{n} \tag{1.19}$$

1.9.3 Stored Energy in an Inductor

An inductor stores energy in the magnetic field. Let dw be the energy stored in the inductor in the time interval dt, then

$$p = \frac{dw}{dt}$$

$$dw = pdt$$

$$W = \int_0^I p\,dt = \int_0^I vi\,dt = \int_0^I Li\frac{di}{dt}dt = L\int_0^I i\,di = \frac{1}{2}LI^2 \qquad (1.20)$$

Problem 1.6 Find the equivalent inductance between the terminals A and B in the circuit.

Solution:

The parallel combination of 6 H inductances can be reduced to $\frac{6}{2} = 3\text{ H}$. So the given circuit can be reduced to,

The equivalent inductance between the terminals A and B

$L_{AB} = 3 + 3 + 4 = 10\text{ H}$

Problem 1.7 Find the equivalent inductance between the terminals A and B in the circuit.

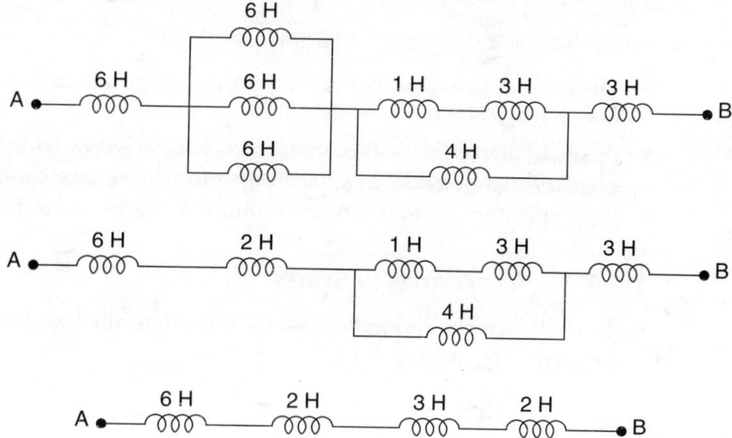

Solution:

The parallel combination of 6 H inductances can be reduced to $\frac{6}{3} = 2\text{ H}$. So the given circuit can be reduced to,

The above circuit can be further reduced to that shown below.

The equivalent inductance between the terminals A and B

$L_{AB} = 6 + 2 + 3 + 2 = 13\text{ H}$

1.10 CAPACITANCE PARAMETER

The capacitance is the property of an element or matter by which it opposes the change in charge or voltage. Since charge is a physical quantity it cannot change from one value to another value instantaneously. Whenever charge exists at a point, there should be some voltage at that point. Hence in an element with capacitive property, the voltage cannot change instantaneously, that is, the change in voltage will be delayed. Any two conducting surfaces separated by an insulating medium exhibit the property of a capacitor. The conducting surfaces are called electrodes and the insulating medium is called a dielectric.

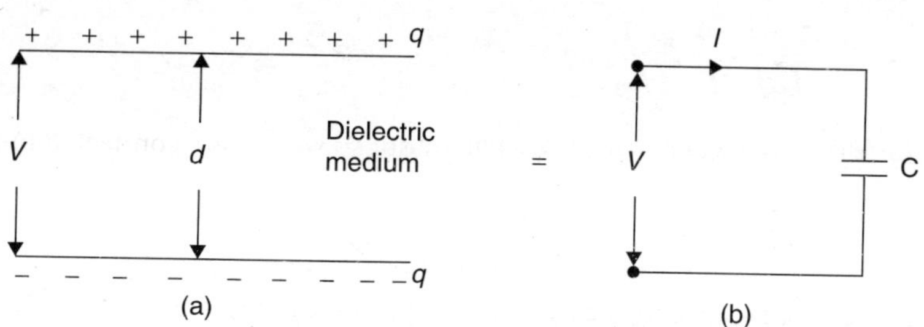

Fig. 1.13 Capacitor across a source

Charge on a capacitor

$$q \propto V \Rightarrow q = CV \tag{1.21}$$

where q = charge in coulombs and V = voltage in volts.

The unit of capacitance is Farad and the circuit symbol is ●—C—●

From Eq. 1.21,

$$\frac{dq}{dt} = C\frac{dv}{dt}$$

$$\Rightarrow \quad i = C\frac{dv}{dt}$$

The v–i relationship in the case of a pure capacitor is

$$i = C\frac{dv}{dt} \Rightarrow v = \frac{1}{C}\int i dt \tag{1.22}$$

From the above discussion we can conclude that

- The current in a capacitor is zero, if the voltage across it is constant, that is, the capacitor acts as an open circuit to DC.
- A small change in voltage across a capacitor gives an infinite current through the capacitor, which is physically impossible. In a fixed capacitor the voltage cannot change abruptly.
- The capacitor can store a finite amount of energy, even if the current through it is zero.

1.10.1 Capacitors in Series

In the case of a series connection, the same current will flow through all the elements that are connected in series.

From the circuit (Fig. 1.14),

$$V = V_1 + V_2$$

$$\frac{dV}{dt} = \frac{dV_1}{dt} + \frac{dV_2}{dt}$$

$$\frac{i}{C_{eq}} = \frac{i}{C_1} + \frac{i}{C_2}$$

$$\frac{1}{C_{eq}} = \frac{1}{C_1} + \frac{1}{C_2} \tag{1.23}$$

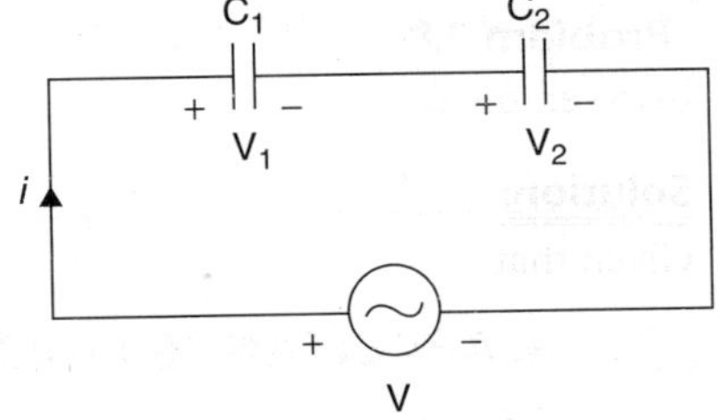

Fig. 1.14 Capacitances are connected in series

Similarly if n capacitors, with capacitances of C_1, C_2 … C_n respectively, are connected in series, then

$$\frac{1}{C_{eq}} = \frac{1}{C_1} + \frac{1}{C_2} + \cdots + \frac{1}{C_n} \tag{1.24}$$

If n identical capacitors, each with a capacitance of C, are connected in series then,

$$C_{eq} = \frac{C}{n} \tag{1.25}$$

1.10.2 Capacitors in Parallel

In a parallel circuit, the voltage across each branch connected in parallel is the same.

From the circuit (Fig. 1.15),

$$i = i_1 + i_2$$

$$C_{eq}\frac{dV}{dt} = C_1\frac{dV_1}{dt} + C_2\frac{dV_2}{dt}$$

$$C_{eq} = C_1 + C_2 \tag{1.26}$$

Similarly n capacitors, with capacitances of $C_1, C_2 \ldots C_n$ respectively, are connected in parallel, then

Fig. 1.15 Capacitances are connected in parallel

$$C_{eq} = C_1 + C_2 + \cdots + C_n \tag{1.27}$$

If n identical capacitors, each with a capacitance of C are connected in parallel then

$$C_{eq} = nC \tag{1.28}$$

1.10.3 Stored Energy in a Capacitor

The capacitor stores energy in an electric field. Let dw be the energy stored in the capacitor in the time interval dt, then

$$p = \frac{dw}{dt}$$

$$dw = pdt$$

$$W = \int_0^V pdt = \int_0^V vidt = \int_0^V vC\frac{dv}{dt}dt = C\int_0^V vdv = \frac{1}{2}CV^2 \tag{1.29}$$

Problem 1.8 Find the equivalent capacitance between the terminals A and B in the circuit.

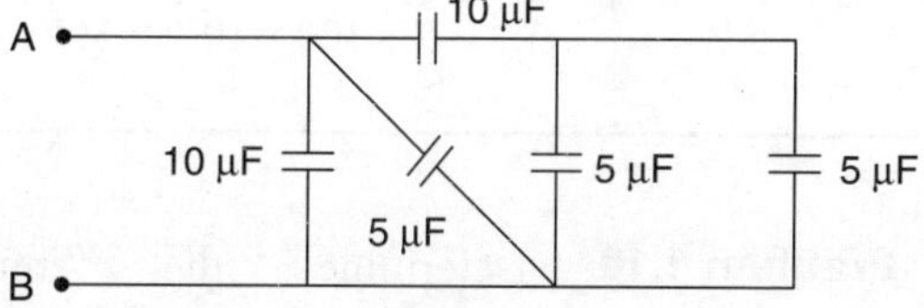

Solution:

Given that

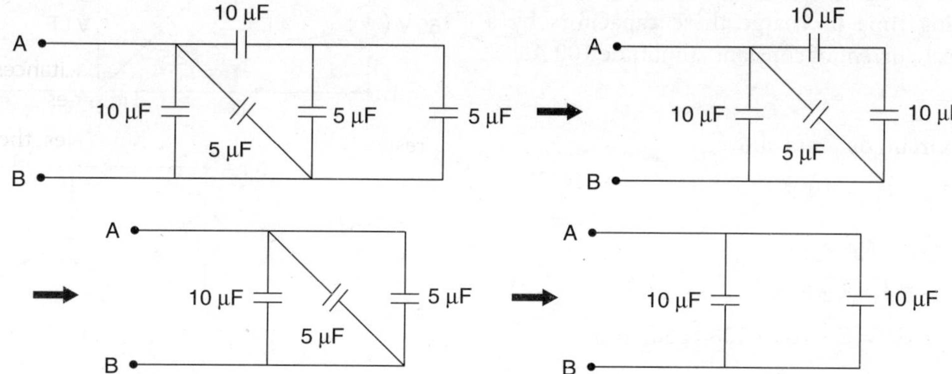

The equivalent capacitance between the terminals A and B is

$$C_{AB} = 10 + 10 = 20\ \mu F$$

Problem 1.9 A voltage of 60 V DC is applied across two capacitors, each of 100 μF. Find the voltage sharing between them if they are connected in series. What is the energy stored in each of the capacitors?

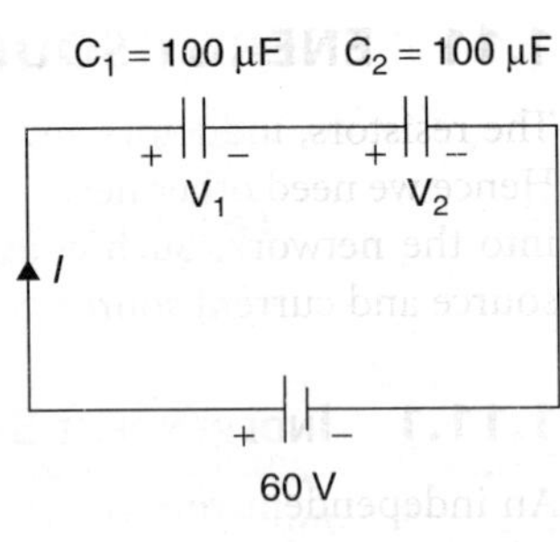

Solution:

Since the capacitors are connected in series, the charge through each capacitor is the same.

But $\quad q = C_1 V_1 = C_2 V_2$

$$\Rightarrow \quad \frac{V_1}{V_2} = \frac{C_2}{C_1} = \frac{100}{100} = 1$$

$$\Rightarrow \quad V_1 = V_2 \qquad (1)$$

$$V_1 + V_2 = 60 \qquad (2)$$

Adding Eqs (1) and (2),

$$2V_1 = 60$$

$$\Rightarrow \quad V_1 = 30 \text{ V}$$

$$\therefore \quad V_1 = V_2 = 30 \text{ V}$$

Energy stored in capacitor C_1

$$W_1 = \frac{1}{2} C_1 V_1^2 = \frac{1}{2} \times 100 \times 10^{-6} \times 30^2 = 0.045 \text{ W}$$

Energy stored in capacitor C_2

$$W_2 = \frac{1}{2} C_2 V_2^2 = \frac{1}{2} \times 100 \times 10^{-6} \times 30^2 = 0.045 \text{ W}$$

Problem 1.10 Determine the equivalent capacitance across the terminals A and B. Also find the charging time to charge these capacitors by a steady direct current of constant amplitude 100 A.

Solution:

Given the circuit diagram above,

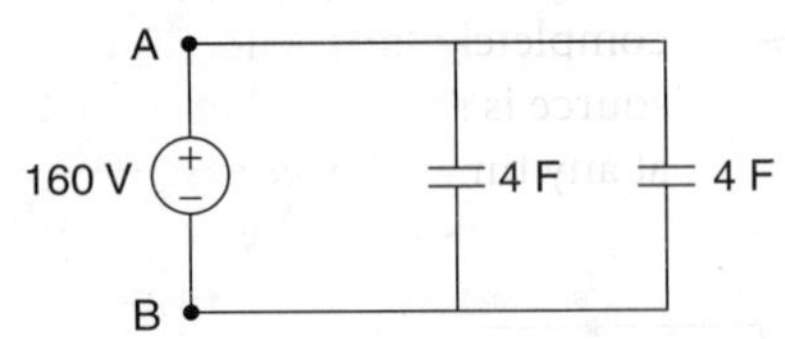

$$C_{EF} = 1 + 3 = 4 \text{ F}$$

$$C_{CF} = 2 + 2 = 4 \text{ F}$$

$$C_{AB} = 4 + 4 = 8 \text{ F}$$

$$Q = CV = 8 \times 160 = 1280 \text{ coulombs}$$

$$\text{Charging time, } t = \frac{Q}{I} = \frac{1280}{100} = 12.8 \text{ s}$$

1.11 ENERGY SOURCES

The resistors, inductors and capacitors are incapable of generating voltage, current or power of their own. Hence we need other network components capable of generating voltage or current and transferring energy into the network. Such components are called sources. There are two principal types of source—voltage source and current source. Sources can be either independent or dependent upon some other quantities.

1.11.1 INDEPENDENT SOURCES

An independent voltage source maintains a voltage (fixed or varying with time) that is not affected by any other quantity. Similarly an independent current source maintains a current (fixed or time-varying), which is unaffected by any other quantity. The usual symbols used for independent sources are shown in Fig. 1.16.

There are two independent energy sources:

- ideal voltage source/practical voltage source, and
- ideal current source/practical current source.

V_1 or $v(t)$ V_1 or $v(t)$ I_1 or $i(t)$ I_1 or $i(t)$

Independent voltage source   Independent current source

Fig. 1.16 Independent sources

(i) *Ideal voltage source* An ideal voltage source is a two terminal element in which the voltage V_s is completely independent of the current I_s, through its terminals. The representation of an ideal voltage source is shown in Fig. 1.17. If we observe *v–i* characteristics of an ideal voltage source (Fig. 1.17), at any given time the value of the terminal voltage V_s is constant with respect to the current value I_s.

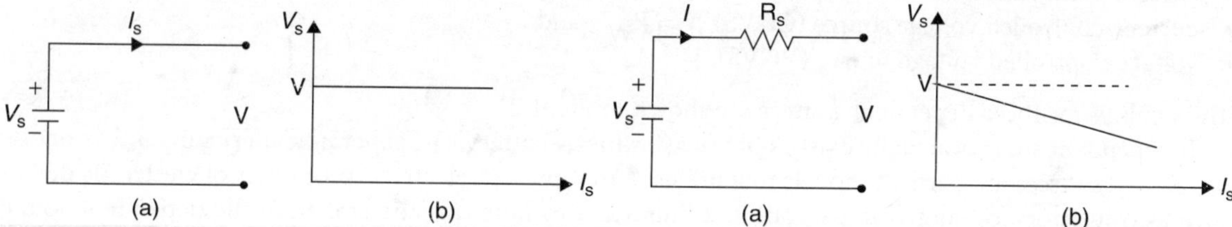

Fig. 1.17 Ideal voltage source

Fig. 1.18 Practical voltage source

The practical voltage source can be considered as a series combination of an ideal voltage source and a resistance, which is referred to as *source resistance* (Fig. 1.18). The reduction in voltage across the terminals with increasing load current is due to the voltage drop in the source resistance. When the value of the source resistance is zero, ideal conditions are achieved in the voltage source. Hence the source resistance or internal resistance of an ideal voltage source is zero.

(ii) *Ideal current source* An ideal current source is a two terminal element in which the current I_s is completely independent of the voltage V_s, across its terminals. The representation of an ideal current source is shown in Fig. 1.19. If we observe the *v–i* characteristics of an ideal current source (Fig. 1.19), at any time the value of the current I_s is constant with respect to the voltage V_s across it.

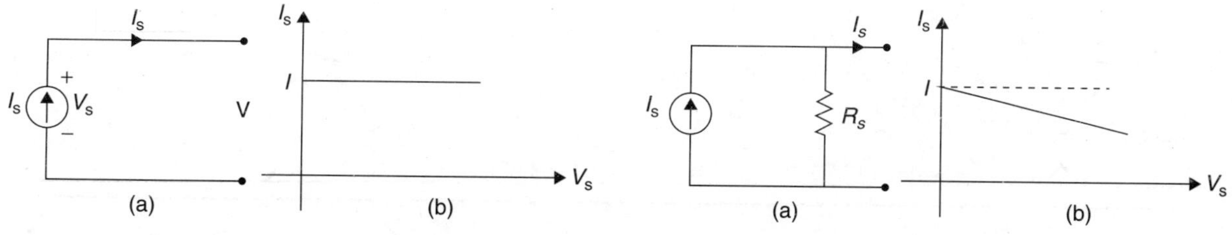

Fig. 1.19 Ideal current source

Fig. 1.20 Practical current source

The practical current source can be considered as a parallel combination of an ideal current source and a resistance, referred to as *source resistance* (Fig. 1.20). The reduction in current delivered by the source is due to the current drawn by the parallel source resistance. When the value of the source resistance is infinite, the ideal condition is achieved in the current source. Hence the source resistance or internal resistance of an ideal current source is infinity.

1.11.2 Dependent Sources

If the voltage or current of a source depends in turn upon some other voltage or current in the network, it is called *dependent source* or *controlled source*. Such a source is represented by a diamond shaped symbol. There are four types of dependent sources:

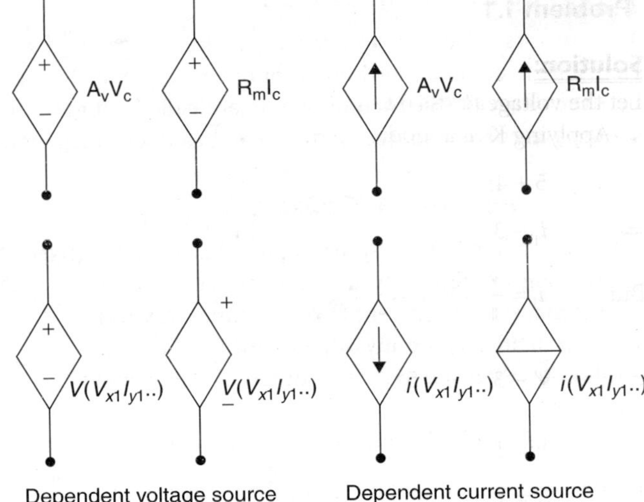

Fig. 1.21 Symbols for dependent sources. Variables in brackets are the controlling variables whose values affect the value of the source

- voltage-controlled current source (VCCS), $I = G_m V_c$
- current-controlled current source (CCCS), $I = A_i I_c$
- current-controlled voltage source (CCVS), $V = R_m I_c$, and
- voltage-controlled voltage source (VCVS), $V = A_v V_c$.

The symbols for these dependent sources are shown in Fig. 1.21.

Independent sources actually exist as physical entities—battery, DC generator, alternator, and so on. But dependent sources are parts of models that are used to represent electrical properties of electronic devices such as transistors, op-amps, and so on. It is important to note that the emf V_s of the dependent voltage source will be zero if the variable V_x or I_x becomes zero, under this condition it can be represented by short circuit. Similarly the current I_s of the dependent current source will be zero if the variable V_x or I_x becomes zero, under this condition it can be represented by open circuit.

Problem 1.11 Obtain the numerical value of the voltage dependent current source.

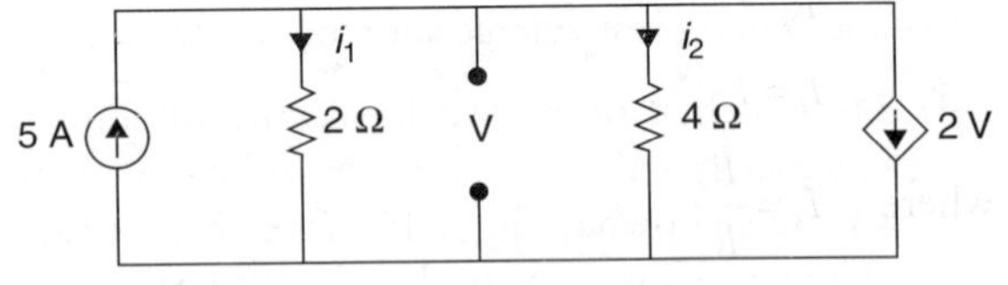

Solution:

Applying KCL to the circuit

$$5 = i_1 + i_2 + 2\text{ V}$$

But, $$i_1 = \frac{V}{2},\ i_2 = \frac{V}{4}$$

Therefore, $$5 = 0.5\text{ V} + 0.25\text{ V} + 2\text{ V}$$

$$\Rightarrow \quad V = \frac{5}{2.75} = 1.8181\text{ V}$$

$\therefore$ Numerical value of VDCS = 2 V = 2 × 1.8181 = 3.636 A

Problem 1.12 Find the currents i_1 and i_2.

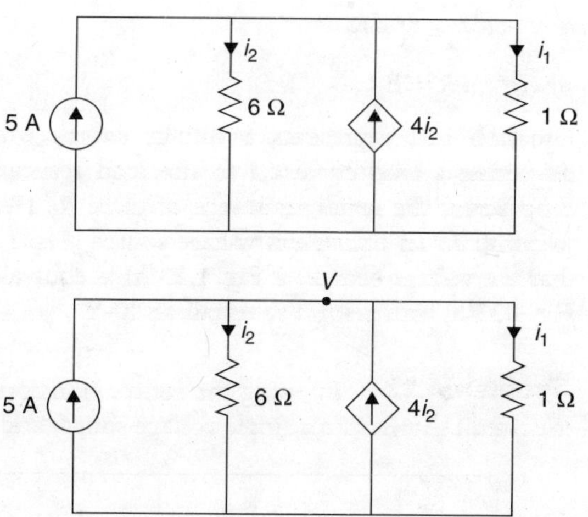

Solution:

Let the voltage across 6 Ω or 1 Ω resistor be V volts.

Applying KCL at node V,

$$5 + 4i_2 = i_1 + i_2$$

$$\Rightarrow \quad i_1 - 3i_2 = 5$$

But $$i_1 = \frac{V}{1} = V, \; i_2 = \frac{V}{6}$$

$$\therefore \quad V - 3 \times \frac{V}{6} = 5$$

$$V = 10 \text{ volts}$$

$$\therefore \quad i_1 = V = 10 \text{ A}$$

$$i_2 = \frac{V}{6} = \frac{10}{6} = 1.67 \text{ A}$$

1.12 NETWORK REDUCTION METHODS

1.12.1 Source Transformation

By using the source transformation technique, we can convert a practical voltage source into a practical current source and vice versa without changing the terminal behaviour of the network.

According to the source transformation technique, a voltage source in series with a resistance can be converted into a current source in parallel with a resistance and vice versa.

Applying KVL to Fig. 1.22(a),

$$E_s = IR_s + V$$

$$\frac{E_s}{R_s} = I + \frac{V}{R_s}$$

$$I_s = I + I_{sh} \tag{1.30}$$

where $$I_s = \frac{E_s}{R_s}, \quad I_{sh} = \frac{V}{R_s}$$

Fig. 1.22 Conversion of voltage source into current source

Equation 1.30 represents a current source with a source current I_s and delivering a load current I to the load resistance R_L and I_{sh} to the parallel resistance R_s connected across the current source. Hence, Eq. 1.30 can be used to construct an equivalent current source [Fig. 1.22(b)]. It can be observed that the current source of Fig. 1.22(b) is equivalent to the voltage source of Fig. 1.22(a) with respect to terminals X–Y.

Applying KCL to Fig. 1.23(a),

$$I_s = \frac{V}{R_s} + I$$

$$I_s R_s = IR_s + V$$

$$E_s = V + IR_s \tag{1.31}$$

where $I_s R_s = E_s$

Equation 1.31 represents a voltage source with source voltage E_s and delivering a load current I to the load resistance R_L. IR_s is the voltage drop across the series resistance of value R_s. Hence, Eq. 1.31 can be used to construct an equivalent voltage source [Fig. 1.23(b)]. It can be observed that the voltage source of Fig. 1.23(b) is equivalent to a current source of Fig. 1.23(a) with respect to terminals X–Y.

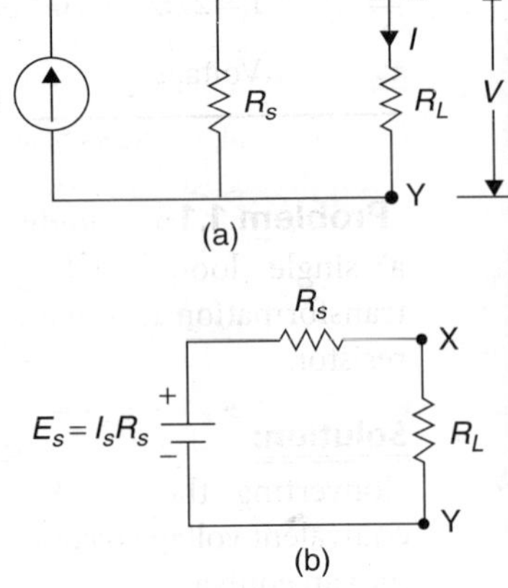

Fig. 1.23 Conversion of current source into voltage source

Problem 1.13 By using the source transformation technique, convert the circuit shown into a single voltage source and single resistance.

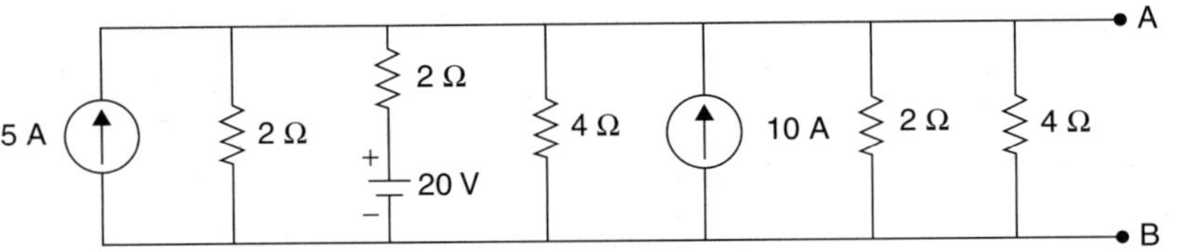

Solution:

By converting a 20 V voltage source into an equivalent current source, the circuit diagram reduced to

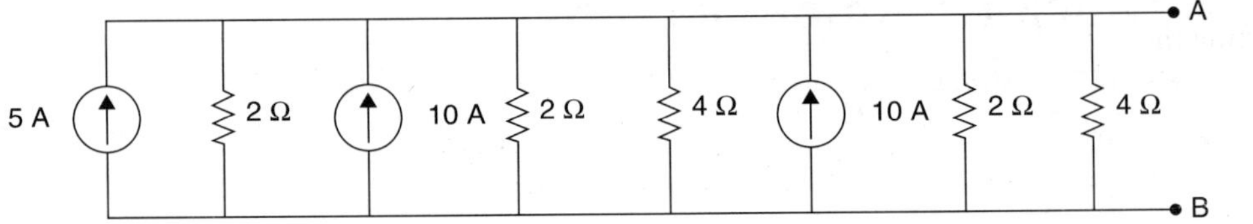

The above circuit diagram can be reduced to

where $I_T = 5 + 10 + 10 = 25$ A

$$\frac{1}{R_T} = \frac{1}{2} + \frac{1}{2} + \frac{1}{4} + \frac{1}{2} + \frac{1}{4} = 2$$

$\Rightarrow$ $R_T = 0.5\ \Omega$

The above circuit diagram can be redrawn as shown (by using source transformation).

I_T, R_T, A, B = $R_T = 0.5\ \Omega$, $V_T = 25 \times 0.5 = 12.5$ V

Problem 1.14 For the circuit shown, compute the voltage V across the 1 MΩ resistor using repeated source transformation.

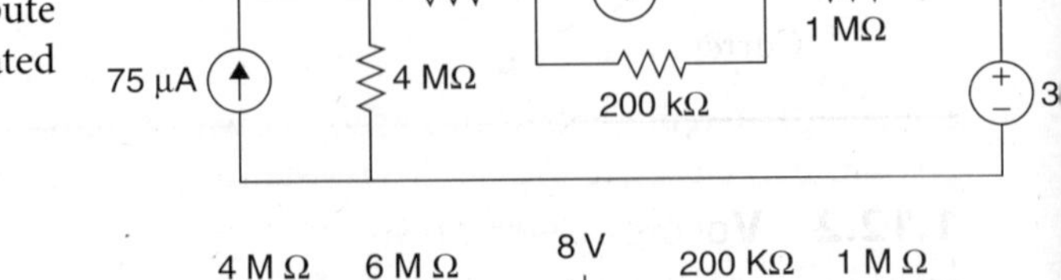

Solution:

Using current source transformation, the above network can be written as

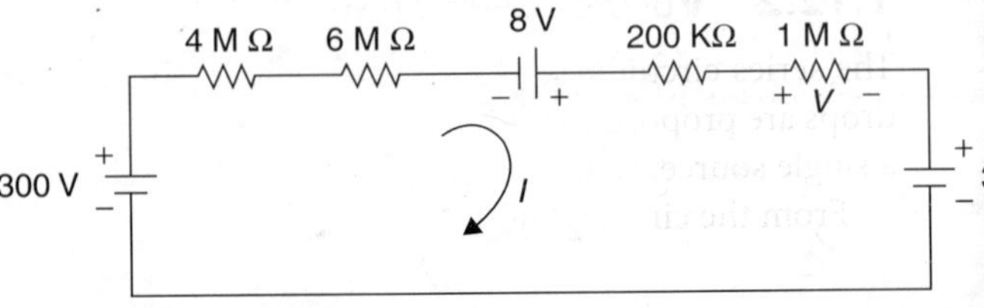

Applying KVL to the circuit

$$300 + 8 - 3 - (4 + 6 + 0.2 + 1)10^6 I = 0$$

$$\Rightarrow \quad 11.2 \times 10^6 I = 305$$

$\Rightarrow \qquad I = 27.23 \times 10^{-6}$ A

$\therefore \qquad$ Voltage across 1 MΩ resistance, $V = 27.23 \times 1 = 27.23$ V

Problem 1.15 Reduce the network shown to a single loop network by successive source transformation to obtain the current in the 12 Ω resistor.

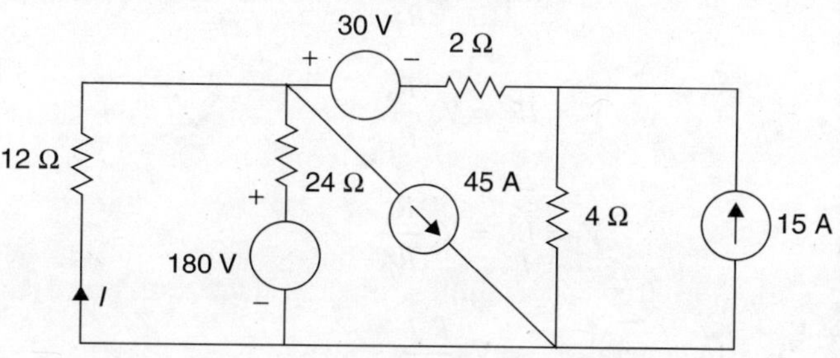

Solution:

Converting the 15 A current source into an equivalent voltage source and 180 V voltage source into an equivalent current source, we have

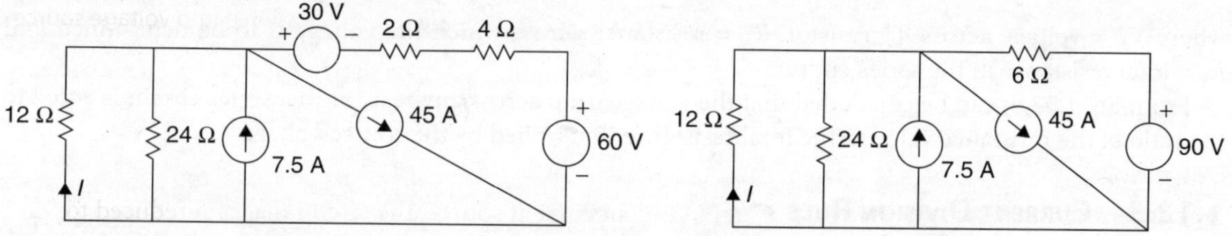

Converting the 90 V voltage source into an equivalent current source,

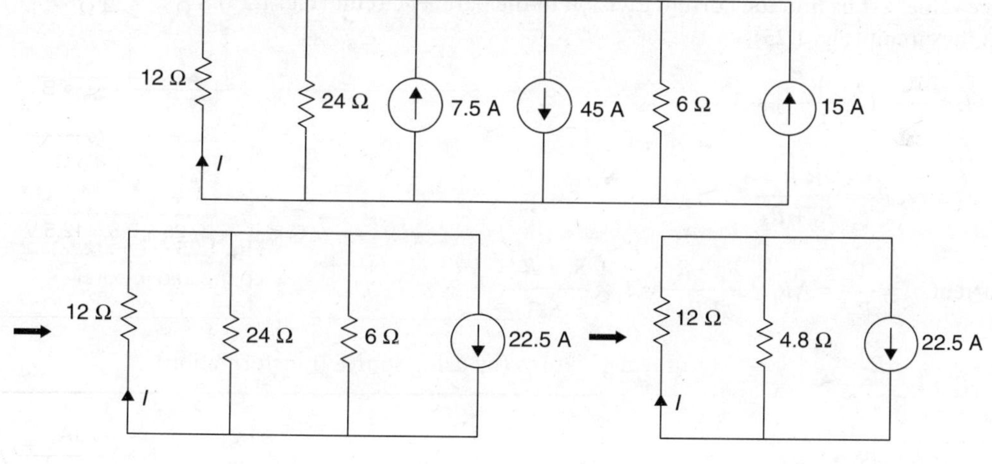

$$\text{Current in the 12 Ω resistor, } I = 22.5 \times \frac{4.8}{4.8 + 12} = 6.43 \text{ A}$$

1.12.2 Voltage Division Rule

The series circuit acts as a voltage divider. Since the same current flows through each resistor, the voltage drops are proportional to the value of resistors. Using this principle, different voltages can be obtained from a single source, called a voltage divider.

From the circuit (Fig. 1.24),

$$I = \frac{V_S}{R_1 + R_2 + R_3} = \frac{V_S}{R_T}$$

$$V_1 = IR_1 = V_S \frac{R_1}{R_T}$$

$$V_2 = IR_2 = V_S \frac{R_2}{R_T}$$

$$V_3 = IR_3 = V_S \frac{R_3}{R_T}$$

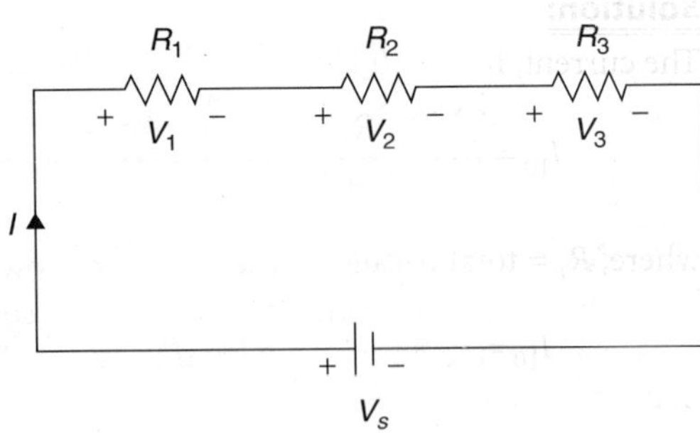

Fig. 1.24 Three resistances are connected in series

In general, $V_N = V_S \dfrac{R_N}{R_T}$ (1.32)

where V_N = voltage across n^{th} resistor, R_N = resistance across which the voltage is to be determined and R_T = total resistance in the series circuit.

From Eq. 1.32, it can be concluded that the voltage drop across any resistor in a series circuit is equal to the ratio of the resistance value to the total resistance, multiplied by the source voltage.

1.12.3 Current Division Rule

In a parallel circuit the current divides into all the branches. Thus a parallel circuit acts as a current divider. The total current entering into the parallel branches is divided into branch currents according to the resistance value. Let us find the current division in the parallel circuit (Fig. 1.25).

From the circuit (Fig. 1.25),

$$I_1 = \frac{V}{R_1}, \; I_2 = \frac{V}{R_2}$$

Fig. 1.25 Two resistances are connected in parallel

Total resistance, $R_T = \dfrac{R_1 R_2}{R_1 + R_2}$

Total current, $I = \dfrac{V}{R_T} = I_1 R_1 \times \dfrac{R_1 + R_2}{R_1 R_2} = I_1 \times \dfrac{R_1 + R_2}{R_2}$

$$\Rightarrow \quad I_1 = I \frac{R_2}{R_1 + R_2}$$

Similarly $I_2 = I \dfrac{R_1}{R_1 + R_2}$

In general $I_N = I \dfrac{R_T}{R_N + R_T}$ (1.33)

where I_N = current in the nth branch, R_N = resistance of the nth branch and R_T = total parallel resistance to the nth branch. From the above equation, it can be concluded that the current in any branch is equal to the ratio of the opposite branch resistance to the total resistance value, multiplied by total current in the circuit.

Problem 1.16 Determine the current in the 10 Ω resistor and find V in the circuit.

Solution:

The current, in the 10 Ω resistor,

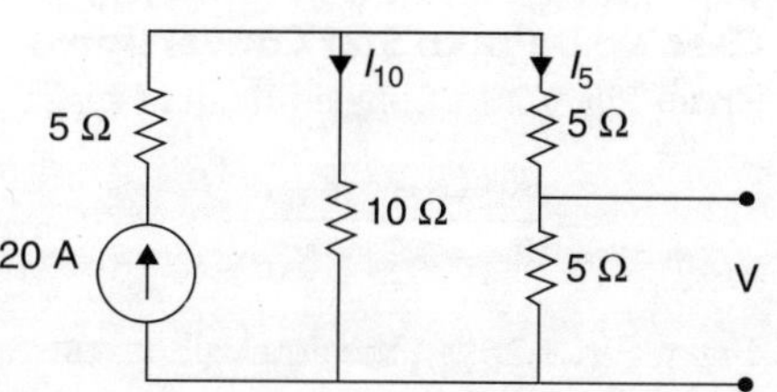

$$I_{10} = I_T \times \frac{R_T}{R_T + 10}$$

where, R_T = total parallel resistance = 5 + 5 = 10 Ω

$$I_{10} = 20 \times \frac{10}{10 + 10} = 10$$

$$I_5 = 20 - I_{10} = 20 - 10 = 10 \text{ A}$$

$$V = 5 \times I_5 = 5 \times 10 = 50 \text{ V}$$

Problem 1.17 Use voltage and current division rules to find V_0 and i_0 for the circuit below.

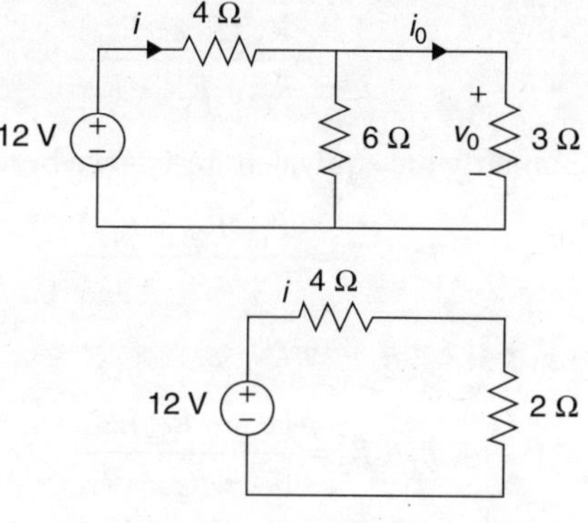

Solution:

The equivalent resistance of the parallel combination 6 Ω and 3 Ω is $\frac{6 \times 3}{6 + 3} = 2\,\Omega$. So the given circuit is reduced to

$$i = \frac{12}{4 + 2} = 2 \text{ A}$$

$$i_0 = i \times \frac{6}{6 + 3} = 2 \times \frac{6}{6 + 3} = 1.333 \text{ A}$$

$$V_0 = 3i_0 = 3 \times 1.333 = 4 \text{ V}$$

Problem 1.18 Find I_1, I_2 and V for the circuit.

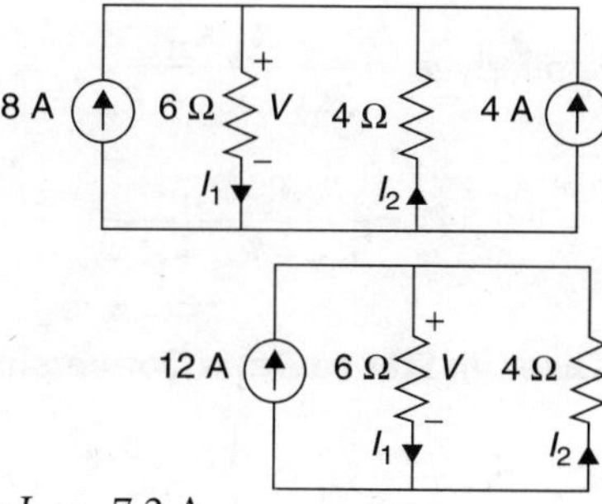

Solution:

The total current in the circuit = 8 + 4 = 12 A. So the above circuit can be reduced to the circuit shown below.

$$I_1 = I \times \frac{4}{6 + 4} = 12 \times \frac{4}{10} = 4.8 \text{ A}$$

$I_2 = I \times \frac{6}{6 + 4} = 12 \times \frac{6}{10} = 7.2$ A, but the direction is reversed, so $I_2 = -7.2$ A

$$V = 6I_1 = 6 \times 4.8 = 28.8 \text{ volts}$$

1.12.4 Star–delta Transformation

Delta–star and star–delta transformations are quite useful to simplify certain network problems. If three elements meet at a node then the three elements are said to be in star connection, whereas if three elements form a closed path then they are said to be in delta connection (Fig. 1.26).

Case (i): Delta to Star Conversion

From Fig. 1.26(a), the equivalent resistance between terminals 1 and 2

$$= \frac{R_{12}(R_{23}+R_{31})}{R_{12}+R_{23}+R_{31}} \tag{1.34}$$

From Fig. 1.26(b), the equivalent resistance between terminals 1 and 2

$$= R_1 + R_2 \tag{1.35}$$

From Eqs 1.34 and 1.35,

$$R_1 + R_2 = \frac{R_{12}(R_{23}+R_{31})}{R_{12}+R_{23}+R_{31}} \tag{1.36}$$

Similarly the equivalent resistance between terminals 2 and 3

$$R_3 + R_2 = \frac{R_{23}(R_{12}+R_{31})}{R_{12}+R_{23}+R_{31}} \tag{1.37}$$

Similarly the equivalent resistance between terminals 1 and 3

$$R_3 + R_1 = \frac{R_{13}(R_{23}+R_{12})}{R_{12}+R_{23}+R_{31}} \tag{1.38}$$

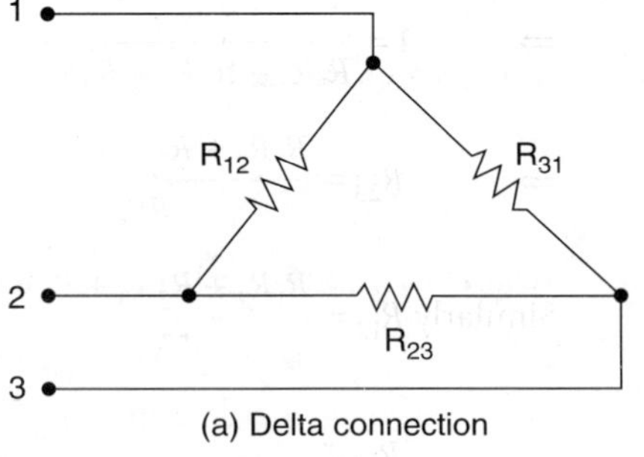

(a) Delta connection

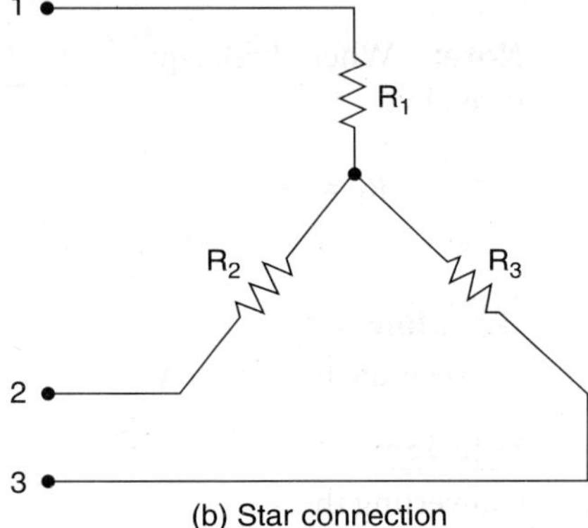

(b) Star connection

Fig. 1.26 Star–delta conversion

Eq. 1.36 – Eq. 1.37

$$R_1 - R_3 = \frac{(R_{12}-R_{23})R_{31}}{R_{12}+R_{23}+R_{31}} \tag{1.39}$$

Eq. 1.38 + Eq. 1.39

$$2R_1 = \frac{2R_{12}R_{31}}{R_{12}+R_{23}+R_{31}} \Rightarrow R_1 = \frac{R_{12}R_{31}}{R_{12}+R_{23}+R_{31}} \tag{1.40}$$

$$\text{Similarly } R_2 = \frac{R_{23}R_{21}}{R_{12}+R_{23}+R_{31}} \tag{1.41}$$

$$R_3 = \frac{R_{32}R_{31}}{R_{12}+R_{23}+R_{31}} \tag{1.42}$$

Case (ii): Star to Delta Conversion

$$\frac{\text{Eq. 1.40}}{\text{Eq. 1.41}} \Rightarrow \frac{R_1}{R_2} = \frac{R_{31}}{R_{23}} \Rightarrow R_{13} = \frac{R_1}{R_2}R_{23} \tag{1.43}$$

$$\frac{\text{Eq. 1.40}}{\text{Eq. 1.42}} \Rightarrow \frac{R_1}{R_3} = \frac{R_{12}}{R_{23}} \Rightarrow R_{12} = \frac{R_1}{R_3}R_{23} \tag{1.44}$$

Substituting Eqs 1.43 and 1.44 into Eq. 1.40, we obtain

$$R_1 = \frac{\frac{R_1}{R_3}R_{23}\frac{R_1}{R_2}R_{23}}{\frac{R_1}{R_3}R_{23} + R_{23} + \frac{R_1}{R_2}R_{23}}$$

$$\Rightarrow \qquad 1 = \frac{R_1 R_{23}}{R_1R_2 + R_2R_3 + R_3R_1}$$

$$\Rightarrow \qquad R_{23} = \frac{R_1R_2 + R_2R_3 + R_3R_1}{R_1} \tag{1.45}$$

$$\text{Similarly } R_{12} = \frac{R_1R_2 + R_2R_3 + R_3R_1}{R_3} \tag{1.46}$$

$$R_{31} = \frac{R_1R_2 + R_2R_3 + R_3R_1}{R_2} \tag{1.47}$$

Note: When three equal resistances are connected in delta [Fig. 1.26(a)], the equivalent star resistance is given by

$$R_Y = \frac{R_\Delta R_\Delta}{R_\Delta + R_\Delta + R_\Delta} = \frac{R_\Delta}{3} \Rightarrow R_\Delta = 3R_Y$$

Problem 1.19 Find the equivalent resistance between the terminals A and B.

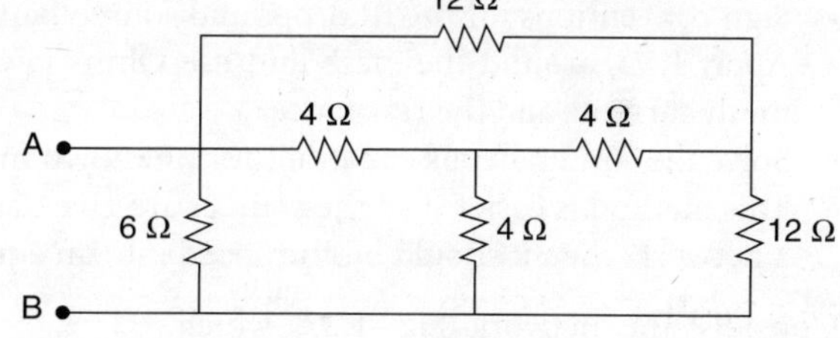

Solution:

Converting the 4 Ω star into equivalent delta

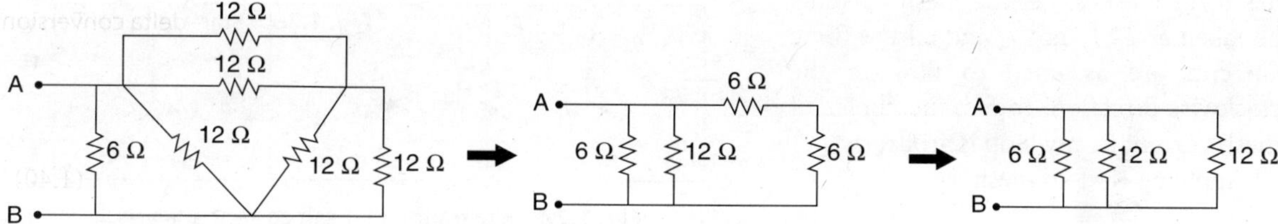

Equivalent resistance between the terminals AB is

$$\frac{1}{R_{AB}} = \frac{1}{6} + \frac{1}{12} + \frac{1}{12}$$

$$\Rightarrow \qquad R_{AB} = 3\ \Omega$$

Problem 1.20 Find the current delivered by the source.

Solution:

Converting the 9 Ω delta into equivalent star,

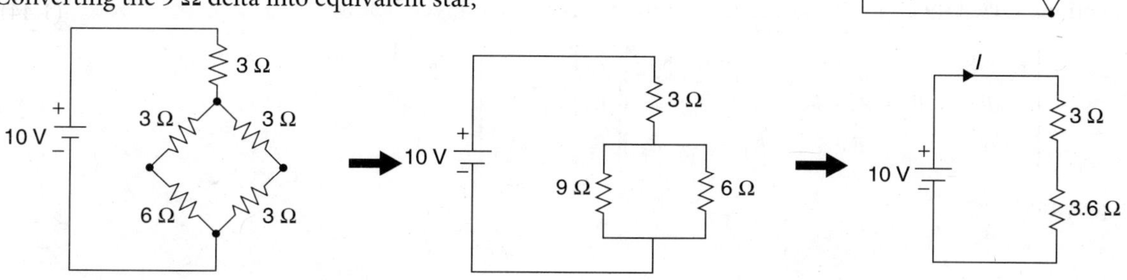

∴ Current delivered by the source

$$I = \frac{10}{3+3.6} = 1.515 \text{ A}$$

1.12.5 Mesh Analysis

Any closed electrical path is called a loop. A *mesh* is defined as a loop which does not contain any other loops within it. If a network has a large number of voltage sources, it is useful to use mesh analysis, which mainly depends on KVL. If the network contains B branches and N nodes then the number of mesh currents is given by $M = B - N + 1$.

Steps to be followed in mesh analysis

- Identify all the meshes in the network and select loop/mesh currents. Here, loop currents are assumed to flow in the clockwise direction.
- Sign conventions for the IR drops and source/battery emfs are the same as for Kirchhoff's law.
- Apply KVL around the mesh and use Ohm's law to express the branch voltages in terms of unknown mesh currents and the resistance.
- Solve the simultaneous equations for unknown mesh currents.
- This method is easier if all the sources are given as voltage sources. If there is a current source present in a network, then it should be converted into an equivalent voltage source.

Consider the network Fig. 1.27, which has three meshes. Let the mesh currents be taken as I_1, I_2 and I_3 and all the three currents are assumed to flow in the clockwise direction. In fact the choice of mesh current in any loop is arbitrary.

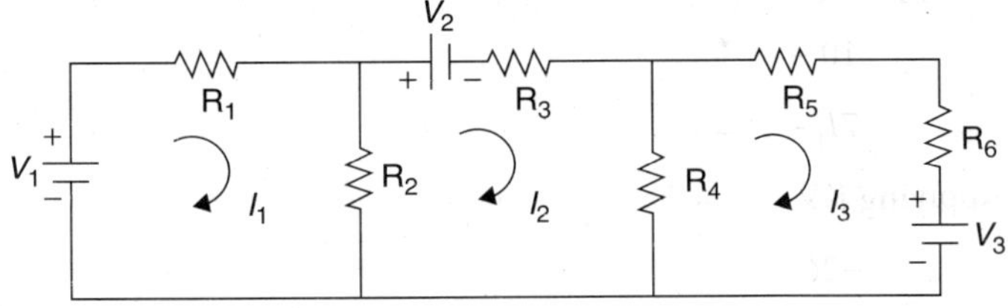

Fig. 1.27 Illustration of mesh current analysis

Applying KVL to mesh-1,

$$V_1 - I_1R_1 - (I_1 - I_2)R_2 = 0$$

$$I_1(R_1 + R_2) - I_2R_2 = V_1 \tag{1.48}$$

Applying KVL to mesh-2

$$-V_2 - I_2R_3 - (I_2 - I_3)R_4 - (I_2 - I_1)R_2 = 0$$

$$-I_1R_2 + I_2(R_2 + R_3 + R_4) - I_3R_4 = -V_2 \tag{1.49}$$

Applying KVL to mesh-3

$$-I_3R_5 - I_3R_6 - V_3 - (I_3 - I_2)R_4 = 0$$

$$-I_2R_4 + I_3(R_4 + R_5 + R_6) = -V_3 \tag{1.50}$$

Equations 1.48, 1.49 and 1.50 are rearranged in matrix form as given below:

$$\begin{bmatrix} R_1 + R_2 & -R_2 & 0 \\ -R_2 & R_2 + R_3 + R_4 & -R_4 \\ 0 & -R_4 & R_4 + R_5 + R_6 \end{bmatrix} \begin{bmatrix} I_1 \\ I_2 \\ I_3 \end{bmatrix} = \begin{bmatrix} V_1 \\ -V_2 \\ -V_3 \end{bmatrix} \tag{1.51}$$

In general,

$$\begin{bmatrix} R_{11} & \pm R_{12} & \pm R_{13} \\ \pm R_{21} & R_{22} & \pm R_{23} \\ \pm R_{31} & \pm R_{32} & R_{33} \end{bmatrix} \begin{bmatrix} I_1 \\ I_2 \\ I_3 \end{bmatrix} = \begin{bmatrix} V_1 \\ V_2 \\ V_3 \end{bmatrix} \quad (1.52)$$

where R_{11}, R_{22}, R_{33} are the sum of the resistances in their respective meshes/loops. $R_{12} = R_{21}$ is the mutual resistance or sum of all the resistances connected between meshes 1 and 2. $R_{13} = R_{31}$ is the mutual resistance or sum of all the resistances connected between meshes 1 and 3. $R_{23} = R_{32}$ is the mutual resistance or sum of all the resistances connected between meshes 2 and 3.

If the directions of the currents passing through the common resistance are the same, the mutual resistance will have a positive sign, and if the directions of the currents passing through the common resistance are opposite then the mutual resistance will have a negative sign.

The voltages V_1, V_2 and V_3 are the algebraic sum of the voltages in the respective loops, which are taken as positive, if the loop current directions are the same as the direction of the sources (that is, negative terminal of the source to positive terminal), otherwise (that is, positive terminal of the source to negative terminal) it is taken as negative.

Problem 1.21 Find the mesh currents for the circuit.

Solution:

Let us assume the mesh currents as I_1, I_2 and I_3 as shown.

Applying KVL to mesh-1

$$10 - 6I_1 - 1(I_1 - I_2) = 0$$

$$7I_1 - I_2 = 10 \quad (1)$$

Applying KVL to mesh-2

$$-2I_2 - 3(I_2 - I_3) - 1(I_2 - I_1) = 0$$

$$-I_1 + 6I_2 - 3I_3 = 0 \quad (2)$$

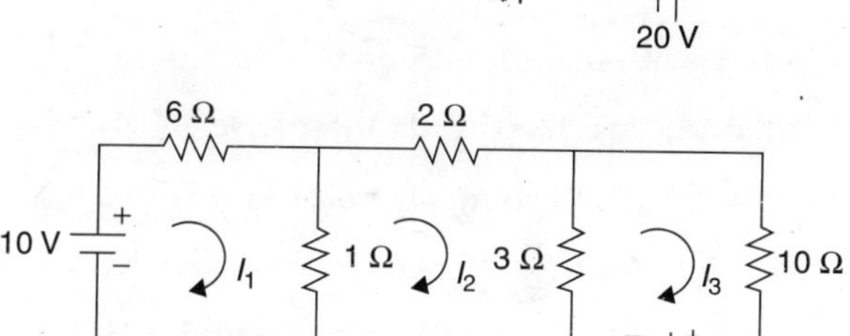

Applying KVL to mesh-3

$$-10I_3 - 20 - 3(I_3 - I_2) = 0$$

$$-3I_2 + 13I_3 = -20 \quad (3)$$

Solving Eqs (1), (2) and (3), we have

$$I_1 = 1.34 \text{ A}, \quad I_2 = -0.62 \text{ A}, \quad I_3 = -1.68 \text{ A}$$

Problem 1.22 Find the mesh current I_1 and I_2 for the circuit.

Solution:

Applying KVL to mesh-1

$$5 - 2I_1 - 2(I_1 - I_2) = 0$$

$$4I_1 - 2I_2 = 5 \quad (1)$$

Applying KVL to mesh-1

$$-4I_2 - 6I_2 + 10 - 2(I_2 - I_1) = 0$$

$$-2I_1 + 12I_2 = 10 \quad (2)$$

Solving Eqs (1) and (2), we have $I_1 = 1.82$ A, $I_2 = 1.136$ A

Problem 1.23 Find the current and power supplied by the source.

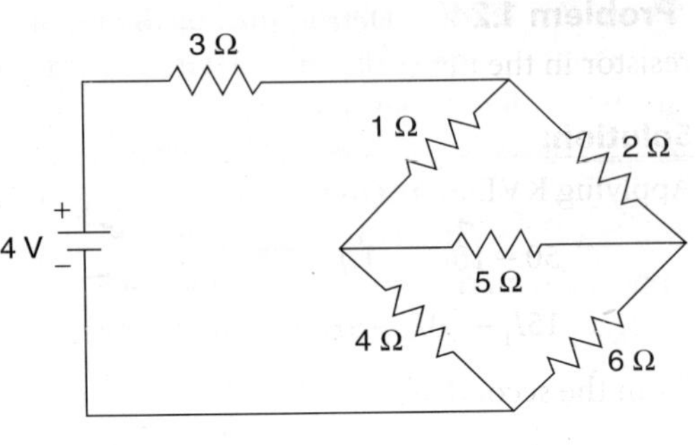

Solution:

Let us assume the mesh currents as I_1, I_2 and I_3 as shown.

Applying KVL to mesh-1

$$4 - 3I_1 - 1(I_1 - I_2) - 4(I_1 - I_3) = 0$$

$$8I_1 - I_2 - 4I_3 = 4 \quad (1)$$

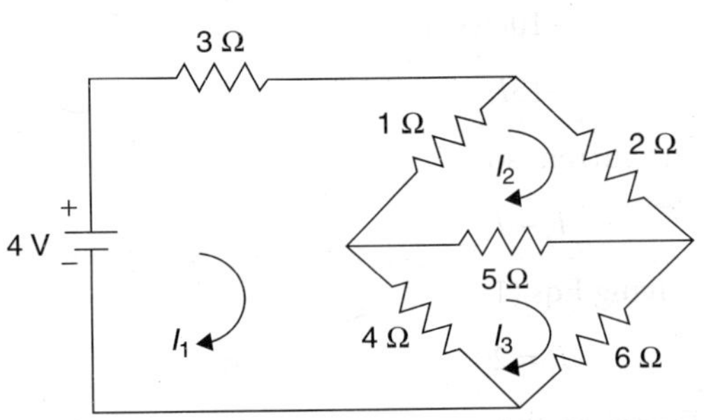

Applying KVL to mesh-2

$$-2I_2 - 5(I_2 - I_3) - 1(I_2 - I_1) = 0$$

$$-I_1 + 8I_2 - 5I_3 = 0 \quad (2)$$

Applying KVL to mesh-3

$$-6I_3 - 4(I_3 - I_1) - 5(I_3 - I_2) = 0$$

$$-4I_1 - 5I_2 + 15I_3 = 0 \quad (3)$$

Solving Eqs (1), (2) and (3), we have

$$I_1 = 0.66 \text{ A}, \quad I_2 = 0.24 \text{ A}, \quad I_3 = 0.26 \text{ A}$$

Current supplied by the source $= I_1 = 0.66$ A

Power supplied by the source $= 4I_1 = 4 \times 0.66 = 2.64$ W

1.12.6 Supermesh Analysis

Suppose any of the branches in the network has a current source, then it is slightly difficult to apply mesh analysis. This difficulty can be overcome by using supermesh technique. A supermesh is constituted by two adjacent loops that have a common current source.

Consider the circuit (Fig. 1.28). Here the current source I is in the common boundary for two loops (1) and (2). This current source creates a supermesh, which is nothing but a combination of meshes (1) and (2).

Applying combined KVL to meshes 1 and 2

$$V_1 - I_1R_1 - (I_2 - I_3)R_3 = 0$$

$$I_1R_1 + I_2R_3 - I_3R_3 = V_1 \quad (1.53)$$

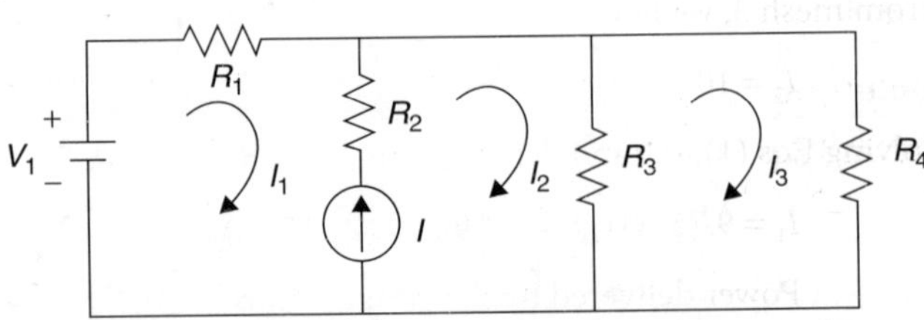

Fig. 1.28 Illustration of supermesh current analysis

Applying KVL to mesh 3

$$-(I_3 - I_2)R_3 - I_3R_4 = 0$$

$$-I_2R_3 + (R_3 + R_4)I_3 = 0 \quad (1.54)$$

From the supermesh

$$I_2 - I_1 = I \quad (1.55)$$

Solving Eqs 1.53, 1.54 and 1.55, we can get the values of I_1, I_2 and I_3.

Problem 1.24 Determine the current in the 5 Ω resistor in the network.

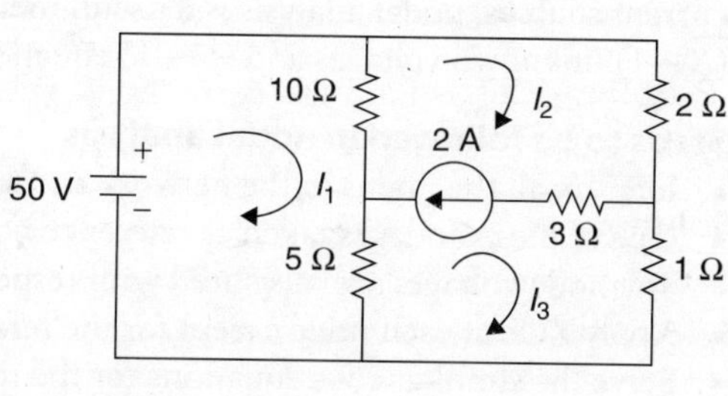

Solution:

Applying KVL to mesh-1

$$50 - 10(I_1 - I_2) - 5(I_1 - I_3) = 0$$

$$15I_1 - 10I_2 - 5I_3 = 50 \quad (1)$$

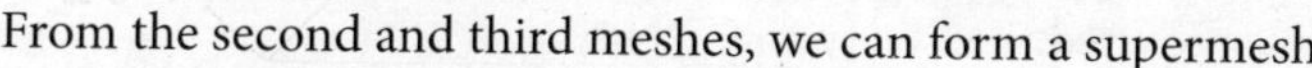

From the second and third meshes, we can form a supermesh

$$-10(I_2 - I_1) - 2I_2 - 1I_3 - 5(I_3 - I_1) = 0$$

$$-15I_1 + 12I_2 + 6I_3 = 0 \quad (2)$$

The current source is equal to the difference between the 2nd and 3rd mesh currents

$$I_2 - I_3 = 2 \quad (3)$$

Solving Eqs (1), (2) and (3), we have

$$I_1 = 20 \text{ A}, \quad I_2 = 17.33 \text{ A}, \quad I_3 = 15.33 \text{ A}$$

Therefore, the current in the 5 Ω resistor $= I_1 - I_3 = 20 - 15.33 = 4.67$ A

Problem 1.25 Determine the power delivered by the voltage source and the current in the 10 Ω resistor for the circuit.

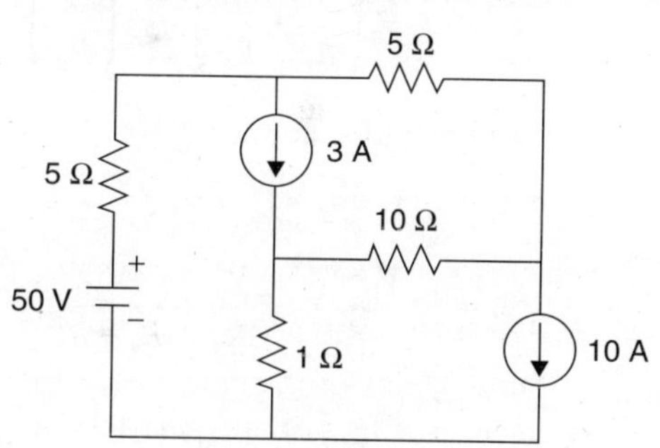

Solution:

Let us assume the mesh currents as I_1, I_2 and I_3.

Meshes 1 and 2 will form a supermesh, so by writing the current equation for supermesh, we have

$$I_1 - I_3 = 3 \quad (1)$$

Applying KVL to the outer path of the supermesh

$$50 - 5I_1 - 5I_2 - 10(I_2 - I_3) - 1(I_1 - I_3) = 0$$

$$6I_1 + 15I_2 - 11I_3 = 50 \quad (2)$$

From mesh 3, we have

$$I_3 = 10 \quad (3)$$

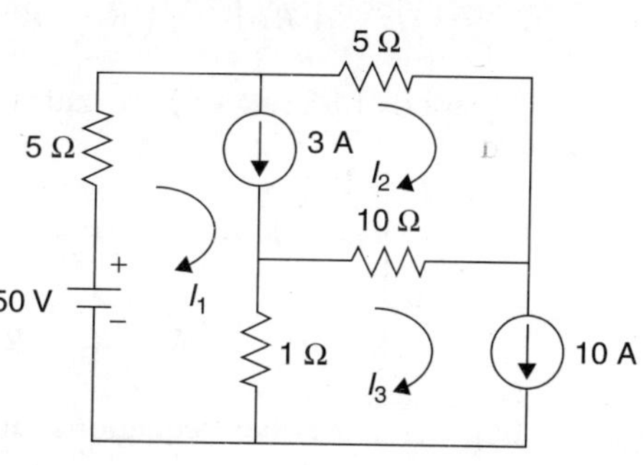

Solving Eqs (1), (2) and (3), we have

$$I_1 = 9.76 \text{ A}, \quad I_2 = 6.76 \text{ A}, \quad I_3 = 10 \text{ A}$$

Power delivered by the voltage source $= 50I_I = 50 \times 9.76 = 488$ W

Current in the 10 Ω resistor $= I_3 - I_2 = 10 - 6.76 = 3.24$ A

1.12.7 Nodal Analysis

A node is a point in a network common to two or more circuit elements. If three or more elements meet at a node, that node is called the *principle node*. A *node voltage* is the voltage of a given node with respect to one particular node, called the *reference node*, which we assume at zero potential. If the network has more current sources, nodal analysis is a useful method; mainly depends on KCL. An N node circuit will require $(N-1)$ unknown voltages and $(N-1)$ equations.

Steps to be followed in nodal analysis

- Identify all the nodes in the network and select node voltages.
- One of these nodes is taken as reference node, which is at zero potential.
- The node voltages are measured with respect to the reference node.
- Apply KCL at each node except for the reference node and apply Ohm's law to the branch currents.
- Solve the simultaneous equations for the unknown node voltages.
- Using these voltages, find any branch currents required.
- This method is easier if all the current sources are present. If there is any voltage source, convert it to a current source.

Consider the circuit (Fig. 1.29) which has three nodes, out of which one of the nodes is taken as a reference node. Let the other two node voltages be V_1 and V_2.

Applying KCL at node 1

$$I = I_1 + I_2$$

$$I = \frac{V_1}{R_1} + \frac{V_1 - V_2}{R_2}$$

$$V_1\left(\frac{1}{R_1} + \frac{1}{R_2}\right) - V_2\left(\frac{1}{R_2}\right) = I \qquad (1.56)$$

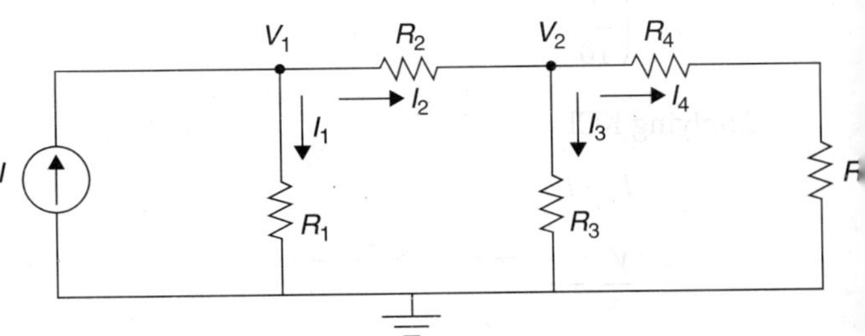

Fig. 1.29 Illustration of node voltage analysis

Applying KCL at node 2

$$I_2 = I_3 + I_4$$

$$\frac{V_1 - V_2}{R_2} = \frac{V_2}{R_3} + \frac{V_2}{R_4 + R_5}$$

$$-V_1\left(\frac{1}{R_2}\right) + V_2\left(\frac{1}{R_2} + \frac{1}{R_3} + \frac{1}{R_4 + R_5}\right) = 0 \qquad (1.57)$$

Equations 1.56 and 1.57 are rearranged in matrix form:

$$\begin{bmatrix} \frac{1}{R_1} + \frac{1}{R_2} & -\frac{1}{R_2} \\ -\frac{1}{R_2} & \frac{1}{R_2} + \frac{1}{R_3} + \frac{1}{R_4 + R_5} \end{bmatrix} \begin{bmatrix} V_1 \\ V_2 \end{bmatrix} = \begin{bmatrix} I_1 \\ 0 \end{bmatrix} \qquad (1.58)$$

In general, the above equations can be written as

$$\begin{bmatrix} G_{11} & -G_{12} \\ -G_{21} & G_{22} \end{bmatrix} \begin{bmatrix} V_1 \\ V_2 \end{bmatrix} = \begin{bmatrix} I_1 \\ I_2 \end{bmatrix} \qquad (1.59)$$

where, G_{11} = self conductance or sum of the conductances connected to node 1, G_{22} = self conductance or sum of the conductances connected to node 2, $G_{12} = G_{21}$ = sum of the mutual conductances connected to node 1 and 2. Here, all the mutual conductances have negative signs.

The currents I_1 and I_2 are the sum of the source currents at nodes 1 and 2 respectively. The current which drives into the node has a positive sign, while the current that drives away from the node has a negative sign.

Problem 1.26 Write the node voltage equations and determine the current in each branch for the network.

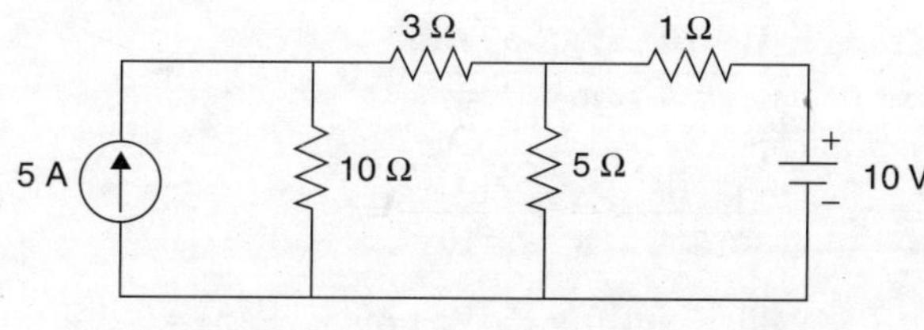

Solution:

Let us assume the node voltages as V_1 and V_2.

Applying KCL at node 1,

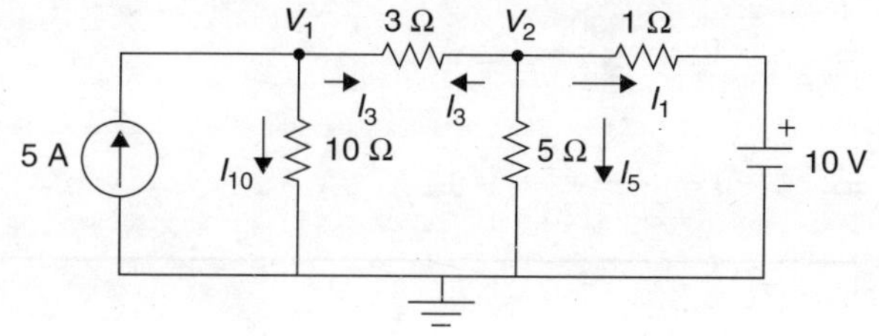

$$5 = I_{10} + I_3$$

$$5 = \frac{V_1}{10} + \frac{V_1 - V_2}{3}$$

$$\left(\frac{1}{10} + \frac{1}{3}\right)V_1 - \frac{V_2}{3} = 5 \qquad (1)$$

Applying KCL at node 2,

$$I_5 + I_3 + I_1 = 0$$

$$\frac{V_2}{5} + \frac{V_2 - V_1}{3} + \frac{V_2 - 10}{1} = 0$$

$$-\frac{V_1}{3} + \left(\frac{1}{3} + \frac{1}{5} + 1\right)V_2 = 10 \qquad (2)$$

Solving Eqs (1) and (2), we have

$$V_1 = 19.55 \text{ V}, \quad V_2 = 10.9 \text{ V}$$

The currents in various branches are as given below:

$$I_{10} = \frac{V_1}{10} = \frac{19.85}{10} = 1.985 \text{ A}$$

$$I_3 = \frac{V_1 - V_2}{3} = \frac{19.85 - 10.9}{3} = 2.98 \text{ A}$$

$$I_5 = \frac{V_2}{5} = \frac{10.9}{5} = 2.18 \text{ A}$$

$$I_1 = \frac{V_2 - 10}{1} = 10.9 - 10 = 0.9 \text{ A}$$

Problem 1.27 For the circuit, find the current through the 20 Ω resistor.

Solution:

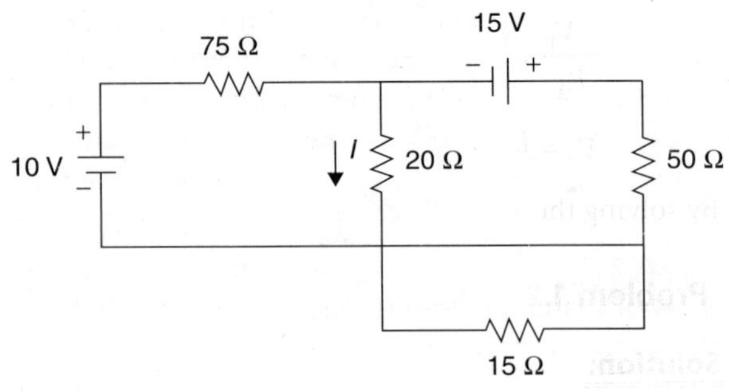

A resistance in parallel with a wire (that is, short circuit) will not have any effect on the circuit, so we can neglect that resistance. So, the above circuit can be redrawn as shown below.

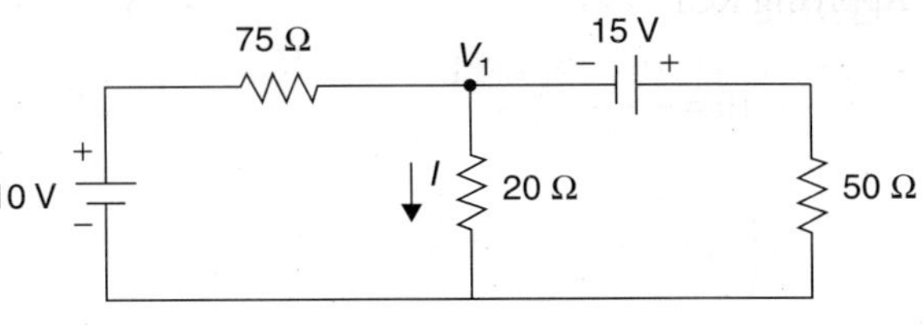

Applying KCL at node 1

$$\frac{V_1-10}{75}+\frac{V_1}{20}+\frac{V_1+15}{50}=0$$

$$\Rightarrow \quad \frac{V_1-10}{15}+\frac{V_1}{4}+\frac{V_1+15}{10}=0$$

$$40(V_1-10)+150V_1+60(V_1+15)=0$$

$$40V_1+150V_1+60V_1=400-900=-500$$

$$\Rightarrow \quad V_1=\frac{-500}{250}=-2\text{ V}$$

$$\Rightarrow \quad I=\frac{V_1}{20}=\frac{-2}{20}=-0.1\text{ A}$$

1.12.8 Supernode Analysis

If a network has a single voltage source in any branch, then it is slightly difficult to apply nodal analysis. This difficulty can be overcome by using *supernode analysis*. In this method, the two adjacent nodes that are connected by a voltage source are reduced to a single node and then the equations are formed as usual by applying KCL.

Consider the circuit in Fig. 1.30. Here, the voltage source V_k is in the common boundary for the two nodes (1) and (2). This voltage source creates a supernode, which is nothing but a combination of nodes (1) and (2).

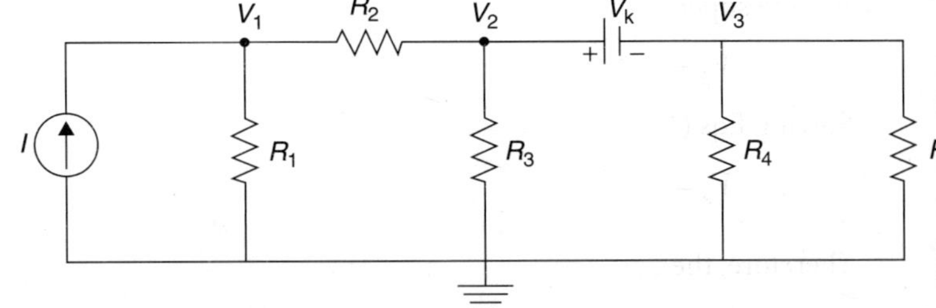

Fig. 1.30 Illustration of supernode voltage analysis

Applying KCL at node 1

$$I=\frac{V_1}{R_1}+\frac{V_1-V_2}{R_2}$$

$$V_1\left(\frac{1}{R_1}+\frac{1}{R_2}\right)-V_2\left(\frac{1}{R_2}\right)=I \tag{1.60}$$

Due to the presence of the voltage source V_k between nodes 2 and 3, it is slightly difficult to find out the current. The super node technique can be conveniently applied in this case. Accordingly, we can write the combined equations for nodes 2 and 3 as given below:

$$\frac{V_2-V_1}{R_2}+\frac{V_2}{R_3}+\left(\frac{1}{R_4}+\frac{1}{R_5}\right)V_3=0$$

$$\frac{-V_1}{R_2}+\left(\frac{1}{R_2}+\frac{1}{R_3}\right)V_2+\left(\frac{1}{R_4}+\frac{1}{R_5}\right)V_3=0 \quad (1.61)$$

$$V_2-V_3=V_k \quad (1.62)$$

By solving the above three equations, we can get the values of I_1, I_2 and I_3.

Problem 1.28 Determine the current in the 5 Ω resistor for the circuit.

Solution:

Applying KCL at node 1

$$10=\frac{V_1}{3}+\frac{V_1-V_2}{2}$$

$$\left(\frac{1}{2}+\frac{1}{3}\right)V_1-\frac{V_2}{2}=10 \quad (1)$$

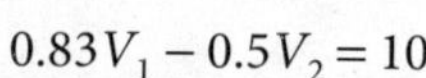

$$0.83V_1-0.5V_2=10$$

Nodes 2 and 3 form a supernode, so

$$\frac{V_2-V_1}{2}+\frac{V_2}{1}+\frac{V_3-10}{5}+\frac{V_3}{2}=0$$

$$-\frac{V_1}{2}+\left(\frac{1}{2}+1\right)V_2+\left(\frac{1}{5}+\frac{1}{2}\right)V_3=0$$

$$-0.5V_1+1.5V_2+0.7V_3=0 \quad (2)$$

For the supernode,

$$V_2-V_3=20 \quad (3)$$

Solving Eqs (1), (2) and (3), we have

$$V_3=-8.42\text{ V}$$

Therefore, the current in the 5 Ω resistor $=\frac{V_3-10}{5}=\frac{-8.82-10}{5}=-3.68$ A

Problem 1.29 Find the node voltages V_1, V_2 and V_3 for the circuit.

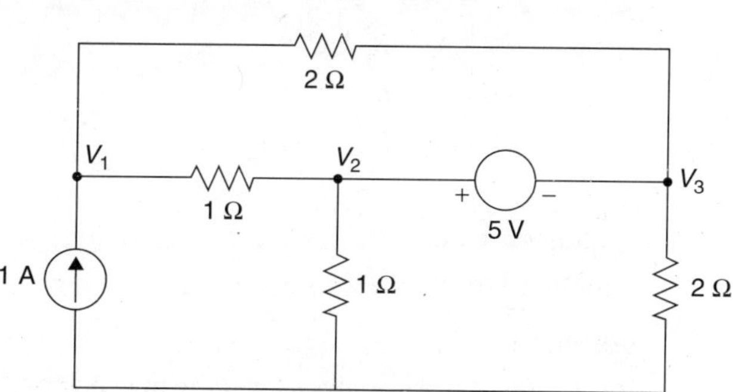

Solution:

Applying KCL at node 1

$$1=\frac{V_1-V_2}{1}+\frac{V_1-V_3}{2}$$

$$3V_1-2V_2-V_3=2 \quad (1)$$

The combination of nodes 2 and 3 forms a supernode, so these two nodes are taken as a single node. So writing KCL for this supernode

$$\frac{V_2 - V_1}{1} + \frac{V_2}{1} + \frac{V_3 - V_1}{2} + \frac{V_3}{2} = 0$$

$$-3V_1 + 4V_2 + 2V_3 = 0 \tag{2}$$

From the supernode, we have

$$V_2 - V_3 = 5 \tag{3}$$

Solving Eqs (1), (2) and (3), we have

$$V_1 = 1.333 \text{ V}, \quad V_2 = 2.333 \text{ V}, \quad V_3 = -2.667 \text{ V}$$

1.13 SOLUTION OF MESH AND NODAL EQUATIONS

The mesh or nodal equations have to be solved for finding loop currents or node voltages as the case may be. These equations are algebraic equations of the form [A][X] = [B], where [X] is unknown. Cramer's rule is a simple method used for solving these equations. It is also known as *method of determinants.*

Consider the equations

$$A_1x + B_1y + C_1z = D_1$$

$$A_2x + B_2y + C_2z = D_2$$

$$A_3x + B_3y + C_3z = D_3$$

The above equations can be written matrix form as

$$\begin{bmatrix} A_1 & B_1 & C_1 \\ A_2 & B_2 & C_2 \\ A_3 & B_3 & C_3 \end{bmatrix} \begin{bmatrix} x \\ y \\ z \end{bmatrix} = \begin{bmatrix} D_1 \\ D_2 \\ D_3 \end{bmatrix} \tag{1.63}$$

Using Cramer's rule x, y and z are obtained as

$$x = \frac{\Delta_1}{\Delta}, \quad y = \frac{\Delta_2}{\Delta}, \quad z = \frac{\Delta_3}{\Delta}$$

Where $\Delta_1 = \begin{vmatrix} D_1 & B_1 & C_1 \\ D_2 & B_2 & C_2 \\ D_3 & B_3 & C_3 \end{vmatrix}, \Delta_2 = \begin{vmatrix} A_1 & D_1 & C_1 \\ A_2 & D_2 & C_2 \\ A_3 & D_3 & C_3 \end{vmatrix}, \Delta_3 = \begin{vmatrix} A_1 & B_1 & D_1 \\ A_2 & B_2 & D_2 \\ A_3 & B_3 & D_3 \end{vmatrix}$

$$\Delta = \begin{vmatrix} A_1 & B_1 & C_1 \\ A_2 & B_2 & C_2 \\ A_3 & B_3 & C_3 \end{vmatrix}$$

Problem 1.30 Determine the mesh currents I_1, I_2 and I_3 in the circuit.

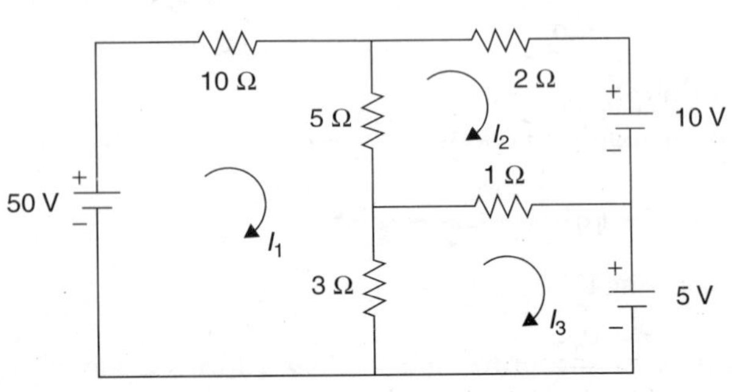

Solution:

Inspection of mesh analysis gives the matrix loop equation as:

$$\begin{bmatrix} 18 & -5 & -3 \\ -5 & 8 & -1 \\ -3 & -1 & 4 \end{bmatrix} \begin{bmatrix} I_1 \\ I_2 \\ I_3 \end{bmatrix} = \begin{bmatrix} 50 \\ -10 \\ -5 \end{bmatrix}$$

$$\Delta = \begin{vmatrix} 18 & -5 & -3 \\ -5 & 8 & -1 \\ -3 & -1 & 4 \end{vmatrix} = 18(32-1) + 5(-20-3) - 3(5+24) = 356$$

$$\Delta_1 = \begin{vmatrix} 50 & -5 & -3 \\ -10 & 8 & -1 \\ -5 & -1 & 4 \end{vmatrix} = 50(32-1) + 5(-40-5) - 3(10+40) = 1175$$

$$\Delta_2 = \begin{vmatrix} 18 & 50 & -3 \\ -5 & -10 & -1 \\ -3 & -5 & 4 \end{vmatrix} = 18(-40-5) - 50(-20-3) - 3(25-30) = 355$$

$$\Delta_3 = \begin{vmatrix} 18 & -5 & 50 \\ -5 & 8 & -10 \\ -3 & -1 & -5 \end{vmatrix} = 18(-40-10) + 5(25-30) + 50(5+24) = 525$$

Using Cramer's rule, the mesh currents are

$$I_1 = \frac{\Delta_1}{\Delta} = \frac{1175}{356} = 3.3 \text{ A}$$

$$I_2 = \frac{\Delta_2}{\Delta} = \frac{355}{356} = 0.997 \text{ A}$$

$$I_3 = \frac{\Delta_3}{\Delta} = \frac{525}{356} = 1.474 \text{ A}$$

Problem 1.31 Find the node voltages V_1, V_2 and V_3 in the network and hence determine the current I_x.

Solution:

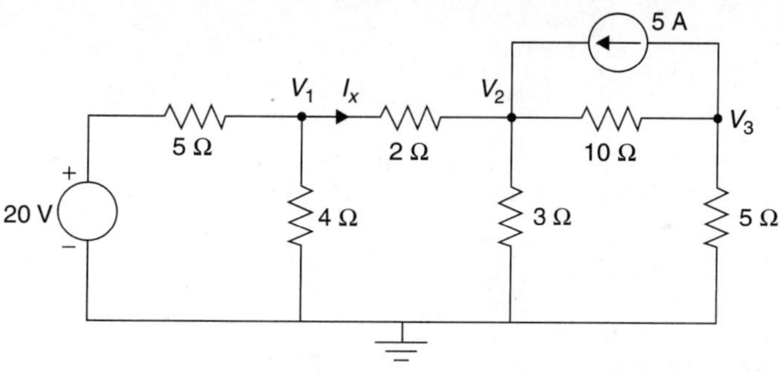

Applying KCL at node 1

$$\frac{V_1 - 20}{5} + \frac{V_1 - V_2}{2} + \frac{V_1}{4} = 0$$

$$\left(\frac{1}{5} + \frac{1}{2} + \frac{1}{4}\right)V_1 - \frac{V_2}{2} = 4$$

$$19V_1 - 10V_2 = 80 \qquad (1)$$

Applying KCL at node 2

$$\frac{V_2 - V_1}{2} + \frac{V_2}{3} + \frac{V_2 - V_3}{10} - 5 = 0$$

$$-\frac{V_1}{2}+\left(\frac{1}{2}+\frac{1}{3}+\frac{1}{10}\right)V_2-\frac{V_3}{10}=5$$

$$-15V_1+28V_2-3V_3=150 \tag{2}$$

Applying KCL at node 3

$$\frac{V_3-V_2}{10}+\frac{V_3}{5}+5=0$$

$$-V_2+3V_3=-50 \tag{3}$$

The above three equations can be written in the matrix form as given below:

$$\begin{bmatrix} 19 & -10 & 0 \\ -15 & 28 & -3 \\ 0 & -1 & 3 \end{bmatrix}\begin{bmatrix} V_1 \\ V_2 \\ V_3 \end{bmatrix}=\begin{bmatrix} 80 \\ 150 \\ -50 \end{bmatrix}$$

$$\Delta=\begin{vmatrix} 19 & -10 & 0 \\ -15 & 28 & -3 \\ 0 & -1 & 3 \end{vmatrix}=19(81)+10(-45)-0(15)=1089$$

$$\Delta_1=\begin{vmatrix} 80 & -10 & 0 \\ 150 & 28 & -3 \\ -50 & -1 & 3 \end{vmatrix}=80(81)+10(300)-0(1250)=9480$$

$$\Delta_2=\begin{vmatrix} 19 & 80 & 0 \\ -15 & 150 & -3 \\ 0 & -150 & 3 \end{vmatrix}=19(300)-80(-45)-=9300$$

$$\Delta_3=\begin{vmatrix} 19 & -10 & 80 \\ -15 & 28 & 150 \\ 0 & -1 & -50 \end{vmatrix}=19(-1250)+10(750)-80(15)=-15050$$

Using Cramer's rule, the node voltages are

$$V_1=\frac{\Delta_1}{\Delta}=\frac{9480}{1089}=8.7\text{ V}$$

$$V_2=\frac{\Delta_2}{\Delta}=\frac{9300}{1089}=8.54\text{ V}$$

$$V_3=\frac{\Delta_3}{\Delta}=\frac{-15050}{1089}=-13.82\text{ V}$$

$$I_x=\frac{V_1-V_2}{2}=\frac{8.7-8.54}{2}=0.0826\text{ A}$$

ADDITIONAL SOLVED PROBLEMS

1.1 Find the current and power supplied by the battery to the circuit, in the following cases

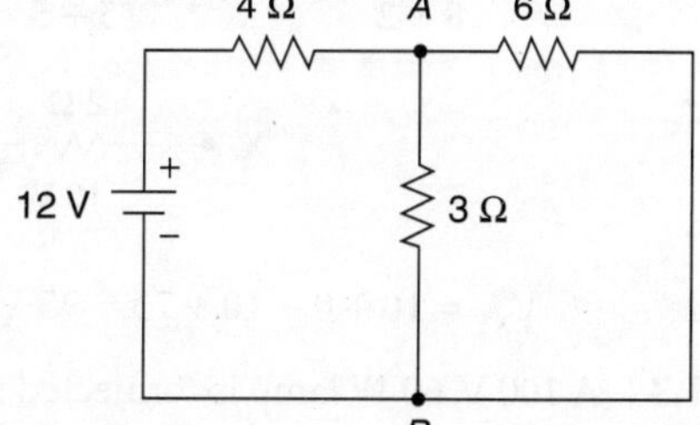

(i) Under normal condition.
(ii) When a short circuit occurs between terminals A–B.

Solution:

(i) Under normal condition

$$R_{eq} = 4 + \frac{6 \times 3}{6+3} = 4 + 2 = 6\,\Omega$$

$\therefore$ Current supplied by the source or battery, $I = \frac{V}{R_{eq}} = \frac{12}{6} = 2$ A

Power supplied by the battery, $P = VI = 12 \times 2 = 24$ W

(ii) When a short circuit occurs between terminals A–B

When there is a short circuit across any resistor, that resistor should be ignored. Therefore, the given circuit can be reduced to following form

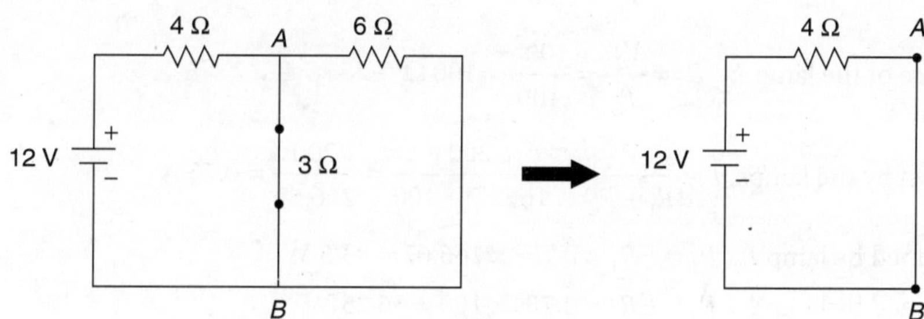

$\therefore$ Current supplied by the source or battery, $I = \frac{V}{R} = \frac{12}{4} = 3$ A

Power supplied by the battery, $P = VI = 12 \times 3 = 36$ W

1.2 Obtain the potential difference V_{XY} in the circuit using Kirchhoff's laws.

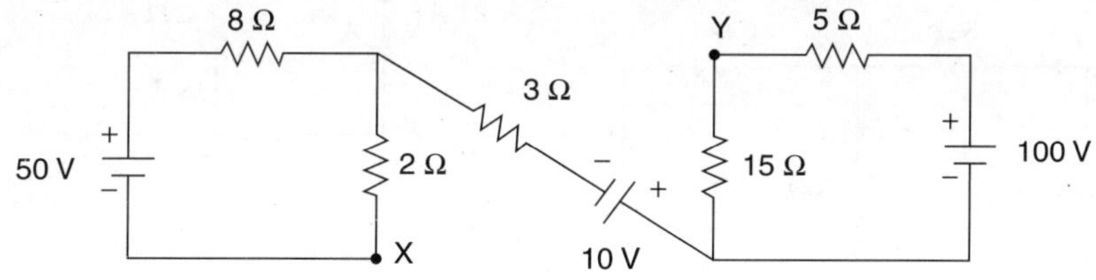

Solution: Given that

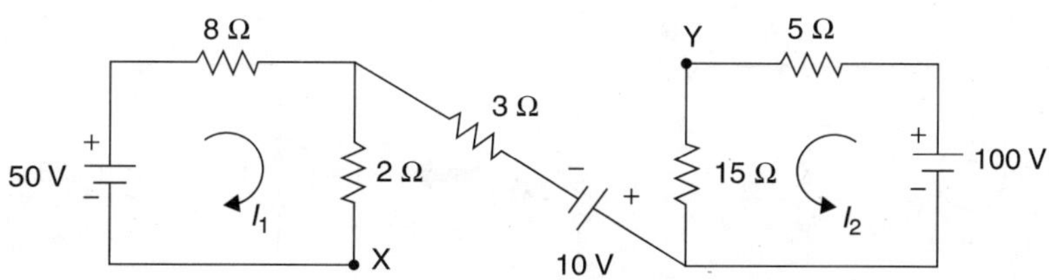

From the above circuit

$$I_1 = \frac{50}{8+2} = 5\text{ A}\,;\; I_2 = \frac{100}{15+5} = 5\text{ A}$$

$$V_{XY} = 10 + 0 + 10 + 75 = 95\text{ V}$$

1.3 A 100 V, 60 W lamp is connected in series with a 100 V, 100 W lamp across 200 V supply. What will be the current drawn by the lamps? What will be the power consumed by each lamp and will such a combination work?

Solution: The network diagram for the given system can be drawn as follows:

$V_1 = 100$ V, $P_1 = 60$ W

$V_2 = 100$ V, $P_2 = 100$ W

Supply voltage, $V = 200$ V

$$\text{Resistance of the lamp } L_1,\; R_1 = \frac{V_1^2}{P_1} = \frac{100^2}{60} = 166.67\ \Omega$$

$$\text{Resistance of the lamp } L_2,\; R_2 = \frac{V_2^2}{P_2} = \frac{100^2}{100} = 100\ \Omega$$

(i) Current drawn by the lamps, $I = \dfrac{V}{R_1 + R_2} = \dfrac{200}{166.67 + 100} = \dfrac{200}{266.67} = 0.75$ A

(ii) Power consumed by lamp L_1, $P_1 = I^2R_1 = 0.75^2 \times 166.67 = 93.5$ W

Power consumed by lamp L_2, $P_2 = I^2R_2 = 0.75^2 \times 100 = 56.25$ W

If a 100 V, 60 W lamp is connected, then it draws a power of 93.75 W, so its filament will get overheated and as a result it will burn out. So, this combination doesn't work.

1.4 Determine the current through the 6 Ω resistor and power supplied by the current source for the circuit.

Solution: Given that

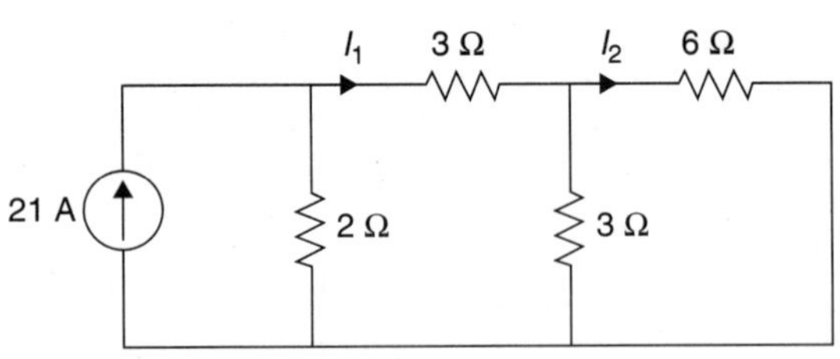

The above circuit can be reduced to following form

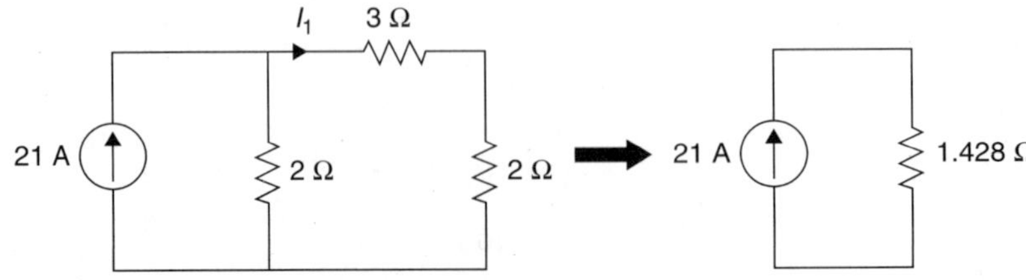

According to current division rule

$$I_1 = 21 \times \frac{2}{2+(3+2)} = 21 \times \frac{2}{7} = 6\text{ A}$$

$$I_2 = I_1 \times \frac{3}{3+6} = 6 \times \frac{3}{9} = 2\text{ A}$$

The current through 6 Ω resistor, $I_2 = 2$ A

Power supplied by the current source $= 21^2 \times 1.428 = 629.75$ watts

1.5 A resistor R is connected in series with two lamps of 12 V, 9 W across 220 V supply. Find the value of R so that both the lamps operate at the rated conditions. If one lamp is short circuited, find the current through the circuit and power dissipated in each lamp and the resistance R.

Solution: The network diagram for the given system can be drawn as follows:

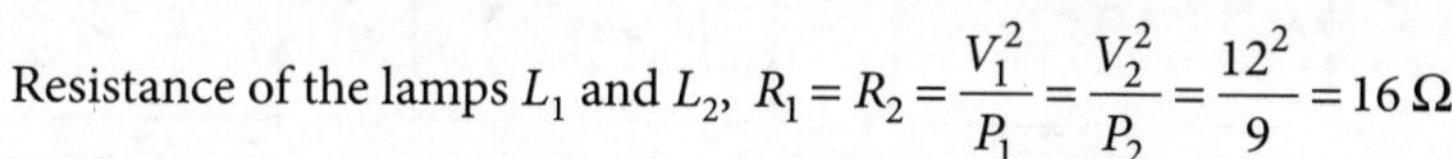

$V_1 = 12$ V, $P_1 = 9$ W

$V_2 = 12$ V, $P_2 = 9$ W

Supply voltage, $V = 200$ V

Rated current of the lamps L_1 and L_2, $I = \frac{P_1}{V} = \frac{9}{12} = 0.75$ A

Resistance of the lamps L_1 and L_2, $R_1 = R_2 = \frac{V_1^2}{P_1} = \frac{V_2^2}{P_2} = \frac{12^2}{9} = 16\ \Omega$

Voltage across the resistor R, $V_3 = 220 - 12 - 12 = 196$ V

(i) The value of resistance, $R = \frac{V_3}{I} = \frac{196}{0.75} = 261.33\ \Omega$

(ii) Current through the circuit, if the lamp L_1 is short circuited: If the lamp L_1 is short circuited, resistance across the terminals of L_1 is zero, so the new current through the circuit is

$$I' = \frac{V}{R_1 + R_2 + R_3} = \frac{220}{0 + 16 + 261.33} = \frac{220}{277.33} = 0.7933\text{ A}$$

(iii) Power dissipated in each lamp if the lamp L_1 is short circuited:

Power dissipated in lamp L_1, $P_1 = I'^2 R_1 = 0.7993^2 \times 0 = 0$ W

Power dissipated in lamp L_2, $P_2 = I'^2 R_2 = 0.7933^2 \times 16 = 10.07$ W

Power dissipated in resistance R, $P_R = I'^2 R = 0.7933^2 \times 261.33 = 164.46$ W

1.6 Find the current delivered by the 12 V source.

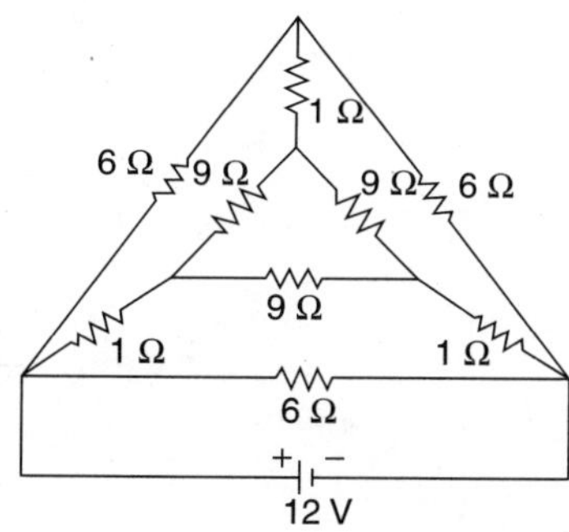

Solution: Convert the inner delta (9 Ω delta) into an equivalent star.

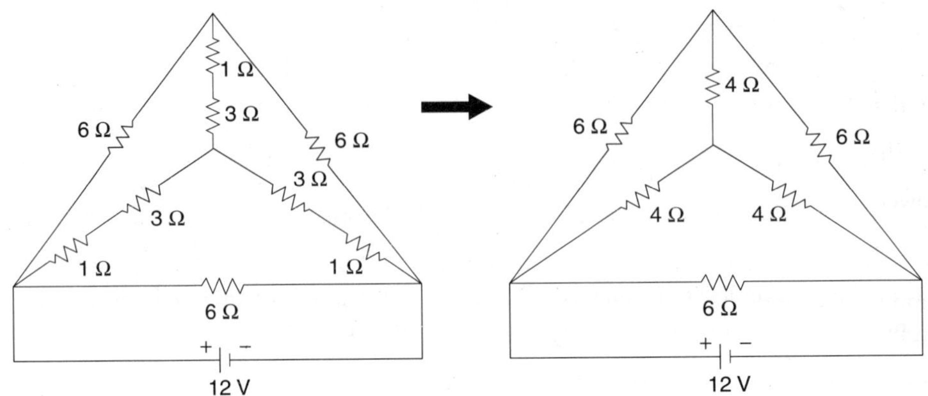

Convert the 4 Ω star into an equivalent delta.

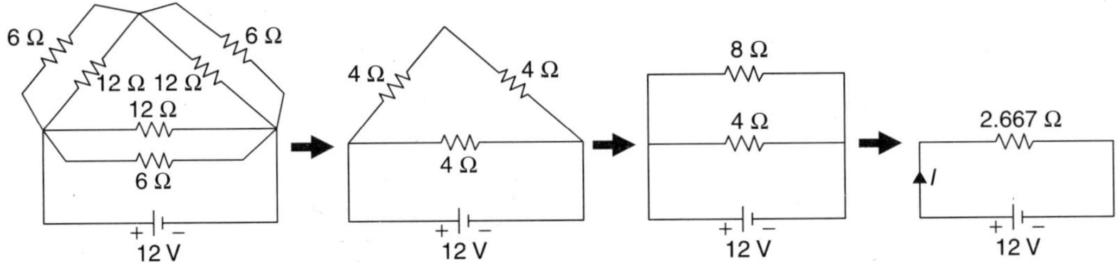

Current delivered by the source, $I = \dfrac{12}{2.667} = 4.5\text{ A}$

1.7 A circuit consisting of three resistances 12 Ω, 18 Ω and 36 Ω respectively joined in parallel is connected in series with a fourth resistance. The whole circuit is applied with 60 V and it is found that the power dissipated in the 12 Ω resistor is 36 W. Determine the value of the fourth resistance and the total power dissipated in the circuit.

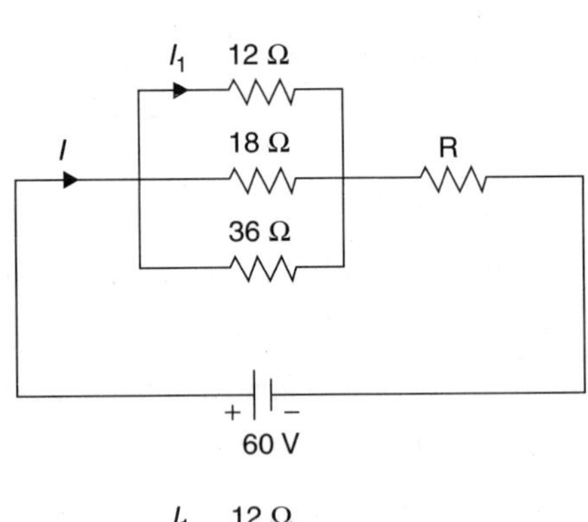

Solution: From the given data the circuit diagram can be drawn as shown on the right.

$$P_{12} = 36\text{ W}$$

$$I_1^2 \times 12 = 36 \Rightarrow I_1 = 1.732\text{ A}$$

The above circuit can be reduced to

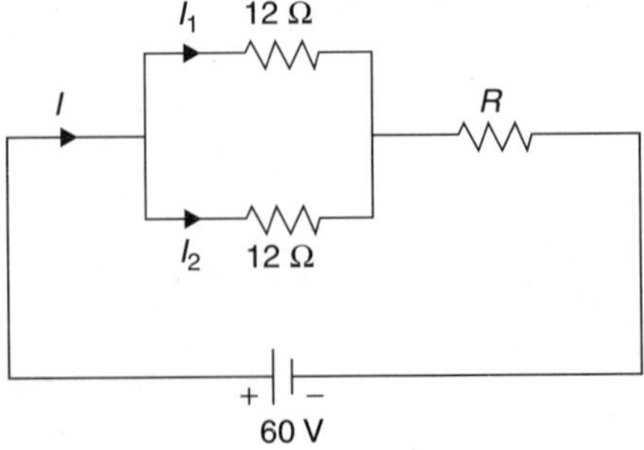

$$I_1 = I \times \frac{12}{12+12} = \frac{I}{2}$$

$$\Rightarrow \quad I = 2I_1 = 2 \times 1.732 = 3.464\text{ A}$$

Total current, $I = 3.464$ A

Total resistance of the circuit, $R_T = 6 + R$

$$R_T = \frac{60}{I} = \frac{60}{3.464} = 17.32$$

$\Rightarrow \quad R + 6 = 17.32$

$\Rightarrow \quad R = 17.32 - 6 = 11.32\ \Omega$

$\therefore$ The value of fourth resistance, $R = 11.32\ \Omega$

Total power dissipated in the circuit

$$P = VI = 60 \times 3.464 = 207.84\ \text{W}$$

1.8 Find the power delivered by the 60 V voltage source, using source transformation shown below.

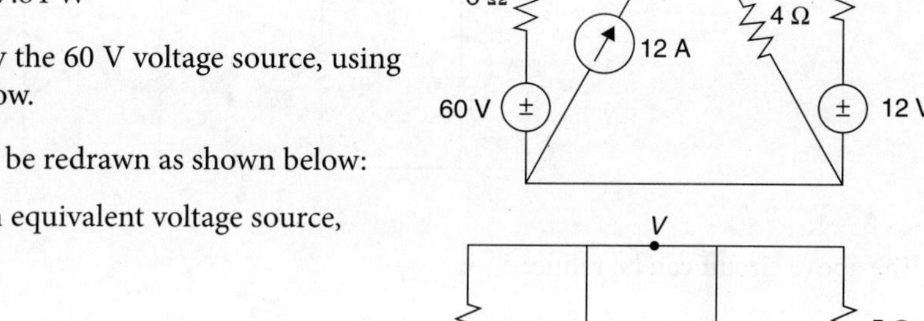

Solution: The given circuit can be redrawn as shown below:

Replacing the current source with equivalent voltage source, $= IR = 12 \times 4 = 48$ V

Applying KCL at node V,

$$\frac{V-60}{6} + \frac{V-48}{4} + \frac{V-12}{5} = 0$$

$$20V - 1200 + 30V - 1440 + 24V - 288 = 0$$

$$74V = 2928$$

$$V = 39.57 \text{ volts}$$

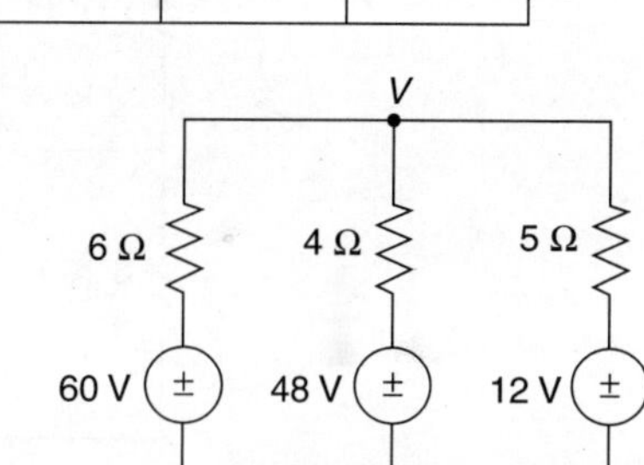

Current delivered by the 60 V voltage source, $I = \dfrac{60 - 39.57}{6} = 3.4$ A

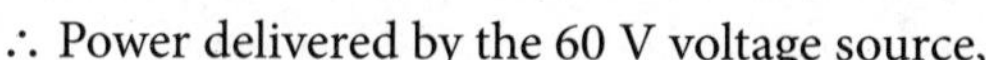

$\therefore$ Power delivered by the 60 V voltage source,

$$P = VI = 60 \times 3.4 = 204.3\ \text{W}$$

1.9 Using source transformation, reduce the network between A and B into an equivalent voltage source.

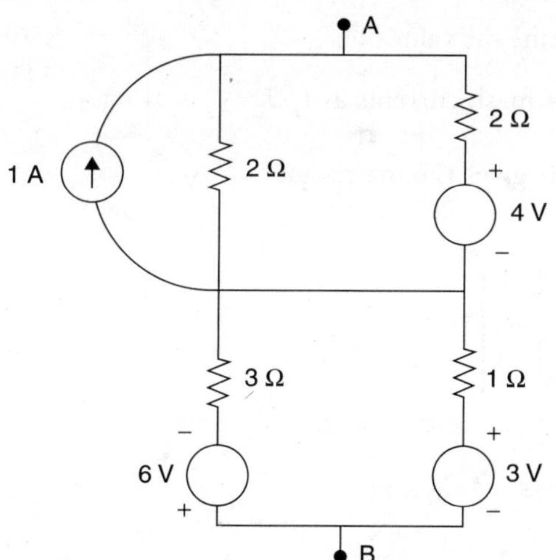

Solution: Using the source transformation technique, the voltage sources can be converted into equivalent current sources.

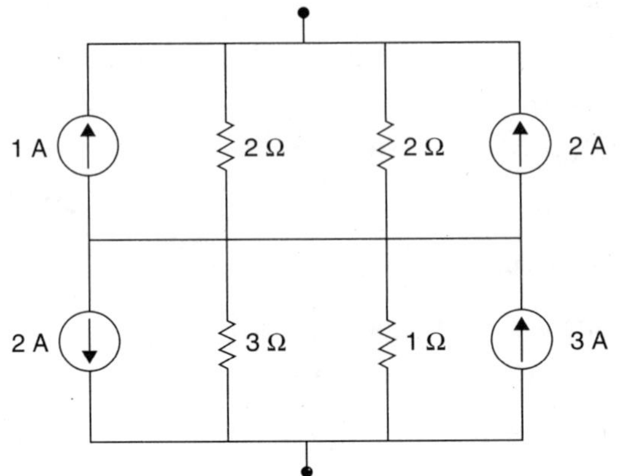

The above circuit can be reduced to:

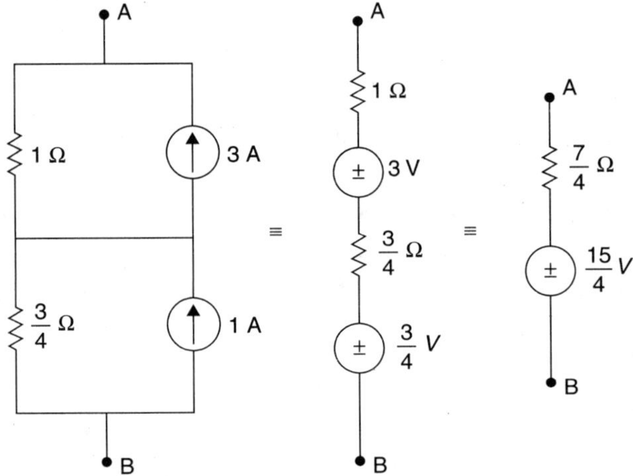

1.10 In the network, determine the value of i.

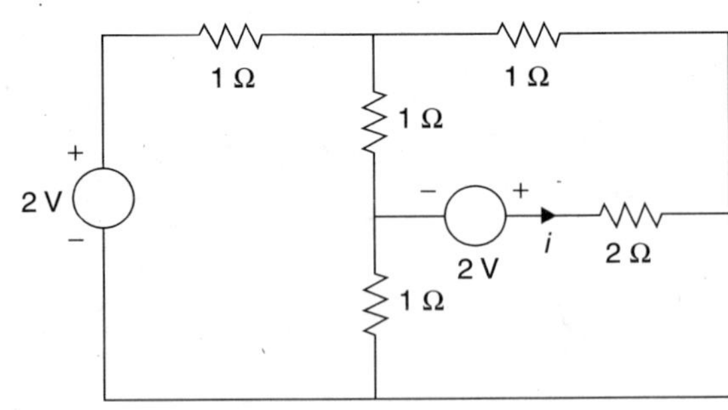

Solution: Let us assume the mesh currents as I_1, I_2 and I_3 as given below.

Inspection of mesh analysis gives the matrix loop equation as

$$\begin{bmatrix} 3 & -1 & -1 \\ -1 & 4 & -2 \\ -1 & -2 & 3 \end{bmatrix} \begin{bmatrix} I_1 \\ I_2 \\ I_3 \end{bmatrix} = \begin{bmatrix} 2 \\ -2 \\ 2 \end{bmatrix}$$

$$\Delta = \begin{vmatrix} 3 & -1 & -1 \\ -1 & 4 & -2 \\ -1 & -2 & 3 \end{vmatrix} = 24 - 5 - 6 = 13$$

$$\Delta_2 = \begin{vmatrix} 3 & 2 & -1 \\ -1 & -2 & -2 \\ -1 & 2 & 3 \end{vmatrix} = -6 + 10 + 4 = 8$$

$$\Delta_3 = \begin{vmatrix} 3 & -1 & 2 \\ -1 & 4 & -2 \\ -1 & -2 & 2 \end{vmatrix} = 12 - 4 + 12 = 20$$

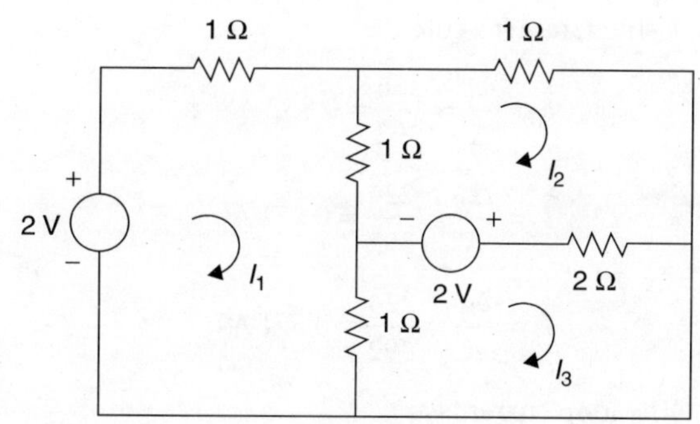

Using Cramer's rule

$$I_2 = \frac{\Delta_2}{\Delta} = \frac{8}{13} = 0.615 \text{ A}$$

$$I_3 = \frac{\Delta_3}{\Delta} = \frac{20}{13} = 1.538 \text{ A}$$

The value of current i is

$$i = I_3 - I_2 = 1.538 - 0.615 = 0.923 \text{ A}$$

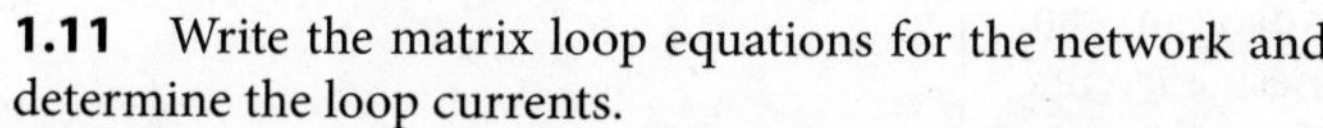

1.11 Write the matrix loop equations for the network and determine the loop currents.

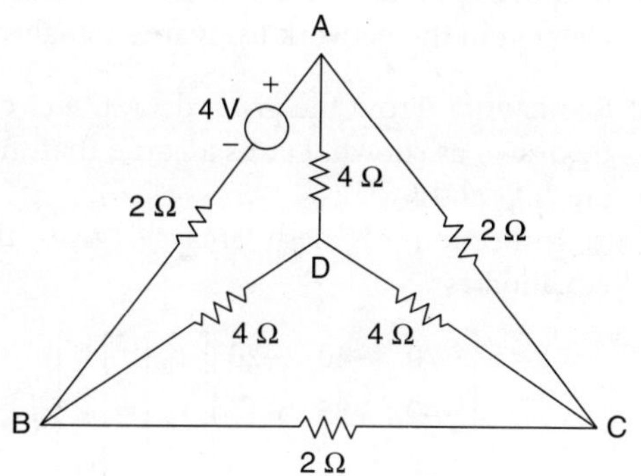

Solution: Let us assume the loop currents as I_1, I_2 and I_3.
Inspection of mesh analysis gives the matrix loop equation as

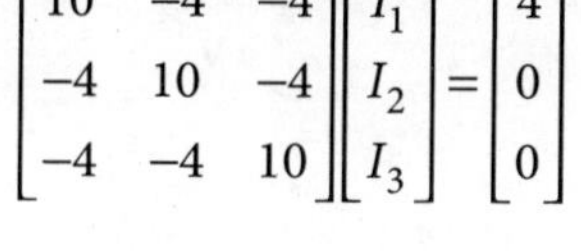

$$\begin{bmatrix} 10 & -4 & -4 \\ -4 & 10 & -4 \\ -4 & -4 & 10 \end{bmatrix} \begin{bmatrix} I_1 \\ I_2 \\ I_3 \end{bmatrix} = \begin{bmatrix} 4 \\ 0 \\ 0 \end{bmatrix}$$

$$\Delta = \begin{vmatrix} 10 & -4 & -4 \\ -4 & 10 & -4 \\ -4 & -4 & 10 \end{vmatrix} = 10(100 - 16) + 4(-40 - 16) - 4(16 + 40) = 392$$

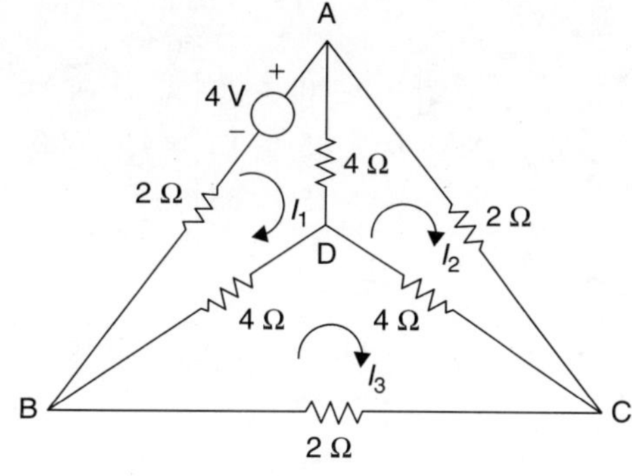

$$\Delta_1 = \begin{vmatrix} 4 & -4 & -4 \\ 0 & 10 & -4 \\ 0 & -4 & 10 \end{vmatrix} = 4(100 - 16) = 336$$

$$\Delta_2 = \begin{vmatrix} 10 & 4 & -4 \\ -4 & 0 & -4 \\ -4 & 0 & 10 \end{vmatrix} = -4(-40 - 16) = 224$$

$$\Delta_3 = \begin{vmatrix} 10 & -4 & 4 \\ -4 & 10 & 0 \\ -4 & -4 & 0 \end{vmatrix} = 4(16 + 40) = 224$$

Using Cramer's rule

$$I_1 = \frac{\Delta_1}{\Delta} = \frac{336}{392} = 0.857 \text{ A}$$

$$I_2 = \frac{\Delta_2}{\Delta} = \frac{224}{392} = 0.571 \text{ A}$$

$$I_3 = \frac{\Delta_3}{\Delta} = \frac{224}{392} = 0.571 \text{ A}$$

The loop currents are

$$I_1 = 0.857 \text{ A}, I_2 = 0.571\text{A}, I_3 = 0.571 \text{ A}$$

1.12 A bridge network ABCD is arranged as follows. Resistances between terminals AB, BC, CD, DA and BD are 10 Ω, 30 Ω, 15 Ω, 20 Ω and 40 Ω respectively. A 4 V battery is connected with negligible internal resistance between terminals A and C. Determine the current through each element in the network using mesh analysis.

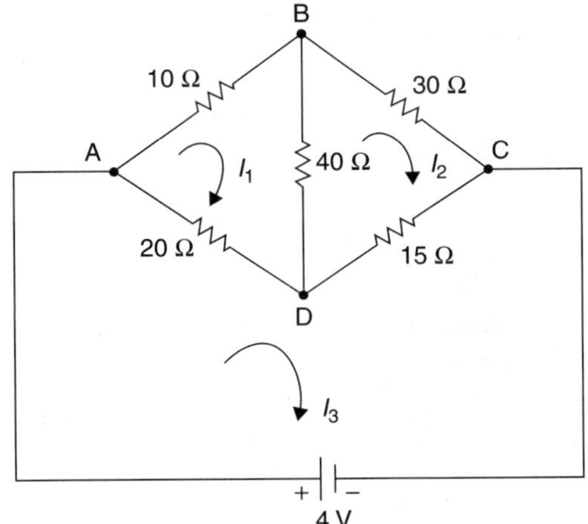

Solution: From the given data, the circuit diagram can be drawn as shown. Let us assume that the mesh currents are I_1, I_2 and I_3.

Inspection of mesh analysis gives the matrix loop equation as

$$\begin{bmatrix} 70 & -40 & -20 \\ -40 & 85 & -15 \\ -20 & -15 & 35 \end{bmatrix} \begin{bmatrix} I_1 \\ I_2 \\ I_3 \end{bmatrix} = \begin{bmatrix} 0 \\ 0 \\ 4 \end{bmatrix}$$

$$\Delta = \begin{vmatrix} 70 & -40 & -20 \\ -40 & 85 & -15 \\ -20 & -15 & 35 \end{vmatrix} = 70 \times 2750 - 40 \times 1700 - 20 \times 2300 = 78500$$

$$\Delta_1 = \begin{vmatrix} 0 & -40 & -20 \\ 0 & 85 & -15 \\ 4 & -15 & 35 \end{vmatrix} = 4 \times 2300 = 9200$$

$$\Delta_2 = \begin{vmatrix} 70 & 0 & -20 \\ -40 & 0 & -15 \\ -20 & 4 & 35 \end{vmatrix} = 4 \times 1850 = 7400$$

$$\Delta_3 = \begin{vmatrix} 70 & -40 & 0 \\ -40 & 85 & 0 \\ -20 & -15 & 4 \end{vmatrix} = 4 \times 4350 = 17400$$

Using Cramer's rule

$$I_1 = \frac{\Delta_1}{\Delta} = \frac{9240}{78500} = 0.118 \text{ A}$$

$$I_2 = \frac{\Delta_2}{\Delta} = \frac{7400}{78500} = 0.0938 \text{ A}$$

$$I_3 = \frac{\Delta_3}{\Delta} = \frac{17400}{78500} = 0.2216 \text{ A}$$

∴ Current through branch AB, $I_{AB} = I_1 = 0.118$ A

Current through branch BC, $I_{BC} = I_2 = 0.0938$ A

Current through branch CD, $I_{CD} = I_3 - I_2 = 0.127$ A

Current through branch DA, $I_{DA} = I_3 - I_1 = 0.1036$ A

Current through branch BD, IBD $= I_1 - I_2 = 0.0232$ A

1.13 For the network, determine the power dissipated in the 9 Ω resistor using mesh analysis.

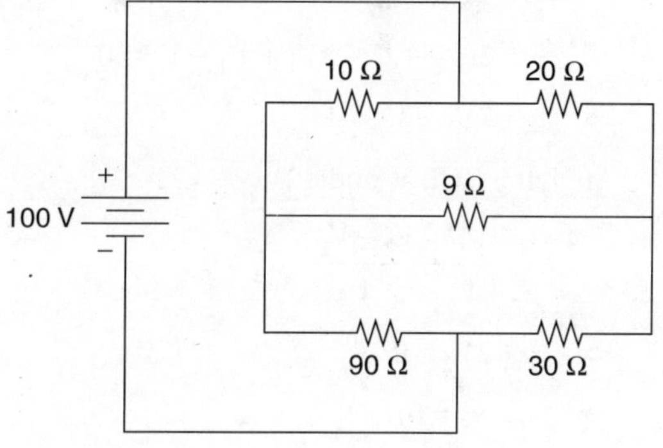

Solution: Let us assume that the mesh currents are I_1, I_2 and I_3.

Inspection of mesh analysis gives the matrix loop equation as

$$\begin{bmatrix} 100 & -10 & -90 \\ -10 & 39 & -9 \\ -90 & -9 & 129 \end{bmatrix} \begin{bmatrix} I_1 \\ I_2 \\ I_3 \end{bmatrix} = \begin{bmatrix} 100 \\ 0 \\ 0 \end{bmatrix}$$

$$\Delta = \begin{vmatrix} 100 & -10 & -90 \\ -10 & 39 & -9 \\ -90 & -9 & 129 \end{vmatrix} = 70 \times 4950 - 10 \times 2100 - 90 \times 3600 = 150000$$

$$\Delta_1 = \begin{vmatrix} 100 & -10 & -90 \\ 0 & 39 & -9 \\ 0 & -9 & 129 \end{vmatrix} = 100 \times 4950 = 495000$$

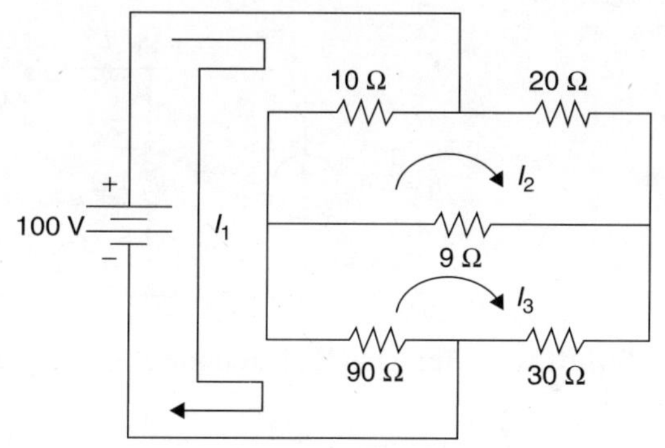

$$\Delta_2 = \begin{vmatrix} 100 & 100 & -90 \\ -10 & 0 & -9 \\ -90 & 0 & 129 \end{vmatrix} = 100 \times 2100 = 210000$$

$$\Delta_3 = \begin{vmatrix} 100 & -10 & 100 \\ -10 & 39 & 0 \\ -90 & -9 & 0 \end{vmatrix} = 100 \times 3600 = 360000$$

Using Cramer's rule

$$I_1 = \frac{\Delta_1}{\Delta} = \frac{495000}{150000} = 3.3 \text{ A}$$

$$I_2 = \frac{\Delta_2}{\Delta} = \frac{210000}{150000} = 1.4 \text{ A}$$

$$I_3 = \frac{\Delta_3}{\Delta} = \frac{360000}{150000} = 2.4 \text{ A}$$

Power dissipated in the 9 Ω resistor $= (I_3 - I_2)^2 \times 9 = (2.4 - 1.4)^2 \times 9 = 9$ W

1.14 Find the node voltages V_1 and V_2 for the circuit.

Solution: Applying KCL at node-1

$$\frac{V_1 - 2}{0.5} + \frac{V_1}{0.25} + \frac{V_1 - V_2}{1} = 0$$

$$2(V_1 - 2) + 4V_1 + V_1 - V_2 = 0$$

$$\Rightarrow \quad 7V_1 - V_2 = 4 \qquad (1)$$

Applying KCL at node-2

$$\frac{V_2}{1} + \frac{V_2 - V_1}{1} + V_1 = 0$$

$$\Rightarrow \quad 2V_2 = 0$$

$$\Rightarrow \quad V_2 = 0 \qquad (2)$$

Solving Eqs (1) and (2), we have

$$V_1 = 0.57 \text{ V}, \quad V_2 = 0 \text{ V}$$

1.15 For the network, determine the node voltages V_1 and V_2. Determine the power dissipated in each resistor.

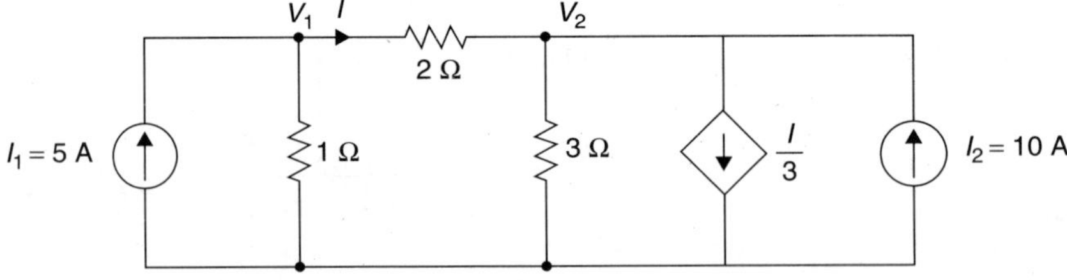

Solution: Applying KCL at node 1

$$\frac{V_1}{1} + \frac{V_1 - V_2}{2} = 5$$

$$\Rightarrow \quad 3V_1 - V_2 = 10 \qquad (1)$$

Applying KCL at node 2

$$\frac{V_2}{3} + \frac{V_2 - V_1}{2} + \frac{I}{3} = 10$$

$$\Rightarrow \qquad -3V_1 + 5V_2 = 60 - 2I \qquad (2)$$

Also

$$\frac{V_1 - V_2}{2} = I \qquad (3)$$

From Eqs (2) and (3),

$$-3V_1 + 5V_2 = 60 - (V_1 - V_2)$$

$$-V_1 + 2V_2 = 30 \qquad (4)$$

$$6V_1 - 2V_2 = 20 \text{ [Eq. (1)} \times 2]$$

From the above two equations

$$5V_1 = 50 \Rightarrow V_1 = 10 \text{ V}$$

From Eq. (1), $V_2 = 3V_1 - 10 = 30 - 10 = 20$ V

$\therefore$ The node voltages are $V_1 = 10$ V, $V_2 = 20$ V

Power dissipated in the 1 Ω resistor $= \dfrac{V_1^2}{1} = \dfrac{10^2}{1} = 100$ W

Power dissipated in the 2 Ω resistor $= \dfrac{(V_1 - V_2)^2}{2} = \dfrac{(10 - 20)^2}{2} = 50$ W

Power dissipated in 3 Ω resistor $= \dfrac{V_2^2}{3} = \dfrac{20^2}{3} = 133.33$ W

1.16 Find the node voltages V_1 and V_2 for the circuit.

Solution: Applying KCL at node 1

$$\frac{V_1}{1} + V_1 + \frac{V_1 - V_2}{2} = 5$$

$$2.5V_1 - 0.5V_2 = 5$$

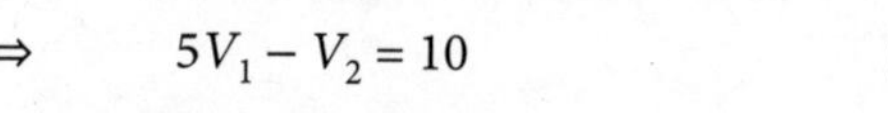

$$\Rightarrow \qquad 5V_1 - V_2 = 10 \qquad (1)$$

Applying KCL at node 2

$$\frac{V_2}{1} + \frac{V_2 - V_1}{2} - V_1 + 2I_1 = 0$$

$$\Rightarrow \qquad -1.5V_1 + 1.5V_2 = -2I_1 \qquad (2)$$

From the circuit diagram

$$\frac{V_1 - V_2}{2} = I_1$$

$$V_1 - V_2 = 2I_1 \qquad (3)$$

From Eqs (2) and (3), we have

$$-1.5V_1 + 1.5V_2 = -V_1 + V_2$$

$$\Rightarrow \quad V_1 - V_2 = 0 \qquad (4)$$

Solving Eqs (1) and (4), we have

$$V_1 = 2.5 \text{ V}, \quad V_2 = 2.5 \text{ V}$$

1.17 Find the currents I_1 and I_2 in the circuit using nodal analysis.

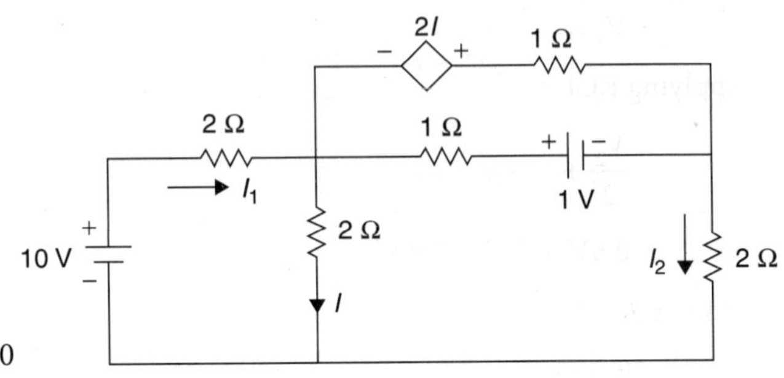

Solution: Let us assume the node voltages as V_1 and V_2.

Applying KCL at node 1

$$\frac{V_1 - 10}{2} + \frac{V_1}{2} + \frac{V_1 - 1 - V_2}{1} + \frac{V_1 + 2I - V_2}{1} = 0$$

$$\Rightarrow \quad 3V_1 - 2V_2 = 6 - 2I \qquad (1)$$

Applying KCL at node 2

$$\frac{V_2}{2} + \frac{V_2 + 1 - V_1}{1} + \frac{V_2 - 2I - V_1}{1} = 0$$

$$\Rightarrow \quad -2V_1 + 2.5V_2 = 2I - 1 \qquad (2)$$

From the circuit diagram

$$I = \frac{V_1}{2}$$

$$\Rightarrow \quad 2I = V_1 \qquad (3)$$

From Eqs (1) and (3), we have

$$3V_1 - 2V_2 = 6 - V_1$$

$$\Rightarrow \quad 4V_1 - 2V_2 = 6$$

$$\Rightarrow \quad 2V_1 - V_2 = 3 \qquad (4)$$

From Eqs (2) and (3), we have

$$-2V_1 + 2.5V_2 = V_1 - 1$$

$$\Rightarrow \quad 3V_1 - 2.5V_2 = 1 \qquad (5)$$

Solving Eqs (4) and (5), we have

$$V_1 = 3.25 \text{ V}, \quad V_2 = 3.5 \text{ V}$$

$$\therefore \quad I_1 = \frac{10 - V_1}{2} = \frac{10 - 3.25}{2} = 3.375 \text{ A}$$

$$I_2 = \frac{V_2}{2} = \frac{3.5}{2} = 1.75 \text{ A}$$

1.18 Find the currents I_1 and I_2 and V in the circuit using nodal analysis.

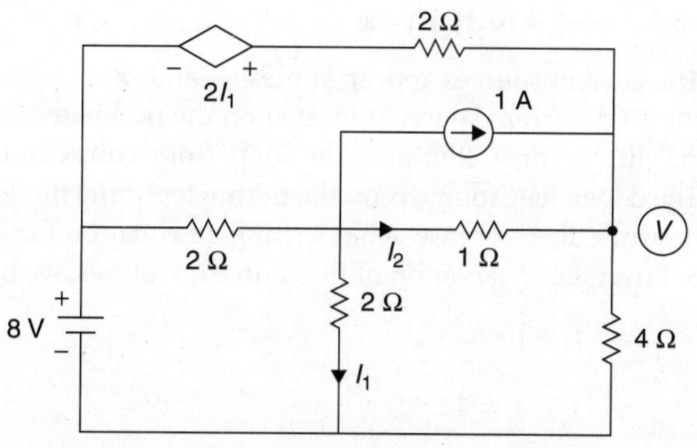

Solution: Let us assume the node voltages as V_1, V_2 and V.

From the above circuit diagram

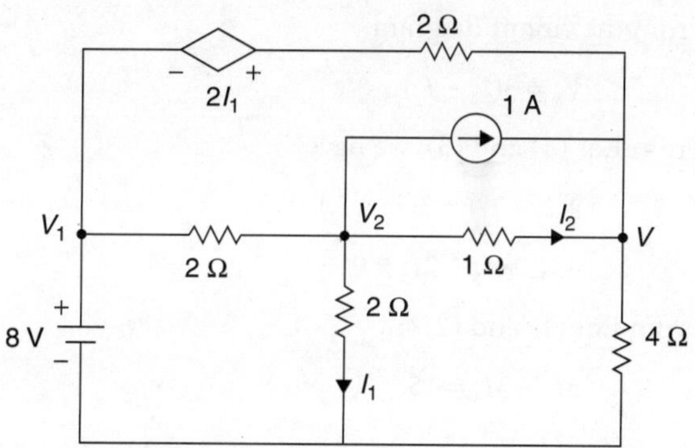

$$V_1 = 8 \quad (1)$$

Applying KCL at node 2

$$\frac{V_2}{2} + \frac{V_2 - V_1}{2} + \frac{V_2 - V}{1} + 1 = 0$$

$$\Rightarrow \quad 0.5V_1 - 2V_2 + V = 1 \quad (2)$$

From Eqs (1) and (2), we have

$$0.5 \times 8 - 2V_2 + V = 1$$

$$\Rightarrow \quad 2V_2 - V = 3 \quad (3)$$

Applying KCL at node 2

$$\frac{V}{4} + \frac{V - V_2}{1} + \frac{V - 2I_1 - V_1}{2} - 1 = 0$$

$$\Rightarrow \quad -V_2 + 1.75\text{ V} - I_1 = 5 \quad (4)$$

But from the circuit

$$I_1 = \frac{V_2}{2} = 0.5\,V_2 \quad (5)$$

From Eqs (4) and (5), we have

$$-V_2 + 1.75V - 0.5V_2 = 5$$

$$\Rightarrow \quad -1.5V_2 + 1.75V = 5 \quad (6)$$

Solving Eqs (3) and (6), we have

$$V_2 = 5.125, \quad V = 7.25$$

$$\therefore \quad I_1 = 0.5V_2 = 2.5625\text{ A}$$

$$I_2 = \frac{V_2 - V}{1} = \frac{5.125 - 7.25}{1} = -2.125\text{ A}$$

$$V = 7.25\text{ V}$$

1.19 Using the loop method of analysis, determine the current in the 2 Ω resistor.

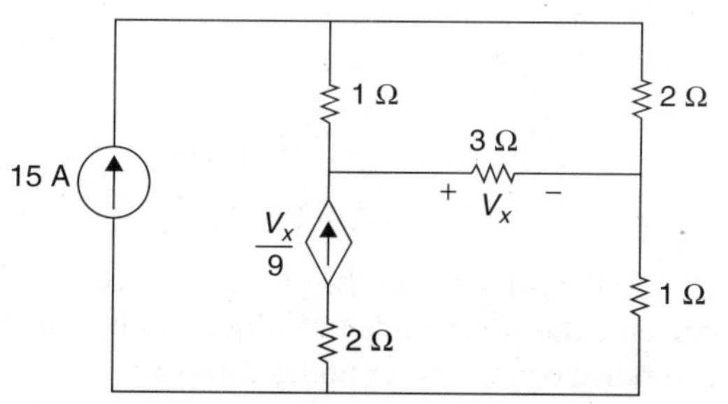

Solution: Let us assume that the loop currents are I_1, I_2 and I_3 as shown below:

Applying KVL to loop (2)

$$(I_2 - I_1) + 2I_2 + 3(I_2 - I_3) = 0$$

$$\Rightarrow \qquad -I_1 + 6I_2 - 3I_3 = 0 \qquad (1)$$

The current sources appear in mesh 1 and mesh 3. Since, the 15 A current source is located on the perimeter of the circuit, we may eliminate the loop from consideration. The dependent source is on the perimeter of the modified network, therefore we avoid writing an equation for loop 3. From the observation of the source quantities, we have

$$I_1 = 15 \text{ A} \qquad (2)$$

$$I_3 - I_1 = \frac{V_x}{9} \qquad (3)$$

From the circuit diagram

$$V_x = 3(I_3 - I_2) \qquad (4)$$

From Eqs (4) and (5), we have

$$9(I_3 - I_1) = 3(I_3 - I_2)$$

$$-3I_1 + I_2 + 2I_3 = 0 \qquad (5)$$

From Eqs (1) and (2)

$$6I_2 - 3I_3 = 15$$

$$2I_2 - I_3 = 5 \qquad (6)$$

From Eqs (2) and (5)

$$-3 \times 15 + I_2 + 2I_3 = 0$$

$$I_2 + 2I_3 = 45 \qquad (7)$$

Solving Eqs (3) and (6), we have

$$I_2 = 11 \text{ A}, \quad I_3 = 17 \text{ A}$$

$\therefore$ Current flowing through the 2 Ω resistor $= I_3 - I_1 = 17 - 15 = 2$ A

1.20 Using the nodal method, find the current through the 5 Ω resistor in the circuit.

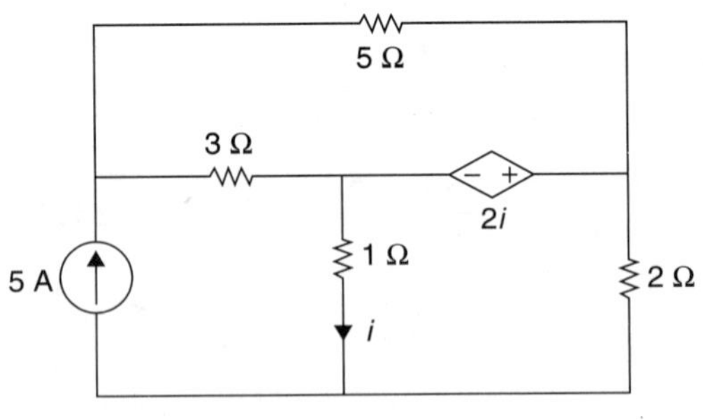

Solution: Let us assume the node voltages are V_1, V_2 and V_3 as shown below.

Applying KCL at node-1

$$\frac{V_1 - V_2}{3} + \frac{V_1 - V_3}{5} = 5$$

$$5(V_1 - V_2) + 3(V_1 - V_3) = 75$$

$$\Rightarrow \qquad 8V_1 - 5V_2 - 3V_3 = 75 \qquad (1)$$

Due to the presence of the voltage source ($2i$) between nodes 2 and 3 it is slightly difficult to find out the current. The super node technique can be conveniently applied in this case. Accordingly, we can write the combined equations for nodes 2 and 3:

$$\frac{V_2 - V_1}{3} + \frac{V_2}{1} + \frac{V_3}{2} + \frac{V_3 - V_1}{5} = 0$$

$$10(V_2 - V_1) + 30V_2 + 15V_3 + 6(V_3 - V_1) = 0$$

$$\Rightarrow \quad -8V_1 + 20V_2 + 10.5V_3 = 0 \qquad (2)$$

$$V_2 - V_3 = -2i \qquad (3)$$

But from the circuit

$$i = \frac{V_2}{1} = V_2 \qquad (4)$$

From Eqs (3) and (4), we have

$$V_2 - V_3 = -2V_2$$

$$\Rightarrow \quad V_3 = 3V_2 \qquad (5)$$

From Eqs (2) and (5), we have

$$-8V_1 + 20V_2 + 10.5 \times 3V_2 = 0$$

$$-8V_1 + 51.5V_2 = 0$$

$$V_1 = 6.4375V_2 \qquad (6)$$

Substituting Eqs (5) and (6) in Eq. (1),

$$8 \times 6.437V_2 - 5V_2 - 3 \times 3V_2 = 75$$

$$37.5V_2 = 75$$

$$\Rightarrow \quad V_2 = 2\text{ V} \qquad (7)$$

From Eqs (5) and (7), we have

$$V_3 = 3V_2 = 3 \times 2 = 6\text{ V}$$

From Eqs (6) and (7), we have

$$V_1 = 6.4375V_2 = 6.4375 \times 2 = 12.875\text{ V}$$

$$\therefore \quad \text{Current through the } 5\ \Omega \text{ resistor} = \frac{V_1 - V_3}{5} = \frac{12.875 - 6}{5} = 1.375\text{ A}$$

1.21 Using mesh analysis determine the voltage V which gives a voltage of 50 V across the 10 Ω resistor.

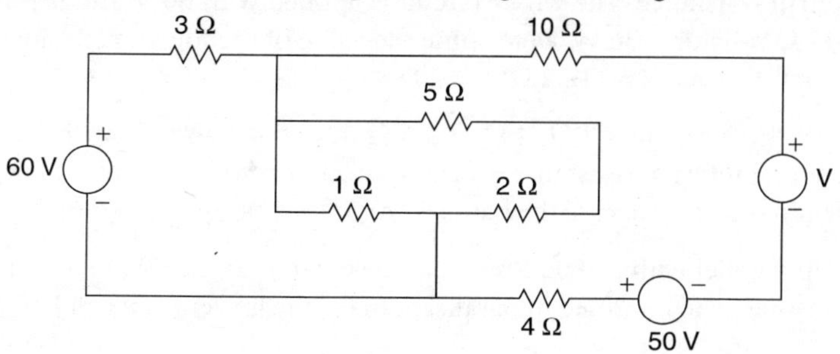

Solution: The given circuit can be redrawn as shown. Let us assume that the loop currents are I_1, I_2 and I_3.

Inspection of mesh analysis gives the matrix loop equation as

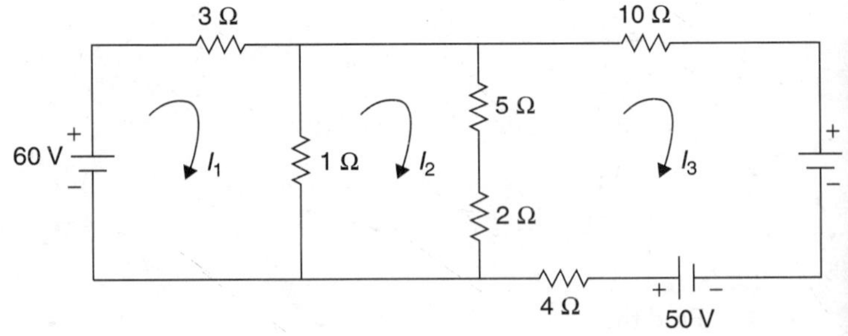

$$\begin{bmatrix} 4 & -1 & 0 \\ -1 & 8 & -7 \\ 0 & -7 & 21 \end{bmatrix}\begin{bmatrix} I_1 \\ I_2 \\ I_3 \end{bmatrix} = \begin{bmatrix} 60 \\ 0 \\ 50-V \end{bmatrix}$$

$$\Delta = \begin{vmatrix} 4 & -1 & 0 \\ -1 & 8 & -7 \\ 0 & -7 & 21 \end{vmatrix} = 4\times 119 - 1\times 21 = 455$$

$$\Delta_3 = \begin{vmatrix} 4 & -1 & 60 \\ -1 & 8 & 0 \\ 0 & -7 & 50-V \end{vmatrix} = 32(50-V) + 1(V-50) + 60\times 7 = 1970 - 31V$$

Using Cramer's rule

$$I_3 = \frac{\Delta_3}{\Delta} = \frac{1970-31V}{455}$$

But according to the given data, the voltage across the 10 Ω resistor = 50 volts.

$$10I_3 = 50$$

$$I_3 = 5 = \frac{1970-31V}{455}$$

$$V = -9.84 \text{ V}$$

EXERCISE PROBLEMS

1. Two resistances when they are in series have an equivalent resistance of 9 Ω and when connected in parallel have an equivalent resistance of 2 Ω. Find the individual resistances. [**Ans:** $R_1 = 6$ Ω, $R_2 = 3$ Ω]
2. A circuit consisting of three resistances 12 Ω, 18 Ω and 36 Ω respectively joined in parallel, is connected in series with a fourth resistance. The whole circuit is applied with 60 V and it is found that the power dissipated in the 12 Ω resistor is 36 W. Determine the value of the fourth resistance and the total power dissipated in the circuit. [**Ans:** $R = 11.32$ Ω, $P = 207.84$ W]
3. A circuit consists of three resistors 3 Ω, 4 Ω and 6 Ω in parallel and a fourth resistor 4 Ω in series. A battery of emf 12 V and internal resistance 6 Ω is connected across the circuit. Find the total current in the circuit and terminal voltage across the battery. [**Ans:** $I = 1.06$ A, $V_{ter.} = 5.63$ V]
4. A 50 Ω resistor is in parallel with a 100 Ω resistor. The current in the 50 Ω resistor is 7.2 A. What is the value of the third resistance to be added in parallel to make the line current as 12.1A? [**Ans:** $R = 276.92$ Ω]
5. Find the current delivered by the source for the network using network reductions technique. [**Ans:** 5 A]

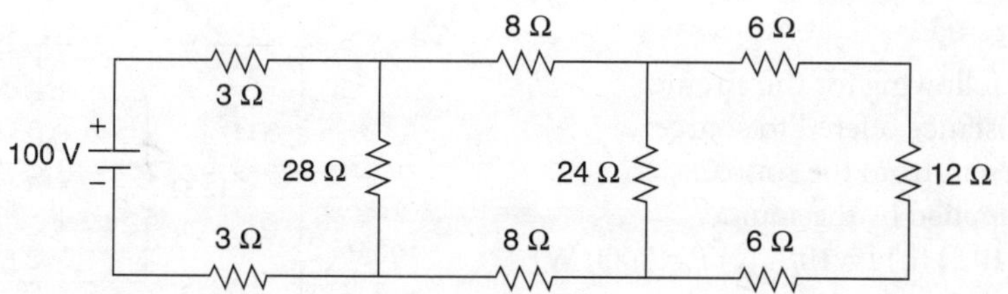

6. Find the voltage and current source equivalent representation of the following network across AB. [**Ans:** A voltage source of 4 V in series with a resistance of 1 Ω]

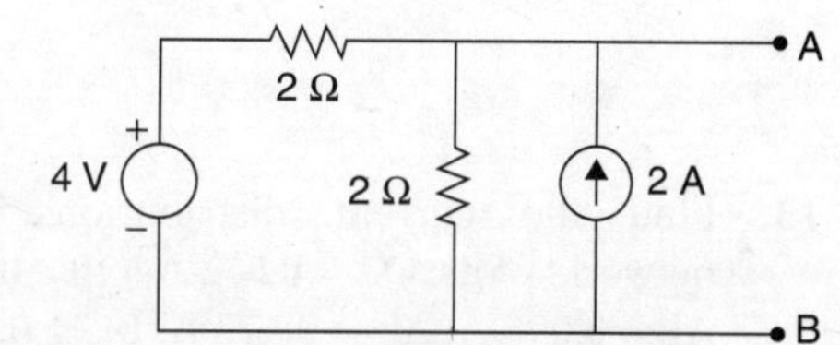

7. A bridge network ABCD is arranged as follows: Resistance between terminals AB, BC, CD, DA and BD are 10 Ω, 30 Ω, 15 Ω, 20 Ω and 40 Ω respectively. A 4 V battery is connected with negligible internal resistance between terminals A and C. Determine the current through each element in the network using network reduction techniques. [**Ans:** $I_{AB} = 0.118$ A, $I_{BC} = 0.094$ A, $I_{CD} = 0.127$ A, $I_{DA} = 0.1036$ A, $I_{BD} = 0.0232$ A]

8. Using star delta conversion find the current I in the circuit. [**Ans:** $I = 24$ A]

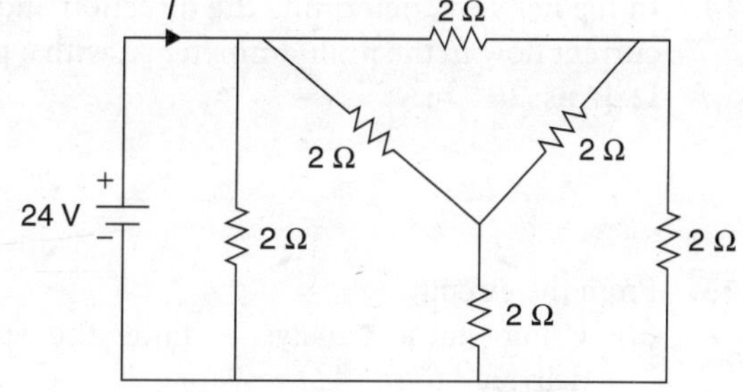

9. Determine the currents through the resistances in the network using source transformation. [**Ans:** $I_{4\Omega} = 3.89$ A, $I_{5\Omega} = 3.111$ A]

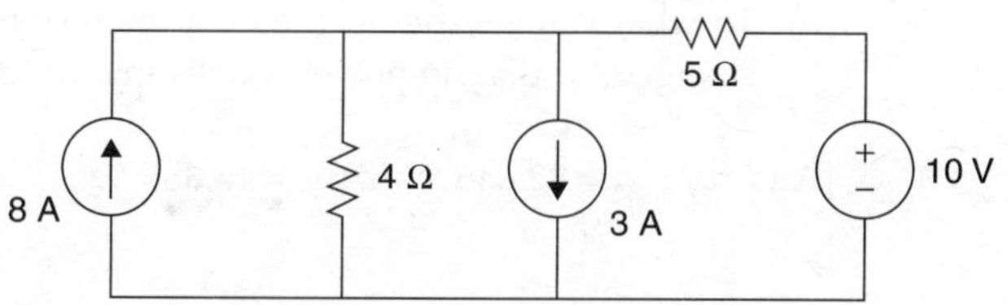

10. In the network, determine the value of i. [**Ans:** $i = 0.923$ A]

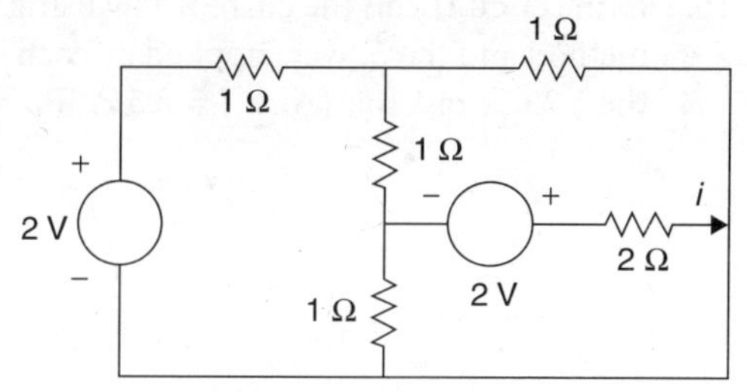

11. Find the potential difference V_{AB} in the circuit using Kirchhoff's laws. [**Ans:** $V_{AB} = 21.8$ V]

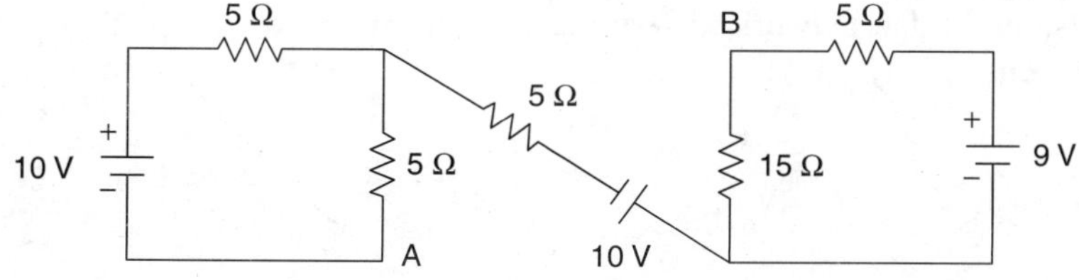

12. Calculate the following for the circuit.
    (a) Total resistance offered to source.
    (b) Total current from the source.
    (c) Power supplied by the source.
    [**Ans:** (a) $R = 10\ \Omega$ (b) $I = 10$ A (c) $P = 1000$ W]

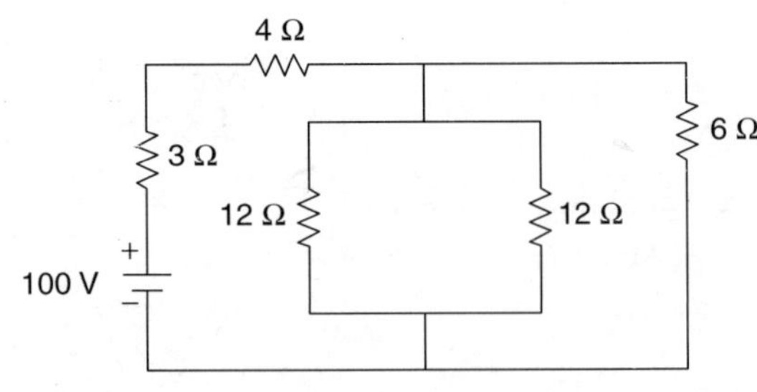

13. Find the current distribution in the network. [**Ans:** OA = 0.572 A, OB = 0.428 A, AB = 0.095 A, AC = 0.477 A, BC = 0.523 A]

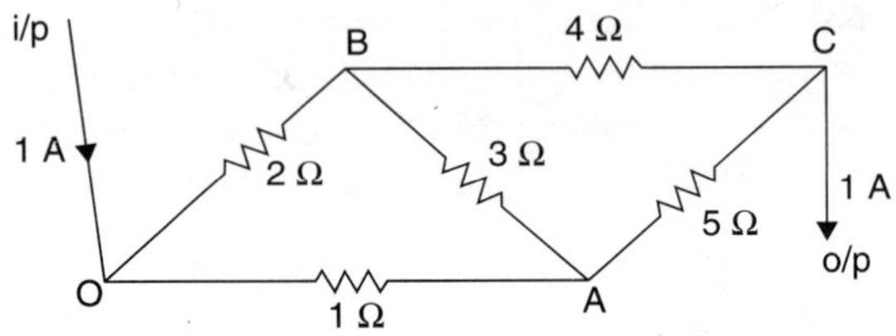

14. In the network, determine the direction and magnitude of current flow in the milli-ammeter A, with a resistance of 10 Ω. [**Ans:** 26.7 mA]

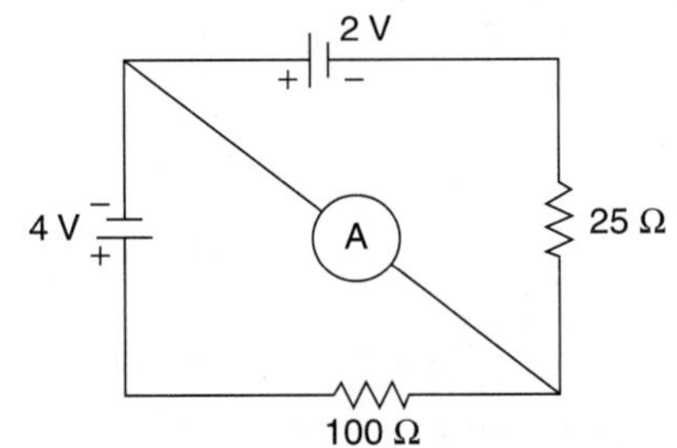

15. From the circuit,
    (a) Using mesh analysis, find the power delivered to the 4 Ω resistor.
    (b) To what voltage should the 80 V battery be changed, so that no power is delivered to the 4 Ω resistor.
    [**Ans:** (a) $P_{4\Omega} = 82.646$ W (b) $V = 46.667$ V]

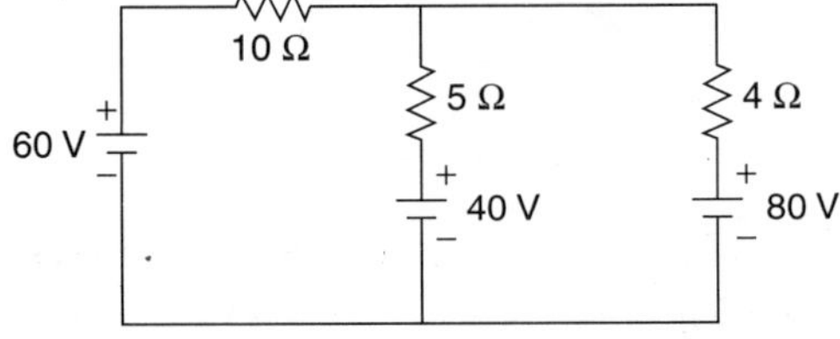

16. In the circuit, find the current I by using the mesh method and the power supplied by each battery to the 1.25 Ω resistor. [**Ans:** $I = 2.5$ A, $P_{10} = 2.38$ W, $P_{20} = 1.6$ W]

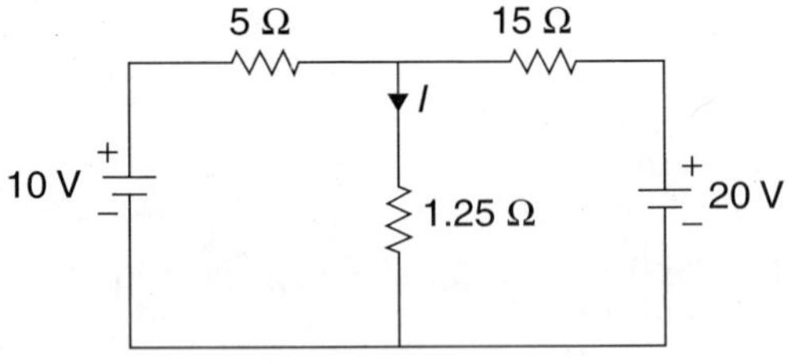

17. In the Wheatstone bridge network, determine the current in the galvanometer. [**Ans:** $I_G = 17.4$ uA]

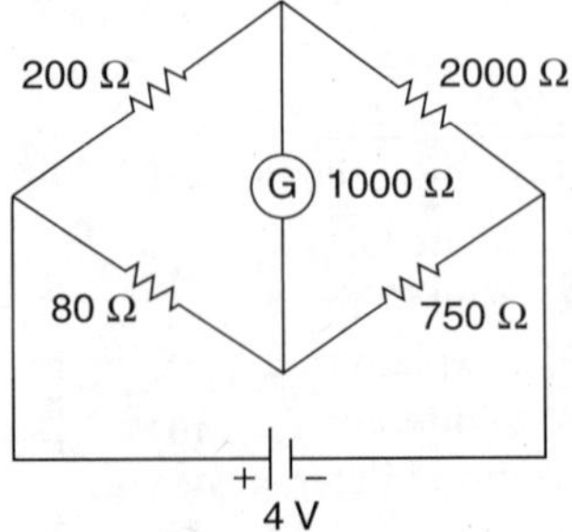

18. Find the current in 12 Ω resistor using mesh analysis. [**Ans:** $I_{12} = -1.667$ A]

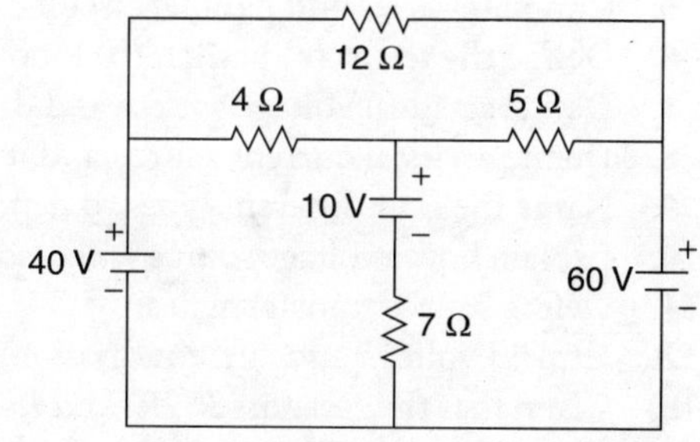

19. Find the current through 4 Ω resistor in the circuit by using nodal analysis. [**Ans:** $I_{4\Omega} = 30$ A]

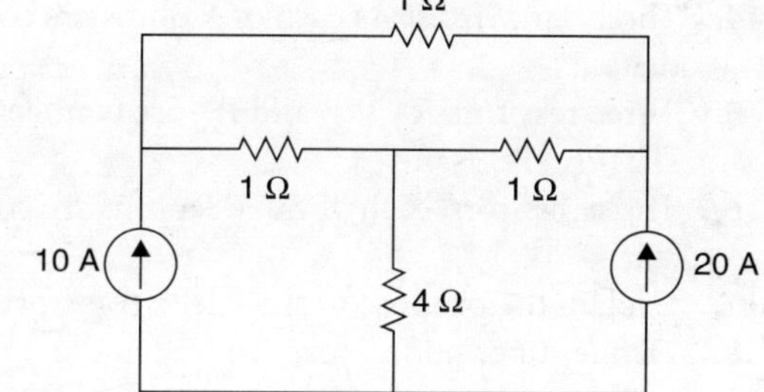

20. Find the node voltages V_1, V_2 in the circuit. [**Ans:** $V_1 = 7.058$ V, $V_2 = 9.41$ V]

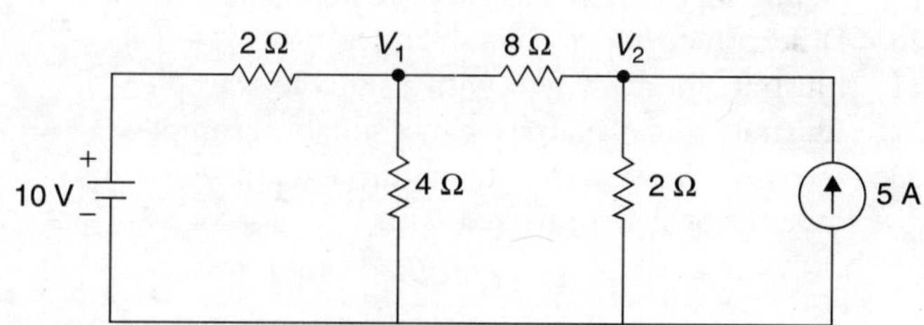

21. Find the current I through 20 Ω resistor using source transformation for the circuit. [**Ans:** $I = 1.6154$ A]

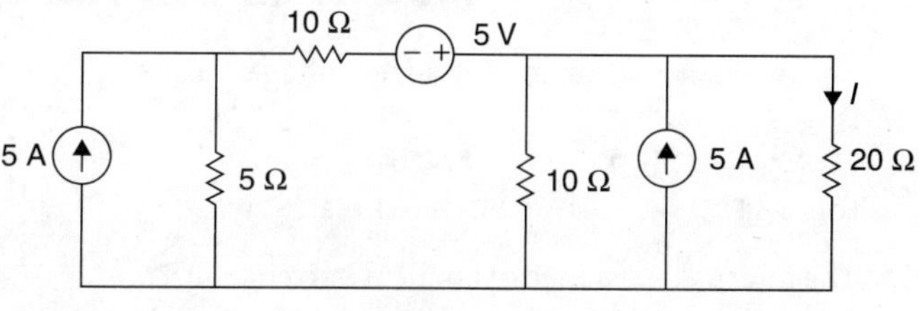

22. Using the source transformation technique, convert the circuit into a single current source in parallel with a single resistance. [**Ans:** 3.25 A in parallel with 1 Ω]

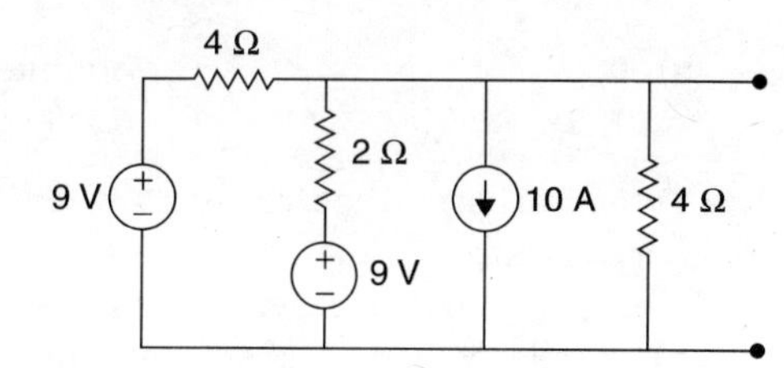

REVIEW QUESTIONS

1. State Ohm's law and mention its limitations.
2. State Kirchhoff's laws.
3. Explain the classifications of circuit elements.
4. Differentiate between (a) linear and nonlinear elements, (b) active and passive elements, (c) unilateral and bilateral elements.

5. Compare series and parallel circuits.
6. Define the terms (a) branch (b) loop (c) node (d) mesh.
7. Define an ideal voltage source and draw its V–I characteristics.
8. Define an ideal current source and draw its V–I characteristics.
9. Name the four different types of dependent sources in electric circuits.
10. Explain how a voltage source with a source resistance can be converted into an equivalent current source.
11. Define source transformation.
12. Explain voltage and current division rules.
13. Given that the resistors R_a, R_b and R_c are connected electrically in star, write the equations for resistors in equivalent delta.
14. Three equal resistors each of R ohms are connected in star. Find the value of resistors in the equivalent delta.
15. Three resistors R_{ab}, R_{bc} and R_{ca} are connected in delta. Write the expression for resistors in equivalent star.
16. Three resistors, each of value R ohms are connected in delta. Find the value of resistors in its equivalent star.
17. Explain the purpose of star–delta transformation.
18. Define super node. How can we handle it while applying Kirchhoff's laws?
19. Define super mesh. How can we handle it while applying Kirchhoff's laws?
20. Differentiate between mesh and loop.
21. Illustrate mesh analysis with a suitable example.
22. Illustrate nodal analysis with a suitable example.
23. Derive expressions for star connected arms in terms of delta connected arms and delta connected arms in terms of star connected arms.

MULTIPLE CHOICE QUESTIONS

1. The internal resistance of an ideal voltage source is
   (a) 0 (b) infinite
   (c) 1 Ω (d) can't say

2. The internal resistance of an ideal current source is
   (a) 0 (b) infinite
   (c) 1 Ω (d) can't say

3. A practical current source is usually represented by a resistance in
   (a) series with an ideal current source
   (b) parallel with an ideal current source
   (c) series with an ideal voltage source
   (d) parallel with an ideal voltage source

4. A practical voltage source is usually represented by a resistance in
   (a) series with an ideal current source
   (b) parallel with an ideal current source
   (c) series with an ideal voltage source
   (d) parallel with an ideal voltage source

5. If $R_A = R_B = R_C = R$ in star network, $R_{AB} = R_{BC} = R_{CA} =$ __________, in its equivalent delta network.
   (a) $R/3$ (b) $3R$
   (c) R (d) $2R/3$

6. The number of 2 μF , 400 V capacitors needed to obtain a capacitance value of 1.5 μF rated for 1600 V is
   (a) 3 (b) 8
   (c) 6 (d) 4

7. When a resistor R is connected to a current source, it consumes a power of 18 W. When the same R is connected to a voltage source having the same magnitude as the current source, the power absorbed by R is 4.5 W. The magnitude of the current source and the value of R are

(a) $\sqrt{18}$ A and 1 Ω (b) 3 A and 2 Ω
(c) 1 A and 18 Ω (d) 8 A and 0.5 Ω

8. Two incandescent bulbs of 40 W and 60 W rating are connected in series across the mains. Then
(a) the bulbs together consume 100 W
(b) the bulbs together consume 50 W
(c) the 60 W bulb glows brighter
(d) the 40 W bulb glows brighter

9. Five inductors are connected in series. The lowest value is 10 mH. If the value of each inductor is twice that of the preceding one, and if the inductors are connected in order ascending values, what is the total inductance?
(a) 210 mH (b) 165 mH
(c) 50 mH (d) None of the above

10. Five capacitors are connected in parallel. The lowest value is 20 F. If the value of each capacitor is twice that of the preceding one, and if the capacitors are connected in order of ascending values, what is the total capacitance?
(a) 210 F (b) 165 F
(c) 50 F (d) 620 F

11. Six incandescent bulbs are connected across 200 V. Each bulb is rated at 100 W. How much current flows through each bulb?
(a) 0.5 A (b) 2 A
(c) 6 A (d) 7 A

12. If a 20 V battery is connected across parallel resistors of 4 Ω, 8 Ω, 16 Ω, how much voltage is there across the 8 Ω resistor?
(a) 5 V (b) 20 V
(c) 10 V (d) 40 V

13. A 10 V source is connected to a resistor R = 10 Ω. How much resistance should be added in series with R in order to reduce the current to 1/3rd of its original value?
(a) 5 Ω (b) 20 Ω
(c) 10 Ω (d) 15 Ω

14. If a network contains B branches and N nodes, then the number of mesh current equations are
(a) $B - N + 1$ (b) $B - N - 1$
(c) $N - B + 1$ (d) $N - B - 1$

15. A 2 H inductor carrying a current of 1 A will store energy equal to
(a) 1 J (b) 2 J
(c) 3 J (d) 4 J

16. When five identical capacitors each having a capacitance of 5 F are connected in parallel, then the equivalent capacitance is
(a) 5 F (b) 25 F
(c) 10 F (d) 15 F

17. An inductor stores energy in the
(a) magnetic field
(b) electric field
(c) electromagnetic field
(d) all

18. A capacitor stores energy in the
(a) magnetic field
(b) electric field
(c) electromagnetic field
(d) all

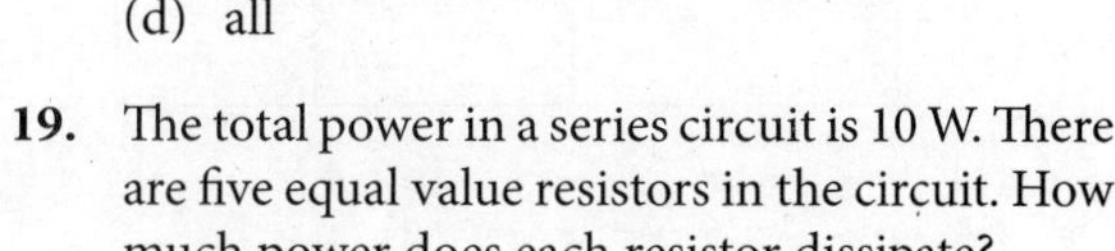

19. The total power in a series circuit is 10 W. There are five equal value resistors in the circuit. How much power does each resistor dissipate?
(a) 2 W (b) 4 W
(c) 6 W (d) 8 W

20. Mesh analysis mainly depends on
(a) KVL (b) KCL
(c) KVL and KCL (d) None of the above

21. Nodal analysis mainly depends on
(a) KVL (b) KCL
(c) KVL and KCL (d) None of the above

22. In an electrical network, if the number of nodes are N, then the number of node voltages are
(a) N (b) $N - 1$
(c) $N + 1$ (d) None of the above

23. If three equal resistances of 9 Ω are connected in star, then the equal resistance in one of the arms of the delta circuit is
(a) 3 Ω (b) 9 Ω
(c) 15 Ω (d) 27 Ω

24. If a circuit consists of two resistances 10 Ω and 20 Ω in parallel and the total current passing through the circuit is 100 A, then the current passing through 20 Ω is
(a) 22.22 A (b) 33.33 A
(c) 44.44 A (d) 55.55 A

25. Identify the passive element among the following
(a) voltage source (b) current source
(c) inductor (d) transistor

26. A battery has an emf of 12.9 V and supplies a current of 3.5 A. What is the resistance of the circuit?
(a) 5.5 (b) 16.4
(c) 3.69 (d) 45.15

27. Sign convention used for potential rise taken as
(a) negative (b) zero
(c) equal to fall in potential
(d) positive

28. In the circuit shown, the potential of E_2 is

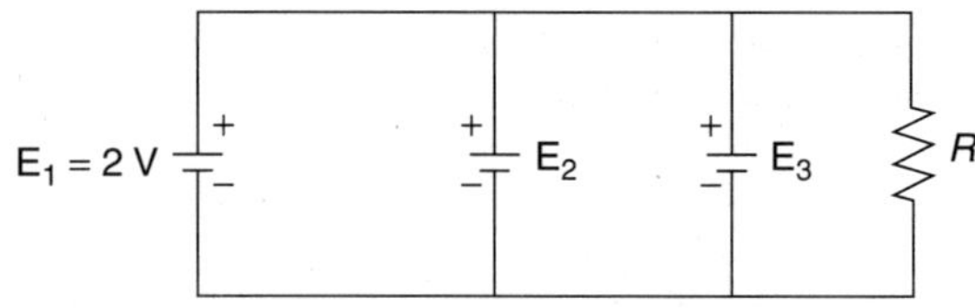

(a) 0 V (b) 4 V
(c) 2 V (d) 1 V

29. For the circuit shown, R_{ab} =

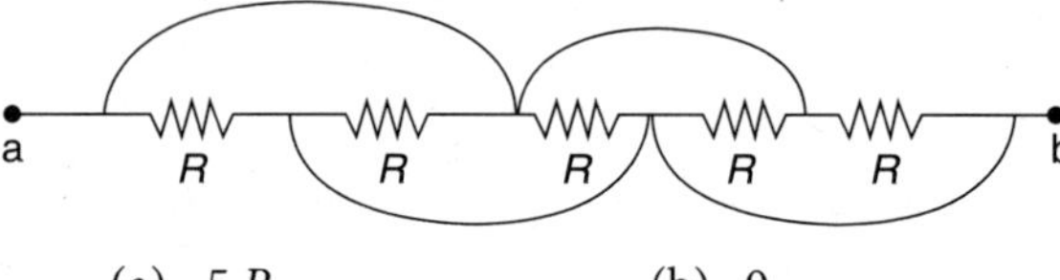

(a) 5 R (b) 0
(c) R/5 (d) R/2

30. A resistor takes 0.3 A at 230 V. If the voltage is reduced to 100 V, What is the current taken by the resistor?
(a) 0.13 A (b) 0.69 A
(c) 0.18 A (d) 0.3 A

31. The following voltage drops are measured across each of three resistors in series: 5.2 V, 8.5 V, 12.3 V. What is the value of the source voltage to which these resistors are connected?
(a) 26 V (b) 5.2 V
(c) 8.2 V (d) 12.3 V

32. Power in a parallel circuit is equal to
(a) product of all powers
(b) sum of all resistors in parallel
(c) sum of all powers in parallel
(d) product of all resistors in parallel

33. A cell of emf 2 V and internal resistance 1 Ω is connected with two wires of resistances 2 and 5 in parallel. Find the current through the circuit
(a) 100/12 A (b) 17/14 A
(c) 0 A (d) 14/17 A

34. In a series circuit, which of the statements is correct?
(a) total power = sum of powers of each resistor in series
(b) total power = zero
(c) total power = $VI \cos\phi$
(d) total power = infinity

35. For a parallel circuit, which statement is incorrect?
(a) $P_T = V_s^2 / R_T$
(b) $P_T = P_1 + P_2 + \cdots P_m$
(c) $I_1 + I_2 + I_3 = 0$
(d) $I_i = I_T R_T / (R_i + R_T)$

36. A battery of emf 1.8 V and internal resistance 1.2 Ω is connected to a pair of resistances of 4 Ω and 6 Ω in parallel. Calculate the potential difference of the battery.
(a) 100 V (b) 10 V
(c) 1.2 V (d) 1 V

37. In the circuit shown, the current coming to node A from the 2 Ω resistor is

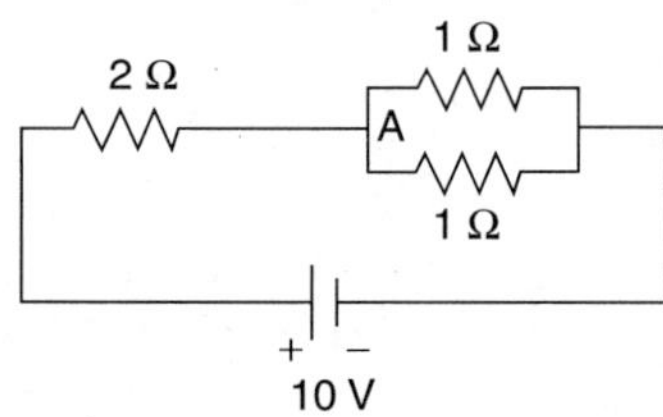

(a) 4 A (b) 2 A
(c) 10 A (d) 1 A

38. The voltage drop across the 2 Ω resistor in the circuit shown is

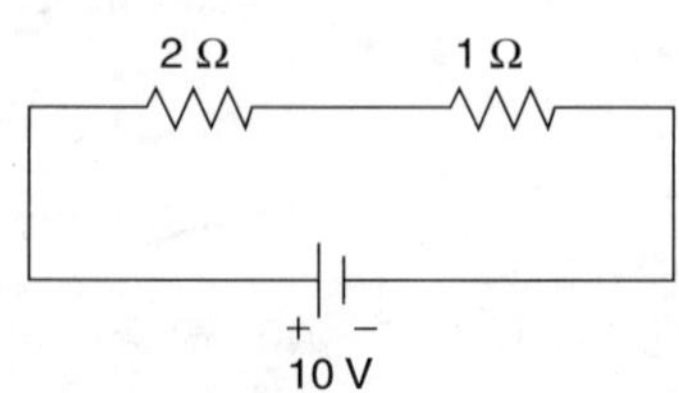

(a) 6.66 V (b) 0.66 V
(c) 0.066 V (d) 66.66 V

39. A battery of emf 12 V is connected to an external resistance of 20 Ω and it is found to have a potential difference of 10 V. Find its internal resistance.
(a) 400 Ω (b) 40 Ω
(c) 0.4 Ω (d) 4 Ω

40. Kirchhoff's current law is based on the
(a) law of conservation of energy
(b) law of conservation of electric charge
(c) law of conservation of current
(d) law of conservation of power

41. When a 1.2 kΩ resistor, 100 Ω resistor, 1 kΩ resistor and 50 Ω resistor are in parallel, the total resistance is less than
(a) 1.2 kΩ (b) 100 Ω
(c) 1 kΩ (d) 50 Ω

42. For the circuit shown, R_{AB} =

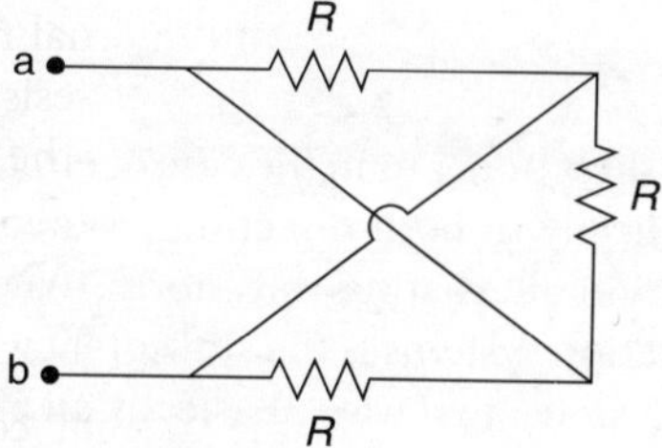

(a) 1 (b) 0
(c) $R/3$ (d) $3R$

43. For the circuit shown, I_2 =

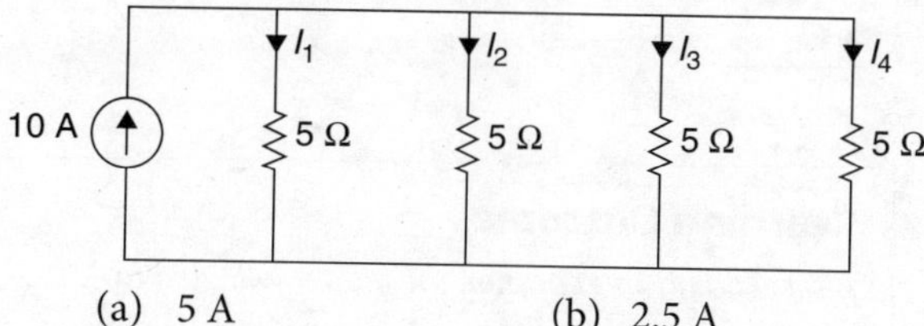

(a) 5 A (b) 2.5 A
(c) 2 A (d) 10 A

44. 1 KWh =
(a) 3.6×10^8 J (b) 3.6×10^5 J
(c) 3.6×10^7 J (d) 3.6×10^6 J

45. For the circuit shown, I_3 =

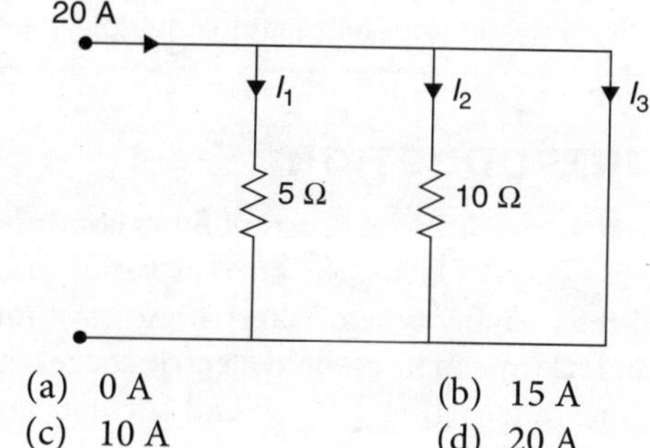

(a) 0 A (b) 15 A
(c) 10 A (d) 20 A

ANSWERS

1. a	2. b	3. b	4. c	5. b	6. a	7. b	8. d	9. a	10. d
11. a	12. b	13. b	14. a	15. a	16. b	17. a	18. b	19. a	20. a
21. b	22. b	23. d	24. b	25. c	26. c	27. d	28. c	29. b	30. a
31. a	32. c	33. d	34. a	35. c	36. c	37. a	38. a	39. d	40. a
41. d	42. b	43. b	44. a	45. d					

2 AC Fundamentals

Learning Outcomes

After reading this chapter, the reader will able to

- ➢ Define a phasor
- ➢ Define RMS and average values
- ➢ Evaluate form factor and peak factor for different periodic wave forms
- ➢ Analyse the angular relationship of a sine wave along with its equation
- ➢ Explain the concept of *j*-notation
- ➢ Represent a given phasor into polar as well as rectangular forms
- ➢ Identify a suitable form for mathematical operations in complex notation
- ➢ Organise addition, subtraction, multiplication and division on given phasors

2.1 INTRODUCTION

In an electric circuit, direct current flows continuously in only one direction, but in the case of circuits where alternating current flows, the current varies in magnitude periodically in both directions. When it is AC, it could refer to any type of alternating wave form. A very common alternating wave form that we come across in real time in household electric sockets and in communication systems is the sinusoidal wave form. Many times, alternating voltages and currents are represented by a sinusoidal wave. Basically an alternating voltage (or current) wave form is defined as the voltage (or current) that varies periodically with time, with a change in magnitude and direction. Thus, an alternating quantity – either current or voltage – is one which periodically passes through definite cycles, each consisting of two half cycles, one of which is in the positive direction and the other is in the opposite direction.

In general, the sine wave is more useful than other waveforms such as pulse, saw tooth, square, and so on, due to the following reasons:

- if we consider any second order system, the response of this system is sinusoidal,
- any periodic waveform can be written in terms of a sinusoidal function according to the Fourier theorem,
- derivatives and integrals of sine functions are again sinusoidal functions,
- it can be easily generated and analysed, and
- the properties of sinusoidal functions are well defined.

2.2 ADVANTAGES AND DISADVANTAGES OF AC OVER DC

2.2.1 Advantages

- Generation of AC is cheaper and easier than DC.
- AC can easily step-up or step-down using transformers, but it is not possible in the case of DC.
- AC machines are simple, robust and do not require much attention for their repairs and maintenance during their use.
- When AC is supplied at higher voltages in long distance transmission, the line losses are small compared to a DC transmission.

- AC can easily be converted into DC with the help of rectifiers.
- The value or magnitude of AC can be decreased easily without the loss of excess energy using choke coil.

2.2.2 Disadvantages

- Peak value of AC is high and it is dangerous to use, so better insulation is required.
- AC attracts a person who touches it unlike DC, which gives a repelling shock.
- AC is transmitted from the surface of the conductor and hence needs several strands of thin wires insulated from each other.
- AC resistance is always greater than DC resistance (1.2 to 1.5 times) so copper losses are more in AC.
- In an AC system, due to *skin effect*, the cross-sectional area of conductors is more since the current wave travels on the outer periphery of cross-section up to the skin depth. However, in DC, it flows through the entire area and therefore, the cost of the conductor is less.

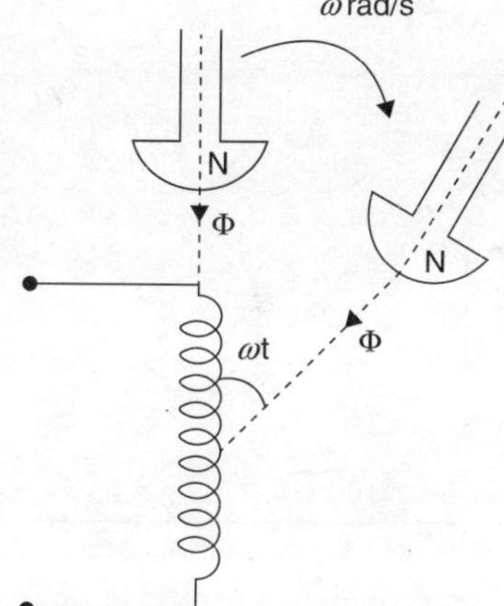

Fig. 2.1 Generation of emf in a rotating coil

2.3 GENERATION OF A SINUSOIDAL VOLTAGE

Consider a coil of N turns (Fig. 2.1). A pole of flux Φ mWb initially at $t = 0$, is kept along the coil axis and then rotated with uniform angular velocity of ω rad/s. At any instant t seconds later, the pole moves through an angle $\theta = \omega t$ radians. Now, flux Φ passes through the coil at an angle $\theta = \omega t$.

So, linkage flux = flux along axis of coil = $\Phi \cos \omega t$

$\therefore$ Flux linkages = $N\Phi \cos \omega t$

According to Faraday's law of electromagnetic induction, instantaneous induced voltage at an instant t is $v(t)$ and is given by

$$v(t) = -\frac{d}{dt}(\text{flux linkages}) = -\frac{d}{dt}(N\Phi \cos \omega t) = -N\Phi \frac{d}{dt}(\cos \omega t) = N\Phi\omega \sin \omega t$$

$$\Rightarrow \quad v(t) = N\Phi\omega \sin \omega t \tag{2.1}$$

As per Eq. 2.1, the instantaneous induced voltage is a function of ωt or θ and changing sinusoidally. $v(t)$ is calculated for various θ values and sketched (Fig. 2.2). It is found that $v(t)$ is alternating in nature, that is, for the first half period it is positive and for the next half period it is negative. Such a voltage is known as AC voltage. Variations of $v(t)$ are as per the sine curve, hence, it is known as sinusoidal AC voltage.

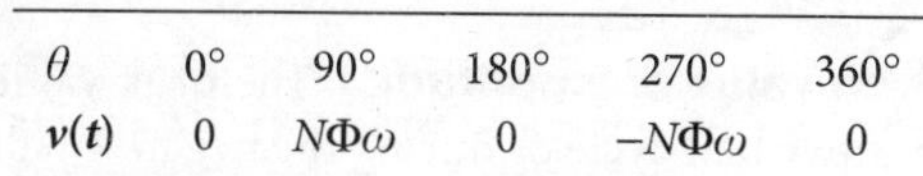

θ	0°	90°	180°	270°	360°
$v(t)$	0	$N\Phi\omega$	0	$-N\Phi\omega$	0

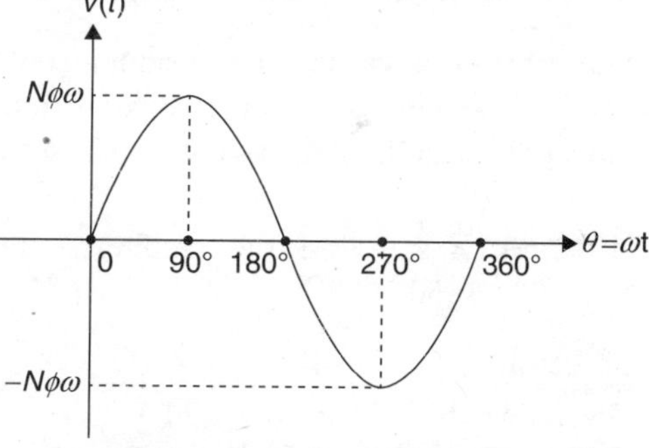

Fig. 2.2 Sinusoidal wave form

2.4 DEFINITION OF TERMS ASSOCIATED WITH PERIODIC FUNCTIONS

Periodic functions are those which repeat regularly at equal intervals of time. A function $f(t)$ is said to be periodic function if

$$f(t \pm K\,T) = f(t) \tag{2.2}$$

where T is the time period and K is an integer. A common example of a periodic function is a sine function. Some examples are shown in Fig. 2.3 (T is the period).

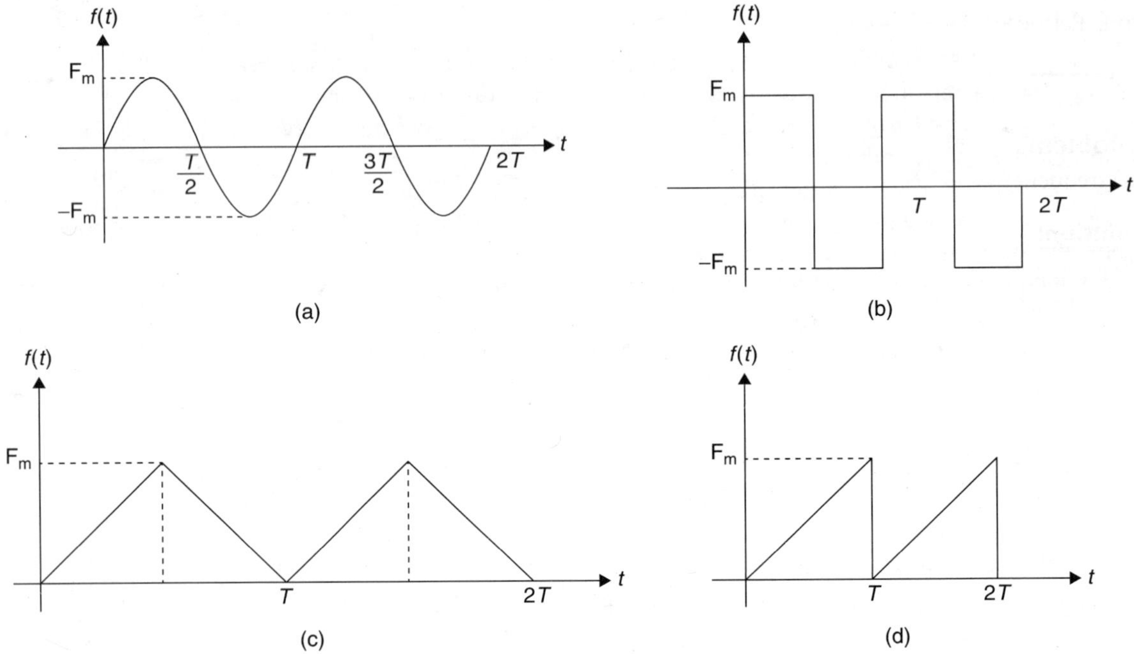

Fig. 2.3 Some periodic waveforms

Cycle One complete set of positive and negative values of an alternating quantity is called a cycle.

Frequency (*f*) Number of cycles completed per second by an alternating quantity is known as frequency. Units are cycles/s or hertz.

Time period (*T*) It is defined as the time taken by an alternating quantity to complete one cycle.

That is, $T = \dfrac{1}{f}$ (2.3)

Peak value or **amplitude** The peak value of a sine wave is the maximum value of the wave during the positive half cycle or during the negative half cycle.

Peak to peak value The peak to peak value of a sine wave is the value from the positive to the negative peak.

Instantaneous value The instantaneous value of an AC signal is the value of voltage or current at one particular instant. This value changes with time and would be positive in the positive half cycle and negative during the negative half cycle.

Problem 2.1 Find the amplitude, phase, period and frequency of the sinusoid as given by $v(t) = 20\cos(50t + 70°)$.

Solution:

Given that $v(t) = 20\cos(50t + 70°)$

Comparing with $v(t) = V_m\cos(\omega t + \phi)$

(i) Amplitude, $V_m = 20$ V
(ii) Phase, $\phi = 70°$
(iii) Angular frequency, $\omega = 50$ rad/s
(iv) Period, $T = \dfrac{2\pi}{\omega} = \dfrac{2\pi}{50} = \dfrac{\pi}{25}$ s

---

Problem 2.2 An alternating current $i(t)$ is given by $i(t) = 141.4\sin(314t)$. Find (i) the maximum value, (ii) frequency, (iii) time period, and (iv) the instantaneous value when $t = 3$ ms.

Solution:

Given that $i(t) = 141.4\sin(314t)$

Comparing with $i(t) = I_m \sin(\omega t)$

(i) Maximum current, $I_m = 141.1$ A

$$\omega = 2\pi f = 314 \text{ rad/s}$$

$$\Rightarrow f = \frac{\omega}{2\pi} = \frac{314}{2\pi} = 50 \text{ Hz}$$

(iii) Time period, $T = \dfrac{1}{f} = \dfrac{1}{50} = 0.02$ s

(ii) Frequency = 50 Hz

(iv) The instantaneous value when $t = 3$ ms is

$$i(t) = 141.4\sin(314t)$$

$$= 141.4\sin\left(314 \times 3 \times 10^{-3} \times \frac{180}{\pi}\right)$$

$$= 114.4 \text{ A}$$

2.5 AVERAGE VALUE

In AC circuit applications we are interested in finding out the average value of a waveform; the wave could be sinusoidal, triangular, trapezoidal or any other shape. It is also known as DC value. The following are the definitions for average value.

(i) *Average value* is defined as that constant value, which produces the same amount of flux in the case of voltage or same amount of charge in the case of current as produced by alternating voltage or current when both are applied to the same circuit for the same period.
(ii) The average value of an AC current or voltage is the average of all the instantaneous values during one complete cycle. They are actually DC values.
(iii) The average value is the amount of voltage that would be indicated by a DC voltmeter if it were connected across the load resistor.

For symmetrical waveforms (having identical +ve and –ve half cycles) the average value over the full cycle is zero. Hence, the average value is determined over a half cycle only. For an unsymmetrical waveform, the average value is calculated over the full cycle.

2.5.1 MID-ORDINATE METHOD

The average value of an alternating wave (both sinusoidal and non-sinusoidal) can be determined graphically by taking the arithmetic mean of the ordinates at equal intervals over a half cycle of the wave. In these intervals, let the currents be approximated by average values $i_1, i_2, \ldots i_n$. From Fig. 2.4, the average value of the current is given by

$$I_{\text{avg}} = \frac{i_1 + i_2 + i_3 + \cdots + i_n}{n} \tag{2.4}$$

2.5.2 Analytical Method

This method is more convenient for the sinusoidal waveform. The average value of a periodic function $f(t)$ with period T is given by

$$F_{\text{Avg}} = \frac{1}{T}\int_0^T f(t)dt \qquad (2.5)$$

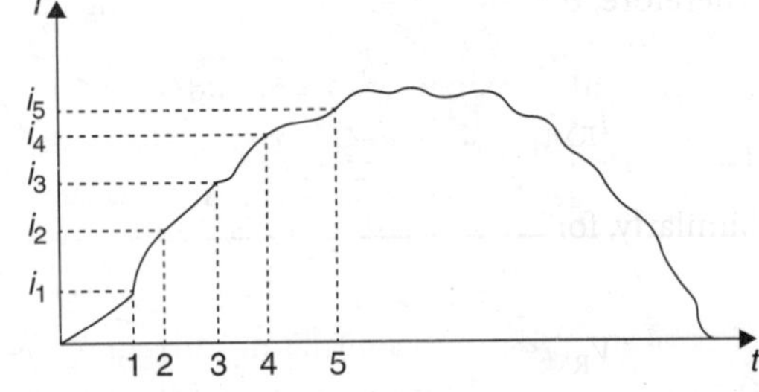

Fig. 2.4 Sinusoidal alternating quantity

Let us consider a sinusoidal voltage

$$v(t) = V_m \sin\omega t = V_m \sin\theta$$

$$V_{\text{Avg}} = \frac{1}{T}\int_0^T v(t)dt = \frac{1}{\pi}\int_0^\pi V_m \sin\theta d\theta = \frac{V}{\pi}[-\cos\theta]_0^\pi = \frac{2V_m}{\pi}$$

$$\Rightarrow \qquad V_{\text{Avg}} = \frac{2V_m}{\pi} \qquad (2.6)$$

The average value of a sine wave over one complete cycle is always zero. So the average value of a sine wave is defined over a half cycle, and not a full cycle.

2.6 RMS OR EFFECTIVE VALUE

While calculating the RMS value of an alternating quantity, heat energy is compared, produced by constant voltage and AC voltage. *The RMS value of an AC voltage is defined as that constant voltage, which produces the same amount of heat energy as produced by AC voltage, when both are applied to the same circuit for the same period.* It is possible to compute the effective value of a sine wave of current to a good degree of accuracy by taking equally spaced instantaneous values of current along the curve and extracting the square root of the average of the sum of the squared values. For this reason, the effective value is often called the *root-mean square* (RMS) value.

The RMS value of an alternating current is of considerable importance in practice because the ammeters and voltmeters record the RMS value of alternating current and voltage respectively.

2.6.1 Mid-ordinate Method

Consider an alternating waveform (Fig. 2.4). The wave is divided into n equal parts with the instantaneous currents during these intervals being i_1, i_2, … i_n. Let this be the current allowed through a circuit having a resistance of R ohms. The average power dissipated in the resistor in the interval is

$$P = \frac{i_1^2R + i_2^2R + i_3^2R + \cdots + i_n^2R}{n} = \frac{(i_1^2 + i_2^2 + i_3^2 + \cdots + i_n^2)R}{n} \qquad (2.7)$$

If a direct current of I amps flows through the same resistance R for the same time, the power dissipated is I^2R. If both the currents produce the same amount of heat, then

$$I^2R = \frac{(i_1^2 + i_2^2 + i_3^2 + \cdots + i_n^2)R}{n}$$

$$I^2 = \frac{(i_1^2 + i_2^2 + i_3^2 + \cdots + i_n^2)}{n}$$

Therefore, the RMS value of an alternating current is

$$I_{RMS} = \sqrt{\frac{i_1^2 + i_2^2 + i_3^2 + \cdots + i_n^2}{n}} \tag{2.8}$$

Similarly, for an alternating voltage

$$V_{RMS} = \sqrt{\frac{v_1^2 + v_2^2 + v_3^2 + \cdots + v_n^2}{n}} \tag{2.9}$$

2.6.2 Analytical Method

The RMS value of a periodic function $f(t)$ with period T is given by

$$F_{RMS} = \sqrt{\frac{1}{T}\int_0^T f(t)^2\, dt} \tag{2.10}$$

Let us consider a sinusoidal voltage

$$v(t) = V_m \sin \omega t = V_m \sin \theta$$

$$V_{RMS} = \sqrt{\frac{1}{2\pi}\int_0^T [v(t)]^2\, dt} = \sqrt{\frac{1}{2\pi}\int_0^{2\pi} [V_m \sin \theta]^2\, d\theta} = \sqrt{\frac{V_m^2}{2\pi}\int_0^{2\pi}\left[\frac{1-\cos 2\theta}{2}\right] d\theta} = \sqrt{\frac{V_m^2}{4\pi} \times (2\pi - 0)} = \frac{V_m}{\sqrt{2}}$$

$$\Rightarrow \quad V_{RMS} = \frac{V_m}{\sqrt{2}} \tag{2.11}$$

If the function consists of a number sinusoidal terms,

$$f(t) = a_0 + (a_1 \sin \omega t + a_2 \sin 2\omega t + \ldots) + (b_1 \cos \omega t + b_2 \cos 2\omega t + \ldots)$$

The RMS or effective value is given by

$$F_{RMS} = \sqrt{a_0^2 + \frac{1}{2}(a_1^2 + a_2^2 \cdots + a_n^2) + \frac{1}{2}(b_1^2 + b_2^2 \cdots + b_n^2)} \tag{2.12}$$

2.7 FORM FACTOR

It is defined as the ratio of the RMS value to the average value of the wave.

$$\text{Form factor} = \frac{\text{RMS value}}{\text{Average value}}$$

For a sinusoidal alternating voltage

$$\text{Form factor} = \frac{V_{RMS}}{V_{Avg}} = \frac{V_m/\sqrt{2}}{2V_m/\pi} = 1.11 \tag{2.13}$$

2.8 PEAK OR CREST FACTOR

It is defined as the ratio of the peak value to the RMS value of the wave.

$$\text{Peak factor} = \frac{\text{Peak value}}{\text{RMS value}}$$

For a sinusoidal alternating voltage

$$\text{Peak factor} = \frac{V_m}{V_{\text{RMS}}} = \frac{V_m}{V_m/\sqrt{2}} = 1.414 \quad (2.14)$$

Problem 2.3 The equation of an alternating current is $i(t) = 42.42 \sin(628t)$. Determine the

(i) RMS value (ii) average value (iii) form factor (iv) peak factor.

Solution:

Given that $i(t) = 42.42\sin(628t)$

Comparing with $i(t) = I_m \sin\omega t$

$$I_m = 42.42 \text{ A}, \omega = 628 \text{ rad/s}$$

(i) RMS value, $I_{\text{RMS}} = \dfrac{I_m}{\sqrt{2}} = \dfrac{42.42}{\sqrt{2}} = 30 \text{ A}$

(ii) Average value, $I_{\text{Avg}} = \dfrac{2I_m}{\pi} = \dfrac{2 \times 42.42}{\pi} = 27 \text{ A}$

(iii) Form factor $= \dfrac{\text{RMS value}}{\text{Average value}} = \dfrac{30}{27} = 1.111$

(iv) Peak factor $= \dfrac{\text{Peak value}}{\text{RMS value}} = \dfrac{42.42}{30} = 1.414$

Problem 2.4 Find the average and effective values, form factor and peak factor of the saw-tooth waveform.

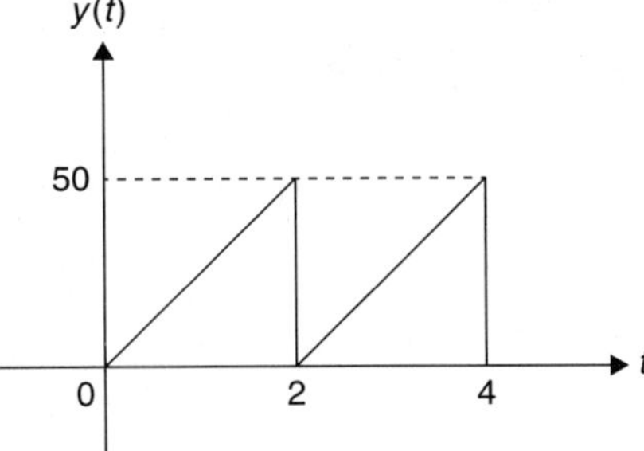

Solution:

For $0 < t < 2,\ y - 0 = \dfrac{50-0}{2-0}(t-0)$

$\Rightarrow \quad y = 25t$

$$Y_{\text{Avg}} = \frac{1}{T}\int_0^T y(t)dt = \frac{1}{2}\int_0^2 25t dt = \frac{25}{2}\int_0^2 t dt = 25$$

$$Y_{\text{RMS}} = \sqrt{\frac{1}{T}\int_0^T y(t)^2\, dt} = \sqrt{\frac{1}{2}\int_0^2 25^2 t^2 dt} = \sqrt{\frac{625}{2}\int_0^2 t^2 dt} = 28.86$$

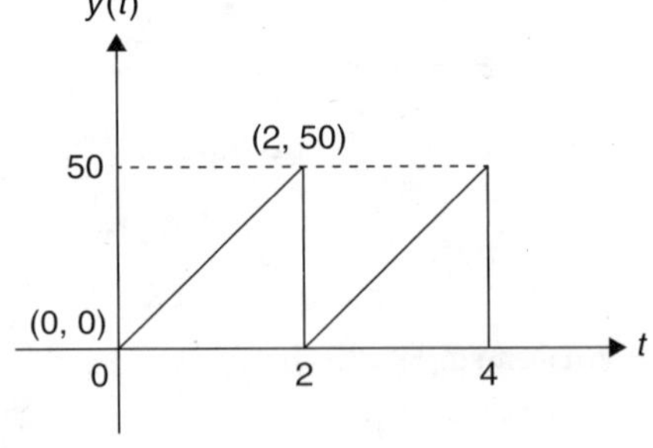

$$\text{Form factor} = \frac{Y_{\text{RMS}}}{Y_{\text{Avg}}} = \frac{28.86}{25} = 1.15$$

$$\text{Peak factor} = \frac{Y_m}{Y_{\text{RMS}}} = \frac{50}{28.86} = 1.732$$

Problem 2.5 Find the average and effective values, form factor and peak factor for the given waveform.

Solution:

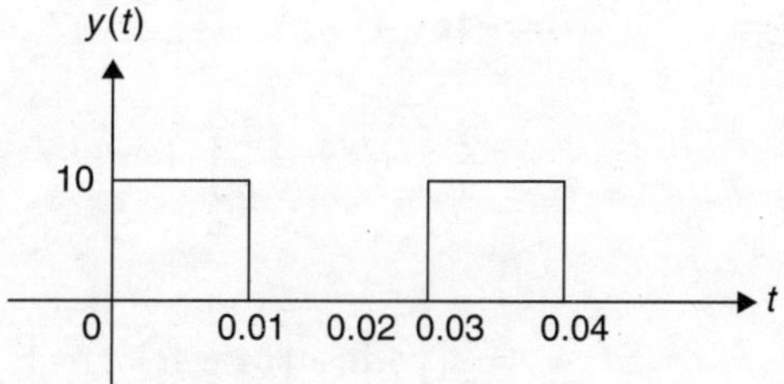

For $0 < t < 0.01, y(t) = 10$

For $0.01 < t < 0.03, y(t) = 0$

$$Y_{\text{Avg}} = \frac{1}{T}\int_0^T y(t)dt = \frac{1}{0.03}\int_0^{0.01} 10dt = 10 \times \frac{0.01}{0.03} = 3.333$$

$$Y_{\text{RMS}} = \sqrt{\frac{1}{T}\int_0^T y(t)^2\, dt} = \sqrt{\frac{1}{0.03}\int_0^{0.01} 10^2\, dt} = \sqrt{100 \times \frac{0.01}{0.03}} = 5.773$$

$$\text{Form factor} = \frac{Y_{\text{RMS}}}{Y_{\text{Avg}}} = \frac{5.773}{3.33} = 1.733$$

$$\text{Peak factor} = \frac{Y_m}{Y_{\text{RMS}}} = \frac{10}{5.773} = 1.732$$

Problem 2.6 Calculate the RMS and average values for the wave from.

y(t)
100
$\frac{T}{4}$
T
t
–20

Solution:

For $0 < t < \frac{T}{4}, y = 100$

$\frac{T}{4} < t < T, y = -20$

$$Y_{\text{avg}} = \frac{1}{T}\int_0^T y(t)dt = \frac{1}{T}\left[\int_0^{T/4} 100dt + \int_{T/4}^{T} -20dt\right] = 10$$

$$Y_{\text{RMS}}^2 = \frac{1}{T}\int_0^T [y(t)]^2\, dt = \frac{1}{T}\left[\int_0^{T/4} 100^2\, dt + \int_{T/4}^{T} 20^2\, dt\right] = 2800$$

$\Rightarrow \quad Y_{\text{RMS}} = \sqrt{2800} = 52.9$

Problem 2.7 Calculate the RMS and average values of the voltage waveform.

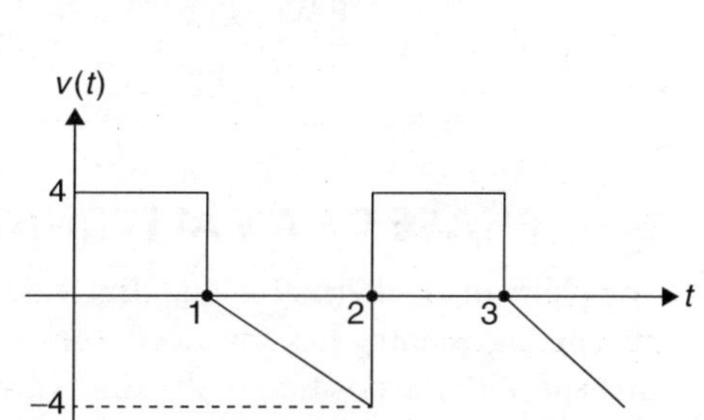

Solution:

For $0 < t < 1, v(t) = 4$

For $1 < t < 2, v(t) - 0 = \frac{-4 - 0}{2 - 1}(t - 1)$

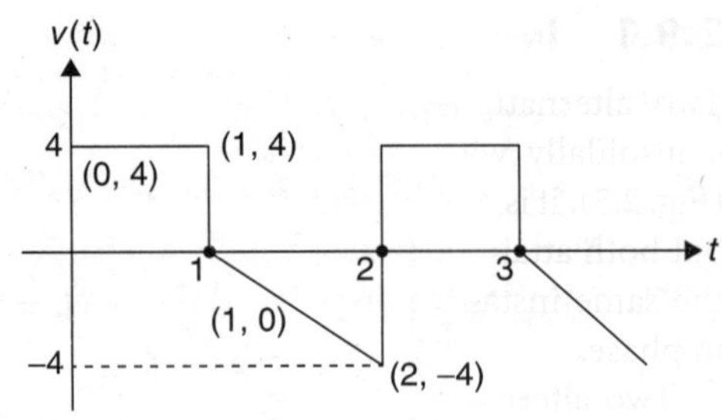

$\Rightarrow \quad v(t) = -4t + 4$

$$V_{\text{Avg}} = \frac{1}{T}\int_0^T v(t)dt = \frac{1}{2}\int_0^2 v(t)dt$$

$$= \frac{1}{2}[\int_0^1 4dt + \int_1^2 (4-4t)dt] = 1$$

$$V_{\text{RMS}}^2 = \frac{1}{2}\int_0^2 v(t)^2 dt = \frac{1}{2}[\int_0^1 4^2 dt + \int_1^2 (4-4t)^2 dt] = 10.66$$

$\Rightarrow \quad V_{\text{RMS}} = \sqrt{10.66} = 3.264$

Problem 2.8 A current has the following steady values (in amperes) for equal intervals of time changing suddenly from one value to the next: 0, 10, 20, 30, 20, 10, 0, –10, –20, –30... Calculate (i) RMS value (ii) average value (iii) form factor (iv) peak factor.

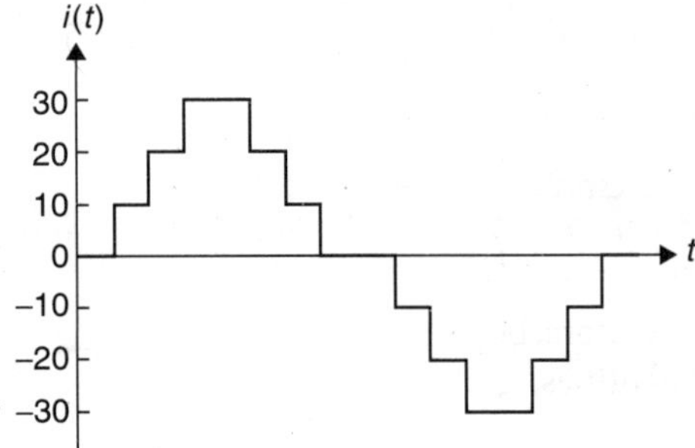

Solutions:

The wave form of the above alternating quantity is as shown.

(i) RMS value of an alternating current is

$$I_{\text{RMS}} = \sqrt{\frac{i_1^2 + i_2^2 + i_3^2 + \cdots + i_n^2}{n}} = \sqrt{\frac{0^2 + 10^2 + 20^2 + 30^2 + 20^2 + 10^2}{6}} = \sqrt{\frac{1900}{6}} = 17.8 \text{ A}$$

The RMS value is the same for either a half cycle or a full cycle, since the wave is symmetrical.

(ii) Average value of an alternating current is

$$I_{\text{avg}} = \frac{i_1 + i_2 + i_3 + \cdots + i_n}{n} = \frac{0 + 10 + 20 + 30 + 20 + 10}{6} = \frac{90}{6} = 15 \text{ A}$$

The average value is calculated for a half cycle only, since the wave is symmetrical.

(iii) $\text{Form factor} = \dfrac{\text{RMS value}}{\text{Average value}} = \dfrac{17.8}{15} = 1.187$

(iv) $\text{Peak factor} = \dfrac{\text{Peak value}}{\text{RMS value}} = \dfrac{30}{17.8} = 1.68$

2.9 PHASE OF AN ALTERNATING QUANTITY

The phase of an alternating quantity is defined as the fractional part of a period or cycle through which the alternating quantity has advanced from a chosen value. The phase of a sine wave is an angular measurement that specifies the position of the sine wave relative to a reference.

2.9.1 In-phase Alternating Quantities

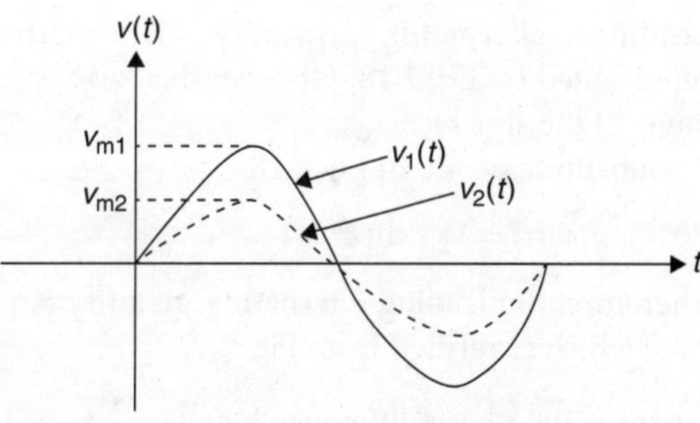

Fig. 2.5 In-phase alternating quantities

Two alternating voltages $v_1(t)$ and $v_2(t)$ are changing sinusoidally with amplitudes V_{m1} and V_{m2} respectively (Fig. 2.5). It is observed that their amplitudes are different, but both attain their zero values and maximum values at the same instant. Hence, they are said to be alternating in phase.

Two alternating quantities are said to be in-phase, if they obtain their zero values and maximum values at the same instant.

Inphase sinusoidal voltages are mathematically represented as

$$v_1(t) = V_{m1} \sin \omega t \tag{2.15}$$

$$v_2(t) = V_{m2} \sin \omega t \tag{2.16}$$

Substitute $\omega t = 0$ in Eqs 2.15 and 2.16.

$$\therefore \quad v_1(t) = 0 \text{ and } v_2(t) = 0$$

Therefore, both become zero at the same instant t. Put $\omega t = 90°$, corresponding to some other t.

$$\therefore \quad v_1(t) = V_{m1} \text{ and } v_2(t) = V_{m2}$$

Therefore, both become maximum at the same instant. Hence, in mathematical equations for two alternating quantities, if $\sin \omega t$ appears in both the equations then we have to understand that both are in same phase.

2.9.2 Out of Phase Alternating Quantities (Lagging)

In Fig. 2.6, $v_1(t)$ and $v_2(t)$ both are alternating, but they are not in phase. Here, $v_1(t) = 0$ at $\omega t = 0$, hence, $v_1(t)$ is taken as reference to compare the alternating of $v_2(t)$. It is observed that $v_2(t)$ will appear after a delay of ϕ compared to $v_1(t)$. Hence, $v_2(t)$ is said to be lagging $v_1(t)$ in time.

$$v_2(t) = V_{m2} \sin(\omega t - \phi) \tag{2.17}$$

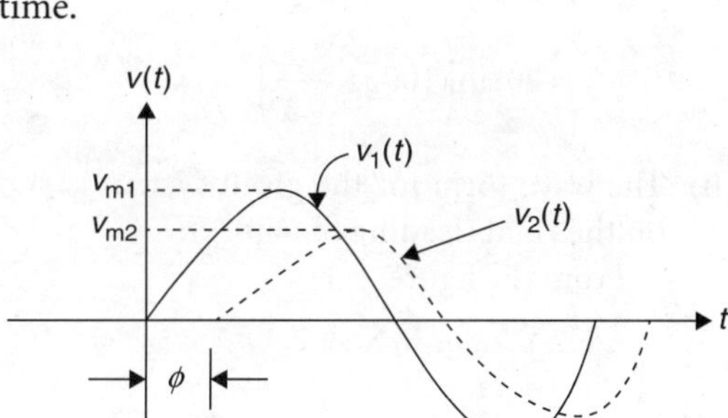

Fig. 2.6 Out of phase alternating quantities (lagging)

The lagging alternating quantity is mathematically represented by Eq. 2.17. Observe that $-\phi$ appears in the angle of sine term.

Substitute $\omega t = 0$ in Eq. 2.17.

$$v_2(t) = V_{m2} \sin(-\phi) = -V_{m2} \sin(\phi)$$

Therefore, the lagging quantity is negative at $t = 0$, which is clear from Fig. 2.6. Hence, there is a relation between mathematical equations and time diagrams of alternating quantity.

2.9.3 Out of Phase Alternating Quantities (Leading)

In Fig. 2.7, $v_1(t)$ is a reference quantity, because it is zero at $t = 0$. $v_2(t)$ becomes zero and maximum earlier than $v_1(t)$ in time, hence, $v_2(t)$ is said to be leading $v_1(t)$ in time.

$$v_2(t) = V_{m2} \sin(\omega t + \phi) \tag{2.18}$$

Leading alternating quantity is mathematically represented by Eq. 2.18. Observe that $+\phi$ appears in the angle of the sine term.

Substitute $\omega t = 0$ in Eq. 2.18.

$$v_2(t) = V_{m2} \sin \phi$$

Therefore, the leading alternating quantity is positive at $t = 0$ which is verified from Fig. 2.7.

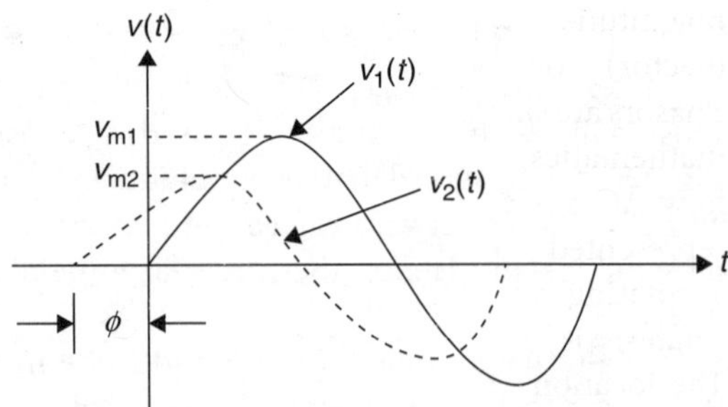

Fig. 2.7 Out of phase alternating quantities (leading)

Note: The phase difference between two or more sine waves can be estimated only if the frequency of the sine waves is the same (or speed of rotation should be same), but the amplitude need not to be same.

Problem 2.9 Draw the wave form and write the expressions of instantaneous value for the following.

(i) Sinusoidal voltage of amplitude 20 V, 50 Hz passing through its zero value at $\omega t = \frac{\pi}{3}$ and increasing positively.

(ii) Sinusoidal voltage of amplitude 15 V, 50 Hz passing through its zero value at $\omega t = -\frac{\pi}{6}$ and increasing positively.

Solution:

(i) The wave form for the given system is shown on the right (lagging in nature).

From the figure,

$$v = V_m \sin(\omega t - \phi)$$

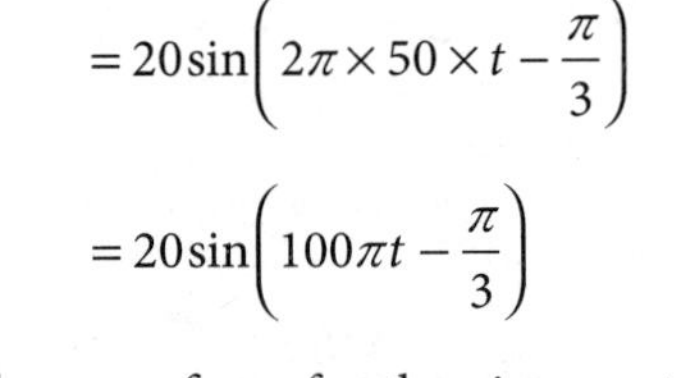

$$= 20\sin\left(2\pi \times 50 \times t - \frac{\pi}{3}\right)$$

$$= 20\sin\left(100\pi t - \frac{\pi}{3}\right)$$

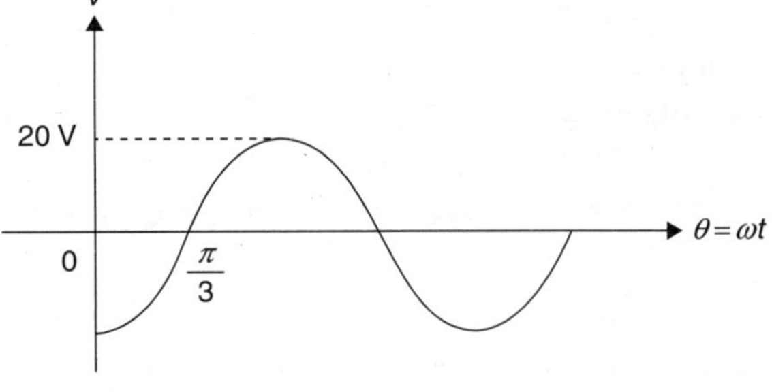

(ii) The wave form for the given system is shown on the right (leading in nature).

From the figure,

$$v = V_m \sin(\omega t + \phi)$$

$$= 15\sin\left(2\pi \times 50 \times t + \frac{\pi}{6}\right)$$

$$= 15\sin\left(100\pi t + \frac{\pi}{6}\right)$$

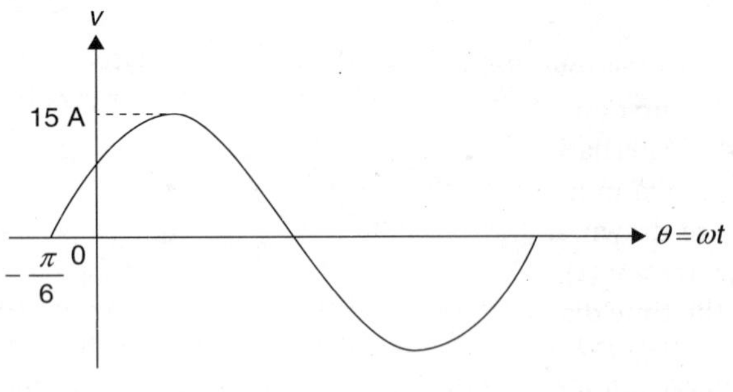

2.10 PHASORS

The amplitude and phase are the two important quantities that determine the way the circuit affects the signal. Accordingly, the signal can be expressed as a linear combination of complex sinusoids. Phase and magnitude defines a phasor (vector) or complex number. Phasors are similar to vectors (from mathematics). Figure 2.8 shows how AC sinusoidal quantities are represented by the position of a rotating vector. As the vector rotates, it generates an angle. The location of the vector on the plane surface is determined by the magnitude (length) of the vector and by the generated angle.

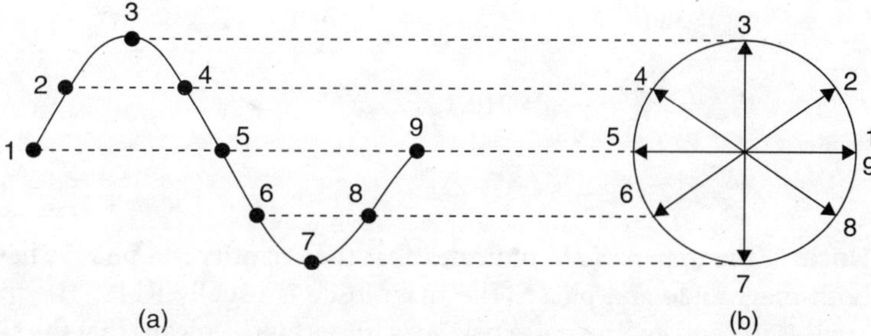

Fig. 2.8 (a) Magnitude of a sine wave. (b) A vector with its end fixed at the origin and rotating in a counter clockwise (ccw) direction representing the varying conditions of the AC signal

Representing sinusoidal signals by phasors is useful since circuit analysis laws such as KVL and KCL and familiar algebraic circuit analysis tools, such as series and parallel equivalence, voltage and current division are applicable in the phasor domain. These have been studied in DC circuits and can be applied. We do not need new analysis techniques to handle circuits in the phasor domain. The only difference is that circuit responses are phasors (complex numbers) rather than DC signals (real numbers).

2.11 VECTOR OR PHASOR DIAGRAM

The vector is a quantity which has both magnitude as well as direction. A vector should only be used to represent the magnitude and direction of a quantity in a plane. The term phasor is used to represent graphically the magnitude and phase of a sinusoidal alternating quantity.

The phase relations between various alternating quantities are represented by diagrams known as *phasor diagrams* or *vector diagrams*. Alternating quantities are represented by line segments whose lengths represent the magnitude of the alternating quantity. For an alternating quantity, a huge magnitude is represented by a longer line and smaller magnitude is represented by a shorter line. The reference alternating quantity is drawn along the positive x-axis with an arrow on its head pointing towards 0°. If the second alternating quantity is in phase with the first one, this is also drawn along the same line.

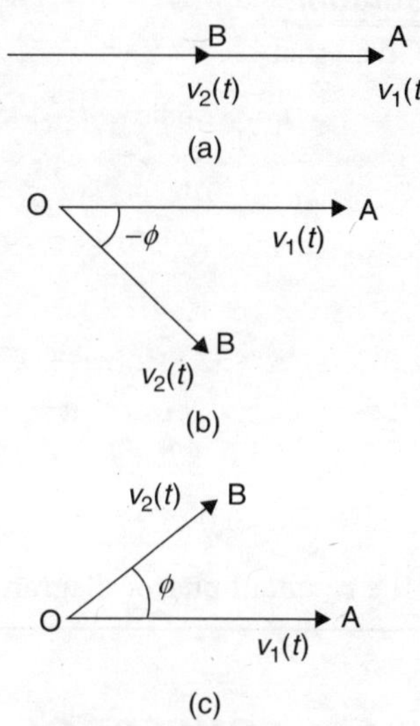

Fig. 2.9 Phasor or vector diagram representation

Alternating quantities $v_1(t)$ and $v_2(t)$ (time diagrams of Fig. 2.5) are shown in a vector diagram [Fig. 2.9(a)]. Both are in phase, hence, they are drawn along the same direction, that is, towards the 0° direction. $v_1(t) > v_2(t)$ in magnitude, hence OA > OB in Fig. 2.9(a). Alternating quantities $v_1(t)$ and $v_2(t)$ as shown in the time diagram of Fig. 2.6 are represented as vectors in Fig. 2.9(b). $v_1(t)$ is taken as reference, represented by line OA towards the 0° direction and $v_2(t)$ lags $v_1(t)$ by an angle ϕ° direction. Alternating quantities $v_1(t)$ and $v_2(t)$ as shown in Fig. 2.7 are represented by lines OA and OB in Fig. 2.9(c), as vectors. $v_1(t)$ is the reference and $v_2(t)$ is leading $v_1(t)$ by a phase angle of ϕ°, hence OB is shown at an angle of ϕ in the positive direction of measurement of angle.

Problem 2.10 Write the phasor form of the given signal and draw the phasor diagram.

$$v(t) = 300\sin(377t - 45°)$$

Solution:

Given that

$$V_m = 300$$

$$V_{rms} = \frac{V_m}{\sqrt{2}} = \frac{300}{\sqrt{2}} = 212.13$$

$$\therefore \quad V = 212.13\angle -45°$$

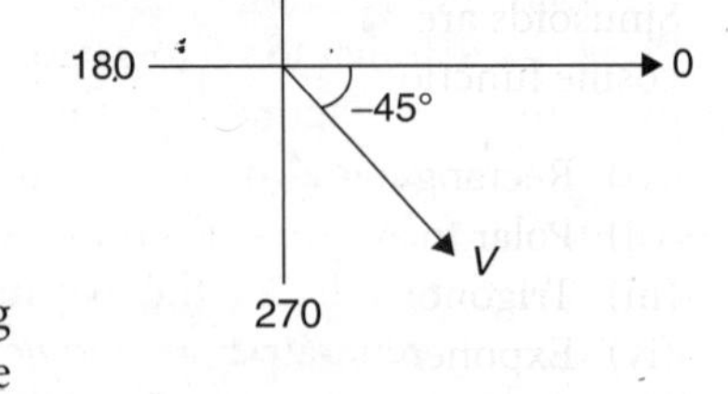

Note: The uppercase V, indicates that the quantity is a phasor, having both magnitude and phase. The magnitude is usually RMS. The phase angle is in degrees. The polarity is very important: + means that the signal leads the reference; while – means that the signal lags the reference.

Problem 2.11 Find the resultant of the following three alternating quantities and draw the phasor diagram for the resultant.

$$i_1 = 32.6\sin(\omega t - 145°)\text{ A},\ i_2 = 32.6\sin(\omega t - 25°)\text{ A} \quad \text{and} \quad i_3 = 32.6\sin(\omega t + 95°)\text{ A}$$

Solution:

Given that

$$i_1 = 32.6\sin(\omega t - 145°)\text{ A} \Rightarrow I_1 = \frac{32.6}{\sqrt{2}}\angle -145° = 23\angle -145° = (-18.8 - j13.2)\text{ A}$$

$$i_2 = 32.6\sin(\omega t - 25°)\text{ A} \Rightarrow I_2 = \frac{32.6}{\sqrt{2}}\angle -25° = 23\angle -25° = (20.8 - j9.71)\text{ A}$$

$$i_3 = 32.6\sin(\omega t + 95)\text{ A} \Rightarrow I_3 = \frac{32.6}{\sqrt{2}}\angle 95° = 23\angle 95° = (-2 + j23)\text{ A}$$

$$\therefore \quad I = I_1 + I_2 + I_3 = (-18.8 - j13.2) + (20.8 - j971) + (-2 + j23) = j0.09\text{ A}$$

$$= 0.09\angle 90°$$

The resultant phasor diagram is shown on the right.

2.12 CONCEPT OF *j* OPERATOR

The *j* operator is a vector operator. When if operates (multiplies) on a given phasor, produces a ccw rotation of the phasor by 90°, without changing its magnitude.

Consider a vector **V** along the real axis (Fig. 2.10). If it is rotated through 90° in counter clockwise (ccw) direction then multiplied by *j*, it becomes *j***V** where $j = \sqrt{-1}$ and it is $V\angle 90°$ in polar form. If the vector is rotated through 90° in the clockwise direction then it becomes –*j***V**. Suppose two vectors **P** and **Q** are at 90° and **P** is acting along the real axis, then the resultant is (**P** + *j***Q**), if **Q** leads **P** by 90°. If **Q** lags **P** by 90°, then the resultant is (**P** – *j***Q**).

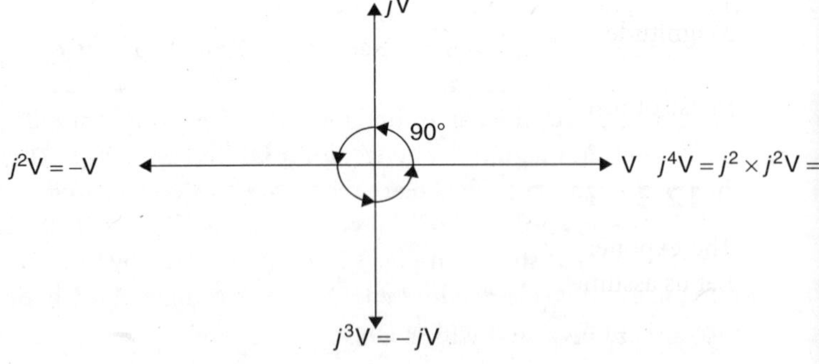

Fig. 2.10 Application of *j* operator

2.12.1 Representation of Phasors in the Complex Plane

Sinusoids are easily expressed in terms of phasors, which are more convenient to work with than sine and cosine functions. Phasors in the complex form can be represented in the following forms:

(i) Rectangular or cartesian or complex form: $z = x \pm jy$
(ii) Polar form: $z = r\angle\pm\theta$
(iii) Trigonometrical form: $z = r(\cos\theta \pm j\sin\theta)$
(iv) Exponential form: $z = re^{\pm j\theta}$

where $r = \sqrt{x^2 + y^2}$ is the magnitude of z, and $\theta = \tan^{-1}\left(\frac{y}{x}\right)$ is the phase of z.

The conversion from rectangular to polar form is given as

$$z = x \pm jy = r\angle\pm\theta \quad \text{where} \quad r = \sqrt{x^2 + y^2} \quad \text{and} \quad \theta = \tan^{-1}\left(\frac{y}{x}\right)$$

The conversion from polar to rectangular form is given as

$$z = r\angle\pm\theta = x \pm jy \quad \text{where} \quad x = r\cos\theta \quad \text{and} \quad y = r\sin\theta.$$

2.12.2 Addition and Subtraction of Phasors

The rectangular or complex form is best suited for addition and subtraction of alternating quantities. Let us assume two vector quantities as

$$z_1 = x_1 + jy_1 \quad \text{and} \quad z_2 = x_2 + jy_2$$

Addition $z = z_1 + z_2 = x_1 + jy_1 + x_2 + jy_2 = x_1 + x_2 + j(y_1 + y_2)$

Magnitude of resultant vector, $r = \sqrt{(x_1 + x_2)^2 + (y_1 + y_2)^2}$

Phase of resultant vector with respect to the x-axis, $\theta = \tan^{-1}\left(\frac{y_2 + y_1}{x_2 + x_1}\right)$

Subtraction $z = z_1 - z_2 = x_1 + jy_1 - x_2 - jy_2 = x_1 - x_2 + j(y_1 - y_2)$

Magnitude of resultant vector, $r = \sqrt{(x_1 - x_2)^2 + (y_1 - y_2)^2}$

Phase of resultant vector with respect to the x-axis, $\theta = \tan^{-1}\left(\frac{y_1 - y_2}{x_1 - x_2}\right)$

2.12.3 Multiplication and Division of Phasors

The exponential and polar forms are best suited for multiplication and division of alternating quantities. Let us assume two vector quantities as

$$z_1 = r_1\angle\theta_1 \quad \text{and} \quad z_2 = r_2\angle\theta_2$$

Multiplication $z = z_1 \times z_2 = r_1\angle\theta_1 \times r_2\angle\theta_2 = r_1 r_2\angle(\theta_1 + \theta_2)$

Division $z = \frac{z_1}{z_2} = \frac{r_1\angle\theta_1}{r_2\angle\theta_2} = \frac{r_1}{r_2}\angle(\theta_1 - \theta_2)$

Problem 2.12 Perform the following operations:

(i) $X+Y$ (ii) $X-Y$ (iii) $X\times Y$ (iv) $X\div Y$

where $X=6+j8$, $Y=3-j4$

Solution:

Given that

$$X=6+j8,\ Y=3-j4$$

(i) $X+Y=6+j8+3-j4=9+j4$

Using rectangular to polar transformation

$$X+Y=9+j4=\sqrt{9^2+4^2}\ \angle\tan^{-1}\left(\frac{4}{9}\right)=9.85\angle 23.94°$$

(ii) $X-Y=6+j8-3+j4=3+j12$

Using rectangular to polar transformation

$$X-Y=3+j12=\sqrt{3^2+12^2}\ \angle\tan^{-1}\left(\frac{12}{3}\right)=12.37\angle 75.96°$$

(iii) $X\times Y=(6+j8)(3-j4)=18-j24+j24+32=50+j0=50$

(iv) $\dfrac{X}{Y}=\dfrac{6+j8}{3-j4}$

Using rectangular to polar transformation

$$\frac{X}{Y}=\frac{6+j8}{3-j4}=\frac{\sqrt{6^2+8^2}\ \angle\tan^{-1}\left(\frac{8}{6}\right)}{\sqrt{3^2+4^2}\ \angle\tan^{-1}\left(\frac{-4}{3}\right)}=\frac{10\angle 53.13}{5\angle -53.13}=2\angle 106.26°$$

Problem 2.13 Evaluate these complex numbers

(i) $\sqrt{40\angle 50°+20\angle -30°}$ (ii) $\dfrac{10\angle -30°+(3-j4)}{(2+j4)(3-j5)^*}$

Solution:

(i) Using polar to rectangular transformation

$$40\angle 50°=40(\cos 50°+j\sin 50°)=25.71+j30.64$$

$$20\angle -30°=20[\cos(-30°)+j\sin(-30°)]=17.32-j10$$

Adding the above two gives

$$40\angle 50°+20\angle -30°=25.71+j30.64+17.32-j10=43.03+j20.64=47.72\angle 25.62°$$

Taking the square root of this

$$\sqrt{40\angle 50°+20\angle -30°^{0}}=\sqrt{47.72\angle 25.62°}=6.91\angle 12.81°$$

(ii) Using polar to rectangular transformation, addition, multiplication and division

$$\frac{10\angle -30^\circ + (3-j4)}{(2+j4)(3-j5)^*} = \frac{8.66 - j5 + (3-j4)}{(2+j4)(3+j5)} = \frac{11.66 - j9}{-14 + j22} = \frac{14.73\angle -37.66^\circ}{26.07\angle 122.47^\circ} = 0.565\angle -160.31^\circ$$

Problem 2.14 A sinusoidal voltage $V = 100\angle 60^\circ$ volts, is applied across a circuit having an impedance of $Z = (3 + j4)$ ohms. Find the magnitude of current and its phase angle with respect to voltage.

Solution:

Given that $V = 100\angle 60^\circ$ volts, $Z = (3 + j4)\ \Omega$

$$\text{Current, } I = \frac{V}{Z} = \frac{100\angle 60^\circ}{3 + j4} = \frac{100\angle 60^\circ}{5\angle 53.13^\circ} = 20\angle 6.87^\circ$$

Magnitude of current, $I = 20$ A

Phase angle $= 60^\circ - 6.87^\circ = 53.13^\circ$

ADDITIONAL SOLVED PROBLEMS

2.1 Find the RMS value of the resultant current in a conductor which simultaneously carries sinusoidal alternating current with a maximum value of 15 A and direct current of 15 A.

Solution: Let I be the RMS value of the resultant current and R be the resistance of the conductor. The heat produced by 1is the sum of heat produced by the DC current and heat produced by AC current.

$$I^2 R = 15^2 R + \left(\frac{15}{\sqrt{2}}\right)^2 R$$

$$I^2 = 225 + 112.5 = 337.5$$

$$I = \sqrt{337.5} = 18.37 \text{ A}$$

∴ The RMS value of the resultant current, $I = 18.37$ A

2.2 A light bulb is rated at 100 W for a 220 V supply. Find the (i) resistance of the bulb, (ii) peak voltage of the source, and (iii) RMS current through the bulb.

Solution: Given that $P = 100$ W, $V = 220$ V

(i) The resistance of the bulb is given by

$$R = \frac{V^2}{P} = \frac{220^2}{100} = 484\ \Omega$$

(ii) The peak voltage of the source

$$V_m = \sqrt{2}V = \sqrt{2} \times 220 = 311 \text{ V}$$

(iii) The RMS current through the bulb

$$I = \frac{100}{220} = 0.45 \text{ A}$$

2.3 Obtain the RMS value, average value, form factor and peak factor of half-wave rectified sine wave.

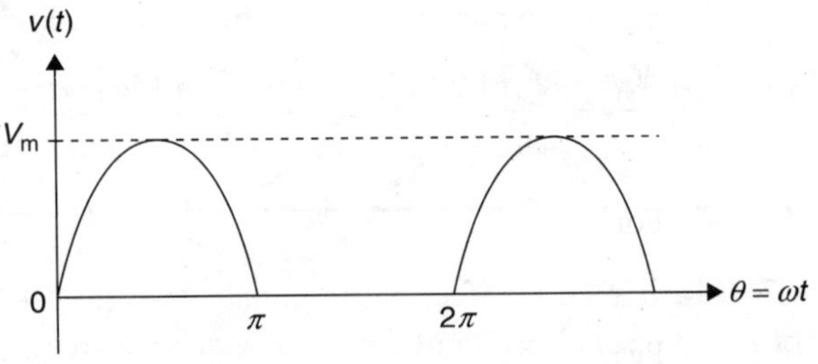

Solution: From the given data, half-wave rectified sine wave can be drawn as shown.

Let us consider a sinusoidal voltage

$$v(t) = V_m \sin\omega t = V_m \sin\theta$$

(i) RMS value, $V_{\text{RMS}} = \sqrt{\dfrac{1}{T}\displaystyle\int_0^T [v(t)]^2\, dt}$

$$V_{\text{RMS}} = \sqrt{\frac{1}{2\pi}\int_0^{\pi} [V_m \sin\theta]^2\, d\theta} = \sqrt{\frac{V_m^2}{2\pi}\int_0^{\pi}\left[\frac{1-\cos 2\theta}{2}\right] d\theta} = \sqrt{\frac{V_m^2}{4\pi}\times(\pi-0)} = \frac{V_m}{2}$$

(ii) Average value, $V_{\text{Avg}} = \dfrac{1}{T}\displaystyle\int_0^T v(t)dt$

$$V_{\text{Avg}} = \frac{1}{2\pi}\int_0^{\pi} V_m \sin\theta d\theta = \frac{V_m}{2\pi}[-\cos\theta]_0^{\pi} = \frac{V_m}{\pi}$$

$$\text{Form factor} = \frac{\text{RMS value}}{\text{Average value}} = \frac{V_{\text{RMS}}}{V_{\text{Avg}}} = \frac{V_m/2}{V_m/\pi} = \frac{\pi}{2} = 1.57$$

$$\text{Peak factor} = \frac{\text{Peak value}}{\text{RMS value}} = \frac{V_{\text{max}}}{V_{\text{RMS}}} = \frac{V_m}{V_m/2} = 2$$

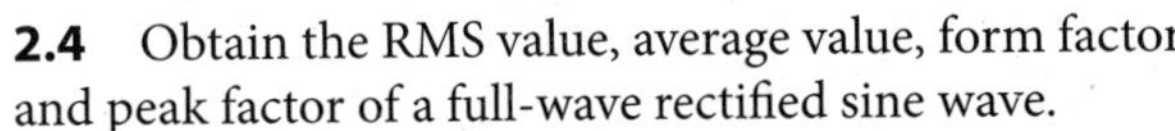

2.4 Obtain the RMS value, average value, form factor and peak factor of a full-wave rectified sine wave.

Solution: From the given data, half-wave rectified sine wave can be drawn as shown.

Let us consider a sinusoidal voltage

$$v(t) = V_m \sin\omega t = V_m \sin\theta$$

(i) RMS value, $V_{\text{RMS}} = \sqrt{\dfrac{1}{T}\displaystyle\int_0^T [v(t)]^2\, dt}$

$$V_{\text{RMS}} = \sqrt{\frac{1}{\pi}\int_0^{\pi} [V_m \sin\theta]^2\, d\theta} = \sqrt{\frac{V_m^2}{\pi}\int_0^{\pi}\left[\frac{1-\cos 2\theta}{2}\right] d\theta} = \sqrt{\frac{V_m^2}{2\pi}\times(\pi-0)} = \frac{V_m}{\sqrt{2}}$$

(ii) Average value, $V_{\text{Avg}} = \dfrac{1}{T}\displaystyle\int_0^T v(t)dt$

$$V_{Avg} = \frac{1}{\pi}\int_0^{\pi} V_m \sin\theta d\theta = \frac{V_m}{\pi}[-\cos\theta]_0^{\pi} = \frac{2V_m}{\pi}$$

$$\text{Form factor} = \frac{\text{RMS value}}{\text{Average value}} = \frac{V_{RMS}}{V_{Avg}} = \frac{V_m/\sqrt{2}}{2V_m/\pi} = \frac{\pi}{2\sqrt{2}} = 1.11$$

$$\text{Peak factor} = \frac{\text{Peak value}}{\text{RMS value}} = \frac{V_{max}}{V_{RMS}} = \frac{V_m}{V_m/\sqrt{2}} = \sqrt{2} = 1.414$$

2.5 Obtain the RMS value, average value, form factor and peak factor for a voltage of symmetrical square shape whose amplitude is 10 V and time period is 40 s.

Solution: From the given data, the symmetrical square wave can be drawn as shown.

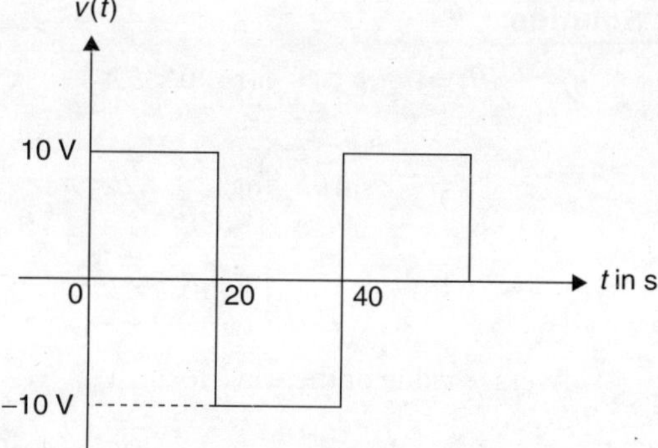

For $0 < t < 20$, $v(t) = 10$

For $20 < t < 40$, $v(t) = -10$

$$\text{RMS value, } V_{RMS} = \sqrt{\frac{1}{T}\int_0^T [v(t)]^2 dt}$$

$$V_{RMS} = \sqrt{\frac{1}{40}\int_0^{40} v(t)^2 dt} = \sqrt{\frac{1}{40}\int_0^{20} 100dt + \int_{20}^{40} 100dt} = \sqrt{\frac{1}{40}(2000 + 2000)} = 10 \text{ V}$$

$$\text{Average value, } V_{Avg} = \frac{1}{T}\int_0^T v(t)dt$$

$$V_{Avg} = \frac{1}{20}\int_0^{20} v(t)dt = \frac{1}{20}\int_0^{20} 10dt = \frac{1}{20}\left[10t\right]_0^{20} = 10$$

$$\text{Form factor} = \frac{\text{RMS value}}{\text{Average value}} = \frac{V_{RMS}}{V_{Avg}} = \frac{10}{10} = 1$$

$$\text{Peak factor} = \frac{\text{Peak value}}{\text{RMS value}} = \frac{V_{max}}{V_{RMS}} = \frac{10}{10} = 1$$

2.6 Calculate the RMS value, average value, form factor and peak factor for the current over one cycle of an alternating voltage $v(t) = 200\sin(314t)$ volts applied to a resistor of 20 Ω, which offers the flow of current in one direction only.

Solution: Given that $v(t) = 200\sin(314t)$ V, $R = 20\ \Omega$, $V_m = 200$ V

$$I_m = \frac{V_m}{R} = \frac{200}{20} = 10 \text{ A}$$

(i) RMS value of current, $I_{RMS} = \frac{I_m}{\sqrt{2}} = \frac{10}{\sqrt{2}} = 7.07 \text{ A}$

(ii) Average value of current, $I_{Avg} = \dfrac{2I_m}{\pi} = \dfrac{20}{\pi} = 6.37$ A

(iii) Form factor $= \dfrac{\text{RMS value}}{\text{Average value}} = \dfrac{7.07}{6.37} = 1.11$

(iv) Peak factor $= \dfrac{\text{Peak value}}{\text{RMS value}} = \dfrac{10}{7.07} = 1.414$

2.7 Find the average and RMS value of the wave form.

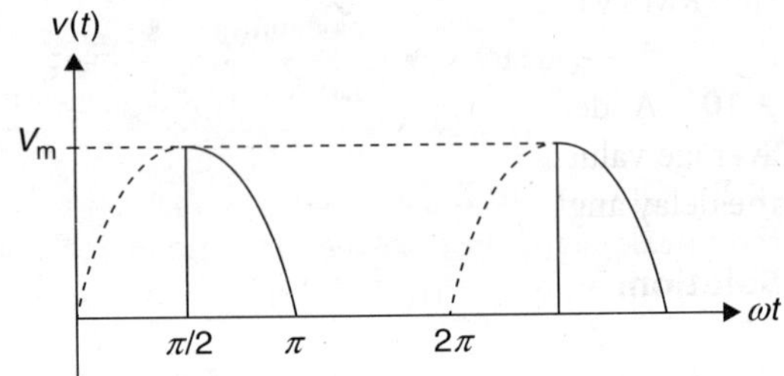

Solution:

$$v(\theta) = 0 \quad \text{for} \quad 0 < \theta < \frac{\pi}{2}$$

$$= V_m \sin\theta \quad \text{for} \quad \frac{\pi}{2} < \theta < \pi$$

$$= 0 \quad \text{for} \quad \pi < \theta < 2\pi$$

(i) Average value of the wave form, $V_{Avg} = \dfrac{1}{T}\displaystyle\int_0^T v(t)dt$

$$V_{Avg} = \frac{1}{2\pi}\int_0^{2\pi} v(\theta)d\theta = \frac{1}{2\pi}\int_{\pi/2}^{\pi} V_m \sin\theta d\theta = \frac{V_m}{2\pi}\left[-\cos\theta\right]_{\pi/2}^{\pi} = \frac{-V_m}{2\pi}[-1-0] = \frac{V_m}{2\pi}$$

(ii) RMS value of the wave form, $V_{RMS} = \sqrt{\dfrac{1}{T}\displaystyle\int_0^T [v(t)]^2 dt}$

$$V_{RMS} = \sqrt{\frac{1}{2\pi}\int_0^{2\pi} [v(\theta)^2 d\theta} = \sqrt{\frac{1}{2\pi}\int_{\pi/2}^{\pi} [V_m \sin\theta]^2 d\theta} = \sqrt{\frac{V_m^2}{2\pi}\int_{\pi/2}^{\pi}\left[\frac{1-\cos 2\theta}{2}\right] d\theta}$$

$$= \sqrt{\frac{V_m^2}{4\pi}\left[\theta - \frac{\sin 2\theta}{2}\right]_{\pi/2}^{\pi}} = \sqrt{\frac{V_m^2}{4\pi} \times \frac{\pi}{2}} = \frac{V_m}{2\sqrt{2}}$$

2.8 Two alternating currents represented as $i_1 = 4\sin\omega t$ and $i_2 = 10\sin(\omega t + 60°)$ are fed into a common conductor. Find the RMS value of the resultant current.

Solution: Given that $i_1 = 4\sin\omega t$ and $i_2 = 10\sin(\omega t + 60°)$

$$i_1 = 4\sin\omega t \;\Rightarrow\; I_1 = \frac{4}{\sqrt{2}} = 2.83 \text{ A}$$

$$i_2 = 10\sin(\omega t + 60°) \Rightarrow I_2 = \frac{10}{\sqrt{2}}\angle 60° = 7.07\angle 60° = 3.535 + j6.123$$

Resultant current, $I = I_1 + I_2 = 2.83 + 3.535 + j6.123 = 6.365 + j6.123 = 8.83\angle 44°$

Therefore, the RMS value of current = 8.83 A

2.9 Find the average and RMS values of the wave form.

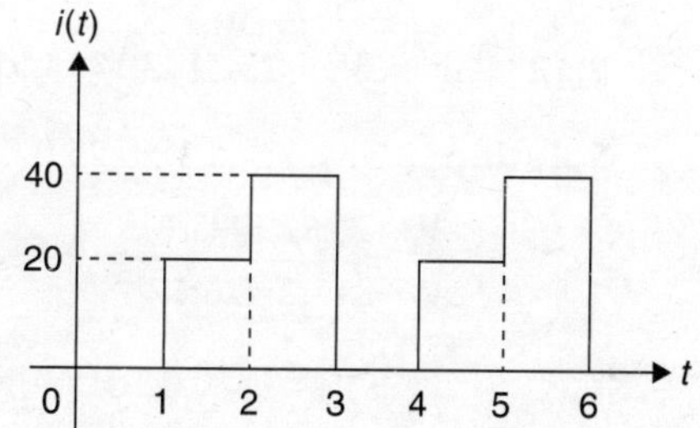

Solution:

(i) Average value, $I_{Avg} = \dfrac{i_1 + i_2 + i_3 + \cdots + i_n}{n} = \dfrac{0 + 20 + 40}{3} = 20 \text{ A}$

(ii) RMS value, $I_{RMS} = \sqrt{\dfrac{i_1^2 + i_2^2 + i_3^2 + \cdots + i_n^2}{n}} = \sqrt{\dfrac{0^2 + 20^2 + 40^2}{3}} = 25.82$

2.10 A delayed full wave rectified current has an average value equal to half of its maximum value. Find the delay angle, θ.

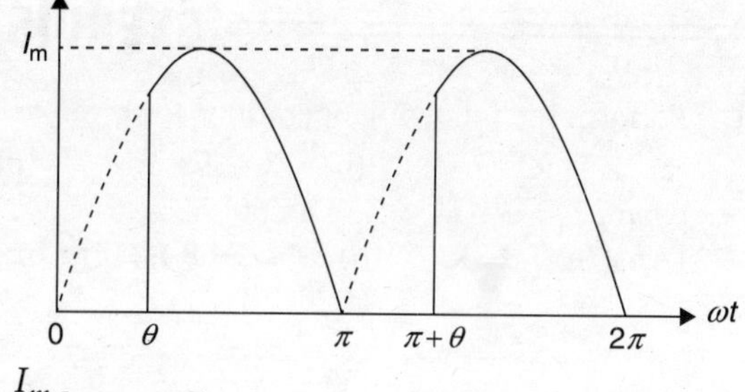

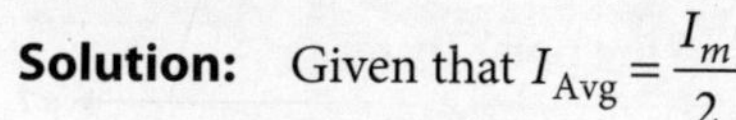

Solution: Given that $I_{Avg} = \dfrac{I_m}{2}$

Average value, $I_{Avg} = \dfrac{1}{T}\displaystyle\int_0^T i(t)dt$

$$I_{Avg} = \frac{1}{\pi}\int_\theta^\pi i(t)dt = \frac{1}{\pi}\int_\theta^\pi I_m \sin\theta = \frac{I_m}{\pi}\left[-\cos\theta\right]_\theta^\pi = \frac{I_m}{\pi}[1 + \cos\theta]$$

But as per data, $I_{Avg} = \dfrac{I_m}{2} = \dfrac{I_m}{\pi}[1 + \cos\theta]$

$\Rightarrow \quad 1 + \cos\theta = \dfrac{\pi}{2}$

$\Rightarrow \quad \cos\theta = \dfrac{\pi}{2} - 1 = 0.57$

$\Rightarrow \quad \theta = \cos^{-1}(0.57) = 55.25°$

2.11 Determine the RMS value of a semi-circular current wave which has a maximum value of r.

Solution: The equation of a semi circuiar wave is

$$x^2 + y^2 = r^2$$

$$y^2 = r^2 - x^2$$

$$I_{RMS} = \sqrt{\frac{1}{2r}\int_{-r}^{r} y^2 dx}$$

$$I_{RMS}{}^2 = \frac{1}{2r}\int_{-r}^{r}(r^2 - x^2)dx = \frac{1}{2r}\left[r^2 x - \frac{x^3}{3}\right]_{-r}^{r}$$

$$= \frac{1}{2r}\left[r^3 - \frac{r^3}{3} + r^3 - \frac{r^3}{3}\right] = r^2 - \frac{r^2}{3} = \frac{2r^2}{3}$$

$\therefore \quad I_{RMS} = \sqrt{\dfrac{2}{3}}\, r = 0.816r$

2.12 Given $V_1 = 25\angle 143.13°$ and $V_2 = 11.2\angle 26.57°$ find the ratio $\dfrac{V_1}{V_2}$ and the sum $V_1 + V_2$.

Solution: Given that $V_1 = 25.0\angle 143.13°$, $V_2 = 11.2\angle 26.57°$

$$\frac{V_1}{V_2} = \frac{25\angle 143.13°}{11.2\angle 26.57°} = 2.23\angle 116.56° = -1.00 + j1.99$$

$$V_1 + V_2 = (-20.0 + j15.0) + (10.0 + j5.0) = -10.0 + j20.0 = 22.36\angle 116.57°$$

EXERCISE PROBLEMS

1. Perform the following operations for given vectors and convert each into the polar form.
(a) $Z_1 + Z_2$ (b) $Z_1 - Z_2$ (c) $\frac{Z_1}{Z_2}$ (d) $Z_1 Z_2$
where $Z_1 = 5 - j4$, $Z_2 = 4\angle 60°$
[**Ans:** (a) $7\angle -4.37°$, (b) $8.04\angle -68.1°$, (c) $1.6\angle -98.7°$, (d) $25.6\angle -21.34°$]

2. Find the average and RMS values of the voltage waveform as shown. Also calculate the form factor of the waveform.
[**Ans:** $V_{RMS} = 0.816$, $V_{Avg} = 0.75$, form factor = 1.088]

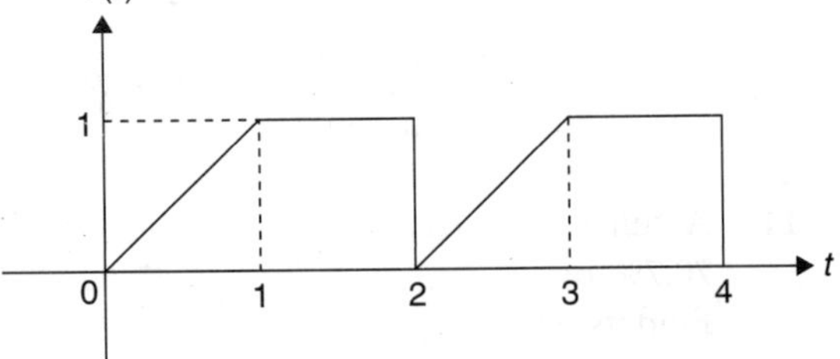

3. Determine the RMS value, average value and form factor of a periodic function as shown.
[**Ans:** $V_{rms} = 4.0825$ V, $V_{avg} = 2.5$ V, Form factor = 1.633]

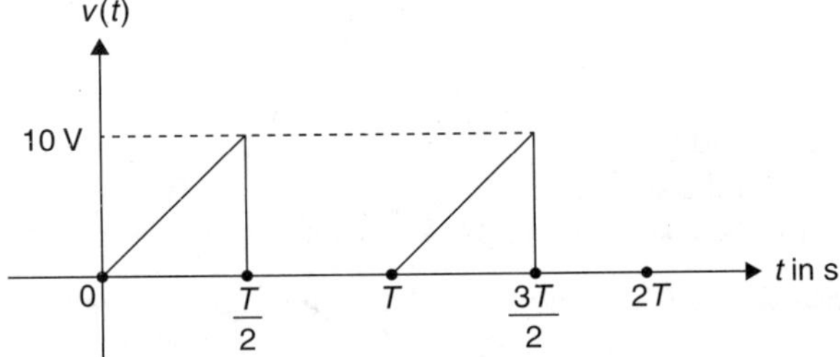

4. Calculate the RMS value for the periodically alternating wave having the following values for equal intervals of time, changing suddenly from one value to the next value 0, 5, 10, 20, 50, 60, 50, 20, 10, 5, 0, –5, –10, –20 V... Also calculate the form factor for the wave [**Ans:** RMS value = 31.06, form factor = 1.35]

5. The equation of an alternating current is $i(t) = 200\sin(318t)$. Find
(a) maximum value (b) RMS value (c) average value (d) form factor (e) peak factor
[**Ans:** (a) 200 A (b) 141.4 A (c) 127.4 A (d) 1.11 (e) 1.414]

6. Represent the following AC voltages by phasors
(a) $v_1 = 100\sin\omega t$ (b) $v_2 = 150\sin(\omega t - 30°)$ (c) $v_3 = 200\sin(\omega t + 120°)$
[**Ans:** (a) $V_1 = 70.7\angle 0$ (b) $V_2 = 106.1\angle -30°$ (c) $V_3 = 141.4\angle 120°$]

7. Find the resultant of the following alternating currents
$i_1 = 10\sin\omega t$ and $i_2 = 14\sin(\omega t + 60°)$
[**Ans:** $i = 20.87\sin(\omega t + 35.5°)$]

8. Determine the RMS value of the current, $i = 10 + 20\sin\omega t + 10\cos\omega t$ [**Ans:** $I = 18.71$ A]

9. Determine the RMS and average values of the saw tooth wave form. [**Ans:** $F_{RMS} = 28.9$, $F_{avg} = 25$]

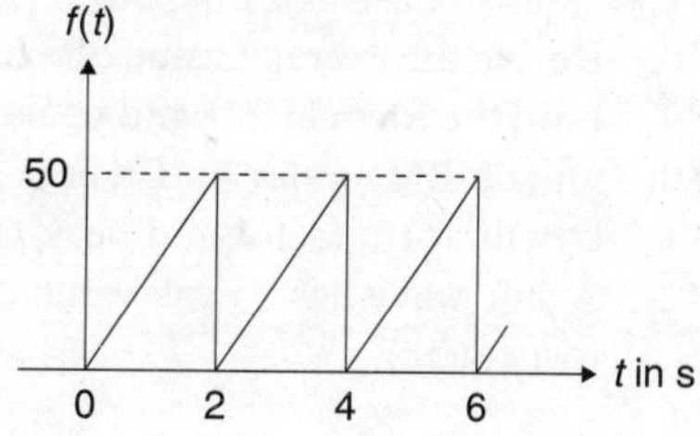

10. Determine the RMS value, average value and form factor of the wave form.
[**Ans:**
$$V_{RMS} = \frac{V_m}{\sqrt{3}},\ V_{Avg} = \frac{V_m}{2},\ \text{form factor} = 1.1547]$$

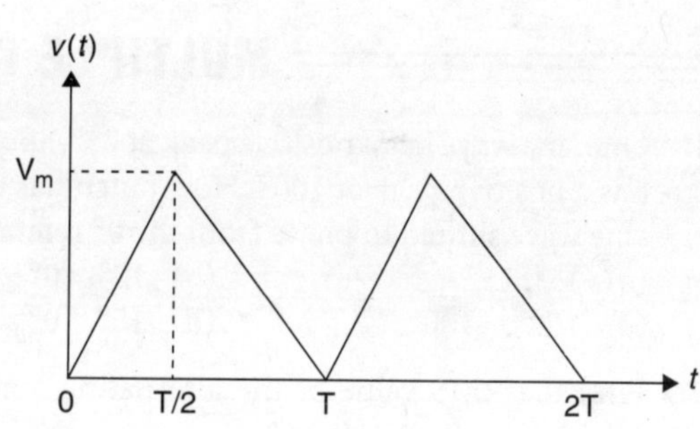

11. A full wave rectified wave is clipped at 70.7% of its maximum value as shown. Find its average and RMS value.
[**Ans:** $V_{Avg} = 0.54V_m$, $V_{RMS} = 0.555V_m$]

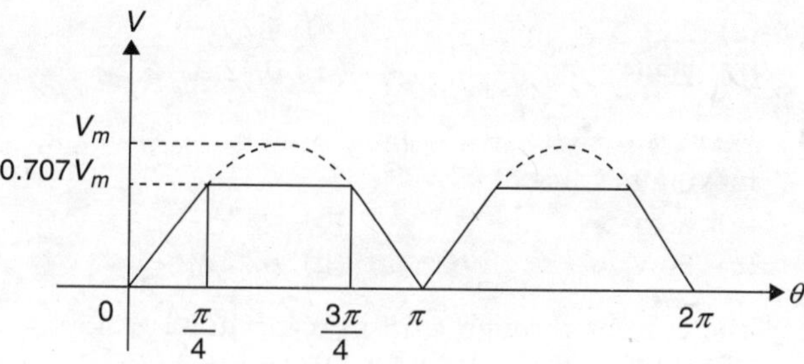

12. Find the effective value of the resultant current which simultaneously carries a direct current of 10 A and a sinusoidally varying current with a peak value of 10 A. [**Ans:** 12.25 A]

13. Find the average and RMS values of the wave form.
[**Ans:** $V_{Avg} = 57.5$ V, $V_{RMS} = 64.42$ V]

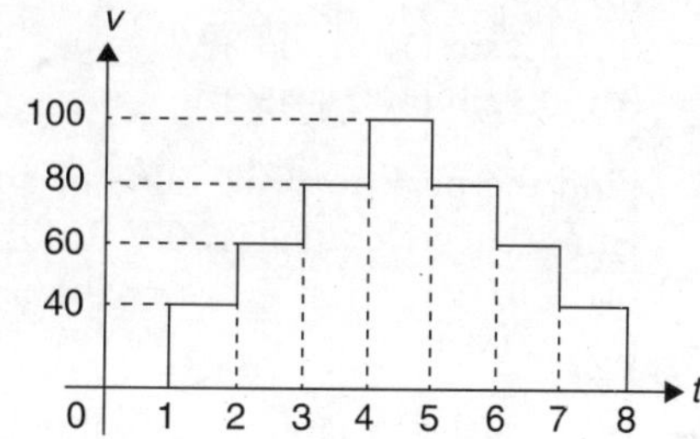

REVIEW QUESTIONS

1. State the advantages of sinusoidal alternating quantity.
2. Define phasor.
3. Define (a) RMS value and derive the expressions for the same of a sinusoidal alternating quantity, (b) average value, (c) form factor, (d) form peak factor.
4. Define amplitude.
5. What is j operator? Explain its significance.

6. What a phasor diagram? Explain its significance.
7. Define phase and phase difference.
8. Derive the average value of a half-wave rectified sine wave.
9. Find the form factor and peak factor of a half-wave rectified sine wave.
10. Obtain RMS value and average values of a full-wave rectified sine wave.
11. Obtain form factor and peak factor of a full-wave rectified sine wave.
12. A sine wave has a peak value of 100 V. Determine (a) RMS value (b) average value (c) peak factor (d) form factor.

MULTIPLE CHOICE QUESTIONS

1. One sine wave has a positive peak at 75°, another has a positive peak at 100°. How much has each sine wave shifted in phase from the 0° reference.
   (a) 15°, 15° (b) 10°, 10°
   (c) 100°, –100° (d) 15°, 10°

2. Find the RMS value of the alternating current $I = 4.2 \sin(5000t + 45°)$ A
   (a) 2.21 A (b) 4.2 A
   (c) 2.9 A (d) 0.42 A

3. What is the effective value of sine wave with a maximum value of 95 V?
   (a) zero (b) 95 V
   (c) 50 V (d) 67.2 V

4. The current through a 15 pF capacitor is 0.45 sin $(10^8t + 45°)$ mA. Write the mathematical expression for the voltage across it.
   (a) 0.45 sin $(10^8t - 0°)$ V
   (b) 0.45 sin $(10^8t - 45°)$ V
   (c) 0.3 sin $(10^8t - 45°)$ V
   (d) 0.3 sin $(10^8t + 45°)$ V

5. Find the peak to peak value of an AC voltage whose effective value is 50 V RMS?
   (a) 7.07 V (b) 707.0 V
   (c) 141.4 V (d) 70.7 V

6. What is the instantaneous value of $v(t) = 5\sin(2\pi \times 10^4 t)$ volts at time, $t = 25\ \mu s$
   (a) –10 V (b) 5 V
   (c) 10 V (d) 0.137 V

7. Average value of sine wave over half a cycle of $v(t) = V_m \sin\omega t$
   (a) $-0.637V_m$ (b) zero
   (c) $0.637V_m$ (d) unity

8. A 318 μF capacitor is connected across a 230 V, 50 Hz system. Find the RMS value of the current.
   (a) 30 A (b) 33 A
   (c) 1 A (d) 23 A

9. The current in a 2.2 kΩ resistor is $I = 5 \sin(2\pi \times 100t + 45°)$ mA. What is the effective value of resistor voltage?
   (a) 778.0 V (b) 7.78 V
   (c) 77.8 V (d) 0.778 V

10. The ratio of RMS value to the average value is called
    (a) peak factor (b) form factor
    (c) power factor (d) all of the above

11. The ratio of maximum value to the RMS value is called
    (a) peak factor (b) form factor
    (c) power factor (d) all of the above

12. The form factor of a sinusoidal wave form is
    (a) 1.11 (b) 1.414
    (c) 1.732 (d) 0

13. The peak factor of a sinusoidal wave form is
    (a) 1.11 (b) 1.414
    (c) 1.732 (d) 0

14. The form factor of a DC voltage is
    (a) 1 (b) 1.414
    (c) infinity (d) 0

15. RMS value and the average value are the same in case of a
    (a) triangular wave (b) square wave
    (c) sine wave (d) rectangular wave

16. The voltage wave consists of two components—a 100 V DC component and a sinusoidal component of maximum value 100 V, the average value of the resultant will be
(a) 100 V (b) 200 V
(c) 50 V (d) 0 V

17. The average value of a sinusoidal wave form over a full cycle is
(a) 1 (b) 1.414
(c) infinity (d) 0

18. If a wire is carrying a direct current of 100 A and a sinusoidal alternating current of peak value 100 A , then the RMS value of resultant current is
(a) 100 V (b) 200 V
(c) 50 V (d) 122.4 V

19. Two alternating emfs are represented by v_1 = 5 sin(ωt + 45°) and v_2 = 10sin(ωt – 45°). The phase angle between them is
(a) 30° (b) 45°
(c) 60° (d) 90°

20. Two currents are represented by $i_1 = 10\sin(\omega t)$ and $i_2 = 10\sin(\omega t - 45°)$, their resultant is
(a) $i = 10\sin(\omega t - 45°)$
(b) $i = 10\sqrt{2}\sin(\omega t + 45°)$
(c) $i = 10\sqrt{2}\sin(\omega t - 45°)$
(d) $i = 10\sqrt{2}\sin(\omega t)$

21. If the peak value of an alternating quantity is 250 V and the peak factor is 1.57, then the RMS value is
(a) 356 V (b) 159 V
(c) 177 V (d) 250 V

22. The average value of a sine wave of current is 10 A. If it is rectified by a half-wave rectifier, the rectified output average current is
(a) 10 A (b) 5 A
(c) $10/\sqrt{2}$ A (d) $10\sqrt{2}$ A

23. The RMS value of a half-wave rectified sine wave is 5 V, then the peak value of the quantity is
(a) 10 V (b) $5\sqrt{2}$ V
(c) 2.5 V (d) $5/\sqrt{2}$ V

24. The RMS value of an alternating current $i(t) = 2 + 5\sin(314t)$
(a) $\sqrt{27}$ A (b) $\sqrt{14.5}$ A
(c) $\sqrt{29}$ A (d) 7 A

25. An alternating quantity has a time period of 0.02 s. If the time period is doubled for the alternating quantity, then the new frequency will be
(a) halved (b) doubled
(c) three times (d) four times

26. A constant current of 2.8 A exists in a resistor. The RMS value of the current is
(a) 1.4 A (b) 2.8 A
(c) 5.6 A (d) undefined

Answers

1. d	**2.** c	**3.** d	**4.** c	**5.** c	**6.** b	**7.** c	**8.** d	**9.** b	**10.** b
11. a	**12.** a	**13.** b	**14.** d	**15.** b	**16.** a	**17.** a	**18.** d	**19.** d	**20.** c
21. b	**22.** b	**23.** a	**24.** b	**25.** a	**26.** b				

3 Steady State Analysis of AC Circuits

Learning Outcomes

After reading this chapter, the reader will able to

- Find the response of pure *R*, *L* and *C* for sinusoidal excitation
- Outline the concept of time and frequency domain response
- Define impedance and admittance
- Explain the concepts instantaneous and complex powers
- Illustrate the power triangle
- Contrast real, reactive and apparent powers
- Define power factor and explain its significance
- Illustrate the response of *RL*, *RC* and *RLC* series circuits for sinusoidal excitation
- Illustrate the response of *RL*, *RC* and *RLC* parallel circuits for sinusoidal excitation

3.1 INTRODUCTION

The behaviour of a pure resistor, inductor and capacitor, and their series and parallel combinations in various circuits is dealt with in this chapter. This also leads us to the concept of complex impedance, admittance, power and power factor.

The alternating voltage source is assumed to be purely sinusoidal in nature and is represented as $v(t) = V_m \sin\omega t$. The corresponding analysis of current, power and phase shift is discussed for each case. The equations for the complex impedance and complex admittance for all possible circuit configurations are developed.

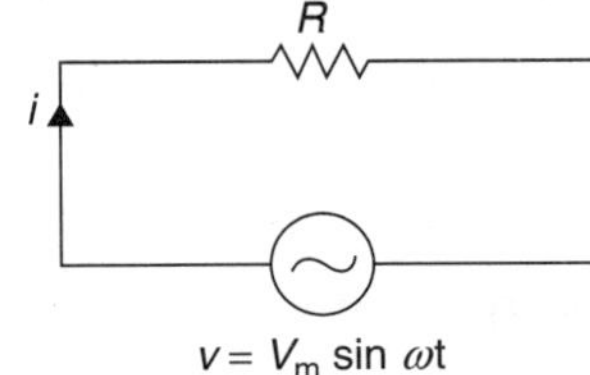

(a) Circuit diagram

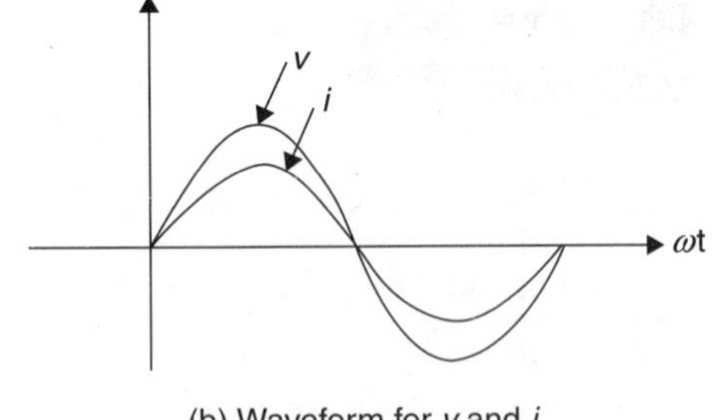

(b) Waveform for *v* and *i*

0 $\quad \bar{I} = I\angle 0° \quad \bar{V} = I\angle 0°$

(c) Phasor diagram

Fig. 3.1 AC through a pure resistor

3.2 RESPONSE TO SINUSOIDAL EXCITATION

3.2.1 AC Through Pure Resistor

Consider an AC circuit with a pure resistance of *R* ohms connected across an alternating voltage $v = V_m \sin\omega t$ [Fig. 3.1(a)]. The current flowing in the circuit is *i*.

Let $\quad v = V_m \sin\omega t$, then

$$i = \frac{v}{R} = \frac{V_m \sin\omega t}{R} = I_m \sin\omega t \qquad (3.1)$$

where $\quad I_m = \dfrac{V_m}{R}$

That is, the phase difference between the voltage and current in case of pure resistor is zero.

$$\phi = 0$$

$\therefore$ Power factor $= \cos\phi = \cos 0 = 1$

Phasor diagram To understand the behaviour of any circuit, it will be useful to draw a phasor diagram. A phasor diagram is one in which all the currents and voltages are known in a single diagram. Usually one of the quantities is taken as reference and is drawn along the *X*-axis. The phasor diagram for AC through pure *R* is shown in Fig. 3.1(c).

Let $v = V_m \sin\omega t$, then

$$\Rightarrow \quad \bar{V} = \frac{V_m\angle 0}{\sqrt{2}} = V\angle 0$$

$$i = I_m \sin\omega t$$

$$\Rightarrow \quad \bar{I} = \frac{I_m\angle 0}{\sqrt{2}} = I\angle 0$$

Instantaneous power

$$p = vi = V_m \sin\omega t \times I_m \sin\omega t = V_m I_m \sin^2\omega t$$

$$= \frac{V_m I_m}{2} - \frac{V_m I_m}{2}\cos 2\omega t$$

Average power

$$P = \frac{1}{2\pi}\int_0^{2\pi} p\,d(\omega t) = \frac{1}{2\pi}\int_0^{2\pi}\left[\frac{V_m I_m}{2} - \frac{V_m I_m}{2}\cos 2\omega t\right] d(\omega t)$$

$$= \frac{V_m I_m}{2} = \frac{V_m}{\sqrt{2}}\frac{I_m}{\sqrt{2}} = V_{RMS} I_{RMS}$$

3.2.2 AC Through Pure Inductor

Consider an AC circuit with a pure inductance of L henrys connected across an alternating voltage $v = V_m \sin\omega t$ [Fig. 3.2(a)]. The current flowing in the circuit is i.

Let $v = V_m \sin\omega t$, then

Voltage across inductor

$$V_L = v = L\frac{di}{dt}$$

$$\Rightarrow \quad \frac{di}{dt} = \frac{v}{L} = \frac{V_m \sin\omega t}{L}$$

$$\Rightarrow \quad \int di = \int \frac{V_m \sin\omega t}{L} dt$$

$$\Rightarrow \quad i = \frac{-V_m \cos\omega t}{L\omega} = \frac{V_m}{\omega L}\sin(\omega t - 90°)$$

∴ $$i = \frac{V_m}{X_L}\sin(\omega t - 90°) = I_m \sin(\omega t - 90°) \quad (3.2)$$

where $X_L = \omega L$ = inductive reactance and $I_m = \dfrac{V_m}{X_L}$.

That is, v leads i by 90° or i lags v by 90°.

So, the phase difference between voltage and current in the case of pure inductor is 90°.

∴ Power factor $= \cos\phi = \cos 90° = 0$

(a) Circuit diagram

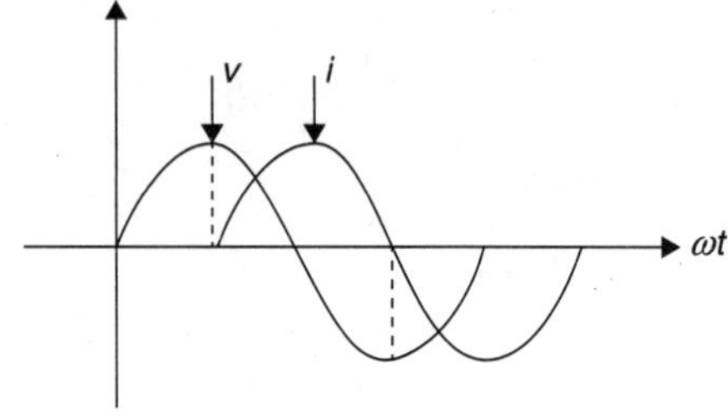

(b) Waveform for v and i

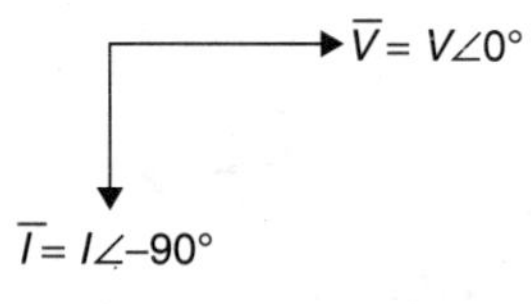

(c) Phasor diagram

Fig. 3.2 AC through a pure inductor

Phasor diagram

$$v = V_m \sin\omega t \quad \Rightarrow \quad \bar{V} = \frac{V_m\angle 0°}{\sqrt{2}} = V\angle 0°$$

$$i = I_m \sin(\omega t - 90°) \quad \Rightarrow \quad \bar{I} = \frac{I_m\angle -90°}{\sqrt{2}} = I\angle -90°$$

Instantaneous power

$$p = vi = V_m \sin\omega t \times I_m \sin(\omega t - 90°)$$

$$= -V_m I_m \sin\omega t \cos\omega t = -\frac{V_m I_m}{2}\sin 2\omega t$$

Average power

$$P = \frac{1}{2\pi}\int_0^{2\pi} p\, d(\omega t) = \frac{1}{2\pi}\int_0^{2\pi}\left[-\frac{V_m I_m}{2}\sin 2\omega t\right] d(\omega t) = 0$$

The power consumed by an inductor is zero, that is, only the inductor stores energy in the magnetic field. The phasor diagram for AC through pure L is shown in Fig. 3.2(c).

3.2.3 AC Through Pure Capacitor

Consider an AC circuit with a pure capacitance C farads connected across an alternating voltage $v = V_m \sin\omega t$ [Fig. 3.3(a)]. The current flowing in the circuit is i.

Let $v = V_m \sin\omega t$, then

Current flowing through the capacitor

$$i = C\frac{dv}{dt} = CV_m \omega \cos\omega t$$

$$= \frac{V_m}{(1/\omega C)}\cos\omega t = \frac{V_m}{X_C}\sin(\omega t + 90°)$$

∴ $$i = \frac{V_m}{X_C}\sin(\omega t + 90°) = I_m \sin(\omega t + 90°) \quad (3.3)$$

where $X_C = \dfrac{1}{\omega C}$ = capacitive reactance and $I_m = \dfrac{V_m}{X_C}$

that is, v lags i by 90° or i leads v by 90°.

So, the phase difference between voltage and current in case of a pure capacitor is 90°.

$\therefore$ Power factor $= \cos\phi = \cos 90° = 0$

Phasor diagram

$$v = V_m \sin\omega t \Rightarrow \bar{V} = \frac{V_m\angle 0}{\sqrt{2}} = V\angle 0$$

$$i = I_m \sin(\omega t + 90°) \Rightarrow \bar{I} = \frac{I_m\angle 90°}{\sqrt{2}} = I\angle 90°$$

Instantaneous power

$$p = vi = V_m \sin\omega t \times I_m \sin(\omega t + 90°)$$

$$= V_m I_m \sin\omega t \cos\omega t = \frac{V_m I_m}{2}\sin 2\omega t$$

Average power

$$P = \frac{1}{2\pi}\int_0^{2\pi} p\, d(\omega t) = \frac{1}{2\pi}\int_0^{2\pi}\left[\frac{V_m I_m}{2}\sin 2\omega t\right] d(\omega t) = 0$$

Thus, the power consumed by a pure capacitor is zero, that is, only the capacitor stores energy in an electric field. The phasor diagram for AC through pure C is shown in Fig. 3.3(c).

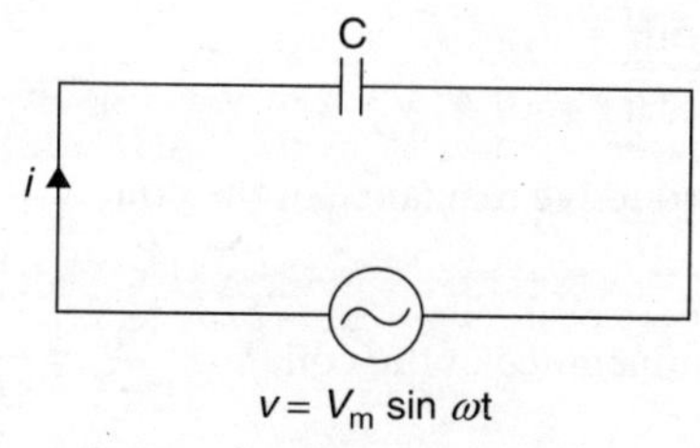

(a) Circuit diagram

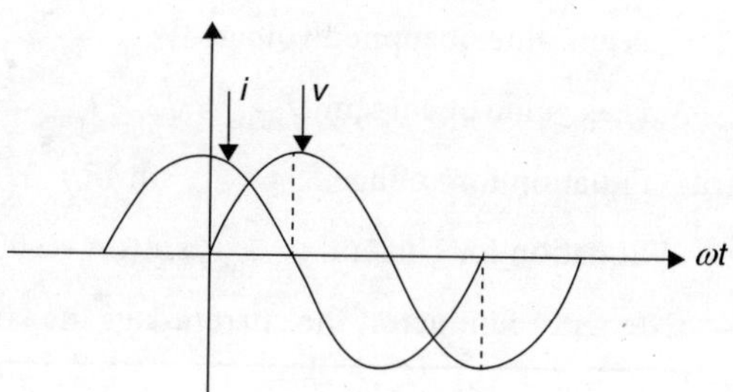

(b) Waveform for v and i

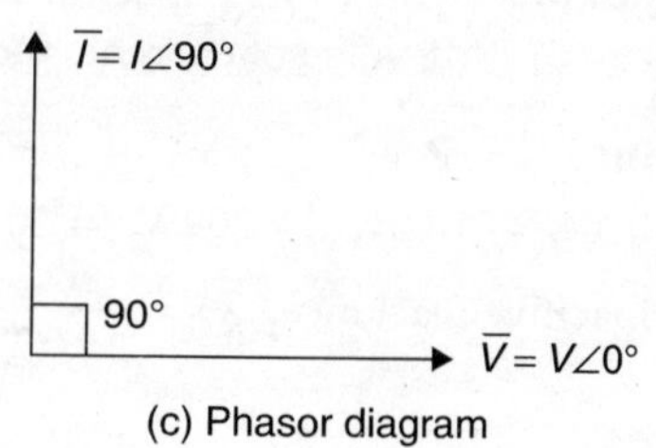

(c) Phasor diagram

Fig. 3.3 AC through a pure capacitor

Problem 3.1 An AC circuit consists of a pure resistance of 20 Ω which is connected to an AC supply of 250 V, 50 Hz. Determine (i) current flowing through the circuit, (ii) power absorbed by the circuit, and (iii) equations for voltage and current.

Solution:

Given that $R = 20\ \Omega$, $V = 250$ V, $f = 50$ Hz

(i) Current flowing through the circuit, $I = \frac{V}{R} = \frac{250}{20} = 12.5$ A

(ii) Power absorbed by the circuit, $P = VI = 250 \times 12.5 = 3125$ W

Peak value of applied voltage, $V_{max} = \sqrt{2} \times V_{rms} = \sqrt{2} \times 250 = 353.6$ V

Peak value of current, $I_{max} = \sqrt{2} \times I_{rms} = \sqrt{2} \times 12.5 = 17.68$ A

(iii) Equation for voltage, $v = V_{max} \sin\omega t = 353.6 \sin(2\pi f t) = 353.6 \sin(314t)$

Equation for current, $i = I_{max} \sin\omega t = 17.68 \sin(2\pi f t) = 17.68 \sin(314t)$

Problem 3.2 A pure inductive coil allows a current of 10 A to flow from a 230 V, 50 Hz supply. Determine (i) inductance of the coil, (ii) power absorbed by the circuit, and (iii) equations for voltage and current.

Solution:

Given that $I = 10$ A, $V = 230$ V, $f = 50$ Hz

(i) Inductive reactance of the coil, $X_L = \dfrac{V}{I} = \dfrac{230}{10} = 23\ \Omega$

Inductance of the coil, $L = \dfrac{X_L}{2\pi f} = \dfrac{23}{100\pi} = 0.073$ H

(ii) Power absorbed by the pure inductor is zero, that is, $P = 0$

Peak value of applied voltage, $V_{\text{max}} = \sqrt{2} \times V_{\text{rms}} = \sqrt{2} \times 230 = 325.3$ V

Peak value of current, $I_{\text{max}} = \sqrt{2} \times I_{\text{rms}} = \sqrt{2} \times 10 = 14.14$ A

(iii) Equation for voltage, $v = V_{\text{max}} \sin \omega t = 325.3 \sin(2\pi ft) = 325.3 \sin(314t)$

Equation for current, $i = I_{\text{max}} \sin(\omega t - 90°) = 14.14 \sin(2\pi ft - 90°) = 14.14 \sin(314t - 90°)$

In a pure inductor, the current lags the voltage by 90°.

Problem 3.3 A 318 μF capacitor is connected across a 200 V, 50 Hz supply. Determine (i) capacitive reactance, (ii) RMS value of current, and (iii) equations for voltage and current.

Solution:

Given that $C = 318$ μF, $V = 200$ V, $f = 50$ Hz

(i) Capacitive reactance, $X_C = \dfrac{1}{2\pi fC} = \dfrac{1}{2\pi \times 50 \times 318 \times 10^{-6}} = 10\ \Omega$

(ii) RMS value of current, $I_{\text{rms}} = \dfrac{V}{X_C} = \dfrac{200}{10} = 20$ A

Peak value of applied voltage, $V_{\text{max}} = \sqrt{2} \times V_{\text{rms}} = \sqrt{2} \times 200 = 282.84$ V

Peak value of current, $I_{\text{max}} = \sqrt{2} \times I_{\text{rms}} = \sqrt{2} \times 20 = 28.28$ A

(iii) Equation for voltage, $v = V_{\text{max}} \sin \omega t = 282.84 \sin(2\pi ft) = 282.84 \sin(314t)$

Equation for current, $i = I_{\text{max}} \sin(\omega t + 90°) = 28.28 \sin(2\pi ft + 90°) = 28.28 \sin(314t + 90°)$

In a pure capacitor, the current leads the voltage by 90°.

3.3 IMPEDANCE AND ADMITTANCE PARAMETERS

The impedance is defined as the ratio of sinusoidal voltage to the sinusoidal current. It is also defined as the total opposition offered to the flow of sinusoidal current. Hence the impedance is measured in ohms. The real part of the impedance is resistance and the imaginary part of impedance is reactance. There are two types of reactances—inductive reactance and capacitive reactance. The inductive reactance is denoted by X_L and is equal to ωL and the capacitive reactance is denoted by X_C and is equal to $1/\omega C$. Since the inductive and capacitive reactances have exact opposite behaviour, one is considered positive and the other is negative. Conventionally the inductive reactance is taken as positive and the capacitive reactance is taken as negative.

The complex impedance for a series RLC circuit is given by

$$Z = R + jX = R + j(X_L - X_C) = \sqrt{R^2 + X^2}\angle\tan^{-1}\left(\frac{X}{R}\right) = Z\angle\phi$$

The right angled triangle formed by R, X and Z is called the impedance triangle [Fig. 3.4(a)].

In parallel circuits the inverse of the parameters will be useful for analysis. The inverse of impedance is admittance and so the admittance is defined as the ratio of sinusoidal current to voltage. The real part of admittance is conductance and imaginary part of the admittance is called susceptance.

$\therefore$ Admittance $Y = \frac{1}{Z}$; Conductance $G = \frac{1}{R}$;

Susceptance $B = \frac{1}{X}$

There are two types of susceptances—inductive and capacitive. Inductive susceptance is denoted by B_L and is equal to $1/\omega L$; capacitive susceptance is denoted by B_C and is equal to ωC. Since the inductive and capacitive susceptances have exact opposite behaviours, one is considered as positive and the other as negative. Conventionally, inductive susceptance is taken as negative and the capacitive susceptance is taken as positive. The complex admittance is given by

$$Y = G + jB = G + j(-B_L + B_C)$$

$$= \sqrt{G^2 + B^2}\angle\tan^{-1}\left(\frac{B}{G}\right) = Y\angle\phi$$

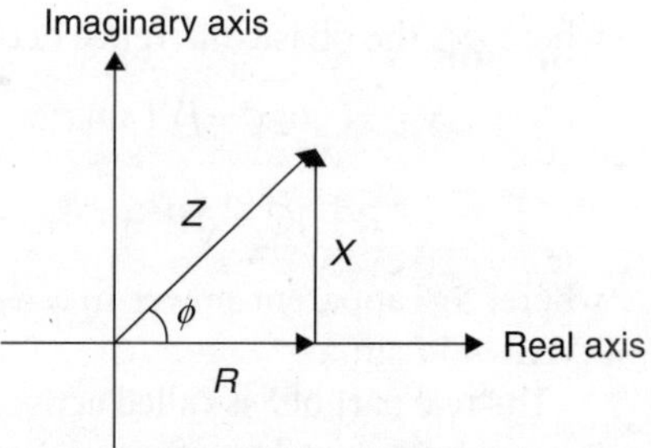

(a) Impedance diagram

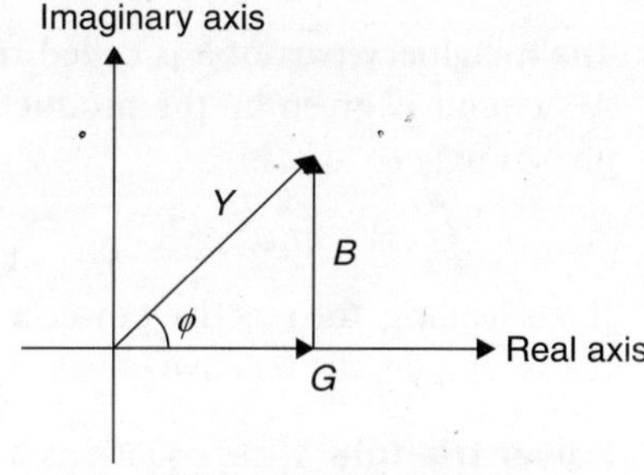

(b) Admittance diagram

Fig. 3.4 Impedance and admittance triangles

The right angled triangle formed by G, B and Y is called the admittance triangle [Fig. 3.4(b)].

3.4 POWER AND POWER FACTOR

3.4.1 Power in AC Circuits

Power is the rate at which work is done; power is the rate of energy transfer. In circuits excited by DC sources, the voltage and current are constant, so the power is constant. This constant power is called average power or power and it is denoted by P.

$\therefore$ Power, $P = VI$ (3.4)

In circuits excited by an AC source, the voltage and current are sinusoidal quantities which vary with time. When voltage and current are time varying quantities the power is also a time varying quantity, is called instantaneous power and is denoted by p.

Instantaneous power, $p = vi$ (3.5)

For time varying quantities, the power is defined as average power over a period of time. Since the average value of sinusoidal voltage and current is zero, we can take the RMS value of voltage and current. We know that the RMS values of voltage and current are complex and so the power is also complex. The complex power is given by

$$S = VI^* = VI\angle\phi \quad (3.6)$$

where ϕ is the phase difference between V and I

$$S = VI\cos\phi + jVI\sin\phi$$

$$= P + jQ = \sqrt{P^2 + Q^2}$$

where, S = apparent power in VA or kVA, P = active power in kW = $VI\cos\phi$ and Q = reactive power in kVAR = $VI\sin\phi$.

The real part of S is called active power. Active power in an AC circuit is given by the product of voltage, current and cosine of the phase angle ϕ.

$$\therefore \quad P = VI\cos\phi, \text{ watts} \tag{3.7}$$

The imaginary part of S is called reactive power. Reactive power in an AC circuit is given by the product of voltage, current and sine of the phase angle ϕ.

$$\therefore \quad Q = VI\sin\phi, \text{ VAR} \tag{3.8}$$

If ϕ is leading, the reactive power is taken as positive and it is capacitive. If ϕ is lagging, the reactive power is taken as negative and it is inductive.

Power triangle The equations associated with the average, apparent and reactive power can be developed geometrically on a right angle triangle called the power triangle (Fig. 3.5).

Active power P = voltage × in-phase component of current = $VI\cos\phi$, reactive power Q = voltage × quadrature component of current = $VI\sin\phi$ and apparent power S = voltage × current = VI.

(a) (b) (c)

Fig. 3.5 Power triangle for inductive load

3.4.2 Power Factor

It is the ratio of watts that are converted to the volt amperes that are fed into the circuit.

$$\therefore \quad \text{Power factor} = \frac{\text{Active power}}{\text{Apparent power}} = \frac{P}{S}$$

It is also defined as the cosine of phase angle (ϕ) between the voltage and current. Depending on whether the current lags or leads the voltage, the power factor is also taken as lagging or leading.

The phase angle ϕ, that is, the phase different between V and I is the same as the impedance angle.

From the impedance triangle (Fig. 3.6),

$$Z = \sqrt{R^2 + X^2}$$

$$\cos\phi = \frac{R}{Z}$$

$$\sin\phi = \frac{X}{Z}$$

$$\therefore \quad \text{Power factor} = \cos\phi = \frac{P}{S} = \frac{R}{Z} \tag{3.9}$$

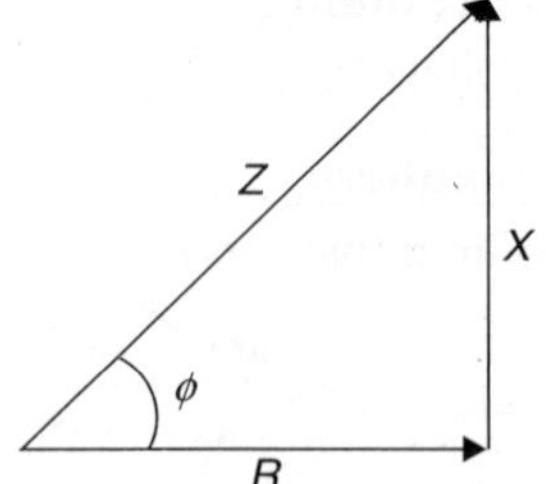

Fig. 3.6 Impedance triangle

Significance of power factor *Power factor* is a measure of the effectiveness of utilisation of available power. The power in an AC circuit is mainly of three types—apparent power, active power and reactive power. *Apparent power* is the total power supplied to the circuit. But actually, the circuit does not utilise the applied power completely (if it is not a purely resistive circuit). The part of the applied power which is actually consumed by the circuit is called *active power*. The rest of the applied power is circulating in the circuit without doing any actual work, is called *reactive power*. Thus, the power factor is the measure of percentage of the power consumed.

In a purely resistive circuit, the power factor is 1, or 100%. This means that, in a pure resistive circuit, the applied power is completely utilised by the circuit (reactive power is zero). If in a circuit, the power factor is 0.5 or 50%, it means that only 50% of the applied power is utilised by the circuit.

A power factor of one or unity is the goal of any electric utility company. This is because, if the power factor is less than one, more current has to be supplied to the user for a given amount of power used. In doing so, they incur more line losses.

Problem 3.4 Find the power delivered from a sinusoidal voltage source with $V = 220$ volts to an impedance of $Z = (6 + j8)\ \Omega$. Also calculate the power factor.

Solution:

Given that $V = 220$ volts, $Z = (6 + j8)\ \Omega = 10\angle 53.13°\ \Omega$

$$I = \frac{V}{Z} = \frac{220}{10\angle 53.13^0} = 22\angle -53.13°\ \text{A}$$

$$\text{Power delivered, } P = VI\cos\phi = 220 \times 22 \times \cos(53.13) = 2904\ \text{W}$$

$$\text{Power factor} = \cos\phi = \cos 53.13° = 0.6$$

Problem 3.5 The voltage and current across a load are given by $V = 110$ V and $I = 20\ \angle -50°$ A. Find active power, reactive power and apparent power.

Solution:

Given that $V = 110$ V, $I = 20\ \angle -50°$, $\phi = 50°$

$$\text{Active power, } P = \text{VIcos}\phi = 110 \times 20 \times \cos 50° = 1414\ \text{W}$$

$$\text{Reactive power, } Q = VI\sin\phi = 110 \times 20 \times \sin 50° = 1685\ \text{VAR}$$

$$\text{Apparent power, } S = VI = 110 \times 20 = 2200\ \text{VA}$$

Problem 3.6 A certain passive network has an equivalent impedance of $Z = (3 + j4)\ \Omega$ and an applied voltage $v(t) = 75\cos(1000t + 30°)$ volts. Give the complete power information.

Solution:

Given that $Z = 3 + j4 = 5\angle 53.13°$

$$v(t) = 75\cos(1000t + 30°) \Rightarrow V = \frac{75}{\sqrt{2}}\angle 30° = 53\angle 30°$$

$$I = \frac{V}{Z} = \frac{53\angle 30°}{5\angle 53.13°} = 10.6\angle -23.13°\ \text{A}$$

$$S = VI^* = 53\angle 30° \times 10.6\angle 23.13° = 562\angle 53.13° = 337.2 + j449.6$$

Hence, $P = 337.2$ W, $Q = 449.6$ VAR (inductive), $S = 562$ VA, and $\phi = \cos^{-1}(53.138) = 0.6$ lagging.

Problem 3.7 Three loads are connected in parallel to a 6 kV AC line, as shown. Given $P_1 = 10$ kW; $p.f_1 = 1$; $P_2 = 20$ kW; $p.f_2 = 0.5$ lagging; $P_3 = 15$ kW; $p.f_3 = 0.6$ lagging. Find P_T, Q_T, S_T, $p.f_T$ and the current I.

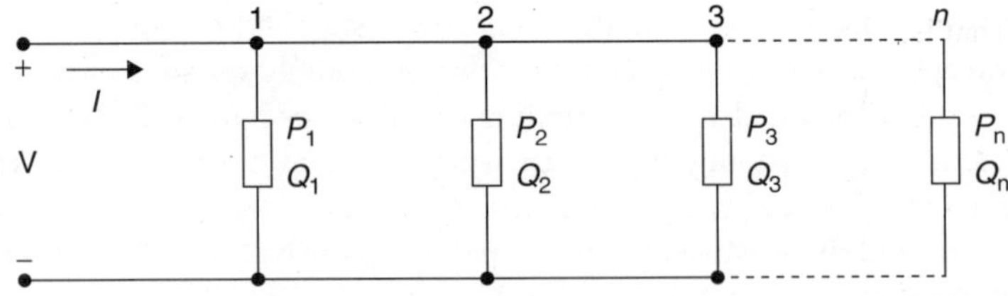

Solution:

Given that $P_1 = 10$ kW, $p.f_1 = 1$, $P_2 = 20$ kW, $p.f_2 = 0.5$ lagging, $P_3 = 15$ kW, $p.f_3 = 0.6$ lagging

The reactive power for each load is given as

$$pf_1 = \cos\phi_1 = 1 \qquad \tan\phi_1 = 0 \qquad Q_1 = P_1 \tan\phi_1 = 0 \text{ kVAR}$$

$$pf_2 = \cos\phi_2 = 0.5 \qquad \tan\phi_2 = 1.73 \qquad Q_2 = P_2 \tan\phi_2 = 34.6 \text{ kVAR}$$

$$pf_3 = \cos\phi_3 = 0.6 \qquad \tan\phi_3 = 1.33 \qquad Q_3 = P_3 \tan\phi_3 = 20 \text{ VAR}$$

Total active power, $P_T = P_1 + P_2 + P_3 = 10 + 20 + 15 = 45$ kW

Total reactive power, $Q_T = Q_1 + Q_2 + Q_3 = 0 + 34.6 + 20 = 54.6$ kVAR

Total power, $S_T = \sqrt{P^2 + Q^2} = \sqrt{45^2 + 54.6^2} = 70.75$ kVA

Total power factor, $pf_T = \dfrac{P_T}{S_T} = 0.64 = \cos\phi$

$\Rightarrow \qquad \phi = 50.5°$ lagging

$$I = \frac{S}{V} = \left(\frac{70.75 \text{ kVA}}{6 \text{ kV}}\right) = 11.8 \text{ A}$$

$\therefore \qquad I = 11.8\angle{-50.5°}$ A

3.5 *RL* CIRCUIT EXCITED BY SINUSOIDAL SOURCE

3.5.1 *RL* Series Circuit

Consider the *RL* series circuit excited by sinusoidal voltage source (Fig. 3.7).

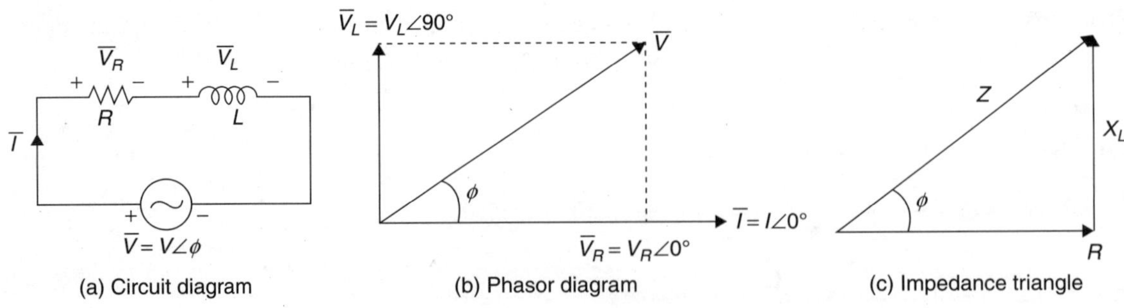

(a) Circuit diagram (b) Phasor diagram (c) Impedance triangle

Fig. 3.7 *RL* series circuit

Let $\overline{I}$ be the reference phasor.

That is, $\bar{I} = I\angle 0$

$$\bar{V}_R = \text{Voltage across the resistor} = \bar{I} \times R = I\angle 0^\circ\ R = IR\angle 0^\circ = V_R\angle 0^\circ$$

$$\bar{V}_L = \text{Voltage across the inductor} = \bar{I} \times jX_L = I\angle 0^\circ \times X_L\angle 90^\circ = IX_L\angle 90^\circ = V_L\angle 90^\circ$$

$$\bar{V} = \text{Applied voltage} = \bar{I} \times \bar{Z} = I\angle 0^\circ \times Z\angle\phi = IZ\angle\phi = V\angle\phi$$

From the circuit diagram [Fig. 3.7(a)],

$$\bar{V} = \bar{V}_R + \bar{V}_L = V_R\angle 0^\circ + V_L\angle 90^\circ = V_R + jV_L$$

$$= \sqrt{V_R^2 + V_L^2}\angle\tan^{-1}\left(\frac{V_L}{V_R}\right)$$

(or) $\quad \bar{I} \times \bar{Z} = IR + IX_L\angle 90^\circ = IR + jIX_L = I(R + jX_L)$

$\therefore \quad \bar{Z} = R + jX_L = \sqrt{R^2 + X_L^2}\ \angle\tan^{-1}\left(\frac{X_L}{R}\right) = Z\angle\phi$

The phasor diagram for the *RL* series circuit with $\bar{I}$ as reference phasor is shown in Fig. 3.7(b). The following observations can be made from the phasor diagram.

- The voltage $\bar{V}$ leads the current $\bar{I}$ when impedance of the circuit is inductive, and the corresponding leading angle is ϕ.
- In the resistor, the voltage and current are in phase.
- In the inductor, the voltage leads the current by 90°.

3.5.2 *RL* Parallel Circuit

Consider the *RL* parallel circuit excited by a sinusoidal voltage source (Fig. 3.8).

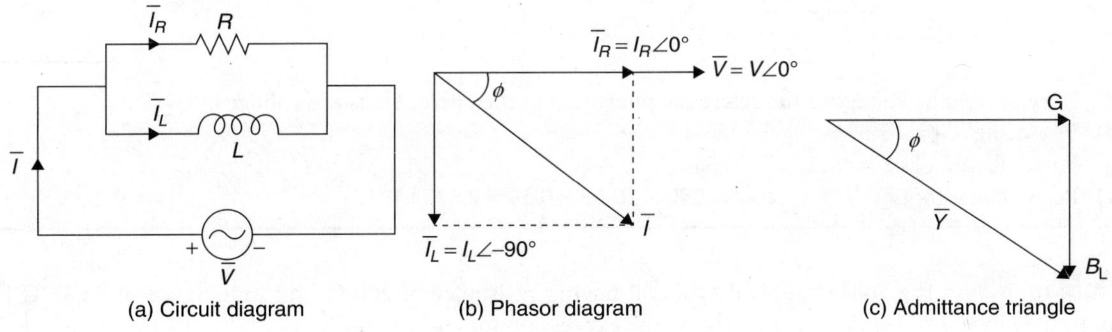

Fig. 3.8 *RL* parallel circuit

Let $\bar{V}$ be the reference phasor.

That is, $\bar{V} = V\angle 0$

$$\bar{I}_R = \text{Current through the resistor} = \frac{\bar{V}}{R} = \frac{V\angle 0^\circ}{R} = VG\angle 0^\circ = I_R\angle 0^\circ$$

$$\bar{I}_L = \text{Current through the inductor} = \frac{\bar{V}}{jX_L} = \frac{V\angle 0^\circ}{X_L\angle 90^\circ} = VB_L\angle -90^\circ = I_L\angle -90^\circ$$

$$\bar{I} = \text{Total current} = \frac{\bar{V}}{\bar{Z}} = \frac{V\angle 0^\circ}{Z\angle\phi} = VY\angle -\phi = I\angle -\phi$$

From the circuit diagram [Fig. 3.17(a)],

$$\bar{I} = \bar{I}_R + \bar{I}_L = I_R\angle 0^\circ + I_L\angle -90^\circ = I_R - jI_L$$

$$= \sqrt{I_R^2 + I_L^2}\angle \tan^{-1}\left(-\frac{I_L}{I_R}\right)$$

(or) $\bar{V}\times\bar{Y} = VG + VB_L\angle -90^\circ = VG - jVB_L = V(G - jB_L)$

$\therefore$ $\bar{Y} = G - jB_L = \sqrt{G^2 + B_L^2}\angle -\tan^{-1}\left(\frac{B_L}{G}\right) = Y\angle -\phi$

The phasor diagram for the *RL* parallel circuit with $\bar{V}$ as reference phasor is shown in Fig. 3.8(b). The following observations can be made from the phasor diagram.

- The current $\bar{I}$ lags the supply voltage $\bar{V}$ in the inductive circuit, and the corresponding lagging angle is ϕ.
- In the resistor, the voltage and current are in phase.
- In the inductor, the current lags the voltage by 90°.

Problem 3.8 A coil having resistance of 6 Ω and inductance of 0.03 H is connected across 230 V, 50 Hz supply. Determine (i) current, (ii) phase angle, (iii) power factor, and (iv) power consumption.

Solution:

Given that $R = 6\ \Omega$, $L = 0.03$ H, $V = 230$ V, $f = 50$ Hz

$$X_L = 2\pi fL = 2\pi\times 50\times 0.03 = 9.42\ \Omega$$

$$Z = R + jX_L = 6 + j9.42 = 11.2\angle 57.5^\circ$$

(i) Current, $I = \frac{V}{Z} = \frac{230}{11.2\angle 57.5^\circ} = 20.53\angle -57.5^\circ$ A

Here, if we take voltage as the reference phasor, then the current lags the voltage by 57.5°.

(ii) Phase angle, $\phi = 57.5^\circ$

(iii) Power factor, $\cos\phi = \cos 57.5^\circ = 0.54$

(iv) Power consumption, $P = VI\cos\phi = 230\times 20.53\times 0.54 = 2.537$ kW

Problem 3.9 The voltage applied to a coil having resistance of 200 Ω and inductance of 0.638 H is represented by $v = 200\sin 100\pi t$. Determine the expression for current and power taken by the coil.

Solution:

Given that $R = 200\ \Omega$, $L = 0.638$ H, $V_m = 200$ V, $f = 50$ Hz

$$X_L = 2\pi fL = 2\pi\times 50\times 0.638 = 200.4\ \Omega$$

$$Z = R + jX_L = 200 + j200.4 = 283.13\angle 45.05^\circ$$

(i) Current, $I_m = \frac{V_m}{Z} = \frac{200}{283.13} = 0.7064$ A

$$I = \frac{V}{Z} = \frac{V_m/\sqrt{2}}{Z} = \frac{200/\sqrt{2}}{283.13\angle 45.05^\circ} = 0.5\angle -45.05^\circ$$

Here, if we take voltage as reference phasor, then the current lags the voltage by 45.05°. Therefore, the expression for current is

$$i = 0.7064\sin(100\pi t - 45.05°)$$

(ii) Power taken by the coil, $P = I^2R = \left(\frac{I_m}{\sqrt{2}}\right)^2 R = \frac{I_m^2 R}{2} = \frac{(0.7064)^2 \times 200}{2} = 49.9\text{ W}$

Problem 3.10 A parallel *RL* circuit consisting of resistance $R = 10\ \Omega$ and inductance $L = 10$ mH is energised by $v = 100\sin(1000t + 36°)$ volts. Determine the instantaneous values of currents through *R* and *L*, hence obtain the total current in terms of RMS values.

Solution:

Given that $R = 10\ \Omega$, $L = 10$ mH

$$v = 100\sin(1000t + 36°)\text{ volts} \Rightarrow V = \frac{100}{\sqrt{2}}\angle 36° = 70.71\angle 36°\text{ V}$$

$$I_R = \frac{V}{R} = \frac{70.71\angle 36°}{10} = 7.071\angle 36°\text{ A}$$

$$X_L = \omega L = 1000 \times 10 \times 10^{-3} = 10\ \Omega$$

$$I_L = \frac{V}{jX_L} = \frac{70.71\angle 36°}{10\angle 90°} = 7.071\angle -54°\text{ A}$$

Total RMS current is given by

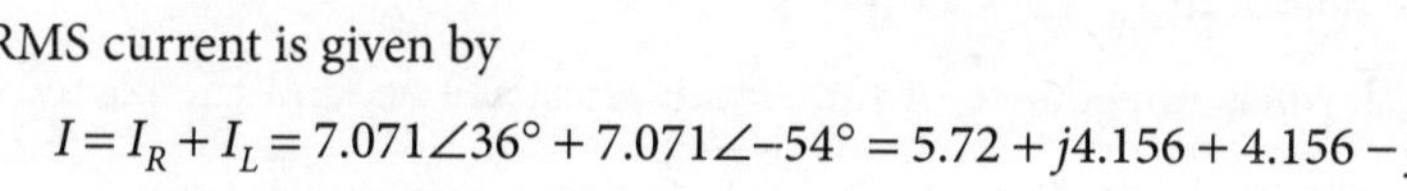

$$I = I_R + I_L = 7.071\angle 36° + 7.071\angle -54° = 5.72 + j4.156 + 4.156 - j5.72$$

$$= 9.876 - j1.564 = 10\angle -9°\text{ A}$$

The instantaneous values various currents are as given below

$$i_R = 7.071 \times \sqrt{2}\sin(1000t + 36°) = 10\sin(1000t + 36°)\text{ A}$$

$$i_L = 7.071 \times \sqrt{2}\sin(1000t - 54°) = 10\sin(1000t - 54°)\text{ A}$$

$$i = 10 \times \sqrt{2}\sin(1000t - 9°) = 14.14\sin(1000t - 9°)\text{ A}$$

3.6 *RC* CIRCUIT EXCITED BY SINUSOIDAL SOURCE

3.6.1 *RC* Series Circuit

Consider an *RC* series circuit excited by a sinusoidal voltage source (Fig. 3.9).

Let $\bar{I}$ be the reference phasor

That is, $\bar{I} = I\angle 0$

$$\bar{V}_R = \text{Voltage across the resistor} = \bar{I} \times R = I\angle 0°\ R = IR\angle 0° = V_R\angle 0°$$

$$\bar{V}_C = \text{Voltage across the capacitor} = -\bar{I} \times jX_C = I\angle 0° \times X_C\angle -90° = IX_C\angle -90° = V_C\angle -90°$$

$$\bar{V} = \text{Applied voltage} = \bar{I} \times \bar{Z} = I\angle 0° \times Z\angle -\phi = IZ\angle -\phi = V\angle -\phi$$

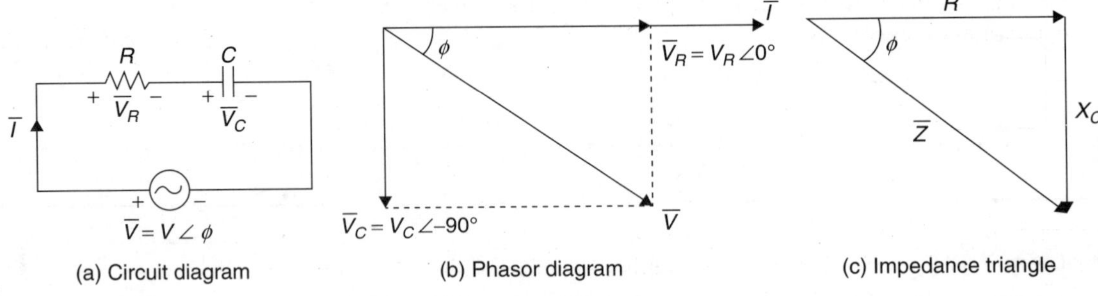

(a) Circuit diagram (b) Phasor diagram (c) Impedance triangle

Fig. 3.9 *RC* series circuit

From the circuit diagram [Fig. 3.9(a)],

$$\overline{V} = \overline{V}_R + \overline{V}_C = V_R\angle 0° + V_C\angle -90° = V_R - jV_C$$

$$= \sqrt{V_R^2 + V_C^2}\ \angle -\tan^{-1}\left(\frac{V_C}{V_R}\right)$$

(or) $$\overline{I} \times \overline{Z} = IR + IX_C\angle -90° = IR - jIX_C = I(R - jX_C)$$

$\therefore$ $$\overline{Z} = R - jX_C = \sqrt{R^2 + X_C^2}\ \angle -\tan^{-1}\left(\frac{X_C}{R}\right) = Z\angle -\phi$$

The phasor diagram for the *RC* series circuit with $\overline{I}$ as reference phasor is shown in Fig. 3.9(b). The following observations can be made from the phasor diagram.

- The voltage $\overline{V}$ lags the current $\overline{I}$ when impedance of the circuit is capacitive, and the corresponding lagging angle is ϕ.
- In the resistor, the voltage and current are in phase.
- In the capacitor, the voltage lags the current by 90°.

3.6.2 *RC* Parallel Circuit

Consider an *RC* parallel circuit excited by a sinusoidal voltage source (Fig. 3.10).

Let $\overline{V}$ be the reference phasor.

That is, $\overline{V} = V\angle 0$

$$\overline{I}_R = \text{Current through the resistor} = \frac{\overline{V}}{R} = \frac{V\angle 0°}{R} = VG\angle 0° = I_R\angle 0°$$

$$\overline{I}_C = \text{Current through the capacitor} = \frac{\overline{V}}{-jX_C} = \frac{V\angle 0°}{X_C\angle -90°} = VB_C\angle 90° = I_C\angle 90°$$

$$\overline{I} = \text{Total current} = \frac{\overline{V}}{\overline{Z}} = \frac{V\angle 0°}{Z\angle -\phi} = VY\angle\phi = I\angle\phi$$

From the circuit diagram [Fig. 3.10(a)],

$$\overline{I} = \overline{I}_R + \overline{I}_C = I_R\angle 0° + I_C\angle 90° = I_R + jI_C$$

$$= \sqrt{I_R^2 + I_C^2}\angle\tan^{-1}\left(\frac{I_C}{I_R}\right)$$

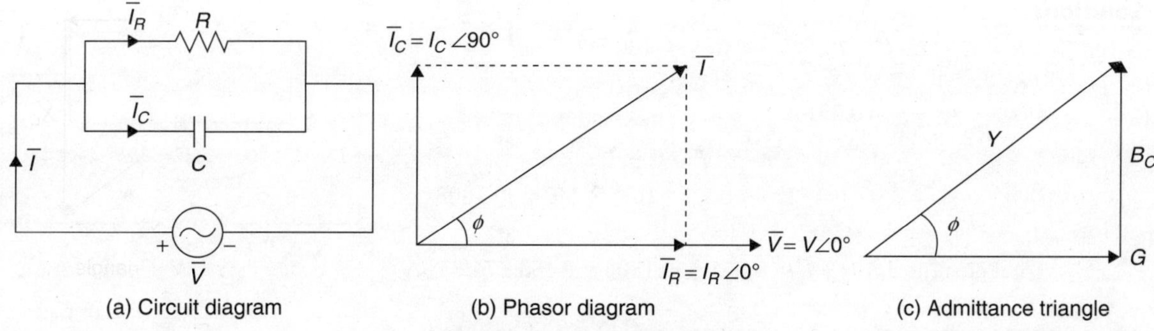

Fig. 3.10 *RC* parallel circuit

(or) $\quad \overline{V} \times \overline{Y} = VG + VB_C\angle 90° = VG + jVB_C = V(G + jB_C)$

$$\therefore \quad \overline{Y} = G + jB_C = \sqrt{G^2 + B_C^2}\angle \tan^{-1}\left(\frac{B_C}{G}\right) = Y\angle\phi$$

The phasor diagram for the *RC* parallel circuit with $\overline{V}$ as reference phasor is shown in Fig. 3.10(b). The following observations can be made from the phasor diagram:

- The current $\overline{I}$ leads the supply voltage $\overline{V}$ in the capacitive circuit, and the corresponding leading angle is ϕ.
- In the resistor, the voltage and current are in phase.
- In the capacitor, the current leads the voltage by 90°.

Problem 3.11 A capacitor having capacitance of 79.5 μF is connected in series with a non-inductive resistance of 30 Ω across a 100 V, 50 Hz supply. Determine (i) impedance, (ii) RMS current, (iii) phase angle, and (iv) equation for the instantaneous value of current.

Solution:

Given that $R = 30\ \Omega$, $C = 79.5\ \mu F$, $V = 100$ V, $f = 50$ Hz

$$X_C = \frac{1}{2\pi fC} = \frac{1}{2\pi \times 50 \times 79.5 \times 10^{-6}} = 40\ \Omega$$

(i) Impedance, $Z = R - jX_C = 30 - j40 = 50\angle -53°\ \Omega$

(ii) Current, $I = \dfrac{V}{Z} = \dfrac{100}{50\angle -53°} = 2\angle 53°$ A

Here, if we take voltage as reference phasor, then the current leads the voltage by 53°

(iii) Phase angle $\phi = 53°$ leading

$$\omega = 2\pi f = 2\pi \times 50 = 314 \text{ rad/s}$$

(iv) Equation for the instantaneous value of current

$$i = 2\sqrt{2}\sin(\omega t + \varphi) = 2.828\sin(314t + 53°)$$

Problem 3.12 A 4700 Ω resistor and 2 μF capacitor are connected in parallel across a 240 V, 60 Hz supply. Determine the circuit impedance and the line current.

Solution:

Given that $R = 4700\ \Omega$, $C = 2\ \mu\text{F}$, $V = 240$ V, $f = 60$ Hz

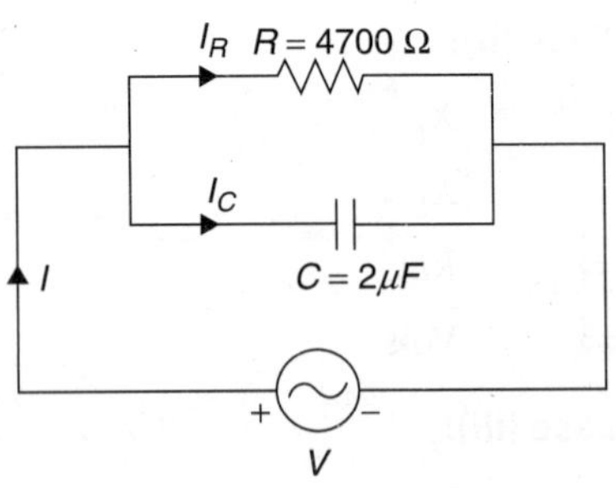

$$I_R = \frac{V}{R} = \frac{240}{4700} = 0.051\text{ A}$$

$$I_C = \frac{V}{-jX_C} = j\omega CV = j2\pi \times 60 \times 2 \times 10^{-6} \times 240 = j0.1808$$

Total current, $I = I_R + I_C = 0.051 + j0.1808 = 0.188\angle 74.25°$ A

Impedance, $Z = \dfrac{V}{I} = \dfrac{240}{0.188\angle 74.25°} = 1276\angle -74.25°\ \Omega$

3.7 *RLC* CIRCUIT EXCITED BY SINUSOIDAL SOURCE

3.7.1 *RLC* Series Circuit

Consider the *RLC* series circuit excited by a sinusoidal voltage source (Fig. 3.11).

Let $\bar{I}$ be the reference phasor

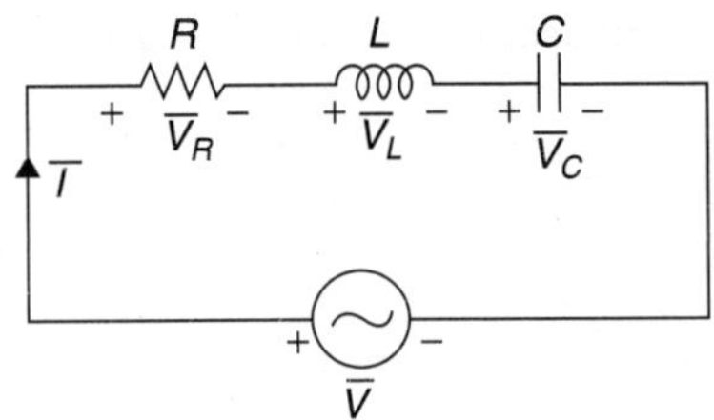

Fig. 3.11 *RLC* series circuit

That is, $\bar{I} = I\angle 0$

$\bar{V}_R =$ Voltage across the resistor $= \bar{I} \times R = I\angle 0°\ R = IR\angle 0° = V_R\angle 0°$

$\bar{V}_L =$ Voltage across the inductor $= \bar{I} \times jX_L = I\angle 0° \times X_L\angle 90° = IX_L\angle 90° = V_L\angle 90°$

$\bar{V}_C =$ Voltage across the capacitor $= -\bar{I} \times jX_C = I\angle 0° \times X_C\angle -90° = IX_C\angle -90° = V_C\angle -90°$

From the circuit diagram (Fig. 3.11),

$$\bar{V} = \bar{V}_R + \bar{V}_L + \bar{V}_C = V_R\angle 0° + V_L\angle 90° + V_C\angle -90° = V_R + jV_L - jV_C$$

$$= \sqrt{V_R^2 + (V_L - V_C)^2}\ \angle \tan^{-1}\left(\frac{V_L - V_C}{V_R}\right)$$

(or) $\quad \bar{I} \times \bar{Z} = IR + IX_L\angle 90° + IX_C\angle -90° = IR + jIX_L - jIX_C = I(R + jX_L - jX_C)$

$$\therefore \quad \bar{Z} = R + j(X_L - X_C) = \sqrt{R^2 + (X_L - X_C)^2}\ \angle \tan^{-1}\left(\frac{X_L - X_C}{R}\right) = \sqrt{R^2 + X^2}\ \angle \tan^{-1}\left(\frac{X}{R}\right)$$

where $X = X_L - X_C$. Here the reactance X may be + ve, −ve or zero.

Case (i): When X is positive,

That is, $X_L - X_C > 0$

$\Rightarrow \quad X_L > X_C$

$\Rightarrow \quad$ *RLC* series circuit behaves like a resistive–inductive circuit.

$\Rightarrow \quad$ Voltage $\bar{V}$ leads the current $\bar{I}$ by an angle ϕ.

Case (ii): When X is negative

i.e. $X_L - X_C < 0$

$\Rightarrow$ $X_L < X_C$

$\Rightarrow$ RLC series circuit behaves like a resistive-capacitive circuit

$\Rightarrow$ Voltage $\overline{V}$ lags the current $\overline{I}$ by an angle ϕ.

Case (iii): When X is zero

That is, $X_L - X_C = 0$

$\Rightarrow$ $X_L = X_C$

$\Rightarrow$ RLC series circuit behaves like a resistive circuit. This condition is called the *resonance condition.*

The phasor diagram of RLC series circuit with $\overline{I}$ as reference phasor is shown in Fig. 3.12.

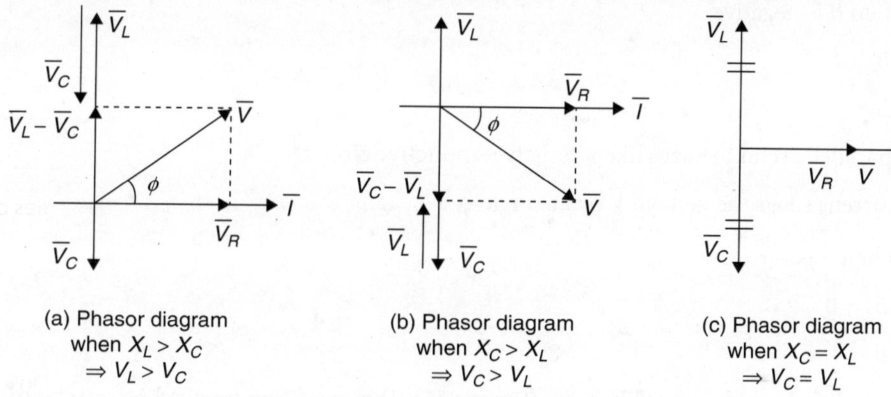

Fig. 3.12 Phasor diagram of *RLC* series circuit

3.7.2 *RLC* PARALLEL CIRCUIT

Consider an RLC parallel circuit excited by a sinusoidal voltage source (Fig. 3.13).

Let $\overline{V}$ be the reference phasor.

That is, $\overline{V} = V\angle 0$

Fig. 3.13 *RLC* parallel circuit

$$\overline{I}_R = \text{Current through the resistor} = \frac{\overline{V}}{R} = \frac{V\angle 0°}{R} = VG\angle 0° = I_R\angle 0°$$

$$\overline{I}_L = \text{Current through the inductor} = \frac{\overline{V}}{jX_L} = \frac{V\angle 0°}{X_L\angle 90°} = IB_L\angle -90° = I_L\angle -90°$$

$$\overline{I}_C = \text{Current through the capacitor} = \frac{\overline{V}}{-jX_C} = \frac{V\angle 0°}{X_C\angle -90°} = VB_C\angle 90° = I_C\angle 90°$$

From the circuit diagram (Fig. 3.13),

$$\overline{I} = \overline{I}_R + \overline{I}_L + \overline{I}_C = I_R\angle 0° + I_L\angle -90° + I_C\angle 90° = I_R - jI_L + jI_C$$

$$= \sqrt{I_R^2 + (I_C - I_L)^2}\,\angle \tan^{-1}\left(\frac{I_C - I_L}{I_R}\right)$$

(or) $\bar{V} \times \bar{Y} = VG + VB_L \angle{-90°} + VB_C \angle 90° = VG - jVB_L + jVB_C = V[G + j(B_C - B_L)]$

$$\therefore \quad \bar{Y} = G + j(B_C - B_L) = \sqrt{G^2 + (B_C - B_L)^2} \angle \tan^{-1}\left(\frac{B_C - B_L}{G}\right) = \sqrt{G^2 + B^2} \angle \tan^{-1}\left(\frac{B}{G}\right)$$

where $B = B_C - B_L$. Here the susceptance B may be + ve, –ve or zero.

Case (i): When B is positive,

That is, $B_C - B_L > 0$

$\Rightarrow$ $B_C > B_L$

$\Rightarrow$ *RLC* parallel circuit behaves like a resistive–capacitive circuit.

$\Rightarrow$ The current $\bar{I}$ leads the voltage $\bar{V}$ by an angle ϕ.

Case (ii): When B is negative

Tht is, $B_C - B_L < 0$

$\Rightarrow$ $B_C < B_L$

$\Rightarrow$ *RLC* parallel circuit behaves like a resistive–inductive circuit.

$\Rightarrow$ The current $\bar{I}$ lags the voltage $\bar{V}$ by an angle ϕ.

Case (iii): When B is zero,

That is, $B_C - B_L = 0$

$\Rightarrow$ $B_C = B_L$

$\Rightarrow$ *RLC* parallel circuit behaves like a resistive circuit. This condition is called resonance condition.

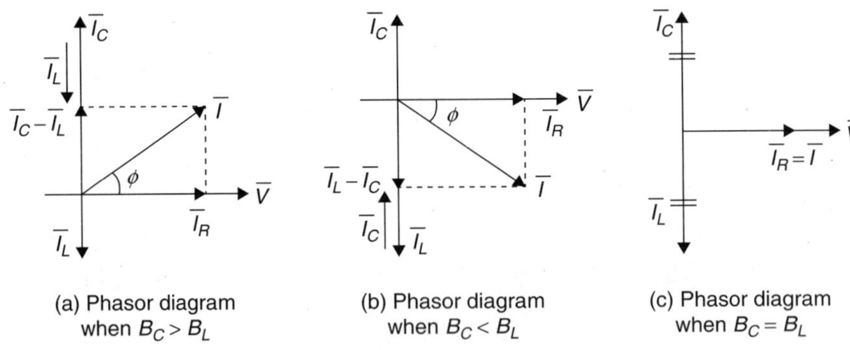

(a) Phasor diagram when $B_C > B_L$

(b) Phasor diagram when $B_C < B_L$

(c) Phasor diagram when $B_C = B_L$

Fig. 3.14 Phasor diagram of *RLC* parallel circuit

Problem 3.13 An inductive coil, having a resistance of 8 Ω and inductance of 80 mH, is connected in series with a capacitance of 100 μF across 150 V, 50 Hz supply. Calculate, (i) the current, (ii) the power factor, and (iii) the voltage drops in the coil and capacitance.

Solution:

Given that $f = 50$ Hz

$$\omega = 2\pi f = 2\pi \times 50 = 314.16 \text{ rad/s}$$

$$R = 8\ \Omega,\ L = 80\ \text{mH},\ C = 100\ \mu\text{F}$$

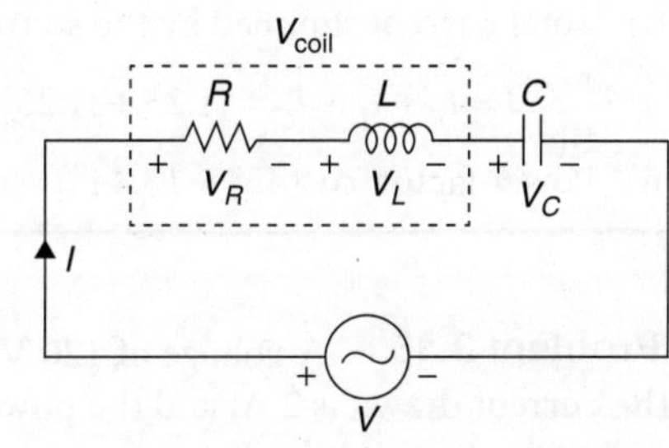

$$X_L = \omega L = 314.16 \times 80 \times 10^{-3} = 25.13\ \Omega$$

$$X_C = \frac{1}{\omega C} = \frac{1}{(314.16 \times 100 \times 10^{-6})} = 31.83\ \Omega$$

The impedance of the coil

$$Z_{\text{coil}} = R + j\,X_L = 8 + j25.13 = 26.375\angle 72.34°$$

The total impedance

$$Z = R + j(X_L - X_C) = 8 + j25.13 - j31.83 = 10.435\angle{-39.95°}\ \Omega$$

(i) The current drawn from the circuit

$$I = \frac{V}{Z} = \frac{150\angle 0°}{10.435\angle{-39.95°}} = 14.375\angle 39.95°\ \text{A}$$

(ii) Power factor, $\cos\phi = \cos(39.95°) = 0.767$ leading

(iii) Voltage drop in the coil

$$V_{\text{coil}} = I\,Z_{\text{coil}} = 14.375\angle 39.95° \times 26.375\angle 72.34° = 379.14\angle 112.2°$$

(iv) Voltage drop in the capacitor

$$V_c = I \times -jX_c = 14.375\angle 39.95° \times 31.83\angle{-90°} = 457.58\angle{-50°}$$

Problem 3.14 The applied voltage in a parallel *RLC* circuit is given by $v = 50\sin(5000t + 45°)$ volts. If the values of *R*, *L* and *C* are given as 20 Ω, 1.6 mH and 20 μF respectively, then find the total current supplied by the source and power factor.

Solution:

Given that $v = 50\sin(5000t + 45°)$ volts

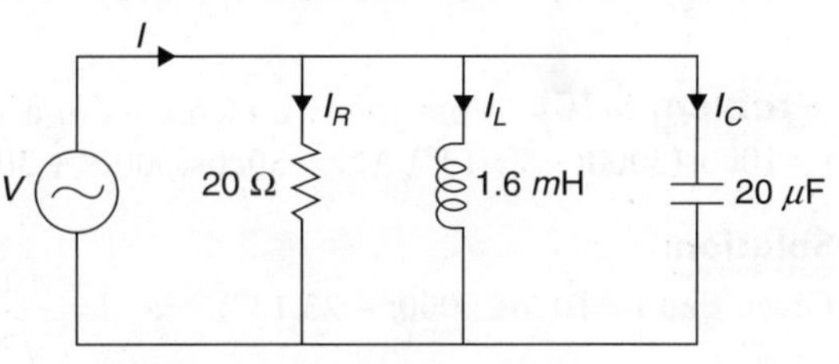

$$\Rightarrow \qquad V = \frac{50}{\sqrt{2}}\angle 45° = 35.35\angle 45°$$

$$V_m = 50\ \text{V},\ \omega = 5000\ \text{rad/s}$$

$$R = 20\ \Omega,\ L = 1.6\ \text{mH},\ C = 20\ \mu\text{F}$$

$$X_L = \omega L = 5000 \times 1.6 \times 10^{-3} = 8\ \Omega$$

$$X_C = \frac{1}{\omega C} = \frac{1}{(5000 \times 20 \times 10^{-6})} = 10\ \Omega$$

$$I_R = \frac{V}{R} = \frac{35.35\angle 45°}{20} = 1.77\angle 45° = (1.25 + j1.25)\ \text{A}$$

$$I_L = \frac{V}{jX_L} = \frac{35.35\angle 45°}{8\angle 90°} = 4.42\angle{-45°} = (3.125 - j3.125)\ \text{A}$$

$$I_C = \frac{V}{-jX_C} = \frac{35.35\angle 45°}{10\angle{-90°}} = 3.535\angle 135° = (-2.5 + j2.5)\ \text{A}$$

(i) Total current supplied by the source

$$I = I_R + I_L + I_C = (1.25 + j1.25) + (3.125 - j3.125) + (-2.5 + j2.5) = 1.875 + j0.625 = 1.976\angle 18.44^\circ$$

(ii) Power factor, $\cos(45^\circ - 18.44^\circ) = \cos(26.56^\circ) = 0.894$

Problem 3.15 A voltage of 120 V at 50 Hz is applied to a resistance, R in series with a capacitance C. The current drawn is 2 A, and the power loss in the resistance is 100 W. Calculate (i) the resistance, (ii) the capacitance and (ii) the power factor.

Solution:

Given that $V = 120$ V, $I = 2$ A, $P = 100$ W, $f = 50$ Hz

$$R = \frac{P}{I^2} = \frac{100}{2^2} = 25\ \Omega$$

$$Z = \sqrt{R^2 + X_C^2} = \frac{V}{I} = \frac{120}{2} = 60\ \Omega$$

$$X_C = \frac{1}{2\pi f \times C} = \sqrt{Z^2 - R^2} = \sqrt{(60)^2 - (25)^3} = 54.54\ \Omega$$

$$C = \frac{1}{2\pi f \times X_C} = \frac{1}{2\pi \times 50 \times 54.54} = 58.36 \times 10^{-6} = 58.36\ \mu\text{F}$$

The power factor is, $\cos\phi = \frac{R}{Z} = \frac{25}{60} = 0.417$ (leading)

The phase angle is $\phi = \cos^{-1}(0.417) = 65.38^\circ$

Problem 3.16 Find the two elements in a series circuit, given that the current and total voltage are $i = 10\cos(5000t - 23.13^\circ)$ A, $v = 50\cos(5000t + 30^\circ)$ V

Solution:

Given that $i = 10\cos(5000t - 23.13^\circ) \Rightarrow I = \frac{10}{\sqrt{2}}\angle -23.13^\circ = 7.07\angle -23.13^\circ$

$$v = 50\cos(5000t + 30^\circ) \Rightarrow V = \frac{50}{\sqrt{2}}\angle 30^\circ = 35.35\angle 30^\circ$$

$$\text{Impedance, } Z = \frac{V}{I} = \frac{35.35\angle 30^\circ}{7.07\angle -23.13^\circ} = 5\angle 53.13^\circ = 3 + j4$$

Comparing with $Z = R + jX_L$, we have

$$R = 3\ \Omega,\ X_L = 4\ \Omega$$

$$L = \frac{X_L}{\omega} = \frac{4}{5000} = 0.8\ \text{mH}$$

The two elements in a series circuit are $R = 3\ \Omega$ and $L = 0.8$ mH.

Problem 3.17 The voltage applied to a load is $V = (200 - j100)$ volts and the current is $I = (60 + j40)$ amperes. Find the load parameters and power dissipated.

Solution:

Given that $V = (200 - j100) = 223.6\angle{-26.56°}$ V

$$I = (60 + j40) = 72.1\angle 33.7° \text{ A}$$

$$\text{Impedance, } Z = \frac{V}{I} = \frac{223.6\angle{-26.56°}}{72.1\angle 33.7°} = 3.1\angle{-60.26°} = 1.54 - j2.69$$

Comparing with $Z = R - jX_C$, we have

$$R = 1.54\ \Omega,\ X_C = 2.69\ \Omega$$

$$C = \frac{1}{2\pi f X_C} = \frac{1}{2\pi \times 50 \times 2.69} = 1.183 \text{ mF}$$

The load parameters are $R = 1.54\ \Omega$ and $C = 1.183$ mF

Power dissipated, $P = I^2R = 72.1^2 \times 1.54 = 8$ kW

Problem 3.18 At what frequency will the current lead the voltage by 30° in a series circuit with $R = 8\ \Omega$ and $C = 30\ \mu$F?

Solution:

Given that $\phi = 30°$, $R = 8\ \Omega$, $C = 30\ \mu$F

For an RC series circuit, $\tan\phi = \dfrac{X_C}{R} = \dfrac{1}{\omega CR}$

$$\Rightarrow \quad \omega = \frac{1}{CR\tan\phi} = \frac{1}{30\times 10^{-6} \times 8 \times \tan 30°} = 7217$$

$$\Rightarrow \quad f = \frac{7217}{2\pi} = 1148.6 \text{ Hz}$$

Problem 3.19 A series RC circuit, with $R = 10\ \Omega$ has an impedance with an angle of 45° at $f_1 = 500$ Hz. Find the frequency for which the magnitude of the impedance is (i) twice that at f_1 (ii) one-half of that at f_1.

Solution:

Given that $10 - jX_C = Z_I\angle 45°$

$$\Rightarrow \quad X_C = 10\ \Omega,\ Z_I = 14.14\ \Omega$$

(i) For twice the magnitude, $10 - jX_C = 28.28\angle\phi°$

$$\Rightarrow \quad X_C = \sqrt{(28.28)^2 - (10)^2} = 26.45\ \Omega$$

Then, since X_C is inversely proportional to f,

That is, $X_C = \dfrac{1}{2\pi fC} \quad \Rightarrow \quad \dfrac{X_{C1}}{X_{C2}} = \dfrac{f_2}{f_1}$

$$\Rightarrow \quad f_2 = \frac{10}{26.45} \times 500 = 189 \text{ Hz}$$

(ii) A magnitude $Z_3 = 7.07\ \Omega$ is impossible; the smallest magnitude possible is $Z = R = 10\ \Omega$

Problem 3.20 A two-element series circuit has voltage $V = 240\angle 0°$ V and current $I = 50\angle -60°$ A. Determine the current which results when the resistance is reduced to (i) 30% (ii) 60 % of its former value.

Solution:

Given that $V = 240\angle 0°$ V, $I = 50\angle -60°$

$$Z = \frac{V}{I} = \frac{240\angle 0°}{50\angle -60°} = 4.8\angle 60° = 2.40 + j4.16\ \Omega$$

(i) 30% of R

$$R' = 30\% \times 2.4 = 0.72$$

$$Z_1 = 0.72 + j4.16 = 4.22\angle 80.2°$$

$$I_1 = \frac{240\angle 0°}{4.22\angle 80.2°} = 56.8\angle -80.2° \text{ A}$$

(ii) 60% of R

$$R' = 60\% \times 2.4 = 1.44$$

$$Z_2 = 1.44 + j4.16 = 54.5\angle 70.9°$$

$$I_2 = \frac{240\angle 0°}{4.40\angle 70.9°} = 54.5\angle -70.9° \text{ A}$$

ADDITIONAL SOLVED PROBLEMS

3.1 In the circuit, determine the voltage V_{AB} to be applied if a current of 2.5 A is required to flow in the capacitor. Determine also total power factor and total active and reactive power. Draw the corresponding phasor diagram.

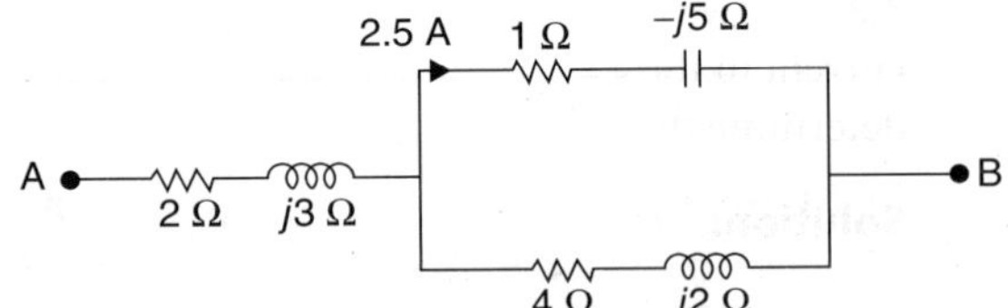

Solution: Given that $V_{CD} = 2.5(1 - j5) = I_1(4 + j2)$

$$I_1 = \frac{2.5(1-j5)}{4+j2} = 2.85\angle -105.25 = -0.75 - j2.75$$

$$I = I_1 + I_2 = -0.75 - j2.75 + 2.5 = 1.75 - j2.75$$

$$= 3.26\angle -57.53°$$

$$V_{AB} = I(2 + j3) + 2.5(1 - j5) = (1.75 - j2.75)(2 + j3) + 2.5(1 - j5) = 14.25 - j12.75$$

$$Z_{AB} = \frac{V_{AB}}{I} = \frac{19.12\angle -41.82°}{3.26\angle -57.53°} = 5.865\angle 15.71°$$

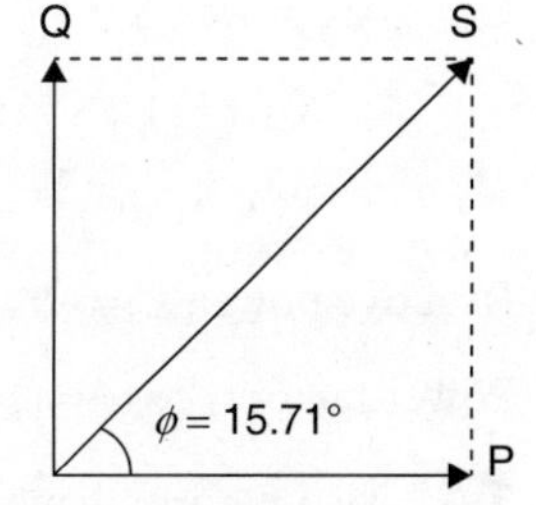

$\Rightarrow \qquad \phi = 15.71°$

Total power factor = $\cos\phi = \cos 15.71° = 0.962$

Total active power, $P = V_{AB} I \cos\phi = 19.12 \times 3.26 \times \cos(15.71°) = 60$ W

Total reactive power, $Q = V_{AB} I \sin\phi = 19.12 \times 3.26 \times \sin(15.71°) = 16.87$ VAR

Apparent power, $S = VI = 19.12 \times 3.26 = 63.33$ VA

3.2 In the circuit, when a 220 V AC is applied across A and B, the current drawn is 20 A and power input is 300 W. Find the value of Z and its parameters.

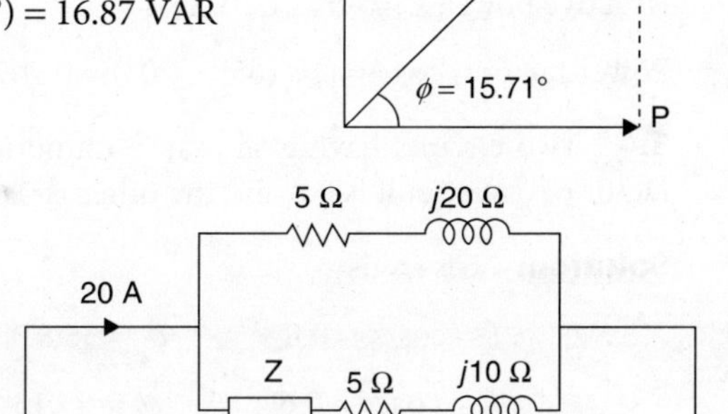

Solution: Given that

But $\qquad i_1 = \dfrac{220}{5 + j20}$

$$i_1 + i_2 = 20$$

$$i_2 = 20 - i_1 = 20 - \frac{220}{5 + j20} \qquad (1)$$

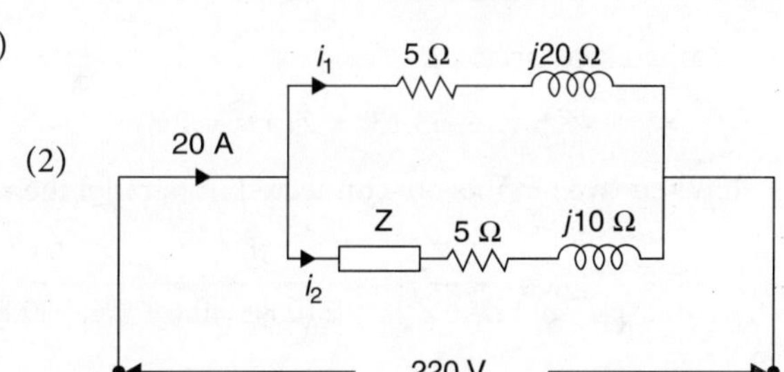

$$i_2 = \frac{220}{Z + 5 + j10} \qquad (2)$$

From Eqs (1) and (2)

$$20 - \frac{220}{5 + j20} = \frac{220}{Z + 5 + j10}$$

$$\Rightarrow \qquad \frac{-120 + j400}{5 + j20} = \frac{220}{Z + 5 + j10}$$

$$\Rightarrow \qquad Z = \frac{5700 + j3600}{-120 + j400} = -44.33 + j15.55 = 16.14\angle 105.56° \ \Omega$$

3.3 A two element series circuit is connected across an AC source given by $v = 200\sqrt{2}\sin(314t + 20°)$. The current in the circuit is found to be $i = 10\sqrt{2}\cos(314t - 25°)$. Determine the parameters of the circuit. Also determine the power factor, real power and reactive power taken by the circuit?

Solution: Given that $V = 200\sqrt{2}\sin(314t + 20°) \Rightarrow V_{rms} = 200\angle 20°$

$$i = 10\sqrt{2}\cos(314t - 25°) = 10\sqrt{2}\sin(90 + 314t - 25°) = 10\sqrt{2}\sin(314t + 65°)$$

$$I_{rms} = 10\angle 65°$$

$$Z = \frac{V_{rms}}{I_{rms}} = \frac{200\angle 20°}{10\angle 65°} = 20\angle -45° = 14.14 - j14.14$$

$$Z = 14.14 - j14.14 = R - jX_C$$

$$\Rightarrow \qquad R = 14.14\ \Omega, \qquad X_C = 14.14\ \Omega$$

$$X_C = \frac{1}{\omega C} = 14.14 \Rightarrow C = \frac{1}{14.14 \times 314} = 225.23\ \mu\text{F}$$

Complex power, $S = VI^* = 200\angle 20° \times 10\angle -65° = 2000\angle -45°$

$$S = 1414.2 - j1414.2 = P + jQ$$

$\therefore$ Real power, $P = 1414.2$ W

Reactive power, $Q = -1414.2$ VAR

Power factor $= \cos\phi = \cos(65° - 20°) = 0.707$ leading.

3.4 Two circuits having the same numerical ohmic impedance value are joined in parallel. The power factor of one circuit is 0.8 and the other is 0.6, both lagging. Calculate the power factor of the combination.

Solution: Given that

$$p.f_1 = \cos\phi_1 = 0.8 \quad \Rightarrow \quad \phi_1 = 36.87°$$

$$p.f_2 = \cos\phi_2 = 0.6 \quad \Rightarrow \quad \phi_2 = 53.13°$$

Impedance circuit 1,

$$Z_1 = Z\angle -36.87° = Z(0.8 - j0.6)$$

Impedance circuit 2,

$$Z_2 = Z\angle -53.13° = Z(0.6 - j0.8)$$

When two circuits are connected in parallel the resultant impedance,

$$Z_T = \frac{Z_1 Z_2}{Z_1 + Z_2} = \frac{Z\angle -36.86° \times Z\angle -53.13°}{Z(0.8 - j0.6 + 0.6 - j0.8)} = \frac{Z\angle -90°}{1.4 - j1.4} = \frac{Z\angle -90°}{2\angle -45°} = \frac{Z}{2}\angle 45°$$

Resultant $p.f. = \cos 45° = 0.707$, lagging.

3.5 Draw the phasor diagram for the circuit, indicating the terminal voltage V_1 and V_2 and total current I. Determine the value of current I, voltage V_1 and V_2 and circuit power factor.

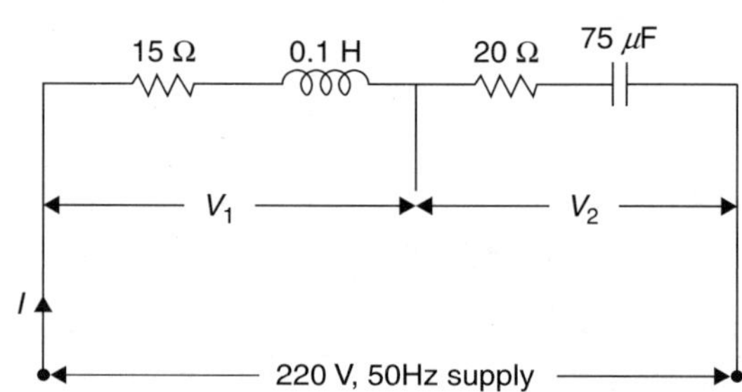

Solution:

$$X_L = 2\pi fL = 2\pi \times 50 \times 0.1 = 31.416\ \Omega$$

$$X_C = \frac{1}{2\pi fC} = \frac{1}{2\pi \times 50 \times 75 \times 10^{-6}} = 42.44\ \Omega$$

$$Z_1 = 15 + j31.416 = 34.8\angle 64.5°$$

$$Z_2 = 20 - j42.44 = 46.92\angle -64.76°$$

Total impedance,

$$Z = Z_1 + Z_2 = 15 + j\,31.46 + 20 - j\,43.44 = 35 - j\,11.024 = 36.71\angle -1\,7.48°$$

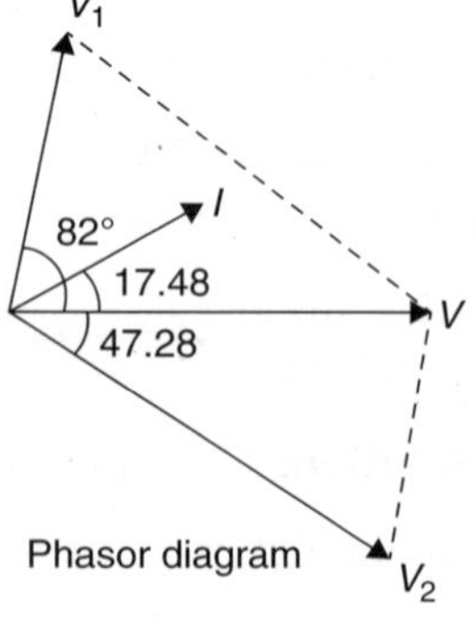

Phasor diagram

Let $V = 220\ \angle 0°$ be taken as reference phasor

Total current

$$I = \frac{V}{Z} = \frac{220\angle 0°}{36.7\angle -17.48°} = 6\angle 17.48°$$

$$V_1 = I.Z_1 = 6\angle 17.48° \times 34.8\angle 64.5° = 208.8\angle 82° \text{ volts}$$

$$V_2 = I.Z_2 = 6\angle 17.48° \times 16.92\angle -64.76° = 281.52\angle -47.28° \text{ volts}$$

3.6 Obtain the branch currents and total current in the circuit, if the applied voltage is $150\angle 45°$ V and draw the phasor diagram.

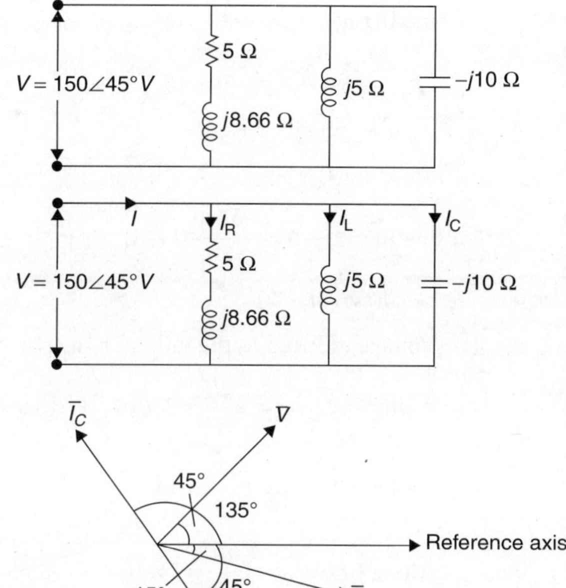

Solution: From the circuit diagram shown on the right,

$$I_R = \frac{V}{5 + j8.66} = \frac{150\angle 45°}{10\angle 60°} = 15\angle -15° = 14.5 - j3.88$$

$$I_L = \frac{V}{j5} = \frac{150\angle 45°}{5\angle 90°} = 30\angle -45° = 21.21 - j21.21$$

$$I_c = \frac{V}{-j10} = \frac{150\angle 45°}{10\angle -90°} = 15\angle 135° = -10.6 + j10.6$$

The total current is

$$I = I_R + I_L + I_C$$

$$= 14.5 - j3.88 + 21.21 - j\,21.21 - 10.6 + j\,10.6$$

$$= 25.11 - j15 = 29.25\angle -30.85°$$

3.7 A voltage $v = 140\cos\omega t$ is connected across an impedance $Z = 5\angle -60°$. Find the instantaneous power, $p(t)$?

Solution: Given that $Z = 5\angle -60°$

$$v = 140\cos\,\omega t \Rightarrow V = \frac{140}{\sqrt{2}}\angle 0° = 99\angle 0°$$

The current I is given by

$$I = \frac{V}{Z} = \frac{99\angle 0°}{5\angle -60} = 19.8\angle 60°$$

Therefore, the instantaneous value of current is given by

$$i = 19.8 \times \sqrt{2}\,\cos(\omega t + 60°) = 28\,\cos(\omega t + 60°)$$

Instantaneous power, $p(t) = v(t)\,i(t) = 140 \times 28\cos\omega t\,\cos\,(\omega t + 60°) = 980 + 1960\,\cos(2\omega t + 60°)$

The instantaneous power has a constant component of 980 W and a sinusoidal component with twice the frequency of the source.

3.8 The following current wave from $i(t)$ is passed through a series RL circuit with $R = 2\ \Omega$ and $L = 2$ mH. Find the voltage across each element and sketch the same.

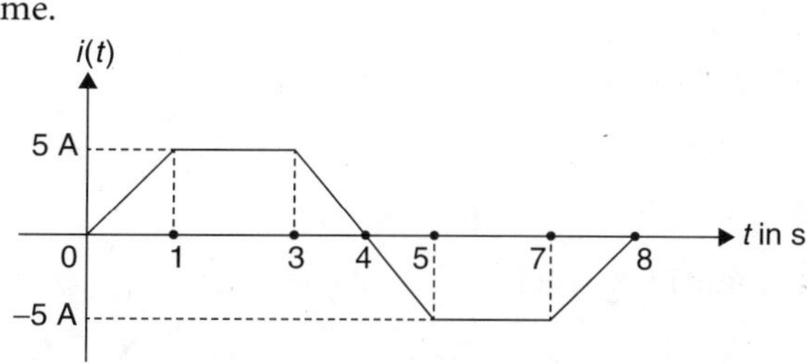

Solution:

For line OA, slope $= \dfrac{5-1}{1-0} = 5$

Equation for line (OA),

$$i(t) - 0 = 5(t - 0)$$

$i(t) = 5t$

For line AB, $i(t) = 5$

For line BD $i(t) - 5 = \dfrac{-5-5}{5-3}(t-3)$

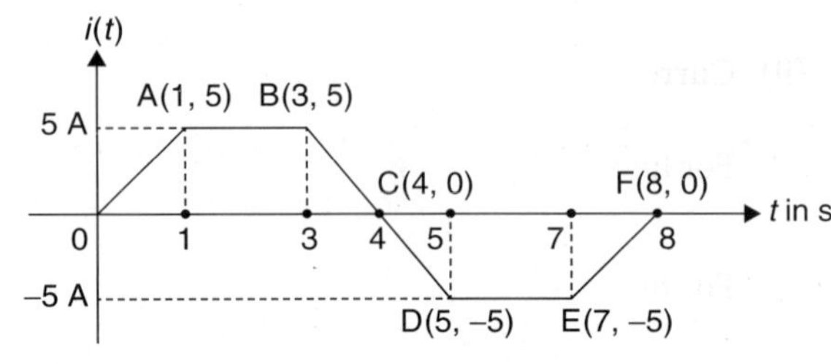

$i(t) - 5 = -5t + 15$

$i(t) = -5t + 20$

For line DE, $i(t) = -5$

For line EF, $i(t) - 0 = \dfrac{-5-0}{7-8}(t-8)$

$i(t) = 5t - 40$

(i) Voltage induced in the inductor $[v_L(t)]$:

Along OA, $v_{OA} = L\dfrac{di}{dt} = 2\times10^{-3}\dfrac{d}{dt}(5t) = 5\times2\times10^{-3} = 10 \text{ mV}$

Along AB, $v_{AB} = L\dfrac{di}{dt} = 0 \text{ V}$

Along BD, $v_{BD} = L\dfrac{di}{dt} = 2\times10^{-3}\times-5 = -10 \text{ mV}$

Along DE, $v_{DE} = L\dfrac{di}{dt} = 0 \text{ V}$

Along EF, $v_{EF} = L\dfrac{di}{dt} = 2\times10^{-3}\times5 = 10 \text{ mV}$

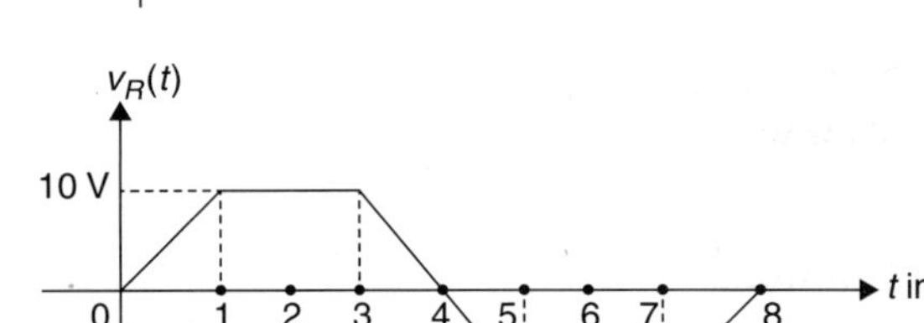

(ii) Voltage across the resistor $[v_R(t)]$
Voltage across the resistor is the same as current through the circuit multiplied by the resistance.
$v_R = IR = 2I$

vR(t)
10 V
t in s
0
1 2 3 4 5 6 7 8
–10 V

3.9 Draw the waveforms for i_R, i_L and i_C for the circuit shown, when it is excited by a voltage source having a waveform as shown.

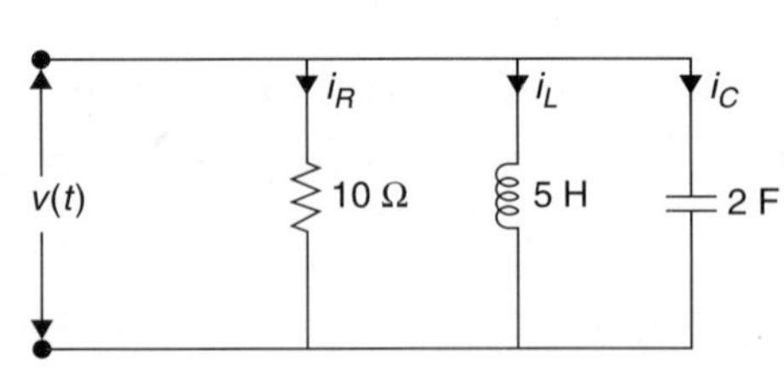

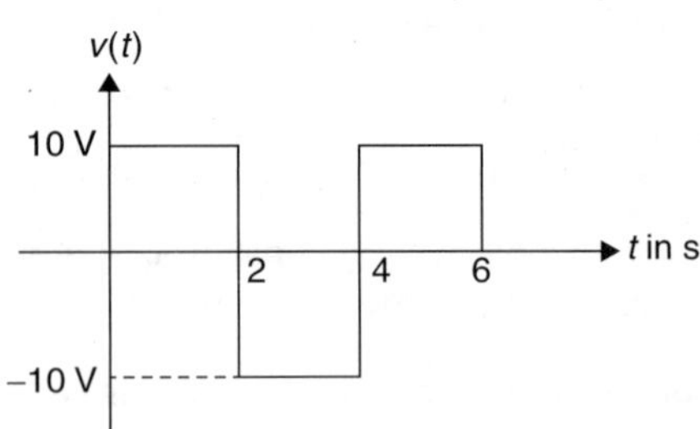

Solution: Given that

For line AB, $v(t) = 10$

For line CD, $v(t) = -10$

For line EF, $v(t) = 10$

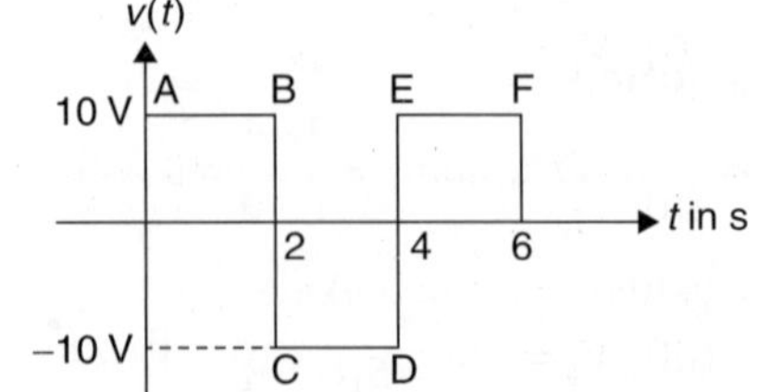

(i) Current through the resistor, i_R

Current through the resistance is the same as the voltage across the circuit divided by the resistance.

$$i_R(t) = \frac{v(t)}{R} = \frac{v(t)}{10}$$

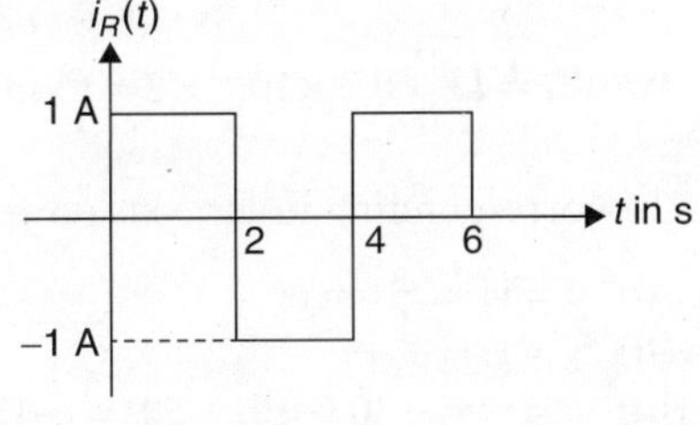

(ii) Current through the capacitance i_C

For line AB, $i_{AB} = C\dfrac{dv}{dt} = 0$

For line CD, $i_{CD} = C\dfrac{dv}{dt} = 0$

For line EF, $i_{EF} = C\dfrac{dv}{dt} = 0$

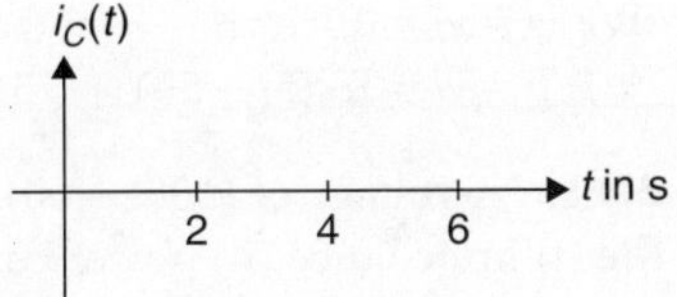

(iii) Current through the inductor, i_L

For line AB, $i_{AB} = \dfrac{1}{L}\displaystyle\int vdt = \dfrac{1}{5}\int 10dt = 2t$

For line CD, $i_{CD} = \dfrac{1}{L}\displaystyle\int vdt = \dfrac{1}{5}\int -10dt = -2t$

For line EF, $i_{EF} = \dfrac{1}{L}\displaystyle\int vdt = \dfrac{1}{5}\int 10dt = 2t$

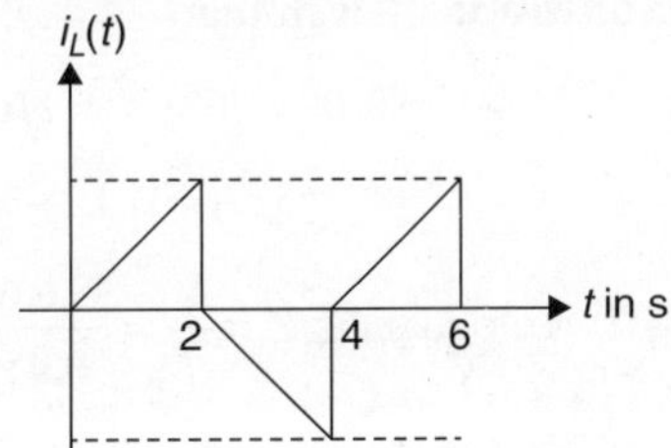

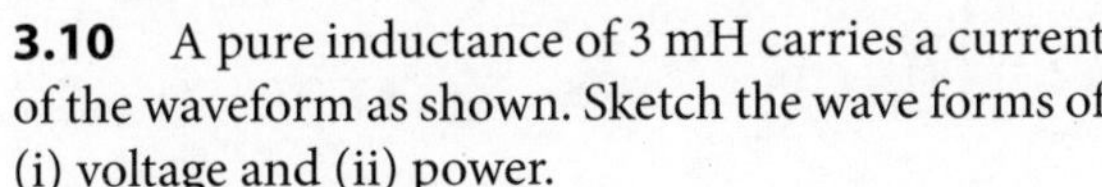

3.10 A pure inductance of 3 mH carries a current of the waveform as shown. Sketch the wave forms of (i) voltage and (ii) power.

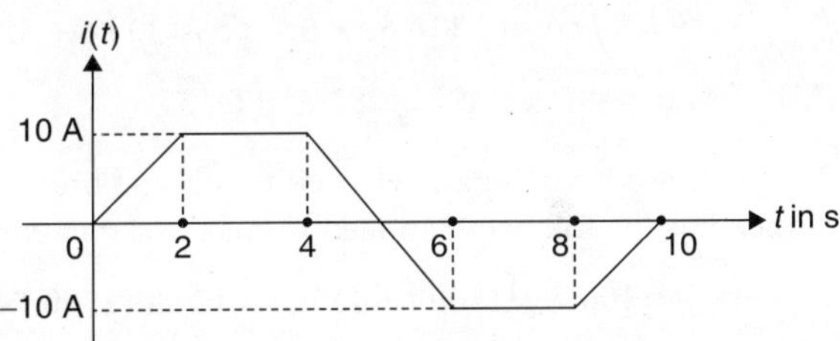

Solution: Given that

The instantaneous current $i(t)$ is given by

(i) For $0 < t < 2$, $i(t) = 5t$

(ii) For $2 < t < 4$, $i(t) = 10$

(iii) For $4 < t < 6$, $i(t) - 10 = \dfrac{-10-10}{6-4}(t-4)$

$$i(t) = -10t + 50$$

(iv) For $6 < t < 8$, $i(t) = -10$

(v) For $8 < t < 10$, $i(t) - 0 = \dfrac{-10-0}{8-10}(t-10)$

$$i(t) = 5t - 50$$

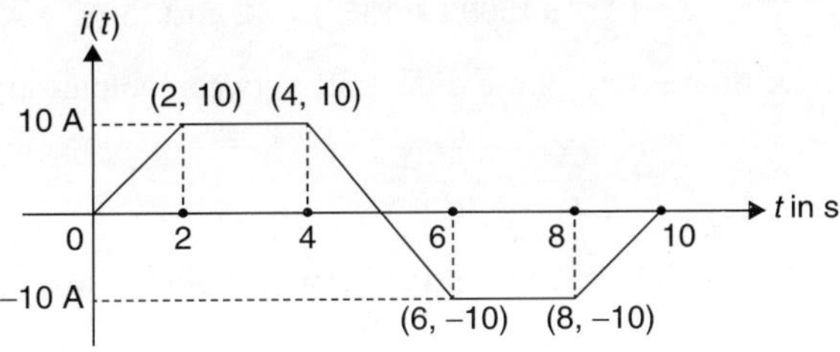

The corresponding voltages are

(i) $V_L = L\dfrac{di}{dt} = 3\times10^{-3}\times5 = 15\text{ mV}$

(ii) $V_L = L\dfrac{di}{dt} = 0$

(iii) $V_L = L\dfrac{di}{dt} = -3\times10^{-3}\times10 = -30\text{ mV}$

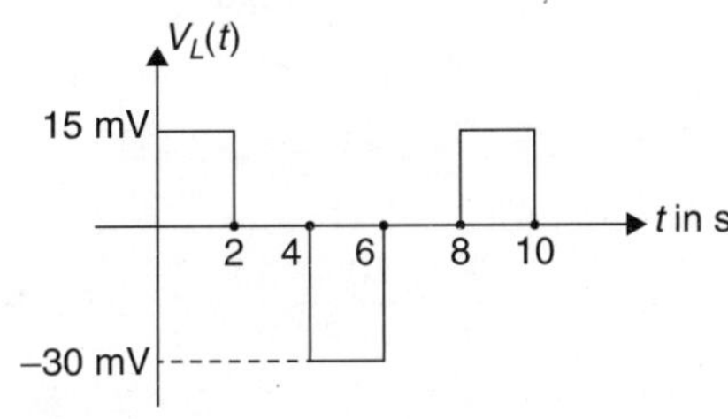

(iv) $V_L = L\dfrac{di}{dt} = 0$

(v) $V_L = L\dfrac{di}{dt} = 3\times10^{-3}\times5 = 15\ \text{mV}$

The corresponding instaneous power values are

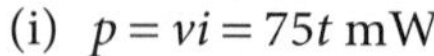

(i) $p = vi = 75t$ mW

(ii) $p = vi = 0$

(iii) $p = vi = -\,30\,(-10t + 50) = (-1500 + 300t)$ mW

(iv) $p = vi = 0$

(v) $p = vi = 15\,(5t - 50) = (75t - 750)$ mW

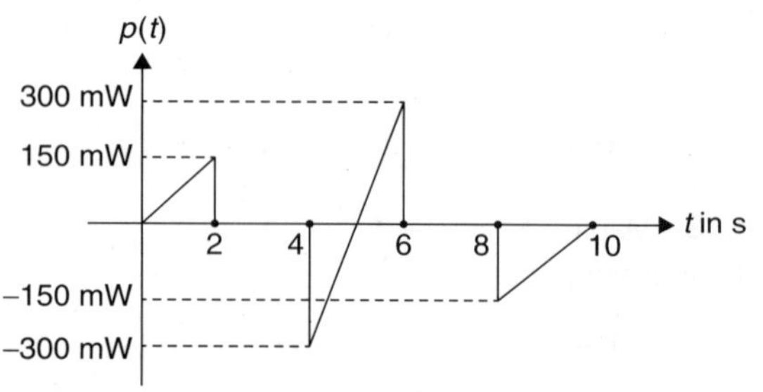

3.11 A voltage of $(100 + j60)$ V drives a current of $(4 - j5)$ A through a series R–L–C circuit. Determine the (i) impedance (ii) power consumed, and (iii) power factor. Draw the phasor diagram.

Solution: Given that

$$V = (100 + j60)\ \text{V} = 116.62\angle 30.96^\circ\ \text{V}$$

$$I = (4 - j5)\ \text{A} = 6.4\angle{-51.34^\circ}\ \text{A}$$

(i) Impedance, $Z = \dfrac{V}{I} = \dfrac{116.62\angle 30.96^\circ}{6.4\angle -51.34^\circ} = 18.22\angle 82.2^\circ$

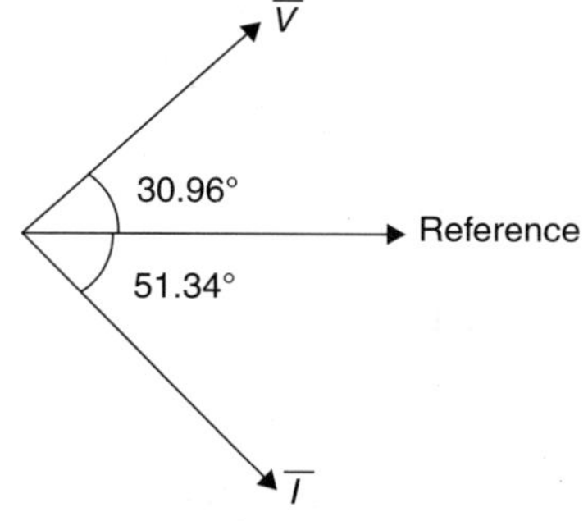

(ii) Power consumed

$$P = VI\cos\phi = 116.62\times6.4\times\cos(30.96 + 51.34) = 100\ \text{W}$$

(iii) Power factor, $\cos\phi = \cos 82.2^\circ = 0.135$

3.12 A two branch parallel circuit with one branch $R = 50\ \Omega$ and a single unknown element in the other branch has the following applied voltage and current:

$$v = 100\cos(1500\,t + 45^\circ),\ i = 12\sin(1500\,t + 135^\circ).\ \text{Find the unknown element.}$$

Solution: Given that $R = 50\ \Omega$, $v = 100\cos(1500t + 45^\circ)$

$$i = 12\sin(1500\,t + 135^\circ) = 12\cos(1500t + 45^\circ)$$

Here, there is no phase difference between voltage and current, so the other element is a resistor. So

$$Z = \frac{RX}{R + X} = \frac{50X}{50 + X} \qquad (1)$$

RMS values of voltage and currents are given as

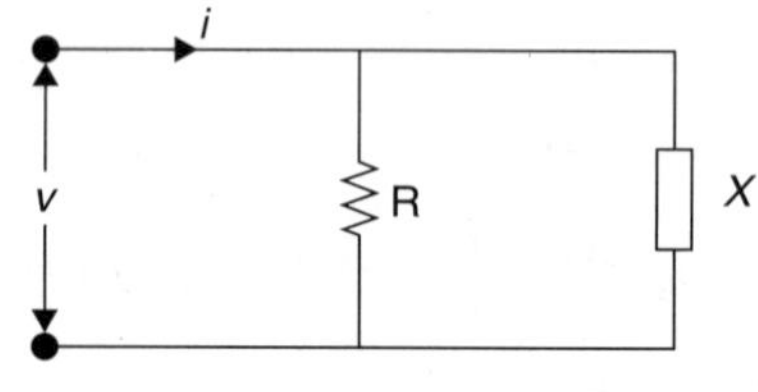

$$V = \frac{100}{\sqrt{2}}\angle 45^\circ = 70.7\angle 45^\circ$$

$$I = \frac{12}{\sqrt{2}}\angle 45^\circ = 8.5\angle 45^\circ$$

$$Z = \frac{V}{I} = \frac{70.7\angle 45^\circ}{8.5\angle 45^\circ} = 8.32\ \Omega \qquad (2)$$

From Eqs (1) and (2),

$$\frac{50X}{50+X} = 8.32$$

$$\Rightarrow \quad 50X = 416.5 + 8.32X$$

$$\Rightarrow \quad X = 10\ \Omega$$

3.13 A parallel circuit with one branch of $R = 5\ \Omega$ and a single unknown element in the other branch has the following applied voltage and total current:

$v = 10\cos(50t + 60°)$ volts, $i = 5.38\cos(50t - 8.23°)$ amperes. Find the unknown element.

Solution: Given that

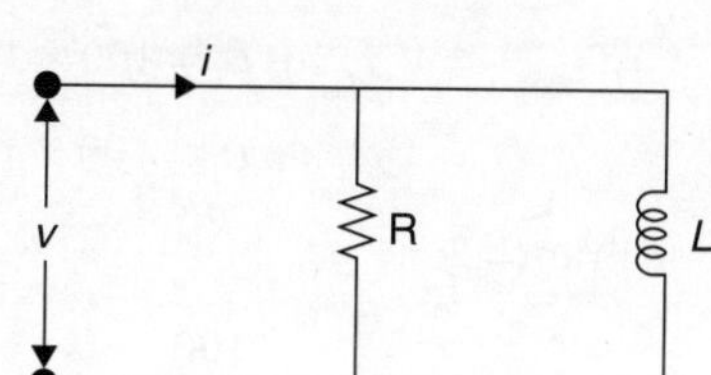

$$R = 5\ \Omega$$

$$V = 10\cos(50t + 60°)$$

$$i = 5.38\cos(50t - 8.23°)$$

Here, v leads i, so the other element is an inductor. So

$$Z = \frac{R \times jX_L}{R + jX_L} = \frac{R \times jX_L(R - jX_L)}{R^2 + jX_L^2} = \frac{RX_L^2}{R^2 + jX_L^2} + j\frac{R^2X_L}{R^2 + jX_L^2} \tag{1}$$

RMS values of voltage and currents are given as

$$V = \frac{10}{\sqrt{2}}\angle 60° = 7.07\angle 60°$$

$$I = \frac{5.38}{\sqrt{2}}\angle{-8.23°} = 3.8\angle{-8.23°}$$

$$Z = \frac{V}{I} = \frac{7.07\angle 60°}{3.8\angle{-8.23°}} = 1.86\angle 68.23° = 0.689 + j1.725 \tag{2}$$

Comparing Eqs (1) and (2),

$$\frac{RX_L^2}{R^2 + jX_L^2} = 0.689 \tag{3}$$

$$\frac{R^2X_L}{R^2 + jX_L^2} = 1.725 \tag{4}$$

$$\frac{\text{Eq. (3)}}{\text{Eq. (4)}} = \frac{X_L}{R} = \frac{0.689}{1.725} = 0.4$$

$$\Rightarrow \quad X_L = 0.4R = 0.4 \times 5 = 2\ \Omega$$

$$\Rightarrow \quad L = \frac{X_L}{\omega} = \frac{2}{50} = 40\text{ mH}$$

3.14 Determine the branch and total real and reactive powers in the parallel circuit as shown.

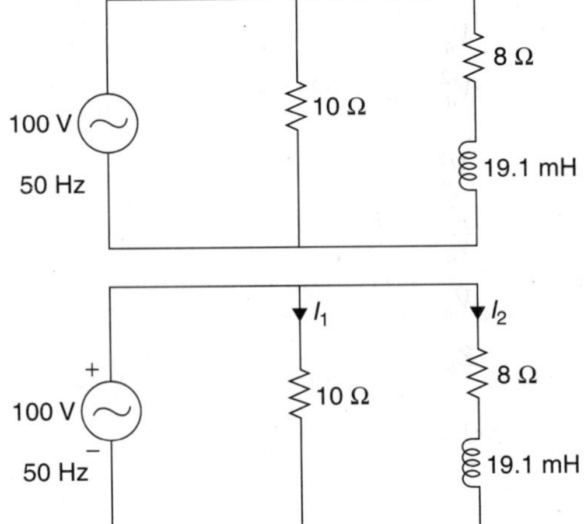

Solution: Given that

$$Z_1 = 10$$

$$Z_2 = R + jX_L = 8 + j2 \times \pi \times 50 \times 19.1 \times 10^{-3}$$

$$= 8 + j6 = 10\angle 36.8^\circ$$

For Branch 1:

$$I_1 = \frac{V_1}{Z_1} = \frac{100}{10} = 10$$

$$\phi_1 = 0$$

$$P_1 = V_1 I_1 \cos\phi_1 = 100 \times 10 \times \cos 0 = 1000 \text{ W}$$

$$Q_1 = V_1 I_1 \sin\phi_1 = 100 \times 10 \times \sin 0 = 0$$

For Branch 2:

$$I_2 = \frac{V_2}{Z_2} = \frac{100}{10\angle 36.8^\circ} = 10\angle -36.8^\circ$$

$\Rightarrow$ $$\phi_2 = 36.8^\circ$$

$$P_2 = V_2 I_2 \cos\phi_2 = 100 \times 10 \times \cos 36.8 = 800 \text{ W}$$

$$Q_2 = V_2 I_2 \sin\phi_2 = 100 \times 10 \times \sin 36.8 = 600 \text{ VAR(lag)}$$

$$\text{Total real power} = P_1 + P_2 = 1800 \text{ W}$$

$$\text{Total reactive power} = Q_l + Q_2 = 600 \text{ VAR (lag)}$$

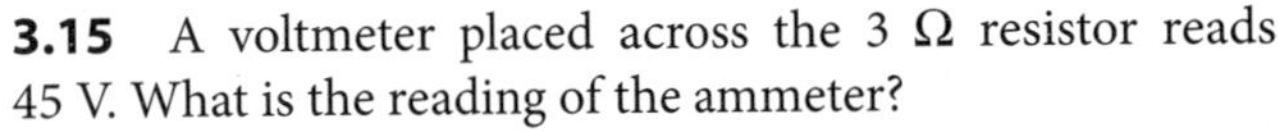

3.15 A voltmeter placed across the 3 Ω resistor reads 45 V. What is the reading of the ammeter?

Solution: Given that

The current flowing through the 3 Ω resistance is

$$I_1 = \frac{V}{R} = \frac{45}{3} = 15 \text{ A}$$

Volt across $(3 + j3)$ Ω impedance $= (3 + j3)15 = 63.63\angle 45^\circ$

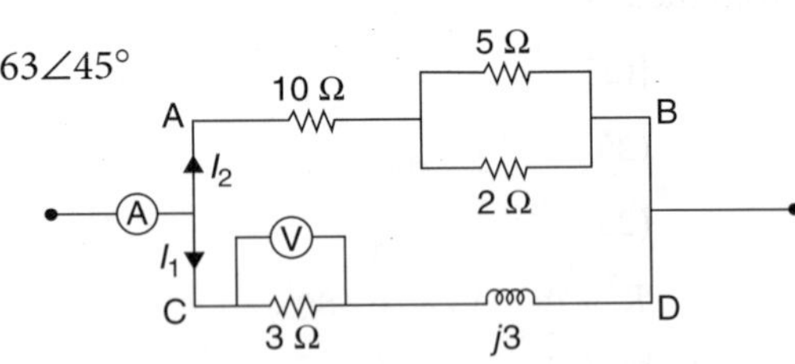

$$R_{AB} = 10 + \frac{5 \times 2}{5 + 2} = 10 + 1.428 = 11.428$$

$$I_2 = \frac{63.63\angle 45^\circ}{11.428} = 5.572\angle 45^\circ = 3.939 + j3.939$$

$$I_1 = I_1 + I_2 = 15 + 3.939 + j3.939 = 18.939 + j3.939 = 19.34\angle 11.74^\circ \text{ A}$$

Therefore, ammeter reading = 19.34 A.

3.16 Find the values of R and C in the circuit shown, so that $V_b = 4V_a$ and V_a and V_b are in phase quadrature?

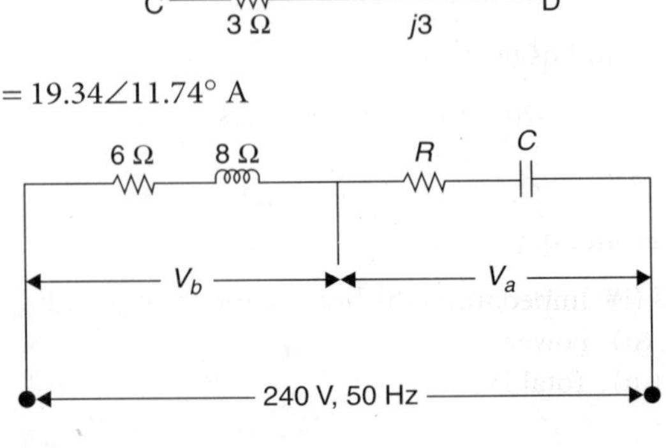

Solution: Given that

$$V_b = 4V_a$$

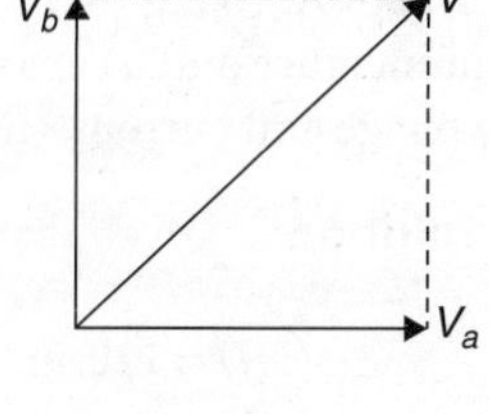

$$V_a^2 + V_b^2 = V^2 \text{ (since } V_a \text{ and } V_b \text{ are in phase quadrature)}$$

$$V_a^2 + 16V_a^2 = V^2$$

$$\Rightarrow \quad V_a^2 = \frac{V^2}{17} = \frac{240^2}{17} = 3388.24$$

$$V_a = 58.2\angle 0^\circ$$

$$\therefore \quad V_b = 4V_a = 232.8\angle 90^\circ$$

$$Z_b = 6 + j8 = 10\angle 53.13^\circ$$

$$I = \frac{V_b}{Z_b} = \frac{232.8\angle 90^\circ}{10\angle 53.13^\circ} = 23.28\angle 36.8^\circ$$

$$Z_a = \frac{V_a}{I} = \frac{58.2\angle 0^\circ}{23.28\angle 36.8^\circ} = 2.5\angle -36.8^\circ = 2 - j1.5 = R - jX_C$$

$$\Rightarrow \quad R = 2\ \Omega,\ X_C = 1.5\ \Omega$$

$$\Rightarrow \quad C = \frac{1}{\omega X_C} = \frac{1}{2\pi \times 50 \times 1.5} = 2.12 \text{ mF}$$

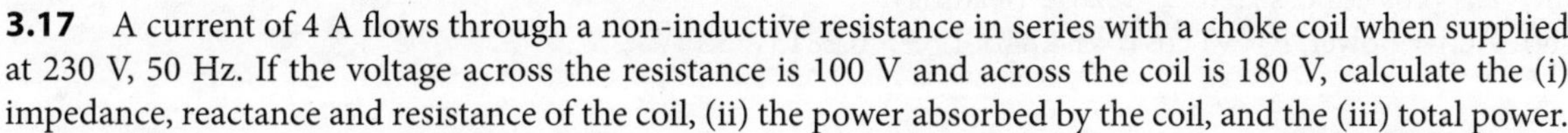

3.17 A current of 4 A flows through a non-inductive resistance in series with a choke coil when supplied at 230 V, 50 Hz. If the voltage across the resistance is 100 V and across the coil is 180 V, calculate the (i) impedance, reactance and resistance of the coil, (ii) the power absorbed by the coil, and the (iii) total power.

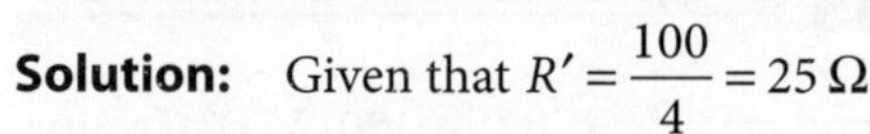

Solution: Given that $R' = \dfrac{100}{4} = 25\ \Omega$

$$Z_{\text{coil}} = \frac{180}{4} = 45 = R + jX_L$$

$$\Rightarrow \quad R^2 + X_L^2 = 45^2 = 2025$$

$$\therefore \quad R^2 + X_L^2 = 2025 \qquad (1)$$

From the circuit diagram

$$[(25 + R) + jX_L]4 = 230$$

$$(25 + R) + jX_L = 57.5$$

$$(25 + R)^2 + X_L{}^2 = 3036.25$$

$$R^2 + X_L^2 + 50R + 625 = 3036.25 \qquad (2)$$

From Eqs (1) and (2),

$$2025 + 50\,R + 625 = 3306.25$$

$$\Rightarrow \quad R = 13.125\ \Omega$$

From Eq. (1) $X_L = \sqrt{(2025 - 172.3)} = 43$

(i) Impedance of the coil, $Z = R + jX_L = (13.125 + j43)\ \Omega$
(ii) Power absorbed, $P = I^2R = 16 \times 13.125 = 210$ W
(iii) Total Power, $PT = I^2R' + 210 = 16 \times 25 + 210 = 610$ W

3.18 A voltage $v(t) = 120\sin 314t$ is applied to a series circuit consisting of 15 Ω resistance, 0.04 H inductance and a capacitance of 50 μF. Calculate the (i) expression for current $i(t)$, (ii) phase angle between voltage and current, (iii) power factor, and (iv) active power.

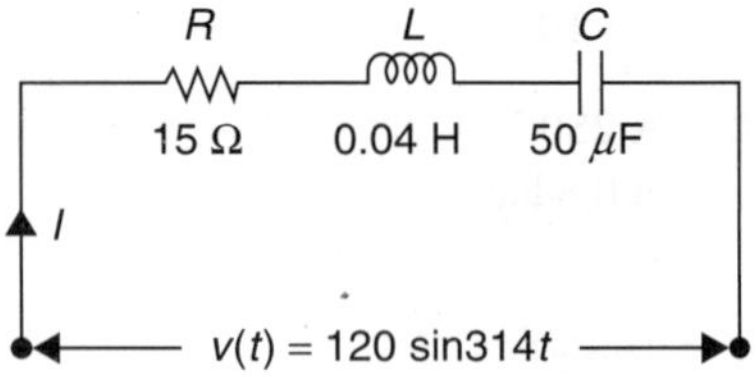

Solution: Given that $R = 15\ \Omega$, $L = 0.04$ H, $C = 50\ \mu$F

$$v(t) = 120\sin 314t \quad \Rightarrow \quad V = \frac{120}{\sqrt{2}} = 84.84\angle 0°,\ \omega = 314$$

$$X_L = \omega L = 314 \times 0.04 = 12.56$$

$$X_C = \frac{1}{\omega C} = \frac{1}{314 \times 50 \times 10^{-6}} = 63.69$$

$$Z = R + j(X_L - X_C) = 15 + j(12.56 - 63.69) = 15 - j51.13 = 53.28\angle -73.65°$$

$$I = \frac{V}{Z} = \frac{84.84\angle 0}{53.28\angle -73.65^0} = 1.59\angle 73.65^0$$

Since $X_C > X_L$, the nature of the circuit is capacitive and hence i leads v by an angle $\phi = 73.65°$.

(i) Expression for $i(t)$, $i(t) = I_m \sin(\omega t + \phi) = \sqrt{2} \times 1.59\sin(314t + 73.65°)$
(ii) Phase angle, $\phi = 73.65°$ with current leading the voltage
(iii) $p.f = \cos\phi = \cos 73.65° = 0.2815$ (leading)
(iv) Active power, $P = VI\cos\phi = 84.84 \times 1.59 \times 0.2815 = 38$ W

EXERCISE PROBLEMS

1. The current in a given circuit is $I = (12 - j5)$ A when the applied voltage is $V = (160 - j120)$ V. Determine (a) the complex expression for power, (b) power factor of the circuit, and (c) the complex expression for impedance of the circuit. [**Ans:** (a) $S = 2520 + j640$, (b) p.f. = 0.97, (c) $Z = 14.9 - j3.786$]

2. A series RL series circuit having a resistance of 4 Ω and 3 Ω inductive reactance is fed by 100 V, $1 - \phi$ supply. Find current, power drawn by the circuit and power factor. [**Ans:** $I = 20\angle -36.87°$ A, $P = 1.6$ kW, p.f. = $\cos\phi = 0.8$]

3. An inductive coil takes 10 A and dissipates 1000 W when connected to a supply of 250 V, 25 Hz. Calculate the (a) impedance, (b) effective resistance, (c) reactance, (d) inductance, and (e) power factor. [**Ans:** (a) $Z = 10 + j23$, (b) $R = 10$, (c) $X_L = 22.9$, (d) $L = 145.8$ mH, (e) p.f = 0.4]

4. A metal filament lamp, rated at 750 W, 100 V is connected in series with capacitor across a 230 V, 60 Hz supply. Calculate the (a) capacitance required, and (b) power factor. [**Ans:** $C = 96\ \mu$F, p.f = 0.4346]

5. Calculate the current, power, power factor and voltage across a resistor of 8 Ω in series with an inductor of 20 H and a capacitor of 14 μF excited by an AC supply of 120 V. [**Ans:** $I = 0.0198\angle -90°$, $P = 0$ W, $\cos\phi = 0$, $V_R = 0.158\angle -90°$ V]

6. A coil having a resistance of 10 Ω and an inductance of 0.2 H is connected in series with a 100×10^{-6} F capacitor across a 230 V, 50 Hz supply. Calculate the (a) active and reactive components of the current, and (b) voltage across the coil. [**Ans.** (a) $I = (2.17 - j6.73)$ A, (b) $V_{coil} = 449.58\angle 8.88°$ V]

7. A 200 V, 50 Hz, $1 - \phi$ supply is impressed across RL Series circuit with $R = 6\ \Omega$ and $L = 25.5$ mH. Find (a) impedance, (b) current, (c) power factor, and (d) power in the circuit. [**Ans:** (a) $Z = 10\angle 53.13\ \Omega$, (b) $I = 20\angle -58.13$, (c) p.f. = 0.6, (d) $P = 2.4$ kW]

8. A current of $i = 4.48\cos(200t - 56.6°)$ produces a potential drop of $v(t) = 150\cos(200t - 30°)$ in the circuit. Find the values of circuit parameters assuming a series combination. [**Ans:** $R = 30\ \Omega$, $L = 0.075$ H]

9. Find the total current to the parallel circuit of $L = 0.05$ H and $C = 0.667$ μF with an applied voltage $v = 100\sin 5000t$ V. [**Ans:** $i = 0.067\sin(5000t - 90°)$ A]

10. A 250 V, 50 Hz single phase supply is impressed across a certain circuit. Current was found to be 25 A at 0.8 lagging. Find the parameters of the circuit and power consumed by the circuit. [**Ans:** $Z = (8 + j6)\ \Omega$, $P = 5$ kW]

11. The EMF whose instantaneous value is $100\sin(314t - 74°)$ V is applied to a circuit and current flowing through the circuit is $20\sin(314t - 1.5708°)$ A. Find the frequency and values of circuit elements assuming series combination of circuit elements. [**Ans:** $f = 50$ Hz, $Z = (1.51 - j4.77)\ \Omega$]

12. An inductive coil draws a current of 2 A when connected to a 230 V, 50 Hz supply. The power taken by the coil is 100 W. Calculate the resistance and inductance of the coil. [**Ans:** $R = 25\ \Omega$, $L = 357.27$ mH]

13. Two impedances $(150 + j157)\ \Omega$ and $(100 - j110)\ \Omega$ are connected in parallel across a 220 V, 50 Hz supply. Find the total current and power factor. [**Ans:** $I = 1.734\angle 12.08°$ A, p.f. = 0.978]

14. A coil of power factor 0.6 is in series with a capacitor of 100 μF. When connected to a 200 V, 50 Hz AC supply, the current was found to be 10 A and the potential difference across the coil is equal to the potential difference across the capacitor. Find the resistance and inductance of the coil. [**Ans:** $R = 19\ \Omega$, $L = 81.2$ mH]

15. An inductive coil is connected in series with a resistance of 50 Ω across a 230 V, 50 Hz, AC supply. The voltage across the coil is 180 V and across the resistance is 130 V. Calculate the (a) resistance and inductance of the coil, and (b) power dissipated in the coil. [**Ans:** (a) $R = 5.33\ \Omega$, $L = 219.7$ mH, (b) $P = 36.03$ W]

16. A resistance of 100 Ω is connected in series with a 100 μF capacitor across a 200 V, 60 Hz supply. Find the impedance, current and power factor. [**Ans:** $Z = 103.45\angle -14.856°\ \Omega$, $I = 1.933\angle 14.856°$ A, p.f. = 0.966]

17. A coil when connected to a 200 V DC supply dissipates 2000 W of power. When connected across a 200 V, $1 - \phi$, 50 Hz supply, it dissipated 800 W of power. Calculate the value of resistance and inductance of the coil. [**Ans:** $R = 20\ \Omega$, $L = 78$ mH]

REVIEW QUESTIONS

1. In the case of a pure resistor, the voltage and current are in phase. Justify.
2. In the case of a pure inductor, the current lags the voltage by 90°. Justify.
3. In the case of a pure inductor, the current leads the voltage by 90°. Justify.
4. What is an impedance diagram? Write the expression for the impedance of a *RLC* series circuit.
5. What is an admittance diagram? Write the expression for the admittance of a *RLC* parallel circuit.
6. Define the terms conductance and susceptance.
7. What is power triangle? List the various powers with their formulae.
8. Define power factor and write the expression for the same.
9. Write the phasor diagram of *RL*, *RC* and *RLC* series circuits.
10. Write the phasor diagram of *RL*, *RC* and *RLC* parallel circuits.
11. List the properties of a series *RLC* circuit.

12. List the properties of a parallel *RLC* circuit.
13. What is the impedance of capacitance and inductance?
14. Define complex power and explain its significance.

MULTIPLE CHOICE QUESTIONS

1. In an *RLC* series circuit, if the difference between X_L and X_C increases, then the total
   (a) impedance remains unchanged
   (b) impedance increases
   (c) impedance reduces
   (d) resistance increases

2. The current through a 15 pF capacitor is 0.45 sin $(10^8 t + 45°)$ mA. Write the mathematical expression for the voltage across it.
   (a) 0.45 sin $(10^8 t - 0°)$ V
   (b) 0.45 sin $(10^8 t - 45°)$ V
   (c) 0.3 sin $(10^8 t - 45°)$ V
   (d) 0.3 sin $(10^8 t + 45°)$ V

3. In an *RLC* circuit, the phase angle is given by
   (a) $\tan^{-1}\left(\frac{X_L - X_C}{R}\right)$ (b) $\sin^{-1}\left(\frac{X_L - X_C}{R}\right)$
   (c) $\cos^{-1}\left(\frac{X_L - X_C}{R}\right)$ (d) $\cot^{-1}\left(\frac{X_L - X_C}{R}\right)$

4. In an RC circuit, the true power is 300 W and reactive power is 1000 VAR. What is the apparent power?
   (a) 1000 VA (b) 1043.9 VA
   (c) 1000 VAR (d) 1000 W

5. What is the instantaneous value of $v = 5\sin(2\pi \times 10^4 t)$ volts at time $t = 25$ μs?
   (a) −10 V (b) 5 V
   (c) 10 V (d) 0.137 V

6. A pure inductive coil allows a current of 10 A to flow from a 230 V, 50 Hz supply. What is the inductance of the coil in henrys?
   (a) $10/\pi$ (b) $26/\pi$
   (c) $0.23/\pi$ (d) $23.5/\pi$

7. The average value of a sine wave over half a cycle of $f(t) = \sin \omega t$ is,
   (a) $-0.637V_m$ (b) zero
   (c) $0.637V_m$ (d) unity

8. A coil of 0.5 H and 10 Ω is connected in series with a 10 μF capacitor. What is the power factor of the circuit?
   (a) 0.99 (b) 0.8
   (c) 0.06 (d) 1

9. What is the capacitance needed to produce 1200 of reactance when the frequency is 3.3 MHz?
   (a) zero (b) 57.7 pF
   (c) 57.7 μF (d) 5.77 pF

10. A coil with a resistance of 7 Ω and an inductance of 31.8 mH is connected to a 230 V, 50 Hz supply. What is the inductive reactance of the coil?
    (a) 25 Ω (b) 15 Ω
    (c) 10 Ω (d) 20 Ω

11. A choke coil takes a current of 3.5 A when connected across a 250 V, 50 Hz mains and consumes 400 W. What is the power factor of the circuit?
    (a) 0.64 lag (b) 0.68 lag
    (c) 0.7 lag (d) 0.67 lag

12. A power factor of 1 indicates a
    (a) purely resistive circuit
    (b) purely reactive circuit
    (c) both a and b
    (d) none

13. A power factor of 0 indicates a
    (a) purely resistive circuit
    (b) purely reactive circuit
    (c) both a and b
    (d) none

14. In a pure resistive circuit the power factor is
    (a) 0 (b) 1
    (c) infinity (d) can't say

15. In a pure inductive circuit the power factor is
    (a) 0 (b) 1
    (c) infinity (d) can't say

16. In a pure capacitive circuit the power factor is
(a) 0 (b) 1
(c) infinity (d) can't say

17. Power factor is defined as
(a) cosine of the phase angle between voltage and current
(b) ratio of active power to apparent power
(c) ratio of resistance to impedance
(d) all

18. In a *RLC* series circuit, $V_R = 3$ V, $V_L = 8$ V and $V_C = 4$ V, the applied voltage is
(a) 15 V (b) 5 V
(c) 8 V (d) 7 V

19. In a *RL* series circuit $V_R = 6$ V, $V_L = 8$ V, the applied voltage is
(a) 4 V (b) 6 V
(c) 8 V (d) 10 V

20. In a *RC* series circuit $V_R = 3$ V, $V_C = 4$ V, the applied voltage is
(a) 15 V (b) 5 V
(c) 8 V (d) 7 V

21. Power in AC circuits is given by
(a) VI (b) $VI \tan\phi$
(c) $VI \cos\phi$ (d) $VI \sin\phi$

22. The phasor combination of resistive power and reactive power is called
(a) true power (b) apparent power
(c) reactive power (d) average power

23. Apparent power is expressed in
(a) volt ampere (b) watts
(c) both a and b (d) VAR

Answers

1. b	2. c	3. a	4. b	5. b	6. c	7. c	8. c	9. d	10. c
11. a	12. a	13. b	14. b	15. a	16. a	17. d	18. b	19. d	20. b
21. c	22. b	23. a							

4 Magnetic and Coupled Circuits

Learning Outcomes

After reading this chapter, the reader will able to

- ➢ Outline the terminology used in magnetic circuits
- ➢ Contrast electric and magnetic circuits
- ➢ Solve series, parallel and composite magnetic circuits
- ➢ Find magnetic field intensity or magnetic flux density from the B–H curve
- ➢ Define magnetic hysteresis and residual magnetism
- ➢ Describe the magnetic properties of common materials
- ➢ Outline magnetic leakage and fringing
- ➢ List Faraday's laws of electromagnetic induction
- ➢ Outline the concepts of self and mutual inductance
- ➢ Outline the concepts of self and mutually induced emfs
- ➢ Define coefficient of coupling and explain its significance
- ➢ Analyse series and parallel coupled inductors
- ➢ Illustrate conductively coupled circuit
- ➢ Illustrate ideal transformer

4.1 INTRODUCTION

Although the lines of magnetic flux have no physical existence, they do form a very convenient and useful basis for explaining various magnetic effects and to calculate the magnitudes of various magnetic quantities. The complete closed path followed by any group of magnetic flux lines is referred to as a *magnetic circuit*. The lines of magnetic flux never intersect, and each line forms a closed path.

Whenever a current flows through a coil, a magnetic flux will be produced and the path followed by the magnetic flux is known as magnetic circuit. The operation of all the electrical devices such as generators, motors, transformers and so on, depend upon the magnetism produced by this magnetic circuit. Therefore, to obtain the required characteristics of these devices, their magnetic circuits have to be designed carefully.

4.2 IMPORTANT TERMS AND DEFINITIONS

Magneto Motive Force (MMF) The magnetic pressure which sets up or tends to set up magnetic flux in a magnetic circuit is known as MMF.

- Magneto motive force is a measure of the ability of a coil to produce flux.
- The magnetic flux is due to the existence of the MMF caused by a current flowing through a coil having a number of turns.
- A coil with N turns carrying a current of I amperes represents a magnetic circuit producing an MMF of NI

$$\therefore \quad \text{MMF} = NI \tag{4.1}$$

- Units of MMF = Ampere turns (AT)

Magnetic flux The number of magnetic lines of force set-up in a magnetic circuit is called magnetic flux.

- The magnetic flux, that is established in a magnetic circuit is proportional to the MMF and the proportional constant is the reluctance of the magnetic circuit.

$\therefore$ Magnetic flux $\propto$ MMF

$$\text{Magnetic flux} = \frac{\text{MMF}}{\text{reluctance}} \Rightarrow \Phi = \frac{NI}{S} \tag{4.2}$$

- The unit of magnetic flux is weber.

Reluctance The opposition offered to the flow of magnetic flux in a magnetic circuit is called *reluctance.*

- Reluctance of a magnetic circuit is defined as the ratio of magneto motive force to the flux established.
- Reluctance depends upon the length (l), area of cross-section (a) and permeability of the material that makes up the magnetic circuit.
  That is, $S \propto l$, $S \propto \frac{1}{a}$; $S \propto \frac{l}{a}$

$$\therefore \quad S = \frac{l}{\mu_0 \, \mu_r a}$$

- $$\text{Magnetic flux} = \frac{\text{MMF}}{\text{Reluctance}} \Rightarrow \Phi = \frac{NI}{l/\mu_0 \, \mu_r a} = \frac{NI}{l} \mu_0 \, \mu_r a \tag{4.3}$$
- The unit of reluctance is AT/ Wb

Magnetic field strength (*H*) If the magnetic circuit is homogeneous, and of uniform cross-sectional area, the magnetic field strength is defined as the magneto motive force per unit length of magnetic circuit.

$$\therefore \quad \text{Magnetic field strength} = \frac{\text{MMF}}{\text{Length}} \Rightarrow H = \frac{NI}{l} \tag{4.4}$$

- The unit of magnetic field strength is AT/m

Magnetic flux density (*B*) The magnetic flux density in any material is defined as the magnetic flux established per unit area of cross-section.

$$\therefore \quad \text{Magnetic flux density} = \frac{\text{Total flux}}{\text{Area of cross-section}} \Rightarrow B = \frac{\Phi}{a} \tag{4.5}$$

- The unit of magnetic flux density is Wb/m^2 or tesla.
- Using the above relations, Ohm's law for magnetic circuit is written as

$$\text{Magnetic flux} = \frac{\text{MMF}}{\text{Reluctance}}$$

$$\Rightarrow \quad \Phi = \frac{NI}{l/\mu_0 \, \mu_r a} = \frac{NI}{l} \mu_0 \, \mu_r a$$

$$\Rightarrow \quad \frac{\Phi}{a} = \frac{NI}{l} \mu_0 \, \mu_r = B$$

$$\Rightarrow \quad B = \mu_0 \, \mu_r \, H = \mu H \tag{4.6}$$

Relative permeability It is defined as the ratio of flux density established in magnetic material to the flux density established in air or vacuum for the same magnetic field strength.

$$\therefore \quad \mu_r = \frac{B_{\text{mater}}}{B_{\text{air}}} = \frac{\mu}{\mu_0} \tag{4.7}$$

4.3 SERIES MAGNETIC CIRCUIT

A series magnetic circuit is analogous to a series electric circuit. A magnetic circuit is said to be in series, if the same flux is flowing through all the elements connected in a magnetic circuit. Consider a circular ring having a magnetic path of l metre, area of cross-section a m^2 with a mean radius of R metres having a coil of N turns carrying a current of I amperes wound uniformly (Fig. 4.1).

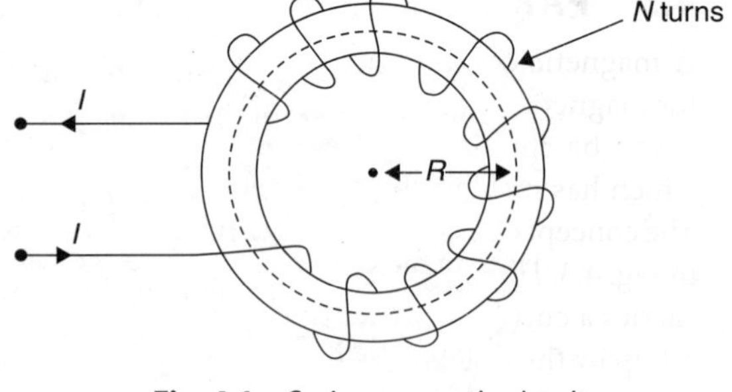

Fig. 4.1 Series magnetic circuit

The flux produced by the circuit is given by

$$\text{Magnetic flux} = \frac{\text{MMF}}{\text{Reluctance}}$$

$$\Rightarrow \quad \Phi = \frac{NI}{l/\mu_0 \mu_r a} = \frac{NI}{l} \mu_0 \mu_r a \tag{4.8}$$

In Eq. 4.8, NI is the MMF of the magnetic circuit, which is analogous to EMF in the electric circuit, $S = \frac{l}{\mu_0 \mu_r a}$ is the reluctance of the magnetic circuit which is analogous to resistance in the electric circuit.

4.4 COMPOSITE MAGNETIC CIRCUIT

A series magnetic circuit that has parts of different dimensions and materials is called a *composite magnetic circuit.* Each part has its own reluctance. Total reluctance is equal to the sum of reluctances of individual parts.

Consider a toroid composed of three different magnetic materials of different permeabilities, areas and lengths excited by a coil of N turns (Fig. 4.2).

$$\text{Total reluctance, } S = \frac{l_1}{\mu_0 \mu_{r1} a_1} + \frac{l_2}{\mu_0 \mu_{r2} a_2} + \frac{l_3}{\mu_0 \mu_{r3} a_3} + \frac{l_g}{\mu_0 a_g} \tag{4.9}$$

$$\text{Total MMF} = \text{Flux} \times \text{Total reluctance}$$

$$= \Phi \left[\frac{l_1}{\mu_0 \mu_{r1} a_1} + \frac{l_2}{\mu_0 \mu_{r2} a_2} + \frac{l_3}{\mu_0 \mu_{r3} a_3} + \frac{l_g}{\mu_0 a_g} \right]$$

$$= \frac{\Phi l_1}{\mu_0 \mu_{r1} a_1} + \frac{\Phi l_2}{\mu_0 \mu_{r2} a_2} + \frac{\Phi l_3}{\mu_0 \mu_{r3} a_3} + \frac{\Phi l_g}{\mu_0 a_g}$$

$$= \frac{\Phi}{a_1} \frac{l_1}{\mu_0 \mu_{r1}} + \frac{\Phi}{a_2} \frac{l_2}{\mu_0 \mu_{r2}} + \frac{\Phi}{a_3} \frac{l_3}{\mu_0 \mu_{r3}} + \frac{\Phi}{a_g} \frac{l_g}{\mu_0}$$

$$= \frac{B_1 l_1}{\mu_0 \mu_{r1}} + \frac{B_2 l_2}{\mu_0 \mu_{r2}} + \frac{B_3 l_3}{\mu_0 \mu_{r3}} + \frac{B_4 l_g}{\mu_0}$$

$$= H_1 l_1 + H_2 l_2 + H_3 l_3 + H_4 l_g$$

$$\therefore \quad \text{MMF} = NI = H_1 l_1 + H_2 l_2 + H_3 l_3 + H_4 l_g \tag{4.10}$$

Fig. 4.2 Composite magnetic circuit

4.5 PARALLEL MAGNETIC CIRCUIT

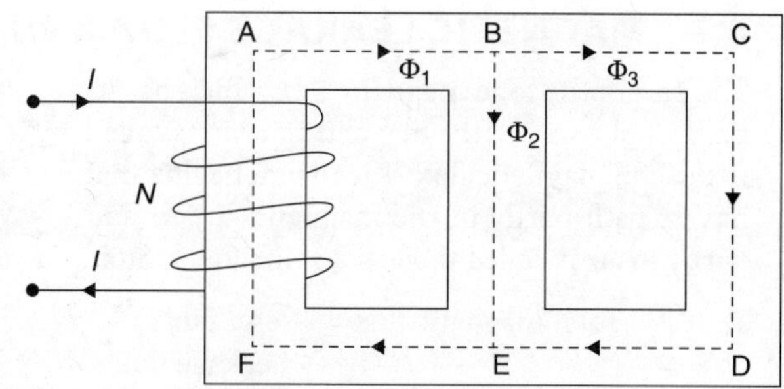

Fig. 4.3 Parallel magnetic circuit

A magnetic circuit which has more than one path for magnetic flux is called a *parallel magnetic circuit*. It can be compared with a parallel electric circuit which has more than one path for electric current. The concept of parallel magnetic circuit is illustrated in Fig. 4.3. Here a coil of N turns wound on limb AF carries a current of I amperes. The magnetic flux ϕ_1 set up by the coil divides at B into two paths namely,

(i) magnetic flux passes Φ_2 along the path BE, and
(ii) magnetic flux passes Φ_3 along the path BCDE.

That is, $\Phi_1 = \Phi_2 + \Phi_3$

The magnetic paths BE and BCDE are in parallel and form a parallel magnetic circuit. The AT required for this parallel circuit is equal to the AT required for any one of the paths.

Let S_1 = reluctance of path EFAB, S_2 = reluctance of path BE and S_3 = reluctance of path BCDE.

$\therefore$ Total MMF = MMF for path EFAB + MMF for path BE or path BCD

That is, $NI = \Phi_1 S_1 + \Phi_2 S_2 = \Phi_1 S_1 + \Phi_3 S_3$ (4.11)

4.6 COMPARISON OF ELECTRIC AND MAGNETIC CIRCUITS

Similarities

S. No	Electric circuit	Magnetic circuit
1	The closed path for electric current	The closed path for magnetic flux
2	Current in amperes	Flux in webers
3	Electro motive force (EMF) in volts	Magneto motive force (MMF) in AT
4	Resistance	Reluctance
5	Current density $J = I / A$	Flux density, $B = \Phi/A$
6	EMF drop = IR	MMF drop = ΦS
7	Conductance, $G = 1/R$	Permeance = $1/S$
8	Resistivity	Reluctivity
9	Electric field intensity, $E = V / d$	Magnetic field intensity, $H = NI/l$

Dissimilarities

S. No	Electric circuit	Magnetic circuit
1	Electric current actually flows in the electric circuit.	Magnetic flux does not flow, but it sets up in the magnetic circuit.
2	Energy must be supplied to the electric circuit to maintain a constant flow of current.	In a magnetic circuit, once established, the flux can be maintained without an energy source.
3	For an electric current, there are a large number of perfect insulators such as rubber, glass, air, and so on.	For magnetic flux, there is no perfect insulator. It can set up even in non-magnetic materials such as rubber, air, glass, and so on, with a reasonable EMF.
4	In an electric circuit, it is possible to precisely point out where the EMF is acting.	In a magnetic circuit, it is difficult to find out exactly where the MMF is acting.
5	The resistance of an electric circuit is almost constant as its value depends upon ρ which is almost constant.	The reluctance of a magnetic circuit is not constant, rather, it varies with the value of B.

4.7 MAGNETIC LEAKAGE FLUX AND FRINGING

The part of the total magnetic flux which has its path wholly within the magnetic circuit is called the useful magnetic flux. The magnetic flux that has its path partly in the magnetic circuit and partly in air is called the leakage magnetic flux.

∴ Total magnetic flux = Useful flux + Leakage flux

Figure 4.4 shows the useful, leakage and fringing fluxes in a magnetic circuit. The ratio of the total flux produced to the useful flux is called the leakage factor or leakage coefficient, which is denoted by λ.

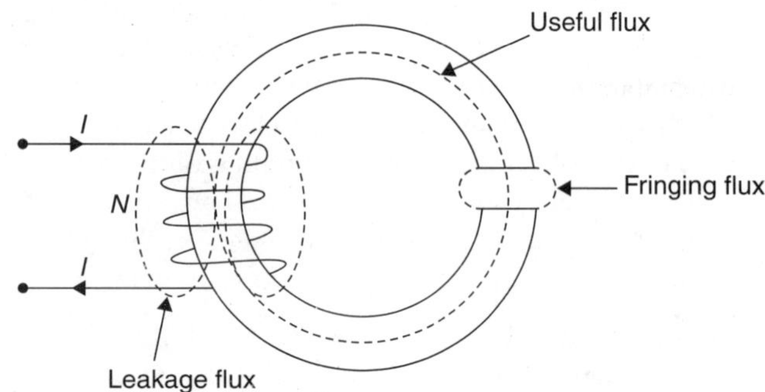

Fig. 4.4 Fringing and leakage flux

$$\therefore \quad \text{Leakage factor } (\lambda) = \frac{\text{Total flux produced}}{\text{Useful flux}} \tag{4.12}$$

The value of λ is always greater than 1; the typical values of the leakage factor are about 1.15–1.24. Leakage is a characteristic of all magnetic circuits and can never be completely eliminated. Air gaps are provided in many practical magnetic circuits. Consider a ring (Fig. 4.4) provided with an air gap. When the flux lines cross the air gap, they tend to bulge out across the edges of the air gap. This effect is called *fringing*. The effect of fringing is to make the effective gap area larger than that of the ring. Consequently the flux density in the air gap is reduced. The effective increase depends upon the length of the air gap. The length of the air gap is kept as small as possible so that the reduction in the flux density is a minimum. If the gap length is small compared to the gap width, the effect of fringing can be neglected.

Problem 4.1 A coil of 200 turns is wound uniformly over a wooden ring with a mean circumference of 600 mm and a uniform cross-sectional area of 500 mm². If the current through the coil is 5 A, calculate the (i) magnetic field strength, (ii) flux density, and (iii) total flux.

Solution:

Given that $N = 200$, $I = 600 \text{ mm} = 0.6 \text{ m}$, $a = 500 \text{ mm}^2 = 500 \times 10^{-6} \text{ m}^2$

(i) Magnetic field strength, $H = NI/l = 200 \times 5/0.6 = 1667$ AT/m
(ii) $B = \mu_0 \mu_r H = 4\pi \times 10^{-7} \times 1 \times 1667 = 20.948 \times 10^{-4}$ Wb/m²
(iii) Flux, $\Phi = Ba = 20.948 \times 10^{-4} \times 500 \times 10^{-6} = 10.478 \times 10^{-7}$ Wb

---

Problem 4.2 An iron ring of mean length 50 cm has an air gap of 1 mm and a winding of 200 turns. If the relative permeability of the iron ring is 400, when a current of 1 A flows in the winding, determine the flux density. Neglect leakage and fringing.

Solution:

Given that $N = 200$, $\mu_r = 400$, $I = 1$

$$\text{MMF} = NI = 200 \times 1 = 200 \text{ AT}$$

Reluctance of air gap:

$$\text{Length } L = 1 \text{ mm} = 1 \times 10^{-3} \text{ m}$$

$$\text{Reluctance, } S_1 = \frac{l}{\mu_0 a} = \frac{10^{-3}}{4\pi \times 10^{-7} \times a} = \frac{10^4}{4\pi \times a}$$

Reluctance of iron ring:

Length, $l = 50$ cm $= 0.5$ m, $\mu_r = 400$

$$\text{Reluctance, } S_2 = \frac{l}{\mu_0 \mu_r a} = \frac{0.5}{4\pi \times 10^{-7} \times 400a} = \frac{1.25 \times 10^4}{4\pi \times a}$$

Total reluctance $S = S_1 + S_2$

$$= \frac{10^4}{4\pi \times a} + \frac{1.25 \times 10^4}{4\pi \times a} = \frac{2.25 \times 10^4}{4\pi \times a}$$

$$\text{Flux} = \frac{\text{MMF}}{\text{Reluctance}} = \frac{2.00 \times 4\pi \times a}{2.25 \times 10^4}$$

$$\text{Flux density, } B = \frac{\Phi}{a} = \frac{2.00 \times 4\pi \times a}{2.25 \times 10^4 \times a} = 0.117 \text{ Wb/m}^2$$

Problem 4.3 An iron ring with a mean diameter of 25 cm and a cross-sectional area of 4 cm² is wound with a coil of 1200 turn. An air gap of 1.5 mm width is cut in the ring. Determine the current required in the coil to produce a flux of 0.48 mWb in the air gap. The relative permeability of iron under this condition is 800. Neglect leakage.

Solution:

Given that Mean diameter, $D = 25$ cm $= 0.25$ m

Mean circumference, $l = \pi \cdot D = \pi \times 0.25 = 0.7854$ m

Area of cross-section, $a = 4 \text{ cm}^2 = 4 \times 10^{-4} \text{ m}^2$

$N = 1200$

$$B = \frac{\Phi}{a} = \frac{0.48 \times 10^{-3}}{4 \times 10^{-4}} = 1.2 \text{ T}$$

Ampere turns for air gap:

$$H = \frac{B}{\mu_0} = \frac{1.20}{4\pi \times 10^{-7}} = \frac{3}{\pi} \times 10^{-6}$$

Width of the air gap $l = 1.5 \times 10^{-3}$ m

$$AT_{\text{air}} = NI = H \times l = \frac{3}{\pi} \times 10^6 \times 1.5 \times 10^{-3} = 1432.4 \qquad \left[\because H = \frac{NI}{l}\right]$$

Ampere turns for iron ring:

$$H = \frac{B}{\mu_0 \mu_r} = \frac{1.2}{4\pi \times 10^{-7} \times 800} = 1193.66$$

$$L = 0.7854\ \text{m}$$

$$\text{AT}_{\text{iron ring}} = NI = H \times L = 1193.66 \times 0.7854 = 937.5$$

$$\text{AT}_{\text{total}} = \text{AT}_{\text{iron ring}} + \text{AT}_{\text{air}} = 937.5 + 1432.4 = 2370\ \text{AT}$$

$$NI = 2370 \quad \Rightarrow \quad I = \frac{2370}{1200} = 1.957\ \text{A}$$

4.8 MAGNETISATION CHARACTERISTICS OF FERROMAGNETIC MATERIALS

4.8.1 Classification of Magnetic Materials

Magnetic materials are classified into the following types depending on their magnetic properties.

- ***Ferromagnetic materials:*** Materials that show excellent magnetic properties are called ferromagnetic materials. The relative permeability of these materials is generally greater than unity. These are used for making permanent and temporary (electro) magnets. For example, iron, nickel and cobalt.
- ***Paramagnetic materials:*** Materials that exhibit very slight magnetic properties and allow the passage of magnetic lines of force slightly are called paramagnetic materials. The relative permeability of these materials is slightly greater than unity. For example, aluminium, platinum and oxygen.
- ***Diamagnetic materials:*** Materials that exhibit a very slight opposition to the magnetic lines of force are called diamagnetic materials. The relative permeability of these materials is slightly less than unity. For example, copper, silver and hydrogen.

Curie point Curie point is the temperature at which ferromagnetic materials lose their magnetic property. This temperature is a characteristic of magnetic materials and differs from material to material. At its curie temperature, iron ceases to be ferromagnetic and becomes paramagnetic.

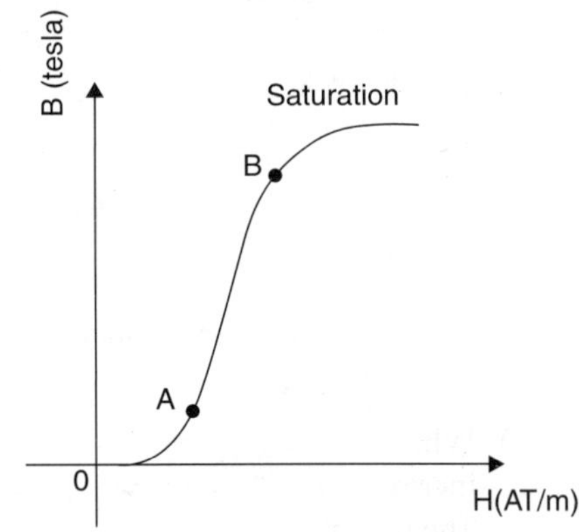

Fig. 4.5 *B–H* curve for a magnetic material

4.8.2 Magnetisation or *B–H* Curve

The curve plotted between flux density *B*, and field intensity *H*, of a magnetic material is called the *magnetisation curve* or *B–H* curve.

The general shape of the *B–H* curve of a magnetic material is non-linear (Fig. 4.5). This indicates that the relative permeability ($\mu_r = B/\mu_0 H$) of a magnetic material is not a constant. In Fig. 4.5, except for a small portion near the origin, the curve is linear from A to B. Over this portion the flux density *B* is proportional to the field intensity *H* and μ_r is constant. For higher values of *H* there is no further increase in *B* with *H*. The curve becomes almost horizontal after the point B. The material is then said to be *saturated* and point B is called the *point of saturation.*

The *B–H* curve for a non-magnetic material is a straight line since $B = \mu_0 H$ or $B \propto H$ as the value of μ_0 is constant (Fig. 4.6).

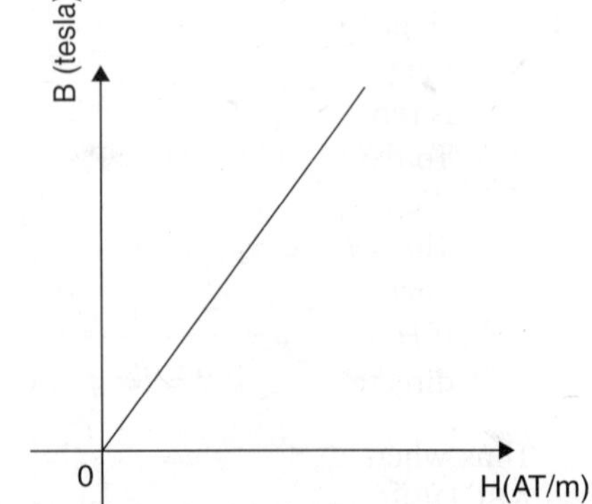

Fig. 4.6 *B–H* curve for a non-magnetic materia

Magnetic calculations from *B–H* curves The solution of magnetic circuits can be easily obtained by the use of *B–H* curves. While solving problems, the following steps are followed.

- Find the value of flux density in the magnetic circuit if not known.

- Determine the magnetic field strength H, corresponding to the magnetic flux density, B from the B–H curve of the material.
- Compute the length of the magnetic path.
- Determine the MMF required [MMF = $H \times l$].

4.9 MAGNETIC HYSTERESIS

When a magnetic material is magnetised first is one direction and then in the other (one cycle of magnetisation), it is found that flux density B in the material lags behind the applied magnetising force H. The phenomenon of flux density B lagging behind the magnetising force H in a magnetic material subjected to a cycle of magnetisation is known as *magnetic hysteresis*.

Consider a coil wound around an iron core [Fig. 4.7(a)] which is completely demagnetised. The field intensity and flux density are increased or decreased by increasing or decreasing the current through the coil. We shall see that when the iron piece is subjected to one cycle of magnetisation, the resultant B–H curve traces a loop ABCDEFA called hysteresis loop [Fig. 4.7(b)].

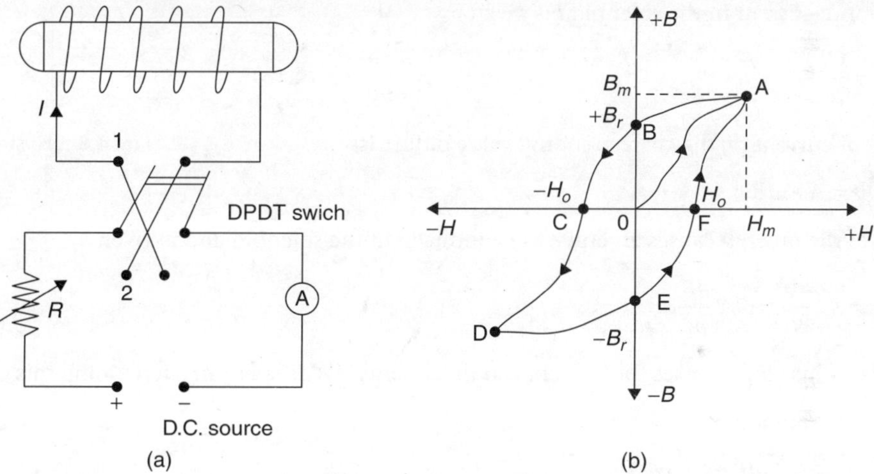

Fig. 4.7 Hysteresis loop

(i) When the current in the solenoid is zero, $H = 0$ and hence B in the iron is zero. As H is increased, by increasing the solenoid current, B also increases until the point of maximum flux density ($+B_m$) is reached. The material is saturated and beyond this point, the magnetic flux density will not increase regardless of any increase in current or magnetising force. Note that the B–H curve of iron follows the path OA.

(ii) If now H is gradually reduced, by reducing solenoid current, the B–H curve will follow the path AB [Fig. 4.7(b)]. At point B, H is zero but B is finite at the value B_r, which indicates the *retentivity* or residual magnetism. This value represents the amount of flux remaining in the core after the magnetising force is removed.

(iii) To demagnetise the iron piece, the magnetising force H is reversed by reversing the current through the coil. When H is gradually increased in the reverse direction, the B–H curve follows the path BC. The amount of magnetising force required to completely demagnetise the core is called the *coercive force* and is designated as $-H_c$ [Fig. 4.7(b)].

(iv) If H is further increased in the negative direction, the material again saturates (point D) in the negative direction. Reducing H to zero and then increasing it in the positive direction completes the curve DEFA.

Thus when an iron piece is subjected to one cycle of magnetisation, the B–H curve traces a closed loop ABCDEFA called the *hysteresis loop*. The word hysteresis means 'lagging behind'. The curve gets its name from the fact that the flux density, B lags behind the magnetic field intensity H.

4.10 HYSTERESIS LOSS

The process of magnetisation and demagnetisation of magnetic material both in the positive and negative direction requires some power for reversing the magnetism of a material; this loss in power is known as *hysteresis loss*. Hysteresis loss occurs in all the magnetic parts of electrical machines where there is a reversal of magnetisation. This loss results in wastage of energy in the form of heat. Consequently, it increases the temperature of the machine, which is undesirable. Therefore, a suitable magnetic material is selected for the construction of such parts, for example, silicon steel.

4.10.1 Expression for Hysteresis Loss

For one cycle of magnetisation, the hysteresis loop of a magnetic material is shown in Fig. 4.8. Consider a strip of small thickness dB on the hysteresis loop.

Let L = length of the iron bar, A = area of cross-section and N = number of turns of wire of the solenoid. Let us suppose that at any instant, the current in the solenoid i is given by

$$i = \frac{Hl}{N} \tag{4.13}$$

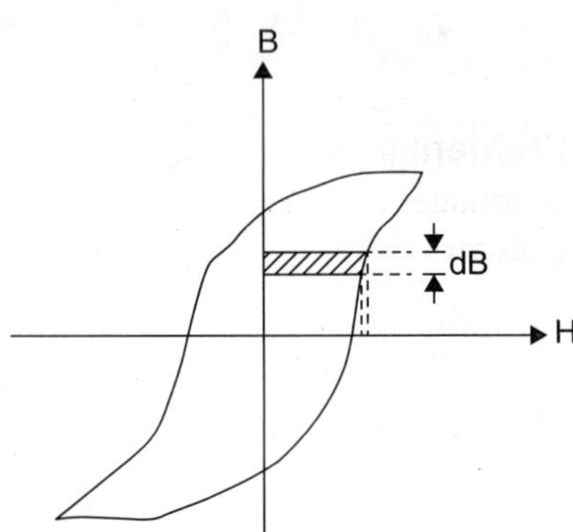

Fig. 4.8 Hysteresis loss

For a value of current di, the corresponding value of flux is

$$d\Phi = A \times dB$$

This value of the flux $d\Phi$ causes an emf e to be induced in the solenoid and is given by

$$e = N\frac{d\Phi}{dt} = NA\frac{dB}{dt} \tag{4.14}$$

By Lenz's law, this emf opposes the current i so that energy dW is spent in overcoming this opposing emf.

$$dW = ei\,dt \text{ joules}$$

$$= \left(NA\frac{dB}{dt}\right) \times \left(\frac{Hl}{N}\right) dt$$

$$dW = H \times (Al) \times dB \text{ joules} \tag{4.15}$$

Integrating both sides, we get the total work done during a complete cycle of magnetisation

$$W = \int H\,Al\,dB = Al\int H \times dB = V\int H \times dB \tag{4.16}$$

where $V = Al$ = volume of the iron bar.

$$\int H \times dB = \text{area of the hysteresis loop}$$

Therefore, hysteresis energy loss/cycle,

$$W_h = V \times (\text{area of hysteresis loop}) \text{ joule}$$

4.11 STEINMETZ HYSTERESIS LAW

In order to calculate the hysteresis loss, we need to find the area of hysteresis loop. To eliminate this, Steinmetz devised an empirical law to calculate the hysteresis loss. According to this law, the area of the hysteresis loop of a magnetic material is directly proportional to the 1.6th power of the maximum flux density established.

$$\therefore \quad \text{Area of hysteresis loop} \propto B_{\text{m}}^{1.6}$$

or $\quad$ hysteresis energy loss $\propto B_m^{1.6}$ J/m³/cycle

or $\quad$ hysteresis energy loss $= \eta B_m^{1.6}$ J/m³/cycle $\quad$ (4.17)

where η is a constant called the hysteresis coefficient. Its value depends upon the nature of the material. The armatures of electrical machines and transformer cores are made up of magnetic material with low hysteresis coefficients in order to reduce the hysteresis loss.

If V is the volume of the material in m³ and f is the frequency of magnetisation, then the hysteresis power loss,

$$P_h = \eta \cdot f \cdot B_m^{1.6}\, V \text{ J/s} \tag{4.18}$$

Problem 4.4 The area of the hysteresis loop obtained with a certain magnetic material is 8.4 cm². The coordinates are such that 1 cm = 1000 AT/m and 1 cm = 0.2 Wb/m². If the density of the given material is 6.7 g/cm³, calculate the hysteresis loss in watt/kg at 50 Hz.

Solution:

Given that Area of hysteresis loop = Area in cm² × scale factors

$$= 8.4 \times (1000 \times 0.2) = 1680 \text{ J/m}^3\text{/cycle}$$

$$\text{Volume of 1 kg of material, } V = \frac{10^3}{6.7} \times 10^{-6} = 1.49 \times 10^{-4} \text{ m}^3$$

$$\text{Hysteresis energy loss, } W_h = V \times (\text{area of hysteresis loop})$$

$$= 1.49 \times 10^{-4} \times 1680 = 0.25 \text{ J/cycle}$$

$$\text{Hysteresis power loss, } P_h = W_h \times f = 0.25 \times 50 = 12.54 \text{ Watt/kg}$$

Problem 4.5 A magnetic circuit consists of a ring of mean diameter 15 cm with a single narrow saw-cut through the ring. The width of the saw-cut is 0.1 cm and the material of the ring has a magnetisation curve given by the following table.

H(AT/m) :	40	80	120	160	800	1600	3200
B(Wb/m²) :	0.37	0.72	0.92	1.04	1.4	1.47	1.55

A coil of 400 turns is uniformly wound on the ring. Estimate the current in the coil required to cause a flux of 0.28 mWb in the air gap formed by the saw-cut. Area of air gap is 4 cm².

Solution:

Given that Mean diameter $D = 15$ cm = 0.15 m

Length of air gap $l_{air} = 0.1$ cm $= 10^{-3}$ m

Area of air gap $a = 4$ cm² $= 4 \times 10^{-4}$ m²

$N = 400, \quad \Phi = 0.28$ mWb

$$B = \frac{\Phi}{a} = \frac{0.28 \times 10^{-3}}{4 \times 10^{-4}} = 0.7 \text{ T}$$

Ampere turns for air gap:

$$H = \frac{B}{\mu_0} = \frac{0.7}{4\pi \times 10^{-7}} = 5.57 \times 10^5 \text{ AT/m}$$

$l = 10^{-3}$ m

$AT_{air} = NI = Hl = 5.57 \times 10^5 \times 10^{-3} = 557$

Ampere turns for iron ring:

The value of H corresponding to $B = 0.7$ T from table is = 0.78 AT/m

$L = \pi D = \pi \times 0.15$

$AT_{iron} = H \times L = 0.78 \times \pi \times 0.15 = 37$

$AT_{total} = AT_{air} + AT_{iron} = 557 + 37 = 594$

$\Rightarrow \quad NI = 594$

$\Rightarrow \quad I = \dfrac{594}{400} = 1.49$ A

Problem 4.6 A ring has a mean diameter of 21 cm and a cross-sectional area of 10 cm². The ring is made up of semicircular sections of cast iron and cast steel, with each joint having an air gap of 0.2 mm. Find the ampere turns required to produce a flux of 8×10^{-4} Wb. The relative permeability of cast iron and cast steel are 166 and 800 respectively. Neglect leakage and fringing.

Solution:

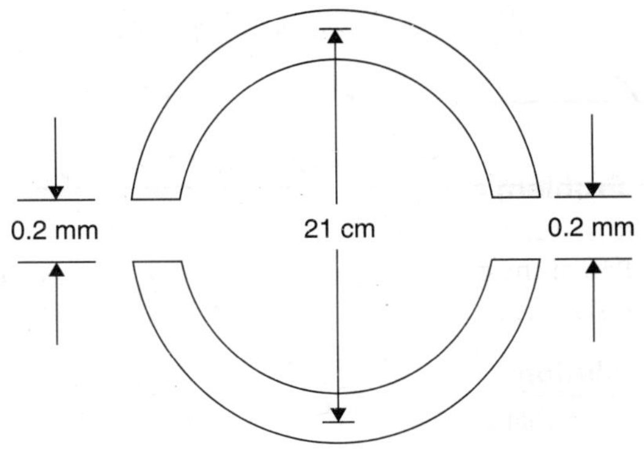

Given that Mean diameter, $D = 21$ cm $= 21 \times 10^{-2}$ m

Area, $a = 10$ cm² $= 10 \times 10^{-4}$ m²

$\Phi = 8 \times 10^{-4}$ Wb

$\mu_r(\text{steel}) = 800, \mu_r(\text{iron}) = 166$

$$B = \frac{\Phi}{a} = \frac{8 \times 10^{-4}}{10 \times 10^{-4}} = 0.8 \text{ T}$$

Ampere turns for air gap:

$$H = \frac{B}{\mu_0} = \frac{0.8}{4\pi \times 10^{-7}} = 6.366 \times 10^5 \text{ AT/m}$$

Total air gap length $= 2 \times 0.2 \times 10^{-3} = 0.4 \times 10^{-3}$ m

$AT_{air} = Hl = 6.366 \times 10^5 \times 0.4 \times 10^{-3} = 255$

Ampere turns for cast iron:

$$H = \frac{B}{\mu_0 \mu_r} = \frac{0.8}{4\pi \times 10^{-7} \times 166} = 3835 \text{ AT/m}$$

$$l = \frac{\pi \cdot D}{2} = 0.33 \text{ m}$$

$AT_{iron} = H \times l = 3835 \times 0.33 = 1265$

Ampere turns for cast steel:

$$H = \frac{B}{\mu_0 \mu_r} = \frac{0.8}{4\pi \times 10^{-7} \times 800} = 796 \text{ AT/m}$$

$$l = \frac{\pi \cdot D}{2} = \frac{\pi \times 21 \times 10^{-2}}{2} = 0.33 \text{ m}$$

$$AT_{steel} = H \times l = 796 \times 0.33 = 263$$

Total ampere turns required

$$AT_{total} = AT_{air\ gap} + AT_{iron} + AT_{steel} = 255 + 1265 + 263 = 1783$$

Problem 4.7 Calculate the loss of energy caused by hysteresis in 1 hour in 75 kg of iron when subjected to cyclic magnetic changes. The frequency is 40 Hz, the area of hysteresis loop is equivalent in area 200 J/m³/cycle and the density of iron is 7.8 g/cm³.

Solution:

Given that The area of hysteresis loop = 200 J/m³/cycle

$$\text{Volume of iron} = \frac{\text{mass}}{\text{density}} = \frac{75 \times 10^3}{7.8} \times 10^{-6} = 9.615 \times 10^{-3}$$

$$\text{No. of cycle/hour} = 40 \times 60 \times 60 = 144 \times 10^3$$

$$\text{Energy loss/hour} = \text{Volume} \times (\text{area of loop}) \times \text{cycle/hour}$$

$$= 9.615 \times 10^{-3} \times 200 \times 144 \times 10^3 = 276912 \text{ J}$$

Problem 4.8 The volume of a transformer core built up of sheet steel laminations is 5000 cm³ and the cross-sectional area is 240 cm². Because of the insulation between the plates, the net cross-sectional area is 90% of the gross. The maximum value of magnetic flux is 20 mWb and the frequency is 50 Hz. Find (i) the hysteresis loss/m³/cycle (ii) power loss in watt. Take hysteresis coefficient as 250.

Solution:

Given that $a = 0.9 \times 240 = 216 \text{ cm}^2$

$$\Phi_m = 20 \times 10^{-3} \text{ Wb}$$

$$B_m = \frac{\Phi_m}{a} = \frac{20 \times 10^{-3}}{216 \times 10^{-4}} = 0.926 \text{ Wb/m}^2$$

(i) Hysteresis energy loss, $W_h = \eta B_{max}^{1.6} = 250 \times (0.9265)^{1.6} = 221.06 \text{ J/m}^3\text{/cycle}$

(ii) Hysteresis power loss, $P_h = \eta \cdot f \cdot B_{max}^{1.6}\ v = 221.06 \times 50 \times 5000 \times 10^{-6} = 55.265 \text{ W}$

4.12 ELECTROMAGNETIC INDUCTION

A magnetic field is set up around a current-carrying conductor. As the current increases, the magnetic field becomes stronger. If the conductor is made into a coil [Fig. 4.9(a)], the magnetic flux at each section of the conductor is added together. Thus, the resultant field becomes stronger [Fig. 4.9(b)]. If the number of turns in the coil increases, the number of fields of individual sections also increases. This results in a stronger field. Whenever the magnetic flux linking a coil or conductor changes, an emf is induced in the coil. If the conductor forms a closed path or circuit, the current will flow in it. This phenomenon is known as *electromagnetic induction*.

4.13 FARADAY'S LAWS OF ELECTROMAGNETIC INDUCTION

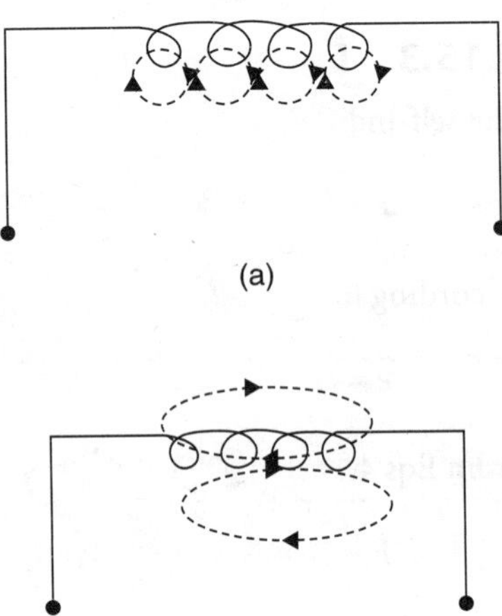

Fig. 4.9 Magnetic field of a coil

There are two principal laws of electromagnetic induction—Faraday's laws. They are stated as follows.

1st law When the magnetic flux linking a conductor or a coil changes, an emf is induced in it.

2nd law The magnitude of the induced emf is directly proportional to the rate of change of flux linkage.

Mathematically, if the flux changes from Φ_1 Wb to Φ_2 Wb in time t s through a coil of N turns, then initial flux linkage = $N\Phi_1$ and final flux linkage = $N\Phi_2$, and the induced emf $= \frac{N\Phi_1 - N\Phi_2}{t} = \frac{N(\Phi_1 - \Phi_2)}{t}$.

In differential form, $e = N\frac{d\Phi}{dt}$

It is the usual practice to use a negative sign in the right-hand side expression. The minus sign comes from Lenz's law and it indicates that the voltage is induced in a direction to oppose the change in flux that is produced.

$$\therefore \qquad e = -N\frac{d\Phi}{dt}$$

4.14 INDUCED EMF

When the magnetic flux linking a conductor (or coil) changes, an emf is induced in the conductor. This emf is of two types.

(i) The conductor is moved in a stationary magnetic field in such a way that the magnetic flux linking changes in magnitude. The emf induced in this way is called *dynamically induced emf* (as in DC or AC generator). It is so called because the emf is induced in a moving conductor.
(ii) The conductor is stationary and the magnetic field is moving or changing. The emf induced in this way is called *statically induced emf* (as in transformer). It is so called because the emf is induced in a stationary conductor.

4.15 INDUCTANCE

It is defined as the property of an electric circuit element that opposes any change of current through it.

4.15.1 Self-Inductance (*L*)

It is defined as the ability of an inductor to induce a voltage into itself. Alternatively, it is the property of a coil by which it opposes the change in the value of current or flux through it due to the production of self-induced emf.

4.15.2 Self-Induced EMF

The emf induced in a coil due to the change of its own magnetic flux linked with it, is called *self-induced emf*. Alternatively, when the current flowing through the coil is changing, then the magnetic flux linking with the coil is also changes, and hence an emf is induced in the coil. This emf is known as self-induced emf.

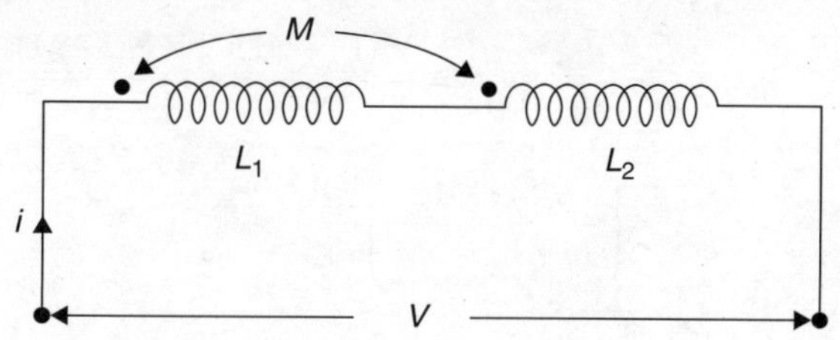

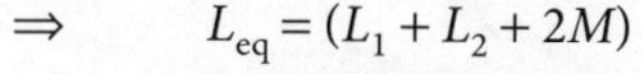

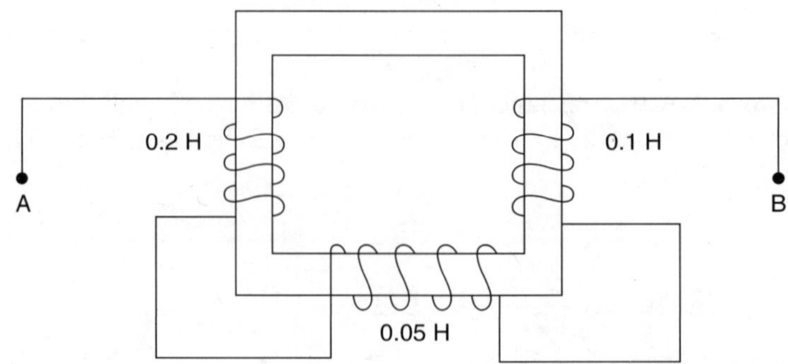

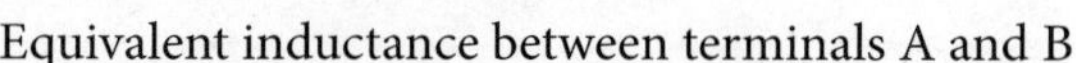

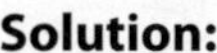

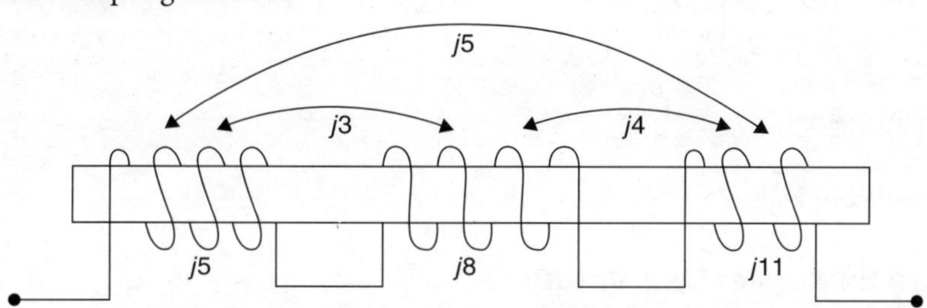

4.15.3 Expressions for Self-Inductance L

The self-induced emf is proportional to the rate of change of current,

$$e \propto \frac{di}{dt} \Rightarrow e = L\frac{di}{dt} \tag{4.19}$$

According to Faraday's law of electromagnetic induction,

$$e = N\frac{d\Phi}{dt} \tag{4.20}$$

From Eqs 4.19 and 4.20,

$$L\frac{di}{dt} = N\frac{d\Phi}{dt} \Rightarrow L = N\frac{d\Phi}{di}$$

If permeability is constant, then

$$L = \frac{N\Phi}{I} \tag{4.21}$$

We know that

$$\text{Magnetic flux} = \frac{\text{MMF}}{\text{Reluctance}}$$

$$\Rightarrow \qquad \Phi = \frac{NI}{l/\mu_0\,\mu_r a} = \frac{NI}{l}\,\mu_0\,\mu_r a$$

Differentiating Φ with respect to i,

$$\frac{d\Phi}{di} = \frac{N}{l}\,\mu_0\,\mu_r a$$

$$\Rightarrow \qquad L = N\frac{d\Phi}{di} = \frac{N^2}{l}\,\mu_0\,\mu_r a = \frac{N^2}{l/\mu_0\,\mu_r a} = \frac{N^2}{S} \tag{4.22}$$

From Eq. 4.22, we observe that the inductance is directly proportional to turns squared and inversely proportional to reluctance of the magnetic path.

4.15.4 Mutual Inductance (M)

It is defined as the ability of one coil or circuit to produce an emf in the other coil placed close to it by induction, when the current in the first coil changes. Alternatively, the two coils so arranged that a change in one coil causes an emf to be induced in the other are said to have mutual inductance.

4.15.5 Mutually Induced EMF

The emf induced in a coil due to the changing current in the neighbouring coil is called *mutually induced emf.*

4.15.6 Expressions for Mutual Inductance M

Consider two coils 1 and 2 close to each other (Fig. 4.10). If a current of I_1 amperes is passed through the coil 1, some of the flux produced by it (Φ_{12}) will be linked with coil 2. So this current will produce not only an emf (called self-induced emf) in coil 1, but also induces an emf (called mutual induced emf) in coil 2. The mutually induced emf is proportional to the rate of change of current in coil 1.

That is, $e_2 \propto \frac{di_1}{dt} \Rightarrow e_2 = M_{12}\frac{di_1}{dt}$ (4.23)

According to Faraday's law of electromagnetic induction

$$e_2 = N_2\frac{d\Phi_{12}}{dt} \quad (4.24)$$

Fig. 4.10 Two coils on a common magnetic core

From Eqs 4.23 and 4.24,

$$M_{12}\frac{di_1}{dt} = N_2\frac{d\Phi_{12}}{dt} \Rightarrow M_{12} = N_2\frac{d\Phi_{12}}{di_1}$$

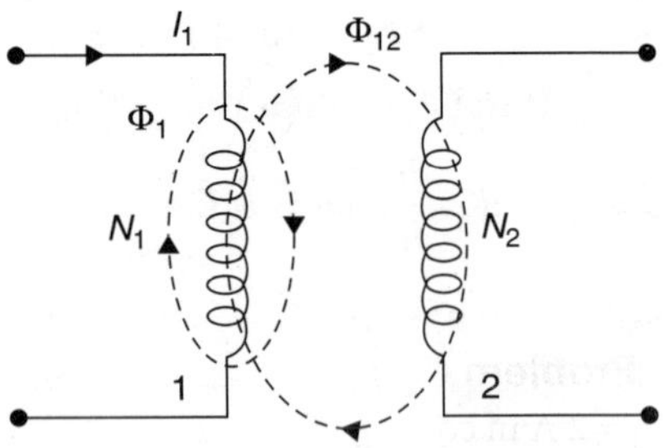

If permeability is constant, then

$$M_{12} = N_2\frac{\Phi_{12}}{I_1} \quad (4.25)$$

Similarly $M_{21} = N_1\frac{\Phi_{21}}{I_2}$ (4.26)

We know that

$$\text{Mutual flux} = \frac{\text{MMF}}{\text{reluctance}}$$

$$\Rightarrow \quad \Phi_{12} = \frac{N_1 I_1}{l/\mu_0\mu_r a} = \frac{N_1 I_1}{l}\mu_0\mu_r a$$

Differentiating Φ_{12} with respect to i_1,

$$\frac{d\Phi_{12}}{di_1} = \frac{N_1}{l}\mu_0\mu_r a$$

$$\Rightarrow \quad M_{12} = N_2\frac{d\Phi_{12}}{di_1} = \frac{N_1N_2}{l}\mu_0\mu_r a = \frac{N_1N_2}{l/\mu_0\mu_r a} = \frac{N_1N_2}{S} \quad (4.27)$$

From Eq. 4.27, we observe that the mutual inductance is inversely proportional to reluctance of the magnetic path.

4.16 COEFFICIENT OF COUPLING (*K*)

The coefficient of coupling between two coils is defined as the ratio of lines of flux produced by coil 1 linking to coil 2 (Φ_{12}), to the total flux produced by coil 1 (Φ_1).

$$\therefore \quad K = \frac{\text{Mutual flux}}{\text{Total flux}} = \frac{\Phi_{12}}{\Phi_1} \text{ (or) } \frac{\Phi_{21}}{\Phi_2}$$

The maximum value of K is unity. If $K = 0$, there is no coupling, if $K = 1$, there is perfect coupling. That is, $0 \le K \le 1$.

4.16.1 Expression for *K*

Mutual inductance is given by $M_{12} = N_2\frac{\Phi_{12}}{I_1}$ and $M_{21} = N_1\frac{\Phi_{21}}{I_2}$

But we know that $M_{12} = M_{21} = M$

$$M^2 = M_{12} \times M_{21} = N_2\frac{\Phi_{12}}{I_1} \times N_1\frac{\Phi_{21}}{I_2}$$

$$= N_2 \frac{K\Phi_1}{I_1} \times N_1 \frac{K\Phi_2}{I_2} = K^2 \frac{N_1\Phi_1}{I_1} \frac{N_2\Phi_2}{I_2} = K^2 L_1 L_2$$

$$\Rightarrow \qquad K = \frac{M}{\sqrt{L_1 L_2}} \tag{4.28}$$

Problem 4.9 Two coils have a coupling coefficient $K = 0.85$ which has 250 turns, with a current $i_1 = 2$ A in coil 1, the total flux Φ_1 is 0.3 mWb. When i_1 is reduced linearly to zero in 2 ms, the voltage induced in coil 2 is 64.75 V. Find L_1, L_2, M and N.

Solution:

Given that $K = 0.85$, $N_1 = 250$, $i_1 = 2$ A

$$\Phi_1 = 0.3 \text{ mWb}, V_2 = 64.75 \text{ V}, t = 2 \text{ ms}$$

$$L_1 = \frac{N_1\Phi_1}{i_1} = \frac{250 \times 0.3 \times 10^{-3}}{2} = 37.5 \text{ mH}$$

$$K = \frac{\Phi_{12}}{\Phi_1} \Rightarrow \Phi_{12} = K\Phi_1 = 0.85 \times 0.3 \times 10^{-3} = 0.255 \text{ mWb}$$

$$V_2 = M\frac{di}{dt} \Rightarrow 63.75 = M \times \frac{2}{2 \times 10^{-3}} \Rightarrow M = 63.75$$

$$M = K\sqrt{L_1 L_2} \Rightarrow L_2 = \frac{M^2}{K^2 L_1} = \frac{63.75^2}{0.85^2 \times 37.5} = 150 \text{ mH}$$

$$M = \frac{N_2\Phi_{12}}{i_1} \Rightarrow N_2 = \frac{Mi_1}{\Phi_{12}} = \frac{63.75 \times 2}{0.255 \times 10^{-3}} = 500$$

Problem 4.10 The magnet is designed to carrry a flux of 1.6 mWb in the air gap. Find the current in the coil of 680 turns wound around the central limb. Assume no leakage, dimensions are given in cm. The relative permeability of the material is 500.

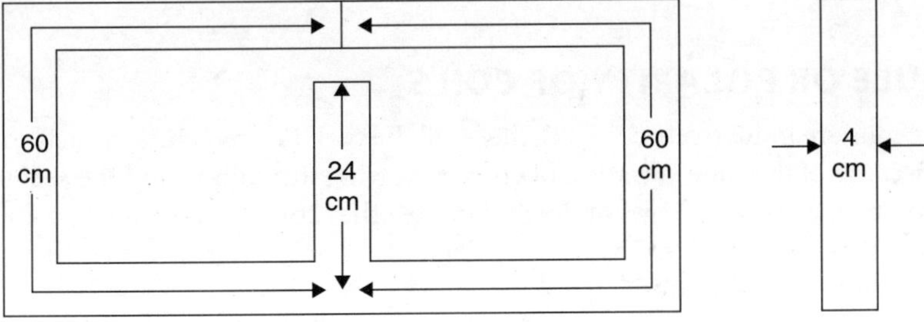

Solution:

Reluctance of central limb:

$$a = 4 \times 4 = 16 \times 10^{-4} \text{ m}^2$$

$$l = 0.24, \mu_r = 500$$

$$S_{\text{centre}} = \frac{l}{a\mu_0\mu_r} = \frac{0.24}{16\times10^{-4}\times4\pi\times10^{-7}\times500} = 23.8\times10^4 = \frac{0.75\times10^6}{\pi}$$

Reluctance of air gap:

$a = 16 \times 10^{-4}$ m^2

$l = 0.1$ cm $= 10^{-3}$

$$S_{\text{air}} = \frac{l}{a\mu_0} = \frac{10^{-3}}{16\times10^{-4}\times4\pi\times10^{-7}} = \frac{100}{64\pi}\times10^6$$

Reluctance of parallel paths:

$l = 0.6$ m

$a = 16 \times 10^{-4}$ m^2

$$S_{\text{parallel}} = \frac{0.6}{4\pi\times10^{-7}\times500\times16\times10^{-4}} = \frac{15}{8\pi}\times10^6$$

Since each parallel path has a reluctance of $\frac{15}{8\pi}\times10^6$, the effective reluctance is $\frac{15}{16\pi}\times10^6$

$$S_{\text{eff}\cdot\text{parallel}} = \frac{15}{16\pi}\times10^6$$

Total reluctance is given by

$$S_{\text{total}} = S_{\text{centre}} + S_{\text{air}} + S_{\text{eff. parallel}}$$

$$= \frac{0.75}{\pi}\times10^6 + \frac{100}{64\pi}\times10^6 + \frac{15}{16\pi}\times10^6 = 1.0345\times10^6$$

$$\text{MMF} = \text{Reluctance} \times \text{Flux}$$

$$= 1.0345 \times 10^6 \times 1.6 \times 10^{-3} = 1655 \text{ AT}$$

$$\text{Current, } I = \frac{\text{MMF}}{N} = \frac{1655}{680} = 2.433 \text{ A}$$

4.17 DOT RULE OR POLARITY OF COILS

When two or more coils are inductively coupled, there will be two induced emfs in each coil—the first is the self-induced emf because of the time variation of current flowing through it, and the second is the mutually induced emf due to time variation of current flowing in the other coil. It is necessary to know whether these induced emfs are additive or opposive. This mainly depends on the sense in which the winding is wound, and the direction of currents in the coils.

This knowledge facilitates the determination of the sign of the mutually induced emf. In case the winding direction is not given, and to give the sign of the mutual inductance this convention is used. To determine the sign of the voltage of mutual inductance in mesh current equations, we use the dot rule which states that:

- When both assumed currents enter or leave a pair of coupled coils at the dotted terminals, the signs of the M terms will be the same as the signs of the L terms.
- If one current enters at a dotted terminal and the other leaves by a dotted terminal, the signs of the M terms are opposite to the signs of the L terms.

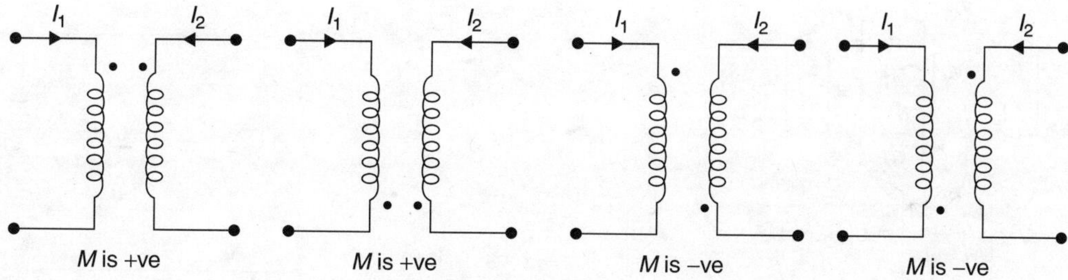

Fig. 4.11 Dot convention

4.18 TWO INDUCTORS OR TWO COILS IN SERIES

Case (i): Series aiding

Two coils 1 and 2 are connected in series with self-inductances L_1 and L_2 and mutual inductance M (Fig. 4.12).

Total induced voltage in the circuit is

$$V = L_1 \frac{di}{dt} + M\frac{di}{dt} + L_2 \frac{di}{dt} + M\frac{di}{dt}$$

$$= (L_1 + L_2 + 2M)\frac{di}{dt}$$

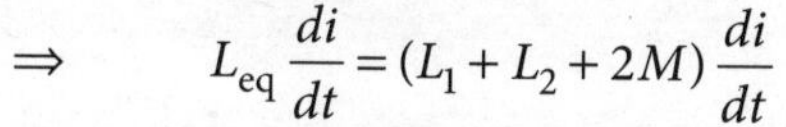

$$\Rightarrow \quad L_{eq}\frac{di}{dt} = (L_1 + L_2 + 2M)\frac{di}{dt}$$

$$\Rightarrow \quad L_{eq} = (L_1 + L_2 + 2M) \tag{4.29}$$

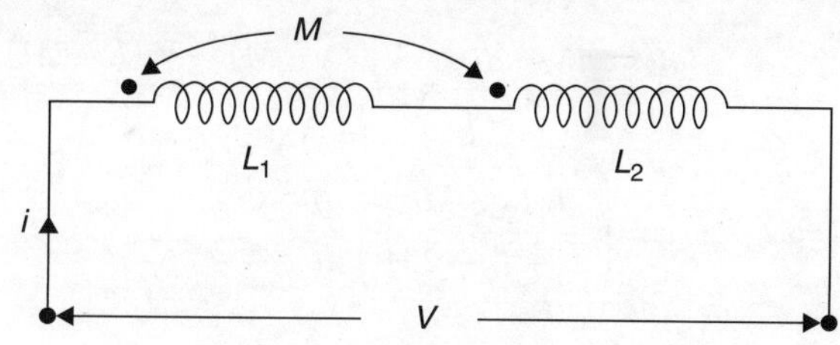

Fig. 4.12 Series aiding magnetic circuit

Case (ii): Series opposing

Two coils 1 and 2 are connected in series with self-inductances L_1 and L_2 and mutual inductance M (Fig. 4.13).

Total induced voltage in the circuit is

$$V = L_1 \frac{di}{dt} - M\frac{di}{dt} + L_2 \frac{di}{dt} - M\frac{di}{dt}$$

$$= (L_1 + L_2 - 2M)\frac{di}{dt}$$

$$\Rightarrow \quad L_{eq}\frac{di}{dt} = (L_1 + L_2 - 2M)\frac{di}{dt}$$

$$\Rightarrow \quad L_{eq} = (L_1 + L_2 - 2M) \tag{4.30}$$

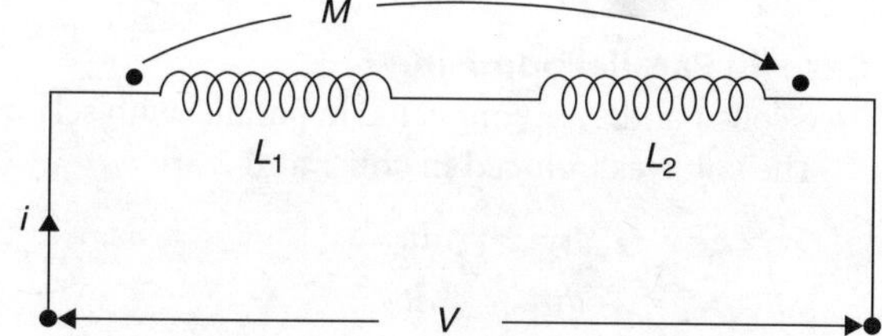

Fig. 4.13 Series opposing magnetic circuit

4.19 TWO INDUCTORS OR TWO COILS IN PARALLEL

Case (i) Parallel aiding

Two coils 1 and 2 are connected in parallel with self-inductances L_1 and L_2 and mutual inductance M (Fig. 4.14).

The voltages induced in coil 1 and 2 are

$$V = L_1 \frac{di_1}{dt} + M\frac{di_2}{dt}$$

$$V = L_2 \frac{di_2}{dt} + M\frac{di_1}{dt}$$

$$\begin{bmatrix} L_1 & M \\ M & L_2 \end{bmatrix} \begin{bmatrix} \dfrac{di_1}{dt} \\ \dfrac{di_2}{dt} \end{bmatrix} = \begin{bmatrix} V \\ V \end{bmatrix}$$

$$\Delta = \begin{vmatrix} L_1 & M \\ M & L_2 \end{vmatrix} = L_1 L_2 - M^2$$

$$\frac{di_1}{dt} = \frac{\begin{vmatrix} V & M \\ V & L_2 \end{vmatrix}}{\Delta} = \frac{V(L_2 - M)}{\Delta}, \quad \frac{di_2}{dt} = \frac{\begin{vmatrix} L_1 & V \\ M & V \end{vmatrix}}{\Delta} = \frac{V(L_1 - M)}{\Delta}.$$

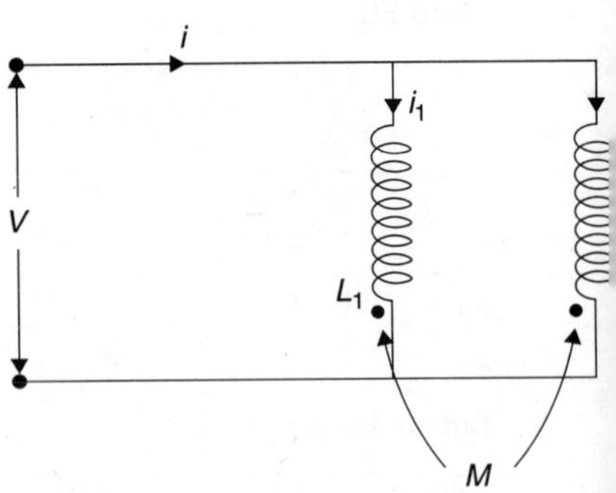

Fig. 4.14 Parallel aiding magnetic circu

From Fig. 4.14,

$$i = i_1 + i_2$$

$$\frac{di}{dt} = \frac{di_1}{dt} + \frac{di_2}{dt} = \frac{V(L_2 - M)}{\Delta} + \frac{V(L_1 - M)}{\Delta} = \frac{V(L_1 + L_2 - 2M)}{\Delta} = \frac{V(L_1 + L_2 - 2M)}{L_1 L_2 - M^2}$$

$$\Rightarrow \quad V = \left(\frac{L_1 L_2 - M^2}{L_1 + L_2 - 2M} \right) \frac{di}{dt}$$

But we know that

$$V = L_{eq} \frac{di}{dt}$$

$$\Rightarrow \quad L_{eq} = \frac{L_1 L_2 - M^2}{L_1 + L_2 - 2M} \tag{4.31}$$

Case (ii) Parallel opposing

Two coils 1 and 2 are connected in parallel with self-inductances L_1 and L_2 and mutual inductance M (Fig. 4.15).

The voltages induced in coil 1 and 2 are

$$V = L_2 \frac{di_2}{dt} - M \frac{di_1}{dt}$$

$$V = L_1 \frac{di_1}{dt} - M \frac{di_2}{dt}$$

$$\begin{bmatrix} L_1 & -M \\ -M & L_2 \end{bmatrix} \begin{bmatrix} \dfrac{di_1}{dt} \\ \dfrac{di_2}{dt} \end{bmatrix} = \begin{bmatrix} V \\ V \end{bmatrix}$$

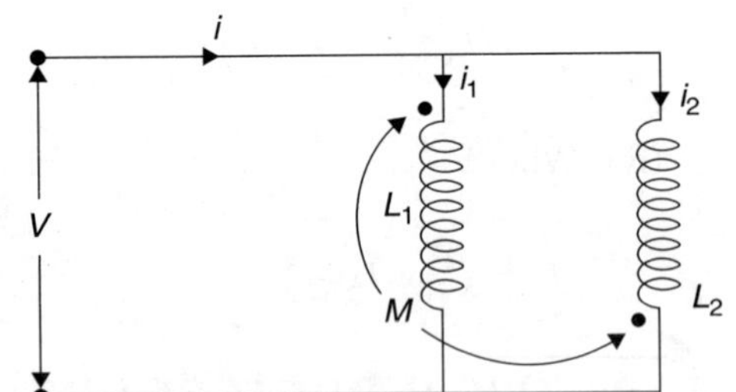

Fig. 4.15 Parallel opposing magnetic circuit

$$\Delta = \begin{vmatrix} L_1 & -M \\ -M & L_2 \end{vmatrix} = L_1 L_2 - M^2$$

$$\frac{di_1}{dt} = \frac{\begin{vmatrix} V & -M \\ V & L_2 \end{vmatrix}}{\Delta} = \frac{V(L_2 + M)}{\Delta}, \quad \frac{di_2}{dt} = \frac{\begin{vmatrix} L_1 & V \\ -M & V \end{vmatrix}}{\Delta} = \frac{V(L_1 + M)}{\Delta}$$

From Fig. 4.15,

$$i = i_1 + i_2$$

$$\frac{di}{dt} = \frac{di_1}{dt} + \frac{di_2}{dt} = \frac{V(L_2+M)}{\Delta} + \frac{V(L_1+M)}{\Delta} = \frac{V(L_1+L_2+2M)}{\Delta} = \frac{V(L_1+L_2+2M)}{L_1L_2-M^2}$$

$$\Rightarrow \qquad V = \left(\frac{L_1L_2-M^2}{L_1+L_2+2M}\right)\frac{di}{dt}$$

But we know that,

$$V = L_{eq}\frac{di}{dt}$$

$$\Rightarrow \qquad L_{eq} = \frac{L_1L_2-M^2}{L_1+L_2+2M} \tag{4.32}$$

Problem 4.11 Two coupled coils with $L_1 = 0.02$ H, $L_2 = 0.01$ H and $K = 0.5$ are connected in four different ways series aiding, series opposing, parallel aiding and parallel opposing. What are the four equivalent inductances?

Solution:

Given that $L_1 = 0.02, H = 20$ mH, $L_2 = 0.01, H = 10$ mH, $K = 0.5$

$$M = K\sqrt{L_1L_2} = 0.5 \times \sqrt{20 \times 10} = 7.07 \text{ mH}$$

(i) When connected in series aiding

$$L_{eq} = L_1 + L_2 + 2M = 20 + 10 + 2 \times 7.07 = 44.14 \text{ mH}$$

(ii) When connected in series opposing

$$L_{eq} = L_1 + L_2 - 2M = 20 + 10 - 2 \times 7.07 = 15.86 \text{ mH}$$

(iii) When connected in parallel aiding

$$L_{eq} = \frac{L_1L_2-M^2}{L_1+L_2-2M} = \frac{20\times 10 - 7.07^2}{15.86} = 9.46 \text{ mH}$$

(iv) When connected in parallel opposing

$$L_{eq} = \frac{L_1L_2-M^2}{L_1+L_2+2M} = \frac{20\times 10 - 7.07^2}{44.14} = 3.4 \text{ mH}$$

Problem 4.12 Two coils with inductances in the ratio of 5:1 have a coupling coefficient $K = 0.4$. When these coils are connected in series aiding, the equivalent inductance is 44.4 mH. Find L_1, L_2 and M.

Solution:

Given that $L_1 : L_2 = 5 : 1 \quad \Rightarrow \quad L_1 = 5L_2$

$$M = K\sqrt{L_1L_2}\,\sqrt{L_1L_2} = 0.5 \times \sqrt{5L_2L_2} = 1.118\, L_2$$

When connected in series aiding

$$L_{eq} = L_1 + L_2 + 2M$$

$$44.4 = 5L_2 + L_2 + 1.18\ L_2 \times 2$$

$$\Rightarrow \quad 44.4 = 8.238\ L_2$$

$$\Rightarrow \quad L_2 = 5.4\ \text{mH}$$

$$L_1 = 5 \times 5.4 = 27\ \text{mH}$$

$$M = 1.118\ L_2 = 1.118 \times 5.4 = 6.026\ \text{mH}$$

Therefore $L_1 = 27$ mH, $L_2 = 5.4$ mH, $M = 6.026$ mH

Problem 4.13 Sketch the dotted equivalent circuit for the coupled coil and find the equivalent inductive reactance.

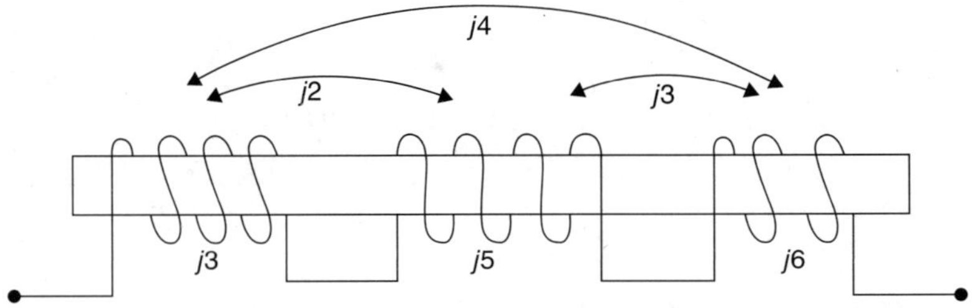

Solution:

The dotted equivalent circuit is

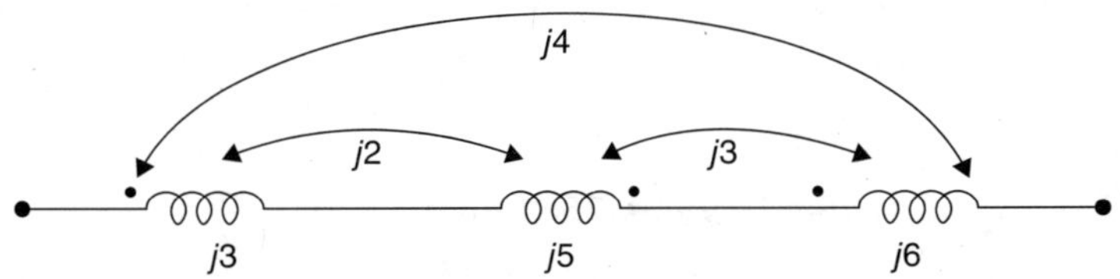

The equivalent inductive reactance is

$$j\,X_{eq} = j3 + j5 + j6 - 2 \times j2 - 2 \times j3 + 2 \times j4) = j14 - j2 = j12$$

Problem 4.14 Sketch the dotted equivalent circuit for the coupled coils and find the equivalent inductance at the terminals AB. All coupling coefficients are 0.5.

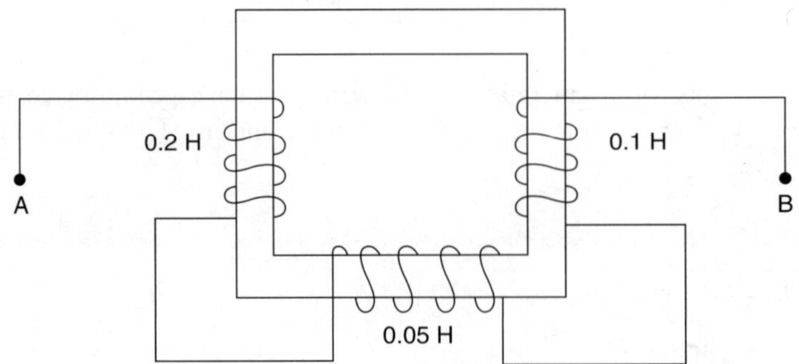

Solution:

The dotted equivalent circuit is

$$M_{12} = 0.5\sqrt{0.2 \times 0.05} = 0.05$$

$$M_{23} = 0.5\sqrt{0.05 \times 0.1} = 0.035$$

$$M_{31} = 0.5\sqrt{0.2 \times 0.1} = 0.0707$$

Equivalent inductance between terminals A and B

$$L_{AB} = 0.2 + 0.05 + 0.1 + 2 \times (0.05 - 0.035 - 0.0707) = 0.2386\ \text{H}$$

Problem 4.15 For the given circuit,

(i) Find the equivalent reactance.
(ii) Draw the transformer coupling circuit.

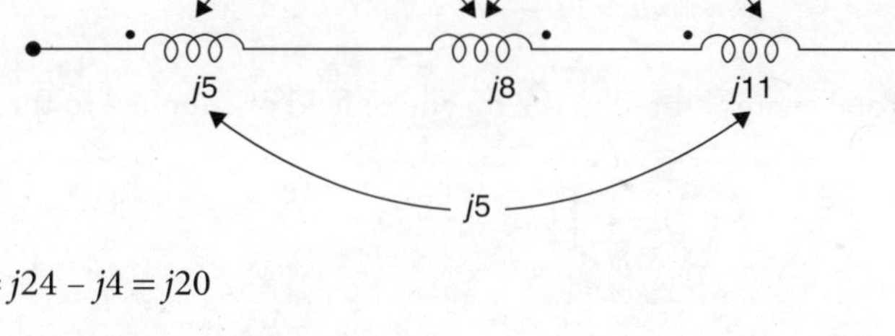

Solution:

(i) The equivalent reactance is

$$j\,X_{eq} = j5 + j8 + j11 + 2(-j3 - j4 + j5) = j24 - j4 = j20$$

(ii) The transformer coupling circuit is

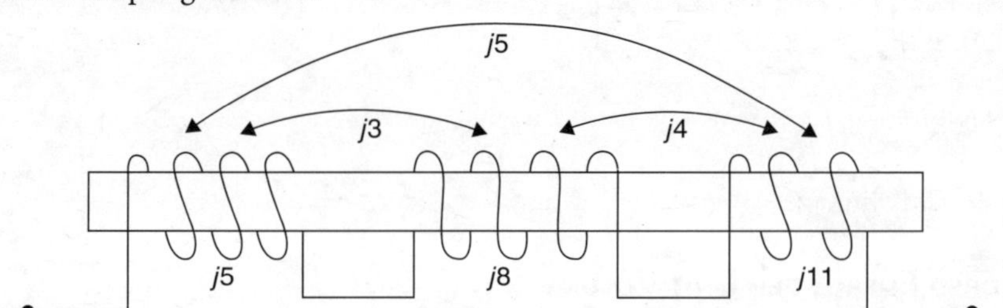

Problem 4.16 Sketch the dotted equivalent circuit for the coupled coils and find the current I.

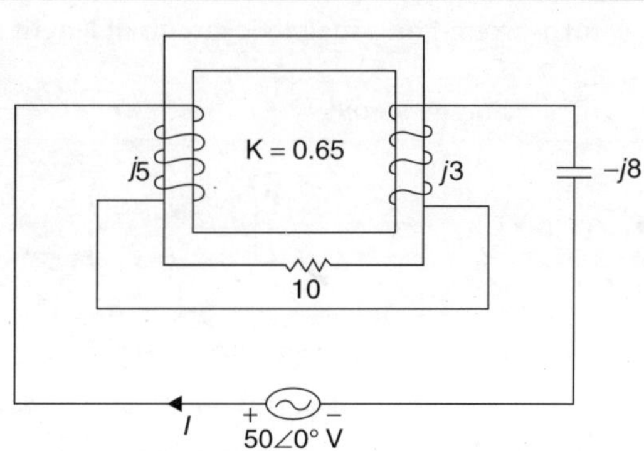

Solution:

The dotted equivalent circuit is shown on the right.

$$jX_M = jK\sqrt{X_{L1} \times X_{L2}} = j\,0.65\sqrt{5 \times 3} = j\,2.5$$

Applying KVL to the circuit

$$10I - j8I + (j5 + j3 - 2 \times j2.5)I = 50$$

$$I \times (10 - j8 + j13) = 50$$

$$\Rightarrow \quad I = \frac{50}{11.18\ \angle -26.56^\circ} = 4.47\ \angle -25.56^\circ\ \text{A}$$

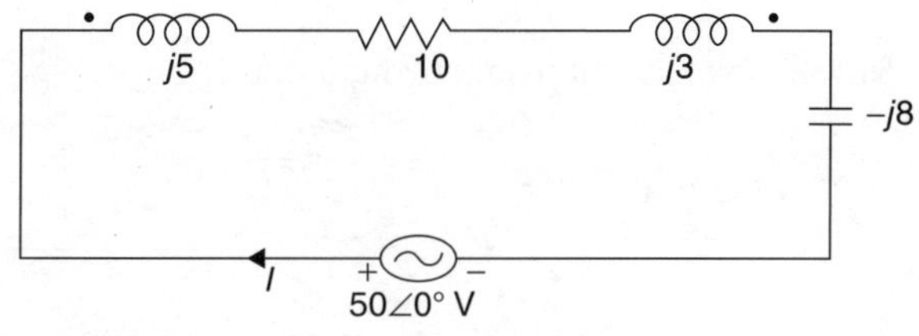

4.20 STORED ENERGY IN A MAGNETIC FIELD

In an electric circuit, energy is required to maintain the flow of current but in a magnetic circuit no energy is required to maintain the magnetic flux. Energy is only required in creating the magnetic flux and energy supplied to create a flux is stored in the magnetic field.

Consider a coil of inductance L henrys. Let us suppose that at any instant the current in the coil is I and increasing at a rate $\frac{di}{dt}$, then the emf e induced is given by

$$e = L\frac{di}{dt}$$

$$\text{Instantaneous power, } P = ei = Li\frac{di}{dt}$$

Energy stored in the magnetic field or energy supplied to the coil during a short interval of time dt

$$d\omega = pdt = Li\frac{di}{dt}\cdot dt = Lidi$$

Total energy stored in the magnetic field or supplied to the coil when current rises from 0 to I.

$$W = \int_0^I dw = \int_0^I Lidi = \frac{1}{2}LI^2 \tag{4.33}$$

or $$W = \frac{1}{2}\left(\frac{N\Phi}{I}\right)I^2 \qquad \left[\because L = \frac{N\Phi}{I}\right]$$

$$= \frac{1}{2}N\Phi I = \frac{1}{2}\psi I$$

where $\psi = N\Phi = \text{flux linkage}$ (4.34)

4.20.1 Stored Energy per Unit Volume

It is sometimes desirable to know the energy stored in a unit volume of the magnetic field. Consider a coil of N turns wound on a magnetic circuit of length l metres and uniform cross-section area of a m^2.

$$\text{Energy stored} = \frac{1}{2}LI^2$$

$$= \frac{1}{2}\left(\frac{N^2 a\mu_0\mu_r}{l}\right)I^2$$

$$= \frac{1}{2}(a\mu_0\mu_r)\,l\left(\frac{NI}{l}\right)^2$$

$$= \frac{1}{2}\mu_0\mu_r(a\times l)\times H^2 \qquad \left[\because H = \frac{NI}{l}\right]$$

Now al = volume of magnetic field in m^3.

$$\text{Energy stored/m}^3 = \frac{1}{2}\mu_0\mu_r H^2 \tag{4.35}$$

$$= \frac{1}{2}\mu_0\mu_r\left(\frac{B}{\mu_0\mu_r}\right)^2 \qquad \left[\because H = \frac{B}{\mu_0\mu_r}\right]$$

$$= \frac{B^2}{2\mu_0\mu_r} \quad \text{(in a medium)}$$

$$= \frac{B^2}{2\mu_0} \quad \text{(in air)}$$

4.20.2 Energy Stored In Two Mutually Coupled Coils

The energy stored in mutually coupled coils is given as

$$W = \int_0^{\psi_1} i_1 d\psi_1 + \int_0^{\psi_2} i_2 d\psi_2 \tag{4.36}$$

For mutually coupled coils, the total flux linkages ψ_1 and $\psi_2$is given as

$$\psi_1 = L_i i_1 + Mi_2$$

$$\psi_2 = L_2 i_2 + Mi_1$$

Differentiating the above equations with respect to current

$$d\psi_1 = L_i di_1 + Mdi_2$$

$$d\psi_2 = L_2 di_2 + Mdi_1$$

By substituting the values of $d\psi_1$ and $d\psi_2$ in Eq. 4.36, the energy stored is

$$W = \int_0^{i_1}(L_1 i_1 di_1 + Mi_1 di_2)\int_0^{i_2}(L_2 i_2 di_2 + Mi_2 di_1) = L_1\frac{i_1^2}{2} + Mi_1 i_2 + L_2\frac{i_2^2}{2} + Mi_2 i_2$$

$$W = \frac{1}{2}L_1 i_1^2 + \frac{1}{2}L_2 i_2^2 + 2Mi_1 i_2 \tag{4.37}$$

4.21 LIFTING POWER OF A MAGNET

Consider two poles, each of area a m² facing each other (Fig. 4.16). Let P be the force of attraction between the two poles. If one of the poles, say the S-pole, is pulled apart through a small distance δx then work will be done against the force of attraction.

Work done $= P \times \delta x$ joule

This work done is stored in the additional volume of the magnetic field created.

Additional volume of magnetic created $= a \times \delta x$ m³

Since energy stored in the magnetic field for medium of air is

$$\frac{B^2}{2\mu_0} \text{ joules/m}^3$$

Increase in stored energy $= \dfrac{B^2}{2\mu_0} \times a\delta x$

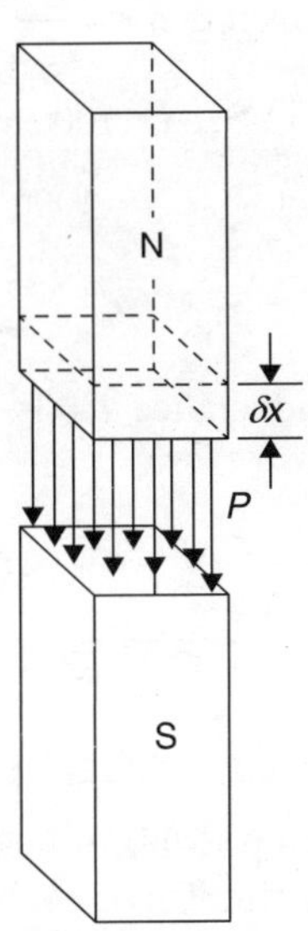

Fig. 4.16 Lifting power of a magnet

$$P \times \delta x = \frac{B^2}{2\mu_0} a\delta x$$

$$\Rightarrow \quad P = \frac{B^2}{2\mu_0} a \text{ newtons} \tag{4.38}$$

Note that P is the force of attraction at each pole. In a practical magnet, there are two poles, so the total force of attraction is $2P$.

Problem 4.17 In a telephone receiver, the since of each pole of the electromagnet is 1.4 cm × 0.4 cm and the flux between each pole and the diaphragm is 6×10^{-6} Wb. With what force is the diaphragm attracted towards the pole?

Solution:

Given that $a = 1.4 \times 0.4 = 0.56$ cm², $\Phi = 6 \times 10^{-6}$ Wb

$$B = \frac{\Phi}{a} = \frac{6 \times 10^{-6}}{0.56 \times 10^{-4}} = 0.107 \text{ Wb/m}^2$$

$$P = \frac{B^2 \times A}{2\mu_0} = \frac{(0.107)^2 \times 0.56 \times 10^{-4}}{2 \times 4\pi \times 10^{-7}} = 0.255 \text{ N}$$

Total force $= 2P = 2 \times 0.255 = 0.51$ N

Problem 4.18 Calculate the inductance and energy stored in the magnetic field of an air-cored solenoid 100 cm long, 7.5 cm in diameter and wound with 1000 turns, if carrying a current of 8 A.

Solution:

Given that $r = \frac{7.5}{2} = 3.75 \times 10^{-2}$ m

$l = 100 \text{ cm} = 100 \times 10^{-2}$

$N = 1000, I = 8$ A

$a = \pi \times r^2 = \pi \times (3.75 \times 10^{-2})^2 = 44.18 \times 10^{-4} \text{ m}^2$

$$\text{Inductance, } L = \frac{N^2 a \mu_0 \mu_r}{l} = \frac{1000^2 \times 44.18 \times 10^{-4} \times 4\pi \times 10^{-7} \times 1}{100 \times 10^{-2}} = 5.55 \text{ mH}$$

$$\text{Energy stored, } W = \frac{1}{2} LI^2 = \frac{1}{2} \times 5.55 \times 10^{-3} \times 8^2 = 0.18 \text{ J}$$

4.22 COUPLED CIRCUIT

It is possible in analysis that a mutually coupled circuit can be replaced by a conductively coupled equivalent circuit. Let us consider a mutually coupled circuit (Fig. 4.17). Let I_1 and I_2 be the loop currents.

Applying KVL to loop-1, for Fig. 4.17,

$$V_1 = R_1 I_1 + j\omega L_1 I_1 - j\omega M I_2 = (R_1 + j\omega L_1) I_1 - j\omega M I_2 \tag{4.39}$$

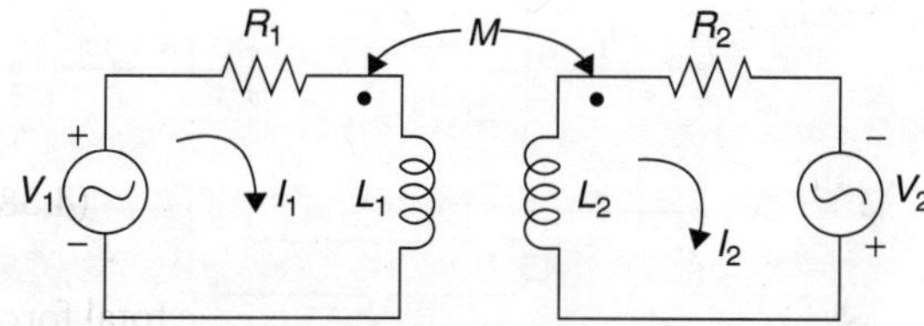

Fig. 4.17 Magnetically coupled circuit

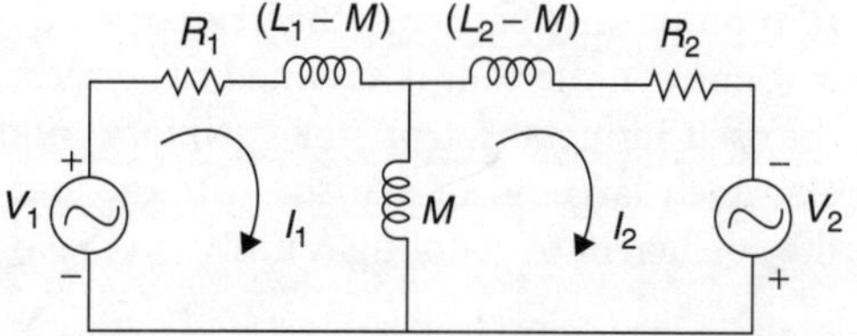

Fig. 4.18 Conductively coupled circuit

Applying KVL to loop-2, for Fig. 4.17,

$$V_2 = R_2 I_2 + j\omega L_2 I_2 - j\omega M I_1$$

$$= -j\omega M I_1 + (R_2 + j\omega L_2)\, I_2 \tag{4.40}$$

Applying KVL to loop-1, for Fig. 4.18,

$$V_1 = R_1 I_1 + j\omega(L_1 - M) I_1 + j\omega M\,(I_1 - I_2)$$

$$= (R_1 + j\omega L_1) I_1 - j\omega M I_2 \tag{4.41}$$

Applying KVL to loop-2, for Fig. 4.18,

$$V_2 = R_2 I_2 + j\omega(L_2 - M) I_2 + j\omega M\,(I_2 - I_1) = -\,j\omega M I_1 + (R_2 + j\omega L_2) I_2 \tag{4.42}$$

The equations for the network (Figs 4.17 and 4.18) are exactly identical. Hence the coupled circuit (Fig. 4.17) and conductively coupled circuit (Fig. 4.18) are equivalent. So a mutually coupled circuit can be replaced by a conductively coupled circuit (Fig. 4.19).

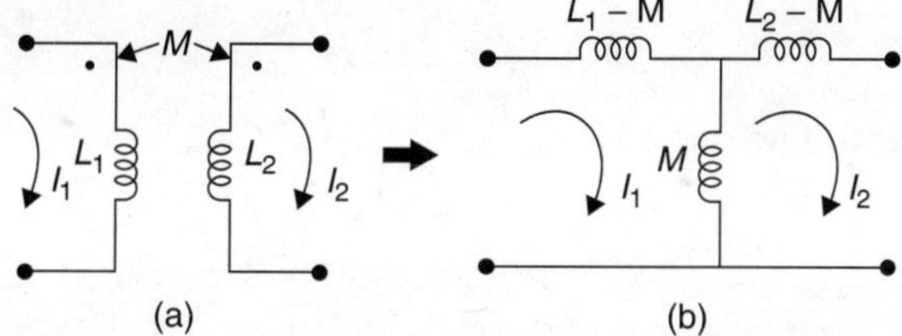

Fig. 4.19 (a) Mutually coupled circuit (b) Conductively coupled circuit

4.23 IDEAL TRANSFORMER

A transformer is a static device that transfers electrical energy from one circuit to another circuit without changing the frequency of the system. It works on the principle of electromagnetic induction.

A transformer is a static apparatus, having two or more windings or coils arranged on a common magnetic core. The transformer winding to which the supply source is connected is called the primary, while the winding connected to the load is called secondary. Accordingly, voltage across the primary is called *primary voltage* and that across the secondary is called *secondary voltage*. Correspondingly I_1 and I_2 are the currents in the primary and secondary windings.

The two inductive coils are electrically separated and magnetically linked (Fig. 4.20). The two coils possess high mutual inductance. If one coil is connected to a source of alternating voltage, an alternating flux is set up in the core, most of which is linked with the other coil, in which it produces mutually induced emf according to Faraday's law of electromagnetic induction. If the second coil circuit is closed, a current flows in it and so electrical energy transfers from the first coil (primary) to the second coil (secondary).

An ideal transformer is characterised by assuming:

- zero power dissipation in the primary and secondary, that is, resistance in the coils is assumed to be zero,
- the self-inductance of the primary and secondary are extremely large in comparison with the load impedance, and
- the coefficient of coupling is unity.

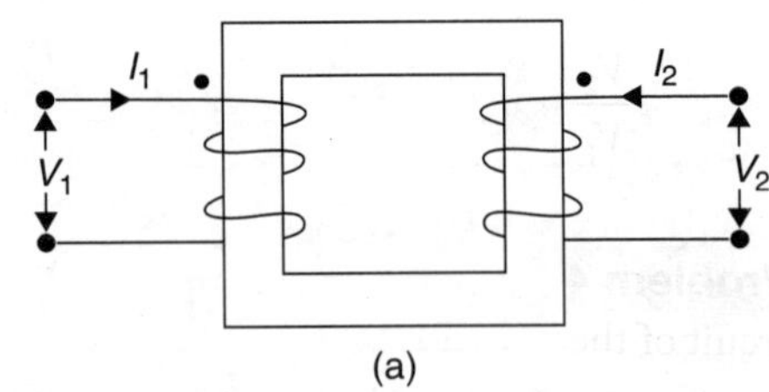

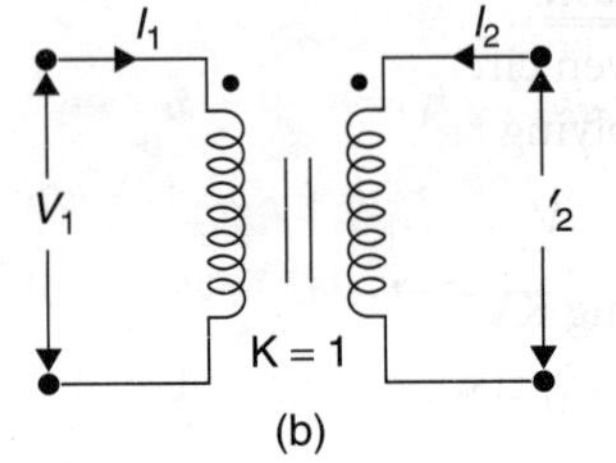

Fig. 4.20 An ideal transformer circuit

The self-induced emf is given by

$$e = L\frac{di}{dt} \tag{4.43}$$

According to Faraday's law of electromagnetic induction

$$e = N\frac{d\Phi}{dt} \tag{4.44}$$

From Eqs 4.43 and 4.44, we have

$$L\frac{di}{dt} = N\frac{d\Phi}{dt} \Rightarrow L = N\frac{d\Phi}{di} \tag{4.45}$$

If permeability is constant, then

$$L = \frac{N\Phi}{I} \tag{4.46}$$

$$\text{Magnetic flux} = \frac{\text{MMF}}{\text{reluctance}}$$

$$\Rightarrow \quad \Phi = \frac{NI}{l/\mu_0\mu_r a} = \frac{NI}{l}\mu_0\mu_r a \tag{4.47}$$

Differentiating Φ with respect to I, we have

$$\frac{d\Phi}{dI} = \frac{N}{l}\mu_0\mu_r a$$

$$L = N\frac{d\Phi}{dI} = \frac{N^2}{l}\mu_0\mu_r a = \frac{N^2}{l/\mu_0\mu_r a} = \frac{N^2}{S}$$

$$\Rightarrow \quad L \propto N^2$$

From the above relation, it follows that

$$\frac{L_2}{L_1} = \frac{N_2^2}{N_1^2} = K^2 \tag{4.48}$$

The turns ratio can also be expressed in terms of primary and secondary voltages. If Φ is the flux through a single turn coil in the core and N_1 and N_2 are the number of turns of the primary and secondary respectively, then the total flux through windings 1 and 2 is

$$\Phi_1 = N_1\Phi, \Phi_2 = N_2\Phi$$

Also,

$$V_1 = \frac{d\Phi_1}{dt}, \quad V_2 = \frac{d\Phi_2}{dt}$$

$$\therefore \quad \frac{V_2}{V_1} = \frac{N_2 d\Phi}{N_1 d\Phi} = \frac{N_2}{N_1} = K \tag{4.49}$$

Problem 4.19 Find the conductively coupled equivalent circuit of the network shown.

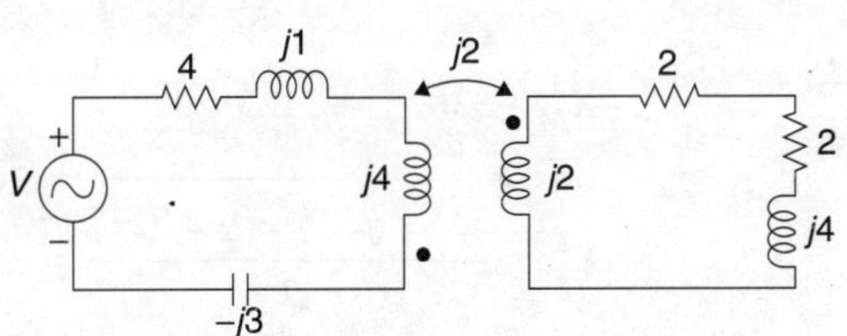

Solution:

The given circuit can be redrawn as

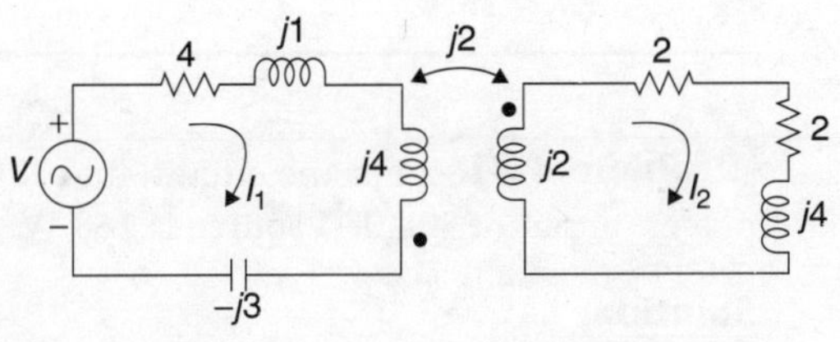

Applying KVL to loop-1

$$V_1 = (4 + j1 + j4 - j3)I_1 + j\,2I_2 = (4 + j2)I_1 - j2I_2 \quad (1)$$

Applying KVL to loop-2

$$0 = (2 + j2 + 2 + j4)I_2 + j2I_1 = j2I_1 + (4 + j6)I_2 \quad (2)$$

Equations (1) and (2) can be written into the matrix form

$$\begin{bmatrix} 4 + j2 & j2 \\ j2 & 4 + j6 \end{bmatrix} \begin{bmatrix} I_1 \\ I_2 \end{bmatrix} = \begin{bmatrix} V_1 \\ 0 \end{bmatrix} \quad (3)$$

From the above matrix equation, the conductively coupled equivalent circuit can be drawn as shown on the right.

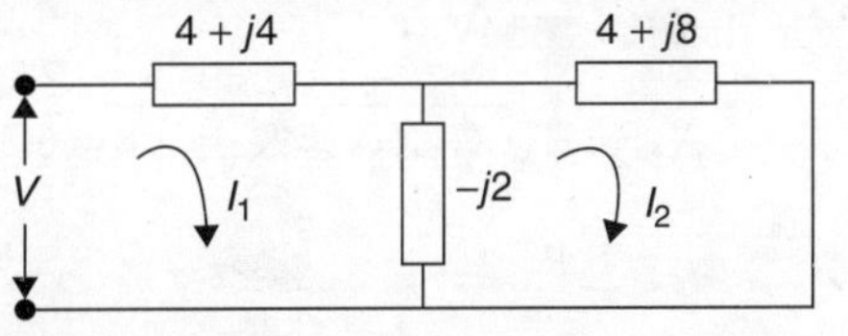

Problem 4.20 In the coupled circuit, find the mutual inductive reactance $j\omega M$ if the power in the 5 Ω resistor is 45.2 W?

50 V
4 Ω
jX_m
I_1
j5
j10
I_2
5 Ω

Solution:

Given that $P_5 = 45.2$ W

$$P_5 = I_2^2 \times 5 = 45.2$$

$$\Rightarrow \quad I_2 = 3.01 \text{ A}$$

Inspection of mesh analysis gives

$$\begin{bmatrix} 4 + j5 & \pm jX_M \\ \pm jX_M & 5 + j10 \end{bmatrix} \begin{bmatrix} I_1 \\ I_2 \end{bmatrix} = \begin{bmatrix} 50 \\ 0 \end{bmatrix}$$

$$\Delta = \begin{vmatrix} 4 + j5 & \pm jX_M \\ \pm jX_M & 5 + j10 \end{vmatrix} = (4 + j5)(5 + j10) + X_M^2 = 20 + j25 + j40 - 50 + X_M^2 = -30 + j65 + X_M^2$$

$$\Delta_2 = \begin{vmatrix} 4 + j5 & 50 \\ \pm jX_M & 0 \end{vmatrix} = \mp 50\,jX_M$$

$$I_2 = \frac{\Delta_2}{\Delta} = \frac{\mp 50\,jX_M}{-30 + j65 + X_M^2} = I_5$$

$$\Rightarrow \quad \frac{50X_M}{\sqrt{(X_M^2 - 30)^2 + 65^2}} = 3.01$$

$$\Rightarrow \quad (X_M^2 - 30)^2 + 65^2 = \left(\frac{50X_M}{3.01}\right)^2$$

$$\Rightarrow \quad X_M^4 - 338X_M^2 + 5125 = 0$$

$$\therefore \quad X_M^2 = \frac{338 \pm \sqrt{338^2 - 4 \times 5125}}{2} = \frac{338 \pm 306.2}{2} = 322.1, 15.9$$

$$\Rightarrow \quad X_M = 18, 4$$

Problem 4.21 For the circuit, find K and place the dots so that the power output of $50\angle 0°$ Vsource is 168 W.

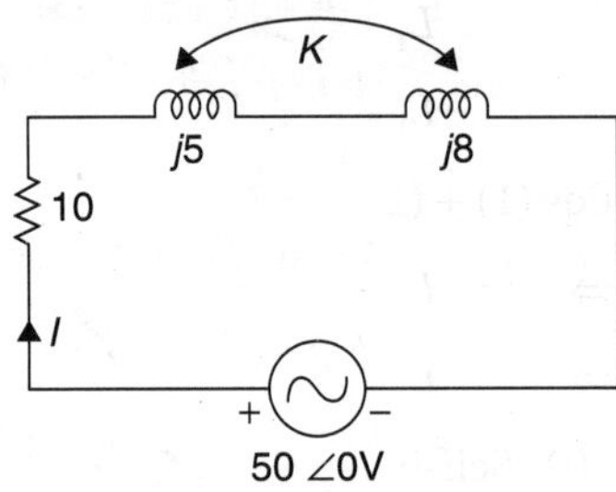

Solution:

Given that $P = 168$ W

$$X_M = K\sqrt{X_{L1}X_{L2}} = K\sqrt{5 \times 8} = 6.324 \text{ K}$$

$$P = I_2^2 R$$

$$\Rightarrow \quad I = \sqrt{\frac{P}{R}} = \sqrt{\frac{168}{10}} = 4.1 \text{ A}$$

From the given circuit

$$I = \frac{50\angle 0°}{10 + j(5 + 8 \pm 2 \times 6.324 \text{ K})}$$

$$\Rightarrow \quad |I| = \frac{50}{\sqrt{100 + (13 \pm 12.648 \text{ K})^2}} = 4.1$$

$$\Rightarrow \quad 100 + (13 \pm 12.648K)^2 = 148.72$$

$$\Rightarrow \quad 13 \pm 12.648K = \sqrt{148.72 - 100} = 6.98$$

$$\Rightarrow \quad \pm 12.648K = 6.98 - 13 = -6.02$$

$$\Rightarrow \quad -12.648K = -6.02$$

$$\Rightarrow \quad K = 0.4759$$

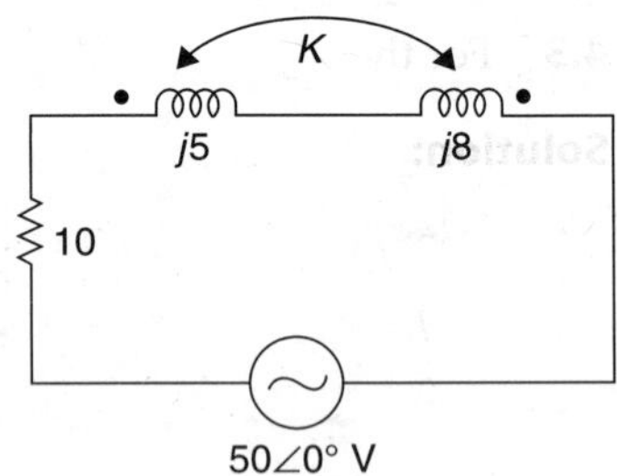

K should be positive, so that the dots are placed as shown.

ADDITIONAL SOLVED PROBLEMS

4.1 The air gap in a magnetic circuit is 1.5 mm long and 2500 mm² in cross-sectional area. Calculate the (i) reluctance of the air gap, and (ii) MMF required to set up a flux of 800×10^{-6} Wb in the air gap.

Solution: Given that $l = 1.5 \text{ mm} = 1.5 \times 10^{-3}$ m

$$a = 2500 \text{ mm}^2 = 2500 \times 10^{-6} \text{ m}^2$$

(i) Reluctance of the air gap

$$S = \frac{l}{\mu_0 \mu_r a} = \frac{1.5 \times 10^{-3}}{4\pi \times 10^{-7} \times 1 \times 250 \times 10^{-6}} = 4.77 \times 10^5 \text{ AT/m}$$

(ii) MMF required $= NI = \Phi S = 800 \times 10^{-6} \times 4.77 \times 10^5 = 381.6$ AT

4.2 The combined inductance of two coils connected in series is 1.2 H or 0.2 H depending on the relative directions of the current in the coils. If one of coil has a self-inductance of 0.4 H, calculate, (i) self-inductance of the second coil, (ii) mutual inductance between the coils, and (iii) the coupling coefficient.

Solution: Given that $L_l = 0.4$ H

$$L_1 + L_2 + 2M = 1 \quad (1)$$

$$L_1 + L_2 - 2M = 1.2 \quad (2)$$

Eqs (1) + (2) $\Rightarrow 2\,(L_l + L_2) = 1.4$

$\Rightarrow \quad L_1 + L_2 = 0.7$

$\Rightarrow \quad L_2 = 0.7 - L_1 = 0.7 - 0.4 = 0.3$

(i) Self-inductance of the second coil $L_2 = 0.3$ H

From Eq. (1), $L_1 + L_2 + 2M = 1.2$

$$M = \frac{1}{2} \times (1.2 - L_1 - L_2)$$

$$= \frac{1}{2} \times (1.2 - 0.4 - 0.3) = 0.25 \text{ H}$$

(ii) Mutual inductance between the coil, $M = 0.25$ H

(iii) The coupling coefficient $K = \dfrac{M}{\sqrt{L_1 L_2}} = \dfrac{0.25}{\sqrt{0.4 \times 0.3}} = 0.723$

4.3 For the circuit, write the inductance matrix.

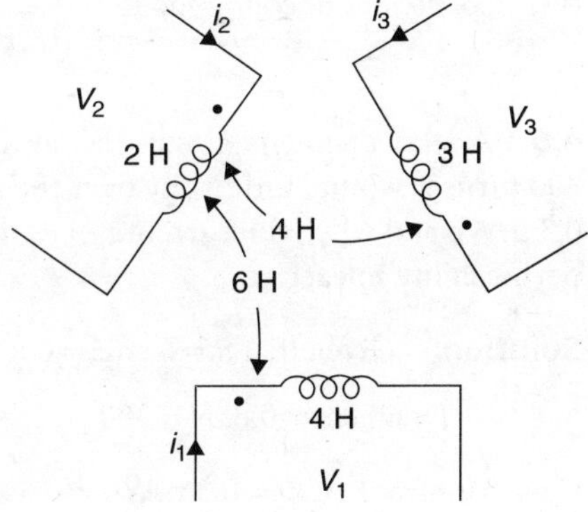

Solution: The inductance matrix is

$$L = \begin{bmatrix} L_{11} & \pm L_{12} & \pm L_{13} \\ \pm L_{21} & L_{22} & \pm L_{23} \\ \pm L_{31} & \pm L_{32} & L_{33} \end{bmatrix} = \begin{bmatrix} 4 & 6 & 0 \\ 6 & 2 & -4 \\ 0 & -4 & 3 \end{bmatrix}$$

4.4 The inductance matrix for the circuit of three series connected coupled coils is given below. Find the inductances and indicate the dots for the coils.

$$L = \begin{bmatrix} 5 & -5 & 2 \\ -5 & 1 & -4 \\ 2 & -4 & 7 \end{bmatrix}$$

Solution: Given that, the inductances are

$$L_{11} = 5, L_{22} = 1, L_{33} = 7, L_{12} = -5, L_{13} = 2, L_{23} = -4$$

The dotted equivalent circuit is

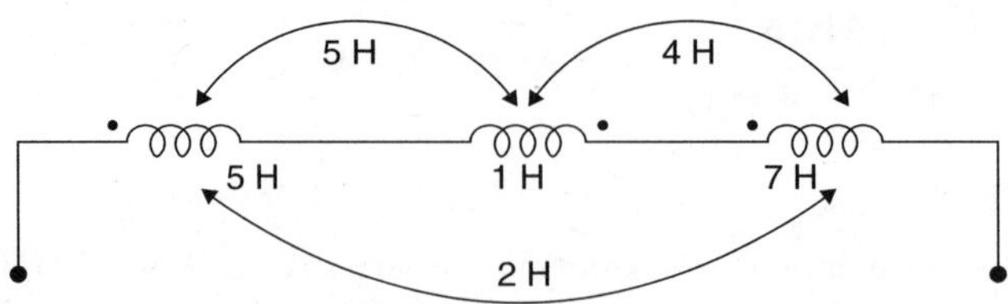

4.5 Two coils of 1500 and 2000 turns are wound on a common magnetic circuit of reluctance 250,000 AT/Wb. Find the mutual inductance when leakage flux is neglected. If the self-inductance of the two coils are 2 H each, calculate the net inductance if the flux in the two coils, (i) oppose each other, (ii) aid each other, and (iii) also determine the coefficient of coupling.

Solution: Given that $N_1 = 1500, N_2 = 2000$

$$S = 250{,}000 \text{ AT/Wb}$$

$$L_1 = L_2 = 2 \text{ H}$$

Mutual inductance, $M_{12} = M = \dfrac{N_1 N_2}{S} = \dfrac{1500 \times 2000}{250000} = 12 \text{ H}$

(i) Fluxes in the two coils opposing each other

$$L_{eq} = L_1 + L_2 - 2M = 2 + 2 - 2 \times 12 = -20 \text{ H}$$

(ii) Fluxes in the two coils aid each other

$$L_{eq} = L_1 + L_2 + 2M = 2 + 2 + 2 \times 12 = 28 \text{ H}$$

(iii) Coefficient of coupling, $K = \dfrac{M}{\sqrt{L_1 L_2}} = \dfrac{12}{\sqrt{2 \times 2}} = 6$

4.6 A steel magnetic circuit has an uniform cross-sectional area of 6 cm² and length 60 cm. A coil of 300 turns is wound uniformly over the magnetic circuit. When the current in the coil is 1 A, the total flux is 0.3 mWb and when the current is 5 A, the flux is 0.6 mWb. Calculate the magnetic field strength and relative permeability in each case.

Solution: Given that $a = 6 \text{ cm}^2 = 6 \times 10^{-4} \text{ m}^2$

$$l = 60 \text{ cm} = 0.6, N = 300$$

Case (i): $I = 1 \text{ A}, \Phi = 0.3 \text{ mWb} = 0.3 \times 10^{-3} \text{ Wb}$

Reluctance, $S = \dfrac{NI}{\Phi} = \dfrac{300 \times 1}{0.0003} = 10^6 \text{ AT/Wb}$

Magnetic field strength, $H = \dfrac{NI}{l} = \dfrac{300 \times 1}{0.6} = 500 \text{ AT/m}$

$$S = \frac{l}{\mu_0 \mu_r a}$$

$$\Rightarrow \quad \mu_r = \frac{l}{\mu_0 S a} = \frac{0.6}{10^6 \times 4\pi \times 10^{-7} \times 6 \times 10^{-4}} = 796$$

Case (ii): $I = 5$ A, $\Phi = 0.6$ mWb $= 0.6 \times 10^{-3}$ Wb

$$\text{Reluctance, } S = \frac{NI}{\Phi} = \frac{300 \times 5}{0.0006} = 2.5 \times 10^6 \text{ AT/Wb}$$

$$\text{Magnetic field strength, } H = \frac{NI}{l} = \frac{300 \times 5}{0.6} = 2500 \text{ AT/m}$$

$$S = \frac{l}{\mu_0 \mu_r a}$$

$$\Rightarrow \quad \mu_r = \frac{l}{\mu_0 S a} = \frac{0.6}{2.5 \times 10^6 \times 4\pi \times 10^{-7} \times 6 \times 10^{-4}} = 318.3$$

4.7 A toroid of a 300 mm mean diameter and 650 mm^2 circular cross-section is wound with a wire 1200 turns uniformly. Calculate the (i) inductance, and (ii) EMF induced in the coil when the current is increasing at the rate of 400 A/s.

Solution:

Mean diameter, $D = 300$ mm $= 300 \times 10^{-3}$ m

Mean circumference, $l = \pi D = \pi \times 0.3 = 0.9425$ m

Area of cross-section, $a = 650$ mm$^2 = 650 \times 10^{-6}$ m^2

$N = 1200$

$$\text{Reluctance, } S = \frac{l}{\mu_0 \mu_r a} = \frac{0.9425}{4\pi \times 10^{-7} \times 1 \times 650 \times 10^{-6}} = 1.1538 \times 10^9$$

(i) Self-inductance

$$L = \frac{N^2}{S} = \frac{1200^2}{1.1538 \times 10^9} = 1.248 \text{ mH}$$

(ii) EMF induced in the coil

$$e = L\frac{di}{dt} = 1.248 \times 10^{-3} \times 400 = 0.5 \text{ volts}$$

4.8 An iron ring has a mean diameter of 25 cm and a cross-sectional area of 4 cm^2. It is wound with a coil of 1200 turns. An air gap of 1.5 mm width is cut in the ring. Determine the current required in the coil to produce a flux of 0.48 mWb in the air gap if the relative permeability of the iron under these conditions is 800. Neglect magnetic leakage and fringing.

Solution: Given that Mean diameter, $D = 25$ cm $= 25 \times 10^{-2}$ m

Mean circumference, $l = \pi D = \pi \times 0.25 = 0.7854$ m

Area, $a = 4$ cm$^2 = 4 \times 10^{-4}$ m^2, $N = 1200$

$\Phi = 0.48 \times 10^{-3}$ Wb

$$B = \frac{\Phi}{A} = \frac{0.48 \times 10^{-3}}{4 \times 10^{-4}} = 1.2 \text{ T}$$

Ampere turns for air gap:

$$H = \frac{B}{\mu_0} = \frac{1.2}{4\pi \times 10^{-7}} = 0.955 \times 10^6 \text{ AT/m}$$

Air gap length, $l = 1.5 \times 10^{-3}$ m

$AT_{air} = NI = Hl = 0.955 \times 10^6 \times 1.5 \times 10^{-3} = 1432.4$

Ampere turns for iron ring:

$$H = \frac{B}{\mu_0 \mu_r} = \frac{1.2}{4\pi \times 10^{-7} \times 800} = 1093.66 \text{ AT/m}$$

$l = 0.7854$ m

$AT_{ring} = NI = Hl = 1193.66 \times 0.7854 = 937.5$

Total ampere turns required,

$AT_{total} = AT_{air} + AT_{ring} = 937.5 + 1432.4 = 2370$

$\Rightarrow$ $NI = 2370$

$\Rightarrow$ $$I = \frac{2370}{N} = \frac{2370}{1200} = 1.975$$

4.9 A coil of 1000 turns of wire uniformly wound on a non-magnetic ring of mean diameter 40 cm and cross-sectional area 20 m², calculate the (i) inductance of the coil, (ii) energy stored in the magnetic field when the coil is carrying a current of 15 A, and (iii) emf induced in the coil if this current is completely interrupted in 0.01 second.

Solution: Given that $N = 1000$

Mean diameter, $D = 40$ cm $= 0.4$ m

Length, $l = \pi D = \pi \times 0.4 = 1.2566$ m

Cross-sectional area $= 20$ cm² $= 20 \times 10^{-4}$ m²

(i) The inductance of the coil is

$$L = \frac{N^2}{l} \mu_0 \mu_r a = \frac{1000 \times 1000}{1.2566} \times 4\pi \times 10^{-7} \times 1 \times 20 \times 10^{-4} = 2 \text{ mH}$$

(ii) The energy stored in the magnetic field is

$$W = \frac{1}{2} Li^2 = \frac{1}{2} \times 2 \times 10^{-3} \times 15^2 = 0.225 \text{ J}$$

(iii) The emf induced in the coil is

$$e = L\frac{di}{dt} = 2 \times 10^{-3} \times \frac{15}{0.01} = 3 \text{ V}$$

4.10 A cast steel ring has a mean diameter of 250 mm and a cross-sectional area 250 mm². Calculate the reluctance of the material if the relative permeability of the material is 800. If a flux of 400×10^{-6} Wb is to be set-up in the material, what should be the MMF?

Solution: Given that Mean diameter, $D = 250$ mm $= 0.25$ m

Cross-sectional area, $a = 250$ mm$^2 = 250 \times 10^{-6}$ m^2

$\mu_r = 800$, $\Phi = 400 \times 10^{-6}$ Wb

Mean circumference, $l = \pi D = \pi \times 0.25 = 0.785$ m

$$\text{Reluctance,} = \frac{l}{\mu_0 \mu_r a} = \frac{0.785}{4\pi \times 10^{-7} \times 800 \times 250 \times 10^{-6}} = 3.123 \times 10^6$$

MMF = Reluctance × Flux $= 3.123 \times 10^6 \times 400 \times 10^{-6} = 1249$ AT

4.11 A cast steel structure is made of a rod of square section 2.5 cm × 2.5 cm. What is the current that should be passed in a 500 turn coil in the left limb, so that a flux of 2.5 mWb is made to pass in the right limb? Assume permeability as 750 and neglect leakage.

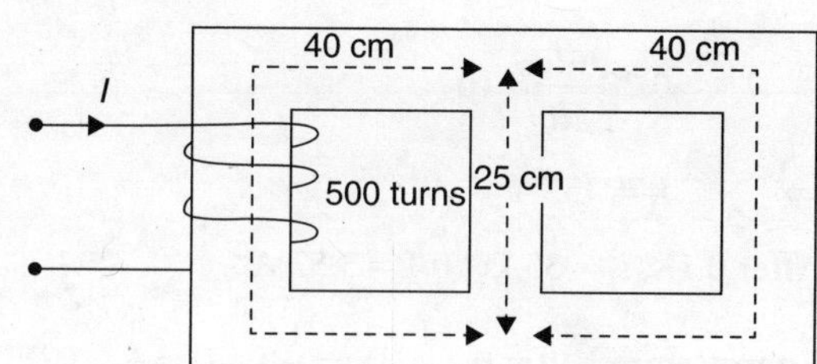

Solution: Given that

Cross-sectional area, $a = 2.5$ cm × 2.5 cm $= 6.25 \times 10^{-4}$ m^2

$N = 500$, $\mu_r = 750$, $\Phi = 2.5 \times 10^{-3}$ Wb

From the figure, length of the total reluctance path, $l = 40$ cm + 40 cm + 25 cm = 105 cm

$$\text{Reluctance, } S = \frac{l}{\mu_0 \mu_r a} = \frac{1.05}{4\pi \times 10^{-7} \times 750 \times 6.25 \times 10^{-4}} = 1.78 \times 10^6 \text{ AT/Wb}$$

$$\text{Reluctance, } S = \frac{\text{MMF}}{\text{Flux}} = \frac{NI}{\Phi}$$

$$\Rightarrow \qquad I = \frac{S\Phi}{N} = \frac{1.78 \times 10^6 \times 2.5 \times 10^{-3}}{500} = 8.91 \text{ A}$$

4.12 In the network, $L_1 = 1$ H, $L_2 = 2$ H, $M = 1.2$ H. Assuming the inductance of coils to be identical, find the amount of energy stored after 0.1 s if the circuit is connected to a DC source of 10 V.

Solution: Given that $L_1 = 1$ H, $L_2 = 2$ H, $M = 1.2$ H

$V_1 = 10$ V (DC voltage)

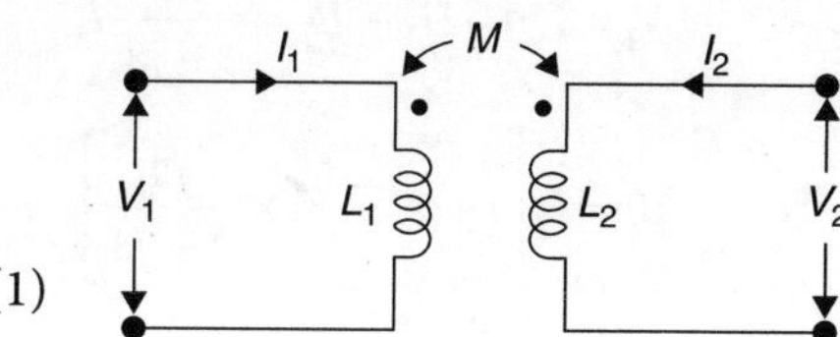

Applying KVL to loop-1

$$10 = L_1 \frac{di_1}{dt} + M \frac{di_2}{dt} \qquad (1)$$

Applying KVL to loop-2

$$0 = M \frac{di_1}{dt} + L_2 \frac{di_2}{dt}$$

$$\Rightarrow \frac{di_2}{dt} = -\frac{M}{L_2} \frac{di_1}{dt} \qquad (2)$$

From Eqs (1) and (2), we have

$$10 = L_1\frac{di_1}{dt} + M\left(-\frac{M}{L_2}\frac{di_1}{dt}\right) = \left(L_1 - \frac{M^2}{L_2}\right)\frac{di_1}{dt} = \left(\frac{L_1L_2 - M^2}{L_2}\right)\frac{di_1}{dt} \quad (3)$$

So, from the above equation, the equivalent inductance is

$$L_{eq} = \frac{L_1L_2 - M^2}{L_2} = \frac{1\times 2 - 1.2^2}{2} = 0.28 \text{ H}$$

From Eq. (3), we have

$$0.28\frac{di_1}{dt} = 10$$

$$\Rightarrow \quad i_1 = 35.7 \text{ t}$$

After 0.1 s, $i_1 = 35.7 \times 0.1 = 3.57$ A

Energy stored after 0.1 s, $W = \frac{1}{2}L_{eq}i_1^2 = \frac{1}{2}\times 0.23 \times 3.57^2 = 1.784$ J

4.13 Solve for the currents I_1 and I_2. Also find the ratio $\frac{V_2}{V_1}$.

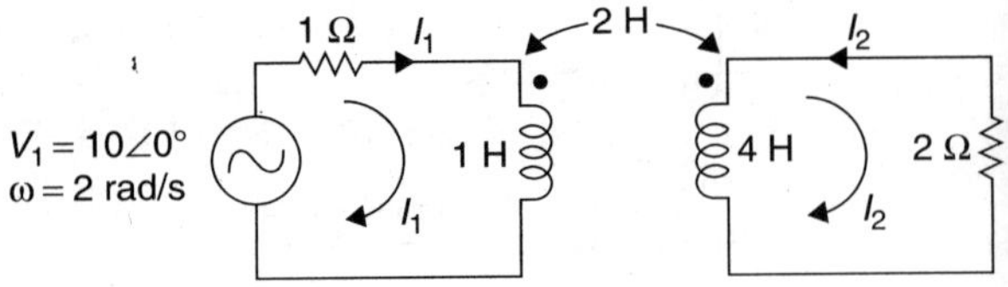

Solution: Applying KVL to loop-1

$$V_1 = I_1 + j2I_1 + j4I_2 = (1 + j2)I_1 + j4I_2 \quad (1)$$

Applying KVL to loop-2

$$0 = 2I_2 + j8I_2 + j4I_1 = j4I_1 + (2 + j8)I_2$$

$$\Rightarrow \quad I_2 = -\frac{j4}{2 + j8}I_1 \quad (2)$$

From the second loop,

$$V_2 = 2I_2 \quad (3)$$

From Eqs (1) and (2), we have

$$V_1 = I_1 + j2I_1 - j4\times\frac{j4}{2 + j8}I_1$$

$$10 = I_1\left[1 + j2 - j4\times\frac{j4}{2 + j8}\right]$$

$$\Rightarrow \quad I_1 = 6.76 - j0.54 = 6.78\ \angle{-4.57°} \text{ A}$$

From Eq. (2), we have

$$\Rightarrow \quad I_2 = -\frac{j4}{2 + j8}\times 6.78\ \angle{-4.57°} = -3.24 - j0.54 = 3.33\ \angle{-170.53°}$$

From Eq. (1), we have

$$V_1 = (1 + j2)I_1 + j4I_2 = (1 + j2)(6.67 - j0.54) + j4(-3.24 - j0.54) = 10\ \angle 0.11°$$

From Eq. (3), we have

$$V_2 = 2I_2 = 2 \times 3.33 \angle{-170.53^\circ} = 6.66 \angle{-170.53^\circ}$$

$$\frac{V_2}{V_1} = \frac{6.66 \angle{-170.53^\circ}}{10 \angle{0.11^\circ}} = 0.66 \angle{-170.64^\circ}$$

4.14 Determine the voltage across the capacitor in the circuit.

Solution: The given circuit diagram can be redrawn as shown below.

Applying KVL to loop-1

$$20\angle 0^\circ = (4 + j4)I_1 - j15(I_1 - I_2) - j2I_2 = (4 - j11)I_1 + j13I_2 \quad (1)$$

Applying KVL to loop-2

$$-20\angle 90^\circ = (4 + j4)I_2 - j15(I_2 - I_1) - j2I_1$$

$$= j13I_1 + (4 - j11)I_2 \quad (2)$$

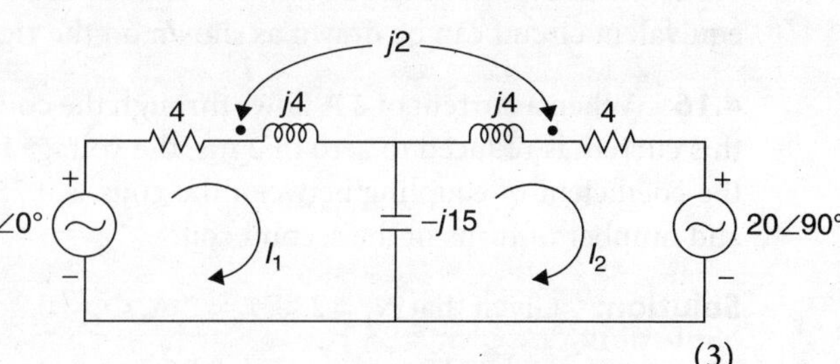

Equations (1) and (2) can be written in matrix form:

$$\begin{bmatrix} 4 - j11 & j13 \\ j13 & 4 - j11 \end{bmatrix} \begin{bmatrix} I_1 \\ I_2 \end{bmatrix} = \begin{bmatrix} 20 \\ -j20 \end{bmatrix}$$

$$\Delta = \begin{vmatrix} 4 - j11 & j13 \\ j13 & 4 - j11 \end{vmatrix} = (4 - j11)^2 - (j13)^2 = 64 - j88 = 108.8 \angle{-54^\circ}$$

$$\Delta_1 = \begin{vmatrix} 20 & j13 \\ -j20 & 4 - j11 \end{vmatrix} = 20\,(4 - j11) + j20 \times j13 = -180 - j220 = 285.25 \angle{-129^\circ}$$

$$\Delta_2 = \begin{vmatrix} 4 - j11 & 20 \\ j13 & -j20 \end{vmatrix} = -\,j20\,(4 - j11) - j13 \times 20 = -220 - j340 = 404.9 \angle{-122.8^\circ}$$

$$I_1 = \frac{\Delta_1}{\Delta} = \frac{285.25 \angle{-129^\circ}}{108.8 \angle{-54^\circ}} = 2.612 \angle{-75.32^\circ}$$

$$I_2 = \frac{\Delta_2}{\Delta} = \frac{404.9 \angle{-122.8^\circ}}{108.8 \angle{-54^\circ}} = 3.72 \angle{-68.92^\circ}$$

Voltage across the capacitor is

$$V_c = -\,j15(I_2 - I_1) = 15\angle{-90^\circ} \times (3.72\angle{-68.92^\circ} - 2.612 \angle{-75.32^\circ}) = 17.49 \angle{-144.56^\circ}$$

4.15 Find the conductively coupled equivalent circuit of the network.

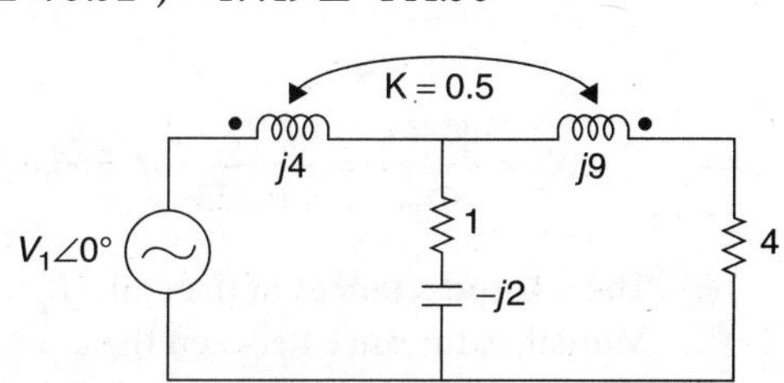

Solution: The given circuit can be redrawn as shown below.

$$X_M = K\sqrt{X_{L1}X_{L2}} = 0.5\sqrt{4 \times 9} = 3$$

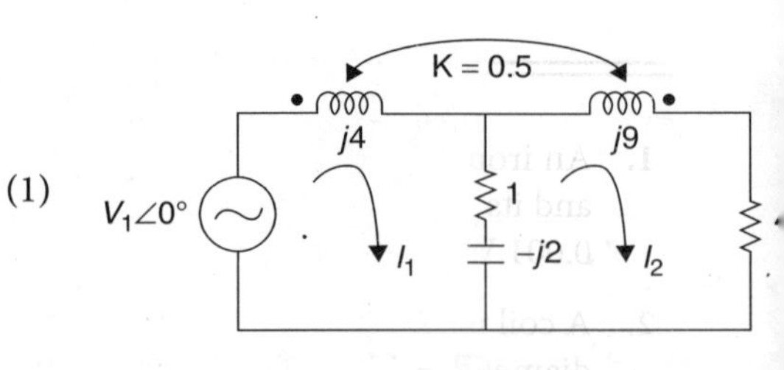

Applying KVL to loop-1

$$V_1 = (j4 + 1 - j2)I_1 + (1 - j2)I_2 - j3I_2$$
$$= (1 + j2)I_1 - (1 + j1)I_2 \quad (1)$$

Applying KVL to loop-2

$$0 = (j9 + 4 - j2 + 1)I_2 - (1 - j2)I_1 - j3I_1$$
$$= -(1 + j1)I_1 + (5 + j7)I_2 \quad (2)$$

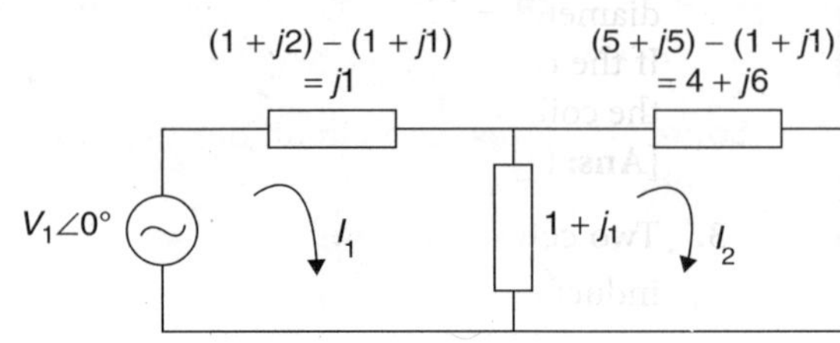

Equations (1) and (2) can be written into matrix form

$$\begin{bmatrix} 1+j2 & -1-j1 \\ -1-j1 & 5+j7 \end{bmatrix}\begin{bmatrix} I_1 \\ I_2 \end{bmatrix} = \begin{bmatrix} V_1 \\ 0 \end{bmatrix} \quad (3)$$

From the above matrix equation, the conductively coupled equivalent circuit can be drawn as shown on the right.

4.16 When a current of 2 A flows through the coil having 250 turns, the flux in the coil is 0.3 m Wb. When this current is reduced to zero in 2 ms, the voltage induced in a coil lying in the vicinity of coil is 63.75 V. If the coefficient of coupling between the coils is 0.75, find self-inductances of two coils, mutual inductance and number of turns in the second coil?

Solution: Given that $N_1 = 250$, $i_1 = 2$ A, $\Phi_1 = 0.3$ mWb

$V_2 = 63.75$ V, $t = 2$ ms, $K = 0.75$

$$L_1 = \frac{N_1\Phi_1}{i_1} = \frac{250 \times 0.3 \times 10^{-3}}{2} = 37.5 \text{ mH}$$

$$K = \frac{\Phi_{12}}{\Phi_1}$$

$$\Rightarrow \quad \Phi_{12} = K\Phi_1 = 0.75 \times 0.3 = 0.225 \text{ mWb}$$

$$V_2 = M\frac{di_1}{dt}$$

$$63.75 = M\frac{2}{2 \times 10^{-3}} \Rightarrow M = 63.75 \text{ mH}$$

$$M = K\sqrt{L_1L_2}$$

$$\Rightarrow \quad L_2 = \frac{M^2}{K^2L_1} = \frac{63.75^2}{0.75^2 \times 37.5} = 192.67 \text{ mH}$$

$$M = \frac{N_2\Phi_{12}}{i_1}$$

$$\Rightarrow \quad N_2 = \frac{M \times i_1}{\Phi_{12}} = \frac{63.75 \times 2}{0.225} = 566.67$$

(i) The self-inductances of the coils, $L_1 = 37.5$ mH and $L_2 = 192.67$ mH
(ii) Mutual inductance between the coils, $M = 63.75$
(iii) Number of turns in the second coil, $N_2 = 567$

EXERCISE PROBLEMS

1. An iron ring with a mean circumference of 400 cm is made from round iron of cross-section 20 cm^2 and its permeability is 500. If it is wound with 400 turns, find the current required to produce a flux of 0.001 Wb. [**Ans:** $I = 7.96$ A]

2. A coil is wound uniformly with 300 turns over a steel ring of relative permeability 900 having a mean diameter of 20 cm. The steel ring is made of a bar having a circular cross-section of diameter 2 cm. If the coil has a resistance of 50 Ω and is connected to a 250 V DC supply, calculate (a) the MMF of the coil, (b) the magnetic field intensity in the ring, (c) reluctance of the magnetic path, (d) total flux. [**Ans:** (a) MMF = 1500 AT (b) $H = 2387$ AT/m (c) $S = 17.684 \times 10^5$ AT/Wb (d) $\Phi = 0.848$ Wb]

3. Two coupled coils of $L_1 = 0.8$ H, and $L_2 = 0.2$ H, have a coupling coefficient $K = 0.9$. Find the mutual inductance M and the turns ratio N_1/N_2. [**Ans:** $M = 0.36$ H, $\frac{N_1}{N_2} = 2$]

4. A core forms a closed magnetic loop with a path length of 32 cm. Half of this path has a cross-sectional area of 2 cm^2 and a relative permeability of 800. The other half has a cross-sectional area of 4 cm^2 and a relative permeability of 400. Find the current required to produce a magnetic flux of 0.4 Wb in the core if it is wound with 1000 turns of insulated wire. Ignore leakage and fringing effects. [**Ans:** $I = 636.8$ A]

5. An iron ring has a mean diameter of 15 cm, a cross-sectional area of 20 cm^2 and a radial gap of 0.5 mm cut in it. It is uniformly wound with 1500 turns of insulated wire and a magnetising current of 1 A produces a flux 1 mWb. Neglecting the effect of magnetic leakage and fringing, calculate (a) reluctance of the magnetic circuit, (b) relative permeability of iron. [**Ans:** (a) $S = 15 \times 10^5$ AT/Wb, (b) $\mu_r = 144$]

6. The hysteresis loop of an iron piece has an area equivalent to 250 J/m^3/cycle. The weight of the iron piece is 12 kg with a specific gravity of 7.16×10^3 kg/m^3 . Determine the loss of energy in kWh in the iron piece in one hour if the frequency of reversal of magnetisation is 50 Hz. [**Ans:** $W_h = 710526$ J (or) 1.974×10^{-3} kWh]

7. In a certain transformer, the hysteresis loss was found to be 160 watts when the maximum flux density was 1.1 Wb/m^2 and the frequency 60 Hz. What will be the loss when the maximum flux density is reduced to 0.9 Wb/m^2 and frequency to 50 Hz? [**Ans:** $P_{h2} = 96.64$ W]

8. A coil wound on an iron core of permeability 400 has 200 turns and a cross-sectional area of 5 cm^2. Calculate the inductance of the coil, if a steady current of 5 mA produces a magnetic field of 10 lines/cm^2 when air is present as the medium. Note: 1 line = 10^{-8} Wb. [**Ans:** $L = 20$ mH]

9. An air-cored solenoid with a diameter of 4 cm and a length of 60 cm is wound with 5000 turns. If a current of 8 A flows in the solenoid, calculate (a) the inductance, (b) the energy stored. [**Ans:** (a) $L = 65.8$ mH, (b) $W = 2.1$ watts]

10. A circuit has 800 turns enclosing a magnetic circuit 20 cm^2 in cross-section. With 5 A, the flux density is 1.2 Wb/m^2 and with 10 A, it is 1.6 Wb/m^2. Find the mean value of inductance between these current limits and the induced emf if the current falls from 10 A to 5 A in 0.05 seconds. [**Ans:** $L = 0.128$ H, $e = 12.8$ V]

11. Two magnetically coupled coils have self-inductances $L_1 = 200$ mH and $L_2 = 800$ mH. If the coefficient of coupling is 0.75, find the value of mutual inductance between the coils. What would be the maximum possible mutual inductance? [**Ans:** $M = 300$ mH, $M_{max} = 400$ mH]

12. An iron ring of cross-sectional area 800 mm^2 and a mean diameter of 340 mm has two windings connected in series, one of 600 turns and the other of 800 turns. If the relative permeability of iron is

1200, find (a) the self-inductance of each coil, (b) mutual inductance, assuming there is no leakage flux. [**Ans:** (a) $L_1 = 0.407$ H, $L_2 = 0.723$ H, (b) $M = 0.5425$ H]

13. Two air-cored coils are placed close to each other so that 80% of the flux of one coil links with the other. Each coil has mean diameter of 2 cm and mean length of 50 cm. If there are 1800 turns of wire on the coil, calculate the number of turns on the other coil to give a mutual inductance of 15 mH.
[**Ans:** $N_2 = 13193$ turns]

14. The combined inductance of two coils connected in series is 0.6 H and 0.1 H depending upon the relative direction of currents in the coil. If one of the coils, when isolated, has a self-inductance of 0.2 H, calculate the mutual inductance of the coil and the self-inductance of the other coil. [**Ans:** $M = 0.125$ H, $L_2 = 0.15$ H]

15. Two coils of self-inductances 3 H and 4 H respectively are connected in series. If the coefficient of coupling between the coils is 0.75, find the inductance of the circuit when the coils are connected in (a) series aiding, (b) series opposing. [**Ans:** (a) 12.2 H, (b) 1.8 H]

16. Two coils of self-inductances 120 mH and 250 mH respectively and mutual inductance of 100 mH are connected in parallel. Determine the equivalent inductances of the combination if (a) mutual flux helps the individual fluxes, (b) mutual flux opposes the individual fluxes. [**Ans:** (a) 117.65 mH, (b) 35.09 mH]

17. When two coils are connected in series their effective inductance is found to be 10 H. When the connection of one coil is reversed, the effective inductance is 6 H. If the coefficient of coupling is 0.6, calculate the self-inductance of each coil and the mutual inductance. [**Ans:** $L_1 = 7.635$ H, $L_2 = 0.365$ H, $M = 1$ H]

18. Two identical coils, when connected in series, have total inductance of 10 H and 6 H depending upon their method of connection. Find (a) self-inductance of the coils, (b) mutual inductance between the coils. [**Ans:** (a) $L_1 = L_2 = 4$ H, (b) $M = 1$ H]

19. A non-magnetic ring with a mean diameter of 30 cm and a cross-sectional area of 4 cm^2 is uniformly wound with two coils A and B one over the other. A has 100 turns and B has 250 turns. Calculate the mutual inductance between the coils. Also, calculate the emf induced in B when a current of 6 A is reversed in 0.02 s. [**Ans:** $M_{AB} = 0.0133$ mH, $E_B = 7.98$ mV]

20. Two coupled coils with $L_1 = 0.03$ H, $L_2 = 0.02$ H and $K = 0.6$ are connected in four different ways—series aiding, series opposing and parallel with both the arrangements of the winding sense. What are the four equal inductances? [**Ans:** 0.079 H, 0.0208 H, 0.0185 H, 0.004884 H]

REVIEW QUESTIONS

1. Compare magnetic and electric circuits.
2. What are coupled circuits?
3. Define (a) self-inductance, (b) self-induced emf, (c) mutual inductance, (d) mutual induced emf, (e) coefficient of coupling.
4. Why does the coefficient of coupling lie between 0 and 1?
5. Write the expression for equivalent inductance of a series connected magnetically coupled coils.
6. Write the expression for equivalent inductance of a parallel connected magnetically coupled coils.
7. Derive the formula for mutual inductance in terms of coefficient of coupling and self-inductance.
8. What is DOT convention?
9. State the dot rule for coupled coils and explain its significance.

10. Two perfectly coupled coils each of 1 H self-inductance are connected in parallel so as to aid each other. Calculate the effective inductance.
11. What is mutual inductance? Derive an expression for the mutual inductance between two magnetically coupled coils having self-inductances L_1 and L_2 respectively.
12. What is an ideal transformer? Explain its operation.

MULTIPLE CHOICE QUESTIONS

1. In case of ideal coupling, the coefficient of coupling is
(a) 1 (b) 0
(c) infinity (d) can't say

2. The maximum value of coefficient of coupling is
(a) 1 (b) 0
(c) infinity (d) can't say

3. The maximum possible mutual inductance of two inductively coupled coils with self-inductance $L_1 = 9$ mH, $L_2 = 16$ mH is
(a) 25 mH (b) 7 mH
(c) 12 mH (d) 24 mH

4. Two coils are connected in series aiding with $L_1 = 4$ H, having an equivalent inductance of 10 H. If the mutual inductance between the coils is 2 H, then L_2 is
(a) 2 H (b) 7 H
(c) 14 H (d) 2 H

5. The mutual inductance between two coupled coils is 40 mH. If the turns in one coil are doubled and that in other are halved, then the mutual inductance will be
(a) 20 mH (b) 10 mH
(c) 40 mH (d) 5 mH

6. Dot convention in the coupled circuit is used
(a) to measure the mutual inductance
(b) to determine the polarity of the mutually induced voltage in the coils
(c) to determine the polarity of the self induced voltage in the coils
(d) none of the above

7. If two perfectly coupled coils each of 1 H self-inductance are connected in parallel so as to oppose each other, then the overall inductance is
(a) 2 H (b) 1 H
(c) 0.5 H (d) 0 H

8. If the number of turns of a coil is increased, its inductance
(a) remains the same (b) is increased
(c) is decreased (d) none of the above

9. A circuit has an inductance of 4 H and the current through it changes at the rate of 10 A/s, then the self-induced emf is
(a) 20 V (b) 40 V
(c) 60 V (d) none of the above

10. If a current of 4 A through a coil sets up a magnetic flux linkage of 12Wb-turn, then the inductance of the coil is
(a) 2 H (b) 3 H
(c) 48 H (d) 8 H

11. If the coefficient of coupling between two coils increased, then the mutual inductance between the coils
(a) remains the same (b) is increased
(c) is decreased (d) none of the above

12. The mutual inductance between two coils, each of N turns, is M. If a current I in the first coil is brought to zero in a time t, then the emf induced in the second coil is
(a) $\frac{MNi}{t}$ (b) $\frac{Mi}{t}$
(c) $\frac{Mt}{iN}$, (d) $\frac{MNt}{i}$

13. The reluctance of the magnetic circuit depends upon
(a) current in the coil
(b) number of turns in the coil
(c) length of the conductor
(d) all of the above

14. Two coupled coils with $L_1 = L_2 = 0.6$ H have a coupling coefficient of 0.8, then the turns ratio N_1/N_2 is
(a) 2 (b) 4
(c) 1 (d) 0.5

15. Given two coupled inductors L_1 and L_2 and their mutual inductance M satisfies
(a) $M=\sqrt{L_1^2+L_2^2}$ (b) $M>\frac{L_1+L_2}{2}$
(c) $M>\sqrt{L_1L_2}$ (d) $M\le\sqrt{L_1L_2}$

16. When two coils connected in series aiding the equivalent inductance is L_1, in series opposing L_2, then the mutual inductance between the two coils is
(a) $\frac{L_1+L_2}{2}$ (b) $\frac{L_1-L_2}{2}$
(c) $\frac{L_1+L_2}{4}$ (d) $\frac{L_1-L_2}{4}$

17. The effective inductance of the circuit shown is:

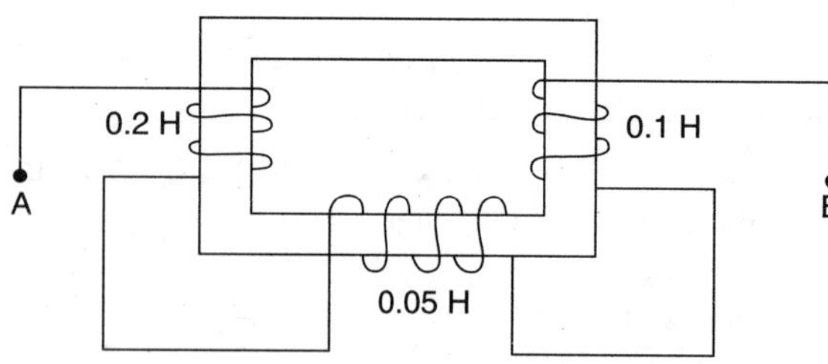

(a) 0.2386 H (b) 1 H
(c) 1.5 H (d) 0.66 H

18. The equivalent inductive reactance for the circuit shown is:

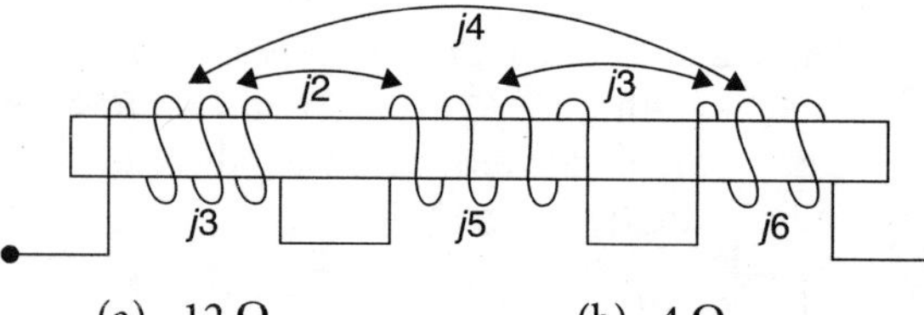

(a) 12 Ω (b) 4 Ω
(c) 10 Ω (d) 25 Ω

19. Mutual inductance is a property associated with
(a) only one coil
(b) two or more coils
(c) two or more coils with magnetic coupling
(d) none of the above

20. A transformer works on the principle of
(a) Faraday's law of electromagnetic induction
(b) Lenz's law
(c) Fleming's law
(d) Coloumb's law

21. The equivalent reactance of the coupled circuit is:

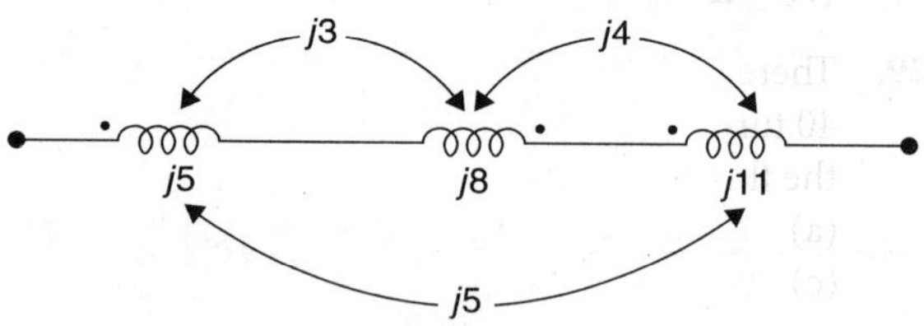

(a) 12 Ω (b) 20 Ω
(c) 10 Ω (d) 25 Ω

22. If the air gap in a magnetic circuit is 1.5 mm long and 2500 mm^2 in cross-sectional area, then the reluctance of the air gap is
(a) 7.5×10^5 AT/m (b) 4.77×10^5 AT/m
(c) 1.77×10^5 AT/m (d) none of the above

23. When the speed at which a conductor is moved through a magnetic field is increased, the induced voltage
(a) increases (b) decreases
(c) remains constant (d) reaches zero

24. The induced voltage across a coil with 250 turns that is located in a magnetic field that is changing at a rate of 8 Wb/s is
(a) 1000 V (b) 2000 V
(c) 3000 V (d) 4000 V

25. For a given wire wound core, an increase in current through the coil
(a) reverses the flux lines
(b) decreases the flux density
(c) increases the flux density
(d) causes no change in flux density

26. If the cross-sectional area of a magnetic field increases, but the flux remains the same, the flux density
(a) increases (b) decreases
(c) remains same (d) doubles

27. When the current through the coil of an electromagnet reverses, the
(a) direction of the magnetic field reverses
(b) magnetic field collapses
(c) magnetic field expands
(d) direction of the magnetic field remains unchanged

28. The unit for reluctance is
(a) tesla (b) AT
(c) AT/m (d) AT/Wb

29. There is 900 mA of current through a wire with 40 turns. What is the reluctance of the circuit if the flux is 400 μWb?
(a) 14,400 AT/Wb (b) 1,440 AT/Wb
(c) 90,000 AT/Wb (d) 9,000 AT/Wb

30. The unit for permeability is
(a) Wb/AT-m (b) AT
(c) AT/m (d) AT/Wb

31. What is the magneto-motive force in a 75-turn coil of wire when there is 4 A of current through it?
(a) 150 AT (b) 300 AT
(c) 450 AT (d) 600 AT

32. The direction of a magnetic field within a magnet is
(a) from south to north
(b) from north to south
(c) back to front
(d) front to back

33. The ability of a material to remain magnetised after removal of the magnetising force is known as
(a) permeability (b) reluctance
(c) hysteresis (d) retentivity

34. The induced voltage across a stationary conductor in a stationary magnetic field is
(a) zero (b) reversed in polarity
(c) increased (d) decreased

35. An electromagnetic field exists only when there is
(a) an increasing current
(b) decreasing current
(c) voltage
(d) current

Answers

1. a	**2.** a	**3.** c	**4.** b	**5.** c	**6.** b	**7.** c	**8.** b	**9.** b	**10.** b
11. b	**12.** b	**13.** d	**14.** c	**15.** d	**16.** d	**17.** a	**18.** a	**19.** c	**20.** a
21. b	**22.** b	**23.** a	**24.** b	**25.** c	**26.** b	**27.** a	**28.** d	**29.** c	**30.** a
31. b	**32.** a	**33.** d	**34.** a	**35.** d					

5 Resonance and Locus Diagrams

Learning Outcomes

After reading this chapter, the reader will able to

- Explain the phenomenon of resonance
- Define resonant frequency, quality factor, bandwidth and selectivity
- Define voltage and current magnification in resonant circuits
- Outline the relation between f_0, f_1 and f_2
- Outline the relation between quality factor and selectivity
- Define dynamic impedance
- Outline the resonant frequency for different circuits
- Compare series and parallel resonant circuits
- Develop locus diagrams for series *RL* and *RC* circuits
- Exemplify the applications of resonance in real life

5.1 INTRODUCTION

Resonance is a particular type of phenomenon inherently found in every kind of system—electrical, mechanical, optical, acoustic and even atomic. Usually resonance occurs in any of these systems, when energy storage elements interchange exactly equal amounts of energy. Resonance cannot take place when only one type of energy storing element is present such as an inductance or a mass. There must be two types of independent energy storing elements capable of interchanging energy between one another – inductance and capacitance in electrical systems and mass and spring in mechanical systems – to get resonance.

In simple terms, resonance may be described as the condition existing in any physical system when a fixed amplitude sinusoidal forcing function produces a response of maximum amplitude. The most frequently used definition of resonance in electrical systems is: the steady state operation of a circuit or a system at that frequency for which the resultant response is in time phase with the forcing function, despite the presence of energy storage elements. Resonance is a phenomenon which enables us to discriminate between different frequencies. Using resonant circuits, it is possible to select a particular frequency from a band of frequencies.

5.2 SERIES RESONANCE

Consider an *RLC* series (Fig. 5.1) connected to a single phase variable frequency (f) supply. The total impedance of the circuit is

$$Z = R + j(X_L - X_C) = R + j\left(\omega L - \frac{1}{\omega C}\right) \tag{5.1}$$

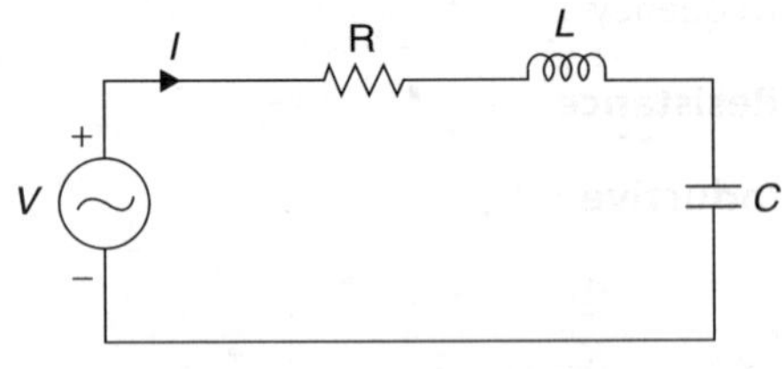

Fig. 5.1 *RLC* series circuit

The circuit is said to be under resonance, when the applied voltage V and the resulting current I are in phase. Thus a series *RLC* circuit under resonance behaves like a pure resistive network and the net reactance of the circuit should be zero.

So, at resonance condition

$$X_L - X_C = 0$$

$$\Rightarrow \qquad \omega_0 L = \frac{1}{\omega_0 C}$$

$$\Rightarrow \qquad \omega_0^2 = \frac{1}{LC}$$

$$\Rightarrow \qquad \omega_0 = \frac{1}{\sqrt{LC}}$$

$$\Rightarrow \qquad f_0 = \frac{1}{2\pi\sqrt{LC}} \tag{5.2}$$

Here f_0 is called the resonant frequency of the circuit. At $f = f_0$, the total impedance of the circuit is $Z = R$. Since the net reactance is zero, the impedance is minimum. The power factor is unity (p.f $= \cos\phi = R/Z = R/R = 1$).

At $f > f_0$, the net reactance is inductive and hence the power factor of the circuit is lagging. At $f < f_0$, the net reactance is capacitive and hence the power factor of the circuit is leading.

Resonant frequency, f_0 It is the frequency at which the inductive and capacitive reactances in the circuit are exactly equal.

Conditions at resonance in a series RLC circuit

- It behaves like a purely resistive circuit since net reactance is equal to zero.
- Inductive reactance and capacitive reactances are exactly equal, that is, the *j* component of the impedance is equal to zero.
- Impedance is minimum and equal to $Z = R$.
- Current is maximum, $I_0 = \frac{V}{R}$.
- The applied voltage and current are in phase and the power factor of the circuit is unity.
- Voltage across the inductor is equal to voltage across the capacitor, $V_L = V_C$.

5.3 CHARACTERISTICS OF A SERIES RESONANT CIRCUIT

The impedance of an RLC series circuit is given by

$$Z = R + j(X_L - X_C) = R + j\left(\omega L - \frac{1}{\omega C}\right)$$

From the above equation, we see that only the imaginary part of the impedance is a function of frequency. The components Z, R, X_L and X_C, and how they vary with frequency are shown in Fig. 5.2.

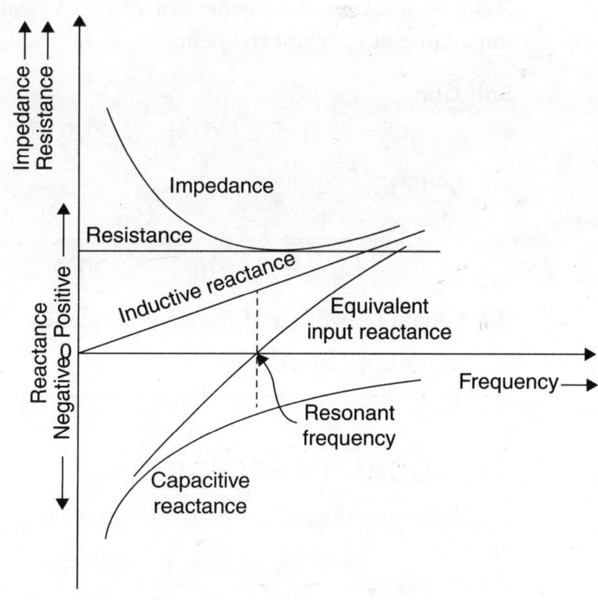

Fig. 5.2 Behaviour of *R*, *L*, *C* and *Z* with frequency

Resistance (*R*) It is independent of frequency.

Inductive reactance (X_L)

$$X_L = \omega L = 2\pi f L$$

$$\Rightarrow \qquad X_L \propto f$$

Inductive reactance is directly proportional to frequency and is positive.

Capacitive reactance (X_C)

$$X_C = \frac{1}{\omega C} = \frac{1}{2\pi f C}$$

$$\Rightarrow \qquad X_C \propto \frac{1}{f}$$

Capacitive reactance is inversely proportional to frequency and is negative.

When the frequency of the source is varied keeping the voltage constant, the inductive reactance varies in a directly proportional manner to the frequency and the capacitive reactance varies inversely with the frequency (Fig. 5.2). At a particular frequency f_0, X_L and X_C are equal and since they are opposite in sign, they cancel each other. The resultant impedance at this frequency is purely resistive and is equal to R.

Net reactance, ($X = X_L - X_C$) It is initially negative, becomes zero and then it becomes positive.

For $f < f_0$, it is capacitive, for $f = f_0$ it is zero and for $f > f_0$, it is inductive.

Impedance (Z) The impedance of an RLC series circuit is given by

$$Z = R + j(X_L - X_C) = \sqrt{R^2 + (X_L - X_C)^2}$$

$$= \sqrt{R^2 + \left(\omega L - \frac{1}{\omega C}\right)^2}$$

If $f < f_0$ then $X_C > X_L$, if $f > f_0$ then $X_C < X_L$.

Current, (I) Since the impedance of the RLC series circuit varies with frequency (Fig. 5.3), the current in the circuit changes accordingly. As the frequency is varied from 0 to ∞ the current increases from 0 to maximum value given by I_{max} at $f = f_0$ and then decreases to zero as $f \to \infty$.

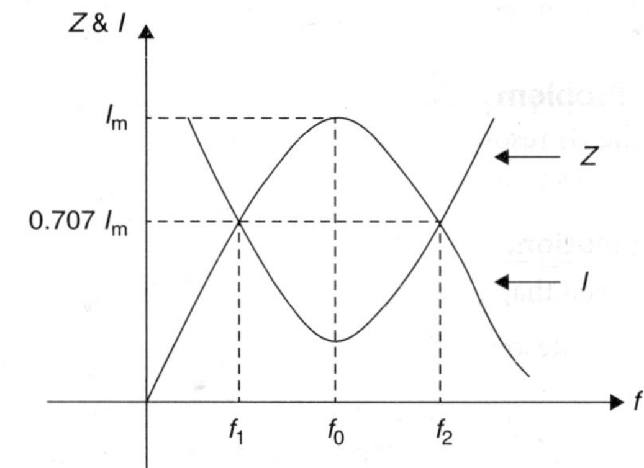

Fig. 5.3 Response of series *RLC* circuit

Problem 5.1 A coil with resistance $R = 80\ \Omega$ and inductance $L = 100$ mH is connected in series with a 500 μF capacitor and a generator of 200 V source. Determine the (i) resonant frequency and (ii) circuit impedance at resonant frequency.

Solution:

Given that $R = 80\ \Omega$, $L = 100$ mH, $C = 500\ \mu$F

(i) Resonant frequency

$$f_0 = \frac{1}{2\pi\sqrt{LC}} = \frac{1}{2\pi\sqrt{0.1 \times 5 \times 10^{-4}}} = 22.5 \text{ Hz}$$

(ii) Circuit impedance at resonant frequency

$$Z = R = 80\ \Omega$$

5.4 QUALITY FACTOR

It is defined as the ratio of either inductive or capacitive reactive power to average power

$$\therefore \qquad Q = \frac{\text{Inductive reactive power}}{\text{Average power}}$$

That is, $$Q = \frac{I^2 X_L}{I^2 R} = \frac{X_L}{R} = \frac{\omega_0 L}{R} \tag{5.3}$$

or $$Q = \frac{\text{Capacitive reactive power}}{\text{Average power}}$$

That is, $$Q = \frac{I^2 X_C}{I^2 R} = \frac{X_C}{R} = \frac{1}{\omega_0 CR} \tag{5.4}$$

$$\Rightarrow \quad Q = \frac{\omega_0 L}{R} = \frac{1}{\sqrt{LC}} \times \frac{L}{R} = \frac{1}{R}\sqrt{\frac{L}{C}} \tag{5.5}$$

It can be observed that, to improve the quality factor (Q) of a coil, it must be designed to have its resistance R, as low as possible. This also results in reduction of bandwidth and losses (for the same value of current).

Problem 5.2 A 40 μF capacitor is connected in series with a coil whose inductance is 8 mH. Determine the (i) resonant frequency, (ii) resistance of the coil if a 100 V source operating at the resonant frequency causes a circuit current of 5.6 A and (iii) quality factor of the coil.

Solution:

Given that $L = 8$ mH, $C = 40$ μF, $V = 100$ V, $I_m = 5.6$ A

(i) Resonant frequency

$$f_0 = \frac{1}{2\pi\sqrt{LC}} = \frac{1}{2\pi\sqrt{40 \times 8 \times 10^{-9}}} = 281.5 \text{ Hz}$$

(ii) $V = 100$ V, $I_m = 5.6$ A

$$\text{Resistance of the coil, } R = \frac{V}{I_m} = \frac{100}{5.6} = 17.86\ \Omega$$

(iii) Quality factor of the coil

$$Q = \frac{\omega_0 L}{R} = \frac{2\pi \times 281.4 \times 8 \times 10^{-3}}{17.86} = 0.8$$

Problem 5.3 A circuit has a resistance of 5 Ω, an inductance of 0.4 H and a variable capacitance in series connected across a 110 V, 50 Hz supply. Calculate the (i) value of capacitance to given resonance, (ii) current flowing through the circuit, (iii) voltage across the inductor, (iv) voltage across the capacitor, and (v) quality factor of the circuit.

Solution:

Given that $R = 5\ \Omega$, $L = 0.4$ H, $V = 110$ volts, $f_0 = 50$ Hz

(i) Value of capacitance to given resonance

$$f_0 = \frac{1}{2\pi\sqrt{LC}}$$

$$\Rightarrow C = \frac{1}{4\pi^2 f_0^2 L} = \frac{1}{4\pi^2 \times 50^2 \times 0.4} = 25.3\ \mu\text{F}$$

(ii) Current flowing through the circuit

$$I_0 = \frac{V}{R} = \frac{110}{5} = 22 \text{ A}$$

(iii) Voltage across the inductor

$$V_L = I_0 \times X_L = I_0 \times 2\pi \times f_0 \times L = 22 \times 2\pi \times 50 \times 0.4 = 2763.4 \text{ V}$$

(iv) Voltage across the capacitor

$$V_C = I_0 X_C = I_0 \times \frac{1}{\omega_0 C} = 22 \times \frac{1}{2\pi \times 50 \times 25.3 \times 10^{-6}} = 2763.4 \text{ V}$$

(v) Quality factor of the circuit

$$Q = \frac{\omega_0 L}{R} = \frac{2\pi \times 50 \times 0.4}{5} = 25.12$$

5.5 BAND WIDTH

It is defined as the band of frequencies which lies between two specified points where power falls to half of its maximum value and current falls to $1/\sqrt{2}$ times of its maximum value.

Bandwidth is given by

$$\Delta\omega = (\omega_2 - \omega_1) \text{ rad/s}$$

Or $$\Delta f = (f_2 - f_1) \text{ Hz}$$

where f_1 is called lower cut-off frequency and f_2 is called upper cut-off frequency, P_1 and P_2 are half-power points.

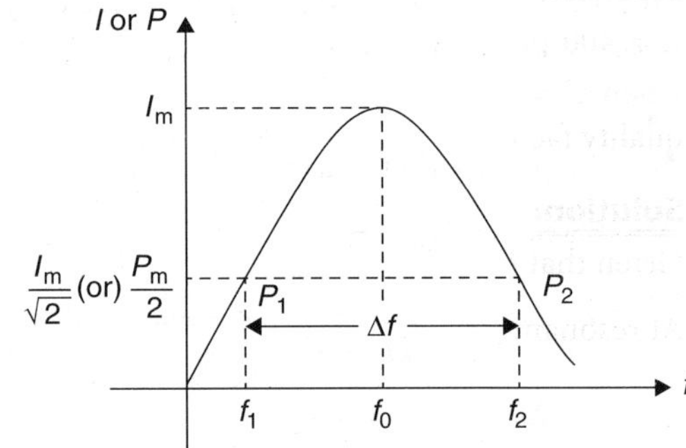

Fig. 5.4 Identification of bandwidth

Half-power frequencies The two frequencies at which the power is half of the maximum power at resonance are called half-power frequencies. The half-power frequency which is greater than resonant frequency is called the *upper half-power frequency* (f_2) and that which is less than resonant frequency is called the *lower half-power frequency* (f_1).

5.6 SELECTIVITY

Selectivity is the ability of a tuned circuit or receiver to accept the frequency to which it is tuned and reject all other frequencies. It is also defined as the ratio of resonant frequency to bandwidth.

$$\text{Selectivity} = \frac{\omega_0}{\Delta\omega} \quad \text{or} \quad \frac{f_0}{\Delta f} = Q$$

$$\Rightarrow \quad \text{selectivity} = Q = \frac{f_0}{\Delta f} \qquad (5.6)$$

This shows that the higher the Q, better the selectivity.

5.7 VOLTAGE MAGNIFICATION

In the case of series resonant circuit, voltage magnification takes place. If we assume that the voltage applied to the series *RLC* circuit is *V*, and the current at resonance is *I*, then the voltage across the inductor is

$$V_L = IX_L = \frac{V}{R} \times \omega_0 L = V\,\frac{\omega_0 L}{R} = VQ$$

Similarly, the voltage across the capacitor is

$$V_C = IX_C = \frac{V}{R} \times \frac{1}{\omega_0 C} = V\,\frac{1}{\omega_0 CR} = VQ$$

That is, the ratio of voltage across either L or C to the applied voltage at resonance can be defined as magnification.

$$\text{Magnification, } Q = \frac{V_L}{V} = \frac{V_C}{V} \tag{5.7}$$

Problem 5.4 A constant voltage of frequency, 1 MHz is applied to a lossy inductor (R in series with L), in series with a variable capacitor, C (as shown). The current drawn is maximum, when $C = 400$ pF; while current is reduced to $1/\sqrt{2}$ of the above value when $C = 450$ pF. Find the values of R and L. Calculate also the quality factor of the coil and the bandwidth.

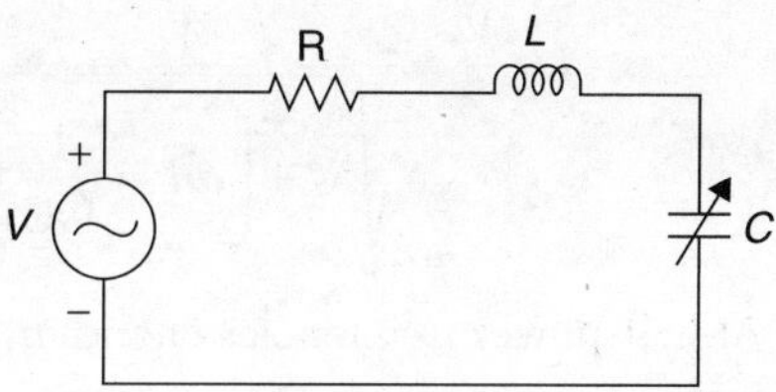

Solution:

Given that $f = 1$ MHz $= 10^6$ Hz, $C = 400$ pF $= 400 \times 10^{-12}$ F

At resonance

$$X_L = X_C = \frac{1}{2\pi fC} = \frac{1}{2\pi \times 10^6 \times 400 \times 10^{-12}} = 398\ \Omega$$

$$X_L = 2\pi \times f \times L = 398\ \Omega \quad \Rightarrow \quad L = \frac{398}{2\pi \times 10^6} = 63.34\ \mu\text{H}$$

$$C_1 = 450\ \text{pF},\ X_{C1} = \frac{1}{2\pi \times 10^6 \times 450 \times 10^{-12}} = 353.7\ \Omega$$

$$Z\angle\phi = R + j(X_L - X_{C1}) = R + j(398.0 - 353.7) = (R + j44.3)\ \Omega$$

$$I = \frac{I_{max}}{\sqrt{2}} = \frac{V}{\sqrt{2} \cdot R} = \frac{V}{Z} = \frac{V}{\sqrt{R^2 + (44.3)^2}}$$

From the above, $\sqrt{2} \cdot R = \sqrt{R^2 + (44.3)^2}$ or $2R^2 = R^2 + (44.3)^2$

Or $\quad R = 44.3\ \Omega$

$$\text{Quality factor, } Q = \frac{X_L}{R} = \frac{398}{44.3} = 8.984$$

$$\text{Bandwidth, } \Delta f = f_2 - f_1 = \frac{R}{2\pi L}$$

$$= \frac{44.3}{2\pi \times 63.34 \times 10^{-6}} = \frac{44.3}{398 \times 10^{-6}} = 0.1113 \times 10^6 = 0.1113\ \text{MHz}$$

5.8 IMPORTANT RELATIONS IN SERIES RESONANCE

(a) $Q = \dfrac{\omega_0}{\Delta\omega}$ or $\dfrac{f_0}{\Delta f}$

(b) $\omega_0 = \sqrt{\omega_1 \omega_2}$ or $f_0 = \sqrt{f_1 f_2}$

The impedance of a series circuit is given by

$$Z = \sqrt{R^2 + (X_L - X_C)^2} = \sqrt{R^2 + \left(\omega L - \frac{1}{\omega C}\right)^2}$$

Therefore, the current drawn by the circuit is

$$I = \frac{V}{Z} = \frac{V}{\sqrt{R^2 + \left(\omega L - \frac{1}{\omega C}\right)^2}} \tag{5.8}$$

At half-power frequencies ω_1 and ω_2

$$I = \frac{I_0}{\sqrt{2}} = \frac{V}{\sqrt{2}R} \tag{5.9}$$

From Eqs 5.8 and 5, 9,

$$\frac{V}{\sqrt{2}R} = \frac{V}{\sqrt{R^2 + \left(\omega L - \frac{1}{\omega C}\right)^2}}$$

$$\Rightarrow \quad R^2 + \left(\omega L - \frac{1}{\omega C}\right)^2 = 2R^2$$

$$\Rightarrow \quad \omega L - \frac{1}{\omega C} = \pm R$$

$$\therefore \quad \omega_2 L - \frac{1}{\omega_2 C} = R \tag{5.10}$$

$$\omega_1 L - \frac{1}{\omega_1 C} = -R \tag{5.11}$$

By adding Eqs 5.10 and 5.11,

$$(\omega_1 + \omega_2) L - \left(\frac{1}{\omega_1} + \frac{1}{\omega_2}\right)\frac{1}{C} = 0$$

$$\Rightarrow \quad \omega_1 \omega_2 = \frac{1}{LC} = \omega_0^2$$

$$\Rightarrow \quad \omega_0 = \sqrt{\omega_1 \omega_2} \text{ or } f_0 = \sqrt{f_1 f_2} \tag{5.12}$$

This shows that the resonant frequency is the geometric mean of two half-power frequencies.

By subtracting Eq. 5.11 from Eq. 5.10,

$$(\omega_2 - \omega_1)L + \left(\frac{1}{\omega_1} - \frac{1}{\omega_2}\right)\frac{1}{C} = 2R$$

$$\Rightarrow \quad (\omega_2 - \omega_1) + \left(\frac{\omega_2 - \omega_1}{\omega_2\omega_1}\right)\frac{1}{LC} = \frac{2R}{L}$$

$$\Rightarrow \quad (\omega_2 - \omega_1)\left[1 + \left(\frac{1}{\omega_2\omega_1}\right)\frac{1}{LC}\right] = \frac{2R}{L}$$

$$\Rightarrow \quad (\omega_2 - \omega_1)\left[1 + \left(\frac{\omega_0^2}{\omega_2\omega_1}\right)\right] = \frac{2R}{L}$$

$$\Rightarrow \quad (\omega_2 - \omega_1)[1 + 1] = \frac{2R}{L}$$

$$\Rightarrow \quad (\omega_2 - \omega_1) = \Delta\omega = \frac{R}{L}$$

$$\Rightarrow \quad (f_2 - f_1) = \Delta f = \frac{R}{2\pi L} \tag{5.13}$$

But $$Q = \frac{\omega_0 L}{R} \Rightarrow \frac{R}{L} = \frac{\omega_0}{Q} \tag{5.14}$$

From Eqs 5.13 and 5.14,

$$\Delta\omega = \frac{\omega_0}{Q} \Rightarrow Q = \frac{\omega_0}{\Delta\omega} \text{ or } Q = \frac{f_0}{\Delta f} \tag{5.15}$$

Hence, the quality factor is the ratio of the resonant frequency and the bandwidth of the circuit.

5.9 FREQUENCIES AT WHICH V_C AND V_L ARE MAXIMUM

Note that V_C and V_L are not maximum at the resonant frequency in the case of series resonance, but they are maximum at some other frequency value. This can be obtained as follows:

Voltage across the capacitor,

$$V_C = IX_C = \frac{V}{\sqrt{R^2 + (X_L - X_C)^2}} X_C = \frac{V}{\sqrt{R^2 + \left(\omega L - \frac{1}{\omega C}\right)^2}} \times \frac{1}{\omega C}$$

$$V_C^2 = \frac{V^2}{\omega^2 C^2 \left[R^2 + \frac{(\omega^2 LC - 1)^2}{\omega^2 C^2}\right]}$$

$$V_C^2 = \frac{V^2}{\omega^2 C^2 R^2 + (\omega^2 LC - 1)^2} \tag{5.16}$$

The frequency at which V_C is maximum can be obtained by differentiating V_C and equating the first derivative to zero. We would differentiate V_C^2 here and proceed as follows:

$$\frac{dV_C^2}{d\omega}=0 \;\Rightarrow\; -V^2\left[\frac{2\omega_0 C^2R^2+2(\omega_0^2LC-1)2\omega_0 LC}{\left[\omega_0^2C^2R^2+(\omega_0^2LC-1)^2\right]^2}\right]=0$$

$$\Rightarrow \qquad 2\omega_0 C^2R^2+2(\omega_0^2LC-1)\,2\omega_0 LC=0$$

$$\Rightarrow \qquad 2\omega_0^2L^2C-2L+CR^2=0$$

$$\Rightarrow \qquad 2\omega_0^2L^2C=2L-CR^2$$

$$\Rightarrow \qquad \omega_0^2=\frac{2L}{2L^2C}-\frac{CR^2}{2L^2C}=\frac{1}{LC}-\frac{R^2}{2L^2}$$

$$\Rightarrow \qquad \omega_0=\sqrt{\frac{1}{LC}-\frac{R^2}{2L^2}}$$

$$\Rightarrow \qquad f_0=\frac{1}{2\pi}\sqrt{\frac{1}{LC}-\frac{R^2}{2L^2}} \tag{5.17}$$

To find the frequency at which V_L is maximum we proceed in the same manner.

Voltage across the inductor,

$$V_L=IX_L=\frac{V}{\sqrt{R^2+\left(\omega L-\dfrac{1}{\omega C}\right)^2}}\,\omega L$$

$$V_L^2=\frac{V^2\omega^2L^2}{R^2+\left(\omega L-\dfrac{1}{\omega C}\right)^2}=\frac{V^2\omega^4L^2C^2}{\omega^2C^2R^2+(\omega^2LC-1)^2} \tag{5.18}$$

By differentiating V_L^2 with respect to ω and setting $\frac{dV_L^2}{d\omega}=0$

$$2\omega_0^2LC-\omega_0^2C^2R^2-2=0$$

$$\Rightarrow \qquad \omega_0^2(2LC-C^2R^2)=2$$

$$\Rightarrow \qquad \omega_0^2=\frac{2}{2LC-C^2R^2}$$

$$\Rightarrow \qquad \omega_0=\frac{1}{\sqrt{LC-\dfrac{C^2R^2}{2}}}$$

$$\Rightarrow \qquad f_0=\frac{1}{2\pi\sqrt{LC-\dfrac{C^2R^2}{2}}} \tag{5.19}$$

5.10 RELATION BETWEEN f_1, f_2 AND BANDWIDTH IN TERMS OF f_0

We know that Bandwidth $= f_2 - f_1 = \dfrac{R}{2\pi L}$ (5.20)

and $f_0^2 = f_1 f_2$ (5.21)

$$\Rightarrow \quad f_2 = \frac{f_0^2}{f_1} \tag{5.22}$$

From Eqs 5.20 and 5.22, Bandwidth $(BW) = \dfrac{f_0^2}{f_1} - f_1$

$$\Rightarrow \quad f_1^2 + f_1 BW - f_0^2 = 0$$

$$\Rightarrow \quad f_1 = \frac{-BW \pm \sqrt{(BW)^2 + 4f_0^2}}{2}$$

By neglecting the negative sign, we have

$$f_1 = \frac{-BW}{2} + \sqrt{\frac{(BW)^2}{4} + f_0^2} \tag{5.23}$$

However, as $\frac{(BW)^2}{4}$ is so small, it can be neglected

$$\therefore \quad f_1 = \frac{-BW}{2} + f_0$$

$$\Rightarrow \quad f_1 = f_0 - \frac{BW}{2} \tag{5.24}$$

Similarly $f_2 = f_0 + \dfrac{BW}{2}$ (5.25)

Problem 5.5 A 220 V, 100 Hz AC source supplies a series RLC circuit with a capacitor and a coil. If the coil has 50 mΩ resistance and 5 mH inductance, what is the value of capacitor at a resonance frequency of 100 Hz? Also calculate the Q-factor and half-power frequencies of the circuit.

Solution:

Given that $V = 220$ V, $f_0 = 100$ Hz

$R = 50\ \text{m}\Omega = 50 \times 10^{-3}\ \Omega$, $L = 5\ \text{mH} = 5 \times 10^{-3}$ H

(i) $f_0 = \dfrac{1}{2\pi\sqrt{LC}}$

$$\Rightarrow C = \frac{1}{4\pi^2 \times f_0^2 \times L} = \frac{1}{4\pi^2 \times 100^2 \times 5 \times 10^{-3}} = 507\ \mu\text{F}$$

(ii) $Q = \dfrac{\omega_0 L}{R} = \dfrac{2\pi \times 100 \times 5 \times 10^{-3}}{50 \times 10^{-3}} = 62.83$

(iii) $BW = \dfrac{f_0}{Q} = \dfrac{100}{62.83} = 1.59$ Hz

(iv) $f_1 = f_0 - \dfrac{BW}{2} = 100 - \dfrac{1.59}{2} = 99.205 \text{ Hz}$

$$f_2 = f_0 + \frac{BW}{2} = 100 + \frac{1.59}{2} = 100.795 \text{ Hz}$$

Problem 5.6 Design a series *RLC* circuit that will resonate at 10 kHz, have a bandwidth of 1 kHz and draws 18.5 W power from a 220 V generator operating at the resonant frequency.

Solution:

Given that $f_0 = 10$ kHz, $P = 18.5$ W, $V = 220$ V

$$BW = f_2 - f_1 = 1 \text{ kHz}$$

(i) $P = I^2 R = \dfrac{V^2}{R}$

$$\Rightarrow R = \frac{V^2}{P} = \frac{220^2}{18.5} = 2.61 \text{ k}\Omega$$

$$Q_0 = \frac{f_0}{\Delta f} = \frac{10}{1} = 10$$

(ii) $Q_0 = \dfrac{\omega_0 L}{R}$

$$\Rightarrow L = \frac{Q_0 R}{\omega_0} = \frac{10 \times 2.61 \times 10^3}{2\pi \times 10 \times 10^3} = 416 \text{ mH}$$

(iii) $f_0 = \dfrac{1}{2\pi\sqrt{LC}}$

$$\Rightarrow C = \frac{1}{4\pi^2 f_0^2 L} = \frac{1}{4\pi^2 \times 10^2 \times 10^6 \times 416 \times 10^{-3}} = 610 \text{ pF}$$

$\therefore$ $R = 2.61$ kΩ, $L = 416$ mH, $C = 610$ pF

Problem 5.7 A series RLC circuit consists of a resistance $R = 20\ \Omega$, inductance $L = 0.01$ H and capacitance $C = 0.04$ µF. Calculate the frequency at resonance. If a voltage of 10 V of frequency equal to the frequency of resonance is applied to this circuit, calculate the values of V_C and V_L across C and L respectively. Find the frequencies at which these voltages V_C and V_L are maximum.

Solution:

Given that $R = 20\ \Omega$, $L = 0.01$ H $C = 0.04$ µF

$$\text{Resonant frequency, } f_0 = \frac{1}{2\pi}\frac{1}{\sqrt{LC}} = \frac{1}{2\pi} \times \frac{1}{\sqrt{0.01 \times 0.04 \times 10^{-6}}} = 7957.7 \text{ Hz}$$

Voltage at resonance, $V = 10$ V

$$\text{Current at resonance, } I_0 = \frac{V}{R} = \frac{10}{20} = 0.5 \text{ A}$$

$$V_C = V_L = I_0 X_L \quad \text{(or)} \quad I_0 X_C = 0.5 \times 2\pi f_0 L = 0.5 \times 2\pi \times 7957.7 \times 0.01 = 250 \text{ V}$$

The frequency at which V_C is maximum is

$$f = \frac{1}{2\pi}\sqrt{\frac{1}{LC} - \frac{R^2}{2L^2}} = \frac{1}{2\pi}\sqrt{\frac{1}{0.01 \times 0.04 \times 10^{-6}} - \frac{400}{2 \times 0.01^2}}$$

$$= \frac{1}{2\pi}\sqrt{2500 \times 10^6 - 2 \times 10^6} = 7954.56 \text{ Hz}$$

The frequency at which V_L is maximum is

$$f = \frac{1}{2\pi\sqrt{LC - \frac{C^2R^2}{2}}} = \frac{1}{2\pi\sqrt{0.01 \times 0.04 \times 10^{-6} - (0.04)^2 \times 10^{-12} \times 200}}$$

$$= \frac{1}{2\pi\sqrt{4 \times 10^{-10} - 0.0032 \times 10^{-10}}} = 7964.97 \text{ Hz}$$

5.11 PARALLEL RESONANCE

5.11.1 Ideal Parallel Circuit

The circuit, with resistance R, inductance L and a capacitance C in parallel, is connected to a single phase variable frequency (f) supply (Fig. 5.5). For this circuit, the condition for resonance occurs when the susceptance part is zero. The total admittance of the circuit is

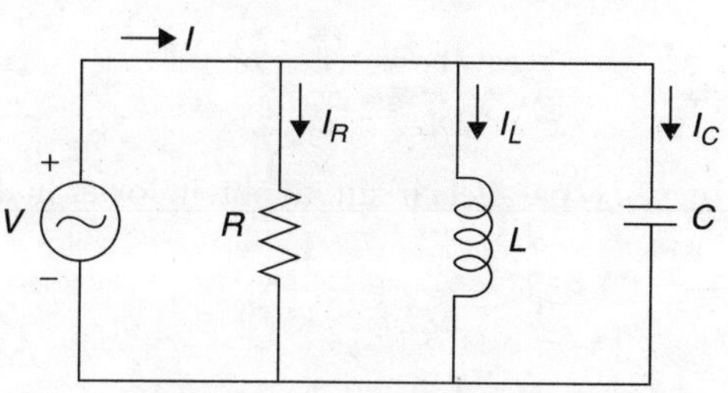

Fig. 5.5 *RLC* parallel circuit

$$Y = Y_R + Y_L + Y_C = \frac{1}{R} + \frac{1}{jX_L} + \frac{1}{-jX_C} = \frac{1}{R} + j\left(\frac{1}{X_C} - \frac{1}{X_L}\right)$$

At resonance condition, the j component of admittance is equal to zero.

$$\frac{1}{X_C} - \frac{1}{X_L} = 0$$

$$\Rightarrow \qquad X_C = X_L$$

$$\Rightarrow \qquad \frac{1}{\omega_0 C} = \omega_0 L \;\Rightarrow\; f_0 = \frac{1}{2\pi\sqrt{LC}} \tag{5.26}$$

The variations of voltage and current with frequency are shown (Fig. 5.6). At resonant frequency, the current is minimum.

Bandwidth, $BW = f_2 - f_1$

The magnitude of the admittance is given by

$$Y = \sqrt{\left[\frac{1}{R^2} + \left(\omega C - \frac{1}{\omega L}\right)^2\right]}$$

The current at resonance condition is $I = VY$

$$V = \frac{I}{Y} = \frac{I}{\sqrt{\frac{1}{R^2} + \left(\omega C - \frac{1}{\omega L}\right)^2}} \quad (5.27)$$

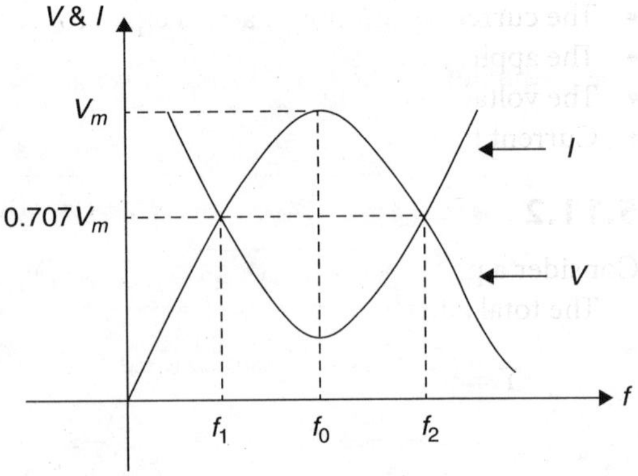

At half-power frequencies

$$V = \frac{V_m}{\sqrt{2}} = \frac{IR}{\sqrt{2}} \quad (5.28)$$

From Eqs 5.27 and 5.28,

$$\frac{IR}{\sqrt{2}} = \frac{I}{\sqrt{\frac{1}{R^2} + \left(\omega C - \frac{1}{\omega L}\right)^2}}$$

$$\Rightarrow \quad \frac{1}{R^2} + \left(\omega C - \frac{1}{\omega L}\right)^2 = \frac{2}{R^2}$$

$$\Rightarrow \quad \omega C - \frac{1}{\omega L} = \pm \frac{1}{R} \quad (5.29)$$

Fig. 5.6 Response of parallel *RLC* circuit

In a *RLC* parallel circuit, to obtain lower half-power frequency,

$$\Rightarrow \quad \omega_1 C - \frac{1}{\omega_1 L} = -\frac{1}{R}$$

$$\Rightarrow \quad \omega_1^2 + \frac{1}{RC}\omega_1 - \frac{1}{LC} = 0$$

$$\Rightarrow \quad \omega_1 = \frac{-1}{2RC} + \sqrt{\frac{1}{4R^2C^2} + \frac{1}{LC}} \quad (5.30)$$

Similarly, the upper half-power frequency can be obtained as

$$\Rightarrow \quad \omega_2 C - \frac{1}{\omega_2 L} = \frac{1}{R}$$

$$\Rightarrow \quad \omega_2^2 - \frac{1}{RC}\omega_2 - \frac{1}{LC} = 0$$

$$\Rightarrow \quad \omega_2 = \frac{1}{2RC} + \sqrt{\frac{1}{4R^2C^2} + \frac{1}{LC}} \quad (5.31)$$

$$\text{Bandwidth, } BW = \omega_2 - \omega_1 = \frac{1}{RC} \quad (5.32)$$

$$\text{Quality factor, } Q = \frac{\omega_0}{BW} = \omega_0 RC \quad (5.33)$$

Conditions at resonance in a parallel RLC circuit

- It behaves like a purely resistive circuit, since net susceptance is equal to zero.
- Inductive and capacitive susceptances are exactly equal.
- Admittance is minimum and equal to conductance, $Y = G$.

- The current is minimum and is equal to VG.
- The applied voltage and current are in phase and power factor of the circuit is unity.
- The voltage is maximum and is equal to $\frac{I}{G}$.
- Current flowing through the inductor is equal to current flowing through the capacitor, $I_L = I_C$.

5.11.2 Practical Parallel Circuit or Tank Circuit

Consider a practical parallel circuit (Fig. 5.7).

The total admittance of the circuit is

$$Y = Y_{RL} + Y_C = \frac{1}{R + jX_L} + \frac{1}{-jX_C}$$

$$= \frac{R - jX_L}{R^2 + X_L^2} + \frac{j}{X_C} = \frac{R}{R^2 + X_L^2} + j\left(\frac{1}{X_C} - \frac{X_L}{R^2 + X_L^2}\right)$$

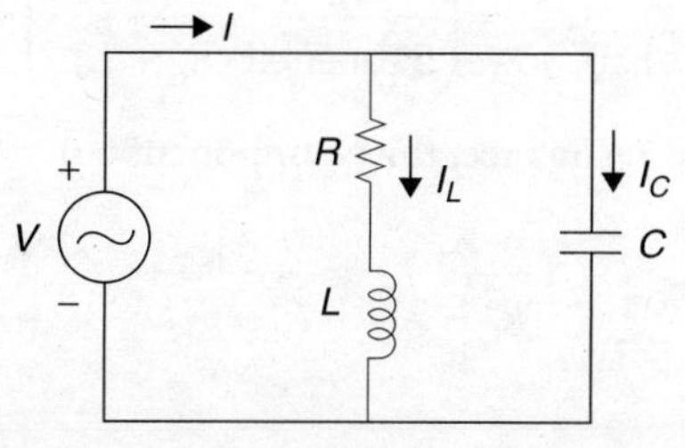

Fig. 5.7 Practical parallel or tank circuit

At resonance condition, the j component of admittance is equal to zero.

$$\frac{1}{X_C} - \frac{X_L}{R^2 + X_L^2} = 0$$

$$\Rightarrow \quad R^2 + X_L^2 = \frac{1}{\omega_0 C} \times \omega_0 L = \frac{L}{C} \tag{5.34}$$

$$\Rightarrow \quad f_0 = \frac{1}{2\pi}\sqrt{\frac{1}{LC} - \frac{R^2}{L^2}} \tag{5.35}$$

To find the current at resonance, $I_{res} = \dfrac{V}{Z_{res}}$

But, $\quad Z_{res} = \dfrac{1}{Y_{res}}$

But, admittance at resonance is the real part of total admittance since at the resonance imaginary part of the admittance is zero.

$$\therefore \quad Y_{res} = \frac{R}{R^2 + X_L^2} \tag{5.36}$$

From Eqs 5.34 and 5.37,

$$Y_{res} = \frac{R}{L/C} = \frac{CR}{L}$$

$$\Rightarrow \quad Z_{res} = \frac{L}{CR} \tag{5.37}$$

The value of impedance of a practical parallel circuit at resonance (Eq. 5.37) is called *dynamic impedance.* The value of current at resonance is minimum; hence L/CR represents the maximum impedance of the circuit and is resistive.

5.11.3 Two Branch Parallel Circuit

Consider a two branch parallel circuit (Fig. 5.8).

Total admittance is given by

$$Y = Y_{RL} + Y_{RC}$$

$$= \frac{1}{R_L + jX_L} + \frac{1}{R_C - jX_C} = \frac{R_L - jX_L}{R_L^2 + X_L^2} + \frac{R_C + jX_C}{R_C^2 + X_C^2}$$

$$= \left(\frac{R_L}{R_L^2 + X_L^2} + \frac{R_C}{R_C^2 + X_C^2}\right) + j\left(\frac{X_C}{R_C^2 + X_C^2} - \frac{X_L}{R_L^2 + X_L^2}\right)$$

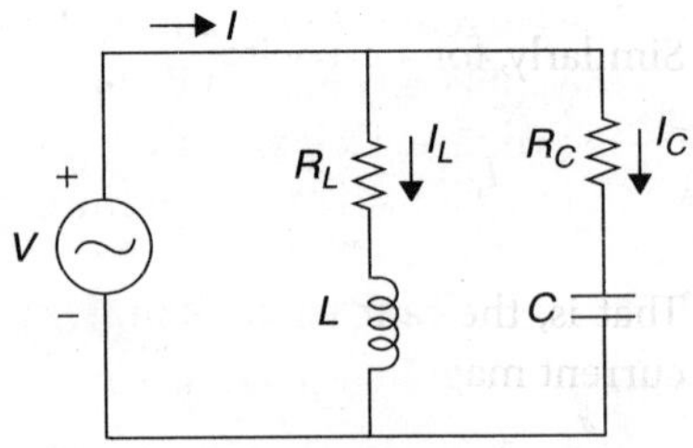

At resonance, the j component = 0

$$\frac{X_C}{R_C^2 + X_C^2} = \frac{X_L}{R_L^2 + X_L^2}$$

$$\Rightarrow \quad \frac{\frac{1}{\omega_0 C}}{R_C^2 + \frac{1}{\omega_0^2 C^2}} = \frac{\omega_0 L}{R_L^2 + \omega_0^2 L^2}$$

$$\Rightarrow \quad \frac{\omega_0 C}{R_C^2 \omega_0^2 C^2 + 1} = \frac{\omega_0 L}{R_L^2 + \omega_0^2 L^2}$$

$$\Rightarrow \quad R_L^2 + \omega_0^2 L^2 = \frac{L}{C}(R_C^2 \omega_0^2 C^2 + 1)$$

$$\Rightarrow \quad R_L^2 + \omega_0^2 L^2 = \omega_0^2 L R_C^2 + \frac{L}{C}$$

$$\Rightarrow \quad \omega_0^2 = \frac{\frac{L}{C} - R_L^2}{L^2 - LCR_C^2} = \frac{R_L^2 - \frac{L}{C}}{LC\left(R_C^2 - \frac{L}{C}\right)}$$

$$\Rightarrow \quad \omega_0 = \frac{1}{\sqrt{LC}}\sqrt{\frac{R_L^2 - \frac{L}{C}}{R_C^2 - \frac{L}{C}}}$$

$$\Rightarrow \quad f_0 = \frac{1}{2\pi\sqrt{LC}}\sqrt{\frac{R_L^2 - \frac{L}{C}}{R_C^2 - \frac{L}{C}}} \qquad (5.38)$$

Fig. 5.8 Two branch parallel circuit

5.12 CURRENT MAGNIFICATION

In the case of a parallel resonant circuit, current magnification takes place. The voltage applied to the parallel circuit is V and is given by

$$V = IR$$

For an inductor

$$I_L = \frac{V}{X_L} = \frac{V}{\omega_0 L} = \frac{IR}{\omega_0 L} = IQ$$

Similarly, for a capacitor

$$I_C = \frac{V}{X_C} = V / \frac{1}{\omega_0 C} = IR\omega_0 C = IQ$$

That is, the ratio of current through either L or C to the applied current at resonance can be defined as current magnification.

$$\text{Magnification, } Q = \frac{I_L}{I} = \frac{I_C}{I} \tag{5.39}$$

Problem 5.8 Determine the value of the capacitance C in order that the circuit is resonant at 6366 Hz.

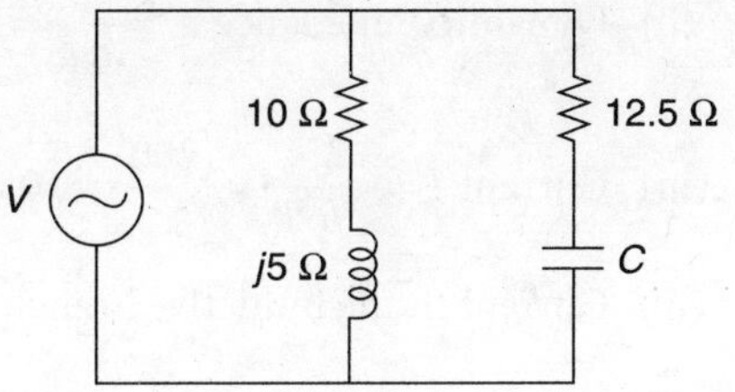

Solution:

Given that $f_0 = 6366$ Hz

$$Z_1 = R_L + jX_L = 10 + j5$$

$$Z_2 = R_C - jX_C = 12.5 - jX_C$$

From the given circuit

$$Y = Y_1 + Y_2 = \frac{1}{R_L + jX_L} + \frac{1}{R_C - jX_C} = \frac{R_L - jX_L}{R_L^2 + X_L^2} + \frac{R_C + jX_C}{R_C^2 - X_C^2}$$

$$= \left(\frac{R_L}{R_L^2 + X_L^2} + \frac{R_C}{R_C^2 - X_C^2}\right) + j\left(\frac{X_C}{R_C^2 + X_C^2} - \frac{X_L}{R_L^2 + X_L^2}\right)$$

At resonance, the j component is zero.

$$\frac{X_C}{R_C^2 + X_C^2} = \frac{X_L}{R_L^2 + X_L^2}$$

$$\Rightarrow \quad \frac{X_C}{12.5^2 + X_C^2} = \frac{5}{10^2 + 5^2} = \frac{5}{125} = \frac{1}{25}$$

$$\Rightarrow \quad X_C^2 - 25X_C + 156.25 = 0$$

$$X_C = \frac{25 \pm \sqrt{25^2 - 4 \times 156.25}}{2} = \frac{25 \pm 0}{2} = 12.5$$

$$X_C = \frac{1}{\omega C} = 12.5$$

$$\Rightarrow \quad C = \frac{1}{12.5 \times 2\pi \times 6366} = 2\ \mu\text{F}$$

The value of capacitance, $C = 2\ \mu$F

Problem 5.9 A coil of 5 Ω resistance and 15 mH inductance is connected in parallel with a capacitor of 160 μF as shown. Calculate the frequency at which resonance occurs. Under this condition, find the value of non-inductive resistance (or dynamic impedance). Also find the total current at resonance when connected to a 200 V supply and the current in each branch.

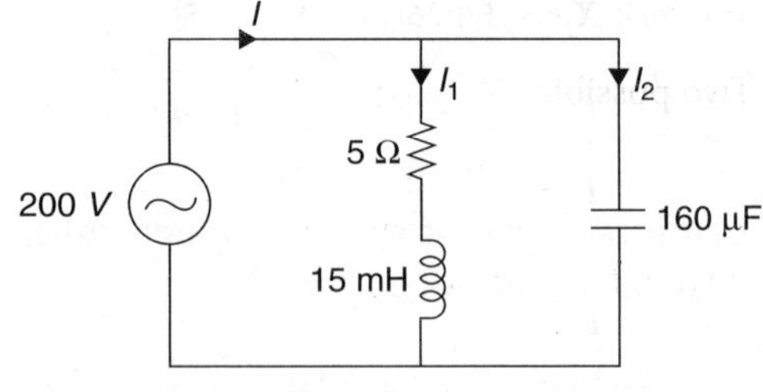

Solution:

Given that $R = 5\ \Omega$, $L = 15$ mH, $C = 160\ \mu$F

(i) For the parallel circuit, resonant frequency is

$$f_0 = \frac{1}{2\pi}\sqrt{\frac{1}{LC} - \frac{R^2}{L^2}} = \frac{1}{2\pi}\sqrt{\frac{1}{15\times10^{-3}\times160\times10^{-6}} - \frac{25}{(15\times10^{-3})^2}} = 87.98 \text{ Hz}$$

(ii) Dynamic impedance $Z = \dfrac{L}{CR} = \dfrac{15\times10^{-3}}{160\times10^{-6}\times5} = 18.75\ \Omega$

(iii) Current $I = \dfrac{V}{L/CR} = \dfrac{200}{18.75} = 10.67$ A

(iv) Current in the inductive branch

$$I_1 = \frac{V}{R + jX_L} = \frac{200}{5 + j8.242} = \frac{200}{9.683\angle 58.91} = 20.655\angle{-58.91°} \text{ A}$$

(v) Current in the capacitive branch

$$I_2 = \frac{V}{-jX_C} = \frac{200}{-j11.306} = 17.69\angle 90° \text{ A}$$

Problem 5.10 Find the values of L such that the circuit is resonant at 100 Hz.

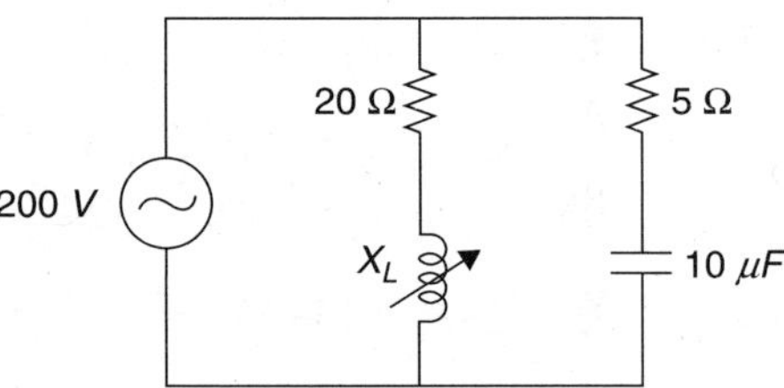

Solution:

$$X_C = \frac{1}{2\pi f_0 C} = \frac{1}{2\pi\times100\times10\times10^{-6}} = 159.155$$

For the given circuit

$$Y = Y_1 + Y_2 = \frac{1}{R_1 + jX_L} + \frac{1}{R_2 - jX_C} = \frac{1}{20 + jX_L} + \frac{1}{5 - jX_C}$$

$$= \frac{1}{20 + jX_L} + \frac{1}{5 - j159.155} = \frac{20 - jX_L}{20^2 + X_L^2} + \frac{5 + j159.155}{5^2 + 159.155^2}$$

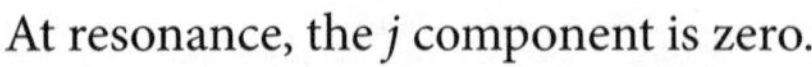

At resonance, the j component is zero.

$$\frac{X_L}{20^2 + X_L^2} = \frac{159.155}{25 + 159.155^2}$$

$$\Rightarrow \quad X_L^2 - 159.312\, X_L + 400 = 0$$

$$X_L = \frac{159.312 \pm \sqrt{159.312^2 - 1600}}{2}$$

$$X_L = 156.76 \quad \text{(or)} \quad 2.556$$

Two possible values of L are

$$L_1 = \frac{156.76}{2\pi \times 100} = 0.25\ \text{H}$$

$$L_2 = \frac{2.556}{2\pi \times 100} = 4.068\ \text{mH}$$

Problem 5.11 Find the active and reactive components of current taken by a series circuit consisting of a coil of inductance 0.1 H, a resistance of 8 Ω and a capacitor of 120 μF connected to a 240 V, 50 Hz supply. Find the value of capacitor that has to be connected in parallel with the above series circuit so that the pf of the entire circuit is unity.

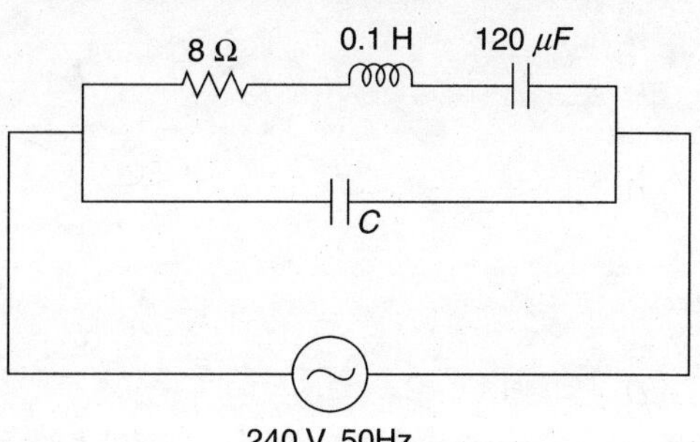

Solution:

Given that $R = 8\ \Omega$, $L = 0.1$ H, $C = 120\ \mu\text{F}$

$$X_L = 2\pi f L = 2\pi \times 50 \times 0.1 = 31.4\ \Omega$$

$$X_C = \frac{1}{2\pi f C} = \frac{1}{2\pi \times 50 \times 120 \times 10^{-6}} = 26.54$$

$$Z_1 = R + j(X_L - X_C) = 8 + j(31.4 - 26.54) = 8 + j4.86$$

$$Y_1 = \frac{1}{Z_1} = \frac{1}{8 + j\,4.86} = 0.1 - j\,0.06$$

$$I_1 = \frac{V}{Z_1} = \frac{240}{8 + j\,4.86} = 25.64\angle -31.3°$$

$$\Rightarrow \quad \phi = 31.3°$$

$$\text{Active component} = I_1 \cos\phi = 25.64 \cos 31.3° = 21.9\ \text{A}$$

$$\text{Reactive component} = I_1 \sin\phi = 25.64 \sin 31.3° = 13.34\ \text{A}$$

$$Y_2 = \frac{1}{Z_2} = \frac{1}{-jX_C}$$

$$Y = Y_1 + Y_2 = 0.1 - j0.06 + \frac{1}{-jX_C} = 0.1 + j\left(\frac{1}{X_C} - 0.06\right)$$

At resonance condition, j component = 0

$$\frac{1}{X_C} - 0.06 = 0$$

$$\Rightarrow \quad X_C = \frac{1}{0.06} = 16.67$$

$$\Rightarrow \quad C = \frac{1}{2\pi \times 50 \times 16.67} = 191.3\ \mu\text{F}$$

5.13 COMPARISON OF SERIES AND PARALLEL RESONANT CIRCUITS

S. no	Particular	Series resonance	Parallel resonance
1	Impedance	Minimum and equal to R	Maximum and equal to L/CR
2	Current	Maximum and equal to $\frac{V}{R}$	Minimum and equal to $\frac{V}{L/CR}$
3	Power factor	Unity	Unity
4	Magnification	Magnifies voltage	Magnifies current
5	Other name	Acceptor circuit	Rejector circuit
6	Magnification is	$\frac{\omega L}{R}$	$\frac{\omega L}{R}$
7	Resonant frequency	$f_0 = \frac{1}{2\pi\sqrt{LC}}$	(i) For ideal parallel circuit $f_0 = \frac{1}{2\pi\sqrt{LC}}$ (ii) For tank circuit $f_0 = \frac{1}{2\pi}\sqrt{\frac{1}{LC} - \frac{R^2}{L^2}}$ (iii) For two branch parallel circuit $f_0 = \frac{1}{2\pi\sqrt{LC}}\sqrt{\frac{R_L^2 - \frac{L}{C}}{R_C^2 - \frac{L}{C}}}$
8	Quality factor	$\frac{\omega_0 L}{R}$ (or) $\frac{1}{\omega_0 CR}$	$\frac{R}{\omega_0 L}$ (or) $\omega_0 CR$
9	Bandwidth	$\frac{f_0}{Q}$	$\frac{f_0}{Q}$
10	Half-power frequencies	$f_0 = \sqrt{f_1 f_2}$	$f_0 = \sqrt{f_1 f_2}$

5.14 APPLICATIONS OF RESONANT CIRCUITS

The common applications of resonant circuits are:

- A resonant circuit is used as an oscillator circuit for tuning radio receivers and television sets.
- A series resonant circuit is used as voltage amplifier.
- A parallel resonant circuit is used as current amplifier.
- Resonant tank circuit serves as stable frequency source in the circuits designed to produce AC signals.
- A resonant circuit is used as filter.
- A parallel resonant circuit is used as load impedance in output circuits of radio frequency amplifiers.
- Series and parallel *LC* circuits are used in induction heating.

5.15 LOCUS DIAGRAMS

An AC circuit is generally analysed presuming the input voltage is constant. If the values of *R*, *L*, *C* and *f* are varied, the current in the AC circuit gets affected in magnitude and phase. The behaviour of the circuit under such conditions can be studied using locus diagrams.

The performance of an induction motor can be determined using the locus or circle diagram. The transmission line performance for different load conditions can be easily evaluated using locus diagrams in power system engineering.

Locus diagrams can also be drawn for reactance, impedance, susceptance and admittance when frequency is variable. The loci of these parameters furnish important information for use in circuit analysis.

5.15.1 Series *RL* Circuit

Case (i): Series *RL* circuit with constant *L* and variable *R*

Consider a series *RL* circuit [Fig. 5.9(a)] excited by a sinusoidal voltage source with constant *L* and variable *R*. The impedance of the circuit is $Z = R + jX_L$ where $X_L = \omega L$.

The current in the circuit is

$$I = \frac{V}{Z} = \frac{V}{R + jX_L} = \frac{V(R - jX_L)}{(R + jX_L)(R - jX_L)} = \frac{VR}{R^2 + X_L^2} - j\frac{VX_L}{R^2 + X_L^2}$$

Let $$\frac{VR}{R^2 + X_L^2} - j\frac{VX_L}{R^2 + X_L^2} = x + jy$$

where $$x = \frac{VR}{R^2 + X_L^2} = \frac{V}{\sqrt{R^2 + X_L^2}} \times \frac{R}{\sqrt{R^2 + X_L^2}} = I\cos\theta$$

$$y = -\frac{VX_L}{R^2 + X_L^2} = -\frac{V}{\sqrt{R^2 + X_L^2}} \times \frac{X_L}{\sqrt{R^2 + X_L^2}} = I\sin\theta$$

$$I^2 = x^2 + y^2 = \frac{V^2}{R^2 + X_L^2} = \frac{-yV}{X_L}$$

$$\Rightarrow \quad x^2 + y^2 + \frac{yV}{X_L} = 0 \tag{5.40}$$

$$x^2 + y^2 + \frac{V}{X_L}y + \left(\frac{V}{2X_L}\right)^2 - \left(\frac{V}{2X_L}\right)^2 = 0$$

$$(x - 0)^2 + \left(y + \frac{V}{2X_L}\right)^2 = \left(\frac{V}{2X_L}\right)^2 \tag{5.41}$$

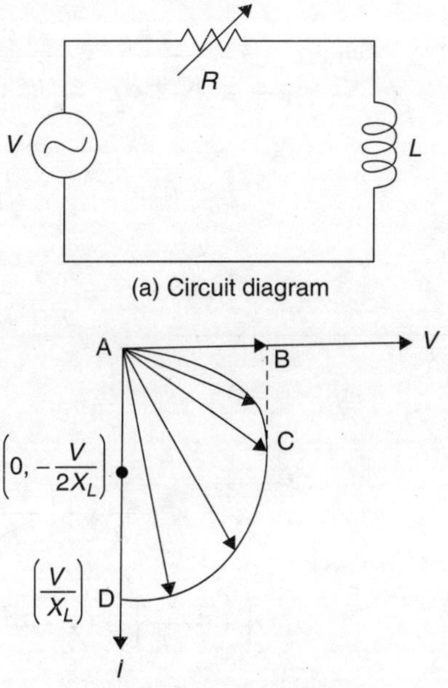

(a) Circuit diagram

(b) Current locus diagram

Fig. 5.9 RL series circuit with variable *R*

Equation 5.41 represents a circle, whose centre is at $\left(0, -\frac{V}{2X_L}\right)$ with radius $\frac{V}{2X_L}$. The locus of current *I* when *R* is varying from 0 to ∞ is a semi circle [Fig. 5.9(b)]. As the resistance is varied from 0 to ∞ the current is traversing along the semicircle ACD. The maximum horizontal component of *I* is AB = $\frac{V}{2X_L}$.

The value of maximum power is

$$P_{\max} = V(I\cos\theta)_{\max} = V \times \frac{V}{2X_L} = \frac{V^2}{2X_L} \text{ W} \tag{5.42}$$

Case (ii): Series RL circuit with constant *R* and variable *L*

Consider a series RL circuit [Fig. 5.10(a)] excited by a sinusoidal voltage source with constant *R* and variable *L*. The impedance of the circuit is $Z = R + jX_L$ where $X_L = \omega L$.

The current in the circuit is

$$I = \frac{V}{Z} = \frac{V}{R + jX_L} = \frac{V(R - jX_L)}{(R + jX_L)(R - jX_L)} = \frac{VR}{R^2 + X_L^2} - j\frac{VX_L}{R^2 + X_L^2}$$

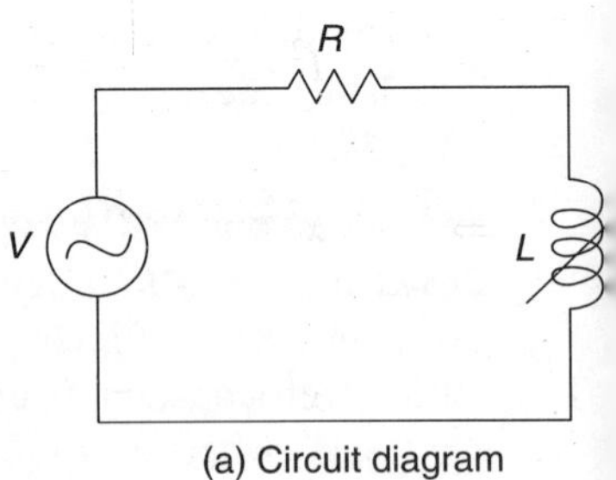

(a) Circuit diagram

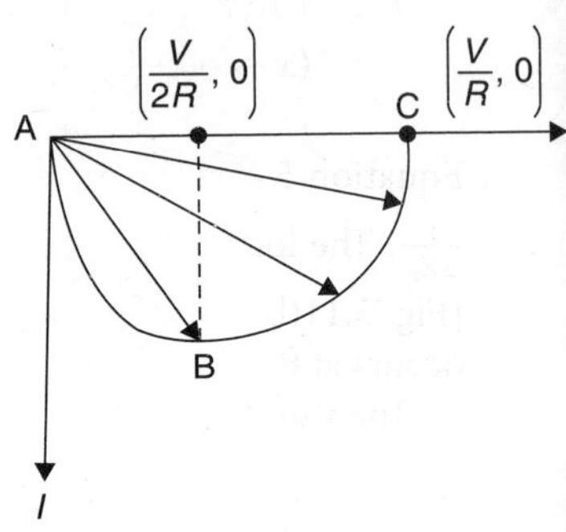

(b) Current locus diagram

Fig. 5.10 RL series circuit with variable L

Let $$\frac{VR}{R^2+X_L^2} - j\frac{VX_L}{R^2+X_L^2} = x + jy$$

where $$x = \frac{VR}{R^2+X_L^2} = \frac{V}{\sqrt{R^2+X_L^2}} \times \frac{R}{\sqrt{R^2+X_L^2}} = I\cos\theta$$

$$y = -\frac{VX_L}{R^2+X_L^2} = -\frac{V}{\sqrt{R^2+X_L^2}} \times \frac{X_L}{\sqrt{R^2+X_L^2}} = I\sin\theta$$

$$I^2 = x^2 + y^2 = \frac{V^2}{R^2+X_L^2} = \frac{V^2}{R^2+X_L^2}\frac{R}{R} = \frac{xV}{R}$$

$$\Rightarrow \quad x^2 + y^2 - \frac{xV}{R} = 0 \tag{5.43}$$

$$x^2 + y^2 - \frac{V}{R}x + \left(\frac{V}{2R}\right)^2 - \left(\frac{V}{2R}\right)^2 = 0$$

$$\left(x - \frac{V}{2R}\right)^2 + (y-0)^2 = \left(\frac{V}{2R}\right)^2 \tag{5.44}$$

Equation 5.44 represents a circle whose centre is at $\left(\frac{V}{2R}, 0\right)$ with radius $\frac{V}{2R}$. The locus of current when L is varying from 0 to ∞ is a semicircle [Fig. 5.10(b)]. As the inductance is varied from 0 to ∞ the current is traversing along the semicircle ABC. The current is maximum when the inductance in the circuit is zero, so $I_{max} = \frac{V}{R}$.

The value of maximum power is

$$P_{max} = V(I\cos\theta)_{max} = V \times \frac{V}{R} = \frac{V^2}{R} \tag{5.45}$$

5.15.2 Series *RC* Circuit

Case (i): Series *RC* circuit with constant *C* and variable *R*

Consider a series *RC* circuit [Fig. 5.11(a)] excited by a sinusoidal voltage source with constant *C* and variable *R*. The impedance of the circuit is $Z = R - jX_C$ where $X_C = 1/\omega C$.

The current in the circuit is

$$I = \frac{V}{Z} = \frac{V}{R - jX_C} = \frac{V(R + jX_C)}{(R + jX_C)(R - jX_C)} = \frac{VR}{R^2+X_C^2} + j\frac{VX_C}{R^2+X_C^2}$$

Let $$\frac{VR}{R^2+X_C^2} + j\frac{VX_C}{R^2+X_C^2} = x + jy$$

where $$x = \frac{VR}{R^2+X_C^2} = \frac{V}{\sqrt{R^2+X_C^2}} \times \frac{R}{\sqrt{R^2+X_C^2}} = I\cos\theta$$

$$y = \frac{VX_C}{R^2+X_C^2} = \frac{V}{\sqrt{R^2+X_C^2}} \times \frac{X_C}{\sqrt{R^2+X_C^2}} = I\sin\theta$$

$$I^2 = x^2 + y^2 = \frac{V^2}{R^2 + X_C^2} = \frac{V^2}{R^2 + X_C^2}\frac{X_C}{X_C} = \frac{yV}{X_C}$$

$$\Rightarrow \quad x^2 + y^2 - \frac{yV}{X_C} = 0 \tag{5.46}$$

$$x^2 + y^2 - \frac{V}{X_C}y + \left(\frac{V}{2X_C}\right)^2 - \left(\frac{V}{2X_C}\right)^2 = 0$$

$$(x-0)^2 + \left(y - \frac{V}{2X_C}\right)^2 = \left(\frac{V}{2X_C}\right)^2 \tag{5.47}$$

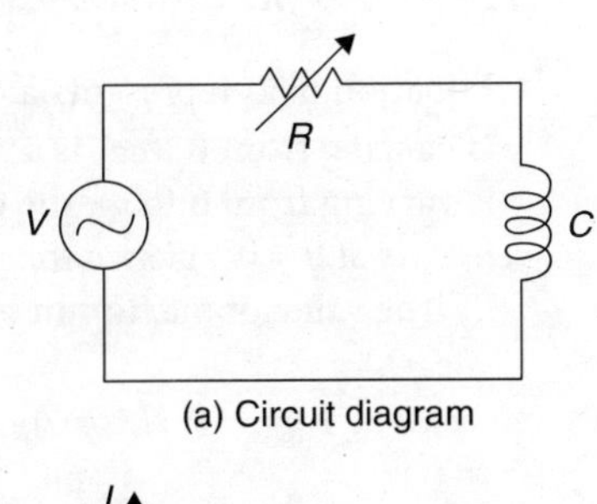

(a) Circuit diagram

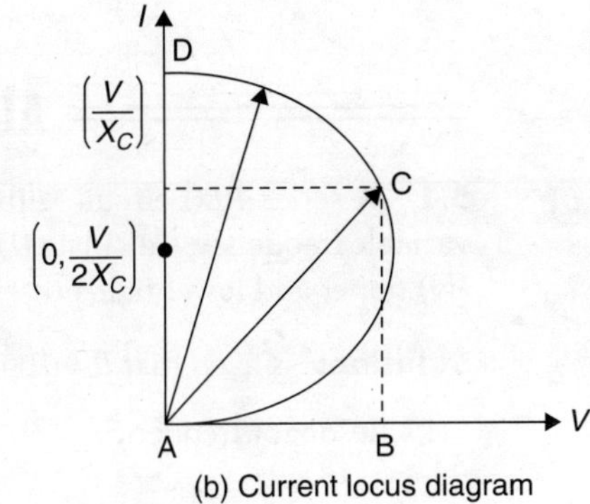

(b) Current locus diagram

Fig. 5.11 RC series circuit with variable R

Equation 5.47 represents a circle, whose centre is at $\left(0, \frac{V}{2X_C}\right)$ with radius $\frac{V}{2X_C}$. The locus of current I when R is varying from 0 to ∞ is a semicircle [Fig. 5.11(b)]. The maximum horizontal component is $AB = \frac{V}{2X_C}$ and this occurs at $\theta = 45°$ leading (here current leads the voltage).

The value of maximum power is

$$P_{max} = V\,(I\cos\theta)_{max} = V \times \frac{V}{2X_C} = \frac{V^2}{2X_C}\ \text{W} \tag{5.48}$$

Case (ii): Series *RC* circuit with constant *R* and variable *C*

Consider a series *RC* circuit [Fig. 5.12(a)] excited by sinusoidal voltage source with constant R and variable C. The impedance of the circuit is $Z = R - jX_C$ where $X_C = 1/\omega C$.

The current in the circuit is

$$I = \frac{V}{Z} = \frac{V}{R - jX_C} = \frac{V\,(R + jX_C)}{(R + jX_C)(R - jX_C)} = \frac{VR}{R^2 + X_C^2} + j\frac{VX_C}{R^2 + X_C^2}$$

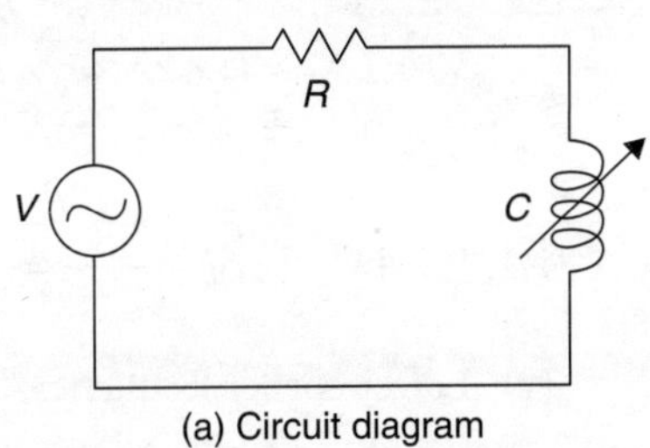

(a) Circuit diagram

Let $\quad \dfrac{VR}{R^2 + X_C^2} + j\dfrac{VX_C}{R^2 + X_C^2} = x + jy$

where $\quad x = \dfrac{VR}{R^2 + X_C^2} = \dfrac{V}{\sqrt{R^2 + X_C^2}} \times \dfrac{R}{\sqrt{R^2 + X_C^2}} = I\cos\theta$

$$y = \frac{VX_L}{R^2 + X_C^2} = \frac{V}{\sqrt{R^2 + X_C^2}} \times \frac{X_C}{\sqrt{R^2 + X_C^2}} = I\sin\theta$$

$$I^2 = x^2 + y^2 = \frac{V^2}{R^2 + X_C^2} = \frac{V^2}{R^2 + X_C^2}\frac{R}{R} = \frac{xV}{R}$$

$$\Rightarrow \quad x^2 + y^2 - \frac{xV}{R} = 0 \tag{5.49}$$

$$x^2 + y^2 - \frac{V}{R}x + \left(\frac{V}{2R}\right)^2 - \left(\frac{V}{2R}\right)^2 = 0$$

$$\left(x - \frac{V}{2R}\right)^2 + (y-0)^2 = \left(\frac{V}{2R}\right)^2 \tag{5.50}$$

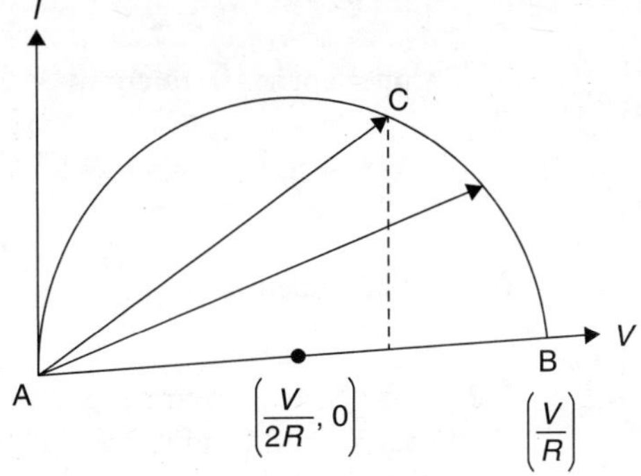

(b) Current locus diagram

Fig. 5.12 *RC* series circuit with variable C

Equation 5.50 represents a circle, whose centre is at $\left(\frac{V}{2R}, 0\right)$ with radius $\frac{V}{2R}$. The locus of current I when C is varying from 0 to ∞ is a semicircle [Fig. 5.12(b)], since the current leads the voltage. As the capacitance is varying from 0 to ∞, the current locus is ACB. The maximum horizontal component is AB = $\frac{V}{R}$ and this occurs at θ = 0°. Hence the power factor is unity and is leading.

The value of maximum power is

$$P_{max} = V\,(I\cos\theta)_{max} = V \times \frac{V}{R} = \frac{V^2}{R} \text{ Watts} \tag{5.51}$$

ADDITIONAL SOLVED PROBLEMS

5.1 A series *RLC* circuit with $R = 100\ \Omega$, $L = 0.5$ H and $C = 40\ \mu$F has an applied voltage of 50 V with variable frequency. Calculate (i) resonant frequency, (ii) current at resonance, (iii) voltage across *R*, *L* and *C*, (iv) upper and lower half-power frequencies, (v) bandwidth, and (vi) *Q*-factor of the circuit.

Solution: Given that $R = 100\ \Omega$, $L = 0.5$ H, $C = 40\ \mu$F, $V = 50$ V

(i) Resonant frequency

$$f_0 = \frac{1}{2\pi\sqrt{LC}} = \frac{1}{2\pi\sqrt{0.5 \times 40 \times 10^{-6}}} = 35.59 \text{ Hz}$$

(ii) Current at resonance, $I_0 = \frac{V}{R} = \frac{50}{100} = 0.5$ A

(iii) $V_R = I_0 R = 0.5 \times 100 = 50$ V

$V_L = I_0 X_L = I_0 \times 2\pi \times f_0 \times L = 0.5 \times 2\pi \times 35.39 \times 0.5 = 55.9$ V

$V_C = V_L = 55.9$ V

(iv) Bandwidth, $\Delta f = \frac{R}{2\pi L} = \frac{100}{2\pi \times 0.5} = 31.8$ Hz

(v) Lower corner frequency,

$$f_1 = f_0 - \frac{\Delta f}{2} = 35.59 - \frac{31.8}{2} = 19.67 \text{ Hz}$$

Upper corner frequency,

$$f_2 = f_0 + \frac{\Delta f}{2} = 35.59 + \frac{31.8}{2} = 51.57 \text{ Hz}$$

(vi) Quality factor, $Q = \frac{\omega_0 L}{R} = \frac{2\pi \times 35.59 \times 0.5}{100} = 1.1182$

5.2 For a two branch parallel circuit $R_L = 6\ \Omega$, $R_C = 9\ \Omega$, $X_C = 12\ \Omega$. Find two values of L and the two values of total current at resonance which connected to a 100 V, 50 Hz supply.

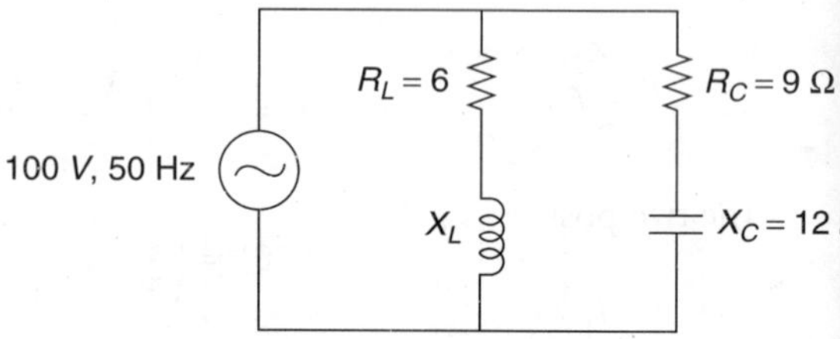

$R_L = 6$, $R_C = 9\ \Omega$, 100 V, 50 Hz, X_L, $X_C = 12$

Solution: Given that

$$Y = Y_1 + Y_2 = \frac{1}{R_L + jX_L} + \frac{1}{R_C - jX_C} = \frac{R_L - jX_L}{R_L^2 + X_L^2} + \frac{R_C + jX_C}{R_C^2 + X_C^2}$$

$$= \left(\frac{R_L}{R_L^2 + X_L^2} + \frac{R_C}{R_C^2 + X_C^2}\right) + j\left(\frac{X_C}{R_C^2 + X_C^2} - \frac{X_L}{R_L^2 + X_L^2}\right)$$

At resonance

$$\frac{X_C}{R_C^2 + X_C^2} = \frac{X_L}{R_L^2 + X_L^2}$$

$$\Rightarrow \quad \frac{12}{9^2 + 12^2} = \frac{X_L}{6^2 + X_L^2}$$

$$\Rightarrow \quad 225X_L = 432 + 12X_L^2$$

$$\Rightarrow \quad X_L^2 - 18.75X_L + 36 = 0$$

$$\Rightarrow \quad X_L = \frac{18.75 \pm \sqrt{18.75^2 - 4 \times 36}}{2}$$

$$\Rightarrow \quad X_L = 16.58, 2.175$$

The two possible values of L are

$$L_1 = \frac{16.58}{2\pi \times 50} = 0.0528 \text{ H}$$

$$L_2 = \frac{2.175}{2\pi \times 50} = 0.00692 \text{ H}$$

To find current at resonance

$$I_{\text{res}} = \frac{V}{Z_{\text{res}}}$$

At resonance, the total admittance

$$Y_{\text{res}} = \frac{R_L}{R_L^2 + X_L^2} + \frac{R_C}{R_C^2 + X_C^2}$$

$$Z_{1\text{res}} = \frac{1}{\dfrac{R_L}{R_L^2 + X_L^2} + \dfrac{R_C}{R_C^2 + X_C^2}} = \frac{1}{\dfrac{6}{6^2 + 16.58^2} + \dfrac{9}{9^2 + 12^2}} = 16.864$$

$$Z_{2\text{res}} = \frac{1}{\dfrac{6}{6^2 + 2.175^2} + \dfrac{9}{9^2 + 12^2}} = 5.339$$

The two possible total currents are

$$I_1 = \frac{100}{16.864} = 5.93 \text{ A}$$

$$I_2 = \frac{100}{5.339} = 18.731 \text{ A}$$

5.3 A series *RLC* circuit has a resistance of 8 Ω and resonates at 250 Hz, the bandwidth of the circuit is 50 Hz. Determine the value of *L* and *C* in the circuit.

Solution: Given that $R = 8\ \Omega, f_0 = 250$ Hz, $BW = \Delta f = 50$ Hz

$$\text{Resonant frequency, } f_0 = \frac{1}{2\pi\sqrt{LC}}$$

$$BW = \Delta f = \frac{R}{2\pi L} = 50$$

$$\Rightarrow \quad L = \frac{R}{2\pi \times 50} = \frac{8}{100\pi} = 25.46 \text{ mH}$$

$$f_0^2 = \frac{1}{4\pi^2 LC}$$

$$\Rightarrow \quad C = \frac{1}{4\pi^2 L f_0^2} = \frac{1}{4\pi^2 \times 25.46 \times 10^{-3} \times 250^2} = 0.0159 \text{ F}$$

5.4 A series *RLC* circuit with $R = 50\ \Omega$, $L = 0.1$ H and C = 10 μF has an applied voltage $V = 100 \angle 0°$. Find the maximum voltage across the inductor and the frequency at which it occurs.

Solution: Given that $R = 50\ \Omega$, $L = 0.1$ H, C = 10 μF, $V = 100$ V.

$$f_L = \frac{1}{2\pi\sqrt{LC - \dfrac{R^2C^2}{2}}} = \frac{1}{2\pi\sqrt{0.1 \times 10 \times 10^{-6} - \dfrac{(50)^2 \times (10)^2 \times 10^{-12}}{2}}} = 170.14$$

$$X_L = \omega L = 2\pi \times (170.14) \times 0.1 = 106.9\ \Omega$$

$$X_C = \frac{1}{\omega C} = \frac{1}{2\pi \times 170.14 \times 10 \times 10^{-6}} = 93.54\ \Omega$$

$$Z = R + j(X_L - X_C) = 50 + j(106.9 - 93.54) = 50 + j13.364 = 51.755\angle 14.96°\ \Omega$$

$$I = \frac{V}{Z} = \frac{100\angle 0°}{51.75\angle 14.96°} = 1.932\angle 14.96° \text{ A}$$

Voltage across the inductor

$$V_L = IX_L = 1.932 \times 106.9 = 206.56 \text{ V}$$

5.5 A series *RLC* circuit has a bandwidth of 600 Hz and quality factor 10. If the value of *L* is 0.01 H, then find the value of *R* and *C*.

Solution: Given that $\Delta f = 600$ Hz, $Q = 10$, $L = 0.01$ H

$$Q = \frac{f_0}{\Delta f} \Rightarrow f_0 = Q \times \Delta f = 10 \times 600 = 6000 \text{ Hz}$$

But $$f_0 = \frac{1}{2\pi\sqrt{LC}}$$

$$\Rightarrow \quad C = \frac{1}{4\pi^2 f_0^2 L} = \frac{1}{4\pi^2 \times 6000^2 \times 0.01} = 7.036 \times 10^{-8}\ \text{F}$$

But $$R = \frac{\omega_0 L}{Q} = \frac{2\pi \times 6000 \times 0.01}{10} = 37.7\ \Omega$$

5.6 It is desired that the impedance Z_T of the circuit be a resistance of 60 kΩ at resonance. Find (i) X_L, (ii) X_C, (iii) the resonance frequency if $L = 18$ mH , and (iv) C.

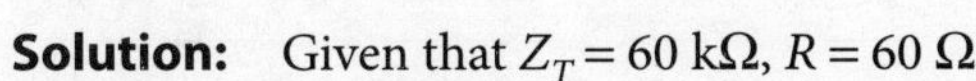

Solution: Given that $Z_T = 60$ kΩ, $R = 60\ \Omega$

The impedance at resonance frequency

$$Z_T \text{ at } \omega_0 = \frac{L}{RC} = \frac{\omega_0 L}{R} \times \frac{1}{\omega_0 CR} \times R = Q^2 R$$

$$\therefore \quad Q^2 = \frac{60 \times 10^3}{60} = 1000$$

$$\Rightarrow \quad Q = 31.62$$

But $$Q = \frac{\omega_0 L}{R} = \frac{X_L}{R}$$

(i) $X_L = QR = 31.62 \times 60 = 1897\ \Omega$
(ii) At resonance $X_C = X_L = 1897\ \Omega$
(iii) $Q > 10$, hence

$$f_0 = \frac{1}{2\pi\sqrt{LC}} = \frac{1}{2\pi\sqrt{18 \times 10^{-3} \times 5 \times 10^{-9}}} = 16.776\ \text{kHz}$$

(iv) $$Z_T \text{ at } \omega_0 = \frac{L}{RC}$$

$$60 \times 10^3 = \frac{18 \times 10^{-3}}{60 \times C} \Rightarrow C = \frac{18 \times 10^{-3}}{60 \times 60 \times 10^3} = 5 \times 10^{-9} = 5\ \text{nF}$$

5.7 A coil of 10 Ω resistance and 0.2 H inductance is connected in parallel with a variable capacitor of across a 220 V, 50 Hz supply. Calculate the (i) value of capacitance at resonance, (ii) dynamic impedance of the circuit, and (iii) supply current.

Solution: Given that $R = 10\ \Omega$, $L = 0.2$ H, $V = 220$ V, $f_o = 50$ Hz

(i) Value of capacitance at resonance

$$f_0 = \frac{1}{2\pi}\sqrt{\frac{1}{LC} - \frac{R^2}{L^2}} = \frac{1}{2\pi}\sqrt{\frac{1}{0.2C} - \frac{10^2}{0.2^2}}$$

$$\Rightarrow C = 49.41\ \mu\text{F}$$

(ii) Dynamic impedance of the circuit

$$Z = \frac{L}{RC} = \frac{0.2}{10 \times 49.41 \times 10^{-6}} = 405\ \Omega$$

(iii) Supply current $I = \frac{V}{Z} = \frac{220}{405} = 0.543$ A

5.8 Design a series *RLC* circuit that will resonate at 10 kHz, have a bandwidth of 1 kHz and draw 15.3 W power from a 200 V generator operating at the resonant frequency of the current.

Solution: Given that $f_0 = 10$ kHz, $\Delta f = 1$ kHz

$$P = 15.3 \text{ W}, V = 200 \text{ V}$$

$$\text{Power, } P = \frac{V^2}{R}$$

$$\Rightarrow \quad R = \frac{V^2}{P} = \frac{200^2}{15.3} = 2614\ \Omega$$

$$\text{Quality factor, } Q = \frac{f_0}{\Delta f} = \frac{10}{1} = 10$$

And $$Q = \frac{\omega_0 L}{R}$$

$$\Rightarrow \quad L = \frac{QR}{\omega_0} = \frac{10 \times 2614}{2\pi \times 10 \times 10^3} = 416 \text{ mH}$$

$$Q = \frac{1}{\omega_0 CR}$$

$$\Rightarrow \quad C = \frac{1}{Q\omega_0 R} = \frac{1}{10 \times 2\pi \times 10 \times 10^3 \times 2614} = 610 \text{ pF}$$

5.9 A 400 V, 50 Hz supply feeds energy to a parallel circuit consisting of $10\angle 30°\ \Omega$ and $10\angle -60°\ \Omega$ branch. Determine the impedance of a circuit element such that if connected in series with the source, the system comes at resonance.

Solution: Given that

$$Z_1 = 10\angle 30°\ \Omega,\ Z_2 = -10\angle -60°\ \Omega$$

$$Z_p = \frac{Z_1 Z_2}{Z_1 + Z_2} = \frac{10\angle 30° \times 10\angle -60°}{10\angle 30° + 10\angle -60^0}° = 7.07\angle -15° = 6.83 - j1.83$$

$$Z_T = Z + Z_p = Z + 6.83 - j1.83$$

At resonance, the *j* component of the impedance is zero. Therefore

$$Z - j1.83 = 0$$

$$\Rightarrow \quad Z = j1.83 = jX_L$$

$$X_L = 1.83 = 2\pi f L$$

$$\Rightarrow \qquad L = \frac{1.83}{2\pi \times 50} = 5.82 \text{ mH}$$

5.10 A series *RLC* circuit has $Q = 5.1$ at its resonant frequency of 100 kHz. Assuming the power dissipation of the circuit is 100 W, when drawing a current of 0.8 A. Find the (i) circuit elements *R*, *L*, *C*, (ii) bandwidth Δf, and (iii) half-power frequencies.

Solution: Given that $f_0 = 100$ kHz, $Q = 5.1$, $P = 100$ W, $I = 0.8$ A

(i) Circuit elements *R*, *L*, *C*

Power, $P = I^2R$

$$\Rightarrow R = \frac{P}{I^2} = \frac{100}{0.8^2} = 156\ \Omega$$

$$Q = \frac{\omega_0 L}{R}$$

$$\Rightarrow L = \frac{QR}{\omega_0} = \frac{5.1 \times 156}{2\pi \times 100 \times 10^3} = 1.265 \text{ mH}$$

$$Q = \frac{1}{\omega_0 CR}$$

$$\Rightarrow C = \frac{1}{Q\omega_0 R} = \frac{1}{2\pi \times 100 \times 10^3 \times 156 \times 5.1} = 2.01 \text{ nF}$$

(ii) Bandwidth, Δf

$$\text{Quality factor, } Q = \frac{f_0}{\Delta f}$$

$$\Rightarrow \Delta f = \frac{f_0}{Q} = \frac{100}{5.1} = 19.6 \text{ kHz}$$

$$\therefore \ BW = \Delta f = 19.6 \text{ kHz}$$

(iii) Half-power frequencies

$$\text{Lower corner frequency } f_1 = f_0 - \frac{BW}{2} = 100 - \frac{19.6}{2} = 90.2 \text{ kHz}$$

$$\text{Upper corner frequency, } f_2 = f_0 + \frac{BW}{2} = 100 + \frac{19.6}{2} = 109.8 \text{ kHz}$$

5.11 For the network, determine the coefficient coupling for which the network is in series resonance.

Solution: For series resonance, total inductive reactance = total capacitive reactance

$$j3 + j27 + 2j\omega M = j20 + j13.6$$

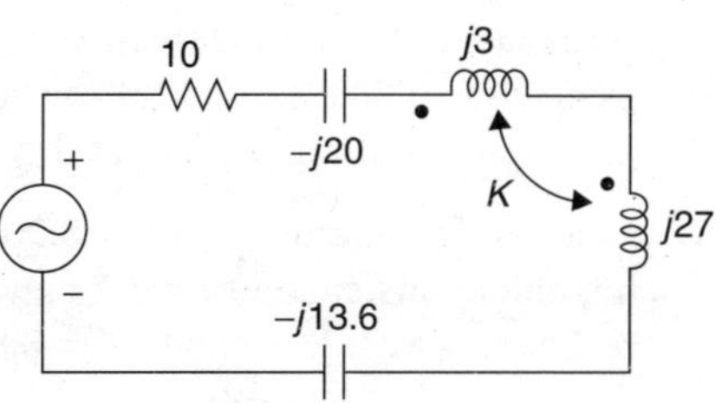

$$\Rightarrow \qquad 2j\omega M = j3.6$$

$$\Rightarrow \qquad 2\omega K\sqrt{L_1L_2} = 3.6$$

$$\Rightarrow \qquad 2K\sqrt{\omega L_1 \times \omega L_2} = 3.6$$

But $\quad \omega L_1 = 3, \omega L_2 = 27$

$\therefore \quad 2K\sqrt{3\times 27} = 3.6$

$\Rightarrow \quad K = 0.2$

5.12 A coil of 400 Ω resistance and 318 μH inductance is connected in parallel with a capacitor and the circuit resonates at 1 MHz. If a second capacitor of 23.5 pF capacitance is connected in parallel with the first capacitor, find the frequency at which the circuit resonates.

Solution: Given that $R = 400\ \Omega$, $L = 318\ \mu\text{H}$, $f_0 = 1$ MHz, $C_2 = 23.5$ pF

$$f_0 = \frac{1}{2\pi}\sqrt{\frac{1}{LC_1} - \frac{R^2}{L^2}}$$

$$\Rightarrow \quad 10^6 = \frac{1}{2\pi}\sqrt{\frac{1}{318\times 10^{-6}\times C_1} - \frac{400^2}{(318\times 10^{-6})^2}}$$

$$\Rightarrow \quad C_1 = 76.59 \text{ pF}$$

When capacitor of 23.5 pF is connected in parallel with $C_1 = 76.59$ pF

$$C_T = C_1 + C_2 = 76.59 + 23.5 = 100.1 \text{ pF}$$

The new resonant frequency is

$$f_0' = \frac{1}{2\pi}\sqrt{\frac{1}{LC_T} - \frac{R^2}{L^2}} = \frac{1}{2\pi}\sqrt{\frac{1}{318\times 10^{-6}\times 100.1\times 10^{-12}} - \frac{400^2}{(318\times 10^{-6})^2}} = 869.34 \text{ kHz}$$

5.13 Find the resonant frequency for the given series circuit.

Solution: Here the two inductors are connected in series opposing. So the mutual inductance is negative.

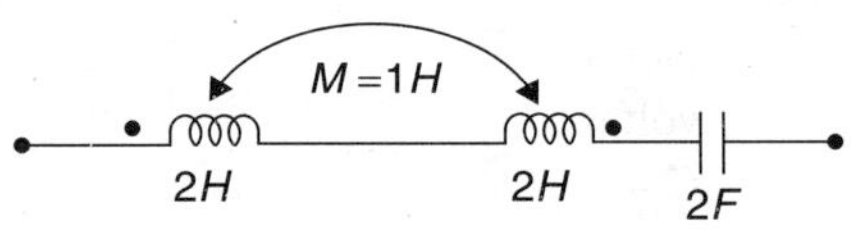

$$L_{eq} = L_1 + L_2 - 2M = 2 + 2 - 2\times 1 = 2$$

Resonant frequency

$$f_0 = \frac{1}{2\pi\sqrt{L_{eq}C}} = \frac{1}{2\pi\sqrt{2\times 2}} = 0.0795 \text{ Hz}$$

EXERCISE PROBLEMS

1. An *RLC* circuit has $R = 1$ kΩ, $L = 100$ mH, $C = 10$ pF. If a voltage of 100 V is applied across the series combination. Determine (a) resonant frequency (b) Q-factor and (c) half-power frequencies. [**Ans:** (a) $f_0 = 159$ kHz (b) Q = 100 (c) $f_1 = 158.2$ kHz $f_2 = 159.8$ kHz]

2. A circuit consisting of a resistance, an inductance of 0.4 H and a capacitance in series is connected across a 200 V, variable frequency supply. The current in the circuit has a maximum value of 40 A at a frequency of 50 c/s. Find (a) the value of resistance, (b) the capacitance, and (c) the voltage across the inductance and capacitance at this frequency. [**Ans:** (a) $R = 5\ \Omega$ (b) $C = 25.2\ \mu$F (c) $V_L = V_C = 5027$ V]

3. A series *RLC* circuit with $L = 0.5$ H has an instantaneous voltage $v = 70.7\sin(500t + 30°)$ V = and an instantaneous current $i = 1.5\sin(500t)$ A. Find the value of R and C. At what ω_0 will the circuit be resonant? [**Ans:** $R = 40.8\ \Omega$, $C = 8.83\ \mu$F, $\omega_0 = 476$ rad/s]

4. A series RLC circuit with $R = 25\ \Omega$ and $L = 0.6$ H results in a leading phase angle of 60° at a frequency of 40 Hz. At what frequency will the circuit be resonant? [**Ans:** $f_0 = 45.4$ Hz]

5. A coil of 20 Ω resistance has an inductance of 0.2 H and is connected in parallel with a 100 μF capacitor. Calculate the frequency at which the circuit will act as a non-inductance resistance of R Ω. Find also the value of R. [**Ans:** $f_0 = 31.8$ Hz, $Z_T = R = 100\ \Omega$]

6. Find the value of R_L for which the parallel circuit is resonant? [**Ans:** $R_L = 12.25\ \Omega$]

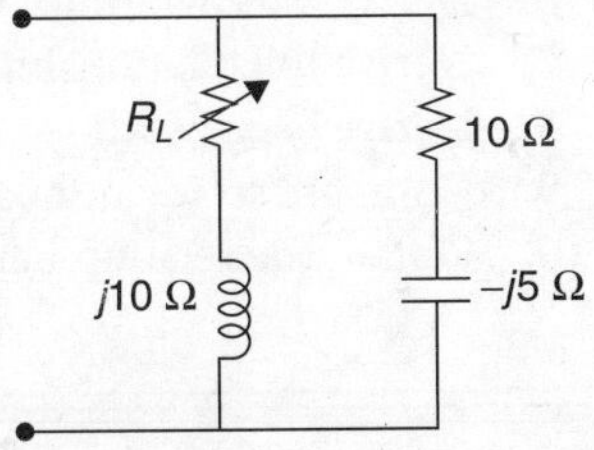

R_L 10 Ω
$j10\ \Omega$ $-j5\ \Omega$

7. For the circuit, find the value of capacitance so that the circuit resonates at $\omega_0 = 5$ krad/s. [**Ans:** $C = 21.32$ μF]

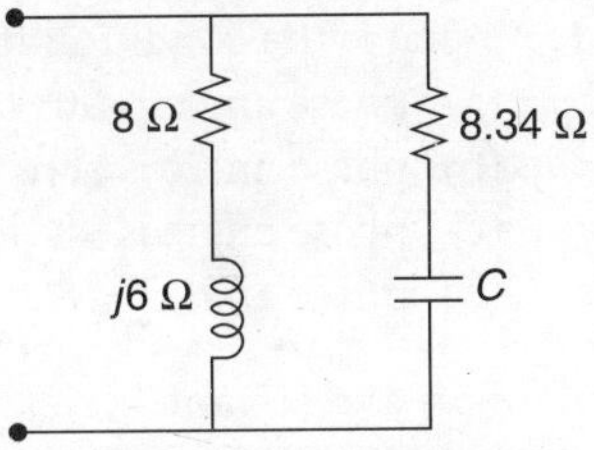

8 Ω 8.34 Ω
$j6\ \Omega$ C

8. A coil having a 2 Ω resistance is connected in series with a 50 μF capacitor. The circuit resonates at 100 Hz. What is the inductance of the coil? If the circuit is connected across a 100 V, 100 Hz AC source, find the power dissipated in the coil. Calculate the voltage across the capacitor and the coil. [**Ans:** $L = 50.66$ mH, $P = 5$ kW, $V_C = 1591.5$ V, $V_{coil} = 1594.6$ V]

9. A series RLC circuit has $R = 200\ \Omega$, $L = 1$ H and $C = 1$ μF. Find the resonant frequency, voltage magnification at resonance and bandwidth in rad/s. [**Ans:** $f_0 = 159.155$ Hz, $Q = 5$, $\Delta\omega = 200$ rad/s]

10. A coil of resistance R and inductance L is connected in series with a capacitance of 1 μF. The quality factor of this series resonant circuit is 10 and the bandwidth is 500 Hz. Find the circuit constant and voltage across the coil at resonance if the supply voltage is 20 V. [**Ans:** $R = 3.183\ \Omega$, $L = 1.013$ mH, $C = 1$ μF, $V_{coil} = 201$ V]

11. Two impedances $Z_1 = 20 + j10$ and $Z_2 = 10 - j30$ are connected in parallel and this combination is connected in series with $Z_3 = 30 + jX$. Find the value of X which will produce resonance. [**Ans:** $X = 3.85\ \Omega$]

12. A series RLC circuit takes a maximum current of 0.3 A at 200 V, 50 Hz. If the voltage across the capacitor is 290 V at resonance, determine R, L, C and Q of the coil. [**Ans:** $R = 666.7\ \Omega$, $L = 3.1$ H, $C = 3.29$ μF, $Q = 1.45$]

13. A series RLC circuit has $R = 30\ \Omega$, $L = 80$ mH and $C = 80$ μF. Find the resonant frequency, under resonance condition. Obtain the current, power and voltage drops across the various elements if the applied voltage equals 150 V. [**Ans:** $f_0 = 62.9$ Hz, $I = 5$ A, $P = 750$ W, $V_R = 150$ V, $V_L = V_C = 158$ V]

14. Given a series RLC circuit with $R = 100\ \Omega$, $L = 0.5$ H and $C = 40$ μF. Calculate the resonance, lower and upper half-power frequencies. [**Ans:** $f_0 = 35.7$ Hz, $\omega_1 = 123$ rad/s, $\omega_2 = 322$ rad/s]

REVIEW QUESTIONS

1. Define (a) resonance, (b) resonant frequency, (c) quality factor and bandwidth, (d) half-power frequency, (e) dynamic impedance, (f) bandwidth and selectivity, and (g) voltage and current magnification.

2. List the characteristics of series resonance.
3. In a series resonant circuit, prove that resonant frequency is the geometric mean of two half-power frequencies.
4. What is anti resonance?
5. List the characteristics of parallel resonance.
6. Derive bandwidth for a series *RLC* circuit as a function of resonant frequency.
7. Derive the relationship between bandwidth and half-power frequencies of an *RLC* series circuit.
8. Derive bandwidth for a series *RLC* circuit as a function of resonant frequency.
9. Compare series and parallel resonant circuits.
10. Obtain the relation between f_0, f_1 and f_2.

MULTIPLE CHOICE QUESTIONS

1. What is the condition for resonance?
   (a) phase angle is 90° lag
   (b) phase angle is zero
   (c) phase angle is 90° lead
   (d) phase angle is 180°

2. For a resonant series circuit, for $f < f_r$, the behaviour of the circuit is
   (a) resistive (b) *R–L–C*
   (c) capacitive (d) inductive

3. A coil of resistance 100 Ω and 100 μH is connected in series with a 100 PF is connected to a 10 V, variable frequency supply. What is the current through the circuit at resonance?
   (a) 1 A (b) 10 A
   (c) 0.01 A (d) 0.1 A

4. The *Q*-factor of a series resonant circuit is
   (a) voltage/current
   (b) voltage across *L* or *C*/applied voltage
   (c) power factor
   (d) *L*/*C*

5. In a series *RLC* circuit $R = 2$ kΩ , $L = 1$ H and $C = 2.5$ nF, the resonant frequency is:
   (a) 1083 Hz (b) 2183 Hz
   (c) 3183 Hz (d) 4123 Hz

6. For a series *RLC* circuit, the power factor at lower half-power frequency is:
   (a) 0.5 lagging (b) 0.65 leading
   (c) 0.707 leading (d) unity

7. In *RLC* parallel circuit, the impedance at resonance is
   (a) maximum (b) minimum
   (c) zero (d) infinity

8. The value of current at resonance in a series *RLC* circuit is governed by
   (a) *R* (b) *L*
   (c) *C* (d) all

9. On increasing the *Q* of the coil
   (a) its power factor increases
   (b) its power factor decreases
   (c) its power factor remains unaltered
   (d) none of the above

10. What type of magnification occurs in a series resonant *RLC* circuit?
    (a) voltage magnification
    (b) current magnification
    (c) both (d) none of the above

11. How many minimum storage elements are required to apply the resonance condition?
    (a) 4 (b) 3
    (c) 2 (d) 0

12. What type of magnification occurs in a parallel resonant *RLC* circuit?
    (a) voltage magnification
    (b) current magnification
    (c) both (d) can't say

13. In a series resonant *RLC* circuit, if frequency increases then resistance will
    (a) increase (b) decrease
    (c) remain constant (d) none of the above

14. The power in a series *RLC* circuit will be half of that at resonance when the magnitude of the current is equal to
    (a) $\frac{V}{2R}$ (b) $\frac{V}{\sqrt{3}R}$
    (c) $\frac{V}{\sqrt{2}R}$ (d) $\frac{V}{R}$

15. Which of the following statements is correct?
(a) $f_1 = f_0 - BW/2$ (b) $f_2 = f_0 + BW/2$
(c) $f_0^2 = f_1 f_2$ (d) all

16. What is the relation between f_0, BW and Q-factor?
(a) $f_0 = BW/Q$-factor
(b) $f_0 =$ BW – Q-factor
(c) $f_0 = BW + Q$-factor
(d) $f_0 = BW \times Q$-factor

17. In a series RLC circuit the resonant frequency is f_r. If all the component values are now doubled, the new resonant frequency is:
(a) $2f_r$ (b) f_r
(c) $f_r/4$ (d) $f_r/2$

18. The relation between f_0, f_1 and f_2 is
(a) $f_0 = f_1 + f_2$ (b) $f_0 = f_1 - f_2$
(c) $f_0^2 = f_1 f_2$ (d) $f_0 = f_1 f_2$

19. For an RLC series circuit
(a) selectivity = quality factor
(b) selectivity = 1/quality factor
(c) selectivity = bandwidth
(d) none of the above

20. The dynamic impedance of an RLC parallel circuit is:
(a) R (b) L/CR
(c) R/LC (d) C/LR

21. In a series RLC circuit, the half-power frequencies are f_1 = 40 Hz and f_2 = 90 Hz. Then the resonant frequency is
(a) 50 Hz (b) 130 Hz
(c) 60 Hz (d) 90 Hz

22. In a series RLC circuit, R = 10 Ω and bandwidth = 31.8 Hz, then inductance in the circuit is
(a) 2 H (b) 0.15 H
(c) 0.1 Hz (d) 0.05 H

23. The locus of impedance of a series RL circuit with variable R is
(a) a straight line parallel to the resistance axis
(b) a straight line parallel to the reactance axis
(c) a semi-circle with the centre on the resistance axis
(d) a semi-circle with the centre on the reactance axis

24. The locus of admittance of a series RC circuit with a variable C is
(a) a straight line parallel to the resistance axis
(b) a straight line parallel to the reactance axis
(c) a semi-circle with the centre on the resistance axis
(d) a semi-circle with the centre on the reactance axis

25. The locus of impedance of a series RL circuit with a variable L is
(a) a straight line parallel to the resistance axis
(b) a straight line parallel to the reactance axis
(c) a semi-circle with the centre on the resistance axis
(d) a semi-circle with the centre on the reactance axis

26. The coordinates of the centre of the locus of current in a series RC circuit when R is varied is
(a) $\left(\frac{C}{2X_C}, 0\right)$ (b) $\left(\frac{V}{2R}, 0\right)$
(c) $\left(\frac{V}{R}, 0\right)$ (d) $\left(0, \frac{V}{2X_C}\right)$

Answers

1. b	**2.** c	**5.** d	**5.** b	**5.** b	**6.** c	**7.** a	**8.** d	**9.** b	**10.** a
11. c	**12.** b	**15.** c	**15.** c	**15.** d	**16.** d	**17.** d	**18.** c	**19.** a	**20.** b
21. c	**22.** d	**23.** a	**25.** c	**25.** d	**26.** d				

6 Three Phase Circuits

Learning Outcomes

After reading this chapter, the reader will able to

- ➢ Define phase sequence, balanced load and balanced supply system
- ➢ List the advantages of the 3-phase system over the 1-phase system
- ➢ Define phase and line voltages
- ➢ Relate line and phase voltages and currents in star and delta connections
- ➢ Summarise star to delta and delta to star transfromations
- ➢ Contrast star and delta connections in 3-phase systems
- ➢ Analyse balanced and unbalanced 3-phase circuits
- ➢ Apply different power measurement methods for 3-phase balanced and unbalanced loads
- ➢ Find the power factor of unbalanced and balanced systems

6.1 INTRODUCTION

In an AC system, it is possible to connect two or more number of individual circuits to a common polyphase source. Though it is possible to have any number of sources in a polyphase system, the increase in the available power is not significant beyond the 3-phase system. The power generated by the same machine increases 41.4% from single phase to two phase and increase in the power is 50% from single phase to three phase. Beyond 3-phase, the maximum possible increase is only 7%, but complications are many. So an increase beyond 3-phase is not justified, but in some exceptional cases more than three phases are used. For example, in high power radio transmitter stations, six, twelve and more phases are used.

A 3-phase electrical system may be considered as three separate single phase systems, phase displaced from each other by 120°. The common configurations of interconnections in a 3-phase system are either star or delta connections. Three-phase voltages are generated and the voltage in all phases is equal in magnitude but shifted in phase by 120°.

6.2 ADVANTAGES OF THE 3-PHASE SYSTEM OVER THE SINGLE-PHASE SYSTEM

The polyphase, especially 3-phase system, has many advantages over the 1-phase system, both from a utility point of view as well as from the consumer point of view. Some of the advantages are:

- The output from a poly-phase machine is greater than a single phase machine of the same size.
- A 3-phase transmission circuit requires less conductor material than a 1-phase circuit to transmit a given amount of power over a given length. So, it is economical.
- Voltage regulation of a 3-phase system is better than that of a 1-phase system.
- 3-phase machines start more easily than 1-phase machines.
- The torque produced by a 3-phase motor is more when compared to a 1-phase motor.
- To transmit a given amount of power at a specified voltage, the poly-phase system has higher efficiency when compared to a 1-phase system.
- The power factor of a poly-phase machine is greater than a 1-phase machine of the same rating.
- Three-phase machines have less vibrations when compared to 1-phase machines.

6.3 IMPORTANT TERMS AND DEFINITIONS

Phase sequence The phase sequence is the time order in which the voltages pass through their respective maximum values. Alternatively, it is the order in which the alternating quantity in various phases (R, Y and B) attains the maximum value.

$$V_{RN} = V_{ph}\angle 0° \text{ (reference)}$$

$$V_{YN} = V_{ph}\angle -120°$$

$$V_{BN} = V_{ph}\angle -240°$$

Positive phase sequence If the voltage in the Y-phase reaches the maximum value 120° after the R phase and the voltage in the B-phase reaches the maximum value 120° after the Y phase, it is called positive phase sequence (RYB).

Negative phase sequence If the maximum value of voltage reached by various phases is in the order RBY, then it is called negative phase sequence.

Balanced Supply system If the voltage in all the 3-phases is equal in magnitude and displaced by 120°, then the system is called a balanced supply system.

Balanced load If the loads in all the 3-phases are equal in magnitude and phase, then they are called balanced loads.

Unbalanced load If the loads in all the 3-phases are not identical to each other, that is, unequal in magnitude and phase, then they are called unbalanced loads.

6.4 THREE-PHASE BALANCED SYSTEM

Three equal voltages which differ by in phase by 120° to each other, constitute a 3-phase balanced system. Their mathematical equations can be written as given below:

$$v_{RN} = V_m \sin\theta \text{ (reference)} \tag{6.1}$$

$$v_{YN} = V_m \sin(\theta - 120°) \tag{6.2}$$

$$v_{BN} = V_m \sin(\theta - 240°) = V_m \sin(\theta + 120°) \tag{6.3}$$

The time diagram of a 3-phase balanced voltage is sketched (Fig. 6.1). Here, V_{RN} is taken as reference, hence it is zero at $\theta = \omega t = 0°$, V_{YN} lags V_{RN} by 120° and V_{BN} lags V_{RN} by 240° or leads V_{RN} by 120°. In this case, the phase sequence is said to be RYB. The vector diagram of 3-phase balanced voltages for both RYB and RBY phase sequence is shown in Fig. 6.2.

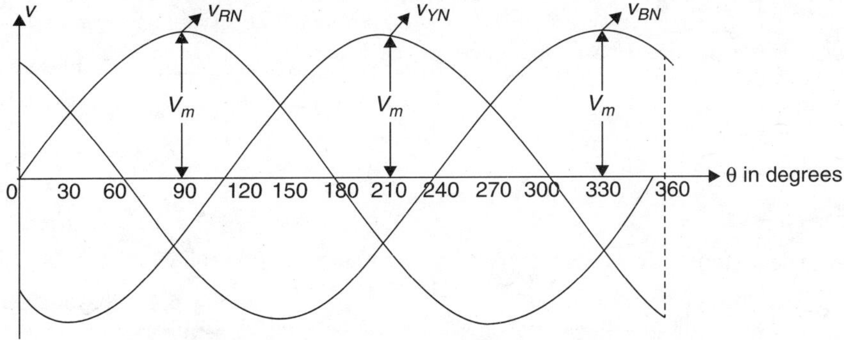

Fig. 6.1 Time diagram of a 3-phase balanced voltage

Balanced 3-phase voltages can be written in polar form as shown.

$$V_{RN} = V_{ph}\angle 0° \text{ (reference)}$$
$$V_{YN} = V_{ph}\angle -120°$$
$$V_{BN} = V_{ph}\angle -240°$$

Note: In a 3-phase system, selection of one voltage as the reference with a phase angle of zero determines the phase angles of all other voltages in the system.

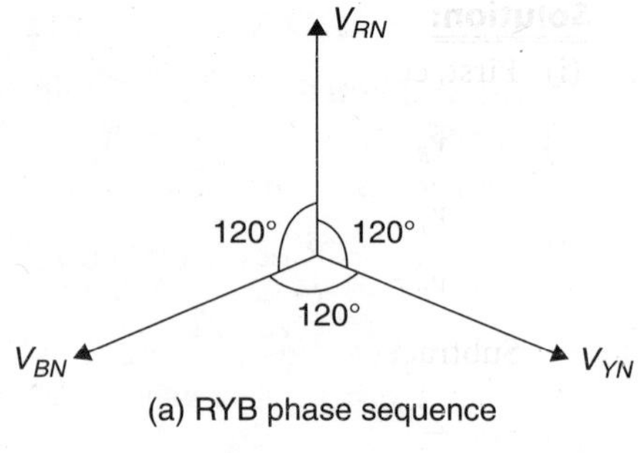

(a) RYB phase sequence

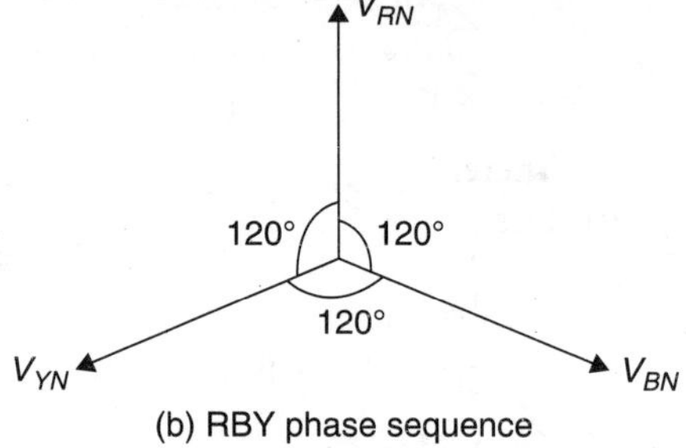

(b) RBY phase sequence

Fig. 6.2 Phasor diagram of a 3-phase balanced system

Case (i) RYB, YBR and BRY (positive phase) sequence

Let V_{RY} be taken as reference.

$$\therefore \quad V_{RY} = V_L\angle 0°,\ V_{YB} = V_L\angle -120°,\ V_{BR} = V_L\angle 120°$$

$$V_{RN} = V_{ph} = \frac{V_L}{\sqrt{3}}\angle -30°,\ V_{YN} = \frac{V_L}{\sqrt{3}}\angle -150°,\ V_{BN} = \frac{V_L}{\sqrt{3}}\angle 90°$$

Let V_{YB} be taken as reference.

$$\therefore \quad V_{YB} = V_L\angle 0°,\ V_{RY} = V_L\angle 120°,\ V_{BR} = V_L\angle -120°$$

$$V_{YN} = V_{ph} = \frac{V_L}{\sqrt{3}}\angle -30°,\ V_{RN} = \frac{V_L}{\sqrt{3}}\angle 90°,\ V_{BN} = \frac{V_L}{\sqrt{3}}\angle -150°$$

The phasor diagram for RYB phase sequence is shown in Fig. 6.3.

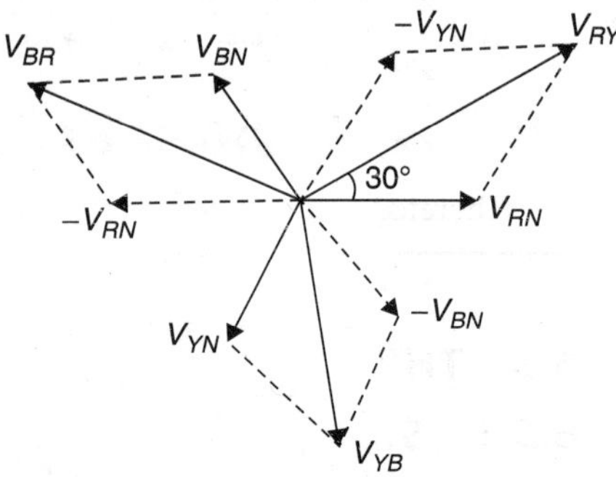

Fig. 6.3 Phasor diagram for RYB phase sequence

Case (ii) BYR, RBY and YRB (negative phase) sequence

Let V_{RY} be taken as reference.

$$\therefore \quad V_{RY} = V_L\angle 0°,\ V_{YB} = V_L\angle 120°,\ V_{BR} = V_L\angle -120°$$

$$V_{RN} = V_{ph} = \frac{V_L}{\sqrt{3}}\angle 30°,\ V_{YN} = \frac{V_L}{\sqrt{3}}\angle 150°,\ V_{BN} = \frac{V_L}{\sqrt{3}}\angle -90°$$

Let V_{YB} be taken as reference.

$$\therefore \quad V_{YB} = V_L\angle 0°,\ V_{RY} = V_L\angle -120°,\ V_{BR} = V_L\angle 120°$$

$$V_{YN} = V_{ph} = \frac{V_L}{\sqrt{3}}\angle 30°,\ V_{RN} = \frac{V_L}{\sqrt{3}}\angle -90°,\ V_{BN} = \frac{V_L}{\sqrt{3}}\angle 150°$$

The phasor diagram for RBY phase sequence is shown in Fig. 6.4.

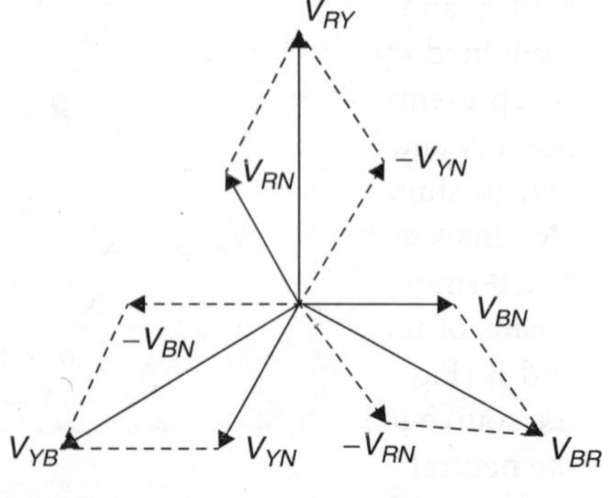

Fig. 6.4 Phasor diagram for RBY phase sequence

Problem 6.1 What is the phase sequence of each of the following sets of voltages?

(i) $v_R = 208\cos(\omega t + 27°)$

$v_Y = 208\cos(\omega t + 147°)$

$v_B = 208\cos(\omega t - 93°)$

(ii) $v_{an} = 200\cos(\omega t + 10°)$

$v_{bn} = 200\cos(\omega t - 230°)$

$v_{cn} = 200\cos(\omega t - 110°)$

Solution:

(i) First, convert the cosine waveforms into phasors

$$v_R = 208\cos(\omega t + 27°) \Rightarrow V_R = 208\angle 27°$$

$$v_Y = 208\cos(\omega t + 147°) \Rightarrow V_Y = 208\angle 147°$$

$$v_B = 208\cos(\omega t - 93°) \Rightarrow V_B = 208\angle -93°$$

Subtract all the phase angles from the R-phase.

$$\angle V_R' = 27° - 27° = 0°$$

$$\angle V_Y' = 27° - 147° = -120°$$

$$\angle V_B' = 27° + 93° = 120°$$

Therefore, the phase sequence is 'RYB'

(ii) First, convert the cosine waveforms into phasors

$$v_{an} = 200\cos(\omega t + 10°) \Rightarrow V_{an} = 200\angle 10°$$

$$v_{bn} = 200\cos(\omega t - 230°) \Rightarrow V_{bn} = 200\angle -230°$$

$$v_{cn} = 200\cos(\omega t - 110°) \Rightarrow V_{cn} = 200\angle -110°$$

Subtract all the phase angles from the a-phase.

$$\angle V_{an}' = 10° - 10° = 0°$$

$$\angle V_{bn}' = 10° + 230° = 240°$$

$$\angle V_{cn}' = 10° + 110° = 120°$$

Therefore, the phase sequence is 'abc'.

6.5 THREE-PHASE BALANCED SYSTEM CONNECTIONS

6.5.1 STAR CONNECTION

Three similar polarity terminals of three sources connected at a single point (Fig. 6.5), is known as *star connection*. The point of connection is known as source neutral and is represented by *N*. Similarly, three loads are joined at a single point known as *load neutral* and is represented by *n*. The wire joining source neutral point *N* and load neutral point *n* is known as *neutral wire* or simply *neutral*. After connecting three similar terminals at the neutral point, the remaining three free terminals of the source are joined to the load by means of individual condcutors known as lines R, Y and B (Fig. 6.5). Three lines carry the currents from the source to the load and the neutral carries all the return currents from the load to the source. Therefore, the neutral current I_N is the sum of the three currents.

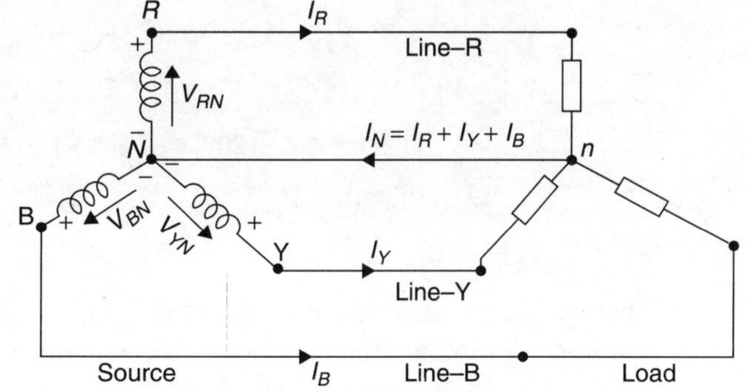

Fig. 6.5 Star connection

$$\therefore \quad I_N = I_R + I_Y + I_B \tag{6.4}$$

In a three-phase balanced system, if the loads in all the three phases are balanced, then three currents I_R, I_Y, I_B constitute a balanced system of currents.

$$\therefore \quad I_R = I\angle 0°,\ I_Y = I\angle{-120°},\ I_B = I\angle 120°$$

$$I_N = I_R + I_Y + I_B = I\angle 0° + I\angle{-120°} + I\angle 120° = 0$$

From the above calculations, it is clear that neutral current I_N is zero. Hence, in a balanced system, a neutral wire is not required. Such a system is known as 3-phase 3-wire system.

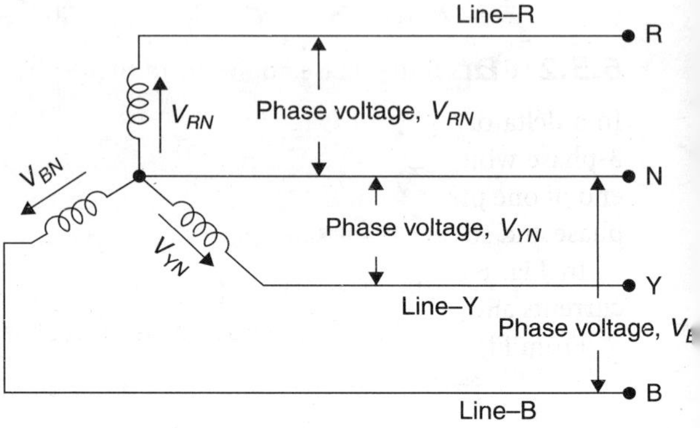

Line voltages and phase voltages Phase voltage is a voltage measured between any line conductor and the neutral. Thus, in Fig. 6.6, three phase voltages V_{RN}, V_{YN} and V_{BN} are shown.

Line voltage is a voltage measured between any two line conductors. Thus in Fig. 6.7, three line voltages V_{RY}, V_{YB} and V_{BR} are shown.

Applying KVL to the loop consisting of V_{RN}, V_{RY} and V_{YN}, we have,

Fig. 6.6 Three phase voltages V_{RN}, V_{YN} and V_{BN}

$$V_{RN} - V_{RY} - V_{YN} = 0$$

$$\Rightarrow \quad V_{RY} = V_{RN} - V_{YN} \tag{6.5}$$

Similarly, $$V_{YB} = V_{YN} - V_{BN} \tag{6.6}$$

$$V_{BR} = V_{BN} - V_{RN} \tag{6.7}$$

The above equations give the relation between line voltages and phase voltages.

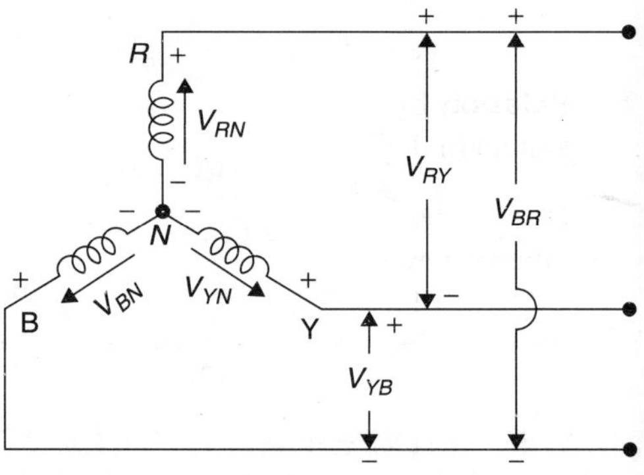

Fig. 6.7 Three line voltages V_{RY}, V_{YB} and V_{BR}

Relation between line and phase values Let $V_{RN} = V_{YN} = V_{BN}$ be the phase voltage of balanced system in star connection.

$$\therefore \quad V_{RN} = V_{ph}\angle 0°,\ V_{YN} = V_{ph}\angle{-120°},\ V_{BN} = V_{ph}\angle{+120°}$$

$$\therefore \quad V_{RY} = V_L = V_{RN} - V_{YN} = V_{ph}\angle 0° - V_{ph}\angle{-120°}$$

$$= V_{ph}[1\angle 0° - 1\angle{-120°}] = V_{ph}[1.5 + j0.866]$$

$$= 1.732\angle 30° \times V_{ph}$$

$$\Rightarrow \quad V_L = \sqrt{3}V_{ph} \tag{6.8}$$

Therefore, the magnitude of the line voltage V_{RY} is $\sqrt{3}$ times the magnitude of the phase voltage V_{RN}, and V_{RY} leads V_{RN} by 30°. The same is the case with the other two line voltages. From the star connected 3-phase system, it is clearly observed that whatever currents flows through the lines R,Y and B also flows through the respective phase windings or coils. Hence in a star connected system the phase currents and line currents are equal.

$$\text{For a star connected system, } I_L = I_{ph} \tag{6.9}$$

Power in star-connection In a balanced star connected system, the power in each phase is the same. Therefore 3-phase power

$$P = 3 \times \text{Per phase power} = 3 \times V_{ph} I_{ph} \cos\phi$$

$$= 3 \times \frac{V_L}{\sqrt{3}} \times I_L \cos\phi = \sqrt{3} V_L I_L \cos\phi$$

$$P = \sqrt{3} V_L I_L \cos\phi \quad (6.10)$$

6.5.2 Delta or Mesh Connection

In a delta or mesh connection, the dissimilar ends of the 3-phase windings are joined together, that is, the starting end of one phase is joined to the finishing end of the other phase and so on (Fig. 6.8).

In Fig. 6.8, I_{RY}, I_{YB} and I_{BR} represent phase values of currents and I_R, I_Y and I_B represent line values of currents.

From Fig. 6.8, by applying KCL at node R,

$$-I_{BR} - I_R + I_{RY} = 0$$

$$\Rightarrow \quad I_R = I_{RY} - I_{BR} \quad (6.11)$$

Similarly $I_Y = I_{YB} - I_{RY}$ (6.12)

$$I_B = I_{BR} - I_{YB} \quad (6.13)$$

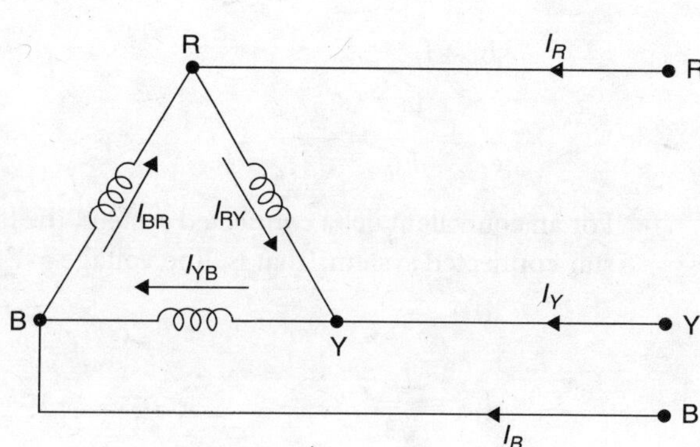

Fig. 6.8 Delta connection

Relation between line and phase values Let $I_{RY} = I_{YB} = I_{BR} = I_{ph}$ be the phase currents of a balanced system in delta connection.

$$\therefore \quad I_{RY} = I_{ph}\angle 0°, I_{YB} = I_{ph}\angle -120°, I_{BR} = I_{ph}\angle +120°$$

Line current flowing through the R-phase

$$I_R = I_L = I_{RY} - V_{BR} = I_{ph}\angle 0° - I_{ph}\angle 120°$$

$$= I_{ph}[1\angle 0° - 1\angle 120°] = I_{ph}[1.5 - j0.866]$$

$$= 1.732\angle -30° \times I_{ph}$$

$$\therefore \quad I_L = \sqrt{3} I_{ph} \quad (6.14)$$

From Eq. 6.14, it is clear that the line current I_L is $\sqrt{3}$ times the phase current and current I_R lags I_{RY} by 30°.

From the delta connected 3-phase system, it is clearly observed that the voltage that exists between the lines, appears across the phases also. Hence in a delta connected system, the phase and line voltages are equal. Therefore,

$$V_L = V_{ph} \quad (6.15)$$

Power in a delta-connection In a balanced 3-phase delta connected system, the power in each phase is the same. Therefore 3-phase power

$$P = 3 \times \text{per phase power} = 3 \times V_{ph} I_{ph} \cos\phi$$

$$= 3 \times V_L \times \frac{I_L}{\sqrt{3}} \cos\phi = \sqrt{3} V_L I_L \cos\phi$$

$$P = \sqrt{3} V_L I_L \cos\phi \quad (6.16)$$

From Eqs 6.10 and 6.16, it is clear that irrespective of star connection or delta connection

3-phase power, $P = \sqrt{3} V_L I_L \cos\phi$ (6.17)

6.5.3 Balanced Star/Delta and Delta/Star Conversions

Any balanced star connected system can be converted into an equivalent delta connected system and vice versa. For a balanced star connected load, let line voltage = V_L, line current = I_L and impedance per phase = Z_Y.

$$V_{ph} = \frac{V_L}{\sqrt{3}}$$

$$I_{ph} = I_L$$

$$Z_Y = \frac{V_{ph}}{I_{ph}} = \frac{V_L}{\sqrt{3}I_L} \tag{6.18}$$

For an equivalent delta connected system, the line voltages and currents must have the same values as in the star connected system. That is, line voltage = V_L, line current = I_L and impedance per phase = Z_Δ.

$$V_{ph} = V_L$$

$$I_{ph} = \frac{I_L}{\sqrt{3}}$$

$$Z_\Delta = \frac{V_{ph}}{I_{ph}} = \frac{V_L}{I_L/\sqrt{3}} = \frac{\sqrt{3}V_L}{I_L} \tag{6.19}$$

From Eqs 6.18 and 6.19, we have

$$Z_Y = \frac{V_L}{\sqrt{3}I_L} = \frac{Z_\Delta}{\sqrt{3}\times\sqrt{3}} = \frac{Z_\Delta}{3} \tag{6.20}$$

Thus, when three equal impedances are connected in delta, the equivalent star impedance is one third of the delta impedance.

6.5.4 Relation Between Power in Delta and Star Systems

Let a balanced load be connected in star having an impedance per phase as Z_{ph}.

For a star connected load,

$$V_{ph} = \frac{V_L}{\sqrt{3}}$$

$$I_{ph} = \frac{V_{ph}}{Z_{ph}} = \frac{V_L}{\sqrt{3}Z_{ph}}$$

$$I_L = I_{ph} = \frac{V_L}{\sqrt{3}Z_{ph}}$$

Now $\quad P_Y = \sqrt{3}V_L I_L \cos\phi = \sqrt{3}V_L \times \dfrac{V_L}{\sqrt{3}Z_{ph}} \times \cos\phi = \dfrac{V_L^2}{Z_{ph}} \times \cos\phi$

$$\Rightarrow \quad P_Y = \frac{V_L^2}{Z_{ph}} \times \cos\phi \tag{6.21}$$

For a delta connected load,

$$V_{ph} = V_L$$

$$I_{ph}=\frac{V_{ph}}{Z_{ph}}=\frac{V_L}{Z_{ph}}$$

$$I_L=\sqrt{3}I_{ph}=\sqrt{3}\times\frac{V_L}{Z_{ph}}$$

Now $$P_\Delta=\sqrt{3}V_LI_L\cos\phi=\sqrt{3}V_L\times\sqrt{3}\frac{V_L}{Z_{ph}}\times\cos\phi=3\frac{V_L^2}{Z_{ph}}\times\cos\phi$$

$\Rightarrow$ $$P_\Delta=3\frac{V_L^2}{Z_{ph}}\times\cos\phi \tag{6.22}$$

From Eqs 6.21 and 6.22, we have

$$P_Y=\frac{P_\Delta}{3}\quad\Rightarrow\quad P_\Delta=3P_Y \tag{6.23}$$

Thus, the power consumed by a balanced delta connected load is three times that in the case of a star connected load.

6.5.5 Comparison Between Star and Delta Connections

S. no	Star connection	Delta connection
1	Similar ends are joined	Dissimilar ends are joined
2	$V_L=\sqrt{3}V_{ph}$ and $I_L=I_{ph}$	$V_L=V_{ph}$ and $I_L=\sqrt{3}I_{ph}$
3	Possible to carry neutral current	Neutral wire is not available
4	Provides 3-phase 4-wire arrangement	Provides 3-phase 3-wire arrangement
5	The phasor sum of all the phase currents is zero	The phasor sum of all the phase voltages is zero
6	Can be used for lighting as well as power loads	Can be used for power loads only

Problem 6.2 A balanced delta connected load of $(8+j6)\ \Omega$ per phase is connected to a 3-phase, 50 Hz, 230 V supply. Calculate (i) line current, (ii) power factor, (iii) reactive volt-ampere, and (iv) total volt-ampere.

Solution:

Given that $Z_{ph}=8+j6=10\angle 36.87°$

$V_L=230$ V

In the case of delta connection, $V_L=V_{ph}=230$ V

Phase current, $I_{ph}=\frac{V_{ph}}{Z_{ph}}=\frac{230}{10}=23$

(i) Line current, $I_L=\sqrt{3}I_{ph}=\sqrt{3}\times 23=39.84$ A

(ii) Power factor, $\cos\phi=\frac{R_{ph}}{Z_{ph}}=\frac{8}{10}=0.8$

(iii) Reactive volt-ampere, $Q=\sqrt{3}V_LI_L\sin\phi=\sqrt{3}\times 230\times 39.84\times 0.6=9523$ VAR

(iv) Total volt-ampere, $S=\sqrt{3}V_LI_L=\sqrt{3}\times 230\times 39.84=15.87$ kVA

Problem 6.3 A balanced 3-phase star connected load of 150 kW takes a leading current of 100 A with a line voltage of 1100 V, 50 Hz. Find the circuit constants of the load per phase.

Solution:

Given that Power, $P = 150$ kW

Current, $I_L = 100$ A

Line voltage, $V_L = 1100$ V

3-phase star connected balanced load

$$\text{Impedance } Z_{ph} = \frac{V_{ph}}{I_{ph}} = \frac{1100}{\sqrt{3} \times 100} = 6.35\ \Omega$$

Power consumed in the load

$$P = 3\, I_{ph}^2 R_{ph}$$

$$150 \times 10^3 = 3 \times 100^2 \times R_{ph}$$

$$\Rightarrow \quad R_{ph} = 5\ \Omega$$

$$\text{Impedance, } Z_{ph} = \sqrt{R_{ph}^2 + X_{ph}^2}$$

$$\Rightarrow \quad X_{ph} = \sqrt{Z_{ph}^2 - R_{ph}^2} = \sqrt{6.35^2 - 5^2} = 3.91\ \Omega$$

Since it is given that input current is leading, X_{ph} must be capacitive.

$$\therefore \quad X_{ph} = \frac{1}{2\pi fC} = 3.91$$

$$\Rightarrow \quad C = \frac{1}{2\pi f X_{ph}} = \frac{1}{2\pi \times 50 \times 3.91} = 814.1\ \mu\text{F}$$

Therefore, the circuit constants are $R = 5\ \Omega$, $C = 814.1\ \mu\text{F}$

Problem 6.4 Three equal impedance of each $(5 + j8.66)\ \Omega$ are connected in star to a 400 V, 3-phase, 50 Hz supply system. Calculate the (i) line current, (ii) power factor, (iii) active power consumed. (iv) If the same three impedances are connected in delta to the same source of supply, what is the active power consumed?

Solution:

Given that $Z_{ph} = 5 + j8.66 = 10\angle 60^\circ\ \Omega$, $V_L = 400$ V

$$\text{Phase voltage, } V_{ph} = \frac{V_L}{\sqrt{3}} = \frac{400}{\sqrt{3}} = 231\ \text{V}$$

$$\text{Phase current, } I_{ph} = \frac{V_{ph}}{Z_{ph}} = \frac{231}{10} = 23.1\ \text{A}$$

(i) Line current, $I_L = I_{ph} = 23.1$ A

(ii) Power factor, $\cos\phi = \dfrac{R_{ph}}{Z_{ph}} = \dfrac{5}{10} = 0.5$ lag

(iii) Active power consumed, $P = \sqrt{3}V_L I_L \cos\phi = \sqrt{3} \times 400 \times 23.1 \times 0.5 = 8$ kW

(iv) Active power consumed for delta connected load

$$Z_{ph} = 5 + j8.66 = 10\angle 60°,\ V_L = 400 \text{ V}$$

$$V_L = V_{ph} = 400 \text{ V}$$

$$I_{ph} = \frac{V_{ph}}{Z_{ph}} = \frac{400}{10} = 40 \text{ A}$$

$$I_L = \sqrt{3}I_{ph} = \sqrt{3} \times 40 = 69.28$$

$$P = \sqrt{3}V_L I_L \cos\phi = \sqrt{3} \times 400 \times 69.28 \times 0.5 = 24 \text{ kW}$$

Problem 6.5 Three identical resistances are connected in a star fashion against a balanced three phase voltage supply. If one of the resistance is removed, how much power is to be reduced?

Solution:

Three identical resistors each of resistance R are connected in star as shown in Fig. (a).

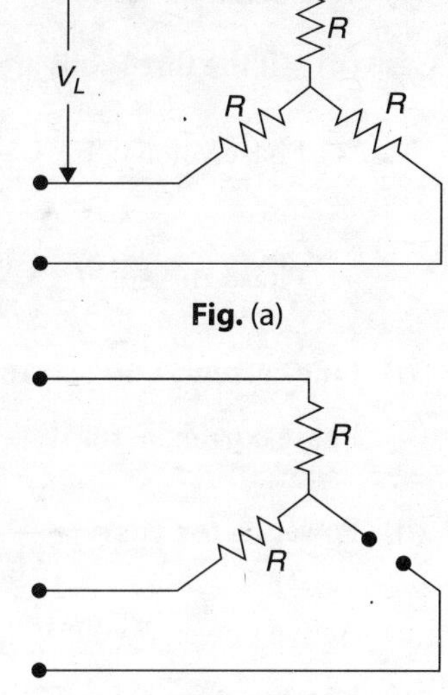

Fig. (a)

Fig. (b)

Power consumed by the load

$$P_1 = 3\frac{V_{ph}^2}{R} = 3\left(\frac{V_L}{\sqrt{3}}\right)^2 \times \frac{1}{R} = \frac{V_L^2}{R} \text{ watts} \quad (1)$$

When one of the phase resistance is removed [Fig. (b)], then the power consumed is given by

$$P_2 = 2\frac{V_{ph}^2}{R} = 2\left(\frac{V_L}{2}\right)^2 \times \frac{1}{R} = \frac{V_L^2}{2R} \text{ watts} \quad (2)$$

[∵ Voltage across each resistance is $V_L/2$ only]

Reduction in power is given by

$$\Delta P = \frac{\frac{V_L^2}{R} - \frac{V_L^2}{2R}}{\frac{V_L^2}{R}} \times 100 = 50\%$$

Hence, removing a resistance from the circuit reduces the power by 50%.

Problem 6.6 Three similar coils R, Y and B each having an impedance of $15\angle 53.13°$ are connected in delta across a 440 V, 3-phase, 50 Hz supply system. Calculate (i) phase and line currents, (ii) power factor, (iii) active power, (iv) reactive power, and (v) total kVA. If the same three impedances are connected in star across the same source of supply, calculate the above quantities.

Solution:

Given that $Z_{ph} = 15\angle 53.13°\ \Omega = (9 + j12)\ \Omega$, $V_L = 440$ V

Case (i) If the three coils are connected in delta connection

$$V_{ph} = V_L = 440 \text{ V}$$

(i) Phase current, $I_{ph} = \dfrac{V_{ph}}{Z_{ph}} = \dfrac{440}{15} = 29.33 \text{ A}$

Line current, $I_L = \sqrt{3}I_{ph} = \sqrt{3} \times 29.33 = 50.8 \text{ A}$

(ii) Power factor, $\cos\phi = \dfrac{R_{ph}}{Z_{ph}} = \dfrac{9}{15} = 0.6 \text{ lag}$

(iii) Active power, $P = \sqrt{3}V_L I_L \cos\phi = \sqrt{3} \times 440 \times 50.8 \times 0.6 = 23.23 \text{ kW}$

(iv) Reactive power, $S = \sqrt{3}V_L I_L \sin\phi = \sqrt{3} \times 440 \times 50.8 \times 0.8 = 30.98 \text{ kVAR}$

(v) Total kVA, $S = \sqrt{3}V_L I_L = \sqrt{3} \times 440 \times 50.8 = 38.7 \text{ kVA}$

Case (ii) If the three coils are connected in star connection

Phase voltage, $V_{ph} = \dfrac{V_L}{\sqrt{3}} = \dfrac{440}{\sqrt{3}} = 254 \text{ V}$

Phase current, $I_{ph} = \dfrac{V_{ph}}{Z_{ph}} = \dfrac{254}{15} = 16.94 \text{ A}$

(i) Line current, $I_L = I_{ph} = 16.94 \text{ A}$

Phase current = 16.94 A

(ii) Power factor, $\cos\phi = \dfrac{R_{ph}}{Z_{ph}} = \dfrac{9}{15} = 0.6 \text{ lag}$

(iii) Active power, $P = \sqrt{3}V_L I_L \cos\phi = \sqrt{3} \times 440 \times 16.94 \times 0.6 = 7.74 \text{ kW}$

(iv) Reactive power, $S = \sqrt{3}V_L I_L \sin\phi = \sqrt{3} \times 440 \times 16.94 \times 0.8 = 10.32 \text{ kVAR}$

(v) Total kVA, $S = \sqrt{3}V_L I_L = \sqrt{3} \times 440 \times 16.94 = 12.91 \text{ kVA}$

Problem 6.7 A 3-phase 220 V supply is applied to a balanced 3-phase delta connected load of $(6 + j8)\ \Omega$ in each phase. Determine the phase currents and line currents. Take phase sequence as RYB. Draw the phasor diagram.

Solution:

Given that Load impedance, $Z = (6 + j8)\ \Omega = 10\angle 53.13°$

Let us take V_{RY} as reference phasor

$$V_{RY} = 220\angle 0° \text{ V},\ V_{YB} = 220\angle -120° \text{ V},\ V_{BR} = 220\angle -240° \text{ V}$$

$$I_{RY} = \frac{V_{RY}}{Z} = \frac{220}{10\angle 53.13°} = 22\angle -53.13° = 13.178 - j17.616$$

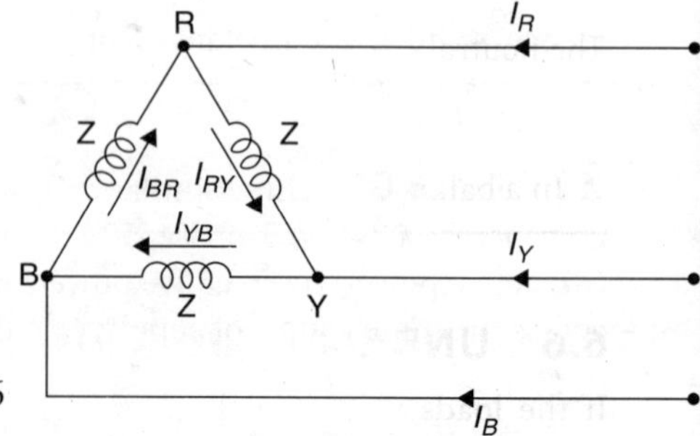

Fig. 1: Circuit diagram

$$I_{YB} = \frac{V_{YB}}{Z} = \frac{220\angle{-120^\circ}}{10\angle 53.13^\circ} = 22\angle{-173.2^\circ} = -21.845 - j2.6$$

$$I_{BR} = \frac{V_{BR}}{Z} = \frac{220\angle{-240^\circ}}{10\angle 53.13^\circ} = 22\angle{-293.13^\circ} = 8.667 + j20.2$$

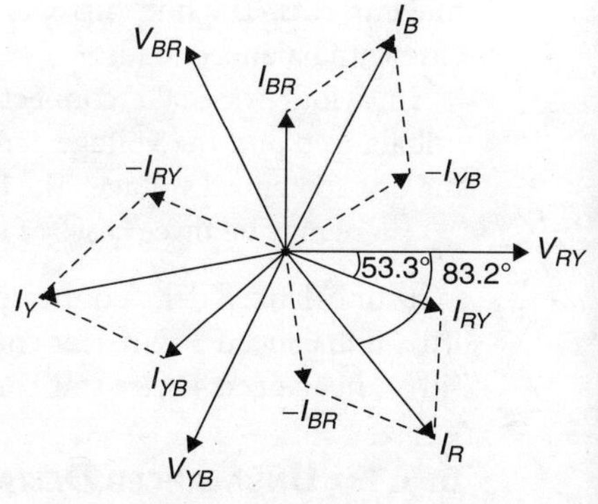

Fig. 2 Phasor diagram

By applying KCL at node R

$$I_R + I_{BR} = I_{RY}$$

$$\Rightarrow \quad I_R = I_{RY} - I_{BR} = 22\angle{-53.13^\circ} - 22\angle{-293.13^\circ} = 38.1\angle{-83.2^\circ}\text{ A}$$

By applying KCL at node Y

$$I_Y = I_{YB} - I_{RY} = 22\angle{-173.2^\circ} - 22\angle{-53.2^\circ} = 38.1\angle{-203.2^\circ}$$

By applying KCL at node B

$$I_B = I_{BR} - I_{YB} = 22\angle{-293.2^\circ} - 22\angle{-173.2^\circ} = 38.1\angle{-323.2^\circ}$$

Problem 6.8 A 3-phase, 4-wire 220 V supply is applied to a balanced 3-phase star connected load of $20\angle 30^\circ\ \Omega$ in each phase. Find the line currents and draw the phasor diagram. Take phase sequence as RBY.

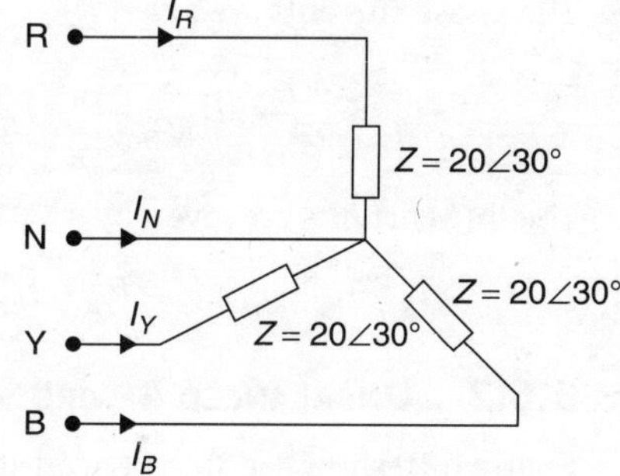

Fig. 1 Circuit diagram

Solution:

Given that $V_{ph} = \frac{V_L}{\sqrt{3}} = \frac{220}{\sqrt{3}} = 127$

$$V_{RN} = 127\angle 30^\circ,\ V_{YN} = 127\angle 150^\circ,\ V_{BN} = 127\angle{-90^\circ}$$

The line currents are

$$I_R = \frac{V_{RN}}{Z} = \frac{127\angle 30^\circ}{20\angle 30^\circ} = 6.35$$

$$I_Y = \frac{V_{YN}}{Z} = \frac{127\angle 150^\circ}{20\angle 30^\circ} = 6.35\angle 120^\circ$$

$$I_B = \frac{V_{BN}}{Z} = \frac{127\angle{-90^\circ}}{20\angle 30^\circ} = 6.35\angle{-120^\circ}$$

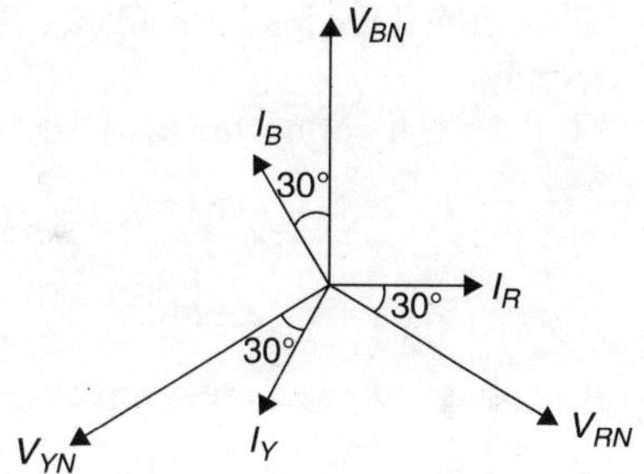

Fig. 2 Phasor diagram

The neutral current is

$$I_N = -(I_R + I_Y + I_B) = -[6.35 + 6.35\angle 120^\circ + 6.35\angle{-120^\circ}] = 0$$

$\therefore$ In a balanced 3-phase system the neutral current is zero.

6.6 UNBALANCED 3-PHASE SYSTEMS

If the loads in all the three phases are not identical to each other, that is, unequal in magnitude and phase, then it is called unbalanced load. The solution of the unbalanced delta-connected load consists of computing the phase currents and then applying Kirchhoff's current law to the junctions to obtain the three line currents. The line currents will not be equal and they will not have a 120° phase difference as was the case with balanced loads.

In a four-wire star connected system, the neutral conductor will carry a current when the load is unbalanced and the voltage across each of the load impedance remains fixed with the same magnitude as the line to neutral voltage. The line currents are unequal and do not have a 120° phase difference.

There may be three cases of unbalanced load:

(i) unbalanced delta connected load,
(ii) unbalanced 3-wire star connected load, and
(iii) unbalanced 4-wire star connected load.

6.6.1 Unbalanced Delta Connected Load

Figure 6.9 shows an unbalanced delta connected load connected to a balanced 3-phase supply.

For a delta connected load, let

$$V_L = V_{ph};\ V_{RY} = V_{ph}\angle 0°;\ V_{YB} = V_{ph}\angle -120°;$$

$$V_{BR} = V_{ph}\angle -240°$$

The phase currents are given by

$$I_{RY} = \frac{V_{RY}}{Z_{RY}};\ I_{YB} = \frac{V_{YB}}{Z_{YB}};\ I_{BR} = \frac{V_{BR}}{Z_{BR}}$$

The line currents are given by

$$I_R = I_{RY} - I_{BR};\ I_Y = I_{YB} - I_{RY};\ I_B = I_{BR} - I_{YB}$$

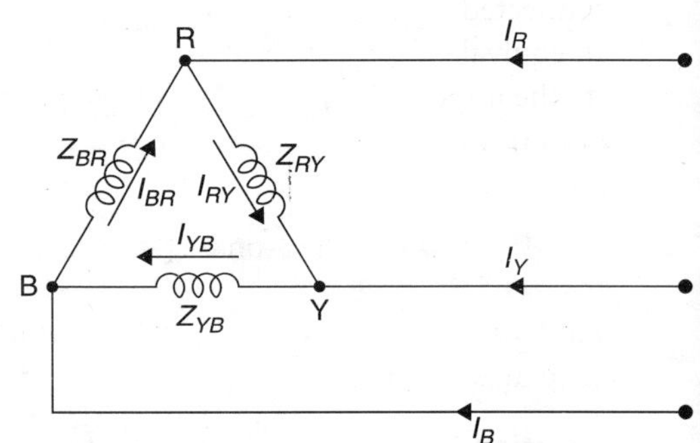

Fig. 6.9 Unbalanced delta connected load

6.6.2 Unbalanced 4-wire Star Connected Load

Figure 6.10 shows an unbalanced star connected load connected to a balanced 3-phase, 4-wire supply. The neutral point N of the load is connected to neutral point O of the supply. Hence voltage across the three load impedances is equal to phase voltage of the supply.

For a star connected load, let

$$V_L = \sqrt{3}V_{ph};\ V_{RN} = V_{ph}\angle 0°;\ V_{YN} = V_{ph}\angle -120°;$$

$$V_{BN} = V_{ph}\angle -240°$$

The phase currents are given by

$$I_R = \frac{V_{RN}}{Z_R};\ I_Y = \frac{V_{YN}}{Z_Y};\ I_B = \frac{V_{BN}}{Z_B}$$

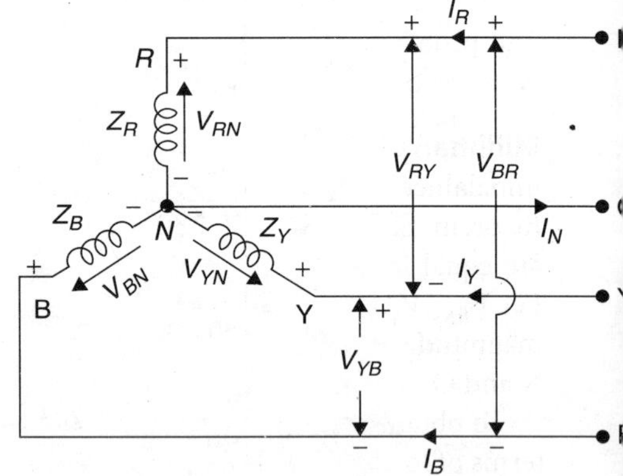

Fig. 6.10 Unbalanced 4-wire star connected load

For a star connected load, phase currents are equal to line currents. The current in the neutral wire is given by

$$I_N = I_R + I_Y + I_B \tag{6.24}$$

6.6.3 Unbalanced 3-wire Star Connected Load

In the case when a star-connected load is unbalanced and if there is no neutral wire, then its star-point is isolated from the star-point of the generator. The potential of the load star-point is different from that of the generator star-point. The potential of the former is subject to variations according to the unbalance of the load and under certain conditions of loading, the potentials of the two star-points may differ considerably. Such an isolated load star-point or neutral point is called a *floating neutral point* because its potential is always changing and not fixed. All star-connected unbalanced load supplied from polyphase systems without a neutral wire, have floating neutral points. Any unbalancing of the load causes variations not only of the potential of star-point but also of voltages across the different branches of the load. Hence in that case, phase voltage is not of the line voltage. In general, the phase voltages are not only unequal in magnitude but also subtend angles other than 120° with one another.

The following methods are used to tackle unbalanced star-connected loads having isolated neutral points.

- Star-delta conversion.
- Milliman's theorem or displacement neutral method.

Star-delta conversion In the case of an unbalanced star-connected load, it is somewhat more convenient to convert it into an equivalent delta-connected load and solve it. If Z_R, Z_Y and Z_B are the impedances of the given star-connected load and Z_{RY}, Z_{YB}, Z_{BR} are the impedances of the equivalent delta-connected load (Fig. 6.11), then

$$Z_{RY} = Z_R + Z_Y + \frac{Z_R Z_Y}{Z_B} = \frac{Z_R Z_Y + Z_Y Z_B + Z_R Z_B}{Z_B}$$

$$Z_{YB} = Z_Y + Z_B + \frac{Z_Y Z_B}{Z_R} = \frac{Z_R Z_Y + Z_Y Z_B + Z_R Z_B}{Z_R}$$

$$Z_{BR} = Z_B + Z_R + \frac{Z_B Z_R}{Z_Y} = \frac{Z_R Z_Y + Z_Y Z_B + Z_R Z_B}{Z_Y}$$

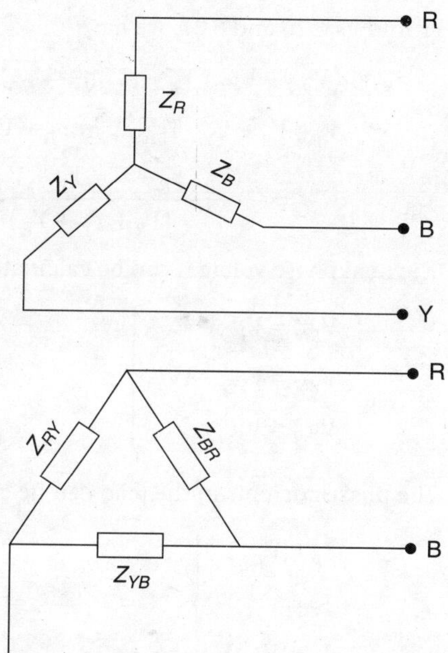

Fig. 6.11 Star-delta conversion

The problem is solved as an unbalanced delta connected load. Now the phase currents and line currents can be determined.

Milliman's method/displacement neutral method An unbalalnced 3-wire star connected load can also be solved by Millman's theorem. Let V_{RO}, V_{YO} and V_{BO} be the phase voltages of the supply which are equal in magnitude but differ in phase from one another by 120°. Let V_{RN}, V_{YN} and V_{BN} be the load phase voltages which are unequal in magnitude as well as phase angles. The voltage between the neutral point N and O, that is, V_{NO} can be determined using the following procedure.

To obtain the displacement neutral voltage write the line currents in terms of load voltages and load admittances.

$$\left.\begin{aligned} I_R &= V_{RO} Y_R \\ I_Y &= V_{YO} Y_Y \\ I_B &= V_{BO} Y_B \end{aligned}\right\} \tag{6.25}$$

where Y_R, Y_Y and Y_B are admittances of the branches of the unbalanced star connected load. Applying KCL at node O,

$$I_R + I_Y + I_B = 0$$

$$V_{RO}\,Y_R + V_{YO}\,Y_Y + V_{BO}\,Y_B = 0 \tag{6.26}$$

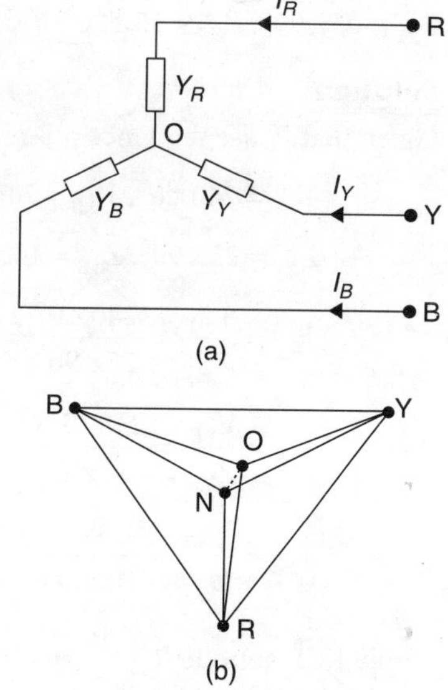

Fig. 6.12 Displacement neutral method (a) circuit diagram (b) voltage triangle

From Fig. 6.12(b), we have

$$\left.\begin{aligned} V_{RO} &= V_{RN} + V_{NO} \\ V_{YO} &= V_{YN} + V_{NO} \\ V_{BO} &= V_{BN} + V_{NO} \end{aligned}\right\} \quad (6.27)$$

From Eqs 6.26 and 6.27, we have

$$(V_{RN} + V_{NO})\, Y_R + (V_{YN} + V_{NO})\, Y_Y + (V_{BN} + V_{NO})\, Y_B = 0$$

$$V_{RN}\, Y_R + V_{YN}\, Y_Y + V_{BN}\, Y_B + V_{NO}(Y_R + Y_Y + Y_B) = 0$$

$$\therefore \quad V_{NO} = -\frac{(V_{RN}Y_R + V_{YN}Y_Y + V_{BN}Y_B)}{(Y_R + Y_Y + Y_B)} \quad (6.28)$$

The load phase voltages can be calculated as

$$\left.\begin{aligned} V_{RN} &= V_{RO} - V_{NO} \\ V_{YN} &= V_{YO} - V_{NO} \\ V_{BN} &= V_{BO} - V_{NO} \end{aligned}\right\} \quad (6.29)$$

The phase currents in the load can be calculated as

$$\left.\begin{aligned} I_R &= V_{RO}Y_R \\ I_Y &= V_{YO}Y_Y \\ I_B &= V_{BO}Y_B \end{aligned}\right\} \quad (6.30)$$

Problem 6.9 A 3-phase, 3-wire, 240 V BYR system supplied a delta connected load in which $Z_{RY} = 25\angle 90°$, $Z_{YB} = 15\angle 30°$ and $Z_{BR} = 20\angle 0°$. Find the line currents and total power.

Solution:

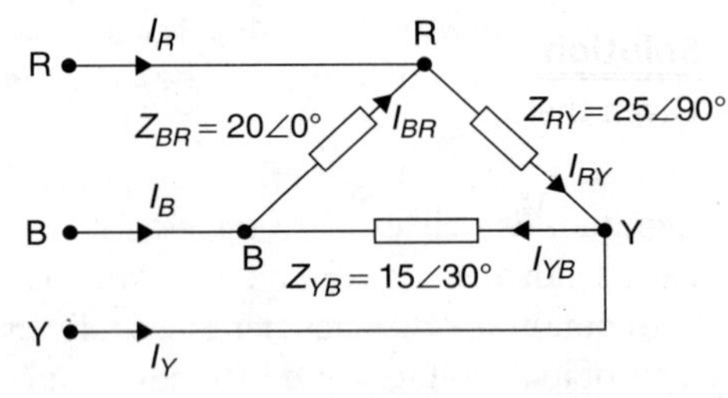

Given that Phase sequence = BYR, So

$$V_{RY} = 240\angle 0°,\ V_{YB} = 240\angle 120°\ V_{BR} = 240\angle -120°$$

$$Z_{RY} = 25\angle 90°,\ Z_{YB} = 15\angle 30°,\ Z_{BR} = 20\angle 0°$$

$$I_{RY} = \frac{V_{RY}}{Z_{RY}} = \frac{240\angle 0°}{25\angle 90°} = 9.6\ \angle -90°\ \text{A}$$

$$I_{YB} = \frac{V_{YB}}{Z_{YB}} = \frac{240\angle 120°}{15\angle 30°} = 16\ \angle 90°\ \text{A}$$

$$I_{BR} = \frac{V_{BR}}{Z_{BR}} = \frac{240\angle -120°}{20\angle 0°} = 12\angle -120°$$

Apply KCL at node R

$$I_R + I_{BR} = I_{RY}$$

$$\Rightarrow \quad I_R = I_{RY} - I_{BR} = 9.6\angle -90° - 12\angle -120° = -j9.6 - (-6 - j10.39) = 6 + j0.99$$

Apply KCL at node Y

$$I_Y + I_{RY} = I_{YB}$$

$$\Rightarrow \quad I_Y = I_{YB} - I_{RY} = 16\angle 90° - 9.6\angle -90° = j16 + j\,9.6 = j\,25.6$$

Apply KCL at node B

$$I_B + I_{YB} = I_{BR}$$

$$\Rightarrow \quad I_B = I_{BR} - I_{YB} = 12\angle -120° - 16\angle 90° = (-6 - j10.39) - j16 = -6 - j\,26.39$$

The power in each phase is calculated as follows:

$$Z_{RY} = 25\angle 90° = 0 + j25$$

$$\Rightarrow \quad R_{RY} = 0 \quad \text{and} \quad I_{RY} = 9.6 \text{ A}$$

$$P_{RY} = I_{RY}^2 \; R_{RY} = 9.6^2 \times 0 = 0 \text{ W}$$

$$Z_{YB} = 15\angle 30° = 13 + j7.5$$

$$\Rightarrow \quad R_{YB} = 13\ \Omega \quad \text{and} \quad I_{YB} = 16 \text{ A}$$

$$P_{YB} = I_{YB}^2 \; R_{YB} = 16^2 \times 13 = 3328 \text{ W}$$

$$Z_{BR} = 20\angle 0° = 20 + j0$$

$$\Rightarrow \quad R_{BR} = 20 \quad \text{and} \quad I_{BR} = 12 \text{ A}$$

$$P_{BR} = I_{BR}^2 \times R_{BR} = 12^2 \times 20 = 2880 \text{ W}$$

Total power, $P_T = P_{RY} + P_{YB} + P_{BR} = 0 + 3328 + 2880 = 6208$ W

Problem 6.10 A 3-phase, 4-wire, 208 V RYB system supplies a star connected load with $Z_R = 10\angle 0°$, $Z_Y = 15\angle 30°$ and $Z_B = 10\angle -30°$. Find the line currents, the neutral current and total power.

Solution:

Given that Phase sequence = RYB, so

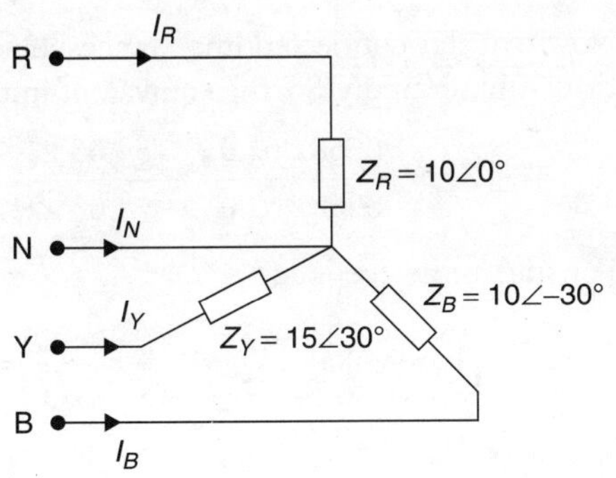

$$V_{RN} = \frac{V_L}{\sqrt{3}}\angle -30° = \frac{208}{\sqrt{3}}\angle -30° = 120\angle -30°$$

$$V_{YN} = 120\angle -150°, \; V_{BN} = 120\angle 90°$$

$$Z_R = 10\angle 0°, \; Z_Y = 15\angle 30°, \; Z_C = 10\angle -30°$$

$$I_R = \frac{V_{RN}}{Z_R} = \frac{120\angle -30°}{10\angle 0°} = 12\angle -30° = 10.4 - j6$$

$$I_Y = \frac{V_{YN}}{Z_Y} = \frac{120\angle -150°}{15\angle 30°} = 8\angle -180° = -8$$

$$I_B = \frac{V_{BN}}{Z_B} = \frac{120\angle 90°}{10\angle -30°} = 12\angle 120° = -6 + j10.39$$

The neutral current is

$$I_N = -(I_R + I_Y + I_B) = -(10.4 - j6 - 8 - 6 + j10.39) = (3.6 - j4.39) \text{ A}$$

The power in each phase is calculated as follows

$$Z_R = 10\angle 0° = 10 + j0$$

$$R_R = 10, I_R = 12$$

$$P_R = 12^2 \times 10 = 144 \times 100 = 1440 \text{ W}$$

$$Z_Y = 15\angle 30° = 13 + j7.5$$

$$R_Y = 13, I_Y = 8$$

$$P_Y = 8^2 \times 13 = 64 \times 13 = 832 \text{ W}$$

$$Z_B = 10\angle -30° = 8.66 - j5$$

$$R_B = 8.66, I_B = 12$$

$$P_B = 12^2 \times 8.66 = 144 \times 8.66 = 1247 \text{ W}$$

Total power, $P_T = P_R + P_Y + P_B = 1440 + 832 + 1247 = 3519$ W

Problem 6.11 Three star connected impedances $Z_Y = (20 + j37.7)\ \Omega$ per phase are connected in parallel with three delta connected impedances $Z_\Delta = (30 - j159.3)\ \Omega$ per phase. The line voltage is 400 V. Find the (i) line current, (ii) power factor, (iii) active power, and (iv) reactive power taken by the combination.

Solution:

Given that $Z_Y = (20 + j37.7)\ \Omega = 42.68\angle 62.05°\ \Omega$

$$Z_\Delta = (30 - j159.3)\ \Omega = 162.1\angle -79.3°\ \Omega$$

$$V_L = 400 \text{ V}$$

Three identical delta connected impedances can be converted into equivalent star impedances

$$Z'_Y = \frac{Z_\Delta}{3} = \frac{162.1\angle -79.3°}{3} = 54.03\ \angle -79.3°$$

Now two star connected impedances $42.68\angle 62.05°$ and $54.03\angle -79.3°$ are connected in parallel across the three-phase supply. So, the equivalent impedance is,

$$Z_{eq} = \frac{42.68\angle 62.05° \times 54.03\ \angle -79.3°}{42.68\angle 62.05° + 54.03\ \angle -79.3°} = 68.33\angle 10°$$

For star connected load

$$\text{Phase voltage, } V_{ph} = \frac{V_L}{\sqrt{3}} = \frac{400}{\sqrt{3}} = 231 \text{ V}$$

(i) Phase current, $I_{ph} = \dfrac{V_{ph}}{Z_{ph}} = \dfrac{V_{ph}}{Z_{eq}} = \dfrac{231}{68.33} = 3.38$ A

Line current, $I_L = I_{ph} = 3.38$ A

(ii) Power factor, $\cos\phi = \cos 10° = 0.985$ lag

(iii) Active power, $P = \sqrt{3} V_L I_L \cos\phi = \sqrt{3} \times 400 \times 3.38 \times 0.985 = 2306.6$ W

(iv) Reactive power, $Q = \sqrt{3} V_L I_L \sin\phi = \sqrt{3} \times 400 \times 3.38 \times \sin 10° = 406.6$ VAR

Problem 6.12 A 3-phase, 3-wire, 208 V BYR system has a star connected load with $Z_R = 6\angle 0°$, $Z_Y = 6\angle 30°$ and $Z_B = 5\angle 45°$. Obtain the line currents and phase voltages across each impedance. Construct the voltage triangle and determine the displacement neutral voltage V_{NO}.

Solution:

Given that $Z_R = 6\angle 0°$, $Z_Y = 6\angle 30°$ and $Z_B = 5\angle 45°$

Phase sequence = BYR

Let us take V_{YB} as reference phasor, then

$$V_{YB} = 208\angle 0°,\ V_{RY} = 208\angle 240°,\ V_{BR} = 208\angle 120°$$

By inspection of mesh analysis, the matrix loop equation can be written as

$$\begin{bmatrix} 6\angle 0° + 6\angle 30° & -6\angle 30° \\ -6\angle 30° & 6\angle 30° + 5\angle 45° \end{bmatrix}\begin{bmatrix} I_1 \\ I_2 \end{bmatrix} = \begin{bmatrix} 208\angle 240° \\ 208\angle 0° \end{bmatrix}$$

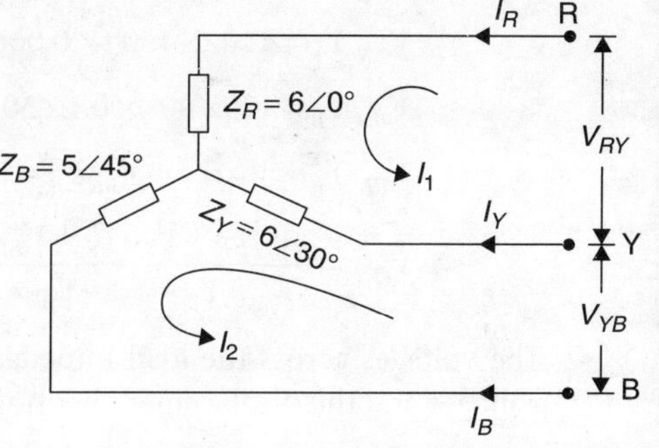

Fig. 1 Circuit diagram

After solving the above martix equation, we get the values of I_1 and I_2 as given below:

$$I_1 = 23.3\angle 261°\ \text{A} \quad \text{and} \quad I_2 = 26.5\angle -63.4°\ \text{A}$$

The line currents are given by

$$I_R = I_1 = 23.3\angle 261°\ \text{A}$$

$$I_Y = I_2 - I_1 = 26.5\angle -63.4° - 23.3\angle 261° = 15.45\angle -2.5°\ \text{A}$$

$$I_B = -I_2 = -26.5\angle -63.4° = 26.5\angle 116.6°\ \text{A}$$

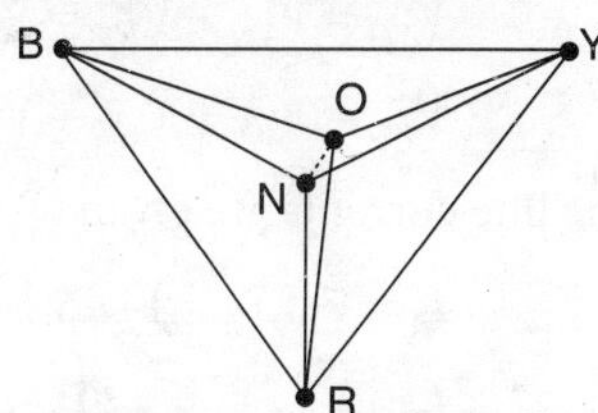

Fig. 2 Voltage triangle

The voltages across the impedances are given by

$$V_{RO} = I_R Z_R = 23.3\angle 261° \times 6\angle 0° = 140\angle 261°\ \text{V}$$

$$V_{YO} = I_Y Z_Y = 15.45\angle -2.5° \times 6\angle 30° = 92.7\angle 27.5°\ \text{V}$$

$$V_{BO} = I_B Z_B = 26.5\angle 116.6° \times 5\angle 45° = 132\angle 161.6°\ \text{V}$$

From the voltage triangle

$$V_{RO} = V_{RN} + V_{NO}$$

$$\Rightarrow \quad V_{NO} = V_{RO} - V_{RN} = 140\angle 261° - 120\angle -90° = 28.1\angle 40°\ \text{V}$$

Problem 6.13 A 3-phase, 3-wire, 208 V, RYB system supplies a star connected load in which $Z_R = 10\angle 0°$, $Z_Y = 15\angle 30°$ and $Z_B = 10\angle -30°$. Find the line currents and voltage across the load impedances using the displacement neutral method.

Solution:

Given that $Z_R = 10\angle 0°$, $Z_Y = 15\angle 30°$ and $Z_B = 10\angle -30°$

Phase sequence = RYB, So

$$V_{RY} = 208\angle 0°,\ V_{YB} = 208\angle -120°,\ V_{BR} = 208\angle 120°$$

$$V_{RN} = \frac{V_L}{\sqrt{3}}\angle -30° = \frac{208}{\sqrt{3}}\angle -30° = 120\angle -30°$$

$$V_{YN} = 120\angle -150°,\ V_{BN} = 120\angle 90°$$

The line admittances are

$$Y_R = \frac{1}{Z_R} = \frac{1}{10\angle 0°} = 0.1$$

$$Y_Y = \frac{1}{Z_Y} = \frac{1}{15\angle 30°} = 0.066\angle -30° = 0.0577 - j0.033$$

$$Y_B = \frac{1}{Z_B} = \frac{1}{10\angle -30°} = 0.1\angle 30° = 0.0866 + j0.05$$

$$Y_R + Y_Y + Y_B = 0.1 + 0.0577 - j0.033 + 0.0866 + j0.05 = 0.244 + j0.0167 = 0.2441\angle 3.93°$$

$$V_{RN}\, Y_R = 120\angle -30° \times 0.1 = 12\angle -30° = 10.39 - j6$$

$$V_{YN}\, Y_Y = 120\angle -150° \times 0.066\angle -30° = 8\angle -180° = -8$$

$$V_{BN}\, Y_B = 120\angle 90° \times 0.1\angle 30° = 12\angle 120° = -6 + j10.4$$

$$V_{RN}\, Y_R + V_{YN} Y_Y + V_{BN} Y_B = 10.39 - j6 - 8 - 6 + j10.4 = -3.61 + j4.39 = 5.68\angle 129.43°$$

$$V_{ON} = \frac{V_{RN} Y_R + V_{YN} Y_Y + V_{BN} Y_B}{Y_R + Y_Y + Y_B} = \frac{5.68\angle 129.43°}{0.2441\angle 3.93°} = 23.3\angle 125.5° = -13.5 + j18.97$$

The voltages across the load impedances can be expressed in terms of the corresponding line to neutral voltages and the displacement neutral voltages as follows:

$$V_{RO} = V_{RN} + V_{NO} = V_{RN} - V_{ON} = 120\angle -30° - 23.3\angle 125.5° = 141.5\angle -33.92° \text{ V}$$

$$V_{YO} = V_{YN} + V_{NO} = V_{YN} - V_{ON} = 120\angle -150° - 23.3\angle 125.5° = 120\angle -138.86° \text{ V}$$

$$V_{BO} = V_{BN} + V_{NO} = V_{BN} - V_{ON} = 120\angle 90° - 23.3\angle 125.5° = 102\angle 82.39° \text{ V}$$

The line currents are given by

$$I_R = V_{RO} Y_R = 141.5\angle -33.92° \times 0.1 = 14.15\angle -33.92° \text{ A}$$

$$I_Y = V_{YO}\, Y_Y = 120\angle -138.86° \times 0.066\angle -30° = 8\angle -169° \text{ A}$$

$$I_B = V_{BO}\, Y_B = 102\angle 82.39° \times 0.1\angle 30° = 10.2\angle 112.4° \text{ A}$$

6.7 MEASUREMENT OF POWER IN A THREE PHASE CIRCUIT

The power in a 3-phase circuit can be measured using the following methods:

- three-wattmeter method,
- two-wattmeter method, and
- one-wattmeter method.

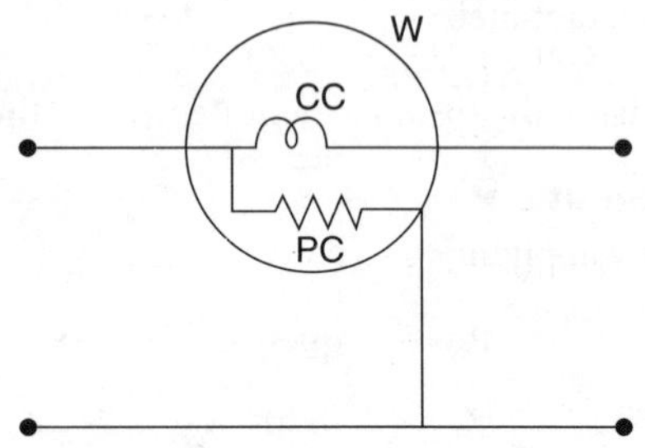

Fig. 6.13 Wattmeter connection

Wattmeter A wattmeter consists of two coils (Fig. 6.13). The first one is a current coil possessing a low resistance and the second one is a pressure coil possessing a high resistance. The current coil (CC) is connected in series with the line carrying the current and the pressure coil (PC) is connected across two points whose potential difference is to be measured. Thus, a wattmeter shows a reading which is proportional to the product of the current through its current coil, the potential different across its pressure coil and cosine of the angle between the voltage and current.

6.7.1 Three-Wattmeter Method

In this method, three wattmeters are connected in each of the three phases of the load whether star or delta connection. Figure 6.14 shows the connection diagram of the three wattmeter method for both star and delta connection loads. The current coil of each wattmeter carries the current of one phase and the pressure coil measures the phase voltage of that particular phase only. Hence each wattmeter measures the power in a single phase. The total power in the load is given by the algebraic sum of the readings of the three wattmeters.

This method has the following disadvantages:

- in the case of star connected load, the neutral point may not always be available,
- in the case of delta connected load, it is not feasible to break into the phase of the load under normal conditions.

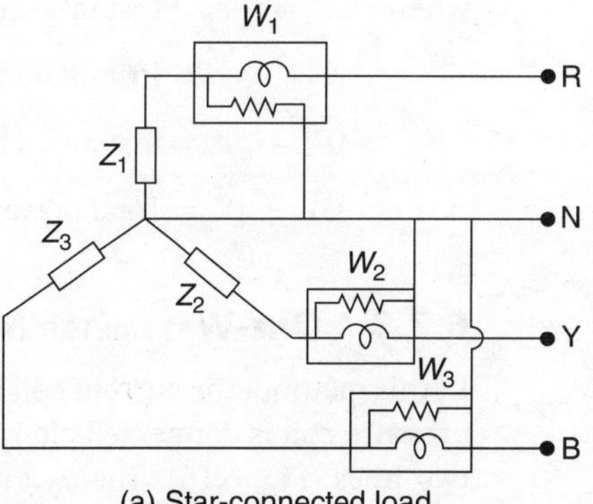

(a) Star-connected load

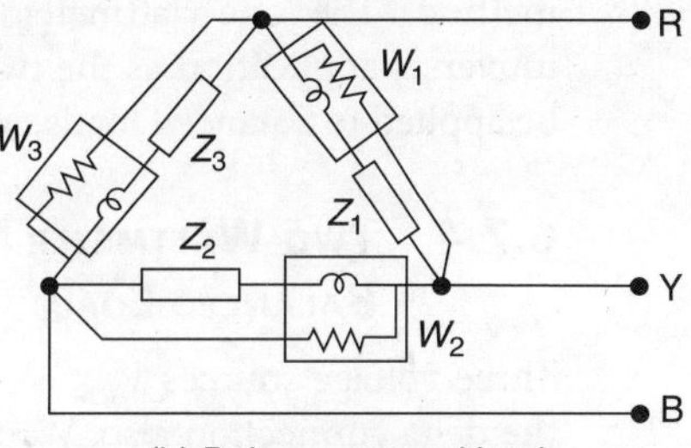

(b) Delta connected load

Fig. 6.14 Three-wattmeter method

6.7.2 Two-Wattmeter Method

In this method the current coils of the two wattmeters connected in any two lines and the pressure coil of each wattmeter is joined to the third line. Figure 6.15 shows the connection diagram of the two-wattmeter method applied to both star and delta connected loads. In this method it can be proved that the sum of the instantaneous powers indicated by W_1 and W_2 gives the instantaneous power absorbed by the three loads Z_1, Z_2 and Z_3.

Let us consider a star connected load (although it can be equally applied to a delta connected load which can also be replaced by an equivalent star connected load).

Instantaneous current through $W_1 = i_R$

Instantaneous potential difference across $W_1 = e_{RB} = (e_R - e_B)$

Instantaneous power read by $W_1 = i_R(e_R - e_B)$

Instantaneous current through $W_2 = i_Y$

Instantaneous potential difference across $W_2 = e_{YB} = (e_Y - e_B)$

Instantaneous power read by $W_2 = i_Y(e_Y - e_B)$

$$W_1 + W_2 = i_R(e_R - e_B) + i_Y(e_Y - e_B)$$

$$= i_R e_R + i_Y e_Y - e_B(i_R + i_Y) \tag{6.31}$$

By applying KCL at node ,

$$(i_R + i_Y + i_B) = 0$$

$$\Rightarrow \quad (i_R + i_Y) = -i_B \tag{6.32}$$

From Eqs 6.31 and 6.32,

$$W_1 + W_2 = i_R e_R + i_Y e_Y + i_B e_B = P_1 + P_2 + P_3$$

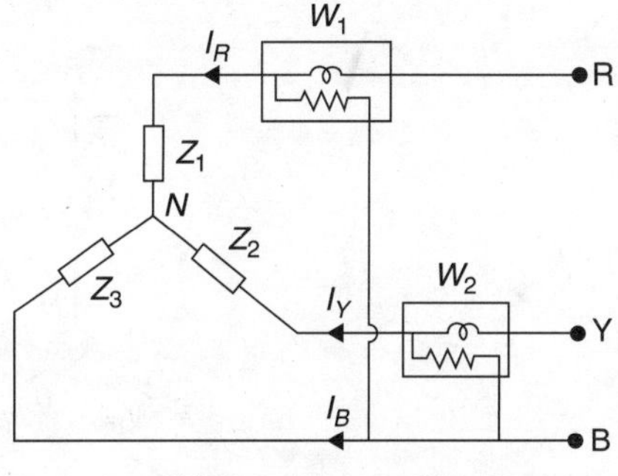

(a) Star-connected load

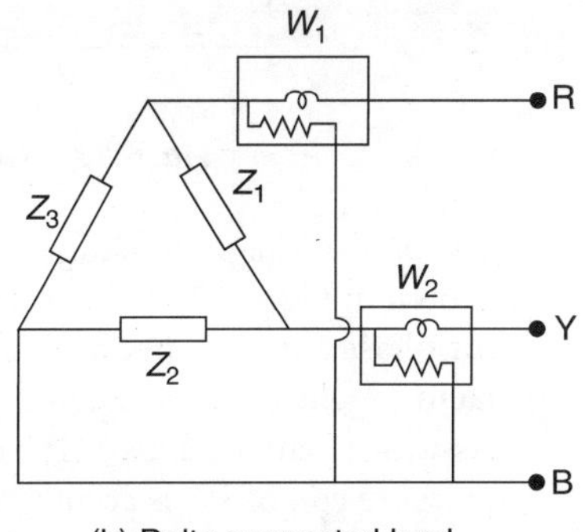

(b) Delta connected load

Fig. 6.15 Two-wattmeter method

where $P_1 = i_R\, e_R$ = Instantaneous power absorbed by load Z_1

$P_2 = i_Y\, e_Y$ = Instantaneous power absorbed by load Z_2

$P_3 = i_B\, e_B$ = Instantaneous power absorbed by load Z_3

$$\therefore \quad W_1 + W_2 = \text{Total power absorbed by load} = P_1 + P_2 + P_3 \tag{6.33}$$

6.7.3 One-Wattmeter Method

In this method, the current coil is connected in any one line and the pressure coil is connected alternatively between this and the other two lines (Fig. 6.16). The two readings so obtained, for a balance load, correspond to those obtained by the normal two-wattmeter method. The one-wattmeter method does not have as much universal application as the two-wattmeter method because it can be applied to balanced loads only.

Fig. 6.16 One-wattmeter method

6.7.4 Two-Wattmeter Method Applied to Balanced Load

Three voltage sources V_{RN}, V_{YN}, V_{BN} are connected in star (Fig. 6.17). This theory holds good equally for the delta connection also. Wattmeter W_1 is connected in Line-R and wattmeter W_2 is connected in line-Y. The other ends of both the pressure coils of both the meters are connected to Line B, where no meters are connected. Two wattmeters can be connected in any two lines. Care should be taken that other ends of both the wattmeters should be connected to the third line which has no wattmeters.

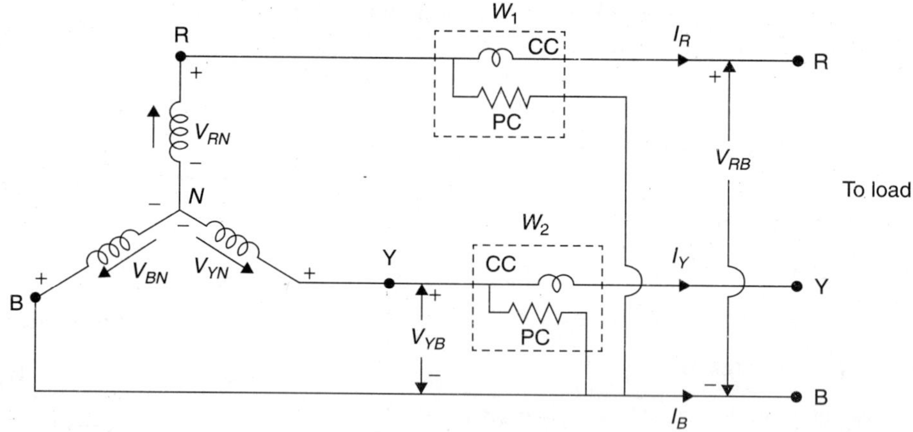

Fig. 6.17 Two-wattmeter method of power measurement for balanced load

The phasor diagram using the two-wattmeter method, for a three-phase balanced star connected circuit is shown in Fig. 6.17. In Fig. 6.18, vectors of V_{RN}, V_{YN} and V_{BN} are shown, I_R, I_Y and I_B are three line currents (or phase currents, because in star connection line current is the same as phase current) and ϕ is the power factor angle. Assume lagging p.f. Therefore I_R, I_Y and I_B lag by angle ϕ respectively with V_{RN}, V_{YN} and V_{BN}. Assume a balanced load. The current coil of W_1 is connected in line R, hence the current involved is I_R and pressure coil of W_1 is connected between lines R and B, hence the voltage involved is V_{RB}.

$$\therefore \quad W_1 = V_{RB}\, I_R \cos (\text{of angle between } V_{RB}\, I_R)$$

From Fig. 6.18, angle between V_{RB} and I_R is $(30° - \phi)$

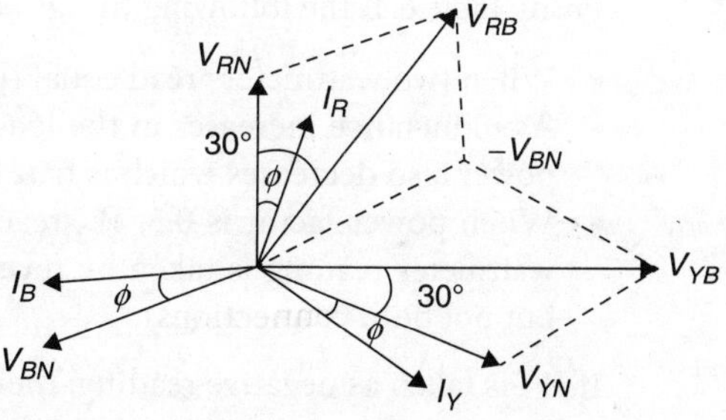

Fig. 6.18 Phasor diagram of two-wattmeter method for balanced load

$$\therefore \quad W_1 = V_{RB} \cdot I_R \cos(30° - \phi) = V_L \cdot I_L \cos(30° - \phi) \tag{6.34}$$

Similarly

$$W_2 = V_{YB} \cdot I_Y \cos(30° + \phi) = V_L \cdot I_L \cos(30° + \phi) \tag{6.35}$$

The sum of the two wattmeter readings is,

$$W_1 + W_2 = V_L I_L [\cos(30° + \phi) + \cos(30 - \phi)]$$
$$= 2V_L I_L \cos 30° \cos\phi$$
$$= \sqrt{3} V_L I_L \cos\phi$$
$$P = W_1 + W_2 = \sqrt{3} V_L I_L \cos\phi \tag{6.36}$$

So, $(W_1 + W_2)$ is equal to the total power consumed by the balanced load.

Determination of power factor for the balanced load The difference of the two wattmeter readings is,

$$W_1 - W_2 = V_L I_L [\cos(30° - \phi) - \cos(30 + \phi)] = 2V_L I_L \sin 30° \sin\phi$$
$$= V_L I_L \sin\phi$$
$$\therefore \quad W_1 - W_2 = V_L I_L \sin\phi \tag{6.37}$$

Dividing Eq. 6.37 with Eq. 6.36,

$$\frac{W_1 - W_2}{W_1 + W_2} = \frac{1}{\sqrt{3}} \tan\phi$$

$$\tan\phi = \frac{\sqrt{3}(W_1 - W_2)}{W_1 + W_2}$$

$$\therefore \quad \phi = \tan^{-1}\left(\frac{\sqrt{3}(W_1 - W_2)}{W_1 + W_2}\right) \tag{6.38}$$

Therefore, the power factor, $\cos\phi$ of the balanced load can be obtained as

$$\cos\phi = \frac{1}{\sqrt{(1 + \tan^2\phi)}} = \frac{1}{\sqrt{\left[1 + 3\left(\frac{W_1 - W_2}{W_1 + W_2}\right)^2\right]}} \tag{6.39}$$

Table 6.1 Variation of wattmeter readings with change in power factor of the load current

Wattmeter readings		**$\phi = 0°$ (or) $\cos\phi = 1$**	**$\phi = 30°$ (or) $\cos\phi = 0.866$**	**$\phi = 60°$ (or) $\cos\phi = 0.5$**	**$\phi = 90$ (or) $\cos\phi = 0$**
W_1	$V_L I_L \cos(30° - \phi)$	$\frac{\sqrt{3}}{2} V_L I_L$	$V_L I_L$	$\frac{\sqrt{3}}{2} V_L I_L$	$0.5\ V_L I_L$
W_2	$V_L I_L \cos(30° + \phi)$	$\frac{\sqrt{3}}{2} V_L I_L$	$0.5\ V_L I_L$	0	$-0.5\ V_L I_L$
$W_1 + W_2$		$\sqrt{3}\ V_L I_L$	$1.5\ V_L I_L$	$\frac{\sqrt{3}}{2} V_L I_L$	0

From Table 6.1, the following things are clear.

- When two wattmeters read equal readings, the power factor is 1. This indicates resisitive load.
- As inductance increases in the load, power factor decreases and wattmeter readings decrease and total power also decreases which is true as per AC fundamentals.
- When power factor is 0.5, W_2 reads zero and if p.f. < 0.5, W_2 reads negative. Under this situation, the wattmeter reading is taken by reversing the connections of either current coil or pressure coil (anyone but not both connections).

If W_2 is taken as negative reading, then

$$P = W_1 + (-W_2) = W_1 - W_2 \tag{6.40}$$

$$\phi = \tan^{-1}\left(\frac{\sqrt{3}\,(W_1 - (-W_2))}{W_1 + (-W_2)}\right) = \tan^{-1}\left(\frac{\sqrt{3}\,(W_1 + W_2)}{W_1 - W_2}\right) \tag{6.41}$$

When the connections are reversed, Eqs 6.40 and 6.41 should be used instead of Eqs 6.36 and 6.38.

Problem 6.14 Two wattmeters are connected to measure the input power to a 3-phase, 20 HP, 50 Hz induction motor which works at a full load efficiency of 90% and a power factor of 0.85. Find the readings of the two wattmeters.

Solution:

Given that Output = 20 HP = 20 × 746 W = 14.92 kW

Full load efficiency = 90%

Power factor = 0.85

$$\text{Electrical input} = \frac{\text{Output}}{\text{Efficiency}} = \frac{14.92}{0.9} = 16.57 \text{ kW}$$

$$W_1 + W_2 = 16.57 \text{ kW} \tag{1}$$

$$\cos\phi = 0.85$$

$$\Rightarrow \quad \phi = \cos^{-1}(0.85) = 31.788°$$

$$\therefore \quad \tan\phi = \frac{\sqrt{3}\,(W_1 - W_2)}{W_1 + W_2}$$

$$\tan 31.788 = \frac{\sqrt{3}\,(W_1 - W_2)}{16.375}$$

$$\Rightarrow \quad W_1 - W_2 = 5.859 \tag{2}$$

Adding Eqs (1) and (2), we have

$$2W_1 = 16.57 + 5.859$$

$$W_1 = 11.21 \text{ kW}$$

$$W_1 - W_2 = 5.859 \quad \Rightarrow \quad W_2 = 5.35 \text{ kW}$$

Problem 6.15 Estimate the power factor in each of the following cases of two-wattmeter method of measuring three-phase power: (i) wattmeter readings are equal, (ii) wattmeter readings are equal and opposite, (iii) wattmeter readings are in the ratio 1 : 2, and (iv) one wattmeter reading is zero.

Solution:

We know that $\phi = \tan^{-1}\left(\dfrac{\sqrt{3}(W_1 - W_2)}{W_1 + W_2}\right)$

(i) Wattmeter readings are equal

$W_1 = W_2$

$$\phi = \tan^{-1}\left(\frac{\sqrt{3}(W_1 - W_2)}{W_1 + W_2}\right) = \tan^{-1}\left(\sqrt{3}\times 0\right) = \tan^{-1} 0^\circ = 0$$

$p.f = \cos\phi = \cos 0^\circ = 1$

(ii) Wattmeter readings are equal and opposite

$W_1 = -W_2$

$$\phi = \tan^{-1}\left(\frac{\sqrt{3}(W_1 - W_2)}{W_1 + W_2}\right) = \tan^{-1}(\infty) = 90^\circ$$

$p.f = \cos\phi = \cos 90^\circ = 0$

(iii) Wattmeter readings are in the ratio 1 : 2

$\dfrac{W_1}{W_2} = \dfrac{1}{2} \Rightarrow 2W_1 = W_2$

$$\phi = \tan^{-1}\left(\frac{\sqrt{3}(W_1 - 2W_1)}{W_1 + 2W_1}\right) = \tan^{-1}\left(-\frac{1}{\sqrt{3}}\right) = -30^\circ$$

$p.f = \cos\phi = \cos(-30^\circ) = 0.866$

(iv) One wattmeter reading zero

$W_2 = 0$

$$\phi = \tan^{-1}\left(\frac{\sqrt{3}(W_1 - 0)}{W_1 + 0}\right) = \tan^{-1}\left(\sqrt{3}\right) = 60^\circ$$

$p.f = \cos\phi = \cos 60^\circ = 0.5$

Problem 6.16 Each of the two wattmeters connected to measure the input to a 3-phase circuit reads 20 kW. What does each wattmeter read when the load p.f is 0.866 lagging with the total three phase power remaining the same?

Solution:

Given that $W_1 + W_2 = 20$ kW (1)

$\cos\phi = 0.85 \Rightarrow \phi = \cos^{-1}(0.866) = 30^\circ$

$\therefore \quad \tan\phi = \dfrac{\sqrt{3}(W_1 - W_2)}{W_1 + W_2}$

$$\tan 30° = \frac{\sqrt{3}(W_1 - W_2)}{20}$$

$$\Rightarrow \quad W_1 - W_2 = 6.667 \text{ kW} \qquad (2)$$

By adding Eqs (1) and (2),

$$2W_1 = 20 + 6.667 = 26.667$$

$$W_1 = 13.335 \text{ kW}$$

$$W_1 - W_2 = 6.667 \quad \Rightarrow \quad W_2 = 6.665 \text{ kW}$$

Problem 6.17 Three indentical coils are connected in star to a 400 V, 3-phase AC supply and each coil takes 100 W. If the power factor is 0.6 lagging, calculate (i) the line current, (ii) impedance of the coil, and (iii) resistance and inductance of the coil.

Solution:

Given that Line voltage $V_L = 400$ V

Power taken by each coil $P_{ph} = 100$ W

Power factor $\cos\phi = 0.6$

Phase voltage $V_{ph} = V_L = 400$ V

Per phase power, $P_{ph} = V_{ph} I_{ph} \cos\phi$

$$\therefore \quad I_{ph} = \frac{P_{ph}}{V_{ph}\cos\phi} = \frac{100}{400 \times 0.6} = 0.417 \text{ A}$$

(i) Line current $I_L = \sqrt{3} I_{ph} = \sqrt{3} \times 0.417 = 0.722$ A

(ii) Impedance of the coil, $Z_{ph} = \dfrac{V_{ph}}{I_{ph}} = \dfrac{400}{0.417} = 959.2\ \Omega$

(iii) Resistance of the coil $R_{ph} = Z_{ph}\cos\phi = 959.2 \times 0.6 = 575.5\ \Omega$

Reactance of the coil $X_{ph} = Z_{ph}\sin\phi = 959.2 \times 0.8 = 767.36\ \Omega$

Inductance of the coil $L_{ph} = \dfrac{X_{ph}}{2\pi f} = \dfrac{767.36}{2\pi \times 50} = 2.44$ H

ADDITIONAL SOLVED PROBLEMS

6.1 Three indentical coils are connected in star to a 400 V, 3-phase AC supply and each coil takes 300 W. If the power factor is 0.8 lagging, calculate (i) the line current, (ii) impedance of the coil, and (iii) resistance and inductance of the coil.

Solution: Given that $V_L = 400$ V, $P_{ph} = 300$ W, $\cos\phi = 0.8$

Phase voltage, $V_{ph} = \dfrac{V_L}{\sqrt{3}} = \dfrac{400}{\sqrt{3}} = 231$ V

$$P_{ph} = V_{ph} I_{ph} \cos\phi = 300$$

$$\Rightarrow \quad I_{ph} = \frac{300}{V_{ph}\cos\phi} = \frac{300}{231\times 0.8} = 1.623 \text{ A}$$

(i) Line current, $I_L = I_{ph} = 1.623$ A

(ii) Impedance of the coil, $Z_{ph} = \dfrac{V_{ph}}{I_{ph}} = \dfrac{231}{1.623} = 142.3\ \Omega$

(iii) Resistance of the coil, $R_{ph} = Z_{ph}\cos\phi = 142.3 \times 0.8 = 114\ \Omega$

Reactance of the coil, $X_{ph} = Z_{ph}\sin\phi = 142.3 \times 0.6 = 85.5\ \Omega$

Inductance of the coil, $L_{ph} = \dfrac{X_{ph}}{2\pi f} = \dfrac{85.5}{2\pi \times 50} = 272$ mH

6.2 Three identical coils connected in delta across 400 V, 50 Hz, 3-phase supply takes a line current of 15 A at 0.8 p.f lagging. Calculate the (i) phase current, (ii) impedance, resistance and reactance of the coil.

Solution: Given that $V_L = 400$ V, $I_L = 15$ A, $\cos\phi = 0.8$

In delta connection, $V_L = V_{ph} = 400$ V

(i) Phase current, $I_{ph} = \dfrac{I_L}{\sqrt{3}} = \dfrac{15}{\sqrt{3}} = 8.66$ A

(ii) Impedance of the coil, $Z_{ph} = \dfrac{V_{ph}}{I_{ph}} = \dfrac{400}{8.66} = 46.2\ \Omega$

Resistance of the coil, $R_{ph} = Z_{ph}\cos\phi = 46.2 \times 0.8 = 36.95\ \Omega$

Reactance of the coil, $X_{ph} = Z_{ph}\sin\phi = 46.2 \times 0.6 = 27.7\ \Omega$

6.3 Two resistors each of 100 Ω are connected in series. The phases a and c of the three phase 400 V supply are connected to the two ends and phase b is connected to the junction of the two resistors. Find the line currents.

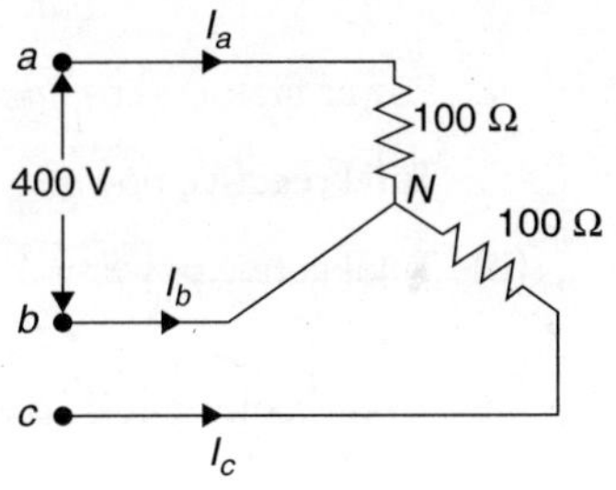

Solution: Given that $R_{ph} = Z_{ph} = 100\ \Omega$, $V_L = 400$ V

The geometry of the circuit will be as shown.

Consider acb as the phase sequence assuming V_{ac} as the reference phasor.

$$V_{ac} = 400\angle 0°,\ V_{cb} = 400\angle -120°,\ V_{ba} = 400\angle +120°$$

Because of the short circuit, the terminals N and b are at the same potential. The lines a, c and b, therefore, carry unequal currents.

$$\text{Currents in line } a,\ I_a = \frac{-V_{ba}}{Z_{ph}} = \frac{-400\angle 120°}{100} = -4\angle 120° \text{ A}$$

$$\text{Currents in line } c,\ I_c = \frac{V_{cb}}{Z_{ph}} = \frac{400\angle -120°}{100} = 4\angle -120 \text{ A}$$

By applying KCL at node N

$$I_a + I_b + I_c = 0$$

$\Rightarrow \qquad I_b = -(I_a + I_c) = -(-4\angle 120° + 4\angle -120°) = 6.93\angle 90°$

Therefore the line currents are

$$I_a = -4\angle 120° \text{ A}, I_b = 6.93\angle 90° \text{ A}, I_c = 4\angle -120° \text{ A}$$

6.4 Two wattmeters are used to measure power input to a 1.5 kV, 50 Hz, 3-phase motor running on full load at an efficiency of 85%. Their readings are 250 kW and 80 kW respectively. Calculate (i) input, (ii) power factor, (iii) line current, and (iv) output.

Solution: Given that $W_1 = 250$ kW, $W_2 = 80$ kW

(i) Input = Total active power = $W_1 + W_2 = 250 \text{ kW} + 80 \text{ kW} = 330$ kW

(ii) Power factor angle, $\phi = \tan^{-1}\left[\sqrt{3}\,\dfrac{(W_1 - W_2)}{(W_1 + W_2)}\right] = \tan^{-1}\left[\sqrt{3}\,\dfrac{(250-80)}{(250+80)}\right] = 41.74$

Power factor $= \cos\phi = \cos 41.74 = 0.746$

(iii) Power $P = \sqrt{3}\, V_L I_L \cos\phi$

$$\Rightarrow I_L = \frac{P}{\sqrt{3}V_L \cos\phi} = \frac{330 \times 1000}{\sqrt{3} \times 1.5 \times 1000 \times 0.746} = 170.2 \text{ A}$$

Line current = 170.2 A

(iv) Output = Input × Efficiency = 330 × 0.85 = 280.5 kW

6.5 The power measurement in a 3-phase circuit is made by using two wattmeters and their readings are (i) $W_1 = 2$ kW, $W_2 = 1.5$ kW, (ii) $W_1 = 2$ kW, $W_2 = 2$ kW, after the reversal of the current coil connections. Find the total active power, power factor and reactive power.

Solutions:

(i) Total active power = $W_1 + W_2 = 2 + 1.5 = 3.5$ kW

Power factor angle, $\phi = \tan^{-1}\left[\sqrt{3}\,\dfrac{(W_1 - W_2)}{(W_1 + W_2)}\right] = \tan^{-1}\left[\sqrt{3}\,\dfrac{(2-1.5)}{(2+1.5)}\right] = 13.89°$

Power factor $= \cos\phi = \cos 13.89° = 0.97$

Total reactive power $= \sqrt{3}\,(W_1 - W_2) = \sqrt{3}(2 - 1.5) = 0.866$ kVAR

(ii) Total active power = $W_1 + W_2 = 2 - 2 = 0$ kW

Power factor angle, $\phi = \tan^{-1}\left[\sqrt{3}\,\dfrac{(W_1 - W_2)}{(W_1 + W_2)}\right] = \tan^{-1}\left[\sqrt{3}\,\dfrac{(2+2)}{(2-2)}\right] = 90°$

Power factor $= \cos\phi = \cos 90° = 0$

Total reactive power $= \sqrt{3}\,(W_1 - W_2) = \sqrt{3}(2 + 2) = 6.928$ kVAR

6.6 A 3-phase, 440 V load has a power factor of 0.4. Two wattmeters are connected to measure the power. If the input power is 10 kW, find the reading of each instrument.

Solution: Given that

$$V_L = 440 \text{ V, power factor} = 0.4$$

$$\text{Total active power} = W_1 + W_2 = 10 \text{ kW} \quad (1)$$

$$\cos\phi = 0.4 \quad \Rightarrow \quad \phi = \cos^{-1}(0.4) = 66.42°$$

$$\phi = \tan^{-1}\left[\sqrt{3}\,\frac{(W_1 - W_2)}{(W_1 + W_2)}\right] = 66.42°$$

$$\Rightarrow \quad W_1 - W_2 = 13.23 \text{ kW} \quad (2)$$

Adding Eqs (1) and (2),

$$2\,W_1 = 23.23 \quad \Rightarrow \quad W_1 = 11.61\,4 \text{ kW}$$

$$W_2 = 10 - W_1 = -1.614 \text{ kW}$$

6.7 A star connected 3-phase load consists of three similar impedances. When the load is connected to a 3-phase, 400 V, 50 Hz supply, it takes 30 A line current at a p.f of 0.8 lagging. Calculate the (i) total power taken by the load, (ii) resistance and reactance of each phase of the load and (iii) readings of each wattmeter, if the power is measured by the two-wattmeter method.

Solution: Given that

$$V_L = 400 \text{ V}, f = 50 \text{ Hz}, I_L = I_{ph} = 30 \text{ A}, \text{p.f} = \cos\phi = 0.8$$

(i) Total power taken by the load

$$P = \sqrt{3}\,V_L I_L \cos\phi = \sqrt{3} \times 400 \times 30 \times 0.8 = 16.627 \text{ kW}$$

(ii) Resistance and reactance of each phase of the load

$$V_{ph} = \frac{V_L}{\sqrt{3}} = \frac{400}{\sqrt{3}} = 230.95 \text{ V}$$

$$\text{Impedance of each phase of the load, } Z_{ph} = \frac{V_{ph}}{I_{ph}} = \frac{230.95}{30} = 7.7\,\Omega$$

$$R_{ph} = Z_{ph}\cos\phi = 7.7 \times 0.8 = 6.16\,\Omega$$

$$X_{ph} = Z_{ph}\sin\phi = 7.7 \times 0.6 = 4.62\,\Omega$$

(iii) Readings of each wattmeter

$$\cos\phi = 0.8 \quad \Rightarrow \quad \phi = 36.9°$$

$$W_1 = V_L I_L \cos(30 + \phi) = 400 \times 30 \times \cos(66.9) = 6.708 \text{ kW}$$

$$W_2 = V_L I_L \cos(30 - \phi) = 400 \times 30 \times \cos(-6.9) = 11.9 \text{ kW}$$

6.8 Three impedances of $(7 + j4)\,\Omega$, $(3 + j2)\,\Omega$ and $(9 + j2)\,\Omega$ are connected between neutral and R, Y and B phases. If the line voltage is 440 V, calculate (i) the line currents, (ii) the currents in the neutral wire, and (iii) the power consumed in each phase and the total power drawn by the circuit.

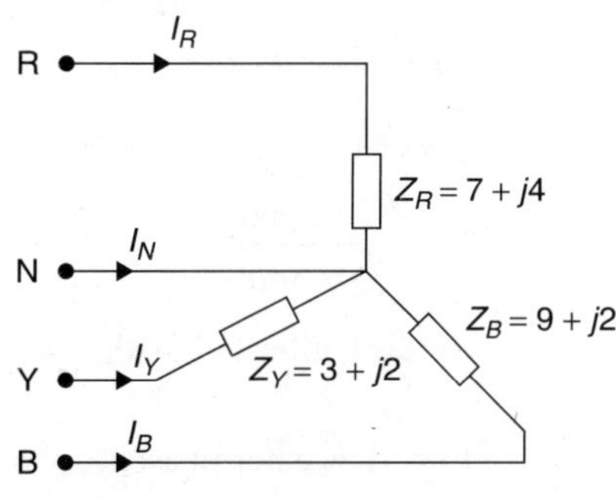

Solution: Given that $V_L = 440$ V

$$Z_R = 7 + j4 = 8.06\angle 29.74°\,\Omega$$

$$Z_Y = 3 + j\,2 = 3.6\angle 33.69°\,\Omega$$

$$Z_B = 9 + j2 = 9.22\angle 12.53°\,\Omega$$

Let us consider the phase sequence as RYB

$$V_{RN} = \frac{V_L}{\sqrt{3}} \angle -30° = \frac{440}{\sqrt{3}} \angle -30° = 254\angle -30°$$

$$V_{YN} = 254\angle -150°, \; V_{BN} = 254\angle 90°$$

The line currents are

$$I_R = \frac{V_{RN}}{Z_R} = \frac{254\angle -30°}{8.06\angle 29.74°} = 31.514\angle -59.74° = 15.88 - j27.22$$

$$I_Y = \frac{V_{YN}}{Z_Y} = \frac{254\angle -150°}{3.6\angle 33.69°} = 70.56\angle -183.69° = -70.4 + j4.54$$

$$I_B = \frac{V_{BN}}{Z_B} = \frac{254\angle 90°}{9.22\angle 12.53°} = 27.55\angle 77.47° = 6 + j26.89$$

The neutral current is

$$I_N = (I_R + I_Y + I_B) = (15.88 - j27.22 - 70.4 + j4.54 + 6 + j26.89) = (-48.52 + j4.21) \text{ A}$$

The power in each phase is calculated as follows

$$Z_R = 7 + j4$$

$$R_R = 7, I_R = 31.514$$

$$P_R = 31.514^2 \times 7 = 6.952 \text{ kW}$$

$$Z_Y = 3 + j2$$

$$R_Y = 3, I_Y = 70.57$$

$$P_Y = 70.5^2 \times 3 = 14.936 \text{ kW}$$

$$Z_B = 9 + j2$$

$$R_B = 9, I_B = 27.55$$

$$P_B = 27.55^2 \times 9 = 6.831 \text{ kW}$$

Total power $P_T = P_R + P_Y + P_B = 6.952 + 14.936 + 6.831 = 28.72$ kW

6.9 Three equal star connected inductors take 8 kW at a p.f of 0.8 when connected to a 460 V, 3-phase, 3-wire supply. Find the line currents, if one conductor is short circuited.

Solution: Given that Line voltage $V_L = 460$ V

Power consumed by load $P = 8$ kW

Power factor $\cos\phi = 0.8$

$$P = \sqrt{3} V_L I_L \cos\phi = 8000$$

$$\Rightarrow \quad I_L = \frac{8000}{\sqrt{3} \times 460 \times 0.8} = 12.55 \text{ A}$$

In star connected load, $I_L = I_{ph} = 12.55$ A

Impedance per phase, $Z_{ph} = \dfrac{V_{ph}}{I_{ph}} = \dfrac{460/\sqrt{3}}{12.55} = 21.16\,\Omega$

$$\cos\phi = 0.8 \Rightarrow \phi = 36.87°$$

$$\therefore \quad Z_{ph} = 21.16\angle 36.87°$$

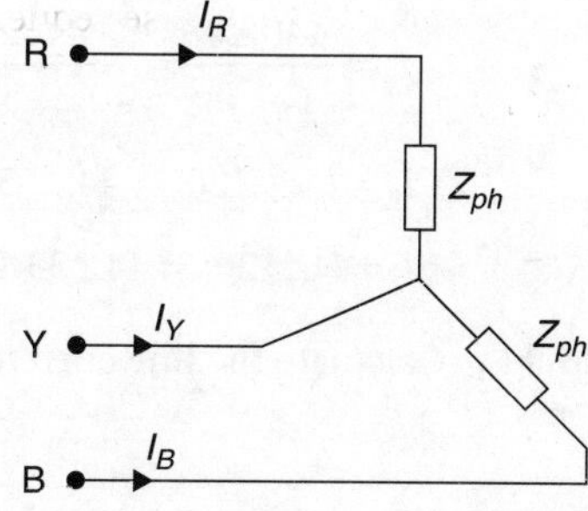

If one of the impedances is short circuited, then the circuit diagram is as shown on the right

Let the phase sequence be RYB

$$V_{RY} = 460\angle 0°$$

$$V_{YB} = 460\angle -120°$$

$$V_{BR} = 460\angle 120°$$

Because of the short circuit, the termainals N and Y are at the same potential. The lines *R*, *Y* and *B* therefore carry unequal currents. Current in the line *R*

$$I_R = -\frac{V_{BR}}{Z_{ph}} = -\frac{460\angle 120°}{21.16\angle 36.87°} = -21.739\angle 83.13° \text{ A}$$

Current in the line *Y*

$$I_Y = -\frac{V_{YB}}{Z_{ph}} = -\frac{460\angle -120°}{21.16\angle 36.87°} = 21.739\angle -156.87° \text{ A}$$

Applying KCL at node N

$$I_R + I_Y + I_B = 0$$

$$\Rightarrow \quad I_B = -(I_R + I_Y) = 21.739\angle 83.13° - 21.739\angle -156.87°$$

$$= 2.6 + j21.58 + 20 + j8.54 = 22.6 + j30.12 = 37.67\angle 53.13°$$

The line currents are

$$I_R = -21.739\angle 83.13° \text{ A}, I_Y = 21.739\angle -156.87° \text{ A and } I_B = 37.67\angle 53.13°$$

6.10 Obtain the line currents in the three-phase circuit.

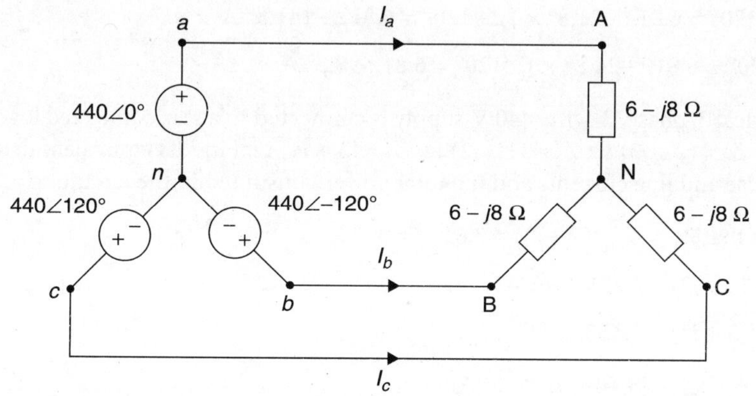

Solution: This is a balanced 3-phase system and the phase sequence is '*abc*'. The per phase circuit of the above system is as shown.

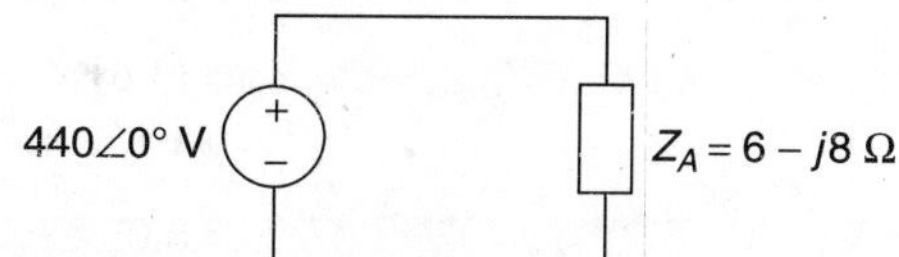

From the above per phase circuit

$$I_a = \frac{440\angle 0^\circ}{6 - j8} = \frac{440\angle 0^\circ}{10\angle -53.13^\circ} = 44\angle 53.13^\circ \text{ A}$$

$$I_b = I_a\angle -120^\circ = 44\angle 53.13^\circ \times 1\angle -120^\circ = 44\angle -66.87^\circ \text{ A}$$

$$I_c = I_a\angle 120^\circ = 44\angle 53.13^\circ \times 1\angle 120^\circ = 44\angle 173.13^\circ \text{ A}$$

6.11 Calculate the line currents in the three-wire Y–Y system.

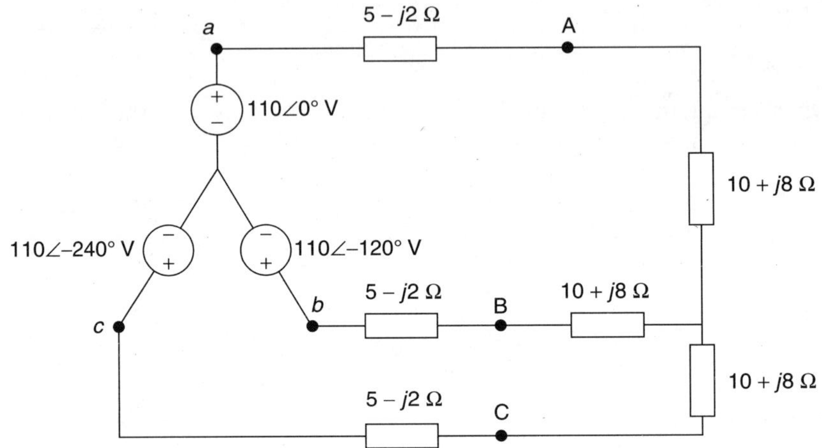

Solution: This is a balanced 3-phase system and the phase sequence is '*abc*'. The per phase circuit of the above system is as shown below:

$$Z_A = (5 - j2) + (10 + j8) = 15 + j6 = 16.2\angle 21.8^\circ$$

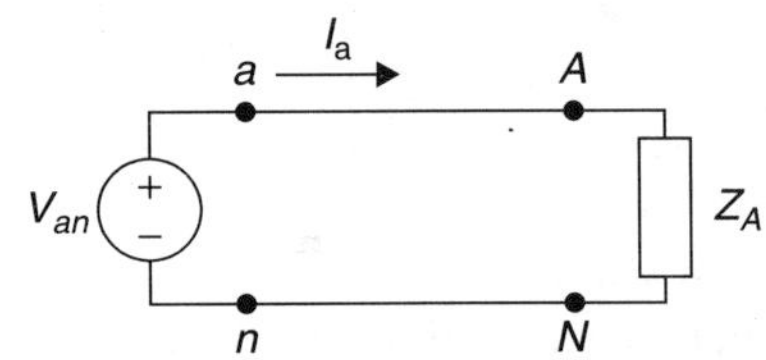

From the above per phase circuit

$$I_a = \frac{V_{an}}{Z_A} = \frac{110\angle 0^\circ}{16.2\angle 21.8^\circ} = 6.81\angle -21.8^\circ \text{ A}$$

$$I_b = I_a\angle -120^\circ = 6.81\angle -21.8^\circ \times 1\angle -120^\circ = 6.81\angle -141.8^\circ \text{ A}$$

$$I_c = I_a\angle 120^\circ = 6.81\angle -21.8^\circ \times 1\angle 120^\circ = 6.81\angle 98.2^\circ \text{ A}$$

6.12 A symmetrical 3-phase, 3-wire, 440 V supply is connected to a star connected load. The impedances in each branch are $Z_1 = (2 + j3)$ Ω, $Z_2 = (1 - j2)$ Ω, $Z_3 = (3 + j4)$ Ω. Find its equivalent delta connected load. Hence find the phase and line currents and the total power consumed in the circuit.

Solution: Given that $Z_1 = Z_R = (2 + j3) = 3.61\angle 56.31^\circ\ \Omega$

$$Z_2 = Z_Y = (1 - j2) = 2.236\angle -63.435^\circ\ \Omega$$

$$Z_3 = Z_B = (3 + j4) = 5\angle 53.13^\circ\ \Omega$$

The equivalent network can be drawn as shown.

The impedance of the delta network can be calculated as follows

$$\begin{aligned} Z_R Z_Y + Z_Y Z_B + Z_B Z_R &= (3.61\angle 56.31^\circ)(2.236\angle -63.435^\circ) + (2.236\angle -63.435^\circ)(5\angle 53.13^\circ) \\ &\quad + (5\angle 53.13^\circ)(3.61\angle 56.31^\circ) \\ &= 8.05\angle -7.1^\circ + 11.15\angle -10.27^\circ + 18.05\angle 109.43^\circ = 19.10\angle 47.3^\circ \end{aligned}$$

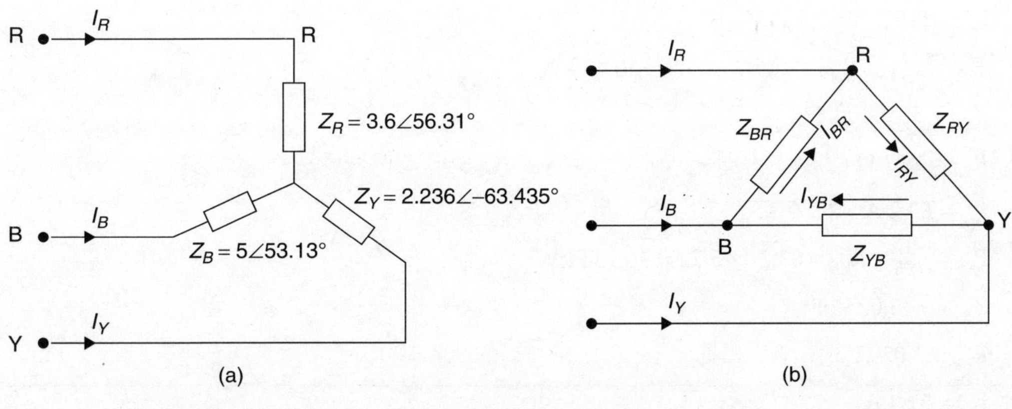

$$Z_{RY} = \frac{Z_R Z_Y + Z_Y Z_B + Z_B Z_R}{Z_B} = \frac{19.10\angle 47.3°}{5\angle 53.13°} = 3.8\angle -5.83° = 3.8 - j0.38$$

$$Z_{YB} = \frac{Z_R Z_Y + Z_Y Z_B + Z_B Z_R}{Z_R} = \frac{19.10\angle 47.3°}{3.61\angle 56.31°} = 5.29\angle -9° = 5.22 - j0.82$$

$$Z_{BR} = \frac{Z_R Z_Y + Z_Y Z_B + Z_B Z_R}{Z_Y} = \frac{19.10\angle 47.3°}{2.236\angle -63.435°} = 8.56\angle 110.70° = -3.02 + j8$$

The unbalanced star connected load and its equivalent delta load is as shown in Figs (a) and (b).

Taking V_{RY} as the reference, we have

$$V_{RY} = 440\angle 0° \text{ V}$$

$$V_{YB} = 440\angle -120° \text{ V}$$

$$V_{BR} = 440\angle -240° \text{ V}$$

The three phase currents in the equivalent delta load are

$$I_{RY} = \frac{V_{RY}}{Z_{RY}} = -\frac{440\angle 0°}{3.82\angle -5.83°} = 115.2\angle 5.83° = 114.6 + j11.7$$

$$I_{YB} = \frac{V_{YB}}{Z_{RB}} = -\frac{440\angle -120°}{5.29\angle -9°} = 83.2\angle -111° = -29.8 - j77.673$$

$$I_{BR} = \frac{V_{BR}}{Z_{BR}} = -\frac{440\angle -240°}{8.56\angle 110.7°} = 51.4\angle -350.7° = 50.7 + j8.3$$

The line currents are

$$I_R = (I_{RY} - I_{BR}) = 63.9 + j3.4$$

$$I_Y = (I_{YB} - I_{RY}) = -114.4 - j89.373$$

$$I_B = (I_{BR} - I_{YB}) = 80.5 - j86$$

The power in each phase is calculated as follows

$$Z_{RY} = 3.8 - j0.38$$

$$R_{RY} = 3.8\ \Omega$$

$I_{RY} = 115.2$ A

$P_{RY} = I_{RY}^2 \times R_{RY} = 115.2^2 \times 3.8 = 50.43$ kW

$Z_{YB} = 5.22 - j0.82$

$R_{YB} = 5.22\ \Omega$

$I_{RY} = 83.2$ A

$P_{YB} = I_{YB}^2 \times R_{YB} = 83.2^2 \times 5.22 = 36.134$ kW

$Z_{BR} = -(3.02 - j8)$

$R_{BR} = 3.02\ \Omega$

$I_{BR} = 51.4$ A

$P_{BR} = I_{BR}^2 \times R_{BR} = 51.4^2 \times 3.02 = 7.98$ kW

Total power , $P_T = P_{RY} + P_{YB} + P_{BR} = 50.43 + 36.134 + 7.98 = 94.544$ kW

6.13 Find the reading of wattmeter when the network is connected to a symmetrical 440 V, 3-phase supply. The phase sequence is RYB.

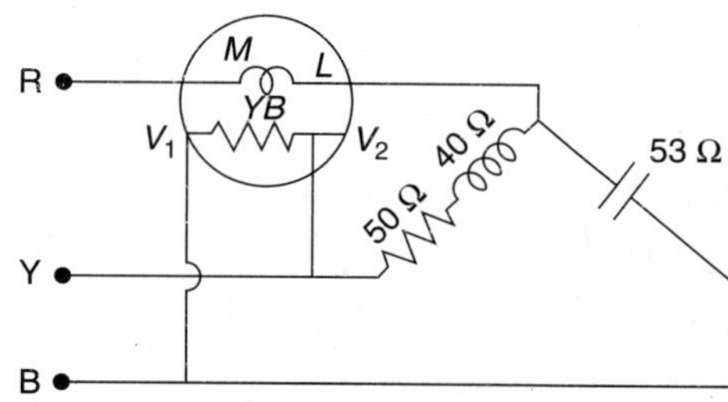

Solution: Given that

$V_L = 440$ V

Phase sequence is RYB

$V_{RY} = 440\angle 0°$ V

$V_{YB} = 440\angle -120°$ V

$V_{BR} = 440\angle -240°$ V

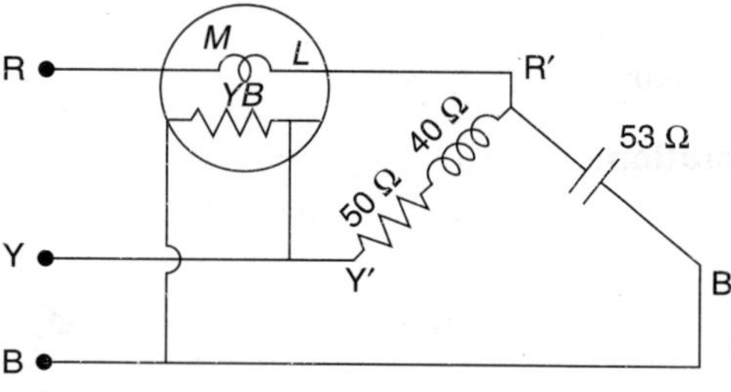

$Z_{R'Y'} = 50 + j40 = 64.03\angle 38.66°$

$Z_{R'B'} = -j53 = 53\angle -90°$

We know that from the circuit

$$I_{R'Y'} = \frac{V_{RY}}{Z_{R'Y'}} = \frac{440\angle 0°}{64.03\angle 38.66°} = 6.87\angle -38.66°$$

$$I_{R'B'} = \frac{V_{RB}}{Z_{R'B'}} = \frac{-440\angle 120°}{53\angle -90°} = -8.3\angle 210° = 29.8 - j77.673$$

$$I_{RR'} = I_{R'Y'} + I_{R'B'} = 6.87\angle 38.66° - 8.3\angle 210° = 12.55\angle -0.65° \text{ A}$$

The current through the current coil of wattmeter = 12.55

Voltage across the wattmeter, $V_{YB} = 440\angle -120°$V

Therefore, reading of the wattmeter is

$$W = I_{RR'} V_{YB} \cos\phi = 12.55 \times 400 \times \cos(-120 + 0.65) = 2706.6 \text{ W}$$

6.14 On a symmetrical 3-phase system phase sequence RYB, a capacitive reactance of 8 Ω is connected across YB and a coil $(R + jX)$ across RY. Find R and X such that $I_Y = 0$.

Solution: Given that

$$X_C = 8\ \Omega = -j8,\ I_Y = 0$$

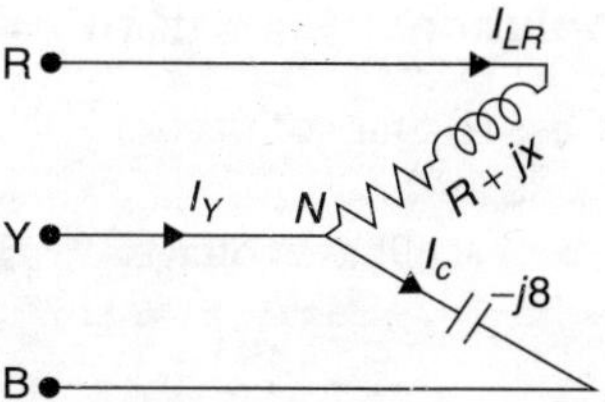

Phase sequence is RYB. The geometry of the circuit is as shown.

Since the phase sequence is RYB,

$$V_{RY} = V\angle 0°\ \text{V}$$

$$V_{YB} = V\angle -120°\ \text{V}$$

$$V_{BR} = V\angle -240°\ \text{V}$$

Let the current through the capacitor be I_C

$$\therefore \quad I_C = \frac{V_{YB}}{X_C} = \frac{V\angle -120°}{8\angle -90°} = \frac{V}{8}\angle -30°$$

Applying KCL at point N

$$I_Y = I_{RL} - I_C = 0$$

$$\Rightarrow \quad I_{RL} = I_C$$

$$\Rightarrow \quad \frac{V_{RY}}{R + jX} = \frac{V}{8}\angle -30°$$

$$\Rightarrow \quad \frac{V}{R + jX} = \frac{V}{8}\angle -30°$$

$$\Rightarrow \quad R + jX = 8\angle 30° = 6.94 + j4$$

$$\therefore \quad R = 6.94\ \Omega \quad \text{and} \quad X = 4\ \Omega$$

6.15 Three equal impedances each having a resistance of 25 Ω and reactance of 40 Ω are connected in star to a 400 V, 3-phase, 50 Hz system. Calculate (i) the line current, (ii) power factor, and (iii) power consumed.

Solution: Given that

$$R_{ph} = 25\ \Omega,\ X_{ph} = 40\ \Omega,\ V_L = 400\ \text{V}$$

$$Z_{ph} = R_{ph} + jX_{ph} = 25 + j40 = 47.17\angle 58°$$

$$\text{Phase voltage, } V_{ph} = \frac{V_L}{\sqrt{3}} = \frac{400}{\sqrt{3}} = 231\ \text{V}$$

$$\text{Phase current, } I_{ph} = \frac{V_{ph}}{Z_{ph}} = \frac{231}{47.17} = 4.9\ \text{A}$$

(i) Line current, $I_L = I_{ph} = 4.9$ A

(ii) Power factor, $\cos\phi = \dfrac{R_{ph}}{Z_{ph}} = \dfrac{25}{47.17} = 0.53$ lag

(iii) Power consumed, $P = \sqrt{3}V_L I_L \cos\phi = \sqrt{3} \times 400 \times 4.9 \times 0.53 = 1800$ W

6.16 Three 100 Ω resistors are connected in star and in delta across a 415 volts, 50 Hz, 3-phase supply. Calculate the line and phase currents, power factor and power consumed in each case.

Solution: Given that $V_L = 415$ V, $f = 50$ Hz, $Z_{ph} = R_{ph} = 100\ \Omega$

Case (i) Star connection

$$\text{Phase voltage, } V_{ph} = \frac{V_L}{\sqrt{3}} = \frac{415}{\sqrt{3}} = 239.6 \text{ V}$$

(i) Phase current, $I_{ph} = \dfrac{V_{ph}}{Z_{ph}} = \dfrac{239.6}{100} = 2.4$ A

Line current, $I_L = I_{ph} = 2.4$ A

Phase current = 2.4 A

(ii) Power factor $\cos\phi = \dfrac{R_{ph}}{Z_{ph}} = \dfrac{100}{100} = 1$

(iii) Power consumed, $P = \sqrt{3} V_L I_L \cos\phi = \sqrt{3} \times 415 \times 2.4 \times 1 = 1.725$ kW

Case (ii) Delta connection

$$V_{ph} = V_L = 415 \text{ V}$$

(i) Phase current, $I_{ph} = \dfrac{V_{ph}}{Z_{ph}} = \dfrac{415}{100} = 4.15$ A

Line current, $I_L = \sqrt{3}\ I_{Ph} = \sqrt{3} \times 4.15 = 7.2$ A

(ii) Power factor, $\cos\phi = \dfrac{R_{ph}}{Z_{ph}} = \dfrac{100}{100} = 1$

(iii) Power consumed, $P = \sqrt{3} V_L I_L \cos\phi = \sqrt{3} \times 415 \times 7.2 \times 1 = 5.175$ kW

EXERCISE PROBLEMS

1. A balanced star connected load of $(5 + j\,4)$ Ω/phase is connected to a 3-phase, 400V, 50 Hz supply. Find the line current, power factor, real and reactive power. [**Ans:** I_L = 36.1 A, $\cos\phi$ = 0.7808 lag, P = 19.53 kW, Q = 15.62 kVAR]

2. A balanced star connected load of 100 kW is connected to a balanced 3-ϕ supply system at 400 V and 50 Hz. The line current taken from the supply is 150 A lagging. Find the circuit constants of the load per phase. [**Ans:** R = 1.482 Ω, L = 1.334 mH]

3. A balanced delta connected load of $20\angle 40°$ Ω is connected to a balanced 3-ϕ, 400 V supply system. Find the line current, power factor and total power. [**Ans:** I_L = 34.64 A, $\cos\phi$ = 0.766 lag, P = 18.358 kW]

4. A balanced delta connected load takes a leading line current of 60 A when connected to a 3-ϕ, 415 V, 50 Hz supply system. Find the circuit constants of the load per phase when the total power taken is 10 kW. [**Ans:** R = 2.78 Ω, C = 273.23 μF]

5. Three identical impednaces of $42\angle -35°$ Ω are connected in delta to a 3-phase, 3 wire, 350 V, *ABC* system. Find the line currents and the total power. [**Ans:** $14.4\angle 125°$ A, $14.4\angle 5°$ A, $14.4\angle -115°$ A, 7.13 kW]

6. A balanced star connected load with impedance of $65\angle -20°$ Ω is connected to a 3-phase, 3-wire, 480 V, BYR system. Find the line currents and the total power. [**Ans:** $4.26\angle -70°$ A, $4.26\angle 50°$ A, $4.26\angle 170°$ A, 3.32 kW]

7. Find the reading of the two wattmeters used on a 3-wire, 240 V system with a balanced delta connected load of 20∠80° Ω. [**Ans:** –1710 W, 3210 W]

8. Calculate the total power input and reading of the two wattmeters connected to measure power in a 3-phase balanced load, if reactive power input is 15 kVAR and the load p.f is 0.8. [**Ans:** P_{in} = 36.641 kW, W_1 = 12.99 kW, W_2 = 21.650 kW]

9. Two wattmeters are connected to measure power in a 3-phase circuit. The reading of one of the wattmeters is 5 kW when the load power factor is unity. If the power factor of the load is changed to 0.707 lagging, without changing the total input power, calculate the readings of the two wattmeters. [**Ans:** W_1 = 2.113 kW, W_2 = 7.886 kW]

10. A 3-phase load having a resistance of 10 Ω in each phase is connected in (i) star and (ii) delta against a 400 V, 3-phase supply. Compare the power consumed in both the cases. [**Ans:** (i) 16 kW, (ii) 48 kW]

11. The input power to a 3-phase AC motor is measured as 5 kW. If the voltage and current to the motor are 400 V and 8.6 A respectively, determine the power factor of the system. [**Ans:** p.f = 0.84]

12. Two wattmeters are connected to measure the input power to a balanced 3-phase load by the two-wattmeter method. If the instrument readings are 8 kW and 4 kW, determine (i) the total power input and (ii) the load power factor. [**Ans:** P = 12 kW, p.f = 0.866]

13. Two wattmeters connected to a 3-phase motor indicate the total power input to be 12 kW. The power factor is 0.6. Determine the readings of each wattmeter. [**Ans:** W_1 = 10.62 kW, W_2 = 1.38 kW]

14. Three loads, each of resistance 30 Ω, are connected in star to a 415 V, 3-phase supply. Determine (i) the system phase voltage, (ii) the phase current and (iii) the line current. [**Ans:** V_{ph} = 240 V, I_{ph} = I_L = 8 A]

15. Three identical coils, each of resistance 10 Ω and inductance 42 mH are connected (i) in star and (ii) in delta to a 415 V, 50 Hz, 3-phase supply. Determine the total power dissipated in each case. [**Ans:** P_Y = 6.3 kW, P_Δ = 18.87 kW]

16. A 415 V, 3-phase AC motor has a power output of 12.75 kW and operates at a power factor of 0.77 lagging and with an efficiency of 85%. If the motor is delta-connected, determine the (i) power input (ii) line current and (iii) phase current. [**Ans:** P = 15 kW, I_{ph} = 15.65 A, I_L = 27.1 A]

17. A 400 V, 3-phase star connected alternator supplies a delta-connected load, each phase of which has a resistance of 30 Ω and inductive reactance 40 Ω. Calculate the (i) current supplied by the alternator and (ii) output power and the kVA of the alternator, neglecting losses in the line between the alternator and load. [**Ans:** I = 13.86 A, P = 5.76 kW, S = 9.6 kVA]

REVIEW QUESTIONS

1. Define (a) balanced voltage, (b) balanced impedance, and (c) neutral shift voltage.
2. Define phase sequence. Explain its significance.
3. Compare RYB and RBY phase sequences.
4. Find the relation between the line and phase value of voltage and current in a balanced star connected load.
5. Find the relation between the line and phase voltage of voltage and current in a balanced delta connected load.
6. Compare three phase star and delta connected systems.
7. Find the relation between the power factor and wattmeter readings in the two-wattmeter method of power measurement.
8. List the methods available for the analysis of unbalanced star connected load.
9. In a three-phase circuit, what do you mean by balanced load?

10. When is a three phase supply system called balanced supply system?
11. List any four advantages of the 3-phase system over the 1-phase system.
12. Derive the expression for the total power in a 3-phase balanced circuit using the two-wattmeter method.
13. How can a wattmeter be used to measure reactive power?
14. List the methods available for measuring in a 3-phase balanced load.
15. Derive the relationship between line and phase quantities in a 3-phase balanced (a) star connected system (b) delta connected system.
16. With a neat circuit and phasor diagram explain three phase power measurement by the two-wattmeter method and also derive the expression for power factor.

MULTIPLE CHOICE QUESTIONS

1. In a balanced delta connection, $I_L =$
   (a) $\frac{I_{ph}}{\sqrt{3}}$ (b) I_{ph}
   (c) $\sqrt{2}I_{ph}$ (d) $\sqrt{3}I_{ph}$
2. In a two-phase system, the phase voltages differ by
   (a) 60° (b) 90°
   (c) 120° (d) 180°
3. In a three-phase system the emfs are
   (a) 30° apart (b) 40° apart
   (c) 90° apart (d) 120° apart
4. Three 50 Ω resistors are connected in star across a 400 V, 3-phase supply. The phase current is
   (a) 6.5 A (b) 6.62 A
   (c) 4 A (d) 5 A
5. In a balanced phase star connected system, the phase difference between line and phase voltage is
   (a) 90° (b) 60°
   (c) 30° (d) 120°
6. In a balanced 3-phase star connected load, the power consumed/ph is 500 W, the power factor of the load is 0.8 lag. The total reactive power taken by the load is
   (a) 1875 var (b) 375 var
   (c) 625 var (d) 1125 var
7. A 3-phase, 4-wire supply is connected to a balanced star connected load. The current in the neutral wire is
   (a) $\sqrt{3}I_{ph}$ (b) I_{ph}
   (c) $\frac{I_{ph}}{\sqrt{3}}$ (d) zero
8. Three equal resistors of 10 Ω each are connected in star. The resistances of an equivalent delta connected load are equal to
   (a) 20 Ω (b) $\frac{10}{3}$ Ω
   (c) 30 Ω (d) 15 Ω
9. Three inductors of 20 mH each are connected in delta. The inductance of an equivalent star connected load is
   (a) 20 mH (b) 60 mH
   (c) 6.66 mH (d) $\frac{20}{3}$ mH
10. Three capacitors of 6 μF each are connected in delta. The capacitance of an equivalent star connected load is
    (a) $\frac{2}{3}$ μF (b) 18 μF
    (c) 36 μF (d) 2 μF
11. The sum of the three line current in a 3-phase 3-wire system is equal to
    (a) zero (b) unity
    (c) infinity (d) can't say
12. In a balanced wye connection, the total 3-phase power in terms of phase quantities is
    (a) $V_{ph} I_{ph}$ (b) $3V_{ph} I_{ph} \cos \phi$
    (c) $3V_{ph} I_{ph} \sin \phi$ (d) $V_{ph} I_{ph} \cos \phi$
13. In the case of a delta connected load, if one resistor is removed, the power will become
    (a) zero (b) one-third
    (c) two-third (d) none of the above
14. Three identical impedances are connected in delta to a 3-phase supply of 400 V. The line-current is 36.65 A and the total power taken is 16.4 kW. The resistance of the load in each phase (in ohm) is

(a) 20 (b) 16
(c) 12 (d) 10

15. The power in a 3-phase system is given by $\sqrt{3}\, V_L I_L \cos\phi$ where ϕ is the phase angle between
(a) line voltage and line current
(b) phase voltage and phase current
(c) line voltage and phase current
(d) phase voltage and line current

16. In a phase 4-wire system, the line currents are $I_a = (5 + j8)$ A, $I_b = (-6 - j9)$ A, $I_c = (3 + j5)$ A. Then the current in the neutral wire is
(a) $-2 + j4$ (b) zero
(c) $2 - j4$ (d) $-2 - j4$

17. The expression for total reactive power in a 3-phase balanced load is
(a) $V_L I_L \sin\phi$ (b) $\sqrt{3}\, V_L I_L \sin\phi$
(c) $3 V_L I_L \sin\phi$ (d) $\sqrt{2}\, V_L I_L \sin\phi$

18. In a balanced star connection, $V_L =$
(a) $\frac{V_{ph}}{\sqrt{3}}$ (b) V_{ph}
(c) $\sqrt{2} V_{ph}$ (d) $\sqrt{3} V_{ph}$

19. In the two-wattmeter method of measurement of power in a balanced load, the readings are $W_1 = 400$ W, $W_2 = 200$ W, the p.f of the load is
(a) 0.5 lag (b) 0.866 lag
(c) 0.866 lead (d) 0.5 lead

20. In a 2-wattmeter method, one of the wattmeters reads zero, and the other reads 1000 W in a balanced 3-phase load. The reactive power taken by the load is
(a) 1000 VAR (b) $\sqrt{3} \times 1000$ VAR
(c) zero (d) 3000 VAR

21. In a balanced 3-phase star connected system E_{RY} lags behind E_B by ______ electrical degrees
(a) 60° (b) 90°
(c) 120° (d) 150°

22. If the R-phase of a 3-phase star connected alternator becomes reversely connected by mistake, it will affect
(a) V_{RY} and V_{YB} (b) V_{YB} and V_{BR}
(c) V_{RY} and V_{BR} (d) V_{RY}, V_{YB} and E_{BR}

23. The relationship between the line and phase voltage of a delta-connected circuit is
(a) $V_L = V_P$ (b) $V_L = \sqrt{3}\, V_P$
(c) $V_L = \frac{V_P}{\sqrt{2}}$ (d) $V_L = \frac{2}{\pi} V_P$

24. A 400 V, 3-phase induction motor takes a no load current of 5 A. The phase angle of the current is 75°. The readings of wattmeters in the two-wattmeter method of measurement of power are
(a) 2000 cos105°, 2000 cos45°
(b) $\sqrt{3} \times 2000$ cos45°, $\sqrt{3} \times 2000$ cos75°
(c) $\sqrt{3} \times 2000$ cos 75° each
(d) 2000 cos 75°, 2000 sin 45°

25. A single wattmeter is employed to measure reactive power in a balanced 3-phase load. If the reading of wattmeter is 500, then total reactive power taken by the three-phase load is
(a) $\frac{500}{\sqrt{3}}$ VAR (b) 1500 VAR
(c) 500 VAR (d) $\sqrt{3} \times 500$ VAR

26. Three equal impedances are first connected in delta across a 3-phase balanced supply. If the same impedances are connected in star across the same supply
(a) phase currents will be one-third
(b) line currents will be one-third
(c) power consumed will be one-third
(d) none of the above

27. A 3-phase star connected symmetrical load consumes P watts of power from a balanced supply. If the same load is connected in delta to the same supply, the power consumption will be
(a) P (b) $\sqrt{3}\, P$
(c) $3P$
(d) not possible to determine from the given data

28. The minimum number of wattmeters required to measure power in a 3-phase unbalanced star connected load is
(a) one (b) two
(c) three (d) four

29. The power measurement in a balanced 3-phase circuit can be done by
(a) one-wattmeter method only
(b) two-wattmeter method only
(c) three-wattmeter method only
(d) any one of the above

30. A balanced delta connected load of $(2 + j3)$ ohms per phase is connected to a balanced 3-phase 440 V supply. The phase current is 10 A. Find the active power.
(a) 50 kW (b) 100 kW
(c) 7.26 kW (d) 10 kW

31. The angle between line current and the corresponding line voltage in a star connection is
(a) 30° (b) $30° + \phi$
(c) $30° - \phi$ (d) 45°

32. The angle between line voltage and the respective phase voltage in a star connection is
(a) 30° (b) $30° + \phi$
(c) $30° - \phi$ (d) 45°

33. The angle between line current and the corresponding line voltage in a delta connection is
(a) 30° (b) $30° + \phi$
(c) $30° - \phi$ (d) 45°

34. The angle between line current and the respective phase current in a delta connection is
(a) 30° (b) $30° + \phi$
(c) $30° - \phi$ (d) 45°

35. A 3-phase, 3-wire supply feeds a load consisting of three equal resistors connected in star. If one of the resistors is open circuited, then the percentage reduction in the load will be
(a) 25 (b) 50
(c) 33.33 (d) 66.66

36. In the measurement of 3-phase power by the two-wattmeter method, if the two wattmeter readings are equal, the power factor of the circuit is
(a) 0.8 lagging (b) 0.8 leading
(c) zero (d) unity

37. In the two-wattmeter method of measuring power in a 3-phase system one of the wattmeters reads negative implying that the
(a) wattmeter connection is faulty
(b) load is unbalanced
(c) power flow is in the reverse direction
(d) power factor is less than 0.5

38. In the two-wattmeter method of power measurement, one of the wattmeters will show a negative reading when the load power factor angle is strictly
(a) less than 30° (b) less than 60°
(c) greater than 30° (d) greater than 60°

39. While measuring power in a three-phase load by the two-wattmeter method, the readings of the two wattmeters will be equal and opposite when
(a) pf is unity (b) load is balanced
(c) phase angle is between 60° and 90°
(d) the load is purely inductive

40. In the two-wattmeter method of power measurement, if one of the wattmeter shows a zero reading, then it can be concluded that the
(a) power factor is unity
(b) power factor is 0.5
(c) power factor is 0.5 lagging
(d) power factor is 0.5 leading

41. The two-wattmeter method is employed to measure power in a 3-phase balanced system with the current coils connected in the A and C lines. The phase sequence is ABC. If the wattmeter with its current coil in A-phase line reads zero, then the power factor of the 3-ϕ load will be
(a) zero lagging (b) zero leading
(c) 0.5 lagging (d) 0.5 leading

42. The ratio of the readings of two wattmeters connected to measure power in a balanced 3-phase load is 5 : 3 and the load is inductive. The power factor of the load is
(a) 0.917 lead (b) 0.917 lag
(c) 0.6 lead (d) 0.6 lag

43. If W_1 and W_2 are the readings of two wattmeters used to measure the power of a 3-phase balanced load, then the reactive power drawn by the load is
(a) $W_1 + W_2$ (b) $W_1 - W_2$
(c) $\sqrt{3}\,(W_1 + W_2)$ (d) $\sqrt{3}\,(W_1 - W_2)$

46. In India, electrical power is transmitted by
(a) 1-phase AC system
(b) 3-wire DC system
(c) 3-phase 3-wire AC system
(d) 2-wire DC system

45. If the readings of the two wattmeters in the 2-wattmeter method of power measurement are 6.5 kW and 3.5 kW respectively and the latter reading has been obtained after reversing the current coil of the wattmeter, what will be the total power in kW?

(a) 1 (b) 3.5
(c) 6.5 (d) 8

46. The minimum number of wattmeters required to measure power in a 3-phase balanced system is

(a) one (b) two
(c) three (d) four

47. If W_1 and W_2 are the readings of two wattmeters used to measure the power of a 3-phase balanced load, then the active power drawn by the load is

(a) $W_1 + W_2$ (b) $W_1 - W_2$
(c) $\sqrt{3}\,(W_1 + W_2)$ (d) $\sqrt{3}\,(W_1 - W_2)$

Answers

1. d	**2.** b	**3.** d	**4.** b	**5.** c	**6.** d	**7.** d	**8.** c	**9.** d	**10.** b
11. a	**12.** b	**13.** c	**14.** c	**15.** b	**16.** d	**17.** b	**18.** d	**19.** b	**20.** b
21. b	**22.** c	**23.** a	**24.** a	**25.** d	**26.** c	**27.** c	**28.** b	**29.** d	**30.** c
31. b	**32.** a	**33.** b	**34.** a	**35.** b	**36.** d	**37.** d	**38.** d	**39.** d	**40.** b
41. c	**42.** b	**43.** d	**44.** c	**45.** a	**46.** a	**47.** a			

7 Network Theorems

Learning Outcomes

After reading this chapter, the reader will able to

- Outline different network theorems
- Solve the DC or AC network using Superposition Theorem
- Solve the DC or AC network using Thevenin's/Norton's Theorem
- Solve the DC or AC network using Maximum Power Transfer Theorem
- Solve the DC or AC network using Reciprocity Theorem
- Solve the DC or AC network using Milliman's Theorem
- Solve the DC or AC network using Tellegen's Theorem
- Solve the DC or AC network using Substitution Theorem
- Solve the DC or AC network using Compensation Theorem

7.1 INTRODUCTION

The loop current method and node voltage method are used to solve all the network problems. It is possible to determine all the branch currents and voltages by using these methods. However, in the analysis of electrical circuits, the voltage or current of only one specific branch is required. The application of mesh or nodal analysis yields simultaneous equations which involves other voltages and currents in addition to the required one. It is highly desirable to find the required quantity without finding the solution for the complete network. In such cases, network theorems are useful which simplifies the method of solution.

7.2 SUPERPOSITION THEOREM

This theorem is very useful to find the response (voltage or current) at a particular point which is excited by more than one independent source. This theorem is applicable to only linear networks. Power cannot be determined by this theorem, since the relationship between power and current/voltage is not linear.

Statement It states that in any linear network containing two or more sources, the response in any element is equal to the algebraic sum of responses caused by an individual source acting alone, while the other sources are kept at zero.

Fig. 7.1 V_1 and V_2 both acting

Verification In the network (Fig. 7.1), the current flows through resistance R_3. Let the node voltage be V.

Applying KCL to Fig. 7.1,

$$\frac{V-V_1}{R_1}+\frac{V}{R_3}+\frac{V-V_2}{R_2}=0 \tag{7.1}$$

But $\quad V = IR_3 \quad$ (7.2)

$$\therefore \quad \frac{IR_3 - V_1}{R_1} + I + \frac{IR_3 - V_2}{R_2} = 0$$

$$I\left(\frac{R_3}{R_1} + \frac{R_3}{R_2} + 1\right) = \frac{V_1}{R_1} + \frac{V_2}{R_2}$$

$$I = \frac{V_1R_2 + V_2R_1}{R_1R_2 + R_2R_3 + R_3R_1} \tag{7.3}$$

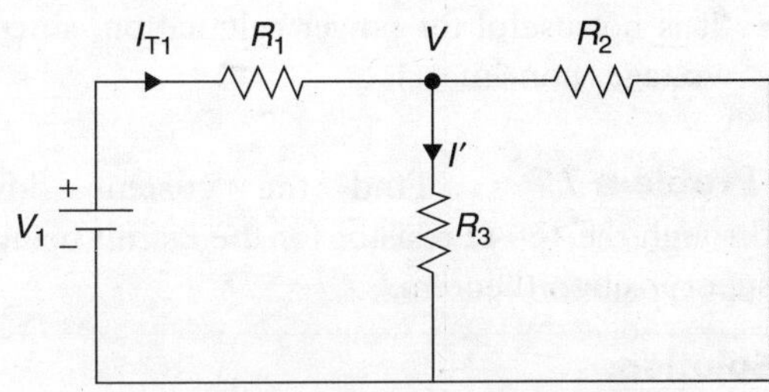

Fig. 7.2 V_1 acting alone

Let us consider V_1 acting alone:
From Fig. 7.2,

$$I_{T1} = \frac{V_1}{R_1 + \dfrac{R_2R_3}{R_2 + R_3}} = \frac{V_1(R_2 + R_3)}{R_1R_2 + R_2R_3 + R_3R_1}$$

$$I' = I_{T1}\frac{R_2}{R_2 + R_3} = \frac{V_1R_2}{R_1R_2 + R_2R_3 + R_3R_1} \tag{7.4}$$

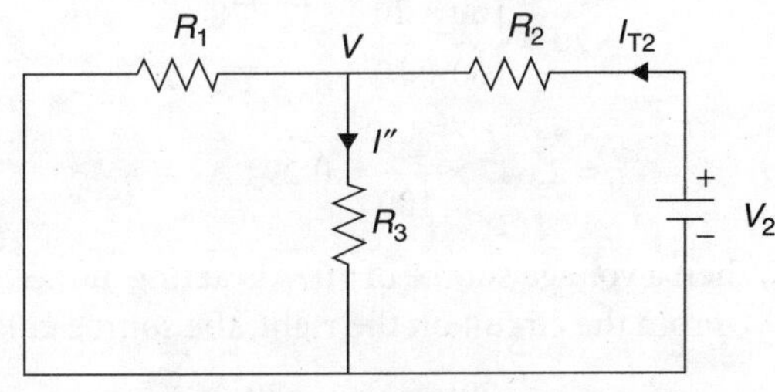

Fig. 7.3 V_2 acting alone

Let us consider V_2 acting alone:
From Fig. 7.3,

$$I_{T2} = \frac{V_2}{R_2 + \dfrac{R_1R_3}{R_1 + R_3}} = \frac{V_2(R_1 + R_3)}{R_1R_2 + R_2R_3 + R_3R_1}$$

$$I'' = I_{T2}\frac{R_1}{R_1 + R_3} = \frac{V_2R_1}{R_1R_2 + R_2R_3 + R_3R_1} \tag{7.5}$$

According to the superposition theorem

$$I = I' + I''$$

$$= \frac{V_1R_2}{R_1R_2 + R_2R_3 + R_3R_1} + \frac{V_2R_1}{R_1R_2 + R_2R_3 + R_3R_1}$$

$$\therefore \quad I = \frac{V_1R_2 + V_2R_1}{R_1R_2 + R_2R_3 + R_3R_1} \tag{7.6}$$

Equations 7.3 and 7.6 represent the same and hence the superposition theorem is verified.

7.2.1 Steps to be Followed in the Superposition Theorem

The following steps have to be followed for the determination of response using the superposition theorem.

- Find the current through the resistance when only one independent source is acting, by replacing all other independent sources by respective internal resistances. That is, voltage sources are replaced with short circuits and current sources are replaced with open circuits.
- Find the current through the resistance for each of the independent sources.
- Find the resultant current through the resistance by the superposition theorem considering magnitude and direction of each current.

Note: The dependent sources are not sources but dissipative components; hence they are active at all times. A dependent source has zero value only when its control voltage or current is zero.

7.2.2 Limitations of the Superposition Theorem

- It is not applicable to circuits consisting of non-linear elements such as semiconductor devices, gas tubes and so on.
- It is not applicable to the circuits consisting of only dependent sources.
- It is not useful to the circuits consisting of less than two independent sources.
- It is not useful for power calculation, since the power is proportional to the square of the current or voltage (non-linear).

Problem 7.1 Find the current flowing through the 160 Ω resistor for the circuit using the superposition theorem.

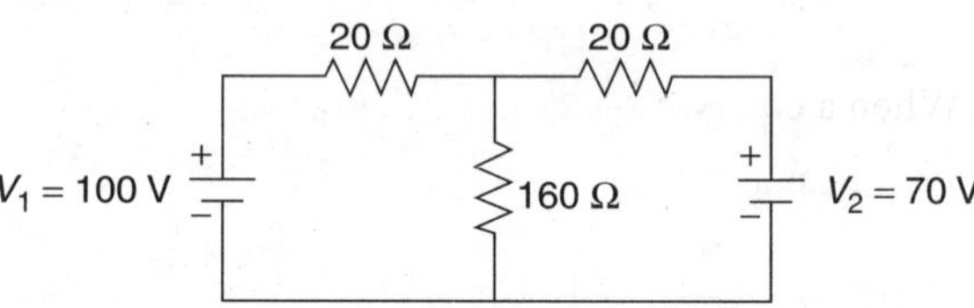

Solution:

When a voltage source of 100 V is acting alone:

Form the circuit on the right, the source current

$$= \frac{100}{20 + \frac{160 \times 20}{160 + 20}} = \frac{100}{37.778} = 2.647 \text{ A}$$

$$\therefore \quad i_1 = 2.647 \times \frac{20}{180} = 0.294 \text{ A}$$

When a voltage source of 70 V is acting alone:

From the circuit on the right, the source current

$$= \frac{70}{20 + \frac{160 \times 20}{160 + 20}} = \frac{70}{37.778} = 1.853 \text{ A}$$

$$\therefore \quad i_2 = 1.853 \times \frac{20}{180} = 0.206 \text{ A}$$

According to the superposition theorem, the current flowing through the 160 Ω resistor

$$i = i_1 + i_2 = 0.294 + 0.206 = 0.5 \text{ A}$$

Problem 7.2 Determine the voltage across the terminals AB in the circuit using the superposition theorem.

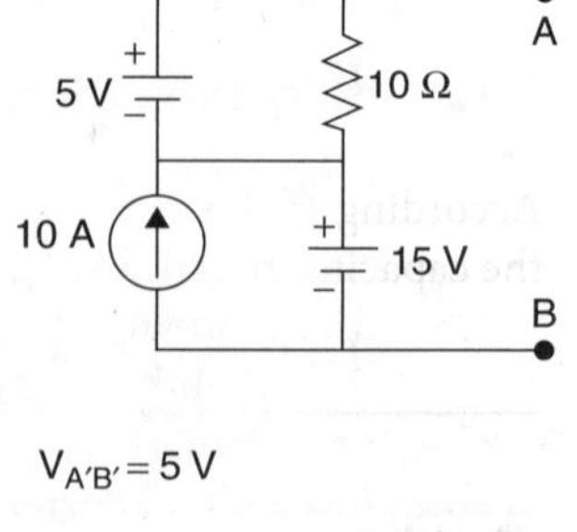

Solution:

When a voltage source of 5 V is acting alone:

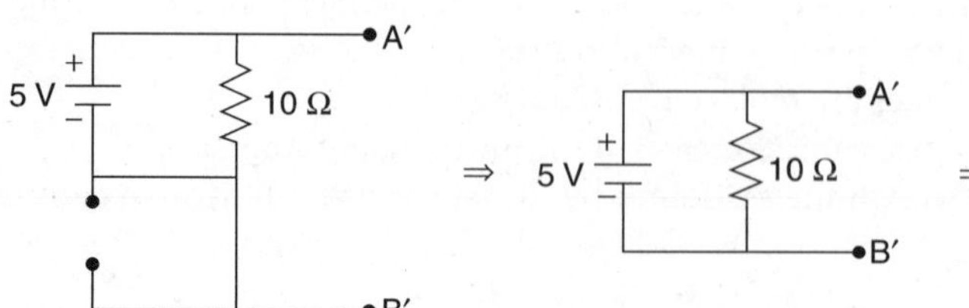

When a voltage source of 15 V is acting alone:

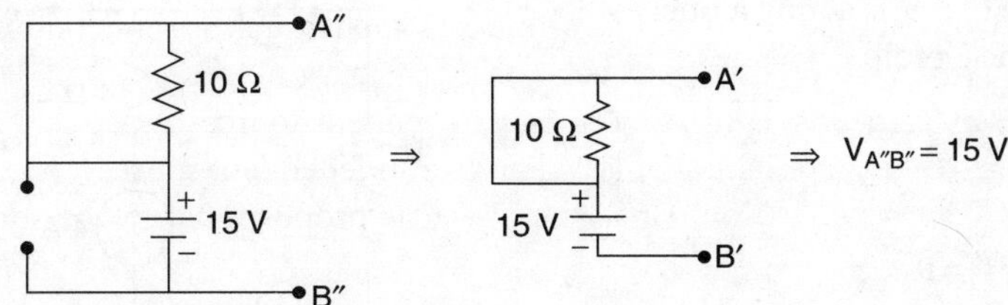

When a current source of 10 A is acting alone:

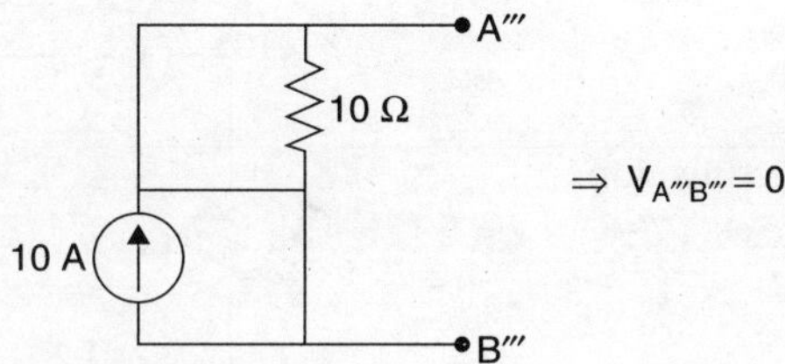

Hence according to the superposition theorem

$$V_{AB} = V_{A'B'} + V_{A''B''} + V_{A'''B'''} = 5 + 15 + 0 = 20 \text{ V}$$

Problem 7.3 Determine the current in the capacitor branch for the circuit using the superposition theorem.

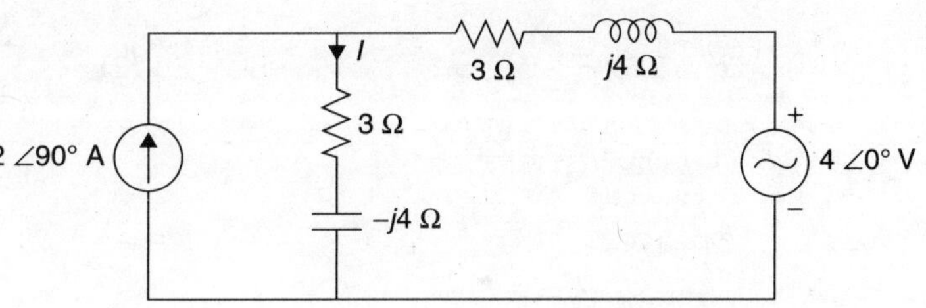

Solution:

When a current source of $2\angle 90°$ A is acting alone:

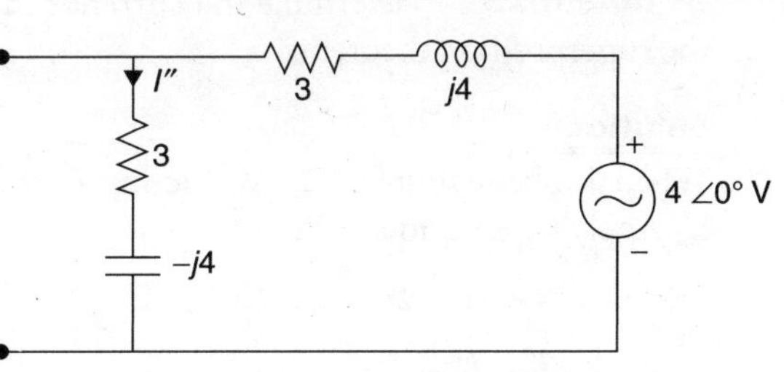

$$I' = 2\angle 90° \times \frac{(3+j4)}{(3+j4)+(3-j4)}$$

$$= 2\angle 90° \times \frac{(3+j4)}{6} = \frac{2\angle 90° \times 5\angle 53.13°}{6}$$

$$= 1.667\angle 143.13° = (-1.333 + j1) \text{ A}$$

When a voltage source of $4\angle 0°$ V acting alone:

$$I'' = \frac{4\angle 0°}{(3+j4)+(3-j4)} = \frac{4}{6} = 0.667 \text{ A}$$

According to the superposition theorem, the current in the capacitor branch,

$$I = I' + I'' = -1.333 + j1 + 0.667 = (-0.664 + j1) \text{ A}$$

Problem 7.4 Determine the current through the 2 Ω resistor for the circuit using the superposition theorem.

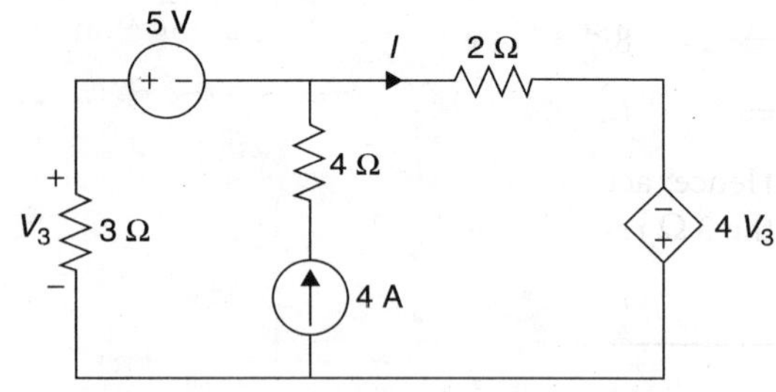

Solution:

When a voltage source of 5 V is acting alone:

Applying KVL to the circuit

$$3I' + 5 + 2I' - 4V_3' = 0$$

Also $\quad V_3' = -3I'$

$\therefore \quad 5I' + 5 + 4 \times 3I' = 0$

$$5 + 7I' = 0$$

$\Rightarrow \quad I' = \dfrac{-5}{7} = -0.294 \text{ A}$

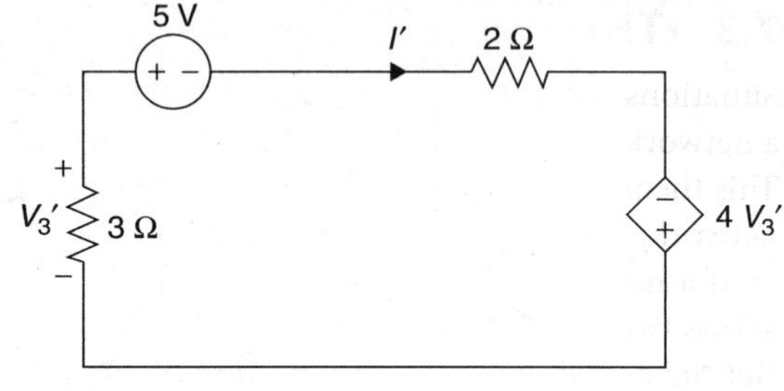

When a current source of 4 A is acting alone:

Let us assume the node voltage as V_3''

Applying KCL at the node,

$$4 = \frac{V_3''}{3} + \frac{V_3'' + 4V_3''}{2} \quad (1)$$

Also $\quad I'' = \dfrac{V_3'' + 4V_3''}{2} = \dfrac{5V_3''}{2}$

$\therefore \quad I'' = 2.5V_3'' \quad (2)$

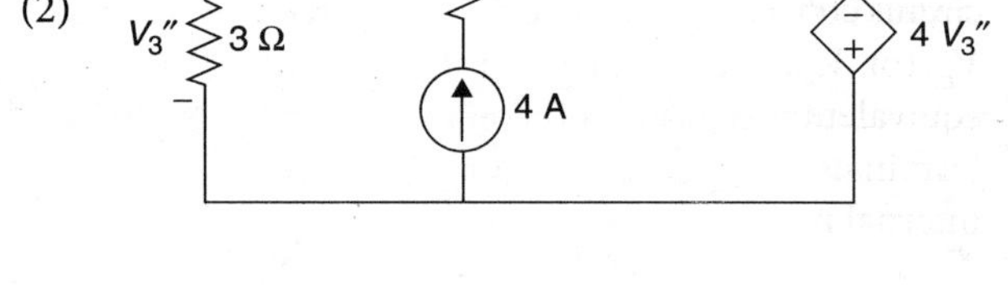

From Eq. (1) $\quad 4 = \dfrac{V_3''}{3} + \dfrac{5V_3''}{2}$

$\Rightarrow \quad 24 = 17V_3''$

$\Rightarrow \quad V_3'' = 1.41176 \text{ V} \quad (3)$

From Eqs (2) and (3), $I'' = 2.5 \times 1.41176 = 3.5294$ A

Hence, according to the superposition theorem, total current in 2 Ω resistor is

$$I = I' + I'' = -0.294 + 3.5394 = 3.235 \text{ A}$$

Problem 7.5 Determine the current i in the circuit using the superposition theorem.

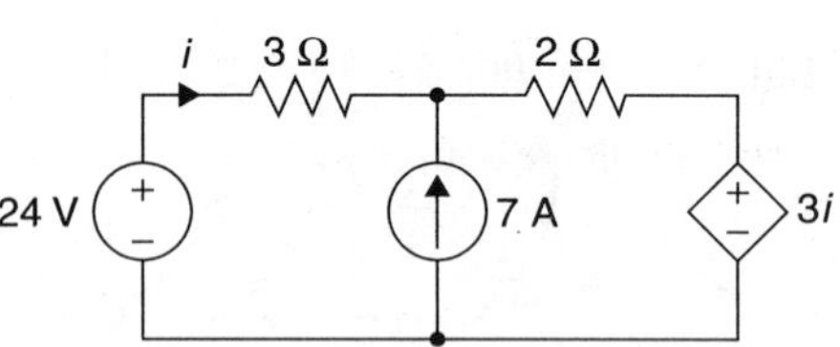

Solution:

When a voltage source of 24 V is acting alone:

Applying KVL to the circuit

$$24 - 3i_1 - 2i_1 - 3i_1 = 0$$

$\Rightarrow \quad 8i_1 = 24$

$\Rightarrow \quad i_1 = 3 \text{ A}$

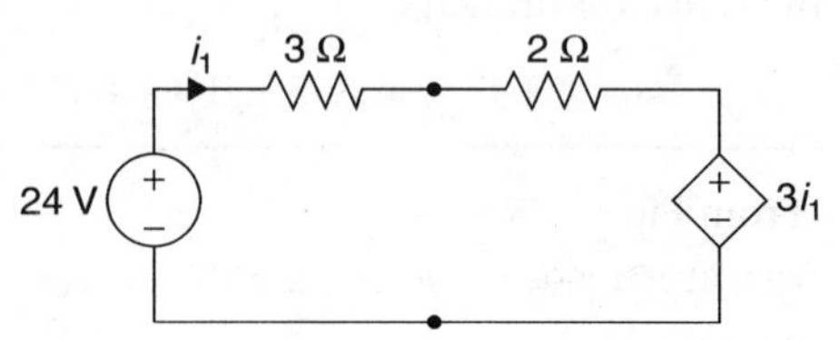

When a current source of 7 A is acting alone:

Applying KVL to the outer loop

$$3i_2 + 2\,(7 + i_2) + 3i_2 = 0$$

$$\Rightarrow \qquad 8i_2 = -14$$

$$\Rightarrow \qquad i_2 = -1.75 \text{ A}$$

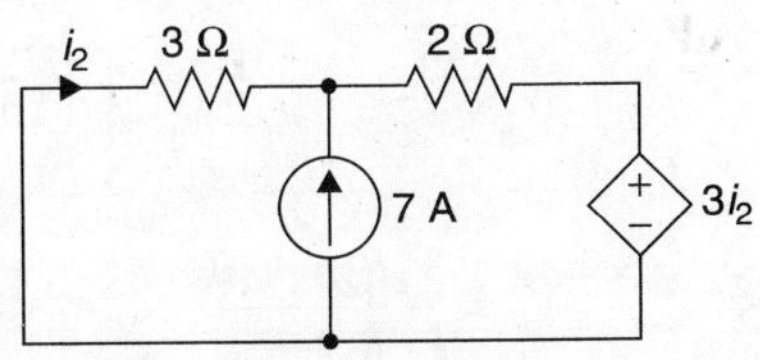

Hence, according to the superposition theorem, the total current in the 3 Ω resistor is

$$i = i_1 + i_2 = 3 - 1.75 = 1.25 \text{ A}$$

7.3 THEVENIN'S THEOREM

Situations sometimes occur in electrical engineering in which it is desirable to find a particular current in a network as the resistance of that branch is varied while all other resistances and sources remain constant. This theorem helps in reducing the given network into a simple equivalent network with respect to a given network.

If a network is to be solved for the current through different load impedances (resistances) connected across two specified points in the network, we can apply either the loop current or nodal voltage methods. But the network should be solved as many number of times as there are different load impedances. In such cases, it will be convenient to reduce the network to an equivalent network with respect to load terminals by applying Thevenin's theorem and calculate the current flowing through each load impedance.

Statement Any two terminal linear bilateral networks (AC or DC) can be replaced by an equivalent circuit consisting of an equivalent source, V_{th} (or V_{oc}) in series with a resistance R_{th} (impedance, Z_{th}). Here V_{th} (or V_{oc}) is the open circuited voltage measured between the load terminals and R_{th} is the Thevenin's equivalent resistance measured across the load terminals when all the sources are replaced by their internal resistances.

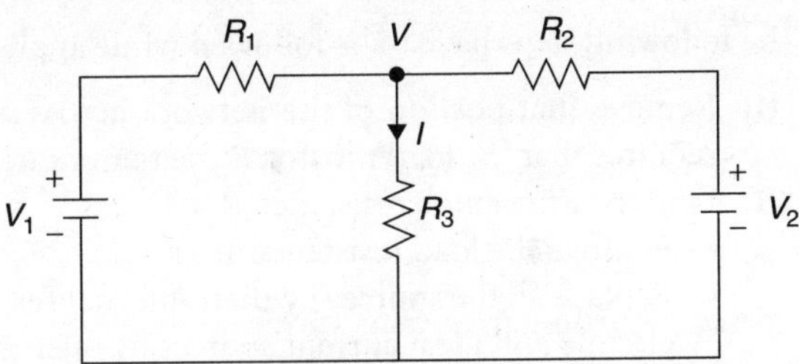

Fig. 7.4 *T*-network

Verification Consider the network (Fig. 7.4). Let us find the current flowing through resistance R_3. Let the node voltage be V.

By applying KCL to Fig. (7.4)

$$\frac{V - V_1}{R_1} + \frac{V}{R_3} + \frac{V - V_2}{R_2} = 0$$

But $\qquad V = IR_3$

$$\therefore \qquad \frac{IR_3 - V_1}{R_1} + I + \frac{IR_3 - V_2}{R_2} = 0$$

$$I\left(\frac{R_3}{R_1} + \frac{R_3}{R_2} + 1\right) = \frac{V_1}{R_1} + \frac{V_2}{R_2}$$

$$I = \frac{V_1 R_2 + V_2 R_1}{R_1 R_2 + R_2 R_3 + R_3 R_1} \qquad (7.7)$$

From Fig. 7.5(a)

$$I_1 = \frac{V_1 - V_2}{R_1 + R_2} \qquad (7.8)$$

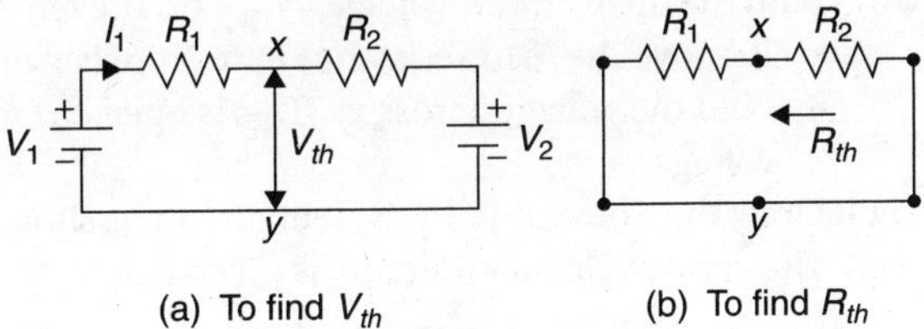

(a) To find V_{th} (b) To find R_{th}

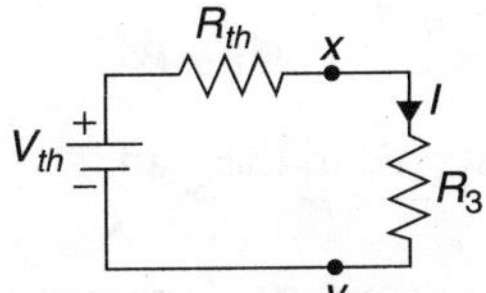

(c) Thevenin's equivalent circuit

Fig. 7.5 Illustration of Thevenin's theorem

$$V_{th} = V_1 - I_1R_1 = V_1 - \left(\frac{V_1 - V_2}{R_1 + R_2}\right)R_1$$

$$\therefore \quad V_{th} = \frac{V_1R_2 + V_2R_1}{R_1 + R_2} \tag{7.9}$$

From Fig. 7.5(b)

$$R_{th} = \frac{R_1R_2}{R_1 + R_2} \tag{7.10}$$

From Fig. 7.5(c)

$$I = \frac{V_{th}}{R_{th} + R_3} = \frac{\dfrac{V_1R_2 + V_2R_1}{R_1 + R_2}}{\dfrac{R_1R_2}{R_1 + R_2} + R_3} = \frac{V_1R_2 + V_2R_1}{R_1R_2 + R_2R_3 + R_3R_1}$$

$$\therefore \quad I = \frac{V_1R_2 + V_2R_1}{R_1R_2 + R_2R_3 + R_3R_1} \tag{7.11}$$

Equations 7.7 and 7.11 represent the same and hence Thevenin's theorem is verified.

7.3.1 Steps to be Followed in Thevenin's Theorem

The following steps have to be followed while applying Thevenin's theorem.

(i) Remove that portion of the network across which Thevenin's equivalent circuit is to be found. This requires that the load resistor R_L be temporarily removed from the network (Fig. 7.6).

(ii) Find the Thevenin's resistance R_{th}.
- Remove the load resistance at *xy*.
- Replace all the sources by their internal resistances (ideal voltage sources are to be replaced by short circuits and ideal current sources by open circuits).
- Find the equivalent resistance of the network between the terminals *x* and *y*. This is Thevenin's resistance, R_{th}.

(iii) Find the open circuit voltage (V_{OC}) or Thevenin's voltage (V_{th}).
- Remove the load resistance at terminals x and y.
- Find the voltage across *xy*. This is open circuit or Thevenin's voltage.

(iv) Draw the Thevenin's equivalent circuit as shown in Fig. 7.6.

(v) The various calculations are as given below:

Load current, $I_L = \dfrac{V_{th}}{R_{th} + R_L}$

Power delivered to the load, $P_L = I_L^2 R_L$

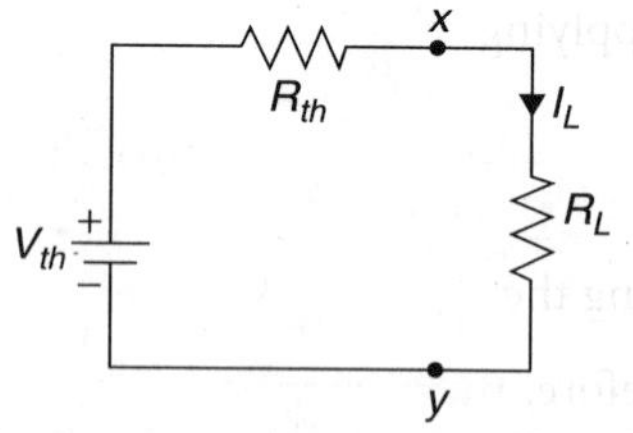

Fig. 7.6 Thevenin's equivalent circuit

7.3.2 Limitations of Thevenin's Theorem

(i) It is not applicable to circuits consisting of non-linear elements such as semiconductor devices, gas tubes and so on.

(ii) It is not applicable to the circuits consisting of magnetic coupling between the load and any other circuit element.

(iii) It is not applicable to the circuit consisting of load series or parallel with dependent sources.

Problem 7.6 Find the current flowing through a 160 Ω resistor for the circuit using Thevenin's theorem.

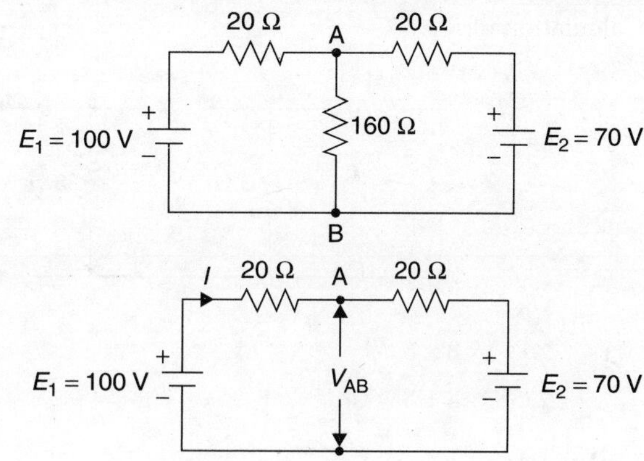

Solution:

Calculation of V_{th} or V_{AB}

Under open circuit conditions, current flowing is

$$I = \frac{100 - 70}{40} = 0.75 \text{ A}$$

$$V_{AB} = 100 - 0.75 \times 20 = 85 \text{ V}$$

$$\therefore \quad V_{th} = 85 \text{ V}$$

Calculation of R_{th}

$$R_{th} = \frac{20 \times 20}{20 + 20} = 10$$

Therefore the Thevenin's equivalent circuit may be drawn with branch AB reintroduced as shown on the right.

$$\text{Load current, } I_L = \frac{V_{th}}{R_{th} + R_L} = \frac{85}{10 + 160} = 0.5 \text{ A}$$

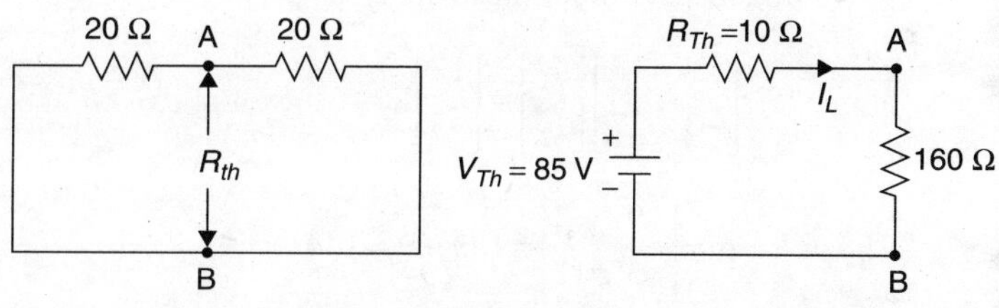

Problem 7.7 For the following circuit find the Thevenin equivalent circuit.

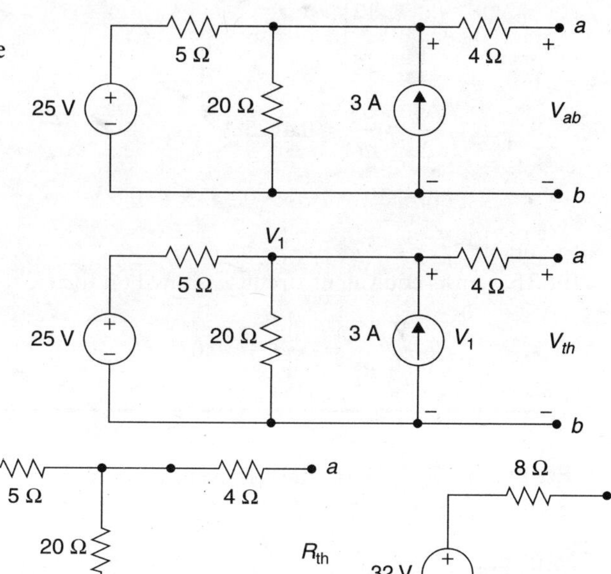

Solution:

Calculation of V_{th}

Let us assume the node voltage as V_1

Applying KCL to the circuit on the right,

$$\frac{V_1 - 25}{5} + \frac{V_1}{20} - 3 = 0$$

Solving the above equation, we have $V_1 = 32$ V.

Therefore, the Thevenin voltage V_{th} for the circuit is $V_{th} = 32$ V

Calculation of R_{th}

$$R_{th} = 4 + \frac{5 \times 20}{5 + 20} = 4 + 4 = 8 \ \Omega$$

Therefore the Thevenin equivalent circuit is shown on the right.

Problem 7.8 Draw the Thevenin's equivalent of the circuit and hence find the load current.

Solution:

Calculation of R_{th}

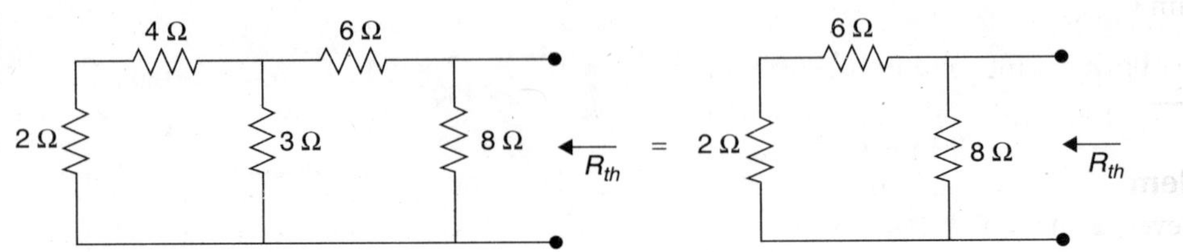

$$R_{th} = \frac{8 \times 8}{8+8} = 4\ \Omega$$

Calculation of V_{th}

Using inspection of mesh analysis

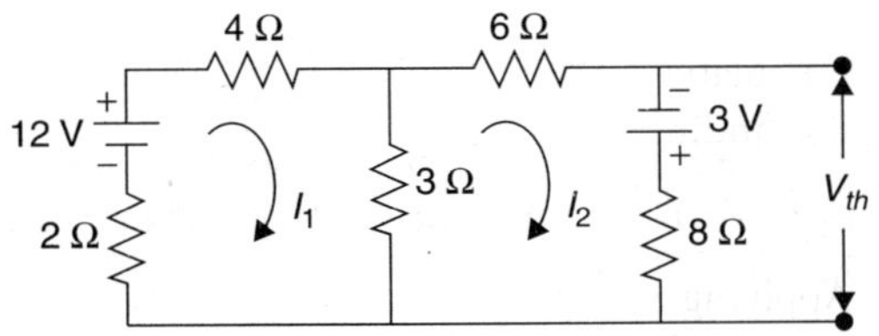

$$\begin{bmatrix} 9 & -3 \\ -3 & 17 \end{bmatrix} \begin{bmatrix} I_1 \\ I_2 \end{bmatrix} = \begin{bmatrix} 12 \\ 3 \end{bmatrix}$$

$$\Delta = \begin{vmatrix} 9 & -3 \\ -3 & 17 \end{vmatrix} = 153 - 9 = 144$$

$$\Delta_2 = \begin{vmatrix} 9 & 12 \\ -3 & 3 \end{vmatrix} = 27 + 36 = 63$$

$$I_2 = \frac{\Delta_2}{\Delta} = \frac{63}{144} = 0.4375\ \text{A}$$

$$V_{th} = 3 - 8I_2 = 3 - 8 \times 0.4375 = -0.5\ \text{V}$$

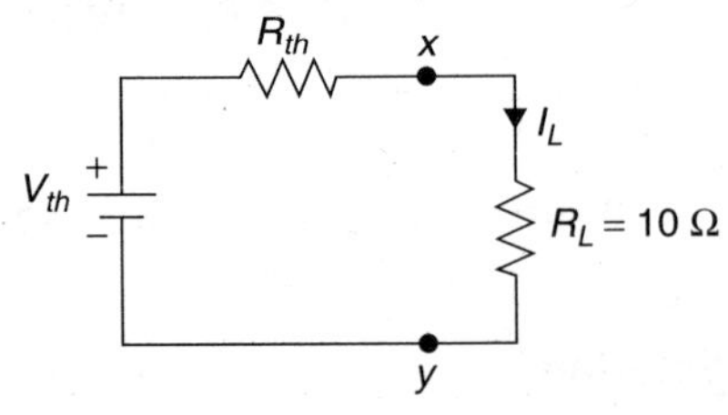

To find out I_L

The Thevenin's equivalent circuit is shown on the right.

$$I_L = \frac{V_{th}}{R_{th} + R_L} = \frac{0.5}{4+10} = 0.0357\ \text{A}$$

Problem 7.9 Find the Thevenin voltage between the terminals a–b.

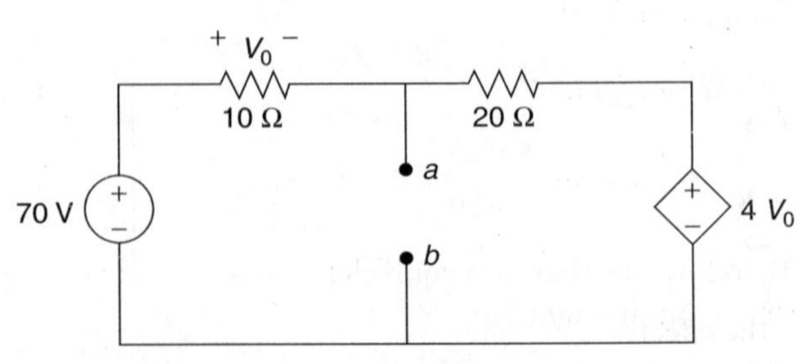

Solution:

Let us assume that the current flowing through the circuit is i.

Applying KVL to the circuit

$$70 - 10i - 20i - 4V_0 = 0$$

$$70 - 30i - 4V_0 = 0$$

But $\quad V_0 = 10i$

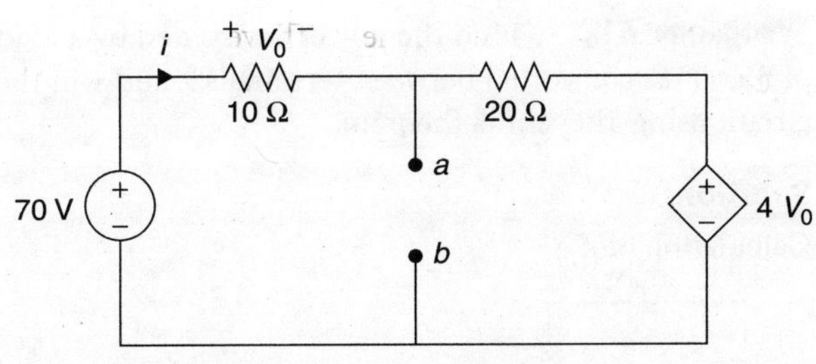

$\therefore \quad 70 - 30i - 40i = 0$

$\Rightarrow \quad i = 1\text{ A}$

Thevenin voltage across the terminals a–b is

$$V_{th} = 70 - 10i = 70 - 10 = 60\text{ V}$$

Problem 7.10 For the circuit find the value of Thevenin voltage and Thevenin resistance.

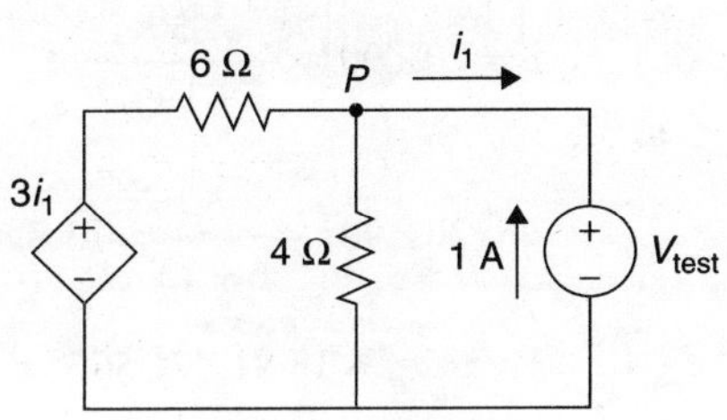

Solution:

Calculation of V_{th}

Circuit does not have any independent source, So, $V_{th} = 0\text{ V}$

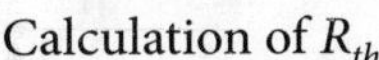
Calculation of R_{th}

For finding R_{th} connect a test voltage source V_{test} at terminals XY supplying 1 A.

$\therefore \quad i_1 = -1\text{ A}$

Applying KCL at node P, we have

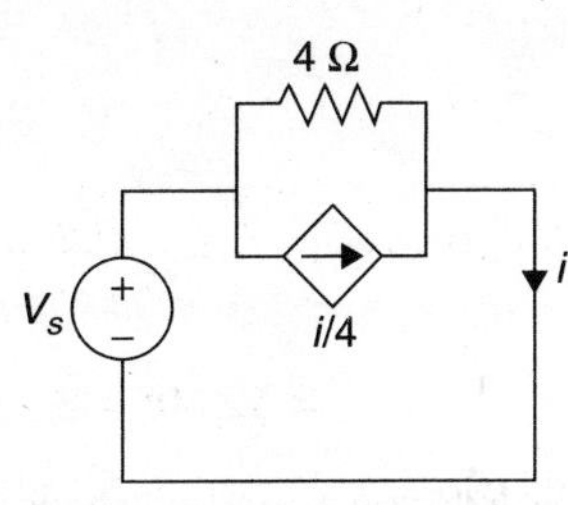

$$\frac{V_{test}}{4} + \frac{V_{test} - 3i_1}{6} + i_1 = 0$$

$$6V_{test} + 4V_{test} - 12i_1 + 24i_1 = 0$$

$$10V_{test} = -12i_1 = 12$$

$$V_{test} = 1.2\text{ V}$$

$$\therefore \quad R_{th} = \frac{V_{test}}{1} = \frac{1.2}{1} = 1.2\,\Omega$$

Problem 7.11 In the circuit, find the effective resistance faced by the voltage source.

4 Ω

V_s $i/4$ i

Solution:

From the given circuit

$$i = \frac{V_s}{4} + \frac{i}{4}$$

$$\Rightarrow \quad \frac{3i}{4} = \frac{V_s}{4}$$

$$\Rightarrow \quad i = \frac{V_s}{3}$$

The effective resistance faced by the voltage source is 3 Ω.

Problem 7.12 Find the power consumed by a load of $5\angle 60°\ \Omega$ connected between terminals x and y in the circuit using Thevenin's theorem.

Solution:

Calculation of Z_{th}

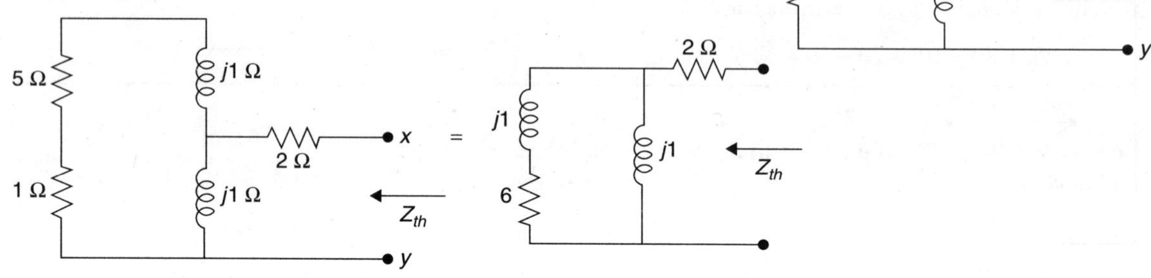

$$Z_{th} = \frac{(6+j1)\times j1}{6+j1+j1} + 2 = 2.15 + j0.95 = 2.35\angle 23.86°\ \Omega$$

Calculation of V_{th}

$$I_1 = 20\angle 90° \times \frac{5}{5+1+j2}$$

$$= 20\angle 90° \times \frac{5}{6+j2} = 15.8\angle 71.565°$$

$$V_{xy} = V_{th} = 15.81\angle 71.565° \times j1 = 15.81\angle 161.6°\ \text{V}$$

Thevenin's equivalent circuit is

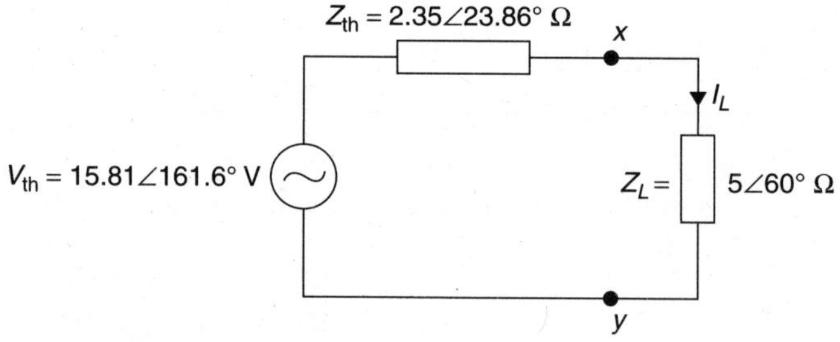

$$\text{Load current, } I_L = \frac{V_{th}}{Z_{th}+Z_L} = \frac{15.81\angle 161.6°}{2.35\angle 23.86° + 5\angle 60°} = 2.247\angle 112.97°\ \text{A}$$

$$Z_L = 5\angle 60° = 2.5 + j4.33$$

Power consumed by the load,

$$P_L = I_L^2 R_L = 2.247^2 \times 2.5 = 12.62\ \text{W}$$

Problem 7.13 Find the Thevenin's equivalent circuit at the terminals x and y of the given network.

Solution:

To find out R_{th}

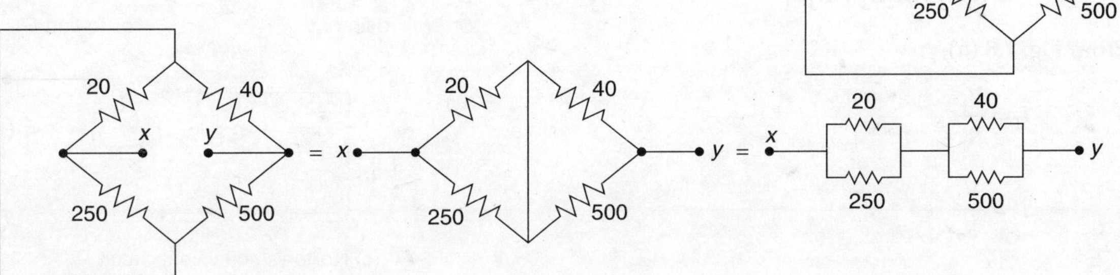

$$R_{xy} = R_{th} = \frac{20 \times 250}{20 + 250} + \frac{40 \times 500}{40 + 500} = \frac{500}{27} + \frac{1000}{27} = 55.55\ \Omega$$

To find out V_{th}

It is a Wheatstone bridge network, in which the product of the resistances in opposite arms are equal. Hence the bridge is balanced.

$$\therefore \quad V_{th} = V_{xy} = 0$$

The Thevenin's equivalent circuit is shown on the right.

7.4 NORTON'S THEOREM

It is the dual of the Thevenin's theorem.

Statement Any two terminal linear bilateral networks (AC or DC) can be replaced by an equivalent circuit consisting of an equivalent source I_{sc}, in parallel with a resistance R_N (impedance, Z_N), where I_{sc} is the short circuited current measured through the load terminals and R_N is the Norton's equivalent resistance measured across the load terminals when all the sources are replaced by their internal resistances.

The Norton equivalent circuit contains an independent current source which is parallel to the Norton equivalent resistance. It can be derived from the Thevenin equivalent circuit by using source transformation. Therefore, the Norton current is equivalent to the short circuit current at the terminal being studied, and Norton resistance is equivalent to Thevenin resistance.

Verification Let us find the current flowing through resistance R_3 in the network (Fig. 7.7). Let the node voltage be V.

Applying KCL to Fig. 7.7,

$$\frac{V - V_1}{R_1} + \frac{V}{R_3} + \frac{V - V_2}{R_2} = 0$$

But $\quad V = IR_3$

$$\therefore \quad \frac{IR_3 - V_1}{R_1} + I + \frac{IR_3 - V_2}{R_2} = 0$$

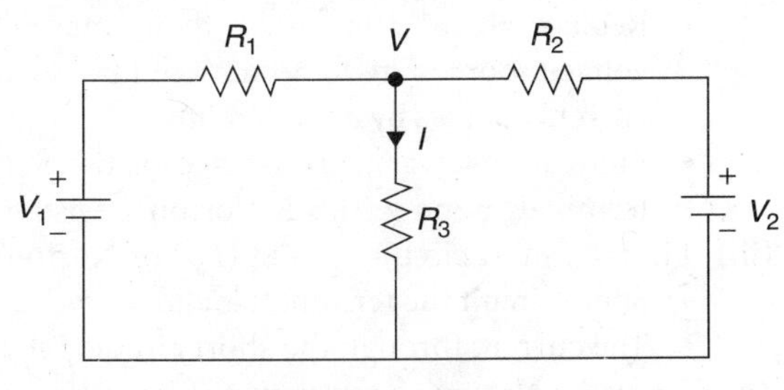

Fig. 7.7 T-network

$$I\left(\frac{R_3}{R_1}+\frac{R_3}{R_2}+1\right)=\frac{V_1}{R_1}+\frac{V_2}{R_2}$$

$$I=\frac{V_1R_2+V_2R_1}{R_1R_2+R_2R_3+R_3R_1} \tag{7.12}$$

(a) To find I_{sc}

(b) To find R_N

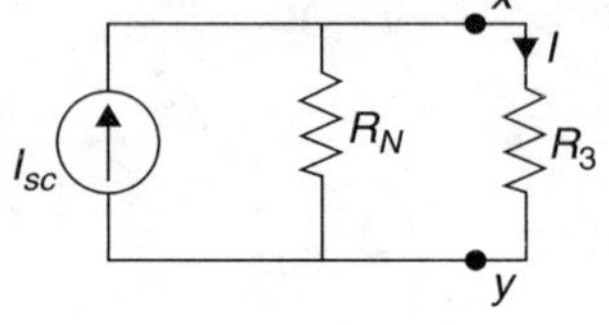

(c) Norton's equivalent circuit

Fig. 7.8 Illustration of Norton's theorem

From Fig. 7.8 (a),

$$I_1=\frac{V_1}{R_1}$$

$$I_2=\frac{V_2}{R_2}$$

$$I_{sc}=I_N=I_1+I_2=\frac{V_1}{R_1}+\frac{V_2}{R_2} \tag{7.13}$$

From Fig. 7.8 (b),

$$R_N=\frac{R_1R_2}{R_1+R_2} \tag{7.14}$$

From Fig. 7.8 (c),

$$I=I_{sc}\times\frac{R_N}{R_N+R_3}=\left[\frac{V_1}{R_1}+\frac{V_2}{R_2}\right]\times\frac{\dfrac{R_1R_2}{R_1+R_2}}{\dfrac{R_1R_2}{R_1+R_2}+R_3}=\frac{V_1R_2+V_2R_1}{R_1R_2+R_2R_3+R_3R_1}$$

$$\therefore \quad I=\frac{V_1R_2+V_2R_1}{R_1R_2+R_2R_3+R_3R_1} \tag{7.15}$$

Equations 7.12 and 7.15 represent the same and hence the Thevenin's theorem is verified.

7.4.1 Steps to be Followed in Norton's Theorem

The following steps have to be followed while applying Norton's theorem.

(i) Remove that portion of the network across which the Norton's equivalent circuit is to be found. In Fig. 7.9, this requires that the load resistor R_L be temporarily removed from the network.

(ii) Find the Norton's resistance R_N.
- Remove the load resistance at *xy*.
- Replace all the sources by their internal resistances (ideal voltage sources are to be replaced by short circuits and ideal current sources by open circuits).
- Find the equivalent resistance of the network between the terminals *x* and *y*. This is Norton's resistance R_N.

(iii) Find the short circuit current (I_{SC}) or Norton's current (I_N).
- Short circuit the terminals *x* and *y*.
- The current through the short circuit path is known as I_{SC} or I_N.

Fig. 7.9 Norton's equivalent circuit

(iv) Draw the Norton's equivalent circuit as shown in Fig. 7.9.

(v) The various calculations are as given below:

$$\text{Load current, } I_L = I_N \frac{R_N}{R_N + R_L}$$

$$\text{Power delivered to the load, } P_L = I_L^2 R_L$$

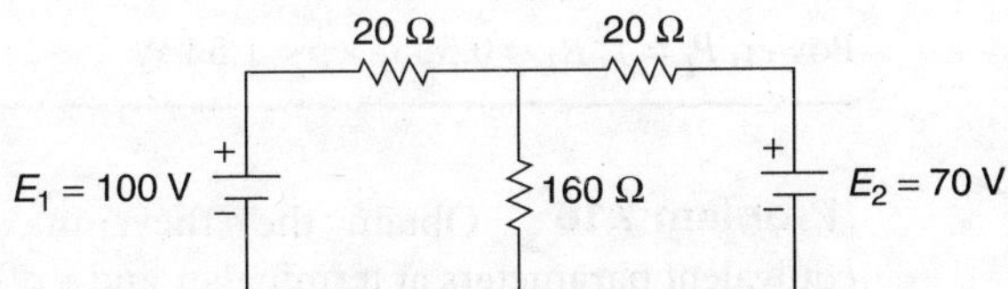

Problem 7.14 Find the current flowing through the 160 Ω resistor for the circuit using Norton's theorem.

Solution

Calculation of I_{SC} or I_{AB}

Since we wish to calculate the current in the 160 Ω resistor, let us find the Norton's equivalent circuit across the terminals after short-circuiting the 160 Ω resistor.

The short circuit current I_{sc} is given by

$$I_{sc} = \frac{100}{20} + \frac{70}{20} = 8.5 \text{ A}$$

$$\therefore \quad I_N = 8.5 \text{ A}$$

Calculation of R_N

$$R_N = \frac{20 \times 20}{20 + 20} = 10\,\Omega$$

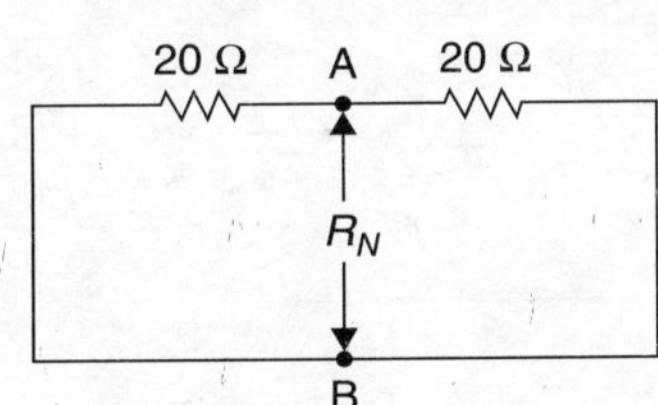

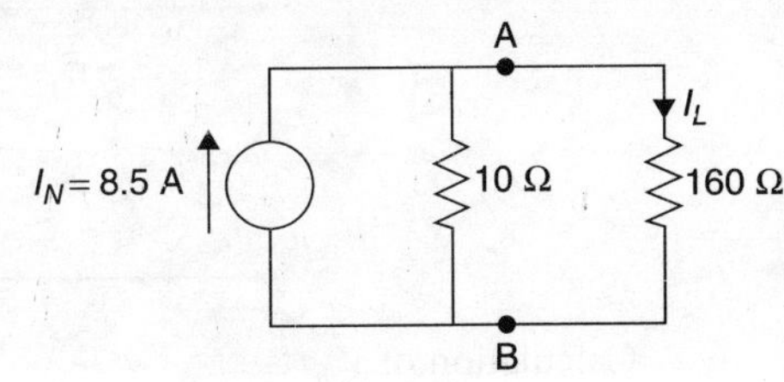

Therefore the Norton's equivalent circuit may be drawn with branch AB reintroduced as shown above.

$$\text{Load current, } I_L = I_N \frac{R_N}{R_N + R_L} = 8.5 \times \frac{10}{10 + 160} = 0.5 \text{ A}$$

Problem 7.15 Find the current and power through the load in the circuit using Norton's theorem.

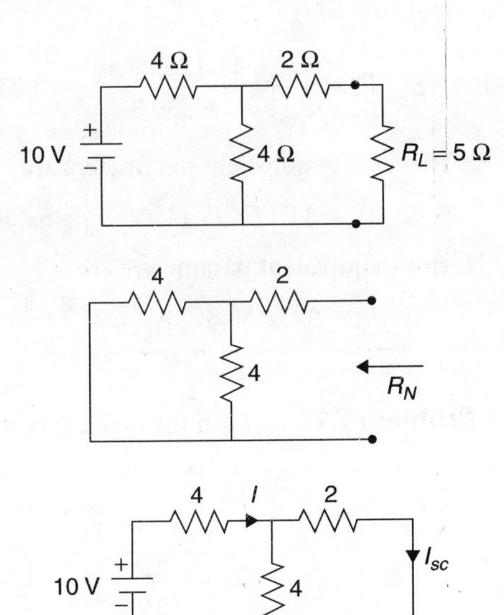

Solution:

Calculation of R_N

$$R_N = 2 + \frac{4 \times 4}{4 + 4} = 4\,\Omega$$

Calculation of I_{sc}

$$R_{eq} = 4 + \frac{2 \times 4}{2 + 4} = 5.333\,\Omega$$

$$I = \frac{10}{R_{eq}} = \frac{10}{5.333} = 1.875 \text{ A}$$

$$I_{sc} = I \times \frac{4}{2 + 4} = 1.25 \text{ A}$$

Norton's equivalent circuit is shown below.

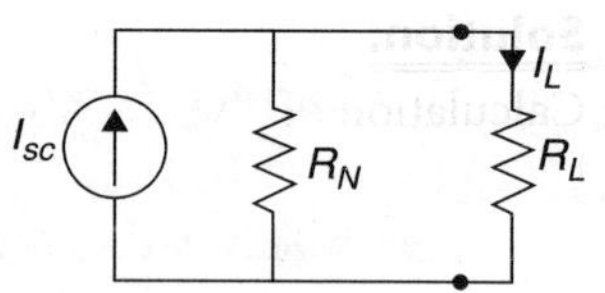

Load current, $I_L = I_{sc}\dfrac{R_N}{R_N + R_L} = 1.25 \times \dfrac{4}{4+5} = 0.555$ A

Power, $P_L = I_L^2 R_L = 0.555^2 \times 5 = 1.53$ W

Problem 7.16 Obtain the Thevenin's and Norton's equivalent parameters at terminals *x* and *y* of the circuit.

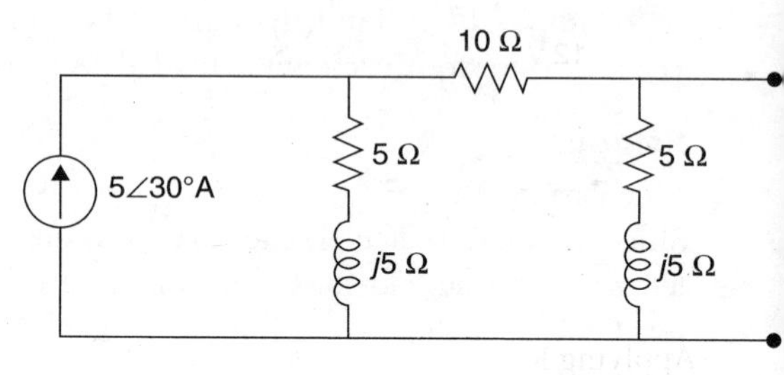

Solution:

Calculation of Z_{th}

$$Z_{th} = \frac{(15 + j5)(5 + j5)}{15 + j5 + 5 + j5} = 5\angle 36.87^\circ\ \Omega$$

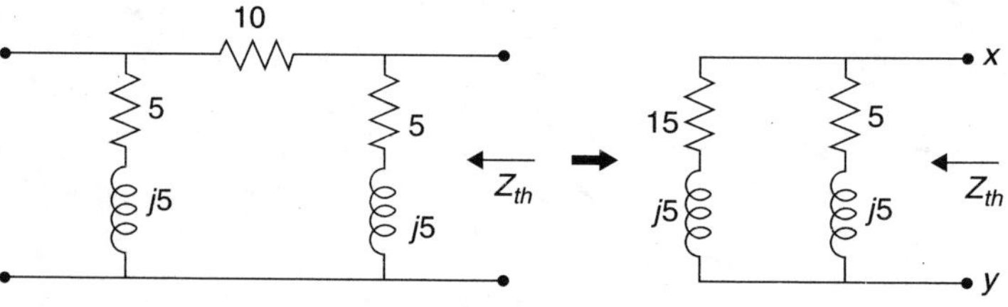

Calculation of V_{th}

$$I = 5\angle 30^\circ \times \frac{5 + j5}{(5 + j5) + (15 + j5)} = 1.58\angle 48.44^\circ \text{ A}$$

$$V_{th} = (5 + j5)\,I = 7.07\angle 45^\circ \times 1.58\angle 48.44^\circ = 11.17\angle 93.44^\circ \text{ V}$$

Calculation of I_{sc}

$$I_{sc} = \frac{V_{th}}{Z_{th}} = \frac{11.17\angle 93.44^\circ}{5\angle 36.87^\circ} = 2.23\angle 56.57^\circ \text{ A}$$

∴ Thevenin's equivalent parameters are

$$V_{th} = 11.17\angle 93.44^\circ \text{ V},\ Z_{th} = 5\angle 36.87^\circ\ \Omega$$

Norton's equivalent parameters are

$$I_{sc} = 2.23\angle 56.57^\circ \text{ A},\ Z_{th} = 5\angle 36.87^\circ\ \Omega$$

Problem 7.17 Find the load current for the circuit using Norton's theorem.

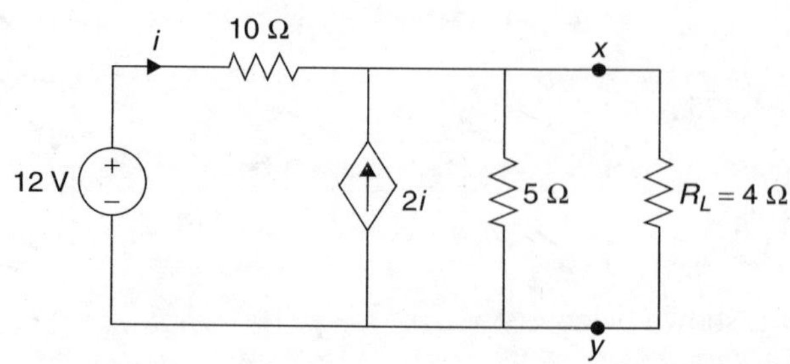

Solution:

Calculation of I_{sc}

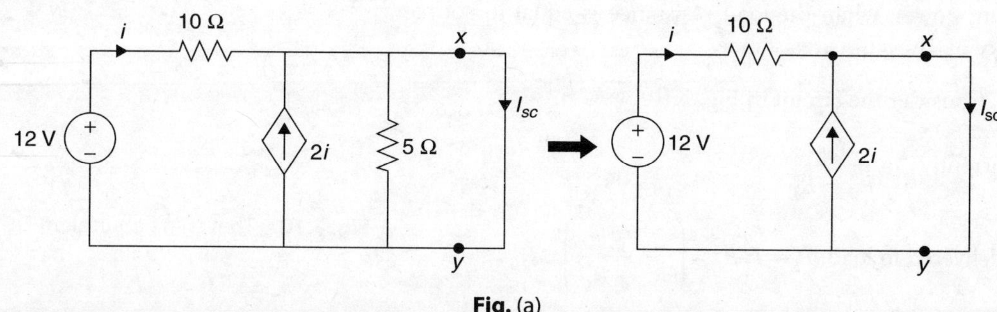

Fig. (a)

Applying KVL to the circuit as shown in Fig. (a).

$$12 = 10i$$

$$\Rightarrow \quad i = 1.2 \text{ A}$$

Applying KCL at node x

$$i + 2i = I_{sc}$$

$$\Rightarrow \quad I_{sc} = 3i = 3 \times 1.2 = 3.6 \text{ A}$$

Calculation of V_{th}

$$V_{th} = 5 \times I_1 = 5 \times 3i = 15i$$

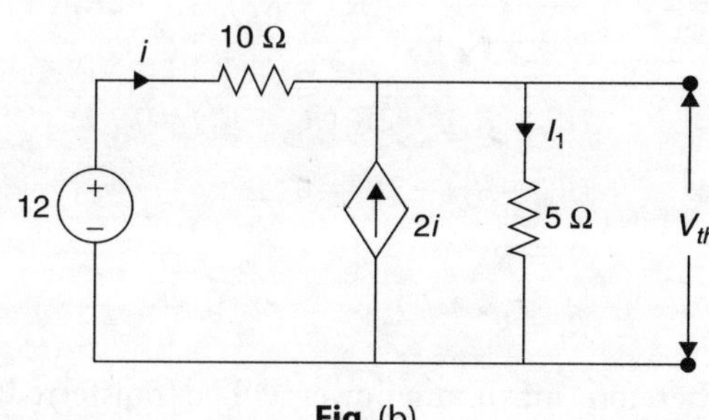

Fig. (b)

Applying KVL to the circuit as shown in Fig. (b).

$$12 = 10i + 5\,(i + 2i)$$

$$\Rightarrow \quad 12 = 25i$$

$$\Rightarrow \quad i = \frac{12}{25}$$

$$\therefore \quad V_{th} = 15i = 15 \times \frac{12}{25} = 7.2 \text{ V}$$

Therefore, $R_{th} = \dfrac{V_{th}}{I_{sc}} = \dfrac{7.2}{3.6} = 2\,\Omega$

Norton's equivalent circuit is as shown on the right.

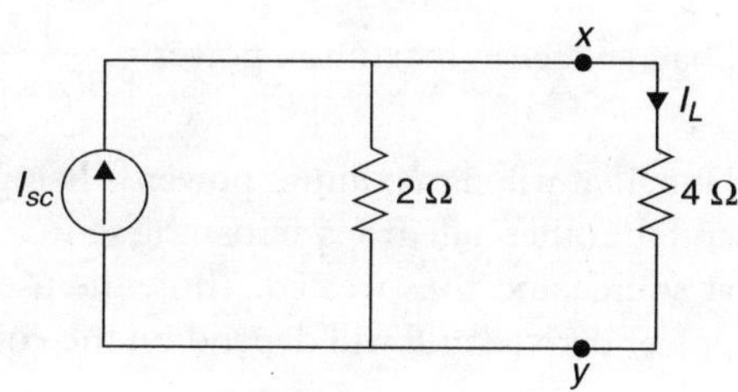

$$\therefore \quad \text{Load current, } I_L = I_{sc} \times \frac{R_{th}}{R_{th} + R_L} = 3.6 \times \frac{2}{4+2} = 3.6 \times \frac{2}{6} = 1.2 \text{ A}$$

7.5 MAXIMUM POWER TRANSFER THEOREM

For many engineering applications, an important consideration is to determine the load impedance which will allow the maximum power to be transferred to the load from some generating source; for example, maximum power transfer is desirable from the output amplifier to the speaker of an audio system. In such cases the maximum power transfer theorem is very useful.

Case (i) Statement for DC network

In any linear bilateral DC network, the load will receive maximum power, when the load resistance is equal to source resistance or Thevenin's resistance.

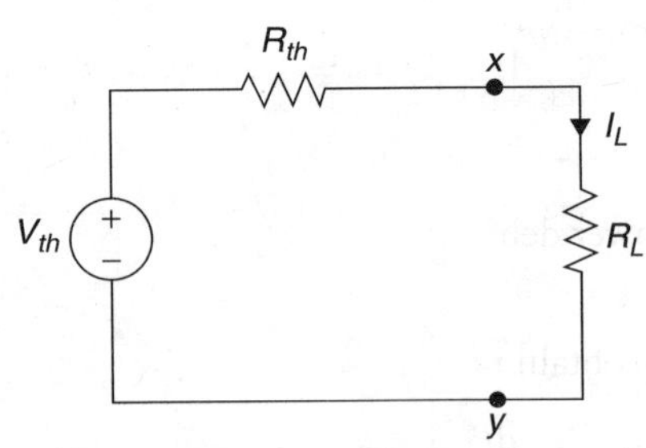

Fig. 7.10 Thevenin's equivalent DC circuit

Proof Consider the circuit in Fig. 7.10.

Load current, $I_L = \dfrac{V_{th}}{R_{th} + R_L}$

Power delivered to load, $P_L = I_L^2 R_L = \left(\dfrac{V_{th}}{R_{th} + R_L}\right)^2 \cdot R_L$

To obtain maximum power transfer to the load, let us differentiate P_L with respect to R_L and equate it to zero.

That is, $\dfrac{dP_L}{dR_L} = 0$

$$\Rightarrow \quad \frac{V_{th}^2}{(R_{th} + R_L)^4} \cdot [(R_{th} + R_L)^2 \times 1 - 2R_L\,(R_{th} + R_L)] = 0$$

$$\Rightarrow \quad (R_{th} + R_L)^2 - 2R_L(R_{th} + R_L) = 0$$

$$\Rightarrow \quad (R_{th} + R_L) - 2R_L = 0$$

$$\Rightarrow \quad R_L = R_{th}$$

$$\therefore \quad R_L = R_{th} \tag{7.16}$$

Therefore, maximum power will be transferred from source to load, if $R_L = R_{th}$.

$$\text{Value of maximum power, } P_{\max} = \left(\frac{V_{th}}{R_L + R_L}\right)^2 \times R_L = \frac{V_{th}^2}{4R_L} \tag{7.17}$$

$$\text{Load voltage at maximum power} = \frac{V_{th}}{R_L + R_{th}} \cdot R_L = \frac{V_{th}}{R_L + R_L} R_L = \frac{V_{th}}{2} \tag{7.18}$$

Note that when maximum power is being transferred, only half the applied voltage is available to the load, and the other half drops across the source. Also, under these conditions, half the power supplied is dissipated at source and thus wasted. Thus, the useful maximum power will be less than the theoretical maximum power derived and will depend on the voltage required to be maintained at the load.

Case (ii) Statement for AC network

In any linear bilateral AC network, the load will receive maximum power, when the load impedance is equal to the complex conjugate of source impedance or Thevenin's impedance.

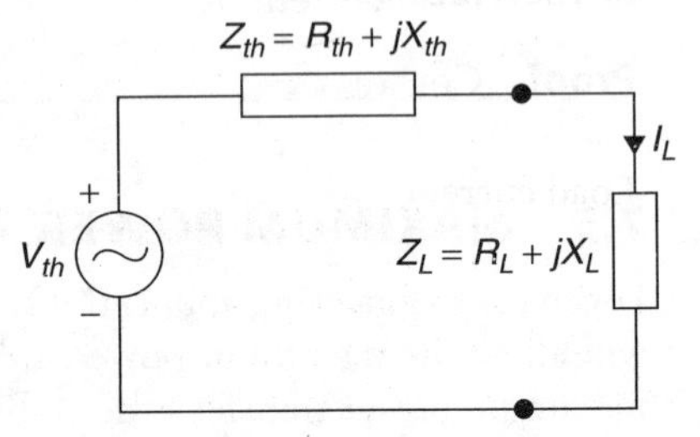

Fig. 7.11 Thevenin's equivalent AC circuit

Proof Consider the circuit in Fig. 7.11.

Load current, $I_L = \dfrac{V_{th}}{Z_{th} + Z_L}$

$$= \frac{V_{th}}{R_{th} + jX_{th} + R_L + jX_L} = \frac{V_{th}}{R_{th} + R_L + j\,(X_{th} + X_L)}$$

$$|I_L| = \frac{V_{th}}{\sqrt{(R_{th}+R_L)^2+(X_{th}+X_L)^2}}$$

Power delivered to load, $P_L = I_L^2 R_L = \dfrac{V_{th}^2}{(R_{th}+R_L)^2+(X_{th}+X_L)^2} \cdot R_L$

To obtain maximum power

$$\frac{\partial P_L}{\partial X_L} = 0$$

$$\Rightarrow \quad V_{th}^2 R_L \times \frac{-1}{[(R_{th}+R_L)^2+(X_{th}+X_L)^2]^2} \times 2\,(X_{th}+X_L) = 0$$

$$\Rightarrow \quad (X_{th}+X_L) = 0$$

$$\Rightarrow \quad X_{th} = -X_L \tag{7.19}$$

Putting $X_{th} = -X_L$

$$P_L = I_L^2 R_L = \left(\frac{V_{th}}{R_{th}+R_L}\right)^2 \cdot R_L$$

Again for maximum power, $\dfrac{dP_L}{dR_L} = 0$

$$\Rightarrow \quad \frac{V_{th}^2}{(R_{th}+R_L)^4} \times [(R_{th}+R_L)^2 \times 1 - 2R_L\,(R_{th}+R_L)] = 0$$

$$\Rightarrow \quad (R_{th}+R_L)^2 - 2R_L\,(R_{th}+R_L) = 0$$

$$\Rightarrow \quad (R_{th}+R_L) - 2R_L = 0$$

$$\Rightarrow \quad R_{th} = R_L$$

$$\therefore \quad R_{th} = R_L \tag{7.20}$$

$$Z_L = R_L + jX_L = R_{th} - jX_{th} = Z_{th}^* \tag{7.21}$$

Therefore maximum power will be transferred from source to load when the load impedance is equal to the complex conjugate of the source or Thevenin's impedance.

Case (iii) When the source has impedance and the load is purely resistive

The maximum power will be transferred from source to resistive load R_L, if the value of R_L is the magnitude of Thevenin's impedance.

Proof Consider the network shown in Fig. 7.12.

Load current, $I_L = \dfrac{V_{th}}{Z_{th}+R_L}$

$$= \frac{V_{th}}{R_{th}+jX_{th}+R_L} = \frac{V_{th}}{R_{th}+R_L+jX_{th}}$$

$$|I_L| = \frac{V_{th}}{\sqrt{(R_{th}+R_L)^2 + X_{th}^2}}$$

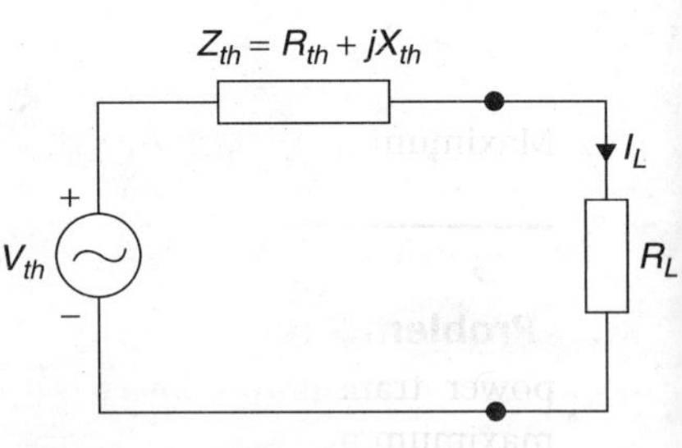

Fig. 7.12 Thevenin's equivalent circuit when the source has impedance and the load is purely resistive

Power delivered to load, $P_L = I_L^2 R_L = \dfrac{V_{th}^2}{(R_{th}+R_L)^2 + X_{th}^2} \times R_L$

To obtain maximum power, $\dfrac{dP_L}{dR_L} = 0$

$$\Rightarrow \quad \frac{V_{th}^2}{[(R_{th}+R_L)^2 + X_{th}^2]^2} \times [(R_{th}+R_L)^2 + X_{th}^2 - 2R_L(R_{th}+R_L)] = 0$$

$$\Rightarrow \quad (R_{th}+R_L)^2 + X_{th}^2 - 2R_L(R_{th}+R_L) = 0$$

$$\Rightarrow \quad R_{th}^2 + R_L^2 + 2R_{th}R_L + X_{th}^2 - 2R_{th}R_L - 2R_L^2 = 0$$

$$\Rightarrow \quad R_L^2 = R_{th}^2 + X_{th}^2$$

$$\Rightarrow \quad R_L = \sqrt{R_{th}^2 + X_{th}^2} = |Z_{th}| \tag{7.22}$$

Therefore maximum power will be transferred from source to load when the load resistance is equal to the magnitude of source or Thevenin's impedance.

7.5.1 Steps to be Followed in Maximum Power Transfer Theorem

The steps to be followed while applying maximum power transfer theorem are given below.

(i) Remove the variable load resistance/impedance, that is, R_L or Z_L.
(ii) Find the open circuit or Thevenin voltage across the removed load terminals, V_{oc} or V_{th}.
(iii) Find the equivalent resistance/impedance between the open circuited load terminals, R_{th} or Z_{th}.
(iv) Find the resistance/impedance (R_L or Z_L) for maximum power transfer, that is, $R_L = R_{th}$ or $Z_L = Z_{th}^*$.

Find the maximum power, $P_{max} = \dfrac{V_{th}^2}{4R_{th}}$.

Problem 7.18 Find the value of load resistance R_L to receive the maximum power and also find the value of maximum power.

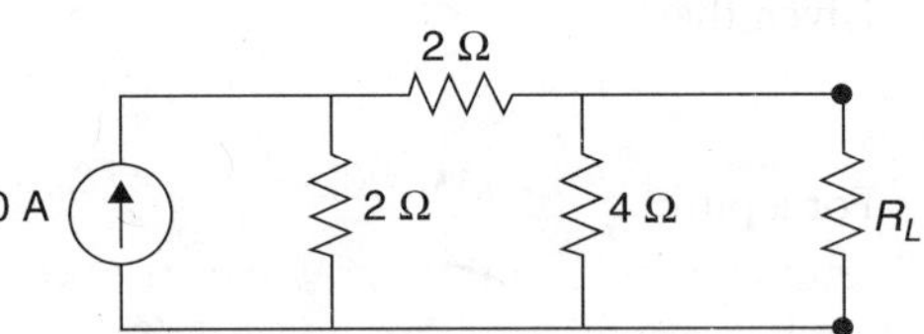

Solution:

Calculation of R_{th}

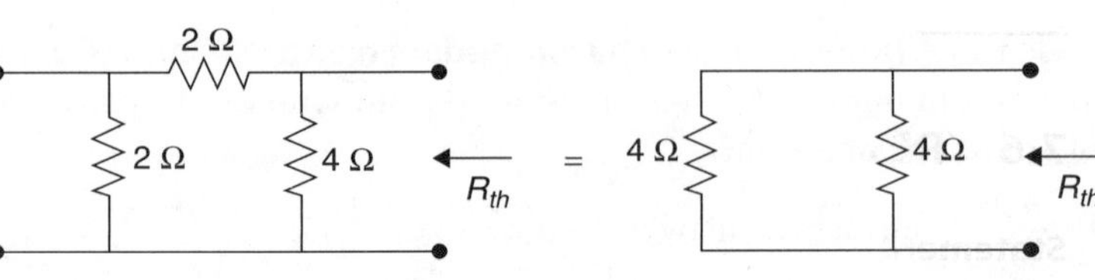

$$\therefore \quad R_{th} = \frac{4 \times 4}{4+4} = 2\ \Omega$$

When $R_L = R_{th} = 2\ \Omega$, the load will receive maximum power.

Calculation of V_{th}

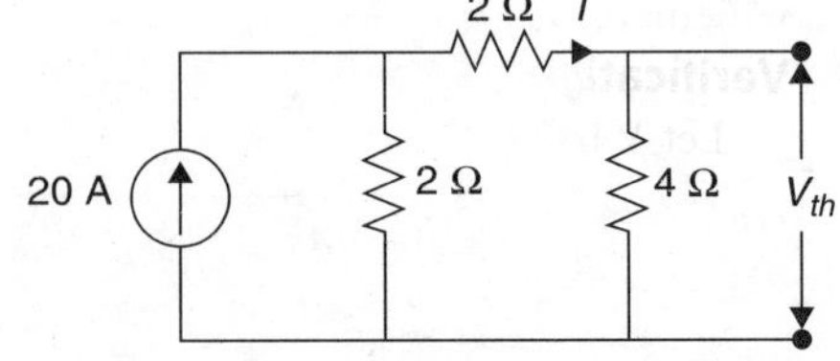

$$I = 20 \times \frac{2}{2+6} = 5\ \text{A}$$

$$V_{th} = 4I = 4 \times 5 = 20 \text{ V}$$

Maximum power received by the load, $P_{max} = \dfrac{V_{th}^2}{4R_{th}} = \dfrac{20^2}{4 \times 2} = 50 \text{ W}$

Problem 7.19 Find Z_L for maximum power transfer and find the corresponding maximum power.

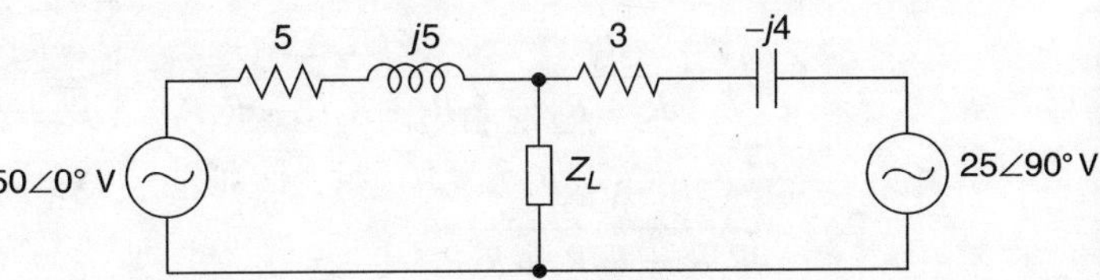

Solution:

Calculation of Z_{th}

$$Z_{th} = \frac{(5 + j5)(3 - j4)}{(5 + j5) + (3 - j4)} = 4.385\angle{-15.25°} = (4.23 - j1.154)$$

Calculation of V_{th}

$$I = \frac{50\angle 0° - 25\angle 90°}{8 + j1} = \frac{50 - j25}{8 + j1} = 6.934\angle{-33.69°}$$

$$V_{th} = 50 - 6.934\angle{-33.69°} \times (5 + j5) = 9.81\angle{-78.7°}$$

The load will receive maximum power when, $Z_L = Z_{th}^* = (4.23 + j1.154)\ \Omega$

Maximum power received by the load, $P_{max} = \dfrac{V_{th}^2}{4R_{th}} = \dfrac{9.81^2}{4 \times 4.23} = 5.69 \text{ W}$

Problem 7.20 A source $v_s(t) = V\cos 100\pi t$ has an internal impedance of $(4 + j3)\ \Omega$. If a purely resistive load connected to this source has to extract the maximum power out of the source, find its value.

Solution:

Given that $v_s(t) = V\cos 100\pi t$

$$Z_{th} = (4 + j3)\ \Omega$$

For a pure resistive load R_L, to extract the maximum power,

$$R_L = |Z_{th}| = \sqrt{R_{th}^2 + X_{th}^2} = \sqrt{4^2 + 3^2} = 5\ \Omega$$

7.6 RECIPROCITY THEOREM

Statement This theorem states that in a linear bilateral single source network, the ratio of excitation to response is constant when the position of excitation and response are interchanged.

Verification Consider the network shown in Fig. 7.13.

Let V be the applied voltage and I be the current response.

$$R_T = R_1 + \frac{R_2 R_3}{R_2 + R_3} = \frac{R_1 R_2 + R_2 R_3 + R_3 R_1}{R_2 + R_3}$$

$$I_T = \frac{V}{R_T} = \frac{V(R_2 + R_3)}{R_1R_2 + R_2R_3 + R_3R_1}$$

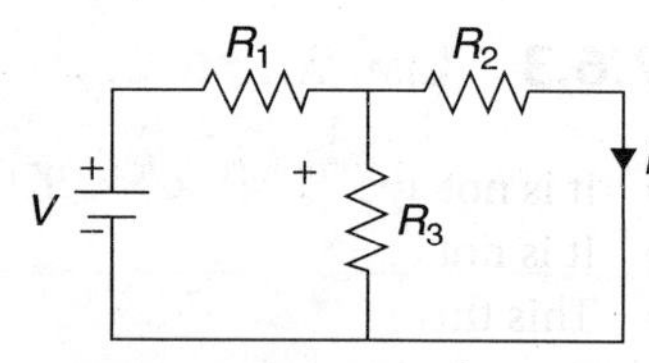

Fig. 7.13 Before V and I are interchanged

By applying current division rule

$$I = I_T \times \frac{R_3}{R_3 + R_2} = \frac{V(R_2 + R_3)}{R_1R_2 + R_2R_3 + R_3R_1} \times \left(\frac{R_3}{R_3 + R_2}\right)$$

$$I = \frac{VR_3}{R_1R_2 + R_2R_3 + R_3R_1}$$

$$\Rightarrow \quad \frac{V}{I} = \frac{R_1R_2 + R_2R_3 + R_3R_1}{R_3} \tag{7.23}$$

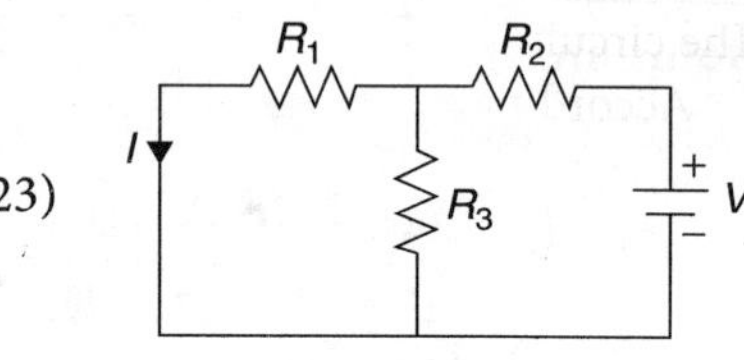

Fig. 7.14 After V and I are interchanged

When the positions of excitation and response are interchanged

$$R'_T = R_2 + \frac{R_1R_3}{R_1 + R_3} = \frac{R_1R_2 + R_2R_3 + R_3R_1}{R_1 + R_3}$$

$$I'_T = \frac{V}{R'_T} = \frac{V(R_1 + R_3)}{R_1R_2 + R_2R_3 + R_3R_1}$$

By applying current division rule

$$I = I'_T \times \frac{R_3}{R_3 + R_1} = \frac{V(R_1 + R_3)}{R_1R_2 + R_2R_3 + R_3R_1} \times \left(\frac{R_3}{R_3 + R_1}\right)$$

$$I = \frac{VR_3}{R_1R_2 + R_2R_3 + R_3R_1}$$

$$\Rightarrow \quad \frac{V}{I} = \frac{R_1R_2 + R_2R_3 + R_3R_1}{R_3} \tag{7.24}$$

Therefore, Eqs 7.23 and 7.24 represent the same and hence the reciprocity theorem is verified.

7.6.1 Steps to be Followed in the Reciprocity Theorem

The following steps have to be followed while applying the reciprocity theorem.

- Identify the branches between which the reciprocity theorem is to be applied.
- Find the current in the branch when excitation and response are not interchanged.
- Find the current in the branch when excitation and response are interchanged.

7.6.2 Assumptions Made in the Reciprocity Theorem

We make the following assumptions for the theorem to be applicable to the network.

- There is only one source of excitation in the network and that the network is initially relaxed (all initial conditions are zero).
- The network is linear.
- We exclude dependent (or controlled) sources in the network, even if they are linear.

7.6.3 Limitations of Reciprocity Theorem

- It is not applicable to the network consisting of non-linear elements such as diodes, transistors and so on.
- It is not applicable to a network consisting of any dependent source, even if it is linear.
- This theorem is not applicable to a network consisting of any time varying element.

Problem 7.21 Verify reciprocity theorem for the network.

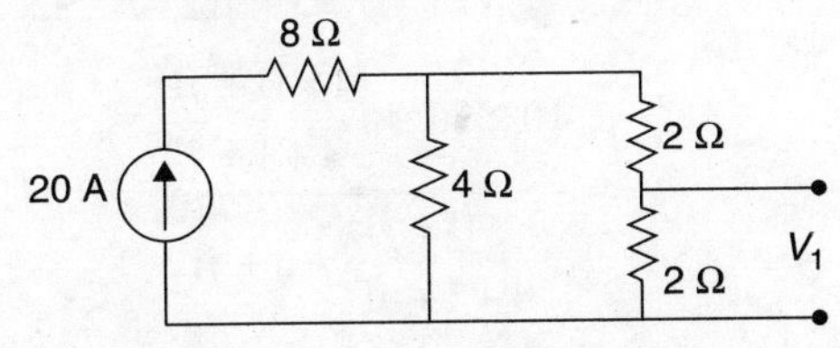

Solution:

The circuit is redrawn as shown in Fig. (a).

According to current division rule

$$I_2 = 20 \times \frac{4}{4+2+2} = 20 \times \frac{4}{8} = 10 \text{ A}$$

$$V_1 = 2I_2 = 2 \times 10 = 20 \text{ V}$$

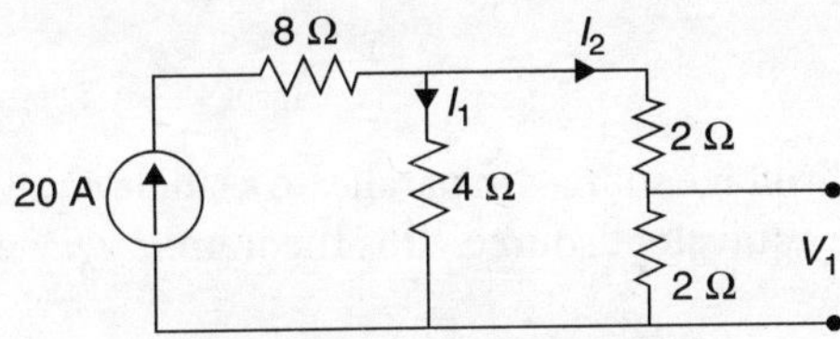

Fig. (a) Before interchanging

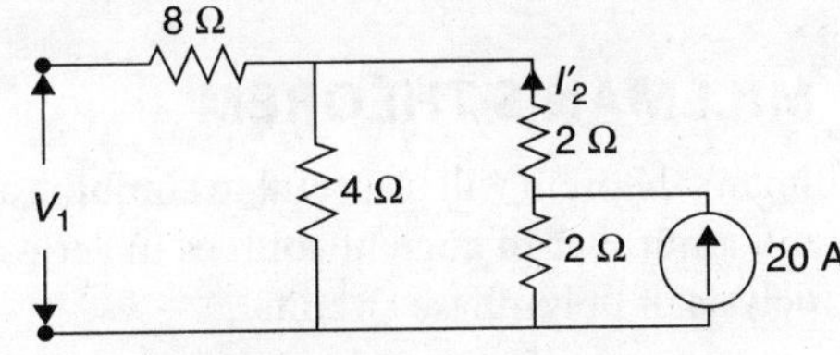

Fig. (b) After interchanging

Interchanging the positions of excitation and response:

According to current division rule

$$I_2' = 20 \times \frac{2}{2+2+4} = 20 \times \frac{2}{8} = 5 \text{ A}$$

$$V_1 = 4I_2' = 4 \times 5 = 20 \text{ V}$$

Hence, reciprocity theorem is verified.

Problem 7.22 Find V in the circuit and verify reciprocity theorem.

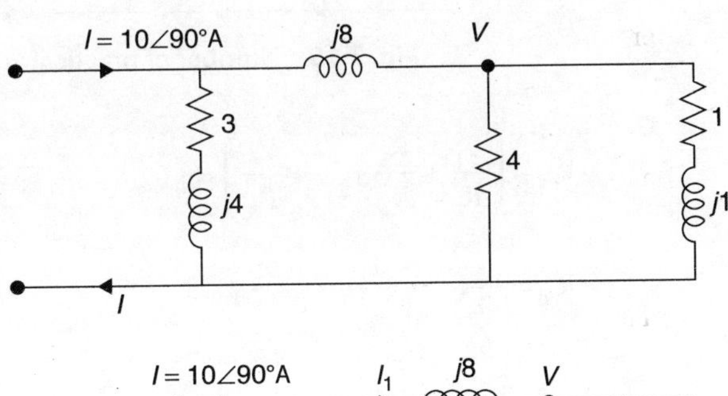

Solution:

The circuit is redrawn as shown in Fig. (a).

$$I_1 = \frac{10\angle 90°(3+j4)}{(3+j4) + \dfrac{(1+j1)\times 4}{(1+j1)+4} + j8}$$

$$= \frac{10\angle 90°(3+j4)}{(3+j12) + \dfrac{(1+j1)\,4}{5+j1}} = 3.785\angle 70.4° \text{ A}$$

By applying current division rule

$$I_2 = I_1 \frac{(1+j1)}{1+j1+4} = 3.785\angle 70.4° \times \frac{(1+j1)}{5+j1} = 1.05\angle 104.1° \text{ A}$$

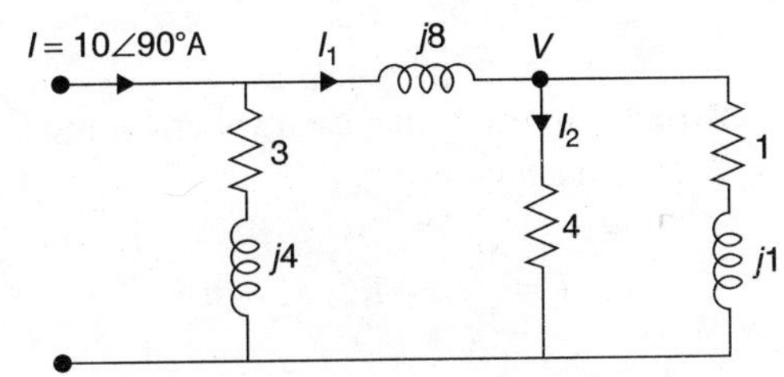

Fig. (a) Before interchanging

$$V = I_2 \times 4 = 4 \times 1.05\angle 104.5^\circ = 4.2\angle 104.1^\circ \text{ V}$$

Now interchanging the positions of excitation and response

Current through impedance $(3 + j4)$ Ω is

$$I_3 = \frac{10\angle 90^\circ \times 4 \,||\, (1 + j1)}{4 \,||\, (1 + j1) + 3 + j12}$$

$$= \frac{10\angle 90^\circ \times \dfrac{4 \times (1 + j1)}{4 + 1 + j1}}{\dfrac{4 \times (1 + j1)}{4 + 1 + j1} + 3 + j12} = 0.84\angle 50.96^\circ \text{ A}$$

$$V = 0.84\angle 50.96^\circ \times (3 + j4) = 4.2\angle 104.1^\circ \text{ V}$$

Hence the reciprocity theorem is verified.

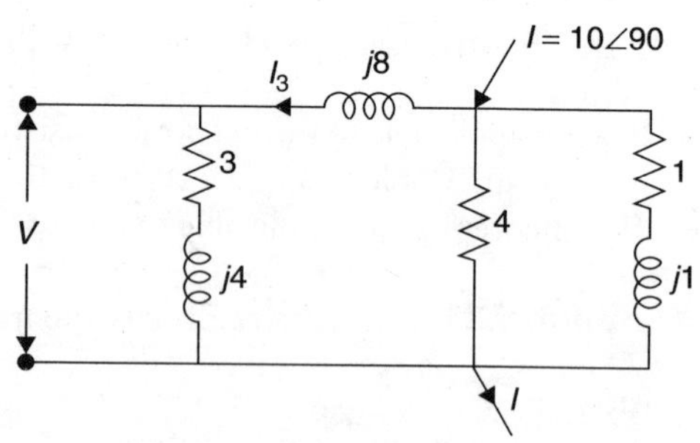

Fig. (b) After interchanging

7.7 MILLMAN'S THEOREM

The Millman's theorem will be useful to combine a number of voltage sources in parallel to a single equivalent source and a number of current sources in series to a single equivalent source. This theorem is very useful in the analysis of poly-phase circuits.

Statements It states that in any network, if the voltage sources V_1, V_2, V_3, ..., V_n in series with internal resistances R_1, R_2, R_3, ..., R_n (or internal impedances Z_1, Z_2, Z_3, ..., Z_n) respectively are in parallel, then these sources may be replaced by a single voltage source V_{eq} in series with R_{eq}.

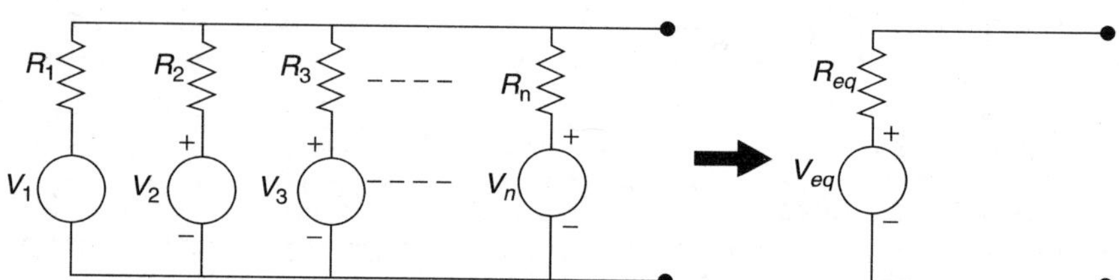

Fig. 7.15 Number of practical voltage sources connected in parallel

$$V_{eq} = \left(\frac{V_1}{R_1} + \frac{V_2}{R_2} + \cdots + \frac{V_n}{R_n} \right) R_{eq} \tag{7.25}$$

$$R_{eq} = \frac{1}{\dfrac{1}{R_1} + \dfrac{1}{R_2} + \cdots + \dfrac{1}{R_n}} \tag{7.26}$$

Proof To prove that each voltage source in Fig. 7.15 can be transformed into an equivalent current source as shown below using,

$$I_i = \frac{V_i}{R_i}, i = 1, 2, 3, \ldots, n$$

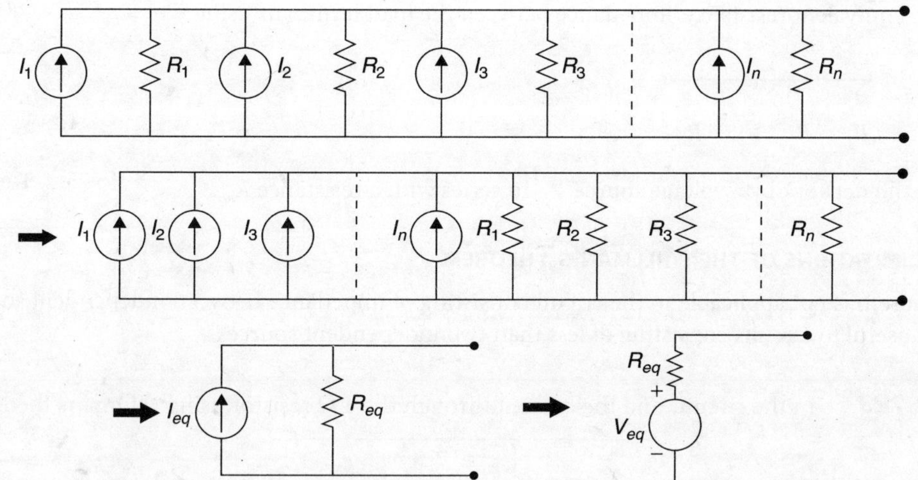

where $I_{eq} = I_1 + I_2 + \cdots + I_n = \dfrac{V_1}{R_1} + \dfrac{V_2}{R_2} + \cdots + \dfrac{V_n}{R_n}$

$$R_{eq} = \frac{1}{\dfrac{1}{R_1} + \dfrac{1}{R_2} + \cdots + \dfrac{1}{R_n}}$$

$$V_{eq} = I_{eq} R_{eq} = \left(\frac{V_1}{R_1} + \frac{V_2}{R_2} + \cdots + \frac{V_n}{R_n} \right) R_{eq}$$

Hence the theorem is proved.

Note: A similar theorem can be stated for n current sources having internal resistances, which can be replaced by a single current source I_{eq} in parallel with an equivalent resistance R_{eq}.

Here $$I_{eq} = \frac{I_1 R_1 + I_2 R_2 + \cdots + I_n R_n}{R_1 + R_2 + \cdots + R_n} \tag{7.27}$$

$$R_{eq} = R_1 + R_2 + \cdots + R_n \tag{7.28}$$

7.7.1 Steps to be Followed in the Millman's Theorem

The steps to be followed while applying Millman's theorem are given below.

- Remove the load resistance/impedance, that is, R_L or Z_L.
- Find Millman's or equivalent voltage across the load terminals using

$$V_{eq} = \left(\frac{V_1}{R_1} + \frac{V_2}{R_2} + \cdots + \frac{V_n}{R_n} \right) R_{eq}$$

- Find the equivalent resistance/impedance between the load terminals using

$$R_{eq} = \frac{1}{\frac{1}{R_1} + \frac{1}{R_2} + \cdots + \frac{1}{R_n}}$$

- Replace the network by a voltage source V_{eq} in series with a resistance R_{eq}.

7.7.2 Limitations of the Millman's Theorem

- This theorem is not applicable to the circuit consisting of impedance between independent sources.
- It is not useful to circuits consisting of less than two independent sources.

Problem 7.23 In the circuit, find the current through the 4 Ω resistor using Millman's theorem.

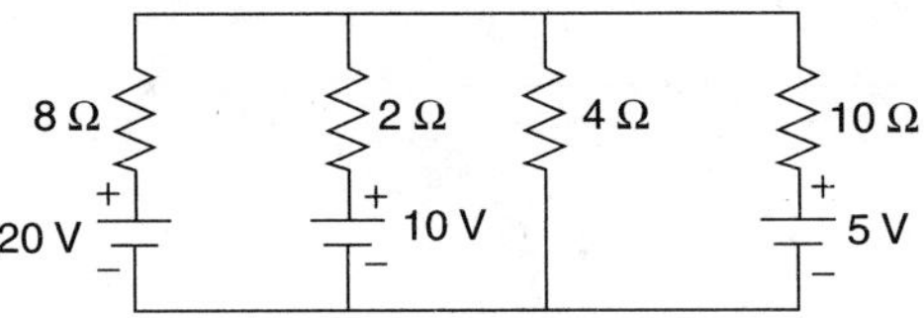

Solution:

The above circuit can be redrawn as

Here, $R_{eq} = \dfrac{1}{\frac{1}{R_1} + \frac{1}{R_2} + \frac{1}{R_3}} = \dfrac{1}{\frac{1}{8} + \frac{1}{2} + \frac{1}{10}} = \dfrac{1}{0.725} = 1.379$

$$V_{eq} = \left(\frac{V_1}{R_1} + \frac{V_2}{R_2} + \frac{V_3}{R_3}\right) R_{eq} = \left(\frac{20}{8} + \frac{10}{2} + \frac{5}{10}\right) \times 1.3793 = 11.04 \text{ V}$$

$\therefore$ Current through the 4 Ω resistor $I = \dfrac{V_{eq}}{R_{eq} + 4} = \dfrac{11.04}{1.379 + 4} = 2.0513$ A

Problem 7.24 In the circuit, determine V_0 using Millman's theorem.

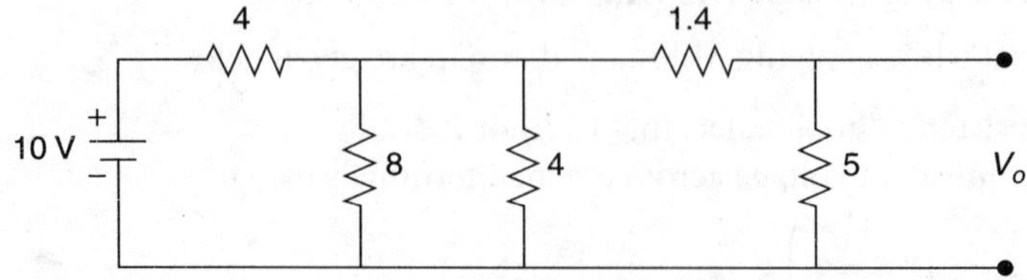

Solution:

The above circuit can be redrawn as

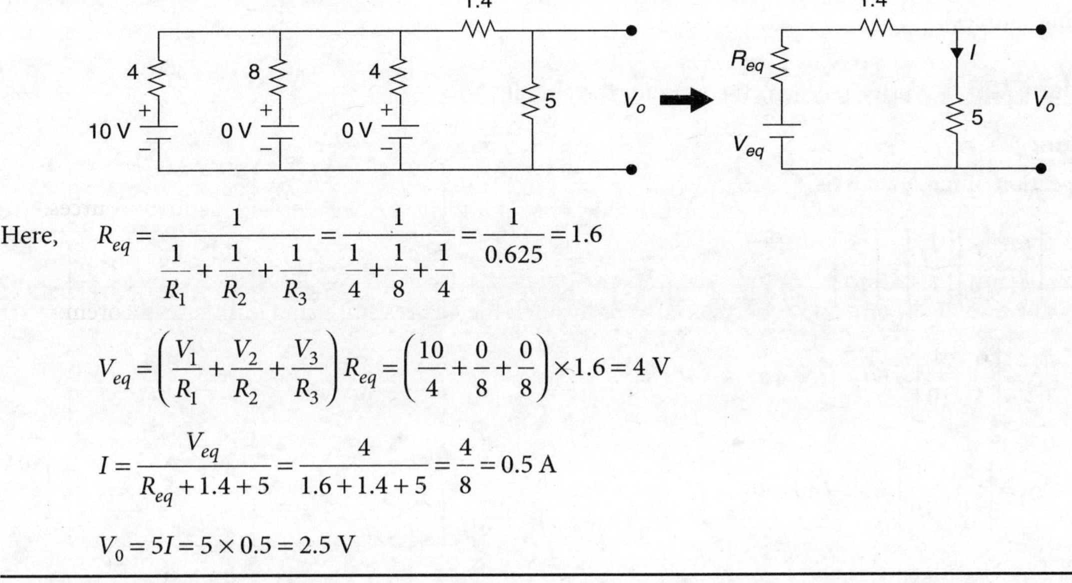

Here, $R_{eq} = \dfrac{1}{\dfrac{1}{R_1}+\dfrac{1}{R_2}+\dfrac{1}{R_3}} = \dfrac{1}{\dfrac{1}{4}+\dfrac{1}{8}+\dfrac{1}{4}} = \dfrac{1}{0.625} = 1.6$

$$V_{eq} = \left(\frac{V_1}{R_1}+\frac{V_2}{R_2}+\frac{V_3}{R_3}\right)R_{eq} = \left(\frac{10}{4}+\frac{0}{8}+\frac{0}{8}\right)\times 1.6 = 4\text{ V}$$

$$I = \frac{V_{eq}}{R_{eq}+1.4+5} = \frac{4}{1.6+1.4+5} = \frac{4}{8} = 0.5\text{ A}$$

$$V_0 = 5I = 5\times 0.5 = 2.5\text{ V}$$

7.8 TELLEGEN'S THEOREM

It is one of the most general theorems of network theory. It has a number of applications in the study of electric circuits. It is valid for any type of network such as linear or non-linear, active or passive, time varying or time invarying.

Statement This theorem states that the sum of all the products of branch voltage and its current of a circuit is zero. Since the product of voltage and current of a branch is equal to the power in the branch, it can also be stated as, the sum of instantaneous power or complex power in a circuit is zero. This implies that the power delivered by the independent source is equal to the power absorbed by various elements in the circuit.

Let a circuit have N nodes and B branches with branch voltage v_k and the branch current i_k, k ranging from 1 to B. Now, by Tellegen's theorem,

$$\sum_{k=1}^{B} v_k i_k = 0 \tag{7.29}$$

Note: In the case of circuits excited by sinusoidal sources, the product of current and voltage of a branch is a complex quantity and it is called complex power. Hence, we have to consider the complex power of the branches. Consider a circuit with B branches. Let S_1, S_2, ... S_B, be the complex powers in the B-branches of the circuit. Now, by Tellegen's theorem,

$$\sum_{k=1}^{B} V_k I_k^* = \sum_{k=1}^{B} S_k = 0 \tag{7.30}$$

While applying Tellegen's theorem, the branch currents should be selected such that they satisfy KCL and the branch voltages should be assigned such that they obey KVL. In order to verify Tellegen's theorem for a circuit, assign arbitrary branch currents and fix the polarity of branch voltages such that the current entry point is positive (for all the elements including sources). Alternatively, assign arbitrary branch voltages and fix the direction of current such that the current enters the branch at the positive end (for all the elements including sources).

Problem 7.25 Verify Tellegen's theorem for the circuit.

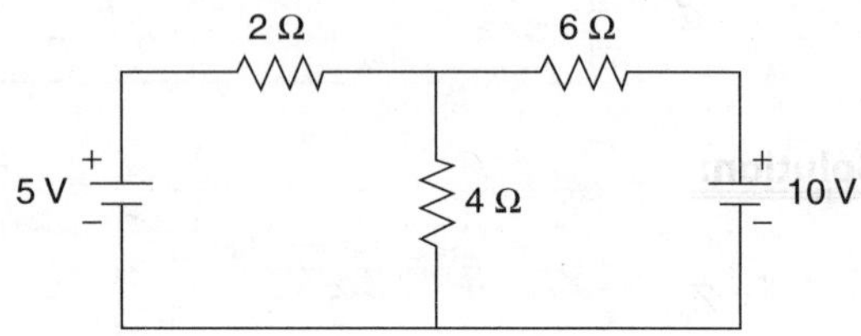

Solution:

By inspection of mesh analysis

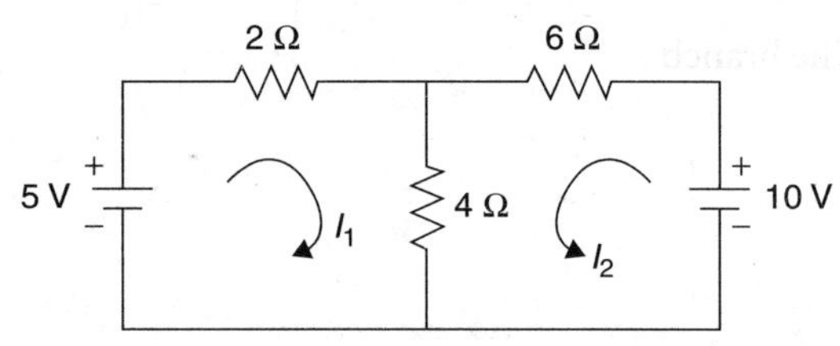

$$\begin{bmatrix} 6 & 4 \\ 4 & 10 \end{bmatrix}\begin{bmatrix} I_1 \\ I_2 \end{bmatrix} = \begin{bmatrix} 5 \\ 10 \end{bmatrix}$$

$$\Delta = \begin{vmatrix} 6 & 4 \\ 4 & 10 \end{vmatrix} = 60 - 16 = 44$$

$$\Delta_1 = \begin{vmatrix} 5 & 4 \\ 10 & 10 \end{vmatrix} = 50 - 40 = 10$$

$$\Delta_2 = \begin{vmatrix} 6 & 5 \\ 4 & 10 \end{vmatrix} = 60 - 20 = 40$$

$$I_1 = \frac{\Delta_1}{\Delta} = \frac{10}{44} = 0.227 \text{ A}$$

$$I_2 = \frac{\Delta_2}{\Delta} = \frac{40}{44} = 0.909 \text{ A}$$

Current flowing through 2 Ω $= I_1 = 0.227$ A

Current flowing through 4 Ω $= I_1 + I_2 = 1.136$ A

Current flowing through 6 Ω $= I_2 = 0.909$ A

Current supplied by 5 V source = 0.227 A

Current supplied by 10 V source = 0.909 A

Voltage across 2 Ω $= 2 \times 0.227 = 0.454$ V

Voltage across 4 Ω $= 4 \times 1.136 = 4.544$ V

Voltage across 6 Ω $= 6 \times 0.909 = 5.454$ V

Power delivered by the sources $= 0.227 \times 5 + 0.909 \times 10 = 10.22$ W

Power dissipated in the resistors $= 0.227^2 \times 2 + 1.136^2 \times 4 + 0.909^2 \times 6 = 10.222$ W

Therefore, the power delivered by the sources is equal to the power dissipated in the resistors, and hence Tellegen's theorem is verified.

Problem 7.26 Verify Tellegen's theorem for the circuit.

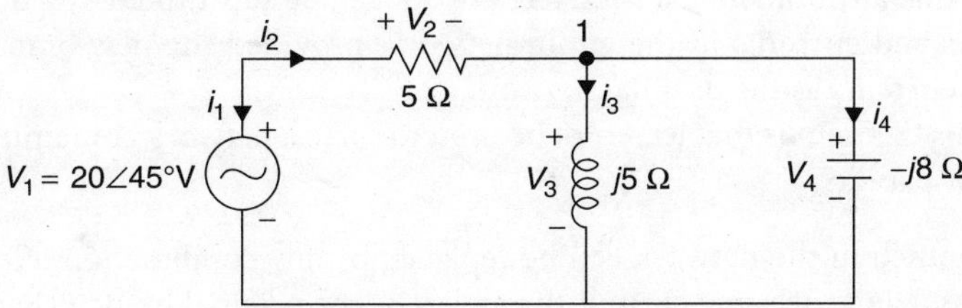

Solution:

$$Z_{eq} = 5 + \frac{j5 \times -j8}{j5 - j8} = 5 + \frac{40}{-j3} = 5 + j13.33 = 14.24\angle 69.4^\circ\ \Omega$$

The branch currents are

$$i_2 = \frac{V_1}{Z_{eq}} = \frac{20\angle 45^\circ}{14.24\angle 69.4^\circ} = 1.404\angle -24.6^\circ\ \text{A}$$

$$i_1 = -i_2 = -1.404\angle -24.6^\circ = 1.404\angle 155.6^\circ\ \text{A}$$

Using current division rule

$$i_3 = i_2 \times \frac{-j8}{-j8 + j5} = 1.404\angle -24.6^\circ \times \frac{8}{3} = 3.745\angle -24.6^\circ\ \text{A}$$

Now, applying KCL at node 1,

$$i_4 = i_2 - i_3 = 1.404\angle -24.6^\circ - 3.745\angle -24.6^\circ = 2.341\angle 155.6^\circ\ \text{A}$$

Now, the branch voltages are

$$V_2 = 5i_2 = 5 \times 1.404\angle -24.6^\circ = 7.02\angle -24.6^\circ\ \text{V}$$

Applying KVL to first loop

$$V_1 - V_2 - V_3 = 0$$

$$\Rightarrow \quad V_3 = V_1 - V_2 = 20\angle 45^\circ - 7.02\angle -24.6^\circ = 18.72\angle 65.5^\circ\ \text{V}$$

$$V_4 = V_3 = 18.72\angle 65.5^\circ\ \text{V}$$

$$\sum_{k=1}^{4} V_k i_k^* = V_1 i_1^* + V_2 i_2^* + V_3 i_3^* + V_4 i_4^*$$

$$= 20\angle 45^\circ \times 1.404\angle -155.4^\circ + 7.02\angle -24.6^\circ \times 1.404\angle 24.6^\circ + 18.72\angle 65.5^\circ \times 3.745\angle 24.6^\circ$$

$$+ 18.72\angle 65.5^\circ \times 2.341\angle -155.6^\circ$$

$$= 28.08\angle -110.6^\circ + 9.86\angle 0^\circ + 70.1\angle 90^\circ + 43.82\angle -90^\circ$$

$$= -9.87 - j26.28 + 9.86 + j70.1 - j43.82 = 0$$

Therefore, Tellegen's theorem is verified.

7.9 SUBSTITUTION THEOREM

Statement It states that any branch in a DC/AC network can be substituted by a different branch without disturbing the voltages and currents in the entire network, provided the new branch has the same set of terminal voltages and currents as the original network.

The limitation of this theorem is that it cannot be used to solve a network containing two or more sources that are not in series or parallel.

Explanation Any branch in the network can be replaced by any combination of elements that will have the same voltage across it and the same current through it as the original branch (Fig. 7.16).

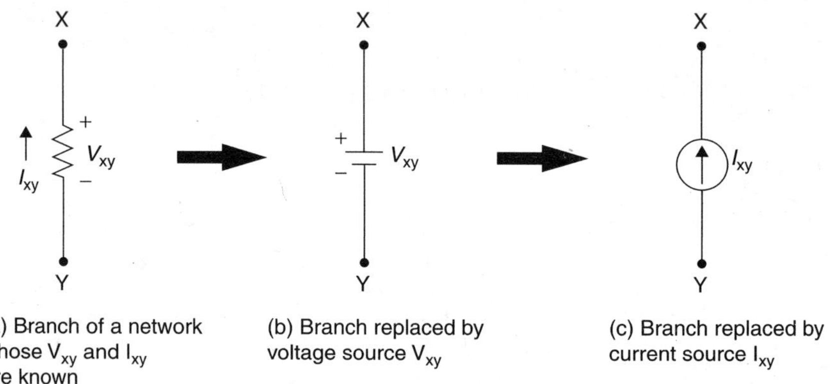

Fig. 7.16 Substitution theorem

7.9.1 Steps to be Followed in the Substitution Theorem

The steps to be followed while applying the substitution theorem are given below.

- First obtain the concerned branch voltage and current in the network.
- Replace the branch by an independent voltage source and obtain the voltages and currents in the network.
- Replace the branch by an independent current source and obtain the voltages and currents in the network.

Problem 7.27 For the circuit verify the substitution theorem by replacing the 6 Ω resistor with (i) a voltage source, (ii) a current source.

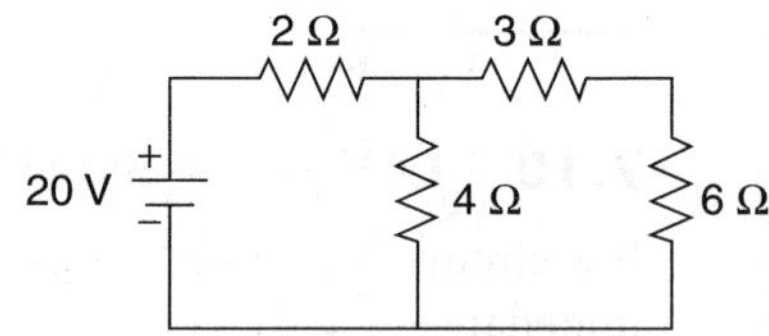

Solution:

Calculate the current through the 6 Ω resistor in the original network.

Applying KVL to mesh-1,

$$20 - 2I_1 - 4(I_1 - I_2) = 0$$

$$3I_1 - 2I_2 = 10 \qquad (1)$$

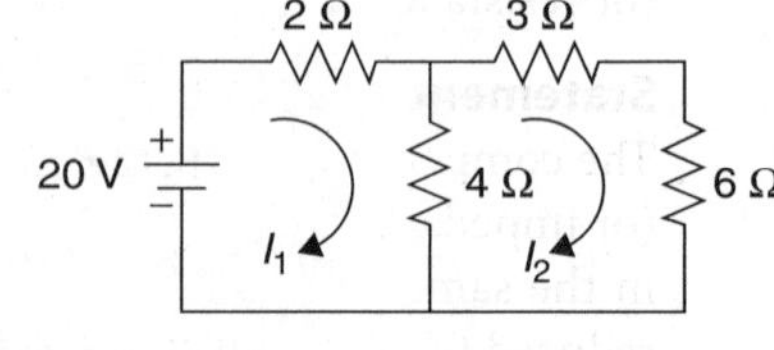

Applying KVL to mesh-2

$$-3I_2 - 6I_2 - 4(I_2 - I_1) = 0$$

$$-4I_1 + 13I_2 = 0 \qquad (2)$$

Solving Eqs (1) and (2), we have

$$I_1 = 4.193 \text{ A}, I_2 = 1.29 \text{ A}$$

Therefore, current through the 6 Ω resistor, $I_{6\Omega} = I_2 = 1.29$ A

Voltage across the 6 Ω resistor, $V_{6\Omega} = 6 \times I_2 = 6 \times 1.29 = 7.74$ V

(i) When the 6 Ω resistor is replaced by a voltage source of 7.74 V.

Applying KVL to mesh-1,

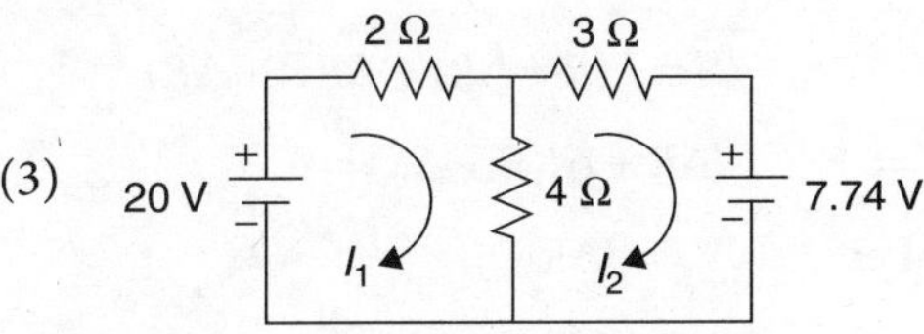

$$20 - 2I_1 - 4(I_1 - I_2) = 0$$

$$3I_1 - 2I_2 = 10 \quad (3)$$

Applying KVL to mesh-2

$$-3I_2 - 7.74 - 4(I_2 - I_1) = 0$$

$$4I_1 - 7I_2 = 7.74 \quad (4)$$

Solving Eqs (3) and (4), we have,

$$I_1 = 4.193 \text{ A}, I_2 = 1.29 \text{ A}$$

So, by replacing the 6 Ω resistor with a voltage source of 7.74 V, the currents I_1 and I_2 obtained in the new network are the same as in the original network and hence the substitution theorem is verified.

(ii) When the 6 Ω resistor is replaced by current source of 1.29 A.

Applying KVL to mesh-1,

$$20 - 2I_1 - 4(I_1 - I_2) = 0$$

$$3I_1 - 2I_2 = 10 \quad (5)$$

From mesh-2

$$I_2 = 1.29 \quad (6)$$

Solving Eqs (5) and (6), we have

$$I_1 = 4.193 \text{ A}, I_2 = 1.29 \text{ A}$$

So, by replacing the 6 Ω resistor with a current source of 1.29 A, the currents I_1 and I_2 obtained in the new network are the same as in the original network and hence the substitution theorem is verified.

7.10 COMPENSATION THEOREM

If a circuit has certain distribution of voltages and currents across and through various branches, if the impedance (or resistance) of one of the branch changes (due to some factors), the voltages and currents in other branches get affected. To nullify this effect, the voltage sources should be changed accordingly. This application occurs in bridge and potentiometer circuits where a slight change in one impedance (or resistance) results in a shift from the null condition.

Statement Let I (or $\bar{I}$) be the current through a resistance R (or impedance Z) in a branch of a circuit. The compensation theorem states that the change in current ΔI (or $\Delta\bar{I}$) due to change in the resistance ΔR (or impedance ΔZ) in a branch will be produced by a compensation voltage source $V_C = I\Delta R$ (or $V_C = \bar{I}\Delta Z$) in the same branch with the polarity opposing the original current I, with all the sources in the network reduced to zero.

Proof Consider a voltage source V connected to a resistance R [Fig. 7.16(a)]. Let I be the current through the circuit and let the resistance R be increased by an amount ΔR [Fig. 7.16(b)]. Now the current in the circuit might have changed by an amount ΔI and so that the current through the circuit is $I + \Delta I$.

From Fig. 7.17(a),

$$V = IR \tag{7.31}$$

From Fig. 7.17(b),

$$V = (I + \Delta I)\,(R + \Delta R)$$

$$V = I\,(R + \Delta R) + \Delta I(R + \Delta R)$$

$$\Rightarrow \quad I\Delta R + \Delta I(R + \Delta R) = 0 \tag{7.32}$$

Let $\quad V_C = I\Delta R$

$$V_C + \Delta I\,(R + \Delta R) = 0$$

$$\Rightarrow \quad \Delta I = \frac{-V_C}{R + \Delta R} \tag{7.33}$$

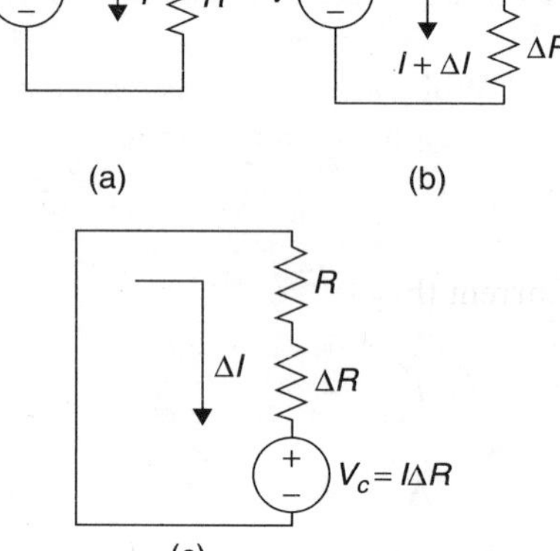

Fig. 7.17 Illustration of compensation theorem

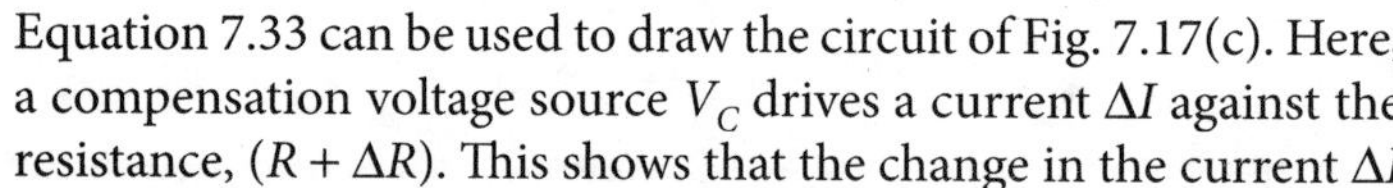

Equation 7.33 can be used to draw the circuit of Fig. 7.17(c). Here, a compensation voltage source V_C drives a current ΔI against the resistance, $(R + \Delta R)$. This shows that the change in the current ΔI due to a change in a branch resistance in a linear network can be computed by determining the current in that branch from the original network and by nullifying the independent source and placing a compensation voltage in series with the branch. The value of compensation voltage source $V_C = I\Delta R$ where I is the current through the branch before its resistance changed and ΔR is the change in the resistance (defined as the new value minus the previous value). From Eq. 7.33, we can say that the compensation voltage $V_C = I\Delta R$ introduced in the branch of R produces the change in current ΔI. Hence, the compensation theorem is verified.

7.10.1 Limitations of the Compensation Theorem

- This theorem is not applicable to the circuit consisting of only dependent sources.
- It is not applicable to the circuit consisting of non-linear elements such as diodes and transistors.

Problem 7.28 In the circuit, the 10 Ω resistor is changed to 15 Ω. Find the current through the 4 Ω resistance before and after the change in resistance. Determine the change in current ΔI through the 4 Ω resistance using the compensation theorem.

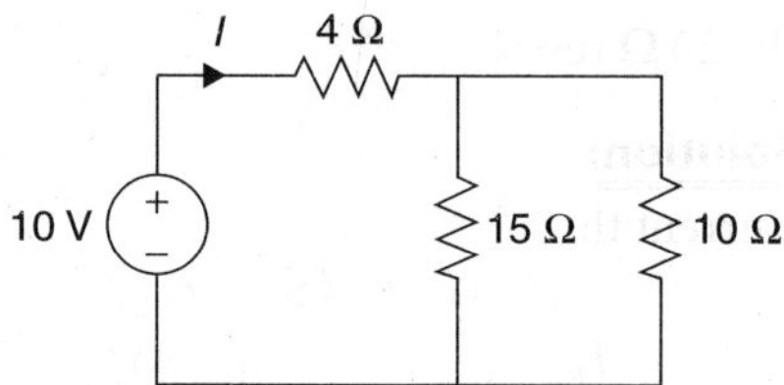

Solution:

Current through the 4 Ω resistance before change is I'.

$$\therefore \quad I' = \frac{10}{10} = 1\text{ A}$$

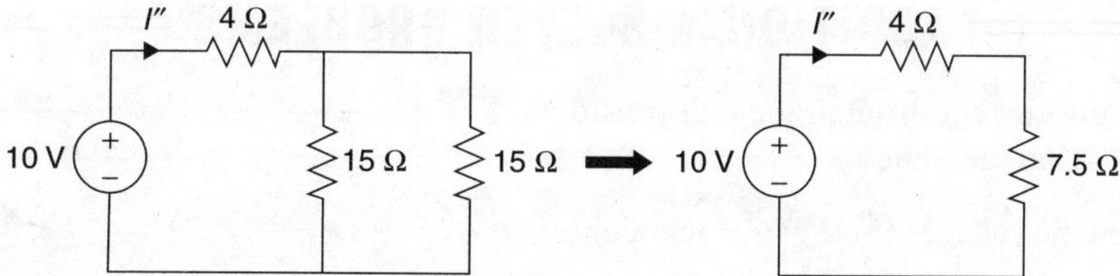

Current through the 4 Ω resistance after the change is I''.

$$\therefore \qquad I'' = \frac{10}{11.5} = 0.8696 \text{ A}$$

$$\Delta I = I' - I'' = 0.1304 \text{ A}$$

To determine ΔI using the compensation theorem, replace the 10 Ω resistance by a 15 Ω resistance in series with compensation voltage $I\Delta R$ where I is the current through the 10 Ω resistance.

$$I = 1 \times \frac{15}{15+10} = 0.6 \text{ A}$$

Compensation voltage, $V_C = I\Delta R = 0.6 \times 5 = 3$ V

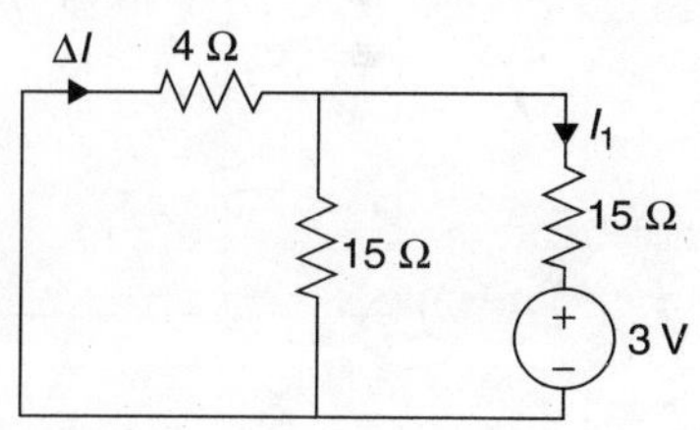

$$I_1 = \frac{3}{15 + \frac{4 \times 15}{4+15}} = \frac{3}{18.16} = 0.165 \text{ A}$$

$$\Delta I = I_1 \times \frac{15}{15+4} = 0.165 \times \frac{15}{19} = 0.13 \text{ A}$$

Problem 7.29 In the circuit, find the compensation voltage and change in current through AB, when the 20 Ω resistance is changed to 10 Ω.

Solution:

Current through the 20 Ω resistance (from B to A),

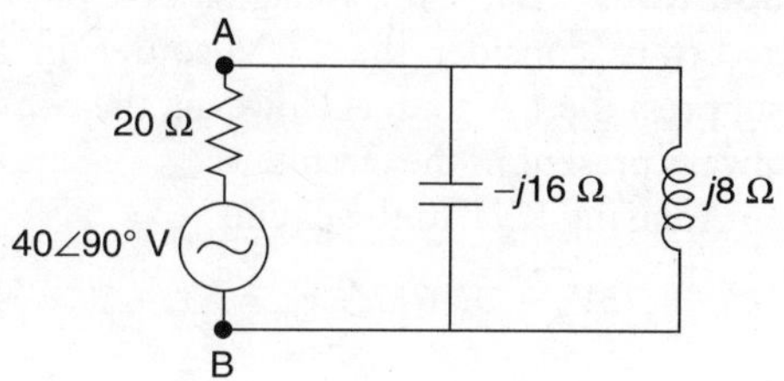

$$I_{BA} = \frac{40\angle 90^\circ}{20 + \frac{j8 \times -j16}{j8 - j16}} = 1.562\angle 51.34^\circ \text{ A}$$

Compensation voltage

$$V_C = 1.562\angle 51.34^\circ \times (10 - 20) = -15.62\angle 51.34^\circ \text{ V}$$

Change in current through AB (from B to A)

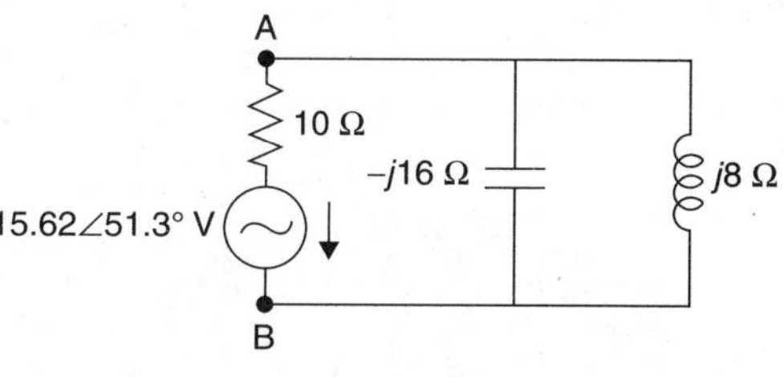

$$\Delta I_{BA} = \frac{15.62\ \angle 51.37^\circ}{10 + \frac{j8 \times -j16}{j8 - j16}} = 0.8278\angle -6.655^\circ \text{ A}$$

ADDITIONAL SOLVED PROBLEMS

7.1 Determine the current through the 4 Ω resistor using the superposition theorem.

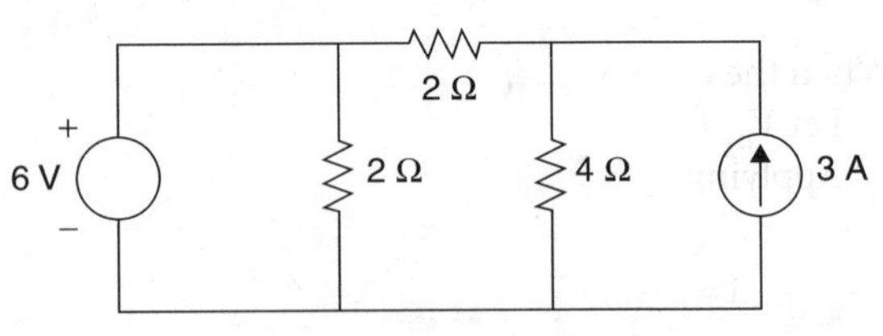

Solution: When the voltage source of 6 V acts alone.

$$R_T = \frac{2\times 6}{2+6} = 1.5$$

$$I_T = \frac{V}{R_T} = \frac{6}{1.5} = 4\text{ A}$$

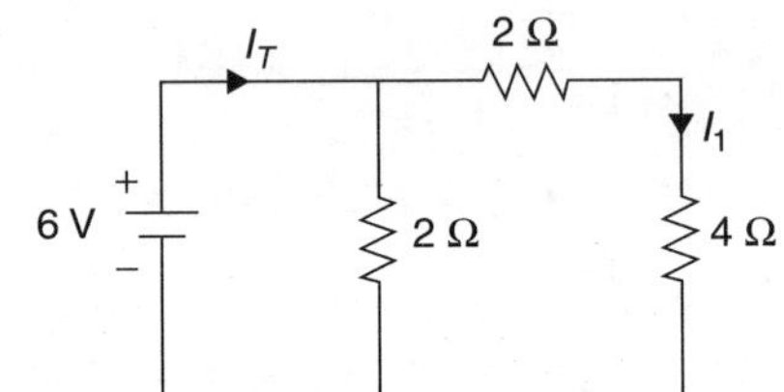

$$I_1 = I_T \times \frac{2}{2+6} = 1\text{ A}$$

When the current source of 3 A acts alone.

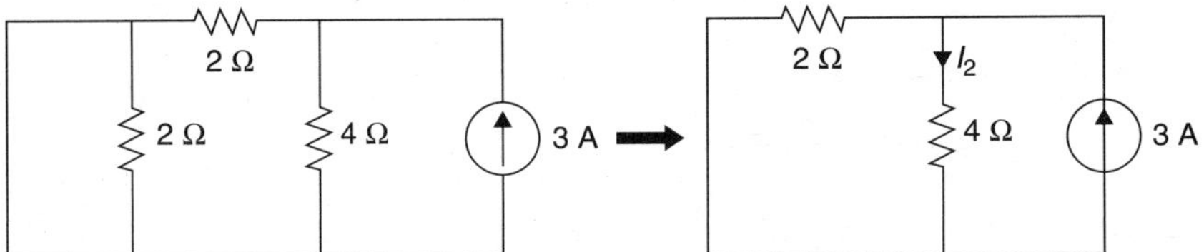

$$I_2 = 3\times\frac{2}{2+4} = 1\text{ A}$$

According to the superposition theorem, the current flowing through the 4 Ω resistance

$$= I_1 + I_2 = 1 + 1 = 2\text{ A}$$

7.2 Find V_a using the superposition principle.

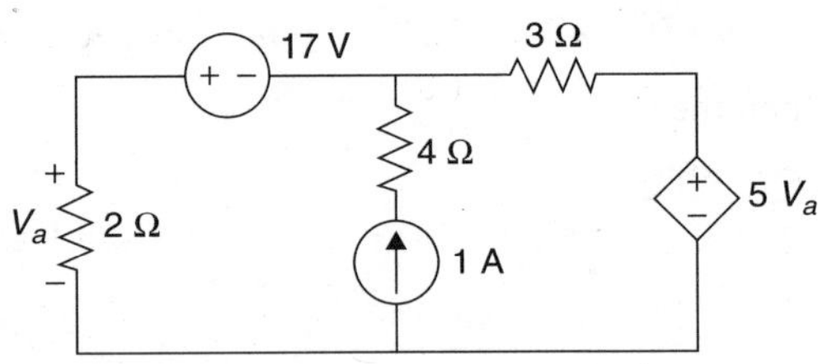

Solution: When the voltage source of 17 V acts alone.

Let us consider the 17 V source in the circuit and suppress the 1 A source. However, the controlled source is always present in the circuit.

Applying KVL to the circuit

$$5V_{a_1} - 3I + 17 - V_{a_1} = 0$$

$$\Rightarrow \quad 4V_{a_1} = 3I - 17$$

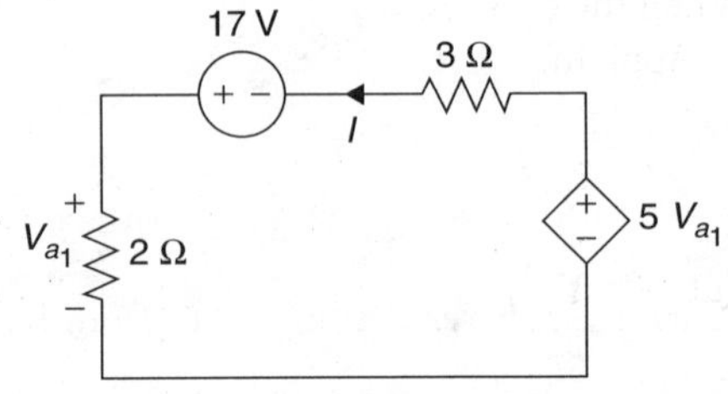

But from the circuit

$$\Rightarrow \quad I = \frac{V_{a_1}}{2}$$

$$\therefore \quad 4V_{a_1} = \frac{3V_{a_1}}{2} - 17$$

$$4V_{a_1} - 1.5V_{a_1} = -17$$

$$\Rightarrow \quad 2.5V_{a_1} = -17$$

$$\Rightarrow \quad V_{a_1} = \frac{-17}{2.5} = -6.8 \text{ V}$$

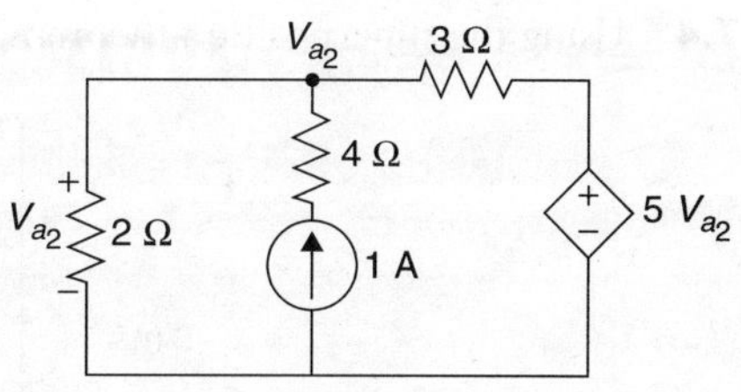

When the current source of 1 A acts alone.

Let V_{a_2} be the node voltage,

Applying KCL at node V_{a_2}

$$1 = \frac{V_{a_2} - 5V_{a_2}}{3} + \frac{V_{a_2}}{2}$$

$$1 = \frac{-4V_{a_2}}{3} + \frac{V_{a_2}}{2}$$

$$1 = \frac{-8V_{a_2} + 3V_{a_2}}{6}$$

$$\Rightarrow \quad -5V_{a_2} = 6$$

$$\Rightarrow \quad V_{a_2} = \frac{-6}{5} = -1.2 \text{ V}$$

Applying the superposition theorem, the resultant voltage is

$$V_a = V_{a_1} + V_{a_2} = -6.8 - 1.2 = -8 \text{ V}$$

7.3 Calculate the current i_y using the superposition theorem.

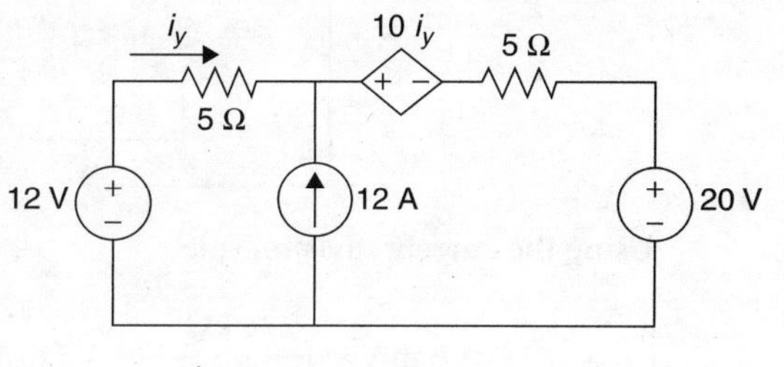

Solution: When the voltage source of 12 V acts alone.

$$12 = 5i_{y1} + 10i_{y1} + 5i_{y1}$$

$$\Rightarrow \quad i_{y1} = \frac{12}{20} = 0.6 \text{ A}$$

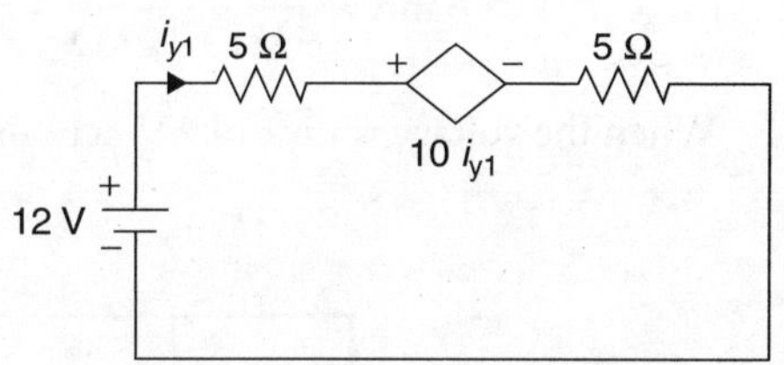

When the voltage source of 20 V acts alone.

$$-20 = 5i_{y2} + 10i_{y2} + 5i_{y2}$$

$$\Rightarrow \quad i_{y2} = -\frac{20}{20} = -1 \text{ A}$$

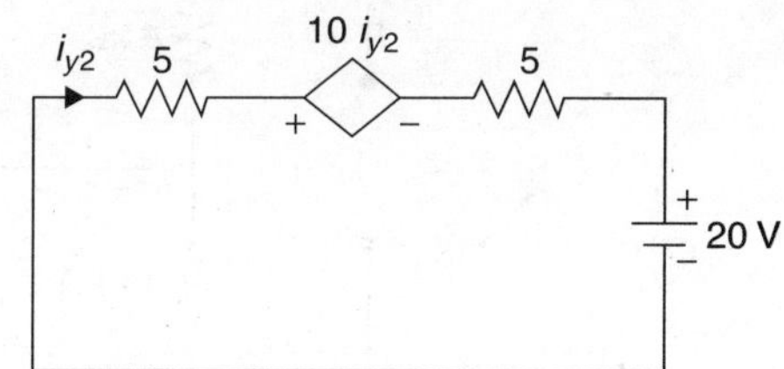

When the current source of 12 A acts alone.

Applying KCL at node (1)

$$i_{y3} + 12 = \frac{V_1 - 10i_{y3}}{5}$$

But $\quad V_1 = 5i_{y3}$

$$\therefore \quad 5i_{y3} + 60 = 5i_{y3} - 10i_{y3}$$

$$i_{y3} = -\frac{60}{10} = -6 \text{ A}$$

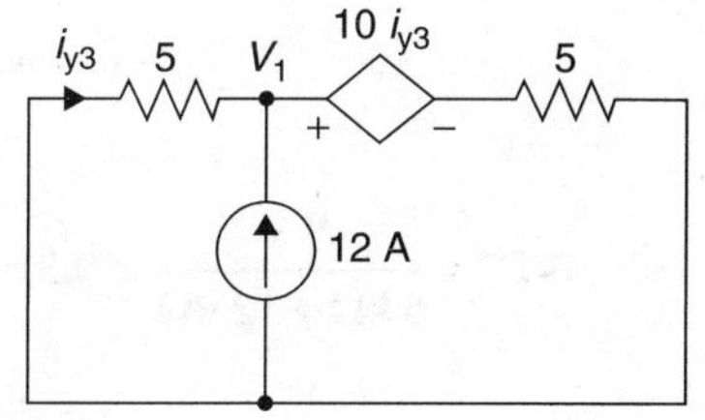

Applying superposition theorem, the resultant current is

$$i_y = i_{y1} + i_{y2} + i_{y3} = 0.6 - 1 - 6 = -6.4 \text{ A}$$

7.4 Using the superposition theorem, determine the current I for the network.

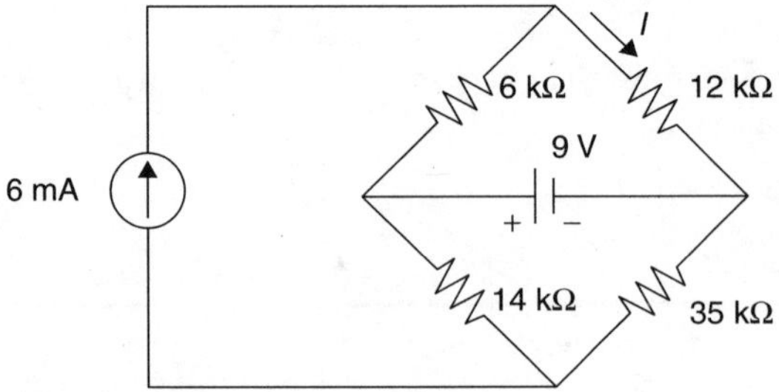

Solution: When the current source of 6 mA acts alone.

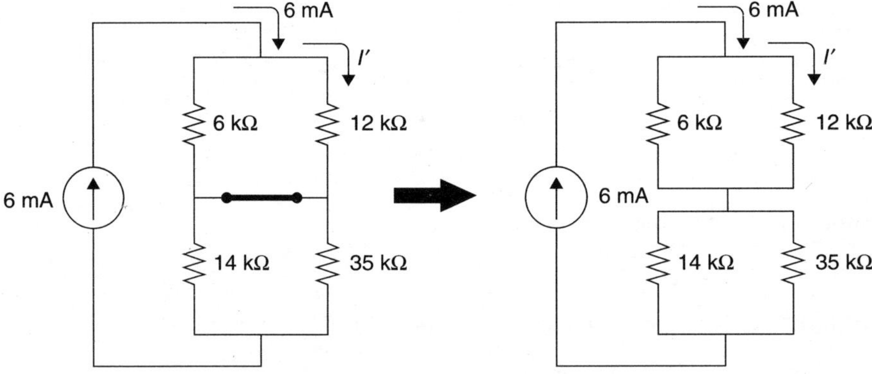

Using the current division rule

$$I' = 6\text{ mA} \times \frac{6\text{ k}\Omega}{6\text{ k}\Omega + 12\text{ k}\Omega} = 2\text{ mA}$$

When the voltage source of 9 V acts alone.

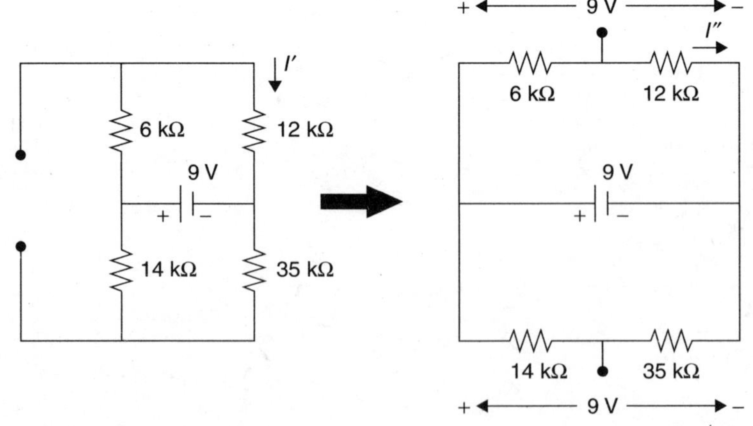

$$I'' = \frac{9\text{ V}}{6\text{ k}\Omega + 12\text{ k}\Omega} = 0.5\text{ mA}$$

According to the superposition theorem, the current I_1 is given by

$$I = I' + I'' = 2 \text{ mA} + 0.5 \text{ mA} = 2.5 \text{ mA}$$

7.5 Using Thevenin's Theorem, find the current through the 1 Ω resistor.

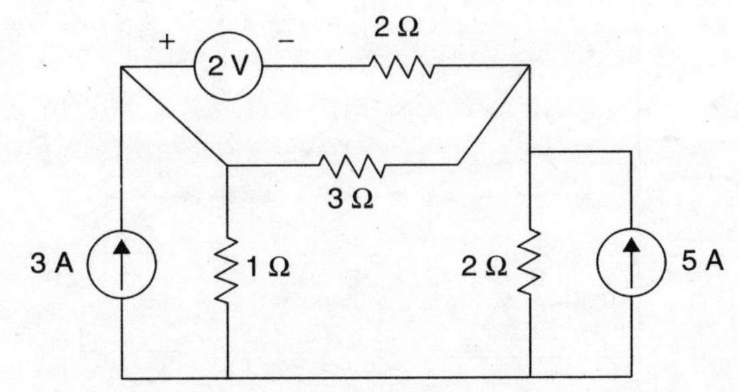

Solution:

Calculation of R_{th}

$$R_{th} = 2 + \frac{2 \times 3}{2+3} = 2 + \frac{6}{5} = \frac{16}{5}$$

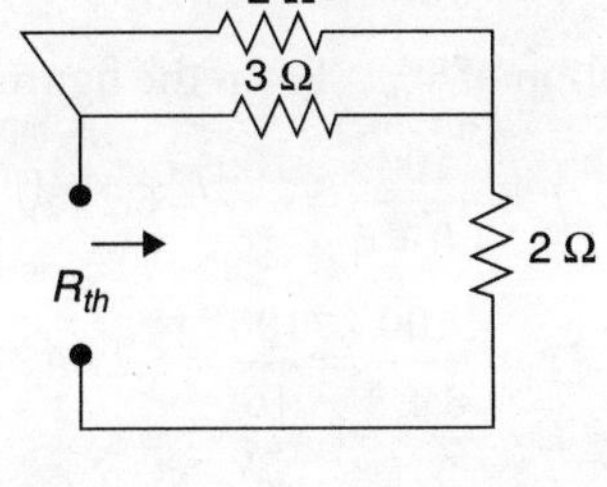

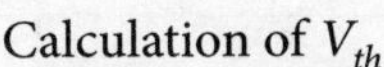

Calculation of V_{th}

Transforming the current source of 5 A to a voltage source, the circuit reduces to

Applying KCL to node (1)

$$\frac{V_1 - V_2 - 2}{2} + \frac{V_1 - V_2}{3} = 3$$

$$3V_1 - 3V_2 - 6 + 2V_1 - 2V_2 = 18$$

$$5V_1 - 5V_2 = 24 \qquad (1)$$

Applying KCL to node (2)

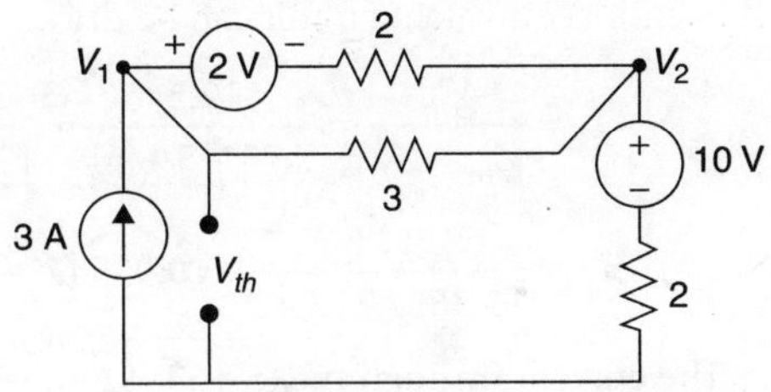

$$\frac{V_2 - V_1 + 2}{2} + \frac{V_2 - V_1}{3} + \frac{V_2 + 10}{2} = 0$$

$$3V_2 - 3V_1 + 6 + 2V_2 - 2V_1 + 3V_2 + 30 = 0$$

$$5V_1 - 8V_2 = 36 \qquad (2)$$

Subtracting Eq. (1) from Eq. (2)

$$-3V_2 = 12$$

$$\Rightarrow \qquad V_2 = -4$$

From Eq. (2)

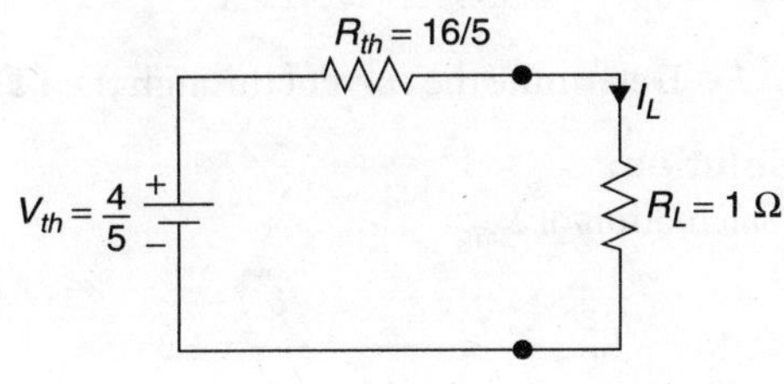

$$5V_1 = 36 + 8\ V_2 = 36 - 32 = 4$$

$$\Rightarrow \qquad V_1 = \frac{4}{5}$$

Thevenin's voltage, $V_{th} = V_1 = \frac{4}{5}$ V

Thevenin's equivalent circuit is shown on the right.

$$I_L = \frac{V_{th}}{R_{th} + R_L} = \frac{4/5}{1 + 16/5} = 0.1904 \text{ A}$$

7.6 Use Thevenin's theorem to find the current through the $(5 + j4)$ Ω impedance.

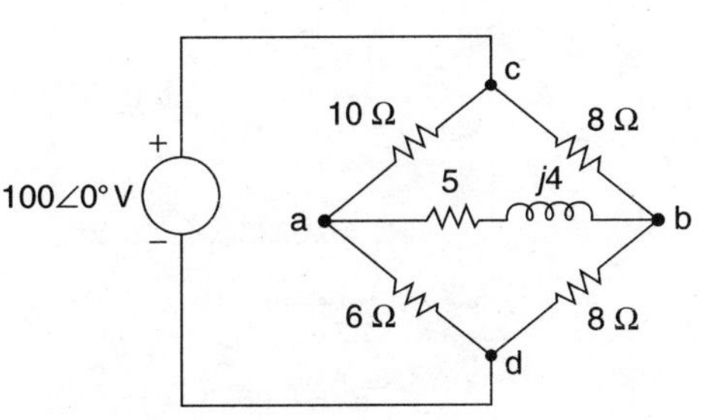

Solution:

Calculation of Z_{th}

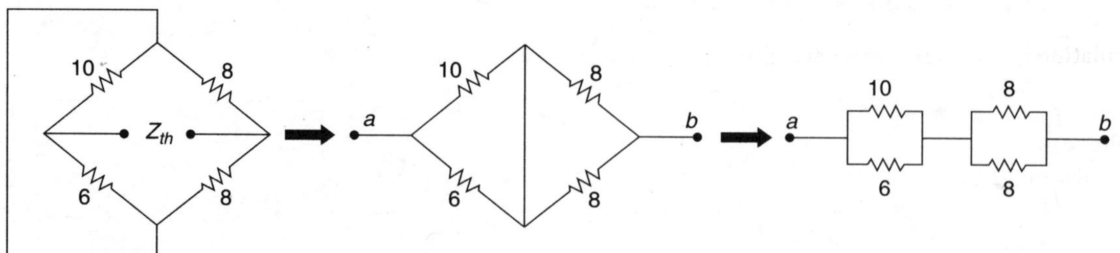

$$Z_{th} = Z_{ab} = \frac{10 \times 6}{10+6} + \frac{8 \times 8}{8+8} = 3.75 + 4 = 7.75\ \Omega$$

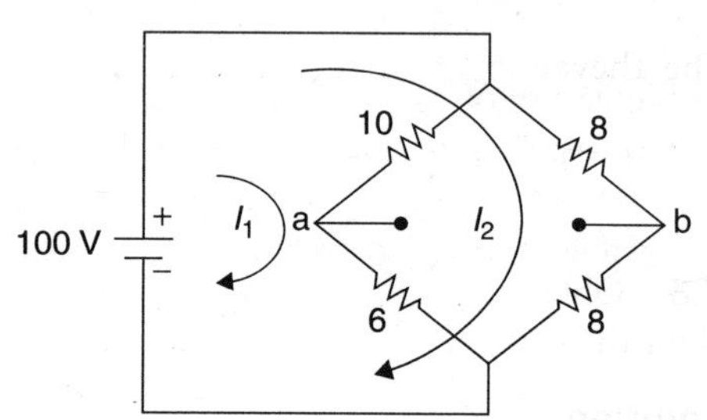

Calculation of V_{th} From the figure,

$$I_1 = \frac{100}{10+6} = \frac{100}{16} = 6.25\ \text{A}$$

$$I_2 = \frac{100}{8+8} = \frac{100}{16} = 6.25\ \text{A}$$

$$V_{th} = V_{ab} = 10I_1 - 8I_2 = (10-8) \times 6.25 = 12.5\ \text{V}$$

Thevenin's equivalent circuit can be drawn as shown on the right.

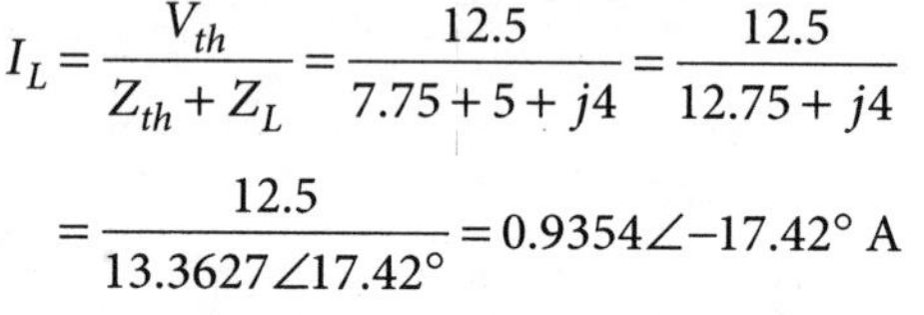

$$I_L = \frac{V_{th}}{Z_{th} + Z_L} = \frac{12.5}{7.75 + 5 + j4} = \frac{12.5}{12.75 + j4}$$

$$= \frac{12.5}{13.3627\angle 17.42^\circ} = 0.9354\angle -17.42^\circ\ \text{A}$$

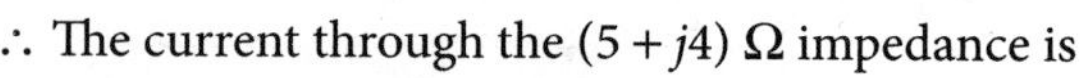

∴ The current through the $(5 + j4)\ \Omega$ impedance is

$$I_L = 0.9354\angle -17.42^\circ\ \text{A}$$

7.7 Determine the current through the 1 Ω resistor using Thevenin's theorem.

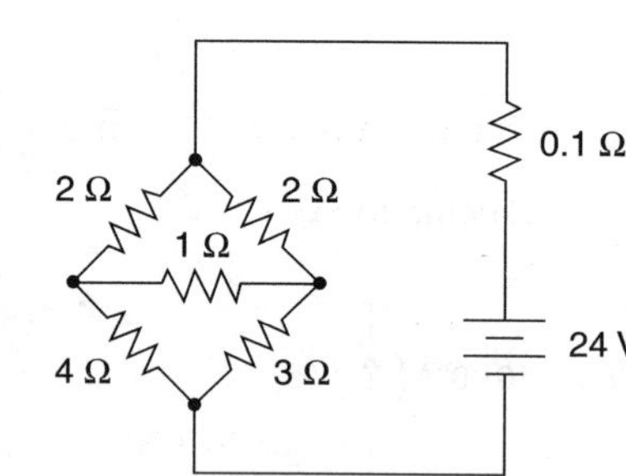

Solution:

Calculation of R_{th}

$$R_1 = \frac{2 \times 4}{2+4+0.1} = \frac{8}{6.1} = 1.31$$

$$R_2 = \frac{2 \times 0.1}{2+4+0.1} = \frac{0.2}{6.1} = 0.0328$$

$$R_3 = \frac{4 \times 0.1}{2+4+0.1} = \frac{0.4}{6.1} = 0.0655$$

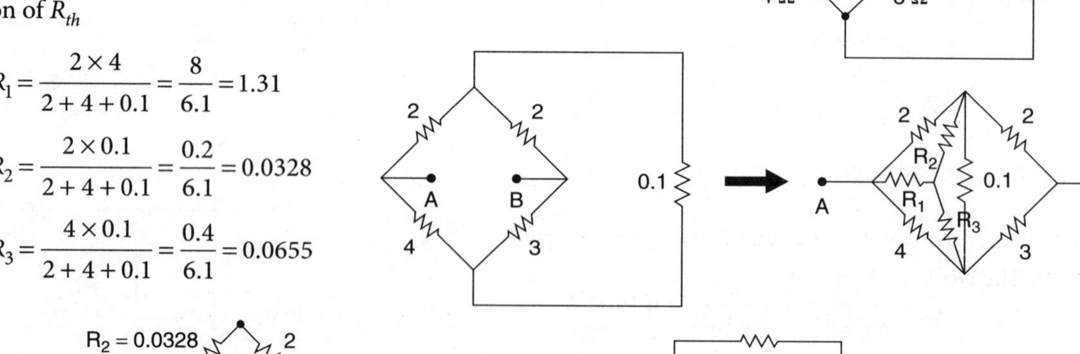

$R_2 = 0.0328$, $R_1 = 1.31$, $R_3 = 0.0655$; 1.31, 2.0328, 3.0655

$$R_{th} = R_{AB} = 1.31 + \frac{2.0328 \times 3.0655}{2.0328 + 3.0655} = 2.53 \quad \frac{2.033}{3.0655} = 2.53$$

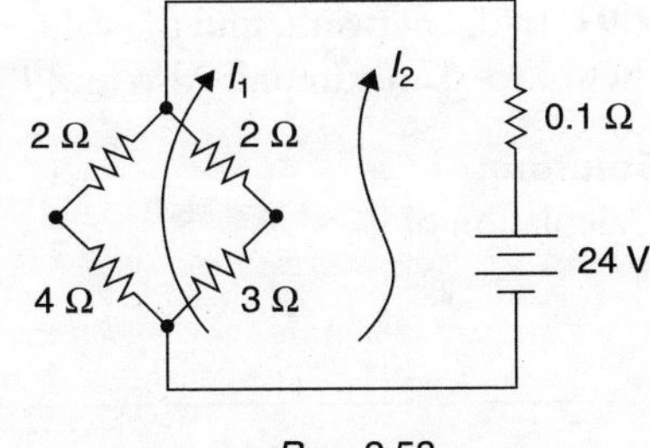

Calculation of V_{th}

$$I_1 = \frac{24}{2+4+0.1} = 3.934$$

$$I_2 = \frac{24}{2+3+0.1} = 4.706$$

$$V_{th} = 4I_1 - 3I_2 = 4 \times 3.934 - 3 \times 4.706 = 1.62 \text{ V}$$

The Thevenin's equivalent circuit is as shown on the right.

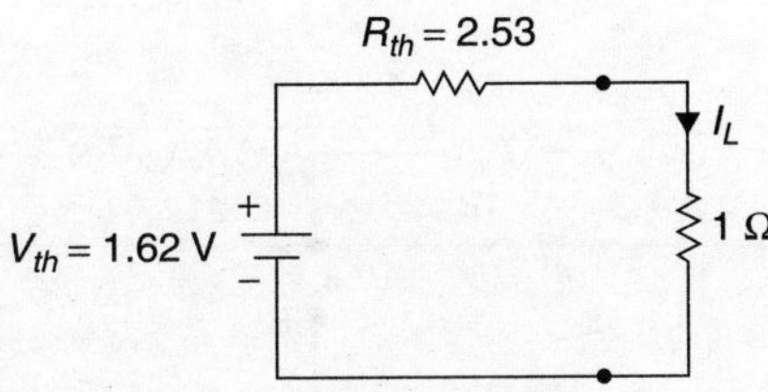

$$I_L = \frac{V_{th}}{R_{th} + R_L} = \frac{1.62}{2.53+1} = 0.459 \text{ A}$$

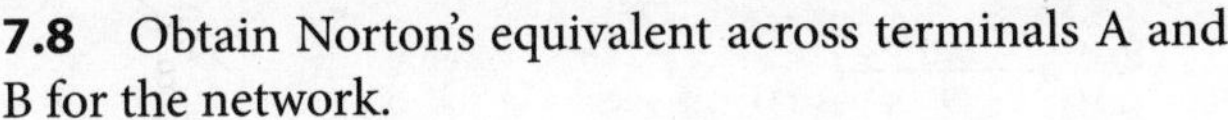

7.8 Obtain Norton's equivalent across terminals A and B for the network.

Solution:

Calculation of Z_N or Z_{AB}

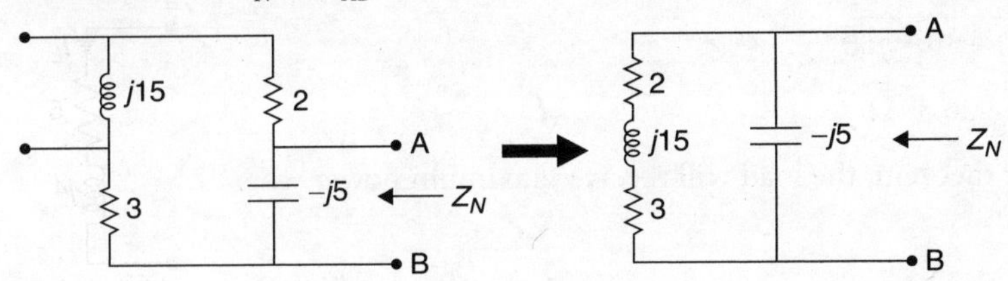

$$Z_N = \frac{(5+j15) \times -j5}{5+j5-j5} = \frac{-j5\,(5+j15)}{5+j10} = \frac{15-j5}{1+j2} = \frac{15.8\angle -18.43^\circ}{2.236\angle 63.42^0} = 7\angle 81.86^\circ$$

Calculation of I_{sc}

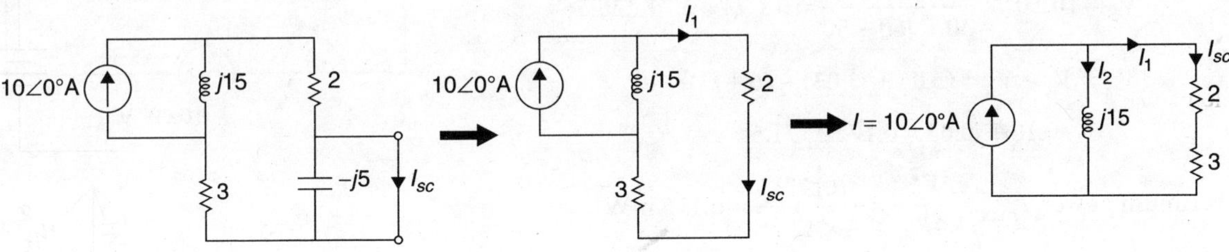

$$I_1 = I_{sc} = I\,\frac{j15}{j15+2+3} = \frac{10 \times j15}{5+j15} = \frac{j30}{1+j3} = \frac{30\angle 90^\circ}{3.16\angle 71.56^\circ} = 9.49\angle 18.435^\circ$$

∴ The Norton's equivalent circuit across terminals AB is shown.

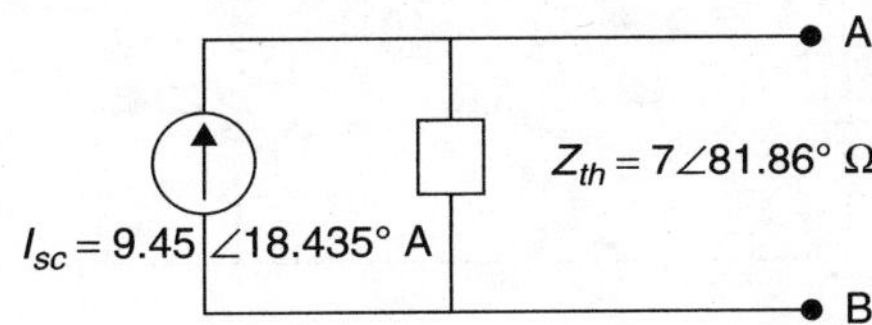

7.9 In the network, find the value of Z_L so that the power transfer from the source is maximum. Also find P_{max}.

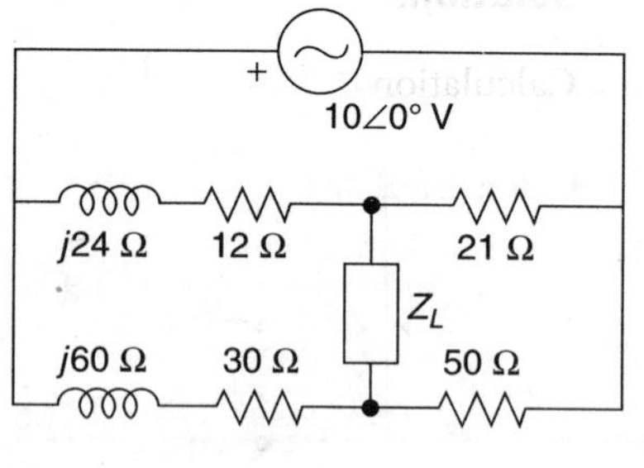

Solution:

Calculation of Z_{th}

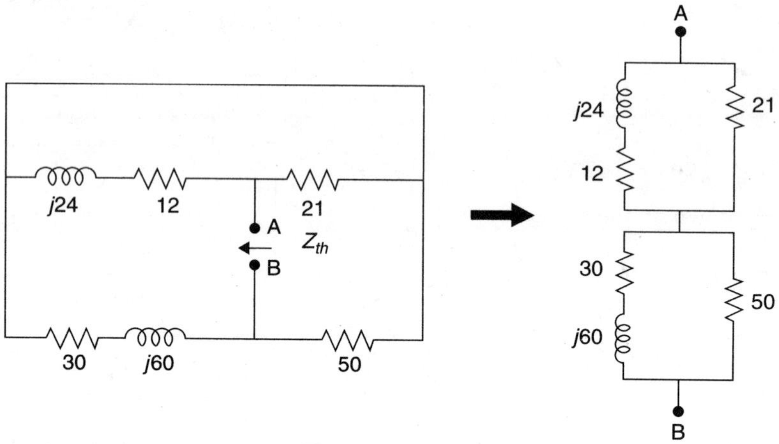

$$Z_{AB} = Z_{th} = \frac{21(12 + j24)}{21 + 12 + j24} + \frac{50(30 + j60)}{50 + 30 + j60}$$

$$= (42.26 + j21.36) = 47.35\angle 26.8°\ \Omega$$

According to maximum power transfer theorem, the load will receive maximum power when $Z_L = Z_{th}^*$.

$\therefore \quad Z_L = (42.26 - j21.36)\ \Omega$

Calculation of V_{th} According to voltage division rule

$$V_A = 10\angle 0° \times \frac{(12 + j24)}{21 + 12 + j24} = 5.84 + j3.03 = 6.57\angle 27.42°$$

$$V_B = 10\angle 0° \times \frac{(30 + j60)}{30 + j60 + 50} = 6 + j3 = 6.71\angle 26.56°$$

$$V_{th} = V_A - V_B = (5.84 + j3.03) - (6 + j3)$$

$$= -0.16 + j0.03 = 0.172\angle 171.5°$$

Maximum power, $P_{max} = \dfrac{V_{th}^2}{4R_{th}} = \dfrac{(0.172)^2}{4 \times 42.26} = 0.175 \text{ mW}$

7.10 Find the value of R_L so that maximum power is delivered to the load resistance R_L as shown, and find the maximum power.

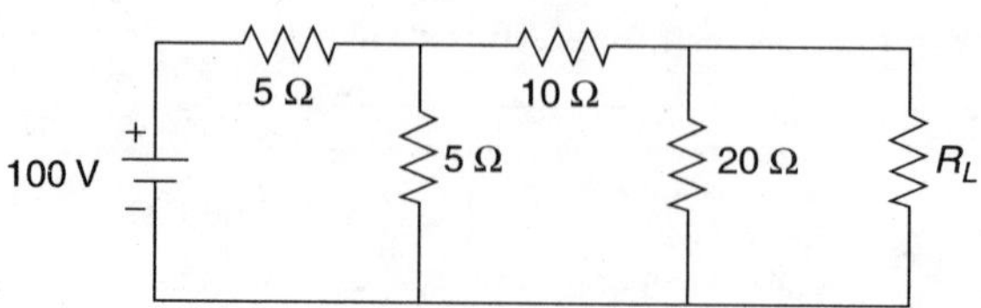

Solution: The load will receive maximum power when $R_L = R_{th}$.

Calculation of R_{th}

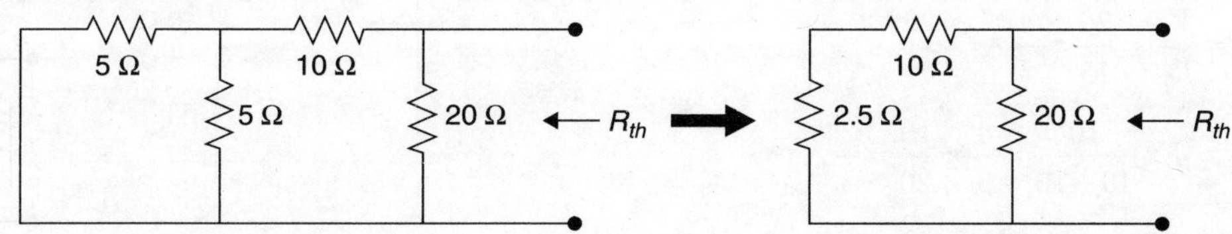

$$R_{th} = \frac{12.5 \times 20}{12.5 + 20} = 11.11\,\Omega$$

$$\therefore \quad R_L = R_{th} = 11.11\,\Omega$$

Calculation of V_{th}

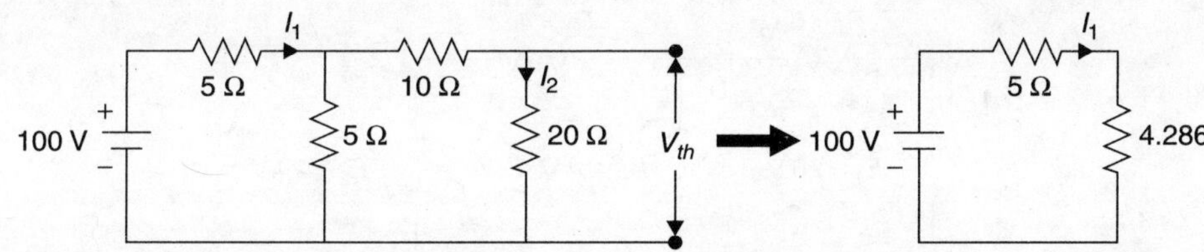

$$I_1 = \frac{100}{5 + 4.286} = 10.77\text{ A}$$

$$I_2 = I_1 \times \frac{5}{5 + 30} = 1.54\text{ A}$$

$$V_{th} = I_2 \times 20 = 1.54 \times 20 = 30.77\text{ V}$$

Maximum power received by the load

$$P_{\max} = \frac{V_{th}^2}{4R_{th}} = \frac{30.77^2}{4 \times 11.11} = 20.304\text{ W}$$

7.11 Verify the reciprocity theorem for the network.

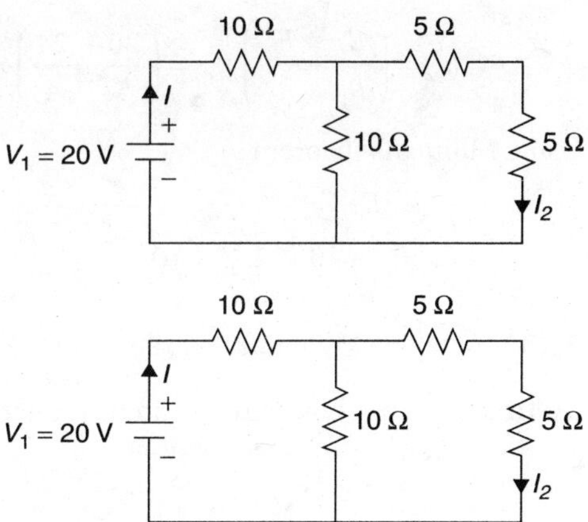

Solution: Without interchanging V_1 and I_2:

$$R_T = 10 + \frac{10 \times 10}{10 + 10} = 10 + 5 = 15$$

$$I = \frac{V_1}{R_T} = \frac{20}{15} = \frac{4}{3}\text{ A}$$

$$I_2 = I \times \frac{10}{10 + 10} = \frac{4}{3} \times \frac{10}{20} = \frac{2}{3}\text{ A}$$

$$\frac{V_1}{I_2} = \frac{20}{2/3} = \frac{60}{2} = 30$$

After interchanging V_1 and I_2:

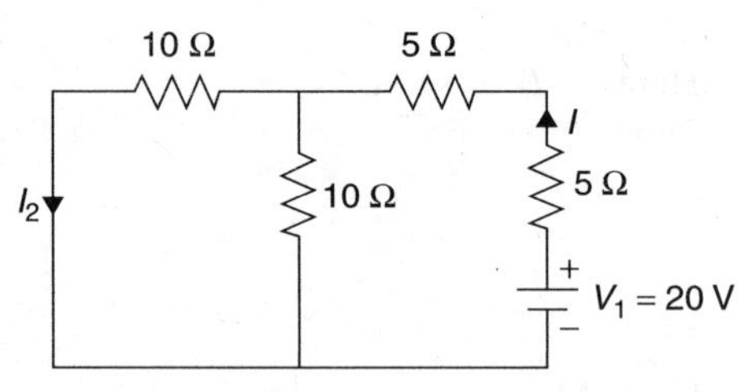

$$R_T = 10 + \frac{10 \times 10}{10 + 10} = 10 + 5 = 15$$

$$I = \frac{V_1}{R_T} = \frac{20}{15} = \frac{4}{3}\text{ A}$$

$$I_2 = I \times \frac{10}{10 + 10} = \frac{4}{3} \times \frac{10}{20} = \frac{2}{3}\text{ A}$$

$$\frac{V_1}{I_2} = \frac{20}{2/3} = \frac{60}{2} = 30$$

Therefore, the ratio of excitation to response when only one excitation is applied is constant when the positions of excitation and response are interchanged. Hence the reciprocity theorem is verified.

7.12 Applying Millman's theorem, find the current in resistor R_3.

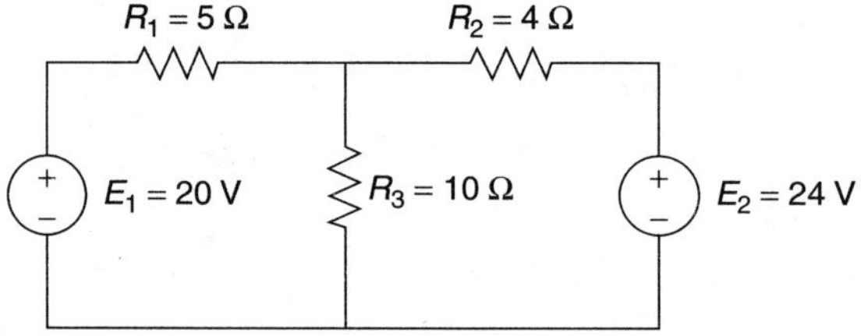

Solution: The above circuit can be redrawn as

Here
$$R_{eq} = \frac{1}{\frac{1}{R_1} + \frac{1}{R_2}} = \frac{1}{\frac{1}{5} + \frac{1}{4}} = \frac{20}{5 + 4} = 2.22\ \Omega$$

$$E_{eq} = \left(\frac{E_1}{R_1} + \frac{E_2}{R_2}\right) R_{eq} = \left(\frac{20}{5} + \frac{24}{4}\right) \times 2.22 = 10 \times 2.22 = 22.2\text{ V}$$

Using Millman's theorem

$$I = \frac{E_{eq}}{R_{eq} + 10} = \frac{22.2}{2.22 + 10} = 1.818\text{ A}$$

7.13 Applying Millman's theorem, find the current in load resistor R_L.

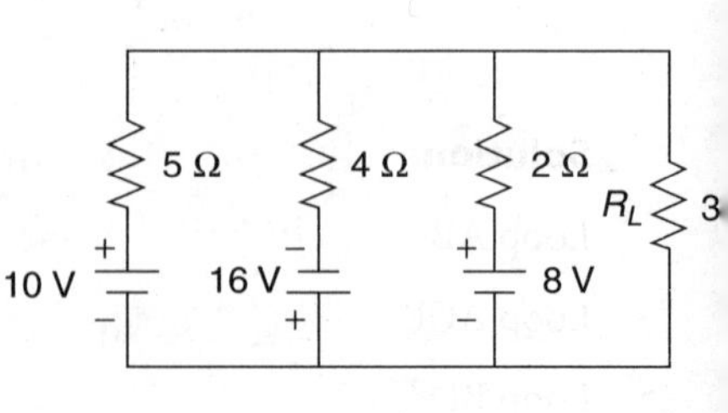

Solution: The above circuit can be reduced to

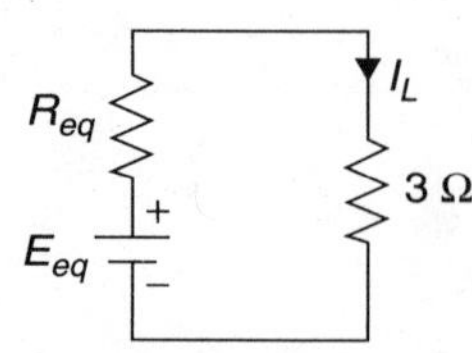

Here $R_{eq} = \dfrac{1}{\dfrac{1}{R_1} + \dfrac{1}{R_2} + \dfrac{1}{R_2}} = \dfrac{1}{\dfrac{1}{5} + \dfrac{1}{4} + \dfrac{1}{2}} = \dfrac{20}{5+4+10} = 1.05\,\Omega$

$$E_{eq} = \left(\frac{E_1}{R_1} + \frac{E_2}{R_2} + \frac{E_3}{R_3}\right) R_{eq} = \left(\frac{10}{5} - \frac{16}{4} + \frac{8}{2}\right) \times 1.05 = 2 \times 1.05 = 2.1\text{ V}$$

Using Millman's theorem

$$I_L = \frac{E_{eq}}{R_{eq} + 3} = \frac{2.1}{1.05 + 3} = 0.52\text{ A}$$

$$V_L = 3 \times I_L = 3 \times 0.52 = 1.56\text{ V}$$

7.14 Verify Tellegen's theorem in the network.

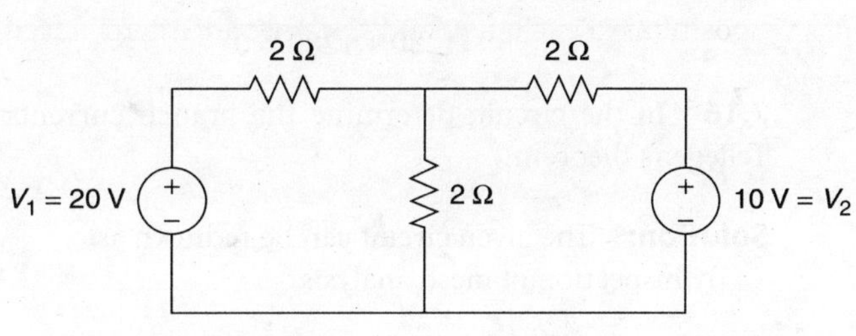

Solution: Let us assume the mesh currents as I_1 and I_2, as shown.

Applying KVL to loop (1)

$$4I_1 + 2I_2 = 20$$

$$2I_1 + I_2 = 10 \qquad (1)$$

Applying KVL to loop (2)

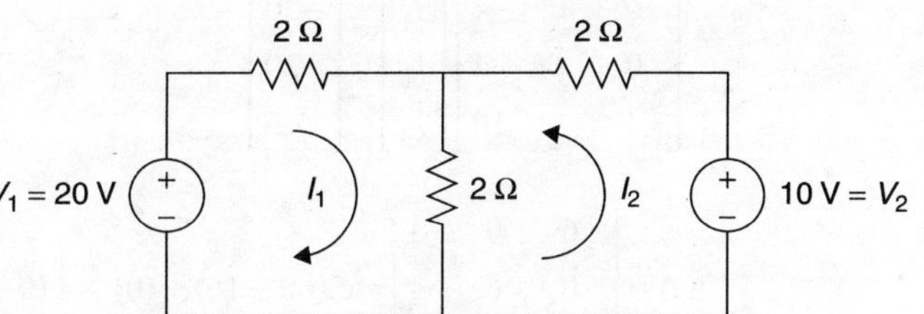

$$2I_1 + 4I_2 = 10$$

$$I_1 + 2\,I_2 = 5 \qquad (2)$$

Solving Eqs (1) and (2)

$$I_1 = 5\text{ A}, I_2 = 0$$

According to Tellegen's theorem, the algebraic sum of the powers in all branches must be zero. There are five branches in the circuit, and hence

$$\sum_{k=1}^{5} V_k I_k = -V_1 I_1 + 2I_1^2 + 2\,(I_1 - I_2)^2 + 2I_2^2 - V_2 I_2 = -100 + 50 + 50 + 0 - 0 = 0$$

∴ Hence the theorem is verified.

7.15 Verify Tellegen's theorem for the circuit in which the branch voltages and currents have the following values:

$$V_0 = 40\text{ V}, V_1 = 32\text{ V}, V_2 = 4\text{ V}, V_3 = 8\text{ V}, V_4 = 28\text{ V}, V_5 = 12\text{ V}$$

$$i_0 = -32\text{ A}, i_1 = 24\text{ A}, i_2 = 4\text{ A}, i_3 = 28\text{ A}, i_4 = 8\text{ A}, i_5 = 4\text{ A}$$

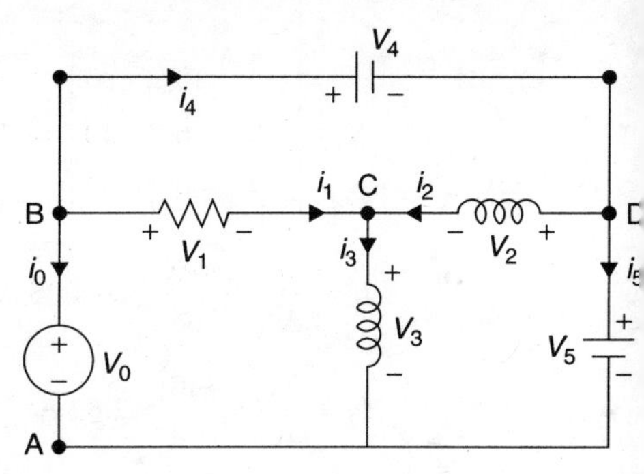

Solution: The KVL equations are

Loop ABCA: $V_0 - V_1 - V_3 = 40 - 32 - 8 = 0$

Loop ACDA: $V_2 + V_3 - V_5 = 4 + 8 - 12 = 0$

Loop BDCB: $V_4 + V_2 - V_1 = 28 + 4 - 32 = 0$

∴ The loops satisfy KVL

The KCL equations at various nodes are

Node B: $i_0 + i_1 + i_4 = -32 + 24 + 8 = 0$

Node C: $-i_1 - i_2 + i_3 = -24 - 4 + 28 = 0$

Node D: $-i_4 + i_5 + i_2 = -8 + 4 + 4 = 0$

$\therefore$ The nodes satisfy KCL.

Now, $$\sum_{K=0}^{5} V_K i_K = (40)(-32) + (32)(24) + (4)(4) + (8)(28) + (28)(8) + (12)(4)$$

$$= -1280 + 768 + 16 + 224 + 224 + 48$$

$$= -1280 + 1280 = 0$$

7.16 In the circuit, determine the branch currents and voltages and verify Tellegen's theorem.

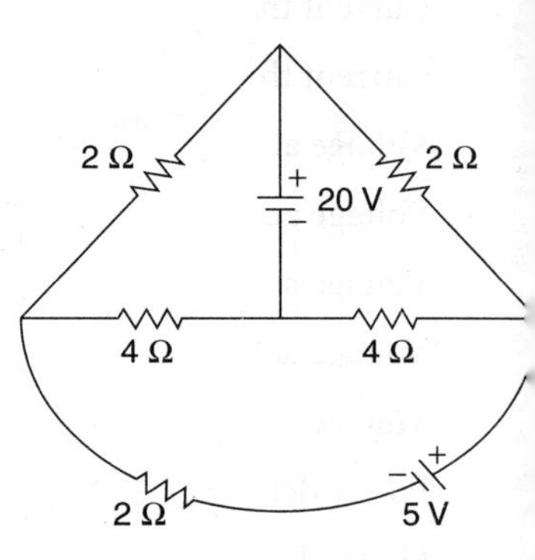

Solution: The given circuit can be redrawn as

By inspection of mesh analysis

$$\begin{bmatrix} 6 & 0 & -4 \\ 0 & 6 & -4 \\ -4 & -4 & 10 \end{bmatrix}\begin{bmatrix} I_1 \\ I_2 \\ I_3 \end{bmatrix} = \begin{bmatrix} -20 \\ 20 \\ -5 \end{bmatrix}$$

$$\Delta = \begin{vmatrix} 6 & 0 & -4 \\ 0 & 6 & -4 \\ -4 & -4 & 10 \end{vmatrix} = 6(60-16) + (0) - 4(0+24) = 168$$

$$\Delta_1 = \begin{vmatrix} -20 & 0 & -4 \\ 20 & 6 & -4 \\ -5 & -4 & 10 \end{vmatrix} = -20(60-16) + (0) - 4(-80+30) = -680$$

$$\Delta_2 = \begin{vmatrix} 6 & -20 & -4 \\ 0 & 20 & -4 \\ -4 & -5 & 10 \end{vmatrix} = 6(200-20) + (0) - 4(80+80) = 440$$

$$\Delta_3 = \begin{vmatrix} 6 & 0 & -20 \\ 0 & 6 & 20 \\ -4 & -4 & -5 \end{vmatrix} = 6(-30+80) + (0) - 20(0+24) = -180$$

$$I_1 = \frac{\Delta_1}{\Delta} = \frac{-680}{168} = -4.05 \text{ A}$$

$$I_2 = \frac{\Delta_2}{\Delta} = \frac{440}{168} = 2.62 \text{ A}$$

$$I_3 = \frac{\Delta_3}{\Delta} = \frac{-180}{168} = -1.07 \text{ A}$$

That is, we have to change the directions of the currents I_1 and I_3

Current through AB = I_1 = 4.05 A

Current through AD = I_2 = 2.62

Current through BC = $I_1 - I_3$ = 4.05 – 1.07 = 2.98 A

Current through CD = $I_2 + I_3$ = 2.62 + 1.07 = 3.69 A

Current through BD = I_3 = 1.07 A

Current through AC = $I_1 + I_2$ = 4.05 + 2.62 = 6.67 A

Voltage across AB = 8.0952 V

Voltage across AD = 5.238 V

Voltage across BC = 11.9048 V

Voltage across CD = 14.7616 V

Voltage across BFD = 2.428 V

Power delivered by the sources = 20 × 6.67 + 5 × 1.07 = 138.7 W

Power dissipated in the resistors

$$= 2(4.05^2 + 2.62^2 + 1.07^2) + 4(2.976^2 + 3.69^2)$$

$$= 48.7802 + 89.9072 = 139.7 \text{ W}$$

Power delivered by the sources is equal to the power dissipated in the resistors. Hence, Tellegen's theorem is verified.

7.17 In the circuit, if the 4 Ω resistance changes to 6 Ω, then calculate the change in current (i) by direct computation, (ii) by compensation theorem.

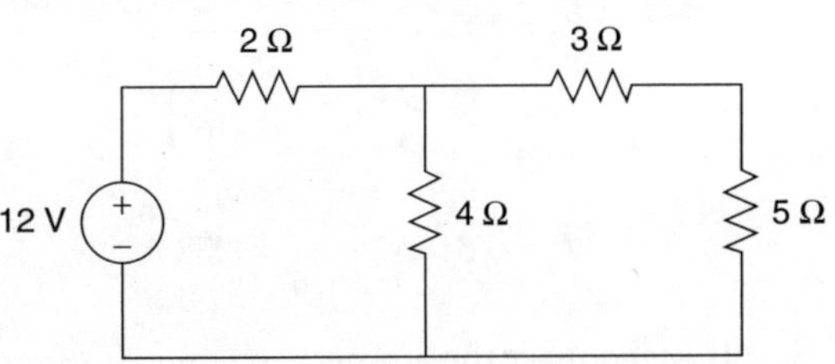

Solution:

(i) By direct computation

$$\text{Total current, } I_1 = \frac{12}{2 + \dfrac{4 \times 8}{4 + 8}} = \frac{12}{2 + 2.667} = 2.57 \text{ A}$$

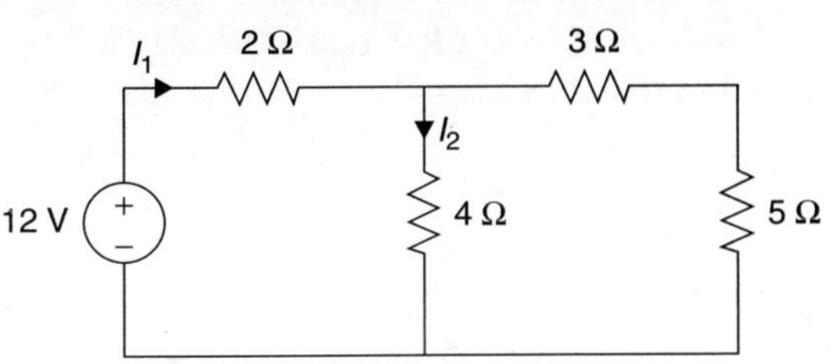

Current through the 4 Ω resistance

$$I_2 = I_1 \times \frac{8}{8+4} = 2.57 \times \frac{8}{12} = 1.7146 \text{ A}$$

When the 4 Ω resistance is changed to 6 Ω, the circuit is shown below:

$$I_1' = \frac{12}{2 + \dfrac{6 \times 8}{6 + 8}} = \frac{12}{2 + 3.428} = 2.21 \text{ A}$$

Current through the 6 Ω resistance

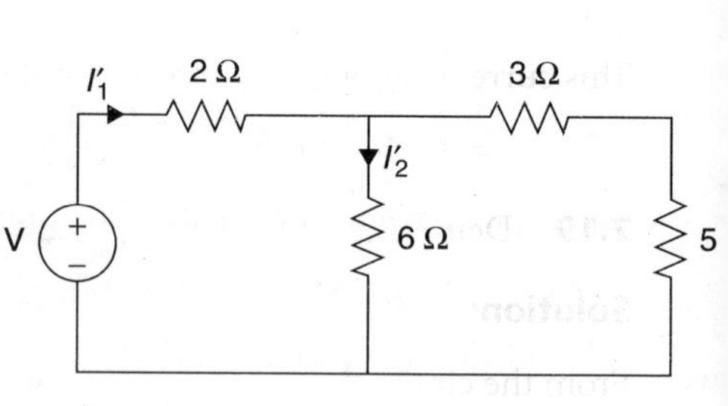

$$I'_2 = I'_1 \times \frac{8}{8+6} = 2.21 \times \frac{8}{14} = 1.263 \text{ A}$$

$\therefore$ Change in current, $\Delta I = I'_2 - I_2 = 1.263 - 1.7143 = -0.451$ A

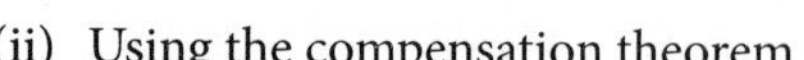

(ii) Using the compensation theorem

Compensation voltage, $V_C = I_2 \Delta R = 1.7143 \times (6-4) = 3.4286$ V

The compensation voltage source and the new circuit are as shown below:

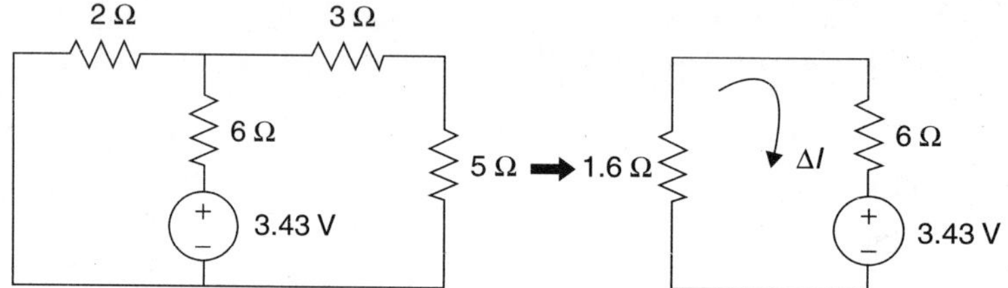

$$\Delta I = \frac{-3.43}{1.6+6} = \frac{-3.43}{7.6} = -0.451 \text{ A}$$

7.18 Using the compensation theorem, determine the ammeter reading where it is connected to the 6 Ω resistor as shown. The internal resistance of the ammeter is 2 Ω.

Solution:

$$I_5 = 20 \times \frac{3}{3 + \left(5 + \frac{2\times 6}{2+6}\right)} = \frac{60}{3+5+1.5} = \frac{60}{9.5} = 6.315 \text{ A}$$

$$I_6 = 6.315 \times \frac{2}{2+6} = 1.58 \text{ A}$$

If we connect the ammeter having 2 Ω internal resistance to the 6 Ω branch, there is a change in resistance. The changes in current in other branches results if a voltage source of voltage $V_C = I_6 \, \Delta R = 1.58 \times 2 = 3.16$ V is inserted in the 6 Ω branch as shown.

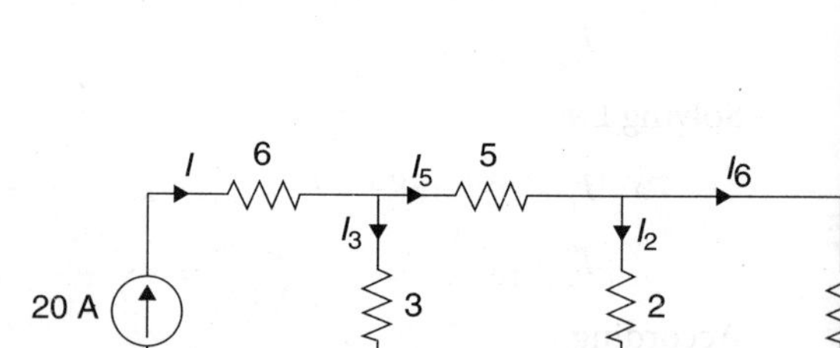

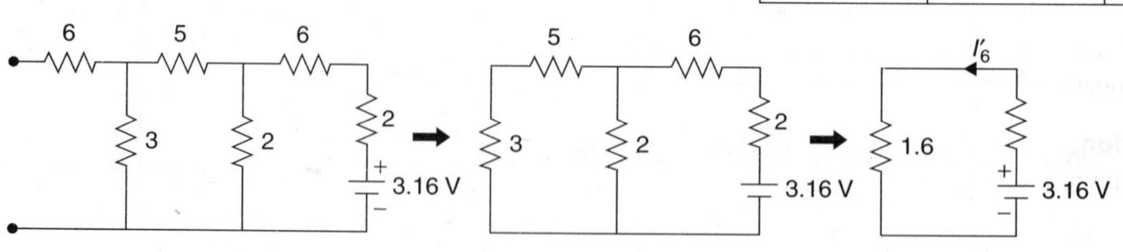

$$I'_6 = \frac{3.16}{8+1.6} = 0.33 \text{ A}$$

This current is opposite to the current I_6 in the 6 Ω branch. Hence, the ammeter reading

$$= 1.58 - 0.33 = 1.251 \text{ A}$$

7.19 Determine the current through the 10 Ω resistor using the superposition theorem.

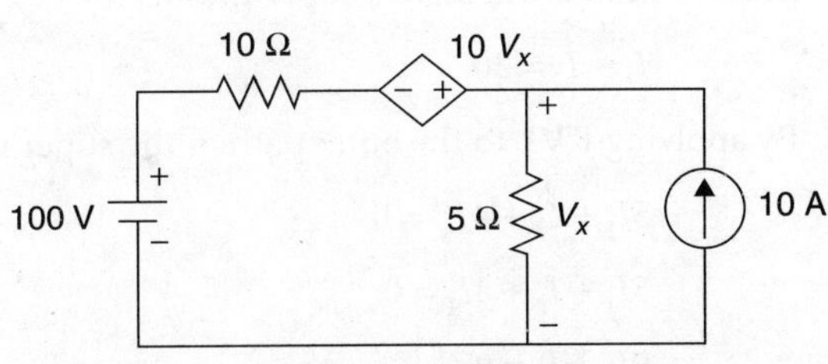

Solution: When a voltage source of 100 V acts alone.

From the circuit, $V_x = 5I'$ (1)

Applying KVL to the circuit, we have

$$100 - 10I' + 10V_x - 5I' = 0$$

$$100 - 15I' + 10V_x = 0 \quad (2)$$

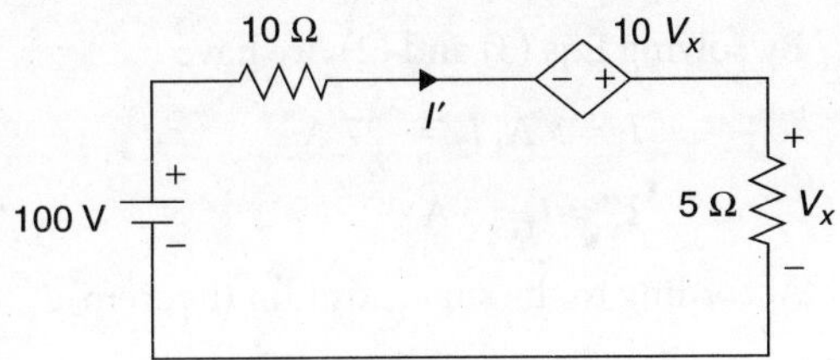

From Eqs (1) and (2)

$$100 - 15I' + 10 \times 5I' = 0$$

$$\Rightarrow \quad 35I' = -100$$

$$\Rightarrow \quad I' = -2.86 \text{ A}$$

When a current source of 10 A acts alone.

From the circuit, $V_x = 5\,(I_1 - I_2)$ (3)

Applying KVL to loop 1, we have

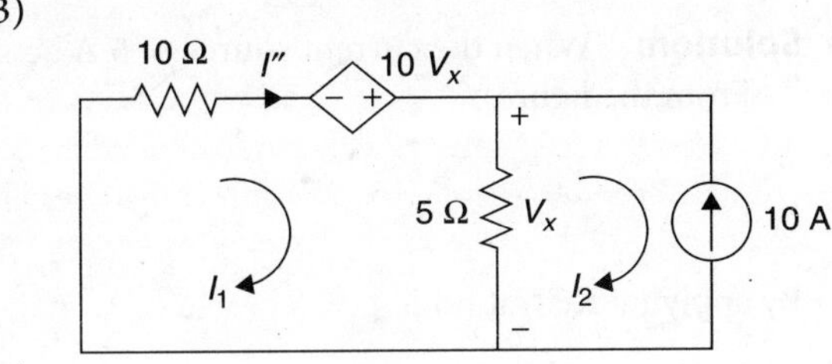

$$-10I_1 + 10V_x - 5\,(I_1 - I_2) = 0$$

$$-15I_1 + 50(I_1 - I_2) + 5I_2 = 0$$

$$35I_1 - 45I_2 = 0$$

$$7I_1 - 9I_2 = 0 \quad (4)$$

From loop 2, we have

$$I_2 = -10 \quad (5)$$

Solving Eqs (4) and (5), we have

$$I_1 = -12.86,\ I_2 = -10$$

$$I'' = I_1 = -12.86 \text{ A}$$

According to the superposition theorem,

$$I = I' + I'' = -2.86 - 12.86 = -15.72 \text{ A}$$

7.20 Find the current through the 10 Ω resistor using the superposition theorem.

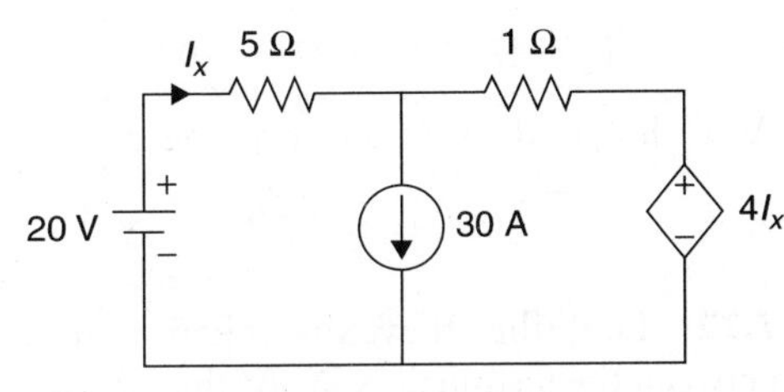

Solution: When a voltage source of 20 V is acting alone:
Applying KVL to the circuit

$$20 - 5I'_x - 1I'_x - 4I'_x = 0$$

$$20 - 10I'_x = 0$$

$$\Rightarrow \quad I'_x = 2 \text{ A}$$

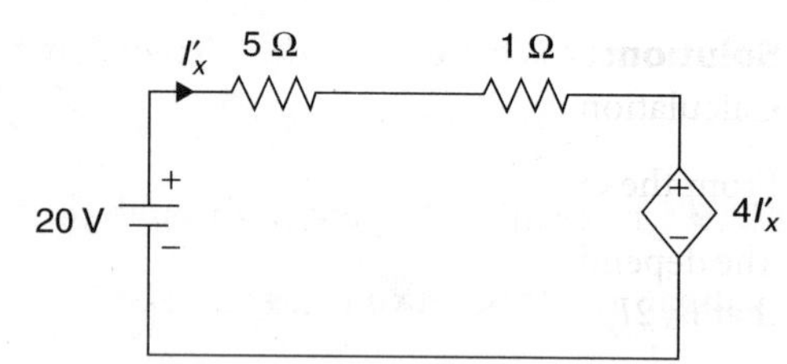

When a current source of 30 A is acting alone:

From the circuit diagram

$$I''_x = I_1 \qquad (1)$$

Meshes 1and 2 will form a super mesh, so

$$I_1 - I_2 = 30 \qquad (2)$$

By applying KVL to the outer path of the super mesh

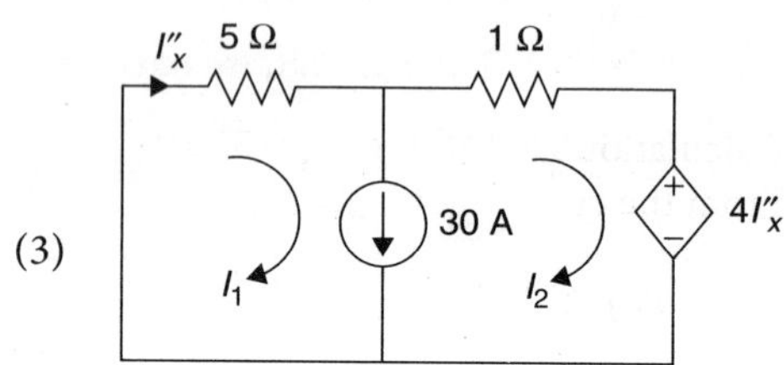

$$5I_1 + I_2 + 4I''_x = 0$$

$$5I_1 + I_2 + 4I_1 = 0$$

$$9I_1 + I_2 = 0 \qquad (3)$$

By solving Eqs (3) and (2), we have

$$I_1 = 3 \text{ A}, I_2 = -27 \text{ A}$$

$$I''_x = I_1 = 3 \text{ A}$$

According to the superposition theorem, $I_x = I'_x + I''_x = 2 + 3 = 5$ A

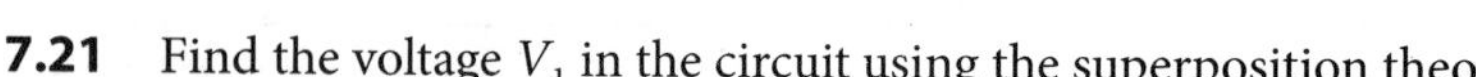

7.21 Find the voltage V_1 in the circuit using the superposition theorem.

Solution: When the current source of 5 A acts alone.

From the figure,

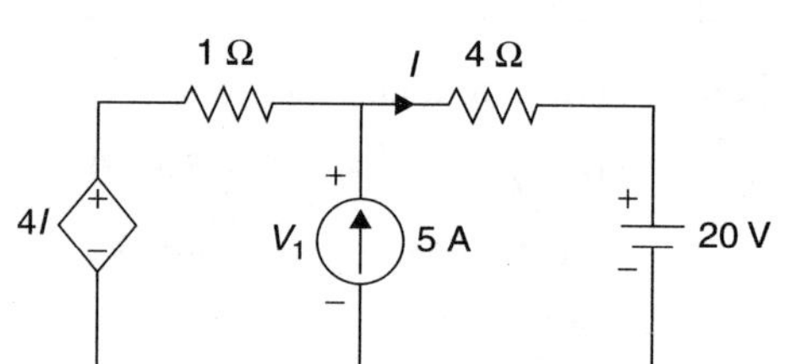

$$I = \frac{V'_1}{4}$$

By applying KCL at node 1

$$5 = \frac{V'_1 - 4I}{1} + \frac{V'_1}{4}$$

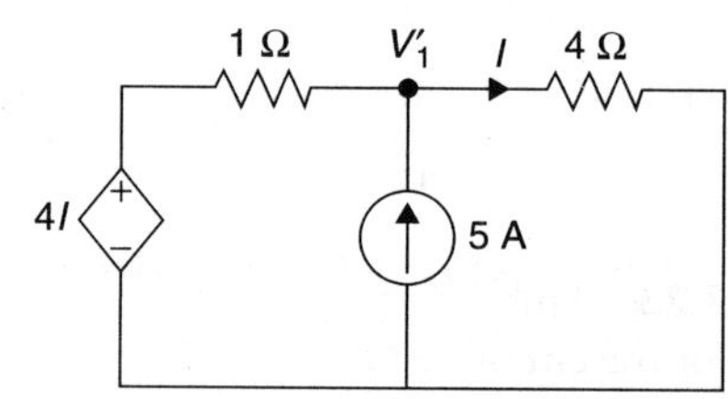

$$5 = \frac{V'_1 - V'_1}{1} + \frac{V'_1}{4}$$

$$\Rightarrow \qquad V'_1 = 20 \text{ V}$$

When the voltage source of 20 V acts alone.

By applying KVL to the circuit

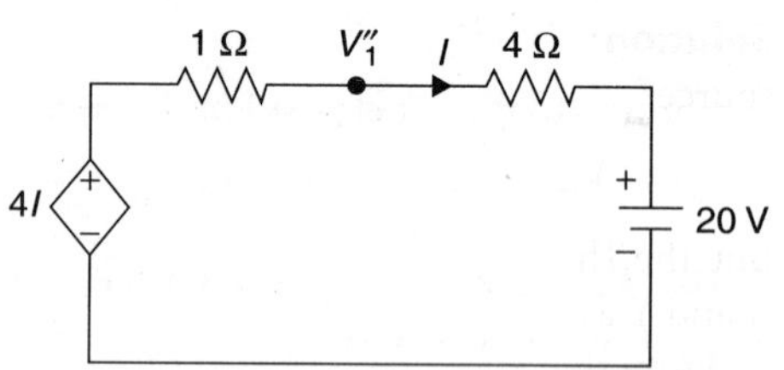

$$4I - I - 4I - 20 = 0$$

$$\Rightarrow \qquad I = -20 \text{ A}$$

$$V''_1 = 4I - 1(I) = 3I = -60 \text{ V}$$

According to the superposition theorem,

$$V_1 = V'_1 + V''_1 = 20 - 60 = -40 \text{ V}$$

7.22 Find the Thevenin voltage and resistance between the terminals X–Y for the circuit.

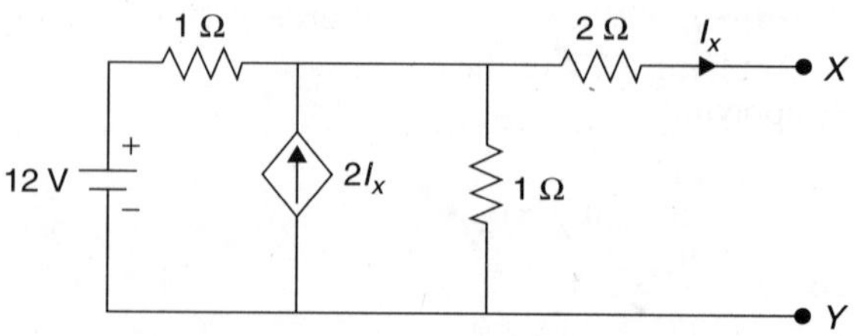

Solution:

Calculation of V_{th}

From the circuit, $I_x = 0$

The dependent source $2I_x$ depends on the controlling variable I_x. When $I_x = 0$, the dependent source vanishes, that is, $2I_x = 0$ as shown.

$$V_{th} = \frac{12}{1+1} \times 1 = 6\text{ V}$$

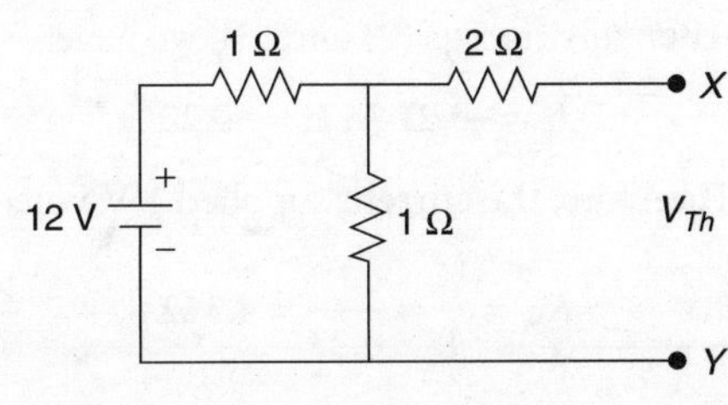

Calculation of I_N

From the circuit diagram,

$$I_x = \frac{V_1}{2}$$

By applying KCL at node 1

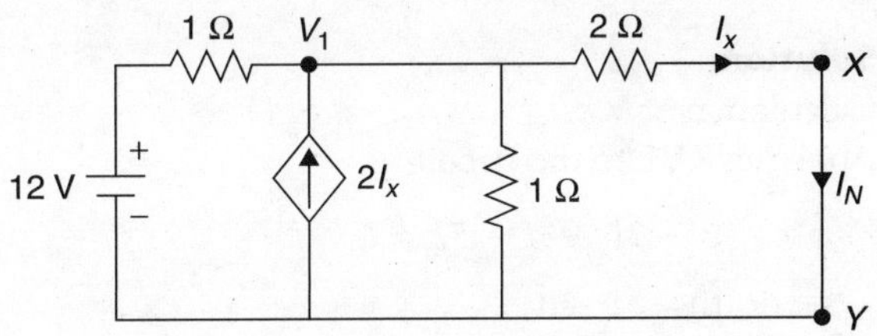

$$2I_x = \frac{V_1 - 12}{1} + \frac{V_1}{2} + \frac{V_1}{1}$$

$$2\left(\frac{V_1}{2}\right) = \frac{V_1 - 12}{1} + \frac{V_1}{2} + \frac{V_1}{1}$$

$\Rightarrow \quad V_1 = 2.5\ V_1 - 12$

$\Rightarrow \quad V_1 = 8\text{ V}$

$$I_N = I_x = \frac{V_1}{2} = 4\text{ A}$$

Calculation of R_{th}

$$R_{th} = \frac{V_{th}}{I_N} = \frac{6}{4} = 1.5\ \Omega$$

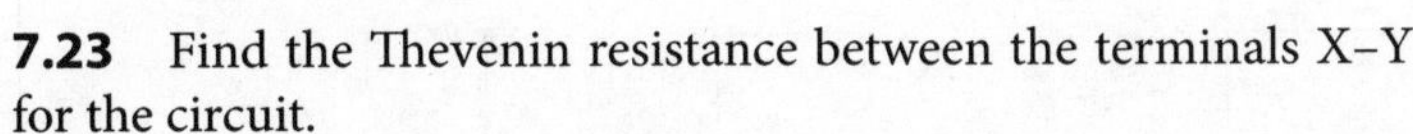

7.23 Find the Thevenin resistance between the terminals X–Y for the circuit.

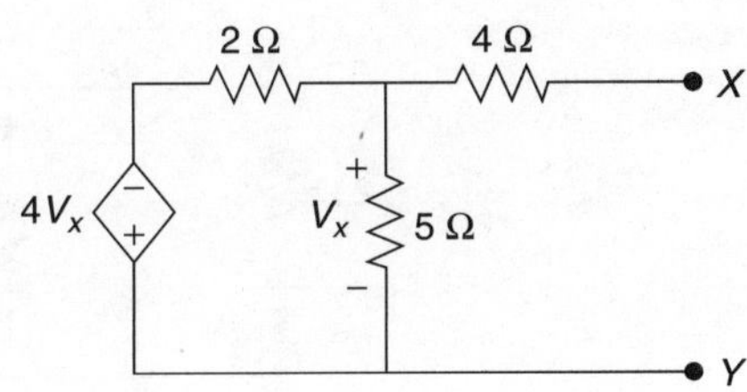

Solution: Since the network does not contain any independent source

$$V_{th} = 0,\ I_N = 0$$

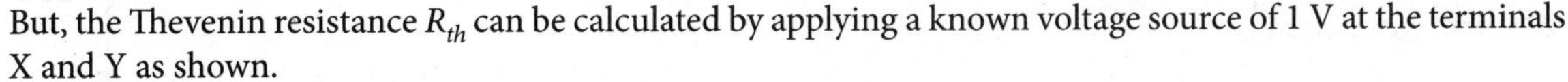

But, the Thevenin resistance R_{th} can be calculated by applying a known voltage source of 1 V at the terminals X and Y as shown.

From the circuit diagram

$$V_x = 5(I_1 - I_2) \qquad (1)$$

By applying KVL to loop 1

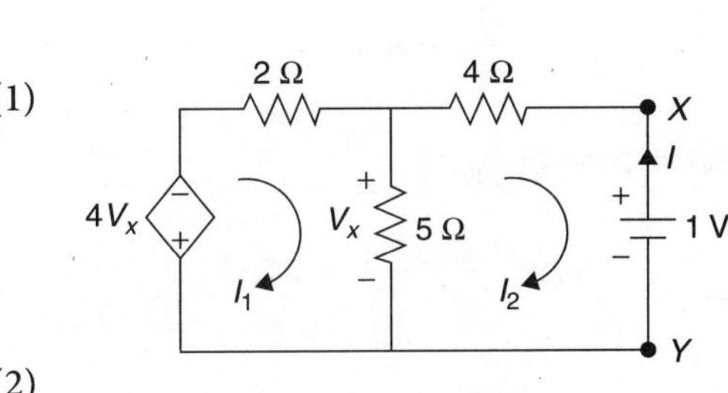

$$4V_x + 2I_1 + 5(I_1 - I_2) = 0$$

$$20(I_1 - I_2) + 2I_1 + 5(I_1 - I_2) = 0$$

$$27I_1 - 25I_2 = 0 \qquad (2)$$

By applying KVL to loop 2

$$4I_2 + 1 + 5(I_2 - I_1) = 0$$

$$-5I_1 + 9I_2 + 1 = 0$$

$$5I_1 - 9I_2 = 1 \qquad (3)$$

After solving Eqs (2) and (3), we have

$$I_1 = -0.21 \text{ A}, I_2 = -0.23 \text{ A}$$

Therefore, the current supplied 1 V voltage source is 0.23 A

$$\therefore \quad R_{th} = \frac{V}{I} = \frac{1}{0.23} = 4.3\ \Omega$$

7.24 Find the current through the 10 Ω resistor using the Norton's theorem.

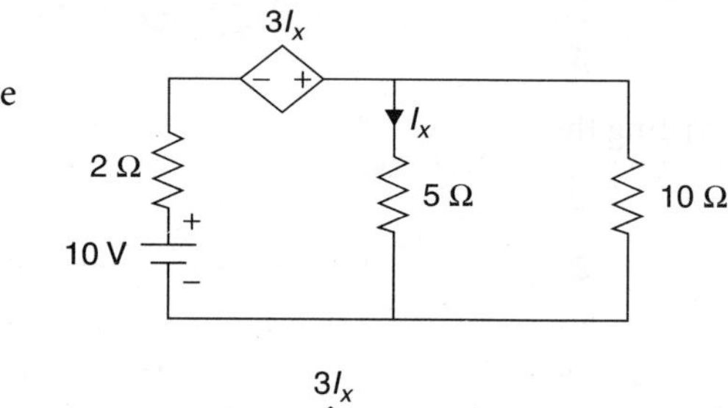

Solution:

Calculation of V_{th}

Applying KVL to the circuit

$$10 - 2I_x + 3I_x - 5I_x = 0$$

$$10 - 4I_x = 0$$

$$\Rightarrow \quad I_x = 2.5 \text{ A}$$

$$V_{th} = 5I_x = 5 \times 2.5 = 12.5 \text{ V}$$

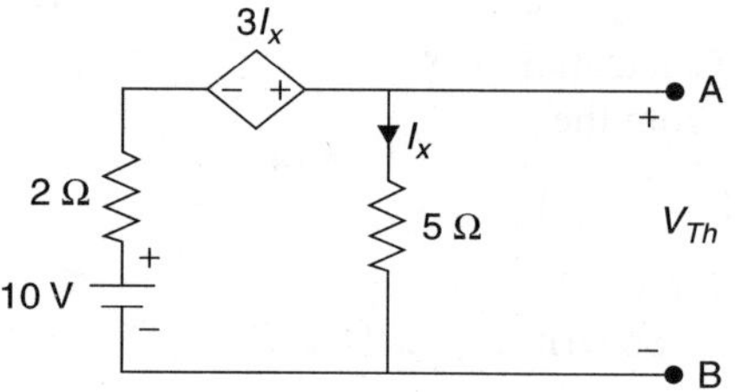

Calculation of I_N

From the figure, $I_x = 0$

The dependent source $3I_x$ depends on the controlling variable I_x. When $I_x = 0$, the dependent source vanishes, that is, $3I_x = 0$ as shown.

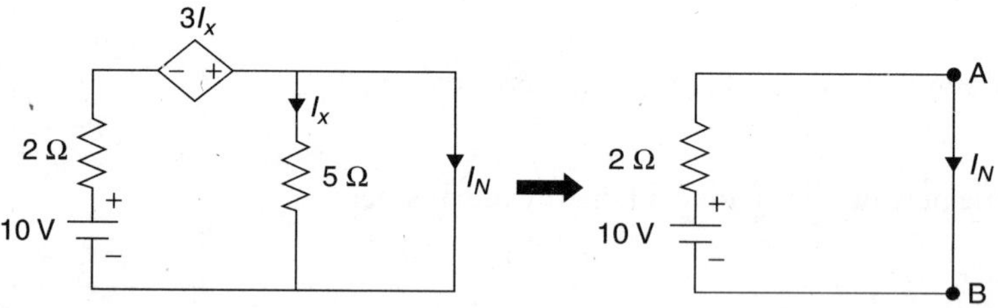

From the above circuit

$$I_N = \frac{10}{2} = 5 \text{ A}$$

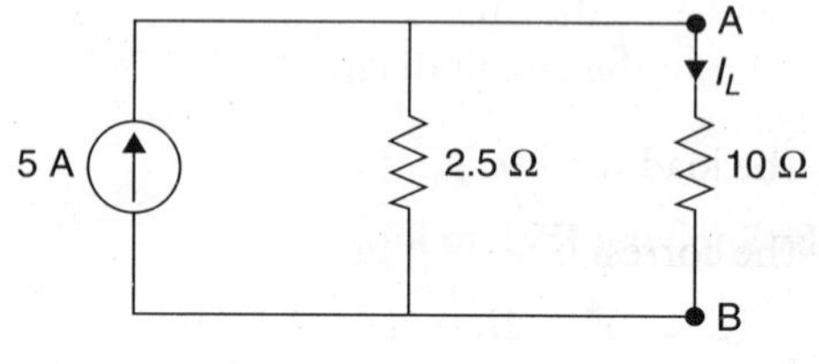

Calculation of R_{th}

$$R_{th} = \frac{V_{th}}{I_N} = \frac{12.5}{5} = 2.5\ \Omega$$

Calculation of I_L

$$I_L = I_N \times \frac{R_{th}}{R_{th} + R_L} = 5 \times \frac{2.5}{2.5 + 10} = 1\text{ A}$$

7.25 For the network, find the value of R_L for maximum power transfer. Also calculate the maximum power.

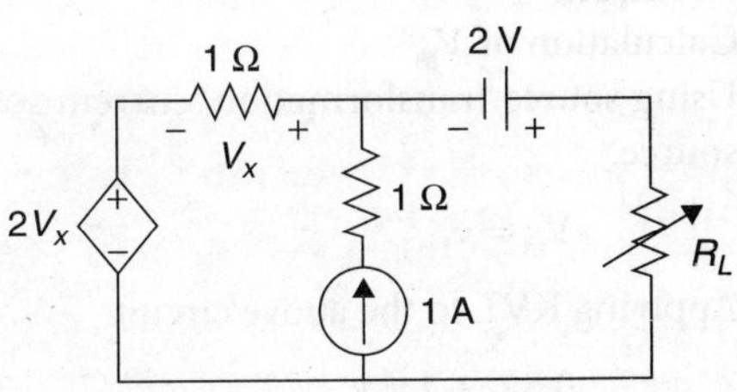

Solution:

Calculation of V_{th}

From the circuit shown below,

$$I = -1\text{ A}$$

$$V_x = -1 \times I = 1\text{ V}$$

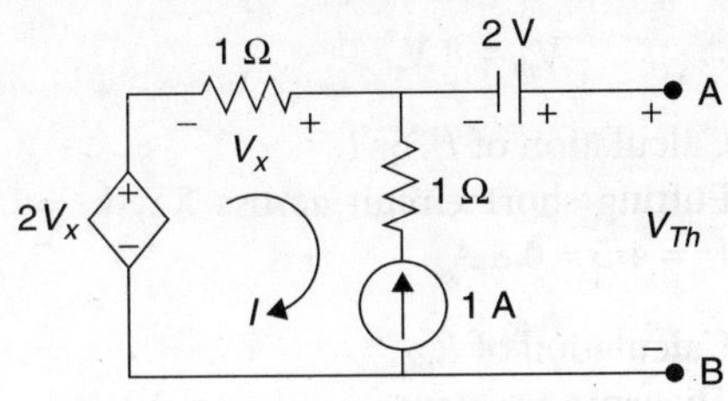

Writing the V_{th} equation

$$2V_x + V_x + 2 - V_{th} = 0$$

$$2 + 1 + 2 - V_{th} = 0$$

$$\Rightarrow \quad V_{th} = 5\text{ V}$$

Calculation of I_N

From the circuit on the right,

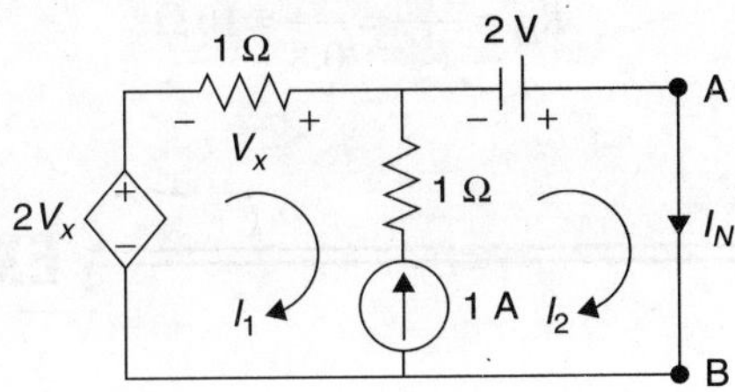

$$V_x = -1 \times I_1 = -I_1 \qquad (1)$$

Meshes 1 and 2 will form a super mesh.

So writing the current equation for super mesh, we have

$$I_2 - I_1 = 1 \qquad (2)$$

By applying KVL to the outer path of the super mesh, we have

$$2V_x + V_x + 2 = 0$$

$$3V_x + 2 = 0$$

$$-3I_1 + 2 = 0$$

$$\Rightarrow \quad I_1 = 0.67\text{ A}$$

From Eq. (2), $I_2 = 1.67$ A

$$\therefore \quad I_N = I_2 = 1.67\text{ A}$$

Calculation of R_{th}

$$R_{th} = \frac{V_{th}}{I_N} = \frac{5}{1.67} = 3\ \Omega$$

The load will receive maximum power, when $R_L = R_{th} = 3\ \Omega$

The corresponding maximum power is given by

$$P_{\max} = \frac{V_{th}^2}{4R_{th}} = \frac{5^2}{4 \times 3} = 2.08\text{ W}$$

7.26 For the circuit, find the value of the Thevenin voltage, Norton current and Thevenin resistance.

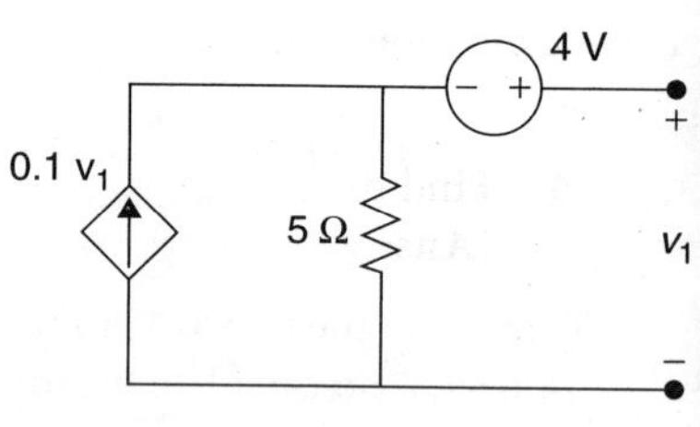

Solution:

Calculation of V_{th}

Using source transformation, current source can be converted into voltage source.

$$V_{th} = v_1$$

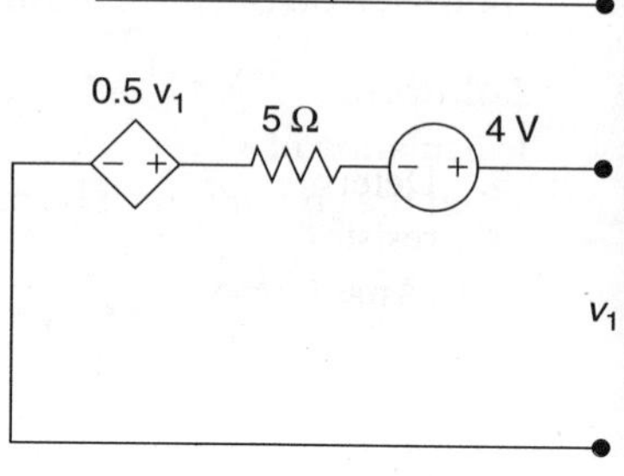

Applying KVL to the above circuit

$$0.5v_1 + 4 = v_1$$

$$\Rightarrow \quad v_1 = 8 \text{ V}$$

$$\therefore \quad V_{th} = 8 \text{ V}$$

Calculation of I_{sc} or I_N

Putting short circuit across XY, $v_1 = 0$, so dependent source 0.5 $v_1 = 0$. So the short circuit current is $I_{sc} = 4/5 = 0.8$ A.

Calculation of R_{th}

Thevenin resistance can be calculated using

$$R_{th} = \frac{V_{th}}{I_{sc}} = \frac{8}{0.8} = 10\,\Omega$$

EXERCISE PROBLEMS

1. For the resistive network, find the current in each resistor using the superposition theorem. [**Ans:** $I_{3\,\Omega} = 5.26$ A, $I_{10\,\Omega} = 3.41$ A, $I_{5\,\Omega} = 1.84$ A]

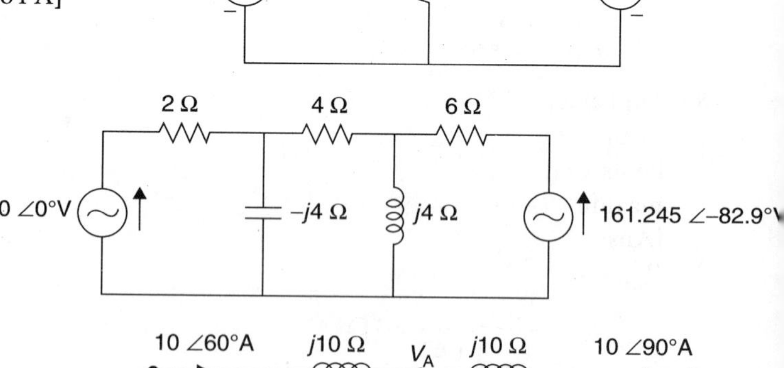

2. Find the current through the 4 Ω resistor using the superposition theorem. [**Ans:** $I_{4\,\Omega} = 0$ A]

3. Find the V_A in the circuit using the superposition theorem. [**Ans:** $V_A = 61.16\angle 56.56°$ V]

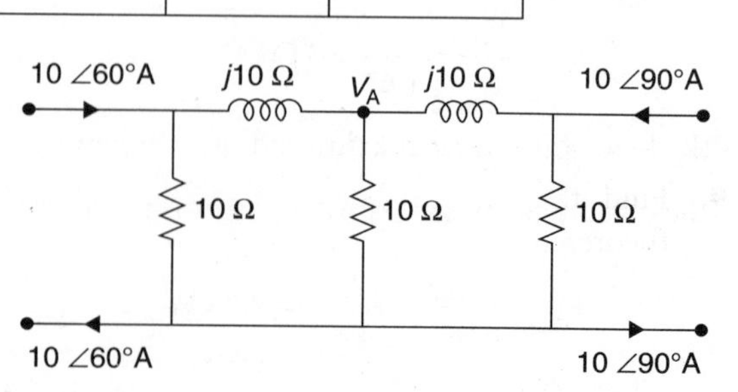

4. Find the Thevenin's equivalent circuit for the circuit. [**Ans:** $V_{th} = 25$ V, $R_{th} = 6.75$ Ω]

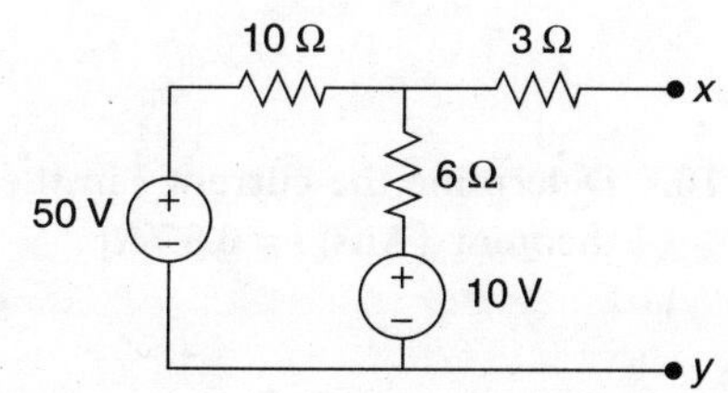

5. Determine the current flowing through the 5 Ω resistor in the circuit as using Norton's theorem. [**Ans:** $I_{sc} = 30$ A, $R_{th} = 1.67$ Ω, $I_{5\,\Omega} = 7.51$ A]

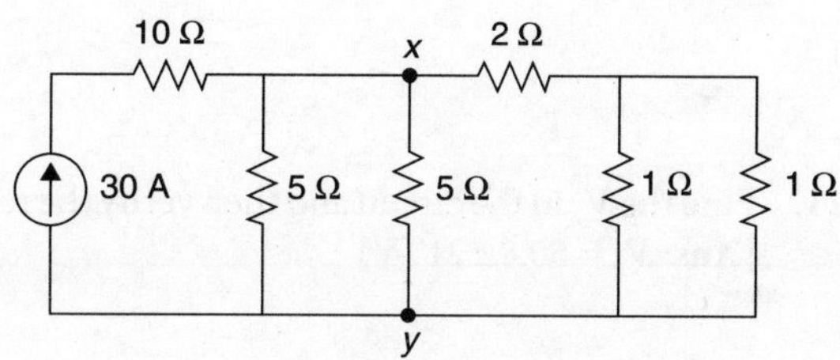

6. Find the current through the 10 Ω resistance in the circuit using Thevenin's theorem. [**Ans:** $V_{th} = 47.23$ V, $R_{th} = 3.14$ Ω, $I_{10\,\Omega} =$ 3.594 A]

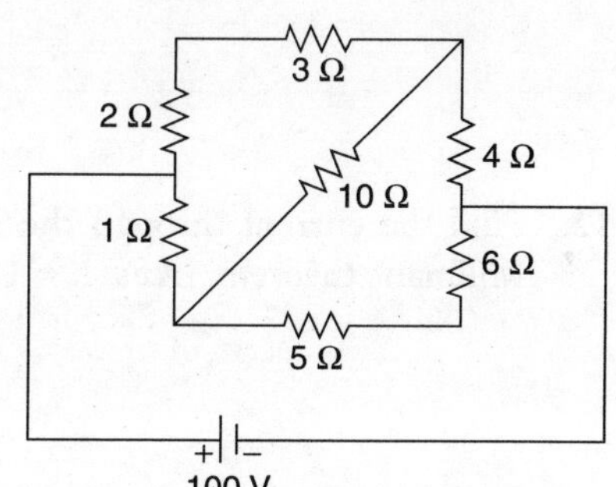

7. Using Norton's theorem, find the current through the load impedance Z_L for the network. [**Ans:** $I_L = 7.44\angle 44.1°$A]

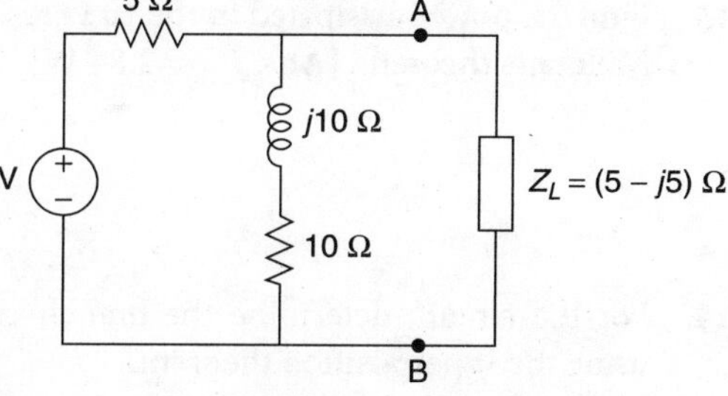

8. Find the load impedance for maximum power transfer in the network. If the load is purely resistive, what will be its value for maximum power transfer? Also, find the maximum power taken by the load in both cases. [**Ans:** (i) $Z_L = (3 - j1)$ Ω, $P_{max} = 0.67$ W, (ii) $R_L = 3.162$ Ω, $P_{max} = 0.6323$ W]

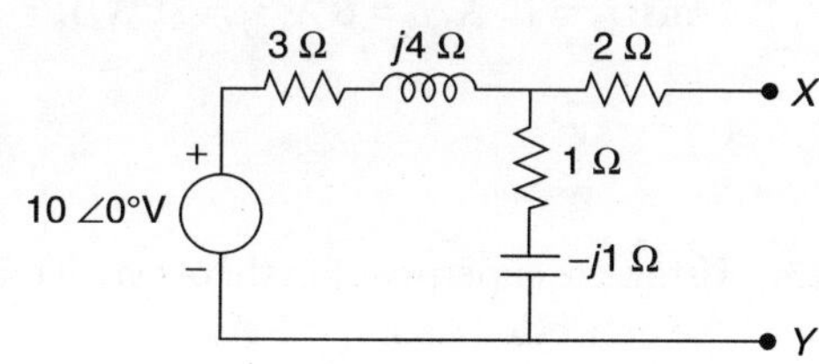

9. Find the voltage across AB by using the superposition theorem. [**Ans:** $V_{AB} = 8.235$ V]

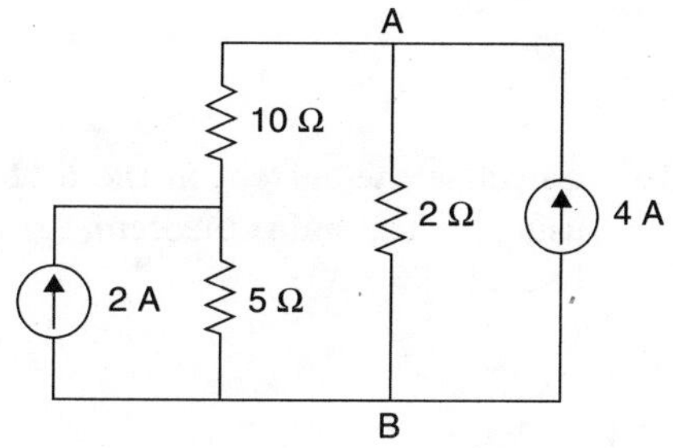

10. Determine the current I in the network by using Thevenin's theorem. [**Ans:** $I = 0.87$ A]

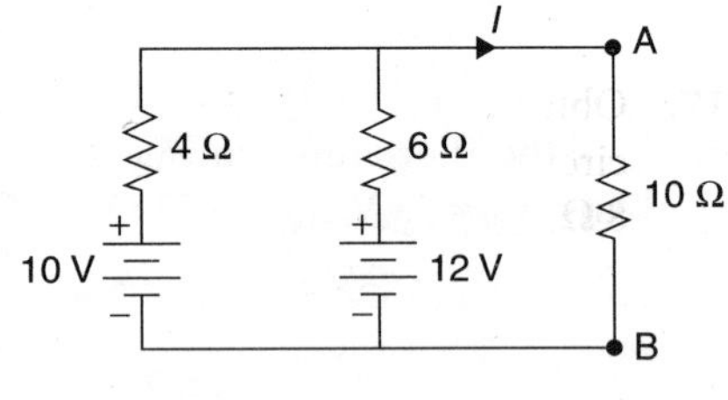

11. Find the V_x in the circuit and then verify the reciprocity theorem. [**Ans:** $V_x = 50.8\angle 21°$ V]

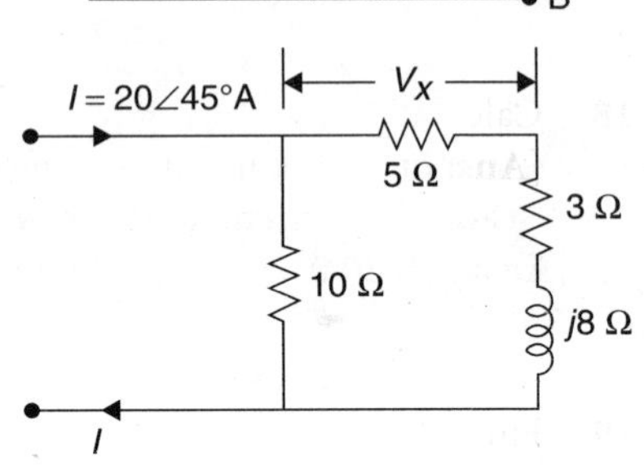

12. Find the current through the 10 Ω resistor using Millman's theorem. [**Ans:** $I_L = 1.41$ A]

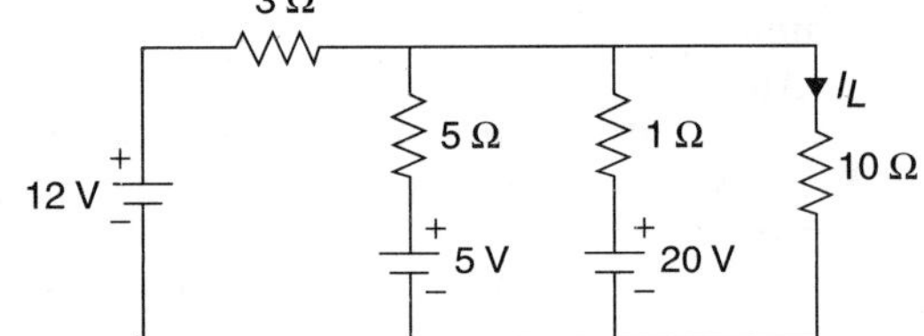

13. Find the power dissipated in the 10 Ω resistor using Millman's theorem. [**Ans:** $P_{10} = 2.84$ W]

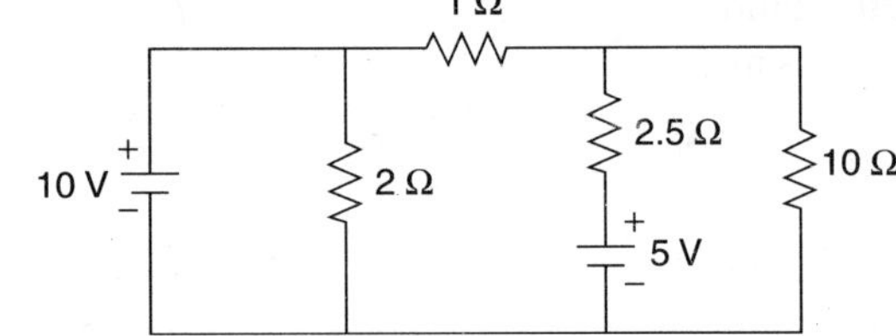

14. For the circuit, determine the branch currents using the superposition theorem. [**Ans:** $i_1 = 17$ A, $i_2 = 6$ A, $i_3 = 11$ A, $i_4 = -1$ A]

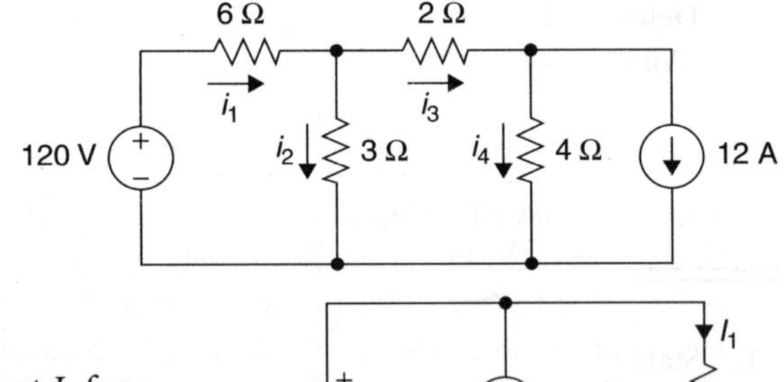

15. Using the superposition theorem, determine current I_1 for the network. [**Ans:** $I_1 = 5$ A]

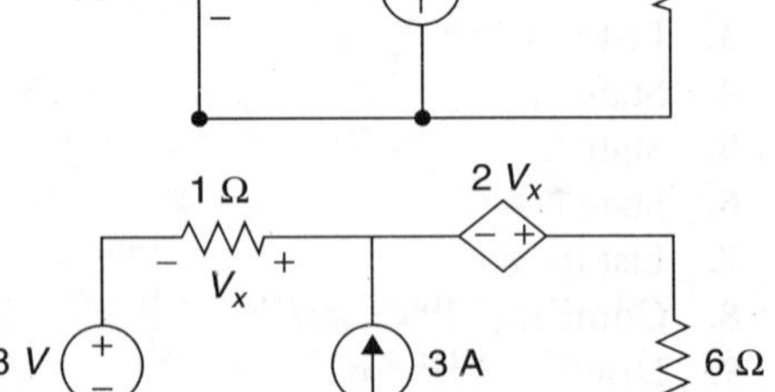

16. Calculate the current in the 6 Ω resistor for the circuit using (a) Thevenin's theorem, (b) superposition theorem. [**Ans:** $I_{6\,\Omega} = 3$ A]

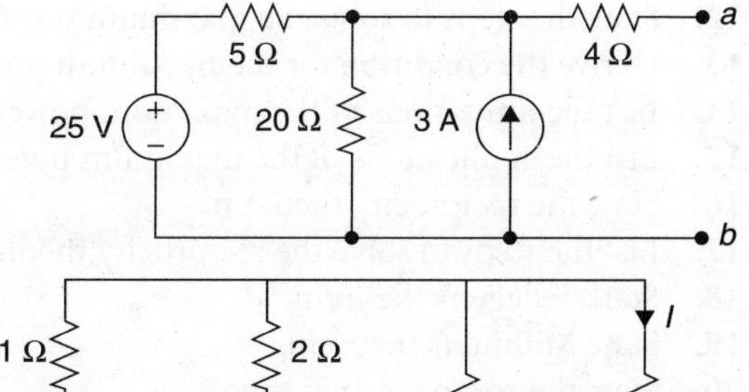

17. Obtain the Thevenin and Norton equivalent circuits for the circuit. [**Ans:** 32 V in series with 8 Ω, 4 A in parallel with 8 Ω]

18. Calculate the load current I by Millman's theorem. [**Ans:** I = 0.129 A]

19. Find the value of Z_L to have maximum power transfer from the 10∠0°V voltage source. Also determine the amount of maximum power. [**Ans:** $Z_L = (0.72 - j5.46)\ \Omega$, $P_{max} = 25.32$ W]

20. Find the value of R_L such that the power transferred to R_L is maximum. [**Ans:** $R_L = 15\ \Omega$]

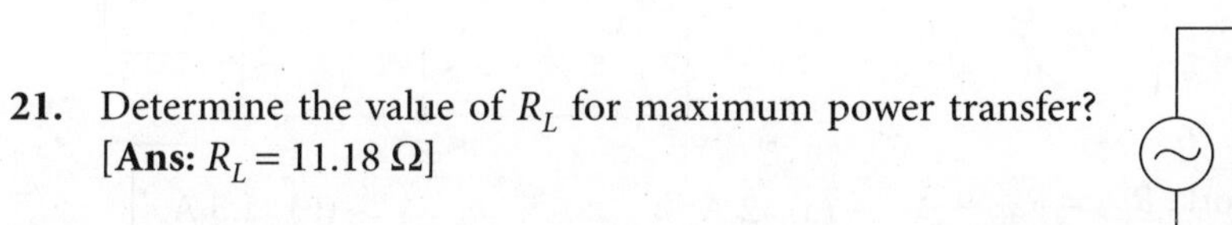

21. Determine the value of R_L for maximum power transfer? [**Ans:** $R_L = 11.18\ \Omega$]

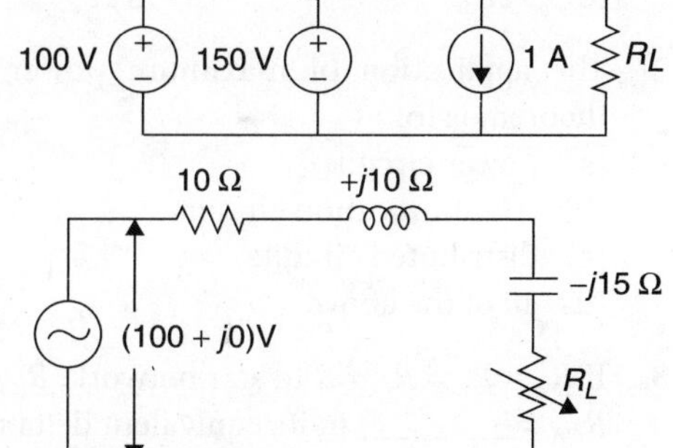

REVIEW QUESTIONS

1. State the superposition theorem.
2. State the steps to solve the superposition theorem.
3. List the limitations of the superposition theorem.
4. State Thevenin's theorem.
5. State the steps to solve Thevenin's theorem.
6. State Norton's theorem.
7. List the steps to solve Norton's theorem.
8. Compare Thevenin's and Norton's theorems.
9. Draw the Thevenin's and Norton's equivalent circuits.
10. State maximum power transfer theorem for an AC network.
11. State and explain maximum power transfer theorem for a variable pure resistive load.

12. State the steps to solve the maximum power transfer theorem.
13. Derive the condition for the maximum power transfer theorem.
14. List the limitations of the maximum power transfer theorem.
15. List the applications of the maximum power transfer theorem.
16. State the reciprocity theorem.
17. List the steps to solve the reciprocity theorem.
18. State Tellegen's theorem.
19. State Millman's theorem.
20. State the compensation theorem.

MULTIPLE CHOICE QUESTIONS

1. For the network, Thevenin's impedance between terminals A and B is:

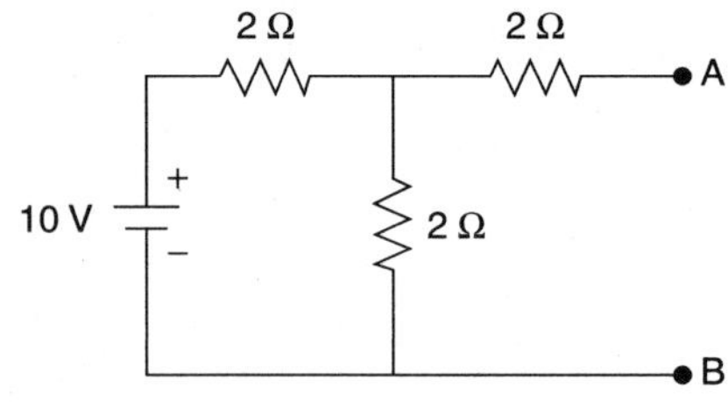

(a) 4 Ω (b) 2 Ω
(c) 3 Ω (d) 6 Ω

2. The application of maximum power transfer theorem is to:
(a) power circuits
(b) communication circuits
(c) distributed circuits
(d) all of the above

3. If $R_A = R_B = R_C = R$ in star network, $R_{AB} = R_{BC} = R_{CA} =$ ________ in its equivalent delta network.
(a) $R/3$ (b) $3R$
(c) R (d) $2R/3$

4. Superposition theorem is not valid for
(a) current responses (b) voltage responses
(c) linear responses (d) power responses

5. Thevenin's voltage between terminal A and B will be:

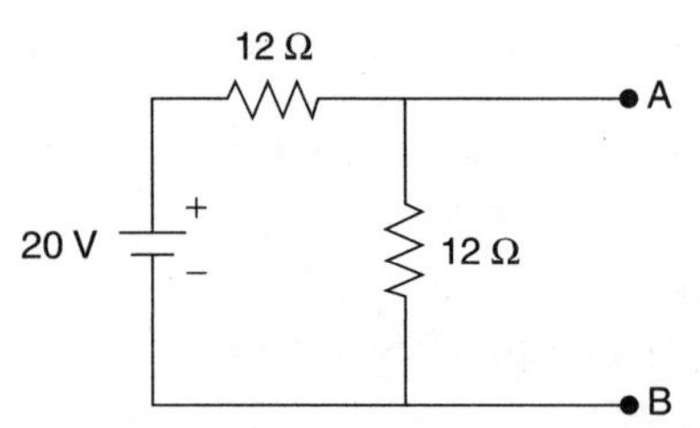

(a) 10 V (b) 20 V
(c) 5 V (d) 24 V

6. Maximum power is transferred where load resistance is
(a) equal to source resistance
(b) equal to zero
(c) equal to half of the source resistance
(d) equal to source conductance

7. The current through AB due to a 10 V voltage source only for the network is

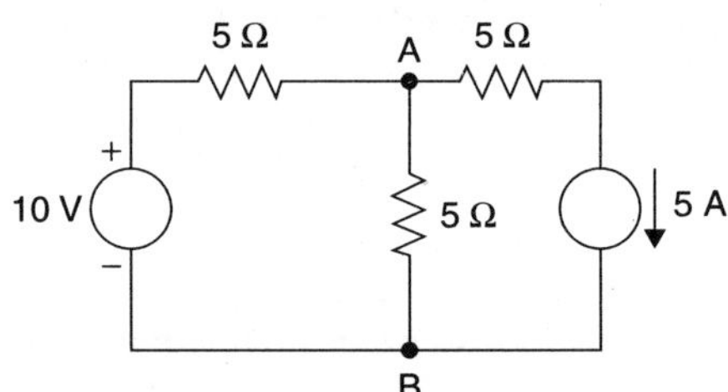

(a) 2 A (b) 1.5 A
(c) 1 A (d) 2.5 A

8. In any lumped network with elements in b branches, $\sum_{k=1}^{b} v_k(t)\, i_k(t) = 0$ for all t, holds good according to:
(a) Norton's theorem
(b) Thevenin's theorem
(c) Millman's theorem
(d) Tellegen's theorem

9. When a source is delivering maximum power to a load, the efficiency of the circuit is
(a) dependent on the circuit parameters
(b) always 75%
(c) always 50% or lower
(d) equals 60%

10. Determine the current I in the circuit.

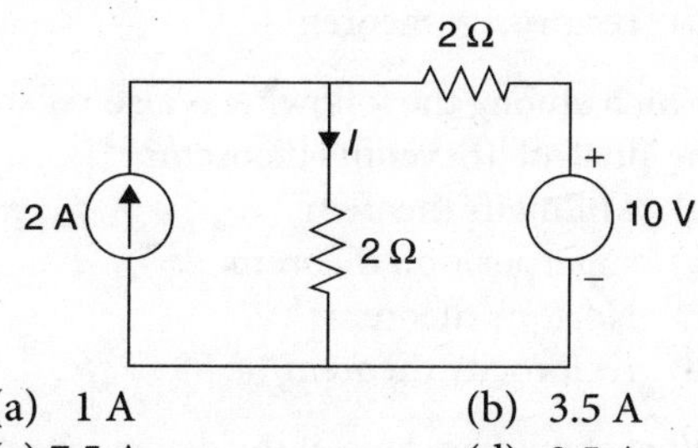

(a) 1 A (b) 3.5 A
(c) 7.5 A (d) 2.5 A

11. The Thevenin's voltage between the terminal A and B in the network is:

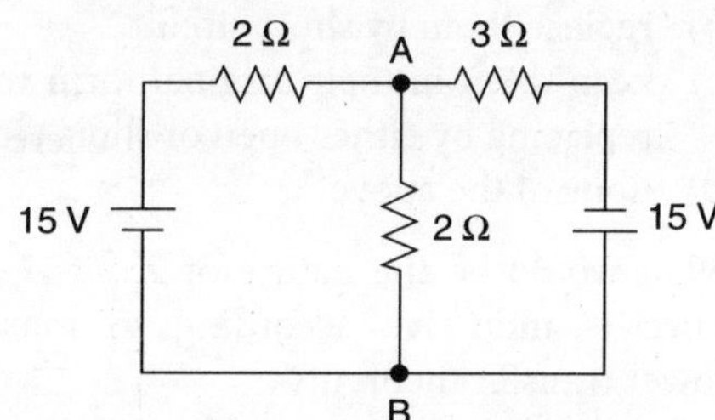

(a) 7.5 V (b) zero
(c) 30 V (d) 15 V

12. In the circuit, what is the maximum power transferred to the load?

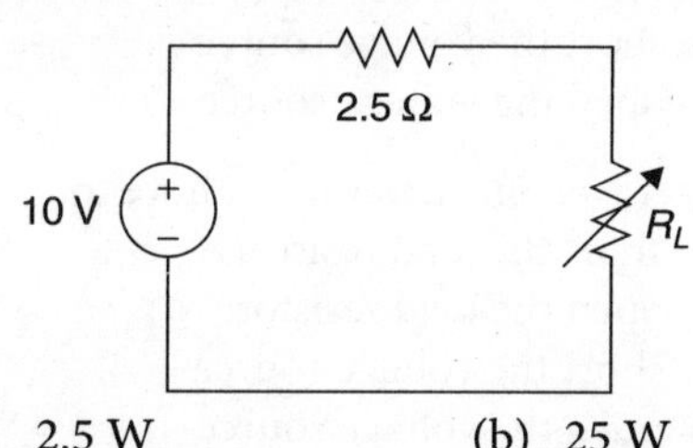

(a) 2.5 W (b) 25 W
(c) 10 W (d) 5 W

13. Under the condition of maximum power transfer for the load, the voltage across load and efficiency are __________ and __________ respectively.
(a) 50% and 25% (b) 100% and 50%
(c) 50% and 50% (d) 50% and 100%

14. Superposition theorem is valid only for
(a) linear circuits (b) passive circuits
(c) non-linear circuits (d) active circuits

15. Under the conditions of maximum power transfer, a voltage source is delivering a power of 30 W to the load. The power produced by the source is __________
(a) 45 W (b) 60 W
(c) 30 W (d) 90 W

16. Norton's theorem is the dual of
(a) Thevenin's theorem
(b) superposition theorem
(c) reciprocity theorem
(d) Millman's theorem

17. In a circuit $V_{th} = 20$ V, $R_{th} = 4\ \Omega$ and $R_L = 6\ \Omega$. The value of load current is
(a) 4 A (b) 6 A
(c) 5 A (d) 2 A

18. In the Thevenin's equivalent network, V_{th} is
(a) short circuit terminal voltage
(b) open circuit terminal voltage
(c) total voltage in the circuit
(d) source voltage

19. The Norton resistance of a network is 20 Ω and the shorted-load current is 2 A. If the network is loaded by a resistance equal to 20 Ω, the current through the load will be __________
(a) 2 A (b) 0.5 A
(c) 4 A (d) 1 A

20. If $R_A = R_B = R_C = R$ in star network, $R_{AB} = R_{BC} = R_{CA} =$ __________, in its equivalent delta network.
(a) $R/3$ (b) $3R$
(c) R (d) $2R/3$

21. An independent voltage source in series with an impedance $Z_S = R + jX$, delivers maximum power to a load impedance Z_L, when
(a) $Z_L = R + jX$ (b) $Z_L = R - jX$
(c) $Z_L = R$ (d) $Z_L = jX$

22. The superposition theorem cannot be applied to circuits containing
(a) non-linear elements
(b) dependent voltage sources
(c) dependent current sources
(d) transformers

23. If all the elements in a particular network are linear, then the superposition theorem would hold, when the excitation is
(a) DC only
(b) AC only
(c) either AC or DC
(d) none of the above

24. In a linear circuit, the superposition theorem can be applied to calculate
(a) voltage and power
(b) voltage and current
(c) current and power
(d) voltage, current and power

25. The open-circuited voltage at the terminals of load R_L in a network is 30 V. Under the conditions of maximum power transfer, the load voltage will be ________
(a) 30 V (b) 10 V
(c) 5 V (d) 15 V

26. Superposition theorem can be applied only to circuits having
(a) resistive elements
(b) passive elements
(c) non-linear elements
(d) linear bilateral elements

27. In a 3-phase, 3-wire system if a unbalanced load is present, then for analysis, the following theorem is needed
(a) Millman's theorem
(b) superposition theorem
(c) Norton's theorem
(d) none of the above

28. In any linear bilateral network, if a source of emf E in any branch produces a current I in any other branch, then the same emf acting in the second branch would produce the same current in the first branch. The above statement is associated with
(a) Millman's theorem
(b) superposition theorem
(c) Norton's theorem
(d) reciprocity theorem

29. Which among the following is also regarded as the 'dual' of Thevenin's theorem?
(a) Millman's theorem
(b) superposition theorem
(c) Norton's theorem
(d) reciprocity theorem

30. What should be done, if the dependent current and voltage sources are present in a circuit while applying the superposition theorem?
(a) replace them by open circuit
(b) replace them by short circuit
(c) keep them in their original form without replacing by either open or short circuits
(d) none of the above

31. What would be the nature of Z_L, if Z_{eq} reactance is inductive according to maximum power transfer theorem?
(a) inductive (b) capacitive
(c) resistive (d) all of the above

32. To get Thevenin voltage, you have to:
(a) short the load resistor
(b) open the load resistor
(c) short the voltage source
(d) open the voltage source

33. To get Norton current, you have to:
(a) short the load resistor
(b) open the load resistor
(c) short the voltage source
(d) open the voltage source

Answers

1. c	**2.** d	**3.** b	**4.** d	**5.** a	**6.** a	**7.** c	**8.** d	**9.** c	**10.** b
11. b	**12.** c	**13.** c	**14.** a	**15.** b	**16.** a	**17.** d	**18.** b	**19.** d	**20.** b
21. b	**22.** a	**23.** c	**24.** b	**25.** d	**26.** d	**27.** a	**28.** d	**29.** c	**30.** c
31. b	**32.** b	**33.** a							

8 Network Topology

Learning Outcomes

After reading this chapter, the reader will able to

- ➢ Define graph, tree, co-tree, fundamental tie-set and fundamental cut-set
- ➢ Illustrate graph, tree and co-tree for a given network
- ➢ Explain incidence matrix along with its properties
- ➢ Explain tie-set matrix along with its properties
- ➢ Find branch currents in terms of link currents or loop currents
- ➢ Explain cut-set matrix along with its properties
- ➢ Find branch voltages in terms of tree branch voltages
- ➢ Illustrate the dual network for the given electrical system

8.1 INTRODUCTION

An electrical circuit or network is an interconnection of electrical elements such as resistors, inductors, capacitors, transmission lines, voltage sources, current sources and switches. The analysis of an electrical circuit should result in knowing the voltage across and current through all the circuit elements. In circuit analysis, all the elements in a network must satisfy Kirchhoff's laws, beside their own characteristics.

Network topology is a generic name that refers to all properties arising from the structure of geometry of a network. If each element or a branch of a network is represented on a diagram by a line irrespective of the characteristics of the elements, we get a graph. Hence various elements are interconnected at their terminals without considering the properties and type of elements connected. This method is considered to be a more systematic approach to the analysis of large electrical networks.

8.2 TERMINOLOGY USED IN NETWORK TOPOLOGY

Node A node is a junction point or interconnection point of two or more network elements.

Branch A branch is a line segment representing one network element or a combination of network elements connected between two nodes.

Degree of node It is the number of branches incident on a node.

Graph In a network, if the branches are represented by straight line segments and nodes by dots, then the resultant diagrammatic representation is called a graph.

Oriented graph If each line segment of a graph is assigned with a direction, it is called a oriented graph.

Connected graph When there exists at least one path between every pair of nodes, the graph is called a connected graph.

Tree The tree of a network connects all the nodes of a network but contains no closed path.

Twig Each branch of a tree is called a twig.

Co-tree All branches that are present in the network, but not in the tree of the network, together constitute a co-tree.

Link Each branch of a co-tree is called a link or a chord.

Path A path is a traversal from one node to another node of the graph along the branches, such that no node is encountered twice.

Planar graph If a graph contains no cross-over, that is, if it can be represented on a single plane, then it is called a planar graph.

Sub-graph A graph G_s is said to be the sub-graph of a graph G, if every node of G_s is a node of G and every branch of G_s is also a branch of G.

Rank The rank of a connected graph is defined as $(N - 1)$ where N = number of nodes in the graph.

Fig. 8.1 shows all the above clearly.

In the above graph

- degree of node 1 is 2, and
- the rank of the graph is 3.

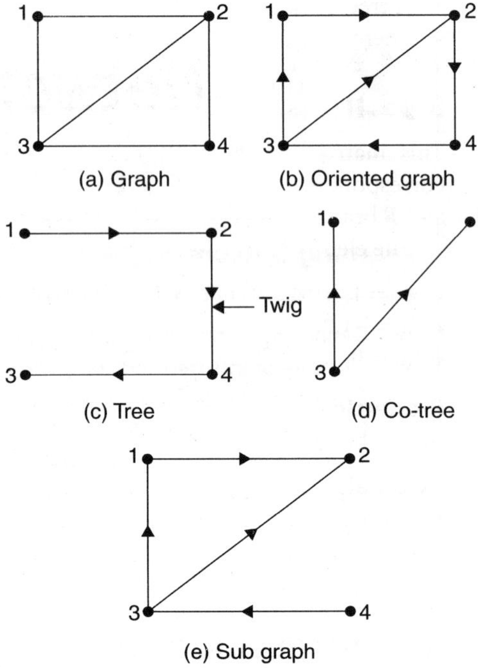

Fig. 8.1 Illustration of graph, tree and co-tree

8.3 TREE OF A GRAPH

A tree is a sub-graph of a network which consists of all nodes as in the graph, but has no closed path. Every graph has at least one tree. The branches of tree are called twigs and the branches removed from the graph in forming the tree are called links or chords.

$$\text{Number of twigs} = \text{Rank of the tree} = (N - 1) \quad \text{where} \quad N = \text{number of nodes.}$$

If the connected graph has B branches and N nodes, then the number of links corresponds to the graph, $l = B - N + 1$.

The set of all links corresponding to the given tree is called a co-tree.

Figure 8.2 shows a tree and co-tree.

Number of trees in a graph The total number of possible trees of a given graph = Determinant of $A \times A^T$ where A = reduced incident matrix.

Note: Since energy sources are replaced by their internal impedances, voltage and current source are replace by short circuit and open circuit respectively.

Properties of a tree The tree of a graph has the following properties:

- It is a connected sub-graph.
- It contains all the nodes of the original graph.
- A graph having N nodes will have $(N - 1)$ branches in its tree.

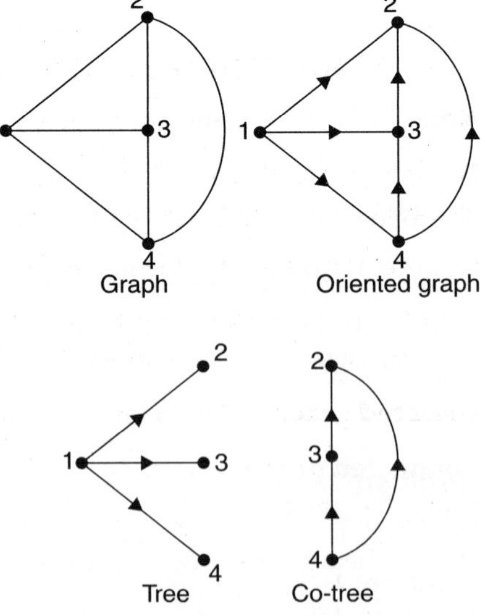

Fig. 8.2 Tree and co-tree

- A tree does not contain any closed path.
- There may be many trees for a given graph.

8.4 INCIDENCE MATRIX

This matrix shows which branch is incident to which node. Each row of the matrix represents the corresponding node of the graph; each column represents the corresponding branch. If there are N nodes and B branches in a graph, then the order of the complete incidence matrix is $N \times B$.

The elements a_{ij} of the complete incidence matrix $[A_C]$ are found as follows.

- $a_{ij} = 1$, if the jth branch is incident at node i and is directed away from node i.
- $a_i = -1$, if the jth branch is incident at node i and is directed towards node i.
- $a_{ij} = 0$, if the jth branch is not incident at node i.

Properties of the complete incidence matrix The complete incidence matrix has the following properties:

- The algebraic sum of the column entries of an incidence matrix is zero.
- The determinant of the complete incidence matrix of a closed loop is zero.
- The rank of the complete incidence matrix of a connected graph is $N - 1$.

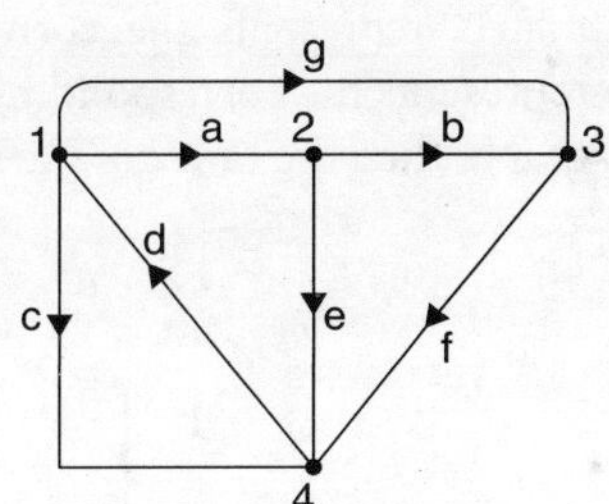

Fig. 8.3 Directed graph

For example, consider the directed graph (Fig. 8.3).

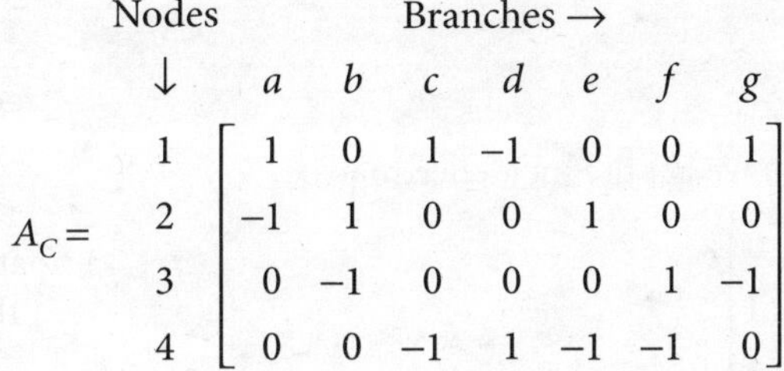

$$\begin{array}{c} \text{Nodes} \\ \downarrow \end{array} \quad \text{Branches} \rightarrow$$

$$A_C = \begin{array}{c} \\ 1 \\ 2 \\ 3 \\ 4 \end{array} \begin{array}{c} \begin{array}{ccccccc} a & b & c & d & e & f & g \end{array} \\ \begin{bmatrix} 1 & 0 & 1 & -1 & 0 & 0 & 1 \\ -1 & 1 & 0 & 0 & 1 & 0 & 0 \\ 0 & -1 & 0 & 0 & 0 & 1 & -1 \\ 0 & 0 & -1 & 1 & -1 & -1 & 0 \end{bmatrix} \end{array}$$

If any one row of the complete incidence matrix is removed, then the matrix is called the reduced incidence matrix. The dimension of this matrix is $(N - 1) \times$ B and the rank is $(N - 1)$. In the graph (Fig. 8.3), by eliminating the last row from A_C, we get the reduced incidence matrix A as

$$A = \begin{bmatrix} 1 & 0 & 1 & -1 & 0 & 0 & 1 \\ -1 & 1 & 0 & 0 & 1 & 0 & 0 \\ 0 & -1 & 0 & 0 & 0 & 1 & -1 \end{bmatrix}$$

The following equations are satisfied in the case of an incidence matrix:

$$AJ = 0 \qquad \text{(KCL)} \tag{8.1}$$

$$V = A^T e \qquad \text{(KVL)} \tag{8.2}$$

where A = incidence matrix, J = branch current vector, V = branch voltage vector and e = node to the datum voltage vector.

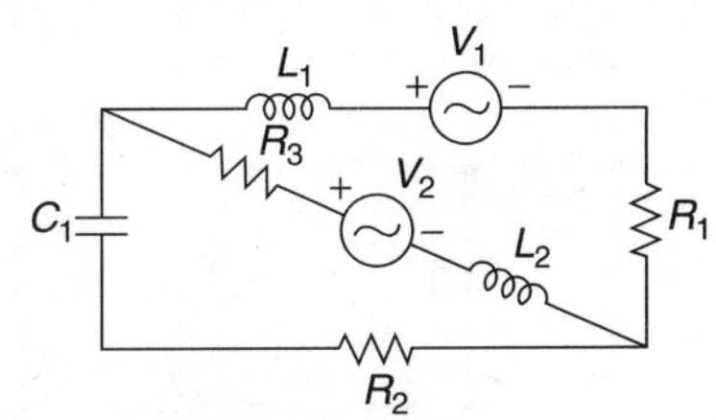

Problem 8.1 For the network, draw the graph, direct graph, tree, co-tree and connected graph.

Solution:

For the network shown, the graph, direct graph, tree, co-tree and connected graph are as given below:

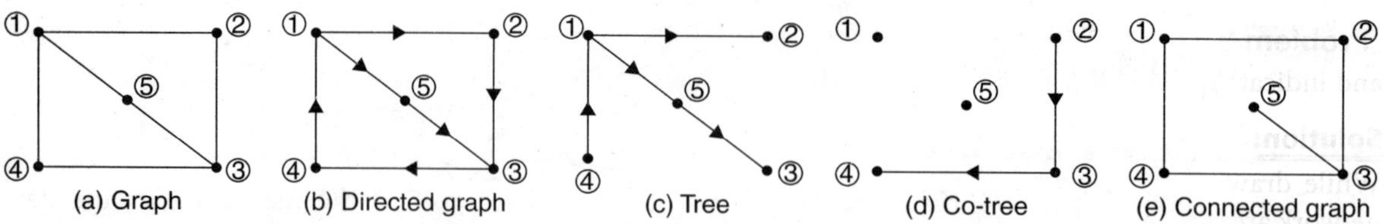

Problem 8.2 Obtain the incidence matrix of the graph as shown.

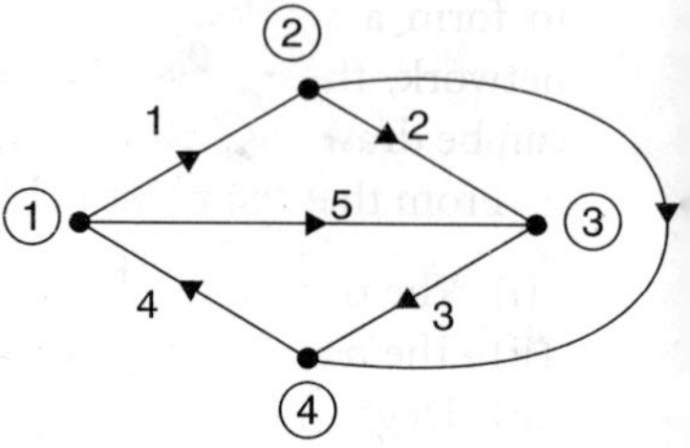

Solution:

This matrix shows which branch is incident to which node. Each row of the matrix represents the corresponding node of the graph and each column represents the corresponding branch. If there are N nodes and B branches in a graph, then the order of the incidence matrix is $(N-1) \times B$

Nodes ↓, Branches →

$$[A_C] = \begin{array}{c} \\ 1 \\ 2 \\ 3 \\ 4 \end{array} \begin{array}{c} \begin{array}{cccccc} 1 & 2 & 3 & 4 & 5 & 6 \end{array} \\ \begin{bmatrix} 1 & 0 & 0 & -1 & 1 & 0 \\ -1 & 1 & 0 & 0 & 0 & 1 \\ 0 & -1 & 1 & 0 & -1 & 0 \\ 0 & 0 & -1 & 1 & 0 & -1 \end{bmatrix} \end{array}$$

If any one row is deleted from the above matrix, then we get the incidence matrix.

$$\text{Incidence matrix} = \begin{bmatrix} 1 & 0 & 0 & -1 & 1 & 0 \\ -1 & 1 & 0 & 0 & 0 & 1 \\ 0 & -1 & 1 & 0 & -1 & 0 \end{bmatrix}$$

Problem 8.3 For the following incidence matrices, draw the directed graph.

(i) Nodes ↓, Branches →

$$\begin{array}{c} \\ a \\ b \\ c \\ d \end{array} \begin{array}{c} \begin{array}{ccccccc} 1 & 2 & 3 & 4 & 5 & 6 & 7 \end{array} \\ \begin{bmatrix} -1 & 0 & -1 & 1 & 0 & 0 & 1 \\ 0 & -1 & 0 & -1 & 0 & -1 & 0 \\ 1 & 1 & 0 & 0 & -1 & 1 & 0 \\ 0 & 0 & 1 & 0 & 1 & 0 & -1 \end{bmatrix} \end{array}$$

(ii) Nodes ↓, Branches →

$$\begin{array}{c} \\ a \\ b \\ c \end{array} \begin{array}{c} \begin{array}{cccc} 1 & 2 & 3 & 4 \end{array} \\ \begin{bmatrix} 1 & 0 & 0 & 1 \\ -1 & 1 & 1 & 0 \\ 0 & -1 & -1 & -1 \end{bmatrix} \end{array}$$

Solution:

(i) The directed graph for the given incidence matrices is as follows:

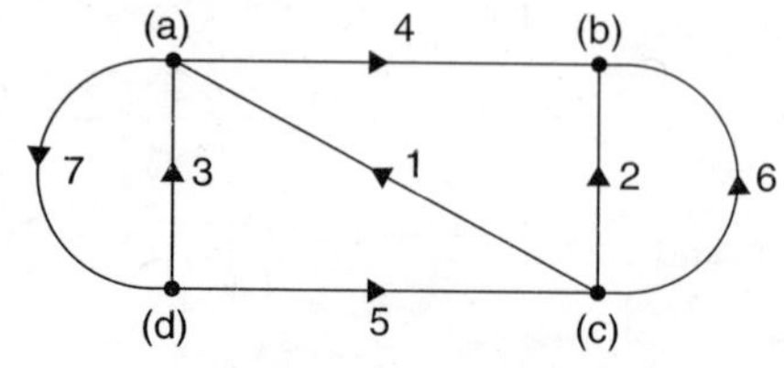

(ii) The directed graph for the given incidence matrices is as follows:

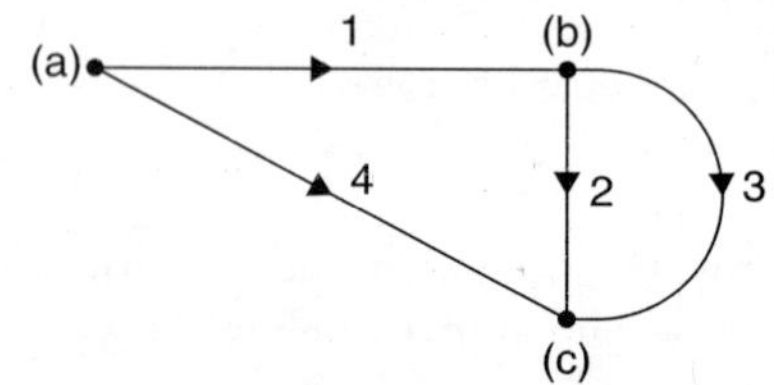

Problem 8.4 For the circuit shown, draw the graph and tree and indicate (i) branch (ii) node (iii) degree of node (iv) links.

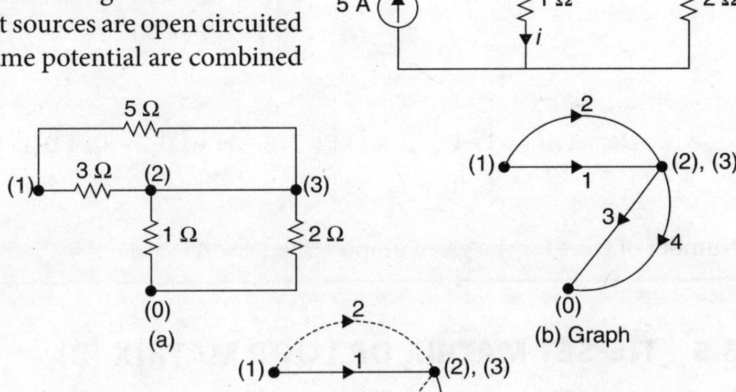

Solution:

While drawing the oriented graph, all the voltage sources in the network are short circuited, all the current sources are open circuited and points which are electrically at the same potential are combined to form a single node. For the given network, the oriented graph and tree can be drawn as shown below.

From the figure,

(i) The tree branches are 1 and 4

(ii) The nodes are (1), (2) and (0)

(iii) Degree of node = Number of branches incident on that node

Degree of node (1) = 2

Degree of node (2) = 4

Degree of node (0) = 2

(iv) The links are 2 and 3.

Problem 8.5 Find the number of trees for the given graph.

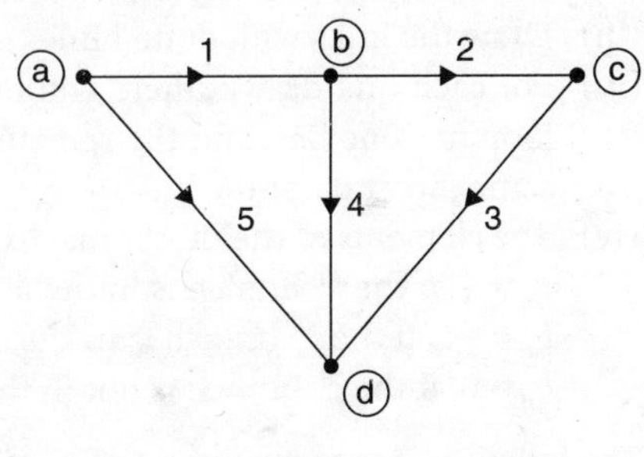

Solution:

The complete incident matrix is given by:

$$\begin{array}{cc} \text{Nodes} & \text{Branches} \rightarrow \\ \downarrow & \begin{array}{ccccc} 1 & 2 & 3 & 4 & 5 \end{array} \end{array}$$

$$[A_C] = \begin{array}{c} a \\ b \\ c \\ d \end{array} \begin{bmatrix} 1 & 0 & 0 & 0 & 1 \\ -1 & 1 & 0 & 1 & 0 \\ 0 & -1 & 1 & 0 & 0 \\ 0 & 0 & -1 & -1 & -1 \end{bmatrix}$$

If any one row is deleted from the above matrix (last row) then, we get the reduced incidence matrix or simply incidence matrix.

$$A = \begin{bmatrix} 1 & 0 & 0 & 0 & 1 \\ -1 & 1 & 0 & 1 & 0 \\ 0 & -1 & 1 & 0 & 0 \end{bmatrix}$$

$$A^T = \begin{bmatrix} 1 & -1 & 0 \\ 0 & 1 & -1 \\ 0 & 0 & 1 \\ 0 & 1 & 0 \\ 1 & 0 & 0 \end{bmatrix}$$

$$A \times A^T = \begin{bmatrix} 1 & 0 & 0 & 0 & 1 \\ -1 & 1 & 0 & 1 & 0 \\ 0 & -1 & 1 & 0 & 0 \end{bmatrix} \times \begin{bmatrix} 1 & -1 & 0 \\ 0 & 1 & -1 \\ 0 & 0 & 1 \\ 0 & 1 & 0 \\ 1 & 0 & 0 \end{bmatrix} = \begin{bmatrix} 2 & -1 & 0 \\ -1 & 3 & -1 \\ 0 & -1 & 2 \end{bmatrix}$$

$$\text{Det}\,[A A^T] = \begin{vmatrix} 2 & -1 & 0 \\ -1 & 3 & -1 \\ 0 & -1 & 2 \end{vmatrix} = 2\,(6-1) + 1\,(-2-0) + 0\,(1-0) = 10 - 2 = 8$$

Number of trees for the given graph = Det($A \times A^{\mathrm{T}}$) = 8

8.5 TIE-SET MATRIX OR LOOP MATRIX (B)

It is the matrix that is used to find the branch currents in terms of the link currents or lop currents. Tie-set is a set of branches which forms a closed path or loop. A basic tie-set or a fundamental tie-set has one and only one link branch, the other elements being tree branched. From the tie-set matrix, we can frame the voltage loop equations for each loop.

8.5.1 Procedure to Form Tie-set Matrix

The following procedure is adopted to form the tie-set matrix for the given oriented graph:

(i) Draw the direct graph and choose the possible tree for the given graph.
(ii) Draw the links with dotted lines.
(iii) For each link drawn, there will be a fundamental loop formed. Mark the loop currents such that the loop has one link and the remaining are twigs. The directions of the loop currents are chosen in the same direction of the link.
(iv) The elements of the tie-set matrix [B] are found as follows:
$b_{ij} = 1$, if the jth branch is in the ith loop and its direction is the same as the loop direction.
$b_{ij} = -1$, if the jth branch is in the ith loop and its direction is opposite to that of the loop direction.
$b_{ij} = 0$, if the jth branch is not in the ith loop.

The following equations are satisfied in the case of a tie-set matrix:

$$BV = 0 \qquad \text{(KVL)} \tag{8.3}$$

$$J = B^{\mathrm{T}} i \qquad \text{(KCL)} \tag{8.4}$$

where B = tie-set matrix, V = branch voltage vector, J = branch current vector and i = loop current vector.

For example, consider the graph [Fig. 8.4(a)] and select a tree for the graph [Fig. 8.4(b)].

In this graph there are 5 nodes and 8 branches. 1, 2, 3, 4 are links and 5, 6, 7, 8 are tree branches. Each link branch forms a closed loop or a basic tie-set. Mark the loop current as i_1, i_2, i_3 and i_4; since there are 4 links and 4 loops. The basic loops or basic tie-sets associated with each of the above link branches are listed below:

Link	Basic tie-set
1	156
2	276
3	387
4	458

Now the tie-set matrix can be formed as shown below:

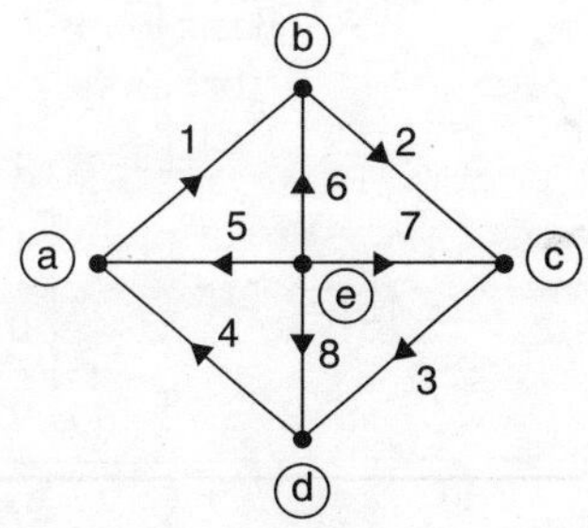

(a) Directed graph

Basic loops (or links) ↓   Branches →

$$[B] = \begin{array}{c} \\ 1 \\ 2 \\ 3 \\ 4 \end{array} \begin{array}{c} \begin{array}{cccccccc} 1 & 2 & 3 & 4 & 5 & 6 & 7 & 8 \end{array} \\ \begin{bmatrix} 1 & 0 & 0 & 0 & 1 & -1 & 0 & 0 \\ 0 & 1 & 0 & 0 & 0 & 1 & -1 & 0 \\ 0 & 0 & 1 & 0 & 0 & 0 & 1 & -1 \\ 0 & 0 & 0 & 1 & -1 & 0 & 0 & 1 \end{bmatrix} \end{array}$$

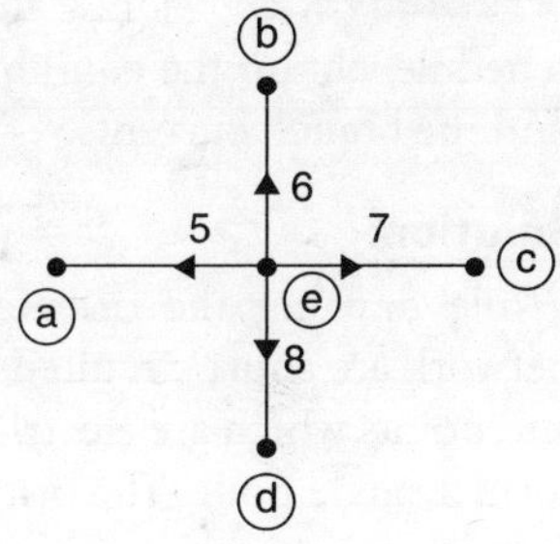

(b) Tree

From the above matrix, we can obtain the loop equations applying KVL for each of the basic loops. If V_1, V_2, ... V_8 are the branch voltages, then from the rows of the above matrix, we can write the loop equations of the network as

$$V_1 + V_5 - V_6 = 0$$
$$V_2 + V_6 - V_7 = 0$$
$$V_3 + V_7 - V_8 = 0$$
$$V_4 - V_5 + V_8 = 0$$

From the column of the above matrix we can obtain branch currents as

$$j_1 = i_1$$
$$j_2 = i_2$$
$$j_3 = i_3$$
$$j_4 = i_4$$
$$j_5 = i_1 - i_4$$
$$j_6 = -i_1 + i_2$$
$$j_7 = -i_2 + i_3$$
$$j_8 = -i_3 + i_4$$

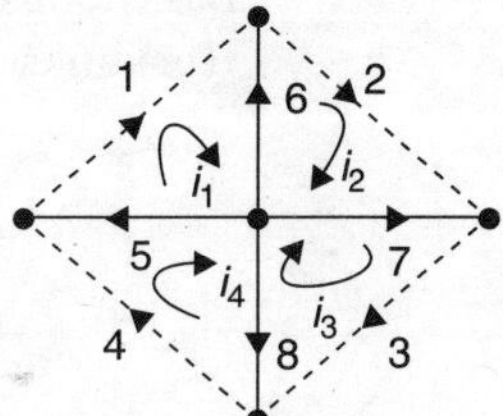

(c) Basic loops or tie sets

Fig. 8.4 Tree and basic loops

Problem 8.6 Write the tie-set schedule for the network.

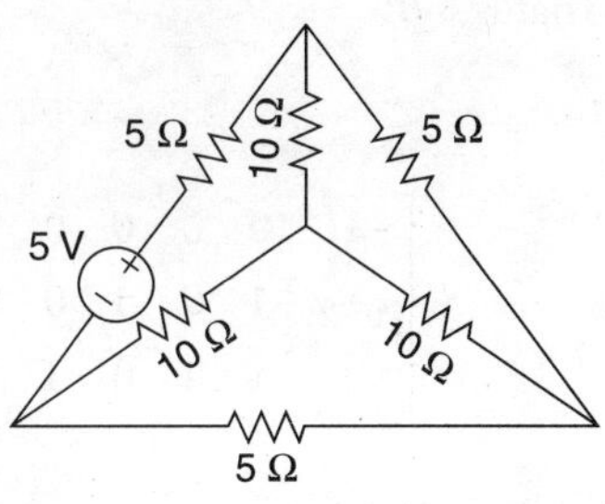

Solution:

While drawing the oriented graph, all the voltage sources in the network are short circuited and all the current sources are open circuited and points which are electrically at the same potential are combined to form a single node. The oriented graph and tree for the given network are shown.

No. of nodes, $N = 4$

No. of tree branches, $N_T = 4 - 1 = 3$

No. of branches $B = 6$

No. of independent loops, $l = B - N + 6 = 6 - 4 + 1 = 3$

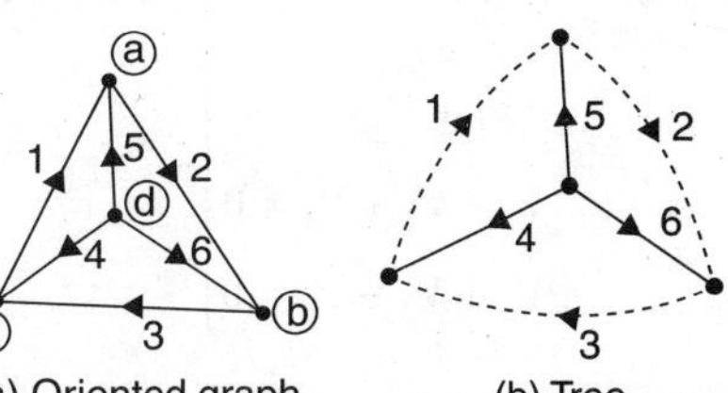

(a) Oriented graph   (b) Tree

Basic loops (or) links ↓   Branches →

$$[B] = \begin{array}{c} \\ 1 \\ 2 \\ 3 \end{array} \begin{array}{c} \begin{array}{cccccc} 1 & 2 & 3 & 4 & 5 & 6 \end{array} \\ \begin{bmatrix} 1 & 0 & 0 & 1 & -1 & 0 \\ 0 & 1 & 0 & 0 & 1 & -1 \\ 0 & 0 & 1 & -1 & 0 & 1 \end{bmatrix} \end{array}$$

(c) Basic loops or basic tie-sets

Problem 8.7 Draw the graph of the network. Find the tie-set schedule, obtain the equilibrium equations on loop current basic and find the branch currents.

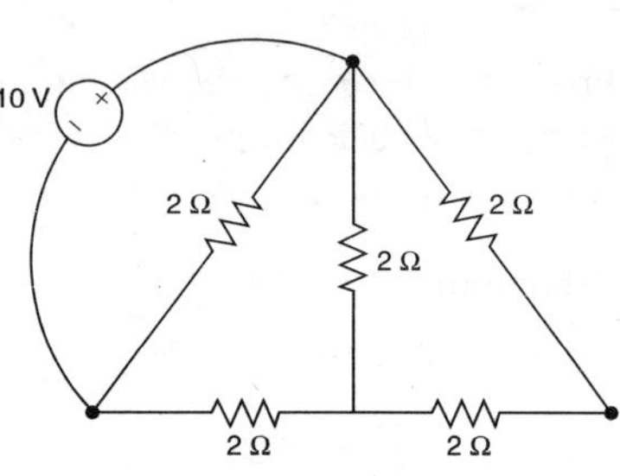

Solution:

While drawing the oriented graph, all the voltage sources in the network are short circuited, all the current sources are open circuited and points which are electrically at the same potential are combined to form a single node. The oriented graph and tree for the given network is as given below:

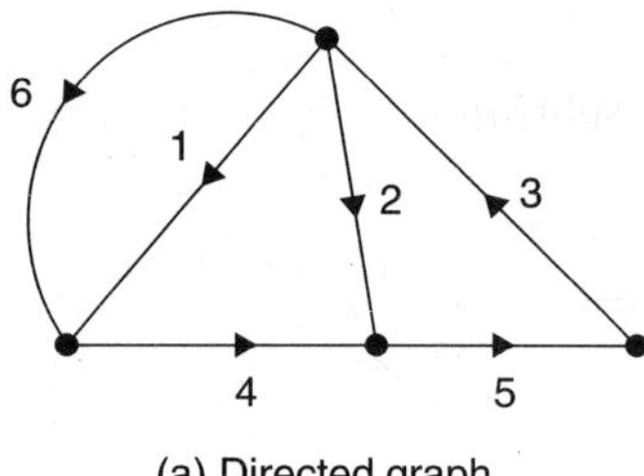

(a) Directed graph

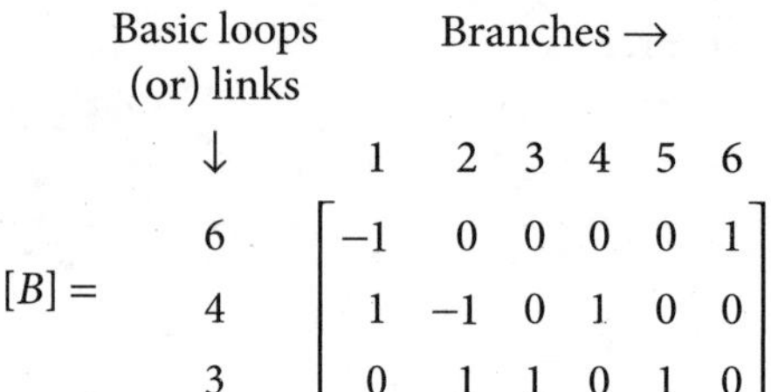

Basic loops (or) links ↓   Branches →

$$[B] = \begin{array}{c} \\ 6 \\ 4 \\ 3 \end{array} \begin{array}{c} \begin{array}{cccccc} 1 & 2 & 3 & 4 & 5 & 6 \end{array} \\ \begin{bmatrix} -1 & 0 & 0 & 0 & 0 & 1 \\ 1 & -1 & 0 & 1 & 0 & 0 \\ 0 & 1 & 1 & 0 & 1 & 0 \end{bmatrix} \end{array}$$

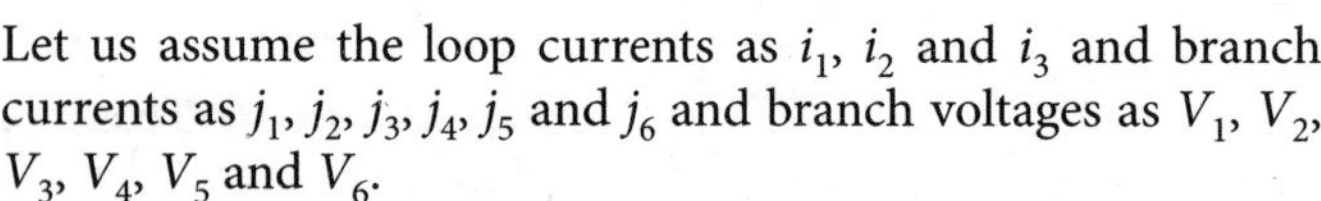

Let us assume the loop currents as i_1, i_2 and i_3 and branch currents as j_1, j_2, j_3, j_4, j_5 and j_6 and branch voltages as V_1, V_2, V_3, V_4, V_5 and V_6.

The rows of the schedule yield the voltage law equations.

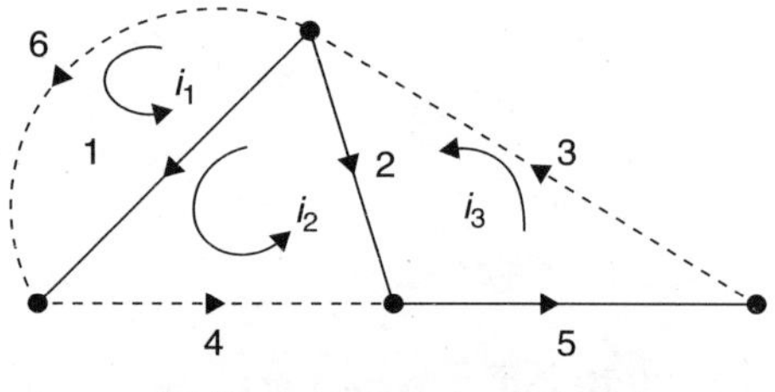

(b) Basic loops or basic tie-sets

That is, $BV = 0$

$$\begin{bmatrix} -1 & 0 & 0 & 0 & 0 & 1 \\ 1 & -1 & 0 & 1 & 0 & 0 \\ 0 & 1 & 1 & 0 & 1 & 0 \end{bmatrix} \times \begin{bmatrix} V_1 \\ V_2 \\ V_3 \\ V_4 \\ V_5 \\ V_6 \end{bmatrix} = 0$$

$$\left. \begin{aligned} -V_1 + V_6 &= 0 \\ V_1 - V_2 + V_4 &= 0 \\ V_2 + V_3 + V_5 &= 0 \end{aligned} \right\} \qquad (1)$$

The columns of this schedule give the branch currents in terms of loop currents, that is, $J = B^T i$

$$\begin{bmatrix} j_1 \\ j_2 \\ j_3 \\ j_4 \\ j_5 \\ j_6 \end{bmatrix} = \begin{bmatrix} -1 & 1 & 0 \\ 0 & -1 & 1 \\ 0 & 0 & 1 \\ 0 & 1 & 0 \\ 0 & 0 & 1 \\ 1 & 0 & 0 \end{bmatrix} \times \begin{bmatrix} i_1 \\ i_2 \\ i_3 \end{bmatrix}$$

$$\left.\begin{array}{ll} j_1 = -i_1 + i_2 & j_4 = i_2 \\ j_2 = -i_2 + i_3 & j_5 = i_3 \\ j_3 = i_3 & j_6 = i_1 \end{array}\right\} \quad (2)$$

The branch voltages are given by

$$\left.\begin{array}{ll} V_1 = 2j_1, & V_4 = 2j_4 \\ V_2 = 2j_2, & V_5 = 2j_5 \\ V_3 = 2j_3, & V_6 = 10 \end{array}\right\} \quad (3)$$

Substituting Eq. (3) in Eq. (1),

$$-2(-i_1 + i_2) + 10 = 0$$

$$\Rightarrow \quad i_1 - i_2 = -5$$

$$2(-i_1 + i_2) - 2(-i_2 + i_3) + 2i_2 = 0$$

$$\Rightarrow \quad -i_1 + 3i_2 - i_3 = 0$$

$$2(-i_2 + i_3) + 2i_3 + 2i_3 = 0$$

$$\Rightarrow \quad -i_2 + 3i_3 = 0$$

$$\left.\begin{array}{l} i_1 - i_2 = -5 \\ i_1 - 3i_2 + i_3 = 0 \\ -i_2 + 3i_3 = 0 \end{array}\right\} \quad (4)$$

Equation (4) can be written into the matrix form as:

$$\begin{bmatrix} 1 & -1 & 0 \\ 1 & -3 & 1 \\ 0 & -1 & 3 \end{bmatrix} \times \begin{bmatrix} i_1 \\ i_2 \\ i_3 \end{bmatrix} = \begin{bmatrix} -5 \\ 0 \\ 0 \end{bmatrix}$$

$$\Delta = \begin{bmatrix} 1 & -1 & 0 \\ 1 & -3 & 1 \\ 0 & -1 & 3 \end{bmatrix} = 1(-9+1) + 1(3-0) + 0(-1-0) = -8 + 3 = -5$$

$$\Delta_1 = \begin{bmatrix} -5 & -1 & 0 \\ 0 & -3 & 1 \\ 0 & -1 & 3 \end{bmatrix} = -5(-9+1) = 40$$

$$\Delta_2 = \begin{bmatrix} 1 & -5 & 0 \\ 1 & 0 & 1 \\ 0 & 0 & 3 \end{bmatrix} = 1(0-0) + 5(3-0) + 0 = 15$$

$$\Delta_3 = \begin{bmatrix} 1 & -1 & -5 \\ 1 & -3 & 0 \\ 0 & -1 & 0 \end{bmatrix} = 1(0-0) + 1(0-0) - 5(-1-0) = 5$$

$$i_1 = \frac{\Delta_1}{\Delta} = \frac{40}{-5} = -8$$

$$i_2 = \frac{\Delta_2}{\Delta} = \frac{15}{-5} = -3$$

$$i_3 = \frac{\Delta_3}{\Delta} = \frac{5}{-5} = -1$$

The various branch currents are

$$j_1 = -i_1 + i_2 = 8 - 3 = 5 \text{ A}$$

$$j_2 = -i_2 + i_3 = 3 - 1 = 2 \text{ A}$$

$$j_3 = i_3 = -1 \text{ A}$$

$$j_4 = i_2 = -3 \text{ A}$$

$$j_5 = i_3 = -1 \text{ A}$$

$$j_6 = i_1 = -8 \text{ A}$$

8.6 CUT-SET MATRIX

The cut-set matrix is used to find the branch voltages in terms of tree branch voltages. A fundamental cut-set of a graph with respect to a tree is a cut-set formed by one and only one twig and a set of links, which must be cut to divide the network graph into two parts. The conventional direction for the fundamental cut-set is taken to be the same as the direction of the tree branch that defines the particular cut-set. From the cut-set matrix, we can frame the current balance equations.

The number of basic cut-sets = number of twigs = $N - 1$

where N = number of nodes

8.6.1 Procedure to Form Cut-set Matrix

The following procedure is adopted to form the cut-set matrix for the given oriented graph:

(i) Draw the direct graph and choose one possible tree for the given graph.

(ii) Draw the links with dotted lines.
(iii) For each twig, form a fundamental cut-set oriented in the same direction as the twig.
(iv) The elements of the cut-set matrix [C] are found as follows:
$C_{ij} = 1$, if branch j has the same orientation as the cut-set i.
$C_{ij} = -1$, if branch j has the opposite orientation as the cut-set i.
$C_{ij} = 0$, if branch j is not in the cut-set i.

The following equations are satisfied in the case of a cut-set matrix:

$$Cj = 0 \qquad \text{(KCL)} \tag{8.5}$$

$$V = C^T e \qquad \text{(KVL)} \tag{8.6}$$

where C = cut-set matrix, V = branch voltage vector, j = branch current vector and e = tree branch voltage vector.

Note: A cut-set should cross only one twig at a time.

For example, consider the following graph and select a tree for the graph (Fig. 8.5). Links are shown by dotted lines. Since there are three twigs, there should be three fundamental cut-sets. The fundamental cut-sets are drawn such that each fundamental cut-set cuts only one twig.

Cut-set C_1: Twig a, link d

Cut-set C_2: Twig b, link d and e

Cut-set C_3: Twig c, link e

Now the cut-set matrix can be formed as given below

Basic cut-sets ↓ Branches →

$$[C] = \begin{matrix} & a & b & c & d & e \\ C_1 \\ C_2 \\ C_3 \end{matrix} \begin{bmatrix} 1 & 0 & 0 & 1 & 0 \\ 0 & 1 & 0 & -1 & 1 \\ 0 & 0 & 1 & 0 & -1 \end{bmatrix}$$

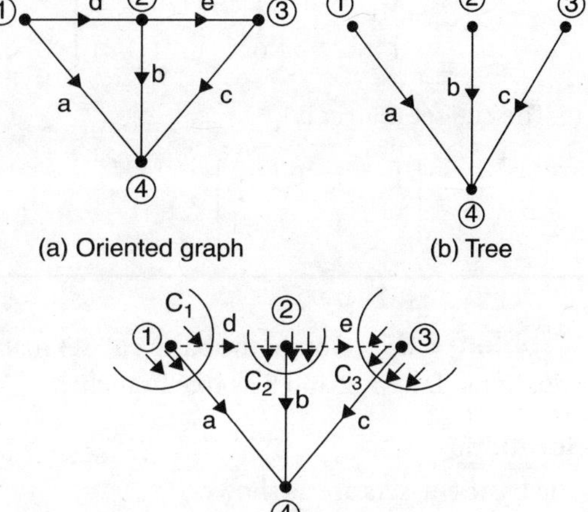

Fig. 8.5 Tree and corresponding basic cut-sets

From the rows of the above matrix, we can obtain the current balance (KCL) equation as follows:

$$j_a + j_d = 0$$

$$j_b - j_d + j_e = 0$$

$$j_c - j_e = 0$$

Let V_a, V_b, V_c, V_d and V_e be branch voltages and e_a, e_b and e_c be tree branch voltages, then

$$V = C^T e$$

$$\begin{bmatrix} V_a \\ V_b \\ V_c \\ V_d \\ V_e \\ V_f \end{bmatrix} = \begin{bmatrix} 1 & 0 & 0 \\ 0 & 1 & 0 \\ 0 & 0 & 1 \\ 1 & -1 & 0 \\ 0 & 1 & -1 \end{bmatrix} \begin{bmatrix} e_a \\ e_b \\ e_c \end{bmatrix} = \begin{bmatrix} e_a \\ e_b \\ e_c \\ e_a - e_b \\ e_b - e_c \end{bmatrix}$$

∴ The branch voltages are

$$V_a = e_a,\ V_b = e_b,\ V_c = e_c$$

$$V_d = e_a - e_b,\ V_e = e_b - e_c$$

Problem 8.8 For the network, draw the oriented graph and frame the cut-set matrix.

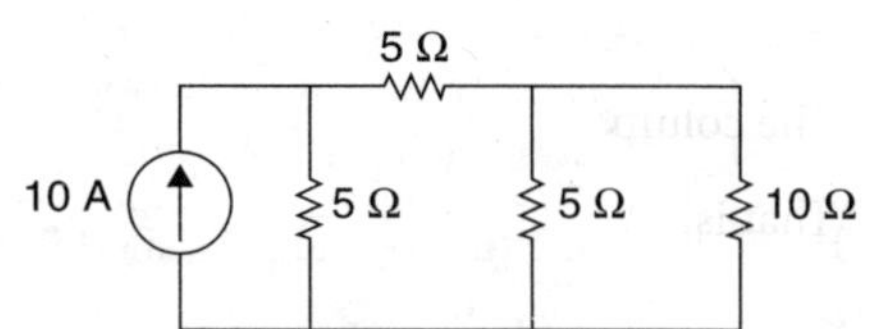

Solution:

While drawing the oriented graph, all the voltage sources in the network are short circuited, all the current sources are open circuited and points which are electrically at the same potential are combined to form a single node. The oriented for the given network is

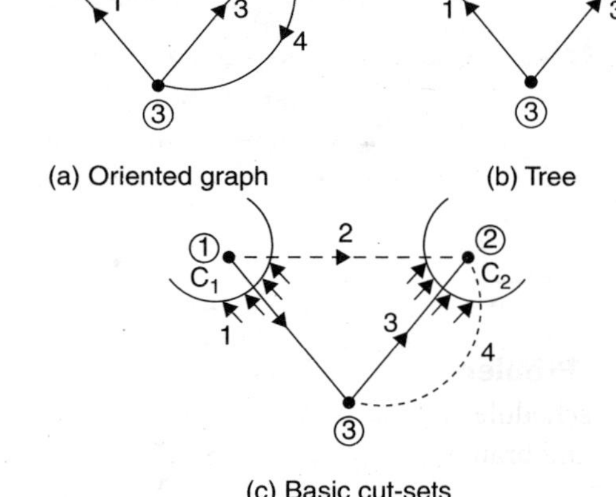

(a) Oriented graph

(b) Tree

(c) Basic cut-sets

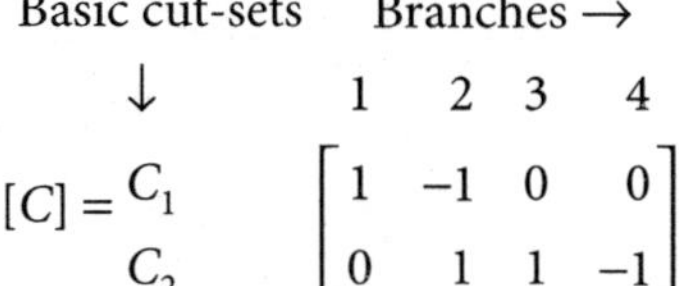

Basic cut-sets ↓ Branches →

$$[C] = \begin{matrix} C_1 \\ C_2 \end{matrix} \overset{\begin{matrix} 1 & 2 & 3 & 4 \end{matrix}}{\begin{bmatrix} 1 & -1 & 0 & 0 \\ 0 & 1 & 1 & -1 \end{bmatrix}}$$

∴ The cut-set matrix is

$$C = \begin{bmatrix} 1 & -1 & 0 & 0 \\ 0 & 1 & 1 & -1 \end{bmatrix}$$

Problem 8.9 Obtain the basic cut-set matrix for the network graph and hence write down the network equations. Take 1, 2 and 3 as tree branches.

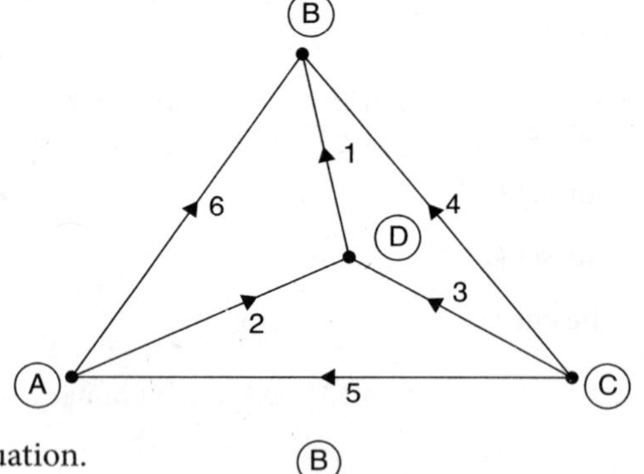

Solution:

The basic cut-sets are as shown.

Basic cut-sets ↓ Branches →

$$[C] = \begin{matrix} C_1 \\ C_2 \\ C_3 \end{matrix} \overset{\begin{matrix} 1 & 2 & 3 & 4 & 5 & 6 \end{matrix}}{\begin{bmatrix} 1 & 0 & 0 & 1 & 0 & 1 \\ 0 & 1 & 0 & 0 & -1 & 1 \\ 0 & 0 & 1 & 1 & 1 & 0 \end{bmatrix}}$$

The rows of this schedule yield the Kirchhoff's current law equation.

That is, $CJ = 0$

$$\begin{bmatrix} 1 & 0 & 0 & 1 & 0 & 1 \\ 0 & 1 & 0 & 0 & -1 & 1 \\ 0 & 0 & 1 & 1 & 1 & 0 \end{bmatrix} \times \begin{bmatrix} j_1 \\ j_2 \\ j_3 \\ j_4 \\ j_5 \\ j_6 \end{bmatrix} = 0$$

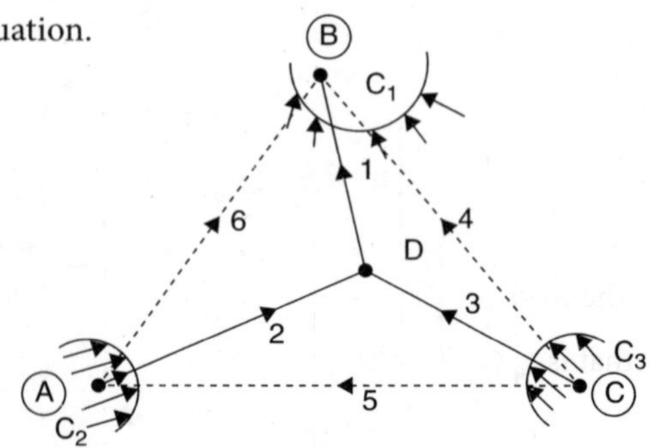

$$j_1 + j_4 = 0$$

$$j_2 - j_5 + j_6 = 0$$

$$j_3 + j_4 + j_5 = 0$$

The column of this schedule gives branch voltages in terms of the tree branch voltages.

That is, $V = C^T e$

$$\begin{bmatrix} V_1 \\ V_2 \\ V_3 \\ V_4 \\ V_5 \\ V_6 \end{bmatrix} = \begin{bmatrix} 1 & 0 & 0 \\ 0 & 1 & 0 \\ 0 & 0 & 1 \\ 1 & 0 & 1 \\ 0 & -1 & 1 \\ 0 & 1 & 0 \end{bmatrix} \times \begin{bmatrix} e_1 \\ e_2 \\ e_3 \end{bmatrix}$$

$V_1 = e_1,\quad V_2 = e_2,\quad V_3 = e_3$

$V_4 = e_1 + e_3,\quad V_5 = -e_2 + e_3,\quad V_6 = e_2$

Problem 8.10 For the network, draw the graph, tree and obtain cut-set schedule and equilibrium equations on voltage basics. Hence obtain voltages and branch currents.

Solution:

While drawing the oriented graph, all the voltage sources in the network are short circuited, all the currents sources are open circuited and points which are electrically at the same potential are combined to form a single node. The oriented graph and tree for the given network are given below:

From the graph, we can find the fundamental cut-sets as

Cut-set C_1: Twig 3, links1 and 5

Cut-set C_2: Twig 4, links 2 and 5

Cut-set C_3: Twig 6, links 1 and 2

The cut-set matrix for the above graph is given below:

Basic cut-set (or tree branches) ↓   Branches →

$$[C] = \begin{matrix} C_1 \\ C_2 \\ C_3 \end{matrix} \begin{bmatrix} -1 & 0 & 1 & 0 & 1 & 0 \\ 0 & -1 & 0 & 1 & 1 & 0 \\ 1 & -1 & 0 & 0 & 0 & 1 \end{bmatrix}$$

(columns: branches 1 2 3 4 5 6)

The rows of this schedule yield the current's law equation,

that is, $Cj = 0$

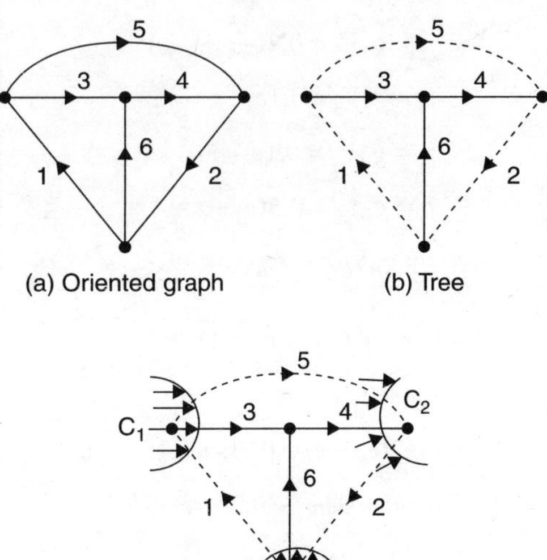

(a) Oriented graph

(b) Tree

(c) Basic cut-sets

$$\begin{bmatrix} -1 & 0 & 1 & 0 & 1 & 0 \\ 0 & -1 & 0 & 1 & 1 & 0 \\ 1 & -1 & 0 & 0 & 0 & 1 \end{bmatrix}\begin{bmatrix} j_1 \\ j_2 \\ j_3 \\ j_4 \\ j_5 \\ j_6 \end{bmatrix} = 0$$

$$\left.\begin{aligned} -j_1 + j_3 + j_5 &= 0 \\ -j_2 + j_4 + j_5 &= 0 \\ j_1 - j_2 + j_6 &= 0 \end{aligned}\right\} \quad (1)$$

The column of this schedule gives branch voltages in terms of tree branch voltages.

That is, $V = C^T e$

$$\begin{bmatrix} V_1 \\ V_2 \\ V_3 \\ V_4 \\ V_5 \\ V_6 \end{bmatrix} = \begin{bmatrix} -1 & 0 & 1 \\ 0 & -1 & -1 \\ 1 & 0 & 0 \\ 0 & 1 & 0 \\ 1 & 1 & 0 \\ 0 & 0 & 1 \end{bmatrix}\begin{bmatrix} e_3 \\ e_4 \\ e_6 \end{bmatrix}.$$

$$\left.\begin{aligned} V_1 &= -e_3 + e_6, & V_3 &= e_3 \\ V_2 &= -e_4 - e_6, & V_4 &= e_4 \\ V_5 &= e_3 + e_4, & V_6 &= e_6 \end{aligned}\right\} \quad (2)$$

From the given network, the branch currents are obtained as

$$\left.\begin{aligned} j_1 &= g_1(V_1 - 910) = 0.2(e_6 - e_3 - 910) \\ j_2 &= g_2 V_2 = 0.2(-e_4 - e_6) \\ j_3 &= g_3 V_3 = 0.1 e_3 \\ j_4 &= g_4 V_4 = 0.1 e_4 \\ j_5 &= g_5 V_5 = 0.5(e_3 + e_4) \\ j &= g_6 V_6 = 0.1 e_6 \end{aligned}\right\} \quad (3)$$

Substituting Eq. (3) in Eq. (1)

$$-j_1 + j_3 + j_5 = 0$$

$$-0.2(e_6 - e_3 - 910) + 0.1e_3 + 0.5(e_3 + e_4) = 0$$

$$\Rightarrow \quad 0.8e_3 + 0.5e_4 - 0.2e_6 = -182$$

$$-j_2 + j_4 + j_5 = 0$$

$$0.2(e_4 + e_6) + 0.1e_4 + 0.5(e_3 + e_4) = 0$$

$$\Rightarrow \quad 0.5e_3 + 0.8e_4 + 0.2e_6 = 0$$

$$j_1 - j_2 + j_6 = 0$$

$$0.2(e_6 - e_3 - 910) + 0.2(e_4 + e_6) + 0.1e_6 = 0$$

$$\Rightarrow \quad -0.2e_3 + 0.2e_4 + 0.5e_6 = 182$$

$$\therefore \quad \left.\begin{aligned} 0.8e_3 + 0.5e_4 - 0.2e_6 &= -182 \\ 0.5e_3 + 0.8e_4 + 0.2e_6 &= 0 \\ -0.2e_3 + 0.2e_4 + 0.5e &= 182 \end{aligned}\right\} \qquad (4)$$

After solving the above equations, we get

$$e_3 = -200 \text{ V}, \qquad e_4 = 60 \text{ V}, \qquad e_6 = 260 \text{ V}$$

From Eq. (2), we get the branch voltages as

$$V_1 = -e_3 + e_6 = 200 + 260 = 460 \text{ V}$$

$$V_2 = -e_4 - e_6 = -60 - 260 = -320 \text{ V}$$

$$V_3 = e_3 = -200 \text{ V}$$

$$V_4 = e_4 = 60 \text{ V}$$

$$V_5 = e_3 + e_4 = -200 + 60 = -140 \text{ V}$$

$$V_6 = e_6 = 260 \text{ V}$$

From Eq. (3) we get the branch currents as

$$j_1 = 0.2(e_6 - e_3 - 910) = 0.2(260 + 200 - 910) = -90 \text{ A}$$

$$j_2 = 0.2(-e_4 - e_6) = 0.2(-60 - 260) = -64 \text{ A}$$

$$j_3 = 0.1e_3 = 0.1 \times -200 = -20 \text{ A}$$

$$j_4 = 0.1e_4 = 0.1 \times 60 = 6 \text{ A}$$

$$j_5 = 0.5(e_3 + e_4) = 0.5(-200 + 60) = -70 \text{ A}$$

$$j_6 = 0.1e_6 = 0.1 \times 260 = 26 \text{ A}$$

8.7 V-SHIFT AND I-SHIFT METHOD

A voltage source in series with a passive branch is called an accompanied voltage source. Similarly a current source in parallel with a passive branch is called an accompanied current source. Figure 8.6 shows both accompanied voltage and current sources.

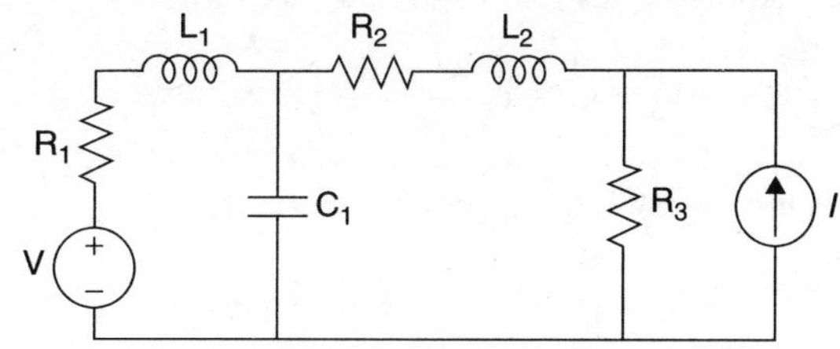

Fig. 8.6 Network containing both accompanied voltage and current sources

To draw a graph for the given network, the accompanied sources are replaced by their internal resistances/impedances. If the internal resistances/impedances are not given, then replace voltage source with short circuit and current source with open circuit.

But if the network contains unaccompanied sources, then it is very difficult to select the number of unknowns in terms of number of branches, if the sources are treated as separate branches.

Figure 8.7 shows networks with unaccompanied sources along with its voltage and current sources shifted network. We can get some equivalence between the networks with and without accompanied sources by using the source shifting technique in the network with unaccompanied sources.

The voltage drops across various elements in one network are analogous to the branch currents in the other network. In one network, equations are written as a summation of voltage drops and in the other network, the equations are written by summing up the current at a node. Thus the basic Kirchhoff's laws give the property of duality.

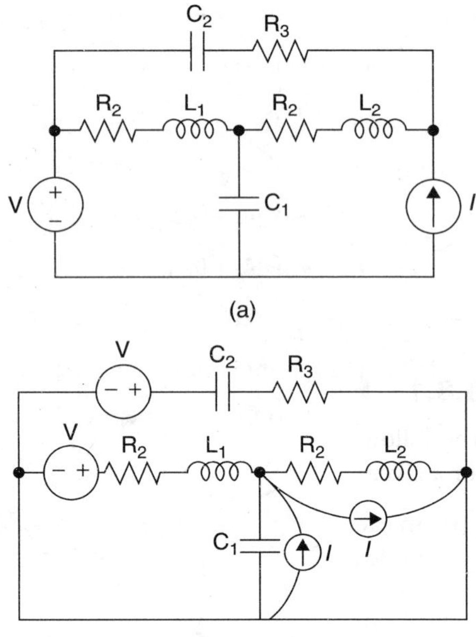

Fig. 8.7 (a) Network with unaccompanied sources and (b) Network with voltage and current source shifted

8.8 DUALITY AND DUAL NETWORKS

In an electrical circuit, there are pairs of terms that can be interchanged to get a new circuit. Such pairs are known as duals. If the mesh equations of one network have the same form as the nodal equations of another network, then the two networks are called dual networks. The concept of dual networks can be extended to the network graph. Two graphs G_1 and G_2 are said to be duals of each other, if and only if there is one to one correspondence between the circuit of one to the cut-set of the other.

The planar network has no dual if it contains mutual inductance. The following are the topological dual in graphs:

Loop = cut-set

Twig = link

Mesh = node

Series = parallel

Short circuit = open circuit

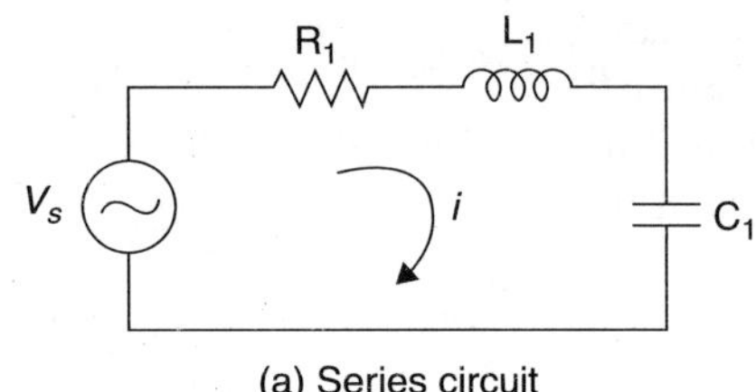

(a) Series circuit

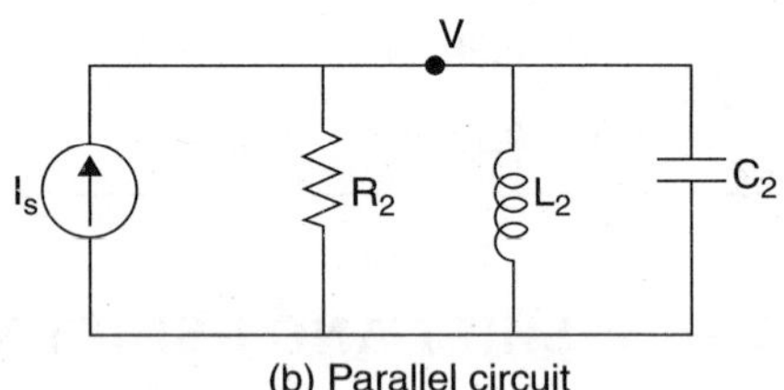

(b) Parallel circuit

Fig. 8.8 *RLC* circuit

For example, consider the two networks (series RLC and parallel RLC networks, Fig. 8.8). They are entirely different networks in physical appearance.

Applying KVL to Fig. 8.6(a), we have,

$$V_S = R_1 i + L_1 \frac{di}{dt} + \frac{1}{C_1}\int idt \tag{8.7}$$

Applying KCL to Fig. 8.6(b), we have

$$I_s = \frac{V}{R_2} + C_2 \frac{dV}{dt} + \frac{i}{L_2}\int Vdt \tag{8.8}$$

Consider the forms of Eqs 8.7 and 8.8. They look exactly similar in their mathematical operations. Only the symbols used for variables and coefficients in the equations are different. In Eq. 8.7, if we make $i = V$, $R_1 = G_2$, $L_1 = C_2$, $C_1 = L_2$, $V_s = I_s$, then we get Eq. 8.8. Thus, if the solution of Eq. 8.7 is known, the solution for Eq. 8.8 can be easily obtained by making the changes as indicated. So the above two circuits are duals of each other. The following table gives the dual pairs:

Table 8.1 Dual pairs

S. No	Element	Dual element	S. No	Element	Dual element
01	Current	Voltage	07	Short circuit	Open circuit
02	Voltage	Current	08	Mesh current	Node voltage
03	Resistance	Conductance	09	Impedance	Admittance
04	Inductance	Capacitance	10	KCL	KVL
05	Capacitance	Inductance	11	Charge	Flux linkage
06	Series branch	parallel branch	12	Link	Twig

8.8.1 Procedure for Finding Dual Network

The following procedure is adopted to draw the dual network for a given network.

(i) In each loop of a network place a node, and place an extra node (called the reference node) outside the network.

(ii) Connect all the nodes by dotted lines through the elements travelling only one element at a time. For each element traversed in the original network, replace each element by its dual element.

(iii) When sources are included, then the line joining the dots should intersect the source also. Between these two nodes the dual of the sources is included.

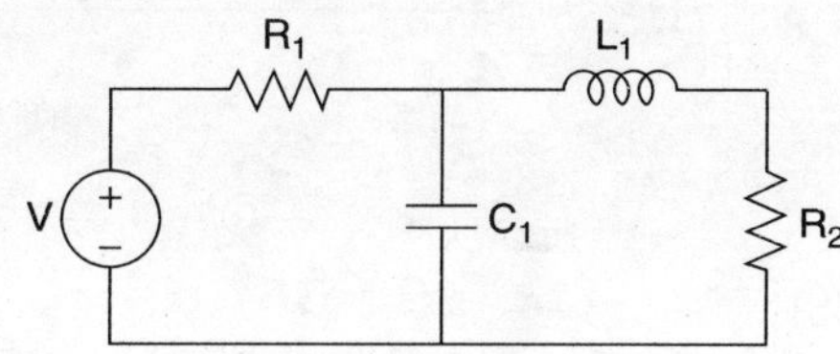

Fig. 8.9 An electrical circuit

For example, consider the network in Fig. 8.9.

Since there are two meshes, one node is placed in each mesh and one reference node 0 outside the network. Draw three nodes—1, 2 and 0 for dual network separately. Join nodes-1, 2 and 0 through each element [Fig. 8.10(a)] and therefore in the dual network draw dual elements between nodes 1, 2 and 0 [Fig. 8.10(b)].

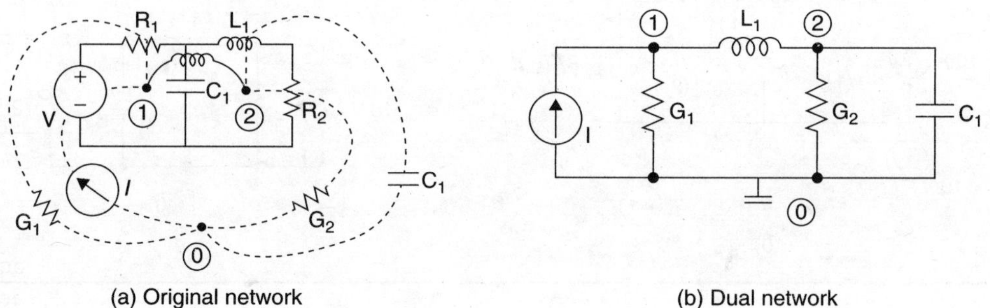

Fig. 8.10 Networks

Problem 8.11 Draw the dual network for the given circuits.

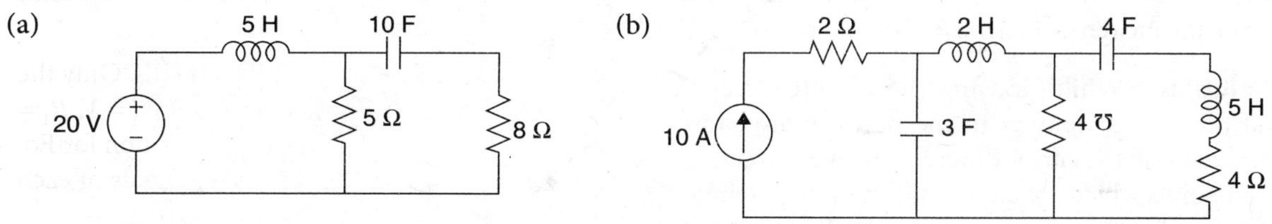

(c)

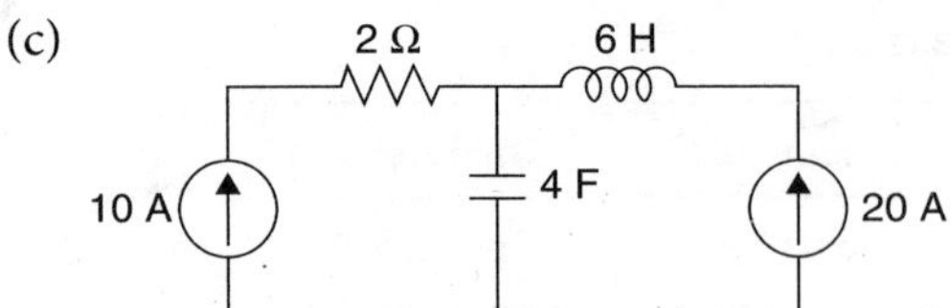

Solution:

(a)

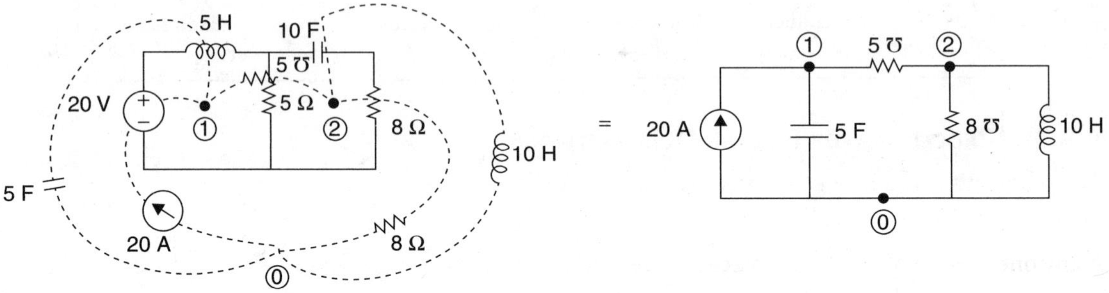

(b)

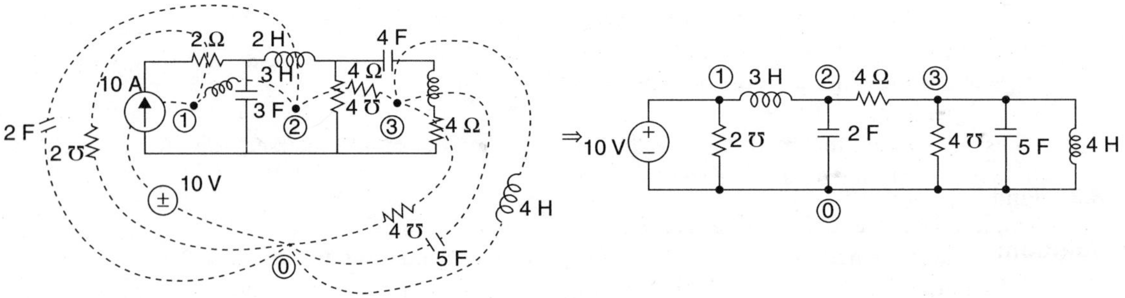

(c)

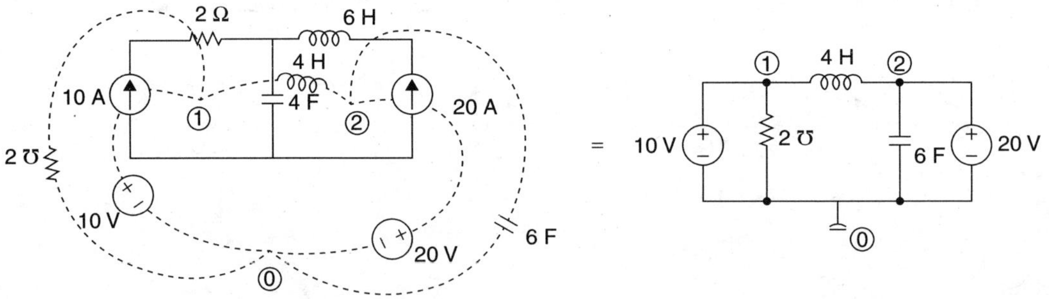

ADDITIONAL SOLVED PROBLEMS

8.1 Draw the oriented graph of the network and write the incidence matrix.

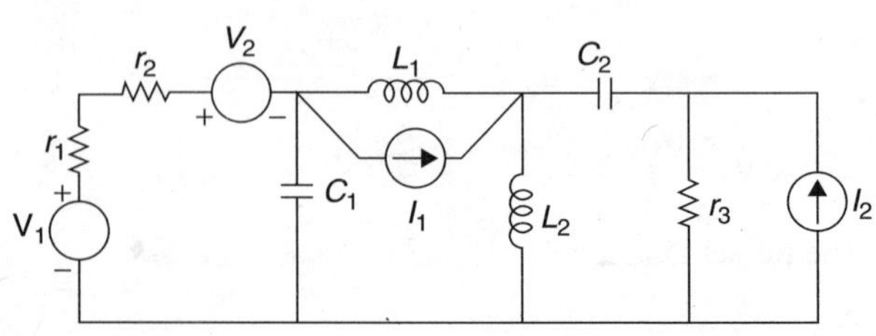

Solution: While drawing the oriented graph, all the voltage sources in the network are short circuited, all the current sources are open circuited and points which are electrically at same potential are combined to form a single node. Therefore the given network is changed to the following form.

The oriented graph of the above network is shown.

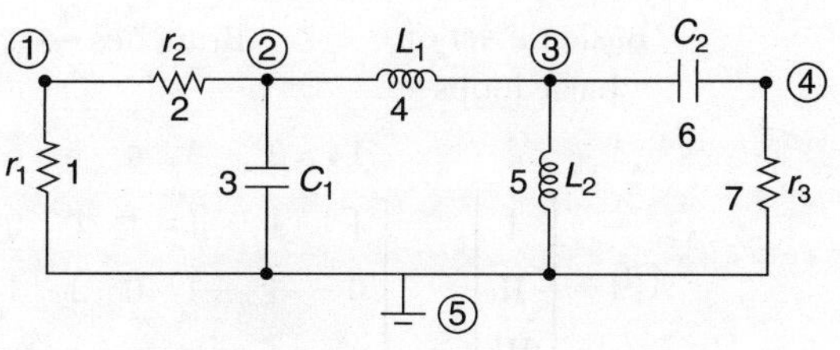

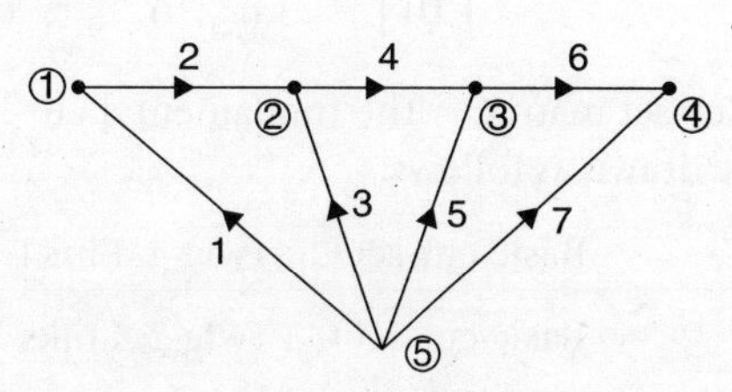

The order of the incidence matrix $= (N-1) \times B = 4 \times 7$

The complete incidence matrix for the above graph is

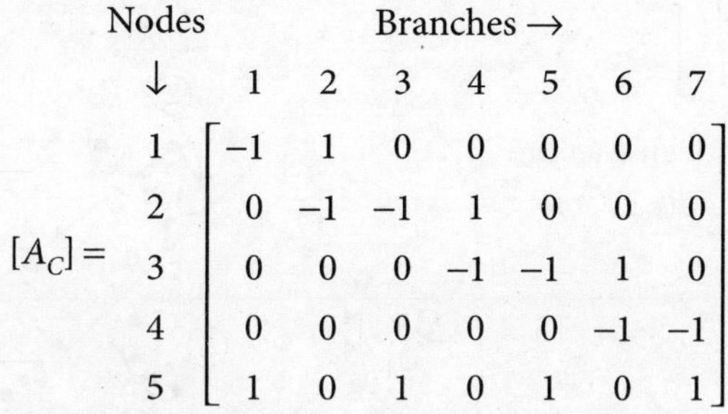

Nodes ↓   Branches →

$$[A_C] = \begin{array}{c} \\ 1 \\ 2 \\ 3 \\ 4 \\ 5 \end{array} \begin{array}{c} \begin{array}{ccccccc} 1 & 2 & 3 & 4 & 5 & 6 & 7 \end{array} \\ \begin{bmatrix} -1 & 1 & 0 & 0 & 0 & 0 & 0 \\ 0 & -1 & -1 & 1 & 0 & 0 & 0 \\ 0 & 0 & 0 & -1 & -1 & 1 & 0 \\ 0 & 0 & 0 & 0 & 0 & -1 & -1 \\ 1 & 0 & 1 & 0 & 1 & 0 & 1 \end{bmatrix} \end{array}$$

If any one row (last row) is removed from the above matrix, then we get the incidence matrix:

$$[A] = \begin{bmatrix} -1 & 1 & 0 & 0 & 0 & 0 & 0 \\ 0 & -1 & -1 & 1 & 0 & 0 & 0 \\ 0 & 0 & 0 & -1 & -1 & 1 & 0 \\ 0 & 0 & 0 & 0 & 0 & -1 & -1 \end{bmatrix}$$

8.2 Find the fundamental tie-set matrix for the graph and for the tree.

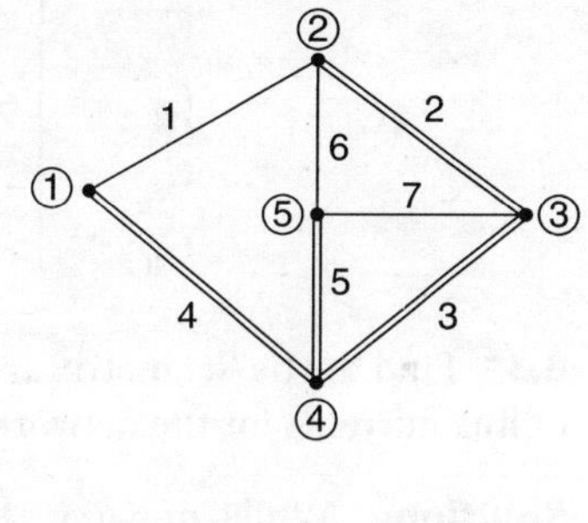

Solution:

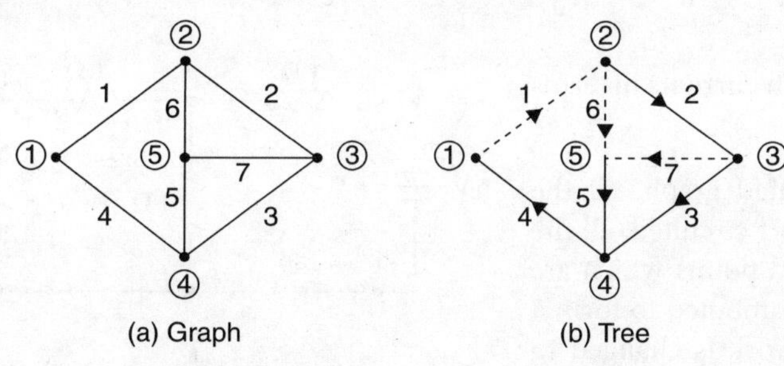

(a) Graph   (b) Tree

Tie-set matrix: The fundamental tie-sets or fundamental loops of the given tree can be drawn as follows:

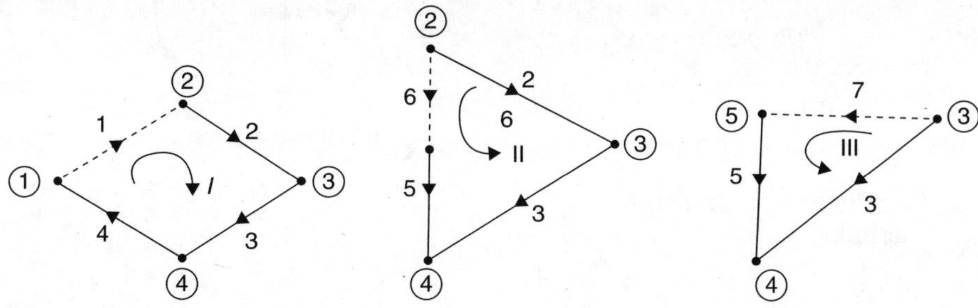

The tie-set matrix for the given graph is

$$
\begin{array}{c}
\text{Basic tie-set or basic loops} \\
\downarrow
\end{array}
\qquad
\text{Branches} \rightarrow
$$

$$
[B] = \begin{bmatrix} \text{I} \\ \text{II} \\ \text{III} \end{bmatrix}
\begin{array}{c} \begin{array}{ccccccc} 1 & 2 & 3 & 4 & 5 & 6 & 7 \end{array} \\
\begin{bmatrix} 1 & 1 & 1 & 1 & 0 & 0 & 0 \\ 0 & -1 & -1 & 0 & 1 & 1 & 0 \\ 0 & 0 & -1 & 0 & 1 & 0 & 1 \end{bmatrix} \end{array}
$$

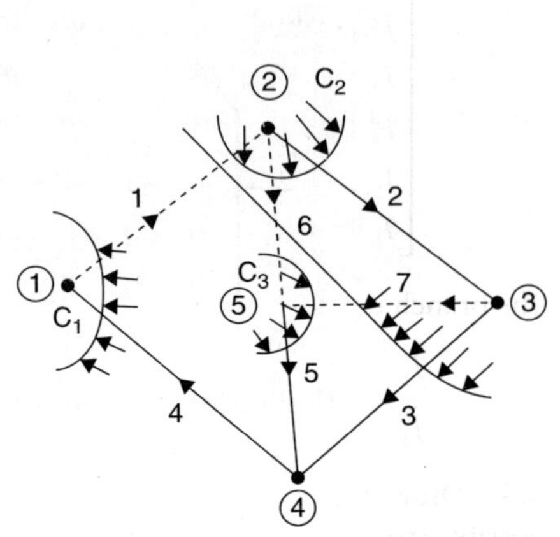

Cut-set matrix: The fundamental cut-sets of the given tree can be drawn as follows:

Basic cut-set C_1: Twig 4, Link1

Basic cut-set C_2: Twig 2, Links 1 and 6

Basic cut-set C_3: Twig 5, Links 6 and 7

Basic cut-set C_4: Twig 3, Links 1, 6 and 7

The cut-set matrix for the given graph is

$$
\begin{array}{c}
\text{Basic cut-set} \\
\downarrow
\end{array}
\qquad
\text{Branches} \rightarrow
$$

$$
[C] = \begin{array}{c} C_1 \\ C_2 \\ C_3 \\ C_4 \end{array}
\begin{array}{c} \begin{array}{ccccccc} 1 & 2 & 3 & 4 & 5 & 6 & 7 \end{array} \\
\begin{bmatrix} -1 & 0 & 0 & 1 & 0 & 0 & 0 \\ -1 & 1 & 0 & 0 & 0 & 1 & 0 \\ 0 & 0 & 0 & 0 & 1 & 1 & -1 \\ -1 & 0 & 1 & 0 & 0 & 1 & 1 \end{bmatrix} \end{array}
$$

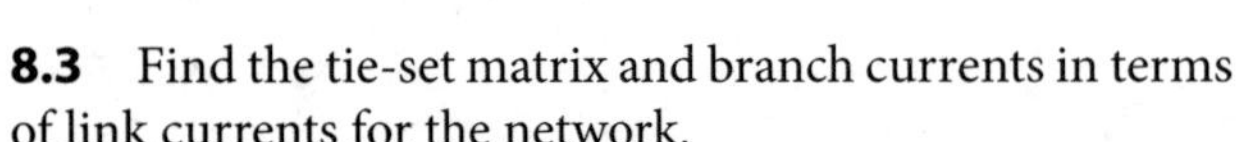

8.3 Find the tie-set matrix and branch currents in terms of link currents for the network.

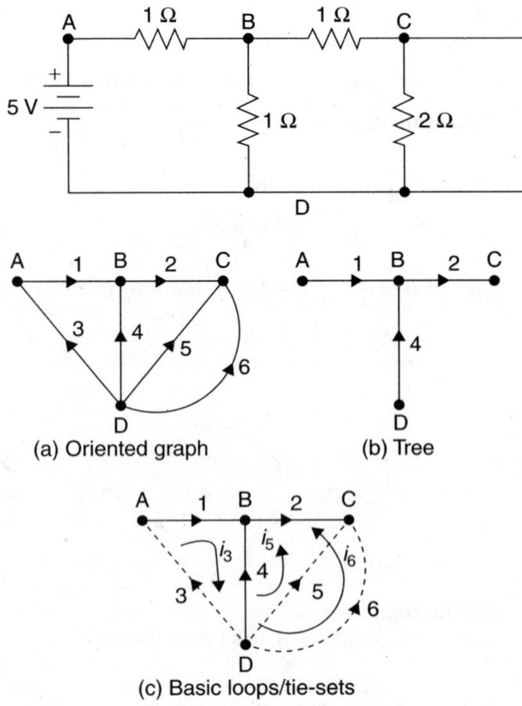

(a) Oriented graph

(b) Tree

(c) Basic loops/tie-sets

Solution: While drawing the oriented graph, all the voltage sources in the network are short circuited, all the current sources are open circuited and points which are electrically at the same potential are combined to form a single node. Therefore the given network is changed to following form. The oriented graph of the above network is shown in Fig. (a).

Link	Basic loop
3	314
5	524
6	624

$$
\begin{array}{c}
\text{Basic loops or links} \\
\downarrow
\end{array}
\qquad
\text{Branches} \rightarrow
$$

$$
[B] = \begin{array}{c} 3 \\ 5 \\ 6 \end{array}
\begin{array}{c} \begin{array}{cccccc} 1 & 2 & 3 & 4 & 5 & 6 \end{array} \\
\begin{bmatrix} 1 & 0 & 1 & -1 & 0 & 0 \\ 0 & -1 & 0 & -1 & 1 & 0 \\ 0 & -1 & 0 & -1 & 0 & 1 \end{bmatrix} \end{array}
$$

In the case of the tie-set matrix, the following equation is satisfied:

$$J = B^T i$$

where J = branch current vector and i = link or loop current vector.

$$\begin{bmatrix} J_1 \\ J_2 \\ J_3 \\ J_4 \\ J_5 \\ J_6 \end{bmatrix} = \begin{bmatrix} 1 & 0 & 0 \\ 0 & -1 & -1 \\ 1 & 0 & 0 \\ -1 & -1 & -1 \\ 0 & 1 & 0 \\ 0 & 0 & 1 \end{bmatrix} \begin{bmatrix} i_3 \\ i_5 \\ i_6 \end{bmatrix} = \begin{bmatrix} i_3 \\ -i_3 - i_5 \\ i_3 \\ -i_3 - i_5 - i_6 \\ i_5 \\ i_6 \end{bmatrix}$$

The branch currents are

$$J_1 = i_3, \quad J_2 = -i_3 - i_5, \quad J_3 = i_3$$

$$J_4 = -i_3 - i_5 - i_6, \quad J_5 = i_5, \quad J_6 = i_6$$

8.4 Draw the graph of the network. Find the number of possible trees and draw them.

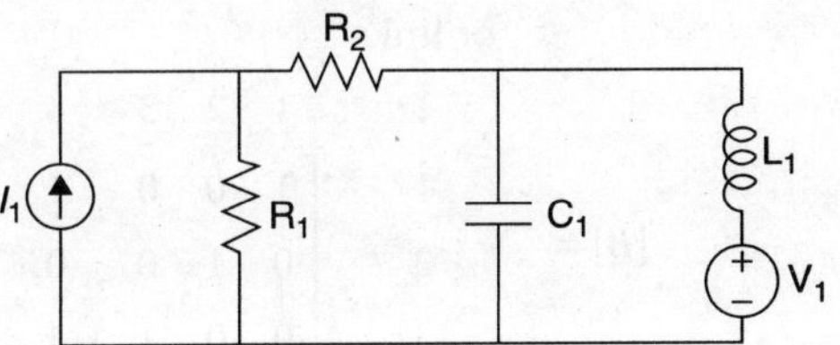

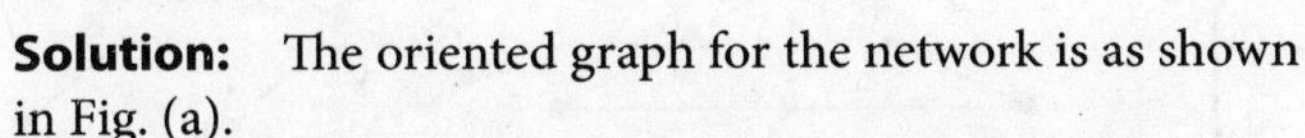

Solution: The oriented graph for the network is as shown in Fig. (a).

The complete incidence matrix for the above graph is

$$\begin{array}{cc} \text{Nodes} & \text{Branches} \rightarrow \\ \downarrow & \begin{array}{cccc} 1 & 2 & 3 & 4 \end{array} \end{array}$$

$$[A_c] = \begin{array}{c} a \\ b \\ c \end{array} \begin{bmatrix} 1 & 1 & 0 & 0 \\ 0 & -1 & 1 & 1 \\ -1 & 0 & -1 & -1 \end{bmatrix}$$

If any one row is deleted from the above matrix, then we can get the incidence matrix (last row) as follows:

$$A = \begin{bmatrix} 1 & 1 & 0 & 0 \\ 0 & -1 & 1 & 1 \end{bmatrix}$$

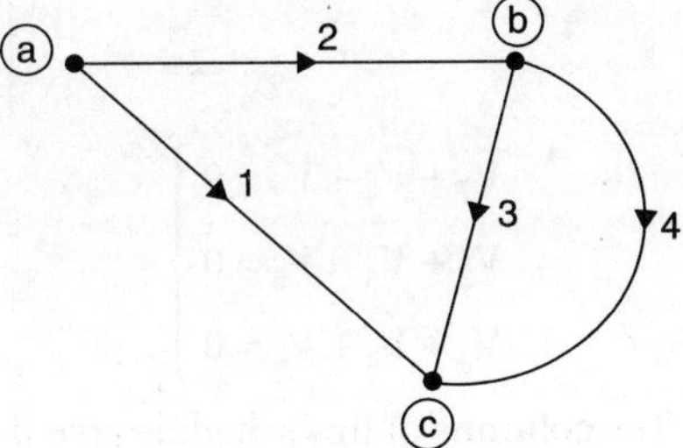

Fig. (a) Oriented graph

$$A \cdot A^T = \begin{bmatrix} 1 & 1 & 0 & 0 \\ 0 & -1 & 1 & 1 \end{bmatrix} \begin{bmatrix} 1 & 0 \\ 1 & -1 \\ 0 & 1 \\ 0 & 1 \end{bmatrix} = \begin{bmatrix} 2 & -1 \\ -1 & 3 \end{bmatrix}$$

$$\det (A \cdot A^T) = \begin{bmatrix} 2 & -1 \\ -1 & 3 \end{bmatrix} = 6 - 1 = 5$$

No. of trees = Det. $(A \cdot A^T) = 5$

All the trees and corresponding co-tree of the above graph are shown in Fig. (b).

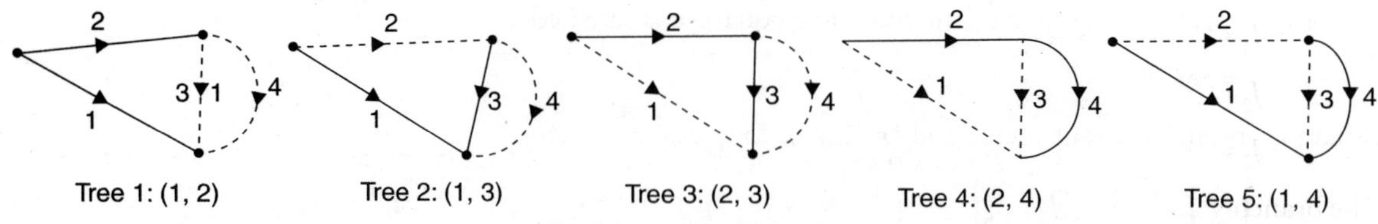

Fig. (b) Trees and co-trees

8.5 For the given resistive network, write the tie-set schedule and obtain equilibrium on the current basics. Solve these equations and hence calculate the values of branch voltages.

Solution: While drawing the oriented graph, all the voltage sources in the network are short circuited, all the current sources are open circuited and points which are electrically at the same potential are combined to form a single node. The oriented graph and tree for the given network is drawn as follows:

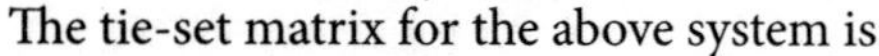
The tie-set matrix for the above system is:

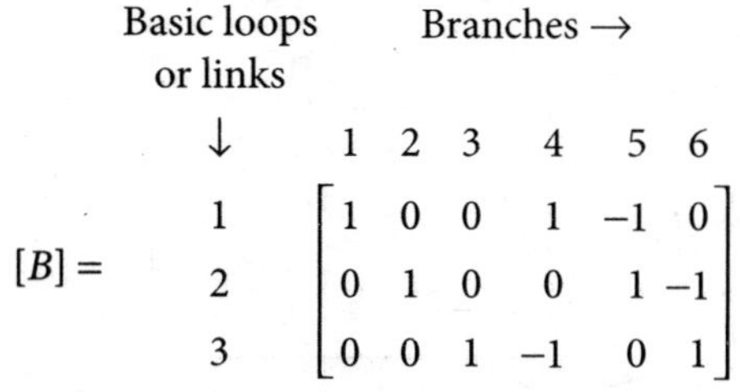

Basic loops or links ↓   Branches →

$$[B] = \begin{array}{c} \\ 1 \\ 2 \\ 3 \end{array} \begin{array}{c} \begin{array}{cccccc} 1 & 2 & 3 & 4 & 5 & 6 \end{array} \\ \begin{bmatrix} 1 & 0 & 0 & 1 & -1 & 0 \\ 0 & 1 & 0 & 0 & 1 & -1 \\ 0 & 0 & 1 & -1 & 0 & 1 \end{bmatrix} \end{array}$$

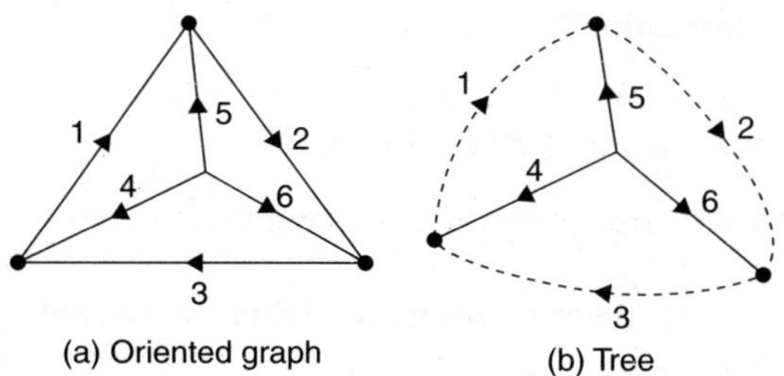

The rows of this schedule yield the voltage law equation.

That is, $BV = 0$

$$\begin{bmatrix} 1 & 0 & 0 & 1 & -1 & 0 \\ 0 & 1 & 0 & 0 & 1 & -1 \\ 0 & 0 & 1 & -1 & 0 & 1 \end{bmatrix} \begin{bmatrix} V_1 \\ V_2 \\ V_3 \\ V_4 \\ V_5 \\ V_6 \end{bmatrix} = 0$$

(c) Basic loops

$$\left.\begin{aligned} V_1 + V_4 - V_5 &= 0 \\ V_2 + V_5 - V_6 &= 0 \\ V_3 - V_4 + V_6 &= 0 \end{aligned}\right\} \tag{1}$$

The columns of this schedule give the branch currents in terms of loop currents.

That is, $J = B^T i$

$$\begin{bmatrix} J_1 \\ J_2 \\ J_3 \\ J_4 \\ J_5 \\ J_6 \end{bmatrix} = \begin{bmatrix} 1 & 0 & 0 \\ 0 & 1 & 0 \\ 0 & 0 & 1 \\ 1 & 0 & -1 \\ -1 & 1 & 0 \\ 0 & -1 & 1 \end{bmatrix} \begin{bmatrix} i_1 \\ i_2 \\ i_3 \end{bmatrix}$$

$$\left.\begin{array}{ll} J_1 = i_1 & J_4 = i_1 - i_3 \\ J_2 = i_2 & J_5 = -i_1 + i_2 \\ J_3 = i_3 & J_6 = -i_2 + i_3 \end{array}\right\} \quad (2)$$

The branch voltages are given by

$$\left.\begin{array}{l} V_1 = 10J_1 - 5 = 10i_1 - 5 \\ V_2 = 10J_2 = 10i_2 \\ V_3 = 10J_3 = 10i_3 \\ V_4 = 5J_4 = 10(i_1 - i_3) \\ V_5 = 5J_5 = 10(i_2 - i_1) \\ V_6 = 5J_6 = 10(i_3 - i_2) \end{array}\right\} \quad (3)$$

Substituting Eq. (3) in Eq. (1)

$$V_1 + V_4 - V_5 = 0$$

$$10i_1 - 5 + 5(i_1 - i_3) - 5(i_2 - i_1) = 0$$

$$4i_1 - i_2 - i_3 = 1$$

$$V_2 + V_5 - V_6 = 0$$

$$10i_2 + 5(i_2 - i_1) - 5(i_3 - i_2) = 0$$

$$-i_1 + 4i_2 - i_3 = 0$$

$$V_3 - V_4 + V_6 = 0$$

$$10i_3 - 5(i_1 - i_3) + 5(i_3 - i_2) = 0$$

$$i_1 + i_2 - 4i_3 = 0$$

$$\therefore \quad \left.\begin{array}{l} 4i_1 - i_2 - i_3 = 1 \\ -i_1 + 4i_2 - i_3 = 0 \\ -i_1 - i_2 + 4i_3 = 0 \end{array}\right\} \quad (4)$$

$$\Delta = \begin{bmatrix} 4 & -1 & -1 \\ -1 & 4 & -1 \\ -1 & -1 & 4 \end{bmatrix} = 4(16-1) + 1(-4-1) + (-1)(1+4) = 50$$

$$\Delta_1 = \begin{bmatrix} 1 & -1 & -1 \\ 0 & 4 & -1 \\ 0 & -1 & 4 \end{bmatrix} = 1(16-1) = 15$$

$$\Delta_2 = \begin{bmatrix} 4 & 1 & -1 \\ -1 & 0 & -1 \\ -1 & 0 & 4 \end{bmatrix} = -1(-4-1) = 5$$

$$\Delta_3 = \begin{bmatrix} 4 & -1 & 1 \\ -1 & 4 & 0 \\ -1 & -1 & 0 \end{bmatrix} = 1(1+4) = 5$$

Using Cramer's rule

$$i_1 = \frac{\Delta_1}{\Delta} = \frac{15}{50} = 0.3 \text{ A}$$

$$i_2 = \frac{\Delta_2}{\Delta} = \frac{5}{50} = 0.1 \text{ A}$$

$$i_3 = \frac{\Delta_3}{\Delta} = \frac{5}{50} = 0.1 \text{ A}$$

∴ The branch currents are

$$j_1 = i_1 = 0.3 \text{ A}$$

$$j_2 = i_2 = 0.1 \text{ A}$$

$$j_3 = i_3 = 0.1 \text{ A}$$

$$j_4 = i_1 - i_3 = 0.3 - 0.1 = 0.2 \text{ A}$$

$$j_5 = i_2 - i_1 = 0.1 - 0.3 = -0.2 \text{ A}$$

$$j_6 = i_3 - i_2 = 0.1 - 0.1 = 0$$

The branch voltages are

$$V_1 = 10j_1 - 5 = 10 \times 0.3 - 5 = -2 \text{ V}$$

$$V_2 = 10j_2 = 10 \times 0.1 = 1 \text{ V}$$

$$V_3 = 10j_3 = 10 \times 0.1 = 1 \text{ V}$$

$$V_4 = 5j_4 = 5 \times 0.2 = 1 \text{ V}$$

$$V_5 = 5j_6 = 5 \times -0.2 = -1 \text{ V}$$

$$V_6 = 5j_6 = 5 \times 0 = 0 \text{ V}$$

8.6 Obtain the dual of the circuit and verify the results by formulating equilibrium equations.

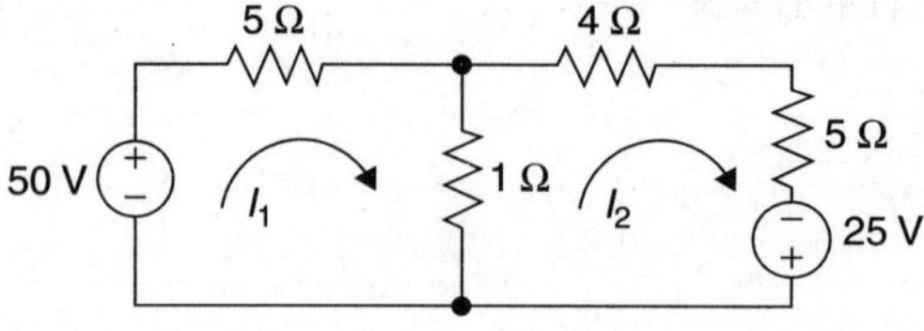

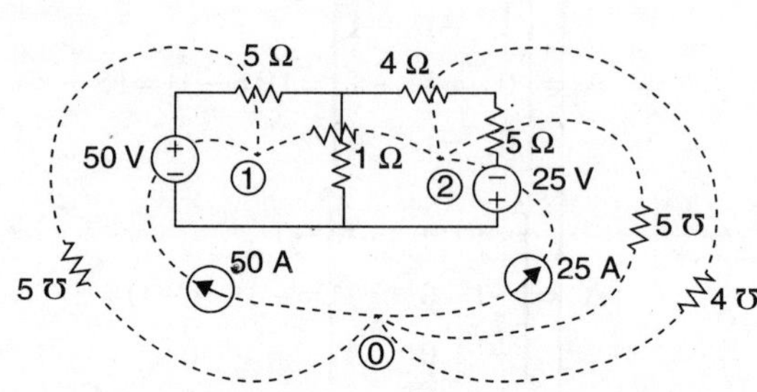

Solution: Mesh equations of the original network are

$$50 = 6I_1 + I_2$$

$$25 = I_1 + 10I_2$$

Nodal equations of the dual network are

$$50 = 6V_1 - V_2$$

$$25 = -V_1 + 10V_2$$

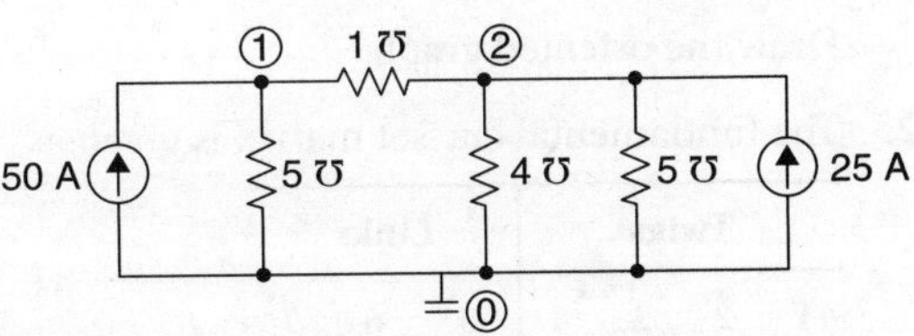

Thus, the mesh equations in the original network have the same form as the nodal equations of the dual network.

8.7 Find the dual of the network.

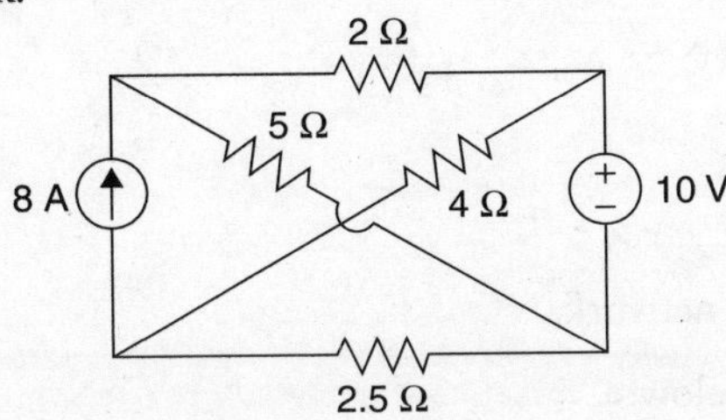

Solution: The given network can be redrawn as

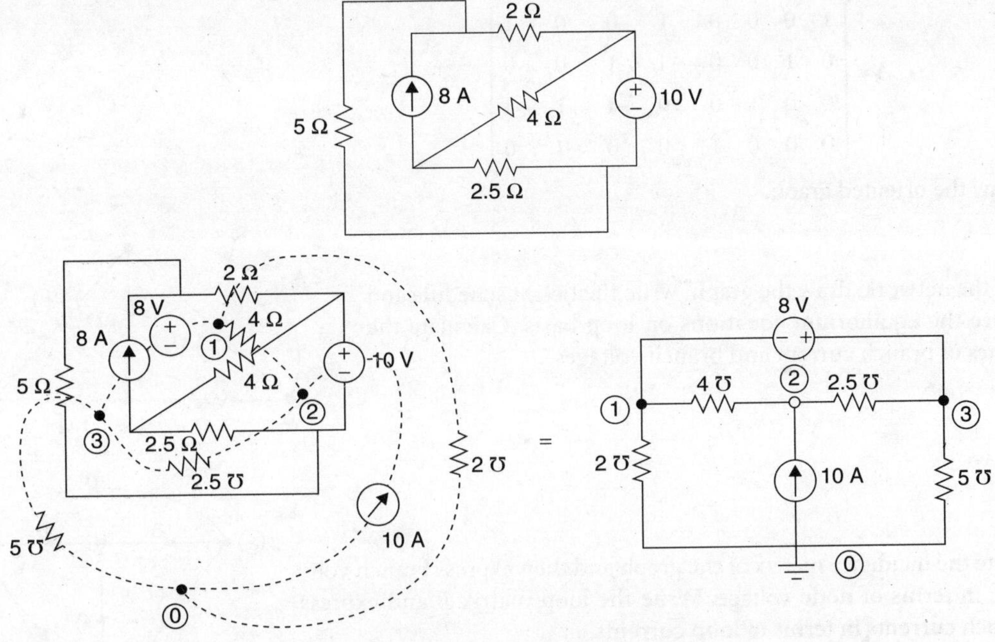

EXERCISE PROBLEMS

1. Branch current and loop current relation are expressed in matrix form as:

$$\begin{bmatrix} i_1 \\ i_2 \\ i_3 \\ i_4 \\ i_5 \\ i_6 \\ i_7 \\ i_8 \end{bmatrix} = \begin{bmatrix} 1 & 0 & 0 & -1 \\ 0 & 1 & 0 & -1 \\ 0 & 1 & 1 & 0 \\ 0 & 1 & 1 & 0 \\ 1 & -1 & 0 & 0 \\ 0 & 0 & -1 & 0 \\ -1 & 0 & 0 & 0 \\ 0 & 0 & 0 & 1 \end{bmatrix} \begin{bmatrix} I_1 \\ I_2 \\ I_3 \\ I_4 \end{bmatrix}$$

Draw the oriented graph.

2. The fundamental cut-set matrix is given as

Twigs				Links		
1	2	3	4	5	6	7
1	0	0	0	–1	0	0
0	1	0	0	1	0	1
0	0	1	0	0	1	1
0	0	0	1	0	1	0

Draw the oriented graph of the network.

3. The incidence matrix is given below:

Branches → 1 2 3 4 5 6 7 8

$$A = \begin{bmatrix} 1 & 0 & 0 & 0 & 1 & 0 & 0 & 1 \\ 0 & 1 & 0 & 0 & -1 & 1 & 0 & 0 \\ 0 & 0 & 1 & 0 & 0 & -1 & 1 & -1 \\ 0 & 0 & 0 & 1 & 0 & 0 & -1 & 0 \end{bmatrix}$$

Draw the oriented graph.

4. For the network, draw the graph, write the tie-set schedule and hence the equilibrium equations on loop basis. Calculate the values of branch current and branch voltages.

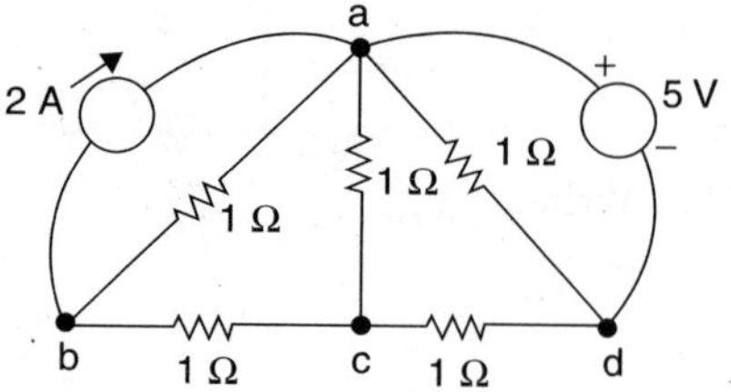

5. Write the incidence matrix of the graph and then express branch voltages in terms of node voltage. Write the loop matrix B and express branch currents in terms of loop currents.

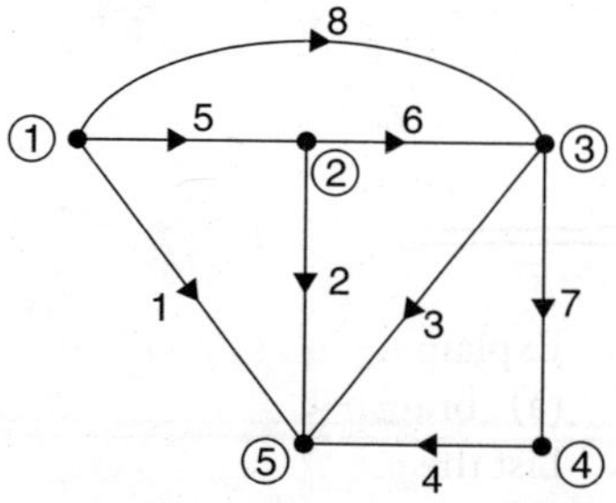

6. Write the basic cut-set matrix for the graph and obtain the relationship between node voltages and branch voltages.

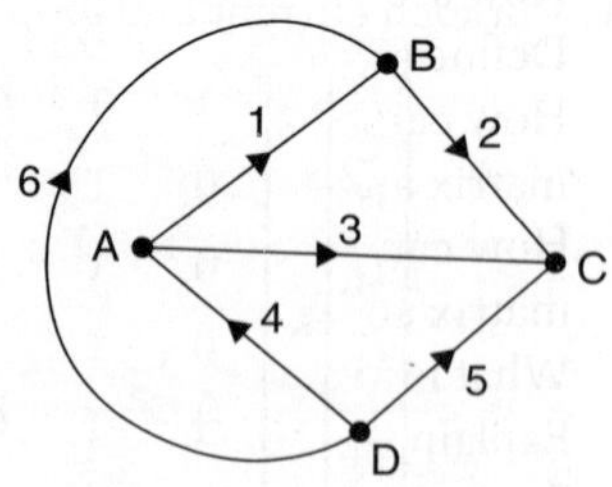

7. Determine the basic cut-set matrix for the oriented graph wherein the elements 1, 2 and 3 are tree branches.

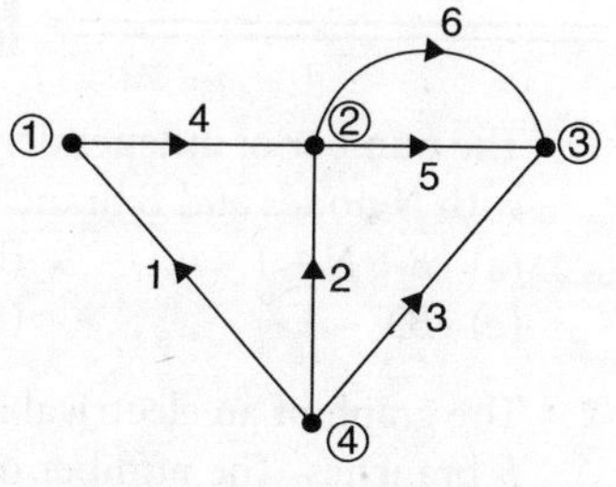

8. Write the tie-set matrix for the graph taking the tree consisting of branches 2, 4 and 5.

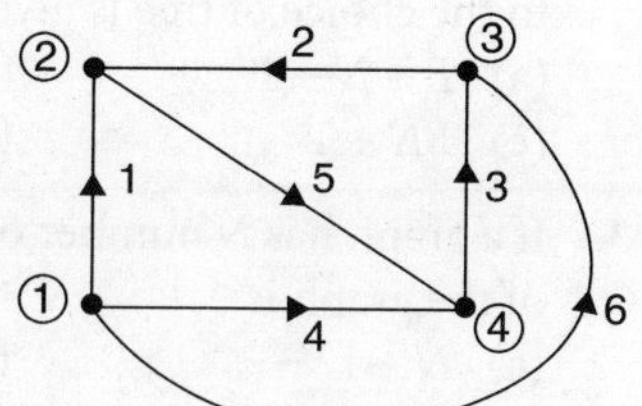

9. For the network graph, write down the fundamental cut-set matrix and fundamental tie-set matrix choosing the tree consisting of branches 5, 6, 7, 8.

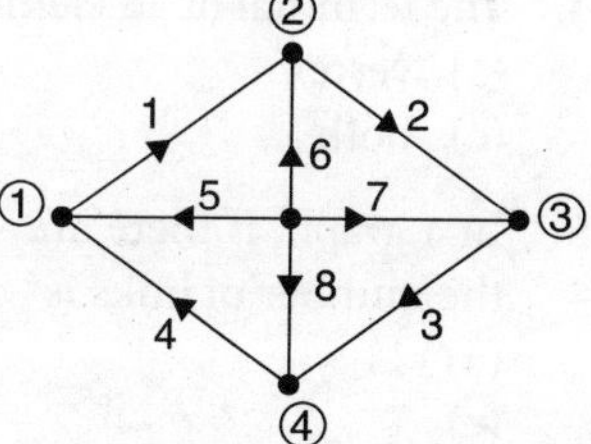

10. Write down the duals of the network using the geometrical procedure.

(a)

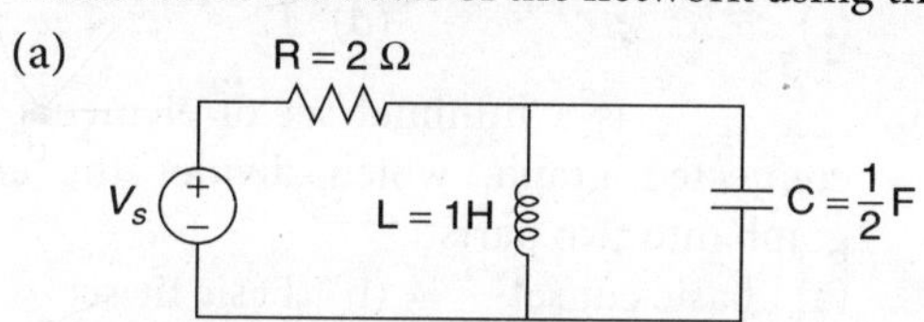

(b)

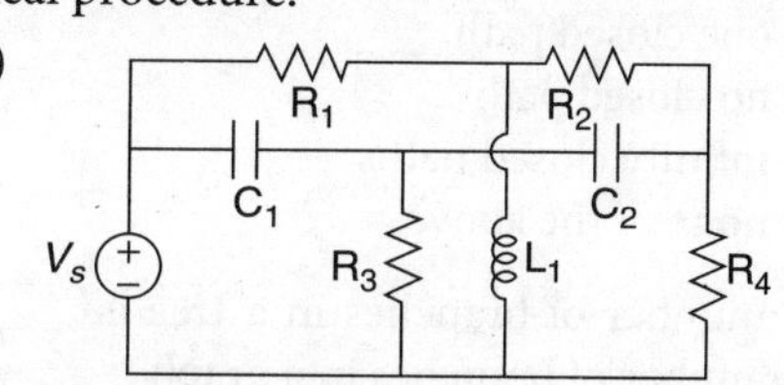

REVIEW QUESTIONS

1. Explain the following with suitable examples
   (a) branch (b) node (c) tree (d) link (e) co-tree (f) loop
2. List the properties of a tree.
3. How are the graphs classified? Explain.
4. Define (a) sub-graph, (b) oriented graph, (d) fundamental cut-set, and (d) fundamental tie-set.
5. How can a cut-set matrix be obtained from an oriented connected graph? What are the entries of this matrix and how are they determined?
6. How can a tie-set matrix be obtained from an oriented connected graph? What are the entries of this matrix and how are they determined?
7. What is a dual network?
8. Explain the procedure of constructing a dual network for the given electrical system.

MULTIPLE CHOICE QUESTIONS

1. The number of independent loops for a network with N nodes and B branches is
(a) $B+N+1$ (b) $B+N-1$
(c) $BN-1$ (d) $B-N+1$

2. The graph of an electrical network has N nodes, B branches. The number of links L with respect to the choice of tree is given by
(a) $B+N-1$ (b) $B+N-1$
(c) $BN+1$ (d) $B-N+1$

3. If a graph has N number of nodes, then the rank of the graph is
(a) $N+1$ (b) $N-1$
(c) N^2-1 (d) N^2+1

4. The terminal of an element is called a
(a) vertex (b) node
(c) both (d) none of the above

5. In a graph, if there are 4 nodes and 7 elements, the number of links is
(a) 11 (b) 4
(c) 7 (d) 3

6. A tree has
(a) one closed path
(b) no closed path
(c) infinity closed paths
(d) none of the above

7. The number of branches in a tree is ________ the number of branches in a graph
(a) less than (b) greater than
(c) equal to (d) none of the above

8. If a network contains B branches and N nodes, then the number of mesh current equations would be
(a) $B+N+1$ (b) $B+N-1$
(c) $BN-1$ (d) $B-N+1$

9. Tree is a sub-graph containing all the ________ of the original graph
(a) vertices (b) elements
(c) both (d) none of the above

10. Co-tree is a complement of a
(a) tree (b) branch
(c) link (d) all of the above

11. The number of loops in a connected graph is equal to the number of
(a) vertices (b) elements
(c) links (d) none of the above

12. The elements of the co-tree are called
(a) vertices (b) branches
(c) links (d) none of the above

13. If a graph consists of n number of nodes, the number of tree branches is
(a) n (b) n^2
(c) $n-1$ (d) $2n$

14. A network has 7 nodes and 5 independent loops. The number of branches in the network is
(a) 11 (b) 7
(c) 5 (d) 12

15. ________ is a minimal set of elements of a connected graph, which divides the entire graph into two parts
(a) basic cut set (b) basic tie set
(c) both (d) none of the above

16. If a graph consists of n number of nodes, the rank of tree is
(a) n (b) $n-1$
(c) $n-2$ (d) $2n$

Answers

1. d	2. d	3. b	4. a	5. b	6. b	7. a	8. d	9. a	10. a
11. c	12. c	13. c	14. a	15. a	16. b				

9 Transient Analysis

Learning Outcomes

After reading this chapter, the reader will able to

- Illustrate transient and steady state behaviour of the network
- Define time constant for RL and RC series circuits
- Explain the significance of time constant
- Outline the initial conditions for resistance, inductance and capacitance
- Analyse *RL*, *RC* and *RLC* series/parallel circuits for DC excitation
- Analyse *RL*, *RC* and *RLC* series circuits for sinusoidal excitation

9.1 INTRODUCTION

When a network is switched from one condition to another by a change in applied voltage (or current) or by a change in one of the circuit elements, during the period of time, the branch currents and voltages change from their initial values to the new one. This time interval is called the *transition period.* The voltages and currents during the transition period are called *transients.* A network in which branch currents and node voltages do not change with respect to time is said to be in a *steady state.* Also, if the voltage and currents in the circuit have constant amplitude and frequency throughout the interval of the time, then such a network is said to be in a steady state. In a network containing energy storage elements, with change in excitation, the currents and voltages change from one state to another state. The behaviour of voltage or current when it is changed from one state to another is called the *transient state* and the corresponding time is called the *transient time.* The response of the system when an external source is applied is called a *forced response.* When no external source is applied, the response of the system due to energy stored in its elements is called a natural or *free response.* The application of Kirchhoff's laws to the network containing energy storage elements such as an inductor or capacitor, result in a differential equation whose solution consists of two parts—the complementary function which represents the transient response or source free response of solution which decays with time, and a particular solution, which represents the steady state response or the forced response of the solution.

9.2 INITIAL CONDITIONS

The conditions obtained in the network immediately after closing or opening of the switch, are known as initial conditions in the network. At $t = 0$, one or more switches are operated which disturb the equilibrium of the circuit. We assume that the switch is operated in zero time. To distinguish time immediately before and immediately after the operation of the switches, we use $t = 0^-$ and $t = 0^+$. The initial conditions will depend on the past history of the network before the time instant $t = 0^+$. These conditions are given in terms of capacitor voltage and inductor current.

9.2.1 BEHAVIOUR OF *R*, *L* AND *C* AT $t = 0$

Resistance The volt–ampere relation for resistance is $V = Ri$. The voltage across the resistance is dependent only on the instantaneous value of the current and hence there is no change in the behaviour or resistance at $t = 0^-$ and $t = 0^+$.

Inductance The voltage across the inductor is given by $V_L = L\frac{di_L}{dt}$. If DC flows through the inductor, $\frac{di_L}{dt} = 0$ as DC current is constant with respect to time. Hence, the voltage across the inductor is zero. Thus, as far as DC quantities are considered, in steady state, the inductor acts as a short circuit. The current in inductor by considering past history is given by

$$i_L(t) = \frac{1}{L}\int_{-\infty}^{t} V_L dt = \frac{1}{L}\int_{-\infty}^{0^-} V_L dt + \frac{1}{L}\int_{0^-}^{t} V_L dt = I_0 + \frac{1}{L}\int_{0^-}^{t} V_L dt \quad (9.1)$$

At $t = 0^+$

$$i_L(0^+) = I_0 + \frac{1}{L}\int_{0^-}^{0^+} V_L dt \quad (9.2)$$

where $I_0 = i_L(0^-) = \frac{1}{L}\int_{-\infty}^{0^-} V_L dt$ is the initial current in the inductor.

If the voltage V_L is finite, since the integral is from 0^- to 0^+, the second term in Eq. 9.2 is equal to zero.

$$\therefore \quad i_L(0^+) = I_0 + 0 = i_L(0^-) \quad (9.3)$$

Thus, current through the inductor cannot change instantaneously. That means the current through the inductor, before and after the switching action, is the same.

If $I_0 = 0$, Eq. 9.3 implies that the inductor behaves like an open circuit since the current is zero. If $I_0 \neq 0$, $i_L(0^+)$ is given as a sum of two currents I_0 and 0, Eq. 9.3 implies that the inductance can be represented by a current source of value I_0 in parallel with an open circuit (Fig. 9.1).

If the initial current $I_0 = 0$, then the inductor behaves like an open circuit at $t = 0^+$.

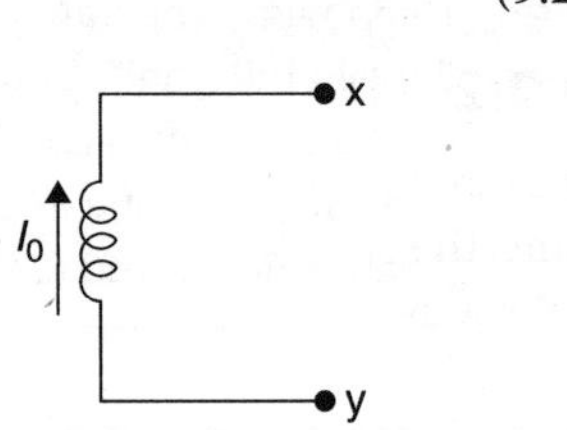

(a) Inductor with initial current I_0

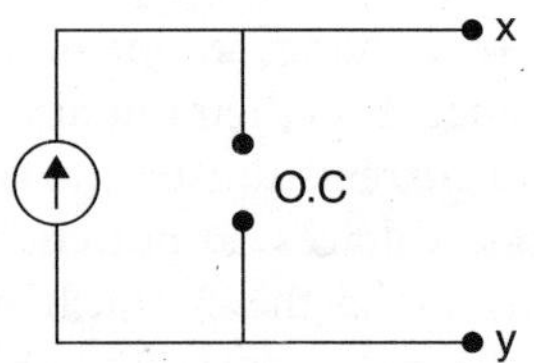

(b) Its equivalent at $t = 0^+$

Fig. 9.1 Behaviour inductor at $t = 0^+$ with initial current I_0

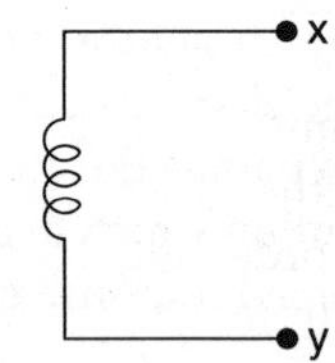

(a) Inductor with zero initial current

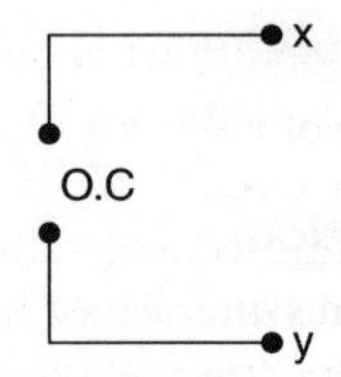

(b) Its equivalent at $t = 0^+$

Fig. 9.2 Behaviour inductor at $t = 0^+$ without initial current

Capacitance The current through the capacitor is given by

$$i_C = C\frac{dv_C}{dt}$$

If DC voltage is applied to the capacitor, $\frac{dv_C}{dt} = 0$, since the DC voltage is constant with respect to time. Hence, the current through the capacitor is zero. Thus, as far as DC quantities are considered, the capacitor acts as an open circuit. The voltage across the capacitor by considering past history is given by,

$$v_C(t) = \frac{1}{C}\int_{-\infty}^{t} i_C dt = \frac{1}{C}\int_{-\infty}^{0^-} i_C dt + \frac{1}{C}\int_{0^-}^{t} i_C dt$$

At $t = 0^+$, $v_C(0^+) = V_0 + \frac{1}{C}\int_{0^-}^{0^+} i_C dt$ (9.4)

where $V_0 = v_C(0^-) = \frac{1}{C}\int_{-\infty}^{0^-} i_C dt$ is the initial voltage across the capacitor.

If the current through the capacitor is finite, the second term in Eq. 9.4 is equal to zero.

$$\therefore \quad v_C(0^+) = V_0 + 0 = v_C(0^-) \tag{9.5}$$

$$\Rightarrow \quad v_C(0^+) = v_C(0^-)$$

Thus, the voltage across the capacitor cannot change instantaneously. Equation 9.5 can be represented as a series circuit consisting of a voltage source of value V_0 and a short circuit as (Fig. 9.3).

If $V_0 = 0$, Eq. 9.5 implies that the capacitor behaves like a short circuit since the voltage is zero.

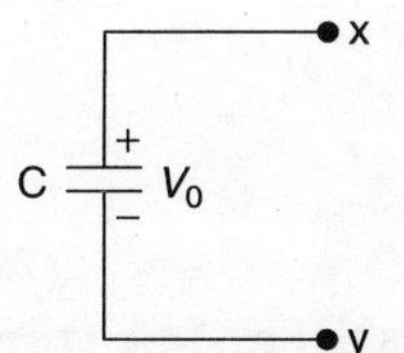

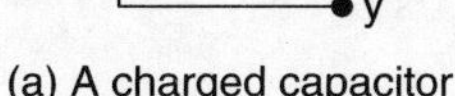
(a) A charged capacitor

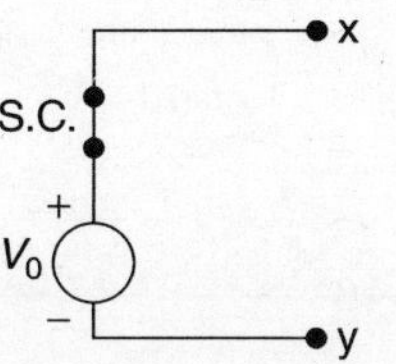

(b) Its equivalent at $t = 0^+$

Fig. 9.3 A charged capacitor and its equivalent at $t = 0^+$

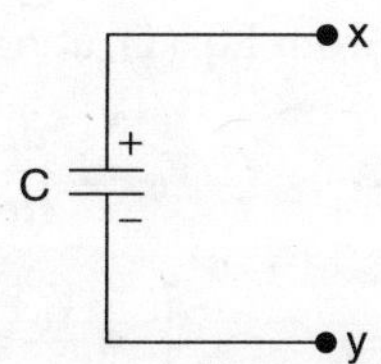

(a) Capacitor with zero initial voltage

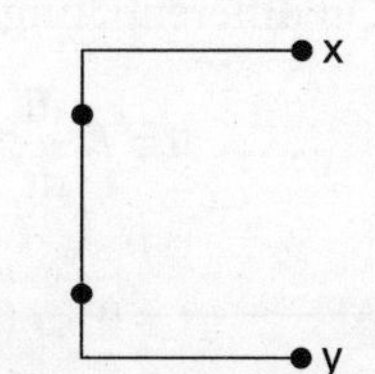

(b) Its equivalent at $t = 0^+$

Fig. 9.4 Uncharged capacitor and its equivalent at $t = 0^+$

9.2.2 Behaviour of *R*, *L* and *C* at $t = \infty$

If a circuit remains in a certain energy state for a long time, the currents and voltages in the network become constants for networks in which the excitations are either constant or decay to zero with time. The currents and voltages are constant, so their derivatives are zero. Hence, the voltages across an inductance and current through a capacitance at $t = \infty$ are given by

$$v_L = L\frac{di}{dt} = 0$$

$$i_C = C\frac{dv}{dt} = 0$$

From the above, it is clear that the inductance behaves like a short circuit and the capacitance behaves like an open circuit. The behaviour of the three elements at $t = 0^+$ and $t = \infty$ is given in Fig. 9.5.

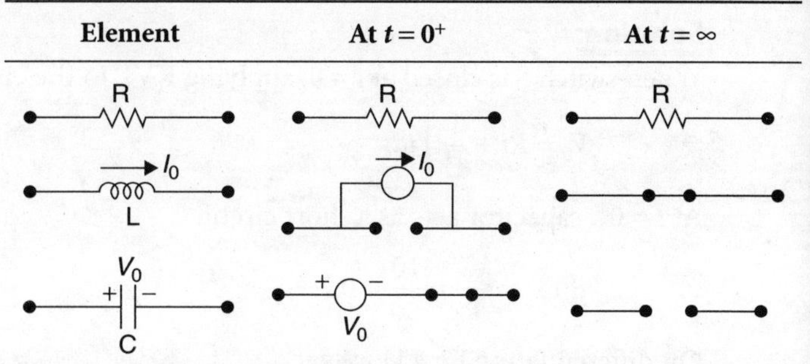

Fig. 9.5 Summary of the behaviour of R, L and C at $t = 0^+$ and $t = \infty$

The $t = \infty$ condition is very useful in determining the initial conditions in a network when the network is in a particular energy state for a long time and the state is changed by a switch at $t = 0$.

In order to calculate the values of currents and voltages at $t = 0^+$, we require the currents and voltages at $t = 0^-$ for the altered network, $t = 0^-$ for the altered network is the same as $t = \infty$ for the original network before the operation of the switch.

Problem 9.1 In the circuit, switch S is closed at $t = 0$. Find the value of i, $\frac{di}{dt}$ and $\frac{d^2i}{dt^2}$ at $t = 0^+$.

S, 100 Ω, 1 H, $V_0 = 10$ V, i

Solution:

When switch S is closed at $t = 0$, applying KVL to the circuit,

$$V_0 = Ri + L\frac{di}{dt} \tag{1}$$

At $t = 0^+$, the inductor acts as an open circuit.

That is, $\quad i(0^+) = 0$

From Eq. (1), at $t = 0^+$, $i(0^+) = 0$

$$\therefore \quad V_0 = L\frac{di}{dt}$$

$$\Rightarrow \quad \frac{di}{dt} = \frac{V_0}{L} = \frac{10}{1} = 10 \text{ A/s}$$

On differentiating (1), we get

$$0 = R\frac{di}{dt} + L\frac{d^2i}{dt^2}$$

At $\quad t = 0^+, i(0^+) = 0, \frac{di}{dt} = 10$

$$\Rightarrow \quad \frac{d^2i}{dt^2} = \frac{-R}{L}\frac{di}{dt} = \frac{-100}{1} \times 10 = -1000 \text{ A/s}^2$$

Problem 9.2 In the circuit, switch S is closed at $t = 0$, find the values of i, $\frac{di}{dt}$ and $\frac{d^2i}{dt^2}$ at $t = 0^+$.

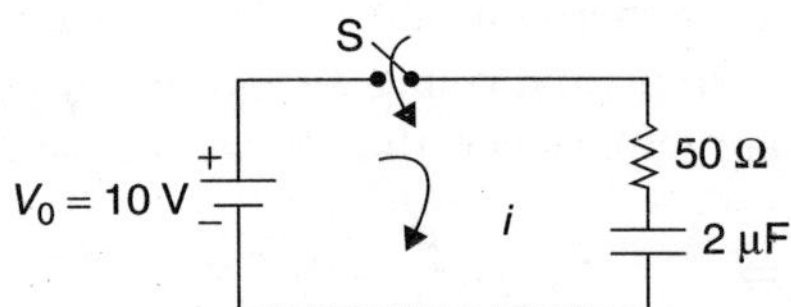

Solution:

When switch S is closed at $t = 0$, applying KVL to the circuit.

$$V_0 = Ri + \frac{1}{C}\int i\,dt \quad (1)$$

At $t = 0^+$, capacitor acts as a short circuit

$$\therefore \quad i(0^+) = \frac{V_0}{R} = \frac{10}{50} = 0.2 \text{ A}$$

On differentiating Eq. (1) we get

$$\Rightarrow \quad 0 = R\frac{di}{dt} + \frac{i}{C} \Rightarrow \frac{di}{dt} = -\frac{i}{RC} \quad (2)$$

$$\left.\frac{di}{dt}\right|_{t=0^+} = -\frac{i(0^+)}{RC} = \frac{-0.2}{50 \times 2 \times 10^{-6}} = -2 \times 10^3 \text{ A/s}$$

On differentiating Eq. (2), we get

$$\frac{d^2i}{dt^2} = \frac{-1}{RC} \times \frac{di}{dt}$$

$$\left.\frac{d^2i}{dt^2}\right|_{t=0^+} = -\frac{1}{RC}\left.\frac{di}{dt}\right|_{t=0^+} = \frac{-1}{50 \times 2 \times 10^{-6}} \times (-2 \times 10^3) = 20 \times 10^6 \text{ A/s}^2$$

Problem 9.3 In the circuit, switch S is closed at time $t = 0$. Find the values of i, $\frac{di}{dt}$ and $\frac{d^2i}{dt^2}$ at $t = 0^+$.

Solution:

When the switch is closed at $t = 0$, applying KVL to the circuit

$$V_0 = Ri + L\frac{di}{dt} + \frac{1}{C}\int idt \qquad (1)$$

At time $t = 0^+$, the inductor acts as an open circuit and the capacitor acts as a short circuit.

That is, $i(0^+) = 0, \frac{1}{C}\int idt = 0$

$\therefore$ From Eq. (1) $V_0 = 0 + L\frac{di}{dt} + 0$

$$\Rightarrow \quad \left.\frac{di}{dt}\right|_{t=0^+} = \frac{V_0}{L} = \frac{10}{2\times 10^{-3}} = 5000 \text{ A/s}$$

On differentiating Eq. (1) we get

$$0 = R\frac{di}{dt} + L\frac{d^2i}{dt^2} + \frac{1}{c}$$

$$\Rightarrow \quad \frac{d^2i}{dt^2} = -\left[\frac{R}{L}\frac{di}{dt} + \frac{i}{LC}\right]$$

$$\left.\frac{d^2i}{dt^2}\right|_{t=0^+} = -\left(\frac{100}{2\times 10^{-3}}\times 5000 + 0\right) = -25\times 10^7 \text{ A/s}^2$$

9.3 DC TRANSIENTS

9.3.1 DC Response of a *RL* Series Circuit

Consider a constant voltage V applied to a RL series circuit at time $t = 0$ (Fig. 9.6).

Applying KVL to the circuit

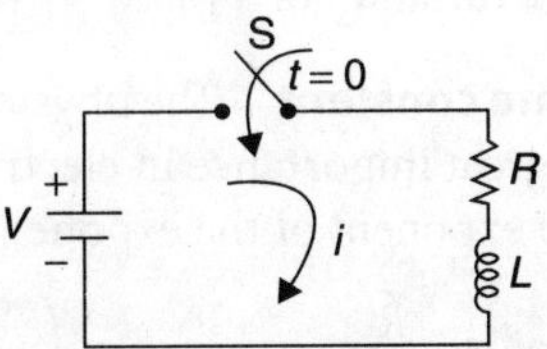

Fig. 9.6 *RL* series circuit excited by a DC voltage source

$$Ri + L\frac{di}{dt} = V$$

$$\frac{di}{dt} + \frac{R}{L}i = \frac{V}{L} \qquad (9.6)$$

Note: Comparing it with a non-homogeneous differential equation $\frac{dx}{dt} + Px = K$, whose solution is

$$x = C_1e^{-Pt} + e^{-Pt}\int Ke^{Pt}dt$$

(C.F.) (P.I.)

Comparing Eq. 9.6 with a non-homogeneous differential equation, the current equation is

$$i = C_1e^{-\frac{R}{L}t} + e^{-\frac{R}{L}t}\int\frac{V}{L}e^{\frac{R}{L}t}dt = C_1e^{-\frac{R}{L}t} + e^{-\frac{R}{L}t}\times\frac{V}{L}e^{\frac{R}{L}t}\times\frac{L}{R} = C_1e^{-\frac{R}{L}t} + \frac{V}{R}$$

$$\Rightarrow \qquad i = C_1 e^{-\frac{R}{L}t} + \frac{V}{R} \qquad (9.7)$$

To determine the value of C_1, we can use the initial condition. In Fig. 9.6, the switch is closed at $t = 0$. At $t = 0^-$, that is, just before closing the switch S, the current in the inductor is zero. Since the inductor does not allow sudden changes in current, at $t = 0^+$, just after the switch is closed, the current remains zero.

That is, at $t = 0$, $i = 0$

∴ From Eq. 9.7, we have

$$0 = C_1 + \frac{V}{R} \Rightarrow C_1 = -\frac{V}{R} \qquad (9.8)$$

∴ The complete solution is

$$i(t) = \frac{V}{R} - \frac{V}{R} e^{-\frac{R}{L}t} = \frac{V}{R}\left(1 - e^{\frac{-R}{L}t}\right) \qquad (9.9)$$

The current $i(t)$ increases exponentially starting from zero to final of $\left(\frac{V}{R}\right)$ (that is, at $t = \infty$, Fig. 9.7). Equation 9.9 consists of two parts—the steady state response/forced response/zero state response $\left(\frac{V}{R}\right)$ and the transient response/natural response/zero input response $\left(\frac{V}{R} e^{\frac{-R}{L}t}\right)$.

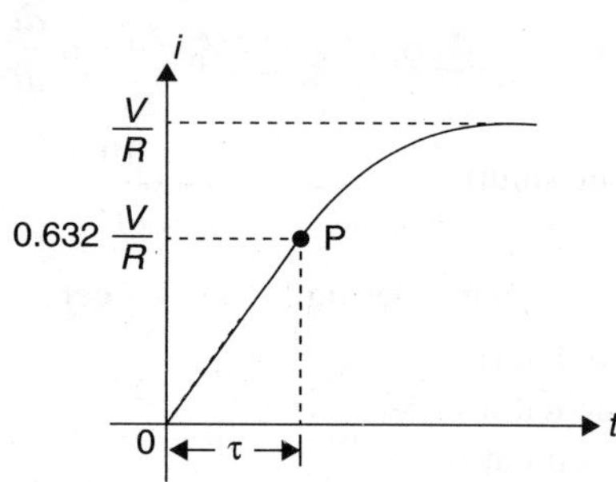

Fig. 9.7 Response of *RL* series circuit

Voltage across the resistor, $V_R = Ri = V\left(1 - e^{-\frac{R}{L}t}\right)$ (9.10)

Voltage across the inductor, $V_L = L\frac{di}{dt} = L \times \frac{V}{R} \times e^{-\frac{R}{L}\times t} \times \frac{R}{L} = Ve^{\frac{-R}{L}t}$ (9.11)

The variation of V_R and V_L with respect to time is shown in Fig. 9.8.

Time constant The physical significance attached to the time constant is of great importance in electrical systems. It is defined as the time at which the exponent of the exponential term is unity.

That is, $\frac{R}{L}t = 1 \Rightarrow t = \frac{L}{R}$

$$\therefore \qquad \text{Time constant } (\tau) = \frac{L}{R} \qquad (9.12)$$

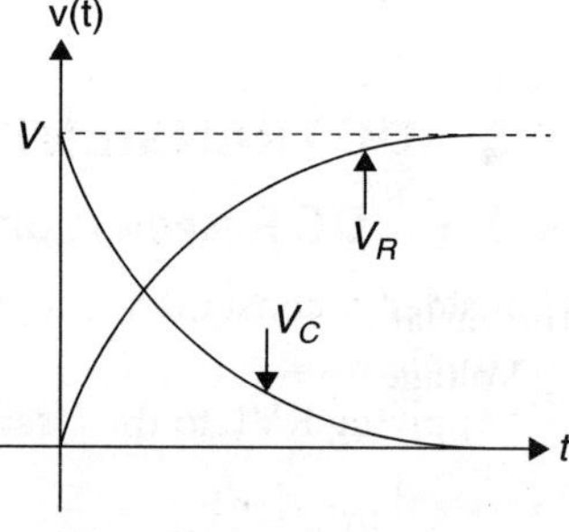

Fig. 9.8 Response of V_R and V_L

The complete solution of current is

$$i(t) = \frac{V}{R}\left(1 - e^{\frac{-R}{L}t}\right) = \frac{V}{R}\left(1 - e^{-\frac{t}{\tau}}\right)$$

$t = 0$	$t = \tau$	$t = 2\tau$	$t = 3\tau$	$t = 4\tau$	$t = 5\tau$
$i = 0$	$0.632\frac{V}{R}$	$0.865\frac{V}{R}$	$0.95\frac{V}{R}$	$0.982\frac{V}{R}$	$0.993\frac{V}{R}$

The current at different instants is shown.

The time constant is also defined as the time required for the current to rise to 0.632 of its final value. For $t > 5\tau$ the current has reached its final value. We will consider that the transient period is about five times the time constant for any circuit. For any circuit, the larger the time constant, slower is the rate of increase of current (response is slower). For circuits with a smaller time constant, the response is faster. The time constant helps in comparing the response with one another.

9.3.2 DC Response of an *RC* Series Circuit

Let a constant voltage V be applied to a RC series circuit at time $t = 0$ (Fig. 9.9).

Applying KVL to the circuit

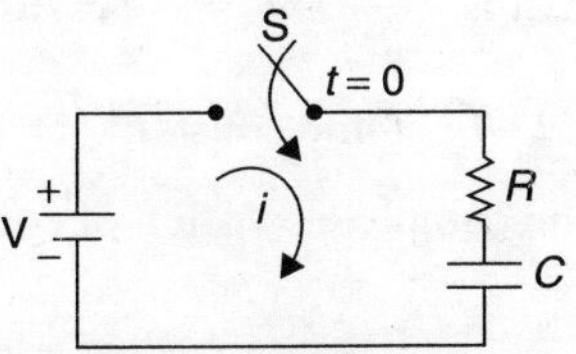

Fig. 9.9 *RL* series circuit excited by a DC voltage source

$$Ri + \frac{1}{C}\int i\,dt = V \tag{9.13}$$

Differentiating Eq. 9.13,

$$R\frac{di}{dt} + \frac{i}{C} = 0$$

$$\frac{di}{dt} + \frac{i}{RC} = 0 \tag{9.14}$$

The solution for Eq. 9.14 is,

$$i = C_1 e^{-\frac{1}{RC}t} \tag{9.15}$$

To determine the value of C_1 we use the initial conditions. In Fig. 9.9, switch S is closed at $t = 0$. Since the capacitor never allows sudden changes in voltage, it will act as a short circuit at $t = 0^+$. So the current in the circuit at $t = 0^+$ is $\frac{V}{R}$.

$\therefore$ At $t = 0, i = \dfrac{V}{R}$

From Eq. 9.15 we have.

$$\frac{V}{R} = C_1 \times e^{-0} = C_1 \Rightarrow C_1 = \frac{V}{R}$$

$\therefore$ The complete solution is

$$i(t) = \frac{V}{R}e^{-\frac{t}{RC}} \tag{9.16}$$

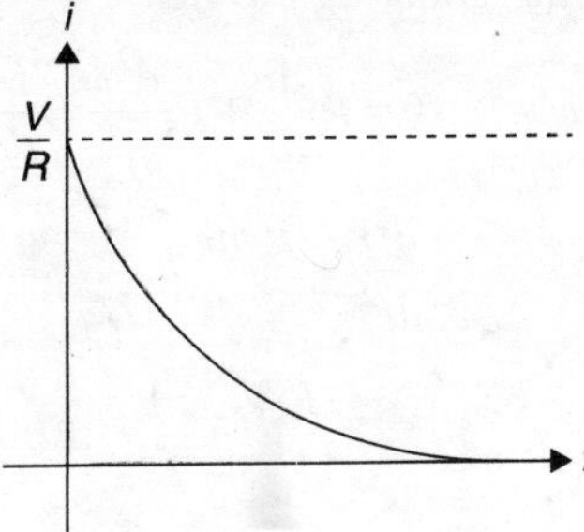

Fig. 9.10 Response of *RL* series circuit

The variation of current $i(t)$ with respect to time decays exponentially (Fig. 9.10).

Voltage across the resistor is

$$V_R = iR = R \times \frac{V}{R}e^{-\frac{t}{RC}} = Ve^{-\frac{t}{RC}} \tag{9.17}$$

Voltage across the capacitor is

$$V_C = \frac{1}{C}\int i\,dt = \frac{1}{C}\int \frac{V}{R}e^{-\frac{t}{RC}} = -\frac{V}{RC}e^{-\frac{t}{RC}} \times RC + K = K - Ve^{-\frac{t}{RC}}$$

At $t = 0$, the voltage across the capacitor is zero

$$0 = -V \times e^{-0} + K \Rightarrow K = V$$

$$\therefore \quad V_C = V - Ve^{-\frac{t}{RC}} = V\left(1 - e^{-\frac{t}{RC}}\right) \tag{9.18}$$

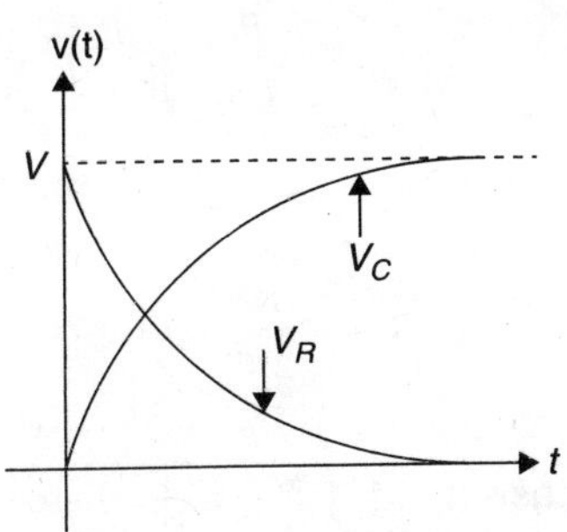

Fig. 9.11 Response of V_R and V_C

The variation of V_R and V_C with respect time is shown in Fig. 9.11. The voltage across the capacitor exponentially increases and the capacitor gets charged.

Time constant It is defined as the time at which the exponent of the exponential term is unity.

That is, $\frac{t}{RC} = 1 \Rightarrow t = RC$

$\therefore$ Time constant $(\tau) = RC$ (9.19)

The complete solution of current is

$$i(t) = \frac{V}{R} e^{-\frac{t}{RC}} = \frac{V}{R} e^{-\frac{t}{\tau}}$$

The current at different instants is shown.

$t=0$	$t=\tau$	$t=2\tau$	$t=3\tau$	$t=4\tau$	$t=5\tau$
$i=\frac{V}{R}$	$0.368\frac{V}{R}$	$0.135\frac{V}{R}$	$0.0498\frac{V}{R}$	$0.0183\frac{V}{R}$	$0.0067\frac{V}{R}$

The time constant is also defined as the time required for the current to reach to 36.8% of its initial value. For $t = 5\tau$, the current has reduced almost to zero, hence transient period is completed.

9.3.3 DC Response of an *RLC* Series Circuit

Let a constant voltage V be applied to a RLC series circuit at time $t = 0$ (Fig. 9.12).

Applying KVL to the circuit

$$V = Ri + L\frac{di}{dt} + \frac{1}{C}\int i\,dt \tag{9.20}$$

Fig. 9.12 *RLC* series circuit excited by a DC voltage source

Differentiating Eq. 9.20,

$$0 = R\frac{di}{dt} + L\frac{d^2i}{dt^2} + \frac{i}{C}$$

$$\frac{d^2i}{dt^2} + \frac{R}{L}\frac{di}{dt} + \frac{1}{LC}i = 0$$

$$s^2 i + \frac{R}{L}si + \frac{1}{LC}i = 0 \quad \text{where} \quad s = \frac{d}{dt}$$

$$\left(s^2 + \frac{R}{L}s + \frac{1}{LC}\right)i = 0 \tag{9.21}$$

The characteristic equation of an RLC circuit is

$$s^2 + \frac{R}{L}s + \frac{1}{LC} = 0 \tag{9.22}$$

The roots of the characteristic equation are

$$s_{1,2} = \frac{-\frac{R}{L} \pm \sqrt{\left(\frac{R}{L}\right)^2 - 4 \times \frac{1}{LC}}}{2} = -\frac{R}{2L} \pm \sqrt{\left(\frac{R}{2L}\right)^2 - \frac{1}{LC}} = \alpha \pm \beta$$

where, $\alpha = -\frac{R}{2L}$ and $\beta = \sqrt{\left(\frac{R}{2L}\right)^2 - \frac{1}{LC}}$

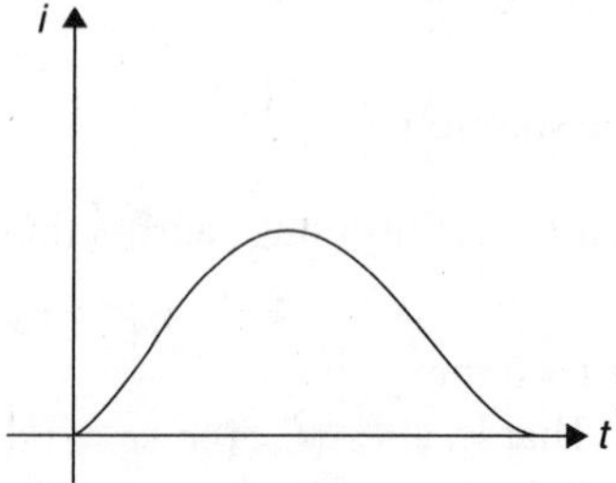

Fig. 9.13 Response of *RLC* series circuit for over damped case

Case (i) If $\left(\frac{R}{2L}\right)^2 > \frac{1}{LC}$ then $s_1 = \alpha + \beta$, $s_2 = \alpha - \beta$. Roots s_1 and s_2 are real and unequal and the solution resulting the over damped case. Then Eq. 9.21 becomes

$$[s-(\alpha+\beta)]\,[s-(\alpha-\beta)]\,i=0 \tag{9.23}$$

The solution of Eq. 9.23 is

$$i=C_1e^{(\alpha+\beta)t}+C_2e^{(\alpha-\beta)t}=e^{\alpha t}(C_1e^{\beta t}+C_2e^{-\beta t}) \tag{9.24}$$

The current characteristics for the over damped case is shown in Fig. 9.13.

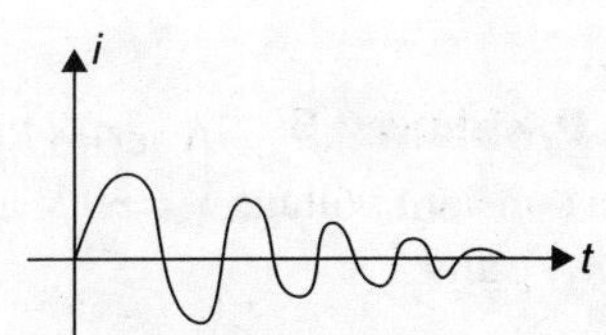

Fig. 9.14 Response of *RLC* series circuit for under damped case

Case (ii) If $\left(\frac{R}{2L}\right)^2<\frac{1}{LC}$ then $s_1=\alpha+j\beta,\ s_2=\alpha-j\beta$

Roots s_1 and s_2 are complex conjugate and the solution results in the under-damped case.

Then, Eq. 9.21 becomes

$$[s-(\alpha+j\beta)]\,[s-(\alpha-j\beta)\,i=0 \tag{9.25}$$

The solution of Eq. 9.25 is,

$$i=C_1e^{(\alpha+\beta)t}+C_2e^{(\alpha-j\beta)t}=e^{\alpha t}(C_1e^{j\beta t}+C_2e^{-j\beta t}) \tag{9.26}$$

The current characteristics for the under damped case is shown in Fig. 9.14.

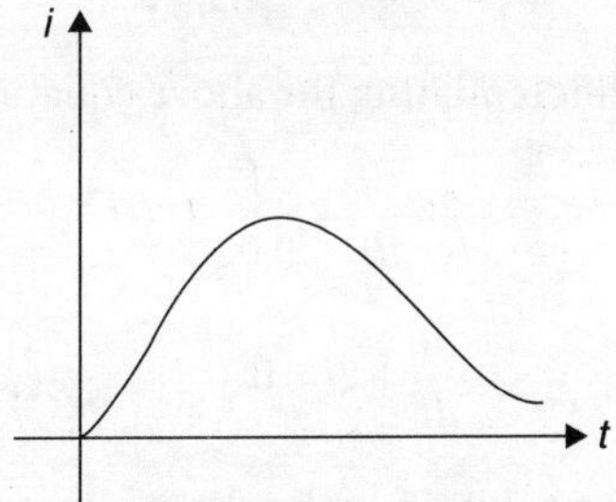

Fig. 9.15 Response of *RLC* series circuit for critically damped case

Case (iii) If $\left(\frac{R}{2L}\right)^2=\frac{1}{LC}$ then the roots are equal and the solution resulting the critically damped case.

Then, Eq. (9.21) becomes

$$(s-\alpha)\,(s-\alpha)\,i=0 \tag{9.27}$$

The solution of Eq. 9.27 is

$$i=C_1e^{\alpha t}+C_2t\cdot e^{\alpha t}=e^{\alpha t}(C_1+C_2t) \tag{9.28}$$

The current curve for the critically damped case is as shown in Fig. 9.15.

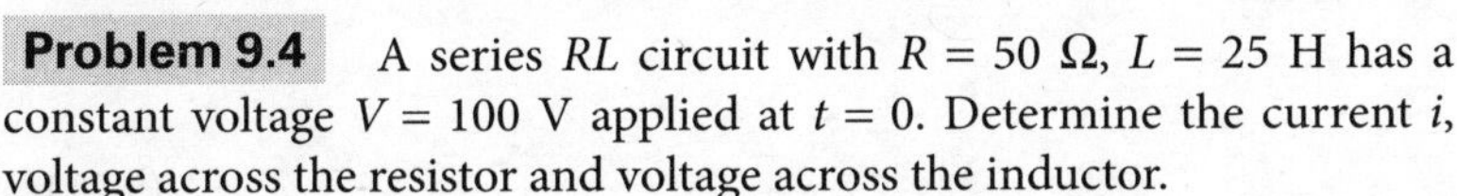

Problem 9.4 A series *RL* circuit with $R=50\ \Omega$, $L=25$ H has a constant voltage $V=100$ V applied at $t=0$. Determine the current i, voltage across the resistor and voltage across the inductor.

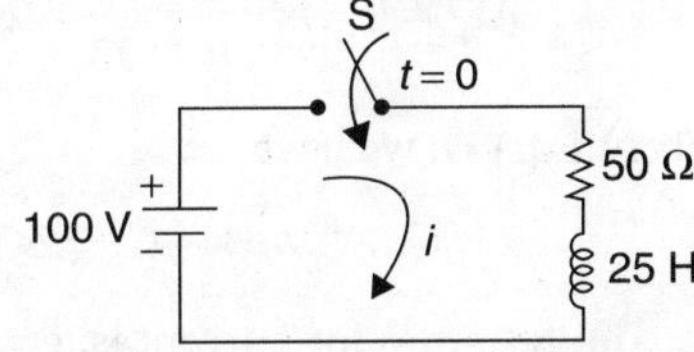

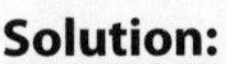

Solution:

Applying KVL to the circuit at $t=0$

$$50i+25\frac{di}{dt}=100$$

$$\frac{di}{dt}+2i=4$$

The solution is

$$i=C_1e^{-2t}+e^{-2t}\int 4e^{2t}dt=C_1e^{-2t}+e^{-2t}\times\frac{4}{2}e^{2t}=C_1e^{-2t}+2$$

At $t=0$ the switch is closed so at $t=0^+$ the inductor acts as an open circuit, so the current is zero.

That is, at $t=0^+$, $i=0$

$\therefore\quad 0=C_1+2\ \Rightarrow\ C_1=-2$

$\therefore$ The current equation is, $i=-2e^{-2t}+2=2(1-e^{-2t})$

Voltage across the resistor is, $V_R = 50\, i = 100\, (1 - e^{-21})$

Voltage across the inductor is, $V_L = L\dfrac{di}{dt} = 25(2 \times 2e^{-2t}) = 100e^{-2t}$ V

Problem 9.5 A series *RC* circuit with $R = 25\ \Omega$, $C = 0.02$ F has a constant voltage $V = 50$ V applied at $t = 0$. Determine the current i, V_R and V_C.

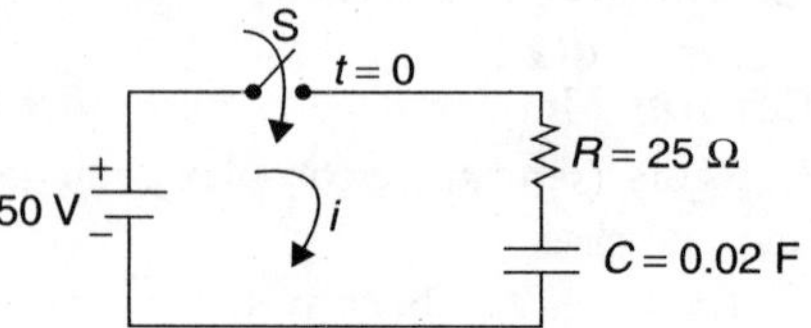

Solution:

Applying KVL to the circuit at $t = 0$

$$50 = 25i + \frac{1}{0.02}\int i\,dt$$

Differentiating the above equation,

$$25\frac{di}{dt} + \frac{1}{0.02}i = 0$$

$$\frac{di}{dt} + 2i = 0$$

The solution of the above equation is

$$i = C_1 e^{-2t} \tag{1}$$

At $t = 0$ the switch is closed and so at $t = 0^+$ the capacitor acts as a short circuit

$$\therefore \quad \text{At } t = 0^+, i = \frac{V}{R} = \frac{50}{25} = 2$$

From Eq. (1), we have

$$2 = C_1\, e^{-0} \;\Rightarrow\; C_1 = 2$$

$\therefore$ The equation for current is, $i = 2e^{-2t}$

$$V_R = Ri = 25 \times 2e^{-2t} = 50e^{-2t}$$

$$V_C = \frac{1}{C}\int_0^t i\,dt = \frac{1}{0.02}\int_0^t 2e^{-2t}\,dt = -\frac{1}{0.02}[e^{-2t}]_0^t = 50\,(1 - e^{-2t})$$

(or) $\quad V_C = V - V_R = 50 - 50e^{-2t} = 50(1 - e^{-2t})$

Problem 9.6 A series *RLC* circuit consists of a 100 V DC source when the switch is closed at $t = 0$. Find the current transient.

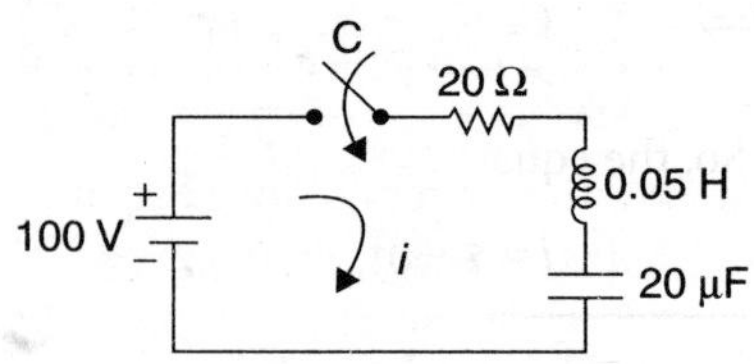

Solution:

Applying KVL to the circuit at $t = 0$

$$20i + 0.05\frac{di}{dt} + \frac{1}{20 \times 10^{-6}}\int i\,dt = 100$$

Differentiating the above equation,

$$20\frac{di}{dt}+0.05\frac{d^2i}{dt^2}+5\times10^4 i=0$$

$$\frac{d^2i}{dt^2}+400\frac{di}{dt}+10^6 i=0$$

$$(s^2+400s+10^6)\,i=0,\quad \text{where}\quad s=\frac{di}{dt}$$

$$s_{1,2}=\frac{-400\pm\sqrt{400^2-4\times10^6}}{2\times1}=-200\pm\sqrt{(200)^2-10^6}$$

$\Rightarrow$ $s_1=-200+j980,\ s_2=-200-j980$

The solution for the current is

$$i=e^{K_1 t}(C_1\cos K_2 t+C_2\sin K_2 t)=e^{-200t}(C_1 980t+C_2\sin 980t)$$

At $t=0$, the inductor acts as an open circuit and capacitor acts as a short circuit.

That is, at $t=0,\ i=0$

$\therefore$ $0=e^{-0}\times C_1 \quad\Rightarrow\quad C_1=0$

Therefore, the current equation is,

$$i=e^{-200t}C_2\sin 980\,t$$

Differentiating the above equation,

$$\frac{di}{dt}=C_2[e^{-200t}\cos 980t\times980-\sin 980t\times e^{-200t}\times200] \tag{1}$$

At $t=0$, the voltage across the inductor is 100 V.

That is, at $t=0$ $V_L=100$ V

$$L\frac{di}{dt}=100$$

$$\Rightarrow\quad \frac{di}{dt}=\frac{100}{L}=\frac{100}{0.05}=2000 \tag{2}$$

From Eqs (1) and (2), we have

$$2000=C_2[e^{-0}\times\cos0\times980-200\times\sin0\times e^{-0}]=980\,C_2$$

$$\Rightarrow\quad C_2=\frac{2000}{980}=2.04$$

So, the equation for current is

$$i=2.04e^{-200t}\sin 980t\ \text{A}$$

Problem 9.7 In the circuit, the switch is at position-1 to establish steady state condition and at $t=0$ it is switched to position-2. Find the resulting current.

Solution:

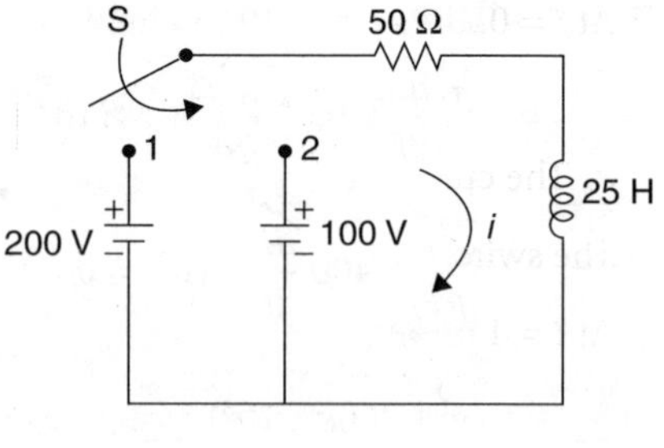

The switch is in position 1 to establish a steady state condition and hence the initial current in the circuit is,

$$i(0) = \frac{V}{R} = \frac{200}{50} = 4 \text{ A} \quad (\therefore \text{ Inductor acts a short circuit})$$

$$\therefore \qquad i(0) = i(0^+) = 4 \text{ A}$$

At $t = 0$, the switch is moved to position 2, so applying KVL to the circuit.

$$50i + 25\frac{di}{dt} = 100$$

$$\frac{di}{dt} + 2i = 4$$

The solution for the current is

$$i = C_1 e^{-2t} + e^{-2t}\int 4e^{2t}\, dt = C_1 e^{-2t} + 2$$

At $t = 0$, $i(0) = 4$

$$4 = C_1 + 2 \quad \Rightarrow \quad C_1 = 2$$

Therefore, the equation for current is

$$i = 2e^{-2t} + 2 = 2(1 + e^{-2t})$$

Problem 9.8 In the circuit the switch S_1 is called at $t = 0$ and switch S_2 is operated at $t = 4$ ms. Obtain i for $t > 0$.

t = 0
50 Ω
S_1
S_2
100 Ω
100 V
i
0.1 H

Solution:

When switch S_1 is closed at $t = 0$,

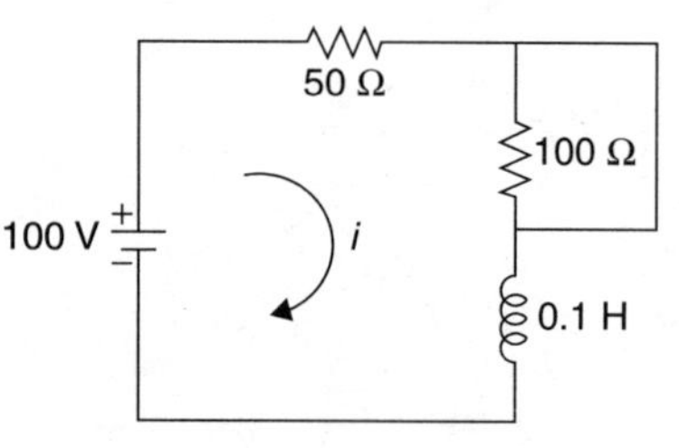

=

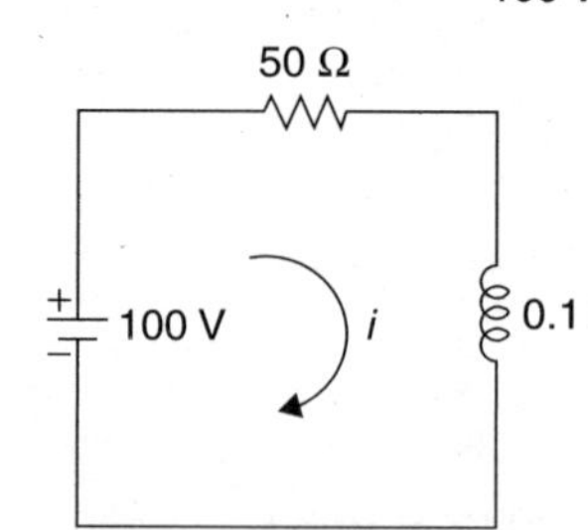

Applying KVL to the circuit

$$50i + 0.1\frac{di}{dt} = 100$$

$$\frac{di}{dt} + 500i = 1000$$

The solution for current is

$$i = C_1 e^{-500} + e^{-500t}\int 1000e^{500t}\, dt = C_1 e^{-500t} + 2$$

At $t = 0$, the switch is closed, so at $t = 0$, $i = 0$

$$0 = C_1 + 2 \quad \Rightarrow \quad C_1 = -2$$

$\therefore$ The current is, $i = 2\,(1 - e^{-500t})$

The switch S_2 is opened at $t = 4$ ms.

At $t = 4$ ms, $i(t) = 2(1 - e^{-500 \times 4 \times 10^{-6}}) = 1.7293$ A

$$i(4\text{ ms}) = 1.7293\text{ A}$$

When switch S_2 is opened, we have

$$50i(t') + 100i(t') + 0.1\frac{di(t')}{dt} = 100$$

$$\frac{di(t')}{dt} + 1500i(t') = 1000$$

The solution for the current is

$$i(t') = C_1 e^{-1500\,t'} + e^{-1500t'}\int 1000 e^{1500t'}dt' = C_1 e^{-1500t'} + \frac{2}{3}$$

At $\quad t' = 4$ ms, $i(t') = i(4\text{ ms}) = 1.7293$

$$1.7293 = C_1 e^{-1500 \times 4 \times 10^{-3}} + \frac{2}{3}$$

$$C_1 e^{-6} = 1.7293 - 0.666 = 1.0626$$

$$C_1 = 1.0626e^{6} = 428.69$$

$\therefore \qquad i(t') = 428.69e^{-1500t'} + \frac{2}{3}$ but $t' = t - 4$ ms

The current transient is

$$i(t) = 2\,(1 - e^{-500t}) \quad \text{for} \quad 0 \le t \le 4\text{ ms}$$

$$i(t - 0.004) = 428.69e^{-1500(t - 0.004)} + \frac{2}{3} \text{ for } t > 4\text{ ms}$$

9.4 AC TRANSIENTS

9.4.1 AC Response of an *RL* Series Circuit

Consider an *RL* series circuit excited by a sinusoidal source (Fig. 9.16).

Applying KVL to the circuit

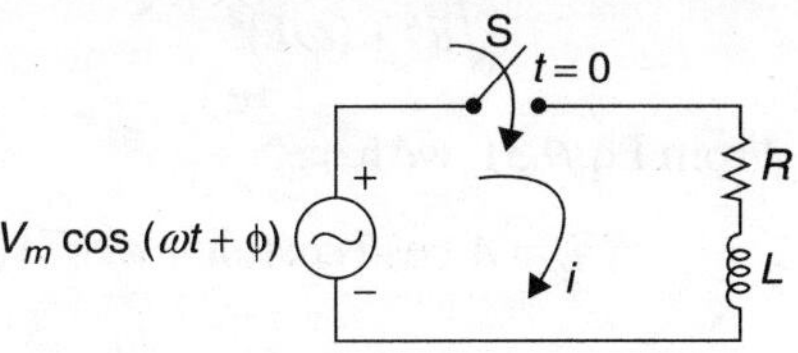

Fig. 9.16 *RL* series circuit excited by a sinusoidal source

$$Ri + L\frac{di}{dt} = V_m \cos(\omega t + \phi)$$

$$\frac{di}{dt} + \frac{R}{L}i = \frac{V_m}{L}\cos(\omega t + \phi) \tag{9.29}$$

(i) The complementary function is

$$i_C = C_1 e^{-\frac{R}{L}t} \tag{9.30}$$

(ii) The particular integral is

$$i_p = e^{-\frac{R}{L}t} \int \frac{V_m}{L} \cos(\omega t + \phi) e^{\frac{R}{L}t} dt = \frac{V_m}{L} e^{\frac{-R}{L}t} \frac{e^{\frac{R}{L}t}}{\left(\frac{R}{L}\right)^2 + \omega^2} \left[\frac{R}{L}\cos(\omega t + \phi) + \omega \sin(\omega t + \phi)\right]$$

$$= \frac{V_m L}{R^2 + (\omega L)^2} \left[\frac{R}{L}\cos(\omega t + \phi) + \omega \sin(\omega t + \phi)\right]$$

$$i_p = \frac{V_m R}{R^2 + (\omega L)^2} \cos(\omega t + \phi) + \frac{V_m \omega L}{R^2 + (\omega L)^2} \sin(\omega t + \phi) \tag{9.31}$$

Let $$A \cos\theta = \frac{V_m R}{R^2 + (\omega L)^2} \tag{9.32}$$

$$A \sin\theta = \frac{V_m \omega L}{R^2 + (\omega L)^2} \tag{9.33}$$

Dividing Eq. 9.33 by Eq. 9.32, we have,

$$\frac{A \sin\theta}{A \cos\theta} = \frac{\omega L}{R}$$

$$\Rightarrow \qquad \tan\theta = \frac{\omega L}{R}$$

$$\Rightarrow \qquad \theta = \tan^{-1}\left(\frac{\omega L}{R}\right)$$

Squaring and adding Eqs 9.33 and 9.32,

$$A^2 = \frac{V_m^2}{[R^2 + (\omega L)^2]^2} \times [R^2 + (\omega L)^2]$$

$$\Rightarrow \qquad A = \frac{V_m}{\sqrt{R^2 + (\omega L)^2}}$$

From Eq. 9.31, we have,

$$i_p = A \cos\theta \cos(\omega t + \phi) + A\,\theta \sin(\omega t + \phi) = A \cos(\omega t + \phi - \theta)$$

$$= \frac{V_m}{\sqrt{R^2 + (\omega L)^2}} \cos\left(\omega t + \phi - \tan^{-1}\frac{\omega L}{R}\right) \tag{9.34}$$

The complete solution is

$$i = i_c + i_p = C_1 e^{-\frac{R}{L}t} + \frac{V_m}{\sqrt{R^2 + (\omega L)^2}} \cos\left(\omega t + \phi - \tan^{-1}\frac{\omega L}{R}\right) \tag{9.35}$$

At $t = 0$, the inductor acts as a open circuit, that is, at $t = 0$, $i = 0$

$$C_1 + \frac{V_m}{\sqrt{R^2 + (\omega L)^2}} \cos\left(\phi - \tan^{-1}\frac{\omega L}{R}\right) = 0$$

$$C_1 = -\frac{V_m}{\sqrt{R^2 + (\omega L)^2}} \cos\left(\phi - \tan^{-1}\frac{\omega L}{R}\right)$$

$\therefore$ The complete solution is

$$i = -\frac{V_m}{\sqrt{R^2 + (\omega L)^2}} e^{-\frac{R}{L}t} \cos\left(\phi - \tan^{-1}\frac{\omega L}{R}\right) + \frac{V_m}{\sqrt{R^2 + (\omega L)^2}} \cos\left(\omega t + \phi - \tan^{-1}\frac{\omega L}{R}\right)$$

$$\Rightarrow \quad i = \frac{V_m}{\sqrt{R^2 + (\omega L)^2}} \left[-e^{-\frac{R}{L}t} \cos\left(\phi - \tan^{-1}\frac{\omega L}{R}\right) + \cos\left(\omega t + \phi - \tan^{-1}\frac{\omega L}{R}\right)\right] \quad (9.36)$$

9.4.2 AC Response of an *RC* Series Circuit

Consider an *RC* series circuit excited by a sinusoidal voltage source (Fig. 9.17).

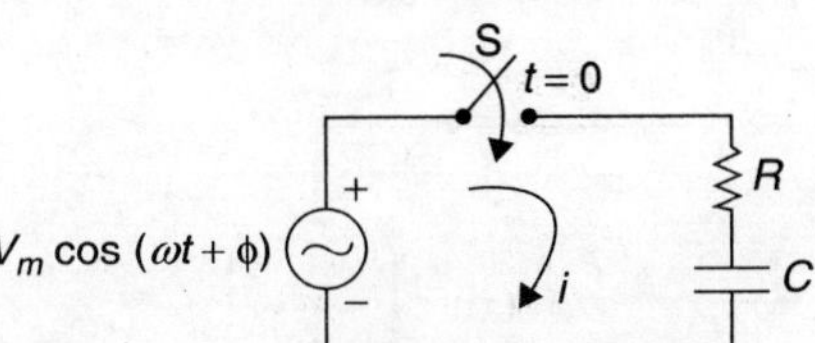

Fig. 9.17 *RC* series circuit excited by a sinusoidal source

Applying KVL to the circuit

$$Ri + \frac{1}{C}\int i dt = V_m \omega \cos(\omega t + \phi)$$

Differentiating the above equation,

$$R\frac{di}{dt} + \frac{1}{C} i = -V_m \omega (\sin \omega t + \theta)$$

$$\frac{di}{dt} + \frac{i}{RC} = \frac{-V_m}{R} \omega \sin(\omega t + \phi) \quad (9.37)$$

(i) The complementary function is

$$i_C = C_1 e^{-\frac{1}{RC}t} \quad (9.38)$$

(ii) The particular integral is

$$i_p = e^{-\frac{t}{RC}} \int e^{\frac{t}{RC}} \left(\frac{-V_m \omega}{R}\right) \sin(\omega t + \phi)\, dt = -\frac{V_m \omega}{R} e^{-\frac{t}{RC}} \int e^{\frac{t}{RC}} \sin(\omega t + \phi)\, dt$$

$$= -\frac{V_m \omega}{R} e^{-\frac{t}{RC}} \times \frac{e^{\frac{t}{RC}}}{\left(\frac{1}{RC}\right)^2 + \omega^2} \left[\frac{1}{RC}\sin(\omega t + \phi) - \omega \cos(\omega t + \phi)\right]$$

$$= -\frac{V_m \omega}{R^2 C} \times \frac{1}{\left[\left(\frac{1}{RC}\right)^2 + \omega^2\right]} \sin(\omega t + \phi) + \frac{V_m \omega^2}{R} \times \frac{1}{\left[\left(\frac{1}{RC}\right)^2 + \omega^2\right]} \cos(\omega t + \phi)$$

$$\therefore \quad i_p = \frac{-V_m/\omega C}{R^2 + \left(\frac{1}{\omega C}\right)^2} \sin(\omega t + \phi) + \frac{V_m R}{R^2 + \left(\frac{1}{\omega C}\right)^2} \cos(\omega t + \phi) \tag{9.39}$$

$$\text{Let } A \sin\theta = \frac{V_m/\omega C}{R^2 + \left(\frac{1}{\omega c}\right)^2} \tag{9.40}$$

$$A \cos\theta = \frac{V_m R}{R^2 + \left(\frac{1}{\omega C}\right)^2} \tag{9.41}$$

Dividing Eq. 9.40 by Eq. 9.41, we have

$$\frac{\sin\theta}{\cos\theta} = \frac{1}{\omega CR}$$

$$\Rightarrow \quad \tan\theta = \frac{1}{\omega CR}$$

$$\Rightarrow \quad \theta = \tan^{-1}\left(\frac{1}{\omega CR}\right)$$

Squaring and adding Eqs 9.40 and 9.41, we have

$$A^2 = \frac{V_m^2}{\left[R^2 + \left(\frac{1}{\omega C}\right)^2\right]^2} \left[\left(\frac{1}{\omega C}\right)^2 + R^2\right] = \frac{V_m^2}{R^2 + \left(\frac{1}{\omega C}\right)^2}$$

$$\Rightarrow \quad A = \frac{V_m}{\sqrt{R^2 + \left(\frac{1}{\omega C}\right)^2}}$$

From Eq. 9.39, we have

$$i_p = -A \sin(\omega t + \phi) \sin\theta + A \cos(\omega t + \phi) \cos\theta = A \cos(\omega t + \phi + \theta)$$

$$i_p = \frac{V_m}{\sqrt{R^2 + \left(\frac{1}{\omega C}\right)^2}} \cos\left(\omega t + \phi + \tan^{-1}\frac{1}{\omega CR}\right) \tag{9.42}$$

The complete solution is

$$i = i_c + i_p = C_1 e^{-\frac{t}{RC}} + \frac{V_m}{\sqrt{R^2 + \left(\frac{1}{\omega C}\right)^2}} \cos\left[\omega t + \phi + \tan^{-1}\frac{1}{\omega CR}\right] \tag{9.43}$$

At $t = 0$, capacitor acts as short circuit, that is, at $t = 0, i = \frac{V_m}{R}\cos\phi$

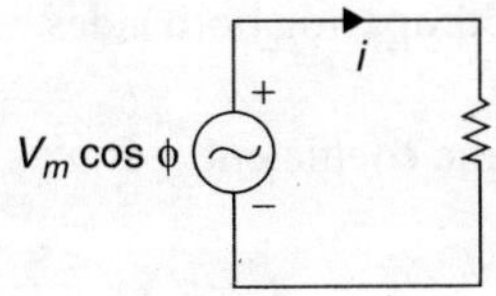

Vm cos ϕ
+
−
i
R

$$\frac{V_m\cos\phi}{R} = C_1 + \frac{V_m}{\sqrt{R^2 + \left(\frac{1}{\omega C}\right)^2}}\cos\left(\phi + \tan^{-1}\frac{1}{\omega CR}\right)$$

$$C_1 = \frac{V_m}{R}\cos\phi - \frac{V_m}{\sqrt{R^2 + \left(\frac{1}{\omega C}\right)^2}}\cos\left(\phi + \tan^{-1}\frac{1}{\omega CR}\right)$$

The complete solution is

$$i = e^{-\frac{t}{RC}}\left[\frac{V_m}{R}\cos\phi - \frac{V_m}{\sqrt{R^2 + \left(\frac{1}{\omega C}\right)^2}}\cos\left(\phi + \tan^{-1}\frac{1}{\omega CR}\right)\right]$$

$$+ \frac{V_m}{\sqrt{R^2 + \left(\frac{1}{\omega C}\right)^2}}\cos\left(\omega t + \phi + \tan^{-1}\frac{1}{\omega CR}\right) \tag{9.44}$$

9.4.3 AC Response of an *RLC* Series Circuit

Consider an *RLC* series circuit excited by a sinusoidal voltage source (Fig. 9.18).

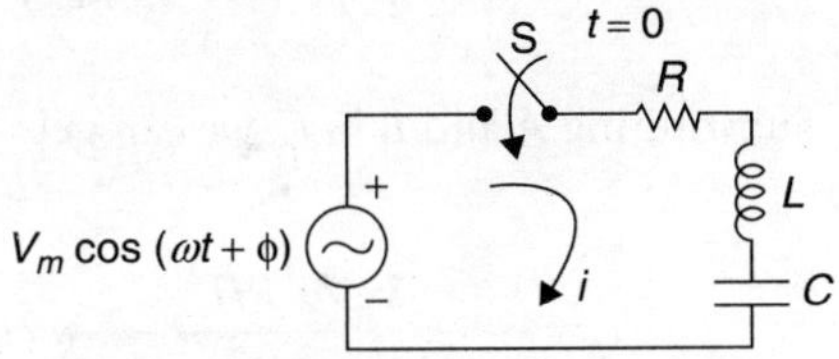

S
t = 0
R
L
C
+
−
Vm cos (ωt + ϕ)
i

Fig. 9.18 *RLC* series circuit excited by a sinusoidal source

Applying KVL to the circuit,

$$Ri + L\frac{di}{dt} + \frac{1}{C}\int i\,dt = V_m\cos(\omega t + \phi) \tag{9.45}$$

Differentiating the above equation with respect to *t*,

$$R\frac{di}{dt} + L\frac{d^2i}{dt^2} + \frac{1}{C}i = -V_m\omega\sin(\omega t + \phi)$$

$$\frac{d^2i}{dt^2} + \frac{R}{L}\frac{di}{dt} + \frac{1}{LC}i = \frac{-V_m\omega}{L}\sin(\omega t + \phi) \tag{9.46}$$

Particular solution can be obtained by using the method of undermined coefficients. Assuming

$$i_p = A\cos(\omega t + \phi) + B\sin(\omega t + \phi) \tag{9.47}$$

$$i'_p = -A\,\omega\sin(\omega t + \phi) + B\omega\cos(\omega t + \phi)$$

$$i''_p = -A\,\omega^2\cos(\omega t + \phi) - B\,\omega^2\sin(\omega t + \phi)$$

Substituting i_p, i'_p, i''_p in Eq. 9.46, we have

$$-A\,\omega^2\cos(\omega t + \phi) - B\,\omega^2\sin(\omega t + \phi) + \frac{R}{L}(-A\omega\sin(\omega t + \phi) + B\cos(\omega t + \phi))$$

$$+ \frac{1}{LC}\{A\cos(\omega t + \phi) + B\sin(\omega t + \phi)\} = \frac{-V_m(t)}{L}\sin(\omega t + \phi) \tag{9.48}$$

Comparing both sides, we have

sine coefficient, $-B\omega^2 - A\omega\dfrac{R}{L} + \dfrac{B}{\omega C} = -\dfrac{V_m\omega}{L}$

$$A\left(\frac{\omega R}{L}\right) + B\left(\omega^2 - \frac{1}{LC}\right) = \frac{V_m\omega}{L} \tag{9.49}$$

cosine coefficients, $-A\omega^2 + B\omega\dfrac{R}{L} + \dfrac{A}{LC} = 0$

$$A\left(\omega^2 - \frac{1}{LC}\right) - B\omega\frac{R}{L} = 0 \tag{9.50}$$

Solving Eqs 9.49 and 9.50, we have,

$$A = \frac{V_m \times \dfrac{\omega^2 R}{L^2}}{\left[\left(\dfrac{\omega R}{L}\right)^2 - \left(\omega^2 - \dfrac{1}{LC}\right)^2\right]}$$

$$B = \frac{\left(\omega^2 - \dfrac{1}{LC}\right)V_m\omega}{L\left[\left(\dfrac{\omega R}{L}\right)^2 - \left(\omega^2 - \dfrac{1}{LC}\right)^2\right]}$$

Substituting A and B in i_p, we can get

$$i_p = \frac{V_m\omega^2 R/L^2}{\left(\dfrac{\omega R}{L}\right)^2 - \left(\omega^2 - \dfrac{1}{LC}\right)^2}\cos(\omega t + \phi) + \frac{\left(\omega^2 - \dfrac{1}{LC}\right)V_m\omega}{L\left(\dfrac{\omega R}{L}\right)^2 - \left(\omega^2 - \dfrac{1}{LC}\right)^2 L}\sin(\omega t + \phi) \tag{9.51}$$

Let $$M\cos\theta = \frac{V_m\omega^2 R/L^2}{\left(\dfrac{\omega R}{L}\right)^2 - \left(\omega^2 - \dfrac{1}{LC}\right)^2} \tag{9.52}$$

$$M\sin\theta = \frac{\left(\omega^2 - \dfrac{1}{LC}\right)^2 V_m\omega}{L\left[\left(\dfrac{\omega}{L}\right)^2 - \left(\omega^2 - \dfrac{1}{LC}\right)^2\right]} \tag{9.53}$$

Dividing Eq. 9.55 by Eq. 9.52,

$$\frac{\sin\theta}{\cos\theta} = \frac{\left(\omega^2 - \dfrac{1}{LC}\right)\omega}{L} \times \frac{L^2}{\omega^2 R} = \frac{\left(\omega^2 - \dfrac{1}{LC}\right)L}{\omega R}$$

$$\Rightarrow \qquad \tan\theta = \frac{\omega L - \frac{1}{\omega C}}{R}$$

$$\Rightarrow \qquad \theta = \tan^{-1}\left(\frac{\omega L - \frac{1}{\omega C}}{R}\right)$$

Squaring and then adding Eqs 9.52 and 9.53,

$$M^2 = \frac{V_m^2\left(\frac{\omega^2 R}{L^2}\right)^2 + V_m^2\left(\frac{\omega^2 - \frac{1}{LC}}{L^2}\right)\omega^2}{\left(\frac{\omega R}{L}\right)^2 - \left(\omega^2 - \frac{1}{LC}\right)^2} = \frac{V_m^2}{R^2 + \left(\frac{1}{\omega C} - \omega L\right)^2}$$

$$\Rightarrow \qquad M = \frac{V_m}{\sqrt{R^2 + \left(\frac{1}{\omega C} - \omega L\right)^2}} \tag{9.54}$$

$\therefore$ The particular current becomes

$$i_p = \frac{V_m}{\sqrt{R^2 + \left(\frac{1}{\omega C} - \omega L\right)^2}} \cos\left[\omega t + \phi + \tan^{-1}\left(\frac{\frac{1}{\omega C} - \omega L}{R}\right)\right] \tag{9.55}$$

The complementary function is similar to that of a DC series circuit. To find out the complementary function, we have the characteristic equation,

$$s^2 + \frac{R}{L}s + \frac{1}{LC} = 0$$

$$s_{1,2} = \frac{-\frac{R}{L} \pm \sqrt{\left(\frac{R}{L}\right)^2 - \frac{4}{LC}}}{2} = \frac{-R}{2L} \pm \sqrt{\left(\frac{R}{2L}\right)^2 - \frac{1}{LC}} = \alpha \pm \beta$$

where $\alpha = \frac{-R}{2L}$ and $\beta = \sqrt{\left(\frac{R}{2L}\right)^2 - \frac{1}{LC}}$

Case (i) If $\left(\frac{R}{2L}\right)^2 > \frac{1}{LC}$, then the roots are real and unequal and result in the over damped case.

$\therefore \qquad s_1 = \alpha + \beta$ and $s_2 = \alpha - \beta$

The complete solution is

$$i = i_c + i_p = e^{\alpha t}(C_1 e^{\beta t} + C_2 e^{-\beta t}) + \frac{V_m}{\sqrt{R^2 + \left(\frac{1}{\omega C} - \omega L\right)^2}} \cos\left[\omega t + \phi + \tan^{-1}\left(\frac{\frac{1}{\omega C} - \omega L}{R}\right)\right] \tag{9.56}$$

Case (ii) If $\left(\frac{R}{2L}\right)^2 < \frac{1}{LC}$, then the roots are complex conjugate and result in the under damped or oscillatory case.

$\therefore \qquad s_1 = \alpha + j\beta$ and $s_2 = \alpha - j\beta$

The complete solution is

$$i = i_C + i_p = e^{\alpha t}[C_1 \cos\beta t + C_2 \sin\beta t] + \frac{V_m}{\sqrt{R^2 + \left(\frac{1}{\omega C} - \omega L\right)^2}} \cos\left[\omega t + \phi + \tan^{-1}\frac{\left(\frac{1}{\omega C} - \omega L\right)}{R}\right] \tag{9.57}$$

Case (iii) If $\left(\frac{R}{2L}\right)^2 = \frac{1}{LC}$, then the roots are real and equal and result in the critically damped case.
The complete solution is

$$i = i_C + i_p = e^{\alpha t}(C_1 + C_2 t) + \frac{V_m}{\sqrt{R^2 + \left(\frac{1}{\omega C} - \omega L\right)^2}} \cos\left[\omega t + \phi + \tan^{-1}\frac{\left(\frac{1}{\omega C} - \omega L\right)}{R}\right] \tag{9.58}$$

Problem 9.9 The circuit consists of a series *RL* circuit with $R = 150\ \Omega$, $L = 0.5$ H, the switch is closed when $\phi = 30°$. Determine the resultant current when voltage $v(t) = 50\cos(100t + \phi)$ is applied to the circuit at $\phi = 30°$.

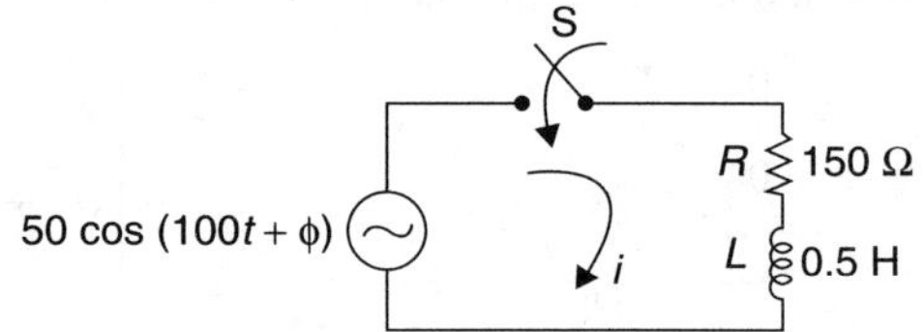

Solution:

Applying KVL to the circuit

$$150i + 0.5\frac{di}{dt} = 50\cos(100t + 30°)$$

$$\frac{di}{dt} + 300i = 100\cos(100t + 30°) \tag{1}$$

The complementary function is

$$i_C = C_1 e^{-300t} \tag{2}$$

To determine the particular current, first we assume the solution as

$$i_p = A\cos(100\,t + 30°) + B\sin(100\,t + 30°)$$

$$i'_p = -100\,A\sin(100t + 30°) + 100\,B\cos(100t + 30°)$$

Substituting i_p and i'_p in Eq. (1), we have,

$$-100\,A\sin(100\,t + 30°) + 100\,B\cos(100\,t + 30°) + 300\,A\cos(100\,t + 30°)$$

$$+ 300\,B\sin(100\,t + 30) = 100\cos(100\,t + 30°)$$

Comparing the corresponding coefficient on both sides, we have

$$-100\,A + 300\,B = 0$$

$$300\,A + 100\,B = 100$$

Solving the above equations, we can get

$$A = 0.3 \quad \text{and} \quad B = 0.1$$

$$\therefore \quad i_p = 0.3\cos(100\,t + 30°) + 0.1\sin(100\,t + 30°)$$

Let $x\cos\theta = 0.3$, $x\sin\theta = 0.1$ then

$$\tan\theta = \frac{0.1}{0.3} \Rightarrow \theta = \tan^{-1}\left(\frac{1}{3}\right) = 18.43°$$

$$x = \sqrt{0.3^2 + 0.1^2} = 0.316$$

$$i_p = x\cos\theta\cos(100\,t + 30°) + x\sin\theta\sin(100\,t + 30°)$$

$$= x\cos(100\,t + 30 - \theta)$$

$$= 0.316\cos(100\,t + 30° - 18.43°)$$

$$= 0.316\cos(100\,t + 11.57°)$$

The complete solution is

$$i = i_C + i_p = C_1 e^{-300t} + 0.316\cos(100\,t + 11.57°)$$

At $t = 0$, the inductor acts as a open circuit, that is, at $t = 0$, $i = 0$

$$0 = C_1 e^{-0} + 0.316\cos 11.57$$

$$0 = C_1 + 0.309$$

$$C_1 = -0.309$$

$$\therefore \quad i = -0.309e^{-300t} + 0.316\cos(100t + 11.57°)\ \text{A}$$

Problem 9.10 The circuit consists of a series of RC elements with $R = 15\ \Omega$ $C = 100\ \mu\text{F}$. A sinusoidal voltage $v(t) = 100\sin(500t + \phi)$ is applied to the circuit at time corresponding to $\phi = 45°$. Obtain the current transient.

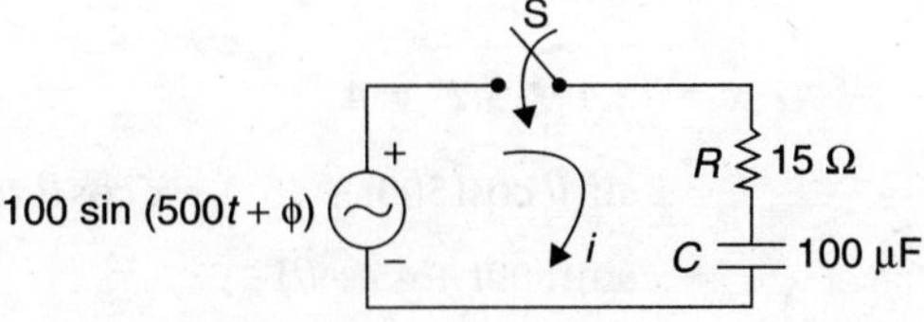

Solution:

Applying KVL to the circuit,

$$15i + \frac{1}{100\times10^{-6}}\int i\,dt = 100\sin(500t + 45°)$$

Differentiating the above equation with respect to t,

$$15\frac{di}{dt} + 10^4 i = 5\times10^4\cos(500t + 45°)$$

$$\frac{di}{dt} + \frac{10^4}{15}i = \frac{5\times10^4}{15}\cos(500t + 45°)$$

$$\frac{di}{dt} + 666.6i = 3333.33\cos(500t + 45°) \qquad (1)$$

The complementary function is

$$i_C = C_1 e^{-666.6t}$$

To determine the particular current we assume the solution as

$$i_p = A\cos(500t + 45°) + B\sin(500t + 45°) \quad (2)$$

$$i'_p = -500A\sin(500t + 45°) + 500B\cos(500t + 45°)$$

Substituting i_p and i'_p in Eq. (1), we have

$$-500A\sin(500t + 45°) + 500B\cos(500t + 45°) + 666.6A\cos(500\,t + 45°)$$
$$+ 666.6B\sin(500t + 45) = 3333.33\cos(500t + 45°)$$

Comparing both sides the corresponding coefficients, we have

$$-500A + 666.6B = 0$$

$$\Rightarrow \quad A = \frac{666.6B}{500} = 1.333\,B$$

$$500B + 666.6A = 3333.33$$

$$\Rightarrow \quad 500B = -666.6 \times 1.333B + 3333.33$$

$$\Rightarrow \quad 1388.79B = 3333.39$$

$$\Rightarrow \quad B = 2.4$$

$$\therefore \quad A = 1.3332 \times 2.4 = 3.2$$

$$\therefore \quad i_p = 3.2\cos(500t + 45°) + 2.4\sin(500\,t + 45°)$$

Let $x\cos\theta = 2.4$, $x\sin\theta = 3.2$ then

$$\tan\theta = \frac{3.2}{2.4} \Rightarrow \theta = \tan^{-1}(1.33) = 53.13°$$

$$x = \sqrt{2.4^2 + 3.2^2} = 4$$

$$i_p = x\sin\theta\cos(500t + 45°) + x\cos\theta\sin(500t + 45°)$$
$$= x\sin(500t + 45 + \theta)$$
$$= 4\sin(500t + 45° + 53.13°)$$
$$= 4\sin(500t + 98.13°)$$

The complete solution is

$$i = i_C + i_p = C_1 e^{-666.6t} + 4\sin(500\,t + 98.13)$$

At $t = 0$, (That is, $\phi = 45°$), the capacitor acts as a short circuit.

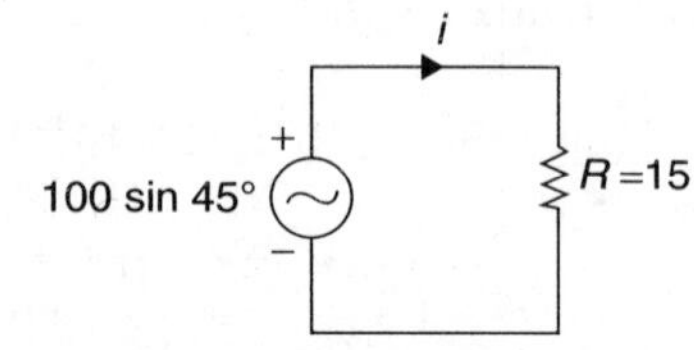

That is, at $t = 0, i = \dfrac{100\sin 45°}{15} = 4.714$

$$4.714 = C_1 + 4\sin 98.13°$$

$$C_1 = 4.714 - 4\sin 98.13° = 0.754$$

$$\therefore \quad i = 0.754e^{-666.6t} + 4\sin(500\,t + 98.13°)$$

Problem 9.11 The circuit consisting of a series *RLC* elements with $R = 10\ \Omega$, $L = 0.5$ H and $C = 200\ \mu$F has a sinusoidal voltage $v(t) = 150\sin(200t + \phi)$. If the switch is closed when = 30°, determine the current transient.

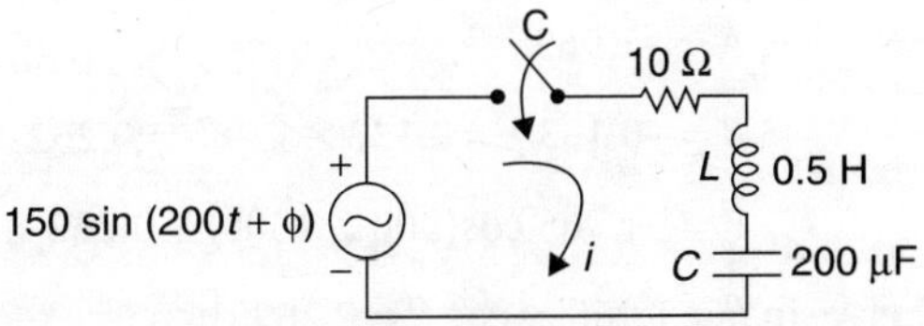

Solution:

Applying KVL to the circuit

$$10i + 0.5\frac{di}{dt} + \frac{1}{200\times 10^{-6}}\int i\,dt = 150\sin(200t + \phi)$$

Differentiating the above equation,

$$10\frac{di}{dt} + 0.5\frac{d^2i}{dt^2} + 5\times 10^3 i = 150\times 200\cos(200t + 30°)$$

$$\frac{d^2i}{dt^2} + 20\frac{di}{dt} + 10^4 i = 6\times 10^4\cos(200t + 30°)$$

The characteristic equation is

$$s^2 + 20s + 10^4 = 0, \quad \text{where} \quad s = \frac{d}{dt}$$

$$s_{1,2} = \frac{-20 \pm \sqrt{20^2 - 4\times 10^4}}{2\times 1} = -10 \pm j99.5$$

$$s_1 = -10 + j99.5$$

$$s_2 = -10 - j99.5$$

The complementary function is

$$i_C = e^{-10t}(C_1\cos 99.5t + C_2\sin 99.5t) \tag{2}$$

We can find the particular current by using the undetermined coefficient method. Let us assume

$$i_p = A\cos(200t + 30°) + B\sin(200t + 30°) \tag{3}$$

$$i'_p = -200A\sin(200t + 30°) + 200B\cos(200t + 30°)$$

$$i''_p = -200^2 A\cos(200t + 30°) - 200^2 B\sin(200t + 30°)$$

Substituting i_p, i'_p and i''_p in Eq. (1) and equating the corresponding coefficients on both sides

$$20[-200A\sin(200t + 30°) + 200B\cos(200t + 30°)] - 200^2 A\cos(200t + 30°)$$

$$-200^2 B\sin(200t + 30°) + 10^4 A\cos(200t + 30°) + 10^4 B\sin(200t + 30°)$$

$$= 6\times 10^4\cos(200t + 30°)$$

Comparing corresponding coefficients on both sides

$$-4000A - 40000B + 10000B = 0$$

$$\Rightarrow \qquad B = -\frac{4000\text{ A}}{30000} = -0.133\text{ A}$$

$$4000B - 40000A + 10000A = 60000$$

$$4000B - 30000A = 60000$$

$$-4000\times 0.133A - 30000A = 60000$$

$\Rightarrow \quad A = -1.965$

$$B = -0.133A = 0.133 \times 1.965 = 0.262$$

$$i_p = -1.965 \cos(200\,t + 30°) + 0.262 \sin(200t + 30°) \tag{4}$$

Let $x \sin\theta = 1.965$, $x \cos\theta = 0.262$ then

$$x = \sqrt{1.965^2 + 0.262^2} = 1.98$$

$$\theta = \tan^{-1}\left(\frac{1.965}{0.262}\right) = 82.4°$$

From Eq. (4), we have

$$i_p = -x \sin\theta \cos(200t + 30°) + x\cos\theta \sin(200t + 30°)$$

$$= x \sin(200t + 30° - \theta)$$

$$= 1.98 \sin(200t + 30° - 82.4°)$$

$$= 1.98 \sin(200t - 52.4°)$$

The complete solution is

$$i = i_C + i_p = e^{-10t}(C_1 \cos 99.5t + C_2 \sin 99.5t) + 1.98 \sin(200t - 52.4°) \tag{5}$$

Applying initial conditions, at $t = 0$, the inductor acts as an open circuit and capacitor acts a short circuit.

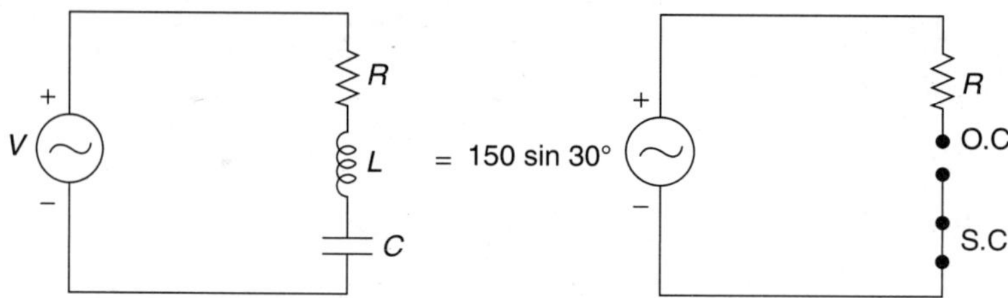

$$V = Ri + L\frac{di}{dt} + \frac{1}{C}\int idt$$

$$150 \sin 30° = 0 + 0.5\frac{di}{dt} + 0$$

$\Rightarrow \quad \frac{di}{dt} = 150$

$\therefore \quad$ At $t = 0, \frac{di}{dt} = 150t$

At $\quad t = 0, i = 0 \;\Rightarrow\; 0 = C_1 + 1.983 \sin(-52.4)$

$\Rightarrow \quad C_1 = 1.57$

Differentiating the current equation [Eq. (5)] with repect to t,

$$\frac{di}{dt} = e^{-10t}(-99.5\,C_1 \sin 99.5t + 99.5\,C_2 \cos 99.5t)$$

$$-10e^{-10t}(C_1 \cos 99.5t + C_2 \sin 99.5) + 200 \times 1.9833 \cos(200t - 52.4°)$$

At $t = 0, \dfrac{di}{dt} = 150, C_1 = 1.57$

$$150 = 99.52C_2 - 10C_1 + 242$$

$$99.5C_2 = -92 + 10C_1 = -76.3$$

$$\Rightarrow \quad C_2 = \frac{-76.3}{99.5} = -0.7668$$

∴ The current transient is

$$i = e^{-10t}(1.57 \cos 99.5t - 0.767 \sin 99.5t) + 1.9833 \sin(200t - 52.4°)$$

ADDITIONAL SOLVED PROBLEMS

9.1 The switch S is closed at $t = 0$ as shown. Find the initial conditions at $t = 0^+$ for $i_1, i_2, V_C, \frac{di_1}{dt}$ and $\frac{di_2}{dt}$.

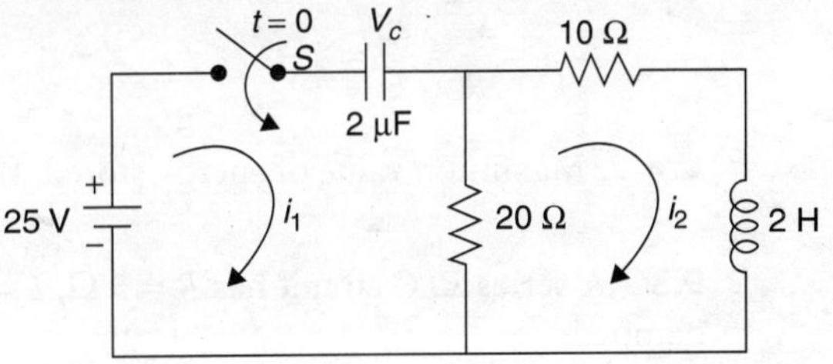

t = 0
S
V_c
2 µF
10 Ω
25 V
i_1
20 Ω
i_2
2 H

Solution: When the switch S is closed at $t = 0$, applying KVL to individual loops:

For loop 1

$$25 = V_C + 20(i_1 - i_2) \quad (1)$$

For loop 2

$$20(i_2 - i_1) + 10i_2 + 2\frac{di_2}{dt} = 0 \quad (2)$$

At time $t = 0^+$, the inductor acts as open circuit and capacitor acts as short circuit.

That is, at $t = 0^+$, $V_C = 0 V$, $i_2 = 0$ A

So, from Eq. (1), we have

$$25 = 0 + 20i_1 \quad \Rightarrow \quad i_1\Big|_{t=0^+} = \frac{25}{20} = 1.25 \text{ A}$$

On differentiating Eq. (1), we have

$$0 = \frac{dV_C}{dt} + 20\frac{di_1}{dt} - 20\frac{di_2}{dt}$$

$$0 = \frac{i_1}{C} + 20\frac{di_1}{dt} - 20\frac{di_2}{dt} \quad (3)$$

Form Eq. (2), we have

$$\frac{di_2}{dt} = 10i_1 - 15i_2$$

$$\frac{di_2}{dt}\Big|_{t=0^+} = 10i_1\Big|_{t=0^+} - 15i_2\Big|_{t=0^+} = 10 \times 1.25 - 0 \times 15 = 12.5 \text{ A/s}$$

From Eq. (3), we have

$$\frac{di_1}{dt} = \frac{di_2}{dt} - \frac{i_1}{20C}$$

$$\left.\frac{di_1}{dt}\right|_{t=0^+} = \left.\frac{di_2}{dt}\right|_{t=0^+} - \frac{1}{20C}\left.i_1\right|_{t=0^+} = 12.5 - \frac{1\times 1.25}{20\times 2\times 10^{-6}} = -31237.5 \text{ A/s}$$

9.2 A DC voltage of 20 V is applied in a *RL* series circuit where $R = 5\ \Omega$ and $L = 10$ H. Find (i) the time constant, (ii) the maximum value of stored energy.

Solution: Given that $R = 5\ \Omega$, $L = 10$ H, $V = 20$ volts

(i) Time constant, $\tau = \frac{L}{R} = \frac{10}{5} = 2$ s

(ii) The steady state current, *I* flowing through the circuit is given by

$$I = \frac{V}{R} = \frac{25}{5} = 4 \text{ A}$$

∴ Maximum value of energy stored, $W = \frac{1}{2}LI^2 = \frac{1}{2}\times 10\times 4^2 = 80$ J

9.3 A series *RLC* circuit has $R = 5\ \Omega$, $L = 3$ H. What value of capacitance will make the circuit critically damped?

Solution: Given that $R = 5\ \Omega$, $L = 3$ H

For critical damping, $\left(\frac{R}{2L}\right)^2 = \frac{1}{LC}$

⇒ $$C = \frac{4L}{R^2} = \frac{4\times 3}{5^2} = 0.48 \text{ F}$$

9.4 A series *RL* circuit with $R = 100\ \Omega$ and $L = 0.4$ H has a sinusoidal voltage source $v(t) = 200\sin(500t + \phi)$ applied at a time when $\phi = 0$. Find the resultant current.

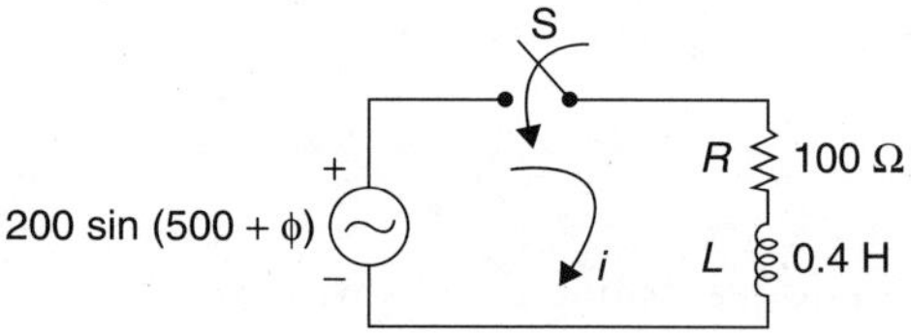

S
200 sin (500 + ϕ)
+
−
i
R 100 Ω
L 0.4 H

Solution: When the switch *S* is closed, applying KVL to the circuit

$$100i + 0.4\frac{di}{dt} = 200\sin 500t$$

$$\frac{di}{dt} + 250i = 500\sin 500t \tag{1}$$

The complementary function is

$$i_C = C_1\, e^{-250t} \tag{2}$$

To determine the particular current, first we assume the solution as

$$i_p = A\cos 500t + B\sin 500t \tag{3}$$

$$i'_p = -500A\sin 500t + 500B\cos 500t$$

Substituting i_p and i'_p in Eq. (1), we have

$$-500A\sin 500t + 500B\cos 500t + 250A\cos 500t + 250B\sin 500t = 500\sin 500t$$

Comparing the corresponding coefficients on both sides

$$-500A + 250B = 500$$

$$500B + 250A = 0$$

Solving the above equations, we can get

$$A = -0.8,\ B = 0.4$$

$$\therefore \quad i_p = -0.8\cos 500t + 0.4\sin 500t$$

Let $x\cos\theta = 0.4$, $x\sin\theta = 0.8$ then

$$\tan\theta = \frac{0.8}{0.4} = 2$$

$$\Rightarrow \quad \theta = \tan^{-1} 2 = 63.43$$

$$x = \sqrt{0.4^2 + 0.82^2} = 0.8944$$

$$\therefore \quad i_p = x\sin 500t\cos\theta - x\cos 500t\sin\theta$$

$$= x\sin(500t - \theta)$$

$$= 0.8944\sin(500t - 63.43°)$$

The complete solution is

$$i = i_C + i_p = C_1 e^{-250t} + 0.8944\sin(500t - 63.43°)$$

At $t = 0$, the inductor acts as an open circuit, i.e., at $t = 0$, $i = 0$

$$0 = C_1 e^{-0} + 0.8944\sin(-63.43°)$$

$$\Rightarrow \quad C_1 = 0.8$$

$$\therefore \quad i = 0.8e^{-250t} + 0.8944\sin(500t - 63.43°)$$

9.5 A series *RC* circuit with R = 200 Ω and C = 25 μF has a sinusoidal voltage source $v(t) = 200\sin(500 + \phi)$ applied at a time when $\phi = 0$. Find the resultant current.

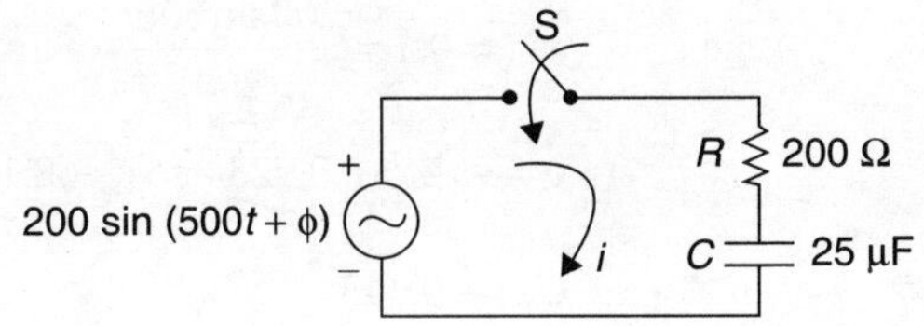

Solution: When the switch *S* is closed, applying KVL to the circuit,

$$200i + \frac{1}{25\times 10^{-6}}\int i\,dt = 200\sin 500t$$

Differentiating the above equation with respect to *t*,

$$200\frac{di}{dt} + 4\times 10^4 i = 200\times 500\cos 500t$$

$$\frac{di}{dt} + 200i = 500\cos 500t \qquad (1)$$

The complementary function is

$$i_C = C_1 e^{-200t}$$

To determine the particular current, we can assume that the solution as

$$i_p = A \cos 500t + B \sin 500t \qquad (2)$$

$$i_p' = -A\, 500 \sin 500t + B\, 500 \cos 500t$$

Substituting i_p and i_p' in Eq. (1), we have,

$$-A\, 500 \sin 500t + B\, 500 \cos 500t + 200\, A \cos 500t + 200\, B \sin 500t = 500 \cos 500t$$

Comparing the corresponding coefficient on both sides, we have

$$-500\, A + 200\, B = 0$$

$$200A + 500B = 500$$

Solving the above equations, we get

$$A = 0.345,\ B = 0.862$$

$$\therefore \qquad i_p = 0.345 \cos 500t + 0.862 \sin 500t$$

Let $x \cos\theta = 0.345$, $x \sin\theta = 0.862$, then

$$\tan\theta = \frac{0.862}{0.345} = 2.5$$

$$\Rightarrow \qquad \theta = 68.19°$$

$$x = \sqrt{0.345^2 + 0.862^2} = 0.9284$$

$$\therefore \qquad i_p = x\cos\theta \cos 500t + x \sin\theta \sin 500t = 0.9284 \cos(500t - 68.19°)$$

The complete solution is

$$i = i_C + i_p = C_1\, e^{-200t} + 0.9284 \cos(500\, t - 68.19°)$$

At $t = 0$, the capacitor acts as a short circuit

$$\text{i.e.,} \qquad \text{at } t = 0, i = \frac{200 \sin 500t}{200} = \sin 0 = 0$$

$$\therefore \qquad 0 = C_1\, e^{-0} + 0.9284 \cos(-68.19°)$$

$$C_1 = -0.345$$

∴ The resultant current is

$$i = -0.345\, e^{-200t} + 0.9284 \cos(500t - 68.19°)$$

9.6 A series *RLC* circuit with $R = 100\ \Omega$, $L = 0.1$ H and $C = 50\ \mu$F has a sinusoidal voltage source $v(t) = 100 \sin (1000 + \phi)$ V volts. If the switch is closed when $\phi = 90°$, find the current assuming zero initial charge on the capacitor.

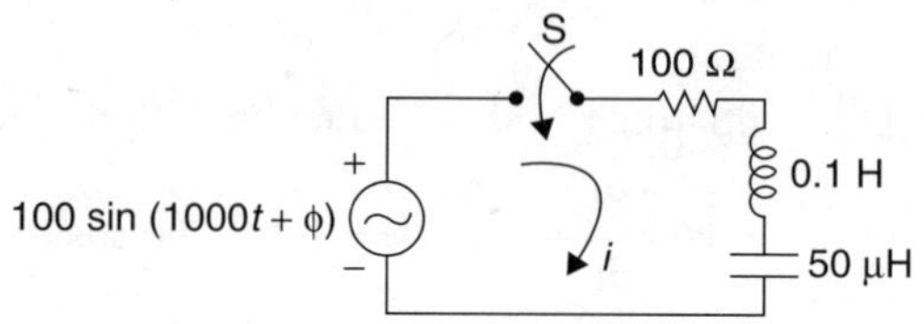

Solution: When the switch *S* is closed, applying KVL to the circuit

$$100i + 0.1\frac{di}{dt} + \frac{1}{50\times10^{-6}}\int i dt = 100\sin(1000t + 90°)$$

Differentiating the above equation with respect to t,

$$100\frac{di}{dt} + 0.1\frac{d^2i}{dt^2} + 2\times10^4 i = 10\times10^4\cos(1000t + 90)$$

$$\frac{d^2i}{dt^2} + 1000\frac{di}{dt} + 2\times10^5 i = -10^6\sin 1000t \quad (1)$$

The characteristic equation is

$$s^2 + 1000s + 2\times10^5 = 0; \quad \text{where,} \quad s = \frac{d}{dt}$$

$$s_{1,2} = \frac{-1000 \pm \sqrt{1000^2 - 4\times2\times10^5}}{2} = \frac{-1000 \pm 447.2}{2}$$

$$s_1 = -723.5, s_2 - 276.5$$

The complementary function is

$$i_C = C_1e^{-276.5t} + C_2e^{-723.5t} \quad (2)$$

We can find the particular current by using the method of undetermined coefficients. Let us assume

$$i_p = A\cos 1000t + B\sin 1000t \quad (3)$$

$$i'_p = -1000A\sin 1000t + 1000B\cos 1000t$$

$$i''_p = -1000^2A\cos 1000t - 1000^2B\sin 1000t$$

Substituting i_p, i'_p, i''_p in Eq. (1), we have

$$-1000^2A\cos 1000t - 1000^2B\sin 1000t + 1000(-1000A\sin 1000t + 1000B\cos 1000t)$$

$$+ 2\times10^5(A\cos 1000t + B\sin 1000t) = -10^6\sin 1000t$$

Comparing the corresponding coefficients on both sides

$$-1000^2A + 1000^2B + 2\times10^5A = 0$$

$$-10A + 10B + 2A = 0$$

$$\Rightarrow \quad B = 0.8A \quad (4)$$

$$-1000^2B - 1000^2A + 2\times10^5B = -10^6$$

$$-B - A + 0.2B = -1$$

$$\Rightarrow \quad 0.8B + A = 1 \quad (5)$$

From Eqs (4) and (5), we have

$$0.8^2A + A = 1$$

$$1.64A = 1 \quad \Rightarrow \quad A = 0.61$$

$$B = 0.8\times0.61 = 0.4888$$

$$\therefore \quad i_p = 0.61\cos 1000t + 0.4888\sin 1000t$$

Let $x\cos\theta = 0.61$, $x\sin\theta = 0.4888$ then

$$\tan\theta = \frac{0.488}{0.61} = 0.8$$

$\Rightarrow$ $$\theta = 38.65°$$

$$x = \sqrt{0.61^2 + 0.488^2} = 0.78$$

$\therefore$ $$i_p = x\cos\theta\cos 1000t + x\sin\theta\ 1000t$$
$$= x\cos(1000t - \theta)$$
$$= 0.78\cos(1000t - 38.65°)$$

The complete solution is

$$i = i_C + i_p = C_1e^{-276.5t} + C_2e^{-723.5t} + 0.78\cos(1000t - 38.65°) \quad (6)$$

Applying initial conditions at $t = 0$, the inductor acts as an open circuit and the capacitor acts as a short circuit.

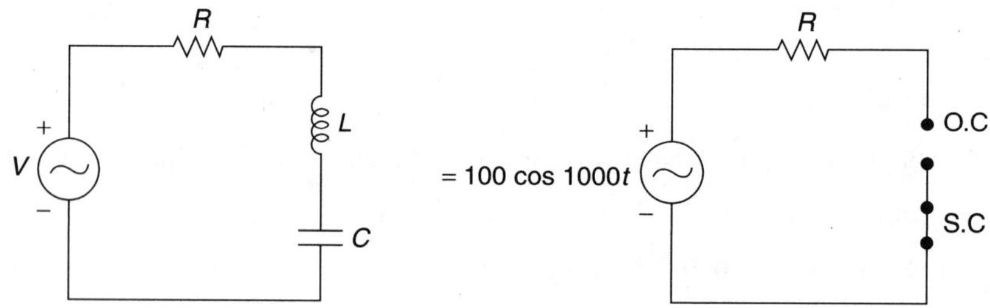

$$V = Ri + L\frac{di}{dt} + \frac{1}{C}\int idt$$

$$100\cos(1000\times 0) = 0 + 0.1\frac{di}{dt} + 0$$

$\Rightarrow$ $$\frac{di}{dt} = 1000$$

At $t = 0, i = 0$

$$0 = C_1 + C_2 + 0.78\cos 38.65°$$

$\Rightarrow$ $$C_1 + C_2 = -0.61 \quad (7)$$

Differentiating Eq. (6), we have

$$\frac{di}{dt} = -276.5C_1e^{-276.5t} - 723.5C_2e^{-723.5t} - 780\sin(1000t - 38.65°)$$

At $t = 0, i = 0, \frac{di}{dt} = 1000$

$$1000 = -276.54C_1 - 723.5C_2 - 780\sin 38.65°$$

$\therefore$ $$276.5C_1 + 723.5C_2 = -512.84$$

$$C_1 + 2.616\, C_2 = -1.856 \qquad (8)$$

After solving the Eqs (7) and (8), we can get

$$C_2 = -0.77,\ C_1 = 0.162$$

∴ The complete solution is

$$i = 0.162e^{-276.5t} - 0.77e^{-723.5t} + 0.78 \cos(1000t - 38.65°)$$

9.7 In the two mesh network, the switch is closed at $t = 0$. Find the transient mesh current i_1 and i_2 and the voltage across the capacitor, V_C.

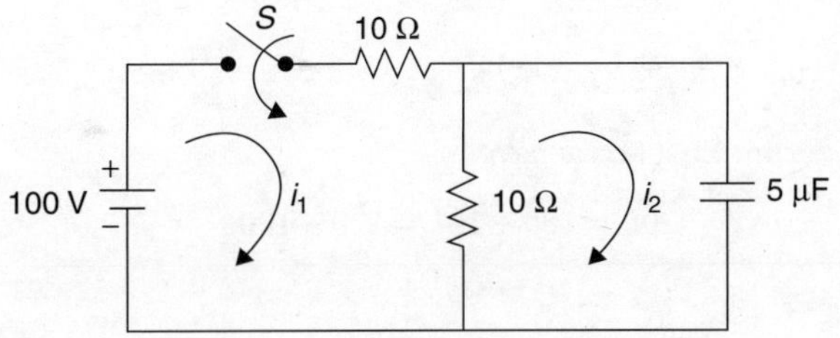

Solution: When the switch S is closed at $t = 0$, applying KVL to the individual loops, we have

For loop 1,

$$100 = 10i_1 + 10(i_1 - i_2)$$

$$100 = 20i_1 - 10i_2 \qquad (1)$$

$$\Rightarrow \quad 20\frac{di}{dt} - 10\frac{di_2}{dt} = 0$$

$$2\frac{di_1}{dt} = \frac{di_2}{dt} \qquad (2)$$

From loop 2,

$$-10i_1 + 10i_2 + \frac{1}{5\times 10^{-6}}\int i_2 dt = 0 \qquad (3)$$

$$-10\frac{di_1}{dt} + 10\frac{di_2}{dt} + 2\times 10^5 i_2 = 0 \qquad (4)$$

From Eqs (2) and (4),

$$-5\frac{di_2}{dt} + 10\frac{di_2}{dt} + 2\times 10^5 i_2 = 0$$

$$5\frac{di_2}{dt} + 2\times 10^5 i_2 = 0$$

$$\frac{di_2}{dt} + 4\times 10^4 i_2 = 0 \qquad (5)$$

$$\Rightarrow \quad i_2 = C_1 e^{-4\times 10^4 t} \qquad (6)$$

Substituting $t = 0$, in Eqs (1) and (3), we can get

$$20i_1 - 10i_2 = 100$$

$$-10i_1 + 10i_2 = 0$$

$$\Rightarrow \quad i_1 = i_2$$

$$10i_1 = 100$$

$\Rightarrow$ $$i_1 = 10, i_2 = 10$$

$\therefore$ At $t = 0$, $t_2 = 10$

From Eq. (6), we have

$$10 = C_1 e^{-0} \Rightarrow C_1 = 10$$

$\Rightarrow$ $$i_2 = 10e^{-4\times 10^4 t}$$

From Eq. (1), we have

$$20i_1 = 100 + 10i_2 = 100 + 100e^{-4\times 10^4 t}$$

$\Rightarrow$ $$i_1 = 5 + 5e^{-4\times 10^4 t}$$

Voltage across the capacitor

$$V_C = \frac{1}{C}\int_0^t i_2 dt = \frac{1}{5\times 10^{-6}}\int_0^t 10e^{-4\times 10^4 t} dt = -2\times 10^5 \times 10\left[\frac{e^{-4}\times 10^4 t}{4\times 10^4}\right]_0^t = 50[1 - e^{-4\times 10^4 t}]$$

$\therefore$ The transient mesh currents are

$$i_1 = 5(1 + e^{-4\times 10^4 t}),\ i_2 = 10e^{-4\times 10^4 t}$$

9.8 In the two mesh networks, the switch is closed at $t = 0$ Find the transient mesh current i_2 and i_2 when $v(t) = 100 \sin 500t$.

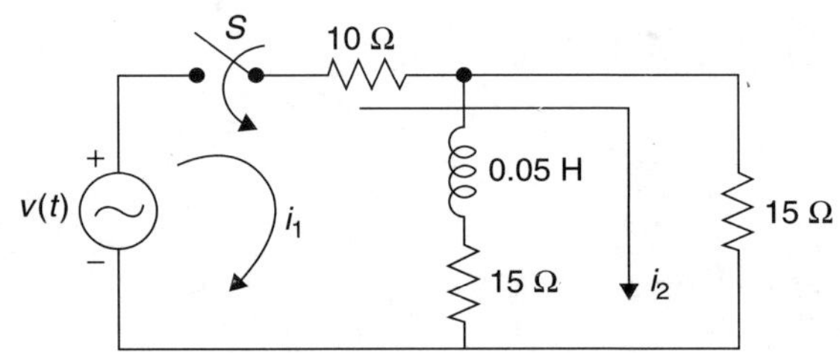

Solution: When the switch S is closed at $t = 0$, applying KVL to the individual loops, we have

For loop 1,

$$25i_1 + 10i_2 + 0.05\frac{di_1}{dt} = 100 \sin 500t \quad (1)$$

For loop 2,

$$25i_2 + 10i_1 = 100 \sin 500t \quad (2)$$

$$i_2 = \frac{1}{25}(-10i_1 + 100 \sin 500t) \quad (3)$$

From Eqs (1) and (3), we have

$$25i_1 + 10\times\frac{1}{25}(-10i_1 + 100 \sin 500t) + 0.05\frac{di_1}{dt} = 100 \sin 500t$$

$$21i_1 + 0.05\frac{di_1}{dt} = 60 \sin 500t$$

$$\frac{di_1}{dt} + 420i_1 = 1200 \sin 500t \quad (4)$$

The complementary function is

$$i_{C_1} = C_1 e^{-420t}$$

Then determine the particular function, we can assume the solution as

$$i_{p1} = A\cos 500t + B\sin 500t$$

$$i''_{P_1} = -A\,500\sin 500t + B\,500\cos 500t$$

Substituting i_{P_1} and $i_{P_2''}$ in Eq. (4), we have

$$-500\,A\sin 500t + 500\,B\cos 500t + 420(A\cos 500t + B\sin 500t) = 1200\sin 500t \quad (5)$$

Comparing the corresponding coefficient on both sides, we have

$$-500\,A + 420\,B = 1200 \quad (6)$$

$$420\,A + 500\,B = 0 \quad (7)$$

After solving Eqs (6) and (7), we get

$$A = -1.4,\ B = 1.182$$

$$\therefore \quad i_p = -1.4\cos 500t + 1.18\sin 500t$$

Let $x\sin\theta = 1.4$, $x\cos\theta = 1.18$ then

$$\tan\theta = \frac{1.4}{1.18} = 1.19 \quad \Rightarrow \quad \theta = 50°$$

$$x = \sqrt{1.4^2 + 1.18^2} = 1.83$$

$$\Rightarrow \quad i_{P_1} = -x\sin\theta\cos 500t + x\cos\theta\sin 500t$$

$$= x\sin(500t - \theta)$$

$$= 1.83\sin(500t - 50°) \quad (8)$$

The complete solution is

$$i_1 = i_{C_1} + i_{P_1} = C_1 e^{-420t} + 1.83\sin(500t - 50°)$$

Applying initial conditions, that is, at $t = 0$, $i_1 = 0$

$$\therefore \quad 0 = C_1 + 1.83\sin(-50) \quad \Rightarrow \quad C_1 = 1.4$$

$$\therefore \quad i_1 = 1.4e^{-420t} + 1.83\sin(500t - 50°) \quad (9)$$

Substituting Eq. (9) in Eq. (3) we have,

$$i_2 = \frac{1}{25}\{-10[1.4e^{-420t} + 1.83\sin(500t - 50°)] + 100\sin 500t\}$$

$$= -0.56e^{-420t} - 0.732\sin(500t - 50°) + 4\sin 500t \quad (10)$$

The transient mesh currents are

$$i_1 = 1.4e^{-420t} + 1.83\sin(500t - 50°)$$

$$i_2 = -0.56e^{-420t} - 0.732\sin(500t - 50°) + 4\sin 500t$$

EXERCISE PROBLEMS

1. For the *RL* circuit, the switch *S* is closed at $t = 0$. Determine the value of i, $\frac{di}{dt}$ and $\frac{d^2i}{dt^2}$ at $t = 0^+$.

[**Ans:** $i(0^+) = 0, \frac{di}{dt}(0^+) = 50 \text{ A/s}, \frac{d^2i}{dt^2}(0^+) = -2500 \text{ A/s}^2$]

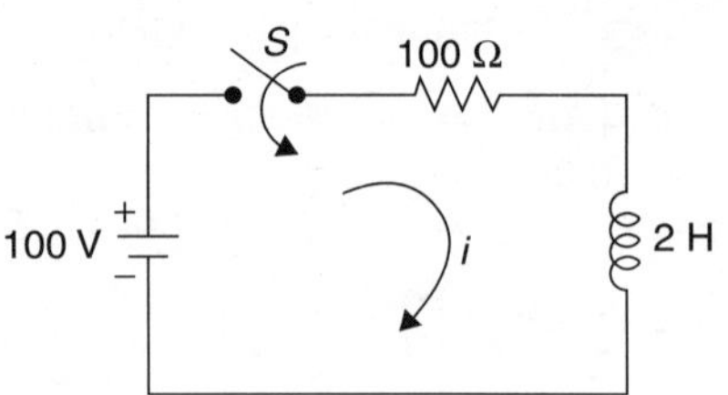

2. For the *RC* circuit, the switch *S* is closed at $t = 0$. Determine the value of i, $\frac{di}{dt}$, $\frac{d^2i}{dt^2}$ at $t = 0^+$.

[**Ans:** $i(0^+) = 4 \text{ A}, \frac{di}{dt}(0^+) = 10^4 \text{ A/s}, \frac{d^2i}{dt^2}(0^+) = 25 \times 10^6 \text{ A/s}$]

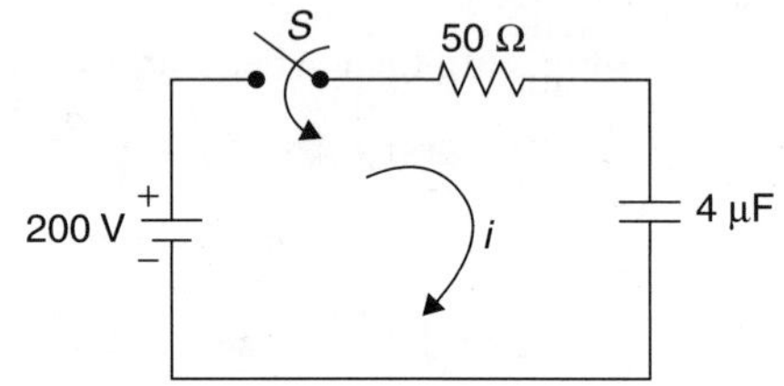

3. In the circuit, find the transient current when the switch is closed at $t = 0$. Assume zero initial conditions.
[**Ans:** $i(t) = 100e^{-5t}$]

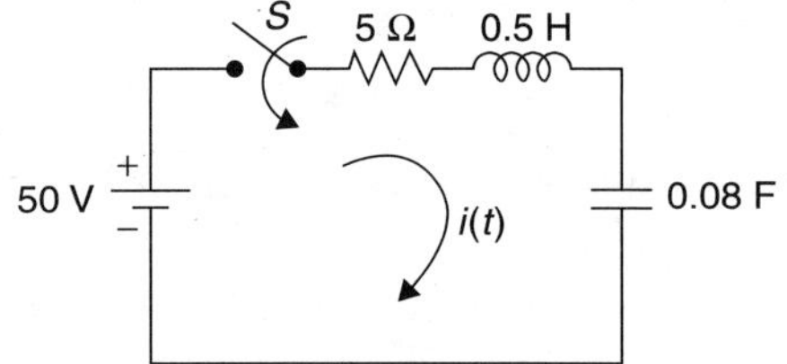

4. In the circuit, the switch *S* is closed at $t = 0$. Find the transient current. The initial conditions are as shown. [**Ans:** $i(t) = 1.52e^{-0.0169t} - 4.52e^{-5t}$]

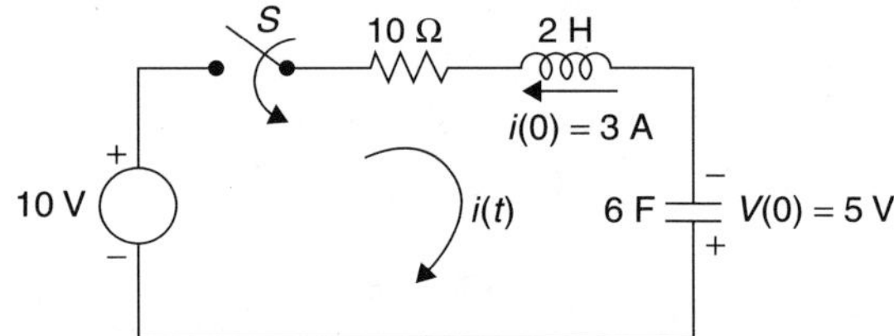

5. Find the natural frequency of a series *RLC* circuit in which $R = 200\ \Omega$, $L = 0.1$ H and $C = 5\ \mu$F.
[**Ans:** 100 rad/s].

6. In the circuit, switch S_1 is closed at $t = 0$ and switch S_2 is opened at $t = 0.2$ s. Find the transient current for the two intervals. [**Ans:** $i = 10(1 - e^{-10t})$ A, $i = 6.97e^{-60(t-0.2)} + 1.67$]

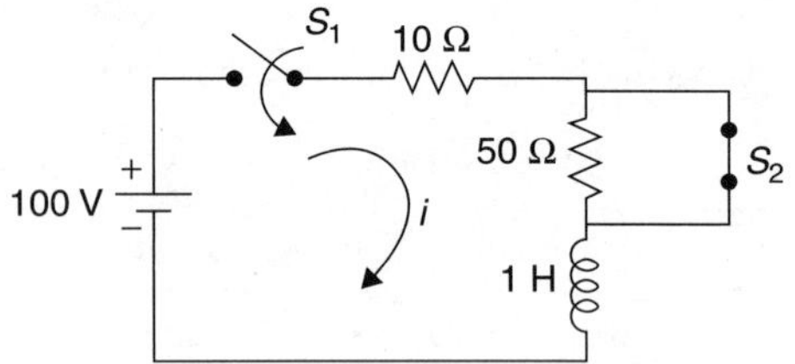

7. In the circuit, the switch *S* is closed on position 1 at $t = 0$, and then moved to position 2 after 1 millisecond. Find the time at which the current is zero and reversing its direction.
[**Ans:** 1.261 ms]

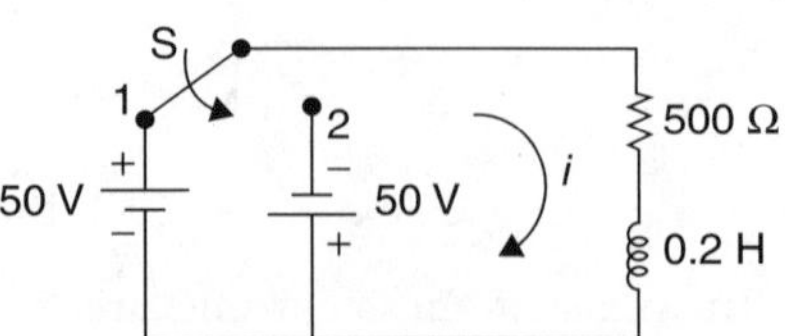

8. An *RL* series circuit with $R = 300\ \Omega$, $L = 1.0$ H has a sinusoidal applied voltage $v(t) = (100 \cos 100t + \phi)$ volts. If the switch is closed when $\phi = 45°$, find the resulting current.
[**Ans:** $i = -0.282e^{-300t} + 0.316 \cos(100t + 26.6°)$]

9. In the two mesh network, find the mesh currents i_1 and i_2 when the switch S is closed at $t = 0$.
[**Ans:** $i_1 = 0.101e^{-100} + 10e^{-9950t}$, $i_2 = -5.05e^{-100t} + 0.05e^{9950t} + 5$]

10. In the two mesh network, find the mesh currents i_1 and i_2 when the switch is closed at $t = 0$.
[**Ans:** $i_1 = 1.67e^{-6.67t} + 5$, $i_2 = -0.555e^{-6.67t} + 5$]

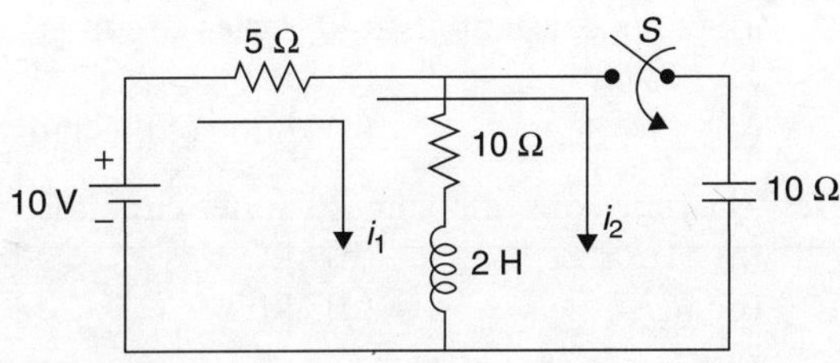

REVIEW QUESTIONS

1. Define (a) transient, (b) time constant of *RL* circuit, (c) time constant of *RC* circuit, (d) damping ratio, (e) free response, (f) forced response.
2. Why do transients occur in electric circuits?
3. What is complementary function?
4. What is particular solution?
5. What is meant by natural frequency?
6. What is critical damping?
7. What is an initial condition?
8. What is the steady state value?
9. What is the significance of time constant of *RL* series circuit?
10. Explain why the current in a pure inductance cannot change in zero time.
11. Explain why the voltage across a capacitor cannot change instantaneously.
12. Distinguish between steady state and transient response.
13. Derive an expression for the current response of an *RL* series circuit transient.
14. Derive an expression for the current response of an *RC* series circuit transient.
15. Derive an expression for the current response of an *RLC* series circuit transient.
16. Write down a few applications of *RL*, *RC* and *RLC* circuits.

MULTIPLE CHOICE QUESTIONS

1. In transient circuit analysis, complementary function gives ________
   (a) transient response
   (b) steady state response
   (c) both (a) and (b)
   (d) none of the above

2. In transient circuit analysis, the particular solution gives ________
   (a) transient response
   (b) steady state response
   (c) both (a) and (b)
   (d) none of the above

3. For a DC voltage, an inductor
   (a) acts as a short-circuit
   (b) acts as an open circuit
   (c) depends on polarity
   (d) depends on voltage value

4. The ________ can't change instantaneously in an inductor.

(a) voltage (b) current
(c) power (d) none of the above

5. The _________ can't change instantaneously in a capacitor.
(a) voltage (b) current
(c) power (d) none of the above

6. The time constant of an *RL* series circuit is
(a) L/R (b) R/L
(c) LR (d) none of the above

7. The time constant of an *RC* series circuit is
(a) $1/RC$ (b) RC
(c) C/R (d) R/C

8. The capacitor at $t = \infty$ for DC voltages will act as _________.
(a) open circuit (b) short circuit
(c) both (d) none of the above

9. The inductor at $t = \infty$ for DC voltages will act as _________
(a) open circuit (b) short circuit
(c) both (d) none of the above

10. The time constant of an *RC* circuit is defined as the time taken by the voltage across the capacitor to become _______ of its final value.
(a) 63.2% (b) 36.8%
(c) 100% (d) none of the above

11. When an *RL* circuit is switched on across a DC source of supply of V volts, the expression of current is given as
(a) $\frac{V}{R}e^{\frac{-Rt}{L}}$ (b) $\frac{V}{R}\left(1-e^{\frac{-Rt}{L}}\right)$
(c) $V\left(1-e^{\frac{-Rt}{L}}\right)$ (d) $V\left(e^{\frac{-Rt}{L}}\right)$

12. In the above expression for current, the steady state component is
(a) $(-e^{(-R/L)t}) \cdot V/R$ (b) V/R
(c) $V/R(e^{(-R/L)t})$ (d) none of the above

13. In the above expression for current, the currents at $t = 0$ and $t = \infty$ will be _______ respectively
(a) V/R and 0 (b) V/R and V/R
(c) 0 and V/R (d) none of the above

14. The voltage across inductance in a series *RL* circuit having $R = 5\ \Omega$ and $L = 0.2$ H, when a DC voltage of 10 V is suddenly applied at $t = 0$ is
(a) $50e^{-25t}$ (b) $2e^{-25t}$
(c) $10\ e^{-25t}$ (d) $20e^{-25t}$

15. A series *RLC* series circuit is energised with a DC source of V volts at $t = 0$. The expression for $i(t)$ when the circuit is critically damped is
(a) $\frac{V}{2L}te^{\frac{-Rt}{L}}$ (b) $\frac{V}{2L}te^{\frac{-Rt}{2L}}$
(c) $\frac{V}{2L}te^{\frac{-Rt}{L}}$ (d) $\frac{V}{2L}te^{\frac{-Rt}{2L}}$

16. Inductance affects the flow of direct current at the time of
(a) turning off
(b) turning on
(c) turning on and off
(d) none of the above

17. The current through an inductor follows
(a) a linear growth
(b) a linear decay
(c) an exponential growth
(d) an exponential decay

18. In an *RL* series circuit excited by a DC voltage V, the initial rate of rise of current is
(a) V/L (b) V/R
(c) V/RL (d) 0

19. In an *RL* series circuit excited by a DC voltage V, the initial rate of rise of current is independent of
(a) resistance, R (b) inductance, L
(c) source voltage (d) none of the above

20. The current in an *RL* circuit at an instant of connecting it (suddenly) to a DC source of V volts will be
(a) V/R (b) V/L
(c) V/LR (d) 0

21. In the discharging of an *RL* circuit, the voltage across the resistor exhibits _________
(a) linear (b) exponential decay
(c) constant (d) none of the above

22. A series *RC* circuit has $R = 5\ \Omega$ and $C = 2.5\ \mu F$. The time constant of the circuit is
(a) 12.5 μs (b) 0.5 μs
(c) 2 μs (d) $\frac{1}{12.5}$ μs

23. The condition for critical damping in a series *RLC* circuit is

(a) $R = 2LC$ (b) $R = 4\frac{L}{C}$
(c) $R^2 = 4\frac{L}{C}$ (d) $R^2 = 4LC$

24. The time constant of a circuit having $R = 5\ \Omega$ $L = 0.2$ H is
(a) 2 s (b) 1 s
(c) 0.04 s (d) 2.5 s

25. A series *RC* circuit having $R = 5\ \Omega$ and $C =$ 0.1 F and a DC voltage of 5 V is suddenly applied at $t = 0$ across the circuit. The circuit is initially relaxed. Then the current at $t = 0^+$ is
(a) 0.5 A (b) 5 A
(c) zero (d) 1 A

26. In an *RC* series circuit excited by a DC voltage of V volts, the initial current is
(a) 0 (b) V/R
(c) V/C (d) $(V/R)C$

27. In an *RC* series circuit excited by a DC source, the circuit current is maximum at
(a) $T = 0^-$ (b) $T = 0^+$
(c) $T = \infty$ (d) $T = CR$

28. A series *RC* circuit has $R = 15\ \Omega$ and $C = 0.2$ F. A constant voltage of 30 V is applied at $t = 0$. The expression for $i(t)$ is
(a) $1.5e^{-t/3}$ (b) $15e^{-t/3}$
(c) $2\,e^{-t/3}$ (d) $30e^{-3t}$

29. In a series *RC* circuit having $R = 10\ \Omega$ and $C = 0.1$ F. A constant voltage of 10 V is applied at $t = 0$. The expression for voltage across capacitor is
(a) $10(1 - e^{-t})$ (b) $5(1 - e^{-10t})$
(c) $10(1 - e^{-t})$ (d) $5e^{-t}$

30. A series *RC* circuit is suddenly connected to a DC voltage of V volts. The current in the series circuit, just after the switch is closed, is equal to
(a) zero (b) V/RC
(c) VC/R (d) V/R

31. An *RC* series circuit is excited by a DC source. After it is switched on
(a) the voltage across the resistance and capacitance are equal
(b) the voltage across the resistance is zero
(c) the voltage across the capacitance is zero
(d) the sum of voltages across *R* and *C* is always equal to the supply voltage

32. The steady state current in the *RC* series circuit, on the application of step voltage of magnitude V will be
(a) zero (b) V/R
(c) $(V/R)e^{(-t/CR)}$ (d) $(V/RC)e^{-t}$

33. The double energy transient occurs in the _______ circuit
(a) *R–L* (b) *R–C*
(c) *L–C* (d) *R–L–C*

34. The current response in an under damped series *RLC* circuit with DC excitation is _________
(a) exponentially rising sinusoid
(b) exponentially decaying sinusoid
(c) either decay or rise
(d) neither rises nor decays

35. A series *RL* circuit having $R = 5\ \Omega$ and $L = 0.1$ H is suddenly connected to a DC voltage of 10V at $t = 0$. The current reaches almost its steady state value in a time of
(a) $10 \times$ time constant
(b) $5 \times$ time constant
(c) $4 \times$ time constant
(d) time constant

36. In the above *RL* circuit, the value of current at $t =$ time constant
(a) 1 A (b) 2 A
(c) 0.632 A (d) 1.264 A

37. In an *RL* circuit connected to an alternating sinusoidal voltage, the magnitude of transient current primarily depends on the
(a) instant in the voltage cycle at which circuits is closed
(b) impedance of the circuit
(c) frequency of the circuit
(d) peak value of steady state current

38. The transient current in a loss free *LC* circuit, when excited from an AC source is _______ sine wave
(a) an under damped (b) an undamped
(c) an over damped (d) critically damped

39. In a loss free *RLC* circuit, the transient current will be
(a) square wave (b) oscillating
(c) sinusoidal (d) non-oscillating

40. The final value steady of current in a series *RLC* circuit when a DC voltage of V volts is applied to it at $t = \infty$ is

(a) zero (b) V/RC
(c) V/RL (d) VC/L

41. A series *RL* circuit with $R = 30\ \Omega$ and $L = 6$ H, is excited by a DC voltage of 20 V at $t = 0$. The circuit is initially relaxed. The voltage across inductor is

(a) $20(1 - e^{-4t})$ (b) $10(1 - e^{-4t})$
(c) $20e^{-4t}$ (d) $10e^{-4t}$

42. A series *RLC* circuit having $R = 10\ \Omega$, $L = 1$ H and $C = 10\ \mu$F is excited by a DC voltage of 10 V at $t = 0$. The circuit is initially relaxed. Then $\frac{di}{dt}$ at $t = 0$ is

(a) 5 A/s (b) 10 A/s
(c) $e^{-t/3}$ (d) e^{-3t}

43. An *RL* series circuit is fed from an AC source of voltage $V_{max}(\sin\omega t + \alpha)$. The transient component of the current, when the circuit is switched on, will be zero if

(a) $\alpha = 0$ (b) $\alpha = 90°$
(c) $\alpha = \tan^{-1}(\omega L/R)$ (d) $\alpha = 135°$

44. If an *RL* circuit having impedance angle ϕ is switched on when the applied sinusoidal voltage wave is passing through an angle θ, there will be no switching transient if

(a) $\theta - \phi = 0$ (b) $\theta + \phi = 0$
(c) $\theta - \phi = 90°$ (d) $\theta + \phi = 90°$

45. An *RC* series circuit with $R = 20\ \Omega$ and $C = 1$ F is connected across an AC supply of voltage $V = 100\cos(t/20)$. The switch is closed at $t = 0$ and the initial charge on the capacitor is zero. The steady state current response for the given input will be

(a) $10\cos(t/20)$ (b) $7.07\cos(t/20 + 45)$
(c) $7.07\cos(t/10)$ (d) $10\cos(t/20 + 45)$

46. In a circuit the response term that tends to zero, when time approaches infinity, is called

(a) transient response
(b) steady state response
(c) forced response
(d) zero state response

47. When a series *RL* circuit is connected to a DC voltage *V* at $t = 0$, the current passing through the inductor *L* at $t = 0^+$ is

(a) V/R amps (b) infinite
(c) zero (d) V/L amps

48. When a series *RC* circuit is connected to a constant voltage *V* volts at $t = 0$, the current passing through the circuit at $t = 0^+$ is

(a) infinite (b) zero
(c) V/R amps (d) $V/C\omega$ amps

49. In under damped circuits, the response

(a) rises or falls very fast
(b) rises or falls very slowly
(c) is a damped sinusoidal
(d) is oscillatory

Answers

1. a	2. b	3. a	4. b	5. a	6. a	7. b	8. a	9. b	10. a
11. b	12. b	13. c	14. c	15. a	16. c	17. c	18. b	19. a	20. d
21. b	22. a	23. c	24. c	25. d	26. b	27. b	28. c	29. a	30. d
31. c	32. a	33. d	34. b	35. b	36. d	37. a	38. b	39. c	40. a
41. c	42. b	43. c	44. a	45. b	46. a	47. c	48. c	49. b	

10 Network Analysis Using Laplace Transforms

Learning Outcomes

After reading this chapter, the reader will able to

- ➢ Outline Laplace and inverse Laplace transforms
- ➢ Illustrate initial and final value theorems
- ➢ Determine Laplace transforms of periodic functions
- ➢ Represent network elements in the *s*-domain
- ➢ Analyse *RL*, *RC* and *RLC* series/parallel circuits for different excitations using Laplace transforms

10.1 INTRODUCTION

The *Laplace transformation* method offers several advantages over the classical methods of solution of differential equations in general and electrical networks in particular. The following advantages make the application of Laplace transformation to network analysis almost compulsive:

- The solution of differential equations becomes systematic, simple and routine. Laplace transforms are used to convert differential equations into algebraic equations, the solution of which is easy and simple.
- The Laplace transform method gives the total solution, that is, the complementary function and particular integral in one stroke.
- Initial conditions are taken into account in the beginning only, instead of at the end as in classical methods.
- It is very difficult to solve multiple node or multiple loop networks using classical methods. By using the Laplace transform method, this difficulty can be overcome.

10.2 THE LAPLACE TRANSFORMATION

If $f(t)$ is a function of t defined for all positive values of t, then the Laplace transform of $f(t)$ is denoted by $L[f(t)]$ and is defined as

$$L[f(t)] = F(s) = \int_0^\infty e^{-st} f(t)\, dt \tag{10.1}$$

where s is a parameter which may be a real or complex number. Some examples are given below.

(i) Laplace transform of e^{at}

$$L[e^{at}] = \int_0^\infty e^{-st} e^{at} dt = \int_0^\infty e^{(a-s)t}\, dt = \int_0^\infty e^{-(s-a)t}\, dt$$

$$= \left[\frac{e^{-(s-a)t}}{-(s-a)}\right]_0^\infty = \frac{1}{a-s}[e^{-\infty} - e^0] = \frac{-1}{a-s} = \frac{1}{s-a}$$

(ii) Laplace transform of cos(*at*)

$$L[\cos at] = \int_0^\infty e^{-st} \cos at \, dt = \left[\frac{e^{-st}}{s^2 + a^2} [-s \cos at + a \sin at] \right]_0^\infty$$

$$= -\frac{1}{s^2 + a^2}(-s) = \frac{s}{s^2 + a^2}$$

(iii) Laplace transform of sin(*h at*)

$$L[\sin h\, at] = L\left(\frac{e^{at} - e^{-at}}{2} \right) = \frac{1}{2} L[e^{at}] - \frac{1}{2} L[e^{-at}] = \frac{1}{2} \times \frac{1}{s-a} - \frac{1}{2} \times \frac{1}{s+a}$$

$$= \frac{1}{2}\left(\frac{1}{s-a} - \frac{1}{s+a} \right) = \frac{1}{2}\left(\frac{s+a-s+a}{s^2 - a^2} \right) = \frac{a}{s^2 - a^2}$$

(iv) Laplace transform of *k*

$$L[k] = \int_0^\infty e^{-st} \times k \, dt = k \left[\frac{e^{-st}}{-s} \right]_0^\infty = \frac{-k}{s}(e^{-\infty} - e^{-0}) = \frac{k}{s}$$

Laplace transforms of some standard functions are given in Table 10.1.

Table 10.1 Some standard Laplace transforms

S. no	Function, $f(t)$	Laplace transform, $F(s)$
1	k	$\frac{k}{s}$
2	t	$\frac{1}{s^2}$
3	t^n	$\frac{n!}{s^{n+1}}$
4	$e^{\pm at}$	$\frac{1}{s \pm a}$
5	$\sin at$	$\frac{a}{s^2 + a^2}$
6	$\cos at$	$\frac{s}{s^2 + a^2}$
7	$\sin h\, at$	$\frac{a}{s^2 - a^2}$
8	$\cos h\, at$	$\frac{s}{s^2 - a^2}$
9	$e^{-at} \cos bt$	$\frac{s+a}{(s+a)^2 + b^2}$
10	$e^{-at} \sin bt$	$\frac{b}{(s+a)^2 + b^2}$
11	$e^{-at}\, t^n$	$\frac{n!}{(s+a)^{n+1}}$
12	$\delta(t)$	1

10.3 PROPERTIES OF LAPLACE TRANSFORMS

Linear property If *a*, *b*, *c* are any constants and *f*, *g*, *h* are any functions of *t*, then

$$L[af(t) + bg(t) + ch(t)] = aL[f(t)] + bL[g(t)] + cL[h(t)] \quad (10.2)$$

First shifting property If $L[f(t)] = \bar{f}(s) = F(s)$ then

$$L[e^{at} f(t)] = \bar{f}(s-a) = F(s-a) \quad (10.3)$$

That is, if we know the Laplace transform $F(s)$ of $f(t)$, we can write the transform of e^{at} simply replacing *s* by $(s - a)$ to get $F(s - a)$.

Time scaling property If $L[f(t)] = F(s)$ then

$$L[f(at)] = \frac{1}{a} F\left(\frac{s}{a} \right) \quad (10.4)$$

Scaling theorem If *k* is a constant then the Laplace transform of $kf(t)$ is given as *k* times the Laplace transform of $f(t)$.

That is, $L[kf(t)] = kL[f(t)] = kF(s)$ (10.5)

Real differentiation: If $F(s)$ is the Laplace transform of $f(t)$, then

$$L\left[\frac{df(t)}{dt}\right] = sF(s) - f(\bar{0}) \tag{10.6}$$

where $f(\bar{0})$ = the value of $f(t)$ at $t = \bar{0}$, that is, just before the instant $t = 0$.

Real integration If $F(s)$ is the Laplace transform of $f(t)$, then

$$L\left[\int_0^t f(t)\,dt\right] = \frac{F(s)}{s} \tag{10.7}$$

Differentiation by s If $F(s)$ is the Laplace transform of $f(t)$ then the differentiation by s in the complex frequency domain corresponds to the multiplication by t in the time domain.

That is, $$L[tf(t)] = -\frac{dF(s)}{ds} \tag{10.8}$$

Real translation or shifting theorem This theorem is useful to obtain the Laplace transform of the shifted or delayed function of time. If $F(s)$ is the Laplace transform of $f(t)$, then the Laplace transform of the function delayed by time T is

$$L[f(t-T)] = e^{-Ts}\,F(s) \tag{10.9}$$

Problem 10.1 Find the Laplace transform of the function $f(t) = \sin^2 t$.

Solution:

$$f(t) = \sin^2(t) = \frac{1-\cos 2t}{2}$$

$$F(s) = L[f(t)] = \frac{1}{2}L(1-\cos 2t) = \frac{1}{2}(L[1] - L[\cos 2t])$$

$$= \frac{1}{2}\left(\frac{1}{s} - \frac{s}{s^2+2^2}\right) = \frac{1}{2}\left[\frac{s^2+4-s^2}{s(s^2+4)}\right] = \frac{2}{s(s^2+4)}$$

Problem 10.2 Find the Laplace transform of the function, $f(t) = 1 - t + 4t^2 + 2t^3$.

Solution:

Given that $f(t) = 1 - t + 4t^2 + 2t^3$

$$F(s) = L[f(t)] = L[1 - t + 4t^2 + 2t^3]$$

$$= L[1] - L[t] + 4L[t^2] + 2L[t^3]$$

$$= \frac{1}{s} - \frac{1}{s^2} + 4\times\frac{2}{s^3} + 2\times\frac{6}{s^4} = \frac{s^3 - s^2 + 8s + 12}{s^4}$$

Problem 10.3 Find the Laplace transform of the function, $f(t) = e^{-3t}\,t^4$.

Solution:

Given that $f(t) = e^{-3t} t^4$

$$L[t^4] = \frac{4!}{s^3}$$

According to first shifting property, if $L[f(t)] = F(s)$ then $L[e^{at} f(t)] = F(s - a)$

$$\therefore \quad L[e^{-3t} t^4] = \frac{4!}{(s+3)^3} = \frac{24}{(s+3)^3}$$

Problem 10.4 Find the Laplace transform of the function, sin $(t - k)$.

Solution:

Let $f(t) = \sin t$, then

$$L[f(t)] = F(s) = \frac{1}{s^2+1}$$

According to real translation or shifting theorem, if $L[f(t)] = F(s)$, then $L[f(t - T) = e^{-Ts} F(s)$

$$\therefore \quad L[\sin(t-k)] = e^{-ks}\frac{1}{s^2+1}$$

Problem 10.5 Find the Laplace transform of the function t sin t.

Solution:

Let $f(t) = \sin t$, then

$$L[f(t)] = F(s) = \frac{1}{s^2+1}$$

According to differentiation by s property, if $L[f(t)] = F(s)$ then $L[tf(t)] = -\frac{dF(s)}{ds}$

$$\therefore \quad L[t\sin t] = -\frac{d}{ds}\left[\frac{1}{s^2+1}\right] = \frac{2s}{(s^2+1)^2}$$

Problem 10.6 If $L[f(t)] = \log\left(\frac{s+2}{s+4}\right)$, find $L[f(3t)]$.

Solution:

Given that $L[f(t)] = \log\left(\frac{s+2}{s+4}\right)$

According to time scaling property, if $L[f(t)] = F(s)$ then $L[f(at)] = \frac{1}{a}F\left(\frac{s}{a}\right)$.

$$\therefore \quad L\left[f(3t)\right] = \frac{1}{3}\log\left(\frac{\frac{s}{3}+2}{\frac{s}{3}+4}\right) = \frac{1}{3}\log\left(\frac{s+6}{s+12}\right)$$

10.4 INITIAL VALUE AND FINAL VALUE THEOREMS

Initial value theorem The Laplace transform is very useful to find the initial value of the time function $f(t)$. Thus, if $F(s)$ is the Laplace transform of $f(t)$, then

$$f(0) = \underset{t \to 0}{Lt}\ f(t) = \underset{s \to \infty}{Lt}\ sF(s) \tag{10.10}$$

Final value theorem The Laplace transform is also useful to find the final value of the time function $f(t)$. Thus, if $F(s)$ is the Laplace transform of $f(t)$ then,

$$f(\infty) = \underset{t \to \infty}{Lt}\ f(t) = \underset{s \to 0}{Lt}\ sF(s) \tag{10.11}$$

Problem 10.7 Verify the initial value and final value theorems for the function $f(t) = e^{-t}(\sin 3t + \cos 5t)$.

Solution:

Given that $f(t) = e^{-t}(\sin 3t + \cos 5t) = e^{-t} \sin 3t + e^{-t} \cos 5t$

$$L[e^{-t} \sin 3t] = \frac{3}{(s+1) + 3^2}$$

$$L[e^{-t} \sin 5t] = \frac{s+1}{(s+1) + 5^2}$$

$$F(s) = L[f(t)] = L[e^{-t} \sin 3t + e^{-t} \cos 5t] = \frac{3}{(s+1)^2 + 3^2} + \frac{s+1}{(s+1) + 5^2}$$

Verification of initial value theorem

$$\underset{t \to 0}{Lt}\ f(t) = \underset{t \to 0}{Lt}\ e^{-t}(\sin 3t + \cos 5t) = e^{-0}(0+1) = 1$$

$$\underset{s \to \infty}{Lt}\ sF(s) = \underset{s \to \infty}{Lt} \left[\frac{3s}{s^2 + 2s + 10} + \frac{s(s+1)}{s^2 + 2s + 26} \right] = 0 + 1 = 1$$

$\underset{t \to 0}{Lt}\ f(t) = \underset{t \to \infty}{Lt}\ sF(s) = 1$, initial value theorem verified.

Verification of final value theorem

$$\underset{t \to \infty}{Lt}\ f(t) = \underset{t \to \infty}{Lt}\ e^{-t}(\sin 3t + \cos 5t) = 0$$

$$\underset{s \to 0}{Lt}\ sF(s) = \underset{s \to 0}{Lt} \left[\frac{3s}{s^2 + 2s + 10} + \frac{s^2 + s}{s^2 + 2s + 26} \right] = 0$$

$\therefore\ \underset{t \to \infty}{Lt}\ f(t) = \underset{S \to 0}{Lt}\ sF(s) = 0$, final value theorem is verified.

Problem 10.8 Find the value of $i(0)$ using the initial value theorem for the Laplace transform given by $I(s) = \frac{2s+3}{(s+1)(s+3)}$. Verify the result by solving it for $i(t)$.

Solution:

Given that $I(s)=\dfrac{2s+3}{(s+1)\,(s+3)}$

According to initial value theorem,

$$i(0)=\underset{t\to 0}{Lt}\ f(t)=\underset{s\to\infty}{Lt}\ sF(s)=\underset{s\to\infty}{Lt}\ \frac{s\,(2s+3)}{(s+1)\,(s+3)}=\frac{2}{1\times 1}=2$$

$$I(s)=\frac{2s+3}{(s+1)(s+3)}=\frac{1/2}{s+1}+\frac{3/2}{s+3}$$

$$i(t)=L^{-1}[I(s)]=L^{-1}\left[\frac{1}{2}\,\frac{1}{s+1}+\frac{3}{2}+\frac{1}{s+3}\right]=\frac{1}{2}e^{-t}+\frac{3}{2}e^{-3t}$$

$\Rightarrow$ $$i(0)=\frac{1}{2}+\frac{3}{2}=\frac{4}{2}=2$$

10.5 INVERSE LAPLACE TRANSFORM

Inverse Laplace transform is calculated by the partial fraction method rather than complex integration evaluation. Let $F(s)$ be the Laplace transform of $f(t)$, then the inverse Laplace transform is denoted as

$$f(t)=L^{-1}[F(s)] \tag{10.12}$$

The following properties will simplify our calculations:

Linear property If a and b are constants, then

$$L^{-1}[aF_1(s)+bF_2(s)]=aL^{-1}[F_1(s)]+bL^{-1}[F_2(s)]$$

Inverse translation property

Given $F(s)=L[f(t)]$, since $L[e^{at}f(t)]=F(s-a)$, $L^{-1}[F(s-a)]=e^{at}f(t)=e^{at}L^{-1}[F(s)]$

Inverse shifting property

Since $L[u_a(t)\,f(t-a)]=e^{-as}\,L[f(t)]=e^{-as}\,F(s)$, then $L^{-1}[e^{-as}\,F(s)]=u_a(t)\,f(t-a)$

The convolution integral The Laplace transforms of the functions $f(t)$ and $g(t)$ are $F(s)$ and $G(s)$ respectively and $L[f(t)\times g(t)]=L[f(t)]\times L[g(t)]=F(s)\,G(s)$ then

$$L^{-1}\big[F(s)\cdot G(s)\big]=f(t)\times g(t)=\int_0^t f(\tau)\,g\,(t-\tau)\,d\tau=\int_0^t g(\tau)\,f\,(t-\tau)\,d\tau$$

Problem 10.9 Find the inverse Laplace transforms of the following functions.

(i) $F(s)=\dfrac{3}{s-5}$ (ii) $F(s)=\dfrac{8}{s^3}$ (iii) $F(s)=\dfrac{4s+1}{s^2+9}$ (iv) $F(s)=\dfrac{4s+1}{s^2-9}$ (v) $F(s)=\dfrac{10}{(s+1)^3}$

Solution:

Given that

(i) $F(s)=\dfrac{3}{s-5}=3\left[\dfrac{1}{s-5}\right]$

Using Table 10.1, we have

$$f(t)=L^{-1}\left[F(s)\right]=L^{-1}\left[3\times\frac{1}{s-5}\right]=3L^{-1}\left[\frac{1}{s-5}\right]=3e^{5t}$$

(ii) $F(s)=\dfrac{8}{s^3}=\dfrac{8}{2!}\times\dfrac{2!}{s^3}=4\times\dfrac{2!}{s^3}$

Using Table 10.1, we have

$$f(t)=L^{-1}[F(s)]=L^{-1}\left[4\times\frac{2!}{s^3}\right]=4L^{-1}\left[\frac{2!}{s^3}\right]=4t^2$$

(iii) $F(s)=\dfrac{4s+1}{s^2+9}=4\left[\dfrac{s}{s^2+9}\right]+\left[\dfrac{1}{s^2+9}\right]$

Using Table 10.1, we have

$$f(t)=L^{-1}\left[F(s)\right]=L^{-1}\left[4\times\frac{s}{s^2+9}+\frac{1}{s^2+9}\right]=4L^{-1}\left[\frac{s}{s^2+9}\right]+L^{-1}\left[\frac{1}{s^2+9}\right]=4\cos 3t+\frac{1}{3}\sin 3t$$

(iv) $F(s)=\dfrac{4s+1}{s^2-9}=4\left[\dfrac{s}{s^2-9}\right]+\left[\dfrac{1}{s^2-9}\right]$

Using Table 10.1, we have

$$f(t)=L^{-1}[F(s)]=L^{-1}\left[4\times\frac{s}{s^2-9}+\frac{1}{s^2-9}\right]=4L^{-1}\left[\frac{s}{s^2-9}\right]+L^{-1}\left[\frac{1}{s^2-9}\right]=4\cos h\ 3t+\frac{1}{3}\sin h\ 3t$$

(v) $F(s)=\dfrac{10}{(s+1)^3}=\dfrac{10}{2!}\times\dfrac{2!}{(s+1)^3}=5\times\dfrac{2!}{(s+1)^3}$

Using Table 10.1, we have

$$f(t)=L^{-1}[F(s)]=L^{-1}\left[5\times\frac{2!}{(s+1)^3}\right]=5L^{-1}\left[\frac{2!}{(s+1)^3}\right]=5t^2e^{-t}$$

Problem 10.10 Find the inverse Laplace transforms of the following functions.

(i) $F(s)=\dfrac{4}{s}-\dfrac{3}{s^2}$ (ii) $F(s)=\dfrac{15}{s^2+4s+13}$ (iii) $F(s)=\dfrac{s+1}{s^2+6s+25}$ (iv) $Y(s)=\dfrac{1}{s\,(s^2+1)}$ (v) $Y(s)=\dfrac{1}{s^2-s-12}$

Solution:

Given that

(i) $F(s)=\frac{4}{s}-\frac{3}{s^2}$

$$f(t)=L^{-1}\left[F(s)\right]=L^{-1}\left[\frac{4}{s}-\frac{3}{s^2}\right]=4L^{-1}\left[\frac{1}{s}\right]-3L^{-1}\left[\frac{1}{s^2}\right]=4-3t$$

(ii) $F(s)=\frac{15}{s^2+4s+13}$

$$F(s)=\frac{15}{s^2+4s+13}=\frac{15}{(s^2+4s+4)+9}=\frac{3\times 5}{(s+2)^2+3^2}=5\times\frac{3}{(s+2)^2+3^2}$$

$$f(t)=L^{-1}[F(s)]=L^{-1}\left[5\times\frac{3}{(s+2)^2+3^2}\right]=5L^{-1}\left[\frac{3}{(s+2)^2+3^2}\right]$$

$$=5L^{-1}\left[\frac{3}{(s-(-2))^2+3^2}\right]=5e^{-2t}L^{-1}\left[\frac{3}{s^2+3^2}\right]=5e^{-2t}\sin 3t$$

(iii) $F(s)=\frac{s+1}{s^2+6s+25}$

$$F(s)=\frac{s+1}{s^2+6s+25}=\frac{s+1}{(s^2+6s+9)+16}=\frac{(s+3)-2}{(s+3)^2+4^2}$$

$$f(t)=L^{-1}[F(s)]=L^{-1}\left[\frac{(s+3)-2}{(s+3)^2+4^2}\right]=L^{-1}\left[\frac{(s+3)}{(s+3)^2+4^2}\right]-L^{-1}\left[\frac{2}{(s+3)^2+4^2}\right]$$

$$=e^{-3t}L^{-1}\left[\frac{s}{s^2+4^2}\right]-\frac{e^{-3t}}{2}L^{-1}\left[\frac{2\times 2}{s^2+4^2}\right]=e^{-3t}\left[\cos 4t-\frac{1}{2}\sin 4t\right]$$

(iv) $Y(s)=\frac{1}{s\,(s^2+1)}$

$$y(t)=L^{-1}[Y(s)]=L^{-1}\left[\frac{1}{s\,(s^2+1)}\right]=L^{-1}\left[\frac{1}{s}\times\frac{1}{(s^2+1)}\right]=f(t)\times g(t)=g(t)\times f(t)$$

Since, $L^{-1}\left[\frac{1}{s}\right]=1,\ L^{-1}\left[\frac{1}{(s^2+1)}\right]=\sin t$

According to convolution integral

$$y(t)=f(t)\times g(t)=\int_0^t \sin\tau\, d\tau=-\cos\tau\Big|_0^t=1-\cos t$$

(v) $Y(s)=\frac{1}{s^2-s-12}$

$$y(t) = L^{-1}[Y(s)] = L^{-1}\left[\frac{1}{s^2 - s - 12}\right] = L^{-1}\left[\frac{1}{s-4} \times \frac{1}{s+3}\right] = f(t) \times g(t) = g(t) \times f(t)$$

Since, $L^{-1}\left[\frac{1}{s-4}\right] = e^{4t}, L^{-1}\left[\frac{1}{s+13}\right] = e^{-3t}$

According to convolution integral,

$$y(t) = f(t) \times g(t) = \int_0^t e^{4(t-\tau)} \times e^{-3\tau} d\tau = e^{4t} \int_0^t e^{-7\tau} d\tau = -\frac{e^{4t}}{7} e^{-7\tau}\Bigg|_0^t = \frac{1}{7}(e^{4t} - e^{-3t})$$

10.6 LAPLACE TRANSFORM OF A PERIODIC FUNCTION

If $f(t)$ is a periodic function with period T, that is, $f(t + nT) = f(t)$, then the Laplace transform is given by

$$F(s) = L[f(t)] = \frac{\int_0^T e^{-st} f(t)\, dt}{1 - e^{-sT}} \tag{10.13}$$

Problem 10.11 Obtain the Laplace transform of the periodic wave form shown.

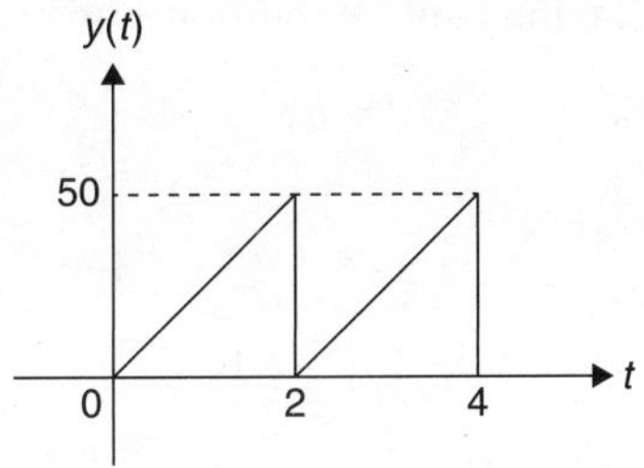

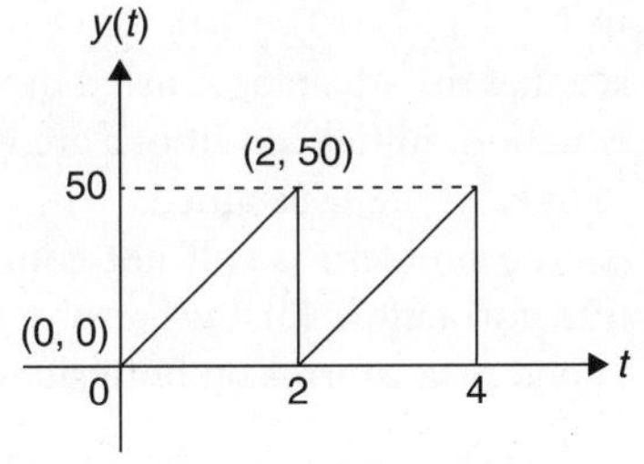

Solution:

For $0 < t < 2,\ y - 0 = \frac{50 - 0}{2 - 0}(t - 0)$

$\Rightarrow \quad y = 25t$

$$Y(s) = L[y(t)] = \frac{1}{1 - e^{-Ts}} \int_0^T y(t) e^{-st}\, dt$$

$$= \frac{1}{1 - e^{-2s}} \int_0^2 25t\, e^{-st}\, dt = \frac{25}{1 - e^{-2s}}\left[t\frac{e^{-st}}{-s} - \frac{e^{-st}}{s^2}\right]_0^2$$

$$= \frac{25}{1 - e^{-2s}}\left[2\frac{e^{-2s}}{-s} - \frac{e^{-2s}}{s^2} + \frac{1}{s^2}\right]$$

$$= \frac{25(-2se^{-2s} - e^{-2s} + 1)}{1 - e^{-2s}}$$

Problem 10.12 Obtain the Laplace transform of the periodic wave form shown.

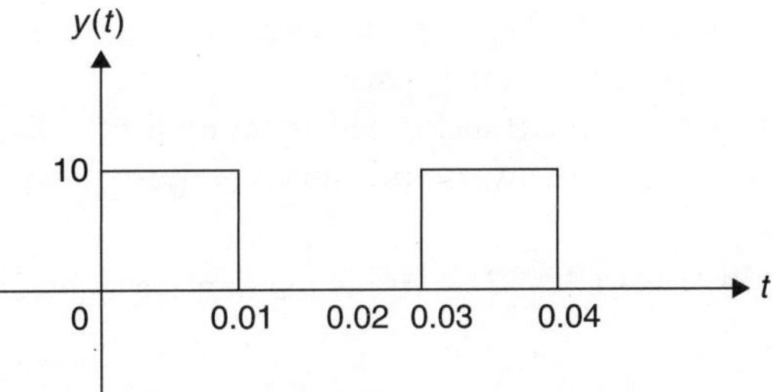

Solution:

For $\quad 0 < t < 0.01, y(t) = 10$

For $\quad 0.01 < t < 0.03, y(t) = 0$

$$Y(s) = L\left[y(t)\right] = \frac{1}{1-e^{-Ts}} \int_0^T y(t)\, e^{-st}\, dt$$

$$= \frac{1}{1-e^{-0.03s}} \int_0^{0.03} y(t)\, e^{-st}\, dt = \frac{1}{1-e^{-0.03s}} \left[\int_0^{0.01} 10e^{-st}\, dt + \int_{0.01}^{0.03} 0 \times e^{-st}\, dt \right]$$

$$= \frac{10}{1-e^{-0.03s}} \left[\frac{e^{-st}}{-s} \right]_0^{0.01} = \frac{10}{1-e^{-0.03s}} \left[\frac{e^{-0.01s}}{-s} + \frac{1}{s} \right]$$

$$= \frac{10(-e^{-0.01s}+1)}{s(1-e^{-0.03s})}$$

10.7 APPLICATION TO SOLUTION OF A DIFFERENTIAL EQUATION

Let us consider the nth order differential equation as

$$\frac{d^n y}{dt^n} + k_1 \frac{d^{n-1}}{dt^{n-1}} + k_2 \frac{d^{n-2} y}{dt^{n-2}} + \cdots + k_{n-1} \frac{dy}{dt} + k_n y = x(t) \tag{10.14}$$

Taking Laplace transform on both sides

$$s^n Y(s) - s^{n-1} y(0) - s^{n-2} y'(0) \ldots -y^{n-1}(0) + k_1[s^{n-1} Y(s) - s^{n-2} y(0) - s^{n-3} y'(0) \ldots y^{n-2}(0)]$$
$$+ \cdots k_n Y(s) = X(s)$$

$$\Rightarrow \quad Y(s)[s^n + a_1 s^{n-1} + a_2 s^{n-2} + \cdots + a_n] = X(s) + s^{n-1} y(0) + \cdots + y^{n-1}(0)$$

$$\Rightarrow \quad Y(s) = \frac{X(s) + s^{n-1} y(0) + s^{n-2} y'(0) + \cdots + y^{n-1}(0)}{s^n + a_1 s^{n-1} + a_2 s^{n-2} + \cdots + a_n} \tag{10.15}$$

In Eq. 10.15, $y(0)$, $y'(0)$, … $y^{n-1}(0)$ are the initial conditions for the given differential equation. Thus, we see that the advantages listed in Section 10.1, namely the differential equation is converted into an algebraic equation, initial conditions are used in the beginning of the problem, the total solution is obtained at one stroke, are well sustained.

The problem is still not completely solved. The time function $y(t)$ is required to be found by inverse transformation. First we resolve the partial fractions to the above equation $Y(s)$, after that by taking inverse Laplace transforms on both sides, we can get the time function $y(t)$.

General procedure of the Laplace method for solving initial value problems Essentially, the Laplace transform converts an initial value problem to an algebraic problem, incorporating initial conditions into the algebraic manipulations. There are three basic steps.

(i) Take the Laplace transform of both sides of the given differential equation, making use of the linearity property of the transform.
(ii) Solve the transformed equation for the Laplace transform of the solution function.
(iii) Find the inverse transform of the expression $F(s)$ found in step (ii).

Problem 10.13 Apply the Laplace transform to solve the initial value problem $y' + 2y = 0$, $y(0) = 1$.

Solution:

Given that $y' + 2y = 0, y(0) = 1$

Applying Laplace transforms on both sides

$$L[y' + 2y] = L[0]$$

$$L[y'] + 2L[y] = 0$$

$$sY(s) - y(0) + 2Y(s) = 0$$

$$Y(s)\ [s + 2] = 1$$

$$Y(s) = \frac{1}{s+2}$$

On taking inverse Laplace transforms on both sides

$$y(t) = L^{-1}[Y(s)] = L^{-1}\left[\frac{1}{s+2}\right] = e^{-2t}$$

Problem 10.14 Solve $y'' + 4y = e^{-t}, y(0) = 2, y'(0) = 1$

Solution:

Given that $y'' + 4y = e^{-t}, y(0) = 2, y'(0) = 1$

Applying Laplace transforms on both sides

$$L[y'' + 4y] = L[e^{-t}]$$

$$L[y''] + 4L[y] = L[e^{-t}]$$

$$sY(s) - sy(0) - y'(0) + 4Y(s) = \frac{1}{s+1}$$

$$Y(s)\,[s+4] - 2s - 1 = \frac{1}{s+1}$$

$$Y(s)\,[s+4] = \frac{1}{s+1} + 2s + 1 = \frac{1 + 2s^2 + 2s + s + 1}{s+1} = \frac{2s^2 + 3s + 2}{s+1}$$

$$Y(s) = \frac{2s^2 + 3s + 2}{(s+1)\,(s+4)}$$

Using partial fraction expansion

$$\frac{2s^2 + 3s + 2}{(s+1)\,(s^2+4)} = \frac{A}{s+1} + \frac{Bs + C}{s^2+4}$$

For which $A = \frac{1}{5}$, $B = \frac{9}{5}$, and $C = \frac{6}{5}$. Thus

$$Y(s) = \frac{1}{5(s+1)} + \frac{9s+6}{5(s^2+4)} = \frac{1}{5(s+1)} + \frac{9s}{5(s^2+4)} + \frac{6}{5(s^2+4)}$$

Taking the inverse transform yields

$$y(t) = \frac{1}{5}e^{-t} + \frac{9}{5}\cos 2t + \frac{3}{5}\sin 2t$$

10.8 HEAVISIDE'S PARTIAL FRACTION EXPANSION TECHNIQUE

Let $$F(s) = \frac{P(s)}{Q(s)} = \frac{\text{Numerator polynomial in } s}{\text{Denominator polynomial in } s}$$

Case (i) Roots of $Q(s)$ are distinct.

In this case, the function $\frac{P(s)}{Q(s)}$ can be written as

$$\frac{P(s)}{Q(s)} = \frac{k_1}{s-s_1} + \frac{k_2}{s-s_2} + \cdots + \frac{k_n}{s-s_n}$$

where $$k_1 = \underset{s \to s_1}{Lt}\ (s-s_1)\frac{P(s)}{Q(s)}$$

$$k_2 = \underset{s \to s_2}{Lt}\ (s-s_2)\frac{P(s)}{Q(s)}$$

$$\vdots \qquad \vdots$$

$$\vdots \qquad \vdots$$

In general $$k_i = \underset{s \to s_i}{Lt}\ (s-s_i)\frac{P(s)}{Q(s)}$$

Case (ii) Repeated roots

$$\frac{P(s)}{Q(s)} = \frac{P(s)}{(s-s_0)^n} = \frac{k_1}{s-s_0} + \frac{k_2}{(s-s_0)^2} + \cdots + \frac{k_n}{(s-s_0)^n}$$

Suppose $n = 3$

$$k_3 = \underset{s \to s_0}{Lt}\left[(s-s_0)^3\frac{P(s)}{Q(s)}\right]$$

$$k_2 = \underset{s \to s_0}{Lt}\left[\frac{d}{ds}(s-s_0)^3\frac{P(s)}{Q(s)}\right]$$

$$k_1 = \underset{s \to s_0}{Lt}\left[\frac{1}{2}\frac{d^2}{ds^2}(s-s_0)^3\frac{P(s)}{Q(s)}\right]$$

In general $$k_m = \underset{s \to s_0}{Lt}\left[\frac{1}{(n-m)!}\frac{d^{n-m}}{ds^{n-m}}(s-s_0)^n\frac{P(s)}{Q(s)}\right]$$

where, n = order of the multiplicity.

Note: The order of the numerator polynomial $P(s)$, should less than the order of the denominator polynomial, $Q(s)$.

Problem 10.15 Find the inverse Laplace transforms for the following functions.

(i) $F(s)=\dfrac{2s+3}{s^2+3s+2}$ (ii) $F(s)=\dfrac{2s^2+3s+2}{(s+1)^3}$ (iii) $F(s)=\dfrac{s+1}{s\,(s^2+4s+4)}$ (iv) $F(s)=\dfrac{s-3}{s^2+4s+13}$

Solution:

(i) $F(s)=\dfrac{2s+3}{s^2+3s+2}$

$$F(s)=\frac{2s+3}{s^2+3s+2}=\frac{2s+3}{(s+1)(s+2)}=\frac{1}{s+1}+\frac{1}{s+2}$$

$$f(t)=L^{-1}[F(s)]=L^{-1}\left[\frac{1}{s+1}+\frac{1}{s+2}\right]=e^{-t}+e^{-2t}$$

(ii) $F(s)=\dfrac{2s^2+3s+2}{(s+1)^3}$

$$F(s)=\frac{2s^2+3s+2}{(s+1)^3}=\frac{k_1}{s+1}+\frac{k_2}{(s+1)^2}+\frac{k_3}{(s+1)^3}$$

$$k_3=\underset{s\to -I}{Lt}\ (s+1)^3\frac{(2s^2+3s+2)}{(s+1)^3}=4-3=1$$

$$k_2=\underset{S\to -1}{Lt}\left\{\frac{d}{ds}\left[(s+1)^3\frac{(2s^2+3s+2)}{(s+1)^3}\right]\right\}=\underset{s\to -1}{Lt}\ [4s+3]=-4+3=-1$$

$$k_1=\underset{S\to -1}{Lt}\left\{\frac{1}{2}\frac{d^2}{ds^2}\left[(s+1)^3\frac{(2s^2+3s+2)}{(s+1)^3}\right]\right\}=\underset{s\to -1}{Lt}\left[\frac{1}{2}\frac{d}{ds}(4s+3)\right]=2$$

$$F(s)=\frac{2s^2+3s+2}{(s-1)^3}=\frac{2}{s+1}-\frac{1}{(s+1)^2}+\frac{1}{(s+1)^3}$$

$$f(t)=L^1[F(s)]=L^{-1}\left[\frac{2}{s+1}-\frac{1}{(s+1)^2}+\frac{1}{(s+1)^3}\right]=2e^{-t}-te^{-t}+\frac{1}{2}t^2e^{-t}$$

(iii) $F(s)=\dfrac{s+1}{s(s^2+4s+4)}$

$$F(s)=\frac{s+1}{s(s^2+4s+4)}=\frac{s+1}{s(s+2)^2}=\frac{k_0}{s}+\frac{k_1}{s+2}+\frac{k_2}{(s+2)^2}$$

$$k_0=\underset{s\to 0}{Lt}\ sF(s)=\underset{s\to 0}{Lt}\left[\frac{s+1}{s^2+4s+4}\right]=\frac{1}{4}$$

$$k_2 = \underset{s \to -2}{Lt}\left[(s+2)^2 \times \frac{(s+1)}{s\,(s+2)^2}\right] = \frac{-2+1}{-2} = \frac{1}{2}$$

$$k_1 = \underset{s \to -2}{Lt}\left\{\frac{d}{ds}\left[(s+2)^2 \times \frac{(s+1)}{s\,(s+2)^2}\right]\right\} = \underset{s \to -2}{Lt}\left\{\frac{d}{ds}\left[\frac{s+1}{s}\right]\right\} = \underset{s \to -2}{Lt}\left[\frac{s-(s+1)}{s^2}\right] = -\frac{1}{4}$$

$$F(s) = \frac{s+1}{s(s+2)^2} = \frac{1}{4}\frac{1}{s} - \frac{1}{4}\frac{1}{s+2} + \frac{1}{2(s+2)^2}$$

$$f(t) = L^{-1}[F(s)] = L^{-1}\left[\frac{1}{4s} - \frac{1}{4(s+2)} + \frac{1}{2(s+2)^2}\right] = \frac{1}{4} - \frac{1}{4}e^{-2t} + \frac{1}{2}te^{-2t}$$

(iv) $F(s) = \dfrac{s-3}{s^2+4s+13}$

$$F(s) = \frac{s-3}{s^2+4s+13} = \frac{(s+2)-5}{(s+2)^2+3^2} = \frac{s+2}{(s+2)^2+3^2} - \frac{5}{(s+2)^2+3^2}$$

$$f(t) = L^{-1}[F(s)] = L^{-1}\left[\frac{s+2}{(s+2)^2+3^2} - \frac{5}{(s+2)^2+3^2}\right]$$

$$= e^{-2t}\cos 3t - \frac{5}{3}e^{-2t}\sin 3t = e^{-2t}\left[\cos 3t - \frac{5}{3}\sin 3t\right]$$

10.9 NETWORK ELEMENTS IN THE *S*-DOMAIN

Resistance The $v - i$ relationship for a resistance is

$$v(t) = i(t)R$$

Taking the Laplace transforms on both sides

$$V(s) = RI(s)$$

$\therefore$ s-domain equivalent of resistance = R

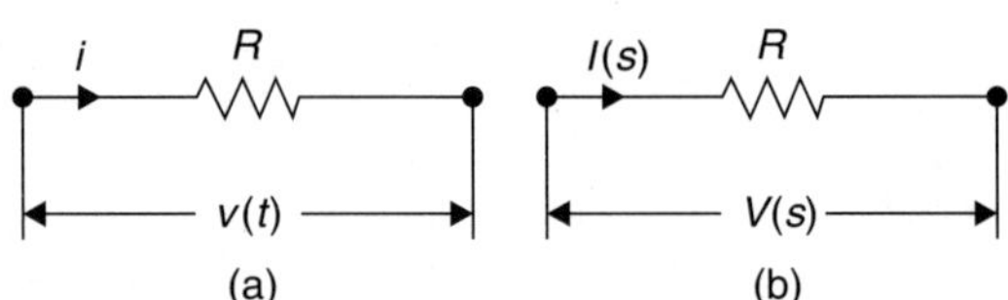

Fig. 10.1 Representation of a resistance in time and s-domains

Figures 10.1(a) and 10.1(b) show the time and frequency domain circuits of the resistance respectively.

Inductance The $v - i$ relationship for an inductance is given by

$$v = L\frac{di}{dt}$$

Taking the Laplace transforms on both sides

$$V(s) = L[sI(s) - i(0)] = sLI(s) - LI_0 \qquad [\because i(0) = I_0] \tag{10.16}$$

$$\Rightarrow \qquad I(s) = \frac{1}{Ls}V(s) + \frac{I_0}{s} \tag{10.17}$$

The time domain and frequency or s-domain network representation of inductance is given in Figs 10.2(a), 10.2(b) and 10.2(c).

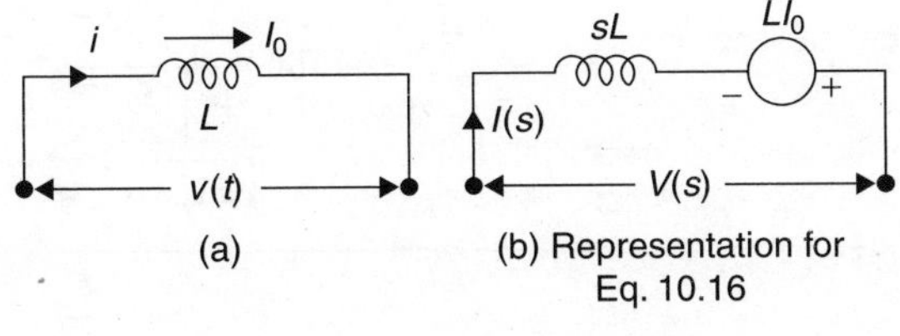

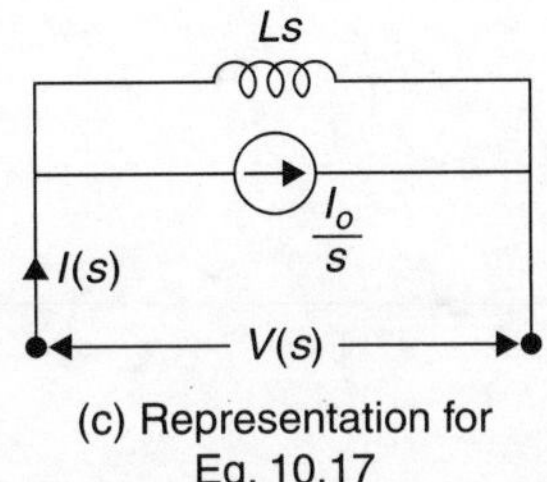

Fig. 10.2 Time domain and *s*-domain representation of the inductance

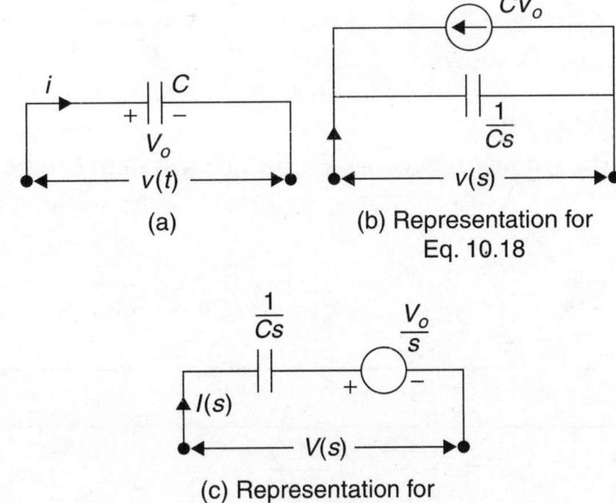

Fig. 10.3 Time domain and *s*-domain representation of the capacitance

Capacitance The $v - i$ relationship for a capacitor is given by

$$i = C\frac{dv}{dt}$$

Taking Laplace transform on both sides

$$I(s) = C[sV(s) - v(\bar{0})]$$

$$I(s) = sCV(s) - CV_0 \qquad [\because v(\bar{0}) = V_0] \tag{10.18}$$

$$\Rightarrow \qquad V(s) = \frac{1}{Cs}I(s) + \frac{V_0}{s} \tag{10.19}$$

The time domain and frequency or *s*-domain network representations of capacitance are given in Figs 10.3(a), 10.3(b) and 10.3(c).

10.10 *S*-DOMAIN NETWORK

Knowing the behaviour of *R*, *L* and *C* in the Laplace domain, the entire time domain network can be converted to the *s*-domain network, assuming zero initial conditions. In the *s*-domain network, each time domain element is represented by its transform impedance. All the associated time domain variables can be represented by the corresponding *s*-domain variables. Table 10.2 gives the transform impedance and transform admittances of three basic elements *R*, *L* and *C*.

Table 10.2 *s*-domain representation of three basic circuit elements

S. no	Element	$Z(s)$	$Y(s)$
1	R	R	$\frac{1}{R}$
2	L	sL	$\frac{1}{sL}$
3	C	$\frac{1}{Cs}$	Cs

The advantage of *s*-domain network is that all the elements *R*, *L* and *C* behave like impedances and lose their individual identity as *R*, *L* and *C* from a mathematical point of view. Hence all such impedances then can be combined and the network can be simplified using series, parallel combinations and other techniques such as star-delta and delta-star transformations. Similarly the voltage drops across all such impedances are of the form $[I(s) \times Z(s)]$ according to Ohm's law. Hence, all the network equations are always simple algebraic in the *s*-domain, without any integral or differential term.

Problem 10.16 Find the driving point impedance of the network shown.

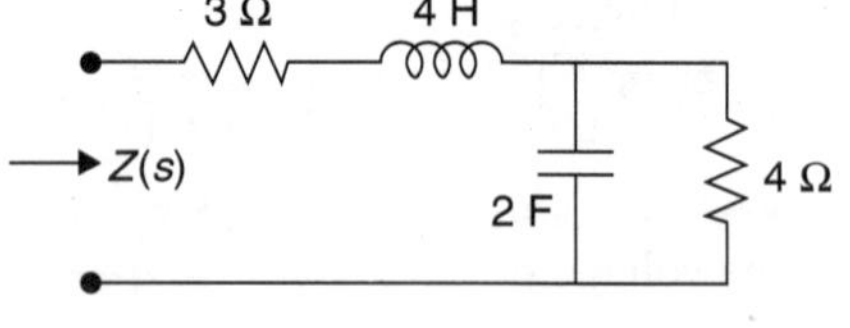

Solution:

The s-domain network for the given system can be drawn as shown.

$$K = \frac{\frac{1}{2s} \times 4}{\frac{1}{2s} + 4} = \frac{4}{1+8s}$$

$$Z(s) = 3 + 4s + \frac{4}{1+8s} = \frac{(3+4s)(1+8s)+4}{1+8s} = \frac{32^2 + 28s + 7}{1+8s}$$

The s-domain network is also called *Laplace domain network.* The total equivalent impedance of the s-domain network, obtained as viewed through the input terminal is called the *driving point impedance* $Z(s)$ of the network.

10.11 APPLICATION TO ELECTRICAL CIRCUITS

10.11.1 Step Response of *RL* Series Circuit

Let us consider a step voltage V applied to an RL series circuit at $t = 0$ (Fig. 10.4).

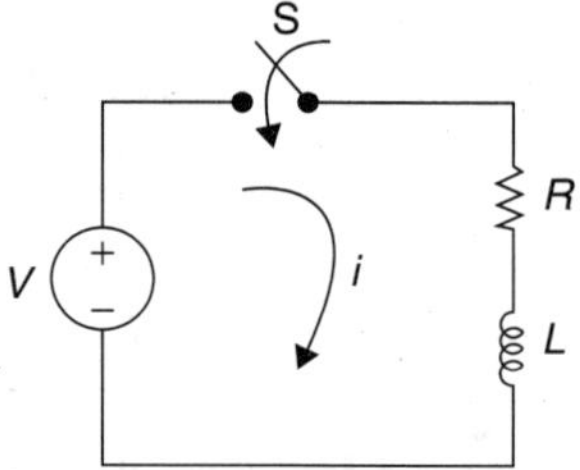

Fig. 10.4 *RL* series circuit excited by DC voltage

Applying KVL to the circuit

$$V = Ri + L\frac{di}{dt}$$

Taking Laplace transforms on both sides, assuming zero initial conditions.

$$RI(s) + LsI(s) = \frac{V}{s}$$

$$\Rightarrow \quad (R + sL)\,I(s) = \frac{V}{s}$$

$$\Rightarrow \quad I(s) = \frac{V}{s(R+sL)} = \frac{V}{L} \times \frac{1}{s(s+R/L)} = \frac{V}{L}\left[\frac{L}{R} \times \frac{1}{s} - \frac{L}{R}\frac{1}{s+R/L}\right]$$

$$\Rightarrow \quad I(s) = \frac{V}{R}\left[\frac{1}{s} - \frac{1}{s+R/L}\right] \tag{10.20}$$

Taking inverse Laplace transform on both sides, we have

$$i(t) = \frac{V}{R}\left(1 - e^{-\frac{R}{L}t}\right) \tag{10.21}$$

The voltage across the resistor is

$$V_R = Ri = R\times\frac{V}{R}\left(i - e^{-\frac{R}{L}t}\right) = V\left(1 - e^{-\frac{R}{L}t}\right) \tag{10.22}$$

The voltage across the insulator is

$$V_L = L\frac{di}{dt} = L\times\frac{V}{R}e^{\frac{-R}{L}t}\left(\frac{R}{L}\right) = Ve^{-\frac{R}{L}t} \tag{10.23}$$

10.11.2 Step Response of *RC* Series Circuit

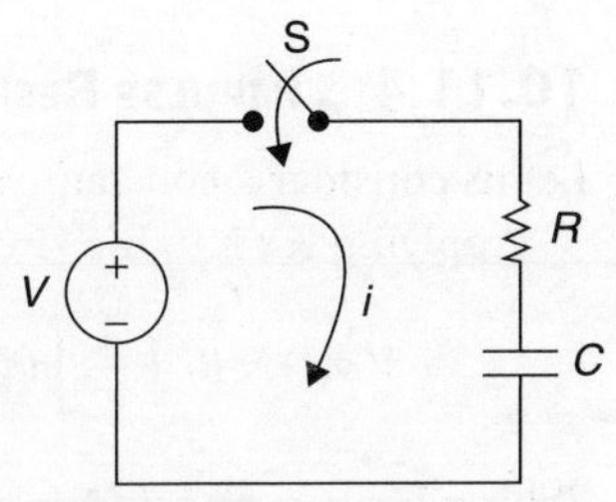

Fig. 10.5 *RC* series circuit excited by DC voltage

Let us consider a step voltage V applied to an RC series circuit (Fig. 10.5).

Applying KVL to the circuit

$$Ri + \frac{1}{C}\int idt = V$$

Taking Laplace transforms on both sides, assuming zero initial conditions,

$$RI(s) + \frac{1}{Cs}I(s) = \frac{V}{s}$$

$$\Rightarrow \quad \frac{I(s)}{Cs}(RCs+1) = \frac{V}{s}$$

$$\Rightarrow \quad I(s) = \frac{VC}{(1+RCs)} = \frac{VC}{RC}\times\frac{1}{(s+1/RC)}$$

$$\Rightarrow \quad I(s) = \frac{V}{R}\times\frac{1}{(s+1/RC)} \tag{10.24}$$

Taking inverse Laplace transform on both sides,

$$i(t) = \frac{V}{R}e^{-t/RC} \tag{10.25}$$

The voltage across the resistor is

$$V_R = Ri = R\times\frac{V}{R}e^{-t/RC} = Ve^{-t/RC} \tag{10.26}$$

The voltage across the capacitor is

$$V_C = \frac{1}{C}\int_0^t idt = \frac{1}{C}\int_0^t \frac{V}{R}e^{-t/RC} = \frac{V}{RC}\times -RC\times[e^{-t/RC}]_0^1 = V(1-e^{-t/RC}) \tag{10.27}$$

10.11.3 Impulse Response of *RL* Series Circuit

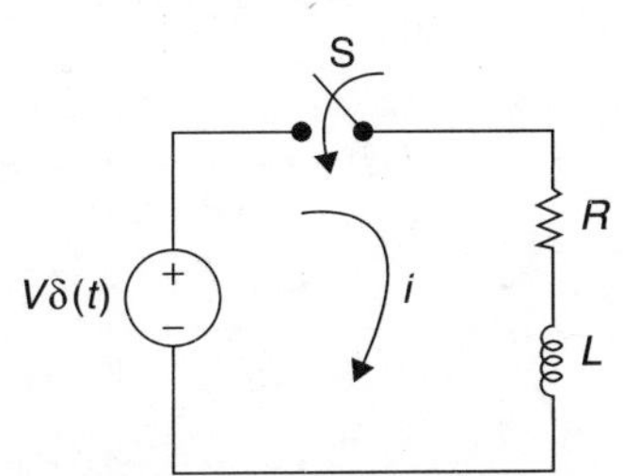

Fig. 10.6 *RL* series circuit excited by impulse voltage

Let us consider a constant voltage $V\delta(t)$ applied to an RL series circuit (Fig. 10.6).

Applying KVL to the circuit

$$V\delta(t) = Ri + L\frac{di}{dt}$$

Taking Laplace transforms on both sides, assuming zero initial conditions,

$$V = RI(s) + Ls\,I(s) = (R + Ls)\,I(s)$$

$$\Rightarrow \quad I(s) = \frac{V}{R + Ls} = \frac{V}{L} \times \frac{1}{(s + R/L)} \tag{10.28}$$

Taking inverse Laplace transforms on both sides,

$$i(t) = \frac{V}{L} e^{\frac{-R}{L}t} \tag{10.29}$$

10.11.4 Impulse Response of an *RC* Series Circuit

Let us consider a constant voltage $V\delta(t)$ applied to an RC series circuit (Fig. 10.7).

Applying KVL to the circuit

$$V\delta(t) = Ri + \frac{1}{C}\int i dt$$

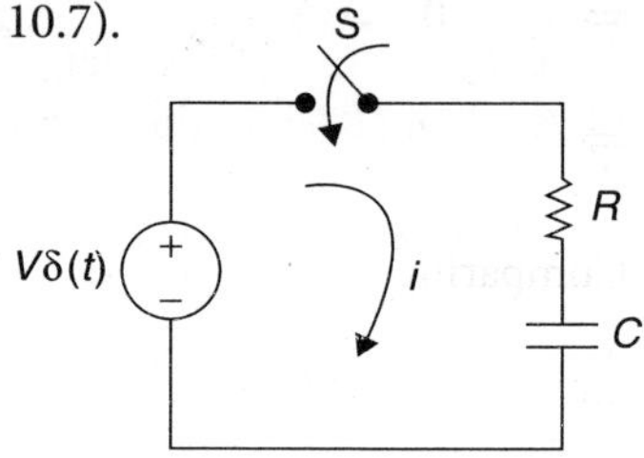

Fig. 10.7 *RC* series circuit excited by impulse voltage

Taking Laplace transforms on both sides, assuming zero initial conditions,

$$V = RI(s) + \frac{1}{Cs} I(s) = \left(R + \frac{1}{Cs}\right) I(s) = \left(\frac{RCs + 1}{Cs}\right) I(s)$$

$$\Rightarrow \quad I(s) = \frac{VCs}{1 + RCs} = \frac{VCs}{RC(s + 1/RC)} = \frac{V}{R}\left(\frac{s}{s + 1/RC}\right)$$

$$\Rightarrow \quad I(s) = \frac{V}{R}\left(1 - \frac{1/RC}{s + 1/RC}\right) \tag{10.30}$$

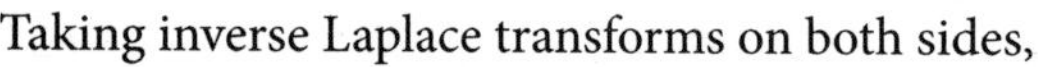

Taking inverse Laplace transforms on both sides,

$$i(t) = \frac{V}{R}\left(\delta(t) - \frac{1}{RC} e^{-t/RC}\right) \tag{10.31}$$

10.11.5 Ramp Response of *RL* Series Circuit

Let us consider a constant voltage Vt applied to an RL series circuit (Fig. 10.8).

Applying KVL to the circuit

$$Vt = Ri + L\frac{di}{dt}$$

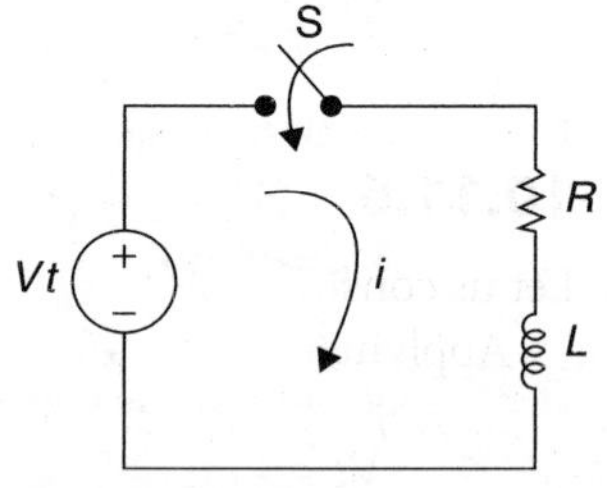

Fig. 10.8 *RL* series circuit excited by ramp voltage

Taking Laplace transforms on both sides, assuming as zero initial conditions,

$$\frac{V}{s^2} = RI(s) + Ls\,I(s) = (R + Ls)\,I(s)$$

$$\Rightarrow \quad I(s) = \frac{V}{s^2(R + Ls)} = \frac{V/L}{s^2(s + R/L)}$$

$$\frac{1}{s^2(s + R/L)} = \frac{A}{s} + \frac{B}{s^2} + \frac{C}{s + R/L}$$

$$\frac{1}{s^2(s + R/L)} = \frac{As(s + R/L) + B(s + R/L) + Cs^2}{s^2(s + R/L)}$$

$$1 = As\left(s + \frac{R}{L}\right) + B\left(s + \frac{R}{L}\right) + Cs^2$$

Put $\quad s = -\dfrac{R}{L} \Rightarrow 1 = C\dfrac{R^2}{L^2} \Rightarrow C = \dfrac{L^2}{R^2}$

$$\Rightarrow \quad 1 = (A + C)s^2 + \left(A\frac{R}{L} + B\right)s + B\frac{R}{L}$$

Comparing s^2 coefficients

$$\Rightarrow \quad 0 = A + C$$

$$\Rightarrow \quad A = -C = \frac{-L^2}{R^2}$$

Comparing constant terms

$$\Rightarrow \quad 1 = \frac{BR}{L}$$

$$\Rightarrow \quad B = \frac{L}{R}$$

$$\therefore \quad I(s) = \frac{V/L}{s^2(s + R/L)} = \frac{V}{L}\left[-\frac{L^2}{R^2}\frac{1}{s} + \frac{L}{R}\frac{1}{s^2} + \frac{L^2}{R^2}\frac{1}{s + R/L}\right]$$

$$= V\left[-\frac{L}{R^2}\frac{1}{s} + \frac{1}{R}\frac{1}{s^2} + \frac{L}{R^2}\frac{1}{s + R/L}\right] \quad (10.32)$$

Taking inverse Laplace transforms on both sides

$$i(t) = V\left[-\frac{L}{R^2} + \frac{1}{R}t + \frac{L}{R}e^{-(R/L)t}\right] \quad (10.33)$$

10.11.6 Ramp Response of *RC* Circuit

Let us consider a constant voltage Vt applied to an RC series circuit (Fig. 10.9).

Applying KVL to the circuit

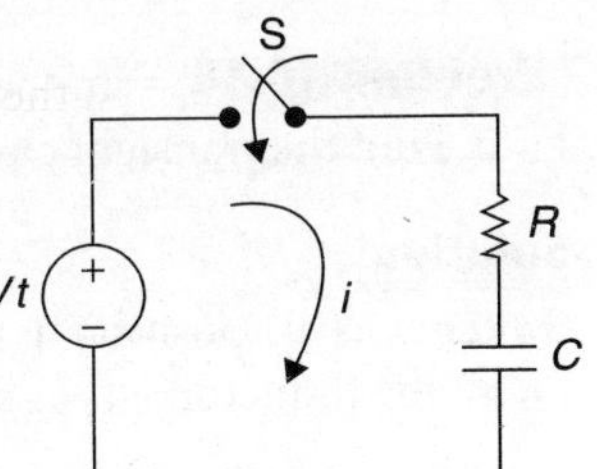

Fig. 10.9 *RC* series circuit excited by ramp voltage

$$Vt = Ri + \frac{1}{C}\int i dt$$

Taking Laplace transforms on both sides, assuming zero initial conditions,

$$\frac{V}{s^2} = RI(s) + \frac{1}{Cs}I(s) = \left[\frac{RCs + 1}{Cs}\right]I(s)$$

$$\Rightarrow \quad I(s) = \frac{VC}{s(1 + RCs)} = \frac{V}{R} \times \frac{1}{s(s + 1/RC)} = \frac{V}{R} \times \left(\frac{RC}{s} - \frac{RC}{s + 1/RC}\right)$$

$$\Rightarrow \quad I(s) = VC\left[\frac{1}{s} - \frac{1}{s + 1/RC}\right] \quad (10.34)$$

Taking inverse Laplace transforms on both sides

$$i(t) = VC[1 - e^{-t/RC}] \tag{10.35}$$

Problem 10.17 In the circuit, find the transient voltage across R and L after the switch is closed at time $t = 0$. Assume the initial current through the inductor before the switch is closed.

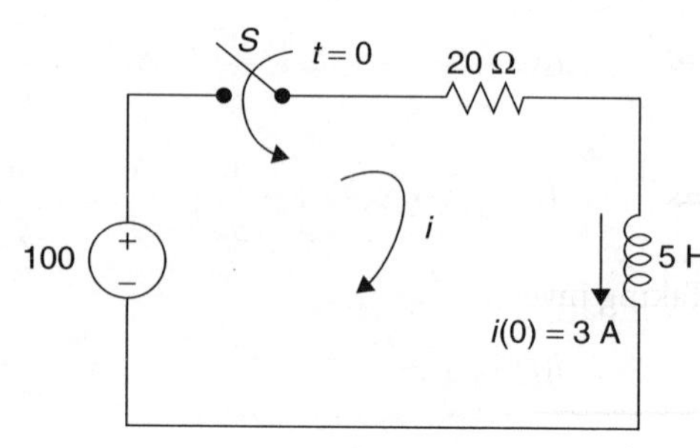

Solution:

Applying KVL to the circuit at $t = 0$,

$$100 = 20i + 5\frac{di}{dt}$$

Taking Laplace transforms on both sides,

$$\frac{100}{s} = 20\,I(s) + 5[sI(s) - i(0)]$$

$$\frac{100}{s} = 20\,I(s) + 5s\,I(s) - 5 \times 3$$

$$\Rightarrow \quad (20 + 5s)\,I(s) = \frac{100}{s} + 15$$

$$\Rightarrow \quad I(s) = \frac{100 + 15s}{s(5s + 20)} = \frac{20 + 3s}{s(s + 4)} = \frac{5}{s} - \frac{2}{s + 4}$$

Taking inverse Laplace transforms on both sides, $i(t) = 5 - 2e^{-4t}$

Voltage across the resistance is $V_R = Ri = 20\,(5 - 2e^{-4t})$

Voltage across the inductance is $V_L = L\dfrac{di}{dt} = 5(2e^{-4t})(4) = 40e^{-4t}$

Problem 10.18 In the circuit, switch S is in position 1 for a long time and brought to position 2 at time $t = 0$. Find the transient current.

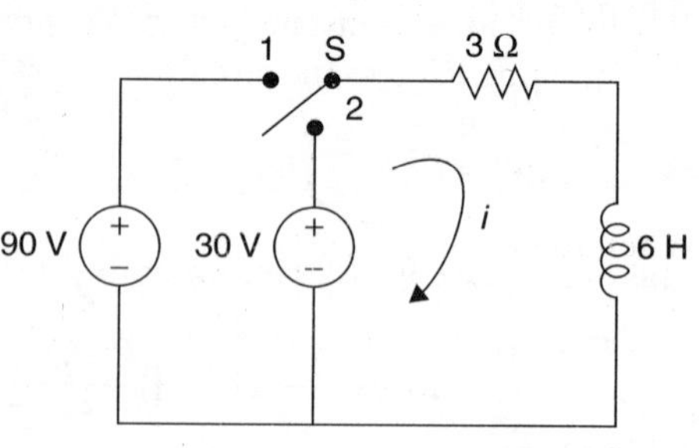

Solution:

Switch S is in position 1 for a long time ($t = \infty$), that is, at $t = \infty$, the inductor acts as short circuit.

$$\therefore \quad i(0) = \frac{90}{3} = 30 \text{ A}$$

When the switch S is in position 2, applying KVL to the circuit,

$$30 = 3i + 6\frac{di}{dt}$$

Taking Laplace transforms on both sides,

$$\frac{30}{s} = 3\,I(s) + 6[sI(s) - i(0)]$$

$$\frac{30}{s} = (3+6s)\,I(s) - 6\times 30$$

$$\Rightarrow \qquad (3+6s)\,I(s) = \frac{30}{s} + 180$$

$$\Rightarrow \qquad I(s) = \frac{30+180s}{s(3+6s)} = \frac{5+30s}{s(s+0.5)} = \frac{10}{s} + \frac{20}{s+0.5}$$

Taking inverse Laplace transforms on both sides,

$$i(t) = 10 + 20e^{-0.5t}$$

Problem 10.19 In the circuit, switch *S* is in position 1 for 1 millisecond and then brought to position 2. Find the transient current in both the intervals.

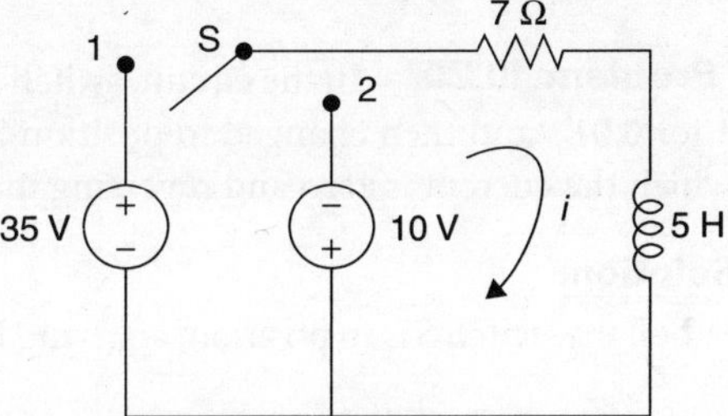

Solution:

When the switch *S* is in position 1, applying KVL to the circuit,

$$35 = 7i + 5\frac{di}{dt}$$

Taking Laplace transforms on both sides, by assuming zero initial conditions,

$$\frac{35}{s} = 7\,I(s) + 5s\,I(s)$$

$$\frac{35}{s} = (7+5s)\,I(s)$$

$$\Rightarrow \qquad I(s) = \frac{35}{s\,(7+5s)} = \frac{7}{s\,(s+1.4)} = \frac{5}{s} - \frac{5}{s+1.4}$$

Taking inverse Laplace transforms on both sides,

$$i(t) = 5 - 5e^{-1.4t}$$

When $t = 1$ ms, the switch is put in position 2.

$$i(t = 1\text{ ms}) = 5 - 5e^{-1.4\times 10^{-3}} = 0.007 \text{ A}$$

$$\Rightarrow \qquad i(0) = 0.007 \text{ A}$$

When the switch *S* is in position 2, applying KVL to the circuit,

$$-10 = 7\,i(t') + 5\frac{di(t')}{dt'}$$

Taking Laplace transforms on both sides,

$$-\frac{10}{s} = 7I(s) + 5\,[sI(s) - i(0)]$$

$$-\frac{10}{s} = (7+5s)\,I(s) - 5\times 0.007$$

$\Rightarrow \qquad (7+5s)\,I(s) = -\dfrac{10}{s} + 0.035$

$\Rightarrow \qquad I(s) = \dfrac{-10+0.035s}{s\,(7+5s)} = \dfrac{-2+0.007s}{s\,(s+1.4)} = \dfrac{-1.43}{s} + \dfrac{1.44}{s+1.4}$

Taking inverse Laplace transforms on both sides,

$$i(t') = -1.43 + 1.44e^{-1.4t'}, \quad \text{where} \quad t' = t - 0.001$$

$\therefore \qquad i(t) = 5(1 - e^{-1.4t}) \quad \text{for} \quad 0 \le t \le 0.001$

$$i(t-0.001) = -1.43 + 1.44e^{-1.4(t-0.001)} \quad \text{for} \quad t > 0.001$$

Problem 10.20 In the circuit, switch S is put in position 1 for 0.01 s and then changed to position 2. Find the time at which the current is zero and reversing its direction.

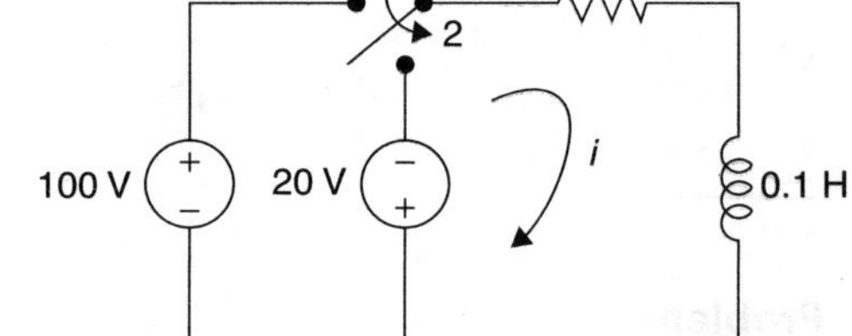

Solution:

When the switch S is in position, applying KVL to the circuit,

$$5i + 0.1\frac{di}{dt} = 100$$

Taking Laplace transforms on both sides, assuming zero initial conditions,

$$5I(s) + 0.1s\,I(s) = \frac{100}{s}$$

$$I(s)\,(5+0.1s) = \frac{100}{s}$$

$$I(s) = \frac{100}{s(0.1s+5)} = \frac{1000}{s(s+50)} = \frac{20}{s} - \frac{20}{s+50}$$

Taking inverse Laplace transforms on both sides,

$$i(t) = 20 - 20e^{-50t}$$

When $t = 0.01$ s, the switch is put in position 2.

$\therefore \qquad i(t=0.01) = 20 - 20e^{-50\times 0.01} = 7.87 \text{ A}$

$\Rightarrow \qquad i(0) = 7.87 \text{ A}$

When the switch S is in position 2, applying KVL to the circuit,

$$5i(t') + 0.1 + \frac{di(t')}{dt'} = -20$$

Taking Laplace transforms on both sides,

$$5I(s) + 0.1[sI(s) - i(0)] = \frac{-20}{s}$$

$$(5+0.1s)\,I(s) - 0.1\times 7.87 = \frac{-20}{s}$$

$$(5+0.1s)\,I(s) = \frac{-20}{s} + 0.787$$

$$I(s) = \frac{-20+0.787s}{s(0.1s+5)} = \frac{-200+7.87s}{s(s+50)} = \frac{-4}{s} + \frac{11.87}{s+50}$$

Taking inverse Laplace transforms on both sides,

$$i(t') = -4 + 11.87e^{-50t'}, \quad \text{where} \quad t' = t - 0.01$$

To find the time at which current is at zero

$$i(t') = 0$$

$$-4 + 11\ 87e^{-50t'}$$

$\Rightarrow \quad t' = 0.0217$ s

$\Rightarrow \quad t - 0.01 = 0.0217$

$\Rightarrow \quad t = 0.01 + 0.0217 = 0.0317$ s

Problem 10.21 In the circuit, switch S_1 is closed at $t = 0$ and switch S_2 is opened at $t = 0.05$ s. Find the transient current.

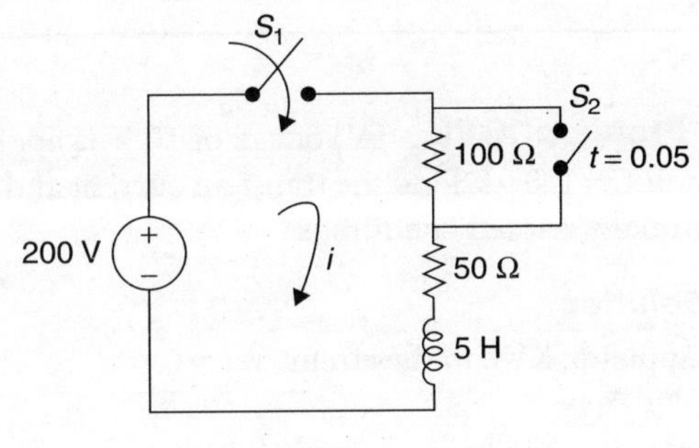

Solution:

When the switch S_1 is closed at $t = 0$

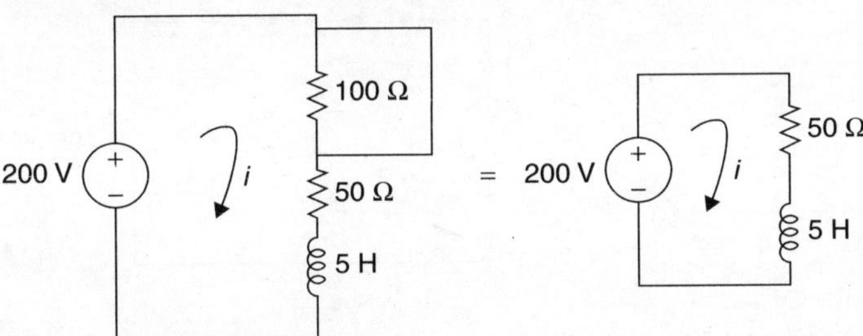

Applying KVL to the circuit,

$$50i + 5\frac{di}{dt} = 200$$

Taking Laplace transforms on both sides, assuming zero initial conditions,

$$50I(s) + 5(s)\,I(s) = \frac{200}{s}$$

$$I(s) = \frac{200}{s(5s+50)} = \frac{40}{s(s+10)} = \frac{4}{s} - \frac{4}{s+10}$$

Taking inverse Laplace transforms on both sides,

$$i(t) = 4 - 4e^{-10t}$$

When the switch S_2 is opened at $t = 0.05$ s,

At $t = 0.05$ s, $i(0.05) = 4 - 4e^{-10 \times 0.05} = 1.574 \text{ A} = i(0)$

When S_2 is opened, applying KVL to the circuit,

$$150i(t') + 5\frac{di(t')}{dt'} = 200$$

Taking Laplace transforms on both sides,

$$150I(s) + 5[sI(s) - i(0)] = 200/s$$

$$(150 + 5s)\, I(s) - 5 \times 1.574 = 200/s$$

$$I(s) = \frac{200 + 5 \times 1.574s}{(5s + 150)s} = \frac{40 + 1.574s}{s(s + 30)} = \frac{1.333}{s} + \frac{0.241}{s + 30}$$

Taking inverse Laplace transforms on both sides,

$$i(t') = 1.333 + 0.241e^{-30t'} \quad \text{where} \quad t' = t - 0.05$$

$\therefore$ $\quad i(t) = 4 - 4e^{-10t} \quad \text{for} \quad 0 \le t \le 0.05$

$$i(t - 0.05) = 1.333 + 0.241e^{-30(t - 0.05)} \quad \text{for} \quad t > 0.05$$

Problem 10.22 A voltage of 10 V is applied through a switch S to an RC series circuit with $R = 3k\ \Omega$ and $C = 100\ \mu\text{F}$. Find the transient current and voltage across R and C after the switch closed at $t = 0$. Assume initially relaxed conditions.

Solution:

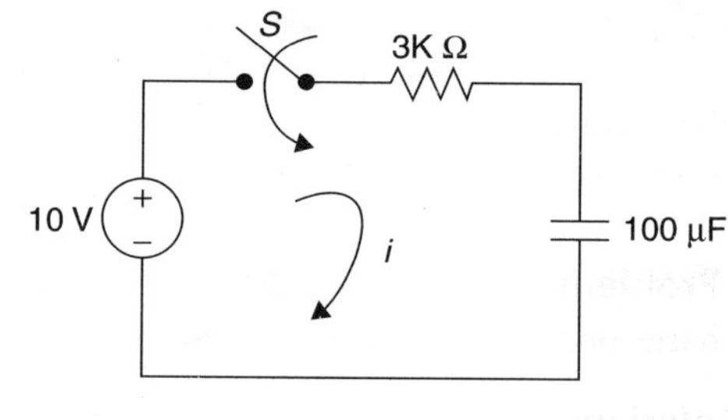

Applying KVL to the circuit at $t = 0$,

$$3000i + \frac{1}{100 \times 10^{-6}} \int_{-\infty}^{t} i\,dt = 10$$

$$3000i + \frac{1}{10^{-4}} \int_{-\infty}^{0} i\,dt + \frac{1}{10^{-4}} \int_{0}^{t} i\,dt = 10$$

Taking Laplace transforms on both sides, assuming zero initial conditions,

$$3000I(s) + 10^4 \frac{I(s)}{s} = \frac{10}{s}$$

$$(3000s + 1000)\, I(s) = 1$$

$$I(s) = \frac{1}{300s + 1000} = \frac{1}{3000}\,\frac{1}{(s + 3.333)}$$

Taking inverse Laplace transforms on both sides, $i(t) = \frac{1}{300} e^{-3.333t}$

Voltage across the resistance is, $V_R = Ri = 3 \times 10^3 \times \frac{1}{300} e^{-3.333t} = 10e^{-3.333t}$

Voltage across the capacitor is, $V_C = V - V_R = 10 - 10e^{-3.333t} = 10(1 - e^{-3.33t})$

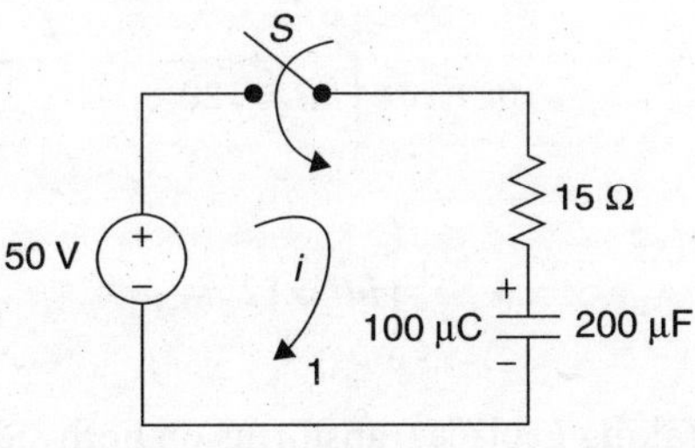

Problem 10.23 In the circuit, find the transient current after the switch is closed at $t = 0$. An initial charge of 100 μC is stored.

Solution:

Initial voltage on the capacitor is

$$V_0 = \frac{q}{C} = \frac{100 \times 10^{-6}}{200 \times 10^{-6}} = 0.5 \text{ V}$$

Applying KVL to the circuit at $t = 0$

$$15i + \frac{1}{200 \times 10^{-6}} \int_{-\infty}^{t} i dt = 50$$

$$15i + \frac{1}{200 \times 10^{-6}} \int_{-\infty}^{0} i dt + \frac{1}{200 \times 10^{-6}} \int_{0}^{t} i dt = 50$$

$$15i + 0.5 + 5000 \int_{0}^{t} i dt = 50$$

Taking Laplace transforms on both sides, $15I(s) + 5000 \frac{I(s)}{s} = \frac{50}{s} - \frac{0.5}{s}$

$$(15s + 5000)\, I(s) = 49.5$$

$$I(s) = \frac{49.5}{15s + 5000} = \frac{3.33}{s + 333.33}$$

Taking inverse Laplace transforms on both sides, $i(t) = 3.33e^{-333.33t}$

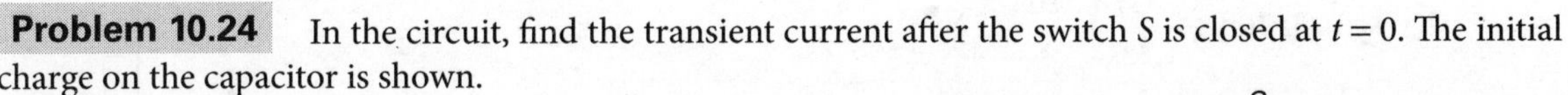

Problem 10.24 In the circuit, find the transient current after the switch S is closed at $t = 0$. The initial charge on the capacitor is shown.

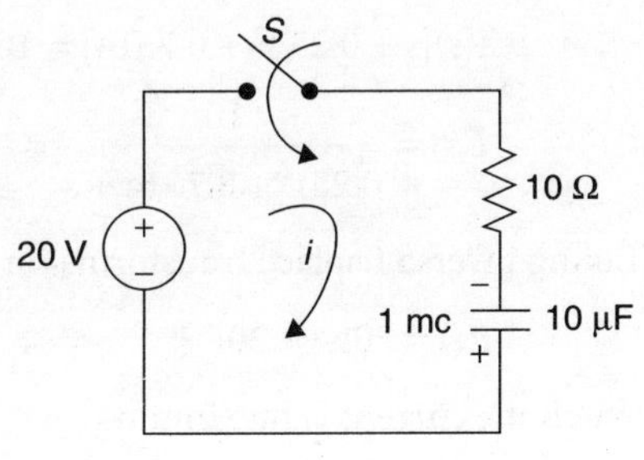

Solution:

Initial voltage on the capacitor

$$V_0 = \frac{q}{C} = \frac{1 \times 10^{-3}}{10 \times 10^{-6}} = 100 \text{ V}$$

Applying KVL to the circuit at $t = 0$,

$$10i + \frac{1}{10 \times 10^{-6}} \int_{-\infty}^{t} i dt = 20$$

$$10i + \frac{1}{10 \times 10^{-6}} \int_{-\infty}^{0} i dt + \frac{1}{10 \times 10^{-6}}\, t \int_{0}^{t} i dt = 20$$

$$10i + (-100) + 10^{5} \int_{0}^{t} i dt = 20$$

$$10i+10^5\int_0^t idt=120$$

$$i+10^4\int_0^t idt=12$$

Taking Laplace transforms on both sides,

$$I(s)+10^4\frac{I(s)}{s}=\frac{12}{s}$$

$$(s+10^4)\,I(s)=12$$

$$I(s)=\frac{12}{s+10^4}$$

Taking inverse Laplace transforms on both sides, $i(t)=12e^{-10^4t}$

Problem 10.25 In the circuit, the switch is closed at time $t=0$. Find the transient current assuming zero initial conditions. Also find the maximum value of current.

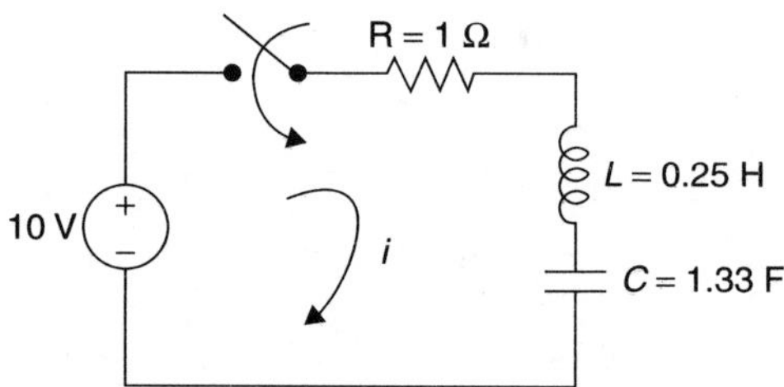

Solution:

Applying KVL to the circuit at $t=0$,

$$i+0.25\frac{di}{dt}+\frac{1}{1.33}\int idt=10$$

Taking Laplace transforms on both sides, assuming zero initial conditions,

$$I(s)+0.25s\,I(s)+\frac{I(s)}{1.33s}=\frac{10}{s}$$

$$\mathrm{I}(s)[s+0.25\,s^2+0.7514]=10$$

$$I(s)=\frac{10}{0.25s^2+0.7514+s}=\frac{40}{s^2+4s+3}=\frac{40}{(s+1)\,(s+3)}=\frac{20}{s+1}-\frac{20}{s+3}$$

Taking inverse Laplace transforms on both sides,

$$i(t)=20e^{-t}-20e^{-3t}$$

When the current is maximum

$$\frac{di}{dt}=0$$

$\Rightarrow \quad 20[e^{-t}(-1)-e^{-3t}(-3)]=0$

$\Rightarrow \quad e^{-t}=3e^{-3t}$

$\Rightarrow \quad t=0.55$ s

$\therefore \quad I_{max}=20^{-0.55}-20e^{-3\times0.55}=7.7$ A

Problem 10.26 In the circuit, find the transient current when the switch is closed at $t = 0$. The initial conditions are shown below.

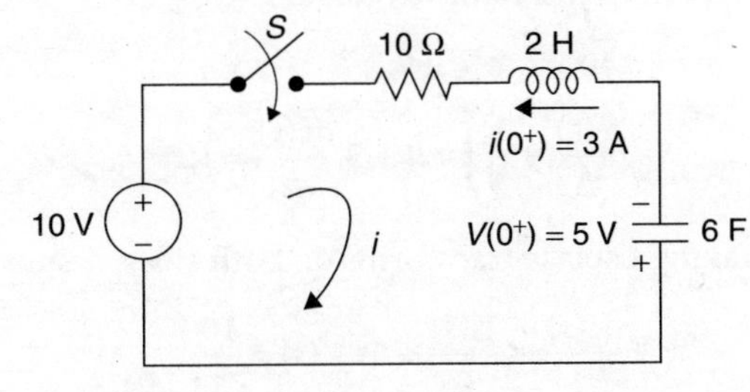

Solution:

Applying KVL to the circuit at $t = 0$,

$$10 = 10i + 2\frac{di}{dt} + \frac{1}{6}\int_{-\infty}^{t} idt$$

$$10 = 10i + 2\frac{di}{dt} + \frac{1}{6}\int_{-\infty}^{0} idt + \frac{1}{6}\int_{0}^{t} idt$$

$$10 = 10i + 2\frac{di}{dt} - 5 + \frac{1}{6}\int_{0}^{t} idt$$

Taking Laplace transforms on both sides,

$$\frac{10}{s} = 10\,I(s) + 2\,[sI(s) - i(0^+)] - \frac{5}{s} + \frac{1}{6s}\,I(s)$$

$$10I(s) + 2s\,I(s) + 6 + \frac{1}{6s}\,I(s) = \frac{10}{s} + \frac{5}{s}$$

$$\frac{(60s + 12s^2 + 1)\,I(s)}{6s} = \frac{15}{s} - 6 = \frac{15 - 6s}{s}$$

$$\Rightarrow \qquad I(s) = \frac{15 \times 6 - 36s}{60s + 12s^2 + 1} = \frac{7.5 - 3s}{s^2 + 5s + 0.0833}$$

The roots of denominator are

$$s^2 + 5s + 0.0833 = 0$$

$$s = \frac{-5 \pm \sqrt{25 - 4 \times 0.0833}}{2} = -2.5 \pm 2.483 = -0.0167 \text{ and } -4.983$$

$$\therefore \qquad s^2 + 5s + 0.0833 = (s + 0.0167)\,(s + 4.983)$$

$$I(s) = \frac{7.5 - 3s}{(s + 0.0167)\,(s + 4.983)} = \frac{1.52}{s + 0.0167} - \frac{4.52}{3 + 4.983}$$

Taking inverse Laplace transforms on both sides,

$$i(t) = 1.52e^{-0.0167t} - 4.52e^{-4.983t}$$

Problem 10.27 Find the voltage across the parallel *RLC* circuit, when the switch is opened at $t = 0$. Assume initially relaxed conditions.

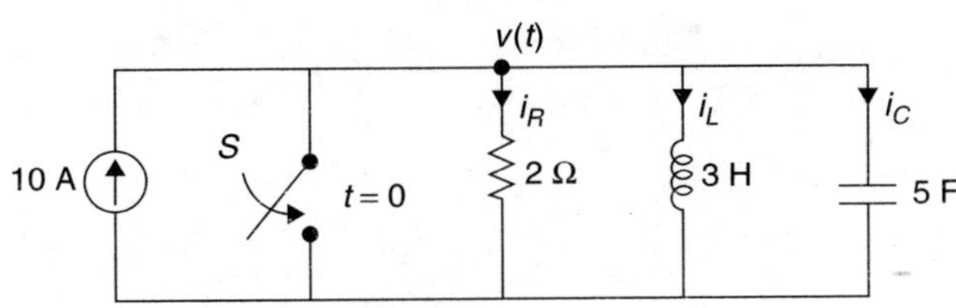

Solution:

Applying KCL to the circuit at $t = 0$,

$$10 = i_R + i_L + i_C$$

$$\frac{v(t)}{2} + \frac{1}{3}\int v dt + 5\frac{dv(t)}{dt} = 10$$

Taking Laplace transforms on both sides, assuming zero initial conditions,

$$\frac{V(s)}{2} + \frac{V(s)}{3s} + 5s\,V(s) = \frac{10}{s}$$

$$V(s)\left[\frac{1}{2} + \frac{1}{3s} + 5s\right] = \frac{10}{s}$$

$$V(s)\left[\frac{3s + 2 + 30s^2}{6s}\right] = \frac{10}{s}$$

$$V(s) = \frac{10 \times 6}{30s^2 + 3s + 2} = \frac{2}{s^2 + 0.1s + 0.066} = \frac{2}{(s + 0.05)^2 + 0.253^2}$$

Taking inverse Laplace transforms on both sides,

$$v(t) = \frac{2}{0.258} e^{-0.05t} \sin 0.253t$$

Problem 10.28 In the circuit, the switch is put in position 1 for 1 ms and then thrown to position 2. Find the transient current in both the intervals.

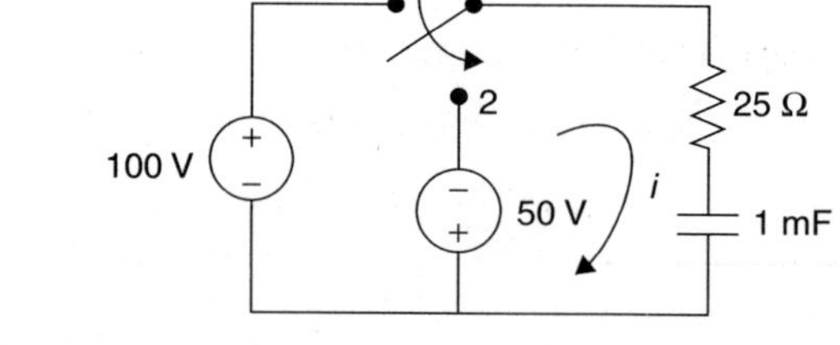

Solution:

When the switch is at position 1

Applying KVL to the circuit,

$$25i + \frac{1}{1 \times 10^{-3}} \int_{-\infty}^{t} i dt = 100$$

$$25i + 10^3 \int_{-\infty}^{0} i dt + 10^3 \int_{0}^{t} i dt = 100$$

Taking Laplace transforms on both sides, assuming as a zero initial conditions

$$25I(s) + 1000\frac{I(s)}{s} = \frac{100}{s}$$

$$I(s)\left(1 + \frac{40}{s}\right) = \frac{4}{s}$$

$$I(s) = \frac{4}{s + 40}$$

Taking inverse Laplace transforms on both sides,

$$i(t) = 4e^{-40t}$$

$$V_R = Ri = 25i = 100e^{-40t}$$

Voltage across the capacitor when $t = 1$ ms

$$V_C = V - V_R = 100 - 100e^{-40t} = 100\,(1 - e^{-40 \times 0.001}) = 3.921 \text{ V}$$

When the switch is at position 2

Applying KVL to the circuit,

$$25i(t') + \frac{1}{1 \times 10^{-3}} \int_{-\infty}^{t'} i(t')\,dt' + 50 = 0$$

$$25i(t') + 1000 \int_{-\infty}^{0} i(t')\,dt' + 1000 \int_{0}^{t'} i(t')\,dt' + 50 = 0$$

$$25i(t') + 3.921 + 1000 \int_{0}^{t'} i(t')\,dt' + 50 = 0$$

Taking Laplace transforms on both sides,

$$25I(s) + \frac{1000}{s} I(s) = \frac{-53.921}{s}$$

$$(25s + 1000)\, I(s) = -53.91$$

$$I(s) = \frac{-53.921}{25s + 1000} = \frac{-2.1568}{s + 40}$$

Taking inverse Laplace transforms on both sides,

$$i(t') = -2.1568e^{-40t'} \quad \text{where} \quad t' = t - 0.001$$

$$\therefore \quad i(t) = 4e^{-40t} \quad \text{for} \quad 0 \le t \le 0.001$$

$$i(t - 0.001) = -2.1568e^{-40(t-0.001)} \quad \text{for} \quad t > 0.001$$

Problem 10.29 In the circuit, find the expression for transient current after the switch is closed at $t = 0$.

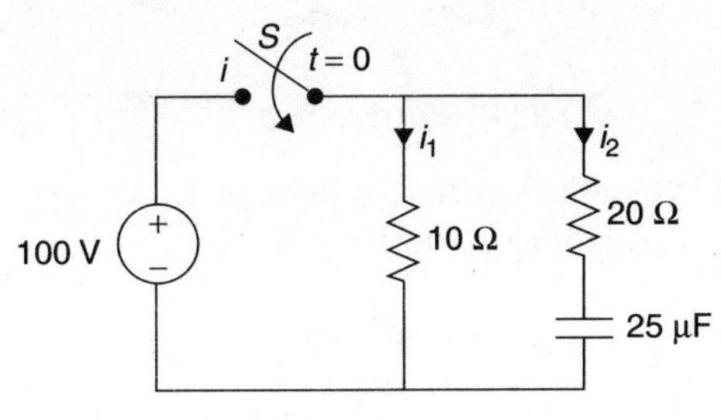

Solution:

When the switch is closed at $t = 0$,

$$i = \frac{100}{10} = 10$$

$$i = i_1 + i_2$$

Applying KVL to the second loop

$$20i_2 + \frac{1}{25 \times 10^{-6}} \int_{0}^{t} i_2\,dt = 100$$

Taking Laplace transforms on both sides, assuming zero initial conditions,

$$2I_2(s) + 4\times 10^4 \times \frac{I_2(s)}{s} = \frac{100}{s}$$

$$I_2(s)\,(s+2000) = 5$$

$$I_2(s) = \frac{5}{s+2000}$$

$$\Rightarrow \qquad i_2 = 5e^{-2000t}$$

Total current, $i = i_1 + i_2 = 10 + 5e^{-2000t}$

Problem 10.30 The switch in the circuit is in position 1 for two time constants and then changed to position 2. Find the transient response.

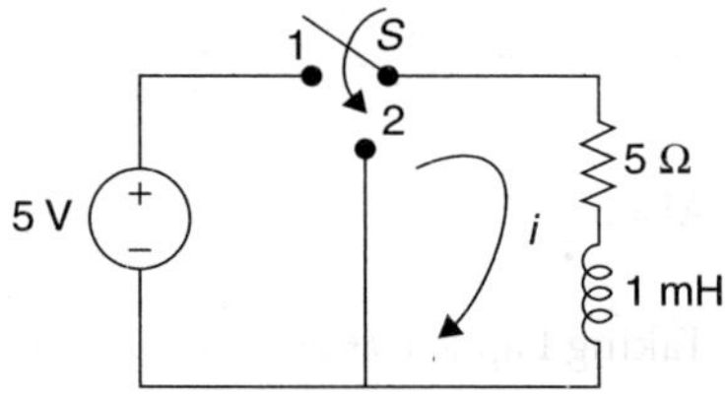

Solution:

When the switch is at position 1

Applying KVL to the circuit,

$$5i + 1\times 10^{-3}\frac{di}{dt} = 5$$

Taking Laplace transforms on both sides, assuming zero initial conditions,

$$5I(s) + \frac{sI(s)}{1000} = \frac{5}{s}$$

$$I(s)\,(s+5000) = \frac{5000}{s}$$

$$I(s) = \frac{5000}{s\,(s+5000)} = \frac{1}{s} - \frac{1}{s+5000}$$

$$\Rightarrow \qquad i(t) = 1 - e^{-5000t}$$

The switch is closed for two time constants, $t = 2T = 2\dfrac{L}{R}$

$$\therefore \qquad i(2T) = i(0) = 1 - e^{-5000\times 2L/R} = 1 - e^{-5000\times\frac{2}{5000}} = 1 - e^{-2} = 0.865$$

When the switch is at position 2

Applying KVL to the circuit

$$5i + 10^{-3}\frac{di}{dt} = 0$$

Taking Laplace transforms on both sides,

$$5I(s) + 10^{-3}\,[sI(s) - i(0)] = 0$$

$$5I(s) + 10^{-3}\,[sI(s) - 0.864] = 0$$

$$5000I(s) + sI(s) - 0.864 = 0$$

$$I(s)\,(s+5000) = 0.864$$

$$I(s) = \frac{0.864}{s+5000}$$

$$\therefore \quad i(t) = 0.864e^{-5000t}$$

Problem 10.31 Determine the $v_C(t)$ and $i_L(t)$ in the circuit; assume zero initial conditions. Use the Laplace transform method.

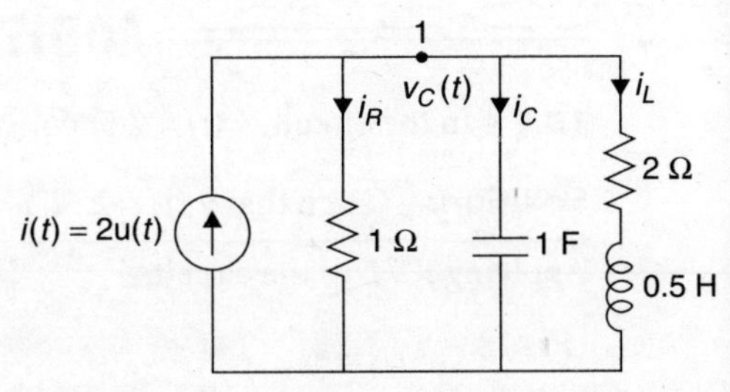

Solution:

Applying KCL at node 1

$$i = i_R + i_L + i_C$$

$$2u(t) = \frac{v_C(t)}{1} + \frac{dv_C(t)}{dt} + i_L \quad (1)$$

Also, $$i_L = \frac{v_C(t)}{2 + j\omega \times 0.5} \quad (2)$$

Taking Laplace transforms on both sides, assuming zero initial conditions,

$$\frac{2}{s} = V_C(s) + sV_C(s) + I_L(s)$$

$$I_L(s) = \frac{V_C(s)}{2+0.5s}$$

$$\therefore \quad \frac{2}{s} = V_C(s) + sV_C(s) + \frac{V_C(s)}{2+0.5s}$$

$$\frac{2}{s} = V_C(s)\left[1+s+\frac{1}{0.5\,(s+4)}\right] = V_C(s)\left[1+s+\frac{2}{s+4}\right]$$

$$\frac{2}{s} = V_C(s)\left[\frac{s+4+s^2+4s+2}{s+4}\right]$$

$$\Rightarrow \quad V_C(s) = \frac{2\times(s+4)}{s(s^2+5s+6)} = \frac{2s+8}{s(s+2)\,(s+3)} = \frac{4}{3}\frac{1}{s} - \frac{2}{s+2} + \frac{4}{3}\frac{1}{s+3}$$

Taking inverse Laplace transforms on both sides,

$$v_C(t) = \frac{4}{3}u(t) - 2e^{-2t} + \frac{4}{3}e^{-3t}$$

$$I_L(s) = \frac{V_C(s)}{2+0.5s} = \frac{2\,(s+4)}{s(s+2)\,(s+3)} \times \frac{1}{0.5\,(s+4)} = \frac{4}{s(s+2)\,(s+3)}$$

$$I_L(s) = \frac{2}{3}\frac{1}{s} - \frac{2}{s+2} + \frac{4}{3}\frac{1}{s+3}$$

Taking inverse Laplace transforms on both sides,

$$i_L(t) = \frac{2}{3}u(t) - 2e^{-2t} + \frac{4}{3}e^{-3t}$$

ADDITIONAL SOLVED PROBLEMS

10.1 In the circuit, $v_g(t) = 2.5t$ volts. What are the values of $i(t)$ and $V_L(t)$ at $t = 4$ seconds?

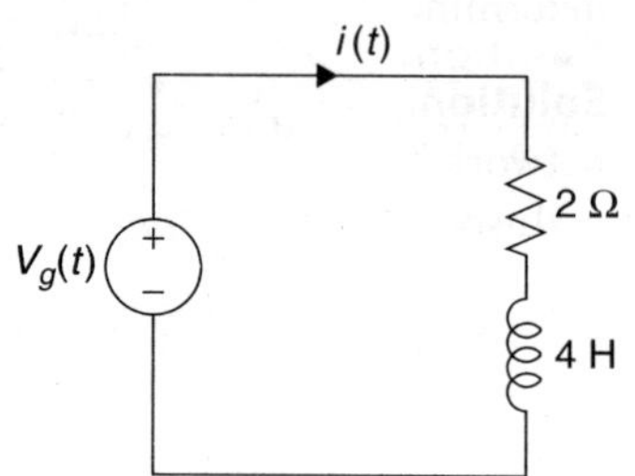

Solution: Given that $v_g(t) = 2.5t$, $t = 4$ s

Applying KVL to the circuit,

$$v_g(t) = 2i + 4\frac{di}{dt}$$

$$2.5t = 2i + 4\frac{di}{dt}$$

Taking Laplace transform on both sides assuming zero initial conditions,

$$\frac{2.5}{s^2} = 2I(s) + 4s\,I(s)$$

$$\Rightarrow \quad I(s) = \frac{2.5}{s^2(4s+2)} = \frac{0.625}{s^2(s+0.5)}$$

$$\frac{0.625}{s^2(s+0.5)} = \frac{A}{s} + \frac{B}{s^2} + \frac{C}{s+0.5} = \frac{As(s+0.5) + B(s+0.5) + Cs^2}{s^2(s+0.5)}$$

$$\Rightarrow \quad 0.625 = As(s+0.5) + B(s+0.5) + Cs^2$$

Put $s = -0.5$

$$0.625 = C \times 0.5^2 \Rightarrow C = \frac{0.625}{0.5^2} = 2.5$$

Comparing s^2 coefficient on both sides,

$$A + C = 0$$

$$\Rightarrow \quad A = -C = -25$$

Comparing s coefficient on both sides,

$$0.5A + B = 0$$

$$B = -0.5\,A = 1.25$$

$$\therefore \quad I(s) = -\frac{2.5}{s} + \frac{1.25}{s^2} + \frac{2.5}{s+0.5}$$

Taking inverse Laplace transforms on both sides,

$$i(t) = -2.5 + 1.25t + 2.5e^{-0.5t}$$

At $t = 4$ s

$$i(t) = i(4) = -2.5 + 1.25 \times 4 + 2.5e^{-0.5 \times 4} = 2.838 \text{ A}$$

$$V_L(t) = L\frac{di}{dt} = 4 \times [1.25 - 2.5 \times 0.5e^{-0.5t}] = 5 - 5e^{-0.5t}$$

At $t = 4$ s, $V_L(t) = V_L(4) = 5 - 5e^{-0.5 \times 4} = 4.323$ V

10.2 The switch in the circuit is closed at $t = 0$. The excitation $v(t) = 0.1e^{-3t}\,u(t)$. Assume relaxed conditions for the circuit; determine $i(t)$ for $t > 0$. Use the Laplace transform method.

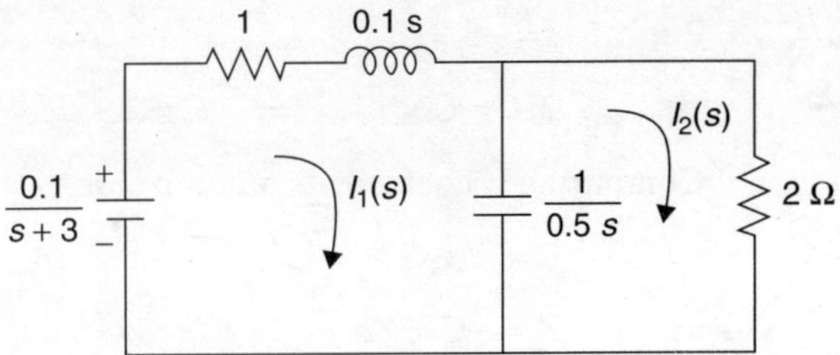

Solution: The s-domain equivalent circuit for the given network at $t = 0$ is

Inspection of mesh analysis gives,

$$\begin{bmatrix} 1+0.1s+\frac{2}{s} & -\frac{2}{s} \\ \frac{-2}{s} & 2+\frac{2}{s} \end{bmatrix}\begin{bmatrix} I_1(s) \\ I_2(s) \end{bmatrix} = \begin{bmatrix} \frac{0.1}{s+3} \\ 0 \end{bmatrix}$$

$$\Delta = \begin{vmatrix} 1+0.1s+\frac{2}{s} & \frac{-2}{s} \\ -\frac{2}{s} & 2+\frac{2}{s} \end{vmatrix} = \left(2+\frac{2}{s}\right)\left(1+0.1s+\frac{2}{s}\right) - \frac{4}{s^2} = \frac{2.2s + 0.2s^2 + 6}{6}$$

$$\Delta_2 = \begin{vmatrix} 1+0.1s+\frac{2}{s} & \frac{0.1}{s+3} \\ -\frac{2}{s} & 0 \end{vmatrix} = \frac{0.2}{s(s+3)}$$

$$I_2(s) = \frac{\Delta_2}{\Delta} = \frac{\frac{0.2}{s\,(s+3)}}{\frac{2.20s + 0.2s^2 + 6}{s}} = \frac{0.2}{(s+3)\,(2.2s + 0.2s^2 + 6)} = \frac{1}{(s+3)\,(s+5)\,(s+6)}$$

$$I_2(s) = I(s) = \frac{1}{(s+3)\,(s+5)\,(s+6)}$$

After resolving into partial fractions,

$$I(s) = \frac{1}{6}\frac{1}{s+3} - \frac{1}{2}\frac{1}{s+5} + \frac{1}{3}\frac{1}{s+6}$$

Taking inverse Laplace transforms on both sides,

$$i(t) = \frac{1}{6}e^{-3t}\,u(t) - \frac{1}{2}e^{-5t}\,u(t) + \frac{1}{3}e^{-6t}$$

10.3 A sinusoidal voltage 25 sin$10t$ is applied at time $t = 0$ to a series RL circuit having $R = 5\ \Omega$ and $L = 1$ H. Find $i(t)$ and assume zero current through the inductor before applying the voltage.

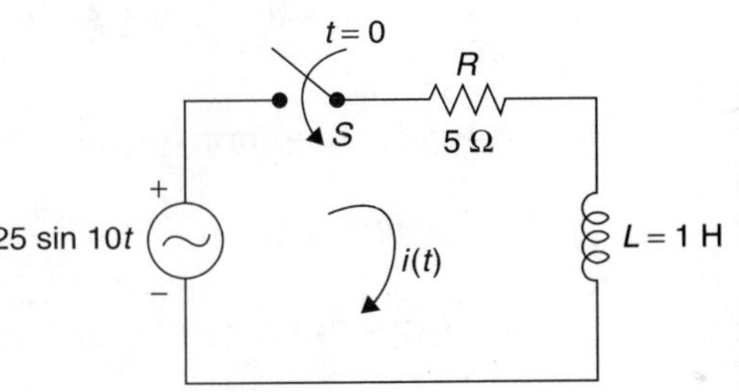

Solution: Applying KVL to the circuit at $t = 0$

$$5i + 1\frac{di}{dt} = 25\sin 10t$$

Taking Laplace transforms on both sides assuming zero initial conditions,

$$5I(s) + sI(s) = 25 \times \frac{10}{s^2 + 10^2}$$

$$I(s) = \frac{250}{(s+5)(s^2+100)} = \frac{As + B}{s^2 + 100} + \frac{C}{s+5}$$

$\Rightarrow$ $250 = (As + B)(s + 5) + C(s^2 + 100)$

Put $s = -5$

$$250 = C \times 125 \quad \Rightarrow \quad C = 2$$

Comparing s^2 coefficients on both sides,

$$0 = A + C$$

$\Rightarrow$ $A = -C = -2$

Comparing s coefficients on both sides,

$$0 = 5A + B$$

$\Rightarrow$ $B = -5A = 10$

$\therefore$ $I(s) = \dfrac{-2s + 10}{s^2 + 100} + \dfrac{2}{s+5} = -\dfrac{2s}{s^2 + 10^2} + \dfrac{10}{s^2 + 10^2} + \dfrac{2}{s+5}$

Taking inverse Laplace transforms on both sides,

$$i(t) = -2\cos 10\,t + \sin 10\,t + 2e^{-5t}$$

10.4 The switch in the circuit is closed on position 1 at $t = 0$ and then moved to position 2 after one time constant $T = 250$ s. Obtain the current $i(t)$ for $t > 0$.

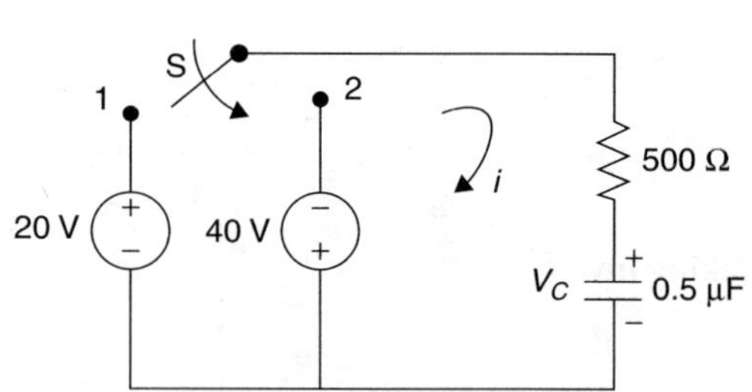

Solution: When the switch S is at position 1, applying KVL to the circuit

$$500i + \frac{1}{0.5 \times 10^{-6}} \int_{-\infty}^{t} i\,dt = 20$$

$$500i + 2 \times 10^{6} \int_{-\infty}^{0} i\,dt + 2 \times 10^{-6} \int_{0}^{t} i\,dt = 20$$

Taking Laplace transforms on both sides, assuming zero initial conditions,

$$500\,I(s) + 2 \times 10^{6}\,\frac{I(s)}{s} = \frac{20}{s}$$

$$I(s)[500s + 2 \times 10^{6}] = 20$$

$$I(s) = \frac{20}{500s + 2\times10^6} = \frac{1}{25}\left[\frac{1}{s+4000}\right]$$

Taking inverse Laplace transforms on both sides,

$$i(t) = \frac{1}{25}e^{-4000t}$$

$$V_R = Ri = 500\times\frac{1}{25}e^{-4000t} = 20e^{-4000t}$$

Voltage across the capacitor when $t = T = 250\times10^{-6}$

$$V_C = V_0 = V - V_R = 20 - 20e^{-400\times25\times10^{-6}} = 12.64\text{ V}$$

When the switch is at position 2, applying KVL to the circuit

$$500i(t') + \frac{1}{0.5\times10^{-6}}\int_{-\infty}^{t'} dt' + 40 = 0$$

$$500i(t') + \frac{1}{0.5\times10^{-6}}\int_{-\infty}^{0} i(t')\,dt' + \frac{1}{0.5\times10^{-6}}\int_{0}^{t'} i(t')\,dt' + 40 = 0$$

$$500i(t') + 12.64 + 2\times10^6\int_{-\infty}^{t'} i(t')\,dt' + 40 = 0$$

Taking Laplace transforms on both sides,

$$500I(s) + \frac{2\times10^6}{s}I(s) = \frac{-52.64}{s}$$

$$I(s) = \frac{-52.64}{500s + 2\times10^6} = \frac{-0.1053}{s+4000}$$

Taking inverse Laplace transforms on both sides,

$$i(t') = -0.1053e^{-4000t'},\quad \text{where}\quad t' = t - 0.000250\text{ s}$$

10.5 Determine the current $i(t)$ in a series RLC circuit consisting of $R = 5\,\Omega$, $L = \frac{1}{2}$ H, $C = \frac{1}{4}$ F, when the applied voltage $v_i(t)$ is a ramp voltage $12r(t-2)$. Assume that the circuit is initially relaxed. Use the Laplace transform method.

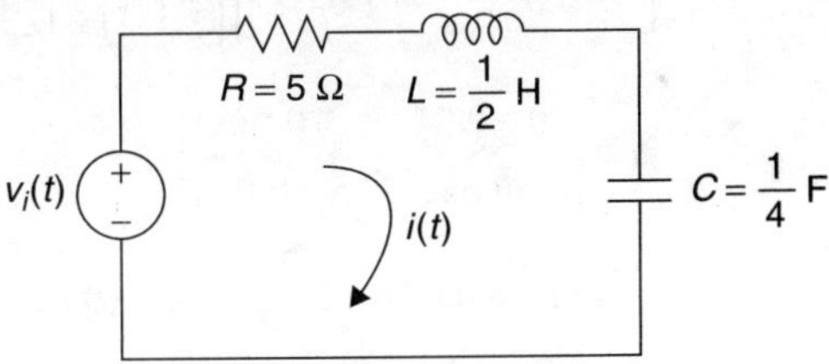

Solution: Applying KVL to the circuit,

$$v_i(t) = Ri + L\frac{di}{dt} + \frac{1}{C}\int i\,dt$$

$$12r(t-2) = 5\,i + \frac{1}{2}\frac{di}{dt} + 4\int i\,dt$$

Taking Laplace transforms on both sides, assuming zero initial conditions,

$$12\times\frac{e^{-2s}}{s^2}=5I(s)+\frac{s}{2}I(s)+\frac{4}{5}I(s) \qquad \left[\because L\,[12r\,(t-2)]=\frac{e^{-2s}}{s^2}\right]$$

$$\frac{12e^{-2s}}{s^2}=(10s+s^2+8)\frac{I(s)}{2s}$$

$$\Rightarrow \qquad I(s)=e^{-2s}\frac{24}{s(s^2+10s+8)}=e^{-2s}\frac{24}{s(s+0.877)\,(s+9.123)}=e^{-2s}\left[\frac{A}{s}+\frac{B}{s+0.877}+\frac{C}{s+9.123}\right]$$

$$A=\left.\frac{24}{(s+0.877)\,(s+9.125)}\right|_{s=0}=\frac{24}{0.877\times 9.123}=3$$

$$B=\left.\frac{24}{s(s+9.125)}\right|_{s=-0.877}=\frac{24}{-0.877(-0.877+9.123)}=-3.32$$

$$C=\left.\frac{24}{s(s+0.877)}\right|_{s=-9.123}=\frac{24}{-9.123(-9.123+0.877)}=0.32$$

$$I(s)=e^{-2s}\left[\frac{3}{s}-\frac{3.32}{s+0.877}+\frac{0.32}{s+9.123}\right]=3\frac{e^{-2s}}{s}-3.32\frac{e^{-2s}}{s+0.877}+0.32\frac{e^{-2s}}{s+9.123}$$

Taking inverse Laplace transforms on both sides,

$$i(t)=3u(t-2)-3.32e^{-0.877(t-2)}+0.32e^{-9.123(t-2)}$$

10.6 In the network, find the currents i_1 and i_2 when the switch is closed at $t=0$.

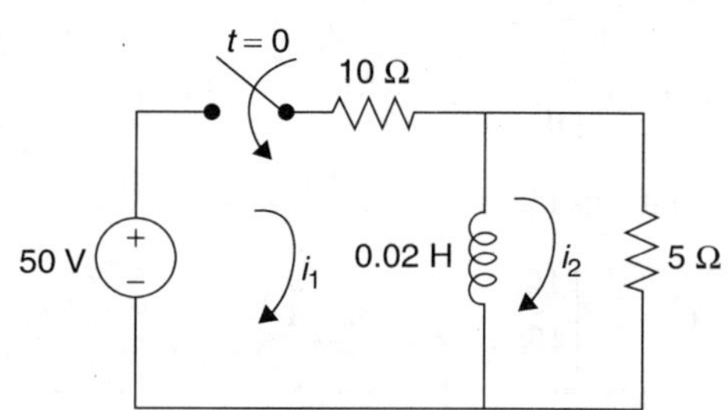

Solution: The *s*-domain equivalent circuit for the given network at $t=0$ is as shown below.

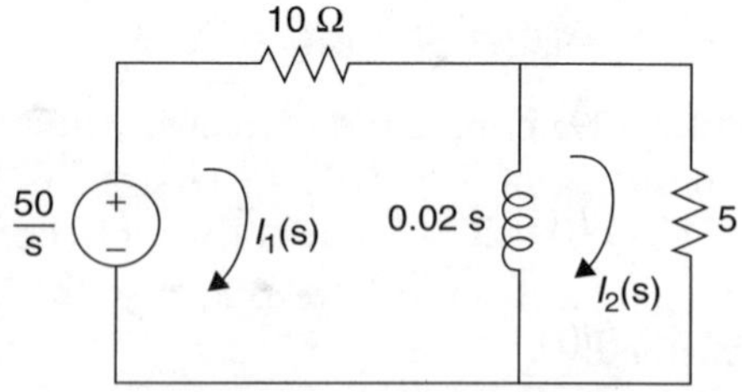

Inspection of mesh analysis gives

$$\begin{bmatrix}10+0.02s & -0.02s\\ -0.02s & 5+0.02s\end{bmatrix}\begin{bmatrix}I_1(s)\\ I_2(s)\end{bmatrix}=\begin{bmatrix}50/s\\ 0\end{bmatrix}$$

$$\Delta=\begin{vmatrix}10+0.02s & -0.02s\\ -0.02s & 5+0.02s\end{vmatrix}$$

$$=(10+0.02s)\,(5+0.02s)-(0.02s)^2$$

$$=50+0.2s+0.1s+(0.02s)^2-(0.02s)^2=0.3s+50$$

$$\Delta_1=\begin{vmatrix}50/s & -0.02s\\ 0 & 5+0.02s\end{vmatrix}=\frac{250+s}{s}$$

$$\Delta_2=\begin{vmatrix}10+0.02s & 50/s\\ -0.02s & 0\end{vmatrix}=50\times 0.02=1$$

$$I_1(s) = \frac{\Delta_1}{\Delta} = \frac{s+250}{s(0.3s+50)} = \frac{3.33s+833.33}{s(s+1.66.67)} = \frac{5}{s} - \frac{1.67}{s+166.67}$$

$\Rightarrow \quad i_1(t) = 5 - 1.66e^{-166.67t}$

$$I_2(s) = \frac{\Delta_2}{\Delta} = \frac{1}{0.3s+50} = \frac{3.33}{s+166.7}$$

$\Rightarrow \quad i_2(t) = 3.33e^{-166.67t}$

10.7 In the two-mesh network, find the mesh currents i_1 and i_2 when the switch is closed at $t = 0$.

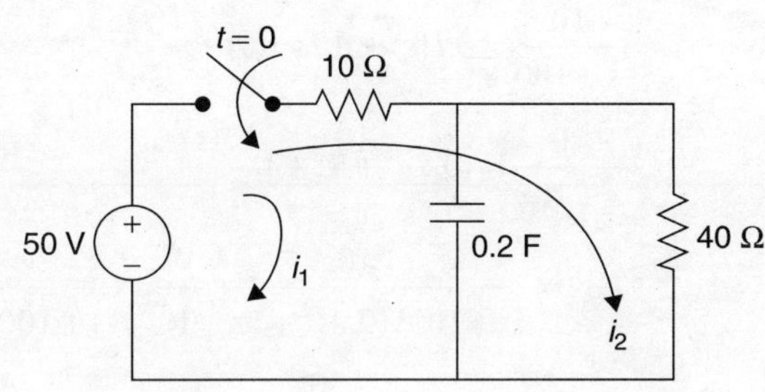

Solution: The s-domain equivalent circuit for the given network at $t = 0$ is as shown below.

Applying KVL to loop-1

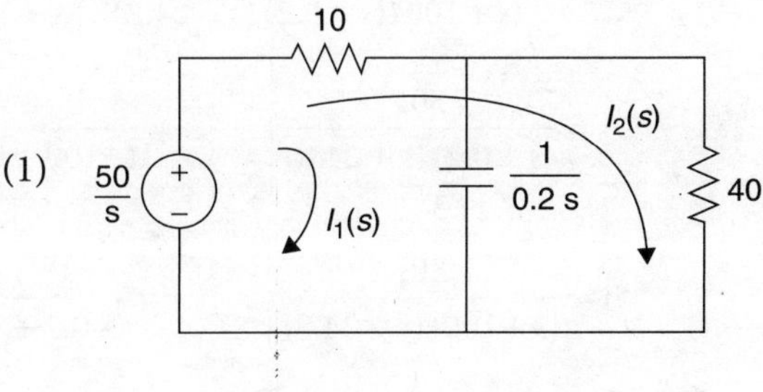

$$\frac{50}{s} = 10[I_1(s) + I_2(s)] + \frac{1}{0.2s} I_1(s)$$

$$\frac{50}{s} = \frac{(10s+5)\, I_1(s) + 10s\, I_2(s)}{s}$$

$$\Rightarrow \quad (10s+5)\, I_1(s) + 10sI_2(s) = 50 \qquad (1)$$

Applying KVL to loop-2

$$\frac{50}{s} = 10\,[I_1(s) + I_2(s)] + 40\, I_2(s)$$

$$50 = 10sI_1(s) + 50s\, I_2(s) \qquad (2)$$

Equations (1) and (2) can be written in the matrix form:

$$\begin{bmatrix} 10s+5 & 10s \\ 10s & 50s \end{bmatrix} \begin{bmatrix} I_1(s) \\ I_2(s) \end{bmatrix} = \begin{bmatrix} 50 \\ 50 \end{bmatrix}$$

$$\Delta = (10s + s)\, 50s - 100s^2 = 500s^2 + 250s - 100s^2 = 400s^2 + 250s$$

$$\Delta_1 = 50\,(50s - 10s) = 2000s$$

$$\Delta_2 = 50\,(10s + 5 - 10s) = 250$$

$$I_1(s) = \frac{\Delta_1}{\Delta} = \frac{2000s}{s(250+400s)} = \frac{5}{s+0.625}$$

$\Rightarrow \quad i(t) = 5e^{-0.625t}$

$$I_2(s) = \frac{\Delta_2}{\Delta} = \frac{250}{s(250+400s)} = \frac{0.625}{s(s+0.625)} = \frac{1}{s} - \frac{1}{s+0.625}$$

$\Rightarrow \quad i_2(t) = 1 - e^{-0.625t}$

10.8 A series RLC circuit with $R = 5\ \Omega$, $L = 0.2$ H and $C = 1$ F has a voltage source $v(t) = 10e^{-100t}$ volts applied at $t = 0$. Find the current in the circuit using the Laplace transform method.

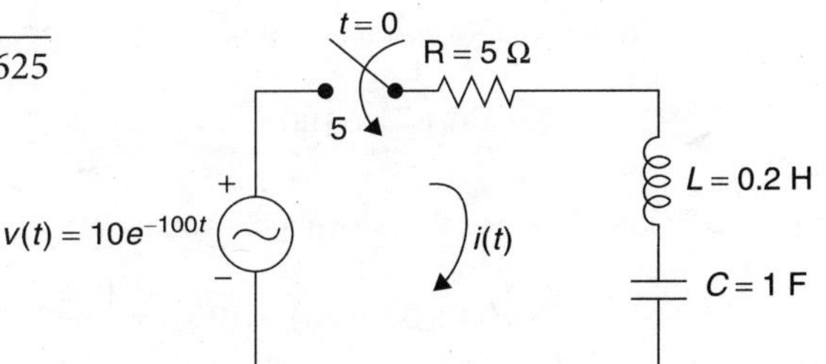

Solution: When the switch is closed at $t = 0$, applying KVL to the circuit,

$$v(t) = Ri + L\frac{di}{dt} + \frac{1}{C}\int idt$$

$$10e^{-100t} = 5\,i + 0.2\frac{di}{dt} + \int idt$$

Taking Laplace transforms on both sides, assuming zero initial conditions,

$$\frac{10}{s+100} = 5\,I(s) + 0.2s\,I(s) + \frac{I(s)}{s}$$

$$\frac{10}{s+100} = (0.2s^2 + 5s + 1)\frac{I(s)}{s}$$

$$\Rightarrow \qquad I(s) = \frac{10s}{(s+100)\,(0.2s^2+5s+1)} = \frac{50s}{(s+100)\,(s^2+25s+5)}$$

$$= \frac{50s}{(s+100)\,(s+0.2)\,(s-24.8)} = \frac{A}{s+100} + \frac{B}{s+0.2} + \frac{C}{s+24.8}$$

$$A = \left.\frac{50s}{(s+0.2)\,(s+24.8)}\right|_{s=-10} = \frac{-5000}{(-100+0.2)\,(-100+24.8)} = -0.666$$

$$B = \left.\frac{50s}{(s+100)\,(s+24.8)}\right|_{s=-0.2} = \frac{-5}{(-0.2+100)\,(-0.2+24.8)} = -0.00204$$

$$C = \left.\frac{50s}{(s+100)\,(s+0.2)}\right|_{s=-24.8} = \frac{-50\times 24.8}{(-24.8+100)\,(-24.8+0.2)} = 0.67$$

$$\therefore \qquad I(s) = \frac{-0.666}{s+100} + \frac{-0.00204}{s+0.2} + \frac{0.67}{s+24.8}$$

Taking inverse Laplace transforms on both sides, we have

$$i(t) = -0.666e^{-100t} - 0.00204e^{-0.2t} + 0.67e^{-24.8t}$$

10.9 A DC voltage of 100 V is applied in the circuit and the switch is kept open. The switch is closed at $t = 0$. Find the complete expression for the current.

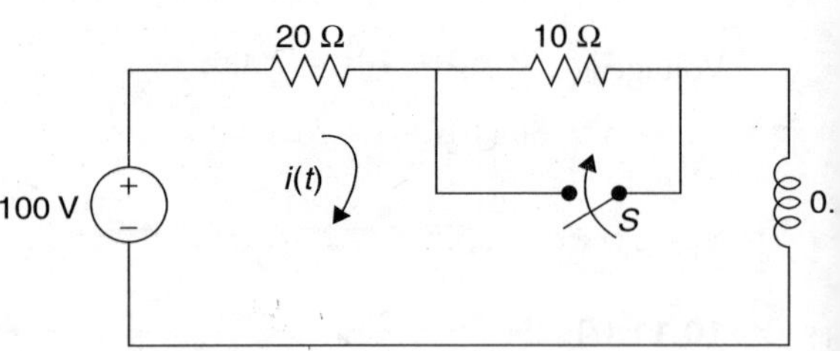

Solution: Current just before closing the switch $i(0^+) = \frac{100}{20+10} = 3.33$ because the inductor acts as a short circuit.

When the switch S is closed at $t = 0$, applying KVL to the circuit

$$20i + 0.1\frac{di}{dt} = 100$$

Taking Laplace transforms on both sides,

$$20I(s) + 0.1[sI(s) - i(0^+)] = \frac{100}{s}$$

$$(20+0.1s)\,I(s)=\frac{100}{s}+0.333$$

$$I(s)=\frac{100+0.333s}{s\,(0.1s+20)}$$

$$I(s)=\frac{1000+3.33s}{s\,(s+200)}=\frac{5}{s}-\frac{1.67}{s+200}$$

Taking inverse Laplace transforms on both sides,

$$i(t)=5-1.67e^{-200t}$$

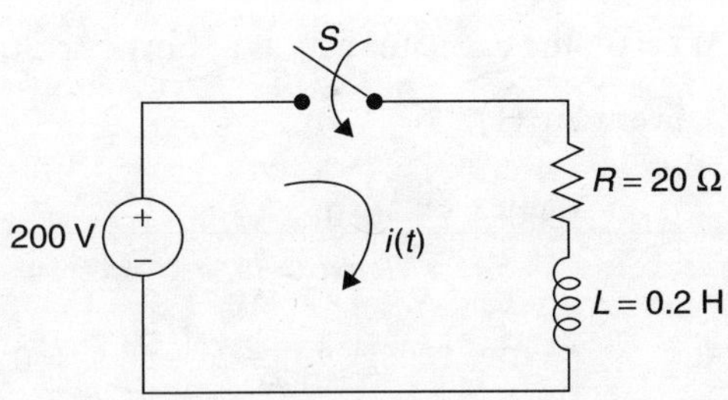

10.10 A direct voltage of 200 V is suddenly applied to a series *RL* circuit having $R = 20\ \Omega$ and inductance $L = 0.2$ H. Determine the voltage drop across the inductor at the instance of switching on and at 0.03 s later.

Solution: When the switch *S* is suddenly closed, the inductor acts as open circuit, that is, $i(0^+) = 0$. Therefore, at the instant of switching, the voltage drop across the inductor is 200 V.

When the switch *S* is closed at $t = 0$, applying KVL to the circuit,

$$200=20i+0.2\frac{di}{dt}$$

Taking Laplace transform on both sides, assuming zero initial conditions,

$$\frac{200}{s}=20I(s)+0.2s\,I(s)$$

$$\frac{200}{s}=(20+0.2s)\,I(s)$$

$$I(s)=\frac{200}{s(0.2s+20)}=\frac{1000}{s(s+100)}=\frac{10}{s}-\frac{10}{s+100}$$

Taking inverse Laplace transform on both sides,

$$i(t)=10\,(1-e^{-100t})$$

Voltage across the inductor

$$V_L=L\frac{di}{dt}=0.2\times10\times100e^{-100t}=200e^{-100t}$$

At $\quad t = 0.03$ s, $V_L = 200\times e^{-100\times0.03} = 200e^{-3} = 10$ V

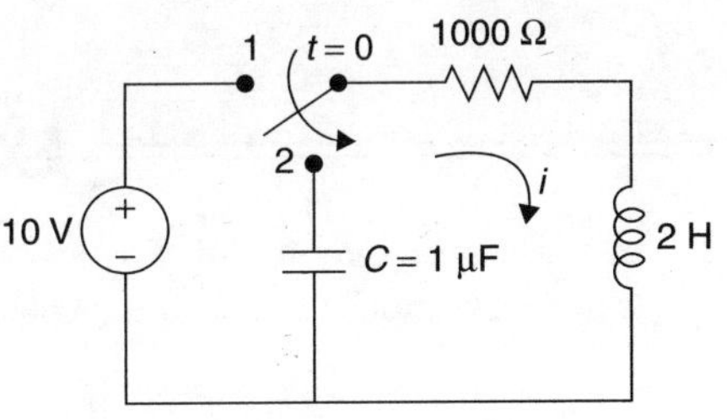

10.11 In the circuit, the switch is changed from position 1 to 2 at $t = 0$. Determine the initial conditions $i, \frac{di}{dt}, \frac{d^2}{dt^2}$ at $t = 0^+$.

Solution: The switch is changed from position 1 to 2 at $t = 0$, which means the switch is kept for a long time at position 1. That is, at $t = \infty$, the inductor acts as a short circuit.

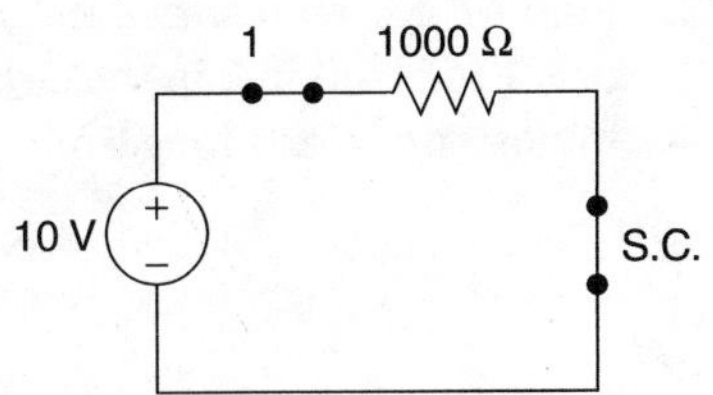

$$\therefore \qquad i(0^+)=\frac{10}{1000}=0.01\text{ A}$$

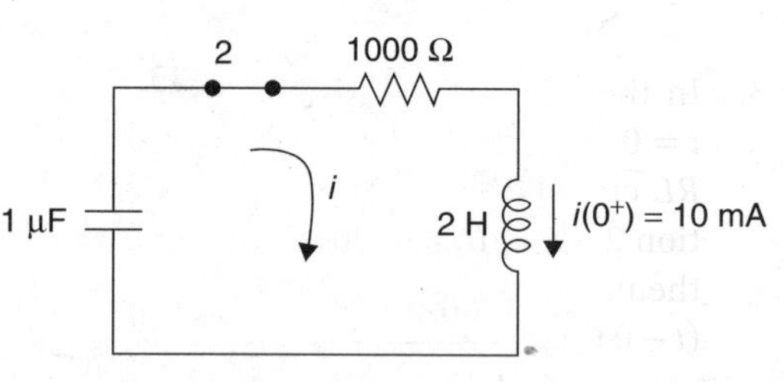

Immediately after closing the switch at position-2, that is, at $t = 0^+$, the capacitor acts as a short circuit.

∴ At $t = 0$ the equivalent circuit is as shown.

Applying KVL to the circuit at $t = 0$,

$$1000i + 2\frac{di}{dt} + \frac{1}{1\times10^{-6}}\int i\,dt = 0 \qquad (1)$$

At $t = 0^+$, the capacitor acts as a short circuit, that is, $V_C = 0$.

∴ From Eq. (1),

$$1000i + 2\frac{di}{dt} = 0$$

At $\quad t = 0^+ \quad 1000i\Big|_{t=0^+} + 2\frac{di}{dt}\Big|_{t=0^+} = 0$

∴ $$\frac{di}{dt}\Big|_{t=0^+} = -500i(0^+) = 500\times0.01 = -5 \text{ A/s}$$

Differentiating Eq. (1) with respect to t,

$$1000\frac{di}{dt} + 2\frac{d^2i}{dt^2} + 10^6\,i = 0$$

$$\frac{d^2i}{dt^2} = \frac{1}{2}\left(-1000\frac{di}{dt} - 10^{-6}\,i\right)$$

$$\frac{d^2i}{dt^2}\Big|_{t=0^+} = \frac{1}{2}\left[-1000\frac{di}{dt}\Big|_{t=0^+} - 10^{-6}\,i(0^+)\right] = \frac{1}{2}[1000\times5 - 10^6\times0.01] = -2500 \text{ A/s}^2$$

∴ $$\frac{d^2i}{dt^2}\Big|_{i=0^+} = -2500 \text{ A/s}^2$$

∴ At $t = 0^+$ (i) $i = 0.01$ A (ii) $\frac{di}{dt} = -5$ A/s (iii) $\frac{d^2i}{dt^2} = -2500$ A/s^2

EXERCISE PROBLEMS

1. In a series RL circuit with $R = 3\ \Omega$ and $L = 1$ H, a DC voltage of $E = 50$ V is applied at $t = 0$. Find the transient response of current. [**Ans:** $i(t) = 16.67\,(1 - e^{-3t})$]

2. Find $i(t)$ for $t > 0$, when the switch is moved from position 1 to position 2 in the circuit at $t = 0$. The switch was in position 1 for a long time. [**Ans:** $i(t) = 2e^{-2.5t}$]

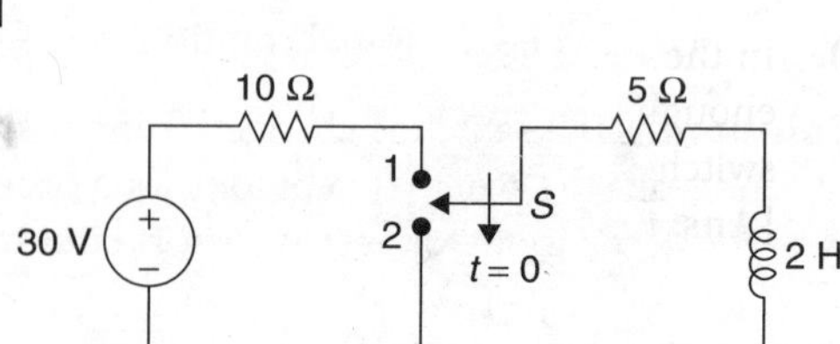

3. In the circuit, the switch is closed on the position 1 at $t = 0$ there by applied a DC voltage of 100 V to a series RL circuit. At t = 500 μs, the switch is moved to position 2. Obtain the expression for current $i(t)$ in the both the intervals. [**Ans:** $i(t) = 1 - e^{-500t}$ for $0 \le t \le 0.0005$ s $i(t - 0.0005) = 0.5 - 0.279e^{-500(t - 0.0005)}$ for $t > 0.0005$]

t = 500 μs
S
100 V
50 V
i(t)
100 Ω
0.2 H

4. A constant voltage of 100 V is applied at $t = 0$ to a series RC circuit having $R = 5$ MΩ and $C = 20$ μF. Assuming no initial charge to the capacitor, find the expression for i, voltage across R and C. [**Ans:** $i(t) = 2 \times 10^{-5}\, e^{-0.01t})\, A$, $V_R = 100e^{-0.01t}\, V$, $V_C = 100\,(1 - e^{-0.01t})$ V]

5. An impulse voltage of magnitude 10 V is applied to a RL series circuit with $R = 10$ Ω and $L = 2$ H at time $t = 0$. Find the transient current by assuming zero initial conditions. [**Ans:** $i(t) = 5e^{-5t}$)]

6. In the circuit shown, find the transient current when the switch S is closed at $t = 0$.
[**Ans:** $i(t) = 25e^{-5t} - 20e^{-6t} - 5e^{-3t}$)]

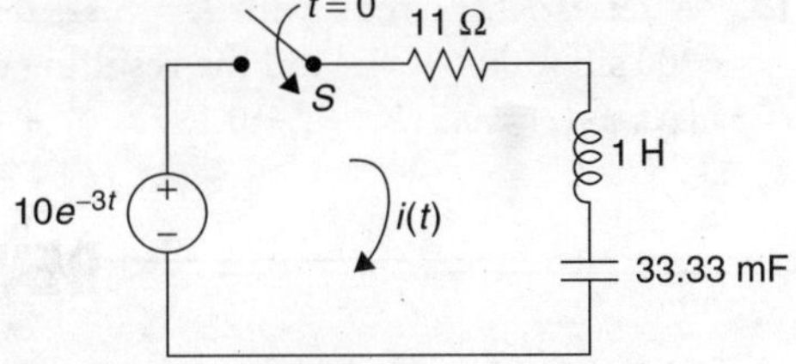

7. A series RL circuit with $R = 60$ Ω, $L = 5$ H has a constant voltage $V = 150$ applied at $t = 0$ by closing the switch. Find (a) $i(t)$ and V_L, (b) the time at which $V_R = V_L$. [**Ans:** (a) $i(t) = 2.5\,(1 - e^{-12t})\, A$, $V_L = 150e^{-12t}$ (b) 0.058 s]

8. In the circuit, find i_2 by assuming zero initial conditions.
[**Ans:** $i_2\,(t) = 3 - 3e^{-t} - 3e^{-2t} + 3e^{-3t}$)]

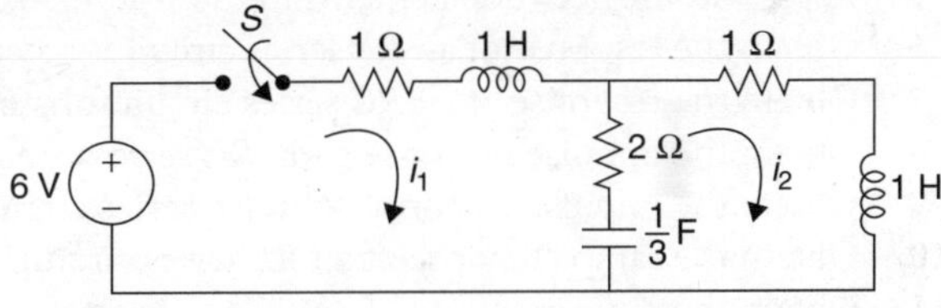

9. In the circuit, find the transient current when the switch S is closed at $t = 0$. [**Ans:** $i(t) = -0.01e^{-0.05t} + 0.01\cos 10t + 2\sin 10t$]

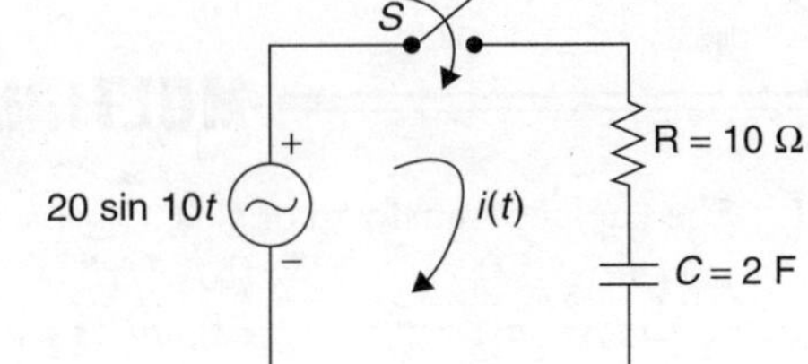

10. In the RL series circuit, the switch S is in position 1 long enough to establish steady state conditions and at $t = 0$ is switched to position 2. Find the resulting current.
[**Ans:** $i(t) = 4 - 6e^{-2500t}$]

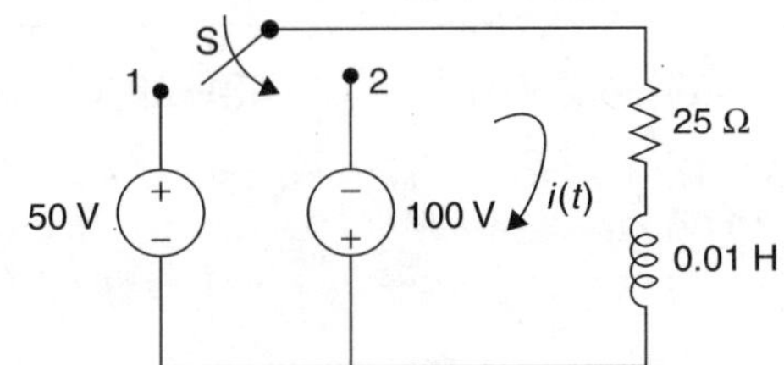

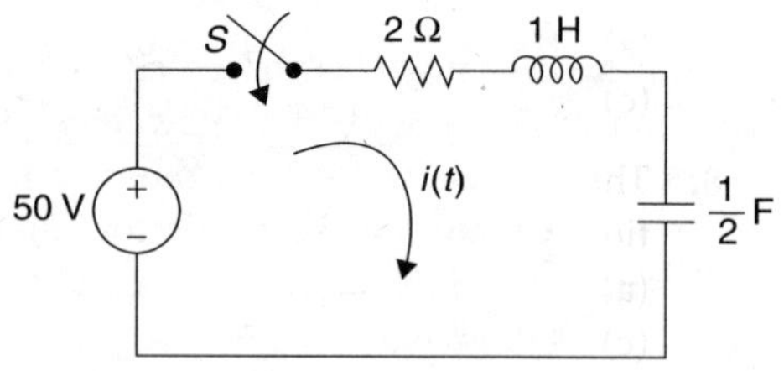

11. In the *RLC* series circuit, there is no initial charge on the capacitor. If the switch is closed at $t = 0$, determine the resulting current. [**Ans:** $i(t) = 50e^{-t} \sin t$]

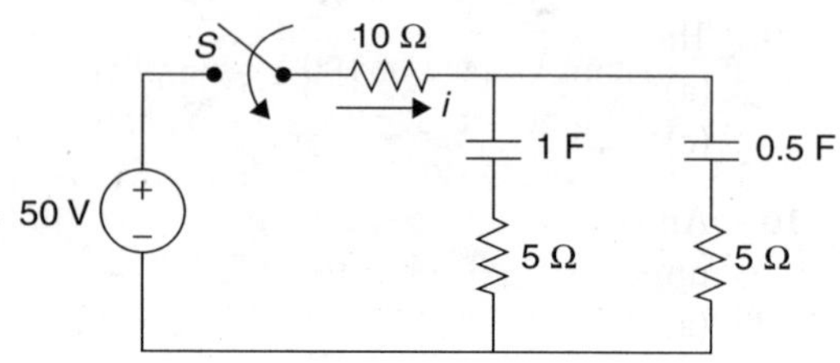

12. In the circuit, the switch is closed at $t = 0$ and there is no initial charge on either of the capacitors. Find the resulting current *i*. [**Ans:** $i(t) = 0.125e^{-0.308t} + 3.875e^{-0.052t}$]

13. A series *RLC* circuit with $R = 5\ \Omega$, $L = 0.5$ H and $C = 100\ \mu$F has a sinusoidal voltage source $v(t) = 300 \sin(500\,t + \phi)$. Find the resulting current, if the switch is closed when $\phi = 30°$.
[**Ans:** $i(t) = 0.51e^{-341.4t} - 0.197e^{-58.6t} + 0.983 \sin(500t - 19°)$]

REVIEW QUESTIONS

1. Define Laplace transform.
2. State initial and final value theorems.
3. Compare the classical and Laplace transform methods of solution of the network.
4. Derive an expression for the current response in *RL* series circuit with a sinusoidal source.
5. Represent the network elements in the *s*-domain.
6. Obtain the response of an *RL* series circuit for step excitation.
7. Obtain the response of an *RC* series circuit for step excitation.
8. Obtain the impulse response of an *RC* series circuit.
9. Obtain the impulse response of an *RL* series circuit.
10. Obtain the ramp response of an *RL* series circuit.
11. Obtain the ramp response of an *RC* series circuit.

MULTIPLE CHOICE QUESTIONS

1. The Laplace transform of t^n is
   (a) $n!/(s^{n+1})$ (b) $1/s^n$
   (c) $n/(s-a)$ (d) $n^2/(s+a)$

2. The Laplace transform of $t^n e^{-at}$ is
   (a) $n!/(s^{n+1})$ (b) $n!/(s+a)^{n+1}$
   (c) $n!/(s^{n+1})$ (d) $n!/(s-a)^{n-1}$

3. The Laplace transform of $t \sin at$ is
   (a) $2as/(s^2+a^2)^2$ (b) $(s^2-a^2)/(s^2+a^2)^2$
   (c) $2as/(s^2-a^2)^2$ (d) $(s^2+a^2)/(s^2-a^2)^2$

4. The Laplace transform of $\cos(\omega_o t + \phi)$ is
   (a) $(s^2+\omega_o^2)/(s \sin\phi + \omega_o \cos\phi)$
   (b) $(s\cos\phi - \omega_o \sin\phi)/(s^2+\omega_o^2)$
   (c) $(s^2+\omega_o^2)/(s \cos\phi - \omega_o \sin\phi)$
   (d) $(s \cos\phi - \omega_o \sin\phi)/(s^2+\omega_o^2)$

5. For which of the following functions will the Laplace transform be $2/s^3$?
   (a) $f(t) = t$ (b) $f(t) = 2t$
   (c) $f(t) = t^2$ (d) $f(t) = 2t^3$

6. Laplace transform of $(e^{-at} - e^{-bt})/(b-a)$ is
   (a) $1/(s+a)(s-b)$ (b) $1/(s-a)(s+b)$
   (c) $1/(s-a)(s-b)$ (d) $1/(s+a)(s+b)$

7. With symbols having usual meanings, the Laplace transform of $u(t-a)$ is

(a) $1/s$ (b) $1/s - a$
(c) $e^{-as}/(1/s)$ (d) $e^{as}/(1/s)$

8. The Laplace transform of unit impulse function is
(a) $1/s$ (b) s
(c) 1 (d) $1/s^2$

9. The Laplace transform of unit step function is
(a) $1/s$ (b) s
(c) 1 (d) $1/s^2$

10. An unit ramp function when integrated gives unit ______ function
(a) ramp (b) parabolic
(c) impulse (d) step

11. The Laplace transform of a unit ramp function is
(a) 1 (b) s
(c) $1/s$ (d) $1/s^2$

12. The Laplace transform of a unit parabolic function is
(a) $2/s^3$ (b) $1/s^2$
(c) $1/s$ (d) s^2

13. Laplace transform of a delayed unit impulse function $u(t-1)$ is
(a) 0 (b) 1
(c) e^{-s} (d) s

14. A non-linear system cannot be analysed by Laplace transform because
(a) it has zero initial conditions
(b) superposition law cannot be determined
(c) non-linearity is generally not well defined
(d) all of the above

15. Given $F(s) = (s+2)/s(s+1)$, the initial and final values of $f(t)$ will be respectively
(a) 1, 2 (b) 2, 1
(c) 1, 1 (d) 2, 2

16. If $F(s) = (s+1)/s(s+k)$ and $f(t) = 1/2$ as $t \to \infty$, then the value of k is
(a) 1/2 (b) 1
(c) 2 (d) ∞

17. The Laplace transform of $f(t)$ is $F(s)$. Given $F(s) = a/(s^2 + a^2)$, the final value of $f(t)$ is
(a) ∞ (b) 0
(c) 1 (d) none of the above

18. $£^{-1}[(s-1)/(s^2+3s+2)]$ is
(a) $3e^{-2t} + 2e^{-t}$ (b) $3e^{-2t} - 2e^{-t}$
(c) $2e^{-3t} - e^{-2t}$ (d) $2e^{-3t} + e^{-2t}$

19. $£^{-1}(6)/(s+a)^4$ is
(a) $t^2(e^{-at})$ (b) $t^3(e^{-at})$
(c) $t^4(e^{-at})$ (d) none of the above

20. $£^{-1}(1)/(s^2+7s+12)$ is
(a) $e^{-2t} - e^{-3t}$ (b) $(e^{-3t} - e^{-4t})/2$
(c) $e^{-3t} - e^{-4t}$ (d) $(e^{-3t} - e^{-2t})/2$

21. The inverse Laplace transform of $1/(s-a)$ is
(a) $\sin at$ (b) $\cos at$
(c) e^{at} (d) e^{-at}

22. The ramp response of an RC series circuit is
(a) $\frac{V}{R}\left(1-e^{\frac{-Rt}{C}}\right)$ (b) $\frac{V}{R}\left(1-e^{\frac{-Rt}{L}}\right)$
(c) $VC\left(1-e^{\frac{-t}{RC}}\right)$ (d) $V\left(e^{\frac{-Rt}{C}}\right)$

23. The impulse response of an RL series circuit is
(a) $\frac{V}{L}e^{\frac{-Rt}{L}}$ (b) $\frac{V}{L}\left(1-e^{\frac{-Rt}{L}}\right)$
(c) $VL\left(1-e^{\frac{-Rt}{L}}\right)$ (d) $V\left(e^{\frac{-Rt}{L}}\right)$

24. The s-domain equivalent of resistance is
(a) R (b) sR
(c) R/s (d) can't say

25. The s-domain equivalent of inductance is
(a) L (b) sL
(c) L/s (d) can't say

26. The s-domain equivalent of capacitance is
(a) C (b) sC
(c) $1/Cs$ (d) can't say

27. The finial value of $£^{-1}(2s+1)/(s^4+16s^3+8s^2+s)$ is
(a) 0 (b) 1
(c) infinity (d) 2

28. The inverse Laplace transform of s is
(a) impulse (b) ramp
(c) step (d) unit doublet

29. The derivate of a step function is
(a) zero
(b) an impulse function
(c) a ramp function
(d) a constant

30. The double integration of a unit step function will result in
(a) a unit step function
(b) a ramp function
(c) impulse
(d) parabola

31. A ramp current flowing through an initially relaxed capacitor will result in a voltage across it that
(a) varies inversely with time
(b) remains constant
(c) varies directly with time twice
(d) varies as the square of time

32. If the step response of an initially relaxed circuit is known, then the ramp response can be obtained by
(a) integrating the step response
(b) differentiating the step response
(c) integrating the step response
(d) differentiating the step response twice

33. The unit step response of system is given by $(1-e^{-\alpha t})u(t)$, its impulse response is
(a) $e^{-\alpha t}(t)$ (b) $\alpha e^{-\alpha t}\, u(t)$
(c) $\frac{1}{\alpha} e^{-\alpha t}\, u(t)$ (d) $-\alpha e^{-\alpha t}\, u(t)$

34. A unit step current source is applied to a parallel *RLC* circuit. Under steady state condition, the input current will
(a) get shared by all the three components
(b) get shared between *R* and *C* only
(c) get shared between *R* and *L* only
(d) flow through lonely

35. The current in a pure inductor with unit step input voltage is
(a) zero
(b) constant but non-zero
(c) a decaying exponential
(d) a ramp function

36. The function is said to be periodic when it
(a) appears for a particular time interval
(b) appears for all time
(c) is of recurring nature
(d) has only linear varying components

37. The steady value of current in a series *RLC* circuit, when a DC voltage of V volts is applied to it at $t = 0$ is
(a) zero (b) *V/RL*
(c) *V/R* (d) *VC/R*

38. In a series circuit consisting of a single resistor, a single inductor and single capacitor, if the resistance is more, the response is
(a) over-damped (b) un-damped
(c) oscillatory (d) under-damped

Answers

1. a	2. b	3. a	4. b	5. c	6. d	7. c	8. c	9. a	10. b
11. d	12. a	13. c	14. a	15. a	16. c	17. b	18. b	19. b	20. c
21. c	22. c	23. a	24. a	25. b	26. c	27. b	28. d	29. b	30. d
31. d	32. a	33. b	34. d	35. d	36. a	37. a	38. a		

11 Two-port Networks

Learning Outcomes

After reading this chapter, the reader will able to

- Explain one-port, two-port and multiple-port networks
- Find impedance and admittance parameters for the given two-port network
- Find transmission and inverse transmission parameters for the given two-port network
- Find hybrid and inverse hybrid parameters for the given two-port network
- Develop the conditions for reciprocity and symmetry for various two-port network parameters
- Outline the interrelationship between different two-port network parameters
- Explain the interconnection of two-port networks
- Develop *T* and π representation for a given two-port network
- Find the driving point impedance at the input and output ports of a terminated two-port network
- Illustrate lattice/bridge networks
- Find the image parameters of a given two-port network

11.1 INTRODUCTION

A port is a pair of terminals at which a signal may enter or leave a network, or, a port is defined as any pair of terminals into which energy is supplied, or from which energy is withdrawn or where the network variables may be measured. A network that has only one pair of terminals is called a two-terminal or one-port network. Figure 11.1(a) shows a one-port network. A network consisting of two pairs of terminals is called a two-port network, usually one pair represents the input and the other represents the output. Figure 11.1(b) shows a two-port network or a two terminal pair network, in which the four terminals have been paired into ports 1–1′ and 2–2′. The terminals 1–1′ together constitute a port and similarly the terminals 2–2′ constitute another port. A voltage and current are assigned to each of the two ports. The voltage and current at the input terminals are V_1 and I_1 and at the output terminals are V_2 and I_2. Figure 11.1(c) represents a network with *n* ports and is called an *n*-port network. In such networks, generally one port is connected to the energy source, one port is connected to the load and other ports may be connected to the different networks.

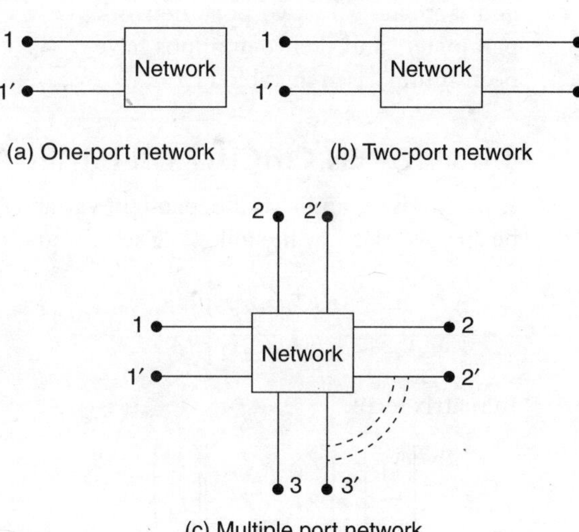

(a) One-port network (b) Two-port network

(c) Multiple port network

Fig. 11.1 Examples of ports

11.2 TWO-PORT NETWORK PARAMETERS

Consider a two-port network (Fig. 11.2). A voltage and current are assigned to each of the two ports. The voltage and current at the input terminals are V_1 and I_1 and at the output terminals are V_2 and I_2. The directions of both the currents, I_I and I_2, are assumed to be flowing into the network. In such networks, only two of the four variables are independent, and the specifications of any two of them determine the remaining two. The dependence of two of the four variables on the other two is described in several ways depending on the choice of independent and dependent variables.

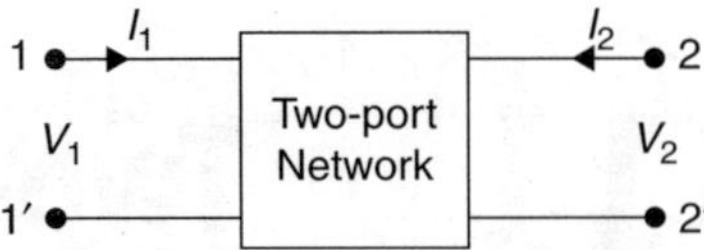

Fig. 11.2 Two-port network

Here we study six combinations of choosing independent and dependent variables giving rise to six sets of parameters:

(i) open circuit or impedance parameter,
(ii) short circuit or admittance parameter,
(iii) hybrid or h-parameters,
(iv) inverse hybrid or g-parameters,
(v) transmission or $ABCD$ parameters, and
(vi) inverse transmission or $A'B'CD'$ parameters.

These different descriptions of two-port networks are useful in designing networks such as filters, attenuators, transmission lines which are inserted between a source and a load. The two-port network parameters and their definitions have been summarised in Table 11.1.

Table 11.1 Various two-port network parameters

S. no	Name of the parameter	Dependent Variables	Independent Variables	Eqs
01	Impedance or Z-parameters	V_1, V_2	I_1, I_2	$V_1 = Z_{11}I_1 + Z_{12}I_2$ $V_2 = Z_{21}I_1 + Z_{22}I_2$
02	Admittance or Y-parameters	I_1, I_2	V_1, V_2	$I_1 = Y_{11}V_1 + Y_{12}V_2$ $I_2 = Y_{21}V_1 + Y_{22}V_2$
03	Hybrid or h-parameters	V_1, I_2	I_1, V_2	$V_1 = h_{11}I_1 + h_{12}V_2$ $I_2 = h_{21}I_1 + h_{22}V_2$
04	Inverse hybrid or g-parameters	I_1, V_2	V_1, I_2	$I_1 = g_{11}V_1 + g_{12}I_2$ $V_2 = g_{21}V_1 + g_{22}I_2$
05	Transmission or $ABCD$ or T-parameters	V_1, I_1	V_2, I_2	$V_1 = AV_2 - BI_2$ $I_1 = CV_2 - DI_2$
06	Inverse transmission or $A'B'C'D'$ or T' parameters	V_2, I_2	V_1, I_1	$V_2 = A'V_1 - B'I_1$ $I_2 = C'V_1 - D'I_1$

11.3 OPEN CIRCUIT OR IMPEDANCE PARAMETERS

If we choose I_1 and I_2 as independent variables and V_1 and V_2 as dependent variables, then the network can be characterised by the following set of equations.

$$\left.\begin{aligned} V_1 &= Z_{11}I_1 + Z_{12}I_2 \\ V_2 &= Z_{21}I_1 + Z_{22}I_2 \end{aligned}\right\} \tag{11.1}$$

In matrix form,

$$\begin{bmatrix} V_1 \\ V_2 \end{bmatrix} = \begin{bmatrix} Z_{11} & Z_{12} \\ Z_{21} & Z_{22} \end{bmatrix} \begin{bmatrix} I_1 \\ I_2 \end{bmatrix} \tag{11.2}$$

By opening the input and output ports of the two-port network, the Z-parameters can be obtained as:

$$Z_{11} = \left.\frac{V_1}{I_1}\right|_{I_2=0} = \text{Driving point impedance at the input port}$$

$$Z_{12} = \left.\frac{V_1}{I_2}\right|_{I_1=0} = \text{Reverse transfer impedance}$$

$$Z_{21} = \left.\frac{V_2}{I_1}\right|_{I_2=0} = \text{Forward transfer impedance}$$

$$Z_{22} = \left.\frac{V_2}{I_2}\right|_{I_1=0} \quad = \text{Driving point impedance at the output port}$$

The coefficients Z_{ij} have the dimension of impedance and are called impedance or Z-parameters of the network. The Z-parameters are also called open-circuit or impedance parameters since they may be measured at one terminal while the other terminal is open. Figure 11.3 shows the equivalent circuit of the two-port network using Z-parameters.

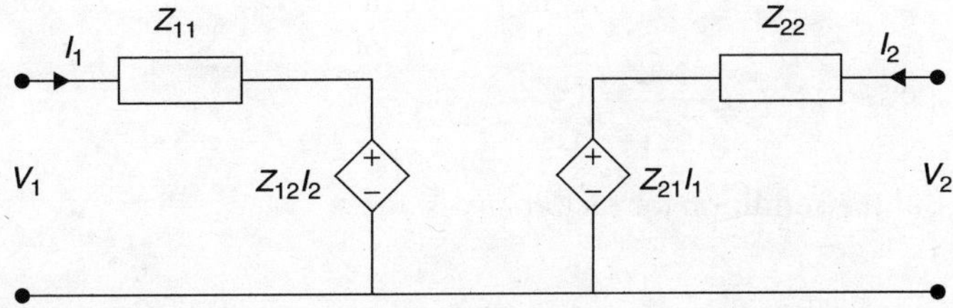

Fig. 11.3 Equivalent circuit of the two-port network using Z-parameters

Condition for reciprocity Using the reciprocity theorem, we can find the condition for reciprocal for the given two-port network. Referring to Figs 11.4(a) and (b), the network is reciprocal if $I_1' = I_2'$.

From Fig. 11.4(a),

$$V_2 = 0, \quad I_2 = -I_2', \quad V_1 = V_s$$

From the Z-parameter equations,

$$V_1 = Z_{11}I_1 + Z_{12}I_2$$

$$V_2 = Z_{21}I_1 + Z_{22}I_2$$

$$V_s = Z_{11}I_1 - Z_{12}I_2' \tag{11.3}$$

$$0 = Z_{21}I_1 - Z_{22}I_2'$$

$$\Rightarrow \quad I_1 = \frac{Z_{22}}{Z_{21}}I_2' \tag{11.4}$$

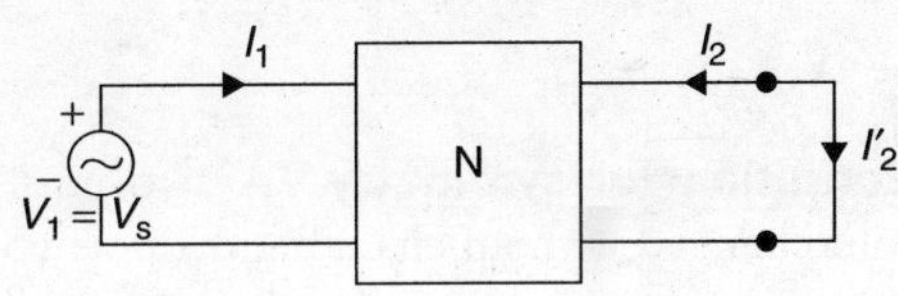

(a)

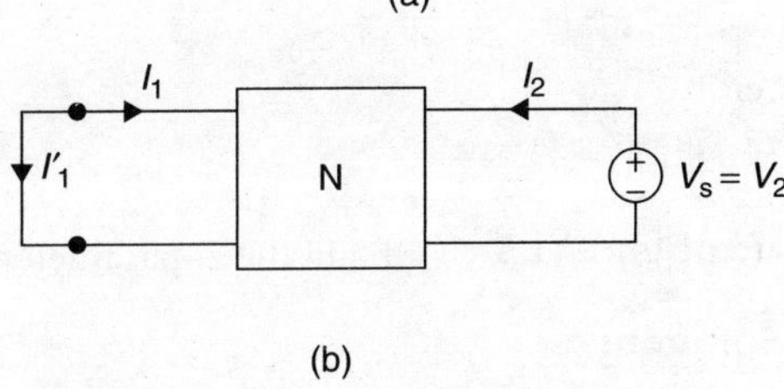

(b)

Fig. 11.4 Network for deriving condition of reciprocity

From Eqs 11.3 and 11.4,

$$V_s = Z_{11}\frac{Z_{22}}{Z_{21}}I_2' - Z_{12}I_2' = \left(\frac{Z_{11}Z_{22} - Z_{12}Z_{21}}{Z_{21}}\right)I_2'$$

$$\Rightarrow \quad I_2' = \frac{Z_{21}}{Z_{11}Z_{22} - Z_{21}Z_{12}}V_s \tag{11.5}$$

From Fig. 11.4(b),

$$V_1 = 0, \quad I_1 = -I_1', \quad V_2 = V_s$$

Substituting the above values in Z-parameters standard equations, we have

$$0 = -Z_{11}I_1' + Z_{12}I_2$$

$$\Rightarrow \quad I_2 = \frac{Z_{11}}{Z_{12}}I_1' \tag{11.6}$$

$$V_s = -Z_{21}I_1' + Z_{22}I_2 \tag{11.7}$$

From Eqs 11.6 and 11.7,

$$V_s = -Z_{21}I_1' + Z_{22}\frac{Z_{11}}{Z_{12}}I_1' = \left(\frac{-Z_{12}Z_{21} + Z_{11}Z_{22}}{Z_{12}}\right)I_1'$$

$$\Rightarrow \quad I_1' = \frac{Z_{12}}{Z_{11}Z_{22} - Z_{12}Z_{21}}V_s \tag{11.8}$$

But the condition for reciprocity is

$$I_1' = I_2'$$

$$\frac{Z_{12}V_s}{Z_{11}Z_{22} - Z_{12}Z_{21}} = \frac{Z_{21}V_s}{Z_{11}Z_{22} - Z_{12}Z_{21}}$$

$$\Rightarrow \quad Z_{12} = Z_{21} \tag{11.9}$$

Condition for symmetry A two-port network is said to be symmetrical if the two-ports can be interchanged without changing the port voltage and currents. This happens if

$$\left.\frac{V_1}{I_1}\right|_{I_2=0} = \left.\frac{V_2}{I_2}\right|_{I_1=0}$$

$$\Rightarrow \quad Z_{11} = Z_{22} \tag{11.10}$$

Problem 11.1 Obtain the Z-parameters for the network.

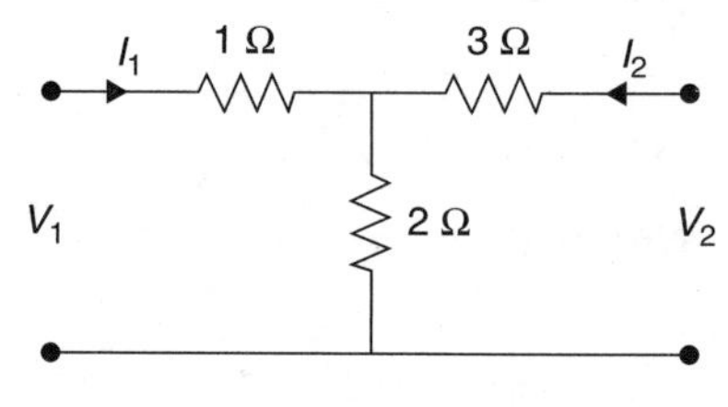

Solution:

The Z-parameters are given by

$$Z_{11} = \left.\frac{V_1}{I_1}\right|_{I_2=0}, Z_{12} = \left.\frac{V_1}{I_2}\right|_{I_1=0}, Z_{21} = \left.\frac{V_2}{I_1}\right|_{I_2=0}, Z_{22} = \left.\frac{V_2}{I_2}\right|_{I_1=0}$$

By putting $I_2 = 0$ in the above circuit, it can be reduced to the circuit shown on the right.

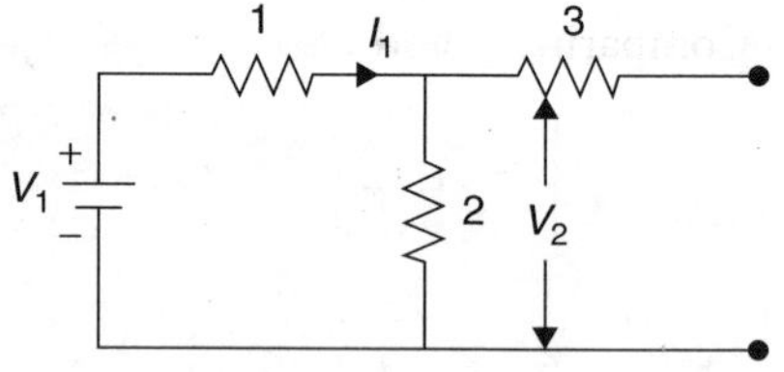

From the above circuit,

$$V_1 = (1+2)I_1 = 3I_1$$

$$\Rightarrow \quad \frac{V_1}{I_1} = 3 = Z_{11}$$

$$V_2 = 2I_1$$

$$\Rightarrow \quad \frac{V_2}{I_1} = 2 = Z_{21}$$

By putting $I_1 = 0$ in the above circuit, it can be reduced to the circuit shown on the right.

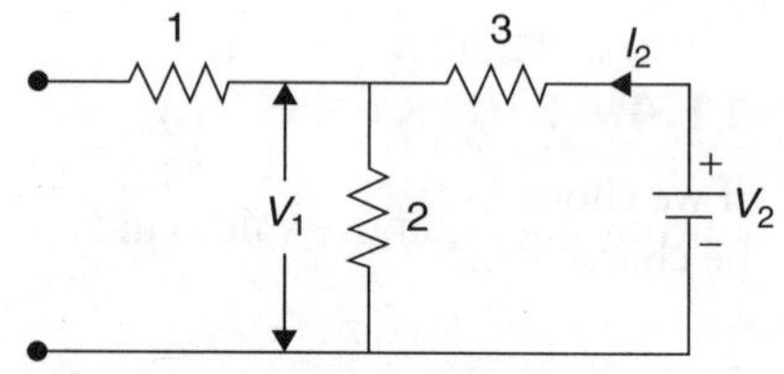

From the above circuit,

$$V_2 = (3+2)I_2 = 5I_2$$

$$\Rightarrow \quad \frac{V_2}{I_2} = 5 = Z_{22}$$

$$V_1 = 2I_2$$

$$\Rightarrow \quad \frac{V_1}{I_2} = 2 = Z_{12}$$

Therefore, the Z-parameters are

$$Z_{11} = 3\ \Omega,\ Z_{12} = 2\ \Omega,\ Z_{21} = 2\ \Omega,\ Z_{22} = 5\ \Omega$$

Problem 11.2 Find the Z-parameters for the two-port circuit.

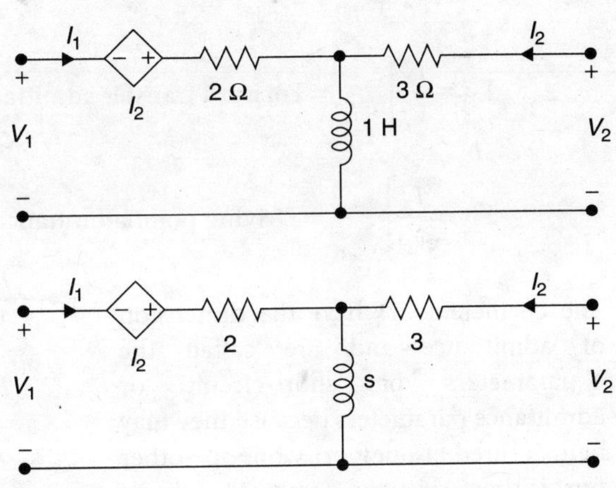

Solution:

The equivalent transformed network for the given circuit is shown on the right.

Applying KVL to loop-1

$$V_1 + I_2 - 2I_1 - s(I_1 + I_2) = 0$$

$$\Rightarrow \quad V_1 = (2 + s)I_1 + (s - 1)I_2$$

Applying KVL to loop-2

$$V_2 - 3I_2 - s(I_1 + I_2) = 0$$

$$\Rightarrow \quad V_2 = sI_1 + (3 + s)I_2$$

Writing the above equations into matrix form, we have

$$\begin{bmatrix} V_1 \\ V_2 \end{bmatrix} = \begin{bmatrix} 2+s & s-1 \\ s & s+3 \end{bmatrix} \begin{bmatrix} I_1 \\ I_2 \end{bmatrix}$$

Comparing with standard Z-parameter equations,

$$\begin{bmatrix} V_1 \\ V_2 \end{bmatrix} = \begin{bmatrix} Z_{11} & Z_{12} \\ Z_{21} & Z_{22} \end{bmatrix} \begin{bmatrix} I_1 \\ I_2 \end{bmatrix}$$

$$Z_{11} = s + 2,\ Z_{12} = s - 1,\ Z_{21} = s,\ Z_{22} = s + 3$$

11.4 SHORT CIRCUIT OR ADMITTANCE PARAMETERS

If we choose V_1 and V_2 as independent variables and I_1 and I_2 as dependent variables then the network can be characterised by the following set of equations.

$$\left.\begin{aligned} I_1 &= Y_{11}V_1 + Y_{12}V_2 \\ I_2 &= Y_{21}V_1 + Y_{22}V_2 \end{aligned}\right\} \qquad (11.11)$$

In matrix form,

$$\begin{bmatrix} I_1 \\ I_2 \end{bmatrix} = \begin{bmatrix} Y_{11} & Y_{12} \\ Y_{21} & Y_{22} \end{bmatrix} \begin{bmatrix} V_1 \\ V_2 \end{bmatrix} \tag{11.12}$$

By short circuiting the input and output ports of the two-port network, the Y-parameters can be obtained as

$$Y_{11} = \left.\frac{I_1}{V_1}\right|_{V_2=0} = \text{Driving point admittance at the input port}$$

$$Y_{12} = \left.\frac{I_1}{V_2}\right|_{V_1=0} = \text{Reverse transfer admittance}$$

$$Y_{21} = \left.\frac{I_2}{V_1}\right|_{V_2=0} = \text{Forward transfer admittance}$$

$$Y_{22} = \left.\frac{I_2}{V_2}\right|_{V_1=0} = \text{Driving point admittance at the output port}$$

The coefficients Y_{ij} have the dimension of admittance and are called the Y-parameters or short-circuit or admittance parameters because they may be measured at one port while the other port is short-circuited. Figure 11.5 shows the equivalent circuit of the two-port network using the Y-parameters.

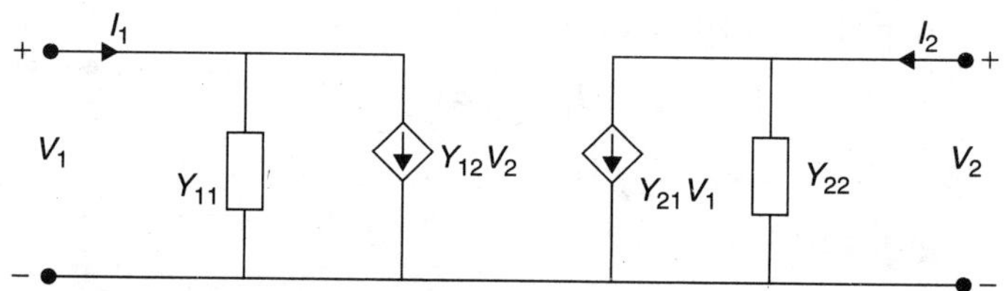

Fig. 11.5 Equivalent circuit of the two-port network using Y-parameters

Condition for reciprocity Using the reciprocity theorem we can find the condition for the reciprocal for the given two-port network. Referring to Figs 11.6(a) and (b), the network is reciprocal, if $I_1' = I_2'$.

From Fig. 11.6(a),

$$I_2 = -I_2', \quad V_2 = 0, \quad V_1 = V_s$$

From the Y-parameter equations,

$$I_1 = Y_{11}V_1 + Y_{12}V_2$$

$$I_2 = Y_{21}V_1 + Y_{22}V_2$$

$$I_1 = Y_{11}V_s$$

$$-I_2' = Y_{21}V_s$$

From Fig. 11.6(b),

$$I_1 = I_1', \quad V_1 = 0, \quad V_2 = V_s$$

$$-I_1' = Y_{12}V_s$$

$$I_2 = Y_{22}V_s$$

But the condition for reciprocity is

$$I_1' = I_2'$$

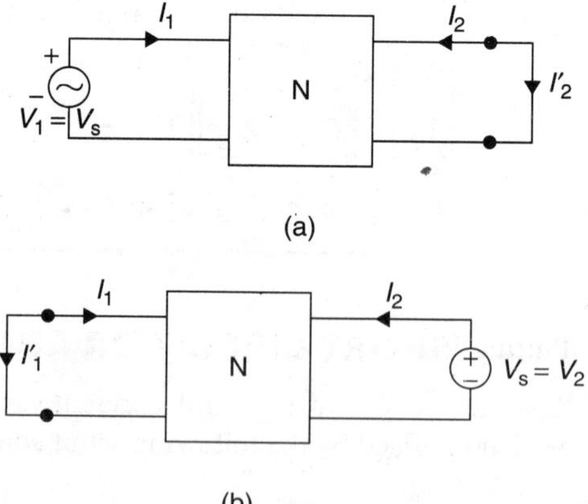

Fig. 11.6 Network for deriving condition of reciprocity

$$-Y_{12}V_s = -Y_{21}V_s$$

$$\Rightarrow \qquad Y_{12} = Y_{21} \tag{11.13}$$

Condition for symmetry A two-port network is said to be symmetrical if the two ports can be interchanged without changing the port voltages and currents. This happens if

$$\left.\frac{I_1}{V_1}\right|_{V_2=0} = \left.\frac{I_2}{V_2}\right|_{V_1=0}$$

$$\Rightarrow \qquad Y_{11} = Y_{22} \tag{11.14}$$

Problem 11.3 Find the Y-parameters for the network.

Solution:

The Y-parameters can be given as

$$Y_{11} = \left.\frac{I_1}{V_1}\right|_{V_2=0}, Y_{12} = \left.\frac{I_1}{V_2}\right|_{V_1=0}, Y_{21} = \left.\frac{I_2}{V_1}\right|_{V_2=0}, Y_{22} = \left.\frac{I_2}{V_2}\right|_{V_1=0}$$

Putting $V_2 = 0$ in the above circuit, it can be reduced to

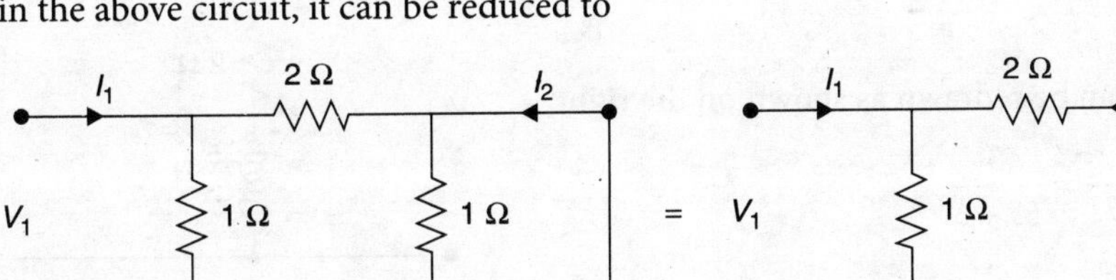

From the above circuit

$$V_1 = I_1 \times \left(\frac{1\times 2}{1+2}\right) = \frac{2}{3}I_1$$

$$\Rightarrow \qquad \frac{I_1}{V_1} = \frac{3}{2} = Y_{11}$$

$$I_2 = -I_1 \times \frac{1}{1+2} = -\frac{3V_1}{2}\times\frac{1}{3} = -\frac{V_1}{2}$$

$$\frac{I_2}{V_1} = -\frac{1}{2} = Y_{21}$$

Putting $V_1 = 0$ in the above circuit, it can be reduced to

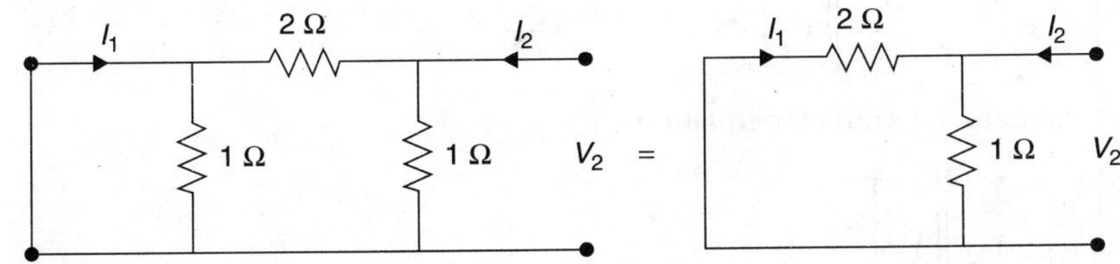

From the above circuit

$$V_2 = I_2 \times \left(\frac{1\times 2}{1+2}\right) = \frac{2}{3}I_2$$

$$\Rightarrow \quad \frac{I_2}{V_2} = \frac{3}{2} = Y_{22}$$

$$I_1 = -I_2 \times \frac{1}{1+2} = -\frac{3V_2}{2}\times\frac{1}{3} = -\frac{V_2}{2}$$

$$\Rightarrow \quad \frac{I_1}{V_2} = -\frac{1}{2} = Y_{12}$$

The Y-parameters are

$$Y_{11} = \frac{3}{2}\text{mho}, Y_{12} = -\frac{1}{2}\text{mho}, Y_{21} = -\frac{1}{2}\text{mho}, Y_{22} = \frac{3}{2}\text{mho}$$

Problem 11.4 Find the Y-parameters of the circuit.

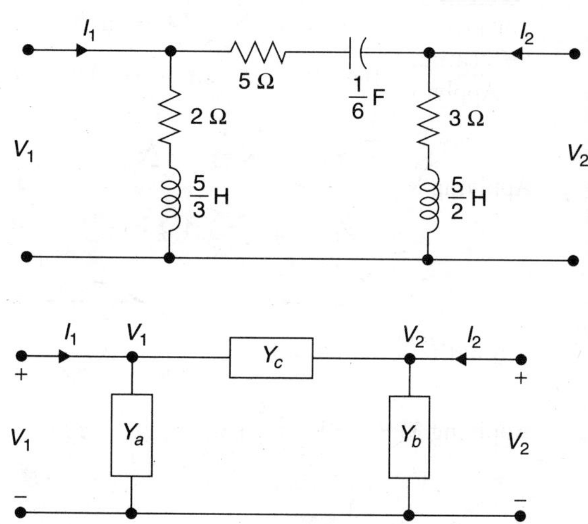

Solution:

The given circuit can be redrawn as shown on the right.

where $$Y_a = \frac{1}{2+\frac{5s}{3}} = \frac{3}{5s+6}$$

$$Y_b = \frac{1}{3+\frac{5s}{2}} = \frac{2}{5s+6}$$

$$Y_c = \frac{1}{5+\frac{6}{s}} = \frac{s}{5s+6}$$

Applying KCL at node-1

$$I_1 = V_1Y_a + (V_1 - V_2)Y_c = (Y_a + Y_c)V_1 - Y_cV_2$$

Applying KCL at node-2

$$I_2 = V_2Y_b + (V_2 - V_1)Y_c = -Y_cV_1 + (Y_b + Y_c)V_2$$

Writing the above equations in the matrix form, we have

$$\begin{bmatrix} I_1 \\ I_2 \end{bmatrix} = \begin{bmatrix} Y_a + Y_c & -Y_c \\ -Y_c & Y_b + Y_c \end{bmatrix}\begin{bmatrix} V_1 \\ V_2 \end{bmatrix}$$

Comparing with standard Y-parameter equations,

$$\begin{bmatrix} I_1 \\ I_2 \end{bmatrix} = \begin{bmatrix} Y_{11} & Y_{12} \\ Y_{21} & Y_{22} \end{bmatrix}\begin{bmatrix} V_1 \\ V_2 \end{bmatrix}$$

$$Y_{11} = Y_a + Y_c$$

$$Y_{12} = Y_{21} = -Y_c$$

$$Y_{22} = Y_b + Y_c$$

Substituting Y_a, Y_b and Y_c values in the above parameters, we have

$$Y_{11} = \frac{3}{5s+6} + \frac{s}{5s+6} = \frac{3+s}{5s+6}$$

$$Y_{12} = Y_{21} = \frac{-s}{5s+6}$$

$$Y_{22} = \frac{s}{5s+6} + \frac{2}{5s+6} = \frac{s+2}{5s+6}$$

Problem 11.5 Find Z and Y-parameters for the network.

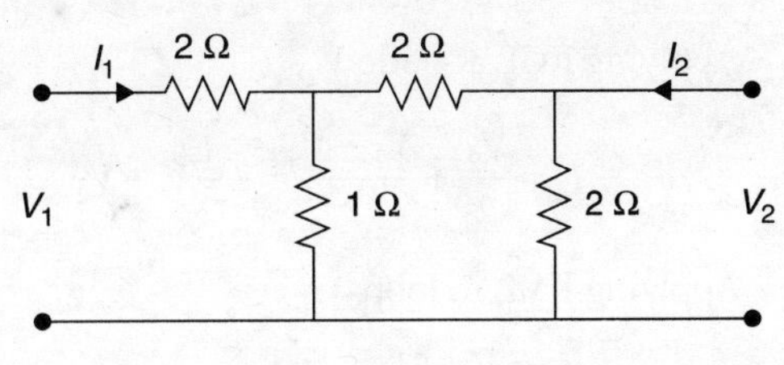

Solution:

The given circuit can be redrawn as shown.

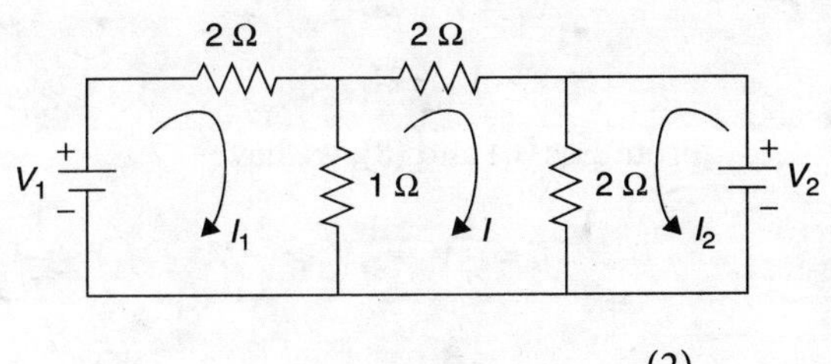

Determination of Z-parameters

Applying KVL to loop-1

$$V_1 = 2I_1 + 1(I_1 - I) = 3I_1 - I \tag{1}$$

Applying KVL to loop-2

$$2I + 2(I_2 + I) + 1(I - I_1) = 0$$

$$5I + 2I_2 - I_1 = 0$$

$$I = \frac{1}{5}(-2I_2 + I_1) \tag{2}$$

Applying KVL to loop-3

$$V_2 = 2I_2 + 2I \tag{3}$$

From Eqs (1) and (2), we have

$$V_1 = 3I_1 - \frac{1}{5}(-2I_2 + I_1)$$

$$V_1 = \frac{14}{5}I_1 + \frac{2}{5}I_2 \tag{4}$$

From Eqs (2) and (3), we have

$$V_2 = 2I_2 + 2 \times \frac{1}{5}(-2I_2 + I_1)$$

$$V_2 = \frac{2}{5}I_1 + \frac{6}{5}I_2 \tag{5}$$

Writing Eqs (4) and (5) in the matrix form, we have

$$\begin{bmatrix} V_1 \\ V_2 \end{bmatrix} = \begin{bmatrix} \frac{14}{5} & \frac{2}{5} \\ \frac{2}{5} & \frac{6}{5} \end{bmatrix} \begin{bmatrix} I_1 \\ I_2 \end{bmatrix}$$

Comparing with standard Z-parameter equations

$$\begin{bmatrix} V_1 \\ V_2 \end{bmatrix} = \begin{bmatrix} Z_{11} & Z_{12} \\ Z_{21} & Z_{22} \end{bmatrix} \begin{bmatrix} I_1 \\ I_2 \end{bmatrix}$$

$$Z_{11} = \frac{14}{5}\,\Omega,\ Z_{12} = Z_{21} = \frac{2}{5}\,\Omega,\ Z_{22} = \frac{6}{5}\,\Omega$$

Determination of Y-parameters

Applying KCL at node V,

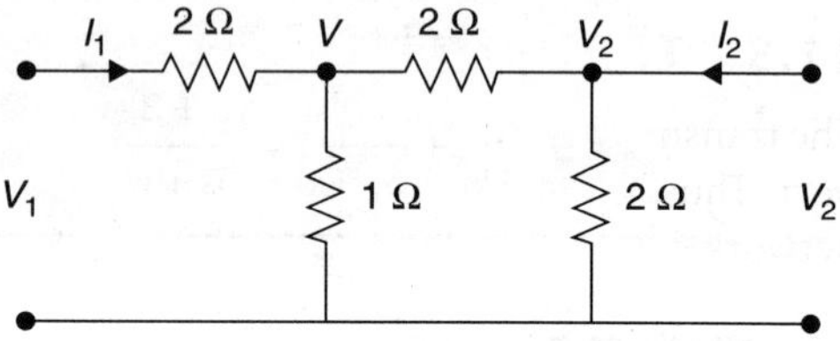

$$I_1 = \frac{V}{1} + \frac{V - V_2}{2} = \frac{3}{2}V - \frac{1}{2}V_2 \tag{6}$$

Applying KCL at node V_2,

$$I_2 = \frac{V_2}{2} + \frac{V_2 - V}{2} = -\frac{1}{2}V + V_2 \tag{7}$$

Applying KVL to loop-1

$$V_1 = V + 2I_1$$

$$V = V_1 - 2I_1 \tag{8}$$

From Eqs (6) and (8), we have

$$I_1 = \frac{3}{2}V - \frac{1}{2}V_2 = \frac{3}{2}(V_1 - 2I_1) - \frac{1}{2}V_2$$

$$4I_1 = \frac{3}{2}V_1 - \frac{1}{2}V_2$$

$$I_1 = \frac{3}{8}V_1 - \frac{1}{8}V_2 \tag{9}$$

From Eqs (7) and (8), we have

$$I_2 = -\frac{1}{2}(V_1 - 2I_1) + V_2 = -\frac{1}{2}V_1 + V_2 + I_1 \tag{10}$$

From Eqs (9) and (10),

$$I_2 = -\frac{1}{2}V_1 + V_2 + \left(\frac{3}{8}V_1 - \frac{1}{8}V_2\right)$$

$$I_2 = -\frac{1}{8}V_1 + \frac{7}{8}V_2 \tag{11}$$

Writing Eqs (9) and (11) in the matrix form, we have

$$\begin{bmatrix} I_1 \\ I_2 \end{bmatrix} = \begin{bmatrix} \frac{3}{8} & -\frac{1}{8} \\ -\frac{1}{8} & \frac{7}{8} \end{bmatrix} \begin{bmatrix} V_1 \\ V_2 \end{bmatrix}$$

Comparing with standard Y-parameter equations,

$$\begin{bmatrix} I_1 \\ I_2 \end{bmatrix} = \begin{bmatrix} Y_{11} & Y_{12} \\ Y_{21} & Y_{22} \end{bmatrix} \begin{bmatrix} V_1 \\ V_2 \end{bmatrix}$$

$$Y_{11} = \frac{3}{8} \mho, \ Y_{12} = Y_{21} = -\frac{1}{8} \mho, \ Y_{22} = \frac{7}{8} \mho$$

11.5 TRANSMISSION, *ABCD* OR *T*-PARAMETERS

The transmission parameters relate the voltage and current at one port to the voltage and current at the other port. Thus, if we choose V_2 and I_2 as independent variables, and V_1 and I_1 as dependent variables then the network can be characterised by the following set of equations.

$$\left. \begin{aligned} V_1 &= AV_2 - BI_2 \\ I_1 &= CV_2 - DI_2 \end{aligned} \right\} \tag{11.15}$$

In matrix form,

$$\begin{bmatrix} V_1 \\ I_1 \end{bmatrix} = \begin{bmatrix} A & B \\ C & D \end{bmatrix} \begin{bmatrix} V_2 \\ -I_2 \end{bmatrix} \tag{11.16}$$

The negative sign in Eq. 11.15 is associated with I_2. These parameters were first used to define transmission line parameters in which the current in ports is always taken going away from the network. Since the reference direction assumed for defining all the two-port network parameters is indicated towards the network, the current I_2 is taken as negative.

By opening and shorting the output ports of the two-port network, the transmission parameters can be obtained as

$$A = \left. \frac{V_1}{V_2} \right|_{I_2=0}, \quad B = -\left. \frac{V_1}{I_2} \right|_{V_2=0}, \quad C = \left. \frac{I_1}{V_2} \right|_{I_2=0}, \quad D = -\left. \frac{I_1}{I_2} \right|_{V_2=0}$$

where, $1/A$ = open circuit voltage gain, $1/B$ = short circuit transfer admittance, $1/C$ = open circuit transfer impedance and $1/D$ = short circuit current gain.

No equivalent circuit exists using the ABCD parameters since the input variables are defined exclusively in terms of output port variables and it is impossible to satisfy both the equations of the *ABCD* parameters simultaneously.

Condition for reciprocity Using the reciprocity theorem, we can find the condition for the reciprocal for the given two-port network. Referring to Figs 11.7(a) and (b), the network is reciprocal if $I_1' = I_2'$.

From Fig. 11.7(a),

$$V_2 = 0, \ I_2 = -I_2', \ V_1 = V_s$$

From the *ABCD* parameter equations,

$$V_1 = AV_2 - BI_2$$

$$I_1 = CV_2 - DI_2$$

$$V_s = BI_2'$$

$$\Rightarrow \quad I_2' = \frac{V_s}{B} \tag{11.17}$$

$$I_1 = DI_2' \tag{11.18}$$

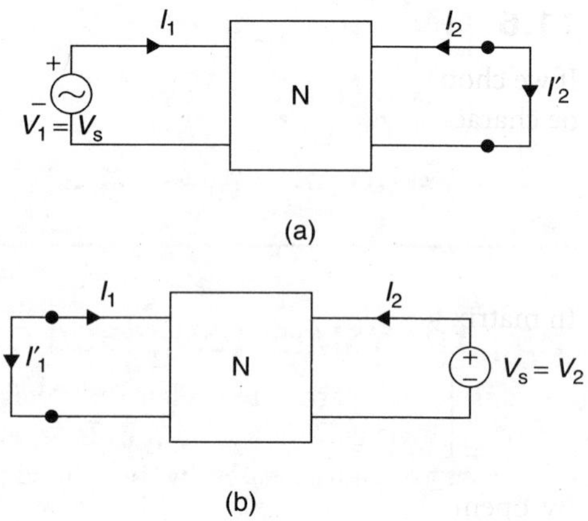

From Fig. 11.7(b),

$$V_1 = 0, \quad I_1 = -I_1', \quad V_2 = V_s$$

Substituting the above values in the standard equations for *ABCD*-parameters, we have

$$0 = AV_s - BI_2$$

$$\Rightarrow \quad I_2 = \frac{A}{B} V_s \tag{11.19}$$

$$-I_1' = CV_s - DI_2 \tag{11.20}$$

Fig. 11.7 Network for deriving condition of reciprocity

From Eqs (11.19) and (11.20),

$$I_1' = -CV_s + D\left(\frac{A}{B} V_s\right) = \left(\frac{AD - BC}{B}\right) V_s. \tag{11.21}$$

But the condition for reciprocity is

$$I_1' = I_2'$$

$$\left(\frac{AD - BC}{B}\right) V_s = \frac{V_s}{B}$$

$$\Rightarrow \quad AD - BC = 1 \tag{11.22}$$

Condition for symmetry A two-port network is said to be symmetrical if the two ports can be interchanged without changing the port voltage and currents. This happens if

$$\left.\frac{V_1}{I_1}\right|_{I_2=0} = \left.\frac{V_2}{I_2}\right|_{I_1=0}$$

$$\left.\frac{V_1}{I_1}\right|_{I_2=0} = \left.\frac{AV_2 - BI_2}{CV_2 - DI_2}\right|_{I_2=0} = \frac{A}{C} \tag{11.23}$$

We know from *ADCD* parameter equations,

$$I_1 = CV_2 - DI_2 = 0$$

$$\Rightarrow \quad \left.\frac{V_2}{I_2}\right|_{I_1=0} = \frac{D}{C} \tag{11.24}$$

The condition for symmetry is

$$\left.\frac{V_1}{I_1}\right|_{I_2=0} = \left.\frac{V_2}{I_2}\right|_{I_1=0}$$

$$\frac{A}{C} = \frac{D}{C} \Rightarrow A = D \tag{11.25}$$

11.6 INVERSE TRANSMISSION OR $A'B'C'D'$ OR T' PARAMETERS

If we choose V_1 and I_1 as independent variables and V_2 and I_2 as dependent variables, then the network can be characterised by the following set of equations:

$$\left.\begin{aligned} V_2 &= A'V_1 - B'I_1 \\ I_2 &= C'V_1 - D'I_1 \end{aligned}\right\} \tag{11.26}$$

In matrix form,

$$\begin{bmatrix} V_2 \\ I_2 \end{bmatrix} = \begin{bmatrix} A' & B' \\ C' & D' \end{bmatrix} \begin{bmatrix} V_1 \\ -I_1 \end{bmatrix} \tag{11.27}$$

By opening and shorting the input ports of the two-port network, the transmission parameters can be obtained as

$$A' = \left.\frac{V_2}{V_1}\right|_{I_1=0} = \text{open circuit voltage gain}$$

$$B' = -\left.\frac{V_2}{I_1}\right|_{V_1=0} = \text{short circuit transfer impedance}$$

$$C' = \left.\frac{I_2}{V_1}\right|_{I_1=0} = \text{open circuit transfer admittance}$$

$$D' = -\left.\frac{I_2}{I_1}\right|_{V_1=0} = \text{short circuit current gain}$$

Condition for reciprocity Using the reciprocity theorem, we can find the condition for the reciprocal for the given two-port network. Referring to Figs 11.8(a) and (b) the network is reciprocal if $I_1' = I_2'$.

From Fig. 11.8(a),

$$V_2 = 0, \; I_2 = -I_2', \; V_1 = V_s$$

From $A'B'C'D'$ parameter equations,

$$V_2 = A'V_1 - B'I_1$$

$$I_2 = C'V_1 - D'I_1$$

$$0 = A'V_s - B'I_1$$

$$\Rightarrow \quad I_1 = \frac{A'}{B'}V_s \tag{11.28}$$

$$-I_2' = C'V_s - D'I_1 \tag{11.29}$$

From Eqs 11.28 and 11.29,

$$I_2' = -C'V_s + D'\left(\frac{A'}{B'}V_s\right)$$

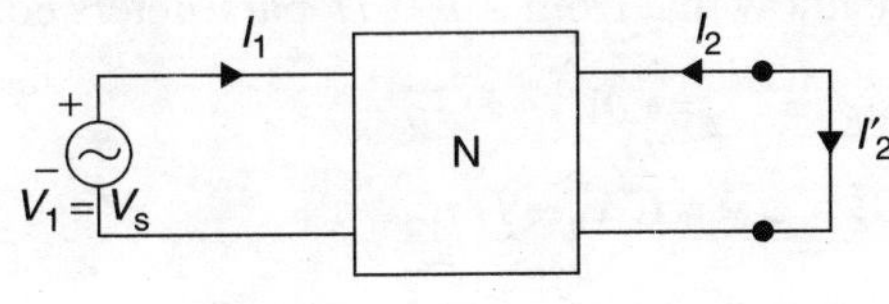

(a)

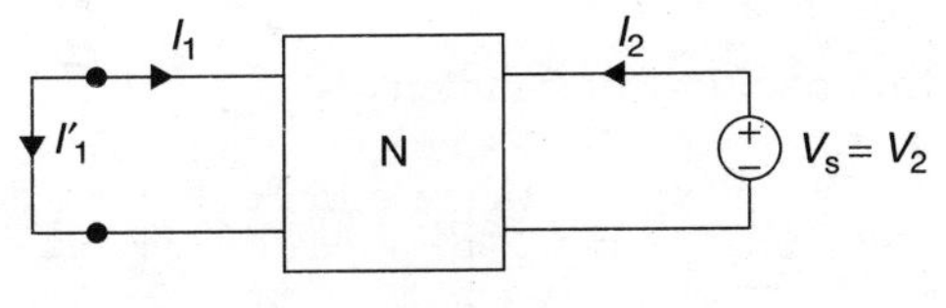

(b)

Fig. 11.8 Network for deriving condition of reciprocity

$$I_2' = \left(\frac{A'D' - B'C'}{B'}\right)V_s \tag{11.30}$$

From Fig. 11.8(b),

$$V_1 = 0, \quad I_1 = -I_1', \quad V_2 = V_s$$

Substituting the above values in the standard equations for $A'B'C'D'$ parameters, we have

$$V_2 = A'V_1 - B'I_1$$

$$V_s = B'I_1'$$

$$\Rightarrow \qquad I_1' = \frac{V_s}{B'} \tag{11.31}$$

But the condition for reciprocity is

$$I_1' = I_2'$$

$$\frac{V_s}{B'} = \left(\frac{A'D' - B'C'}{B'}\right)V_s$$

$$\Rightarrow \qquad A'D' - B'C' = 1 \tag{11.32}$$

Condition for symmetry A two-port network is said to be symmetrical if the two ports can be interchanged without changing the port voltage and currents. This happens if

$$\left.\frac{V_1}{I_1}\right|_{I_2=0} = \left.\frac{V_2}{I_2}\right|_{I_1=0}$$

$$\left.\frac{V_2}{I_2}\right|_{I_1=0} = \left.\frac{A'V_1 - B'I_1}{C'V_1 - D'I_1}\right|_{I_1=0} = \frac{A'}{C'} \tag{11.33}$$

We know that from $A'B'C'D'$ parameters equations,

$$I_2 = C'V_1 - D'I_1$$

$$0 = C'V_1 - D'I_1$$

$$\Rightarrow \qquad \left.\frac{V_1}{I_1}\right|_{I_2=0} = \frac{D'}{C'} \tag{11.34}$$

The condition for symmetry is

$$\left.\frac{V_1}{I_1}\right|_{I_2=0} = \left.\frac{V_2}{I_2}\right|_{I_1=0}$$

$$\frac{A'}{C'} = \frac{D'}{C'} \Rightarrow A' = D' \tag{11.35}$$

Problem 11.6 Find the *ABCD* parameters for the network.

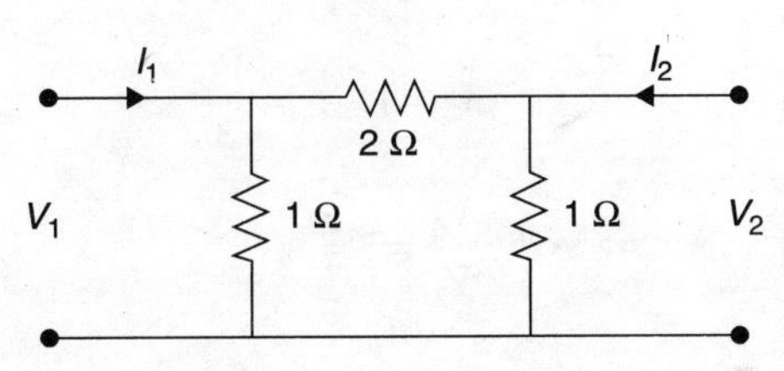

Solution:

The ABCD parameters are given as

$$A = \frac{V_1}{V_2}\bigg|_{I_2=0}, \quad B = -\frac{V_1}{I_2}\bigg|_{V_2=0}, \quad C = \frac{I_1}{V_2}\bigg|_{I_2=0}, \quad D = -\frac{I_1}{I_2}\bigg|_{V_2=0}$$

Putting $V_2 = 0$ in the above circuit, it can be reduced to

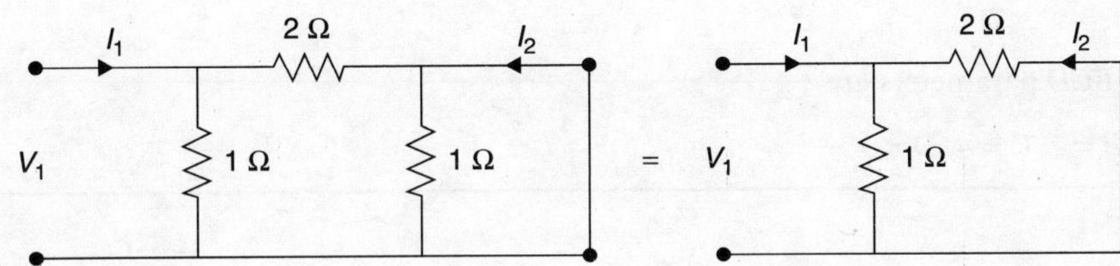

From the above circuit

$$V_1 = I_1 \times \left(\frac{1\times 2}{1+2}\right) = \frac{2}{3}I_1$$

$$\Rightarrow \quad I_1 = \frac{3}{2}V_1$$

$$I_2 = -I_1 \times \frac{1}{1+2} = -\frac{3V_1}{2} \times \frac{1}{3} = -\frac{V_1}{2}$$

$$\frac{V_1}{I_2} = -2 = -B$$

$$\Rightarrow \quad B = 2$$

$$I_2 = -I_1 \times \frac{1}{3}$$

$$\frac{I_1}{I_2} = -3 = -D$$

$$\Rightarrow \quad D = 3$$

Putting $I_2 = 0$ in the above circuit, it can be reduced to

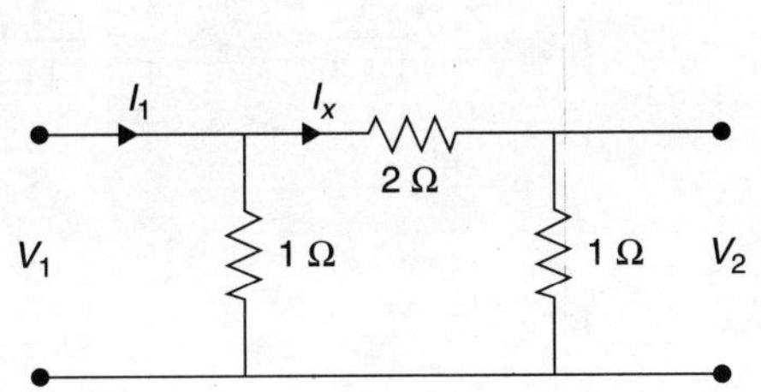

From the above circuit

$$V_1 = I_1 \times \left(\frac{1\times 3}{1+3}\right) = \frac{3}{4}I_1$$

$$\Rightarrow \quad I_1 = \frac{4}{3}V_1$$

$$I_x = I_1 \times \frac{1}{1+3} = \frac{4V_1}{3} \times \frac{1}{4} = \frac{V_1}{3}$$

$$V_2 = 1 \times I_x = \frac{V_1}{3}$$

$$\Rightarrow \quad \frac{V_1}{V_2} = 3 = A$$

Also $\quad V_2 = 1 \times I_x = I_1 \times \frac{1}{4}$

$$\frac{I_1}{V_2} = 4 = C$$

Therefore, the *ABCD* parameters are

$$A = 3,\ B = 2,\ C = 4,\ D = 3$$

Problem 11.7 Find the inverse transmission parameters for the network.

Solution:

The $A'B'C'D'$ parameters are given as

$$A' = \left.\frac{V_2}{V_1}\right|_{I_1=0},\quad B' = -\left.\frac{V_2}{I_1}\right|_{V_1=0},\quad C' = \left.\frac{I_2}{V_1}\right|_{I_1=0},\quad D' = -\left.\frac{I_2}{I_1}\right|_{V_1=0}$$

Putting $V_1 = 0$ in the above circuit, it can be reduced to the network shown below.

From the circuit,

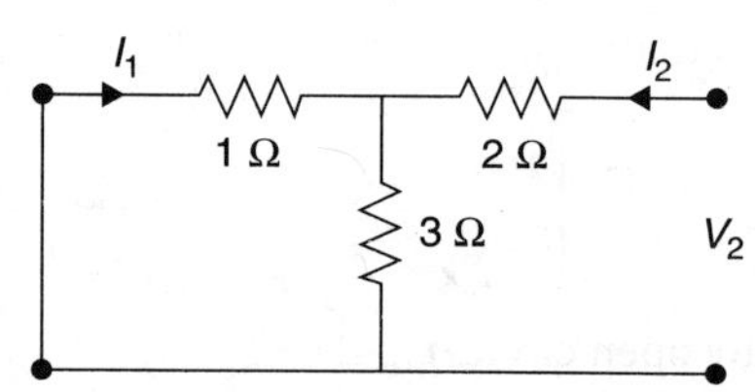

$$V_2 = I_2 \times \left(2 + \frac{1 \times 3}{1+3}\right) = \frac{11}{4} I_2$$

$$\Rightarrow \quad I_2 = \frac{4}{11} V_2$$

$$I_1 = -I_2 \times \frac{3}{1+3} = -I_2 \times \frac{3}{4} = -\frac{4}{11} V_2 \times \frac{3}{4} = -\frac{3}{11} V_2$$

$$\Rightarrow \quad \frac{V_2}{I_1} = -\frac{11}{3} = -B'$$

$$\Rightarrow \quad B' = \frac{11}{3}$$

Also $\quad I_1 = -I_2 \times \frac{3}{4}$

$$\Rightarrow \quad \frac{I_2}{I_1} = -\frac{4}{3} = -D'$$

$$\Rightarrow \quad D' = \frac{4}{3}$$

Putting $I_1 = 0$ in the above circuit, it can be reduced to the circuit shown below.

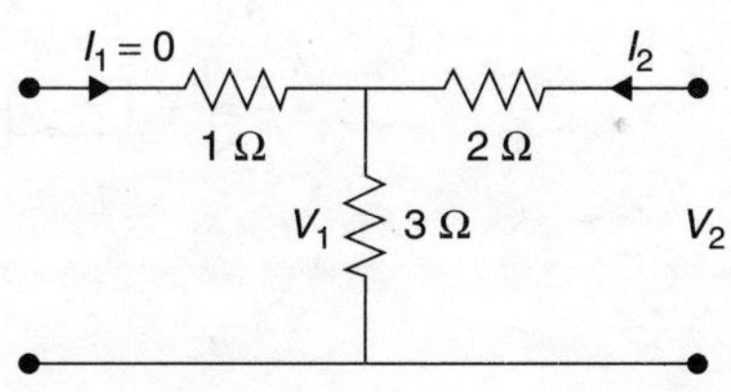

From the circuit,

$$V_2 = I_2 \times (2+3) = 5I_2$$

$$V_1 = 3I_2 = 3 \times \frac{1}{5} V_2$$

$$\Rightarrow \quad \frac{V_2}{V_1} = \frac{5}{3} = A'$$

Also $\quad V_1 = 3I_2$

$$\Rightarrow \quad \frac{I_2}{V_1} = \frac{1}{3} = C'$$

Therefore, the inverse transmission parameters are

$$A' = \frac{5}{3}, B' = \frac{11}{3}, C' = \frac{1}{3}, D' = \frac{4}{3}$$

11.7 HYBRID OR *h*-PARAMETERS

The hybrid parameters find wide usage in electronic circuits especially in constructing models of transistors. If we choose I_1 and V_2 as independent variables and V_1 and I_2 as dependent variables, then the network can be characterised by the following set of equations.

$$\left.\begin{aligned} V_1 &= h_{11}I_1 + h_{12}V_2 \\ I_2 &= h_{21}I_1 + h_{22}V_2 \end{aligned}\right\} \tag{11.36}$$

In matrix form,

$$\begin{bmatrix} V_1 \\ I_2 \end{bmatrix} = \begin{bmatrix} h_{11} & h_{12} \\ h_{21} & h_{22} \end{bmatrix} \begin{bmatrix} I_1 \\ V_2 \end{bmatrix} \tag{11.37}$$

By open circuiting the input and short circuiting the output port of the two-port network, the *h*-parameters can be obtained as

$$h_{11} = \left.\frac{V_1}{I_1}\right|_{V_2=0} = \text{short circuit input impedance}$$

$$h_{12} = \left.\frac{V_1}{V_2}\right|_{I_1=0} = \text{open circuit reverse voltage gain}$$

$$h_{21} = \left.\frac{I_2}{I_1}\right|_{V_2=0} = \text{short circuit current gain}$$

$$h_{22} = \left.\frac{I_2}{V_2}\right|_{I_1=0} = \text{open circuit output admittance}$$

Figure 11.9 shows the equivalent circuit of the two-port network using *h*-parameters.

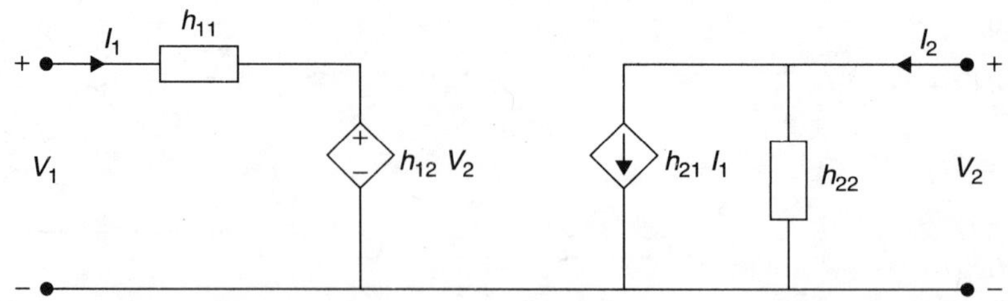

Fig. 11.9 Equivalent circuit of the two-port network using *h*-parameters

Condition for reciprocity Using the reciprocity theorem we can find the condition for the reciprocal for the given two-port network. Referring to Figs 11.10(a) and (b) the network is reciprocal if $I_1' = I_2'$.

From Fig. 11.10(a),

$$V_2 = 0,\quad I_2 = -I_2',\quad V_1 = V_s$$

From the *h*-parameter equations,

$$V_1 = h_{11}I_1 + h_{12}V_2$$

$$I_2 = h_{21}I_1 + h_{22}V_2$$

$$V_s = h_{11}I_1$$

$$\Rightarrow \quad I_1 = \frac{V_s}{h_{11}} \tag{11.38}$$

$$-I_2' = h_{21}I_1 \tag{11.39}$$

From Eqs 11.38 and 11.39,

$$I_2' = -h_{21} \times \frac{V_s}{h_{11}} = -\frac{h_{21}}{h_{11}}V_s \tag{11.40}$$

(a)

(b)

Fig. 11.10 Network for deriving condition of reciprocity

From Fig. 11.10(b),

$$V_1 = 0,\quad I_1 = -I_1',\quad V_2 = V_s$$

Substituting the above values in standard equations for *h*-parameters, we have

$$V_1 = h_{11}I_1 + h_{12}V_2$$

$$0 = -h_{11}I_1' + h_{12}V_s$$

$$\Rightarrow \quad I_1' = \frac{h_{12}}{h_{11}}V_s \tag{11.41}$$

But the condition for reciprocity is

$$I_1' = I_2'$$

$$\frac{h_{12}}{h_{11}}V_s = -\frac{h_{21}}{h_{11}}V_s$$

$$\Rightarrow \quad h_{12} = -h_{21} \tag{11.42}$$

Condition for symmetry A two-port network is said to be symmetrical if the two ports can be interchanged without changing the port voltages and currents. This happens if

$$\left.\frac{V_1}{I_1}\right|_{I_2=0} = \left.\frac{V_2}{I_2}\right|_{I_1=0}$$

From the h-parameter equations, put $I_2 = 0$, we have

$$V_1 = h_{11}I_1 + h_{12}V_2$$

$$0 = h_{21}I_1 + h_{22}V_2$$

$$\Rightarrow \qquad V_2 = -\frac{h_{21}}{h_{22}}I_1$$

$$\therefore \qquad V_1 = h_{11}I_1 - h_{12}\times\frac{h_{21}}{h_{22}}I_1$$

$$\Rightarrow \qquad \frac{V_1}{I_1} = \frac{h_{11}h_{22} - h_{12}h_{21}}{h_{22}} \tag{11.43}$$

From the h-parameter equations, put $I_1 = 0$, we have

$$V_1 = h_{12}V_2$$

$$I_2 = h_{22}V_2$$

$$\Rightarrow \qquad \frac{V_2}{I_2} = \frac{1}{h_{22}} \tag{11.44}$$

But the condition for symmetry is

$$\left.\frac{V_1}{I_1}\right|_{I_2=0} = \left.\frac{V_2}{I_2}\right|_{I_1=0}$$

$$\frac{h_{11}h_{22} - h_{12}h_{21}}{h_{22}} = \frac{1}{h_{22}}$$

$$\Rightarrow \qquad h_{11}h_{22} - h_{21}h_{12} = 1 \tag{11.45}$$

11.8 INVERSE HYBRID OR *g*-PARAMETERS

If we choose V_1 and I_2 as independent variables and I_1 and V_2 as dependent variables, then the network can be characterised by the following set of equations.

$$\left.\begin{aligned} I_1 &= g_{11}V_1 + g_{12}I_2 \\ V_2 &= g_{21}V_1 + g_{22}I_2 \end{aligned}\right\} \tag{11.46}$$

In matrix form,

$$\begin{bmatrix} I_1 \\ V_2 \end{bmatrix} = \begin{bmatrix} g_{11} & g_{12} \\ g_{21} & g_{22} \end{bmatrix}\begin{bmatrix} V_1 \\ I_2 \end{bmatrix} \tag{11.47}$$

By short circuiting the input and open circuiting the output port of the two-port network, the g-parameters can be obtained as

$$g_{11} = \left.\frac{I_1}{V_1}\right|_{I_2=0} = \text{Open circuit input admittance}$$

$$g_{12} = \left.\frac{I_1}{I_2}\right|_{V_1=0} = \text{Short circuit current gain}$$

$$g_{21} = \left.\frac{V_2}{V_1}\right|_{I_2=0} = \text{Open circuit voltage ratio}$$

$$g_{22} = \left.\frac{V_2}{I_2}\right|_{V_1=0} = \text{Short circuit output admittance}$$

Figure 11.11 shows the equivalent circuit of the two-port network using *g*-parameters.

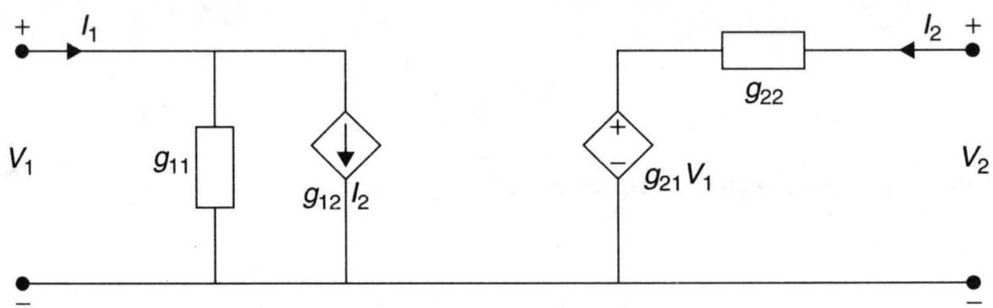

Fig. 11.11 Equivalent circuit of the two-port network using *g*-parameters

Condition for reciprocity Using the reciprocity theorem we can find the condition for the reciprocal for the given two-port network. Referring to Fig. 11.12(a) and (b) the network is reciprocal if $I_1' = I_2'$.

From Fig. 11.12(a),

$$V_2 = 0, \quad I_2 = -I_2', \quad V_1 = V_s$$

From the *g*-parameter equations,

$$I_1 = g_{11}V_1 + g_{12}I_2$$

$$V_2 = g_{21}V_1 + g_{22}I_2$$

$$I_1 = g_{11}V_s - g_{12}I_2'$$

$$0 = g_{21}V_s - g_{22}I_2'$$

$$\Rightarrow \quad I_2' = \frac{g_{21}}{g_{22}}V_s \tag{11.48}$$

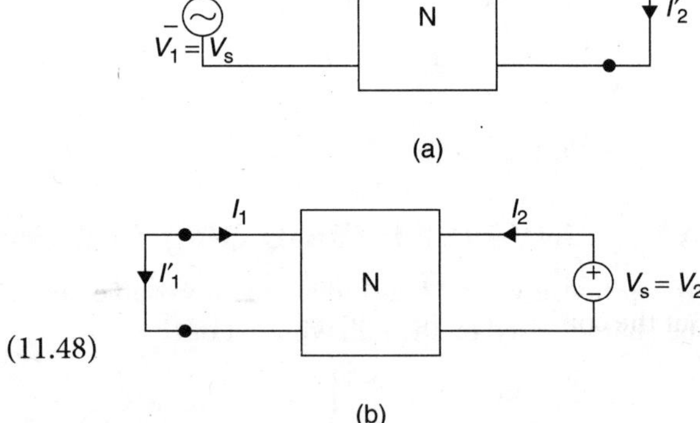

Fig. 11.12 Network for deriving condition of reciprocity

From Fig. 11.12(b),

$$V_1 = 0, \quad I_1 = -I_1', \quad V_2 = V_s$$

Substituting the above values in the standard equations for *g*-parameters, we have

$$-I_1' = g_{12}I_2 \tag{11.49}$$

$$V_s = g_{22}I_2$$

$$\Rightarrow \quad I_2 = \frac{V_s}{g_{22}} \tag{11.50}$$

From Eqs 11.49 and 11.50,

$$I_1' = -g_{12} \times \frac{V_s}{g_{22}} = -\frac{g_{12}}{g_{22}} V_s \tag{11.51}$$

But the condition for reciprocity is

$$I_1' = I_2'$$

$$-\frac{g_{12}}{g_{22}} V_s = \frac{g_{21}}{g_{22}} V_s$$

$$\Rightarrow \quad g_{12} = -g_{21} \tag{11.52}$$

Condition for symmetry A two-port network is said to be symmetrical if the two ports can be interchanged without changing the port voltages and currents. This happens if

$$\left.\frac{V_1}{I_1}\right|_{I_2=0} = \left.\frac{V_2}{I_2}\right|_{I_1=0}$$

From the g-parameter equations, put $I_2 = 0$, we have

$$I_1 = g_{11}V_1 + g_{12}I_2$$

$$V_2 = g_{21}V_1 + g_{22}I_2$$

$$I_1 = g_{11}V_1$$

$$\Rightarrow \quad \frac{V_1}{I_1} = \frac{1}{g_{11}} \tag{11.53}$$

From the g-parameter equations, put $I_1 = 0$, we have

$$0 = g_{11}V_1 + g_{12}I_2$$

$$\Rightarrow \quad V_1 = -\frac{g_{12}}{g_{11}} I_2$$

$$\therefore \quad V_2 = g_{21}V_1 + g_{22}I_2 = -g_{21}\left(\frac{g_{12}}{g_{11}} I_2\right) + g_{22}I_2$$

$$\Rightarrow \quad \frac{V_2}{I_2} = \frac{g_{11}g_{22} - g_{12}g_{21}}{g_{11}} \tag{11.54}$$

But the condition for symmetry is

$$\left.\frac{V_1}{I_1}\right|_{I_2=0} = \left.\frac{V_2}{I_2}\right|_{I_1=0}$$

$$\frac{1}{g_{11}} = \frac{g_{11}g_{22} - g_{12}g_{21}}{g_{11}}$$

$$\Rightarrow \quad g_{11}g_{22} - g_{21}g_{12} = 1 \tag{11.55}$$

Table 11.2 Condition for reciprocity and symmetry

Name of the parameter	Condition for reciprocity	Condition for symmetry
Impedance	$Z_{12} = Z_{21}$	$Z_{11} = Z_{22}$
Admittance	$Y_{12} = Y_{21}$	$Y_{11} = Y_{22}$
Transmission	$AD - BC = 1$	$A = D$
Inverse transmission	$A'D' - B'C' = 1$	$A' = D'$
Hybrid	$h_{12} = -h_{21}$	$h_{11}h_{22} - h_{21}h_{12} = 1$
Inverse hybrid	$g_{12} = -g_{21}$	$g_{11}g_{22} - g_{21}g_{12} = 1$

Problem 11.8 Obtain the h-parameters for the network.

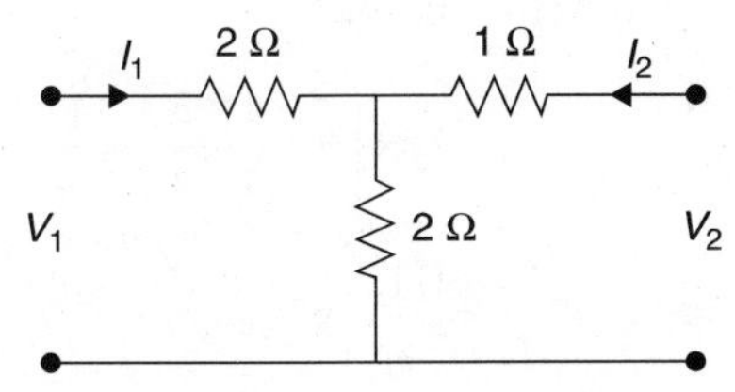

Solution:

The h-parameters are given as

$$h_{11} = \left.\frac{V_1}{I_1}\right|_{V_2=0}, h_{12} = \left.\frac{V_1}{V_2}\right|_{I_1=0}, h_{21} = \left.\frac{I_2}{I_1}\right|_{V_2=0}, h_{22} = \left.\frac{I_2}{V_2}\right|_{I_1=0}$$

Putting $I_1 = 0$ in the above circuit, it can be reduced to

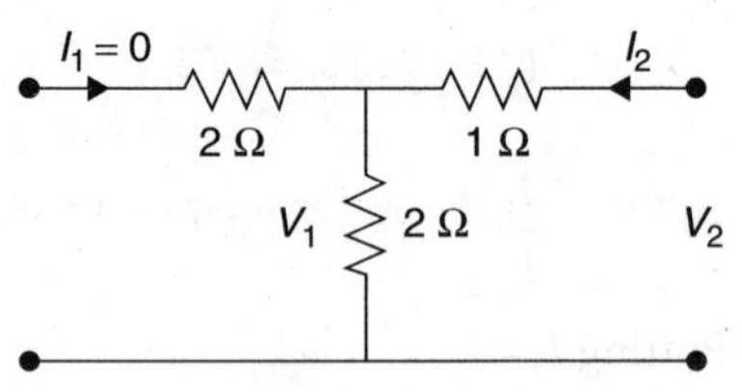

From the circuit,

$$V_2 = I_2 \times (2+1) = 3I_2$$

$$V_1 = 2I_2 = 2\times\frac{1}{3}V_2$$

$$\Rightarrow \quad \frac{V_1}{V_2} = \frac{2}{3} = h_{12}$$

Also $\quad V_2 = 3I_2$

$$\Rightarrow \quad \frac{I_2}{V_2} = \frac{1}{3} = h_{22}$$

Putting $V_2 = 0$ in the above circuit, it can be reduced to

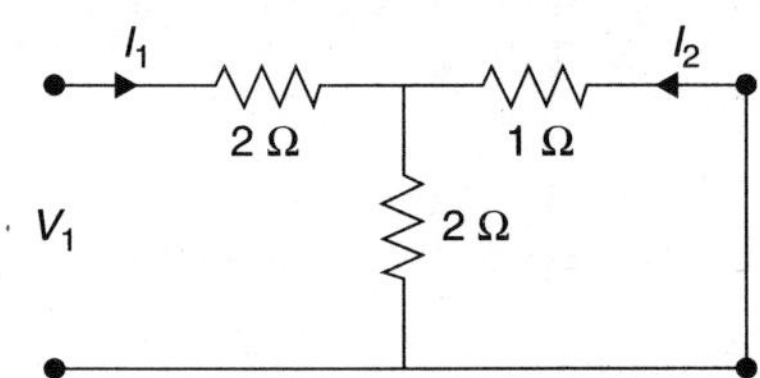

From the circuit,

$$V_1 = I_1 \times \left(2 + \frac{1\times 2}{1+2}\right) = \frac{8}{3}I_1$$

$$\Rightarrow \quad \frac{V_1}{I_1} = \frac{8}{3} = h_{11}$$

$$I_2 = -I_1 \times \frac{2}{1+2} = -I_1 \times \frac{2}{3}$$

$$\Rightarrow \quad \frac{I_2}{I_1} = -\frac{2}{3} = h_{21}$$

Therefore, the hybrid parameters are

$$h_{11} = \frac{8}{3}, h_{12} = \frac{2}{3}, h_{21} = -\frac{2}{3}, h_{22} = \frac{1}{3}$$

Problem 11.9 Obtain the *g*-parameters for the network.

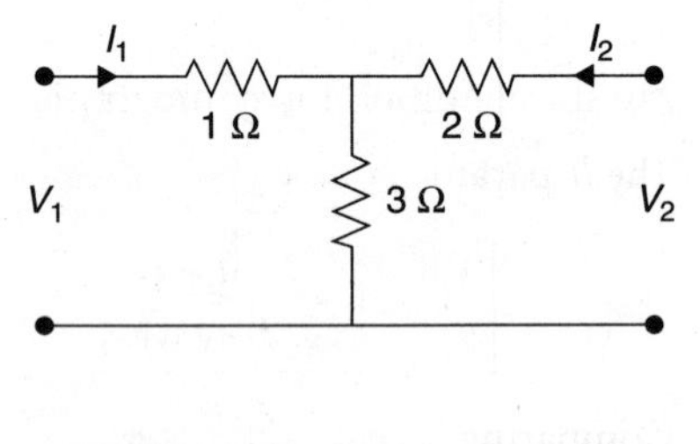

Solution:

The *g*-parameters are given as

$$g_{11} = \left.\frac{I_1}{V_1}\right|_{I_2=0}, g_{12} = \left.\frac{I_1}{I_2}\right|_{V_1=0}, g_{21} = \left.\frac{V_2}{V_1}\right|_{I_2=0}, g_{22} = \left.\frac{V_2}{I_2}\right|_{V_1=0}$$

Putting $V_1 = 0$ in the above circuit, it can be reduced to

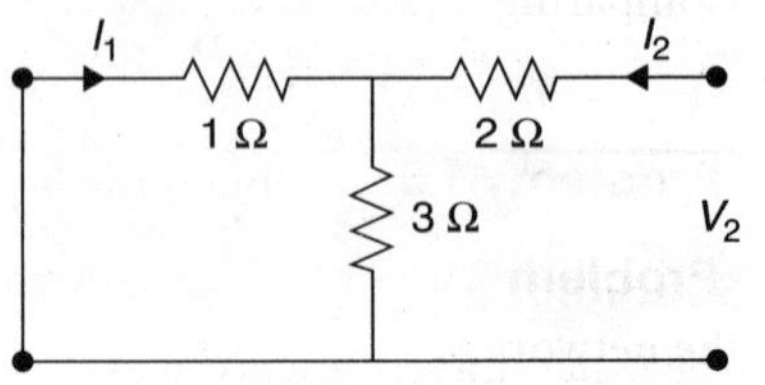

From the circuit,

$$V_2 = I_2 \times \left(2 + \frac{1\times 3}{1+3}\right) = \frac{11}{4}I_2$$

$$\Rightarrow \quad \frac{V_2}{I_2} = \frac{11}{4} = g_{22}$$

$$I_1 = -I_2 \times \frac{3}{1+3} = -I_2 \times \frac{3}{4}$$

$$\Rightarrow \quad \frac{I_1}{I_2} = -\frac{3}{4} = g_{12}$$

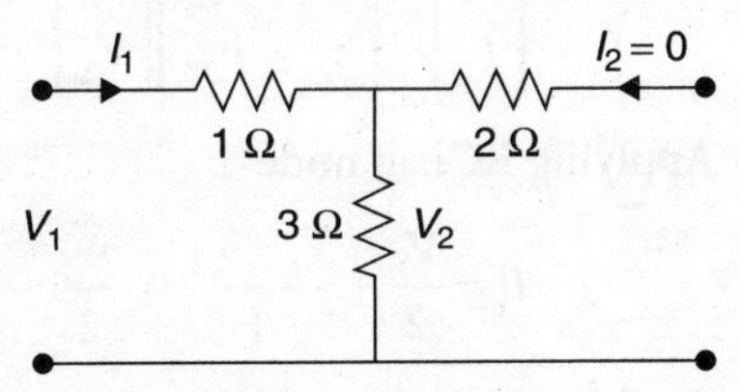

Putting $I_2 = 0$ in the above circuit, it can be reduced to

From the circuit,

$$V_1 = I_1 \times (1+3) = 4I_2$$

$$\Rightarrow \quad \frac{I_1}{V_1} = \frac{1}{4} = g_{11}$$

$$V_2 = 3I_1 = 3 \times \frac{1}{4} V_1$$

$$\frac{V_2}{V_1} = \frac{3}{4} = g_{21}$$

Therefore, the inverse hybrid parameters are $g_{11} = \frac{1}{4}, g_{12} = -\frac{3}{4}, g_{21} = \frac{3}{4}, g_{22} = \frac{11}{4}$

Problem 11.10 Find the hybrid parameters for the network.

Solution:

The given circuit can be redrawn as shown below.

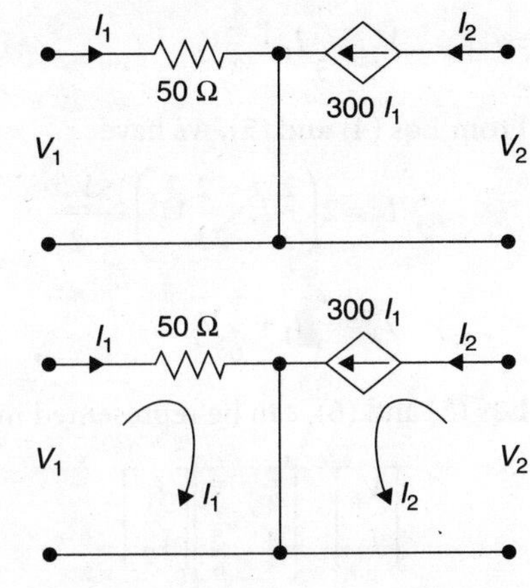

Applying KVL to loop-1

$$V_1 = 50I_1$$

From loop-2, we have

$$I_2 = 300I_1$$

The above equations can be written in the matrix form as follows

$$\begin{bmatrix} V_1 \\ I_2 \end{bmatrix} = \begin{bmatrix} 50 & 0 \\ 300 & 0 \end{bmatrix} \begin{bmatrix} I_1 \\ V_2 \end{bmatrix} \quad (1)$$

The h-parameters are given as

$$\begin{bmatrix} V_1 \\ I_2 \end{bmatrix} = \begin{bmatrix} h_{11} & h_{12} \\ h_{21} & h_{22} \end{bmatrix} \begin{bmatrix} I_1 \\ V_2 \end{bmatrix} \quad (2)$$

Comparing Eqs (1) and (2), we can get

$$h_{11} = 50, h_{12} = 0, h_{21} = 300, h_{22} = 0$$

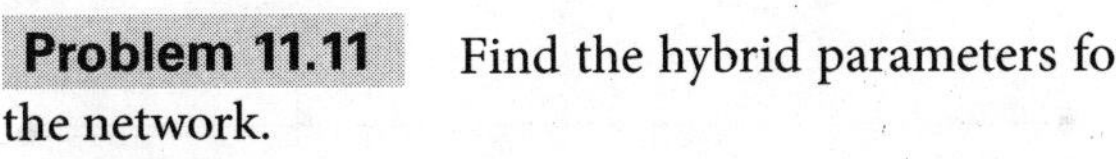

Problem 11.11 Find the hybrid parameters for the network.

Solution:

The given circuit can be redrawn as shown below.

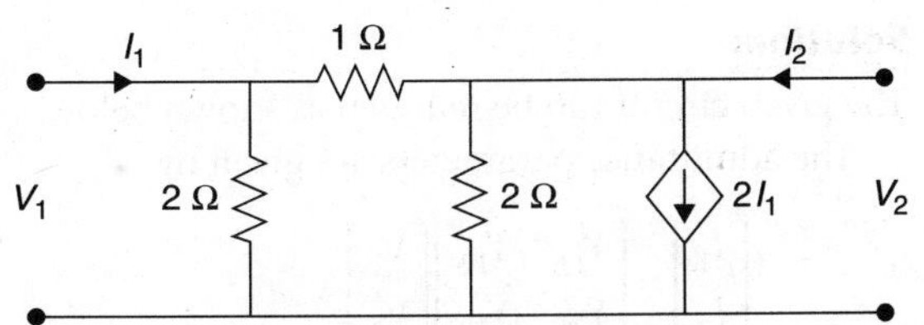

The hybrid parameters are given by

$$\begin{bmatrix} V_1 \\ I_2 \end{bmatrix} = \begin{bmatrix} h_{11} & h_{12} \\ h_{21} & h_{22} \end{bmatrix} \begin{bmatrix} I_1 \\ V_2 \end{bmatrix} \quad (1)$$

Applying KCL at node-1

$$I_1 = \frac{V_1}{2} + \frac{V_1 - V_2}{1} = \frac{3V_1}{2} - V_2 \quad (2)$$

Applying KCL at node-2

$$I_2 = \frac{V_2}{2} + \frac{V_2 - V_1}{1} + 2I_1 = \frac{3V_2}{2} - V_1 + 2I_1 \quad (3)$$

From Eqs (2) and (3), we have

$$I_2 = \frac{3V_2}{2} - V_1 + 2\left(\frac{3V_1}{2} - V_2\right) = 2V_1 - \frac{V_2}{2} \quad (4)$$

From Eq. (2), we have

$$\frac{3V_1}{2} = I_1 + V_2$$

$$\Rightarrow \quad V_1 = \frac{2}{3}I_1 + \frac{2}{3}V_2 \quad (5)$$

From Eqs (4) and (5), we have

$$I_2 = 2\left(\frac{2}{3}I_1 + \frac{2}{3}V_2\right) - \frac{V_2}{2}$$

$$\Rightarrow \quad I_2 = \frac{4}{3}I_1 + \frac{5}{6}V_2 \quad (6)$$

Eqs (5) and (6), can be represented into matrix form

$$\begin{bmatrix} V_1 \\ I_2 \end{bmatrix} = \begin{bmatrix} \frac{2}{3} & \frac{2}{3} \\ \frac{4}{3} & \frac{5}{6} \end{bmatrix} \begin{bmatrix} I_1 \\ V_2 \end{bmatrix} \quad (7)$$

Comparing Eqs (1) and (7), the h-parameters are

$$h_{11} = \frac{2}{3}, h_{12} = \frac{2}{3}, h_{21} = \frac{4}{3}, h_{22} = \frac{5}{6}$$

Problem 11.12 . Determine the admittance parameters for the network.

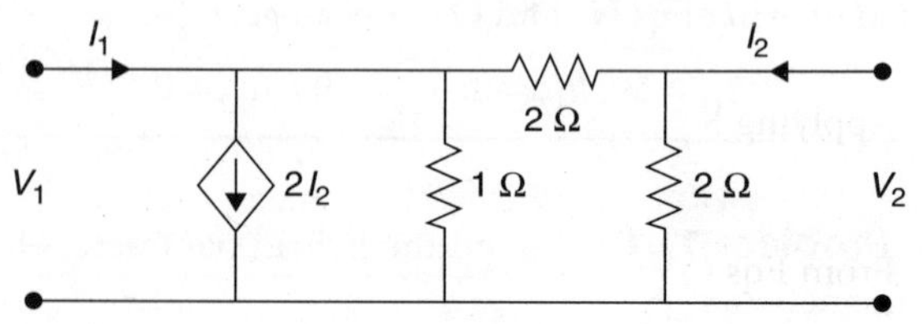

Solution:

The given circuit can be redrawn as shown below.

The admittance parameters are given by

$$\begin{bmatrix} I_1 \\ I_2 \end{bmatrix} = \begin{bmatrix} Y_{11} & Y_{12} \\ Y_{21} & Y_{22} \end{bmatrix} \begin{bmatrix} V_1 \\ V_2 \end{bmatrix} \quad (1)$$

Applying KCL at node-1

$$I_1 = \frac{V_1}{1} + \frac{V_1 - V_2}{2} + 2I_2 = \frac{3V_1}{2} - \frac{V_2}{2} + 2I_2 \quad (2)$$

Applying KCL at node-2

$$I_2 = \frac{V_2}{2} + \frac{V_2 - V_1}{2} = -\frac{V_1}{2} + V_2 \quad (3)$$

From Eqs (2) and (3), we have

$$I_1 = \frac{3V_1}{2} - \frac{V_2}{2} + 2\left(-\frac{V_1}{2} + V_2\right) = \frac{V_1}{2} + \frac{3V_2}{2} \quad (4)$$

Eqs (4) and (3), can be represented into matrix form

$$\begin{bmatrix} I_1 \\ I_2 \end{bmatrix} = \begin{bmatrix} \frac{1}{2} & \frac{3}{2} \\ -\frac{1}{2} & 1 \end{bmatrix} \begin{bmatrix} V_1 \\ V_2 \end{bmatrix} \quad (5)$$

Comparing Eqs (1) and (5), we have

$$Y_{11} = \frac{1}{2}, \quad Y_{12} = \frac{3}{2}, \quad Y_{21} = -\frac{1}{2}, \quad Y_{22} = 1$$

Problem 11.13 Find the Z-parameters for the network.

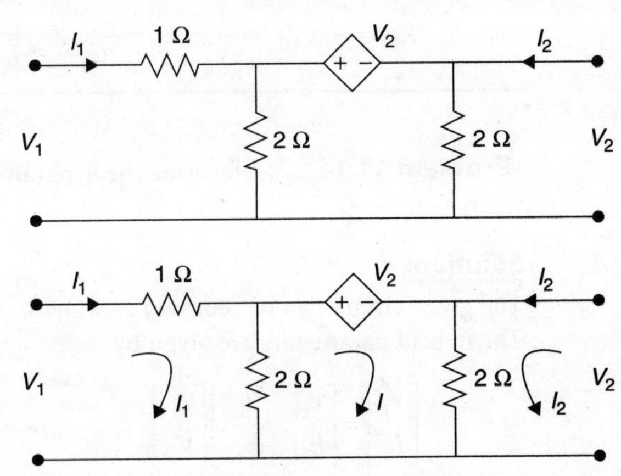

Solution:

The given circuit can be redrawn as

The Z-parameters are given by

$$\begin{bmatrix} V_1 \\ V_2 \end{bmatrix} = \begin{bmatrix} Z_{11} & Z_{12} \\ Z_{21} & Z_{22} \end{bmatrix} \begin{bmatrix} I_1 \\ I_2 \end{bmatrix} \quad (1)$$

Applying KVL to loop-1

$$V_1 = I_1 + 2(I_1 - I) = 3I_1 - 2I \quad (2)$$

Applying KVL to loop-2

$$V_2 + 2(I_2 + I) + 2(I - I_1) = 0$$

$$4I + 2I_2 - 2I_1 + V_2 = 0$$

$$I = \frac{1}{4}(-2I_2 + 2I_1 - V_2) \quad (3)$$

Applying KVL to loop-3

$$V_2 = 2I_2 + 2I \quad (4)$$

From Eqs (3) and (4), we have

$$V_2 = 2I_2 + \frac{2}{4}(-2I_2 + 2I_1 - V_2) = I_2 + I_1 - \frac{1}{2}V_2$$

$$\Rightarrow \qquad V_2 = \frac{2}{3}I_1 + \frac{2}{3}I_2 \tag{5}$$

From Eqs (2) and (3), we have

$$V_1 = 3I_1 - 2 \times \frac{1}{4}(-2I_2 + 2I_1 - V_2)$$

$$\Rightarrow \qquad V_1 = 2I_1 + I_2 + \frac{1}{2}V_2 \tag{6}$$

From Eqs (5) and (6), we have

$$V_1 = 2I_1 + I_2 + \frac{1}{2}\left(\frac{2}{3}I_1 + \frac{2}{3}I_2\right)$$

$$\Rightarrow \qquad V_1 = \frac{7}{3}I_1 + \frac{4}{3}I_2 \tag{7}$$

Writing Eqs (7) and (5) in the matrix form, we have

$$\begin{bmatrix} V_1 \\ V_2 \end{bmatrix} = \begin{bmatrix} \frac{7}{3} & \frac{4}{3} \\ \frac{2}{3} & \frac{2}{3} \end{bmatrix} \begin{bmatrix} I_1 \\ I_2 \end{bmatrix} \tag{8}$$

Comparing Eqs (1) and (8), we have

$$Z_{11} = \frac{7}{3}, \quad Z_{12} = \frac{4}{3}, \quad Z_{21} = \frac{2}{3}, \quad Z_{22} = \frac{2}{3}$$

Problem 11.14 Determine the h-parameters for the network.

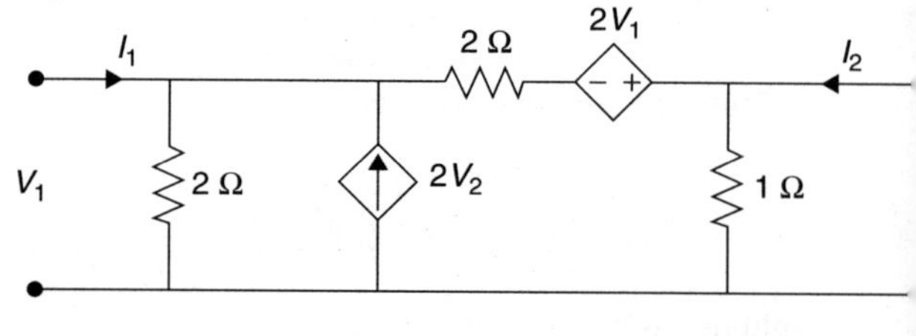

Solution:

The given circuit can be redrawn as shown.
The hybrid parameters are given by

$$\begin{bmatrix} V_1 \\ I_2 \end{bmatrix} = \begin{bmatrix} h_{11} & h_{12} \\ h_{21} & h_{22} \end{bmatrix} \begin{bmatrix} I_1 \\ V_2 \end{bmatrix} \tag{1}$$

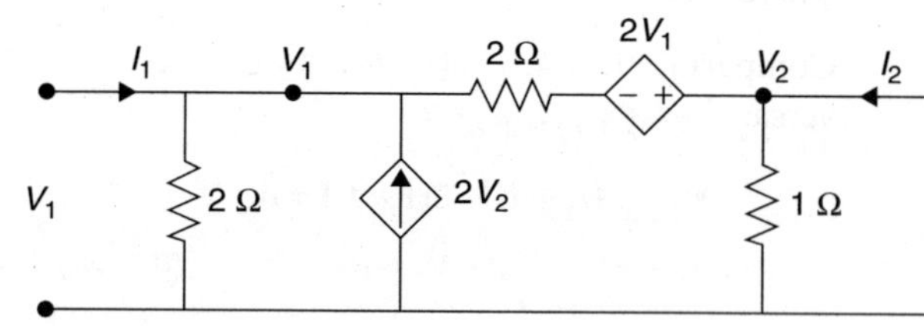

Applying KCL at node-1

$$I_1 + 2V_2 = \frac{V_1}{2} + \frac{V_1 - V_2 + 2V_1}{2}$$

$$\Rightarrow \qquad I_1 = 2V_1 - \frac{5}{2}V_2$$

$$\Rightarrow \qquad V_1 = \frac{1}{2}I_1 + \frac{5}{4}V_2 \tag{2}$$

Applying KCL at node-2

$$I_2 = \frac{V_2}{1} + \frac{V_2 - V_1 - 2V_1}{2} = -\frac{3V_1}{2} + \frac{3V_2}{2} \tag{3}$$

From Eqs (2) and (3), we have

$$I_2 = -\frac{3}{2} \times \left(\frac{1}{2} I_1 + \frac{5}{4} V_2 \right) + \frac{3V_2}{2}$$

$$\Rightarrow \qquad I_2 = -\frac{3}{4} I_1 - \frac{3}{8} V_2 \tag{4}$$

Equations (2) and (4), can be represented in the matrix form

$$\begin{bmatrix} V_1 \\ I_2 \end{bmatrix} = \begin{bmatrix} \frac{1}{2} & \frac{5}{4} \\ -\frac{3}{4} & -\frac{3}{8} \end{bmatrix} \begin{bmatrix} I_1 \\ V_2 \end{bmatrix} \tag{5}$$

Comparing Eqs (1) and (5), the h-parameters are

$$h_{11} = \frac{1}{2}, h_{12} = \frac{5}{4}, h_{21} = -\frac{3}{4}, h_{22} = -\frac{3}{8}$$

11.9 CONVERSION BETWEEN TWO-PORT NETWORK PARAMETERS

Sometimes it becomes necessary to convert one set of parameters to another. This helps in simplifying some electrical network problems easily. We now take various cases of conversion of parameters.

Case (i): Conversion between Z and Y parameters

Since Z and Y parameters are inverse to each other we can write

$$\begin{bmatrix} Z_{11} & Z_{12} \\ Z_{21} & Z_{22} \end{bmatrix} = \begin{bmatrix} Y_{11} & Y_{12} \\ Y_{21} & Y_{22} \end{bmatrix}^{-1} = \frac{1}{\Delta Y} \begin{bmatrix} Y_{22} & -Y_{12} \\ -Y_{21} & Y_{11} \end{bmatrix} \tag{11.56}$$

where $\Delta Y = Y_{11} Y_{22} - Y_{12} Y_{21}$

$$\begin{bmatrix} Y_{11} & Y_{12} \\ Y_{21} & Y_{22} \end{bmatrix} = \begin{bmatrix} Z_{11} & Z_{12} \\ Z_{21} & Z_{22} \end{bmatrix}^{-1} = \frac{1}{\Delta Z} \begin{bmatrix} Z_{22} & -Z_{12} \\ -Z_{21} & Z_{11} \end{bmatrix} \tag{11.57}$$

where $\Delta Z = Z_{11} Z_{22} - Z_{12} Z_{21}$

Comparing the above equations, we can now write the Z-parameters in terms of the Y-parameters and vice versa:

$$Z_{11} = \frac{Y_{22}}{\Delta Y}, \quad Z_{12} = \frac{-Y_{12}}{\Delta Y}, \quad Z_{21} = \frac{-Y_{21}}{\Delta Y}, \quad Z_{22} = \frac{Y_{11}}{\Delta Y} \tag{11.58}$$

$$Y_{11} = \frac{Z_{22}}{\Delta Z}, \quad Y_{12} = \frac{-Z_{12}}{\Delta Z}, \quad Y_{21} = \frac{-Z_{21}}{\Delta Z}, \quad Y_{22} = \frac{Z_{11}}{\Delta Z} \tag{11.59}$$

Case (ii): Conversion between Z and $ABCD$ parameters

The ABCD parameters are given by

$$\left. \begin{aligned} V_1 &= AV_2 - BI_2 \\ I_1 &= CV_2 - DI_2 \end{aligned} \right\} \tag{11.60}$$

$$\Rightarrow \quad CV_2 = I_1 + DI_2$$

$$\Rightarrow \quad V_2 = \frac{1}{C}I_1 + \frac{D}{C}I_2 \tag{11.61}$$

Also $$V_1 = A\left(\frac{1}{C}I_1 + \frac{D}{C}I_2\right) - BI_2 = \frac{A}{C}I_1 + \frac{(AD-BC)}{C}I_2 \tag{11.62}$$

Equations 11.62 and 11.61 can be written in the matrix form

$$\begin{bmatrix} V_1 \\ V_2 \end{bmatrix} = \begin{bmatrix} \frac{A}{C} & \frac{AD-BC}{C} \\ \frac{1}{C} & \frac{D}{C} \end{bmatrix} \begin{bmatrix} I_1 \\ I_2 \end{bmatrix} \tag{11.63}$$

The Z-parameters equations are

$$\begin{bmatrix} V_1 \\ V_2 \end{bmatrix} = \begin{bmatrix} Z_{11} & Z_{12} \\ Z_{21} & Z_{22} \end{bmatrix} \begin{bmatrix} I_1 \\ I_2 \end{bmatrix} \tag{11.64}$$

Comparing Eqs 11.63 and 11.64, we have

$$Z_{11} = \frac{A}{C}, \quad Z_{12} = \frac{(AD-BC)}{C}, \quad Z_{21} = \frac{1}{C}, \quad Z_{22} = \frac{D}{C}$$

Similarly to find ABCD parameters in terms of the Z-parameters, we proceed as follows.

The Z-parameters are given by

$$\left.\begin{aligned} V_1 &= Z_{11}I_1 + Z_{12}I_2 \\ V_2 &= Z_{21}I_1 + Z_{22}I_2 \end{aligned}\right\} \tag{11.65}$$

$$\Rightarrow \quad Z_{21}I_1 = V_2 - Z_{22}I_2$$

$$\Rightarrow \quad I_1 = \frac{1}{Z_{21}}V_2 - \frac{Z_{22}}{Z_{21}}I_2 \tag{11.66}$$

Also

$$V_1 = Z_{11}\left(\frac{1}{Z_{21}}V_2 - \frac{Z_{22}}{Z_{21}}I_2\right) + Z_{12}I_2 = \frac{Z_{11}}{Z_{21}}V_2 - \left(\frac{Z_{11}Z_{22} - Z_{12}Z_{21}}{Z_{21}}\right)I_2 \tag{11.67}$$

Equations 11.67 and 11.66 can be written in the matrix form

$$\begin{bmatrix} V_1 \\ I_1 \end{bmatrix} = \begin{bmatrix} \frac{Z_{11}}{Z_{21}} & \frac{Z_{11}Z_{22} - Z_{12}Z_{21}}{Z_{21}} \\ \frac{1}{Z_{21}} & \frac{Z_{22}}{Z_{21}} \end{bmatrix} \begin{bmatrix} V_2 \\ -I_2 \end{bmatrix} \tag{11.68}$$

The $ABCD$ parameter equations are

$$\begin{bmatrix} V_1 \\ I_1 \end{bmatrix} = \begin{bmatrix} A & B \\ C & D \end{bmatrix} \begin{bmatrix} V_2 \\ -I_2 \end{bmatrix} \tag{11.69}$$

Comparing Eqs 11.68 and 11.69, we have

$$A = \frac{Z_{11}}{Z_{21}}, \quad B = \frac{Z_{11}Z_{22} - Z_{12}Z_{21}}{Z_{21}}, \quad C = \frac{1}{Z_{21}}, \quad D = \frac{Z_{22}}{Z_{21}} \tag{11.70}$$

Case (iii): Conversion between Z and $A'B'C'D'$ parameters

The $A'B'C'D'$ parameters are given by

$$\left.\begin{aligned} V_2 &= A'V_1 - B'I_1 \\ I_2 &= C'V_1 - D'I_1 \end{aligned}\right\} \tag{11.71}$$

$$C'V = I_2 + D'I_1$$

$$V_1 = \frac{D'}{C'}I_1 + \frac{1}{C'}I_2 \tag{11.72}$$

Also,

$$V_2 = A'\left(\frac{D'}{C'}I_1 + \frac{1}{C'}I_2\right) - B'I_1 = \left(\frac{A'D' - B'C'}{C'}\right)I_1 - \frac{A'}{C'}I_2 \tag{11.73}$$

Equations 11.72 and 11.75 can be written in the matrix form

$$\begin{bmatrix} V_1 \\ V_2 \end{bmatrix} = \begin{bmatrix} \frac{D'}{C'} & \frac{1}{C'} \\ \frac{A'D' - B'C'}{C'} & \frac{A'}{C'} \end{bmatrix} \begin{bmatrix} I_1 \\ I_2 \end{bmatrix} \tag{11.74}$$

The Z-parameters equations are

$$\begin{bmatrix} V_1 \\ V_2 \end{bmatrix} = \begin{bmatrix} Z_{11} & Z_{12} \\ Z_{21} & Z_{22} \end{bmatrix} \begin{bmatrix} I_1 \\ I_2 \end{bmatrix} \tag{11.75}$$

Comparing Eqs 11.75 and 11.74, we have

$$Z_{11} = \frac{D'}{C'}, \quad Z_{12} = \frac{1}{C'}, \quad Z_{21} = \frac{A'D' - B'C'}{C'}, \quad Z_{22} = \frac{A'}{C'} \tag{11.76}$$

Similarly to find the $A'B'C'D'$ parameters in terms of the Z-parameters we proceed as follows:

The Z-parameters are given by

$$\left.\begin{aligned} V_1 &= Z_{11}I_1 + Z_{12}I_2 \\ V_2 &= Z_{21}I_1 + Z_{22}I_2 \end{aligned}\right\} \tag{11.77}$$

$$\Rightarrow \quad Z_{12}I_2 = V_1 - Z_{11}I_1$$

$$\Rightarrow \quad I_2 = \frac{1}{Z_{12}}V_1 - \frac{Z_{11}}{Z_{12}}I_1 \tag{11.78}$$

Also, $$V_2 = Z_{21}I_1 + Z_{22}\left(\frac{1}{Z_{12}}V_1 - \frac{Z_{11}}{Z_{12}}I_1\right) = \frac{Z_{22}}{Z_{12}}V_1 - \frac{Z_{12}Z_{21} - Z_{11}Z_{22}}{Z_{12}}I_1 \tag{11.79}$$

Equations 11.79 and 11.78 can be written in the matrix form

$$\begin{bmatrix} V_2 \\ I_2 \end{bmatrix} = \begin{bmatrix} \frac{Z_{22}}{Z_{12}} & \frac{Z_{12}Z_{21} - Z_{11}Z_{22}}{Z_{12}} \\ \frac{1}{Z_{12}} & \frac{Z_{11}}{Z_{12}} \end{bmatrix} \begin{bmatrix} V_1 \\ -I_1 \end{bmatrix} \tag{11.80}$$

The $A'B'C'D'$-parameters equations are

$$\begin{bmatrix} V_2 \\ I_2 \end{bmatrix} = \begin{bmatrix} A' & B' \\ C' & D' \end{bmatrix} \begin{bmatrix} V_1 \\ -I_1 \end{bmatrix} \tag{11.81}$$

Comparing Eqs 11.80 and 11.81, we have

$$A' = \frac{Z_{22}}{Z_{12}}, \quad B' = \frac{Z_{12}Z_{21} - Z_{11}Z_{22}}{Z_{12}}, \quad C' = \frac{1}{Z_{12}}, \quad D' = \frac{Z_{11}}{Z_{12}} \tag{11.82}$$

Case (iv): Conversion between Z and h-parameters

The h-parameters are given by

$$\left.\begin{aligned} V_1 &= h_{11}I_1 + h_{12}I_2 \\ I_2 &= h_{21}I_1 + h_{22}V_2 \end{aligned}\right\} \tag{11.83}$$

$$\Rightarrow \qquad h_{22}V_2 = -h_{21}I_1 + I_2$$

$$\Rightarrow \qquad V_2 = \frac{-h_{21}}{h_{22}}I_1 + \frac{1}{h_{22}}I_2 \tag{11.84}$$

Also, $$V_1 = h_{11}I_1 + h_{12}\left(\frac{-h_{21}}{h_{22}}I_1 + \frac{1}{h_{22}}I_2\right) = \left(\frac{h_{11}h_{22} - h_{12}h_{21}}{h_{22}}\right)I_1 + \frac{h_{12}}{h_{22}}I_2 \tag{11.85}$$

Equations 11.85 and 11.84 can be written in the matrix form

$$\begin{bmatrix} V_1 \\ V_2 \end{bmatrix} = \begin{bmatrix} \dfrac{h_{11}h_{22} - h_{12}h_{21}}{h_{22}} & \dfrac{h_{12}}{h_{22}} \\ \dfrac{-h_{21}}{h_{22}} & \dfrac{1}{h_{22}} \end{bmatrix} \begin{bmatrix} I_1 \\ I_2 \end{bmatrix} \tag{11.86}$$

The Z-parameters equations are

$$\begin{bmatrix} V_1 \\ V_2 \end{bmatrix} = \begin{bmatrix} Z_{11} & Z_{12} \\ Z_{21} & Z_{22} \end{bmatrix} \begin{bmatrix} I_1 \\ I_2 \end{bmatrix} \tag{11.87}$$

Comparing Eqs 11.86 and 11.87, we have

$$Z_{11} = \frac{h_{11}h_{22} - h_{12}h_{21}}{h_{22}}, \quad Z_{12} = \frac{h_{12}}{h_{22}}, \quad Z_{21} = \frac{-h_{21}}{h_{22}}, \quad Z_{22} = \frac{1}{h_{22}} \tag{11.88}$$

Similarly to find h-parameters in terms of Z-parameters we proceed as follows.

The Z-parameters are given by

$$\left.\begin{aligned} V_1 &= Z_{11}I_1 + Z_{12}I_2 \\ V_2 &= Z_{21}I_1 + Z_{22}I_2 \end{aligned}\right\} \tag{11.89}$$

$$\Rightarrow \qquad Z_{22}I_2 = -Z_{21}I_1 + V_2$$

$$\Rightarrow \qquad I_2 = \frac{-Z_{21}}{Z_{22}}I_1 + \frac{1}{Z_{22}}V_2 \tag{11.90}$$

Also, $$V_1 = Z_{11}I_1 + Z_{12}\left(\frac{-Z_{21}}{Z_{22}}I_1 + \frac{1}{Z_{22}}V_2\right) = \left(\frac{Z_{11}Z_{22} - Z_{12}Z_{21}}{Z_{22}}\right)I_1 + \frac{Z_{12}}{Z_{22}}V_2 \tag{11.91}$$

Equations 11.91 and 11.90 can be written in the matrix form

$$\begin{bmatrix} V_1 \\ I_2 \end{bmatrix} = \begin{bmatrix} \dfrac{Z_{11}Z_{22} - Z_{12}Z_{21}}{Z_{22}} & \dfrac{Z_{12}}{Z_{22}} \\ \dfrac{-Z_{21}}{Z_{22}} & \dfrac{1}{Z_{22}} \end{bmatrix} \begin{bmatrix} I_1 \\ V_2 \end{bmatrix} \tag{11.92}$$

The h-parameter equations are

$$\begin{bmatrix} V_1 \\ I_2 \end{bmatrix} = \begin{bmatrix} h_{11} & h_{12} \\ h_{21} & h_{22} \end{bmatrix} \begin{bmatrix} I_1 \\ V_2 \end{bmatrix} \tag{11.93}$$

Comparing Eqs 11.92 and 11.93, we have

$$h_{11} = \frac{Z_{11}Z_{22} - Z_{12}Z_{21}}{Z_{22}}, \quad h_{12} = \frac{Z_{12}}{Z_{22}}, \quad h_{21} = \frac{-Z_{21}}{Z_{22}}, \quad h_{22} = \frac{1}{Z_{22}}$$

Case (v): Conversion between Z and g-parameters

The g-parameters are given by

$$\left.\begin{aligned} I_1 &= g_{11}V_1 + g_{12}I_2 \\ V_2 &= g_{21}V_1 + g_{22}I_2 \end{aligned}\right\} \tag{11.94}$$

$$\Rightarrow \qquad g_{11}V_1 = I_1 - g_{12}I_2$$

$$\Rightarrow \qquad V_1 = \frac{1}{g_{11}}I_1 - \frac{g_{12}}{g_{11}}I_2 \tag{11.95}$$

Also, $$V_2 = g_{21}\left(\frac{1}{g_{11}}I_1 - \frac{g_{12}}{g_{11}}I_2\right) + g_{22}I_2 = \frac{g_{21}}{g_{11}}I_1 + \left(\frac{g_{11}g_{22} - g_{12}g_{21}}{g_{11}}\right)I_2 \tag{11.96}$$

Equations 11.95 and 11.96 can be written into matrix form

$$\begin{bmatrix} V_1 \\ V_2 \end{bmatrix} = \begin{bmatrix} \dfrac{1}{g_{11}} & -\dfrac{g_{12}}{g_{11}} \\ \dfrac{g_{21}}{g_{11}} & \dfrac{g_{11}g_{22} - g_{12}g_{21}}{g_{11}} \end{bmatrix} \begin{bmatrix} I_1 \\ I_2 \end{bmatrix} \tag{11.97}$$

The Z-parameters equations are

$$\begin{bmatrix} V_1 \\ V_2 \end{bmatrix} = \begin{bmatrix} Z_{11} & Z_{12} \\ Z_{21} & Z_{22} \end{bmatrix} \begin{bmatrix} I_1 \\ I_2 \end{bmatrix} \tag{11.98}$$

Comparing Eqs 11.97 and 11.98, we have

$$Z_{11} = \frac{1}{g_{11}}, \quad Z_{12} = -\frac{g_{12}}{g_{11}}, \quad Z_{21} = \frac{g_{21}}{g_{11}}, \quad Z_{22} = \frac{g_{11}g_{22} - g_{12}g_{21}}{g_{11}} \tag{11.99}$$

Similarly to find h-parameters in terms of Z-parameters we proceed as follows.
The Z-parameters are given by

$$\left.\begin{aligned} V_1 &= Z_{11}I_1 + Z_{12}I_2 \\ V_2 &= Z_{21}I_1 + Z_{22}I_2 \end{aligned}\right\} \tag{11.100}$$

$$\Rightarrow \qquad Z_{11}I_1 = V_1 - Z_{12}I_2$$

$$\Rightarrow \qquad I_1 = \frac{1}{Z_{11}}V_1 - \frac{Z_{12}}{Z_{11}}I_2 \tag{11.101}$$

Also,
$$V_2 = Z_{21}\left(\frac{1}{Z_{11}}V_1 - \frac{Z_{12}}{Z_{11}}I_2\right) + Z_{22}I_2 = \frac{Z_{21}}{Z_{11}}V_1 + \left(\frac{Z_{11}Z_{22} - Z_{21}Z_{12}}{Z_{11}}\right)I_2 \tag{11.102}$$

Equations 11.101 and 11.102 can be written in the matrix form

$$\begin{bmatrix} I_1 \\ V_2 \end{bmatrix} = \begin{bmatrix} \frac{1}{Z_{11}} & -\frac{Z_{12}}{Z_{11}} \\ \frac{Z_{21}}{Z_{11}} & \frac{Z_{11}Z_{22}-Z_{21}Z_{12}}{Z_{11}} \end{bmatrix} \begin{bmatrix} V_1 \\ I_2 \end{bmatrix} \tag{11.103}$$

The g-parameter equations are

$$\begin{bmatrix} I_1 \\ V_2 \end{bmatrix} = \begin{bmatrix} g_{11} & g_{12} \\ g_{21} & g_{22} \end{bmatrix} \begin{bmatrix} V_1 \\ I_2 \end{bmatrix} \tag{11.104}$$

Comparing Eqs 11.103 and 11.104, we have

$$g_{11} = \frac{1}{Z_{11}},\quad g_{12} = -\frac{Z_{12}}{Z_{11}},\quad g_{21} = \frac{Z_{21}}{Z_{11}},\quad g_{22} = \frac{Z_{11}Z_{22} - Z_{21}Z_{12}}{Z_{11}} \tag{11.105}$$

In a similar manner we can find one parameter in terms of other parameters. The summary of conversion of parameters is given in Table 11.3.

Table 11.3 Summary of interrelationships between two-port network parameters

In terms of/ Parameter	[Z]	[Y]	[T]	[T′]	[h]	[g]
[Z]	$\begin{matrix} Z_{11} & Z_{12} \\ Z_{21} & Z_{22} \end{matrix}$	$\begin{matrix} \frac{Y_{22}}{\Delta Y} & -\frac{Y_{12}}{\Delta Y} \\ -\frac{Y_{21}}{\Delta Y} & \frac{Y_{11}}{\Delta Y} \end{matrix}$	$\begin{matrix} \frac{A}{C} & \frac{\Delta T}{C} \\ \frac{1}{C} & \frac{D}{C} \end{matrix}$	$\begin{matrix} \frac{D'}{C'} & \frac{1}{C'} \\ \frac{\Delta T'}{C'} & \frac{A'}{C'} \end{matrix}$	$\begin{matrix} \frac{\Delta h}{h_{22}} & \frac{h_{12}}{h_{22}} \\ -\frac{h_{21}}{h_{22}} & \frac{1}{h_{22}} \end{matrix}$	$\begin{matrix} \frac{1}{g_{11}} & -\frac{g_{12}}{g_{11}} \\ \frac{g_{21}}{g_{11}} & \frac{\Delta g}{g_{11}} \end{matrix}$
[Y]	$\begin{matrix} \frac{Z_{22}}{\Delta Z} & -\frac{Z_{12}}{\Delta Z} \\ -\frac{Z_{21}}{\Delta Z} & \frac{Z_{11}}{\Delta Z} \end{matrix}$	$\begin{matrix} Y_{11} & Y_{12} \\ Y_{21} & Y_{22} \end{matrix}$	$\begin{matrix} \frac{D}{B} & -\frac{\Delta T}{B} \\ -\frac{1}{B} & \frac{A}{B} \end{matrix}$	$\begin{matrix} \frac{A'}{B'} & -\frac{1}{B'} \\ \frac{\Delta T'}{B'} & \frac{D'}{B'} \end{matrix}$	$\begin{matrix} \frac{1}{h_{11}} & -\frac{h_{12}}{h_{11}} \\ \frac{h_{21}}{h_{11}} & \frac{\Delta h}{h_{11}} \end{matrix}$	$\begin{matrix} \frac{\Delta g}{g_{22}} & \frac{g_{12}}{g_{22}} \\ -\frac{g_{21}}{g_{22}} & \frac{1}{g_{22}} \end{matrix}$
[T]	$\begin{matrix} \frac{Z_{11}}{Z_{21}} & \frac{\Delta Z}{Z_{21}} \\ \frac{1}{Z_{21}} & \frac{Z_{22}}{Z_{21}} \end{matrix}$	$\begin{matrix} -\frac{Y_{22}}{Y_{21}} & -\frac{1}{Y_{21}} \\ -\frac{\Delta Y}{Y_{21}} & -\frac{Y_{11}}{Y_{21}} \end{matrix}$	$\begin{matrix} A & B \\ C & D \end{matrix}$	$\begin{matrix} \frac{D'}{\Delta T'} & \frac{B'}{\Delta T'} \\ \frac{C'}{\Delta T'} & \frac{A'}{\Delta T'} \end{matrix}$	$\begin{matrix} -\frac{\Delta h}{h_{21}} & -\frac{h_{11}}{h_{21}} \\ -\frac{h_{22}}{h_{21}} & -\frac{1}{h_{21}} \end{matrix}$	$\begin{matrix} \frac{1}{g_{21}} & \frac{g_{22}}{g_{21}} \\ \frac{g_{11}}{g_{21}} & \frac{\Delta g}{g_{21}} \end{matrix}$
[T′]	$\begin{matrix} \frac{Z_{22}}{Z_{12}} & \frac{\Delta Z}{Z_{12}} \\ \frac{1}{Z_{12}} & \frac{Z_{11}}{Z_{12}} \end{matrix}$	$\begin{matrix} -\frac{Y_{11}}{Y_{12}} & -\frac{1}{Y_{12}} \\ -\frac{\Delta Y}{Y_{12}} & -\frac{Y_{22}}{Y_{12}} \end{matrix}$	$\begin{matrix} \frac{D}{\Delta T} & \frac{B}{\Delta T} \\ \frac{C}{\Delta T} & \frac{A}{\Delta T} \end{matrix}$	$\begin{matrix} A' & B' \\ C' & D' \end{matrix}$	$\begin{matrix} \frac{1}{h_{12}} & \frac{h_{11}}{h_{12}} \\ \frac{h_{22}}{h_{12}} & \frac{\Delta h}{h_{12}} \end{matrix}$	$\begin{matrix} -\frac{\Delta g}{g_{12}} & -\frac{g_{22}}{g_{12}} \\ -\frac{g_{11}}{g_{12}} & -\frac{1}{g_{12}} \end{matrix}$
[h]	$\begin{matrix} \frac{\Delta Z}{Z_{22}} & \frac{Z_{12}}{Z_{22}} \\ -\frac{Z_{21}}{Z_{22}} & \frac{1}{Z_{22}} \end{matrix}$	$\begin{matrix} \frac{1}{Y_{11}} & -\frac{Y_{12}}{Y_{11}} \\ \frac{Y_{21}}{Y_{11}} & \frac{\Delta Y}{Y_{11}} \end{matrix}$	$\begin{matrix} \frac{B}{D} & \frac{\Delta T}{D} \\ -\frac{1}{D} & \frac{C}{D} \end{matrix}$	$\begin{matrix} \frac{B'}{A'} & \frac{1}{A'} \\ -\frac{\Delta T'}{A'} & \frac{C'}{A'} \end{matrix}$	$\begin{matrix} h_{11} & h_{12} \\ h_{21} & h_{22} \end{matrix}$	$\begin{matrix} \frac{g_{22}}{\Delta g} & -\frac{g_{12}}{\Delta g} \\ -\frac{g_{21}}{\Delta g} & \frac{g_{11}}{\Delta g} \end{matrix}$
[g]	$\begin{matrix} \frac{1}{Z_{11}} & -\frac{Z_{12}}{Z_{11}} \\ \frac{Z_{21}}{Z_{11}} & \frac{\Delta Z}{Z_{11}} \end{matrix}$	$\begin{matrix} \frac{\Delta Y}{Y_{22}} & \frac{Y_{12}}{Y_{22}} \\ -\frac{Y_{21}}{Y_{22}} & \frac{1}{Y_{22}} \end{matrix}$	$\begin{matrix} \frac{C}{A} & -\frac{\Delta T}{A} \\ \frac{1}{A} & \frac{B}{A} \end{matrix}$	$\begin{matrix} \frac{C'}{D'} & -\frac{1}{D'} \\ \frac{\Delta T'}{D'} & \frac{B'}{D'} \end{matrix}$	$\begin{matrix} \frac{h_{22}}{\Delta h} & -\frac{h_{12}}{\Delta h} \\ -\frac{h_{21}}{\Delta h} & \frac{h_{11}}{\Delta h} \end{matrix}$	$\begin{matrix} g_{11} & g_{12} \\ g_{21} & g_{22} \end{matrix}$

where $\Delta P = P_{11}P_{22} - P_{12}P_{21}$; P may be Z-, Y-, T-, T', h-, and g-parameters

Problem 11.15 The h-parameters of a certain two-port network are $h_{11} = 2\ \Omega$, $h_{12} = 4$, $h_{21} = -4$, $h_{22} = 2\ \mho$. Find the (i) Z-parameters, (ii) Y-parameters, (iii) $ABCD$ parameters, and (vi) $A'B'C'D'$ parameters. And also find whether the network is reciprocal or symmetrical.

Solution:

Given that $h_{11} = 2\ \Omega$, $h_{12} = 4$, $h_{21} = -4$, $h_{22} = 2\ \mho$

So the equations for the h-parameters are given by

$$V_1 = h_{11}I_1 + h_{12}V_2$$

$$I_2 = h_{11}I_1 + h_{22}V_2$$

$$\left.\begin{aligned} V_1 &= 2I_1 + 4V_2 \\ I_2 &= -4I_1 + 2V_2 \end{aligned}\right\} \quad (1)$$

(i) Calculation of Z-parameters

The Z-parameters equations are

$$\begin{bmatrix} V_1 \\ V_2 \end{bmatrix} = \begin{bmatrix} Z_{11} & Z_{12} \\ Z_{21} & Z_{22} \end{bmatrix} \begin{bmatrix} I_1 \\ I_2 \end{bmatrix} \quad (2)$$

From the given h-parameter equations

$$V_1 = 2I_1 + 4V_2$$

$$2V_2 = 4I_1 + I_2$$

$$\Rightarrow \quad V_2 = 2I_1 + 0.5I_2 \quad (3)$$

Also, $V_1 = 2I_1 + 4(2I_1 + 0.5I_2) = 10I_1 + 2I_2$ (4)

Equations (4) and (3), can be represented in the matrix form

$$\begin{bmatrix} V_1 \\ V_2 \end{bmatrix} = \begin{bmatrix} 10 & 2 \\ 2 & 0.5 \end{bmatrix} \begin{bmatrix} I_1 \\ I_2 \end{bmatrix} \quad (5)$$

Comparing Eqs (2) and (5), we have

$$Z_{11} = 10\ \Omega,\ Z_{12} = 2\ \Omega,\ Z_{21} = 2\ \Omega,\ Z_{22} = 0.5\ \Omega$$

Since $Z_{12} = Z_{21} = 2\ \Omega$, the given network is reciprocal.

(ii) Calculation of Y-parameters

The Y-parameters equations are

$$\begin{bmatrix} I_1 \\ I_2 \end{bmatrix} = \begin{bmatrix} Y_{11} & Y_{12} \\ Y_{21} & Y_{22} \end{bmatrix} \begin{bmatrix} V_1 \\ V_2 \end{bmatrix} \quad (6)$$

From the given h-parameters

$$V_1 = 2I_1 + 4V_2$$

$$I_2 = -4I_1 + 2V_2$$

$$\Rightarrow \quad 2I_1 = V_1 - 4V_2$$

$$\Rightarrow \quad I_1 = 0.5V_1 - 2V_2 \quad (7)$$

Also, $I_2 = -4(0.5V_1 - 2V_2) + 2V_2 = -2V_1 + 10V_2$ (8)

Equations (7) and (8) can be represented in the matrix form

$$\begin{bmatrix} I_1 \\ I_2 \end{bmatrix} = \begin{bmatrix} 0.5 & -2 \\ -2 & 10 \end{bmatrix} \begin{bmatrix} V_1 \\ V_2 \end{bmatrix} \quad (9)$$

Comparing Eqs (6) and (9), we have

$$Y_{11} = 0.5\ \mho,\ Y_{12} = -2\ \mho,\ Y_{21} = -2\ \mho,\ Y_{22} = 10\ \mho$$

Since $Y_{12} = Y_{21} = -2\ \mho$, the given network is reciprocal.

(iii) Calculation of ABCD-parameters

The ABCD parameters equations are

$$\begin{bmatrix} V_1 \\ I_1 \end{bmatrix} = \begin{bmatrix} A & B \\ C & D \end{bmatrix} \begin{bmatrix} V_2 \\ -I_2 \end{bmatrix} \quad (10)$$

From the given h-parameters,

$$V_1 = 2I_1 + 4V_2$$

$$I_2 = -4I_1 + 2V_2$$

$$4I_1 = 2V_2 - I_2$$

$$\Rightarrow \quad I_1 = 0.5V_2 - 0.25I_2 \quad (11)$$

Also, $V_1 = 2(0.5V_2 - 0.25I_2) + 4V_2 = 5V_2 - 0.5I_2$ (12)

Equations (12) and (11) can be represented in the matrix form

$$\begin{bmatrix} V_1 \\ I_1 \end{bmatrix} = \begin{bmatrix} 5 & 0.5 \\ 0.5 & 0.25 \end{bmatrix} \begin{bmatrix} V_2 \\ -I_2 \end{bmatrix} \quad (13)$$

Comparing Eqs (10) and (13), we have

$$A = 5,\ B = 0.5,\ C = 0.5,\ D = 0.25$$

Since $AD - BC = 1$, the given network is reciprocal.

(iv) Calculation of $A'B'C'D'$ parameters

The $A'B'C'D'$ parameters equations are

$$\begin{bmatrix} V_2 \\ I_2 \end{bmatrix} = \begin{bmatrix} A' & B' \\ C' & D' \end{bmatrix} \begin{bmatrix} V_1 \\ -I_1 \end{bmatrix} \quad (14)$$

From the given h-parameters

$$V_1 = 2I_1 + 4V_2$$

$$I_2 = -4I_1 + 2V_2$$

$$4V_2 = V_1 - 2I_1$$

$$\Rightarrow \quad V_2 = 0.25V_1 - 0.5I_1 \quad (15)$$

Also, $I_2 = -4I_1 + 2(0.25V_1 - 0.5I_1) = 0.5V_1 - 5I_1$ (16)

Equations (15) and (16) can be represented in the matrix form

$$\begin{bmatrix} V_2 \\ I_2 \end{bmatrix} = \begin{bmatrix} 0.25 & 0.5 \\ 0.5 & 5 \end{bmatrix} \begin{bmatrix} V_1 \\ -I_1 \end{bmatrix} \tag{17}$$

Comparing Eqs (14) and (17), we have

$$A' = 0.25, B' = 0.5, C' = 0.5, D' = 5$$

Since $A'D' - B'C' = 1$, the given network is reciprocal.

11.10 INTERCONNECTION OF TWO-PORT NETWORKS

Two-port networks may be interconnected in various configurations, such as series, parallel, cascade and series–parallel resulting in new two-port networks. For each configuration, a certain set of parameters may be more useful than others to describe the network.

11.10.1 Series Connection of Two-port Networks

Figure 11.13 shows a series connection of two two-port networks X and Y. In series connection, both the networks carry the same input and output currents. The Z-parameters can be used to describe the parameters of the two-port networks connected in series.

If the Z-parameters of network X are $Z'_{11}, Z'_{12}, Z'_{21}, Z'_{22}$ and network Y are $Z''_{11}, Z''_{12}, Z''_{21}, Z''_{22}$, then

For network X,

$$\begin{bmatrix} V'_1 \\ V'_2 \end{bmatrix} = \begin{bmatrix} Z'_{11} & Z'_{12} \\ Z'_{21} & Z'_{22} \end{bmatrix} \begin{bmatrix} I_1 \\ I_2 \end{bmatrix}$$

For network Y,

$$\begin{bmatrix} V''_1 \\ V''_2 \end{bmatrix} = \begin{bmatrix} Z''_{11} & Z''_{12} \\ Z''_{21} & Z''_{21} \end{bmatrix} \begin{bmatrix} I_1 \\ I_2 \end{bmatrix}$$

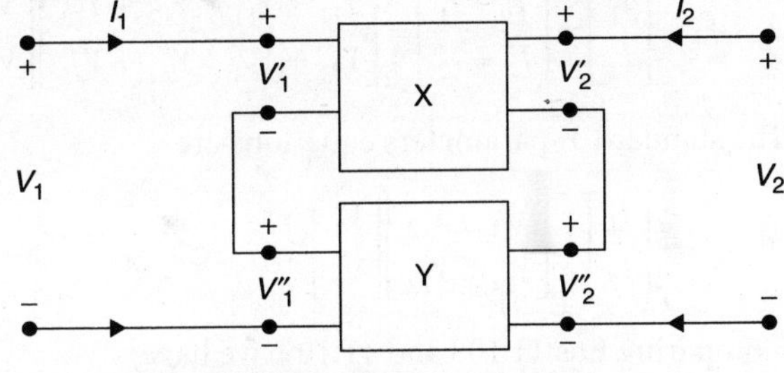

Fig. 11.13 Series connection

For the network diagram shown in Fig. 11.13,

$$V_1 = V'_1 + V''_1$$

$$V_2 = V'_2 + V''_2$$

$$\therefore \quad \begin{bmatrix} V_1 \\ V_2 \end{bmatrix} = \begin{bmatrix} V'_1 + V''_1 \\ V'_2 + V''_2 \end{bmatrix} = \begin{bmatrix} Z'_{11} + Z''_{11} & Z'_{12} + Z''_{12} \\ Z'_{21} + Z''_{21} & Z'_{22} + Z''_{22} \end{bmatrix} \begin{bmatrix} I_1 \\ I_2 \end{bmatrix} \tag{11.106}$$

The standard Z-parameters equations are

$$\begin{bmatrix} V_1 \\ V_2 \end{bmatrix} = \begin{bmatrix} Z_{11} & Z_{12} \\ Z_{21} & Z_{22} \end{bmatrix} \begin{bmatrix} I_1 \\ I_2 \end{bmatrix} \tag{11.107}$$

Comparing Eqs 11.106 and 11.107 we have,

$$Z_{11} = Z'_{11} + Z''_{11}, \quad Z_{12} = Z'_{12} + Z''_{12}$$

$$Z_{21} = Z'_{21} + Z''_{21}, \quad Z_{22} = Z'_{22} + Z''_{22}$$

From the above result we can conclude that the Z-parameters of the series connected two-port network are given as the sum of the corresponding Z-parameters of the individual networks.

11.10.2 Parallel Connection of Two-port Networks

Figure 11.14 shows a parallel connection of two two-port networks X and Y. In parallel connection, both the networks have the same input and output voltages. The Y-parameters can be used to describe the parameters of the parallel connected two-port networks.

If the Y-parameters of network X are $Y'_{11}, Y'_{12}, Y'_{21}, Y'_{22}$ and network Y are $Y''_{11}, Y''_{12}, Y''_{21}, Y''_{22}$, then

For network X,

$$\begin{bmatrix} I'_1 \\ I'_2 \end{bmatrix} = \begin{bmatrix} Y'_{11} & Y'_{12} \\ Y'_{21} & Y'_{22} \end{bmatrix} \begin{bmatrix} V_1 \\ V_2 \end{bmatrix}$$

For network Y,

$$\begin{bmatrix} I''_1 \\ I''_2 \end{bmatrix} = \begin{bmatrix} Y''_{11} & Y''_{12} \\ Y''_{21} & Y''_{22} \end{bmatrix} \begin{bmatrix} V_1 \\ V_2 \end{bmatrix}$$

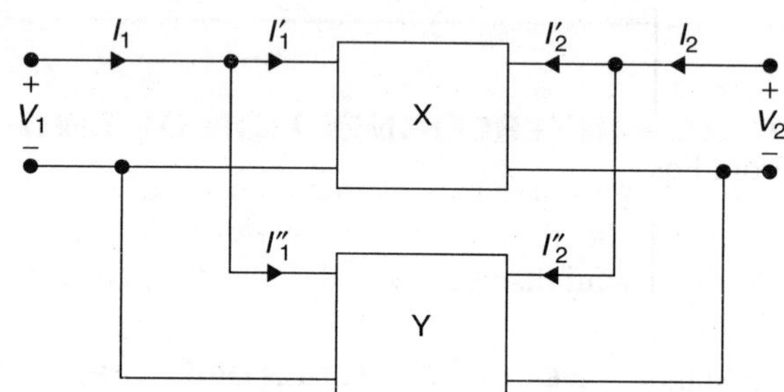

Fig. 11.14 Parallel connection

For the network diagram shown in Fig. 11.14,

$$I_1 = I'_1 + I''_1$$

$$I_2 = I'_2 + I''_2$$

$$\therefore \quad \begin{bmatrix} I_1 \\ I_2 \end{bmatrix} = \begin{bmatrix} I'_1 + I''_1 \\ I'_2 + I''_2 \end{bmatrix} = \begin{bmatrix} Y'_{11} + Y''_{11} & Y'_{12} + Y''_{12} \\ Y'_{21} + Y''_{21} & Y'_{22} + Y''_{22} \end{bmatrix} \begin{bmatrix} V_1 \\ V_2 \end{bmatrix} \tag{11.108}$$

The standard Y-parameters equations are

$$\begin{bmatrix} I_1 \\ I_2 \end{bmatrix} = \begin{bmatrix} Y_{11} & Y_{12} \\ Y_{21} & Y_{22} \end{bmatrix} \begin{bmatrix} V_1 \\ V_2 \end{bmatrix} \tag{11.109}$$

Comparing Eqs 11.108 and 11.109, we have

$$Y_{11} = Y'_{11} + Y''_{11}, \quad Y_{12} = Y'_{12} + Y''_{12}$$

$$Y_{21} = Y'_{21} + Y''_{21}, \quad Y_{22} = Y'_{22} + Y''_{22}$$

From the above result we can conclude that the Y-parameter of the parallel connected two-port network is given as the sum of the corresponding Y-parameters of the individual networks.

11.10.3 Cascade Connection of Two-port Networks

Figure 11.15 shows a cascade connection of two two-port networks X and Y. In the cascade connection, the output port of the first network becomes the input port of the second network. The $ABCD$ parameters can be used to describe the parameters of the cascade connected two-port networks.

If the $ABCD$ parameters of network X are A_1, B_1, C_1, D_1 and network Y are A_2, B_2, C_2, D_1, then

For network X,

$$\begin{bmatrix} V_1 \\ I_1 \end{bmatrix} = \begin{bmatrix} A_1 & B_1 \\ C_1 & D_1 \end{bmatrix} \begin{bmatrix} V'_1 \\ -I'_1 \end{bmatrix} \tag{11.110}$$

For network Y,

$$\begin{bmatrix} V_2' \\ I_2' \end{bmatrix} = \begin{bmatrix} A_2 & B_2 \\ C_2 & D_2 \end{bmatrix} \begin{bmatrix} V_2 \\ -I_2 \end{bmatrix} \quad (11.111)$$

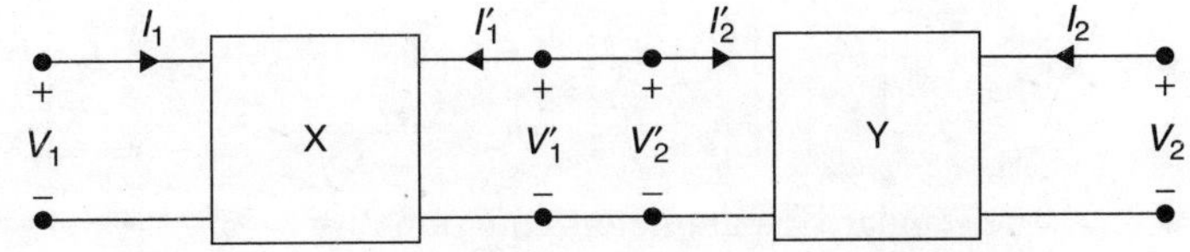

Fig. 11.15 Cascade connection

For the network diagram shown in Fig. 11.15,

$$V_1' = V_2', \quad I_1' = -I_2', \quad (11.112)$$

From Eqs 11.111 and 11.112, we have

$$\begin{bmatrix} V_1' \\ -I_1' \end{bmatrix} = \begin{bmatrix} A_2 & B_2 \\ C_2 & D_2 \end{bmatrix} \begin{bmatrix} V_2 \\ -I_2 \end{bmatrix} \quad (11.113)$$

From Eqs 11.110 and 11.113, we have

$$\begin{bmatrix} V_1 \\ I_1 \end{bmatrix} = \begin{bmatrix} A_1 & B_1 \\ C_1 & D_1 \end{bmatrix} \begin{bmatrix} A_2 & B_2 \\ C_2 & D_2 \end{bmatrix} \begin{bmatrix} V_2 \\ -I_2 \end{bmatrix} \quad (11.114)$$

The standard $ABCD$-parameters equations are

$$\begin{bmatrix} V_1 \\ I_1 \end{bmatrix} = \begin{bmatrix} A & B \\ C & D \end{bmatrix} \begin{bmatrix} V_2 \\ -I_2 \end{bmatrix} \quad (11.115)$$

Comparing Eqs 11.114 and 11.115, we have

$$\begin{bmatrix} A & B \\ C & D \end{bmatrix} = \begin{bmatrix} A_1 & B_1 \\ C_1 & D_1 \end{bmatrix} \begin{bmatrix} A_2 & B_2 \\ C_2 & D_2 \end{bmatrix} \quad (11.116)$$

From Eq. 11.116, we can conclude that the transmission matrix of cascade two-port network is the product of transmission matrices of the individual two-port networks.

11.10.4 Series–Parallel Connection of Two-port Networks

Figure 11.16 shows a series–parallel connection of two two-port networks X and Y. Here the input ports of the two networks are connected in series and the output ports are connected in parallel. The h-parameters can be used to describe the parameters of the series–parallel connected two-port networks.

If the h-parameters of network X are $h_{11}', h_{12}', h_{21}', h_{22}'$ and network Y are $h_{11}'', h_{12}'', h_{21}'', h_{22}''$, then

For network X,

$$\begin{bmatrix} V_1' \\ I_2' \end{bmatrix} = \begin{bmatrix} h_{11}' & h_{12}' \\ h_{21}' & h_{22}' \end{bmatrix} \begin{bmatrix} I_1 \\ V_2 \end{bmatrix}$$

For network Y,

$$\begin{bmatrix} V_1'' \\ I_2'' \end{bmatrix} = \begin{bmatrix} h_{11}'' & h_{12}'' \\ h_{21}'' & h_{22}'' \end{bmatrix} \begin{bmatrix} I_1 \\ V_2 \end{bmatrix}$$

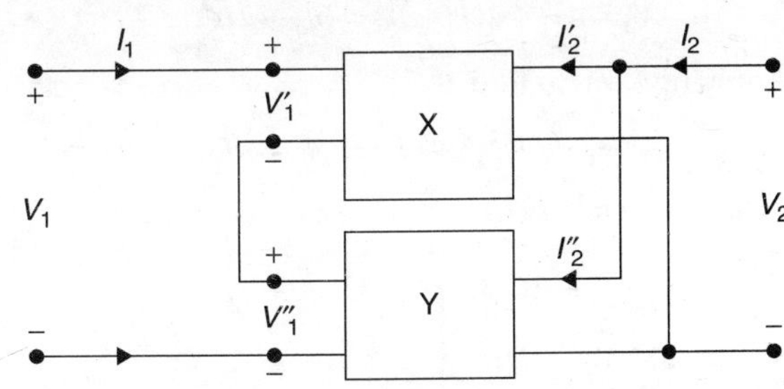

Fig. 11.16 Series–parallel connection

For the network diagram shown in Fig. 11.16,

$$V_1 = V_1' + V_1''$$

$$I_2 = I_2' + I_2''$$

$$\therefore \quad \begin{bmatrix} V_1 \\ I_2 \end{bmatrix} = \begin{bmatrix} V_1' + V_1'' \\ I_2' + I_2'' \end{bmatrix} = \begin{bmatrix} h_{11}' + h_{11}'' & h_{12}' + h_{12}'' \\ h_{21}' + h_{21}'' & h_{22}' + h_{22}'' \end{bmatrix} \begin{bmatrix} I_1 \\ V_2 \end{bmatrix} \quad (11.117)$$

The standard h-parameters equations are

$$\begin{bmatrix} V_1 \\ I_2 \end{bmatrix} = \begin{bmatrix} h_{11} & h_{12} \\ h_{21} & h_{22} \end{bmatrix} \begin{bmatrix} I_1 \\ V_2 \end{bmatrix} \quad (11.118)$$

Comparing Eqs 11.117 and 11.118, we have

$$\begin{bmatrix} h_{11} & h_{12} \\ h_{21} & h_{22} \end{bmatrix} = \begin{bmatrix} h_{11}' + h_{11}'' & h_{12}' + h_{12}'' \\ h_{21}' + h_{21}'' & h_{22}' + h_{22}'' \end{bmatrix} \quad (11.119)$$

From the above result we can conclude that the h-parameter of the series–parallel connected two-port network is given as the sum of the corresponding h-parameters of the individual networks.

Problem 11.16 Two two-port networks are connected in series. Obtain the Z-parameters of the combination. Also verify by direct calculation.

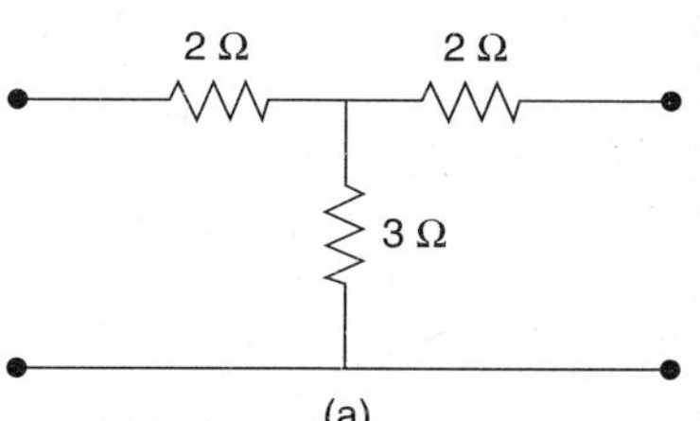

(a)

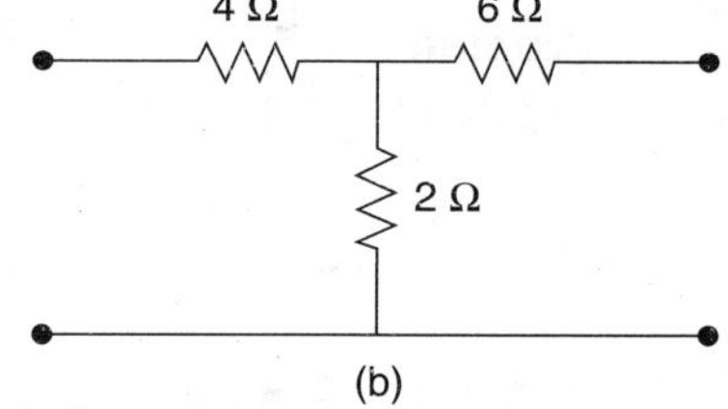

(b)

Solution:

The given circuit diagrams can be redrawn as shown.

From Fig. (c),

Applying KVL to loop 1

$$V_1 = 2I_1 + 3(I_1 + I_2) = 5I_1 + 3I_2 \quad (1)$$

Applying KVL to loop 2

$$V_2 = 2I_2 + 3(I_1 + I_2) = 3I_1 + 5I_2 \quad (2)$$

Comparing Eqs (1) and (2) with standard Z-parameter equations, we have

$$\begin{bmatrix} Z_{11}' & Z_{12}' \\ Z_{21}' & Z_{22}' \end{bmatrix} = \begin{bmatrix} 5 & 3 \\ 3 & 5 \end{bmatrix}$$

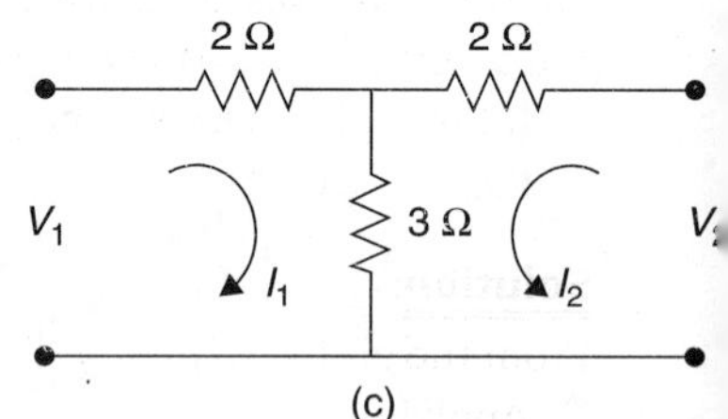

(c)

From Fig. (d),

Applying KVL to loop 1

$$V_1 = 4I_1 + 2(I_1 + I_2) = 6I_1 + 2I_2 \quad (3)$$

Applying KVL to loop 2

$$V_2 = 6I_2 + 2(I_1 + I_2) = 2I_1 + 8I_2 \quad (4)$$

Comparing Eqs (3) and (4) with standard Z-parameter equations, we have

$$\begin{bmatrix} Z_{11}'' & Z_{12}'' \\ Z_{21}'' & Z_{22}'' \end{bmatrix} = \begin{bmatrix} 6 & 2 \\ 2 & 8 \end{bmatrix}$$

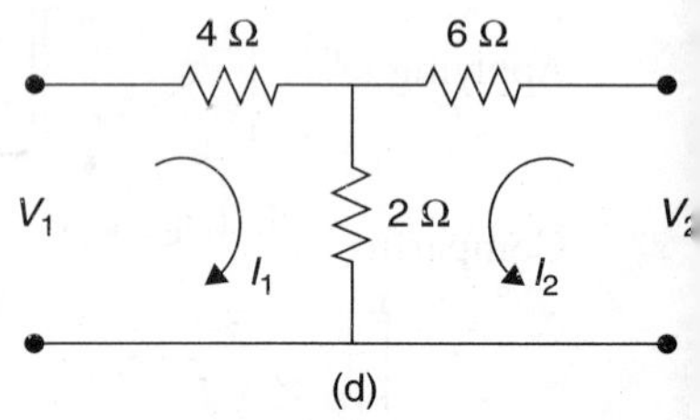

(d)

The Z-parameters of the combined network are

$$\begin{bmatrix} Z_{11} & Z_{12} \\ Z_{21} & Z_{22} \end{bmatrix} = \begin{bmatrix} Z_{11}' & Z_{12}' \\ Z_{21}' & Z_{22}' \end{bmatrix} + \begin{bmatrix} Z_{11}'' & Z_{12}'' \\ Z_{21}'' & Z_{22}'' \end{bmatrix} = \begin{bmatrix} 11 & 5 \\ 5 & 13 \end{bmatrix}$$

Verification: The combined series connected two-port network can be drawn as given below:

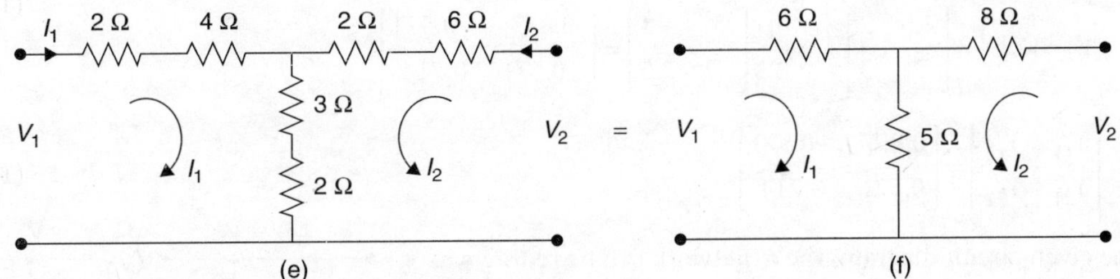

From Fig. (e), applying KVL to individual loops

Applying KVL to loop 1

$$V_1 = 6I_1 + 5(I_1 + I_2) = 11I_1 + 5I_2 \tag{5}$$

Applying KVL to loop 2

$$V_2 = 8I_2 + 5(I_1 + I_2) = 5I_1 + 13I_2 \tag{6}$$

Comparing Eqs (5) and (6) with standard Z-parameter equations, we have

$$\begin{bmatrix} Z_{11} & Z_{12} \\ Z_{21} & Z_{22} \end{bmatrix} = \begin{bmatrix} 11 & 5 \\ 5 & 13 \end{bmatrix}$$

Problem 11.17 The figure shows a resistive T-network and a resistive π-network connected in parallel. Find the overall Y-parameters of the combination. Also verify by direct calculation.

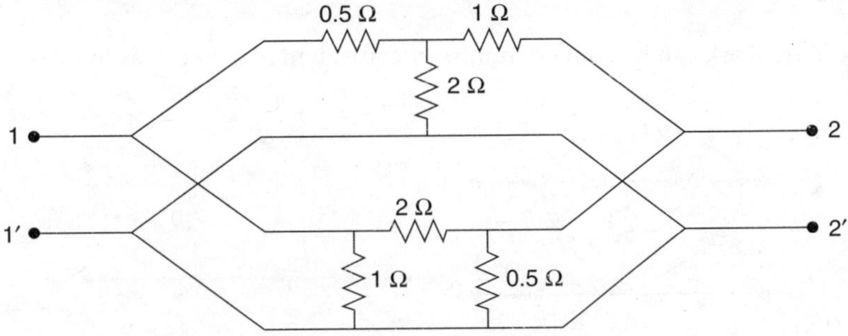

Solution:

From the given circuit diagram, the T-network can be drawn as shown.

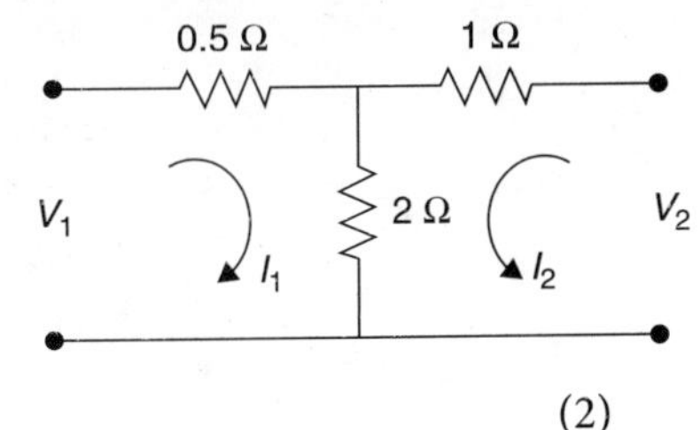

Applying KVL to loop 1

$$V_1 = 0.5I_1 + 2(I_1 + I_2) = 2.5I_1 + 2I_2 \tag{1}$$

Applying KVL to loop 2

$$V_2 = 1I_2 + 2(I_1 + I_2) = 2I_1 + 3I_2 \tag{2}$$

Comparing Eqs (1) and (2) with standard Z-parameter equations, we have

$$\begin{bmatrix} Z'_{11} & Z'_{12} \\ Z'_{21} & Z'_{22} \end{bmatrix} = \begin{bmatrix} 2.5 & 2 \\ 2 & 3 \end{bmatrix}$$

The Y-parameters for the T-network are given by

$$[Y]=[Z]^{-1}=\begin{bmatrix}2.5 & 2\\ 2 & 3\end{bmatrix}^{-1}=\frac{1}{3.5}\begin{bmatrix}3 & -2\\ -2 & 2.5\end{bmatrix}=\begin{bmatrix}0.857 & -0.571\\ -0.571 & 0.714\end{bmatrix}$$

$$\begin{bmatrix}Y'_{11} & Y'_{12}\\ Y'_{21} & Y'_{22}\end{bmatrix}=\begin{bmatrix}0.857 & -0.571\\ 0.571 & 0.714\end{bmatrix} \tag{3}$$

From the given circuit diagram, the π-network can be redrawn as

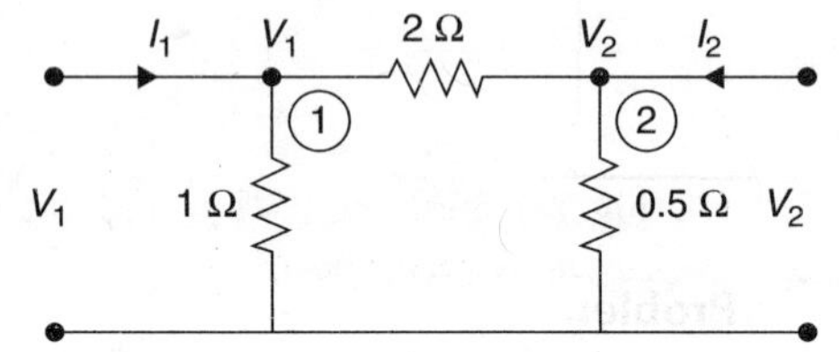

Applying KCL at node 1

$$I_1=\frac{V_1}{1}+\frac{V_1-V_2}{2}=1.5V_1-0.5V_2 \tag{4}$$

Applying KCL at node 2

$$I_2=\frac{V_2}{0.5}+\frac{V_2-V_1}{2}=-0.5V_1+2.5V_2 \tag{5}$$

Comparing Eqs (4) and (5) with standard Y-parameter equations, we have

$$\begin{bmatrix}Y''_{11} & Y''_{12}\\ Y''_{21} & Y''_{22}\end{bmatrix}=\begin{bmatrix}1.5 & -0.5\\ -0.5 & 2.5\end{bmatrix}$$

The Y-parameters of the combined network are

$$\begin{bmatrix}Y_{11} & Y_{12}\\ Y_{21} & Y_{22}\end{bmatrix}=\begin{bmatrix}Y'_{11} & Y'_{12}\\ Y'_{21} & Y'_{22}\end{bmatrix}+\begin{bmatrix}Y''_{11} & Y''_{12}\\ Y''_{21} & Y''_{22}\end{bmatrix}=\begin{bmatrix}2.357 & -1.071\\ -1.071 & 3.214\end{bmatrix}$$

Verification: The T-network can be converted into an equivalent π-network as follows:

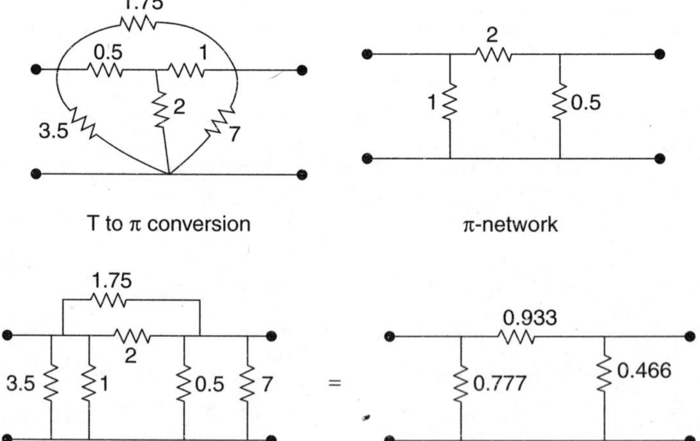

T to π conversion

π-network

The above circuit can be redrawn as

Applying KCL at node-1

$$I_1=\frac{V_1}{0.78}+\frac{V_1-V_2}{0.93}=2.355V_1-1.07V_2 \tag{6}$$

Applying KCL at node-2

$$I_2 = \frac{V_2}{0.47} + \frac{V_2 - V_1}{0.93} = -1.07V_1 + 3.2V_2 \qquad (7)$$

Comparing Eqs (6) and (7) with standard Y-parameter equations, we have

$$\begin{bmatrix} Y_{11} & Y_{12} \\ Y_{21} & Y_{22} \end{bmatrix} = \begin{bmatrix} 2.357 & -1.071 \\ -1.071 & 3.214 \end{bmatrix}$$

Problem 11.18 Determine the transmission parameters for the network.

Solution:

The given network can be considered as a cascade connection of two networks X (Fig. a) and Y (Fig. b).

Applying KVL to loop 1

$$V_1 = 2I_1 + \frac{1}{2s}(I_1 + I_1') = \left(2 + \frac{1}{2s}\right)I_1 + \frac{1}{2s}I_1' \qquad (1)$$

Applying KVL to loop 2

$$V_1' = 2sI_1' + \frac{1}{2s}(I_1 + I_1') = \frac{1}{2s}I_1 + \left(2s + \frac{1}{2s}\right)I_1' \qquad (2)$$

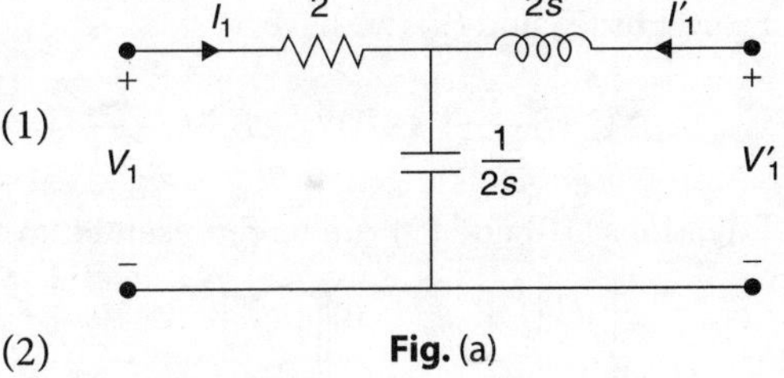

Fig. (a)

From Eq. (2), we have

$$I_1 = 2sV_1' - (4s^2 + 1)I_1' \qquad (3)$$

From Eqs (1) and (3), we have

$$V_1 = \left(2 + \frac{1}{2s}\right)[2sV_1' - (4s^2 + 1)I_1'] + \frac{1}{2s}I_1'$$

$$\Rightarrow \quad V_1 = (4s + 1)V_1' - (8s^2 + 2s + 2)I_1' \qquad (4)$$

Equations (4) and (3) can be represented in the matrix form

$$\begin{bmatrix} V_1 \\ I_1 \end{bmatrix} = \begin{bmatrix} 4s + 1 & 8s^2 + 2s + 2 \\ 2s & 4s^2 + 1 \end{bmatrix} \begin{bmatrix} V_1' \\ -I_1' \end{bmatrix} \qquad (5)$$

Comparing Eq. (5) with standard $ABCD$-parameter equations, we have

$$\begin{bmatrix} A_1 & B_1 \\ C_1 & D_1 \end{bmatrix} = \begin{bmatrix} 4s + 1 & 8s^2 + 2s + 2 \\ 2s & 4s^2 + 1 \end{bmatrix} \qquad (6)$$

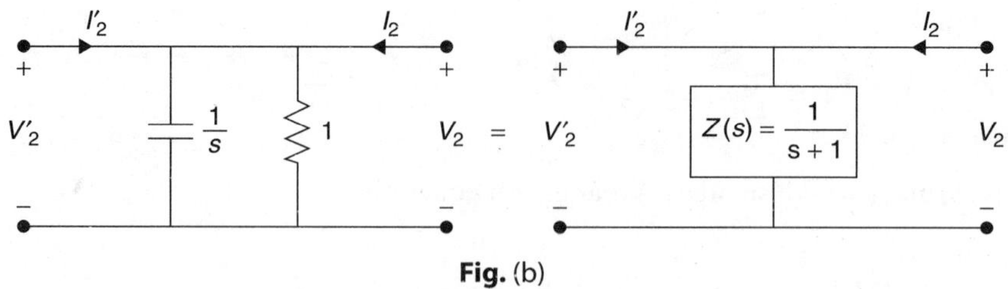

Fig. (b)

Applying KVL to loop 1

$$V_2' = \frac{1}{s+1} I_2' + \frac{1}{s+1} I_2 \tag{7}$$

Applying KVL to loop 2

$$V_2 = \frac{1}{s+1} I_2' + \frac{1}{s+1} I_2 \tag{8}$$

From Eq. (8), we have

$$I_2' = (s+1)V_2 - I_2 \tag{9}$$

From Eqs (7) and (9), we have

$$V_2' = \frac{1}{s+1}[(s+1)V_2 - I_2] + \frac{1}{s+1} I_2 = V_2 \tag{10}$$

Equations (10) and (9) can be represented in the matrix form

$$\begin{bmatrix} V_2' \\ I_2' \end{bmatrix} = \begin{bmatrix} 1 & 0 \\ s+1 & 1 \end{bmatrix} \begin{bmatrix} V_2 \\ -I_2 \end{bmatrix} \tag{11}$$

Comparing Eq. (11) with standard *ABCD* parameter equations, we have

$$\begin{bmatrix} A_2 & B_2 \\ C_2 & D_2 \end{bmatrix} = \begin{bmatrix} 1 & 0 \\ s+1 & -1 \end{bmatrix}$$

The *ABCD* parameters of the combined network are

$$\begin{bmatrix} A & B \\ C & D \end{bmatrix} = \begin{bmatrix} A_1 & B_1 \\ C_1 & D_1 \end{bmatrix} \begin{bmatrix} A_2 & B_2 \\ C_2 & D_2 \end{bmatrix}$$

$$= \begin{bmatrix} 4s+1 & 8s^2+2s+2 \\ 2s & 4s^2+1 \end{bmatrix} \begin{bmatrix} 1 & 0 \\ s+1 & 1 \end{bmatrix} = \begin{bmatrix} 8s^3+10s^2+8s+3 & 8s^2+2s+2 \\ 4s^3+4s^2+3s+1 & 4s^2+1 \end{bmatrix}$$

Problem 11.19 Determine the hybrid parameters for the network.

Solution:

The given network can be considered as a series–parallel connection of two two-port networks X and Y. The network X is shown in Fig. (a) and network Y is shown in Fig. (b).

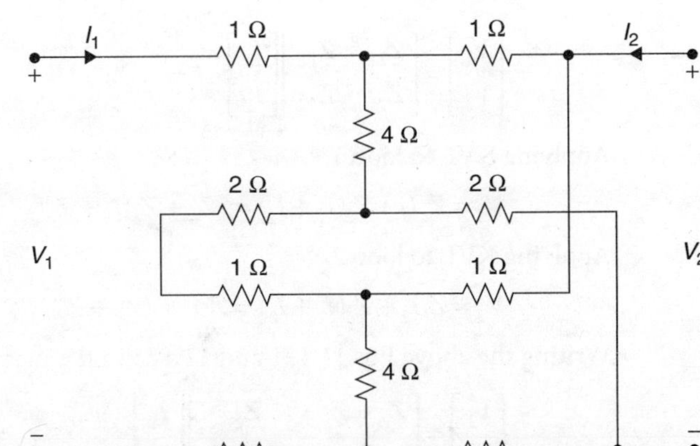

Applying KVL to loop 1

$$V_1 = I_1 + 4(I_1 + I_2) + 2I_1 = 7I_1 + 4I_2 \qquad (1)$$

Applying KVL to loop 2

$$V_2 = I_2 + 2I_2 + 4(I_1 + I_2) = 4I_1 + 7I_2 \qquad (2)$$

From Eq. (2), we have

$$7I_2 = V_2 - 4I_1$$

$$\Rightarrow \qquad I_2 = \frac{-4}{7}I_1 + \frac{1}{7}V_2 \qquad (3)$$

From Eqs (1) and (3), we have

$$V_1 = 7I_1 + 4\left(\frac{-4}{7}I_1 + \frac{1}{7}V_2\right) = \frac{33}{7}I_1 + \frac{4}{7}V_2 \qquad (4)$$

Equations (4) and (3) can be represented in the matrix form

$$\begin{bmatrix} V_1 \\ I_2 \end{bmatrix} = \begin{bmatrix} \frac{33}{7} & \frac{4}{7} \\ -\frac{4}{7} & \frac{1}{7} \end{bmatrix} \begin{bmatrix} I_1 \\ V_2 \end{bmatrix} \qquad (5)$$

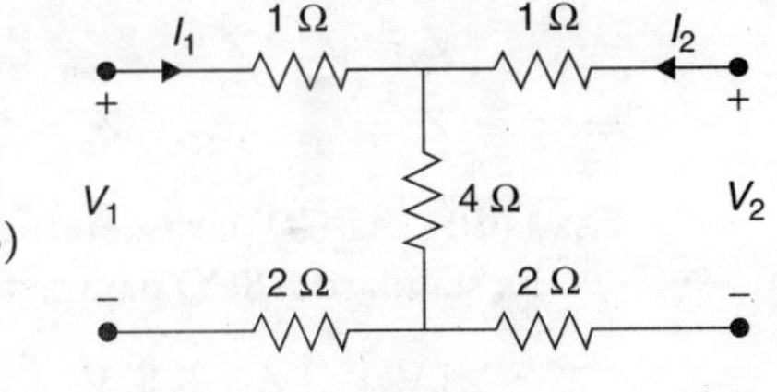

Fig. (a)

Comparing Eq. (5) with standard h-parameter equations, we have

$$\begin{bmatrix} h'_{11} & h'_{12} \\ h'_{21} & h'_{22} \end{bmatrix} = \begin{bmatrix} \frac{33}{7} & \frac{4}{7} \\ -\frac{4}{7} & \frac{1}{7} \end{bmatrix}$$

For network Y, h-parameters will be same as the two networks are identical.

$$\begin{bmatrix} h''_{11} & h''_{12} \\ h''_{21} & h''_{22} \end{bmatrix} = \begin{bmatrix} \frac{33}{7} & \frac{4}{7} \\ -\frac{4}{7} & \frac{1}{7} \end{bmatrix}$$

Fig. (b)

The hybrid parameters of the combined network are

$$\begin{bmatrix} h_{11} & h_{12} \\ h_{21} & h_{22} \end{bmatrix} = \begin{bmatrix} h'_{11} & h'_{12} \\ h'_{21} & h'_{22} \end{bmatrix} + \begin{bmatrix} h''_{11} & h''_{12} \\ h''_{21} & h''_{22} \end{bmatrix} = \begin{bmatrix} \frac{66}{7} & \frac{8}{7} \\ -\frac{8}{7} & \frac{2}{7} \end{bmatrix}$$

11.11 T AND π REPRESENTATION OF A TWO-PORT NETWORK

11.11.1 T-Representation of a Two-port Network

A two-port network with any number of elements may be converted into a two-port three terminal network. Thus, a two-port network may be represented by an equivalent T-network, that is, three impedances are connected together in the form of T (Fig. 11.17). It is possible to express the elements of the T-network in terms of Z-parameters or ABCD parameters as explained below:

Case (i): *Z*-parameters of the network

The Z-parameters are given by

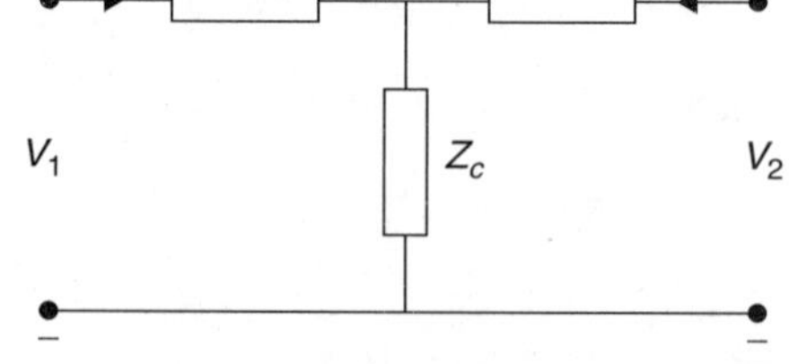

Fig. 11.17 T-network

$$\begin{bmatrix} V_1 \\ V_2 \end{bmatrix} = \begin{bmatrix} Z_{11} & Z_{12} \\ Z_{21} & Z_{22} \end{bmatrix} \begin{bmatrix} I_1 \\ I_2 \end{bmatrix} \tag{11.120}$$

Applying KVL to loop 1

$$V_1 = Z_a I_1 + Z_c(I_1 + I_2) = (Z_a + Z_c)I_1 + Z_c I_2 \tag{11.121}$$

Applying KVL to loop 2

$$V_2 = Z_b I_2 + Z_c(I_1 + I_2) = Z_c I_1 + (Z_b + Z_c)I_2 \tag{11.122}$$

Writing the above Eqs 11.121 and 11.122 in the matrix form, we have

$$\begin{bmatrix} V_1 \\ V_2 \end{bmatrix} = \begin{bmatrix} Z_a + Z_c & Z_c \\ Z_c & Z_b + Z_c \end{bmatrix} \begin{bmatrix} I_1 \\ I_2 \end{bmatrix} \tag{11.123}$$

Comparing Eqs 11.120 and 11.123, the Z-parameters are

$$Z_{11} = Z_a + Z_c, \quad Z_{12} = Z_{21} = Z_c, \quad Z_{22} = Z_b + Z_c$$

$$\Rightarrow \quad Z_a = Z_{11} - Z_{12}, \quad Z_b = Z_{22} - Z_{12}, \quad Z_c = Z_{21} = Z_{12} \tag{11.124}$$

Case (ii): *ABCD* parameters of the network

The standard $ABCD$ parameter equations are

$$\begin{bmatrix} V_1 \\ I_1 \end{bmatrix} = \begin{bmatrix} A & B \\ C & D \end{bmatrix} \begin{bmatrix} V_2 \\ -I_2 \end{bmatrix} \tag{11.125}$$

The Z-parameters equations for the T-network are given by

$$V_1 = (Z_a + Z_c)I_1 + Z_c I_2$$

$$V_2 = Z_c I_1 + (Z_b + Z_c)I_2$$

$$\Rightarrow \quad Z_c I_1 = V_2 - (Z_b + Z_c)I_2$$

$$\Rightarrow \quad I_1 = \frac{1}{Z_c} V_2 - \left(\frac{Z_b + Z_c}{Z_c} \right) I_2 \tag{11.126}$$

Also, $$V_1 = (Z_a + Z_c)\left(\frac{1}{Z_c} V_2 - \frac{(Z_b + Z_c)}{Z_c} I_2 \right) + Z_c I_2$$

$$\Rightarrow \quad V_1 = \left(\frac{Z_a + Z_c}{Z_c} \right) V_2 - \left(\frac{Z_a Z_b + Z_b Z_c + Z_c Z_a}{Z_c} \right) I_2 \tag{11.127}$$

Equations 11.127 and 11.126 can be represented in the matrix form

$$\begin{bmatrix} V_1 \\ I_1 \end{bmatrix} = \begin{bmatrix} \dfrac{Z_a + Z_c}{Z_c} & \dfrac{Z_a Z_b + Z_b Z_c + Z_c Z_a}{Z_c} \\ \dfrac{1}{Z_c} & \dfrac{Z_b + Z_c}{Z_c} \end{bmatrix} \begin{bmatrix} V_2 \\ -I_2 \end{bmatrix} \tag{11.128}$$

Comparing Eqs 11.125 and 11.128, we have

$$A = \frac{Z_a + Z_c}{Z_c}, \quad B = \frac{Z_a Z_b + Z_b Z_c + Z_c Z_a}{Z_c}, \quad C = \frac{1}{Z_c}, \quad D = \frac{Z_b + Z_c}{Z_c} \tag{11.129}$$

From Eq. 11.129, we have

$$Z_c = \frac{1}{C}$$

$$\frac{Z_a}{Z_c} = A - 1$$

$$\Rightarrow \quad Z_a = Z_c(A-1) = \frac{A-1}{C}$$

$$\frac{Z_b}{Z_c} = D - 1$$

$$\Rightarrow \quad Z_b = Z_c(D-1) = \frac{D-1}{C}$$

$$\therefore \quad Z_a = \frac{A-1}{C}, \quad Z_b = \frac{D-1}{C}, \quad Z_c = \frac{1}{C} \tag{11.130}$$

11.11.2 π-Representation of a Two-port Network

A two-port network may be represented by an equivalent π-network, that is, three impedances or admittances are together in the form of π (Fig. 11.18). It is possible to express the elements of the π-network in terms of Y-parameters or $ABCD$ parameters as explained below:

Case (i): *Y*-parameters of the network

The standard Y-parameter equations are

$$\begin{bmatrix} I_1 \\ I_2 \end{bmatrix} = \begin{bmatrix} Y_{11} & Y_{12} \\ Y_{21} & Y_{22} \end{bmatrix} \begin{bmatrix} V_1 \\ V_2 \end{bmatrix} \tag{11.131}$$

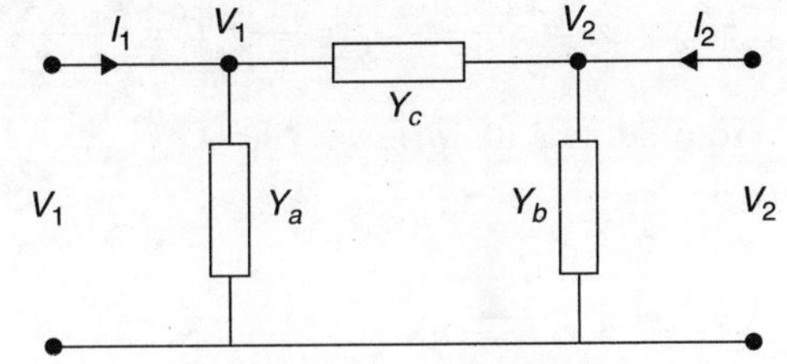

Fig. 11.18 π-network

Applying KCL at node 1

$$I_1 = V_1Y_a + (V_1 - V_2)Y_c = (Y_a + Y_c)V_1 - Y_cV_2 \tag{11.132}$$

Applying KCL at node 2

$$I_2 = V_2Y_b + (V_2 - V_1)Y_c = -Y_cV_1 + (Y_b + Y_c)V_2 \tag{11.133}$$

Equations 11.132 and 11.133 can be represented in the matrix form

$$\begin{bmatrix} I_1 \\ I_2 \end{bmatrix} = \begin{bmatrix} Y_a + Y_c & -Y_c \\ -Y_c & Y_b + Y_c \end{bmatrix} \begin{bmatrix} V_1 \\ V_2 \end{bmatrix} \tag{11.134}$$

On comparing Eqs 11.131 and 11.134, we have

$$Y_{11} = Y_a + Y_c, \quad Y_{12} = Y_{21} = -Y_c, \quad Y_{22} = Y_b + Y_c$$

$$\Rightarrow \quad Y_a = Y_{11} + Y_{12}, \quad Y_b = Y_{22} + Y_{12}, \quad Y_c = -Y_{21} = -Y_{12} \tag{11.135}$$

Case (ii): *ABCD* parameters of the network

The standard $ABCD$ parameter equations are

$$\begin{bmatrix} V_1 \\ I_1 \end{bmatrix} = \begin{bmatrix} A & B \\ C & D \end{bmatrix} \begin{bmatrix} V_2 \\ -I_2 \end{bmatrix} \tag{11.136}$$

The Y-parameters equations for the π-network are given by

$$I_1 = (Y_a + Y_c)V_1 - Y_c V_2$$

$$I_2 = -Y_c V_1 + (Y_b + Y_c)V_2$$

$$\Rightarrow \quad Y_c V_1 = (Y_b + Y_c)V_2 - I_2$$

$$\Rightarrow \quad V_1 = \left(\frac{Y_b + Y_c}{Y_c}\right)V_2 - \frac{1}{Y_c}I_2 \tag{11.137}$$

Also,

$$I_1 = (Y_a + Y_c)\left[\left(\frac{Y_b + Y_c}{Y_c}\right)V_2 - \frac{1}{Y_c}I_2\right] - Y_c V_2$$

$$\Rightarrow \quad I_1 = \left(\frac{Y_a Y_b + Y_b Y_c + Y_c Y_a}{Y_c}\right)V_2 - \left(\frac{Y_a + Y_c}{Y_c}\right)I_2 \tag{11.138}$$

Equations 11.137 and 11.138 can be represented in the matrix form

$$\begin{bmatrix} V_1 \\ I_1 \end{bmatrix} = \begin{bmatrix} \dfrac{Y_b + Y_c}{Y_c} & \dfrac{1}{Y_c} \\ \dfrac{Y_a Y_b + Y_b Y_c + Y_c Y_a}{Y_c} & \dfrac{Y_a + Y_c}{Y_c} \end{bmatrix} \begin{bmatrix} V_2 \\ -I_2 \end{bmatrix} \tag{11.139}$$

Comparing Eqs 11.136 and 11.139, we have

$$A = \frac{Y_b + Y_c}{Y_c}, \quad B = \frac{1}{Y_c}, \quad C = \frac{Y_a Y_b + Y_b Y_c + Y_c Y_a}{Y_c}, \quad D = \frac{Y_a + Y_c}{Y_c} \tag{11.140}$$

From Eq. 11.140, we have

$$Y_c = \frac{1}{B}$$

$$\frac{Y_b}{Y_c} = A - 1$$

$$\Rightarrow \quad Y_b = Y_c(A - 1) = \frac{A - 1}{B}$$

$$\frac{Y_a}{Y_c} = D - 1$$

$$\Rightarrow \quad Y_a = Y_c(D - 1) = \frac{D - 1}{B}$$

$$\therefore \quad Y_a = \frac{D - 1}{B}, \quad Y_b = \frac{A - 1}{B}, \quad Y_c = \frac{1}{B} \tag{11.141}$$

Problem 11.20 The Z-parameters of a two-port network are $Z_{11} = 5\ \Omega$, $Z_{12} = Z_{21} = 4\ \Omega$, $Z_{22} = 8\ \Omega$. Find the equivalent T-network and ABCD parameters.

Solution:

Given that $Z_{11} = 5\ \Omega, \quad Z_{12} = Z_{21} = 4\ \Omega, \quad Z_{22} = 8\ \Omega$

The equivalent T-network is shown,

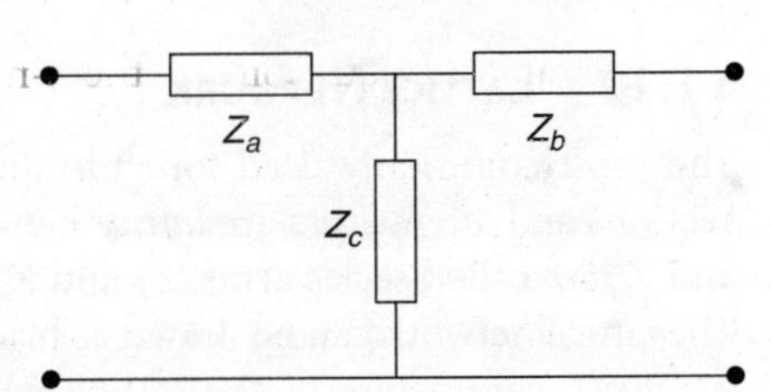

where, $Z_a = Z_{11} - Z_{12} = 5 - 4 = 1\,\Omega$

$Z_b = Z_{22} - Z_{12} = 8 - 4 = 4\,\Omega$

$Z_c = Z_{21} = Z_{12} = 4\,\Omega$

The *ABCD* parameters of the network are

$$A = \frac{Z_a + Z_c}{Z_c} = \frac{1+4}{4} = \frac{5}{4}$$

$$B = \frac{Z_a Z_b + Z_b Z_c + Z_c Z_a}{Z_c} = \frac{1\times 4 + 4\times 4 + 4\times 1}{4} = 6\,\Omega$$

$$C = \frac{1}{Z_c} = \frac{1}{4}\,\mho$$

$$D = \frac{Z_b + Z_c}{Z_c} = \frac{4+4}{4} = 2$$

Problem 11.21 The port currents of a two-port network are given by

$I_1 = 5V_1 - 2V_2,\ I_2 = -2V_1 + 10V_2$

Find the equivalent π-network and ABCD parameters.

Solution:

Given that $Y_{11} = 5\,\mho,\quad Y_{12} = -2\,\mho,\quad Y_{21} = -2\,\mho,\quad Y_{22} = 10\,\mho$

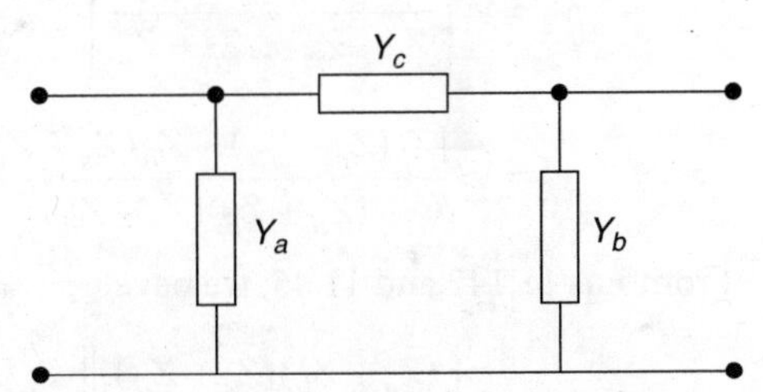

The equivalent π-network parameters are

where, $Y_a = Y_{11} + Y_{12} = 5 - 2 = 3\,\mho$

$Y_b = Y_{22} + Y_{12} = 10 - 2 = 8\,\mho$

$Y_c = -Y_{21} = -Y_{12} = 2\,\mho$

The *ABCD* parameters of the network are

$$A = \frac{Y_b + Y_c}{Y_c} = \frac{8+2}{2} = 5$$

$$B = \frac{1}{Y_c} = \frac{1}{2} = 0.5\,\Omega$$

$$C = \frac{Y_a Y_b + Y_b Y_c + Y_c Y_a}{Y_c} = \frac{3\times 8 + 8\times 2 + 2\times 3}{2} = 23\,\mho$$

$$D = \frac{Y_a + Y_c}{Y_c} = \frac{3+2}{2} = \frac{5}{2} = 2.5$$

11.12 Lattice Network

The most commonly used four terminal two-port network in filter sections and attenuators are *lattice networks* [Fig. 11.19(a)], where Z_a and Z_d are called series arms, Z_b and Z_c are called the diagonal arms. The lattice network can be drawn as bridge network [Fig. 11.19(b)].

The Z-parameters of the lattice network can be determined as follows:

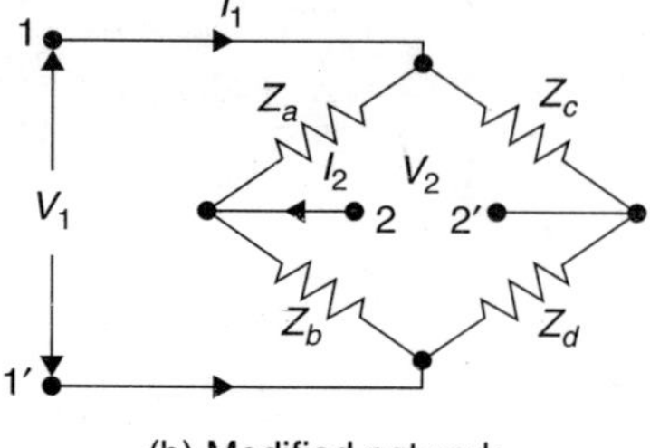

(a) Original network

(b) Modified network

Fig. 11.19 Lattice network

$$Z_{11}=\left.\frac{V_1}{I_1}\right|_{I_2=0}, \quad Z_{21}=\left.\frac{V_2}{I_1}\right|_{I_2=0}$$

When $I_2 = 0$, the circuit of Fig. 11.19(b) can be redrawn as shown in Fig. 11.20(a).

From Fig. 11.20(a), we have

$$V_1=I_1\frac{(Z_a+Z_b)(Z_c+Z_d)}{Z_a+Z_b+Z_c+Z_d} \tag{11.142}$$

$$Z_{11}=\frac{V_1}{I_1}=\frac{(Z_a+Z_b)(Z_c+Z_d)}{Z_a+Z_b+Z_c+Z_d} \tag{11.143}$$

If the network is symmetric, then $Z_a = Z_d, Z_b = Z_c$.

$$Z_{11}=\frac{Z_a+Z_b}{2} \tag{11.144}$$

$$V_2=V_1\left[\frac{Z_b}{Z_a+Z_b}-\frac{Z_d}{Z_c+Z_d}\right]$$

$$\Rightarrow \quad V_2=V_1\frac{[Z_b(Z_c+Z_d)-Z_d(Z_a+Z_b)]}{(Z_a+Z_b)(Z_c+Z_d)} \tag{11.145}$$

From Eqs 11.142 and 11.45, we have

$$V_2=I_1\left[\frac{(Z_a+Z_b)(Z_c+Z_d)}{Z_a+Z_b+Z_c+Z_d}\right]\left[\frac{Z_b(Z_c+Z_d)-Z_d(Z_a+Z_b)}{(Z_a+Z_b)(Z_c+Z_d)}\right]$$

$$\Rightarrow \quad V_2=I_1\left[\frac{Z_bZ_c-Z_aZ_d}{Z_a+Z_b+Z_c+Z_d}\right]$$

$$\Rightarrow \quad Z_{21}=\frac{V_2}{I_1}=\left[\frac{Z_bZ_c-Z_aZ_d}{Z_a+Z_b+Z_c+Z_d}\right] \tag{11.146}$$

If the network is symmetric, $Z_a = Z_d, Z_b = Z_c$

$$Z_{21}=\frac{Z_b-Z_a}{2} \tag{11.147}$$

When $I_1 = 0$, the circuit of Fig. 11.19(b) can be redrawn as shown in Fig. 11.20(b).

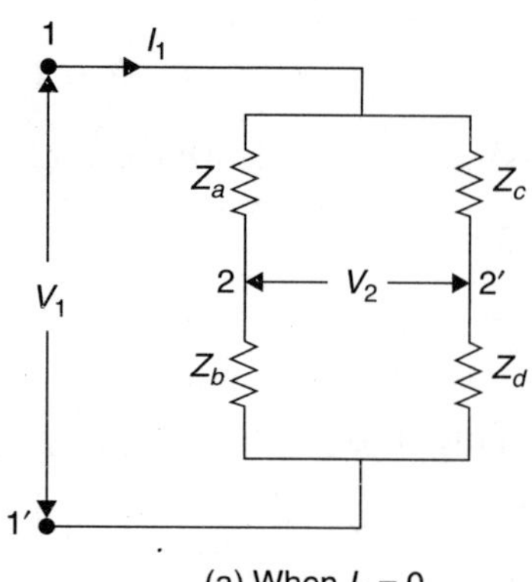

(a) When $I_2 = 0$

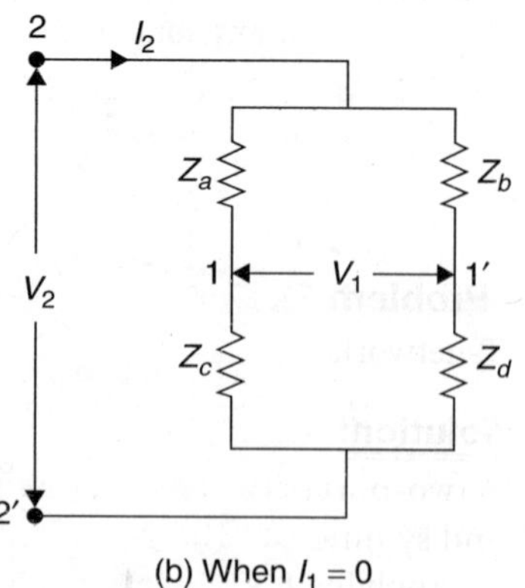

(b) When $I_1 = 0$

Fig. 11.20 Bridge network

From Fig. 11.20(b), we have

$$V_2 = \frac{(Z_a + Z_c)(Z_b + Z_d)}{Z_a + Z_b + Z_c + Z_d} I_2 \quad (11.148)$$

$$\Rightarrow \quad Z_{22} = \frac{V_2}{I_2} = \frac{(Z_a + Z_c)(Z_b + Z_d)}{Z_a + Z_b + Z_c + Z_d} \quad (11.149)$$

If the network is symmetric, $Z_a = Z_d$, $Z_b = Z_c$

$$Z_{22} = \frac{Z_a + Z_b}{2} = Z_{11} \quad (11.150)$$

$$V_1 = V_2 \left[\frac{Z_c}{Z_a + Z_c} - \frac{Z_d}{Z_b + Z_d} \right]$$

$$\Rightarrow \quad V_1 = V_2 \left[\frac{Z_c(Z_b + Z_d) - Z_d(Z_a + Z_c)}{(Z_a + Z_c)(Z_b + Z_d)} \right] \quad (11.151)$$

From Eqs 11.148 and 11.151, we have

$$V_1 = I_2 \left[\frac{(Z_a + Z_c)(Z_b + Z_d)}{Z_a + Z_b + Z_c + Z_d} \right] \left[\frac{Z_c(Z_b + Z_d) - Z_d(Z_a + Z_c)}{(Z_a + Z_c)(Z_b + Z_d)} \right]$$

$$\Rightarrow \quad V_1 = I_2 \left[\frac{Z_c Z_b - Z_d Z_a}{Z_a + Z_b + Z_c + Z_d} \right]$$

$$\Rightarrow \quad Z_{12} = \frac{V_1}{I_2} = \left[\frac{Z_c Z_b - Z_d Z_a}{Z_a + Z_b + Z_c + Z_d} \right] \quad (11.152)$$

If the network is symmetric, then $Z_a = Z_d$, $Z_b = Z_c$.

$$Z_{12} = \frac{Z_b - Z_a}{2} = Z_{21} \quad (11.153)$$

From the above equations, we have

$$Z_{11} = Z_{22} = \frac{Z_b + Z_a}{2}, \quad Z_{12} = Z_{21} = \frac{Z_b - Z_a}{2}$$

$$Z_a = Z_{11} - Z_{12}, \quad Z_b = Z_{22} - Z_{12} \quad (11.154)$$

Problem 11.22 Obtain the lattice equivalent of the symmetrical T-network.

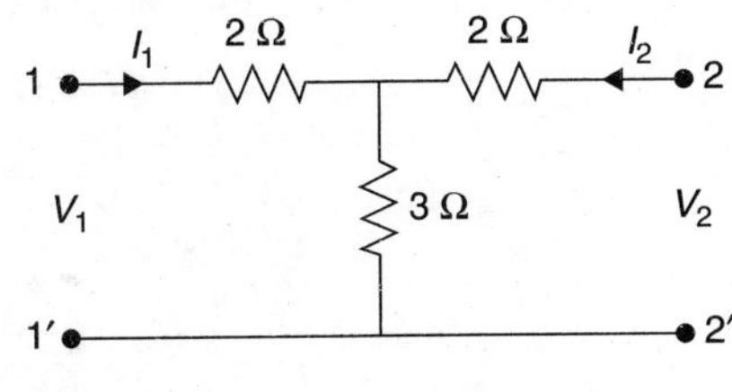

Solution:

A two-port network can be realised as a symmetric lattice if it is reciprocal and symmetric. The given circuit can be redrawn as shown.

Applying KVL to loop 1

$$V_1 = 2I_1 + 3(I_1 + I_2) = 5I_1 + 3I_2 \quad (1)$$

Applying KVL to loop 2

$$V_2 = 2I_2 + 3(I_1 + I_2) = 3I_1 + 5I_2 \quad (2)$$

Comparing Eqs (1) and (2) with standard Z-parameter equations, we have

$$\begin{bmatrix} Z_{11} & Z_{12} \\ Z_{21} & Z_{22} \end{bmatrix} = \begin{bmatrix} 5 & 3 \\ 3 & 5 \end{bmatrix}$$

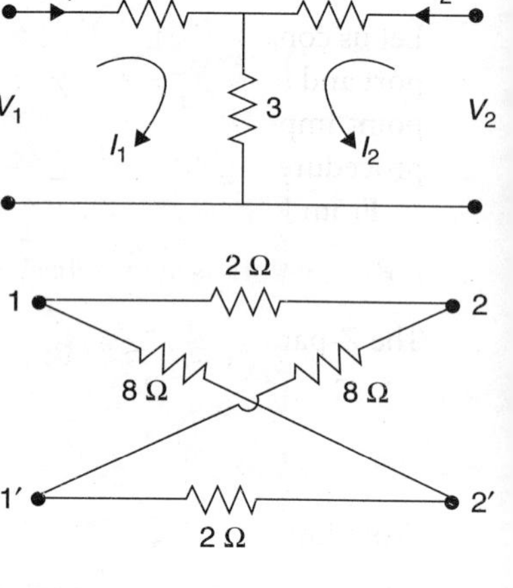

Since $Z_{11} = Z_{22}$, $Z_{12} = Z_{21}$, the given network is symmetrical and reciprocal.
Therefore, the parameters of the lattice network are

$$Z_a = Z_{11} - Z_{12} = 5 - 3 = 2\ \Omega$$

$$Z_b = Z_{22} + Z_{12} = 5 + 3 = 8\ \Omega$$

The lattice network is shown.

11.13 TERMINATED TWO-PORT NETWORKS

11.13.1 Input Impedance of a Terminated Two-port Network

Let us consider a two-port network excited by a voltage source V_S with internal impedance Z_S at the input port and terminated by a load impedance Z_L at the output port (Fig. 11.21). The input impedance or driving point impedance, $Z_{in} = V_1/I_1$, at the input port can be evaluated in terms of the Z-parameters. A similar procedure can be adopted for finding Z_{in} in terms of the other parameters.

From Fig. 11.21, we have

$$V_2 = -I_2 Z_L \quad (11.155)$$

The Z-parameters can be represented as

$$V_1 = Z_{11}I_1 + Z_{12}I_2 \quad (11.156)$$

$$V_2 = Z_{21}I_1 + Z_{22}I_2 \quad (11.157)$$

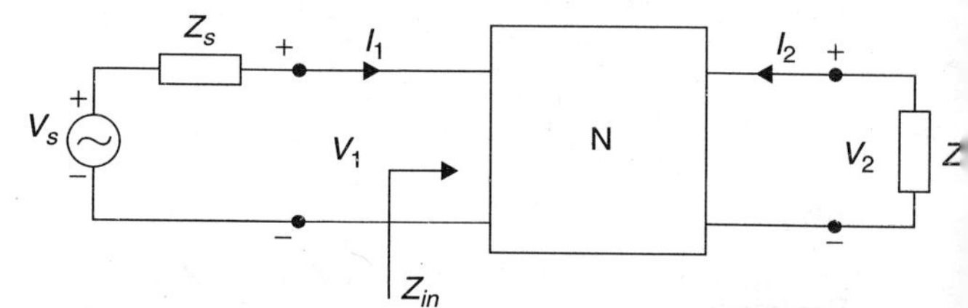

Fig. 11.21 Terminated two-port network

From Eqs 11.155 and 11.157, we have

$$-I_2 Z_L = Z_{21}I_1 + Z_{22}I_2$$

$$\Rightarrow \quad -I_2(Z_L + Z_{22}) = Z_{21}I_1$$

$$\Rightarrow \quad I_2 = -\frac{Z_{21}}{Z_L + Z_{22}} I_1 \quad (11.158)$$

Substituting the value of I_2 in Eq. 11.156, we get

$$V_1 = Z_{11}I_1 - Z_{12}\left(\frac{Z_{21}}{Z_L + Z_{22}} I_1\right) = \left(Z_{11} - \frac{Z_{12}Z_{21}}{Z_L + Z_{22}}\right) I_1$$

$$\therefore \quad Z_{in} = \frac{V_1}{I_1} = \left(Z_{11} - \frac{Z_{12}Z_{21}}{Z_L + Z_{22}}\right) \quad (11.159)$$

This gives the required relation for the input or driving point impedance of the circuit.

11.13.2 Output Impedance of a Terminated Two-port Network

Let us consider a two-port network excited by a voltage sources V_S with internal impedance Z_S at the output port and terminated by an impedance Z_L at the input port (Fig. 11.22), The output impedance or the driving point impedance $Z_0 = V_2/I_2$, at the output port can be evaluated in terms of the Z-parameters. A similar procedure can be adopted for finding Z_0 in terms of the other parameters.

From Fig. 11.22, we have

$$V_1 = -I_1 Z_L \tag{11.160}$$

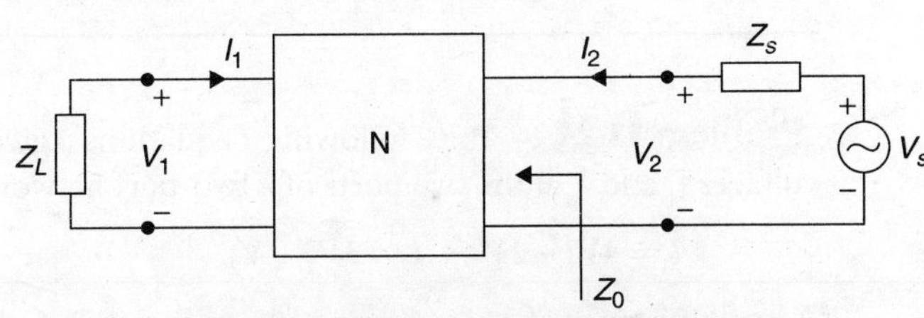

Fig. 11.22 Terminated two-port network

The Z-parameters can be represented as

$$V_1 = Z_{11}I_1 + Z_{12}I_2 \tag{11.161}$$

$$V_2 = Z_{21}I_1 + Z_{22}I_2 \tag{11.162}$$

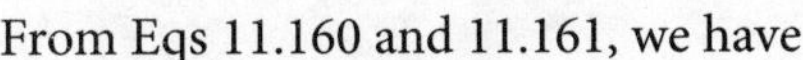

From Eqs 11.160 and 11.161, we have

$$-I_1 Z_L = Z_{11}I_1 + Z_{12}I_2$$

$$\Rightarrow \quad -I_1(Z_L + Z_{11}) = Z_{12}I_2$$

$$\Rightarrow \quad I_1 = -\frac{Z_{12}}{Z_L + Z_{11}} I_2 \tag{11.163}$$

Substituting the value of I_1 in Eq. 11.162, we get

$$V_2 = Z_{21}\left(-\frac{Z_{12}}{Z_L + Z_{11}} I_2\right) + Z_{22}I_2 = \left(Z_{22} - \frac{Z_{12}Z_{21}}{Z_L + Z_{11}}\right) I_2$$

$$\therefore \quad Z_0 = \frac{V_2}{I_2} = \left(Z_{22} - \frac{Z_{12}Z_{21}}{Z_L + Z_{11}}\right) \tag{11.164}$$

This gives the required relation for the output or driving point impedance of the circuit.

Problem 11.23 The following equations give the voltages V_1 and V_2 at the two ports of a two-port network.

$$V_1 = 5I_1 + 2I_2, \quad V_2 = 2I_1 + I_2$$

A load resistance of 3 Ω is connected across port 2. Calculate the input impedance.

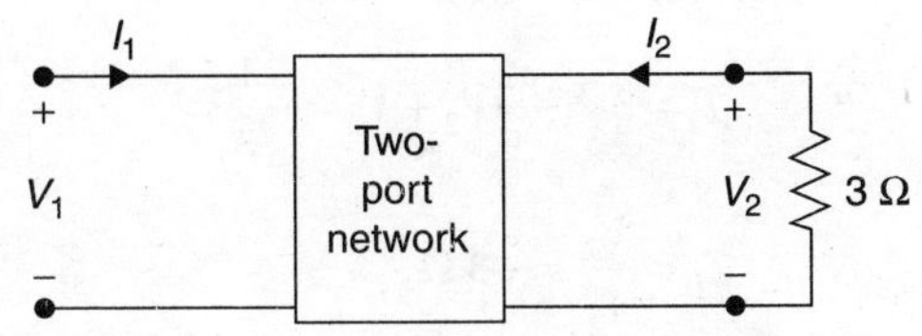

Solution:

Given that $V_1 = 5I_1 + 2I_2$ (1)

$$V_2 = 2I_1 + I_2 \tag{2}$$

From the above circuit diagram

$$V_2 = -3I_2 \tag{3}$$

From Eqs (2) and (3), we have

$$-3I_2 = 2I_1 + I_2$$

$$\Rightarrow \quad I_2 = -\frac{1}{2} I_1 \tag{4}$$

From Eqs (1) and (4), we have

$$V_1 = 5I_1 - 2\times\frac{1}{2}I_1 = 4I_1$$

$$\therefore \quad Z_{in} = \frac{V_1}{I_1} = 4\,\Omega$$

Problem 11.24 The following equations give the voltages I_1 and I_2 at the two ports of a two-port network.

$$I_1 = 4V_1 + 2V_2, \quad I_2 = 3V_1 + V_2$$

A load resistance of 2 Ω is connected across port 1. Calculate the output impedance.

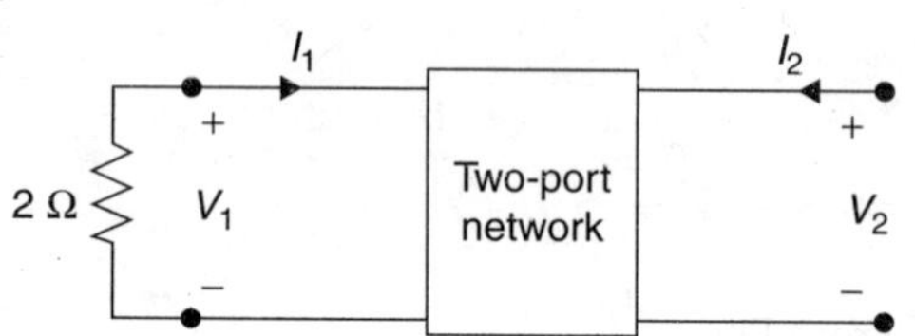

Solution:

Given that $I_1 = 4V_1 + 2V_2$ (1)

$$I_2 = 3V_1 + V_2 \quad (2)$$

From the above circuit diagram

$$V_1 = -2I_1 \Rightarrow I_1 = -\frac{1}{2}V_1 \quad (3)$$

From Eqs (1) and (3), we have

$$-\frac{1}{2}V_1 = 4V_1 + 2V_2$$

$$\Rightarrow \quad V_1 = -\frac{4}{9}V_2 \quad (4)$$

From Eqs (2) and (4), we have

$$I_2 = 3\times -\frac{4}{9}V_2 + V_2 = -\frac{1}{3}V_2$$

$$\therefore \quad Z_0 = \frac{V_2}{I_2} = -3\,\Omega$$

11.14 IMAGE PARAMETERS

Image impedance is a concept used in electronic network design and analysis and most especially in filter design. The term image impedance applies to the impedance seen looking into the port of a network. Usually a two-port network is implied but the concept can be extended to networks with more than two ports. The definition of image impedance for a two-port network is the impedance Z_{i1} seen looking into port 1 when port 2 is terminated with the image impedance Z_{i2} for port 2. In general, the image impedances of ports 1 and 2 will not be equal unless the network is symmetrical (or anti-symmetrical) with respect to the ports.

The image parameters can be conveniently expressed in terms of *ABCD* constants. Figure 11.23(a) shows a two-port network terminated in Z_{i2} at port 2 and Fig. 11.23(b) shows a two-port network terminated in Z_{i1} at port 1.

$$V_1 = AV_2 - BI_2$$
$$I_1 = CV_2 - DI_2$$

From Fig. 11.23(a),

$$V_2 = -Z_{i2} I_2$$

$$Z_{i1} = \frac{V_1}{I_1} = \frac{AV_2 - BI_2}{CV_2 - DI_2} = \frac{-AZ_{i2}I_2 - BI_2}{-CZ_{i2}I_2 - DI_2} = \frac{AZ_{i2} + B}{CZ_{i2} + D}$$

$$\Rightarrow \quad Z_{i1} = \frac{AZ_{i2} + B}{CZ_{i2} + D} \tag{11.165}$$

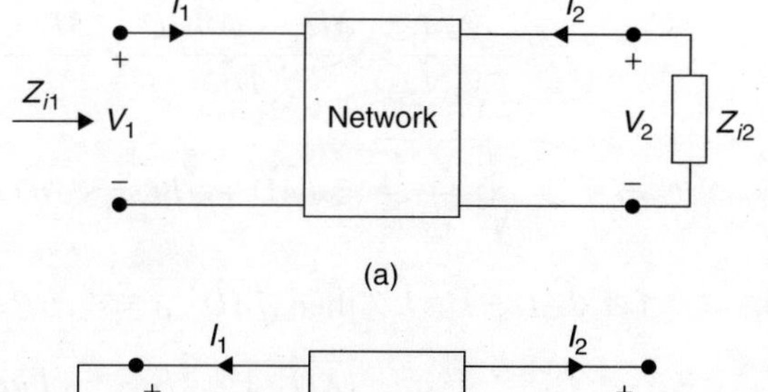

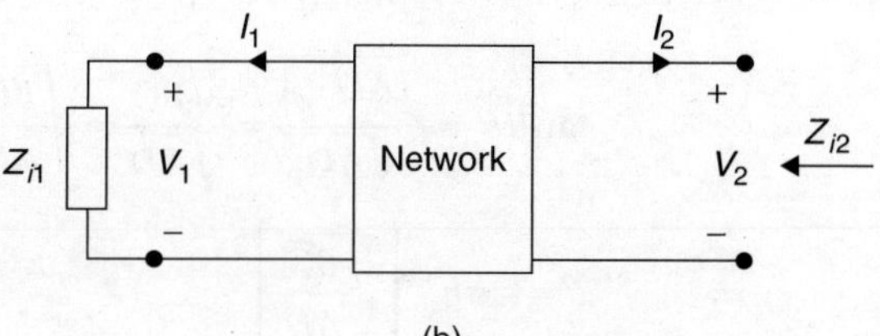

Fig. 11.23 Image impedances

From Fig. 11.23(b),

$$V_1 = -Z_{i1} I_1$$

$$Z_{i2} = \frac{V_2}{I_2} = \frac{V_1\left[\frac{D}{AD - BC}\right] - I_1\left[\frac{B}{AD - BC}\right]}{V_1\left[\frac{C}{AD - BC}\right] - I_1\left[\frac{A}{AD - BC}\right]} = \frac{DV_1 - BI_1}{CV_1 - AI_1} = \frac{-DZ_{i1}I_1 - BI_1}{-CZ_{i1}I_1 - DI_1} = \frac{DZ_{i1} + B}{CZ_{i1} + D}$$

$$\Rightarrow \quad Z_{i2} = \frac{DZ_{i1} + B}{CZ_{i1} + D} \tag{11.166}$$

Solving Eqs 11.165 and 11.166, we have

$$Z_{i1} = \sqrt{\frac{AB}{CD}} \tag{11.167}$$

$$Z_{i2} = \sqrt{\frac{DB}{CD}} \tag{11.168}$$

Equations 11.167 and 11.168 represent the image impedances of *ABCD* network, but do not define the network completely. A third parameter image transfer constant θ is also used to define the network, which can be expressed in terms of *ABCD* parameters. Let the network be terminated in impedance Z_{i2} at port 2.

$$V_2 = -Z_{i2} I_1$$

$$V_1 = AV_2 - BI_2 = AV_2 - B\left[-\frac{V_2}{Z_{i2}}\right] = \left[A + \frac{B}{Z_{i2}}\right]V_2$$

$$\frac{V_1}{V_2} = \left[A + \frac{B}{Z_{i2}}\right] = A + \frac{B}{\sqrt{\frac{BD}{AC}}} = \frac{AD + \sqrt{ABCD}}{D}$$

$$I_1 = CV_2 - DI_2 = -CZ_{i2}I_2 - DI_2$$

$$\Rightarrow \quad \frac{I_1}{I_2} = -CZ_{i2} - D = -C\sqrt{\frac{DB}{CD}} - D = -\frac{\sqrt{ABCD}}{A} - D = \frac{-AD - \sqrt{ABCD}}{A}$$

$$\therefore \qquad -\frac{V_1}{V_2}\frac{I_1}{I_2} = \frac{AD+\sqrt{ABCD}}{D} \times \frac{AD+\sqrt{ABCD}}{A} = \frac{(AD+\sqrt{ABCD})^2}{AD} = (\sqrt{AD}+\sqrt{BC})^2$$

$$\Rightarrow \qquad \sqrt{-\frac{V_1}{V_2}\frac{I_1}{I_2}} = \sqrt{AD}+\sqrt{BC} = \sqrt{AD}+\sqrt{AD-1} \quad (\because AD-BC=1)$$

Let $\sqrt{AD} = \cos h\theta$, then $\sqrt{AD-1} = \sin h\theta\ AD$

$$\tanh\theta = \frac{\sqrt{AD-1}}{\sqrt{AD}} = \frac{\sqrt{BC}}{\sqrt{AD}} = \sqrt{\frac{BC}{AD}}$$

$$\Rightarrow \qquad \theta = \tanh^{-1}\left[\sqrt{\frac{BC}{AD}}\right] \tag{11.169}$$

Also $\sqrt{-\frac{V_1}{V_2}\frac{I_1}{I_2}} = \cosh\theta + \sinh\theta = e^{\theta}$

$$\Rightarrow \qquad \theta = \ln\left[\sqrt{-\frac{V_1}{V_2}\frac{I_1}{I_2}}\right] = \frac{1}{2}\ln\left[-\frac{V_1}{V_2}\frac{I_1}{I_2}\right] \tag{11.170}$$

11.14.1 Relation Between Image Parameters and Open Circuit and Short Circuit Impedances

The *ABCD* parameters are given by

$$V_1 = AV_2 - BI_2$$

$$I_1 = CV_2 - DI_2$$

When the output port is open circuited, $I_2 = 0$.

$$V_1 = AV_2$$

$$I_1 = CV_2$$

Therefore, the impedance measured at input port with output port open circuited is

$$Z_{1OC} = \frac{V_1}{I_1} = \frac{AV_2}{CV_2} = \frac{A}{C} \tag{11.171}$$

When the output port is short circuited, $V_2 = 0$.

$$V_1 = -BI_2$$

$$I_1 = -DI_2$$

Therefore, the impedance measured at input port with output port short circuited is

$$Z_{1SC} = \frac{V_1}{I_1} = \frac{-BI_2}{-DI_2} = \frac{B}{D} \tag{11.172}$$

Similarly, the impedances measured at the output port with input port open circuited and short circuited are

$$Z_{2OC} = \frac{D}{C} \tag{11.173}$$

$$Z_{2SC} = \frac{B}{A} \tag{11.174}$$

The ratio of short circuit to open circuit impedance at two ports is

$$\frac{Z_{1SC}}{Z_{1OC}} = \frac{Z_{2SC}}{Z_{2OC}} = \frac{BC}{AD} \tag{11.175}$$

The image parameters can also be expressed in terms of open circuit and short circuit impedances.

$$Z_{i1} = \sqrt{\frac{AB}{CD}} = \sqrt{Z_{1OC}Z_{1SC}} \tag{11.176}$$

$$Z_{i2} = \sqrt{\frac{DB}{AC}} = \sqrt{Z_{2OC}Z_{2SC}} \tag{11.177}$$

$$\theta = \tanh^{-1}\left[\sqrt{\frac{BC}{AD}}\right] = \tanh^{-1}\left[\sqrt{\frac{Z_{1SC}}{Z_{1OC}}}\right] = \tanh^{-1}\left[\sqrt{\frac{Z_{2SC}}{Z_{2OC}}}\right] \tag{11.178}$$

Problem 11.25 The $ABCD$ parameters of the two-port network are given as $A = 1$, $B = 2$, $C = 0.5$, $D = 4$. Find the image parameters.

Solution:

Given that $A = 1$, $B = 2$, $C = 0.5$, $D = 4$

$$Z_{i1} = \sqrt{\frac{AB}{CD}} = \sqrt{\frac{1\times 2}{0.5\times 4}} = 1\,\Omega$$

$$Z_{i2} = \sqrt{\frac{DB}{ACD}} = \sqrt{\frac{4\times 2}{0.5\times 1}} = 4\,\Omega$$

$$\theta = \tanh^{-1}\left[\sqrt{\frac{BC}{AD}}\right] = \tanh^{-1}\left[\sqrt{\frac{2\times 0.5}{1\times 4}}\right] = \tanh^{-1}(0.5) = 0.55^\circ$$

Problem 11.26 Find the image parameters of the lattice network.

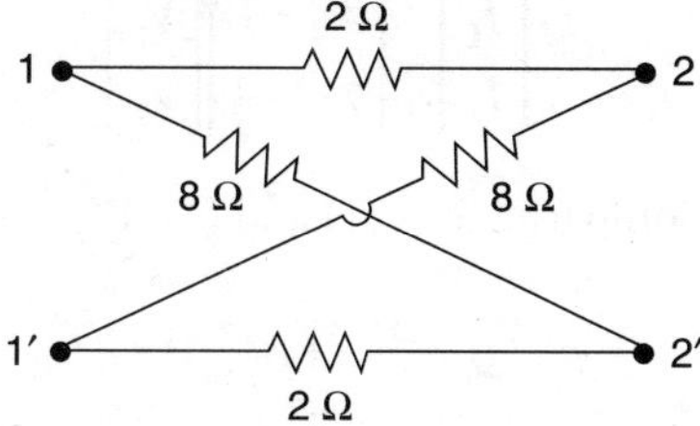

Solution:

The network is redrawn as shown.

$$Z_{1OC} = Z_{2OC} = (2+8)//(2+8) = \frac{10}{2} = 5\,\Omega$$

$$Z_{1SC} = Z_{2SC} = (2//8) + (2//8) = 1.6 + 1.6 = 3.2\,\Omega$$

$$Z_{i1} = \sqrt{Z_{1OC}Z_{1SC}} = \sqrt{5\times 3.2} = 4\,\Omega$$

$$Z_{i2}=\sqrt{Z_{2OC}Z_{2SC}}=\sqrt{5\times 3.2}=4\,\Omega$$

$$\theta=\tanh^{-1}\left[\sqrt{\frac{Z_{1SC}}{Z_{1OC}}}\right]$$

$$=\tanh^{-1}\left[\sqrt{\frac{3.2}{4}}\right]$$

$$=\tanh^{-1}(0.89)=1.422°$$

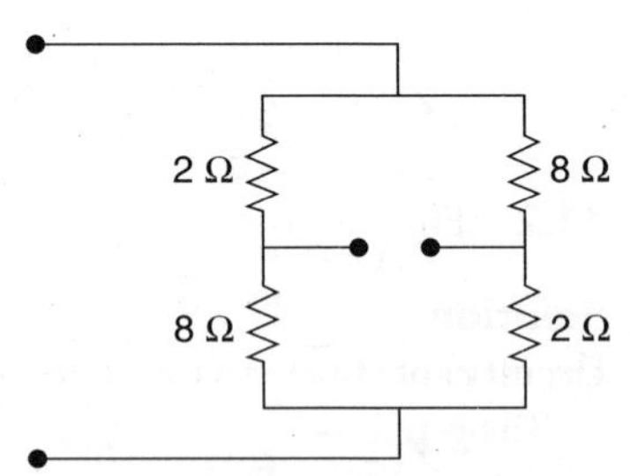

ADDITIONAL SOLVED PROBLEMS

11.1 Obtain the open circuit and short circuit parameters for the network.

Solution: The given circuit can be redrawn as shown.

Determination of Y-parameters:

The admittance parameters are given by

$$\begin{bmatrix} I_1 \\ I_2 \end{bmatrix}=\begin{bmatrix} Y_{11} & Y_{12} \\ Y_{21} & Y_{22} \end{bmatrix}\begin{bmatrix} V_1 \\ V_2 \end{bmatrix} \tag{1}$$

Applying KCL at node 1

$$I_1=\frac{V_1}{1}+\frac{V_1-V_2}{1}=2V_1-V_2 \tag{2}$$

Applying KCL at node 2

$$I_2=\frac{V_2}{2}+\frac{V_2-V_1}{1}+4I_1=\frac{3V_2}{2}-V_1+4I_1 \tag{3}$$

From Eqs (2) and (3), we have

$$I_2=\frac{3V_2}{2}-V_1+4(2V_1-V_2)=7V_1-\frac{5V_2}{2} \tag{4}$$

Equations (2) and (4) can be represented in the matrix form

$$\begin{bmatrix} I_1 \\ I_2 \end{bmatrix}=\begin{bmatrix} 2 & -1 \\ 7 & -\frac{5}{2} \end{bmatrix}\begin{bmatrix} V_1 \\ V_2 \end{bmatrix} \tag{5}$$

Comparing Eqs (1) and (5), Y-parameters are

$$Y_{11}=2,\quad Y_{12}=-1,\quad Y_{21}=7,\quad Y_{22}=-\frac{5}{2}$$

Determination of Z-parameters:

$$[Z]=[Y]^{-1}=\begin{bmatrix} 2 & -1 \\ 7 & -\frac{5}{2} \end{bmatrix}^{-1}=\frac{1}{-5+7}\begin{bmatrix} -\frac{5}{2} & 1 \\ -7 & 2 \end{bmatrix}=\begin{bmatrix} -\frac{5}{4} & \frac{1}{2} \\ \frac{-7}{2} & 1 \end{bmatrix}$$

$$\therefore \qquad Z_{11} = -\frac{5}{4}, \quad Z_{12} = \frac{1}{2}, \quad Z_{21} = -\frac{7}{2}, \quad Z_{22} = 1$$

11.2 Find the g-parameters for the network.

Solution: Using source transformation, the given circuit can be redrawn as shown.

The g-parameters are given by

$$\begin{bmatrix} I_1 \\ V_2 \end{bmatrix} = \begin{bmatrix} g_{11} & g_{12} \\ g_{21} & g_{22} \end{bmatrix} \begin{bmatrix} V_1 \\ I_2 \end{bmatrix} \qquad (1)$$

Applying KVL to loop 1

$$V_1 = I_1 + 1(I_1 + I_2) = 2I_1 + I_2$$

$$\Rightarrow \qquad I_1 = \frac{1}{2}V_1 - \frac{1}{2}I_2 \qquad (2)$$

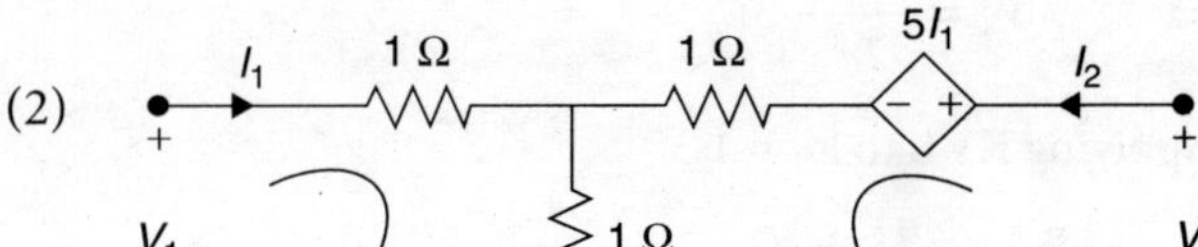

Applying KVL to loop-2

$$V_2 = 5I_1 + I_2 + 1(I_1 + I_2) = 6I_1 + 2I_2 \qquad (3)$$

From Eqs (2) and (3), we have

$$V_2 = 6 \times \left(\frac{1}{2}V_1 - \frac{1}{2}I_2 \right) + 2I_2 = 3V_1 - I_2 \qquad (4)$$

Equations (2) and (4) can be represented in the matrix form

$$\begin{bmatrix} I_1 \\ V_2 \end{bmatrix} = \begin{bmatrix} \frac{1}{2} & -\frac{1}{2} \\ 3 & -1 \end{bmatrix} \begin{bmatrix} V_1 \\ I_2 \end{bmatrix} \qquad (5)$$

Comparing Eqs (1) and (5), the Y-parameters are

$$g_{11} = \frac{1}{2}, \quad g_{12} = -\frac{1}{2}, \quad g_{21} = 3, \quad g_{22} = -1$$

11.3 Determine the $ABCD$ parameters of the network.

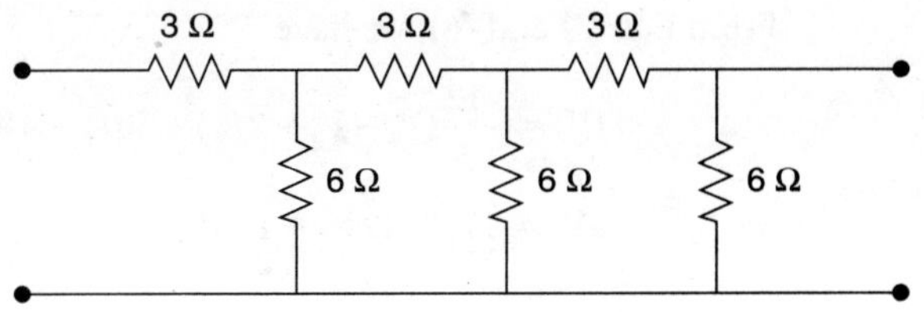

Solution: The given network can be redrawn as shown.

The standard $ABCD$ parameters equations are

$$\begin{bmatrix} V_1 \\ I_1 \end{bmatrix} = \begin{bmatrix} A & B \\ C & D \end{bmatrix} \begin{bmatrix} V_2 \\ -I_2 \end{bmatrix} \qquad (1)$$

Applying KCL at node 1

$$I_1 = \frac{V_x}{6} + \frac{V_x - V_y}{3} = \frac{1}{2}V_x - \frac{1}{3}V_y \qquad (2)$$

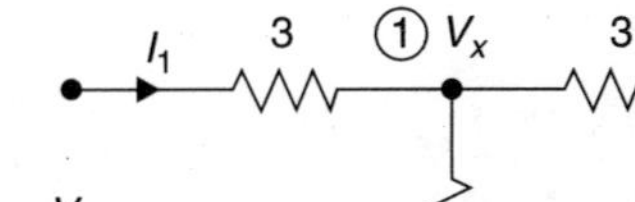

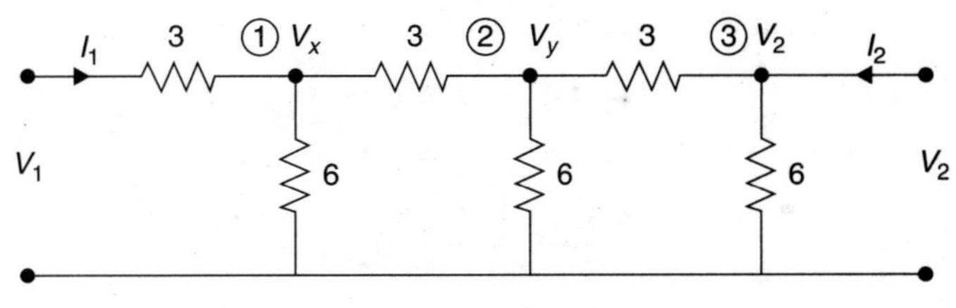

Applying KCL at node 2

$$\frac{V_y}{6} + \frac{V_y - V_X}{3} + \frac{V_y - V_2}{3} = 0$$

$$\Rightarrow \quad \left(\frac{1}{6}+\frac{2}{3}\right)V_y - \frac{V_x}{3} = \frac{V_2}{3}$$

$$\Rightarrow \quad V_2 = \frac{5}{2}V_y - V_x \tag{3}$$

Applying KCL at node 3

$$I_2 = \frac{V_2}{6} + \frac{V_2 - V_y}{3}$$

$$\Rightarrow \quad I_2 = \frac{V_2}{2} - \frac{V_y}{3}$$

$$\Rightarrow \quad V_y = \frac{3V_2}{2} - 3I_2 \tag{4}$$

Applying KVL to loop 1

$$V_1 = 3I_1 + V_x$$

$$\Rightarrow \quad V_x = V_1 - 3I_1 \tag{5}$$

From Eqs (2), (4) and (5), we have

$$I_1 = \frac{1}{2}(V_1 - 3I_1) - \frac{1}{3}\left(\frac{3V_2}{2} - 3I_2\right)$$

$$\Rightarrow \quad 2I_1 = V_1 - 3I_1 - V_2 + 2I_2$$

$$\Rightarrow \quad I_1 = \frac{1}{5}(V_1 - V_2 + 2I_2) \tag{6}$$

From Eqs (3), (4) and (5), we have

$$V_2 = \frac{5}{2}\left(\frac{3V_2 - 6I_2}{2}\right) - (V_1 - 3I_1)$$

$$\Rightarrow \quad 11V_2 = -12I_1 + 30I_2 + 4V_1 \tag{7}$$

From Eqs (7) and (6), we have

$$11V_2 = -\frac{12}{5}(V_1 - V_2 + 2I_2) + 30I_2 + 4V_1 = \frac{8}{5}V_1 + \frac{12}{5}V_2 + \frac{126}{5}I_2$$

$$\Rightarrow \quad 55V_2 = 8V_1 + 12V_2 + 126I_2$$

$$V_1 = \frac{43}{8}V_2 - \frac{126}{8}I_2 \tag{8}$$

From Eqs (6) and (8), we have

$$I_1 = \frac{1}{5}\left(\frac{43V_2}{8} - \frac{126I_2}{8}\right) - \frac{1}{5}V_2 + \frac{2}{5}I_2$$

$$I_1 = \frac{4.375}{5}V_2 - \frac{13.75}{5}I_2 \tag{9}$$

Equations (8) and (9) can be written in the matrix form

$$\begin{bmatrix} V_1 \\ I_1 \end{bmatrix} = \begin{bmatrix} \frac{43}{8} & \frac{126}{8} \\ \frac{4.375}{5} & \frac{13.75}{5} \end{bmatrix} \begin{bmatrix} V_2 \\ -I_2 \end{bmatrix} \tag{10}$$

Comparing Eqs (1) and (10),

$$A = \frac{43}{8}, \quad B = \frac{126}{8}, \quad C = \frac{4.375}{5}, \quad D = \frac{13.75}{5}$$

11.4 Determine the Z and Y-parameters of the network.

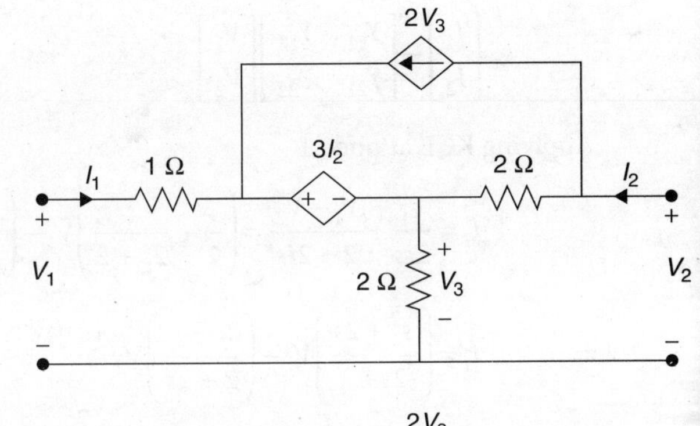

Solution: The given network can be redrawn as shown below.

Determination of Z-parameters

The standard Z-parameter equations are

$$\begin{bmatrix} V_1 \\ V_2 \end{bmatrix} = \begin{bmatrix} Z_{11} & Z_{12} \\ Z_{21} & Z_{22} \end{bmatrix} \begin{bmatrix} I_1 \\ I_2 \end{bmatrix} \tag{1}$$

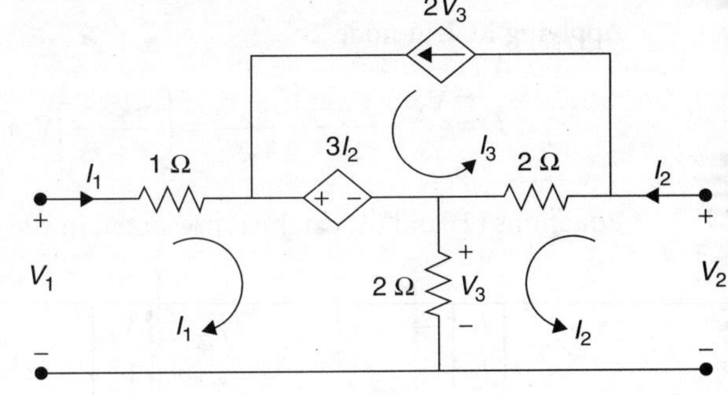

Applying KVL to loop 1

$$V_1 = I_1 + 3I_2 + 2(I_1 + I_2) = 3I_1 + 5I_2 \tag{2}$$

Applying KVL to loop 2

$$V_2 = 2(I_2 - I_3) + 2(I_2 + I_1) = 2I_1 + 4I_2 - 2I_3 \tag{3}$$

From loop 3

$$I_3 = 2V_3 \tag{4}$$

From the given circuit diagram

$$V_3 = 2(I_1 + I_2) \tag{5}$$

From Eqs (4) and (5), we have

$$I_3 = 2V_3 = 2 \times 2(I_1 + I_2) = 4I_1 + 4I_2 \tag{6}$$

From Eqs (3) and (6), we have

$$V_2 = 2I_1 + 4I_2 - 2(4I_1 + 4I_2) = -6I_1 - 4I_2 \tag{7}$$

Writing Eqs (2) and (7) in the matrix form, we have

$$\begin{bmatrix} V_1 \\ V_2 \end{bmatrix} = \begin{bmatrix} 3 & 5 \\ -6 & -4 \end{bmatrix} \begin{bmatrix} I_1 \\ I_2 \end{bmatrix} \tag{8}$$

Comparing Eqs (1) and (8), Z-parameters are

$$Z_{11} = 3, Z_{12} = 5, Z_{21} = -6, Z_{22} = -4$$

Determination of Y-parameters

The Y-parameters are given by the inverse of the Z-parameters.

$$\therefore \quad [Y] = [Z]^{-1} = \begin{bmatrix} 3 & 5 \\ -6 & -4 \end{bmatrix}^{-1} = \frac{1}{-12+30} \begin{bmatrix} -4 & -5 \\ 6 & 3 \end{bmatrix} = \begin{bmatrix} -\frac{2}{9} & -\frac{5}{18} \\ \frac{1}{3} & \frac{1}{6} \end{bmatrix}$$

∴ The Y-parameters are,

$$Y_{11}=-\frac{2}{9},\quad Y_{12}=-\frac{5}{18},\quad Y_{21}=\frac{1}{3},\quad Y_{22}=\frac{1}{6}$$

11.5 Find the admittance parameters of the network.

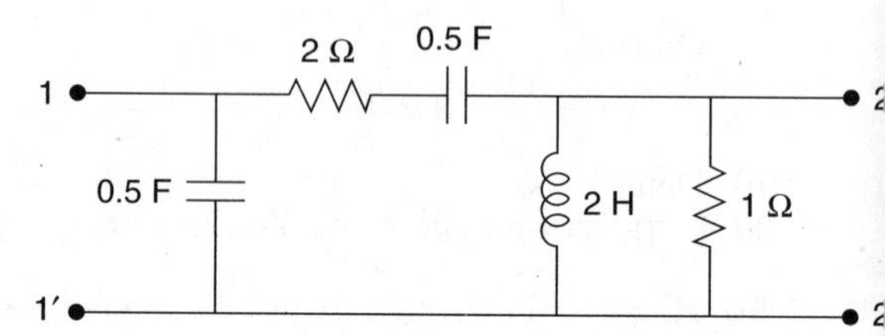

Solution: The s-domain or transformed equivalent circuit for the given network is shown.

The admittance parameters are given by

$$\begin{bmatrix} I_1 \\ I_2 \end{bmatrix}=\begin{bmatrix} Y_{11} & Y_{12} \\ Y_{21} & Y_{22} \end{bmatrix}\begin{bmatrix} V_1 \\ V_2 \end{bmatrix} \qquad (1)$$

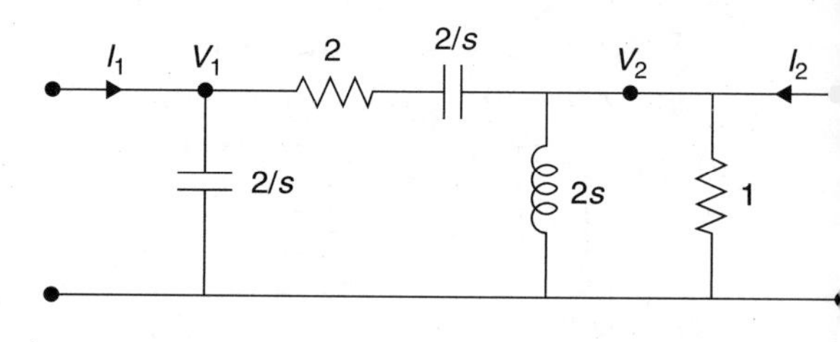

Applying KCL at node 1

$$I_1=\frac{V_1}{2/s}+\frac{V_1-V_2}{2+2/s}=\left(\frac{s}{2}+\frac{s}{2s+2}\right)V_1-\left(\frac{s}{2s+2}\right)V_2$$

$$\Rightarrow \qquad I_1=\left(\frac{s^2+2s}{2s+2}\right)V_1-\left(\frac{s}{2+2s}\right)V_2 \qquad (2)$$

Applying KCL at node 2

$$I_2=\frac{V_2}{2s}+\frac{V_2}{1}+\frac{V_2-V_1}{2+2/s}=\left(\frac{-s}{2+2s}\right)V_1+\left(\frac{3s^2+3s+1}{s(2s+2)}\right)V_2 \qquad (3)$$

Equations (2) and (3) can be represented in the matrix form

$$\begin{bmatrix} I_1 \\ I_2 \end{bmatrix}=\begin{bmatrix} \frac{s^2+2s}{2s+2} & -\frac{s}{2+2s} \\ -\frac{s}{2+2s} & \frac{3s^2+3s+1}{s(2s+2)} \end{bmatrix}\begin{bmatrix} V_1 \\ V_2 \end{bmatrix} \qquad (4)$$

Comparing Eqs (1) and (4), we have

$$Y_{11}=\frac{s^2+2s}{2s+2},\quad Y_{12}=Y_{21}=-\frac{s}{2+2s},\quad Y_{22}=\frac{3s^2+3s+1}{s(2s+2)}$$

11.6 For the two-port network, the currents I_1 and I_2 entering at port 1 and 2 respectively are given by the equations:

$$I_1=0.5V_1-0.2V_2$$
$$I_2=-0.2V_1+V_2$$

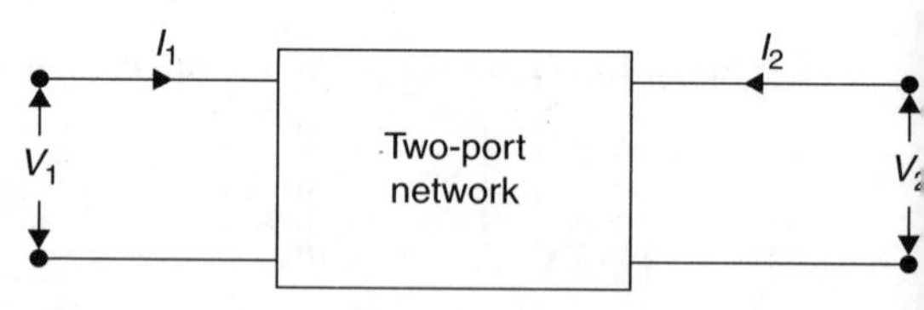

where V_1 and V_2 are the port voltages at port 1 and 2 respectively. Find the Y, Z, $ABCD$, h, g and inverse $ABCD$ parameters for the network.

Solution: Given that

$$\left.\begin{aligned} I_1&=0.5V_1-0.2V_2 \\ I_2&=-0.2V_1+V_2 \end{aligned}\right\} \qquad (1)$$

(i) Determination of Y-parameters

The standard Y-parameter equations are

$$\begin{bmatrix} I_1 \\ I_2 \end{bmatrix} = \begin{bmatrix} Y_{11} & Y_{12} \\ Y_{21} & Y_{22} \end{bmatrix} \begin{bmatrix} V_1 \\ V_2 \end{bmatrix} \tag{2}$$

On comparing Eqs (1) and (2), we have

$$Y_{11} = 0.5, \quad Y_{12} = Y_{21} = -0.2, \quad Y_{22} = 1$$

(ii) Determination of Z-parameters

The Z-parameters are given by

$$[Z] = [Y]^{-1} = \begin{bmatrix} 0.5 & -0.2 \\ -0.2 & 1 \end{bmatrix}^{-1} = \begin{bmatrix} 2.175 & 0.4348 \\ 0.4348 & 1.087 \end{bmatrix}$$

$$Z_{11} = 2.175, \quad Z_{12} = Z_{21} = 0.4348, \quad Z_{22} = 1.087$$

(iii) Determination of $ABCD$ parameters

The standard $ABCD$ parameter equations are

$$\begin{bmatrix} V_1 \\ I_1 \end{bmatrix} = \begin{bmatrix} A & B \\ C & D \end{bmatrix} \begin{bmatrix} V_2 \\ -I_2 \end{bmatrix} \tag{3}$$

The given Y-parameter equations are

$$I_1 = 0.5V_1 - 0.2V_2$$

$$I_2 = -0.2V_1 + V_2$$

$$\Rightarrow \quad 0.2V_1 = V_2 - I_2$$

$$\Rightarrow \quad V_1 = 5V_2 - 5I_2 \tag{4}$$

Also, $I_1 = 0.5(5V_2 - 5I_2) - 0.2V_2 = 2.3V_2 - 2.5I_2$ (5)

Equations (4) and (5) can be represented in the matrix form

$$\begin{bmatrix} V_1 \\ I_1 \end{bmatrix} = \begin{bmatrix} 5 & 5 \\ 2.3 & 2.5 \end{bmatrix} \begin{bmatrix} V_2 \\ -I_2 \end{bmatrix} \tag{6}$$

Comparing Eqs (3) and (6), we have

$$A = 5, \quad B = 5, \quad C = 2.3, \quad D = 2.5$$

(iv) Determination of h-parameters

The standard h-parameter equations are

$$\begin{bmatrix} V_1 \\ I_2 \end{bmatrix} = \begin{bmatrix} h_{11} & h_{12} \\ h_{21} & h_{22} \end{bmatrix} \begin{bmatrix} I_1 \\ V_2 \end{bmatrix} \tag{7}$$

The given Y-parameters equations are

$$I_1 = 0.5V_1 - 0.2V_2$$

$$I_2 = -0.2V_1 + V_2$$

$$\Rightarrow \quad 0.5V_1 = I_1 + 0.2V_2$$

$$\Rightarrow \quad V_1 = 2I_1 + 4V_2 \tag{8}$$

Also, $I_2 = -0.2(2I_1 + 4V_2) + V_2 = -0.4I_1 + 0.2V_2$ (9)

Equations (8) and (9) can be represented in the matrix form

$$\begin{bmatrix} V_1 \\ I_2 \end{bmatrix} = \begin{bmatrix} 2 & 4 \\ -0.4 & 0.2 \end{bmatrix} \begin{bmatrix} I_1 \\ V_2 \end{bmatrix} \quad (10)$$

Comparing Eqs (7) and (10), we have

$$h_{11} = 2, \quad h_{12} = 4, \quad h_{21} = -0.4, \quad h_{22} = 0.2$$

(v) Determination of g-parameters

The standard g-parameter equations are

$$\begin{bmatrix} I_1 \\ V_2 \end{bmatrix} = \begin{bmatrix} g_{11} & g_{12} \\ g_{21} & g_{22} \end{bmatrix} \begin{bmatrix} V_1 \\ I_2 \end{bmatrix} \quad (11)$$

The given Y-parameter equations are

$$I_1 = 0.5V_1 - 0.2V_2$$

$$I_2 = -0.2V_1 + V_2$$

$$\Rightarrow \quad V_2 = 0.2V_1 + I_2 \quad (12)$$

Also, $I_1 = 0.5V_1 - 0.2(0.2V_1 + I_2) = 0.46V_1 - 0.2I_2$ (13)

Equations (13) and (12) can be represented in the matrix form

$$\begin{bmatrix} I_1 \\ V_2 \end{bmatrix} = \begin{bmatrix} 0.46 & -0.2 \\ 0.2 & 1 \end{bmatrix} \begin{bmatrix} V_1 \\ I_2 \end{bmatrix} \quad (14)$$

Comparing Eqs (11) and (14), we have

$$h_{11} = 0.46, \quad h_{12} = -0.2, \quad h_{21} = 0.2, \quad h_{22} = 1$$

(vi) Determination of $A'B'C'D'$ parameters

The standard $A'B'C'D'$ parameter equations are

$$\begin{bmatrix} V_2 \\ I_2 \end{bmatrix} = \begin{bmatrix} A' & B' \\ C' & D' \end{bmatrix} \begin{bmatrix} V_1 \\ -I_1 \end{bmatrix} \quad (15)$$

The given Y-parameter equations are

$$I_1 = 0.5V_1 - 0.2V_2$$

$$I_2 = -0.2V_1 + V_2$$

$$\Rightarrow \quad V_2 = 2.5V_1 - 5I_1 \quad (16)$$

Also, $I_2 = -0.2V_1 + 2.5V_1 - 5I_1 = 2.3V_1 - 5I_1$ (17)

Equations (16) and (17) can be represented in the matrix form

$$\begin{bmatrix} V_2 \\ I_2 \end{bmatrix} = \begin{bmatrix} 2.5 & -5 \\ 2.3 & -5 \end{bmatrix} \begin{bmatrix} V_1 \\ -I_1 \end{bmatrix} \quad (18)$$

Comparing Eqs (15) and (18), we have

$$A' = 2.5, \quad B' = -5, \quad C' = 2.3, \quad D' = -5$$

11.7 The Y-parameters of a two-port network are $Y_{11} = 0.6$, $Y_{22} = 1.2$ and $Y_{12} = -0.3$. Determine the (i) $ABCD$ parameters and (ii) equivalent π-network.

Solution: Given that $Y_{11} = 0.6$, $Y_{22} = 1.2$ and $Y_{12} = -0.3$

Let us assume that the network is reciprocal

$$Y_{12} = Y_{21} = -0.3$$

(i) Determination of $ABCD$ parameters
The standard $ABCD$ parameter equations are

$$\begin{bmatrix} V_1 \\ I_1 \end{bmatrix} = \begin{bmatrix} A & B \\ C & D \end{bmatrix} \begin{bmatrix} V_2 \\ -I_2 \end{bmatrix} \quad (1)$$

The given Y-parameters equations are

$$I_1 = 0.6V_1 - 0.3V_2$$

$$I_2 = -0.3V_1 + 1.2V_2$$

$$\Rightarrow \quad 0.3V_1 = 1.2V_2 - I_2$$

$$\Rightarrow \quad V_1 = 4V_2 - 3.33I_2 \quad (2)$$

Also, $I_1 = 0.6(4V_2 - 3.33I_2) - 0.3V_2 = 2.1V_2 - 2I_2$ (3)

Equations (2) and (3) can be represented in the matrix form

$$\begin{bmatrix} V_1 \\ I_1 \end{bmatrix} = \begin{bmatrix} 4 & 3.33 \\ 2.1 & 2 \end{bmatrix} \begin{bmatrix} V_2 \\ -I_2 \end{bmatrix} \quad (6)$$

Comparing Eqs (3) and (6), we have

$$A = 4, \quad B = 3.33, \quad C = 2.1, \quad D = 2$$

(ii) Equivalent π-network
The equivalent π-network is shown,

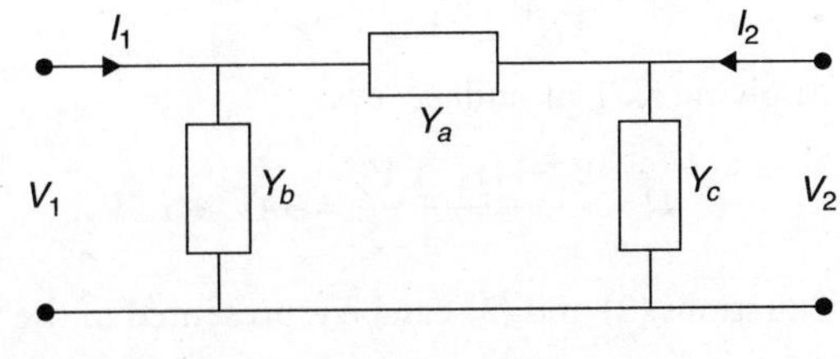

where, $Y_a = -Y_{12} = 0.3$

$$Y_b = Y_{11} + Y_{12} = 0.6 - 0.3 = 0.3$$

$$Y_c = Y_{22} + Y_{12} = 1.2 - 0.3 = 0.9$$

11.8 A typical two-port network is characterised by the equations $2V_1 + 4I_2 = I_1$ and $V_2 + 6V_1 = 8I_2$. Determine the values of (i) Y_{11} (ii) Z_{21} and (iii) h_{21}.

Solution: Given that

$$2V_1 + 4I_2 = I_1 \quad (1)$$

$$V_2 + 6V_1 = 8I_2 \quad (2)$$

From Eq. (1), we have

$$V_1 = 0.5I_1 - 2I_2 \quad (3)$$

From Eqs (2) and (3), we have

$$V_2 + 6(0.5I_1 - 2I_2) = 8I_2$$

$$\Rightarrow \quad V_2 = -3I_1 + 20I_2 \tag{4}$$

Equations (2) and (3) can be represented in the matrix form

$$\begin{bmatrix} V_1 \\ V_2 \end{bmatrix} = \begin{bmatrix} 0.5 & -2 \\ -3 & 20 \end{bmatrix} \begin{bmatrix} I_1 \\ I_2 \end{bmatrix} \tag{5}$$

The standard Y-parameter equations are

$$\begin{bmatrix} V_1 \\ V_2 \end{bmatrix} = \begin{bmatrix} Z_{11} & Z_{12} \\ Z_{21} & Z_{22} \end{bmatrix} \begin{bmatrix} I_1 \\ I_2 \end{bmatrix} \tag{6}$$

Comparing Eqs (5) and (6), we have

$$Z_{11} = 0.5, Z_{12} = -2, Z_{21} = -3, Z_{22} = 20$$

$$\Delta Z = Z_{11}Z_{22} - Z_{12}Z_{21} = 20 \times 0.5 - 2 \times 3 = 10 - 6 = 4$$

(i) $Y_{11} = \dfrac{Z_{22}}{\Delta Z} = \dfrac{20}{4} = 5$ (ii) $Z_{21} = -3$ (iii) $h_{21} = \dfrac{-Z_{21}}{Z_{22}} = \dfrac{3}{20}$

11.9 Find the admittance parameters for the network.

Solution: The given network can be redrawn as shown.

The admittance parameter equations are given by

$$\begin{bmatrix} I_1 \\ I_2 \end{bmatrix} = \begin{bmatrix} Y_{11} & Y_{12} \\ Y_{21} & Y_{22} \end{bmatrix} \begin{bmatrix} V_1 \\ V_2 \end{bmatrix} \tag{1}$$

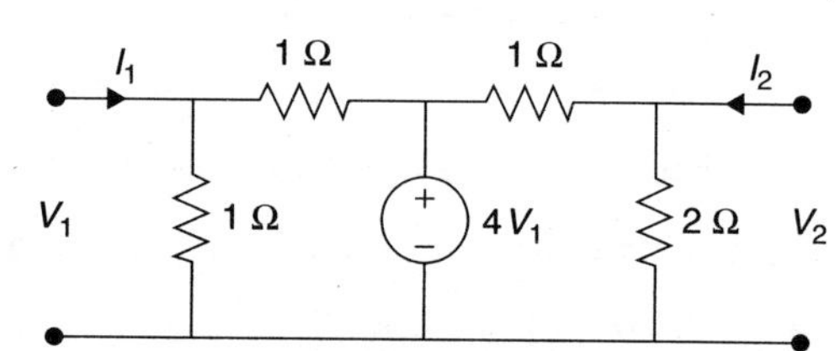

Applying KCL at node 1

$$I_1 = \frac{V_1}{1} + \frac{V_1 - 4V_1}{1} = -2V_1 \tag{2}$$

Applying KCL at node-2

$$I_2 = \frac{V_2 - 4V_1}{1} + \frac{V_2}{2} = -4V_1 + 1.5V_2 \tag{3}$$

Equations (2) and (3) can be represented in the matrix form

$$\begin{bmatrix} I_1 \\ I_2 \end{bmatrix} = \begin{bmatrix} -2 & 0 \\ -4 & 1.5 \end{bmatrix} \begin{bmatrix} V_1 \\ V_2 \end{bmatrix} \tag{4}$$

Comparing Eqs (1) and (4), we have

$$Y_{11} = -2, \quad Y_{12} = 0, \quad Y_{21} = -4, \quad Y_{22} = 1.5$$

11.10 Find the Y-parameters for the bridged T-network.

Solution: The given network can be redrawn as shown on p. 461.

The admittance parameter are given by

$$\begin{bmatrix} I_1 \\ I_2 \end{bmatrix} = \begin{bmatrix} Y_{11} & Y_{12} \\ Y_{21} & Y_{22} \end{bmatrix} \begin{bmatrix} V_1 \\ V_2 \end{bmatrix} \tag{1}$$

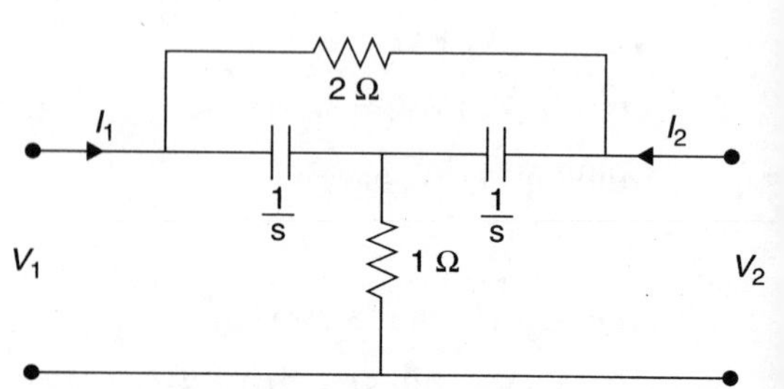

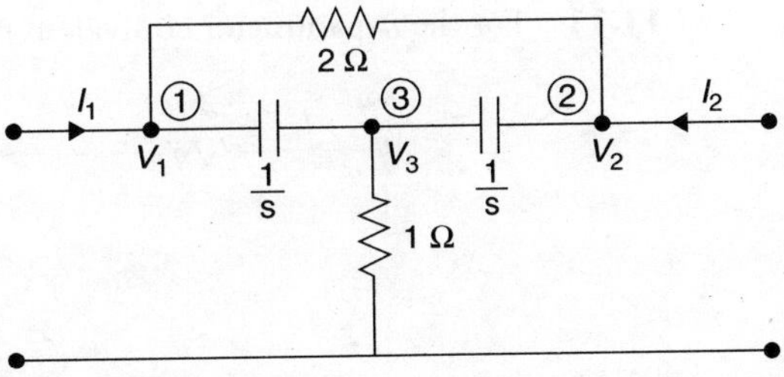

Applying KCL at node 1

$$I_1 = \frac{V_1 - V_3}{1/s} + \frac{V_1 - V_2}{2} = \left(s + \frac{1}{2}\right)V_1 - \frac{1}{2}V_2 - sV_3 \qquad (2)$$

Applying KCL at node 2

$$I_2 = \frac{V_2 - V_1}{2} + \frac{V_2 - V_3}{1/s} = \frac{-1}{2}V_1 + \left(s + \frac{1}{2}\right)V_2 - sV_3 \qquad (3)$$

Applying KCL at node 3

$$\frac{V_3 - V_1}{1/s} + \frac{V_3 - V_2}{1/s} + V_3 = 0$$

$$\Rightarrow \qquad s(V_3 - V_1) + s(V_3 - V_2) + V_3 = 0$$

$$\Rightarrow \qquad V_3 = \frac{sV_1 + sV_2}{2s + 1} \qquad (4)$$

From Eqs (2) and (4), we have

$$I_1 = \left(s + \frac{1}{2}\right)V_1 - \frac{1}{2}V_2 - s\left(\frac{sV_1 + sV_2}{2s + 1}\right)$$

$$= \left(\frac{2s+1}{2}\right)V_1 - \frac{1}{2}V_2 - \left(\frac{s^2V_1 + s^2V_2}{2s + 1}\right)$$

$$\Rightarrow \qquad I_1 = \frac{2s^2 + 4s + 1}{2(2s + 1)}V_1 - \frac{2s^2 + 2s + 1}{2(2s + 1)}V_2 \qquad (5)$$

From Eqs (3) and (4), we have

$$I_2 = \frac{-1}{2}V_1 + \left(s + \frac{1}{2}\right)V_2 - s\left(\frac{sV_1 + sV_2}{2s + 1}\right)$$

$$\Rightarrow \qquad I_2 = -\frac{2s^2 + 2s + 1}{2(2s + 1)}V_1 + \frac{2s^2 + 4s + 1}{2(2s + 1)}V_2 \qquad (6)$$

Equations (5) and (6) can be represented in the matrix form

$$\begin{bmatrix} I_1 \\ I_2 \end{bmatrix} = \begin{bmatrix} \frac{2s^2 + 4s + 1}{2(2s + 1)} & -\frac{2s^2 + 2s + 1}{2(2s + 1)} \\ -\frac{2s^2 + 2s + 1}{2(2s + 1)} & \frac{2s^2 + 4s + 1}{2(2s + 1)} \end{bmatrix} \begin{bmatrix} V_1 \\ V_2 \end{bmatrix} \qquad (7)$$

Comparing Eqs (1) and (7), we have

$$Y_{11} = \frac{2s^2 + 4s + 1}{2(2s + 1)}, \quad Y_{12} = Y_{21} = -\frac{2s^2 + 2s + 1}{2(2s + 1)}, \quad Y_{22} = \frac{2s^2 + 4s + 1}{2(2s + 1)}$$

11.11 For the h-parameter equivalent network, find the voltage gain when the load resistance is R_L.

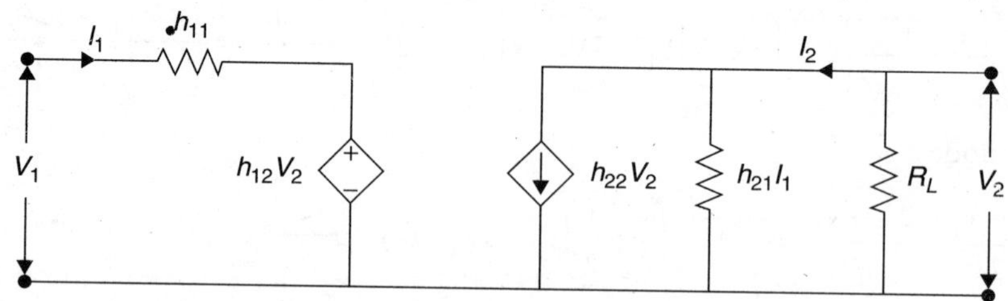

Solution: The current I_1, at the input port is given by

$$I_1 = \frac{V_1 - h_{12}V_2}{h_{11}} \tag{1}$$

The current I_2, at the output port is given by

$$I_2 = h_{21}I_1 + h_{22}V_2 \tag{2}$$

The current I_2 can also given by

$$I_2 = -\frac{V_2}{R_L} \tag{3}$$

From Eqs (2) and (3), we have

$$-\frac{V_2}{R_L} = h_{21}I_1 + h_{22}V_2 \tag{4}$$

From Eqs (1) and (4), we have

$$-\frac{V_2}{R_L} = h_{21}\left(\frac{V_1 - h_{12}V_2}{h_{11}}\right) + h_{22}V_2$$

$$\Rightarrow \quad V_2\left(\frac{h_{21}h_{12}R_L - h_{11}h_{22}R_L - h_{11}}{R_L}\right) = h_{21}V_1$$

$$\Rightarrow \quad \frac{V_2}{V_1} = \frac{h_{21}R_L}{h_{21}h_{12}R_L - h_{11}h_{22}R_L - h_{11}}$$

$$\therefore \quad \text{Voltage gain, } \frac{V_2}{V_1} = \frac{h_{21}R_L}{h_{21}h_{12}R_L - h_{11}h_{22}R_L - h_{11}}$$

11.12 Find the short circuit and open circuit impedances of the network.

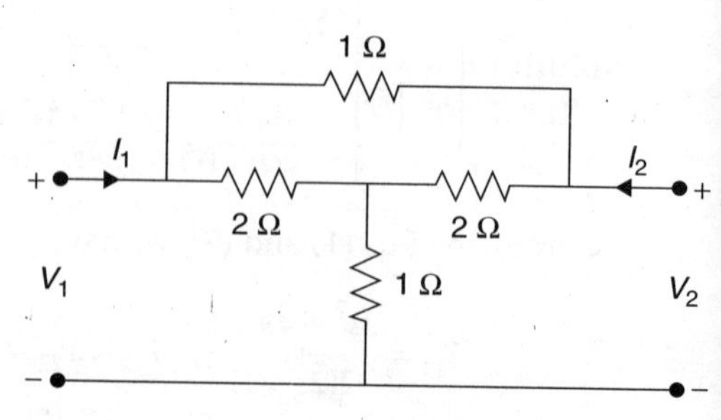

Solution: The given network can be redrawn as shown on p. 463.
Applying KVL to loop 1

$$V_1 = 1(I_1 + I_2) + 2(I_1 - I_3) = 3I_1 + I_2 - 2I_3 \tag{1}$$

Applying KVL to loop 2

$$V_2 = 2(I_2 + I_3) + 1(I_2 + I_1) = I_1 + 3I_2 + 2I_3 \tag{2}$$

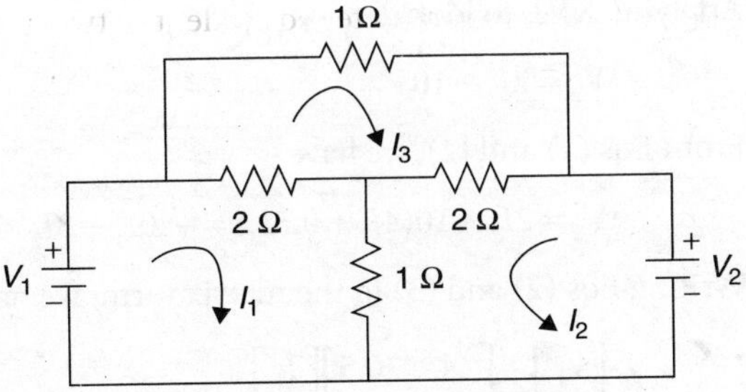

Applying KVL to loop 3

$$I_3 + 2(I_3 + I_2) + 2(I_3 - I_1) = 0$$

$$\Rightarrow \quad -2I_1 + 2I_2 + 5I_3 = 0 \qquad (3)$$

Calculation of Z_{1OC} and Z_{1SC}: When the output port is open circuited, that is, $I_2 = 0$ and eliminating V_2 and I_3 from the above equations, we get

$$I_1 = \frac{5}{11}V_1$$

$$\therefore \quad Z_{1OC} = \left.\frac{V_1}{I_1}\right|_{I_2=0} = \frac{11}{5}$$

When the output port is short circuited, $V_2 = 0$ and eliminating I_3 and I_2 from the above equations, we get

$$I_1 = \frac{11}{8}V_1$$

$$\therefore \quad Z_{1SC} = \left.\frac{V_1}{I_1}\right|_{V_2=0} = \frac{8}{11}$$

Calculation of Z_{2OC} and Z_{2SC}: When the input port is open circuited, $I_1 = 0$. Eliminating V_1 and I_3 from the above equations,

we get $\quad I_2 = \frac{5}{11}V_2$

$$\therefore \quad Z_{2OC} = \left.\frac{V_2}{I_2}\right|_{I_1=0} = \frac{11}{5}$$

When input port is short circuited, $V_1 = 0$; eliminating I_1 and I_3 from above equations, we get

$$I_2 = \frac{11}{8}V_2$$

$$\therefore \quad Z_{2SC} = \left.\frac{V_2}{I_2}\right|_{V_1=0} = \frac{8}{11}$$

11.13 Find impedance and admittance parameters for the network.

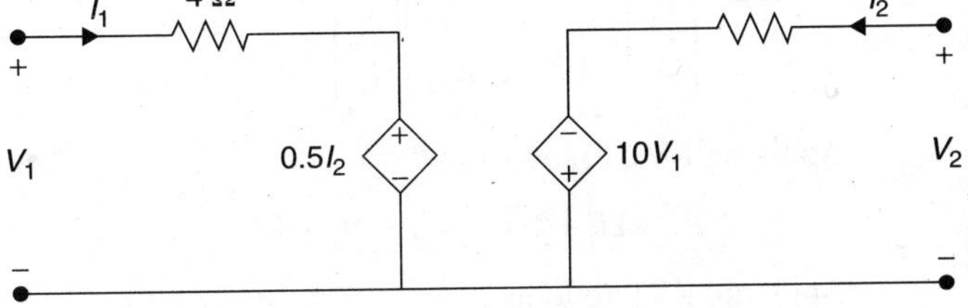

Solution: Determination of Z-parameters:

The Z-parameters are given by

$$\begin{bmatrix} V_1 \\ V_2 \end{bmatrix} = \begin{bmatrix} Z_{11} & Z_{12} \\ Z_{21} & Z_{22} \end{bmatrix} \begin{bmatrix} I_1 \\ I_2 \end{bmatrix} \qquad (1)$$

Applying KVL to loop 1

$$V_1 = 4I_1 + 0.5I_2 \qquad (2)$$

Applying KVL to loop 2

$$V_2 = 2I_2 - 10V_1 \tag{3}$$

From Eqs (1) and (2), we have

$$V_2 = 2I_2 - 10(4I_1 + 0.5I_2) = -40I_1 - 3I_2 \tag{4}$$

Writing Eqs (2) and (3) in the matrix form, we have

$$\begin{bmatrix} V_1 \\ V_2 \end{bmatrix} = \begin{bmatrix} 4 & 0.5 \\ -40 & -3 \end{bmatrix} \begin{bmatrix} I_1 \\ I_2 \end{bmatrix}$$

Comparing Eqs (1) and (2), the Z-parameters are

$$Z_{11} = 4, \quad Z_{12} = 0.5, \quad Z_{21} = -40, \quad Z_{22} = -3$$

Determination of Y-parameters:

The Y-parameters are given by the inverse of the Z-parameters.

$$[Y] = [Z]^{-1} = \begin{bmatrix} 4 & 0.5 \\ -40 & -3 \end{bmatrix}^{-1} = \frac{1}{-12+20} \begin{bmatrix} -3. & -0.5 \\ 40 & 4 \end{bmatrix} = \begin{bmatrix} -\frac{3}{8} & -\frac{1}{16} \\ 5 & \frac{1}{2} \end{bmatrix}$$

∴ The Y-parameters are,

$$Y_{11} = -\frac{3}{8}, \quad Y_{12} = -\frac{1}{16}, \quad Y_{21} = 5, \quad Y_{22} = \frac{1}{2}$$

11.14 Find the Z-parameters for the network. Hence find the Y and h-parameters.

Solution: The network can be redrawn using source transformation as given below:

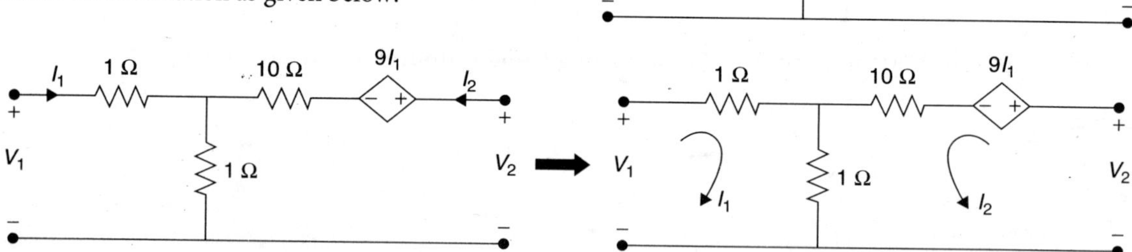

Determination of Z-parameters:

The Z parameter equations are given by

$$\begin{bmatrix} V_1 \\ V_2 \end{bmatrix} = \begin{bmatrix} Z_{11} & Z_{12} \\ Z_{21} & Z_{22} \end{bmatrix} \begin{bmatrix} I_1 \\ I_2 \end{bmatrix} \tag{1}$$

Applying KVL to loop 1

$$V_1 = 1I_1 + 1(I_1 + I_2) = 2I_1 + I_2 \tag{2}$$

Applying KVL to loop 2

$$V_2 = 9I_1 + 10I_2 + 1(I_1 + I_2) = 10I_1 + 11I_2 \tag{3}$$

Equations (2) and (3) can be represented in the matrix form

$$\begin{bmatrix} V_1 \\ V_2 \end{bmatrix} = \begin{bmatrix} 2 & 1 \\ 10 & 11 \end{bmatrix} \begin{bmatrix} I_1 \\ I_2 \end{bmatrix} \tag{4}$$

Comparing Eqs (1) and (4), we have

$$Z_{11} = 2, \quad Z_{12} = 1, \quad Z_{21} = 10, \quad Z_{22} = 11$$

Determination of Y-parameters:

$$[Y] = [Z]^{-1} = \begin{bmatrix} 2 & 1 \\ 10 & 11 \end{bmatrix}^{-1} = \frac{1}{22-10}\begin{bmatrix} 11 & -1 \\ -10 & 2 \end{bmatrix} = \begin{bmatrix} \frac{11}{12} & -\frac{1}{12} \\ -\frac{5}{6} & \frac{1}{6} \end{bmatrix}.$$

$$\therefore \quad Y_{11} = \frac{11}{12}, \quad Y_{12} = -\frac{1}{12}, \quad Y_{21} = -\frac{5}{6}, \quad Y_{22} = \frac{1}{6}$$

Determination of h-parameters:

The h-parameters are given by

$$h_{11} = \left(\frac{Z_{11}Z_{22} - Z_{12}Z_{21}}{Z_{22}} \right) = \frac{2 \times 11 - 1 \times 10}{11} = \frac{12}{11}$$

$$h_{12} = \frac{Z_{12}}{Z_{22}} = \frac{1}{11}$$

$$h_{21} = -\frac{Z_{21}}{Z_{22}} = -\frac{10}{11}$$

$$h_{22} = \frac{1}{Z_{22}} = \frac{1}{11}$$

EXERCISE PROBLEMS

1. Find the Z and transmission line parameters of the network.
[**Ans:** Z-parameters: $Z_{11} = 4/5\ \Omega$, $Z_{12} = 2/5\ \Omega$, $Z_{22} = 6/5\ \Omega$, $Z_{21} = 2/5\ \Omega$ $ABCD$ parameters: $A = 2.5$, $B = 3$, $C = 2$, $D = 2$]

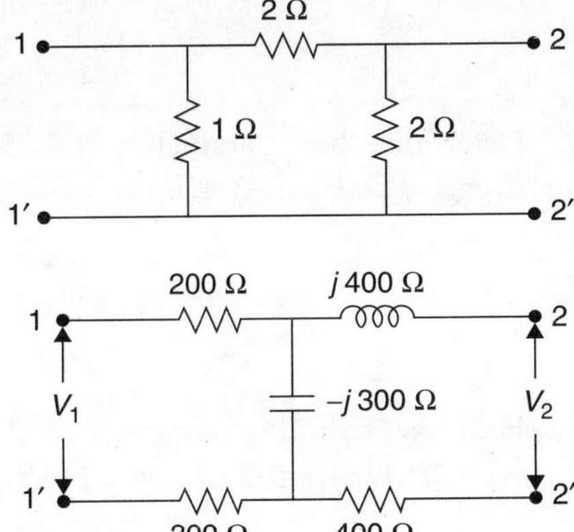

2. Find the Z-parameters of the network.
[**Ans:** $Z_{11} = (500 - j300)\ \Omega$, $Z_{12} = Z_{21} = -j300\ \Omega$, $Z_{22} = (400 + j100)\ \Omega$]

3. Determine the Z-parameters of the network.
[**Ans:** $Z_{11} = 11/5\ \Omega$, $Z_{12} = Z_{21} = 5/3\ \Omega$, $Z_{22} = 35/12\ \Omega$]

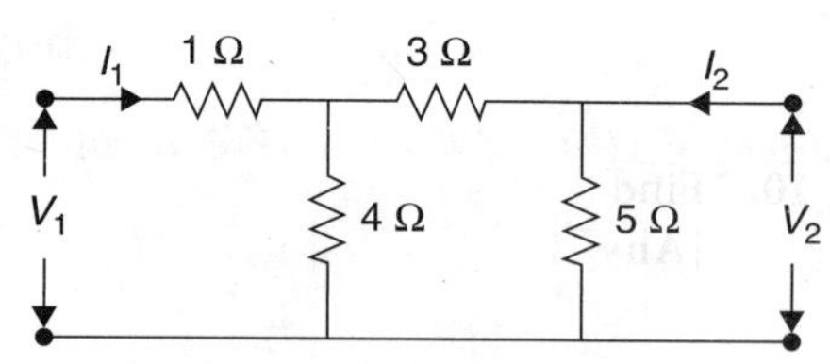

4. Z-parameters for a two-port network are given and $Z_{11} = 25\ \Omega$, $Z_{12} = Z_{21} = 20\ \Omega$, $Z_{22} = 50\ \Omega$. Find the equivalent T-network.

[**Ans:**

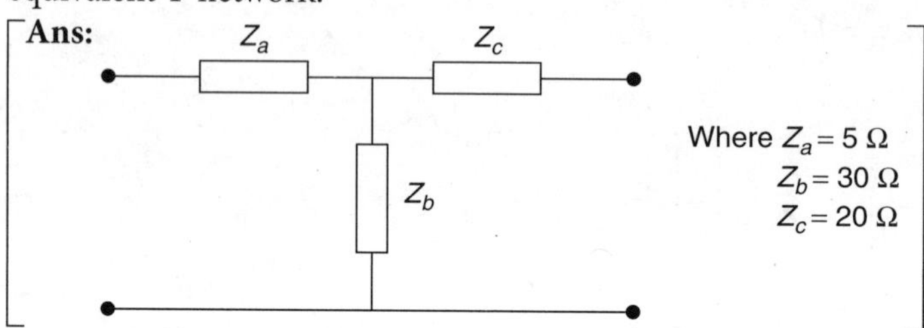

]

5. Determine the $ABCD$ parameters of the network.
[**Ans:** $A = -31/12$, $B = -132.5/13$, $C = -13/24$, $D = -21/12$]

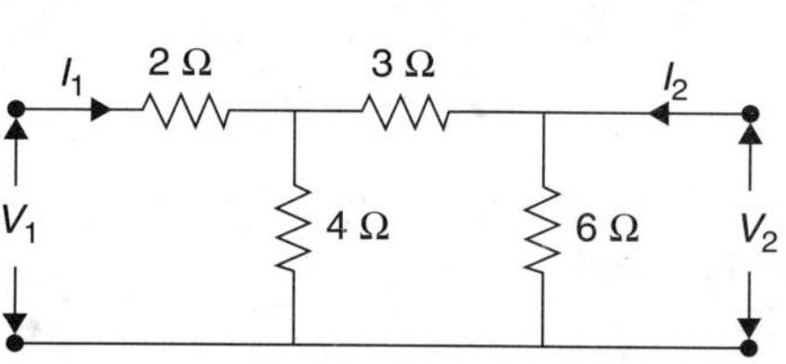

6. Calculate the Y-parameters for the network.

[**Ans:** $Y_{11} = \dfrac{3(2+2s)}{2s+6}$, $Y_{12} = \dfrac{-6}{s(2s+6)}$, $Y_{21} = \dfrac{6}{s(2s+6)}$, $Y_{22} = \dfrac{-3(2+2s)}{2s+6}$]

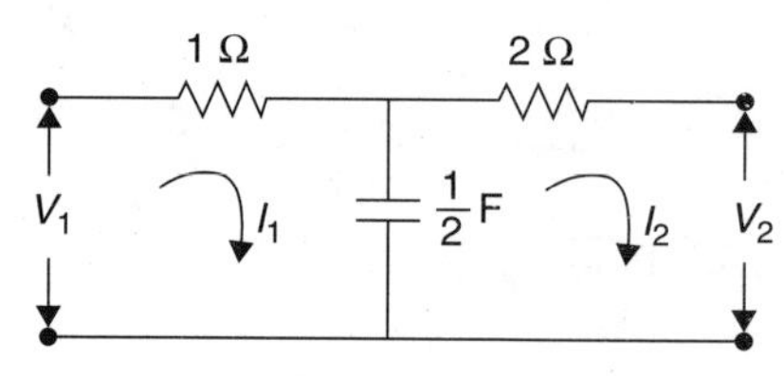

7. Determine the impedance parameters of the network.

[**Ans:** $Z_{11} = \dfrac{2s(5s+1)}{2s^2+5s+1}$, $Z_{12} = \dfrac{2s}{2s^2+5s+1}$, $Z_{21} = \dfrac{2s}{2s^2+5s+1}$,

$Z_{22} = \dfrac{2s^3+5s^2+3s+5}{2s^2+5s+1}$]

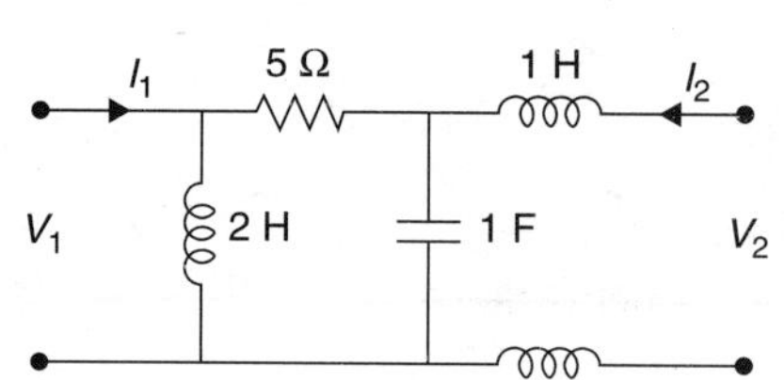

8. Determine the h-parameters of the network. [**Ans:** $h_{11} = 1/4\ \Omega$, $h_{21} = -3/4$, $h_{12} = 3/4\ \Omega$, $h_{22} = -3/4$]

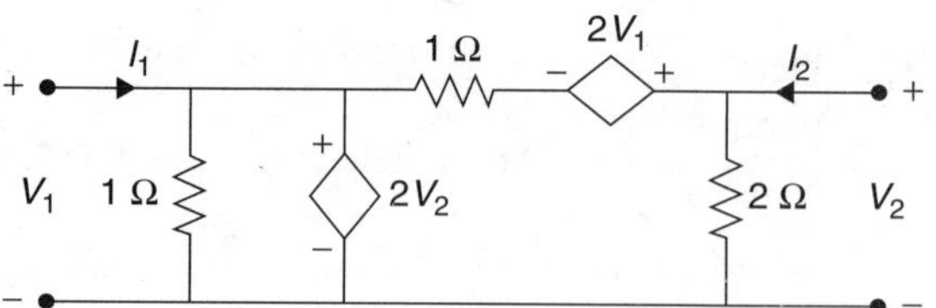

9. Find the hybrid parameters of the network. [**Ans:** $h_{11} = 2/3\ \Omega$, $h_{12} = 1/3$, $h_{21} = 8/3\ \Omega$, $h_{22} = 5/6$]

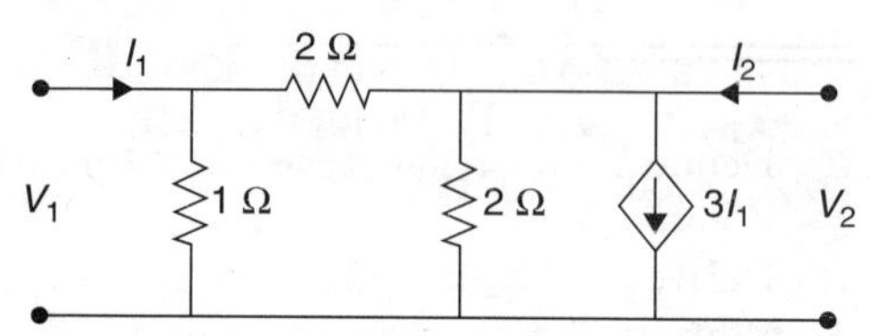

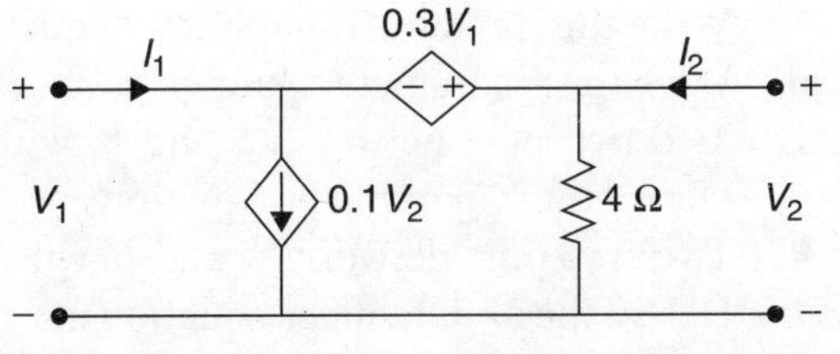

10. Find the transmission parameters for the network.
[**Ans:** $A = 2.115$, $B = 3.846$, $C = 0.35$, $D = -1$]

11. Determine h-parameters, if the Y-parameters are given as $Y = \begin{bmatrix} 0.1 & 0.1 \\ 0.4 & 0.5 \end{bmatrix}$. [**Ans:** $h = \begin{bmatrix} 10 & -1 \\ 4 & 0.1 \end{bmatrix}$]

12. A two-port network has the Z-parameters $Z_{11} = 1$, $Z_{12} = Z_{21} = -0.2$, $Z_{22} = 0.6$. Find the transmission lines parameters. [**Ans:** $A = -5$, $B = -2.8$, $C = -5$, $D = -3$]

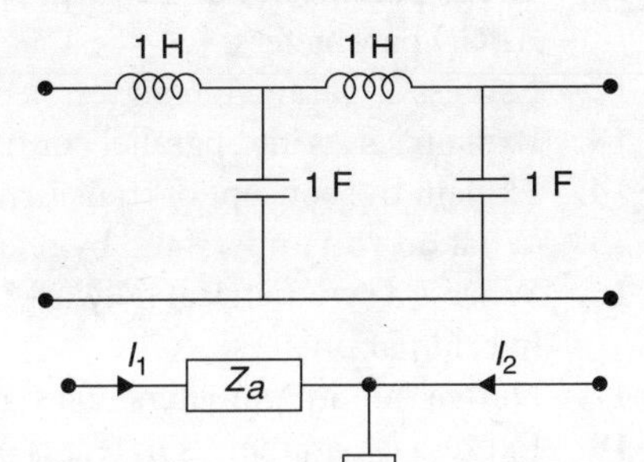

13. Find the transmission line parameters for the network.
[**Ans:** $A = s^4 + 3s^2 + 1$, $B = C = s^3 + 2s$, $D = s^2 + 1$]

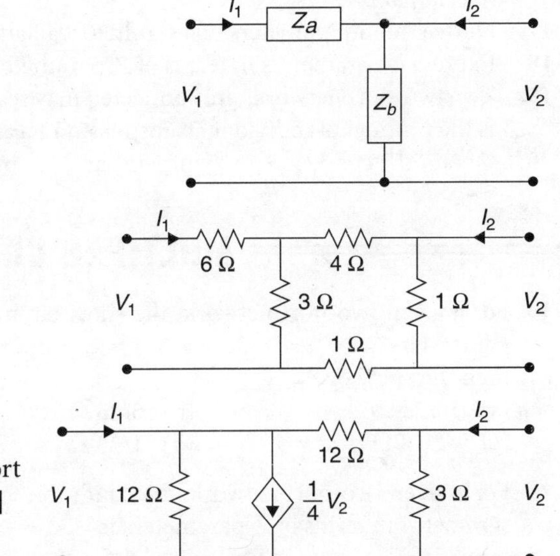

14. Find the T-parameters for the network.
[**Ans:** $A = \frac{Z_a + Z_b}{Z_b}$, $B = \frac{Z_a}{Z_b}$, $C = \frac{1}{Z_b}$, $D = \frac{1}{Z_b}$]

15. Find the Z-parameters of the circuit.
[**Ans:** $Z_{11} = 8\ \Omega$, $Z_{12} = Z_{21} = 1/3\ \Omega$, $Z_{22} = 8/9\ \Omega$]

16. Find the admittance parameters of the two-port network. [**Ans:** $Y_{11} = \frac{1}{6}$, $Y_{12} = \frac{1}{6}$, $Y_{21} = -\frac{1}{12}$, $Y_{22} = \frac{5}{12}$]

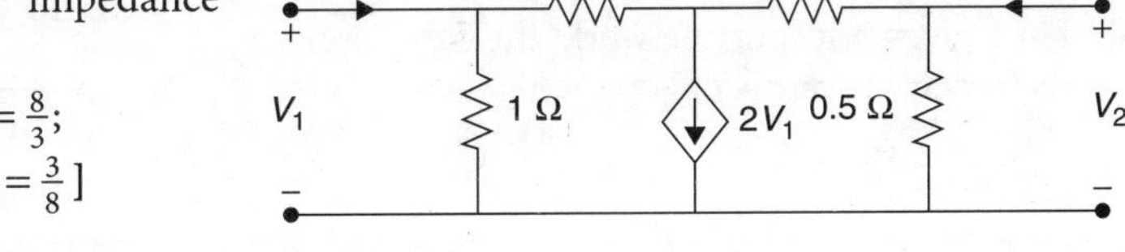

17. Determine the admittance and impedance parameters of the network.
[**Ans:** $Y_{11} = 3$, $Y_{12} = -\frac{2}{3}$, $Y_{21} = 0$, $Y_{22} = \frac{8}{3}$;
$\therefore\ Z_{11} = \frac{1}{3}$, $Z_{12} = \frac{1}{12}$, $Z_{21} = 0$, $Z_{22} = \frac{3}{8}$]

REVIEW QUESTIONS

1. Define Z- and Y-parameters of a typical four-terminal network. Determine the relation between Y- and Z-parameters.
2. Derive *ABCD* parameters from Z parameters and vice versa.
3. Why are Z-parameters known as open circuit parameters?
4. What is the condition for a given network to be reciprocal as well as symmetrical network in terms of *ABCD* parameters?

5. Write the standard Y-parameter equations. Obtain the Y-parameters in terms of h-parameters.
6. Why are Y-parameters known as short circuit parameters?
7. Two two-port networks a and b, with open-circuit impedances Z_a and Z_b, are connected in series. Derive the Z-parameter equations.
8. Two two-port networks a and b, with short-circuit admittances Y_a and Y_b, are connected in parallel. Derive the Y-parameter equations?
9. Explain T and π representations of a two-port network.
10. Obtain the two-port network parameters in the following cases:
    (a) Parallel connection of two-port networks.
    (b) Cascade connection of two-port networks.
11. The Z-parameters of a two-port network are $Z_{11} = 15\ \Omega$, $Z_{22} = 24\ \Omega$, $Z_{12} = Z_{21} = 6\ \Omega$. Determine the $ABCD$ parameters.
12. Express Z-parameters in terms of h-parameters and $ABCD$-parameters.
13. Explain series and parallel connections of two-port networks.
14. Explain the concept of transformed network.
15. What do you understand by reciprocal network?
16. What is a symmetrical network? Write the condition for symmetry in case of inverse transmission and hybrid parameters.
17. Derive the Z-parameters of a symmetrical lattice network?
18. Express h-parameters in terms of Z-parameters for the given two-port network.
19. Two two-port networks are connected in cascade. Prove that the overall transmission parameter matrix is the product of individual transmission parameter matrices.
20. Obtain the condition for symmetry and reciprocity in inverse transmission line parameters.

MULTIPLE CHOICE QUESTIONS

1. For a given two-port network, the short circuit parameters are $Y_{11} = 10$, $Y_{12} = Y_{21} = 2$, $Y_{22} = 5$, then the value of Z_{21} is
   (a) $10/23\ \Omega$ (b) $5/23\ \Omega$
   (c) $-1/23\ \Omega$ (d) $1/23\ \Omega$
2. For a given two-port network, the condition for symmetry in terms of Z-parameters is
   (a) $Z_{11} = Z_{22}$ (b) $Z_{11} = -Z_{22}$
   (c) $Z_{12} = Z_{21}$ (d) $Z_{12} = -Z_{21}$
3. For a given two-port network, the condition for reciprocity in terms of Z-parameters is
   (a) $Z_{11} = Z_{22}$ (b) $Z_{11} = -Z_{22}$
   (c) $Z_{12} = Z_{21}$ (d) $Z_{12} = -Z_{21}$
4. For a given two-port reciprocal network, the o/p open circuit voltage divided by the i/p current is equal to
   (a) Z_{12} (b) $1/Y_{21}$
   (c) B (d) h_{21}
5. A two-port network is defined by the equations $I_1 = 2V_1 + V_2$ and $I_1 = V_1 + V_2$, its open circuit parameters (Z_{11}, Z_{12} Z_{21}, Z_{22}) are given by
   (a) 2, 1, 1, 1 (b) 1, −1, −1, 2
   (c) 1, 1, 1, 2 (d) 2, −1, −1, 1
6. For a given two-port network, the condition for symmetry in terms of Y-parameters is
   (a) $Y_{11} = Y_{22}$ (b) $Y_{11} = -Y_{22}$
   (c) $Y_{12} = Y_{21}$ (d) $Y_{12} = -Y_{21}$
7. For a given two-port network, the condition for s reciprocity in terms of Y-parameters is
   (a) $Y_{11} = Y_{22}$ (b) $Y_{11} = -Y_{22}$
   (c) $Y_{12} = Y_{21}$ (d) $Y_{12} = -Y_{21}$
8. A two-port network is defined by the equations $I_1 = 2V_1 + V_2$ and $I_1 = 2V_1 + 3V_2$, then Z_{12} is
   (a) 2 (b) −1
   (c) −1/2 (d) −1/4
9. If a voltage of 10 V applied at port 1 results in I_1 = 5 A and V_2 = 5 V when port 2 is open circuited, then the open circuit transfer impedance is
   (a) 2 Ω (b) 1 Ω
   (c) 3 Ω (d) 4 Ω
10. For a two-port network $Z_{11} = Z_{22}$ and $Z_{12} = Z_{21}$, then the two-port network is

(a) symmetric only
(b) reciprocal but not symmetrical
(c) symmetric and reciprocal
(d) symmetric but not reciprocal

11. The parameter Y_{11} in terms of Z-parameters is
(a) Z_{22}/Δ_z (b) $-Z_{22}/\Delta_z$
(c) Z_{11}/Δ_z (d) $-Z_{21}/\Delta_z$

12. For a given two-port network, the condition for symmetry in terms of inverse hybrid-parameters is
(a) $g_{11}g_{22}-g_{12}g_{21}=1$ (b) $g_{11}=-g_{22}$
(c) $g_{12}=g_{21}$ (d) $g_{12}=-g_{21}$

13. For a given two-port network, the condition for reciprocity in terms of inverse hybrid-parameters is
(a) $g_{11}g_{22}-g_{12}g_{21}=1$ (b) $g_{11}=-g_{22}$
(c) $g_{12}=g_{21}$ (d) $g_{12}=-g_{21}$

14. With port 1 short circuited, a voltage of 10 V applied at port 2 results in $I_2=4$ A and $I_1=-2$ A. The short circuit dividing point admittance at port 2 is
(a) −0.4 (b) + 0.2
(c) −0.2 (d) 0.4

15. For a given two-port network $Z_{11}=10\ \Omega$; $Z_{22}=8\ \Omega$; $Z_{12}=Z_{21}=3\ \Omega$. A resistance of 5 Ω is connected at port 2. Then the dividing point impedance at port 1 is
(a) 121/3 Ω (b) 7 Ω
(c) 134/13 Ω (d) 108/13 Ω

16. In a two-port network the parameters $A=D=2$ and $B=3\ \Omega$. Then value of parameter C for symmetrical network is
(a) 2 Ω (b) 1 Ω
(c) 1/2 Ω (d) 1/3 Ω

17. For a given two-port network, the condition for symmetry in terms of h-parameters is
(a) $h_{11}h_{22}-h_{12}h_{21}=1$ (b) $h_{11}=-h_{22}$
(c) $h_{12}=h_{21}$ (d) $h_{12}=-h_{21}$

18. For a given two-port network, the condition for reciprocity in terms of h-parameters is
(a) $h_{11}h_{22}-h_{12}h_{21}=1$ (b) $h_{11}=-h_{22}$
(c) $h_{12}=h_{21}$ (d) $h_{12}=-h_{21}$

19. For a given two-port network, the condition for symmetry in terms of transmission parameters is
(a) $AD-BC=1$ (b) $A=D$
(c) $AD-BC=-1$ (d) $A=-D$

20. For a given two-port network, the condition for reciprocity in terms of transmission parameters is
(a) $AD-BC=1$ (b) $A=D$
(c) $AD-BC=-1$ (d) $A=-D$

21. For a two-port network the short circuit parameters are $Y_{11}=5$, $Y_{22}=2$, and $Y_{12}=Y_{21}=1$. The network at port 2 is terminated with an admittance of 5. Then input admittance at port 1 is
(a) 26/7 mhos (b) 30/7 mhos
(c) 34/7 mhos (d) 38/7 mhos

22. In a two-port network , the expression for Z_{11} in terms of $ABCD$ parameters is
(a) D/C (b) $1/C$
(c) B/C (d) A/C

23. If a two-port network has transmission line parameters $A=D=5$, $B=3\ \Omega$ and $C=8$, then the parameter h_{11} for the above network is
(a) 1/5 (b) 8/5
(c) 3/5 (d) 13/5

24. The parameter Y_{11} in terms of h-parameters is
(a) $(h_{11}h_{22}-h_{12}h_{21})/h_{11}$ (b) h_{12}/h_{11}
(c) $1/h_{11}$ (d) $-h_{21}/h_{11}$

25. A two-port network has short circuit parameters $Y_{11}=3/5$, $Y_{12}=Y_{21}=-2/5$, $Y_{22}=13/5$, then the value of parameter B is
(a) 5/2 Ω (b) 13/2 Ω
(c) 3/2 Ω (d) 5 Ω

26. In a passive two-port network, the open circuit impedance matrix is $\begin{bmatrix} 10 & 2 \\ 2 & 5 \end{bmatrix}$. If the *i/p* port is interchanged with the *o/p* port, then the open circuit impedance matrix will be
(a) $\begin{bmatrix} 10 & 2 \\ 5 & 2 \end{bmatrix}$ (b) $\begin{bmatrix} 5 & 2 \\ 2 & 10 \end{bmatrix}$
(c) $\begin{bmatrix} 5 & 10 \\ 2 & 2 \end{bmatrix}$ (d) $\begin{bmatrix} 2 & 5 \\ 10 & 2 \end{bmatrix}$

27. An ideal transformer has a turns ratio of 2:1. Considering high voltage side as port 1 and low voltage side as port 2, the transmission line parameters of the transformer will be

(a) $\begin{bmatrix} 0 & -2 \\ 0.5 & 0 \end{bmatrix}$ (b) $\begin{bmatrix} -2 & 0 \\ 0 & -0.5 \end{bmatrix}$

(c) $\begin{bmatrix} 2 & 0 \\ 0 & 0.5 \end{bmatrix}$ (d) $\begin{bmatrix} 0.5 & 0 \\ 0 & 2 \end{bmatrix}$

28. The Y-parameters of the network are given by the matrix, where Y_s is admittance

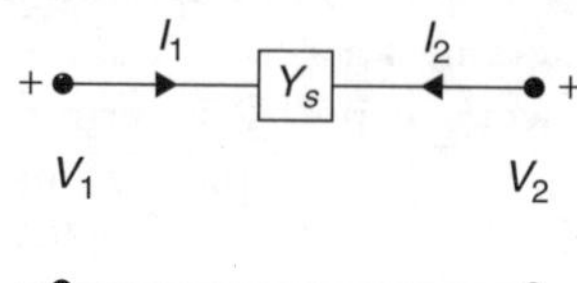

(a) $\begin{bmatrix} Y_s & Y_s \\ Y_s & Y_s \end{bmatrix}$ (b) $\begin{bmatrix} Y_s & -Y_s \\ -Y_s & Y_s \end{bmatrix}$

(c) $\begin{bmatrix} -Y_s & Y_s \\ Y_s & Y_s \end{bmatrix}$ (d) none of the above

29. The Z-parameters of the network are given by the matrix

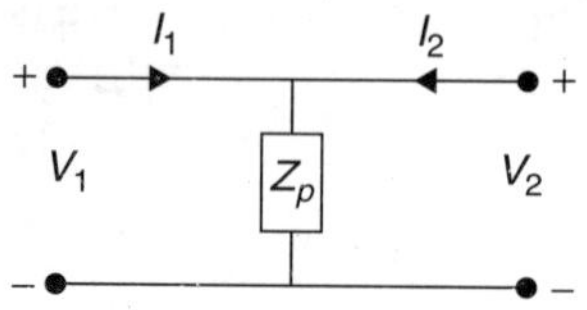

(a) $\begin{bmatrix} Z_P & Z_P \\ Z_P & Z_P \end{bmatrix}$ (b) $\begin{bmatrix} Z_P & -Z_P \\ -Z_P & Z_P \end{bmatrix}$

(c) $\begin{bmatrix} Z_P & 0 \\ 0 & Z_P \end{bmatrix}$ (d) none of the above

30. If the transmission parameters of the network are $A = C = 1$, $B = 2$ and $D = 3$, then the value of Z_{in} in ohms is

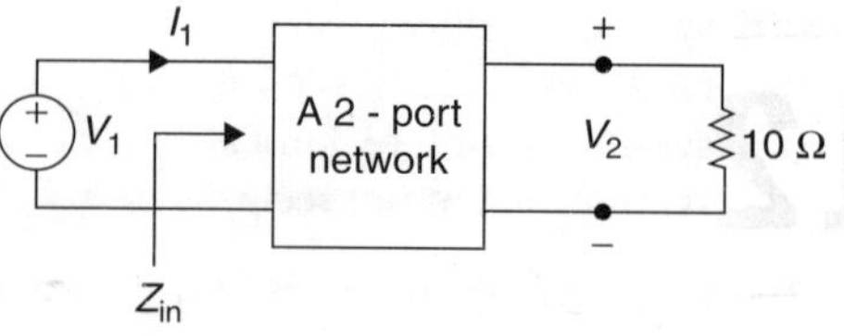

(a) 12/13 (b) 13/12
(c) 3 (d) 4

31. An ideal transformer cannot be described by
(a) h-parameter (b) $ABCD$ parameter
(c) g-parameter (d) Z-parameter

32. Two two-port networks are connected in cascade. The combination is to be represented as a single two-port network. The parameters of the network are obtained by the multiplying the individual's
(a) Z-parameter matrix
(b) h-parameter matrix
(c) Y-parameter matrix
(d) $ABCD$-parameter matrix

33. The impedance matrix of two, two-port networks are given by $\begin{bmatrix} 3 & 2 \\ 2 & 3 \end{bmatrix}$ and $\begin{bmatrix} 15 & 5 \\ 5 & 25 \end{bmatrix}$.
If these two networks are connected in series, then the impedance matrix of the resulting two-port network will be

(a) $\begin{bmatrix} 3 & 5 \\ 2 & 25 \end{bmatrix}$ (b) $\begin{bmatrix} 18 & 7 \\ 7 & 28 \end{bmatrix}$

(c) $\begin{bmatrix} 15 & 2 \\ 5 & 3 \end{bmatrix}$ (d) none of the above

Answers

1. c	**2.** a	**3.** c	**4.** a	**5.** b	**6.** a	**7.** c	**8.** d	**9.** b	**10.** c
11. a	**12.** a	**13.** d	**14.** d	**15.** a	**16.** b	**17.** a	**18.** d	**19.** b	**20.** a
21. c	**22.** d	**23.** c	**24.** c	**25.** a	**26.** b	**27.** c	**28.** b	**29.** a	**30.** a
31. a	**32.** d	**33.** b							

12 Network Functions

Learning Outcomes

After reading this chapter, the reader will able to

- Illustrate the network functions for one-port and two-port networks
- Define transfer function and driving point immittance function
- Find transfer function and driving point immittance function for ladder and non-ladder networks
- Find the poles and zeros of a network function and explain their significance
- List the properties of driving point and transfer functions
- Illustrate time domain response from pole-zero plot

12.1 INTRODUCTION

A network function exhibits the relationship between the transform of the source or excitation to the transform of the response for an electrical network. In this chapter the concept of *transform impedance* and *transform admittance* is extended for one-port and two-port networks. The transform impedance at a port is defined as the ratio of the voltage transform to the current transform in the network for zero state (initial conditions are zero). The voltage transform and current transform that define transform impedance and transform admittance (inverse of impedance) must relate to the same port. The impedance or admittance found at a given port is called driving point impedance or admittance related to the same port. The general term assigned to the driving point impedance and driving point admittance is the *immittance* (a combination of impedance and admittance). Thus, an immittance function represents an impedance function or an admittance function. Furthermore, a function relating currents or voltages at different parts of the network, called a *transfer function*, are found to be mathematically similar to the transform impedance function. These functions are called *network functions*. The definitions and locations (in the s-plane) of poles and zeros are also introduced in this chapter.

12.2 NETWORK FUNCTIONS FOR ONE- AND TWO-PORT NETWORKS

Figure 12.1 represents one-port and two-port networks with the reference directions for the port voltages and currents as indicated. A voltage and current are assigned to each of the two ports. The voltage and current at the input terminals are V_1 and I_1 and at the output terminals are V_2 and I_2.

12.2.1 Driving Point Impedance and Admittance

The driving point impedance and admittance of a one-port network is defined as

$$Z(s) = \frac{V(s)}{I(s)} \qquad (12.1)$$

$$Y(s) = \frac{I(s)}{V(s)} \qquad (12.2)$$

Similarly, for the two-port network, the driving point impedance and admittance at port 1 is defined as

$$Z_{11}(s) = \frac{V_1(s)}{I_1(s)} \tag{12.3}$$

$$Y_{11}(s) = \frac{I_1(s)}{V_1(s)} \tag{12.4}$$

While the driving point impedance and admittance at the port 2 are designated as

$$Z_{22}(s) = \frac{V_2(s)}{I_2(s)} \tag{12.5}$$

$$Y_{22}(s) = \frac{I_2(s)}{V_2(s)} \tag{12.6}$$

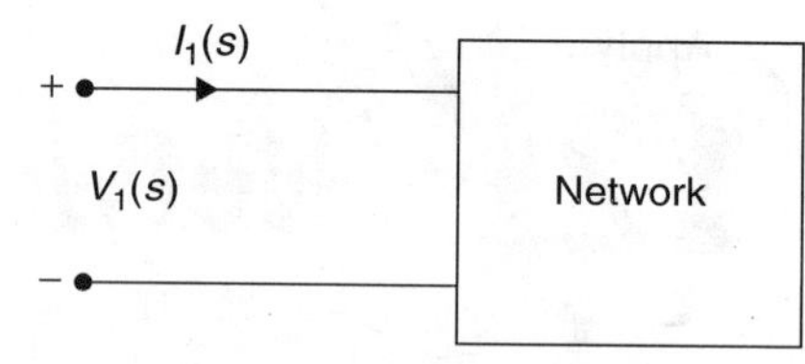

(a) One-port network

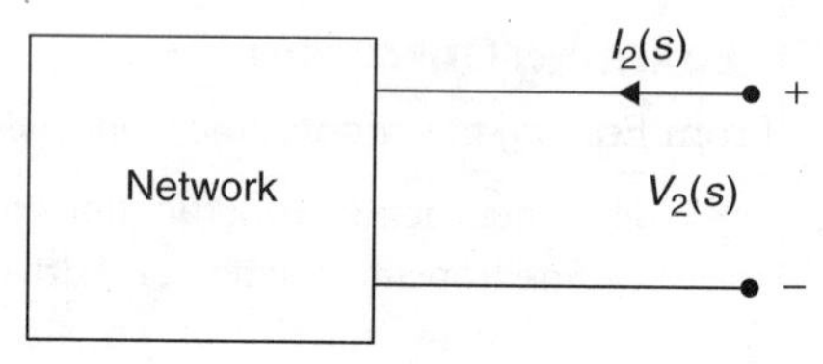

(b) One-port network

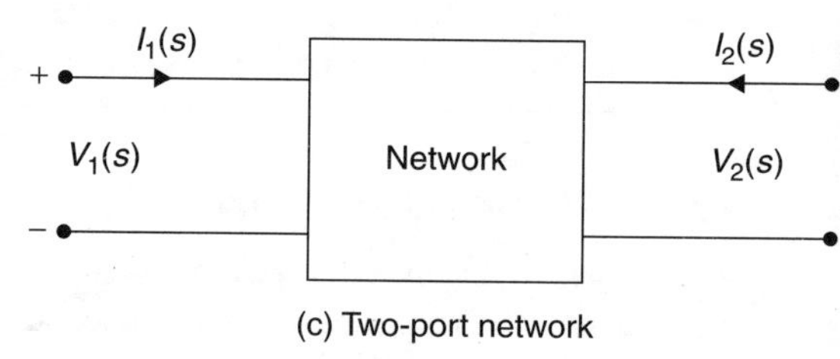

(c) Two-port network

Fig. 12.1 One-port and two-port networks

12.2.2 Transfer Impedance and Admittance

It is defined as the ratio of transformed voltage at output port to the transformed current at the input port of a two-port network. It is given as

$$Z_{12}(s) = \frac{V_2(s)}{I_1(s)} \tag{12.7}$$

Transfer admittance is defined as the ratio of transformed current at the output port to the transformed voltage at the input port of a two-port network. It is given as

$$Y_{12}(s) = \frac{I_2(s)}{V_1(s)} \tag{12.8}$$

12.2.3 Current and Voltage Transfer Ratio

Current and voltage transfer ratios are basically transfer functions.

Current transfer ratio is the ratio of current transform at the output port to the current transform at the input port of a two-port network. It is usually denoted by $\alpha(s)$. Thus,

$$\alpha_{12}(s) = \frac{I_2(s)}{I_1(s)} \tag{12.9}$$

Voltage transfer ratio is the ratio of voltage transform at the output port to the voltage transform at the input port of a two-port network. It is usually denoted by $G(s)$. Thus,

$$G_{12}(s) = \frac{V_2(s)}{V_1(s)} \tag{12.10}$$

Problem 12.1 Find $Z_{11}(s)$, $Z_{12}(s)$ and $G_{12}(s)$ for the network.

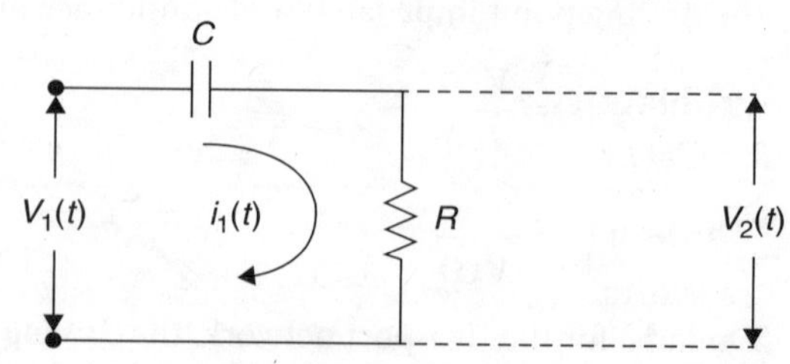

Solution:

Transformed or s-domain equivalent network for the given system is shown below.

Applying KVL to the circuit,

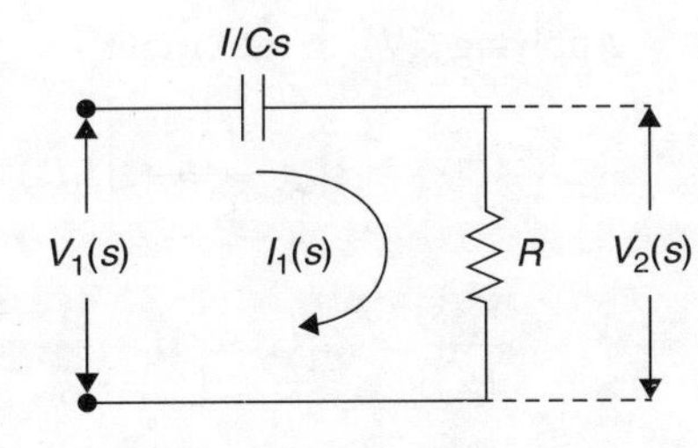

$$V_1(s) = RI_1(s) + \frac{I_1(s)}{sC}$$

$$V_1(s) = I_1(s)\left(\frac{RsC+1)}{sC}\right) \quad (1)$$

$$V_2(s) = RI_1(s) \quad (2)$$

From Eq. (1), we have

$$Z_{11}(s) = \frac{V_1(s)}{I_1(s)} = \frac{sRC+1}{sC}$$

From Eq. (2), we have

$$Z_{12}(s) = \frac{V_2(s)}{I_1(s)} = R$$

$$\frac{\text{Eq. (2)}}{\text{Eq. (1)}} \Rightarrow G_{12}(s) = \frac{V_2(s)}{V_1(s)} = \frac{RI_1(s)}{I_1(s)\left(\frac{RsC+1)}{sC}\right)} = \left(\frac{sRC}{1+sRC}\right)$$

Problem 12.2 Obtain the transfer ratio $\frac{V_2(s)}{V_1(s)}$ for the circuit.

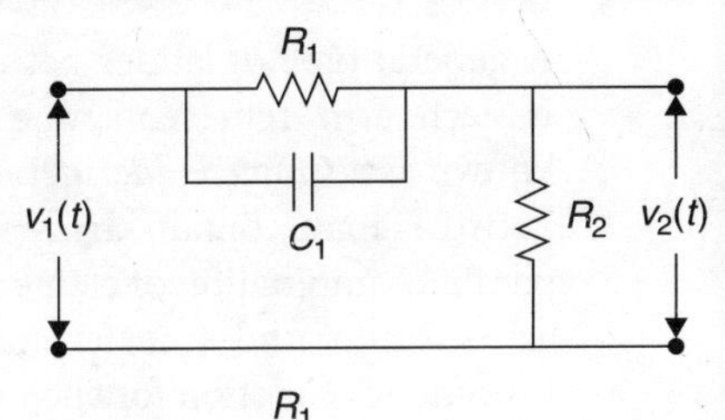

Solution:

The equivalent transformed network for the given system is shown.

Applying KVL to the above circuit

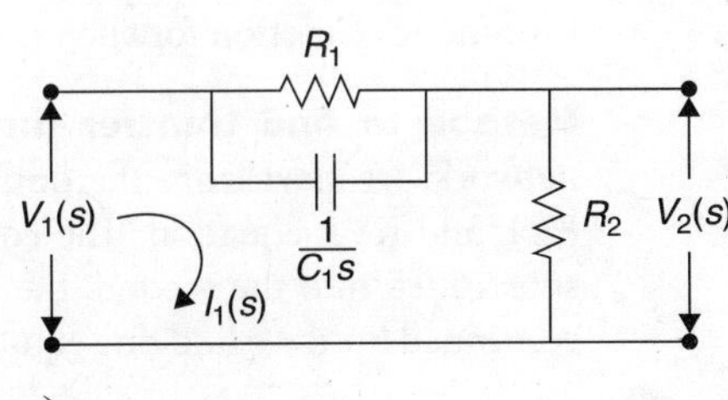

$$V_1(s) = \left[\frac{R_1 \times \frac{1}{sC_1}}{R_1 + \frac{1}{sC_1}}\right] I_1(s) + R_2 I_1(s) = \left[\frac{R_1}{1+sR_1C_1} + R_2\right] I_1(s) \quad (1)$$

$$V_2(s) = R_2 I_1(s) \quad (2)$$

$$\frac{\text{Eq. (2)}}{\text{Eq. (1)}} \Rightarrow \frac{V_2(s)}{V_1(s)} = \frac{R_2 I_1(s)}{\left[\frac{R_1}{1+sR_1C_1} + R_2\right] I_1(s)} = \left(\frac{sR_1R_2C_1 + R_2}{R_1 + R_2 + sR_1R_2C_2}\right)$$

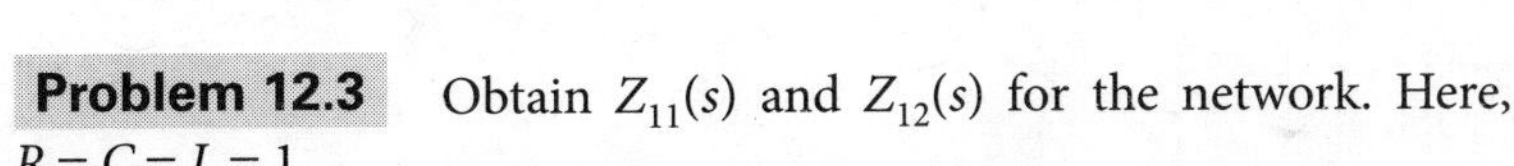

Problem 12.3 Obtain $Z_{11}(s)$ and $Z_{12}(s)$ for the network. Here, $R = C = L = 1$.

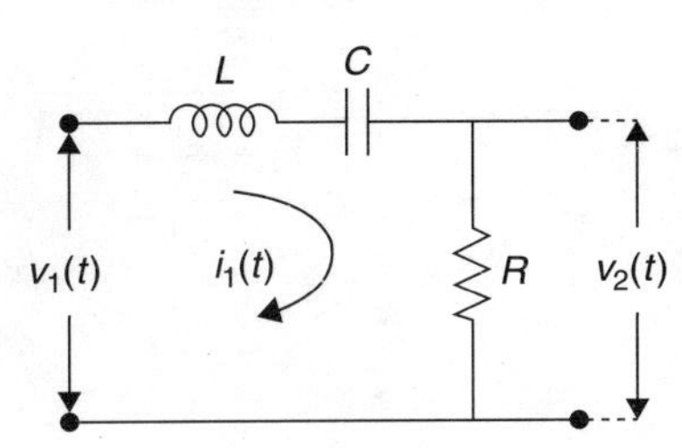

Solution:

Transformed or *s*-domain equivalent network for the given system is shown below.

Applying KVL to the circuit,

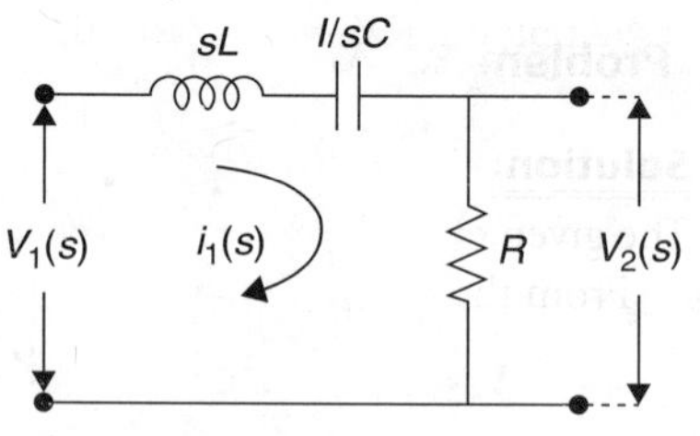

$$V_1(s) = \left[sL + \frac{1}{sC} + R \right] I_1(s)$$

$$\Rightarrow \qquad \frac{V_1(s)}{I_1(s)} = Z_{11}(s) = \left[sL + \frac{1}{sC} + R \right]$$

$$V_2(s) = RI_1(s)$$

$$\Rightarrow \qquad \frac{V_2(s)}{I_1(s)} = Z_{12}(s) = R$$

For $R = C = L = 1$, we have

$$Z_{11}(s) = \left[sL + \frac{1}{sC} + R \right] = s + \frac{1}{s} + 1 = \frac{s^2 + s + 1}{s}$$

$$Z_{12}(s) = R = 1$$

12.3 NETWORK FUNCTIONS OF SOME TYPICAL NETWORKS

12.3.1 Ladder Networks

A general type of ladder network is shown in Fig. 12.2. If each arm represents one element, the network is known as a *simple ladder network*. Otherwise, the ladder network may contain arms which represent a series–parallel combination of elements. The following methods are used to find transfer function and driving point immittance function for such networks.

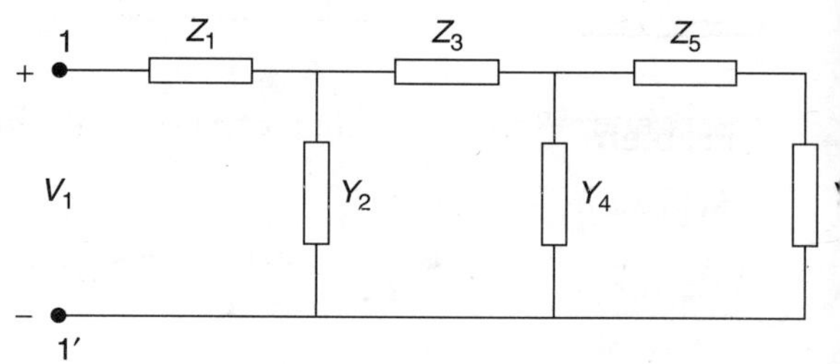

Fig. 12.2 Ladder network

Method to find transfer function For the ladder network, we start from the output port and then work towards the input port, successively applying the KCL and KVL equation. The equations that result are a particularly simple form in that, the first may be substituted into the second, the resulting equation may then be substituted into the third and this process continued until we find one equation which relates output to input. Then the required transfer may be found.

Method to find driving point immittance function To find an open circuited or short circuited parameter, we assume that the appropriate port is organised by being either open or shorted. We begin the calculations at the port other than one for which the driving point immittance is being found.

Referring to Fig. 12.2, we begin with Y_6. It is first inverted and combined with Z_5. Next this sum is inverted and combined with Y_4. This pattern is continued until the process terminates. Thus

$$Z = Z_1 + \cfrac{1}{Y_2 + \cfrac{1}{Z_3 + \cfrac{1}{Y_4 + \cfrac{1}{Z_5 + \cfrac{1}{Y_6}}}}} \qquad (12.11)$$

Problem 12.4 For the network, determine the transfer ratio $\frac{V_2}{V_1}$.

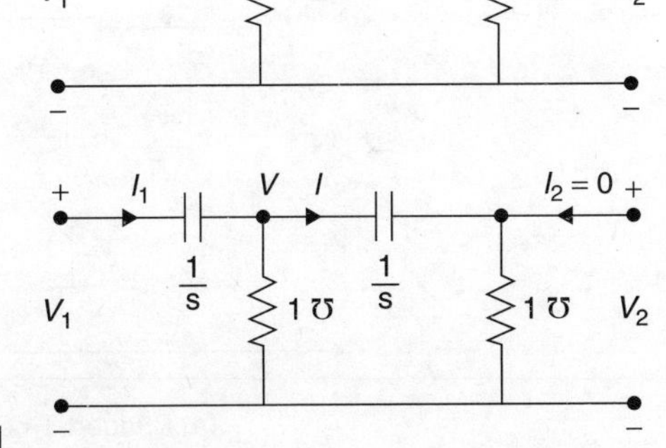

Solution:

The given circuit can be redrawn as shown below.

From the circuit diagram,

$$V_2 = I$$

$$V = V_2 + I \times \frac{1}{s} = V_2 + \frac{I}{s} = V_2 + \frac{V_2}{s}$$

$$I_1 = I + V = V_2 + V_2 + \frac{V_2}{s} = 2V_2 + \frac{V_2}{s} = \left(2 + \frac{1}{s}\right)V_2$$

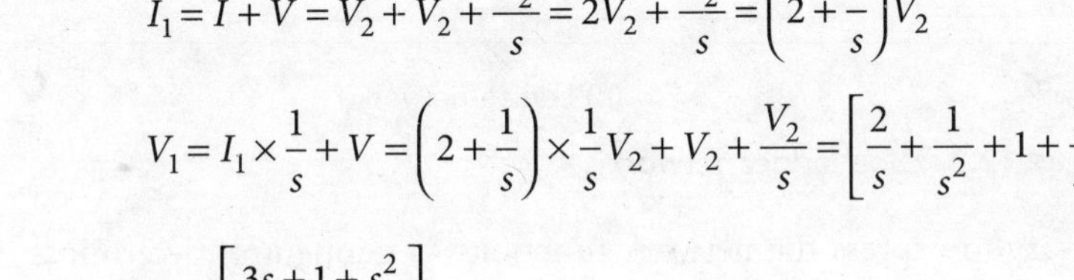

$$V_1 = I_1 \times \frac{1}{s} + V = \left(2 + \frac{1}{s}\right) \times \frac{1}{s}V_2 + V_2 + \frac{V_2}{s} = \left[\frac{2}{s} + \frac{1}{s^2} + 1 + \frac{1}{s}\right]V_2$$

$$\Rightarrow \quad V_1 = \left[\frac{3s + 1 + s^2}{s^2}\right]V_2$$

$$\Rightarrow \quad \frac{V_2}{V_1} = \frac{s^2}{s^2 + 3s + 1}$$

Problem 12.5 For the network, determine the network functions $\frac{V_2}{V_1}$, $\frac{V_2}{I_1}$ and $\frac{V_1}{I_1}$.

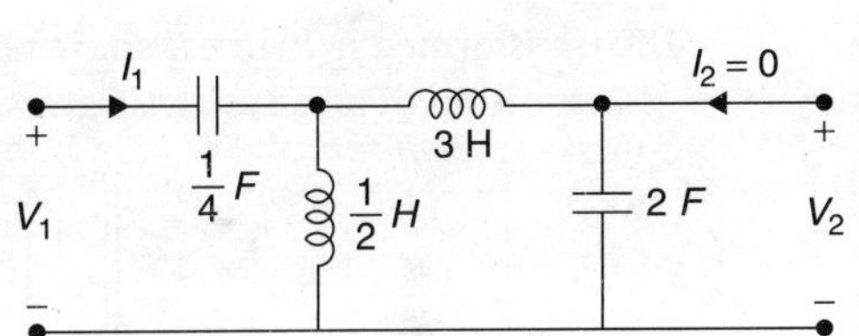

Solution:

The transformed network is as shown.

From the circuit diagram,

$$V_2 = I \times \frac{1}{2s} \quad \Rightarrow I = 2sV_2$$

$$V = V_2 + I \times 3s = V_2 + 3s \times 2sV_2 = (1 + 6s^2)V_2$$

$$I_1 = \frac{V}{s/2} + I = \frac{2V}{s} + 2sV_2 = \frac{2}{s}(1 + 6s^2)V_2 + 2sV_2 = \left(\frac{2 + 14s^2}{s}\right)V_2$$

$$\Rightarrow \quad \frac{V_2}{I_1} = \frac{s}{14s^2 + 2} \tag{1}$$

$$V_1 = I_1 \times \frac{4}{s} + V = \left(\frac{2 + 14s^2}{s}\right) \times \frac{4}{s}V_2 + (1 + 6s^2)V_2 = \left[\frac{8 + 56s^2 + s^2 + 6s^4}{s^2}\right]V_2 = \left[\frac{6s^4 + 57s^2 + 8}{s^2}\right]V_2$$

$$\Rightarrow \quad \frac{V_2}{V_1} = \frac{s^2}{6s^4 + 57s^2 + 8} \tag{2}$$

$$\frac{\text{Eq. (1)}}{\text{Eq. (2)}} \Rightarrow \frac{V_1}{I_1} = \frac{s}{14s^2 + 2} \times \frac{6s^4 + 57s^2 + 8}{s^2} = \frac{6s^4 + 57s^2 + 8}{14s^3 + 2s}$$

12.3.2 Non-Ladder Networks

The above methods are used only for ladder networks. There are other networks for which these methods are not applicable. Some of the non-ladder networks are shown in Fig. 12.3.

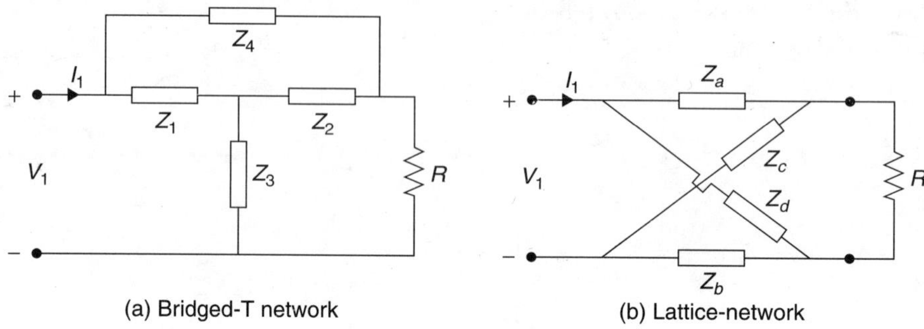

Fig. 12.3 Non-ladder network

For such types of networks, it is necessary to express the network functions as quotient of determinants formulated on KVL and KCL basis.

Problem 12.6 Determine the driving point and transfer admittances of the T-bridge network.

Solution:

The transformed network is shown below.

Inspection of mesh analysis gives,

$$\begin{bmatrix} \frac{1}{s}+1 & 1 & \frac{-1}{s} \\ 1 & \frac{1}{s}+2 & \frac{1}{s} \\ \frac{-1}{s} & \frac{1}{s} & 1+\frac{2}{s} \end{bmatrix} \begin{bmatrix} I_1 \\ I_2 \\ I_3 \end{bmatrix} = \begin{bmatrix} V_1 \\ 0 \\ 0 \end{bmatrix}$$

$$\Delta = \begin{bmatrix} \frac{1}{s}+1 & 1 & \frac{-1}{s} \\ 1 & \frac{1}{s}+2 & \frac{1}{s} \\ \frac{-1}{s} & \frac{1}{s} & 1+\frac{2}{s} \end{bmatrix}$$

$$= \left(\frac{1}{s}+1\right)\left[\left(\frac{1}{s}+2\right)\left(1+\frac{2}{s}\right)-\frac{1}{s^2}\right]-1\left(1+\frac{2}{s}+\frac{1}{s^2}\right)-\frac{1}{s}\left(\frac{1}{s}+\frac{1}{s}\left(\frac{1}{s}+2\right)\right)$$

$$= \left(\frac{1}{s}+1\right)\left(\frac{1}{s}+\frac{2}{s^2}+2+\frac{4}{s}-\frac{1}{s^2}\right)-1-\frac{2}{s}-\frac{1}{s^2}-\frac{1}{s^2}-\frac{1}{s^3}-\frac{2}{s^2}$$

$$= \frac{1}{s^2}+\frac{6}{s}+1 = \frac{s^2+6s+1}{s^2}$$

$$\Delta_1 = \begin{bmatrix} V_1 & 1 & \frac{-1}{s} \\ 0 & \frac{1}{s}+2 & \frac{1}{s} \\ 0 & \frac{1}{s} & 1+\frac{2}{s} \end{bmatrix} = V_1\left[\left(\frac{1}{s}+2\right)\left(1+\frac{2}{s}\right)-\frac{1}{s^2}\right] = V_1\left[\frac{2s^2+5s+1}{s^2}\right]$$

$$\Delta_2 = \begin{bmatrix} \frac{1}{s}+1 & V_1 & \frac{-1}{s} \\ 1 & 0 & \frac{1}{s} \\ \frac{-1}{s} & 0 & 1+\frac{2}{s} \end{bmatrix} = -V_1\left[1+\frac{2}{s}+\frac{1}{s^2}\right] = -V_1\left[\frac{s^2+2s+1}{s^2}\right]$$

According to Cramer's rule,

$$I_1 = \frac{\Delta_1}{\Delta} = V_1\left[\frac{\frac{2s^2+5s+1}{s^2}}{\frac{s^2+6s+1}{s^2}}\right] = V_1\left[\frac{2s^2+5s+1}{s^2+6s+1}\right]$$

$$\therefore \text{ Driving point admittance, } Y_{11} = \frac{I_1}{V_1} = \frac{2s^2+5s+1}{s^2+6s+1}$$

$$I_2 = \frac{\Delta_2}{\Delta} = -V_1\left[\frac{\frac{s^2+2s+1}{s^2}}{\frac{s^2+6s+1}{s^2}}\right] = -V_1\left[\frac{s^2+2s+1}{s^2+6s+1}\right]$$

$$\therefore \text{ Transfer admittance, } Y_{12} = \frac{I_2}{V_1} = -\frac{s^2+2s+1}{s^2+6s+1}$$

Problem 12.7 Find the driving point admittance for the network.

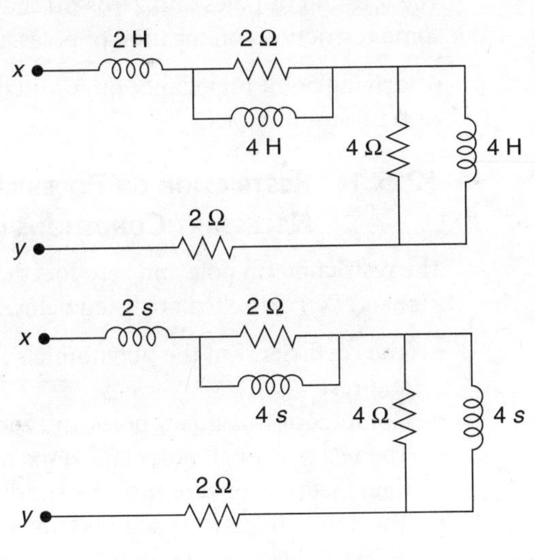

Solution:

The transformed network is shown below.

The driving point impedance $Z(s)$ is

$$Z(s) = 2s + \frac{2\times 4s}{2+4s} + \frac{4\times 4s}{4\times 4s} + 2 = 2s + \frac{8s}{2+4s} + \frac{16s}{4+4s} + 2$$

$$= \frac{(2+2s)(2+4s)(4+4s)+8s(4+4s)+16s(2+4s)}{(2+4s)(4+4s)}$$

$$= \frac{32s^3+56s^2+64s+16+32s+32s^2+32s+62s^2}{8+16s^2+24s}$$

$$= \frac{32s^3+152s^2+128s+16}{16s^2+24s+8}$$

$\therefore$ The driving point admittance is

$$Y(s) = \frac{1}{Z(s)} = \frac{16s^2+24s+8}{32s^3+152s^2+128s+16}$$

12.4 POLES AND ZEROS OF A NETWORK FUNCTION

The network function $N(s)$ for a lumped, linear network is expressed in the form of a ratio of two polynomials in complex frequency s, with real coefficients.

$$N(s)=K\frac{Z(s)}{P(s)}=K\frac{(s-z_1)(s-z_2)\ldots(s-z_m)}{(s-p_1)(s-p_2)\ldots(s-p_n)} \tag{12.12}$$

where K is called the *system gain factor* or *scalar factor.*

Poles The values of s that make the network function $N(s)$ infinite are called poles of network function and are denoted by the '×' symbol.

Therefore, here, the values $p_1, p_2, \ldots p_n$ are called poles of the network function. These poles are nothing but the roots of the equation obtained by equating the denominator of the network function to zero.

Zeros The values of s that make the network function $N(s)$ zero are called zeros of a network function and denoted by the '0' symbol.

Therefore, here, the values $z_1, z_2, z_3 \ldots\ldots\ldots z_m$ are called zeros of the network function.

Poles and zeros may be real or complex conjugates or a combination of both types. Further, poles and zeros may be located at the origin in the s-plane. The representation of poles and zeros in a two dimensional s-plane is called *pole zero plot* (Fig. 12.4).

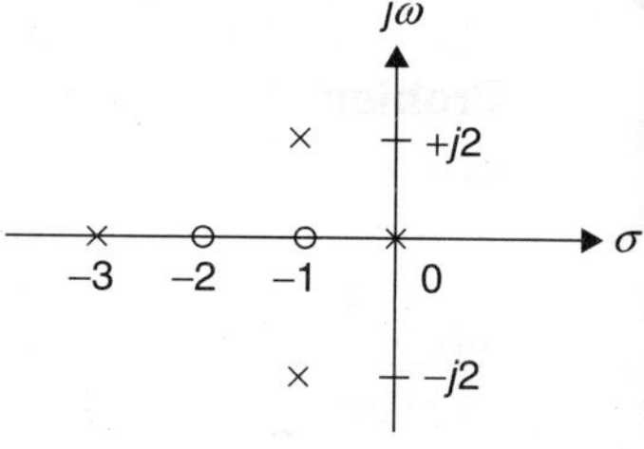

Fig. 12.4 Pole–zero plot

12.5 RESTRICTION ON LOCATION OF POLES AND ZEROS

The location of poles and zeros on the complex s-plane is not arbitrary but follows certain rules. Here are some restrictions on location of poles and zeros for:

- driving point impedance or admittance (immittance) functions, and
- transfer functions.

12.5.1 Restriction on Poles and Zeros of Driving Point Immittance Function (or) Necessary Conditions for Driving Point Immittance Function

The restriction on pole and zero location in the driving point immittance function with common factors in $Z(s)$ and $P(s)$ cancelled are listed below:

- The coefficients in the polynomials $Z(s)$ and $P(s)$ of the network function $N(s)=K\frac{Z(s)}{P(s)}$ must be positive and real.
- Complex or imaginary poles and zeros must occur in conjugate pairs.
- The real part of all poles and zeros must be negative or zero. If the real part of any pole and zero is zero, then that pole or zero must be simple.
- The polynomials $Z(s)$ and $P(s)$ must not have any missing terms between the highest and lowest degrees, unless all even or all odd terms are missing.
- The degree of $Z(s)$ and $P(s)$ may differ by either zero or one only.
- The lowest degree in $Z(s)$ and $P(s)$ may differ in degree at the most by one only.

12.5.2 Restriction on Poles and Zeros of Transfer Function (or) Necessary Conditions for Transfer Function

The restriction on pole and zero location in the transfer function with common factors in $Z(s)$ and $P(s)$ cancelled are listed below.

- The coefficients in the polynomials $Z(s)$ and $P(s)$ of network function $N(s) = K\frac{Z(s)}{P(s)}$ must be real and those for $P(s)$ must be positive.
- Complex or imaginary poles and zeros must occur in conjugate pairs.
- The real part of all poles must be negative or zero. If the real part of any pole is zero, then that pole must be simple.
- The polynomials $P(s)$ must not have any missing terms between the highest and lowest degrees, unless all even or all odd terms are missing.
- The polynomial $Z(s)$ must have any missing terms between the lowest and highest degrees, and some of the coefficients may be negative.
- The degree of $Z(s)$ may be as small as zero, independent of the degree of $P(s)$.
- For voltage and current transfer ratio, the maximum degree of $Z(s)$ must equal to the degree of $P(s)$.
- For the transfer impedance and admittance, the maximum degree of $Z(s)$ must be equal to the degree of $P(s)$ plus one.

Problem 12.8 Derive the transfer function for the network, assuming $R_1 = 5\ \text{M}\Omega$, $R_2 = 5\ \text{M}\Omega$, $C_1 = 0.1\ \mu\text{F}$, $C_2 = 0.1\ \mu\text{F}$.

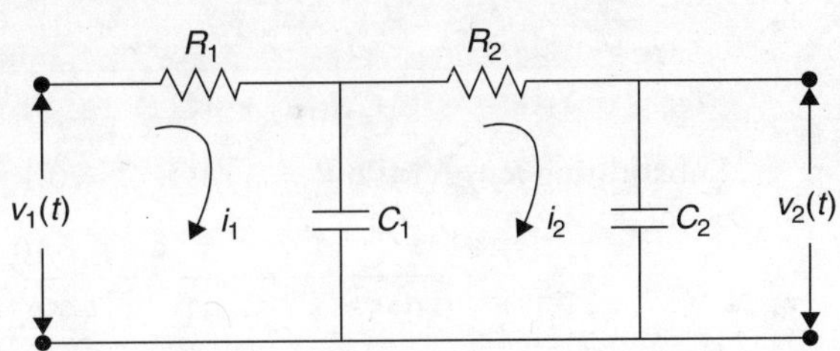

Solution:

The transformed network is shown below.

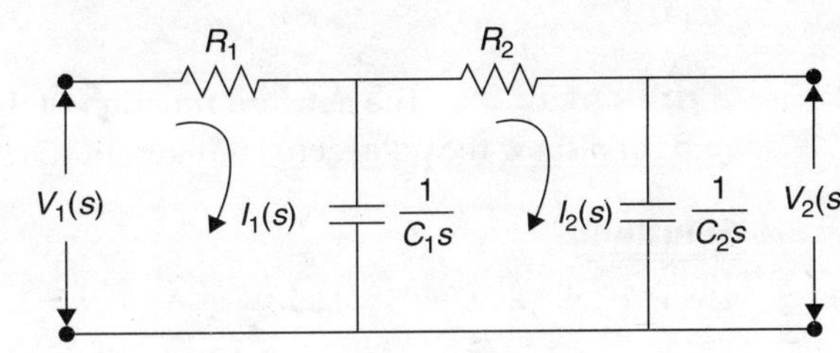

Applying KVL to loop 1

$$V_1(s) = \left(R_1 + \frac{1}{C_1 s}\right) I_1(s) - \frac{1}{C_1 s} I_2(s) \tag{1}$$

Applying KVL to loop 2

$$\left(R_2 + \frac{1}{C_1 s} + \frac{1}{C_2 s}\right) I_2(s) - \frac{1}{C_1 s} I_1(s) = 0$$

$$\Rightarrow \quad I_1(s) = C_1 s\left(R_2 + \frac{1}{C_1 s} + \frac{1}{C_2 s}\right) I_2(s) \tag{2}$$

From Eqs (1) and (2)

$$V_1(s) = \left(R_1 + \frac{1}{C_1 s}\right) C_1 s\left(R_2 + \frac{1}{C_1 s} + \frac{1}{C_2 s}\right) I_2(s) - \frac{1}{C_1 s} I_2(s)$$

$$V_1(s) = \left(\frac{(sC_1R_1 + 1)(sR_2C_1C_2 + C_1 + C_2) - C_2}{sC_1C_2}\right) I_2(s) \tag{3}$$

From the circuit, we know that

$$V_2(s) = \frac{I_2(s)}{C_2 s}$$

$$\Rightarrow \quad I_2(s) = C_2 s V_2(s) \tag{4}$$

Substituting Eq. (4) in Eq. (3), we have

$$V_1(s) = \left(\frac{(sC_1R_1+1)(sR_2C_1C_2+C_1+C_2)-C_2}{sC_1C_2} \right) C_2 s V_2(s)$$

$$\frac{V_2(s)}{V_1(s)} = \frac{C_1}{(sC_1R_1+1)(sR_2C_1C_2+C_1+C_2)-C_2}$$

$$= \frac{C_1}{s^2C_1^2C_2R_1R_2 + sC_1^2R_1 + sC_1C_2R_1 + sR_2C_1C_2 + C_1}$$

$$= \frac{1}{s^2C_1C_2R_1R_2 + s(C_1R_1 + C_2R_1 + R_2C_2) + 1}$$

Hence, the required transfer function of the system is

$$\frac{V_2(s)}{V_1(s)} = \frac{1}{s^2C_1C_2R_1R_2 + s(C_1R_1 + C_2R_1 + R_2C_2) + 1}$$

Substituting $R_1 = 5$ MΩ, $R_2 = 5$ MΩ, $C_1 = 0.1$ μF, $C_2 = 0.1$ μF, we have

$$\frac{V_2(s)}{V_1(s)} = \frac{1}{0.025s^2 + 1.5s + 1} = \frac{40}{s^2 + 60s + 40}$$

Problem 12.9 The network function of the system is $N(s) = \frac{4(s+1)(s+2)}{s(s+3)(s^2+2s+5)}$. Determine the poles and zeros and show the pole–zero configuration in the s-plane.

Solution:

The poles are given by $s(s+3)(s^2+2s+5) = 0$

$$s = 0, \quad s = -3, \quad s = \frac{-2 \pm \sqrt{4-20}}{2} = -1 \pm j2$$

$\therefore$ Poles are $P_1 = 0$, $P_2 = -3$, $P_3 = -1 + j2$, $P_4 = -1 - j2$

The zeros are given by $(s+1)(s+2) = 0$

$$s = -1, \quad s = -2$$

$\therefore$ Zeroes are $Z_1 = -1$, $Z_2 = -2$

The pole–zero configuration is as shown in Fig. (a).

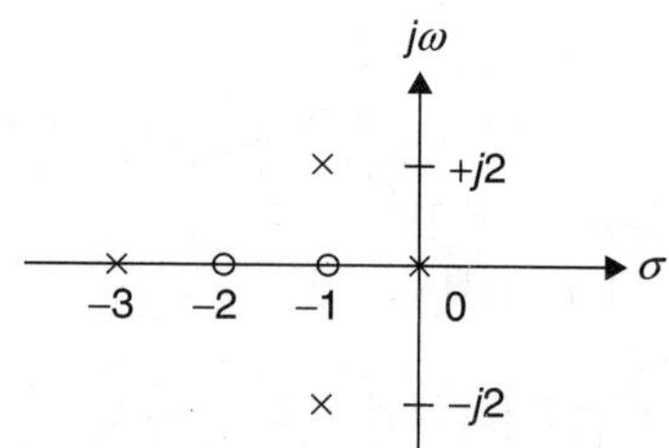

Fig. (a) Pole–zero plot

Problem 12.10 The pole–zero configuration of a system is shown. The value of the transfer function at $s = 1$ is found to be 6.4. Determine the transfer function of the system.

Solution:

The poles of the system are $P_1 = 0$, $P_2 = -2$, $P_3 = -4$

The zeroes of the system are $Z_1 = -3$

The transfer function of the system can be written as

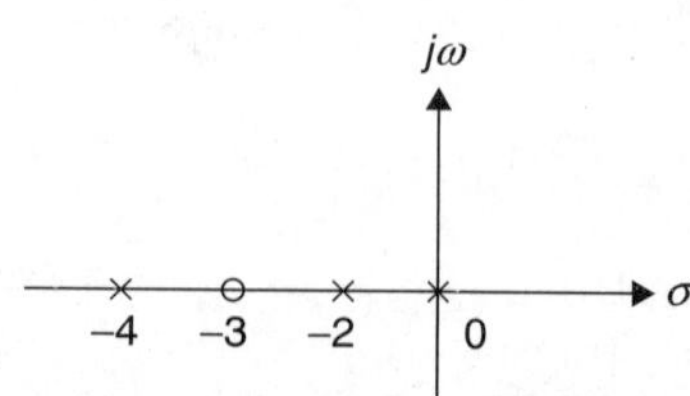

$$N(s) = \frac{K(s+3)}{s(s+2)(s+4)}$$

But as per the given data, at $s = 1$, $N(1) = 6.4$

$$N(s) = 6.4 = \frac{k(1+3)}{1(1+2)(1+4)}$$

$$\Rightarrow K = 24$$

The transfer function of the system is $N(s) = \dfrac{24(s+3)}{s(s+2)(s+4)}$

ADDITIONAL SOLVED PROBLEMS

12.1 Find the driving point impedance of the network.

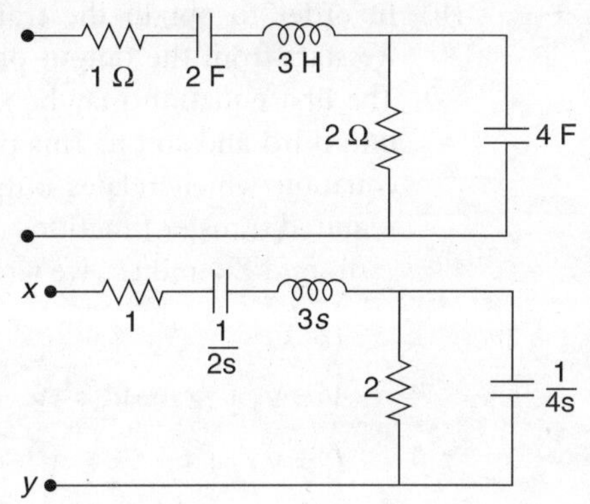

Solution: The transformed network for the given circuit is shown below.
The driving point impedance $Z(s)$ is

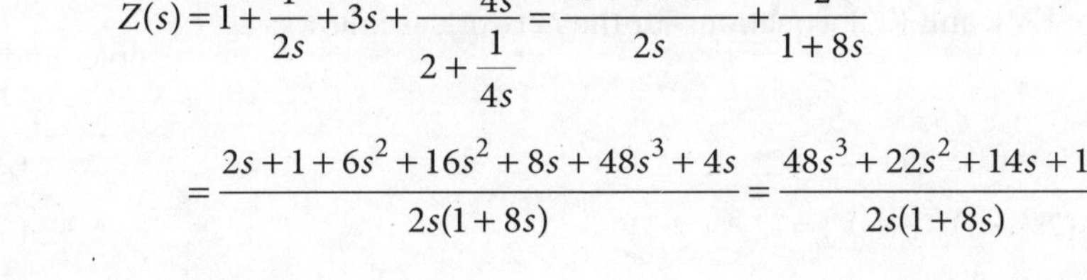

$$Z(s) = 1 + \frac{1}{2s} + 3s + \frac{2 \times \frac{1}{4s}}{2 + \frac{1}{4s}} = \frac{2s + 1 + 6s^2}{2s} + \frac{2}{1+8s}$$

$$= \frac{2s + 1 + 6s^2 + 16s^2 + 8s + 48s^3 + 4s}{2s(1+8s)} = \frac{48s^3 + 22s^2 + 14s + 1}{2s(1+8s)}$$

12.2 Find the operational impedance for the network between the terminals x and y.

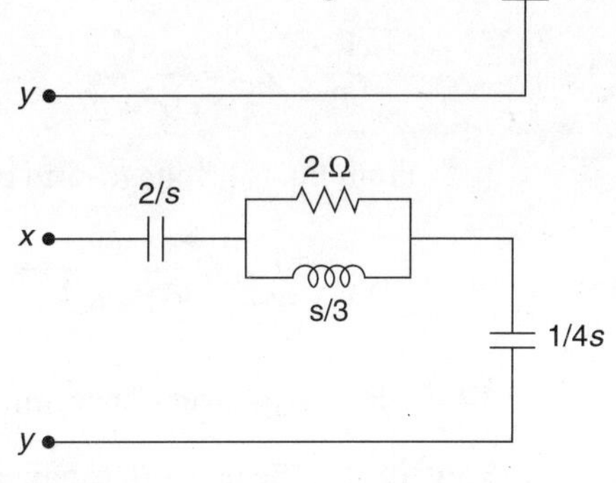

Solution: The transfer network is shown below.
Operational impedance

$$Z_{xy}(s) = \frac{2}{s} + \frac{2 \times \frac{s}{3}}{2 + \frac{s}{3}} + \frac{1}{4s} = \frac{2}{s} + \frac{2s}{s+6} + \frac{1}{4s}$$

$$= \frac{8s(s+6) + 2s^2 \times 4s + s(s+6)}{4s^2(s+6)} = \frac{8s^2 + 48s + 8s^3 + s^2 + 6s}{4s^3 + 24s^2}$$

$$= \frac{8s^2 + 9s + 54}{4s^2 + 24s}$$

12.3 For the ladder network, find

(i) Driving point input impedance
(ii) Transfer impedance function, Z_{12}
(iii) Voltage ratio transfer function G_{12}. Assume $I_2 = 0$.

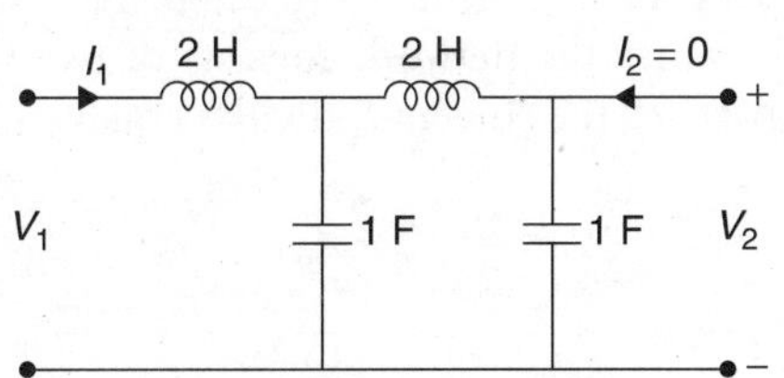

Solution: The transformed network is shown.

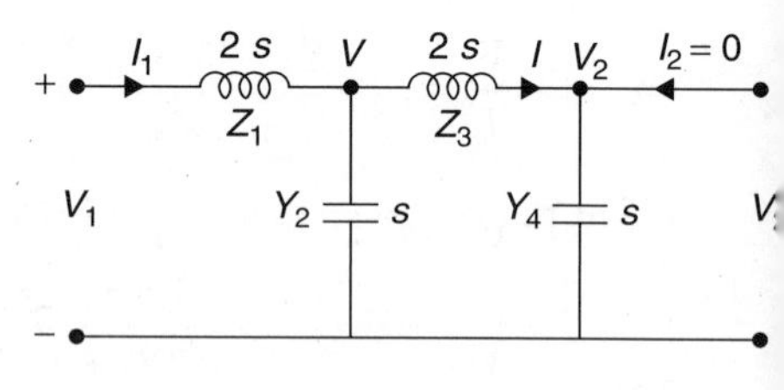

(i) For ladder type of network

$$Z_{11} = Z_1 + \cfrac{1}{Y_2 + \cfrac{1}{Z_3 + \cfrac{1}{Y_4}}} = 2s + \cfrac{1}{s + \cfrac{1}{2s + \cfrac{1}{s}}} = 2s + \cfrac{1}{s + \cfrac{s}{2s^2 + 1}}$$

$$= 2s + \frac{2s^2+1}{2s^3+s+s} = \frac{4s^3+4s^2+2s^2+1}{2s(s^2+1)} = \frac{4s^3+6s^2+1}{2s(s^2+1)}$$

∴ The driving point input impedance is

$$Z_{11} = \frac{4s^3+6s^2+1}{2s(s^2+1)}$$

(ii) In order to obtain the transfer function of a given network we start from the output port using KVL and KCL equations. The first equation may be substituted into the second, second into third and so on. This process is continued till we find one equation which relates output with input and from here the required transfer functions can be obtained.

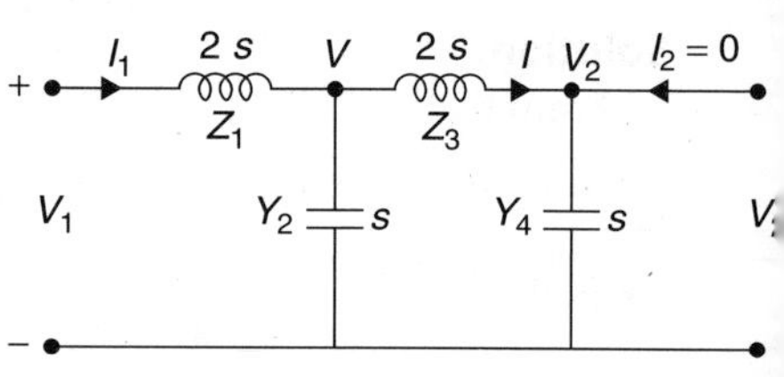

To find Z_{12} and G_{12} we write KVL and KCL equations for the network as follows:

$$I = Y_4 V_2 = sV_2 \quad (1)$$

$$V = V_2 + IZ_3 = V_2 + sV_2 \times 2s = (2s^2+1)V_2 \quad (2)$$

$$I_1 = VY_2 + I = Vs + sV_2 = s(2s^2+1)V_2 + sV_2 = (2s^3+2s)V_2 \quad (3)$$

$$V_1 = V + I_1 Z_1 = (2s^2+1)V_2 + 2sI_1$$

$$= (2s^2+1)V_2 + 2s(2s^3+2s)V_2$$

$$V_1 = (4s^3+6s^2+1)V_2 \quad (4)$$

(iii) From Eq. (3), the transfer impedance is

$$\frac{V_2}{I_1} = Z_{12} = \frac{1}{2s^3+2s}$$

From Eq. (4), voltage ratio transfer function is

$$\frac{V_2}{V_1} = G_{12} = \frac{1}{4s^4+6s^2+1}$$

12.4 For the network, determine the network functions $\frac{V_2}{V_1}$, $\frac{V_2}{I_1}$ and $\frac{V_1}{I_1}$.

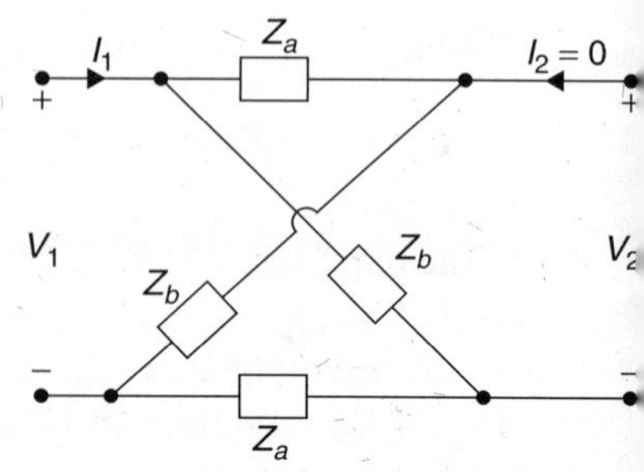

Solution: The network can be redrawn as shown on page 483.

Since the network consists of two identical impedances connected in parallel, the current I_1 divides equally in each branch.

$$V_1 = \frac{I_1}{2}(Z_a + Z_b)$$

$$\Rightarrow \quad \frac{V_1}{I_1} = \frac{Z_a + Z_b}{2}$$

$$V_2 = -\frac{I_1}{2}Z_a + \frac{I_1}{2}Z_b = \frac{I_1}{2}(Z_b - Z_a)$$

$$\Rightarrow \quad \frac{V_2}{I_1} = \frac{Z_b - Z_a}{2}$$

$$\frac{\text{Eq. (2)}}{\text{Eq. (1)}} \Rightarrow \frac{V_2}{V_1} = \frac{Z_b - Z_a}{Z_b + Z_a}$$

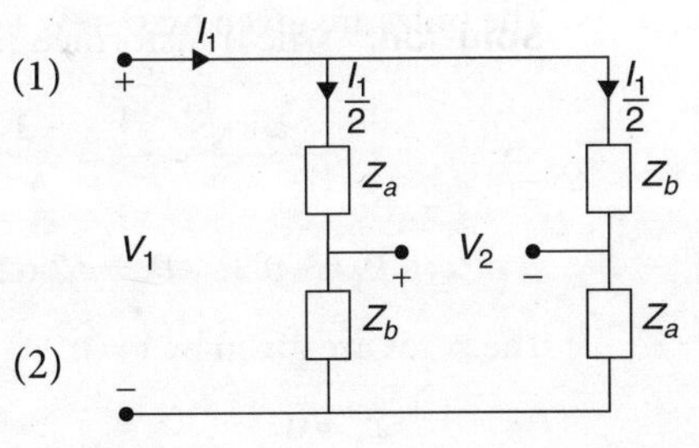

12.5 Find the transfer function of the network, when $R = C = 1$ and draw its pole–zero plot on the *s*-plane.

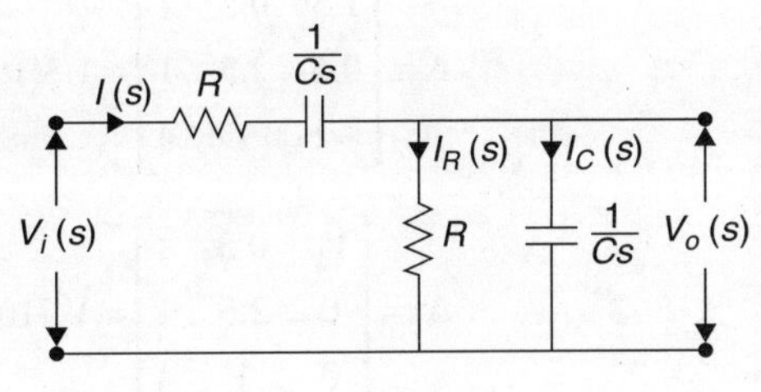

Solution: The transfer network for the given circuit is shown.

From the figure,

$$I(s) = I_R(s) + I_C(s) \tag{1}$$

Applying KVL to loop 1

$$V_i(s) = \left(\frac{R}{1+RCs}\right)I(s) + V_0(s) \tag{2}$$

We know that $V_0(s) = I_R(s)R = \frac{1}{Cs}I_C(s)$

$$I_R(s) = \frac{V_0(s)}{R}, \qquad I_C(s) = CsV_0(s) \tag{3}$$

From Eqs (1) and (3), we have

$$I(s) = \frac{V_0(s)}{R} + CsV_0(s) = \left(\frac{1}{R} + Cs\right)V_0(s) = \left(\frac{1+RCs}{R}\right)V_0(s) \tag{4}$$

From Eqs (2) and (4), we have

$$V_i(s) = \left(\frac{1+RCs}{Cs}\right)\left(\frac{1+RCs}{R}\right)V_0(s) + V_0(s) = \frac{(1+RCs)^2 + RCs}{RCs}V_0(s)$$

$$\frac{V_0(s)}{V_i(s)} = \frac{RCs}{(1+RCs)^2 + RCs}$$

Putting $R = C = 1$, we have

$$G(s) = \frac{V_0(s)}{V_i(s)} = \frac{s}{(1+s)^2 + s} = \frac{s}{s^2 + 3s + 1}$$

∴ The required transfer function is

$$\frac{V_0(s)}{V_i(s)} = \frac{s}{s^2 + 3s + 1}$$

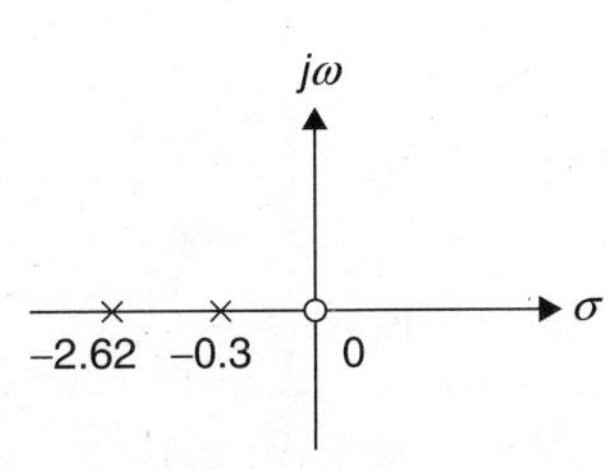

Fig. (a) Pole–zero plot

The poles are given by $s^2 + 3s + 1 = 0$

$$s = \frac{-3 \pm \sqrt{9-4}}{2} = \frac{-3}{2} \pm \frac{\sqrt{5}}{2} = -0.3, -2.62$$

$$P_1 = -0.3, \quad P_2 = -2.62$$

The zeros are given by $s = 0$

$\Rightarrow \qquad Z_1 = 0$

The pole–zero plot is shown in Fig. (a).

12.6 Determine Z_{11}, Z_{12} and G_{12} of the given bridged T-network.

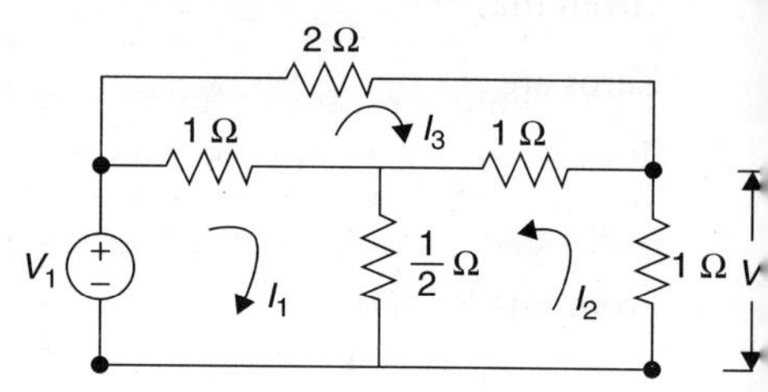

Solution: Inspection of mesh analysis, we have

$$\begin{bmatrix} 1.5 & 0.5 & -1 \\ +0.5 & 2.5 & 1 \\ -1 & 1 & 4 \end{bmatrix} \begin{bmatrix} I_1 \\ I_2 \\ I_3 \end{bmatrix} = \begin{bmatrix} V_1 \\ 0 \\ 0 \end{bmatrix}$$

$$\Delta = \begin{bmatrix} 1.5 & 0.5 & 1 \\ 0.5 & 2.5 & 1 \\ -1 & 1 & 4 \end{bmatrix} = 1.5(10-1) - 0.5(2+1) - 1(0.5+2.5) = 9$$

$$\Delta_1 = \begin{bmatrix} V_1 & 0.5 & 1 \\ 0 & 2.5 & 1 \\ 0 & 1 & 4 \end{bmatrix} = V_1(10-1) = 9V_1$$

$$\Delta_2 = \begin{bmatrix} 1.5 & V_1 & 1 \\ 0.5 & 0 & 1 \\ -1 & 0 & 4 \end{bmatrix} = -V_1(2+1) = -3V_1$$

According to Cramer's rule,

$$I_1 = \frac{\Delta_1}{\Delta} = \frac{9V_1}{9} = V_1$$

$$\Rightarrow \qquad Z_{11} = \frac{V_1}{I_1} = 1$$

$$I_2 = \frac{\Delta_2}{\Delta} = \frac{-3V_1}{9} = -\frac{V_1}{3}$$

$$\Rightarrow \qquad Y_{12} = \frac{I_2}{V_1} = -\frac{1}{3}$$

$$V_2 = -I_2 = \frac{V_1}{3}$$

$$\Rightarrow \qquad G_{12} = \frac{V_2}{V_1} = \frac{1}{3}$$

12.7 The pole and zeros of driving point admittance function of a parallel *RLC* circuit are shown. The pole is at zero 0 and the zeros are at –1 and –4. Find the values of *R*, *L* and *C*.

Solution: The transformed network of a parallel *RLC* circuit is

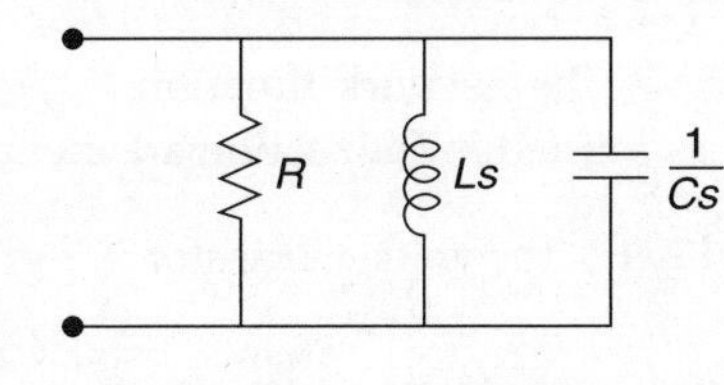

Driving point admittance is

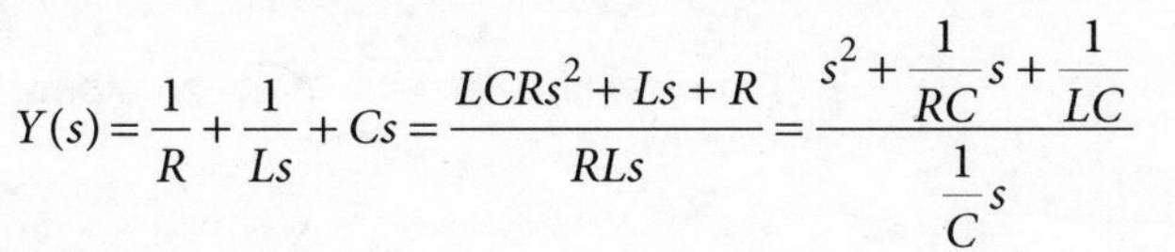

$$Y(s) = \frac{1}{R} + \frac{1}{Ls} + Cs = \frac{LCRs^2 + Ls + R}{RLs} = \frac{s^2 + \frac{1}{RC}s + \frac{1}{LC}}{\frac{1}{C}s} \quad (1)$$

Given that pole at $s = 0$

Zeros are at $s = -1$ and $s = -4$

$$\therefore \quad Y(s) = \frac{(s+1)(s+4)}{s} = \frac{s^2 + 5s + 4}{s} \quad (2)$$

From Eqs (1) and (2),

$$\frac{1}{C} = 1 \;\Rightarrow\; C = 1\,\text{F}$$

$$\frac{1}{RC} = 5 \;\Rightarrow\; R = \frac{1}{5C} = \frac{1}{5} = 0.2\,\Omega$$

$$\frac{1}{LC} = 4 \;\Rightarrow\; L = \frac{1}{4C} = 0.25\,\text{H}$$

12.8 Find whether the following network functions represent driving point immittance functions or not.

(i) $F_1(s) = \dfrac{4s^4 + s^2 - 3s + 1}{s^3 + 2s^2 + 2s + 40}$ (ii) $F_2(s) = \dfrac{s^2 + 4s + 2}{s^6 + s^5 + s^4 + 3s^2 + 4}$ (iii) $F_3(s) = \dfrac{s^2 + s + 2}{2s^2 + s + 1}$

Solution:

(i) $F_1(s) = \dfrac{4s^4 + s^2 - 3s + 1}{s^3 + 2s^2 + 2s + 40}$

$F_1(s)$ does not represent driving point immittance function because of the following errors.

- The coefficient s^3 is missing in the numerator.
- The coefficient of the term *s* is negative in the numerators indicating the presence of zeroes in the right-half of the *s*-plane.
- The denominator $s^3 + 2s^2 + 2s + 40 = (s + 4)(s^2 - 2s + 10)$ has one coefficient negative indicating the presence of two poles in the right half of the *s*-plane.

(ii) $F_2(s) = \dfrac{s^2 + 4s + 2}{s^6 + s^5 + s^4 + 3s^2 + 4}$

$F_2(s)$ does not represent driving point immittance function because of the following errors.

- The coefficient s^3 is missing in the denominator.
- Another coefficient corresponding to *s* is missing in the denominator.
- The highest-power polynomial of the numerator is 2 whereas that of the denominator is 6; a difference of 4 which is not permitted.

(iii) $F_3(s)=\dfrac{s^2+s+2}{2s^2+s+1}$

The network function $F_3(s)$ represents a driving point immittance function since all the properties listed in the section are met.

12.9 The voltage transform is given by $V(s)=\frac{(s+1)(s+2)}{(s+3)(s+4)}$. Find $v(t)$ and draw the pole–zero plot.

Solution: Given that $V(s)=\dfrac{(s+1)(s+2)}{(s+3)(s+4)}$

Poles are $s=-3$, $s=-4$

Zeros are $s=-1$, $s=-2$

$$V(s)=\frac{(s+1)(s+2)}{(s+3)(s+4)}=\frac{A}{s+3}+\frac{B}{s+4}=\frac{2}{s+3}-\frac{6}{s+4}$$

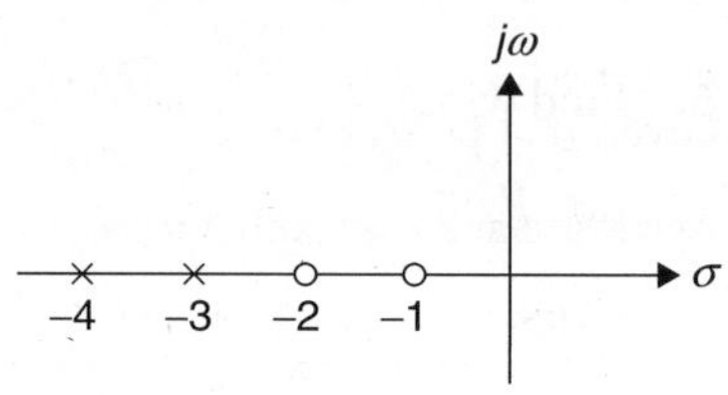

Fig. (a) Pole zero plot

Taking inverse Laplace transform on both sides, we have

$$v(t)=2e^{-3t}-6e^{-4t}$$

The pole–zero plot is shown in Fig. (a).

EXERCISE PROBLEMS

1. For the network shown in the figures, find the driving point input impedances, plot the pole–zero patterns of each network shown. [**Ans:** (a) $Z_{11}(s)=\frac{(s^2+9)(s^2+1)}{s(s^2+4)}$ (b) $Z_{11}(s)=\frac{(s+5)(s+2)}{(s+1)(s+3)}$]

(a)

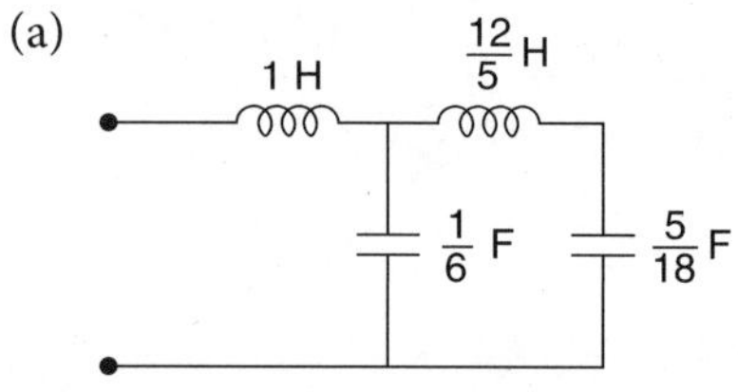

(b)

2. For the two-port *RC* network, find G_{12}.

[**Ans:** $G_{12}=\frac{s^2+1.1s+0.1}{s^2+1.3s+0.1}$]

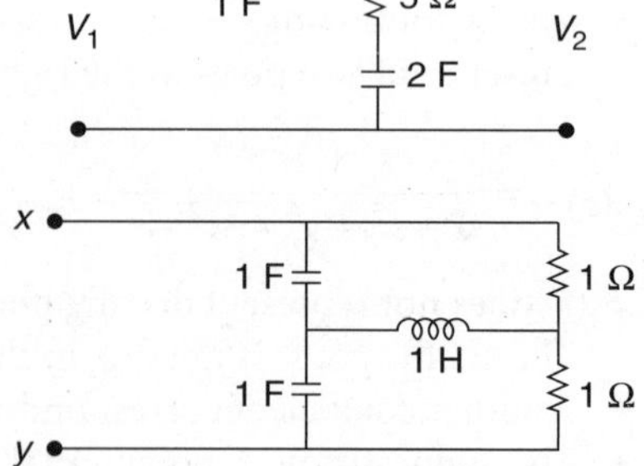

3. Find the poles and zeroes of the impedance seen, looking into the terminals *x* and *y* of the circuit.

[**Ans:** $Z(s)=\frac{2}{s+1}$]

4. A *RLC* series circuit has for its driving point admittance function, the pole–zero diagram is as shown. Find the values of *R*, *L* and *C*. Scale factor = 2. [**Ans:** $R = 2\ \Omega$, $L = 0.5$ H, $C = 0.154$ F]

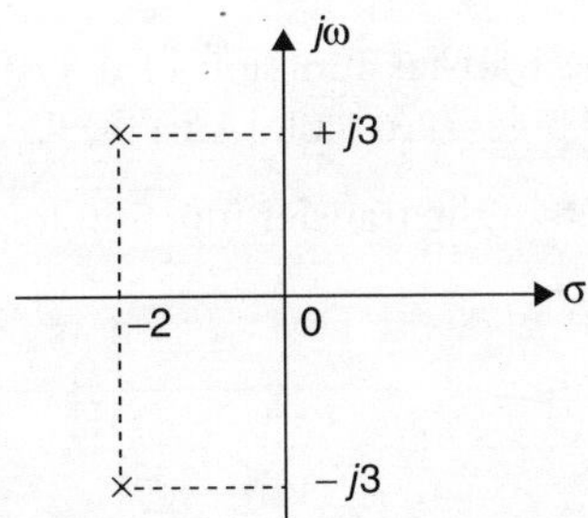

5. Find whether following network functions represent driving point immittance functions or not:

(a) $F_1(s) = \frac{s^2 - s + 1}{s^3 + s^2 + s + 1}$ (b) $F_2(s) = \frac{(s+1)(s+2)(s+3)}{(s^2+1)^2}$ (c) $F_3(s) = \frac{s^2 + s + 2}{s^3 - 2s + 3}$ (d) $F_4(s) = \frac{(s-1)^2}{(s+1)^2}$

[**Ans:** (a) No (b) No (c) No (d) No]

6. Determine the transfer admittance $Y_{12}(s) = \frac{I_2(s)}{V_1(s)}$ for the circuit.

[**Ans:** $Y_{12}(s) = \frac{-3(s+1)}{(s+2)(s+4)}$]

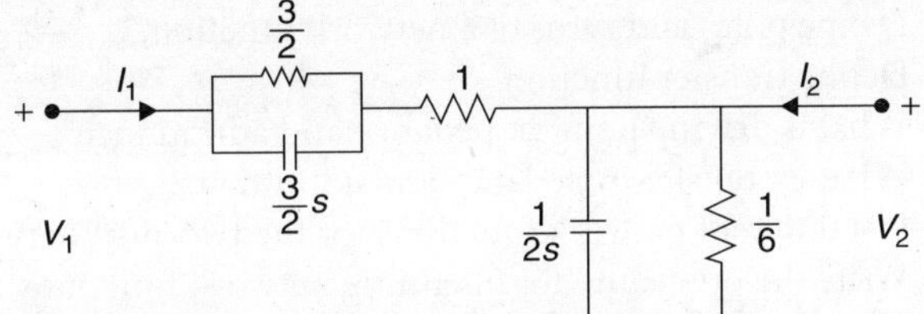

7. For the network, find $G_{12} = \frac{V_2}{V_1}$ and $Z_{12} = \frac{V_2}{I_1}$. [**Ans:** $G_{12} = \frac{1}{41}$ and $Z_{12} = \frac{1}{56}$]

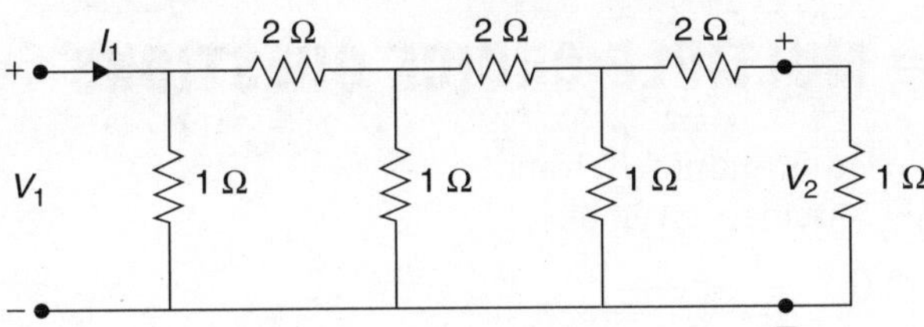

8. Obtain the network functions for the electrical systems.

[**Ans:** (a) $\frac{V_0(s)}{V_i(s)} = \frac{1}{1+RCs}$, (b) $\frac{V_0(s)}{V_i(s)} = \frac{sR_2R_3C_1}{(R_1+R_2)+C_1s(R_1R_2+R_2R_3+R_3R_1)}$ (c) $\frac{V_0(s)}{V_i(s)} = \frac{sL_1(1+sR_2C_1)}{s^2L_1C_1(R_1+R_2)+sL_1+R_1R_2+R_1}$]

(a)

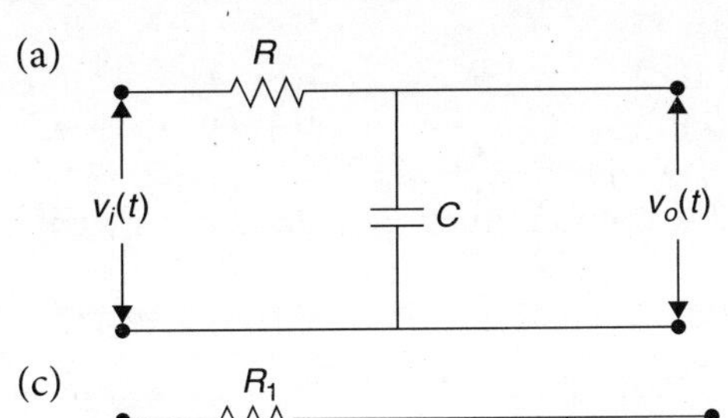

(b)

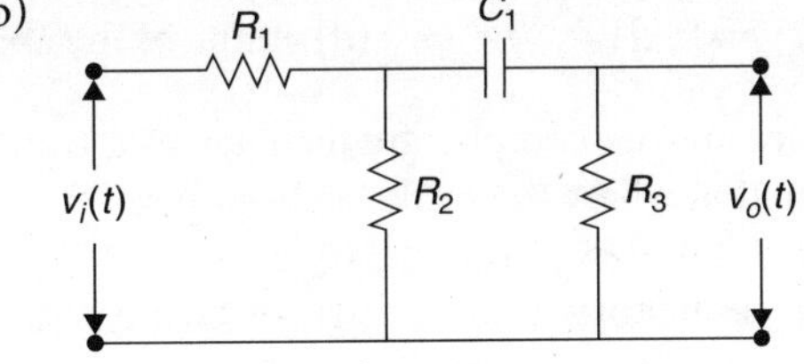

(c)

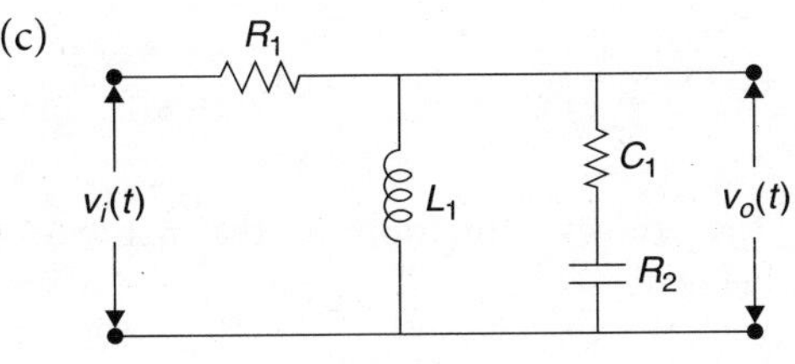

9. The transfer function of a system is given by $N(s) = \frac{10(s+8)}{s(s+4)(s^2+6s+25)}$. Obtain (a) poles, (b) zeros, (c) pole–zero plot. [**Ans:** (a) 0, –4, $-3 \pm j4$, (b) –8]

10. Obtain the transfer function for the system. [**Ans:** $\frac{V_0(s)}{V_i(s)} = \frac{s^2}{(s+1)(s+2)}$]

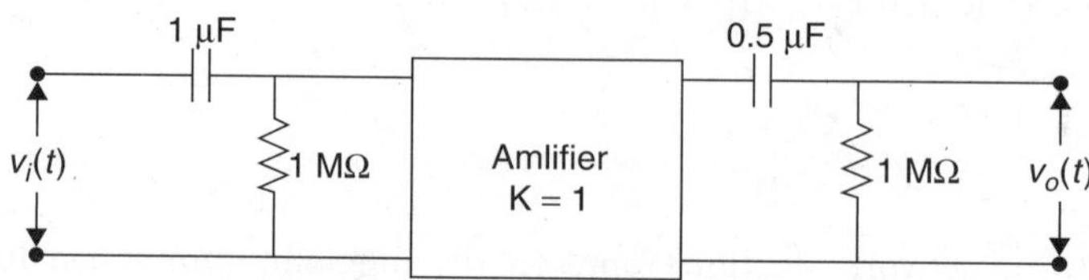

REVIEW QUESTIONS

1. Define poles and zeros of a network function.
2. Define transfer function.
3. What is driving point impedance and admittance?
4. What is transfer impedance and admittance?
5. List different network functions for the two-port network.
6. Write the procedure for obtaining network functions of a ladder network.
7. Write the procedure for obtaining network functions of a non-ladder network.
8. List the restrictions on the location of poles and zeros for the driving point immittance function.
9. List the restriction on the location of poles and zeros for the transfer function.

MULTIPLE CHOICE QUESTIONS

1. The transfer function relating output $I(s)$ and input $V(s)$ in a series RLC circuit is given by
   (a) $\frac{Cs}{LCs^2 + RCs + LC}$ (b) $\frac{Cs}{LCs^2 + RCs + 1}$
   (c) $\frac{Cs}{s^2 + LCs + R}$ (d) none of the above

2. The Laplace transform of df/dt is given by
   (a) $sF(s) - f(0)$ (b) $sF(s) + f(0)$
   (c) $F(s) - f(0)$ (d) none of the above

3. Poles are the complex frequencies of a transfer function where the response becomes
   (a) infinite (b) zero
   (c) oscillatory (d) decaying

4. Zeros are the complex frequencies of a transfer function where the response becomes
   (a) infinite (b) zero
   (c) oscillatory (d) decaying

5. The pole–zero configuration is given below:

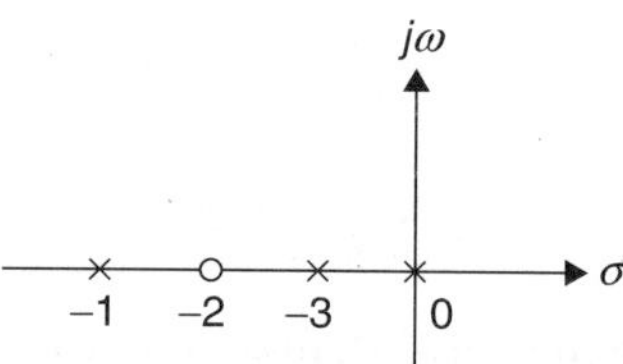

Gain factor, if the value of transfer function at $s = 1$ is:
   (a) 2 (b) 4
   (c) 6 (d) 5.33

6. The transfer function of the above system is:
   (a) $\frac{2(s+2)}{s(s+1)(s+3)}$ (b) $\frac{4(s+2)}{s(s+1)(s+3)}$
   (c) $\frac{5.33(s+2)}{s(s+1)(s+3)}$ (d) $\frac{7.33(s+2)}{s(s+1)(s+3)}$

7. The transfer function of the network given below is

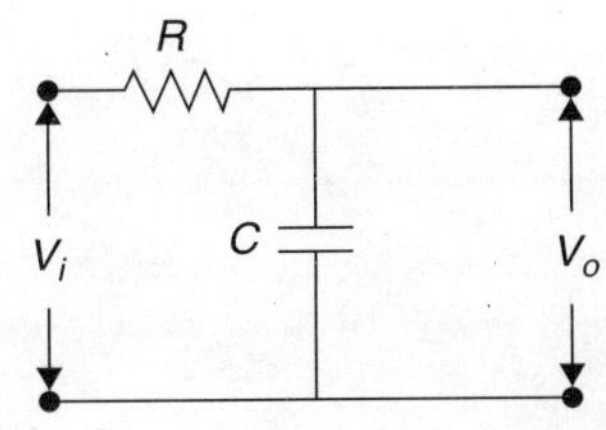

(a) $\frac{1}{1+sRC}$ (b) $\frac{sRC}{1+sRC}$

(c) $\frac{RC}{1+sRC}$ (d) none of the above

8. For a transfer function $T(s) = P(s)/Q(s)$ where $P(s)$ and $Q(s)$ are polynomials of s,
   (a) the degree of $P(s)$ and $Q(s)$ is the same
   (b) the degree of $P(s)$ is always greater than that of $Q(s)$
   (c) the degree of $P(s)$ is independent of the degree of $Q(s)$
   (d) the maximum degrees of $P(s)$ and $Q(s)$ differ by one

9. The magnitude of the function, $F(s) = \frac{s^2-4s+10}{s^2+4s+10}$
   (a) increases with increase in frequency
   (b) decreases with decrease in frequency
   (c) has some relation with the frequency
   (d) is independent of the frequency

10. For the given two-port network, the transfer functions of the network would include

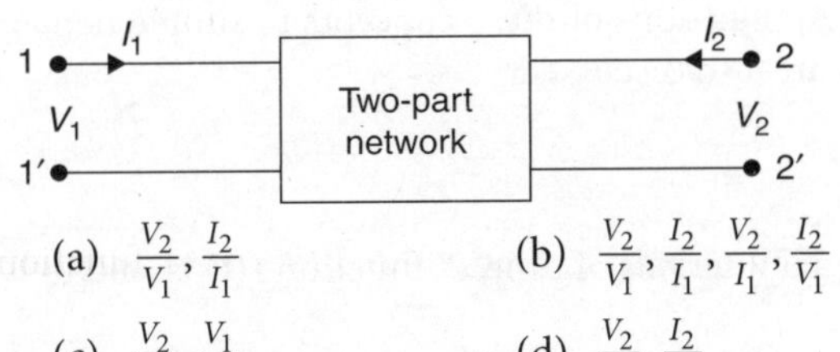

(a) $\frac{V_2}{V_1}, \frac{I_2}{I_1}$ (b) $\frac{V_2}{V_1}, \frac{I_2}{I_1}, \frac{V_2}{I_1}, \frac{I_2}{V_1}$

(c) $\frac{V_2}{I_2}, \frac{V_1}{I_1}$ (d) $\frac{V_2}{I_1}, \frac{I_2}{V_1}$

11. The reciprocal of a network function is
    (a) an immittance function, if the original function is an immittance function
    (b) a transfer function, if the original function is a transfer function
    (c) never an immittance function
    (d) never a transfer function

12. A transient current in a network is, $i(t) = 2e^{-t} - e^{-5t}$. The poles and zeros of the function $I(s)$ are:
    (a) poles, −1, −5; zeros, 2
    (b) poles, −1, −5; zeros, −9
    (c) poles, 1, 5; zeros, 9
    (d) can't define

13. The necessary condition for driving point function is:
    (a) the real part of all poles and zeros must not be zero or negative
    (b) the polynomials $Z(s)$ and $P(s)$ may not have any missing terms between the highest and lowest degree unless all even or all odd terms are missing
    (c) the degree of $Z(s)$ and $P(s)$ may differ by more than one
    (d) the lowest degree in $Z(s)$ and $P(s)$ may differ in degree by more than two

14. The necessary condition for the transfer function is:
    (a) the coefficients in the polynomials $Z(s)$ and $P(s)$ must be real
    (b) the coefficients in $P(s)$ may be negative
    (c) complex or imaginary poles and zeros may not conjugate
    (d) if the real part of the pole is zero, then that pole must be multiple

Answers

1. b	2. a	3. a	4. b	5. d	6. c	7. a	8. c	9. d	10. b
11. a	12. b	13. b	14. a						

13 Fourier Analysis

Learning Outcomes

After reading this chapter, the reader will able to

- ➢ Define periodic function
- ➢ Illustrate different periodic functions
- ➢ State the Fourier theorem
- ➢ Determine the trigonometric Fourier series for any given periodic function
- ➢ Determine the exponential Fourier series for any given periodic function
- ➢ Define Fourier transform along with its properties
- ➢ List the Fourier transforms for standard functions
- ➢ Evaluate the Fourier transforms of periodic functions

13.1 INTRODUCTION

The analysis of networks with sinusoidal inputs is made easy by consideration of frequency domain circuits. The need for analysis of networks with non-sinusoidal periodic signals arises in communications networks. Fourier has shown that any non-sinusoidal periodic signal could be resolved into sinusoidal components of different frequencies. Fourier series are series of sine and cosine terms and are used to represent general periodic signals and as well as non-periodic signals.

Fourier analysis deals with Fourier series and Fourier transforms and has several applications in mathematics, science and engineering, particularly in the area of communication and signal processing. This chapter deals with analysis of non-sinusoidal wave forms using Fourier analysis. The convergence of Fourier series and Fourier transforms is also discussed. Applications of these concepts to simple networks excited by periodic waveforms and aperiodic waveforms are also discussed.

13.2 PERIODIC FUNCTION

Periodic functions are those which repeat regularly at equal intervals of time. A function $f(t)$ is said to be a periodic function if

$$f(t \pm kT) = f(t) \tag{13.1}$$

where T is time period and k is an integer.

If such a periodic signal is given to a linear network, the output or response of the network will also be always periodic. A common example of a periodic function is a sine function. Some examples are shown in Fig. 13.1 (T is the period).

The fundamental frequency of the periodic signal is defined as

$$\omega_0 = \frac{2\pi}{T} \tag{13.2}$$

If n is any integer, then $n\omega_0$ is said to be the nth harmonic of the fundamental frequency ω_0. Thus a periodic wave form will be described in terms of its fundamental frequency, its second harmonic, third harmonic, fourth harmonic, and so on. Each of these frequencies is simply related to the time period T.

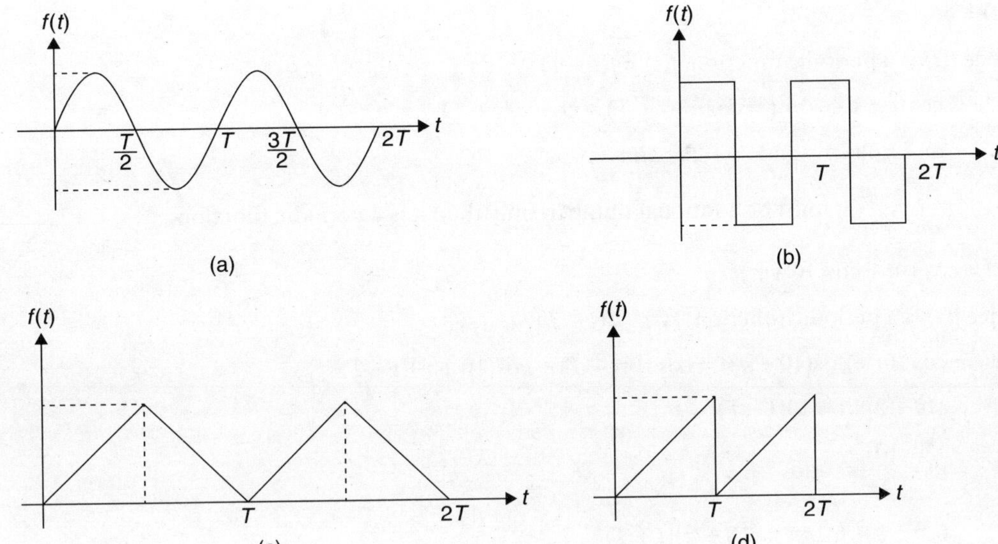

Fig. 13.1 Examples of periodic wave forms

Problem 13.1 Find the period of the following functions.

(i) $f(t) = \cos\frac{t}{3} + \cos\frac{t}{4}$

(ii) $f(t) = \cos\omega_1 t + \cos\omega_2 t$

(iii) $f(t) = \cos 10t + \cos(10 + \pi)t$

Solution:

(i) $f(t) = \cos\frac{t}{3} + \cos\frac{t}{4}$

Since $f(t)$ is a periodic function, $f(t) = f(t + T)$

$$\Rightarrow \quad \cos\frac{t}{3} + \cos\frac{t}{4} = \cos\frac{1}{3}(t+T) + \cos\frac{1}{4}(t+T)$$

Note: $\cos\theta = \cos(\theta + 2n\pi)$

On equating corresponding terms on both sides, we have

$$\frac{t}{3} + 2m\pi = \frac{1}{3}(t+T)$$

$$\Rightarrow \quad 2m\pi = \frac{T}{3}$$

$$\Rightarrow \quad T = 6m\pi \quad \text{and}$$

$$\frac{t}{4} + 2n\pi = \frac{1}{4}(t+T)$$

$$\Rightarrow \quad T = 8m\pi$$

Therefore, smallest period, $T = 24\pi$

(ii) $f(t) = \cos\omega_1 t + \cos\omega_2 t$

Since $f(t)$ is a periodic function, $f(t) = f(t+T)$

$$\cos\omega_1 t + \cos\omega_2 t = \cos\omega_1(t+T) + \cos\omega_2(t+T)$$

$$\omega_1 T = 2m\pi \quad \text{and} \quad \omega_2 T = 2n\pi$$

$\Rightarrow$ $\dfrac{\omega_1}{\omega_2} = \dfrac{m}{n} =$ must be a rational number, only then it is a periodic function.

(iii) $f(t) = \cos 10t + \cos(10+\pi)t$

Since $f(t)$ is a periodic function, $f(t) = f(t+T)$

$$\cos 10t + \cos(10+\pi)t = \cos 10(t+T) + \cos(10+\pi)(t+T)$$

$$10t + 2m\pi = 10(t+T)$$

$\Rightarrow$ $m = \dfrac{10T}{2\pi}$ and

$$(10+\pi)t + 2n\pi = (10+\pi)(t+T)$$

$\Rightarrow$ $n = \dfrac{(10+\pi)T}{2\pi}$

$\therefore$ $\dfrac{m}{n} = \dfrac{10T}{(10+\pi)T} = \dfrac{10}{10+\pi}$ is not a rational number, so it is not a periodic function.

13.3 FOURIER THEOREM

The French mathematician J B J Fourier (1758–1830) established an important theorem called Fourier theorem, which states that, 'A periodic function satisfying the Dirichlet conditions can be represented by an infinite series of sinusoids of harmonically related frequencies. The lowest frequency sinusoid has a periodic time equal to the period of original non-sinusoidal waveform, and this is called the fundamental component of periodic waveform. The other components have the submultiples of the original waveform'.

The Dirichlet conditions that a function $f(t)$ has to satisfy in order that a convergent Fourier series could be written are as follows:

- The function $f(t)$ is single valued everywhere.
- The function $f(t)$ must have a finite number of maxima and minima in the period T.
- In the period T, the function $f(t)$ must be absolutely convergent, that is, $\int_0^T |f(t)|\,dt < \infty$.
- The function $f(t)$ has a finite number of discontinuities in any one time period.

13.4 TRIGONOMETRIC FOURIER SERIES

For any given periodic function $f(t)$, the Fourier series can be represented by

$$f(t) = a_0 + a_1\cos\omega_0 t + a_2\cos 2\omega_0 t + \cdots + b_1\sin\omega_0 t + b_2\sin 2\omega_0 t + \cdots \tag{13.3}$$

In compact form

$$f(t) = a_0 + \sum_{n=1}^{\infty}(a_n\cos n\omega_0 t + b_n\sin n\omega_0 t) \tag{13.4}$$

where a_0, a_n and b_n are constants and the process of determining these constants is called Fourier analysis.

13.4.1 Evaluation of Fourier Coefficients

Evaluation of a_0 The coefficient a_0 can be obtained by integrating Eq. 13.4 over the complete time period *T*. Thus, we have

$$\int_0^T f(t) = \int_0^T a_0 + \int_0^T \sum_{n=1}^{\infty} (a_n \cos n\omega_0 t + b_n \sin n\omega_0 t)dt = \int_0^T a_0 + \int_0^T \sum_{n=1}^{\infty} a_n \cos n\omega_0 t dt + \int_0^T \sum_{n=1}^{\infty} a_n \sin n\omega_0 t dt$$

Since $\int_0^T \sin(n\omega_0 t)dt = 0$; for all *m* and $\int_0^T \cos(n\omega_0 t)dt = 0$; for all $n \neq 0$, the above equation can be written as

$$\int_0^T f(t)dt = a_0 T + 0 + 0$$

$$\Rightarrow \qquad a_0 = \frac{1}{T}\int_0^T f(t)dt \qquad (13.5)$$

We observe that a_0 is the average value of the given function $f(t)$ over a period *T*. Here a_0 is also called the *DC term*.

Evaluation of a_n To determine the coefficient a_n multiplying Eq. 13.4 by $\cos n\omega_0 t$ (since a_n is the cosine coefficient) and integrating with respect to *t* between the limits 0 to *T*, we have

$$\int_0^T f(t)\cos n\omega_0 t dt = \int_0^T a_0 \cos n\omega_0 t dt + \int_0^T \sum_{n=1}^{\infty} a_n \cos n\omega_0 t \cos n\omega_0 t dt + \int_0^T \sum_{n=1}^{\infty} b_n \sin n\omega_0 t \cos n\omega_0 dt$$

$$\int_0^T f(t)\cos n\omega_0 t dt = \int_0^T a_0 \cos n\omega_0 t dt + \int_0^T \sum_{n=1}^{\infty} a_n \cos^2 n\omega_0 t dt + \int_0^T \sum_{n=1}^{\infty} b_n \sin n\omega_0 t \cos n\omega_0 dt \qquad (13.6)$$

According to the orthogonality property of the sine and cosine functions, we have

$$\int_0^T \sin(m\omega_0 t) \times \cos(n\omega_0 t)dt = 0; \quad \text{for all } m,n$$

$$\int_0^T \sin(m\omega_0 t) \times \sin(n\omega_0 t)dt = 0; \quad \text{for } m \neq n$$

$$\int_0^T \cos(m\omega_0 t) \times \cos(n\omega_0 t)dt = 0; \quad \text{for } m \neq n$$

Non-zero values for the integral result when $m = n$. Thus

$$\int_0^T \sin^2(m\omega_0 t)dt = \frac{T}{2}; \quad \text{for all } m$$

$$\int_0^T \cos^2(n\omega_0 t)dt = \frac{T}{2}; \quad \text{for all } n$$

Therefore, Eq. 13.6 can be written as

$$\int_0^T f(t)\cos n\omega_0 t dt = 0 + a_n \frac{T}{2} + 0$$

$$\int_0^T f(t)\cos n\omega_0 t dt = \frac{T}{2} a_n$$

$$\Rightarrow \qquad a_n = \frac{2}{T}\int_0^T f(t)\cos n\omega_0 t dt \qquad (13.7)$$

Evaluation of b_n To determine the coefficient b_n, multiplying Eq. 13.4 by $\sin n\omega_0 t$ (since b_n is the sine coefficient) and integrating with respect to t between the limits 0 to T, we have

$$\int_0^T f(t)\sin n\omega_0 t dt = \int_0^T a_0 \sin n\omega_0 t + \int_0^T \sum_{n=1}^{\infty} a_n \cos n\omega_0 t \sin n\omega_0 t dt + \int_0^T \sum_{n=1}^{\infty} b_n \sin n\omega_0 t \sin n\omega_0 t dt \qquad (13.8)$$

In Eq. 13.8 all the right hand side terms are zero, except the term $\int_0^T b_n \sin^2 n\omega_0 t\, dt$, due to the orthogonality property of the sine and cosine functions. From the orthogonality property, $\int_0^T b_n \sin^2 n\omega_0 t\, dt = b_n \frac{T}{2}$

Therefore from Eq. 13.8, we have

$$\int_0^T f(t)\sin n\omega_0 t dt = 0 + b_n \frac{T}{2} + 0$$

$$\int_0^T f(t)\sin n\omega_0 t dt = b_n \frac{T}{2}$$

$$\Rightarrow \qquad b_n = \frac{2}{T}\int_0^T f(t)\sin n\omega_0 t dt \qquad (13.9)$$

We summarise the result as follows: any sinusoidal periodic function with a period T and fundamental frequency $\omega_0 = \frac{2\pi}{T}$ can be represented by a Fourier series as given by

$$f(t) = a_0 + \sum_{n=1}^{\infty} (a_n \cos n\omega_0 t + b_n \sin n\omega_0 t) \qquad (13.10)$$

where $a_0 = \frac{1}{T}\int_0^T f(t) dt$

$$a_n = \frac{2}{T}\int_0^T f(t)\cos n\omega_0 t dt$$

$$b_n = \frac{2}{T}\int_0^T f(t)\sin n\omega_0 t dt$$

Problem 13.2 Find the trigonometric Fourier series for the waveform.

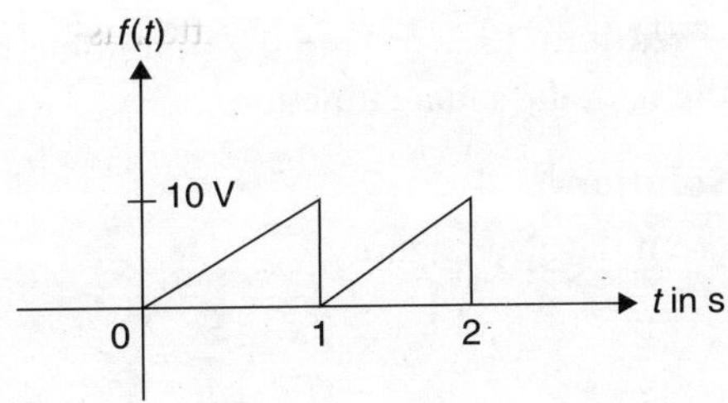

Solution:

From the given figure

$$T = 1, \quad \omega_0 = \frac{2\pi}{T} = \frac{2\pi}{1} = 2\pi$$

Representation of $f(t)$ over one complete cycle is shown.

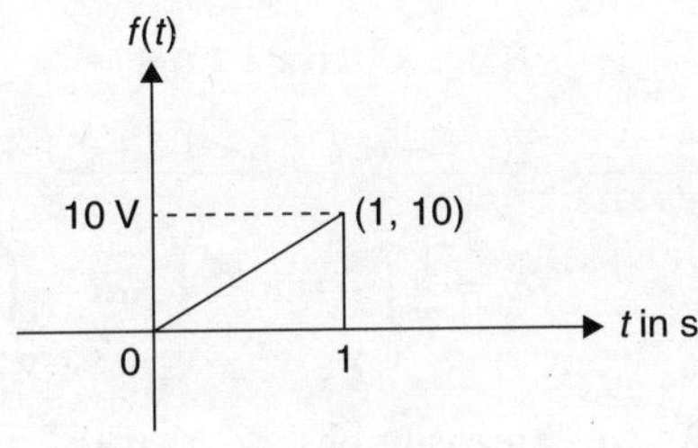

$$f(t) - 0 = \frac{10-0}{1-0}(t-0)$$

$$\Rightarrow \qquad f(t) = 10t; \quad 0 \le t \le 1$$

$$a_0 = \frac{1}{T}\int_0^T f(t)dt = \frac{1}{1}\int_0^1 10t dt = 10\left[\frac{t^2}{2}\right]_0^1 = 5$$

$$a_n = \frac{2}{T}\int_0^T f(t)\cos n\omega_0 dt = \frac{2}{1}\int_0^1 10t\cos(2\pi n)dt = 20\int_0^1 t\cos(2\pi n)dt$$

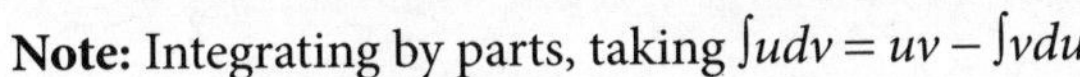
Note: Integrating by parts, taking $\int u dv = uv - \int v du$

$$a_n = 20\left\{\left[\frac{t\sin 2\pi nt}{2\pi n}\right]_0^1 - \int_0^1 \frac{\sin 2\pi nt}{2\pi n}dt\right\} = 20\left[0 + \frac{\cos 2\pi nt}{(2\pi n)^2}\right]_0^1 = 0$$

$$b_n = \frac{2}{T}\int_0^T f(t)\sin n\omega_0 dt = \frac{2}{1}\int_0^1 10t\sin 2\pi n dt = 20\left[\left.\frac{-t\cos 2\pi nt}{2\pi n}\right|_0^1 + \int_0^1 \frac{\cos 2\pi nt}{2\pi n}dt\right]$$

$$= 20\left[\frac{-1}{2\pi n} + \left.\frac{\sin 2\pi nt}{(2\pi n)^2}\right|_0^1\right] = 20\left[\frac{-1}{2\pi n} + 0\right] = \frac{-10}{n\pi}$$

Hence the Fourier series becomes

$$f(t) = a_0 + \sum_{n=1}^{\infty}(a_n\cos n\omega_0 t + b_n \sin n\omega_0 t) = 5 - \sum_{n=1}^{\infty}\frac{10}{n\pi}\sin 2\pi nt = 5 - \frac{10}{\pi}\sum_{n=1}^{\infty}\frac{\sin 2\pi nt}{n}$$

$$= 5 - \frac{10}{\pi}\left[\sin 2\pi t + \frac{\sin 4\pi t}{2} + \frac{\sin 6\pi t}{3} + \cdots\right]$$

$$= 5 - \left[\frac{10\sin 2\pi t}{\pi} + \frac{10\sin 4\pi t}{2\pi} + \frac{10\sin 6\pi t}{3\pi} + \cdots\right]$$

Problem 13.3 Find the trigonometric Fourier series for the periodic square function.

Solution:

From the given figure

$$T = 1, \quad \omega_0 = \frac{2\pi}{T} = \frac{2\pi}{1} = 2\pi$$

The mathematical equation for the function $f(t)$ is given by

$$f(t) = K; \quad 0 < t < 0.5$$

$$f(t) = -K; \quad 0.5 < t < 1$$

$$a_0 = \frac{1}{T}\int_0^T f(t)dt = \int_0^{0.5} Kdt + \int_{0.5}^{1} -Kdt = K\left[t\right]_0^{0.5} - K\left[t\right]_{0.5}^{1} = K(0.5 - 0 - 1 + 0.5) = 0$$

As we can easily observe that the average value of the given function over a period is zero (since it is symmetrical wave form),

$$a_n = \frac{2}{T}\int_0^T f(t)\cos n\omega_0 dt = 2\int_0^1 f(t)\cos 2\pi nt dt = 2\left[\int_0^{0.5} K\cos 2\pi nt dt - \int_{0.5}^{1} K\cos 2\pi nt dt\right]$$

$$= 2K\left[\frac{\sin 2\pi nt}{2\pi n}\Bigg|_0^{0.5} - \frac{\sin 2\pi nt}{2\pi n}\Bigg|_{0.5}^{1}\right] = \frac{2K}{2\pi n}[(\sin n\pi - 0) - (\sin 2n\pi - \sin n\pi)] = 0$$

$$b_n = \frac{2}{T}\int_0^T f(t)\sin n\omega_0 dt = 2\int_0^1 f(t)\sin 2\pi nt dt$$

$$= 2\left[\int_0^{0.5} K\sin 2\pi nt dt - \int_{0.5}^{1} K\sin 2\pi nt dt\right] = 2K\left[\frac{-\cos 2\pi nt}{2\pi n}\Bigg|_0^{0.5} + \frac{\cos 2\pi nt}{2\pi n}\Bigg|_{0.5}^{1}\right]$$

$$= 2K\left[\frac{-\cos n\pi}{2\pi n} + \frac{1}{2\pi n} + \frac{\cos 2\pi n}{2\pi n} - \frac{\cos n\pi}{2\pi n}\right] = \frac{2K}{2\pi n}[2 - 2\cos n\pi] = \frac{2K}{n\pi}[1 - \cos n\pi]$$

$$= \frac{2K}{n\pi}[1 - (-1)^n]$$

$$= \frac{4K}{\pi n} \quad \text{for } n = 1, 3, 5\ldots$$

$$= 0 \quad \text{for } n = 2, 4, 6\ldots$$

Hence the Fourier series becomes

$$f(t) = a_0 + \sum_{n=1}^{\infty}(a_n\cos n\omega_0 t + b_n\sin n\omega_0 t)$$

$$= \sum_{n=1,3,5...}^{\infty} \frac{4K}{\pi n} \sin n\omega t$$

$$= \frac{4K}{\pi}\left[\frac{\sin \omega t}{1} + \frac{\sin 3\omega t}{3} + \frac{\sin 5\omega t}{5} + \cdots\right]$$

13.5 WAVEFORM SYMMETRY

In Problem 13.3, we observed that $a_0 = 0$, $a_n = 0$ for all n. $b_n = 0$ for even n.

Can we predict appropriately which coefficients are going to be zero? If we can do this, it would save a lot of effort in obtaining the Fourier series of a given function. These coefficients are zero because of some symmetry present in the waveform. Usually the symmetry is obvious by inspections of the waveform. Simple mathematical tests are also available to determine the nature of symmetry. There are four types of symmetry, possessed by the waveforms:

(i) even function symmetry,
(ii) odd function symmetry,
(iii) rotational or half-wave symmetry, and
(iv) quarter wave symmetry.

13.5.1 Even Function Symmetry

If a waveform satisfies the condition $f(t) = f(-t)$, the waveform is said to possess *even function symmetry*. An even function is symmetric about the y-axis. The sum of two or more even functions is an even function, and with the addition of a constant the even nature of the function is still preserved. Figure 13.2 shows different examples of an even function symmetry.

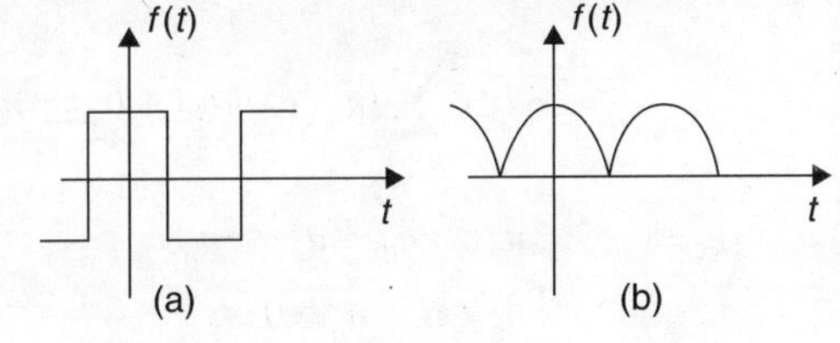

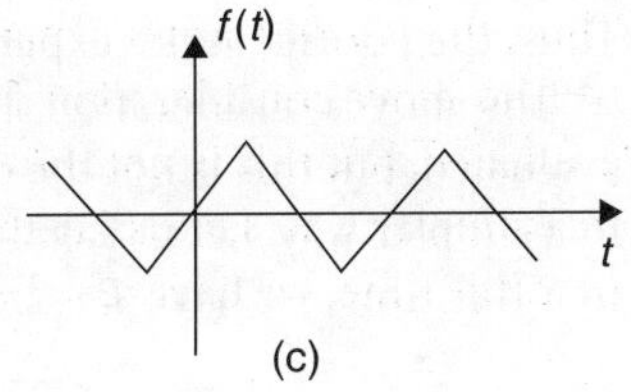

Fig. 13.2 Examples of functions having even symmetry

Now, let us assume that a function $f(t)$ has the following Fourier expansion

$$f(t) = a_0 + \sum_{n=1}^{\infty} (a_n \cos n\omega_0 t + b_n \sin n\omega_0 t)$$

We can write $f(-t) = a_0 + \sum_{n=1}^{\infty} (a_n \cos n\omega_0 t - b_n \sin n\omega_0 t)$

The function is of even symmetry if, $f(t) = f(-t)$

$$a_0 + \sum_{n=1}^{\infty} (a_n \cos n\omega_0 t + b_n \sin n\omega_0 t) = a_0 + \sum_{n=1}^{\infty} (a_n \cos n\omega_0 t - b_n \sin n\omega_0 t)$$

$$\Rightarrow \quad b_n = -b_n$$

$$\Rightarrow \quad 2b_n = 0$$

$$\Rightarrow \quad b_n = 0 \tag{13.11}$$

Thus, the Fourier series expansion of an even periodic function contains only a constant term and a cosine term.

13.5.2 Odd Function Symmetry

If a waveform satisfies the condition, $f(t) = -f(-t)$, the function is said to possess *odd function symmetry*. The sum of two or more odd functions is an odd function, and with the addition of a constant DC term removes the odd nature of the function. The product of two odd functions is an even function. Such functions always have diagonal symmetry. Figure 13.3 shows different examples of odd function symmetry.

f(t) t (a) f(t) (b) f(t) t (c)

Fig. 13.3 Examples of functions having odd symmetry

The function $\cos(n\omega_0 t)$ is even and $\sin(n\omega_0 t)$ is odd.

The function is odd symmetry if,

$$f(t) = -f(-t)$$

$$a_0 + \sum_{n=1}^{\infty}(a_n \cos n\omega_0 t + b_n \sin n\omega_0 t) = -a_0 + \sum_{n=1}^{\infty}(-a_n \cos n\omega_0 t + b_n \sin n\omega_0 t)$$

$$\Rightarrow \quad a_0 = -a_0, \quad a_n = -a_n$$

$$\Rightarrow \quad a_0 = 0, \quad a_n = 0 \tag{13.12}$$

Thus, the Fourier series expansion of an odd periodic function contains only the sine term.

The above consideration shows that odd or even symmetry tells us that terms of only one kind need to be evaluated; but this is not the only thing. Even those coefficients which must be evaluated are now evaluated in a simpler way. Let us say the function is even, then for evaluation of a_n, taking the limit of integration $-\pi$ to π this time, we have $T = 2\pi$, $\omega_0 t = \theta$.

$$a_n = \frac{1}{\pi}\int_{-\pi}^{\pi} f(\theta)\cos n\theta\, d\theta = \frac{1}{\pi}\left[\int_{-\pi}^{0} f(\theta)\cos n\theta\, d\theta + \int_{0}^{\pi} f(\theta)\cos n\theta\, d\theta\right]$$

Now, in the integration $\int_{-\pi}^{0} f(\theta)\cos n\theta\, d\theta$ put $\alpha = -\theta$

$$\Rightarrow \quad d\theta = -d\alpha$$

when $\theta = 0, \quad \alpha = 0$

when $\theta = -\pi, \quad \alpha = \pi$

$$\therefore \quad \int_{-\pi}^{0} f(\theta)\cos n\theta d\theta = -\int_{\pi}^{0} f(-\alpha)\cos(-n\alpha)d\alpha = -\int_{\pi}^{0} f(\alpha)\cos n\alpha\, d\alpha = \int_{0}^{\pi} f(\alpha)\cos n\alpha\, d\alpha$$

[Since for even symmetry, $f(\alpha) = f(-\alpha)$]

$$\therefore \quad a_n = \frac{1}{\pi}\left[\int_{0}^{\pi} f(\alpha)\cos n\alpha\, d\alpha + \int_{0}^{\pi} f(\theta)\cos n\theta\, d\theta\right] = \frac{2}{\pi}\int_{0}^{\pi} f(\theta)\cos n\theta\, d\theta$$

$$\Rightarrow \quad a_n = \frac{2}{\pi}\int_{0}^{\pi} f(\theta)\cos n\theta\, d\theta \tag{13.13}$$

Similarly, $b_n = \frac{2}{\pi}\int_0^{\pi} f(\theta)\sin n\theta\, d\theta$ (13.14)

Or, $$a_n = \frac{4}{T}\int_0^{T/2} f(t)\cos n\omega_0 t\, dt \quad (13.15)$$

$$b_n = \frac{4}{T}\int_0^{T/2} f(t)\sin n\omega_0 t\, dt \quad (13.16)$$

13.5.3 Half Wave Symmetry or Rotational Symmetry

Whenever the positive half cycle of the wave form is exactly the same as the negative half cycle, we have *half wave symmetry*. Mathematically, this can be stated as,

$$f(t) = -f\left(t \pm \frac{T}{2}\right)$$

Clearly, this function is neither completely even, nor completely odd, so it must be both. A typical function having half wave symmetry is shown in Fig. 13.4.

It is observed that, the average value of this wave form is zero. Thus

$$a_0 = 0 \quad (13.17)$$

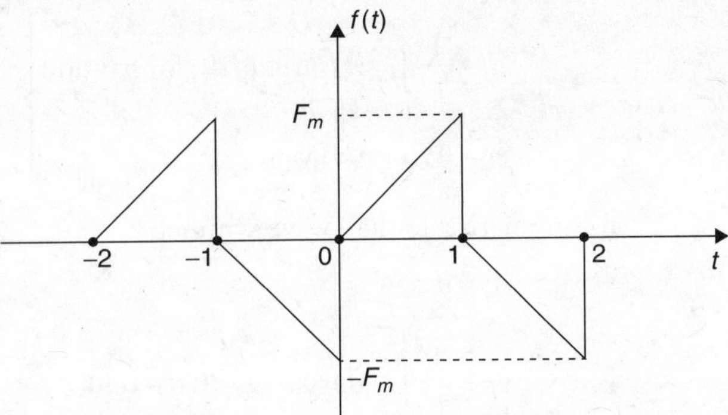

Fig. 13.4 An example of a function with half wave symmetry

The coefficient a_n is given by

$$a_n = \frac{2}{T}\int_0^{T} f(t)\cos n\omega_0 t\, dt = \frac{2}{T}\int_0^{T/2} f(t)\cos n\omega_0 t\, dt + \frac{2}{T}\int_{T/2}^{T} f(t)\cos n\omega_0 t\, dt$$

If t is replaced by $\left(t+\frac{T}{2}\right)$ in the second integral, the limits can be changed to 0 to $\frac{T}{2}$ without changing the value of the integral. Thus we have

$$a_n = \frac{2}{T}\int_0^{T/2} f(t)\cos n\omega_0 t\, dt + \frac{2}{T}\int_0^{T} f\left(t+\frac{T}{2}\right)\cos n\omega_0\left(t+\frac{T}{2}\right)dt$$

But $$f\left(t+\frac{T}{2}\right) = -f(t)$$

$$a_n = \frac{2}{T}\int_0^{T/2} f(t)\cos n\omega_0 t\, dt - \frac{2}{T}\int_0^{T/2} f(t)\left[\cos n\omega_0 t\cdot\cos n\omega_0\frac{T}{2} - \sin n\omega_0 t\cdot\sin n\omega_0\frac{T}{2}\right]dt$$

Since $$T = \frac{2\pi}{\omega_0} \Rightarrow \omega_0 T = 2\pi$$

$$\cos n\omega_0\frac{T}{2} = \cos n\frac{2\pi}{2} = \cos n\pi = (-1)^n$$

$$\sin n\omega_0 \frac{T}{2} = \sin n \frac{2\pi}{2} = \sin n\pi = 0$$

$$\therefore \quad a_n = \frac{2}{T}\int_0^{T/2} f(t)\cos n\omega_0 t\,dt - \frac{2}{T}\int_0^{T/2} f(t)\cdot(-1)^n \cos n\omega_0 (t)\,dt$$

$$\left.\begin{aligned} a_n &= \frac{4}{T}\int_0^{T/2} f(t)\cos n\omega_0 t\,dt; \text{ for } n = \text{odd} \\ &= 0; \text{ for } n = \text{even} \end{aligned}\right\} \tag{13.18}$$

Similarly, we can show that

$$\left.\begin{aligned} b_n &= \frac{4}{T}\int_0^{T/2} f(t)\sin n\omega_0 t\,dt; \text{ for } n = \text{odd} \\ &= 0\,; \text{ for } n = \text{even} \end{aligned}\right\} \tag{13.19}$$

To summarise, for half wave symmetry

$$a_0 = 0$$

$$a_n = \frac{4}{T}\int_0^{T/2} f(t)\cos n\omega_0 t dt; n = \text{odd}$$

$$= 0; \quad n = \text{even}$$

$$b_n = \frac{4}{T}\int_0^{T/2} f(t)\sin n\omega_0 t dt; n = \text{odd}$$

$$= 0; \quad n = \text{even}$$

Thus, the Fourier expansion of a periodic function with half-wave symmetry contains only odd harmonics.

13.5.4 Quarter Wave Symmetry

If a function possesses rotation symmetry in addition to either odd symmetry or even symmetry, the function is said to have quarter wave symmetry. Examples of such functions are shown in Fig. 13.5.

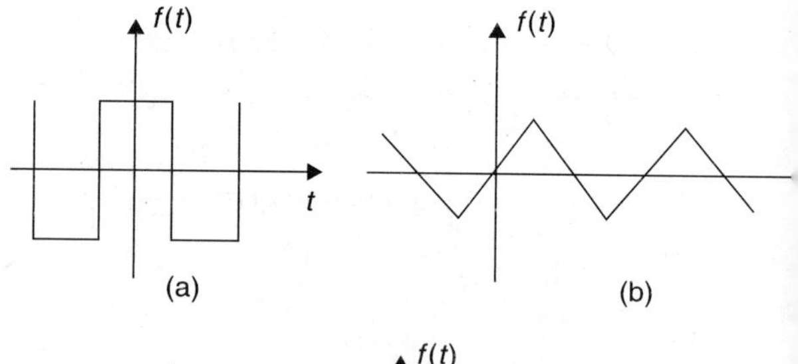

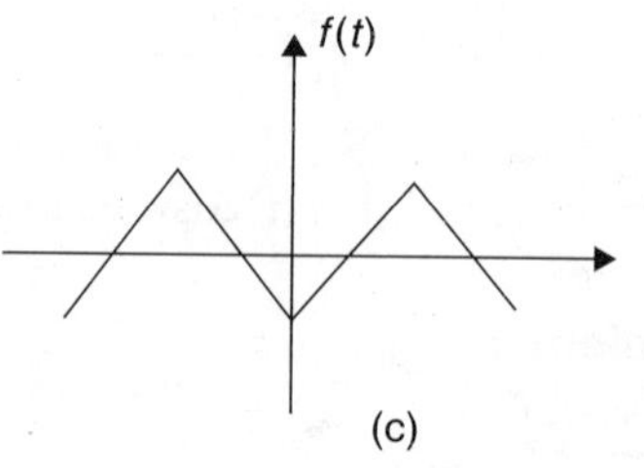

Fig. 13.5 Examples of functions having quarter wave symmetry

Case (i) Even function and rotation symmetry

If $f(t) = f(-t)$ and $f(t) = -f\left(t \pm \frac{T}{2}\right)$

(a) The coefficient $a_0 = 0$
(b) The coefficient $b_n = 0$
(c) The coefficient a_n is given by

$$a_n = \frac{8}{T}\int_0^{T/4} f(t)\cos n\omega_0 t dt; n = \text{odd}$$

$$= 0; \quad n = \text{even}$$

Case (ii) Odd function and rotation symmetry

If $f(t) = -f(-t)$ and $f(t) = -f\left(t \pm \frac{T}{2}\right)$

(a) The coefficient $a_0 = 0$
(b) The coefficient $a_n = 0$
(c) The coefficient b_n is given by

$$b_n = \frac{8}{T}\int_0^{T/4} f(t)\sin n\omega_0 t dt; n = \text{odd}$$

$$= 0; \quad n = \text{even}$$

Problem 13.4 The first half-cycle of a periodic signal is shown; the period is $T = 2$ s. Sketch $y(t)$ clearly for three complete cycles if:

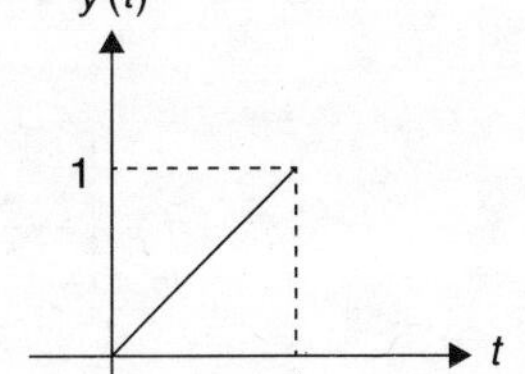

(i) $y(t)$ is an even-symmetrical signal,
(ii) $y(t)$ is an odd-symmetrical signal,
(iii) $y(t)$ is a half-wave symmetrical signal.

Solution:

(i) Even symmetrical signal

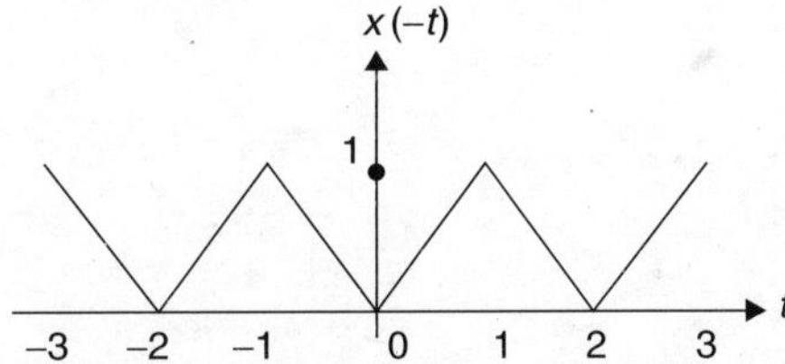

(ii) Odd symmetrical signal

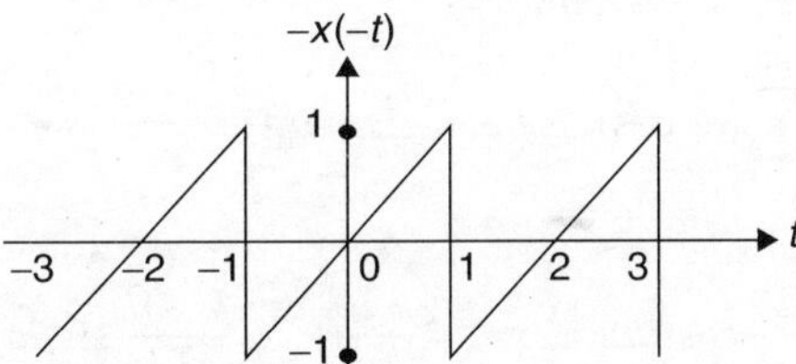

(iii) Half-wave symmetrical signal

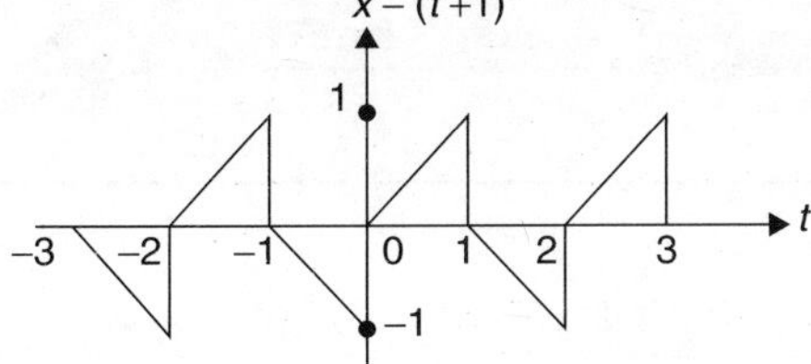

Problem 13.5 Find the trigonometric Fourier series for the waveform.

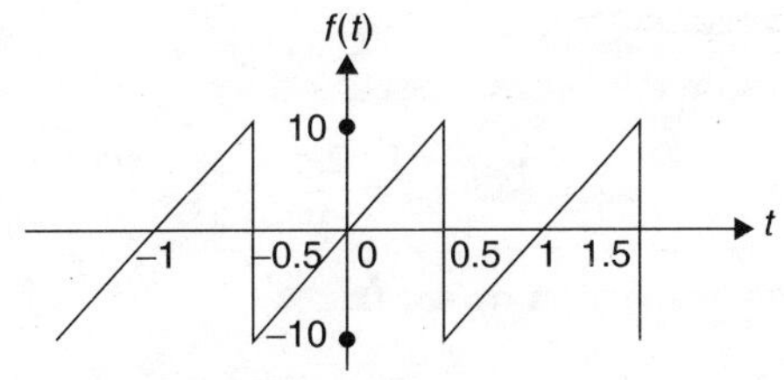

Solution:

From the figure it is clear that $T = 1$ s

$$\omega_0 = \frac{2\pi}{T} = 2\pi$$

By inspection we see that

(i) $f(t)$ has zero average or DC value. Thus $a_0 = 0$
(ii) $f(t)$ has odd wave symmetry, thus $a_n = 0$
(iii) The coefficient b_n can be given by

$$b_n = \frac{4}{T}\int_0^{T/2} f(t)\sin n\omega_0 t dt$$

(iv) The mathematical equation for the function $f(t)$ is given by

$$f(t) - 0 = \frac{10-0}{0.5-0}(t-0)$$

$$f(t) = 20t; \quad \text{for} \quad 0 < t < 0.5$$

$$\therefore \quad b_n = \frac{4}{1}\int_0^{0.5} 20t\sin 2\pi nt dt = 80\int_0^{0.5} t\sin 2\pi nt dt$$

$$= 80\left[-t\frac{\cos 2\pi nt}{2\pi n}\Bigg|_0^{0.5} - \int_0^{0.5}\frac{\cos 2\pi nt}{2\pi n}0.1.dt\right] = 80\left[\frac{-1}{2\pi n}(0.5\cos\pi n - 0) - \frac{\sin 2\pi nt}{(2\pi n)^2}\Bigg|_0^{0.5}\right]$$

$$= 80\left[-0.5\frac{\cos\pi n}{2\pi n} - (0-0)\right] = \frac{-20}{\pi n}\cos\pi n$$

The Fourier series is given by

$$f(t) = a_0 + \sum_{n=1}^{\infty}(a_n\cos n\omega_0 t + b_n\sin n\omega_0 t)$$

$$= \sum_{n=1}^{\infty}\frac{-20}{n\pi}\cos n\pi\sin 2\pi nt = \frac{-20}{\pi}\left[\sum_{n=1}^{\infty}\frac{(-1)^n}{n}\sin 2\pi nt\right]$$

$$= \frac{-20}{\pi}\left[-\sin 2\pi t + \frac{\sin 4\pi t}{2} - \frac{\sin 6\pi t}{3} + \cdots\right]$$

Problem 13.6 Find the trigonometric Fourier series for the waveform.

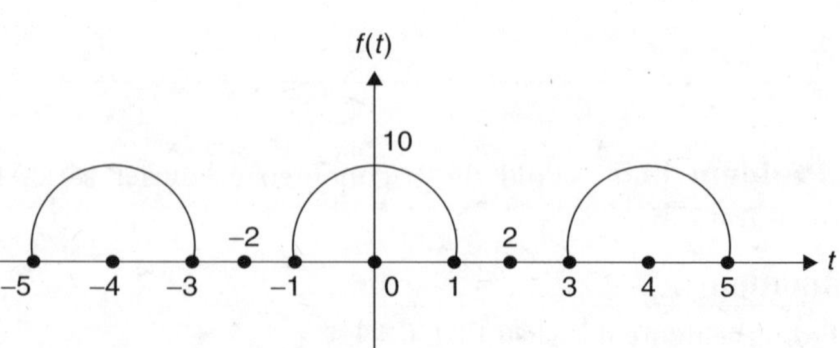

Solution:

From the figure, it is clear that

$$T = 4\text{ s}, \quad \omega_0 = \frac{2\pi}{T} = \frac{2\pi}{4} = \frac{\pi}{2}$$

By inspection we see that

(i) The given function has even symmetry, so $b_n = 0$

(ii) The mathematical equation for the function $f(t)$ is given by

$$f(t) = 10\cos\omega_o t$$

$$= 10\cos\frac{\pi}{2}t; \quad 0 < t < 1$$

$$= 0; \quad 1 < t < 3$$

$$= 10\cos\frac{\pi}{t}t; \quad 3 < t < 4$$

Or, the function $f(t)$ is defined by taking T from -2 to $+2$

$$f(t) = 0; \quad -2 < t < -1$$

$$= 10\cos\frac{\pi}{2}t; \quad -1 < t < 1$$

$$= 0; \quad 1 < t < 2$$

So here we will take the period extending from $t = -2$ to $+2$, which will reduce the number of equations and hence integrals.

(iii) The coefficient a_0 is given by

$$a_0 = \frac{1}{T}\int_0^T f(t)dt = \frac{1}{T}\int_{-T/2}^{-T/2} f(t)dt = \frac{1}{4}\int_{-2}^{2} f(t)dt = \frac{1}{4}\int_{-1}^{1} 10\cos\frac{\pi}{2}tdt$$

$$= \frac{10}{4} \times \sin\frac{\pi/2t}{\pi/2}\Bigg|_{-1}^{1} = \frac{5}{\pi}\left[\sin\frac{\pi}{2} + \sin\frac{\pi}{2}\right] = \frac{10}{\pi}$$

(iv) The coefficient a_n is given by

$$a_n = \frac{4}{T}\int_0^{T/2} f(t)\cos n\omega_0 t dt = \frac{4}{4}\int_0^{2} f(t)\cos\frac{n\pi}{2}tdt = \int_0^{1} 10\cos\frac{\pi}{2}t \cdot \cos\frac{n\pi}{2}tdt$$

$$= 5\int_0^1 \left[\cos\frac{n\pi}{2}(1+n) + \cos\frac{n\pi}{2}(1-n)\right] dt$$

$$= 5\left[\frac{\sin\frac{\pi t(1+n)}{2}}{\frac{\pi}{2}(1+n)} + \frac{\sin\frac{\pi t(1-n)}{2}}{\frac{\pi}{2}(1-n)}\right]_0^1 = 5\left[\frac{\sin\frac{\pi}{2}(1+n)}{\frac{\pi}{2}(1+n)} + \frac{\sin\frac{\pi}{2}(1-n)}{\frac{\pi}{2}(1-n)}\right]$$

$$= \frac{10}{\pi}\left[\frac{\cos\frac{\pi}{2}n}{1+n} + \cos\frac{\frac{\pi}{2}n}{1-n}\right]$$

$$= \frac{10}{(1-n^2)\pi}\left[(1-n)\cos\frac{n\pi}{2} + (1+n)\cos\frac{n\pi}{2}\right]$$

$$= \frac{20}{\pi} \frac{\cos\left(n\frac{\pi}{2}\right)}{1-n^2}$$

Note: $\cos(A+B)+\cos(A-B) = 2\cos A \cos B$

This expression is not valid for $n = 1$. We have to find the coefficient separately. Putting $n = 1$ in the general expression of a_n, we get

$$a_1 = \frac{4}{T}\int_0^{T/2} f(t)\cos\omega_0 t dt = \frac{4}{4}\int_0^2 f(t)\cos\left(\frac{\pi}{2}t\right)dt$$

$$= \int_0^1 10\cos\left(\frac{\pi}{2}t\right)\cdot\cos\left(\frac{\pi}{2}t\right)dt = 10\int_0^1 \cos^2\left(\frac{\pi}{2}t\right)dt$$

$$= 5\int_0^1 (1+\cos\pi t)dt = 5\left[1+\frac{\sin(\pi\cdot t)}{\pi}\right]_0^1 = 5[1+\frac{\sin(\pi)}{\pi} - 0] = 5$$

The Fourier series is given by

$$f(t) = a_0 + \sum_{n=1}^{\infty}(a_n \cos n\omega_0 t + b_n \sin n\omega_0 t)$$

$$= \frac{10}{\pi} + 5\cos\left(\frac{\pi}{2}t\right) + \sum_{n=2}^{\infty}\frac{20}{\pi}\frac{\cos\left(\frac{n\pi}{2}\right)}{1-n^2}\cdot\cos\left(\frac{\pi}{2}t\right)$$

$$= \frac{10}{\pi} + 5\cos\left(\frac{\pi}{2}t)\right) + \frac{20}{3\pi}\cos\pi t - \frac{20}{15}\cos 2\pi t + \cdots$$

13.6 EXPONENTIAL OR COMPLEX FOURIER SERIES

A more suitable and short form of the Fourier series is obtained if the sine and cosine terms in the trigonometric Fourier series are represented as exponential functions with complex multiplying constants. The resulting Fourier series is called the exponential or complex Fourier series.

To find the exponential Fourier series, we start from its trigonometric form:

$$f(t) = a_0 + \sum_{n=1}^{\infty}[a_n \cos n\omega_0 t + b_n \sin n\omega_0 t) \tag{13.20}$$

According to Euler's identity

$$e^{jn\omega_0 t} = \cos n\omega_0 t + j\sin n\omega_0 t$$

$$e^{-jn\omega_0 t} = \cos n\omega_0 t - j\sin n\omega_0 t$$

$$\cos n\omega_0 t = \frac{1}{2}(e^{jn\omega_0 t} + e^{-jn\omega_0 t})$$

$$\sin n\omega_0 t = \frac{1}{2j}(e^{jn\omega_0 t} - e^{-jn\omega_0 t}) = -\frac{j}{2}(e^{jn\omega_0 t} - e^{-jn\omega_0 t})$$

$$f(t) = a_0 + \sum_{n=1}^{\infty}\left[a_n \frac{e^{jn\omega_0 t} + e^{-jn\omega_0 t}}{2} + b_n \frac{-j(e^{jn\omega_0 t} - e^{-jn\omega_0 t})}{2}\right]$$

$$= a_0 + \frac{1}{2}\sum_{n=1}^{\infty} a_n (e^{jn\omega_0 t} + e^{-jn\omega_0 t}) - \frac{j}{2}\sum_{n=1}^{\infty} b_n (e^{jn\omega_0 t} - e^{-jn\omega_0 t})$$

$$= a_0 + \frac{1}{2}\sum_{n=1}^{\infty} a_n (e^{jn\omega_0 t} + e^{-jn\omega_0 t}) - \frac{j}{2}\sum_{n=1}^{\infty} b_n (e^{jn\omega_0 t} - e^{-jn\omega_0 t})$$

$$= a_0 + \sum_{n=1}^{\infty}\left[\frac{1}{2}(a_n - jb_n)e^{jn\omega_0 t} + \frac{1}{2}(a_n + jb_n)e^{-jn\omega_0 t}\right]$$

$$= k_0 + \sum_{n=1}^{\infty}[k_n e^{jn\omega_0 t} + k_{-n} e^{-jn\omega_0 t}]$$

$$\therefore \quad f(t) = k_0 + \sum_{n=1}^{\infty}[k_n e^{jn\omega_0 t} + k_{-n} e^{-jn\omega_0 t}] \tag{13.21}$$

where, $k_0 = a_0$ (13.22)

$$k_n = \frac{1}{2}(a_n - jb_n) \tag{13.23}$$

$$k_{-n} = \frac{1}{2}(a_n + jb_n) \tag{13.24}$$

Therefore, the complex or exponential form of the Fourier series is

$$f(t) = k_0 + \sum_{n=1}^{\infty}[k_n e^{jn\omega_0 t} + k_{-n} e^{-jn\omega_0 t}]$$

$$= \sum_{n=0}^{\infty} k_n e^{jn\omega_0 t} + \sum_{n=-\infty}^{-1} k_n e^{jn\omega_0 t}$$

$$= \sum_{n=-\infty}^{\infty} k_n e^{jn\omega_0 t}$$

Thus we can get a compact form of exponential Fourier series as

$$f(t) = \sum_{n=-\infty}^{\infty} k_n e^{jn\omega_0 t} \tag{13.25}$$

The coefficient k_0 and k_n can be found as follows:

$$k_0 = a_0 = \frac{1}{T}\int_0^T f(t)dt \tag{13.26}$$

$$k_n = \frac{1}{2}(a_n - jb_n)$$

$$= \frac{1}{T}\int_0^T f(t)\cos n\omega_0 t dt - \frac{j}{T}\int_0^T f(t)\sin n\omega_0 t dt$$

$$= \frac{1}{T}\int_0^T f(t)[\cos n\omega_0 t - j\sin n\omega_0 t]dt$$

$$= \frac{1}{T}\int_0^T f(t)e^{-jn\omega_0 t}dt$$

$$\therefore \quad k_n = \frac{1}{T}\int_0^T f(t)e^{-jn\omega_0 t}dt \qquad (13.27)$$

It is clear that the exponential form in the above equations which needs only one formula for all its coefficients is more compact and easier to manipulate rather than the trigonometric form which require two formulae for the coefficients a_n and b_n.

Problem 13.7 Find the exponential Fourier series coefficients of the wave form.

Solution:

From the given figure,

Time period, $T = 8$

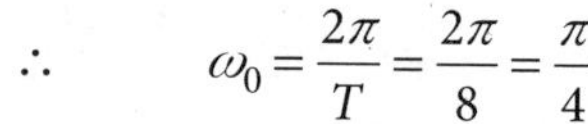

$$\therefore \quad \omega_0 = \frac{2\pi}{T} = \frac{2\pi}{8} = \frac{\pi}{4}$$

The mathematical equation for the function $f(t)$ is given by

$$f(t) = \begin{cases} A \ ; & -2 < t < 2 \\ 0 \ ; & 2 < t < 6 \end{cases}$$

The exponential Fourier series is given by

$$f(t) = \sum_{n=-\infty}^{\infty} k_n e^{jn\omega_0 t} = \sum_{n=-\infty}^{\infty} k_n e^{j\frac{n\pi}{4}t}$$

Hence the exponential Fourier coefficient is

$$k_n = \frac{1}{T}\int_0^T f(t)e^{-jn\omega_0 t}dt = \frac{1}{8}\left[\int_{-2}^{2} Ae^{-jn\pi t/4}dt + \int_2^6 0dt\right]$$

$$= \frac{A}{8}\left[\frac{e^{-j\frac{n\pi}{4}t}}{\left(-j\frac{n\pi}{4}\right)}\right]_{-2}^{2} = \frac{A}{8}\left(\frac{-4}{jn\pi}\right)[e^{-jn\pi/2} - e^{jn\pi/2}]$$

$$= \frac{-A \times 2}{4jn\pi}(e^{-jn\frac{\pi}{2}} - e^{jn\frac{\pi}{2}}) = \frac{A \times 2}{2n\pi}\frac{(e^{jn\frac{\pi}{2}} - e^{-jn\frac{\pi}{2}})}{2j}$$

$$= \frac{2A}{2n\pi}\sin\frac{n\pi}{2} = \frac{A}{2}\left[\frac{\sin\frac{n\pi}{2}}{\frac{n\pi}{2}}\right]; \quad n \neq 0$$

Then for $n = 0$, we have

$$k_0 = \frac{1}{T}\int_0^T f(t)dt = \frac{1}{8}\left[\int_0^2 Adt + \int_2^6 0.dt\right] = \frac{1}{8}A[t]_{-2}^{2} = \frac{A}{8}(2+2) = \frac{A}{2}$$

Therefore, the coefficient of exponential Fourier series is

$$k_n = \begin{cases} \frac{A}{2}\left[\frac{\sin n\pi/2}{n\pi/2}\right]; & n \neq 0 \\ \end{cases}$$

$$= \begin{cases} \frac{A}{2}; & n = 0 \end{cases}$$

13.6.1 Discrete or Line and Phase Spectra

In the exponential Fourier representation, the coefficient k_n is called a line or discrete spectrum since the value of k_n exists only for some discrete values of n (n being an integer). It represents a complex spectrum and has both magnitude and phase spectra.

The Fourier coefficient k_n of the exponential form is a complex quantity and can be represented by

$$k_n = \text{Re}[k_n] + j\text{Im}[k_n] \tag{13.28}$$

The real part of k_n is

$$\text{Re}[k_n] = \frac{1}{T}\int_0^T f(t)\cos\omega_0 dt \tag{13.29}$$

The imaginary part of k_n is

$$\text{Im}[k_n] = \frac{1}{T}\int_0^T f(t)\sin\omega_0 dt \tag{13.30}$$

$\text{Re}[k_n]$ is an even function of n, whereas $\text{Im}[k_n]$ is an odd function of n. Therefore, the amplitude spectrum of Fourier series is given by

$$|k_n| = \sqrt{\text{Re}[k_n]^2 + \text{Im}[k_n]^2} \tag{13.31}$$

While the phase spectrum is given by

$$\angle k_n = \theta_n = \tan^{-1}\left(\frac{\text{Im}[k_n]}{\text{Re}[k_n]}\right) \tag{13.32}$$

13.6.2 Relation Between Trigonometric and Exponential Fourier Coefficients

From the exponential Fourier series representation, we have already found

$$k_n = \frac{1}{2}(a_n - jb_n) \tag{13.33}$$

$$k_{-n} = \frac{1}{2}(a_n + jb_n) \tag{13.34}$$

From Eqs 13.33 and 13.34, we have

$$a_n = k_n + k_{-n} \tag{13.35}$$

$$b_n = j(k_n - k_{-n}) \tag{13.36}$$

To summarise these results, we represent any period waveform $f(t)$ with time period T and fundamental frequency $\omega_0 = \frac{2\pi}{T}$ in terms of exponential Fourier series as

$$f(t) = \sum_{n=-\infty}^{\infty} k_n e^{jn\omega_0 t}$$

where $k_n = \dfrac{1}{T}\displaystyle\int_0^T e^{-jn\omega_0 t} f(t)dt$

and $k_n = \dfrac{1}{2}(a_n - jb_n)$

$$a_0 = k_0, \quad a_n = k_n + k_{-n} \quad \text{and} \quad b_n = j(k_n - k_{-n})$$

Problem 13.8 Find the exponential Fourier series of the wave form. Using the coefficients of this exponential series obtain a_n and b_n. Assume $V = 10$ V, $T = 1$ s.

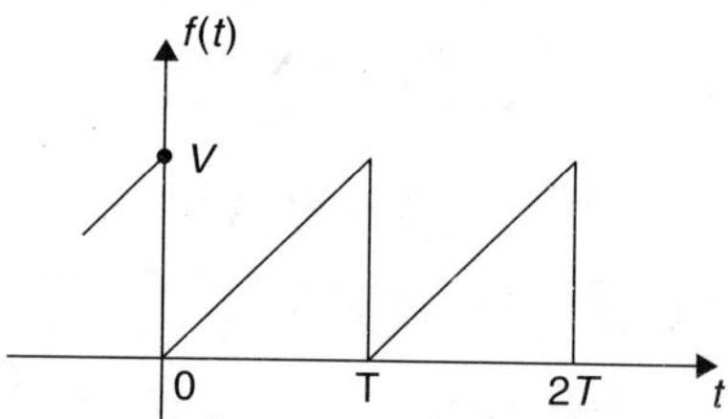

Solution:

From the figure, we know that

$$T = 1, \quad \omega_o = \frac{2\pi}{T} = 2\pi$$

The mathematical equation for the function $f(t)$ is given by

$$f(t) = 10t; \quad 0 < t < 1$$

The exponential Fourier series is given by

$$f(t) = \sum_{n=-\infty}^{\infty} k_n e^{jn\omega_o t}$$

The exponential Fourier coefficient is

$$k_n = \frac{1}{T}\int_0^T e^{-jn\omega_o t} f(t)dt$$

$$= \frac{1}{1}\int_0^1 e^{-j2\pi nt}10t\,dt = \frac{10}{1}\int_0^1 e^{-jn2\pi t}t\,dt$$

$$= 10\left[t\frac{e^{-j2\pi nt}}{-j2\pi n}\Bigg|_0^1 - \int_0^1 \frac{e^{-jn2\pi t}}{-j2\pi n}dt \right]$$

$$= 10\left[\frac{-1}{j2\pi n} + \frac{1}{4\pi^2 n^2}(\cos 2\pi n - j\sin 2\pi n - 1) \right]$$

$$= \frac{-10}{2\pi n} = \frac{j5}{n\pi}$$

Therefore, the exponential Fourier series is given by

$$f(t) = \sum_{n=-\infty}^{\infty} \frac{j5}{n\pi} e^{jn\omega_0 t} = \sum_{n=-\infty}^{\infty} \frac{j5}{n\pi} e^{jn2\pi t}$$

Now $\quad a_n = k_n + k_{-n} = \dfrac{5j}{n\pi} + \dfrac{j5}{-n\pi} = 0$

$$b_n = j(k_n - k_{-n}) = j\left[\frac{5j}{n\pi} - \frac{5j}{-n\pi} \right] = \frac{-10}{n\pi}$$

Thus the trigonometric series contains no cosine terms since $a_n = 0$ for all n, and the sine term coefficients are $(\frac{-10}{n\pi})$.

To find the magnitude and phase line spectra we proceed as follows:

The exponential Fourier coefficient is

$$k_n = \frac{j5}{n\pi}$$

$\therefore \quad$ Magnitude spectrum, $|k_n| = \dfrac{5}{n\pi}; \quad n \neq 0$

For $n = 0$, we have

$$k_n = \frac{1}{T}\int_0^T e^{-jn\omega_0 t} f(t)dt$$

Putting $n = 0$

$$k_0 = \frac{1}{T}\int_0^T f(t)dt = \frac{1}{T}\int_0^T 10t\,dt = 5$$

Hence $|k_0| = 5, |k_1| = \frac{5}{\pi}, |k_2| = \frac{5}{2\pi}$ and so on

The phase spectrum is given by

$$\theta_n = \tan^{-1}\left[\frac{\frac{5}{n\pi}}{0} \right]$$

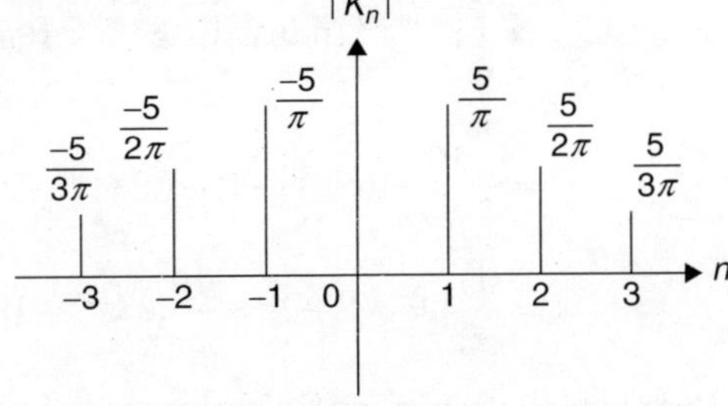

(i) Magnitude spectra

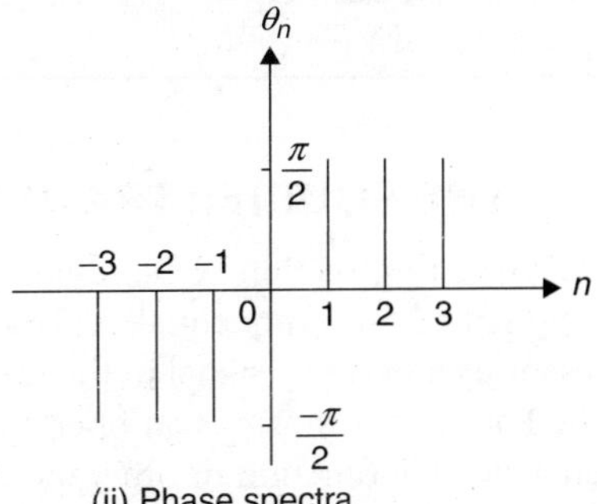

(ii) Phase spectra

Fig. (a) Magnitude and phase spectra

This gives $\frac{\pi}{2}$ for positive n and $-\frac{\pi}{2}$ for negative n.

Magnitude and phase spectra are shown in Fig. (a).

Problem 13.9 Find the exponential Fourier series for the square wave.

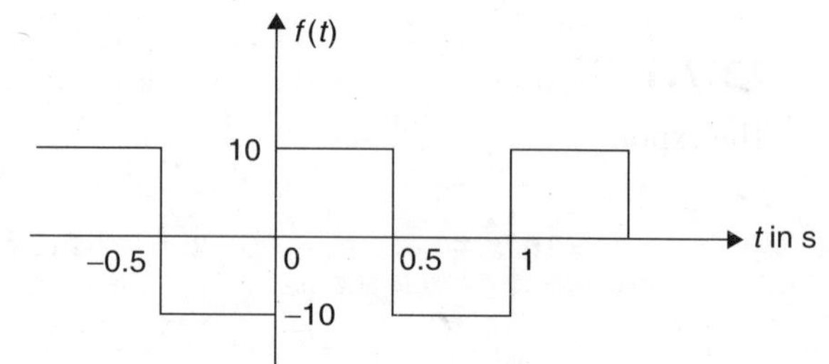

Solution:

From the figure it is clear that

$$T = 1 \text{ s}, \ \omega_0 = \frac{2\pi}{T} = 2\pi$$

The mathematical equation for the function $f(t)$ is given by

$$f(t) = 10; \ 0 < t < 0.5$$
$$= -10; \ 0.5 < t < 1$$

The exponential series is given by

$$f(t) = \sum_{n=-\infty}^{\infty} k_n e^{jn\omega_0 t} dt$$

Hence, the exponential Fourier coefficient is

$$k_n = \frac{1}{T}\int_0^T e^{-jn\omega_o t} f(t)dt$$

$$= \int_0^{0.5} e^{-jn2\pi t} 10dt + \int_{0.5}^{1} -e^{-jn2\pi t} 10dt$$

$$= \frac{10}{-j2\pi n}[(e^{-j\pi n} - 1) - (e^{-j2\pi n} - e^{-jn\pi})]$$

$$= \frac{j5}{\pi n}[2e^{-j\pi n} - 2] = \frac{j10}{\pi n}[e^{-jn\pi} - 1]$$

Therefore, the exponential Fourier series is given by

$$f(t) = \sum_{n=-\infty}^{\infty} \frac{j10}{\pi n}[e^{-jn\pi} - 1]e^{jn\omega_0 t} = \sum_{n=-\infty}^{\infty} \frac{j10}{\pi n}[e^{-jn\pi} - 1]\frac{j5}{n\pi}e^{jn2\pi t}$$

13.7 THE FOURIER TRANSFORM

In the preceding section we studied that any periodic signal that satisfies the Dirichlet conditions can be represented by exponential or trigonometric Fourier series. We will now consider a technique for representing a periodic signal in the frequency domain.

The Fourier transform is an operation that converts a function of time into a function of frequency ω. Given a suitable function of time, there is one and only one Fourier transform that corresponds to it. The Fourier transform is an integral transform which is extremely important in the study of various engineering problems including linear electric circuits.

A non-periodic signal may be assumed as a limiting case of a periodic signal where the period of the signal approaches infinity. We can use this approach to develop the frequency domain representation of a non-periodic signal over an entire interval.

13.7.1 Definition of Fourier Transform

The exponential Fourier series is given by

$$f(t) = \sum_{n=-\infty}^{\infty} k_n e^{jn\omega_0 t} \tag{13.37}$$

where $$k_n = \frac{1}{T}\int_0^T f(t)e^{-jn\omega_0 t}\,dt = \frac{1}{T}\int_{-T/2}^{T/2} f(t)e^{-jn\omega_0 t}\,dt \tag{13.38}$$

and $$\omega_0 = \frac{2\pi}{T} = \text{Fundamental frequency}$$

We now let $T \to \infty$

(i) $\omega_0 = \dfrac{2\pi}{T}$, becomes vanishingly small.

(ii) This limit is then represented by a differential

$$\omega_0 \to d\omega$$

(iii) $\dfrac{1}{T} = \dfrac{\omega_0}{2\pi} \to \dfrac{d\omega}{2\pi}$

(iv) The frequency of any harmonic $n\omega_0$ must now correspond to the general frequency variable which describes the continuous spectrum. In other words, n must tend to infinity as ω_0 approaches zero, so that the product is finite.

That is, $n\omega_0 \to \omega$

If we multiply each side of Eq. 13.38 by the period T and then undertake the limiting process, a non-trival result is obtained:

$$k_n T = \int_{-\infty}^{\infty} f(t)e^{-j\omega t}\,dt \tag{13.39}$$

The right side of this expression is a function of $j\omega$ and we represent it by $F(j\omega)$ as

$$F(j\omega) = \int_{-\infty}^{\infty} f(t)e^{-j\omega t}\,dt \tag{13.40}$$

In order to apply the limiting process to Eq. 13.37, we multiply and divide the summation by T.

$$f(t) = \sum_{n=-\infty}^{\infty} k_n T e^{jn\omega_0 t} \times \frac{1}{T}$$

In the limit, the summation becomes an integral and

$$f(t) = \frac{1}{2\pi}\int_{-\infty}^{\infty} F(j\omega)e^{j\omega t}\,d\omega \tag{13.41}$$

Equations 13.40 and 13.41 are together called the Fourier transform pair. The function $F(j\omega)$ is the Fourier transform or Fourier integral of the signal $f(t)$, and $f(t)$ is the inverse Fourier transform of $F(j\omega)$.

To summarise, we list the transform pair relationship as follows:

$$F(j\omega)=\int_{-\infty}^{\infty} f(t)e^{-j\omega t}\,dt \tag{13.42}$$

$$f(t)=\frac{1}{2\pi}\int_{-\infty}^{\infty} F(j\omega)e^{j\omega t}\,d\omega \tag{13.43}$$

Conditions for existence of Fourier transform A function $f(t)$ is said to be Fourier transformable, if it satisfies the following Dirichlet conditions:

(i) Function $f(t)$ is absolutely integrable. That is, $\int_{-\infty}^{\infty}|f(t)|\,dt<\infty$.

(ii) Function $f(t)$ has a finite number of maxima and minima.

(iii) Function $f(t)$ is single valued and has a finite number of discontinuities.

13.8 FOURIER TRANSFORM OF SOME USEFUL FUNCTIONS

(i) **Fourier transform of single-sided exponential function:** The single-sided exponential function is defined by the equation

$$f(t)=e^{-at}\ ;\ 0<t<\infty$$
$$=0\ ;\ t<0$$

$$F(j\omega)=\int_{-\infty}^{\infty} f(t)e^{-j\omega t}\,dt$$

$$=\int_{-\infty}^{\infty} e^{-at}e^{-j\omega t}\,dt$$

$$=\int_{0}^{\infty} e^{-(a+j\omega)t}\,dt$$

$$=\left[\frac{e^{-(a+j\omega)t}}{-(a+j\omega)}\right]_0^{\infty}=\frac{1}{(a+j\omega)}$$

$$\therefore\quad |F(j\omega)|=\frac{1}{\sqrt{\omega^2+a^2}},\quad \theta(\omega)=-\tan^{-1}\left(\frac{\omega}{a}\right)$$

The magnitude and phase spectra are shown in Fig. 13.6 along with single-sided exponential signal.

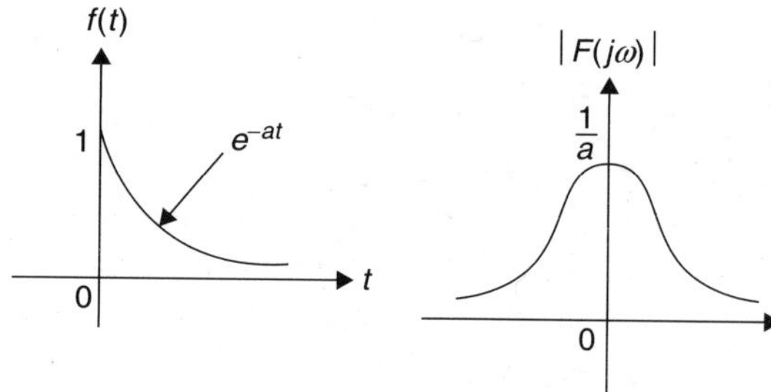

(a) Single sided exponential signal

(b) Magnitude spectrum

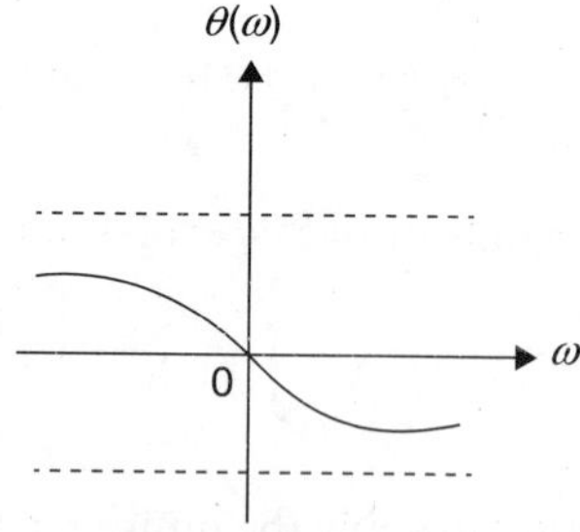

(c) Phase spectrum

Fig. 13.6 Single sided exponential signal along with its magnitude and phase spectra

Note: If $f(t)=e^{-zt}$, z is complex $=a+jb$, then $F(j\omega)=\dfrac{1}{z+j\omega}=\dfrac{1}{a+j(b+\omega)}$

(ii) Fourier transform of double sided exponential function: The double-sided exponential function is defined by the equation

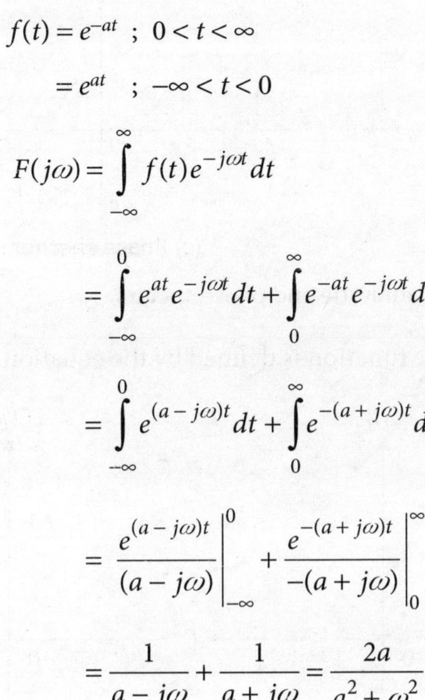

$$f(t) = e^{-at} \;;\; 0 < t < \infty$$

$$= e^{at} \;;\; -\infty < t < 0$$

$$F(j\omega) = \int_{-\infty}^{\infty} f(t)e^{-j\omega t}\,dt$$

$$= \int_{-\infty}^{0} e^{at}e^{-j\omega t}\,dt + \int_{0}^{\infty} e^{-at}e^{-j\omega t}\,dt$$

$$= \int_{-\infty}^{0} e^{(a-j\omega)t}\,dt + \int_{0}^{\infty} e^{-(a+j\omega)t}\,dt$$

$$= \left.\frac{e^{(a-j\omega)t}}{(a-j\omega)}\right|_{-\infty}^{0} + \left.\frac{e^{-(a+j\omega)t}}{-(a+j\omega)}\right|_{0}^{\infty}$$

$$= \frac{1}{a-j\omega} + \frac{1}{a+j\omega} = \frac{2a}{a^2+\omega^2}$$

$$\therefore \quad |F(j\omega)| = \frac{2a}{\omega^2+a^2}, \quad \theta(\omega) = 0$$

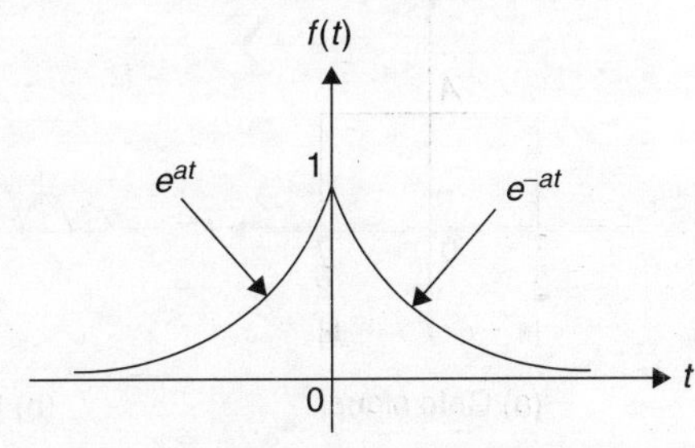

(a) Double sided exponential signal

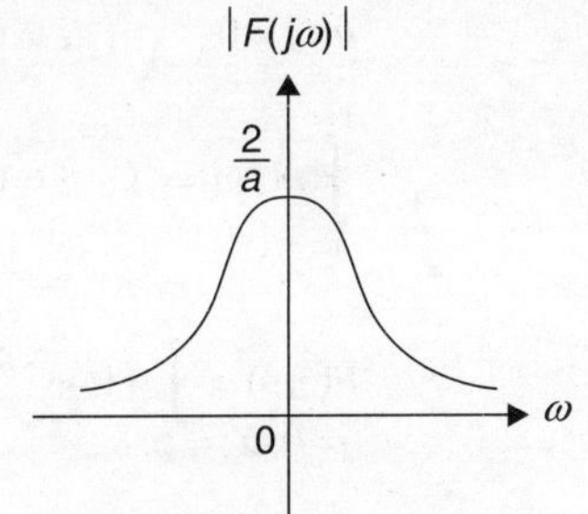

(b) Magnitude spectrum

Fig. 13.7 Double sided exponential signal along with its magnitude spectrum

The magnitude spectrum along with double-sided exponential signal is shown in Fig. 13.7.

(iii) Fourier transform of pulse (or) gate function: The pulse or gate function is defined by the equation

$$f(t) = A \;;\; -\frac{T}{2} < t < \frac{T}{2}$$

$$= 0 \;;\; |t| > \frac{T}{2}$$

$$F(j\omega) = \int_{-\infty}^{\infty} f(t)\,e^{-j\omega t}\,dt$$

$$= \int_{-T/2}^{+T/2} Ae^{-j\omega t}\,dt = A\left.\frac{e^{-j\omega t}}{-j\omega}\right|_{-T/2}^{+T/2} = \frac{-A}{j\omega}\left(e^{-j\omega\frac{T}{2}} - e^{+j\omega\frac{T}{2}}\right)$$

$$= \frac{2A}{\omega}\sin\left(\omega\frac{T}{2}\right) = AT\frac{\sin\left(\omega\frac{T}{2}\right)}{\left(\omega\frac{T}{2}\right)}$$

The magnitude and phase spectra are shown in Fig. 13.8 along with the gate signal.

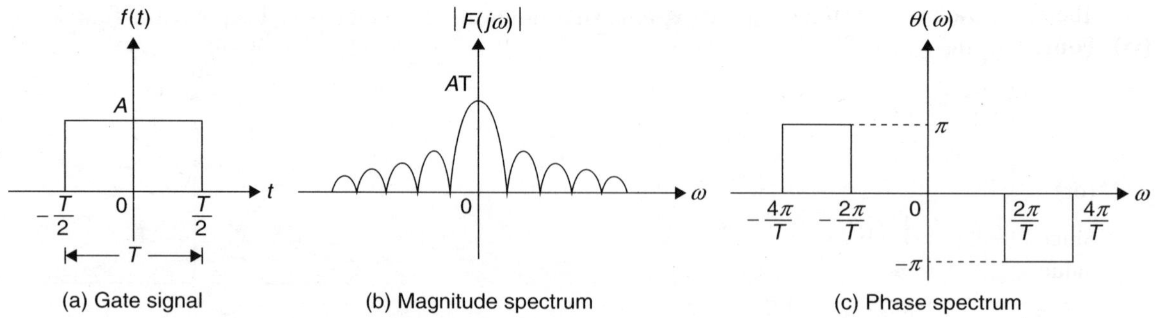

(a) Gate signal (b) Magnitude spectrum (c) Phase spectrum

Fig. 13.8 Gate signal along with its magnitude and phase spectra

(iv) Fourier transform of impulse function: The impulse function is defined by the equation

$$\delta(t) = 0 \quad ; \quad t \neq 0$$

$$\int_{-\infty}^{+\infty} \delta(t)dt = 1; \quad t = 0$$

$$F(j\omega) = \int_{-\infty}^{+\infty} f(t)e^{-j\omega t}dt$$

$$= \int_{-\infty}^{+\infty} \delta(t)e^{-j\omega t}dt$$

$$= e^{-j\omega \times 0}\int_{-\infty}^{+\infty} \delta(t)dt = 1$$

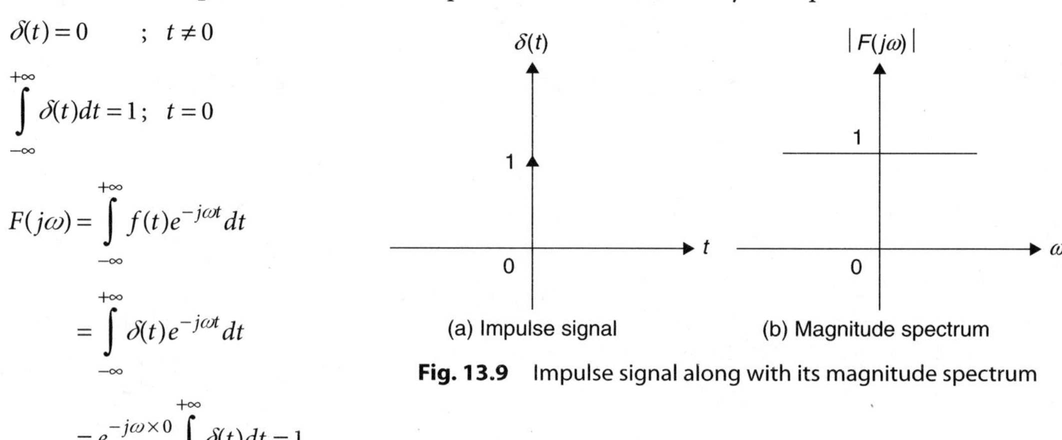

(a) Impulse signal (b) Magnitude spectrum

Fig. 13.9 Impulse signal along with its magnitude spectrum

The magnitude spectrum along with impulse signal is shown in Fig. 13.9.

(v) Fourier transform of a constant function: The impulse function is defined by the equation

$$f(t) = A \quad ; \quad -\infty < t < \infty$$

This function does not satisfy the condition, $\int_{-\infty}^{\infty} |f(t)|\,dt < \infty$

So, since the Fourier transform cannot be obtained directly, it can be evaluated as a limiting value of the Fourier transform of the gate function.

$$f(t) = \underset{T\to\infty}{Lt}[G(t)]$$

$$F(j\omega) = FT[f(t)] = FT\left[\underset{T\to\infty}{Lt}[G(t)]\right]$$

$$= \underset{T\to\infty}{Lt}\ FT[G(t)]$$

$$= \underset{T\to\infty}{Lt}\left[\frac{2A}{\omega}\sin\left(\omega\frac{T}{2}\right)\right]$$

$$= 2\pi A\delta(\omega)$$

(a) Constant signal (b) Magnitude spectrum

Fig. 13.10 Constant signal along with its magnitude spectrum

The magnitude spectrum along with the constant signal is shown in Fig. 13.10.

(vi) Fourier transform of Signum function: The Signum function is defined by the equation

$$f(t) = 1 \quad ; \ t<0$$
$$= -1 \ ; \ t<0$$

(or) $\quad \operatorname{sgn}(t) = u(t) - u(-t)$

Since the Signum function is not absolutely integrable, its Fourier transform is evaluated as limiting value of Fourier transform of an exponential function.

$$f(t) = \underset{a\to\infty}{Lt} \begin{cases} e^{-at} & ; \quad t>0 \\ e^{at} & ; \quad t<0 \end{cases}$$

$$F(j\omega) = \underset{a\to\infty}{Lt}\left[-\int_{-\infty}^{0} e^{at} e^{-j\omega t}\,dt + \int_{0}^{\infty} e^{-at} e^{-j\omega t}\,dt\right]$$

$$= \underset{a\to\infty}{Lt}\left[-\int_{-\infty}^{0} e^{(a-j\omega)t}\,dt + \int_{0}^{\infty} e^{-(a+j\omega)t}\,dt\right]$$

$$= \underset{a\to\infty}{Lt}\left[-\frac{e^{(a-j\omega)t}}{a-j\omega}\Bigg|_{-\infty}^{0} + \frac{e^{-(a+j\omega)t}}{-(a+j\omega)}\Bigg|_{0}^{\infty}\right]$$

$$= \underset{a\to\infty}{Lt}\left[\frac{-1}{a-j\omega} + \frac{1}{a+j\omega}\right] = \underset{a\to\infty}{Lt}\left[\frac{-2j\omega}{a^2+\omega^2}\right] = \frac{2}{j\omega}$$

$$\therefore \quad F|(j\omega)| = \frac{2}{\omega}, \quad \theta(\omega) = -\tan^{-1}\left(\frac{2/\omega}{0}\right)$$

The magnitude and phase spectra are shown in Fig. 13.11 along with the Signum signal.

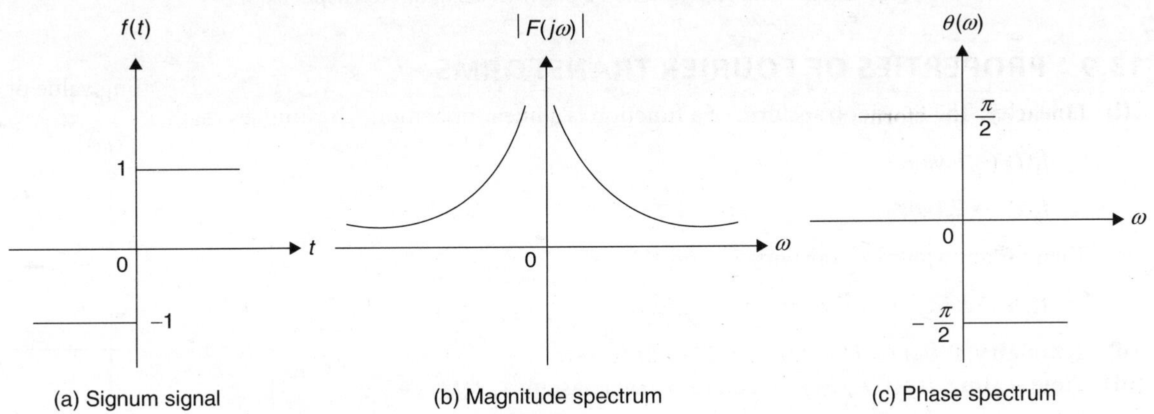

Fig. 13.11 Signum signal along with its magnitude and phase spectra

(vii) Fourier transform of unit step function: The unit step function is defined by the equation

$$u(t) = 1 \;;\; t \geq 0$$
$$= 0 \;;\; t < 0$$

$u(t)$ is not absolutely integrable. It can be easily seen that

$$\text{sgn}(t) = 2u(t) - 1$$

(or) $$u(t) = \frac{1}{2}[1 + \text{sgn}(t)]$$

$$FT[u(t)] = \frac{1}{2}FT[1] + \frac{1}{2}FT[\text{sgn}(t)] = \frac{1}{2}[2\pi\delta(\omega)] + \frac{1}{2}\left[\frac{2}{j\omega}\right] = \pi\delta(\omega) + \frac{1}{j\omega}$$

$\therefore$ $$F(j\omega) = FT[u(t)] = \pi\delta(\omega) + \frac{1}{j\omega}$$

$$|F(j\omega)| = \pi\delta(\omega) + \frac{1}{\omega} \quad \text{and} \quad \theta(\omega) = -\tan^{-1}\left(\frac{1/\omega}{0}\right)$$

The magnitude spectrum along with unit step signal is shown in Fig. 13.12.

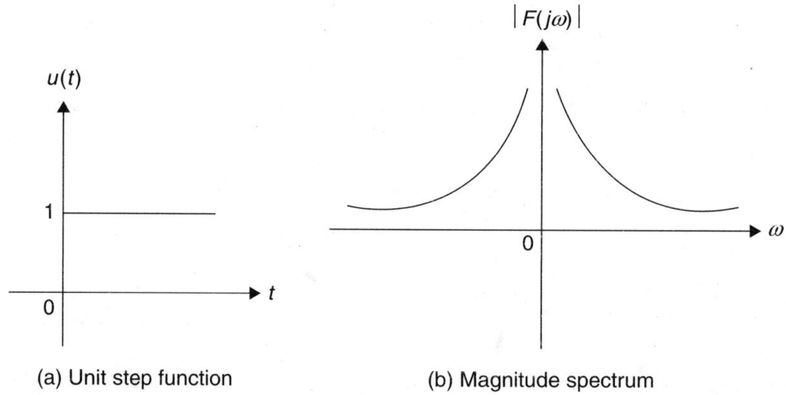

Fig. 13.12 Unit step function along with its magnitude spectrum

13.9 PROPERTIES OF FOURIER TRANSFORMS

(i) Linearity: The Fourier transform of a function is a linear operation. This implies that if

$$f_1(t) \leftrightarrow F_1(j\omega)$$
$$f_2(t) \leftrightarrow F_2(j\omega)$$

Then for any arbitrary constants K_1 and K_2

$$K_1 f_1(t) \pm K_2 f_2(t) = K_1 F_1(j\omega) \pm K_2 F_2(j\omega)$$

(ii) Symmetry: If $f(t) \leftrightarrow F(j\omega)$ then $F(t) \leftrightarrow 2\pi f(-\omega)$

(iii) Time scaling: If $f(t) \leftrightarrow F(j\omega)$ then for a real constant k, $f(kt) \leftrightarrow \frac{1}{|k|} f\left(\frac{j\omega}{k}\right)$

(iv) Time shifting/ translation in time: If $f(t) \leftrightarrow F(j\omega)$ then $f(t - T) \leftrightarrow F(j\omega)e^{-j\omega T}$

(v) Frequency shifting /translation in frequency: If $f(t) \leftrightarrow F(j\omega)$ then $f(t)e^{j\omega_0 t} \leftrightarrow F[j(\omega - \omega_0)]$

(vi) Time differentiation: If $f(t) \leftrightarrow F(j\omega)$ then $\dfrac{df(t)}{dt} = f'(t) \leftrightarrow (j\omega)F(j\omega)$

(vii) Frequency differentiation: If $f(t) \leftrightarrow F(j\omega)$ then $-jf(t) \leftrightarrow \dfrac{dF(j\omega)}{d\omega}$

(viii) Time convolution: If $f_1(t) \leftrightarrow F_1(j\omega)$ and $f_2(t) \leftrightarrow F_2(j\omega)$ then $f_1(t)^* f_2(t) \leftrightarrow F_1(j\omega) \cdot F_2(j\omega)$

(ix) Frequency convolution: If $f_1(t) \leftrightarrow F_1(j\omega)$ and $f_2(t) \leftrightarrow F_2(j\omega)$ then $F_1(j\omega)^* F_2(j\omega) \leftrightarrow 2\pi f_1(t) f_2(t)$

Problem 13.10 Find the Fourier transform of the following functions: (i) $\cos\omega_0 t$, (ii) $\sin\omega_0 t$, (iii) $f(t)\cos\omega_0 t$, and (iv) $f(t)\sin\omega_0 t$.

Solution:

(i) $\cos\omega_0 t$

$$\cos\omega_0 t = \frac{1}{2}[e^{j\omega_0 t} + e^{-j\omega_0 t}]$$

Now $1 \leftrightarrow 2\pi\delta(\omega)$

According to frequency shifting property

$$1 \cdot e^{j\omega_0 t} \leftrightarrow 2\pi\delta(\omega - \omega_0)$$

$$\therefore \quad \cos\omega_0 t \leftrightarrow \frac{1}{2}[2\pi\delta(\omega - \omega_0) + 2\pi\delta(\omega + \omega_0)]$$

$$\leftrightarrow \pi[\delta(\omega - \omega_0) + \delta(\omega + \omega_0)]$$

(ii) $\sin\omega_0 t$

$$\sin\omega_0 t = \frac{1}{2j}[e^{j\omega_0 t} - e^{-j\omega_0 t}]$$

Now $1 \leftrightarrow 2\pi\delta(\omega)$

According to the frequency shifting property

$$1 \cdot e^{j\omega_0 t} \leftrightarrow 2\pi\delta(\omega - \omega_0)$$

$$\therefore \quad \sin\omega_0 t \leftrightarrow \frac{1}{2j}[2\pi\delta(\omega - \omega_0) - 2\pi\delta(\omega + \omega_0)]$$

$$\leftrightarrow j\pi[\delta(\omega + \omega_0) + \delta(\omega - \omega_0)]$$

(iii) $f(t)\cos\omega_0 t$

$$f(t)\cos\omega_0 t = \frac{1}{2}[f(t)e^{j\omega_0 t} + f(t)e^{-j\omega_0 t}]$$

According to frequency shifting property

$$f(t)\cos\omega_0 t \leftrightarrow \frac{1}{2}[FT[j(\omega - \omega_0)] + FT[j(\omega + \omega_0)]]$$

(iv) $f(t)\sin\omega_0 t$

$$f(t)\sin\omega_0 t = \frac{1}{2j}[f(t)e^{j\omega_0 t} - f(t)e^{-j\omega_0 t}]$$

According to the frequency shifting property

$$f(t)\sin\omega_0 t \leftrightarrow \frac{1}{2j}[FT[j(\omega-\omega_0)]-FT[j(\omega+\omega_0)]]$$

13.10 FOURIER TRANSFORM OF A PERIODIC FUNCTION

A periodic function exists from $-\infty$ to ∞. But $\int_{-\infty}^{\infty} f(t)dt = \infty$, that is, $f(t)$ is not absolutely integrable. Strictly speaking, Fourier transform of a periodic function does not exist. But its Fourier transform can be evaluated as a limiting value of Fourier transform of some other functions. A periodic function $f(t)$ with angular frequency ω_0 can be represented in an exponential series as

$$f(t)=\sum_{n=-\infty}^{\infty} k_n e^{jn\omega_0 t}$$

Taking Fourier transform on both sides, we have

$$F(j\omega)=FT\left[\sum_{n=-\infty}^{\infty} k_n e^{jn\omega_0 t}\right]=\sum_{n=-\infty}^{\infty} k_n FT[e^{jn\omega_0 t}] \tag{13.44}$$

Now, according to frequency shifting property

$$FT[e^{jn\omega_0 t}]=FT[1.e^{jn\omega_0 t}]=2\pi\delta(\omega-n\omega_0)$$

$$\therefore \quad F(j\omega)=\sum_{n=-\infty}^{\infty} k_n 2\pi\delta(\omega-n\omega_0)=2\pi\sum_{n=-\infty}^{\infty} k_n\delta(\omega-n\omega_0) \tag{13.45}$$

where k_n are the exponential Fourier coefficients given by

$$k_n=\frac{1}{T}\int_0^T e^{-jn\omega_0 t} f(t)dt=\frac{1}{T}\int_{-T/2}^{T/2} e^{-jn\omega_0 t} f(t)dt \tag{13.46}$$

ADDITIONAL SOLVED PROBLEMS

13.1 Obtain the trigonometric Fourier series for the wave form.

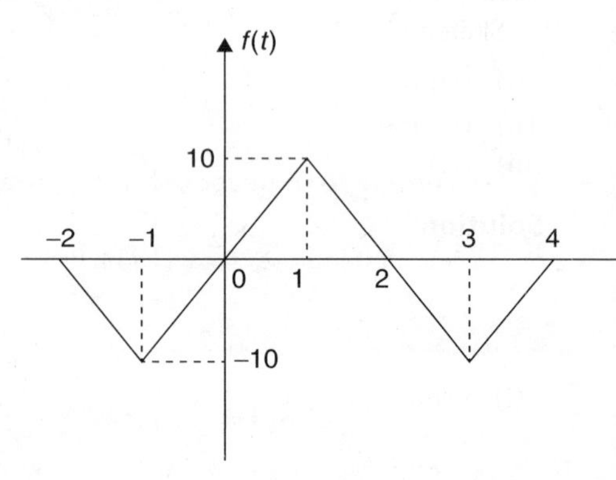

Solution: From this figure, it is clear that

$$T=4, \quad \omega_0=\frac{2\pi}{T}=\frac{2\pi}{4}=\frac{\pi}{2}$$

By inspection we see that

(i) $f(t)$ has zero average or DC value

$$\therefore \quad a_0=0$$

(ii) $f(t)$ has a quarter wave symmetry.

$$\therefore \quad a_n=0$$

(iii) Representation of $f(t)$ over quarter time period as

$$f(t) = 10t \;\; ; \;\; 0 < t < 1$$

$\therefore$ The coefficient b_n is given by

$$b_n = \frac{8}{T}\int_0^{T/4} f(t)\sin\omega_0 t dt = \frac{8}{4}\int_0^1 10t \sin\left(\frac{n\pi}{2}t\right)dt = 20\int_0^1 t\sin\left(\frac{n\pi}{2}t\right)dt$$

$$= 20\left[-t\frac{\cos\frac{n\pi}{2}t}{\frac{n\pi}{2}}\right]_0^1 + 20\int_0^1 \frac{\cos\left(\frac{n\pi}{2}t\right)}{\left(\frac{n\pi}{2}\right)}dt = 20\left[0 + \frac{\sin\left(\frac{n\pi}{2}t\right)}{\left(\frac{n\pi}{2}\right)^2}\right]_0^1$$

$$= 20[0 + \frac{4}{(n\pi)^2}(\sin\left(\frac{n\pi}{2}\right) - \sin 0)] = 20\left[\frac{4}{(n\pi)^2}\right] = \frac{80}{n^2\pi^2}$$

Since $\cos\left(\frac{n\pi}{2}\right) = 0$; n is odd and $\sin\left(\frac{n\pi}{2}\right) = 1$; for $n = 1, 5, 9, 13 \ldots$

$= -1$; for $n = 3, 7, 11, 15 \ldots$

The Fourier series then becomes

$$f(t) = a_0 + \sum_{n=1}^{\infty}(a_n \cos n\omega_0 t + b_n \sin n\omega_0 t)$$

$$= \sum \frac{80}{n^2\pi^2}\sin\left(\frac{n\pi}{2}t\right) \quad \text{For} \quad n = 1, 5, 9 \ldots$$

$$= \sum -\frac{80}{n^2\pi^2}\sin\left(\frac{n\pi}{2}t\right) \quad \text{For} \quad n = 3, 7, 11 \ldots$$

In the expanded form, the Fourier series becomes

$$f(t) = \frac{80}{\pi^2}\left[\sin\frac{\pi}{2}t - \frac{1}{9}\sin\frac{3\pi}{2}t + \frac{1}{25}\sin\frac{5\pi}{2}t + \cdots\right]$$

13.2 The first half-cycle of a periodic signal is shown; the period is $T = 4$ s. Sketch $y(t)$ clearly for three complete cycles if :

(i) $y(t)$ is an even-symmetrical signal,
(ii) $y(t)$ is an odd-symmetrical signal,
(iii) $y(t)$ is a half-wave symmetrical signal.

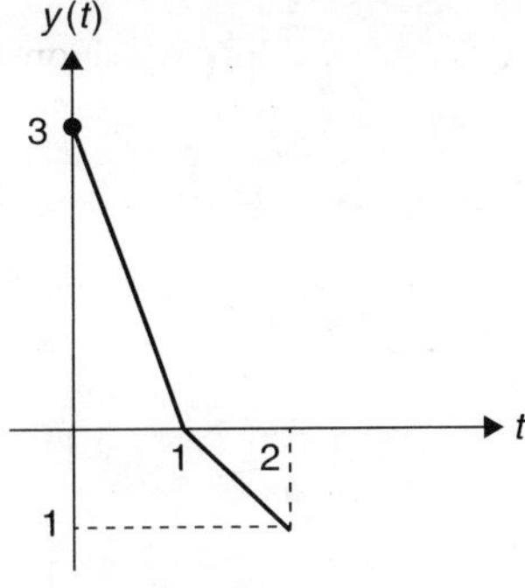

Solution:

(i) Even symmetrical signal

(ii) Odd symmetrical signal

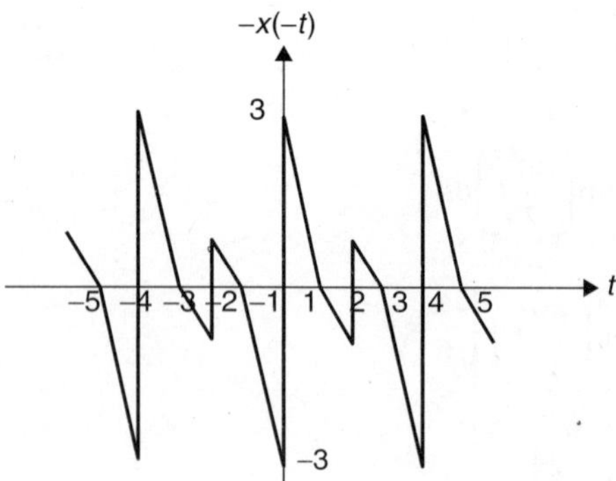

(iii) Half-wave symmetrical signal

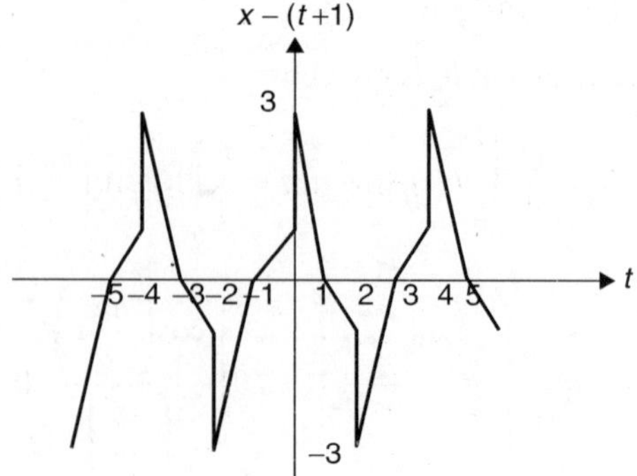

13.3 Determine the exponential Fourier series coefficients for $f(t)$.

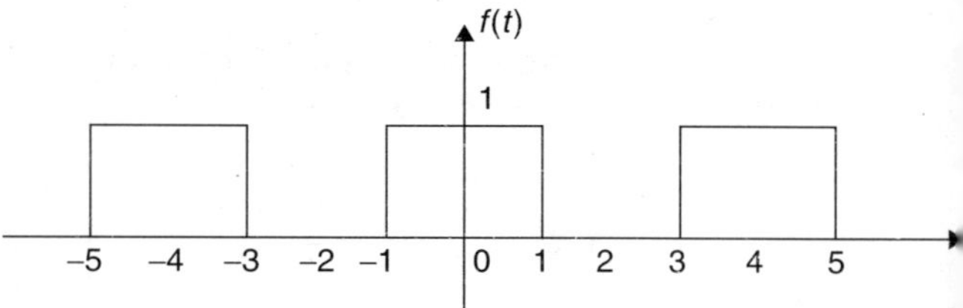

Solution: From the given figure

$$T = 4, \quad \omega_0 = \frac{2\pi}{T} = \frac{2\pi}{4} = \frac{\pi}{2}$$

The mathematical equation for the function $f(t)$ is given by

$$f(t) = 1 \ ; \ -1 < t < 1$$

$$= 0 \ ; \ 1 < t < 3$$

Because of the symmetry of $f(t)$ about the vertical axis or origin and it is convenient to choose $-1 < t < 1$ as the interval over which the integration is performed although any interval of length T is equally valid and thus will lead to the same result. The exponential Fourier series is given by,

$$f(t) = \sum_{n=-\infty}^{\infty} k_n e^{jn\omega_0 t} = \sum_{n=-\infty}^{\infty} k_n e^{j\frac{n\pi}{2}t}$$

Hence the exponential Fourier coefficient is

$$k_n = \frac{1}{T}\int_0^T f(t)e^{-jn\omega_0 t}\,dt = \frac{1}{4}\int_0^4 f(t)e^{-j\frac{n\pi}{2}t}\,dt$$

$$= \frac{1}{4}\left[\int_{-1}^{1} 1 \cdot e^{-j\frac{n\pi}{2}t} + \int_1^3 0 \cdot dt\right] = \frac{1}{4}\left[\frac{e^{-j\frac{n\pi}{2}t}}{\left(-j\frac{n\pi}{2}\right)}\right]_{-1}^{1}$$

$$= \frac{1}{4} \times \left(\frac{-2}{jn\pi}\right)[e^{-j\frac{n\pi}{2}} - e^{j\frac{n\pi}{2}}] = \left(\frac{-1}{2jn\pi}\right)[e^{-j\frac{n\pi}{2}} - e^{j\frac{n\pi}{2}}]$$

$$= \frac{1}{n\pi}\sin\left(\frac{n\pi}{2}\right) \ ; \quad n \neq 0$$

For $n = 0$, we have

$$k_0 = \frac{1}{4}\int_0^4 f(t)e^{-0}dt = \frac{1}{4}\left[\int_{-1}^{1} 1dt + \int_1^3 0dt\right] = \frac{1}{4}[t]_{-1}^{1} = \frac{1}{4}(1+1) = \frac{1}{2}$$

Therefore,

$$k_0 = \frac{1}{2},\quad k_1 = k_{-1} = \frac{1}{\pi},\quad k_2 = k_4 = k_6 = 0$$

$$k_3 = k_{-3} = \frac{-1}{3\pi},\quad k_5 = k_{-5} = \frac{1}{5\pi}$$

13.4 Determine the exponential Fourier series coefficients for $f(t)$.

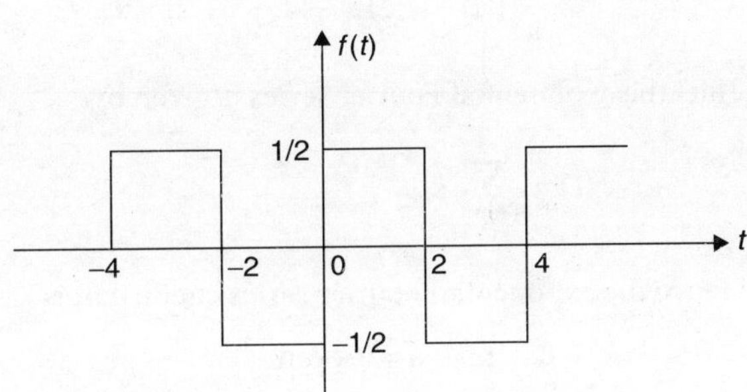

Solution: From the given figure

$$T = 4,\quad \omega_0 = \frac{2\pi}{T} = \frac{2\pi}{4} = \frac{\pi}{2}$$

The mathematical equation for the function $f(t)$ is given by

$$f(t) = \frac{1}{2}\ ;\qquad 0 < t < 2$$

$$= -\frac{1}{2};\qquad 2 < t < 4$$

The exponential Fourier series is given by,

$$f(t) = \sum_{n=-\infty}^{\infty} k_n e^{jn\omega_0 t} = \sum_{n=-\infty}^{\infty} k_n e^{j\frac{n\pi}{2}t}$$

Hence the exponential Fourier coefficient is

$$k_n = \frac{1}{T}\int_0^T f(t)e^{-jn\omega_0 t}dt = \frac{1}{4}\int_0^4 f(t)e^{-j\frac{n\pi}{2}t}dt$$

$$= \frac{1}{4}\left[\int_0^2 \frac{1}{2}e^{-j\frac{n\pi}{2}t}dt + \int_2^4 \left(\frac{-1}{2}\right)e^{-j\frac{n\pi}{2}t}dt\right] = \frac{1}{8}\left[\left.\frac{e^{-j\frac{n\pi}{2}t}}{\left(-j\frac{n\pi}{2}\right)}\right|_0^2 - \left.\frac{e^{-j\frac{n\pi}{2}t}}{\left(-j\frac{n\pi}{2}\right)}\right|_2^4\right]$$

$$= \frac{1}{8}\left(\frac{-2}{jn\pi}\right)[(e^{-jn\pi} - 1) - (-e^{-jn\pi} + e^{-jn2\pi})] = \frac{1}{4jn\pi}[-e^{-jn\pi} + e^{jn2\pi} - e^{-jn\pi} + 1]$$

$$= \frac{1}{4jn\pi}(1 + e^{-j2n\pi} - 2e^{-jn\pi}) = \frac{1}{4jn\pi}(1 + \cos 2n\pi - j\sin 2n\pi - 2e^{-jn\pi})$$

$$= \frac{1}{4jn\pi}(2 - 2e^{-jn\pi}) = \frac{1}{2jn\pi}(1 - e^{-jn\pi})$$

$$= \frac{1}{2jn\pi}(1-\cos n\pi) = \frac{2\sin^2\frac{n\pi}{2}}{2jn\pi} = \frac{1-(-1)^n}{2jn\pi}$$

For $n = 0$, we have

$$K_0 = \frac{1}{4}\int_0^4 f(t)e^0 dt = \frac{1}{4}\left[\int_0^2 \frac{1}{2}dt + \int_2^4 \frac{-1}{2}dt\right]$$

$$= \frac{1}{8}([t]_0^2 - [t]_2^4) = \frac{1}{8}[2-4+2] = 0$$

Thus the exponential Fourier series is given by

$$f(t) = \sum_{n=-\infty}^{\infty} k_n e^{j\frac{n\pi}{2}t}$$

Hence the exponential Fourier series coefficient is

$$k_n = 0 \quad ; \quad n = 0, \text{ even}$$

$$= \frac{1}{jn\pi}; \quad n = \text{odd}$$

13.5 Calculate the exponential Fourier series coefficient for the function $f(t)$

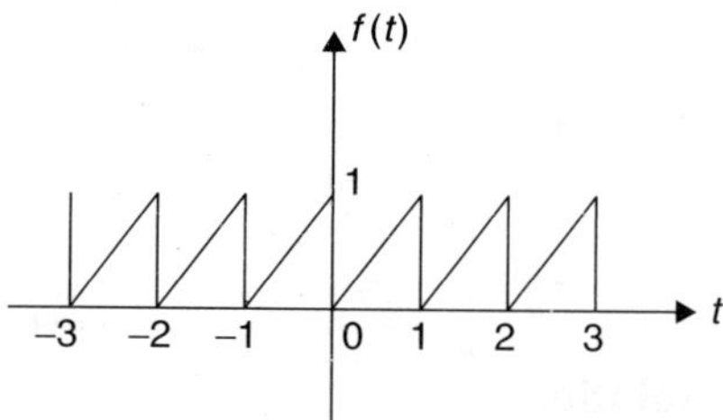

Solution: From the given figure

$$T = 1, \quad \omega_0 = \frac{2\pi}{T} = \frac{2\pi}{1} = 2\pi$$

The mathematical equation for the function $f(t)$ is given by

$$f(t) = t \;;\; 0 < t < 1$$

The exponential Fourier series is given by

$$f(t) = \sum_{n=-\infty}^{\infty} k_n e^{jn\omega_0 t} = \sum_{n=-\infty}^{\infty} k_n e^{jn2\pi t}$$

Hence, the exponential Fourier coefficient is

$$k_n = \frac{1}{T}\int_o^T f(t)e^{-jn\omega_0 t}dt = \frac{1}{1}\int_0^1 te^{-jn2\pi t}dt$$

$$= \left[t \times \frac{e^{-j2\pi t}}{(-j2\pi n)}\right]_0^1 - \left[\int_0^1 \frac{e^{-j2\pi nt}}{(-j2\pi n)}dt\right]$$

$$= \frac{e^{-j2\pi n}}{-j2\pi n} + \frac{1}{j2\pi n}\left[\frac{e^{-j2\pi nt}}{(-j2\pi n)}\right]_0^1 = \frac{e^{-j2\pi n}}{-j2\pi n} + \frac{1}{4\pi^2 n^2}[e^{-j2\pi n} - 1]$$

$$= \frac{1}{-j2\pi n} + \frac{1}{4\pi^2 n^2}[1-1] \quad [\because e^{-j2\pi n} = \cos 2n\pi - j\sin 2n\pi = 1]$$

$$= \frac{1}{-j2\pi n} = \frac{j}{2\pi n}, \quad n \neq 0$$

For $n = 0$, we have

$$K_0 = \frac{1}{1}\int_0^1 t \cdot e^0 dt = \left[\frac{t^2}{2}\right]_0^1 = \frac{1}{2}$$

Hence, the exponential Fourier coefficient is

$$k_n = \frac{j}{2n\pi} \quad ; \quad n \neq 0$$

$$= \frac{1}{2} \quad ; \quad n = 0$$

13.6 Find the Fourier series coefficients for the given saw-tooth wave form.

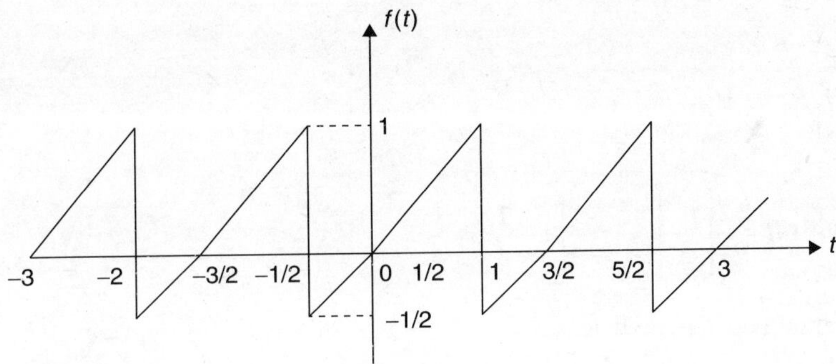

Solution: From the given figure

$$T = \frac{3}{2}, \quad \omega_0 = \frac{2\pi}{T} = \frac{2\pi}{3/2} = \frac{4\pi}{3}$$

The mathematical equation for the function $f(t)$ is given by

$$f(t) = \begin{cases} t \;; & \frac{1}{2} < t < 1 \\ 0 \;; & \text{otherwise} \end{cases}$$

The exponential Fourier series is given by

$$f(t) = \sum_{n=-\infty}^{\infty} k_n e^{jn\omega_0 t} = \sum_{n=-\infty}^{\infty} k_n e^{j\frac{n4\pi}{3}t}$$

Hence the exponential Fourier coefficient is

$$k_n = \frac{1}{T}\int_0^T f(t) e^{-jn\omega_0 t} dt$$

$$=\frac{1}{3/2}\int_{0}^{3/2} f(t)e^{-j4n\pi t/3}dt=\frac{2}{3}\int_{-1/2}^{1} te^{-j4n\pi t/3}dt$$

$$=\frac{2}{3}\left[t\frac{e^{-j4n\pi t/3}}{(-j4n\pi t/3)}\Bigg|_{-1/2}^{1}-\int_{-1/2}^{1}\frac{e^{-j4n\pi t/3}}{(-j4n\pi t/3)}\right]$$

$$=\frac{2}{3}\left[t\frac{e^{-j4n\pi t/3}}{-j4n\pi t/3}\Bigg|_{-1/2}^{1}-\frac{e^{-j4n\pi t/3}}{(-j4n\pi t/3)^2}\Bigg|_{-1/2}^{1}\right]=\frac{2}{3}\left(\frac{-3}{j4n\pi}\right)\left[te^{-j4n\pi t/3}\Big|_{-1/2}^{1}-\frac{e^{-j4n\pi t/3}}{(-j4n\pi t/3)}\Bigg|_{-1/2}^{1}\right]$$

$$=\frac{-2}{j4n\pi}\left[e^{-j4n\pi/3}+\frac{1}{2}e^{j2n\pi/3}+\frac{3}{j4n\pi}(e^{-j4n\pi/3}-e^{j2n\pi/3})\right]$$

$$\therefore \quad k_n=\frac{j}{2n\pi}\left(e^{-j4n\pi/3}+\frac{1}{2}e^{j2n\pi/3}\right)+\frac{3}{8n^2\pi^2}(e^{-j4n\pi/3}-e^{j2n\pi/3}),\ n\neq 0$$

For $n=0$ we have,

$$k_n=\frac{1}{T}\int_{0}^{T} f(t)e^{-jn\omega_0 t}dt$$

$$k_0=\frac{1}{3/2}\int_{-1/2}^{1} tdt=\frac{2}{3}\left[\frac{t^2}{2}\right]_{-1/2}^{1}=\frac{1}{3}\left[1-\frac{1}{4}\right]=\frac{1}{4}$$

Hence, the exponential Fourier coefficient is

$$k_n=\frac{j}{2n\pi}\left(e^{-j4n\pi/3}+\frac{1}{2}e^{j2n\pi/3}\right)+\frac{3}{8n^2\pi^2}(e^{-j4n\pi/3}-e^{j2n\pi/3});\ n\neq 0$$

$$=\frac{1}{4};\ n=0$$

13.7 Find the Fourier series representation of the waveform using complex exponential form.

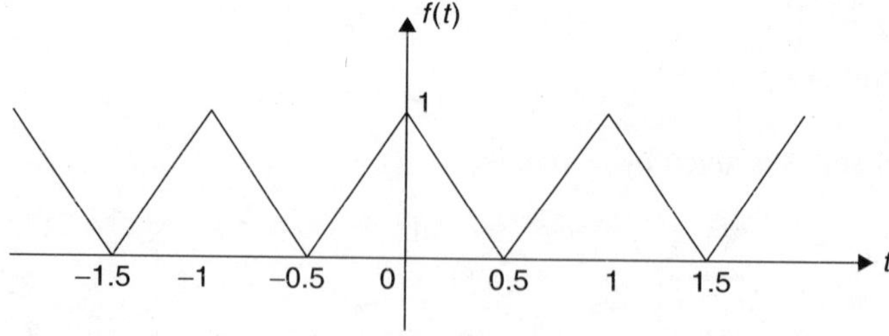

Solution: From the given figure

$$T=1,\quad \omega_0=\frac{2\pi}{T}=\frac{2\pi}{1}=2\pi$$

The mathematical equation for the function $f(t)$ is given by

$$f(t)=\begin{cases} 2t+1\ ; & -0.5<t<0 \\ -2t+1; & 0<t<0.5 \end{cases}$$

The exponential Fourier series is given by,

$$f(t)=\sum_{n=-\infty}^{\infty} k_n e^{jn\omega_0 t}=\sum_{n=-\infty}^{\infty} k_n e^{j2n\pi t}$$

Hence, the exponential Fourier coefficient is

$$k_n=\frac{1}{T}\int_0^T f(t)\cdot e^{-jn\omega_0 t}\,dt$$

$$=\frac{1}{1}\int_0^1 f(t)\cdot e^{-j2\pi nt}\,dt=\int_{-0.5}^{0}(2t+1)e^{-j2\pi nt}\,dt+\int_0^{0.5}(-2t+1)e^{-j2\pi nt}\,dt$$

$$=\left[(2t+1)\frac{e^{-j2\pi nt}}{-j2\pi n}\Bigg|_{0.5}^{0}-\int_{0.5}^{0}2\cdot\frac{e^{-j2\pi nt}}{-j2\pi n}dt\right]+\left[(-2t+1)\frac{e^{-j2\pi nt}}{-j2\pi n}\Bigg|_{0}^{0.5}-\int_0^{0.5}2\cdot\frac{e^{-j2\pi nt}}{-j2\pi n}dt\right]$$

$$=(2t+1)\frac{e^{-j2\pi nt}}{-j2\pi n}\Bigg|_{0.5}^{0}-\frac{2}{(-j2\pi n)^2}e^{-j2\pi nt}\Big|_{-0.5}^{0}+(-2t+1)\frac{e^{-j2\pi nt}}{-j2\pi n}\Bigg|_{0}^{0.5}+\frac{2}{(-j2\pi n)^2}e^{-j2\pi nt}\Big|_{0}^{0.5}$$

$$=\left[1\cdot\frac{1}{-2\pi nj}-(-1+1)\frac{e^{j\pi n}}{-2\pi nj}\right]-\frac{2}{-4\pi^2n^2}[1-e^{j\pi n}]+\left[(-1+1)\frac{e^{-j\pi n}}{-2\pi nj}-\frac{1}{-2\pi nj}\right]+\frac{2}{-4\pi^2n^2}[e^{j\pi n}-1]$$

$$=\frac{1}{-2\pi nj}+\frac{1}{2\pi^2n^2}[1-e^{j\pi n}]+\frac{1}{2\pi nj}-\frac{1}{2\pi^2n^2}[e^{j\pi n}-1]$$

$$=\frac{1}{2\pi^2n^2}[1-e^{j\pi n}-e^{-j\pi n}+1]=\frac{1}{2\pi^2n^2}[2-(e^{j\pi n}+e^{-j\pi n})]$$

$$=\frac{1}{2\pi^2n^2}[2-2\cos\pi n]=\frac{1}{\pi^2n^2}[1-\cos n\pi].$$

$$=\frac{1}{\pi^2n^2}\left(2\sin^2\frac{n\pi}{2}\right)=\frac{1}{\pi^2n^2}[1-(-1^n)];\quad n\neq 0$$

Hence the exponential coefficient for $n=0$

$$k_0=\frac{1}{T}\int_0^T f(t)dt$$

$$=\frac{1}{1}\left[\int_{-0.5}^{0}(2t+1)dt+\int_0^{0.5}(-2t+1)dt\right]=\left[t^2+t\right]_{-0.5}^{0}+\left[-t^2+t\right]_0^{0.5}$$

$$= [-(0.5^2) + 0.5] + [-(0.5)^2 + 0.5] = 0.5 = \frac{1}{2}$$

Hence the exponential Fourier series coefficient

$$k_n = \begin{cases} 0.5 & ; \quad n = 0 \\ 0 & ; \quad n \neq 0 \text{ and } n = \text{even} \\ \dfrac{2}{n^2\pi^2} & ; \quad n = \text{odd} \end{cases}$$

13.8 Determine the exponential form of Fourier series expansion for the periodic waveform.

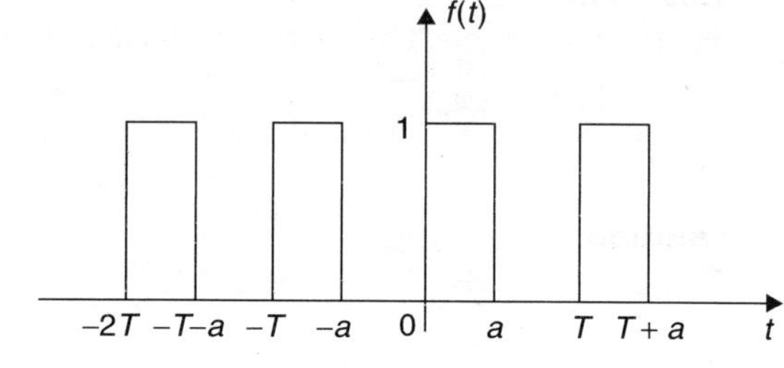

Solution: From the given figure,

Time period, $T = T$

Therefore, $\omega_0 = \dfrac{2\pi}{T}$

The mathematical equation for the function $f(t)$ is given by

$$f(t) = \begin{cases} 1 ; & 0 < t < a \\ 0 ; & a < t < T \end{cases}$$

The exponential Fourier series is given by

$$f(t) = k_0 + \sum_{n=1}^{\infty} (k_n e^{jn\omega_0 t} + k_{-n} e^{-jn\omega_0 t}) = k_0 + \sum_{n=1}^{\infty} \left(k_n e^{j\frac{2n\pi}{T}t} + k_{-n} e^{-j\frac{2n\pi}{T}t}\right)$$

Hence, the exponential Fourier coefficient is

$$k_n = \frac{1}{T}\int_0^T f(t) e^{-jn\omega_0 t} dt = \frac{1}{T}\int_0^T f(t) \cdot e^{-jn\omega_0 t} dt = \frac{1}{T}\left[\int_0^a 1 \cdot e^{-jn\omega_0 t} dt + \int_a^T 0 dt\right]$$

$$= \frac{1}{T}\left[\frac{e^{-jn\omega_0 t}}{-jn\omega_0}\right]_0^a = \frac{1}{T}\left[\frac{e^{-jn\omega_0 a} - 1}{-jn\omega_0}\right]; \quad n \neq 0$$

$$k_{-n} = \frac{1}{T}\int_0^T f(t) e^{jn\omega_0 t} dt = \frac{1}{T}\left[\int_0^a 1 e^{jn\omega_0 t} dt + \int_a^T 0 dt\right]$$

$$= \frac{1}{T}\left[\frac{e^{jn\omega_0 t}}{jn\omega_0}\right]_0^a = \frac{1}{T}\left[\frac{e^{jn\omega_0 a} - 1}{jn\omega_0}\right]; \quad n \neq 0$$

For $n = 0$, we have,

$$k_0 = \frac{1}{T}\int_0^T f(t) dt = \frac{1}{T}\left[\int_0^a 1 dt + \int_a^T 0 dt\right] = \frac{1}{T}[t]_0^a = \frac{a}{T}$$

Hence, the exponential Fourier series is,

$$f(t) = k_0 + \sum_{n=1}^{\infty}\left(k_n e^{jn\omega_0 t} + k_{-n}e^{-jn\omega_0 t}\right)$$

$$= \frac{a}{T} + \sum_{n=1}^{\infty}\left[\frac{1}{T}\left(\frac{e^{-jn\omega_0 a}-1}{-jn\omega_0}\right)e^{jn\omega_0 t} + \frac{1}{T}\left(\frac{e^{jn\omega_0 a}-1}{jn\omega_0}\right)e^{-jn\omega_0 t}\right]$$

13.9 Find the Fourier coefficients and Fourier series of the square-wave function $f(t)$ defined by

$$f(t) = \begin{cases} 0\ ; & -\pi < t < 0 \\ 1\ ; & 0 < t < \pi \end{cases}$$

Solution: Given that

$$T = 2\pi, \quad \omega_0 = \frac{2\pi}{T} = \frac{2\pi}{2\pi} = 1$$

The Fourier coefficients are given by

$$a_0 = \frac{1}{T}\int_{-T/2}^{T/2} f(t)dt = \frac{1}{2\pi}\int_{-\pi}^{\pi} f(t)dt$$

$$= \frac{1}{2\pi}\int_{-\pi}^{0} 0dt + \frac{1}{2\pi}\int_{0}^{\pi} 1dt = 0 + \frac{1}{2\pi}(\pi - 0) = \frac{1}{2}$$

$$a_n = \frac{2}{T}\int_{-T/2}^{T/2} f(t)\cos n\omega_0 t dt = \frac{1}{\pi}\int_{-\pi}^{\pi} f(t)\cos nt dt$$

$$= \frac{1}{\pi}\int_{-\pi}^{0} 0\times \cos nt dt + \frac{1}{\pi}\int_{0}^{\pi} 1\times \cos nt dt$$

$$= 0 + \frac{1}{\pi}\left[\frac{\sin nt}{n}\right]_0^{\pi} = \frac{1}{n\pi}[\sin n\pi - \sin 0] = 0$$

$$b_n = \frac{2}{T}\int_{-T/2}^{T/2} f(t)\sin n\omega_0 t dt = \frac{1}{\pi}\int_{-\pi}^{\pi} f(t)\sin nt dt$$

$$= \frac{1}{\pi}\int_{-\pi}^{0} 0\times \sin nt dt + \frac{1}{\pi}\int_{0}^{\pi} 1\times \sin nt dt$$

$$= 0 + \frac{-1}{\pi}\left[\frac{\cos nt}{n}\right]_0^{\pi} = \frac{-1}{n\pi}[\cos n\pi - \cos 0]$$

$$= \begin{cases} 0\ ; & \text{if } n \text{ is even} \\ \dfrac{2}{n\pi}\ ; & \text{if } n \text{ is odd} \end{cases}$$

The Fourier series then becomes

$$f(t) = a_0 + \sum_{n=1}^{\infty} (a_n \cos n\omega_0 t + b_n \sin n\omega_0 t)$$

$$= \frac{1}{2} + \sum \frac{2}{n\pi} \sin(nt); \quad \text{for} \quad n = 1, 3, 5 \ldots$$

In the expanded form, the Fourier series becomes

$$f(t) = \frac{1}{2} + \frac{2}{\pi}\sin t + \frac{2}{3\pi}\sin 3t + \frac{2}{5\pi}\sin 5t \cdots$$

EXERCISE PROBLEMS

1. Find the Fourier coefficients and Fourier series of the function $f(t)$ defined by

$$f(t) = \begin{cases} 1 \; ; & 0 < t < 2 \\ -1 \; ; & 2 < t < 4 \end{cases}$$

$$\left[\textbf{Ans}: a_0 = 0, a_n = 0, b_n = \begin{cases} 0 \; ; & \text{if } n \text{ is even} \\ \dfrac{4}{n\pi} \; ; & \text{if } n \text{ is odd} \end{cases} \right]$$

2. Find the Fourier series for (periodic extension of)

$$f(t) = \begin{cases} t - 1 \; ; & 0 < t < 2 \\ 3 - 1 \; ; & 2 < t < 4 \end{cases}$$

$$\left[\textbf{Ans}: a_0 = 0, b_n = 0, a_n = \begin{cases} 0 \; ; & \text{if } n \text{ is even} \\ -\dfrac{8}{n^2\pi^2} \; ; & \text{if } n \text{ is odd} \end{cases} \right]$$

3. Find the Fourier series to represent $f(x) = x^2$ in the interval $[0, 2\pi]$ [**Ans:** $a_0 = \frac{8}{3}\pi^2, a_n = \frac{4}{n^2}, b_n = \frac{4\pi}{n}$]

4. Find the Fourier series expansion of the half wave rectified sine wave.

$$\left[\textbf{Ans}: a_0 = \frac{A}{\pi}, b_1 = \frac{A}{2\pi}, a_n = \begin{cases} 0 \; ; & \text{if } n \text{ is odd} \\ \dfrac{2A}{\pi(n^2 - 1)} \; ; & \text{if } n \text{ is even} \end{cases} \right]$$

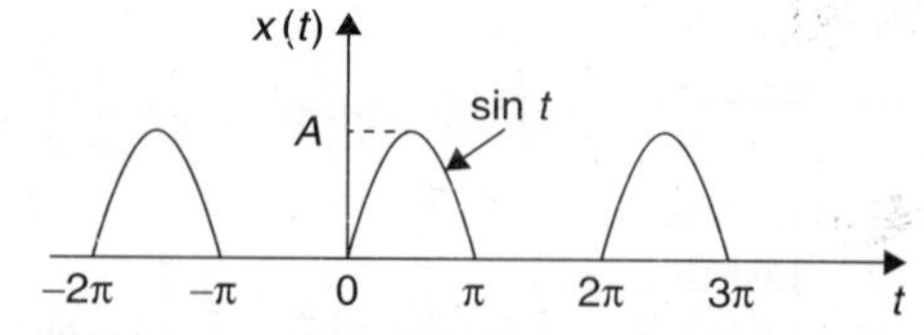

5. Find the trigonometric Fourier series for the waveform. [**Ans:** $a_0 = \frac{A}{2}, a_n = 0, b_n = -\frac{A}{n\pi}$]

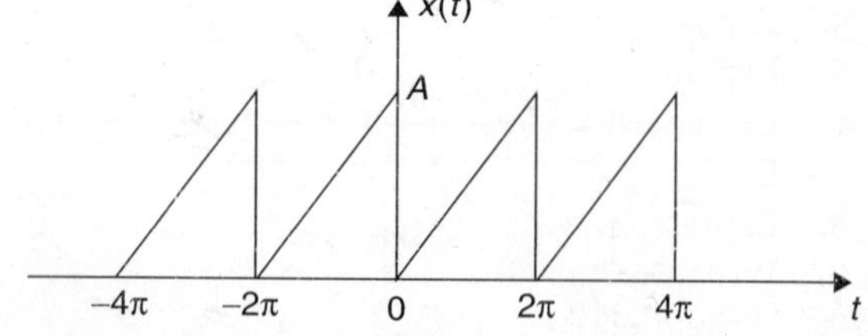

6. Find the Fourier series expansion for the waveform.

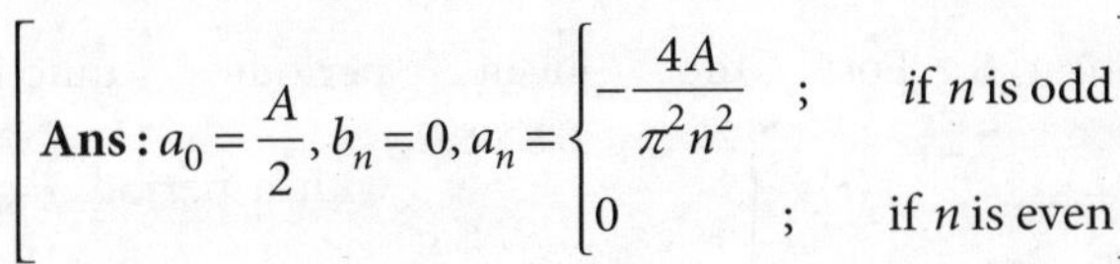

$$\left[\textbf{Ans}: a_0 = \frac{A}{2}, b_n = 0, a_n = \begin{cases} -\frac{4A}{\pi^2 n^2} & ; \quad \text{if } n \text{ is odd} \\ 0 & ; \quad \text{if } n \text{ is even} \end{cases}\right]$$

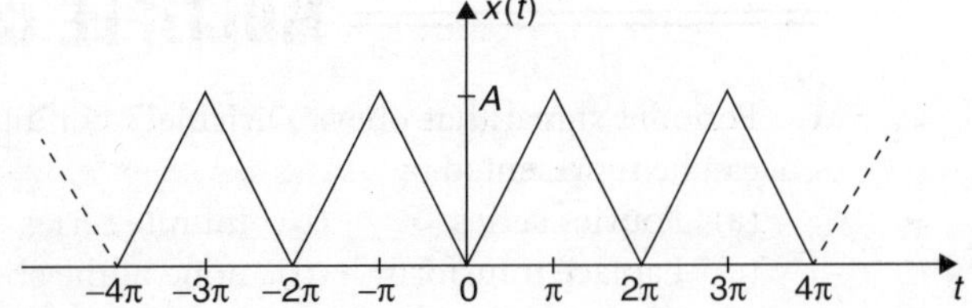

7. Obtain the Fourier components of the periodic rectangular waveform.

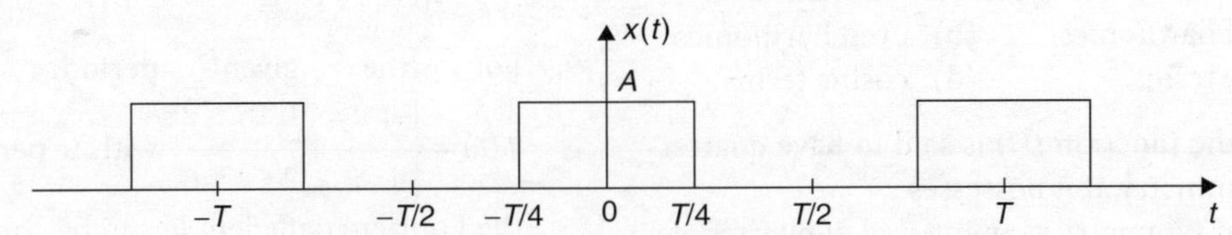

$$\left[\textbf{Ans}: a_0 = \frac{A}{2}, b_n = 0, a_n = \begin{cases} \frac{2A}{\pi n} & ; \quad \text{for } n = 1, 5, 9 \ldots \\ -\frac{2A}{\pi n} & ; \quad \text{for } n = 3, 7, 11 \ldots \\ 0 & ; \quad \text{for } n \text{ even} \end{cases}\right]$$

8. Obtain the exponential Fourier series for the wave form.

$$\left[\textbf{Ans}: x(t) = \sum_{n=-\infty}^{\infty} k_n e^{jn\omega_0 t} = \sum_{n=-\infty}^{\infty} -j\frac{A}{2n\pi} e^{jnt}\right]$$

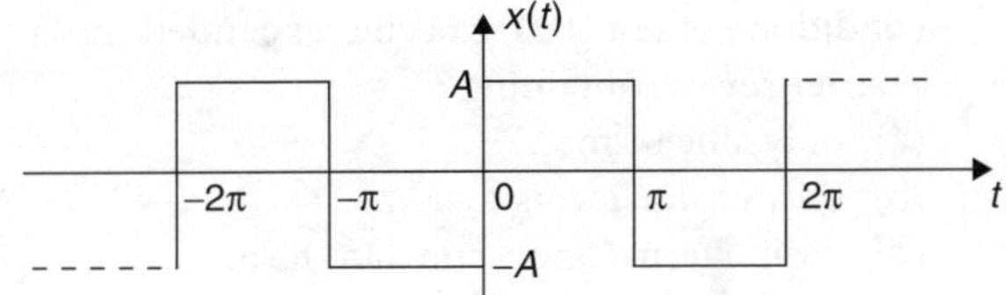

9. Find the exponential Fourier series for the full wave rectified sine wave.

$$\left[\textbf{Ans}: x(t) = \sum_{n=-\infty}^{\infty} k_n e^{jn\omega_0 t} = \sum_{n=-\infty}^{\infty} \frac{2A}{\pi(1-4n^2)} e^{j2nt}\right]$$

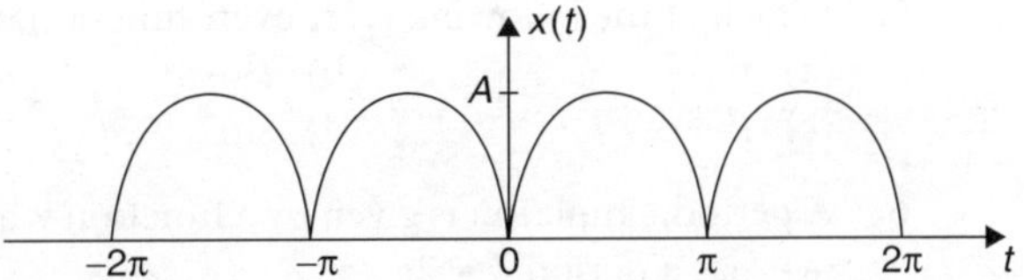

REVIEW QUESTIONS

1. Define Fourier transform of a continuous time function.
2. List the Dirichlet's conditions for a Fourier transform.
3. List the properties of continuous time Fourier transform.
4. Explain the property of even symmetry in Fourier analysis.
5. Explain the property of odd symmetry in Fourier analysis.
6. Explain the property of half-wave symmetry in Fourier analysis.
7. Explain the property of quarter wave symmetry in Fourier analysis.
8. Express the Fourier transform of periodic signal in terms of exponential Fourier series coefficients.
9. Write the formulae for exponential Fourier series coefficients.
10. Write the formulae for trigonometric Fourier series coefficients.

MULTIPLE CHOICE QUESTIONS

1. Periodic signal that obeys Dirichlet's condition can be represented by
   (a) Fourier series (b) infinite series
   (c) Laplace transform (d) none of the above

2. The Fourier series expansion of a periodic function with half-wave symmetry contains only
   (a) odd harmonics (b) even harmonics
   (c) sine terms (d) cosine terms

3. A periodic function $f(t)$ is said to have quarter-wave symmetry, if it possesses
   (a) even symmetry at an interval of quarter of a wave
   (b) even symmetry and half-wave symmetry only
   (c) even and odd symmetry with half-wave symmetry
   (d) even and odd symmetry without half-wave symmetry

4. If $f(t) = -f(-t)$ and $f(t)$ satisfies the Dirichlet's conditions, then $f(t)$ can be expanded in a Fourier series containing
   (a) only sine terms
   (b) only cosine terms
   (c) cosine terms and a constant term
   (d) sine terms and a constant term

5. Which of the following is an 'even' function of t?
   (a) t^2 (b) $t^2 - 4t$
   (c) $t^3 + 6$ (d) $\sin 2t + 3t$

6. A periodic function is given by a function which
   (a) has a period $T = 2\pi$
   (b) has a period $T = \pi$
   (c) satisfies $f(t+T) = -f(t)$
   (d) satisfies $f(t+T) = f(t)$

7. What does the first term a_0 in the expression of a line spectrum indicate?

$$f(t) = a_0 + \sum_{n=1}^{\infty}(a_n \cos n\omega_0 t + b_n \sin n\omega_0 t)$$

   (a) DC component
   (b) fundamental component
   (c) aecond harmonic component
   (d) all of the above

8. For the given periodic function, $f(t) = \begin{cases} 2t\ ; & 0 \le t \le 2 \\ 4\ ; & 2 \le t \le 6 \end{cases}$ with a period $T = 6$, the Fourier coefficient a_1 can be computed as
   (a) −9.2642 (b) −8.1275
   (c) −0.9119 (d) − 0.5116

9. For the given periodic function, $f(t) = \begin{cases} 2t\ ; & 0 \le t \le 2 \\ 4\ ; & 2 \le t \le 6 \end{cases}$ with a period $T = 6$, the Fourier coefficient b_1 can be computed as
   (a) −75.6800 (b) −7.5680
   (c) −6.8968 (d) −0.7468

10. Given the following periodic function, $f(t)$,

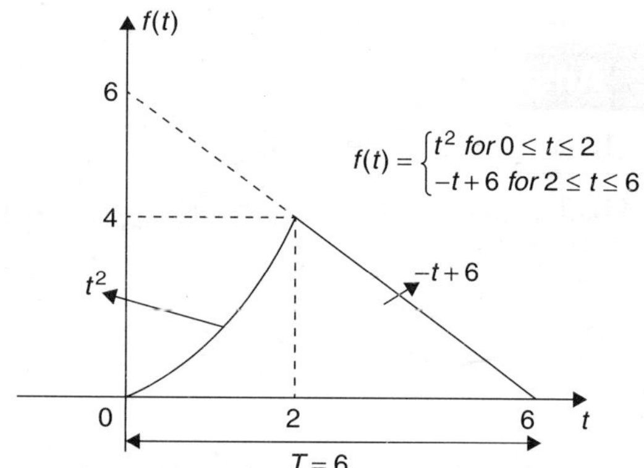

   The coefficient a_0 of the continuous Fourier series associated with the above given function $f(t)$ can be computed as
   (a) 0.9 (b) 2.5
   (c) 1.78 (d) 3.29

11. In a periodic signal, if the period T is doubled, the fundamental frequency ω_0 in the spectrum becomes:
   (a) doubled (b) halved
   (c) increased to 4 times (d) no change

12. A function $f(t)$ is said to be even, if $f(t)$ is equal to:
   (a) $-f(t)$ (b) $f(-t)$
   (c) $f(2t)$ (d) $f(-2t)$

13. A function $f(t)$ is said to be odd if $f(t)$ is equal to:

(a) $-f(t)$ (b) $-f(-t)$
(c) $f(2t)$ (d) $f(-2t)$

14. A function $f(t)$ is said to be half-wave symmetry, if $f(t)$ is equal to
(a) $f\left(t+\frac{T}{2}\right)$ (b) $f\left(t-\frac{T}{2}\right)$
(c) $-f\left(t-\frac{T}{2}\right)$ (d) $f\left(\frac{T}{2}\right)$

15. Fourier transform of the unit impulse $\delta(t)$ is:
(a) 1 (b) 0
(c) π (d) $\delta(\omega)$

16. Fourier transform of the Signum sgn(t) is:
(a) $\frac{2}{j\omega}$ (b) $\frac{1}{j\omega}$
(c) $-\frac{2}{j\omega}$ (d) $j2\omega$

17. Time convolution property states that
(a) $f_1(t) * f_2(t) \leftrightarrow F_1(j\omega) \cdot F_2(j\omega)$
(b) $f_1(t) \cdot f_2(t) \leftrightarrow F_1(j\omega) * F_2(j\omega)$
(c) $f_1(t) * f_2(t) \leftrightarrow -F_1(j\omega) \cdot F_2(j\omega)$
(d) $f_1(t) \cdot f_2(t) \leftrightarrow -F_1(j\omega) * F_2(j\omega)$

18. Frequency convolution property states that
(a) $F_1(j\omega) * F_2(j\omega) \leftrightarrow 2\pi f_1(t) f_2(t)$
(b) $F_1(j\omega) \cdot F_2(j\omega) \leftrightarrow 2\pi f_1(t) * f_2(t)$
(c) $F_1(j\omega) * F_2(j\omega) \leftrightarrow -2\pi f_1(t) f_2(t)$
(d) $F_1(j\omega) \cdot F_2(j\omega) \leftrightarrow -2\pi f_1(t) * f_2(t)$

Answers

1. a	**2.** a	**3.** c	**4.** a	**5.** a	**6.** d	**7.** a	**8.** c	**9.** d	**10.** c
11. b	**12.** b	**13.** b	**14.** c	**15.** a	**16.** a	**17.** a	**18.** a		

14 Filters and Attenuators

Learning Outcomes:

After reading this chapter, the reader will able to

- ➢ Classify filters
- ➢ List the properties of filters
- ➢ Define characteristic impedance and propagation constant
- ➢ Summarise the equations of filter networks
- ➢ Contrast pass-band and stop-band of filter network
- ➢ Analyse constant-*K* or prototype filters
- ➢ Analyse m-derived filters
- ➢ Illustrate terminating half or *L*-section filters
- ➢ Summarise composite filter design
- ➢ Outline various types of attenuators

14.1 INTRODUCTION

A filter is an electrical network that can transmit signals within a specified frequency range and reject all other signals. This frequency range is called pass-band and the other frequency range where the signals are suppressed is called stop-band or attenuation band. But in real world applications, a filter is that which prevents the entry of unwanted things in an output of the system. Some of real world examples are water filter, air filter, cooler filter, and so on.

The frequency that separates the pass-band and stop-band is known as cut-off frequency. For some filter networks, there are two cut-off frequencies in the entire zone of the operation. The cut-off frequency is denoted as f_C if its value is unique, or f_1 and f_2 in case the cut-off frequencies are more than one. Filter networks are generally used in power supplies, radio receivers, electronic circuits, telephone lines, and so on. These are designed to separate different frequency bands available in an alternating current signal. Filters are generally constructed by using T or π networks which are symmetrical. The T and π sections are generally used to construct ladder networks. Symmetrical T and π sections can be generally made up of an unsymmetrical L-section connected in one-way for T-section and the opposite way for a π-section (Fig. 14.1).

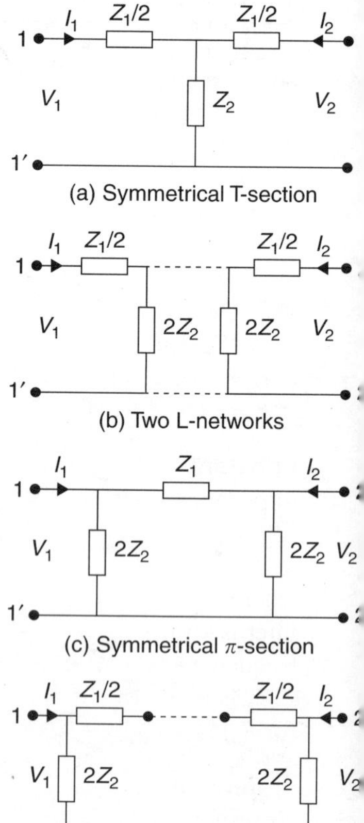

Fig. 14.1 General circuit configuration of filters

14.2 CLASSIFICATION OF FILTERS

Filters may be classified according to the following two philosophies:

(i) Depending upon the frequency response characteristics, the filters are classified as:

- low-pass filters (LPF),
- high-pass filters (HPF),

- band-pass filters (BPF), and
- band stop or band rejection filters (BSF).

Low-pass filters An ideal low pass filter (Fig. 14.2) passes or transmits the signals of all frequencies from zero to cut-off frequency (below the cut-off frequency) and offers very high attenuation at all other higher frequencies.

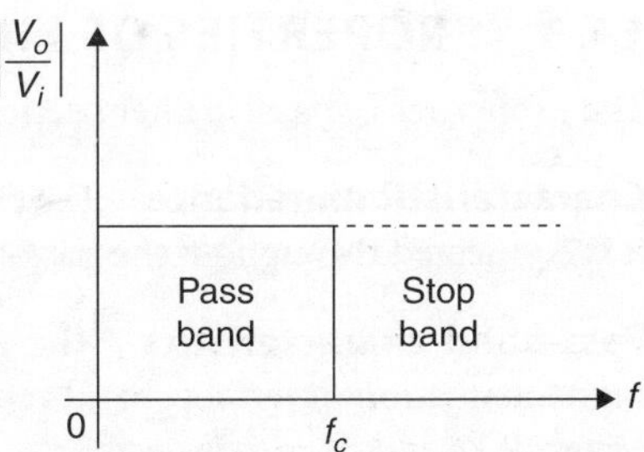

Fig. 14.2 Low-pass filter

High-pass filters An ideal high-pass filter (Fig. 14.3) passes or transmits the signals of the frequencies above the cut-off frequency but attenuates the frequencies below the cut-off frequency.

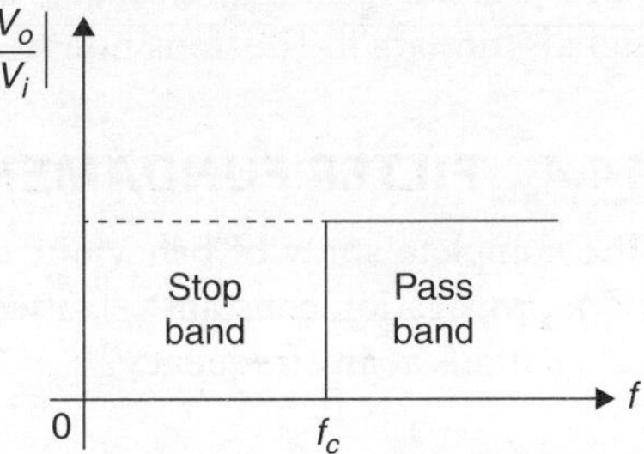

Fig. 14.3 High-pass filter

Band-pass filters An ideal band pass filter (Fig. 14.4) passes or transmits the signals of the frequencies f_1 and f_2 and attenuates all other frequencies. In this filter, all the frequencies below f_1 and above f_2 will be eliminated or attenuated. It will transmit all frequencies from f_1 to f_2 and $(f_2 - f_1)$ is called pass-band.

Band-stop filters An ideal band-rejection filter (Fig. 14.5) rejects all frequencies between the two designed frequencies f_1 and f_2, while it transmits all other frequencies. Here $(f_2 - f_1)$ is called stop-band.

The above discussion is summarised in brief in Table 14.1.

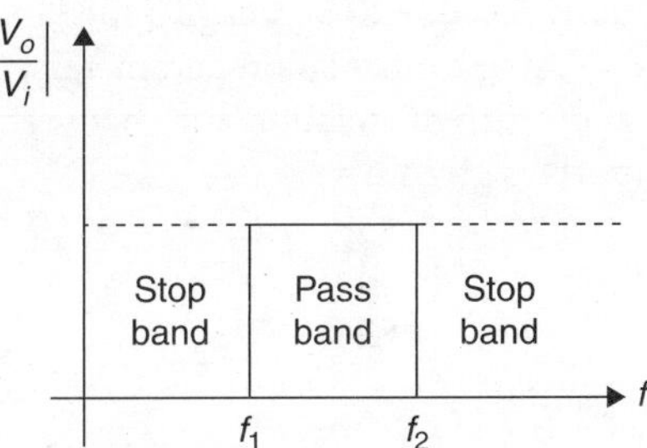

Fig. 14.4 Band-pass filter

Table 14.1 Range of pass-band and stop-band of various filters

Type of filter	Pass-band	Stop-band
Low-pass	$0 \to f_C$	$f_C \to \infty$
High-pass	$f_C \to \infty$	$0 \to f_C$
Band-pass	$f_1 \to f_2$	$0 \to f_1, f_2 \to \infty$
Band-stop	$0 \to f_1, f_2 \to \infty$	$f_1 \to f_2$

(ii) Depending upon the relation between the arm impedances (Z_1 and Z_2), the filters are classified as:
- constant *K* or prototype filters, and
- *m*-derived filters.

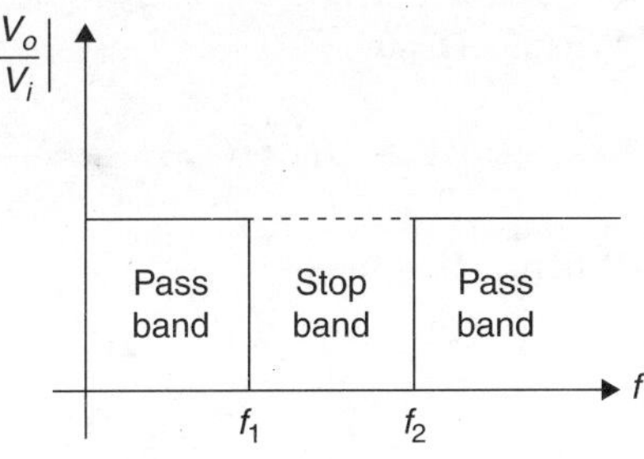

Fig. 14.5 Band-stop filter

Constant *K* or proto-type filter In this filter, the series impedance Z_1 and the shunt impedance Z_2 are related by Eq. 14.1.

$$Z_1 Z_2 = K^2 = R_0^2 \tag{14.1}$$

where *K* is a constant and independent of frequency. The constant *K* filter is known as an inverse network filter and Z_1 and Z_2 vary with frequency in an inverse manner. In almost all the cases, the product $Z_1 Z_2$ is real and has the dimensions of resistance squared, and Z_0 (or R_0) is called the design impedance of the filter.

***m*-derived filter** In this filter, $Z_1 Z_2 \neq K^2$, but will have the same characteristic impedance as the corresponding constant K filter, with much sharper attenuation characteristics.

14.3 PROPERTIES OF FILTERS

The properties of passive filter sections are generally characterised as follows:

Characteristic impedance The characteristic impedance (Z_0) of a filter matches with the circuit to which it is connected throughout the pass-band. This prevents reflection loss in the combination.

Pass-band characteristics The filter should have minimum attenuation in its pass-band range and high attenuation in its stop-band range. The degree of attenuation is generally expressed by the attenuation constant α, and its unit is decibel.

Cut-off frequency characteristics The filter should possess distinguishing property in the pass-band or stop-band. It should be capable of identifying lower as well as higher cut-off frequencies for transmitting signals through it. The transition frequency region between the pass-band and stop-band must be very small.

14.4 FILTER FUNDAMENTALS

The complete study of behaviour of any filter section needs calculations of its characteristic impedance (Z_0), propagation constant (γ), attenuation constant (α) and phase constant (β), using some mathematical calculations at any frequency.

14.4.1 CHARACTERISTIC IMPEDANCE (Z_0)

Consider a two-port network (Fig. 14.6), terminated with its image impedance Z_0.

Using transmission parameters, the voltage and current relationship between the two ports is given by

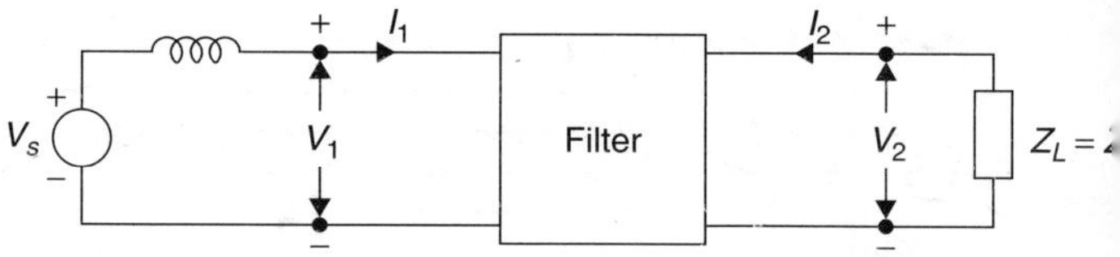

Fig. 14.6 Two-port network

$$V_1 = AV_2 - BI_2$$

$$I_1 = CV_2 - DI_2$$

$$V_2 = Z_0 I_2$$

where $Z_0 = \sqrt{Z_{1OC} Z_{1SC}} = \sqrt{\frac{B}{C}}$. Here Z_{1OC} and Z_{1SC} are open circuit and short-circuit impedances at port 1 respectively.

When $I_1 = 0$

$$CV_2 - DI_2 = 0 \Rightarrow \frac{V_2}{I_2} = \frac{D}{C} = Z_{1OC}$$

When $V_1 = 0$

$$AV_2 - BI_2 = 0 \Rightarrow \frac{V_2}{I_2} = \frac{B}{A} = Z_{1SC}$$

$$\therefore \quad Z_0 = \sqrt{Z_{1OC} Z_{1SC}} = \sqrt{\frac{D}{C} \times \frac{B}{A}} = \sqrt{\frac{B}{C}}$$

$$\Rightarrow \quad Z_0 = \sqrt{\frac{B}{C}} \qquad \text{(Since for a symmetrical network, } A = D\text{)} \qquad (14.2)$$

14.4.2 Propagation Constant (γ)

To easily obtain the change in the voltage or current at the output relative to the input of a cascaded network in terms of individual networks, we had expressed the ratio of magnitudes of currents (or voltages) as exponentials.

The ratio of only magnitudes does not give a complete picture of the performance of the network. The phase angles of the currents and voltages must also be considered to evaluate the performance of the network.

By assuming that the network is terminated in its characteristic impedance Z_0, we can define the ratio of currents expressed in complex or vector form

$$\frac{I_1}{I_1} = e^{\gamma}, \qquad \text{where } \gamma = \alpha + j\beta$$

$$\Rightarrow \quad \frac{I_1}{I_2} = e^{\alpha + j\beta} \tag{14.3}$$

In Eq. 14.3, γ is called the propagation constant. The real part of γ, that is α, is called the attenuation constant and is measured in nepers. Since α is the ratio of I_1 and I_2 or V_1 and V_2, it gives the attenuation produced in the signal as it passes from the input to the output through the network.

The imaginary part of the γ, that is β, is called the phase constant and is measured in radians. β gives the change in phase angle produced by the network between the input and output quantities.

If n networks with propagation constant $\gamma_1, \gamma_2 \dots \gamma_n$ are connected in cascade, the overall propagation constant γ is given by

$$\gamma = \gamma_1 + \gamma_2 + \dots + \gamma_n \tag{14.4}$$

14.5 EQUATIONS OF FILTER NETWORKS

The study of behaviour of any filter requires the calculation of its propagation constant γ, attenuation constant α, phase shift β and its characteristic impedance Z_0.

14.5.1 Equations for T-Network

Characteristic impedance For a symmetrical T-network terminated in impedance Z_0, the input impedance will be equal to Z_0. If several such symmetrical T-networks, each with characteristic impedance Z_0, are connected in cascade or tandem, the input impedance will still be Z_0.

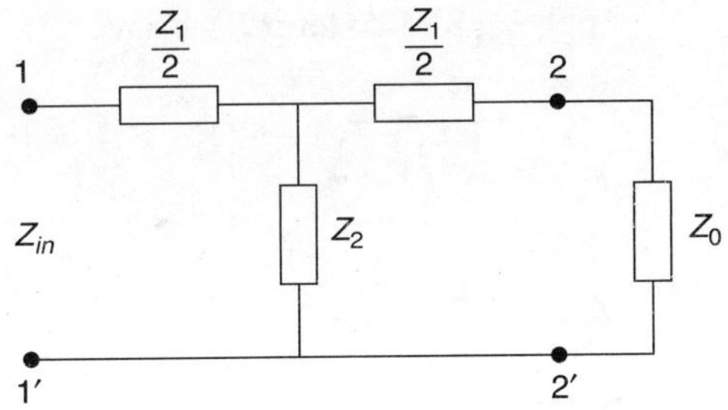

$$Z_{in} = \frac{Z_1}{2} + \frac{Z_2\left(\frac{Z_1}{2} + Z_0\right)}{\frac{Z_1}{2} + Z_0 + Z_2} \tag{14.5}$$

Also we know that

$$Z_{in} = Z_0 \tag{14.6}$$

Fig. 14.7 Symmetrical T-section terminated in Z_0

From Eqs 14.5 and 14.6,

$$Z_0 = \frac{Z_1}{2} + \frac{Z_2(Z_1 + 2Z_0)}{Z_1 + 2(Z_0 + Z_2)} = \frac{Z_1^2 + 2Z_1(Z_0 + Z_2) + 2Z_2(Z_1 + 2Z_0)}{2(Z_1 + 2Z_0 + 2Z_2)}$$

$$\Rightarrow \quad 2Z_1Z_0 + 4Z_0^2 + 4Z_0Z_2 = Z_1^2 + 2Z_0Z_1 + 2Z_1Z_2 + 2Z_1Z_2 + 4Z_0Z_2$$

$$4Z_0^2 = Z_1^2 + 4Z_1Z_2$$

$$Z_0^2 = \frac{Z_1^2}{4} + Z_1Z_2$$

$$Z_0 = \sqrt{\frac{Z_1^2}{4} + Z_1Z_2} \tag{14.7}$$

The characteristic impedance of a symmetrical T-network is

$$Z_{0T} = \sqrt{\frac{Z_1^2}{4} + Z_1Z_2} \tag{14.8}$$

The characteristic impedance Z_{0T} can also be expressed in terms of open circuit impedance Z_{OC} and short circuit impedance Z_{SC} of the T-network. From Fig. 14.7, we have,

$$Z_{OC} = \frac{Z_1}{2} + Z_2 = \frac{Z_1 + 2Z_2}{2} \tag{14.9}$$

$$Z_{SC} = \frac{Z_1}{2} + \frac{Z_2 \times \frac{Z_1}{2}}{Z_2 + \frac{Z_1}{2}} = \frac{Z_1^2 + 2Z_1Z_2 + 2Z_1Z_2}{2(Z_1 + 2Z_2)} = \frac{Z_1^2 + 4Z_1Z_2}{2(Z_1 + 2Z_2)} \tag{14.10}$$

$$Z_{OC} \times Z_{SC} = \frac{Z_1 + 2Z_2}{2} \times \frac{Z_1^2 + 4Z_1Z_2}{2(Z_1 + 2Z_2)} = \frac{Z_1^2}{4} + Z_1Z_2 = Z_{0T}^2$$

$$\Rightarrow \quad Z_{0T} = \sqrt{Z_{OC} \times Z_{SC}} \tag{14.11}$$

Propagation constant Consider the symmetrical T-network terminated in its characteristic impedance (Fig. 14.8). By definition, the propagation constant γ of the network shown in Fig. 14.8 is given by,

$$\gamma = \ln\left(\frac{I_1}{I_2}\right)$$

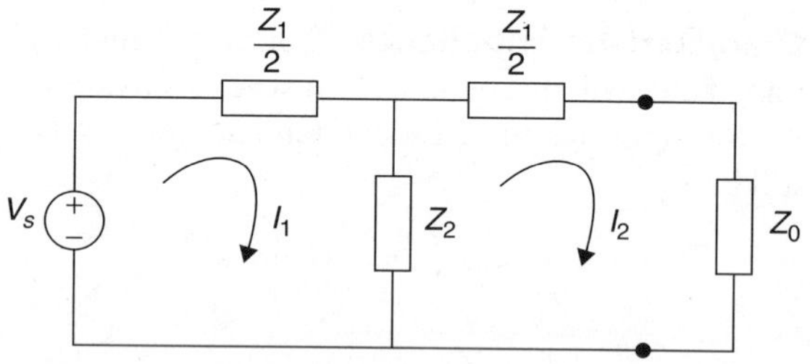

Applying KVL to loop 2, we have

$$\left(Z_0 + Z_2 + \frac{Z_1}{2}\right)I_2 - Z_2I_1 = 0$$

$$\Rightarrow \quad \frac{I_1}{I_2} = \frac{Z_0 + Z_2 + \frac{Z_1}{2}}{Z_2} = e^{\gamma}$$

$$\Rightarrow \quad Z_0 + Z_2 + \frac{Z_1}{2} = Z_2e^{\gamma}$$

$$\Rightarrow \quad Z_0 = Z_2(e^{\gamma} - 1) - \frac{Z_1}{2} \tag{14.12}$$

Fig. 14.8 Asymmetrical T-network terminated in Z_0

The characteristic impedance of the T-network is given by

$$Z_0 = \sqrt{\frac{Z_1^2}{4} + Z_1 Z_2} \tag{14.13}$$

From Eqs 14.12 and 14.13, we have

$$Z_2(-1+e^{\gamma}) - \frac{Z_1}{2} = \sqrt{\frac{Z_1^2}{4} + Z_1 Z_2}$$

$$Z_2^2(-1+e^{\gamma})^2 + \frac{Z_1^2}{4} - Z_1 Z_2(-1+e^{\gamma}) = \frac{Z_1^2}{4} + Z_1 Z_2$$

$$Z_2^2(-1+e^{\gamma})^2 + Z_1 Z_2 - Z_1 Z_2 e^{\gamma} = Z_1 Z_2$$

$$\frac{(e^{\gamma}-1)^2}{e^{\gamma}} = \frac{Z_1}{Z_2}$$

$$\frac{e^{2\gamma}+1-2e^{\gamma}}{e^{\gamma}} = \frac{Z_1}{Z_2}$$

$$\frac{e^{\gamma}+e^{-\gamma}}{2} - 1 = \frac{Z_1}{2Z_2}$$

$$\frac{e^{\gamma}+e^{-\gamma}}{2} = 1 + \frac{Z_1}{2Z_2}$$

$$\Rightarrow \qquad \cosh\gamma = 1 + \frac{Z_1}{2Z_2} \tag{14.14}$$

$$\sinh\gamma = \sqrt{\cosh^2\gamma - 1} = \sqrt{\left(1+\frac{Z_1}{2Z_2}\right)^2 - 1} = \sqrt{\left(\frac{Z_1}{2Z_2}\right)^2 + \frac{Z_1}{Z_2}} = \frac{1}{Z_2}\sqrt{Z_1 Z_2 + \frac{Z_1^2}{4}}$$

$$\Rightarrow \qquad \sinh\gamma = \frac{1}{Z_2}\sqrt{Z_1 Z_2 + \frac{Z_1^2}{4}} = \frac{Z_{0T}}{Z_2} \tag{14.15}$$

$$\frac{\text{Eq. 14.15}}{\text{Eq. 14.14}} \Rightarrow \tanh\gamma = \frac{Z_{0T}}{Z_2} \times \frac{2Z_2}{Z_1 + 2Z_2} = \frac{Z_{0T}}{Z_2 + \frac{Z_1}{2}}$$

But we know that $Z_2 + \frac{Z_1}{2} = Z_{OC}$

$$\Rightarrow \qquad \tanh\gamma = \frac{Z_{0T}}{Z_{OC}} \tag{14.16}$$

Also, we know that from Eq. 14.11,

$$Z_{0T} = \sqrt{Z_{OC} \times Z_{SC}}$$

$$\therefore \qquad \tanh\gamma = \frac{\sqrt{Z_{OC} \times Z_{SC}}}{Z_{OC}} = \sqrt{\frac{Z_{SC}}{Z_{OC}}} \tag{14.17}$$

Also $$\sin\frac{h\gamma}{2}=\sqrt{\frac{\cosh\gamma-1}{2}}=\sqrt{\frac{1}{2}\left(1+\frac{Z_1}{2Z_2}-1\right)}$$

∴ $$\sin\frac{h\gamma}{2}=\sqrt{\frac{Z_1}{4Z_2}} \qquad (14.18)$$

14.5.2 Equations for π-Network

Characteristic impedance Consider a symmetrical π-network (Fig. 14.9). When the network is terminated in Z_0 at port $2-2'$, its input impedance is given by

$$Z_{in}=\frac{2Z_2\left(Z_1+\frac{2Z_2Z_0}{2Z_2+Z_0}\right)}{2Z_2+Z_1+\frac{2Z_2Z_0}{2Z_2+Z_0}}$$

$$=\frac{2Z_2[Z_1(2Z_2+Z_0)+2Z_0Z_2]}{(2Z_2+Z_1)(2Z_2+Z_0)+2Z_2Z_0}$$

$$=\frac{2Z_1Z_2(2Z_2+Z_0)+4Z_0Z_2^2}{4Z_2^2+4Z_0Z_2+2Z_1Z_2+Z_0Z_1}$$

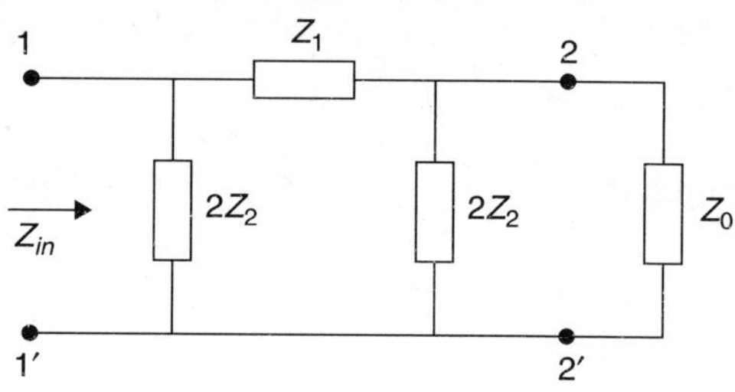

Fig. 14.9 Symmetrical π-network terminated in Z_0

By definition of characteristic impedance,

$$Z_{in}=Z_0$$

∴ $$Z_0=\frac{2Z_1Z_2(2Z_2+Z_0)+4Z_0Z_2^2}{4Z_2^2+4Z_0Z_2+2Z_1Z_2+Z_0Z_1}$$

$$4Z_2^2Z_0+4Z_0^2Z_2+2Z_0Z_1Z_2+Z_0^2Z_1=4Z_1Z_2^2+2Z_0Z_1Z_2+4Z_0Z_2^2$$

$$4Z_0^2Z_2+Z_0^2Z_1=4Z_1Z_2^2$$

$$Z_0^2(Z_1+4Z_2)=4Z_1Z_2^2$$

$$Z_0^2=\frac{4Z_1Z_2^2}{Z_1+4Z_2}=\frac{4Z_2(Z_2Z_1)}{4Z_2\left(1+\frac{Z_1}{4Z_2}\right)}=\frac{Z_1Z_2}{1+\frac{Z_1}{4Z_2}}$$

⇒ $$Z_0=\sqrt{\frac{Z_1Z_2}{1+\frac{Z_1}{4Z_2}}}=\frac{Z_1Z_2}{\sqrt{Z_1Z_2+\frac{Z_1^2}{4}}} \qquad (14.19)$$

∴ The characteristic impedance of the π-network is

$$Z_{0\pi}=\frac{Z_1Z_2}{\sqrt{Z_1Z_2+\frac{Z_1^2}{4}}} \qquad (14.20)$$

From Eq. 14.8, we have

$$Z_{0T} = \sqrt{Z_1Z_2 + \frac{Z_1^2}{4}}$$

$$\therefore \qquad Z_{0\pi} = \frac{Z_1Z_2}{Z_{0T}} \qquad (14.21)$$

The characteristic impedance of the π-network ($Z_{0\pi}$) can be expressed in terms of the open circuit impedance Z_{OC} and short circuit impedance Z_{SC} of the π-network. From Fig. 14.9, the input impedance at port $1 - 1'$ when port $2 - 2'$ is open circuited is,

$$Z_{OC} = \frac{2Z_2(Z_1 + 2Z_2)}{Z_1 + 4Z_2}$$

Similarly, the input impedance at port $1 - 1'$ when port $2 - 2'$ is short circuited is,

$$Z_{SC} = \frac{2Z_1Z_2}{2Z_2 + Z_1}$$

$$\therefore \qquad Z_{OC} \times Z_{SC} = \frac{2Z_1Z_2}{2Z_2 + Z_1} \times \frac{2Z_2(Z_1 + 2Z_2)}{Z_1 + 4Z_2} = \frac{4Z_1Z_2^2}{Z_1 + 4Z_2} = \frac{Z_1Z_2}{1 + \frac{Z_1}{4Z_2}} = Z_{0\pi}^2$$

$$\Rightarrow \qquad Z_{0\pi} = \sqrt{Z_{OC} \times Z_{SC}} \qquad (14.22)$$

Propagation constant By definition, the propagation constant γ of the network (Fig. 14.10) is given by,

$$\gamma = \ln\left(\frac{I_2}{I_1}\right)$$

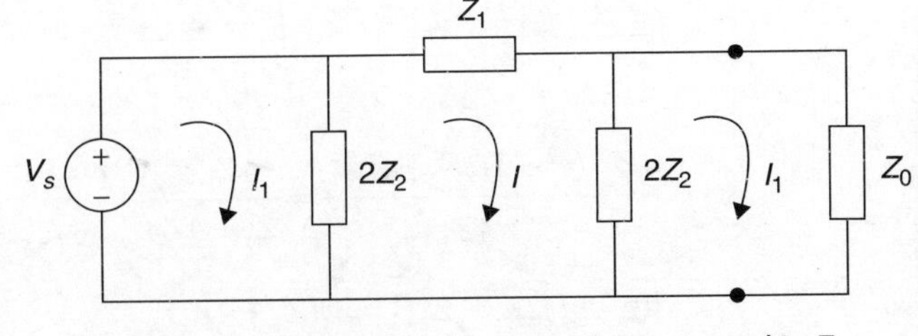

Fig. 14.10 Symmetrical π-network terminated in Z_0

Inspection of mesh analysis gives

$$\begin{bmatrix} 2Z_2 & -2Z_2 & 0 \\ -2Z_2 & Z_1 + 4Z_2 & -2Z_2 \\ 0 & -2Z_2 & 2Z_2 + Z_0 \end{bmatrix} \begin{bmatrix} I_1 \\ I_2 \\ I_3 \end{bmatrix} = \begin{bmatrix} V_S \\ 0 \\ 0 \end{bmatrix}$$

$$\Delta_1 = \begin{vmatrix} V_S & -2Z_2 & 0 \\ 0 & Z_1 + 4Z_2 & -2Z_2 \\ 0 & -2Z_2 & 2Z_2 + Z_0 \end{vmatrix}$$

$$= V_S[(Z_1 + 4Z_2)(2Z_2 + Z_0) - 4Z_2^2]$$

$$= V_S[2Z_1Z_2 + Z_0Z_1 + 4Z_2^2 + 4Z_0Z_2]$$

$$\Delta_3 = \begin{vmatrix} 2Z_2 & -2Z_2 & V_S \\ -2Z_2 & Z_1 + 4Z_2 & 0 \\ 0 & -2Z_2 & 0 \end{vmatrix} = V_S \times 4Z_2^2$$

$$\frac{I_1}{I_2} = \frac{\Delta_1/\Delta}{\Delta_3/\Delta} = \frac{\Delta_1}{\Delta_3} = \frac{V_S[2Z_1Z_2 + Z_0Z_1 + 4Z_2^2 + 4Z_0Z_2]}{V_S \times 4Z_2^2}$$

$$\frac{I_1}{I_2} = e^{\gamma} = \frac{2Z_1Z_2}{4Z_2^2} + \frac{Z_1Z_0}{4Z_2^2} + \frac{4Z_2^2}{4Z_2^2} + \frac{4Z_0Z_2}{4Z_2^2}$$

$$e^{\gamma} = \frac{Z_1}{2Z_2} + \frac{Z_1Z_0}{4Z_2^2} + 1 + \frac{4Z_0Z_2}{4Z_2^2}$$

$$e^{\gamma} - 1 = \frac{Z_1}{2Z_2} + \frac{(Z_1 + 4Z_2)Z_0}{4Z_2^2}$$

$$\left(\frac{Z_1 + 4Z_2}{4Z_2^2}\right)Z_0 = e^{\gamma} - 1 - \frac{Z_1}{2Z_2} = \frac{(e^{\gamma} - 1)2Z_2 - Z_1}{2Z_2}$$

$$Z_0 = \frac{(e^{\gamma} - 1)2Z_2 - Z_1}{2Z_2} \times \frac{4Z_2^2}{Z_1 + 4Z_2} = \frac{2Z_2[(e^{\gamma} - 1)2Z_2 - Z_1]}{Z_1 + 4Z_2} \tag{14.23}$$

The characteristic impedance of the π-network is given by

$$Z_0 = \sqrt{\frac{4Z_1Z_2^2}{Z_1 + 4Z_2}} \tag{14.24}$$

From Eqs 14.23 and 14.24, we have

$$\frac{2Z_2[(e^{\gamma} - 1)2Z_2 - Z_1]}{Z_1 + 4Z_2} = \sqrt{\frac{4Z_1Z_2^2}{Z_1 + 4Z_2}}$$

$$\frac{4Z_2^2[(e^{\gamma} - 1)2Z_2 - Z_1]^2}{(Z_1 + 4Z_2)^2} = \frac{4Z_1Z_2^2}{Z_1 + 4Z_2}$$

$$[(e^{\gamma} - 1)2Z_2 - Z_1]^2 = Z_1(Z_1 + 4Z_2)$$

$$(e^{\gamma} - 1)^2 4Z_2^2 - 4Z_1Z_2(e^{\gamma} - 1) = Z_1^2 + 4Z_1Z_2$$

$$(e^{\gamma} - 1)^2 4Z_2 + Z_1^2 - 4Z_1e^{\gamma} + 4Z_1 = 4Z_1$$

$$(e^{\gamma} - 1)^2 4Z_2 = 4Z_1e^{\gamma}$$

$$\frac{(e^{\gamma} - 1)^2}{e^{\gamma}} = \frac{Z_1}{Z_2}$$

$$\frac{(e^{2\gamma} + 1 - 2e^{\gamma})}{e^{\gamma}} = \frac{Z_1}{Z_2}$$

$$e^{\gamma} + e^{-\gamma} - 2 = \frac{Z_1}{Z_2}$$

$$\frac{e^{\gamma}+e^{-\gamma}}{2}=1+\frac{Z_1}{Z_2}$$

$$\cos h\gamma=1+\frac{Z_1}{Z_2} \tag{14.25}$$

$$\sin h\gamma=\sqrt{\cos h^2\gamma-1}=\sqrt{\left(1+\frac{Z_1}{2Z_2}\right)^2-1}=\sqrt{\left(\frac{Z_1}{2Z_2}\right)^2+\frac{Z_1}{Z_2}}=\frac{1}{Z_2}\sqrt{Z_1Z_2+\frac{Z_1^2}{4}}$$

$$\Rightarrow \quad \sin h\gamma=\frac{1}{Z_2}\sqrt{Z_1Z_2+\frac{Z_1^2}{4}} \tag{14.26}$$

14.6 CLASSIFICATION OF PASS-BAND AND STOP-BAND OR FILTER CHARACTERISTICS

An ideal characteristic of a filter requires that it should transmit the band of frequencies desired, without any loss and should stop or completely attenuate the other frequencies. The ability of any filter network to work as per requirement is decided by the propagation constant (γ) of the network. The propagation constant, being a function of frequency, the pass-band, stop-band and cut-off point (the point of separation between two-bands), can be identified. The propagation constant is given by

$$\frac{I_1}{I_2}=e^{\gamma}=e^{\alpha+i\beta}$$

$$\Rightarrow \quad \left|\frac{I_1}{I_2}\right|=e^{\alpha} \tag{14.27}$$

When $\alpha=0$, the output current of the filter is same as the input current, indicates no attenuation but only the phase shift in the output current. This is the operation of the filter in the pass-band.

When $\alpha>0$, the magnitude of the output current is smaller than the input current, indicating attenuation in the output current. This is due to the operation of the filter in the stop-band. We know that from Eq. 14.18,

$$\sin\frac{h\gamma}{2}=\sqrt{\frac{Z_1}{4Z_2}}$$

Putting $\gamma=\alpha+i\beta$

$$\sin h\left(\frac{\alpha+i\beta}{2}\right)=\left(\sin h\frac{\alpha}{2}\cos\frac{\beta}{2}+i\cos h\frac{\alpha}{2}\sin\frac{\beta}{2}\right)=\sqrt{\frac{Z_1}{4Z_2}} \tag{14.28}$$

From Eq. 14.28, it is clear that the values of α and β also depend on the nature of the two impedances Z_1 and Z_2. We observe that if Z_1 and Z_2 are reactances, the ratio $\frac{Z_1}{4Z_2}$ is positive and real if Z_1 and Z_2 are of same type, and the ratio $\frac{Z_1}{4Z_2}$ is negative and real if they are of opposite type.

Case (i) $\frac{Z_1}{4Z_2}>0$

In this case, the impedances Z_1 and Z_2 are of the same type. The ratio $\frac{Z_1}{4Z_2}$ is real, so the imaginary part of the Eq. 14.28 must be zero. So from Eq. 14.28, we have

$$\cos h\frac{a}{2}\sin\frac{\beta}{2}=0 \tag{14.29}$$

$$\Rightarrow \qquad \sin h\frac{\alpha}{2}\cos\frac{\beta}{2}=\sqrt{\frac{Z_1}{4Z_2}} \tag{14.30}$$

From Eq. 14.29, $\cos h\frac{\alpha}{2}\sin\frac{\beta}{2}=0$

$$\Rightarrow \qquad \sin\frac{\beta}{2}=0$$

$$\Rightarrow \qquad \frac{\beta}{2}=n\pi; \quad \text{For } n = 0, 1, 2 \ldots n$$

$$\Rightarrow \qquad \beta=2n\pi; \quad \text{For } n = 0, 1, 2 \ldots n$$

For these values of β, $\cos\frac{\beta}{2}=\pm 1$

From Eq. 14.30, $\sin h\frac{\alpha}{2}=\sqrt{\frac{Z_1}{4Z_2}}$

$$\Rightarrow \qquad \alpha = 2\sin h^{-1}\sqrt{\frac{Z_1}{4Z_2}} \tag{14.31}$$

Hence, $\frac{Z_1}{4Z_2}>0$ implies that Z_1 and Z_2 are of the same type and it always corresponds to the stop-band or attenuation band.

Case (ii) $\frac{Z_1}{4Z_2}<0$

In this case, the impedances Z_1 and Z_2 are of the opposite type. The ratio $\frac{Z_1}{4Z_2}$ is negative and it makes $\sin h\frac{\gamma}{2}$ purely imaginary. So from Eq. 14.28 we have,

$$\sin h\frac{\alpha}{2}\cos\frac{\beta}{2}=0 \tag{14.32}$$

$$\cos h\frac{\alpha}{2}\sin\frac{\beta}{2}=\sqrt{\frac{Z_1}{4Z_2}} \tag{14.33}$$

From Eq. 14.32, $\sin h\frac{\alpha}{2}=0 \Rightarrow \alpha=0$

$$\Rightarrow \qquad \cos\frac{\beta}{2}=0$$

$$\Rightarrow \qquad \beta=(2n-1)\pi; \quad \text{for} \quad n=0, 1, 2 \ldots n$$

Case (a) $\sin h\frac{\alpha}{2}=0 \Rightarrow \alpha=0, \beta\neq 0$

This corresponds to the pass-band, since $a = 0$. By substituting α in Eq. 14.33,

$$\sin\frac{\beta}{2}=\sqrt{\frac{Z_1}{4Z_2}}$$

$$\Rightarrow \quad \beta=2\sin^{-1}\sqrt{\frac{Z_1}{4Z_2}}$$

Since the limiting value of $\sin\frac{\beta}{2}$ is 1, and $\frac{Z_1}{4Z_2}$ is negative, $\frac{Z_1}{4Z_2}$ must be in the limits $-1<\frac{Z_1}{4Z_2}<0$

Case (b) $\cos\frac{\beta}{2}=0$

$$\Rightarrow \quad \beta=(2n-1)\pi; \quad \text{for} \quad n=0,1,2\ldots n,\ \alpha\neq 0$$

For $\beta=(2n-1)\pi,\ \sin\frac{\beta}{2}=\pm 1$

This corresponds to the stop-band, since $\alpha\neq 0$

Substituting for β in Eq. 14.33,

$$\cosh\frac{\alpha}{2}=\sqrt{\frac{Z_1}{4Z_2}} \tag{14.34}$$

$$\Rightarrow \quad \alpha=2\cosh^{-1}\sqrt{\frac{Z_1}{4Z_2}} \tag{14.35}$$

Since $\cosh\frac{\alpha}{2}$ cannot be less than unity and $\frac{Z_1}{4Z_2}$ is negative, $\frac{Z_1}{4Z_2}$ must be in the limits

$$-\alpha<\frac{Z_1}{4Z_2}<-1$$

To summarise

(i) We have stop-band when $\frac{Z_1}{4Z_2}>0$.

(ii) We have pass-band when $-1<\frac{Z_1}{4Z_2}<0$.

(iii) We have stop-band when $-\alpha<\frac{Z_1}{4Z_2}<-1$.

Case (iii) Cut-off frequency

The two frequencies which separate the pass-band from the two stop-bands are known as cut-off frequencies, which are obtained when $-1<\frac{Z_1}{4Z_2}<0$

$$\frac{Z_1}{4Z_2}=0 \Rightarrow Z_1=0 \tag{14.36}$$

$$\frac{Z_1}{4Z_2}=-1 \Rightarrow Z_1=-4Z_2 \tag{14.37}$$

14.7 CONSTANT *K* OR PROTOTYPE FILTER

A T or π-network in which the series and shunt arm impedances Z_1 and Z_2 satisfy the relationship: $Z_1Z_2 = K^2 = R_0^2$, where R_0 is a real constant is called constant K section. For the same series and shunt arm impedances, the characteristic impedances of T or π-network can be related with each other as:

$$Z_{0\pi} = \frac{Z_1Z_2}{Z_{0T}}$$

For a constant K section, we can write,

$$Z_{0\pi} = \frac{R_0^2}{Z_{0T}}$$

The constant K, either T or π section, are also known as prototype because more complex filters can be derived from them.

14.7.1 Constant *K* Low-pass Filter

A constant K low-pass filter is shown in Fig. 14.11.

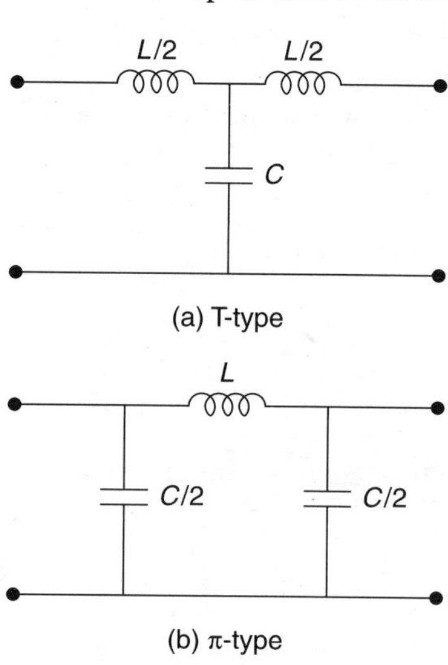

Fig. 14.11 Constant K pass filter

(i) **Design impedance (R_0):** For both T or π section filters,

$$Z_1 = j\omega L = \text{total series arm impedance}$$

$$Z_2 = \frac{1}{j\omega C} = \text{total shunt arm impedance}$$

$Z_1Z_2 = j\omega L \times \dfrac{1}{j\omega C} = \dfrac{L}{C}$, which is real and constant. Hence these filters are constant K filters, so,

$$R_0^2 = Z_1Z_2 = \frac{L}{C}$$

$$\Rightarrow \quad R_0 = \sqrt{\frac{L}{C}} \tag{14.38}$$

(ii) **Cut-off frequency (f_c):** The cut-off frequency is given by

$$Z_1 = 0 \quad \text{for} \quad f = f_c$$

$$\Rightarrow \quad j\omega_c L = 0$$

$$\Rightarrow \quad \omega_c = 0 \quad \Rightarrow \quad f_c = 0$$

$$Z_1 + 4Z_2 = 0, \quad \text{for} \quad f_c = 0$$

$$\Rightarrow \quad j\omega_c L + \frac{4}{j\omega_c C} = 0$$

$$\Rightarrow \quad \omega_c L = \frac{4}{\omega_c C}$$

$$\Rightarrow \quad \omega_c^2 = \frac{4}{LC}$$

$$\Rightarrow \quad \omega_c = \frac{2}{\sqrt{LC}}$$

$$\Rightarrow \quad f_c = \frac{1}{\pi\sqrt{LC}} \tag{14.39}$$

Hence, the pass-band of constant K low-pass filter extends from 0 to $\frac{1}{\pi\sqrt{LC}}$.

(iii) **Attenuation constant (α)** In the pass-band, $\alpha = 0$.

In the stop-band, $\alpha = 2\cosh^{-1}\sqrt{\left|\frac{Z_1}{4Z_2}\right|} = 2\cosh^{-1}\sqrt{\left|\frac{\frac{j\omega L}{4}}{j\omega C}\right|} = 2\cosh^{-1}\sqrt{\frac{\omega^2 LC}{4}}$

$$\Rightarrow \quad \alpha = 2\cosh^{-1}\left(\frac{f}{f_c}\right) \tag{14.40}$$

(iv) **Phase shift (β)**: The phase shift β in pass-band is given by

$$\beta = 2\sin^{-1}\sqrt{\left|\frac{Z_1}{4Z_1}\right|} = 2\sin^{-1}\sqrt{\left|\frac{j\omega L}{4\times\frac{1}{j\omega C}}\right|} = 2\sin^{-1}\sqrt{\frac{\omega^2 LC}{4}}$$

$$\Rightarrow \quad \beta = 2\sin^{-1}\left(\frac{f}{f_c}\right) \tag{14.41}$$

The variations α and β with frequency are shown in Fig. 14.12.

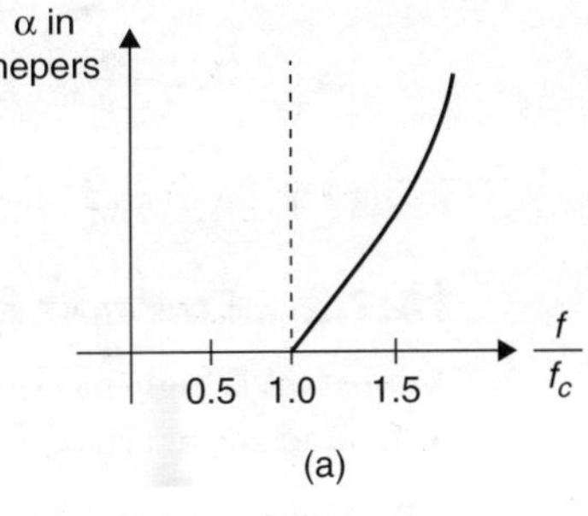

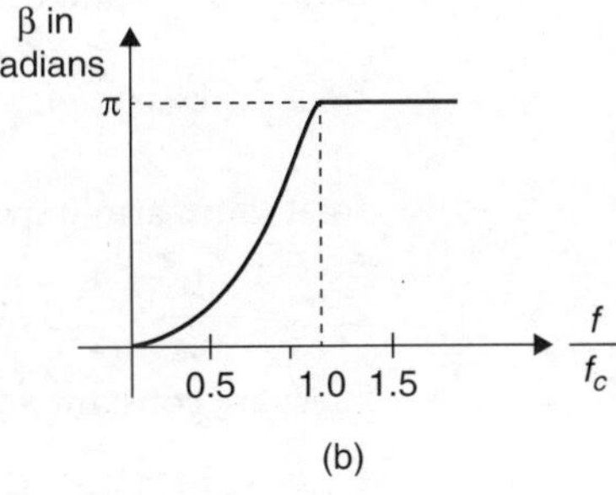

Fig. 14.12 Variation of α and β of constant K low-pass filter with frequency

(v) **Variation of Z_{0T} and $Z_{0\pi}$ with frequency:**

For T section, $Z_{0T} = \sqrt{\frac{Z_1^2}{4} + Z_1 Z_2} = \sqrt{\frac{(j\omega L)^2}{4} + \frac{L}{C}} = \sqrt{\frac{-\omega^2 L^2}{4} + \frac{L}{C}}$

$$= \sqrt{\frac{L}{C}}\sqrt{1 - \frac{\omega^2 LC}{4}} = R_0\sqrt{1 - \frac{4\pi^2 f^2 LC}{4}}$$

$$\Rightarrow \quad Z_{0T} = R_0\sqrt{1 - \left(\frac{f}{f_c}\right)^2} \tag{14.42}$$

Similarly we can write, $Z_{0\pi} = \frac{Z_1 Z_2}{Z_{0T}}$

$$\therefore \quad Z_{0\pi} = \frac{R_0^2}{R_0\sqrt{1 - \left(\frac{f}{f_c}\right)^2}} = \frac{R_0}{\sqrt{1 - \left(\frac{f}{f_c}\right)^2}} \tag{14.43}$$

From Eq. 14.42 it is clear that as frequency increases from 0 to f_c, Z_{0T} decreases from R_0 to 0 in the pass-band. For π-section, from Eq. 14.43 it is clear that in the pass-band, as frequency increases from 0 to f_c, $Z_{0\pi}$ increases from R_0 to ∞. The variations of Z_{0T} and $Z_{0\pi}$ with frequency are shown in Fig. 14.13.

(vi) **Design of constant K Low-pass Filter**: If the cut-off frequency f_c and the design impedance R_0 for a filter are given, we can design the constant K low-pass filter from Eqs 14.38 and 14.39.

From Eq. 14.38, we have

$$R_0 = \sqrt{\frac{L}{C}} \Rightarrow L = CR_0^2 \quad (14.44)$$

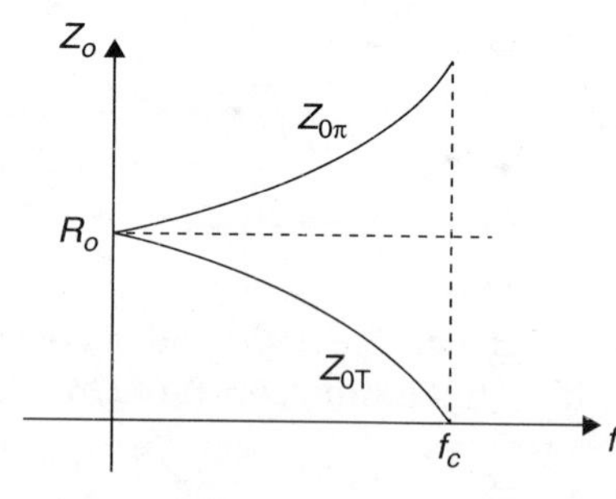

Fig. 14.13 Variation of Z_0 with frequency

From Eq. 14.39, we have

$$f_c = \frac{1}{\pi\sqrt{LC}}$$

$$f_c^2 = \frac{1}{\pi^2 LC} = \frac{1}{\pi^2 C^2 R_0^2}$$

$$\Rightarrow \quad C^2 = \frac{1}{\pi^2 R_0^2 f_c^2}$$

$$\Rightarrow \quad C = \frac{1}{\pi f_c R_0} \quad (14.45)$$

From Eq. 14.44, we have

$$L = CR_0^2 = \frac{1}{\pi f_c R_0} \times R_0^2$$

$$\Rightarrow \quad L = \frac{R_0}{\pi f_c} \quad (14.46)$$

Using Eqs 14.45 and 14.46 we can design the constant K low-pass filter.

14.7.2 Constant *K* High-pass Filter

A constant K high-pass filter using symmetrical T and π-section is shown in Fig. 14.14. By interchanging the series and shunt arms of a constant K low-pass filter, we can get the constant K high-pass filter.

(i) Design impedance (R_0): For both T and π-section filters,

Total series arm impedance $Z_1 = \frac{1}{j\omega C}$

Total shunt arm impedance $Z_2 = j\omega L$

$Z_1 Z_2 = \frac{1}{j\omega C} \times j\omega L$, which is real and constant. Hence these filters are constant K filters, so

$$R_0^2 = Z_1 Z_2 = \frac{L}{C}$$

$$\therefore \quad R_0 = \sqrt{\frac{L}{C}} \quad (14.47)$$

(ii) Cut-off frequency (f_c): The cut off frequencies are given by

$$Z_1 = 0 \quad \text{for} \quad f = f_c$$

$$\therefore \quad \frac{1}{j\omega_c C} = 0$$

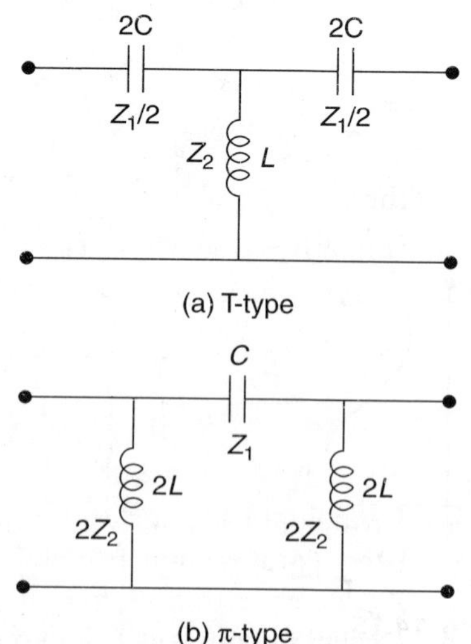

Fig. 14.14 Constant K high-pass filter

$$\Rightarrow \quad \omega_c = \infty \quad \Rightarrow \quad f_c = \infty$$

$$Z_1 + 4Z_2 = 0 \quad \text{for} \quad f = f_c$$

$$\frac{1}{j\omega_c C} = -4j\omega_c L$$

$$\Rightarrow \quad \omega_c L = \frac{1}{4\omega_c C}$$

$$\Rightarrow \quad \omega_c^2 = \frac{1}{4LC}$$

$$\Rightarrow \quad \omega_c = \frac{1}{2\sqrt{LC}}$$

$$\Rightarrow \quad f_c = \frac{1}{4\pi\sqrt{LC}} \tag{14.48}$$

(iii) Attenuation constant (α): In pass-band, $\alpha = 0$

In stop-band, $\alpha = 2\cosh^{-1}\sqrt{\left|\frac{Z_1}{4Z_2}\right|}$

$$\alpha = 2\cosh^{-1}\sqrt{\left|\frac{1}{j\omega C \times 4j\omega L}\right|} = 2\cosh^{-1}\sqrt{\left|\frac{1}{4\omega^2 LC}\right|} = 2\cosh^{-1}\frac{f_c}{f}\left(\because \frac{1}{\sqrt{LC}} = 4\pi f_c\right)$$

$$\Rightarrow \quad \alpha = 2\cosh^{-1}\frac{f_c}{f} \tag{14.49}$$

(iv) Phase Constant (β): In the stop-band, $\beta = \pi$

In the pass-band, $\beta = 2\sin^{-1}\sqrt{\left|\frac{Z_1}{4Z_2}\right|} = 2\sin^{-1}\sqrt{\left|\frac{1}{j\omega C \times 4j\omega L}\right|} = 2\sin^{-1}\sqrt{\left|\frac{1}{4\omega^2 CL}\right|}$

$$\Rightarrow \quad \beta = 2\sin^{-1}\left(\frac{f_c}{f}\right) \tag{14.50}$$

The variations of α and β with frequency are shown in Fig. 14.15.

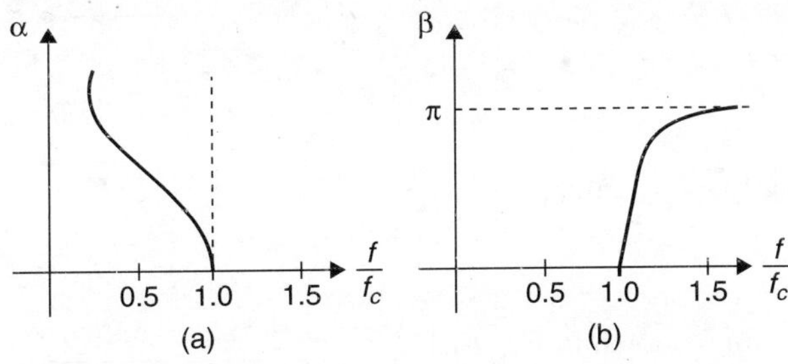

Fig. 14.15 Variation of α and β of constant K high-pass filters with frequency

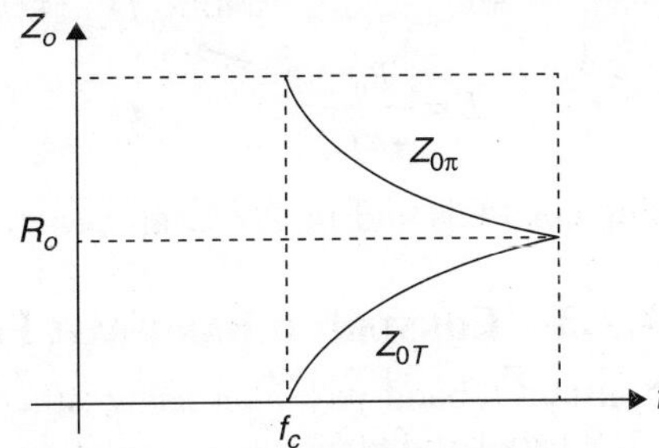

Fig. 14.16 Variation of Z_0 with frequency

(v) **Variation of Z_{0T} and $Z_{0\pi}$ with frequency:** For *T* section filter,

$$Z_{0T} = \sqrt{Z_1 Z_2\left(1+\frac{Z_1}{4Z_2}\right)} = \sqrt{\frac{L}{C}\left(1-\frac{1}{4\omega^2 LC}\right)} = \sqrt{\frac{L}{C}}\sqrt{1-\frac{1}{4\omega^2 LC}} = R_0\sqrt{1-\left(\frac{f_c}{f}\right)^2}$$

$$\Rightarrow \qquad Z_{0T} = R_0\sqrt{1-\left(\frac{f_c}{f}\right)^2} \qquad (14.51)$$

Similarly we can write

$$Z_{0\pi} = \frac{Z_1 Z_2}{Z_{0\text{T}}} = \frac{R_0^2}{R_0\sqrt{1-\left(\frac{f_c}{f}\right)^2}} = \frac{R_0}{\sqrt{1-\left(\frac{f_c}{f}\right)^2}} \qquad (14.52)$$

From Eq. 14.51 it is clear that as frequency increases from f_c to ∞, Z_{0T} also increases from 0 to R_0 in the pass-band. For π-section, from Eq. 14.43, it is clear that as frequency increases from f_c to ∞, $Z_{0\pi}$ decreases from ∞ to R_0 in the pass-band. The variations of $Z_{0\pi}$ and Z_{0T} with frequency is shown in Fig. 14.16.

(vi) **Design of constant *K* high-pass filter:** We know that

From Eq. 14.47, $R_0 = \sqrt{\frac{L}{C}} \;\Rightarrow\; L = R_0^2 C$ (14.53)

From Eq. 14.48, $f_c = \frac{1}{4\pi\sqrt{LC}}$

$$f_c^2 = \frac{1}{16\pi^2 LC} = \frac{1}{16\pi^2 R_0^2 C\times C}$$

$$C^2 = \frac{1}{16\pi^2 R_0^2 f_c^2}$$

$$\Rightarrow \qquad C = \frac{1}{4\pi R_0 f_c} \qquad (14.54)$$

From Eq. 14.53, we have

$$L = R_0^2\times C = R_0^2\times\frac{1}{4\pi R_0 f_c} = \frac{R_0}{4\pi f_c}$$

$$\Rightarrow \qquad L = \frac{R_0}{4\pi f_c} \qquad (14.55)$$

Using Eqs 14.54 and 14.55 we can design a constant *K* high-pass filter.

14.7.3 Constant *K* Band-pass Filter

A constant *K* band-pass filter using either *T* or π-section is shown in Fig. 14.17.

The pass-band filter is a combination of a series resonant circuit in the series arm and parallel resonant circuit in the shunt arm. If the two resonance frequencies are equal, we have

$$\omega_0^2 = \frac{1}{L_1C_1} = \frac{1}{L_2C_2} \quad (14.56)$$

$$\Rightarrow \quad L_1C_1 = L_2C_2$$

L₁/2 2C₁ 2C₁ L₁/2

L₂ C₂

(a) T-network

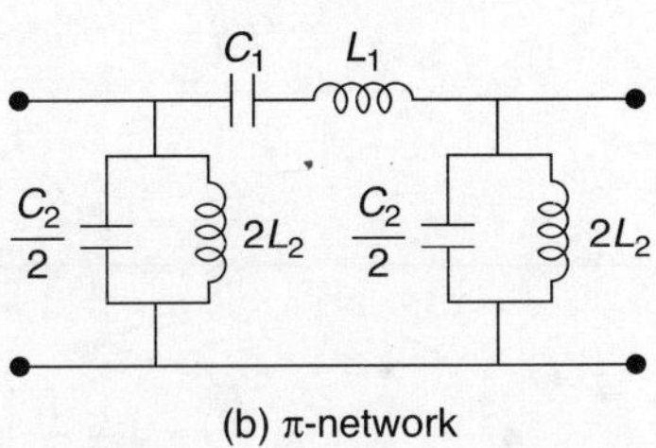

(b) π-network

Fig. 14.17 Constant *K* band-pass filter

(i) **Design impedance (R_0 or Z_0):** The impedance Z_1 and Z_2 of the series and shunt arms are given by,

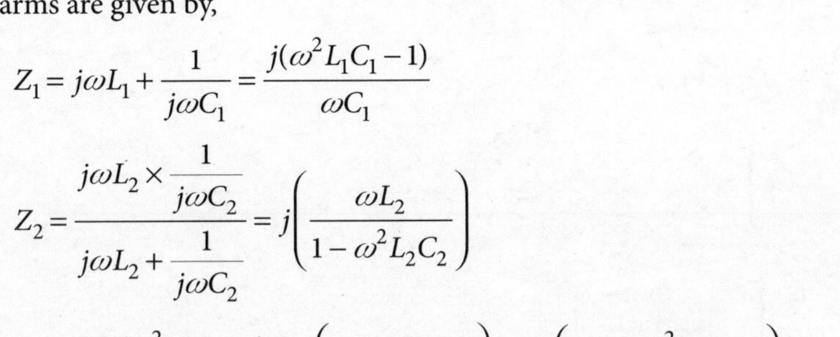

$$Z_1 = j\omega L_1 + \frac{1}{j\omega C_1} = \frac{j(\omega^2 L_1C_1 - 1)}{\omega C_1}$$

$$Z_2 = \frac{j\omega L_2 \times \dfrac{1}{j\omega C_2}}{j\omega L_2 + \dfrac{1}{j\omega C_2}} = j\left(\frac{\omega L_2}{1-\omega^2 L_2C_2}\right)$$

$$Z_1Z_2 = \frac{j(\omega^2 L_1C_1 - 1)}{\omega C_1} \times j\left(\frac{\omega L_2}{1-\omega^2 L_2C_2}\right) = L_2\left(\frac{1-\omega^2 L_1C_1}{C_1(1-\omega^2 L_2C_2)}\right)$$

$$\Rightarrow \quad Z_1Z_2 = \frac{L_2}{C_1} \text{ or } \frac{L_1}{C_2} \quad (\because L_1C_1 = L_2C_2)$$

$Z_1Z_2 = \dfrac{L_2}{C_1}$ or $\dfrac{L_1}{C_2}$ which is real and constant. Hence, the above sections are constant *K* sections. So,

$$R_0^2 = \frac{L_2}{C_1} = \frac{L_1}{C_2}$$

$$\Rightarrow \quad R_0 = \sqrt{\frac{L_2}{C_1}} = \sqrt{\frac{L_1}{C_2}} \quad (14.57)$$

(ii) **Cut-off frequency (f_c):** To find the cut-off frequency we have

$$Z_1 + 4Z_2 = 0$$

$$Z_1 = -4Z_2$$

$$Z_1Z_1 = -4Z_1Z_2$$

$$Z_1^2 = j^2 4Z_1Z_2 = j^2 4Z_0^2$$

$$\Rightarrow \quad Z_1 = \pm j2Z_0 \quad (14.58)$$

From Eq. 14.58, we can get two cut-off frequencies.

At cut-off frequency $f_c = f_1$, $Z_1 = -j2Z_0$

At cut-off frequency $f_c = f_2$, $Z_2 = j2Z_0$

Thus, the impedance Z_1 at f_1 (lower cut-off frequency) is the negative of the impedance Z_1 at f_2 (upper cut-off frequency). Hence we can write,

$$j\left(\omega L_1 - \frac{1}{\omega C_1}\right)_{f_c = f_1} = -j\left(\omega L_1 - \frac{1}{\omega C_1}\right)_{f_c = f_2}$$

$$\omega_1 L_1 - \frac{1}{\omega_1 C_1} = -\left(\omega_2 L_1 - \frac{1}{\omega_2 C_1}\right)$$

$$\frac{\omega_1^2 L_1 C_1 - 1}{\omega_1 C_1} = -\left(\frac{\omega_2^2 L_1 C_1 - 1}{\omega_2 C_1}\right)$$

$$\omega_1^2 L_1 C_1 - 1 = \frac{\omega_1}{\omega_2}(1 - \omega_2^2 L_1 C_1)$$

$$\frac{\omega_1^2}{\omega_0^2} - 1 = \frac{\omega_1}{\omega_2}\left(1 - \frac{\omega_2^2}{\omega_0^2}\right)$$

$$\frac{f_1^2}{f_0^2} - 1 = \frac{f_1}{f_2}\left(1 - \frac{f_2^2}{f_0^2}\right)$$

$$f_1^2 - f_0^2 = \frac{f_1}{f_2}(f_0^2 - f_2^2)$$

$$f_1^2 f_2 - f_0^2 f_2 = f_1 f_0^2 - f_1 f_2^2$$

$$\Rightarrow \quad f_0^2(f_1 + f_2) = f_1 f_2 (f_1 + f_2)$$

$$\Rightarrow \quad f_0 = \sqrt{f_1 f_2} \tag{14.59}$$

Hence, Eq. 14.59 indicates that the frequency of resonance of the individual arms is the geometric mean of two cut-off frequencies.

(iii) Design of constant *K* band-pass filter: Consider that the filter is terminated in design impedance Z_0 and the cut-off frequencies are f_1 and f_2.

From Eq. 14.58,

$$Z_1 = -j2Z_0$$

$$j\omega_1 L_1 - \frac{j}{\omega_1 C_1} = -j2Z_0$$

$$\omega_1 L_1 - \frac{1}{\omega_1 C_1} = -2Z_0$$

$$\Rightarrow \quad \omega_1^2 L_1 C_1 - 1 = -2Z_0 \omega_1 C_1$$

$$\Rightarrow \quad 1 - \frac{\omega_1^2}{\omega_0^2} = 2Z_0 \omega_1 C_1$$

$$\Rightarrow \quad 1 - \frac{f_1^2}{f_0^2} = 2Z_0 2\pi f_1 C_1$$

$$\Rightarrow \quad 1 - \frac{f_1^2}{f_1 f_2} = 4\pi Z_0 f_1 C_1$$

$$\Rightarrow \quad f_2 - f_1 = 4\pi Z_0 f_1 f_2 C_1$$

$$\Rightarrow \quad C_1 = \frac{f_2 - f_1}{4\pi Z_0 f_1 f_2} \tag{14.60}$$

From Eq. 14.56, we have

$$L_1 C_1 = \frac{1}{\omega_0^2} = \frac{1}{4\pi^2 f_1 f_2}$$

$$\Rightarrow \quad L_1 = \frac{1}{4\pi^2 f_1 f_2 C_1} = \frac{1}{4\pi^2 f_1 f_2} \times \frac{4\pi Z_0 f_1 f_2}{f_2 - f_1} = \frac{Z_0}{\pi(f_2 - f_1)}$$

$$\Rightarrow \quad L_1 = \frac{Z_0}{\pi(f_2 - f_1)} \tag{14.61}$$

The other parameters can also be found using

$$Z_0 = \sqrt{\frac{L_1}{C_2}} = \sqrt{\frac{L_2}{C_1}}$$

$$\Rightarrow \quad \frac{L_1}{C_2} = Z_0^2$$

$$\Rightarrow \quad C_2 = \frac{L_1}{Z_0^2} = \frac{Z_0}{\pi(f_2 - f_1)Z_0^2} = \frac{1}{Z_0 \pi(f_2 - f_1)}$$

$$\therefore \quad C_2 = \frac{1}{Z_0 \pi(f_2 - f_1)} \tag{14.62}$$

Also, $\frac{L_2}{C_1} = Z_0^2$

$$\Rightarrow \quad L_2 = C_1 Z_0^2 = \frac{f_2 - f_1}{4\pi Z_0 f_1 f_2} Z_0^2 = \frac{Z_0(f_2 - f_1)}{4\pi f_1 f_2}$$

$$\Rightarrow \quad L_2 = \frac{Z_0(f_2 - f_1)}{4\pi f_1 f_2} \tag{14.63}$$

Using Eqs 14.60–14.63, we can design the constant K band-pass filter.

14.7.4 Constant *K* Band-stop Filters

If the series arm and shunt arm of the band-pass filters are interchanged we can get a band-stop filter. The T and π configuration of a proto type constant K band-stop filter are shown in Fig. 14.18.

The band-stop filter is a combination of a parallel resonant circuit in the series arm and a series resonant circuit in the shunt arm. If the two resonant frequencies are equal, we have

$$\omega_0^2 = \frac{1}{L_1 C_1} = \frac{1}{L_2 C_2} \tag{14.64}$$

$$\Rightarrow \quad L_1 C_1 = L_2 C_2$$

(i) **Design impedance (R_0 or Z_0):** The total series arm impedance is given by

$$Z_1 = \frac{j\omega L_1 \times \dfrac{-j}{\omega C_1}}{j\omega L_1 - \dfrac{j}{\omega C_1}} = \frac{-j\omega L_1}{\omega^2 L_1 C_1 - 1}$$

$$Z_2 = j\omega L_2 - \frac{j}{\omega C_2} = j\left(\omega L_2 - \frac{1}{\omega C_2}\right) = \frac{j(\omega^2 L_2 C_2 - 1)}{\omega C_2}$$

$$Z_1 Z_2 = \left(\frac{-j\omega L_1}{\omega^2 L_1 C_1 - 1}\right) \times \frac{j(\omega^2 L_2 C_2 - 1)}{\omega C_2} = \frac{L_1}{C_2} \times \left(\frac{\omega^2 L_2 C_2 - 1}{\omega^2 L_1 C_1 - 1}\right)$$

$$\Rightarrow \quad Z_1 Z_2 = \frac{L_1}{C_2} \text{ or } \frac{L_2}{C_1} \quad (\because L_1 C_1 = L_2 C_2)$$

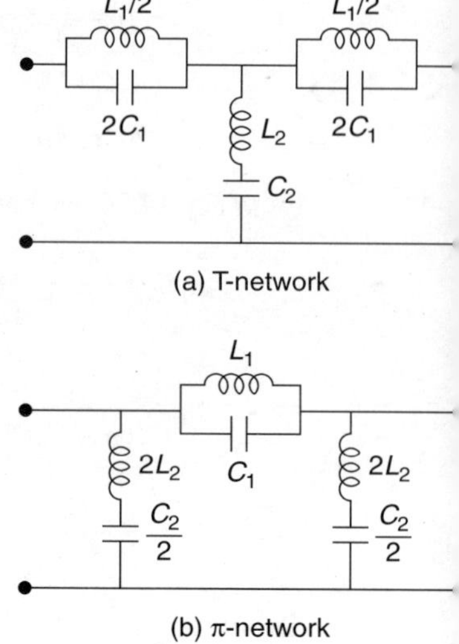

Fig. 14.18 Constant K band-stop filters

$Z_1 Z_2 = \dfrac{L_1}{C_2}$ or $\dfrac{L_2}{C_1}$, which is real and constant. Hence the above sections are constant K sections. So,

$$R_0^2 = \frac{L_2}{C_1} = \frac{L_1}{C_2}$$

$$\Rightarrow \quad R_0 = \sqrt{\frac{L_2}{C_1}} = \sqrt{\frac{L_1}{C_2}} \tag{14.65}$$

(ii) **Cut-off frequency (f_c):** To find the cut-off frequency we have

$$Z_1 + 4Z_2 = 0$$

$$Z_1 = -4Z_2$$

$$Z_1 Z_1 = -4Z_1 Z_2$$

$$Z_1^2 = j^2 4Z_1 Z_2 = j^2 4Z_0^2$$

$$\Rightarrow \quad Z_1 = \pm j2Z_0 \tag{14.66}$$

From Eq. 14.66, we can get two cut-off frequencies.

At cut-off frequency $f_c = f_1$, $Z_1 = j2Z_0$

At cut-off frequency $f_c = f_2$, $Z_2 = -j2Z_0$

Thus, the impedance Z_1 at f_1 (lower cut-off frequency) is the negative of the impedance Z_1 at f_2 (upper cut-off frequency). Hence we can write,

$$\left(\frac{-j\omega L_1}{\omega^2 L_1 C_1 - 1}\right)_{f_c = f_1} = \left(\frac{j\omega L_1}{\omega^2 L_1 C_1 - 1}\right)_{f_c = f_2}$$

$$\frac{\omega_1 L_1}{\omega_1^2 L_1 C_1 - 1} = \frac{-(\omega_2 L_1)}{\omega_2^2 L_1 C_1 - 1}$$

$$1-\omega_2^2 L_1C_1=\frac{\omega_2}{\omega_1}(\omega_1^2 L_1C_1-1)$$

$$1-\frac{\omega_2^2}{\omega_0^2}=\frac{\omega_2}{\omega_1}\left(\frac{\omega_1^2}{\omega_0^2}-1\right)$$

$$\frac{\omega_0^2-\omega_2^2}{\omega_0^2}=\frac{\omega_2}{\omega_1}\left(\frac{\omega_1^2-\omega_0^2}{\omega_0^2}\right)$$

$$\omega_1\omega_0^2-\omega_1\omega_2^2=\omega_1^2\omega_2-\omega_0^2\omega_2$$

$$\omega_0^2(\omega_1+\omega_2)=\omega_1\omega_2(\omega_1+\omega_2)$$

$$\omega_0=\sqrt{\omega_1\omega_2}$$

$$\Rightarrow \quad f_0=\sqrt{f_1f_2} \tag{14.67}$$

(iii) Design of constant *K* band-stop filter: Consider that the filter is terminated in design impedance Z_0 and the cut-off frequencies are f_1 and f_2.

From Eq. 14.66,

$$Z_1=j2Z_0$$

$$\frac{-j\omega_1L_1}{\omega_1^2L_1C_1-1}=j2Z_0$$

$$\frac{\omega_1L_1}{1-\omega_1^2L_1C_1}=2Z_0$$

$$\omega_1L_1=2Z_0\left(1-\frac{\omega_1^2}{\omega_0^2}\right)=2Z_0\left(1-\frac{\omega_1^2}{\omega_1\omega_2}\right)$$

$$\Rightarrow \quad \omega_1L_1=2Z_0\left(\frac{\omega_2-\omega_1}{\omega_2}\right)$$

$$\Rightarrow \quad L_1=\frac{2Z_0 2\pi(f_2-f_1)}{(2\pi)^2 f_1f_2}=\frac{Z_0(f_2-f_1)}{\pi f_1f_2} \tag{14.68}$$

From Eq. 14.64, $\omega_0^2=\frac{1}{L_1C_1}$

$$C_1=\frac{1}{4\pi^2 f_0^2L_1}=\frac{1\times\pi f_1f_2}{4\pi^2 f_0^2Z_0(f_2-f_1)} \quad [\because \text{from Eq. 14.68}]$$

$$\Rightarrow \quad C_1=\frac{1}{4\pi Z_0(f_2-f_1)} \tag{14.69}$$

The other parameters can also be found using

$$Z_0 = \sqrt{\frac{L_1}{C_2}} = \sqrt{\frac{L_2}{C_1}}$$

$$\frac{L_1}{C_2} = Z_0^2$$

$$C_2 = \frac{L_1}{Z_0^2} = \frac{Z_0(f_2 - f_1)}{\pi f_2 f_1 Z_0^2}\frac{1}{4\pi} = \frac{f_2 - f}{\pi Z_0 f_1 f_2}$$

$$\Rightarrow \quad C_2 = \frac{f_2 - f_1}{\pi Z_0 f_1 f_2} \tag{14.70}$$

$$\frac{L_2}{C_1} = Z_0^2$$

$$L_2 = C_1 Z_0^2 = Z_0^2 \frac{1}{4\pi Z_0 (f_2 - f_1)} = \frac{Z_0}{4\pi(f_2 - f_1)}$$

$$\Rightarrow \quad L_2 = \frac{Z_0}{4\pi(f_2 - f_1)} \tag{14.71}$$

Using Eqs 14.68 to 14.71, we can design the constant K band-pass filter.

Problem 14.1 (i) Design a prototype low-pass filter if the design impedance $R_0 = 600\ \Omega$ and cut-off frequency $f_c = 1$ kHz. (ii) Find the frequency at which the filter offers an attenuation of 19.1 dB.

Solution:

(i) Given that $R_0 = 600\ \Omega$, $f_c = 1$ kHz $= 1000$ Hz

For a prototype low-pass filter

$$L = \frac{R_0}{\pi f_c} = \frac{600}{\pi \times 1000} = 191 \text{ mH}$$

$$C = \frac{1}{\pi R_0 f_c} = \frac{1}{\pi \times 600 \times 1000} = 0.5305\ \mu\text{F}$$

Prototype low-pass T and π sections are as given below:

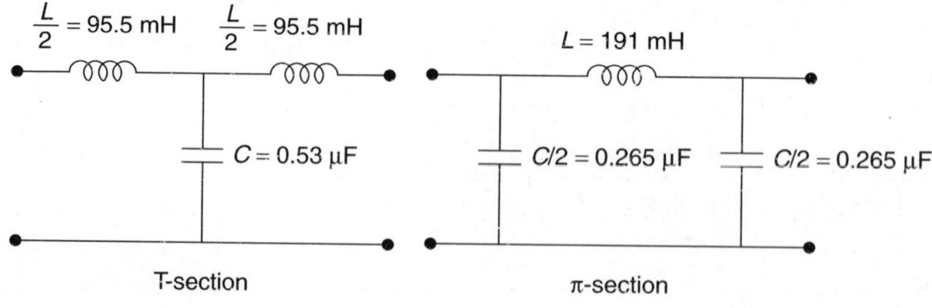

(ii) Attenuation in dB $= 8.686 \times \alpha$

$\therefore \quad 19.1 = 8.686\alpha$

$\Rightarrow \quad \alpha = 2.2$ nepers

For constant K low-pass filter,

$$\alpha = 2\cosh^{-1}\left(\frac{f}{f_c}\right)$$

$$2.2 = 2\cosh^{-1}\left(\frac{f}{1}\right)$$

$$\Rightarrow \quad f = \cosh(1.11) = 1.6685 \text{ kHz}$$

Problem 14.2 (i) Design a prototype high-pass filter, if the design impedance R_0 = 600 Ω and the cut-off frequency f_c = 4 kHz. (ii) Find the characteristic impedance and phase constant of the filter at 25 kHz. (iii) Calculate the attenuation of the filter at 3 kHz.

Solution:

(i) Given that $R_0 = 600\ \Omega, f_c = 4$ kHz

For a prototype high-pass filter

$$L = \frac{R_0}{4\pi f_c} = \frac{600}{4\pi \times 4 \times 1000} = 12 \text{ mH}$$

$$C = \frac{1}{4\pi R_0 f_c} = \frac{1}{4\pi \times 600 \times 4 \times 1000} = 0.03357\ \mu\text{F}$$

Prototype low-pass T and π sections are as given below:

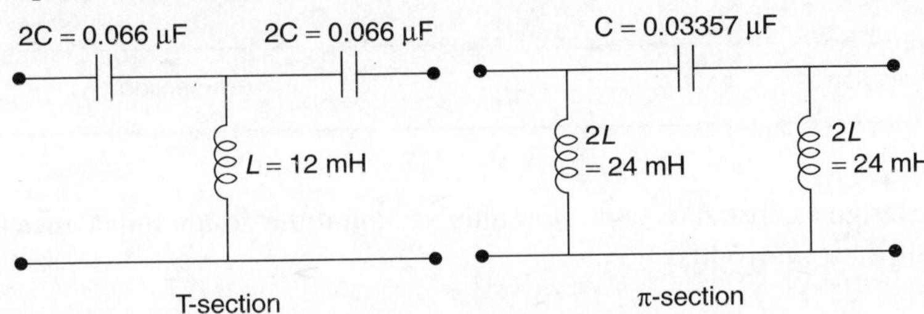

(ii) At f = 25 kHz,

$$Z_{0T} = R_0\sqrt{1-\left(\frac{f_c}{f}\right)^2} = 600\sqrt{1-\left(\frac{4}{25}\right)^2} = 592.2\ \Omega$$

$$Z_{0\pi} = \frac{R_0}{\sqrt{1-\left(\frac{f_c}{f}\right)^2}} = \frac{600}{\sqrt{1-(4/25)^2}} = 607.6\ \Omega$$

$$\text{Phase constant, } \beta = 2\sin^{-1}\left(\frac{f_c}{f}\right) = 2\sin^{-1}\left(\frac{4}{25}\right) = 18.41°$$

(iii) At f = 3 kHz

$$\text{Attenuation constant, } \alpha = 2\cosh^{-1}\left(\frac{f}{f_c}\right) = 2\cosh^{-1}\left(\frac{4}{3}\right) = 1.59 \text{ nepers}$$

Problem 14.3 Design a constant K band-pass filter if the design impedance $R_0 = 4$ kΩ and pass-band between 2 kHz and 3.5 kHz.

Solution:

Given that $R_0 = 4$ kΩ, $f_1 = 2$ kHz, $f_2 = 3.5$ kHz

Resonant frequency, $f_0 = \sqrt{f_1 f_2} = \sqrt{2 \times 3.5} = 2.645$ kHz

Series arm impedance, $L_1 = \dfrac{R_0}{\pi(f_2 - f_1)} = \dfrac{4}{\pi(3.5-2)} = 0.849 = 849$ mH

Shunt-arm impedance, $L_2 = \dfrac{R_0(f_2 - f_1)}{4\pi f_2 f_1} = \dfrac{4 \times (3.5-2)}{4\pi \times 3.5 \times 2} = 68.2$ mH

Series arm capacitance, $C_1 = \dfrac{f_2 - f_1}{4\pi R_0 f_2 f_1} = \dfrac{(3.5-2)}{4\pi \times 4 \times 3.5 \times 2 \times 10^6} = 4.263$ nF

Shunt arm capacitance, $C_2 = \dfrac{1}{\pi R_0 (f_2 - f_1)} = \dfrac{1}{\pi \times 4 \times (3.5-2) \times 10^6} = 53$ nF

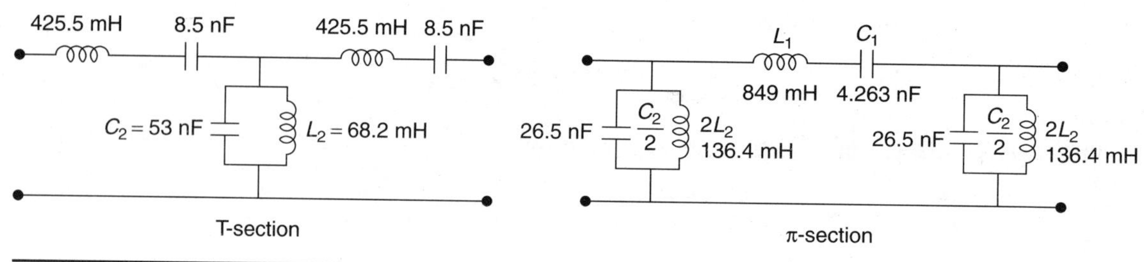

Problem 14.4 Design a constant *K* band stop filter section if the design impedance is $R_0 = 500$ Ω and cut-off frequencies are 2 kHz and 3 kHz.

Solution:

Given that $R_0 = 500$ Ω, $f_1 = 2$ kHz, $f_2 = 3$ kHz

Resonant frequency $f_0 = \sqrt{f_1 f_2} = \sqrt{2 \times 3} = 2.45$ kHz

Series arm-inductance $L_1 = \dfrac{R_0(f_2 - f_1)}{\pi f_1 f_2} = \dfrac{500(3-2) \times 10^3}{\pi \times 3 \times 2 \times 10^3} = 26.5$ mH

Shunt arm inductance $L_2 = \dfrac{R_0}{4\pi(f_2 - f_1)} = \dfrac{500}{4\pi(3-2)1000} = 39.8$ mH

Series arm capacitance $C_1 = \dfrac{1}{4\pi R_0(f_2 - f_1)} = \dfrac{1}{4\pi \times 500(3-2) \times 1000} = 0.159$ μF

Series arm capacitance $C_2 = \dfrac{f_2 - f_1}{\pi R_0 f_1 f_2} = \dfrac{3-2}{\pi \times 500 \times 3 \times 2 \times 1000} = 0.106$ μF

The prototype band stop π and *T*-sections are given below:

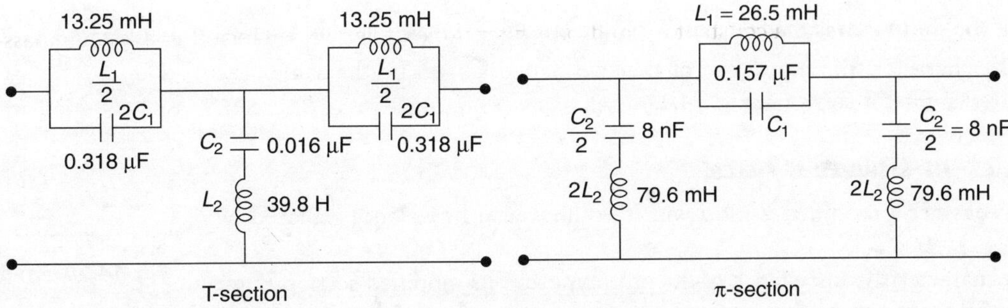

14.7.5 Disadvantages of Constant *K* Filter

There are two disadvantages of the constant *K* filters.

(i) The attenuation does not increase rapidly beyond the cut-off frequency. Hence frequencies just beyond the cut-off frequency are not sufficiently attenuated compared to the frequencies inside the pass-band.

(ii) The characteristic impedance varies widely in the pass-band from the desired value. In order to overcome these disadvantages of constant-*K* filters, a special type of filter called *m-derived filter*, has been implemented.

14.8 *m*-DERIVED FILTERS

An *m*-derived filter is a filter that mostly removes the above two disadvantages in the constant *K* filters. Here, it is possible to derive a filter to have the same impedance throughout the pass-band and stop-band like the constant *K* filter, but with a different degree of attenuation outside the pass-band.

In the *m*-derived filter, it becomes possible to get very rapid attenuation rise in the stop-band and just beyond the cut-off frequency. However, it fails to provide constant characteristic impedance over the entire pass-band.

14.8.1 *m*-Derived T-Filter

Let us consider a modified *T*-filter with the series arm impedance replaced by $\frac{mZ_1}{2}$ (Fig. 14.19). If this network has the same characteristic impedance Z_{0T}, the shunt arm impedance also has to be modified to Z_2'. So the characteristic impedance of the prototype and its modified sections have to be equal for matching.

Fig. 14.19 Modified *T*-filter

$$Z_{0T} = Z'_{0T}$$

$$\sqrt{\frac{Z_1^2}{4} + Z_1 Z_2} = \sqrt{\frac{m^2 Z_1^2}{4} + mZ_1 Z_2'}$$

$$\frac{Z_1^2}{4} + Z_1 Z_2 = \frac{m^2 Z_1^2}{4} + mZ_1 Z_2'$$

$$mZ_1 Z_2' = \frac{Z_1^2}{4}(1 - m^2) + Z_1 Z_2$$

$$Z_2' = \frac{Z_1}{4m}(1 - m^2) + \frac{Z_2}{m} \tag{14.72}$$

Thus, if the shunt arm is made up of two impedances, $\frac{Z_2}{m}$ and $\frac{Z_1}{4m}(1-m^2)$ series, then the characteristic impedance of the two networks will be the same. The m-derived T-filter is shown in Fig. 14.20.

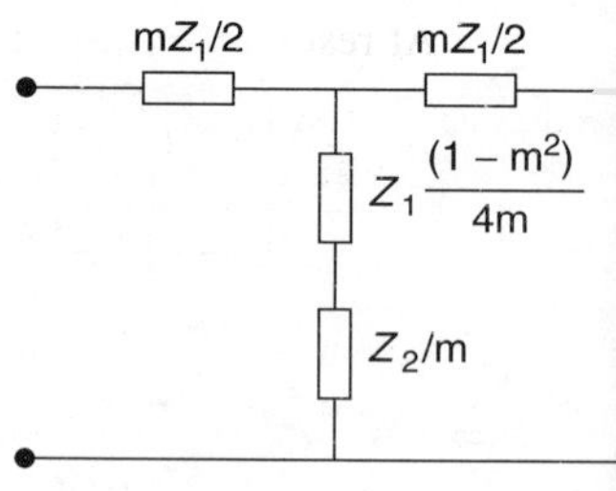

Fig. 14.20 *m*-derived T-filter

14.8.2 *m*-DERIVED π-FILTER

Let us consider a modified π-filter with the shunt arm impedance replaced by $\frac{2Z_2}{m}$ (Fig. 14.21).

The characteristic impedance of the prototype and its modified sections have to be equal for matching.

$$Z_{o\pi} = Z'_{o\pi}$$

$$\sqrt{\frac{Z_1 Z_2}{1+\frac{Z_1}{4Z_2}}} = \sqrt{\frac{Z'_1 \frac{Z_2}{m}}{1+\frac{Z'_1}{4Z_2/m}}}$$

$$\Rightarrow \quad Z_1 Z_2\left(1+\frac{mZ'_1}{4Z_2}\right) = \frac{Z'_1 Z_2}{m}\left(1+\frac{Z_1}{4Z_2}\right)$$

$$Z_1 Z_2 + \frac{mZ_1 Z'_1}{4} = \frac{Z'_1 Z_2}{m} + \frac{Z_1 Z'_1}{4m}$$

$$4Z_1 Z_2 + mZ_1 Z'_1 = \frac{4Z'_1 Z_2 + Z_1 Z'_1}{m}$$

$$Z'_1\left(\frac{4Z_2}{m} + \frac{Z_1}{m} - mZ_1\right) = 4Z_1 Z_2$$

$$Z'_1 = \frac{Z_1 Z_2}{\frac{Z_2}{m} + \frac{Z_1}{4m} - \frac{mZ_1}{4}} = \frac{Z_1 Z_2}{\frac{Z_2}{m} + \frac{Z_1}{4m}(1-m^2)} = \frac{Z_1 Z_2}{\frac{Z_2}{m} + \frac{Z_1}{4m}(1-m^2)} \times \left(\frac{\frac{4m^2}{1-m^2}}{\frac{4m^2}{1-m^2}}\right)$$

$$\Rightarrow \quad Z'_1 = \frac{mZ_1 \times Z_2 \frac{4m^2}{1-m^2}}{Z_2 \frac{4m^2}{1-m^2} + mZ_1} \qquad (14.73)$$

Thus, if the series arm is made up of two impedances mZ_1 and $Z_2\frac{4m^2}{1-m^2}$, in parallel, then the characteristic impedance of the two networks will be the same. The m-derived π-filter is shown in Fig. 14.22.

Fig. 14.21 Modified π-filter

Fig. 14.22 *m*-derived π-filter

14.8.3 *m*-DERIVED LOW-PASS FILTER

Figure 14.23 shows both m-derived low-pass T and π-sections. The shunt-arm in the T-section is chosen as the LC resonant circuit and its impedance is zero at the resonant frequency. Thus, at this frequency it acts like a short circuit which implies that the output will be zero, thus producing infinite attenuation.

At resonance condition

$$X_C = X_L$$

$$\frac{1}{\omega_r mC} = \frac{1-m^2}{4m} L\omega_r$$

$$\Rightarrow \quad \omega_r^2 = \frac{4}{(1-m^2)LC}$$

$$\Rightarrow \quad f_r = \frac{1}{\pi\sqrt{(1-m^2)LC}} = f_\infty$$

But for a prototype low-pass filter

$$f_C = \frac{1}{\pi\sqrt{LC}}$$

$$\therefore \quad f_\infty = \frac{f_C}{\sqrt{1-m^2}} \Rightarrow 1-m^2 = \left(\frac{f_C}{f_\infty}\right)^2$$

$$\Rightarrow \quad m = \sqrt{1-\left(\frac{f_C}{f_\infty}\right)^2} \tag{14.74}$$

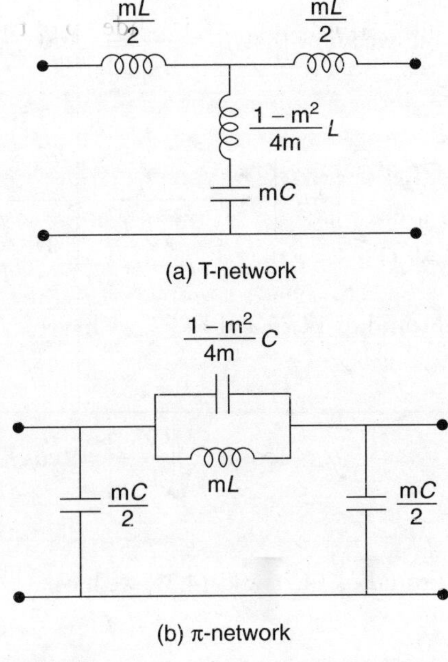

Fig. 14.23 *m*-derived low-pass *T* and *π* filters

Equation 14.74 also holds good for *m*-derived low-pass *π*-section filter. For *π*-section filter parallel combination of *L*, *C* elements from parallel resonant circuit and at resonant frequency, it offers infinite impedance. So it behaves like an open circuit and the signal is zero at the output, thus producing infinite attenuation at this frequency.

The variation of attenuation over the stop-band for a low-pass *m*-derived filter depends on the sign of the impedances. The impedance Z_2' behaves like a capacitance for $f < f_\infty$. Thus, the series and parallel arm impedances are of opposite type *for* $f_C < f < f_\infty$ and are of the same type for $f > f_\infty$. The attenuation in these two cases is given by

$$\alpha = 2\cos h^{-1}\sqrt{\left(\frac{Z_1}{4Z_2}\right)} \quad \text{for} \quad f_C < f < f_\infty \tag{14.75}$$

$$\alpha = 2\sin h^{-1}\sqrt{\left(\frac{Z_1}{4Z_2}\right)} \quad \text{for} \quad f > f_\infty \tag{14.76}$$

For an *m*-derived *T*-filter, we have

$$\left|\frac{Z_1}{4Z_2}\right| = \frac{m\omega L}{4\left[\frac{1}{m\omega C} - \frac{\omega L(1-m^2)}{4m}\right]} = \frac{m\omega L \times m\omega C}{4\left[1-\frac{\omega^2 LC(1-m^2)}{4}\right]} = \frac{m^2\omega^2 LC}{4\left[1-\frac{\omega^2 LC(1-m^2)}{4}\right]}$$

$$= \frac{m^2 4\pi^2 f^2 LC}{4\left[1-\frac{4\pi^2 f^2 LC(1-m^2)}{4}\right]} = \frac{m^2\pi^2 f^2 LC}{1-\pi^2 f^2 LC(1-m^2)}$$

But we know that $f_C = \dfrac{1}{\pi\sqrt{LC}}$ and $f_\infty = \dfrac{f_C}{\sqrt{1-m^2}}$

$$\left|\frac{Z_1}{4Z_2}\right| = \frac{m^2 \times \dfrac{f^2}{f_C^2}}{1-\dfrac{f^2}{f_C^2}\times\dfrac{f_C^2}{f_\infty^2}} = \frac{m^2 \times \dfrac{f^2}{f_C^2}}{1-\dfrac{f^2}{f_\infty^2}} \tag{14.77}$$

From Eqs 14.75 and 14.77, we have

$$\alpha = 2\cos h^{-1}\sqrt{\left|\frac{Z_1}{4Z_2}\right|} = 2\cos h^{-1}\sqrt{\frac{m^2 \times \dfrac{f^2}{f_C^2}}{1-\dfrac{f^2}{f_\infty^2}}} \quad \text{for} \quad f_C < f < f_\infty \tag{14.78}$$

From Eqs 14.76 and 14.77, we have

$$\alpha = 2\sin h^{-1}\sqrt{\left|\frac{Z_1}{4Z_2}\right|} = 2\sin h^{-1}\sqrt{\frac{m^2 \times \dfrac{f^2}{f_C^2}}{1-\dfrac{f^2}{f_\infty^2}}} \quad \text{for} \quad f_C > f_\infty \tag{14.79}$$

The phase shift β in the pass-band is given by

$$\beta = 2\sin^{-1}\sqrt{\left|\frac{Z_1}{4Z_2}\right|} = 2\sin^{-1}\sqrt{\frac{m^2 \times \dfrac{f^2}{f_C^2}}{1-\dfrac{f^2}{f_\infty^2}}} \tag{14.80}$$

In the attenuation band, β has the value π up to, $f = f_\infty$ but β has the value of 0 for $f > f_\infty$. This is because the shunt arm becomes inductive above resonant frequency and the impedances in the series and shunt arms will be of the same type. The characteristic impedance of both low-pass T-section and π-sections are shown to be,

$$Z_{0T} = R_0\sqrt{1-\left(\frac{f}{f_C}\right)^2}$$

$$Z_{0\pi} = \frac{R_0}{\sqrt{1-\left(\dfrac{f}{f_C}\right)^2}}$$

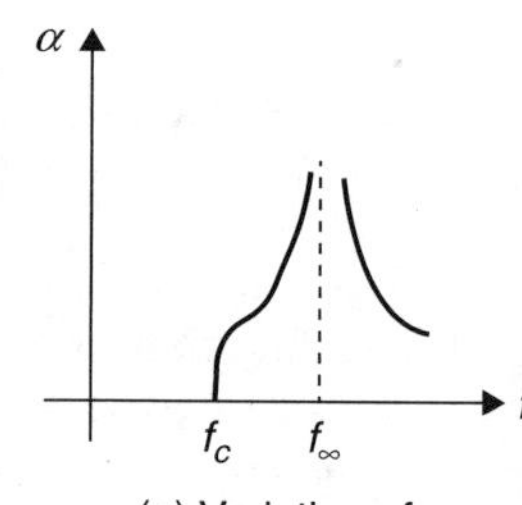

(a) Variation of α

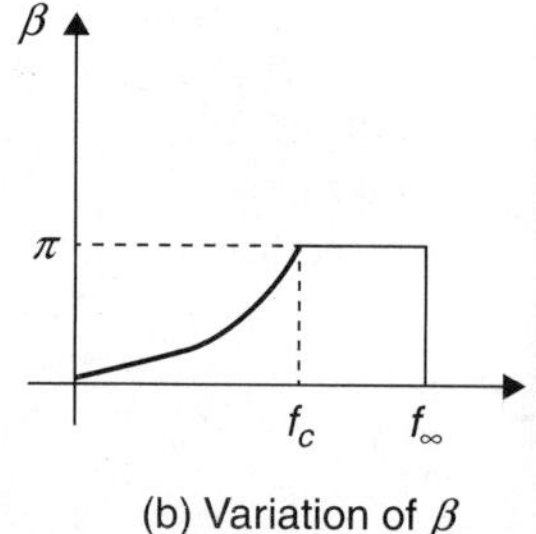

(b) Variation of β

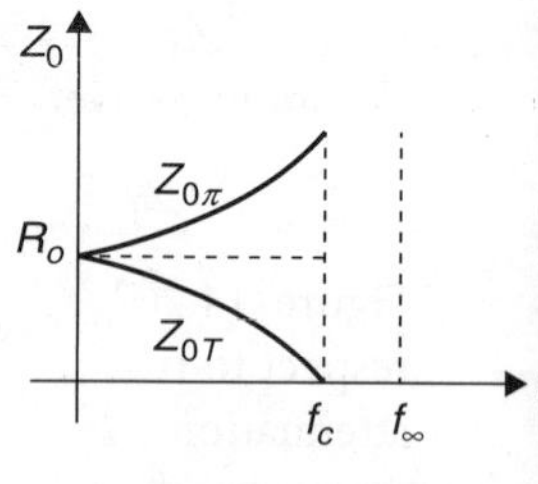

(c) Variation of Z_0

Fig. 14.24 Variation of α, β and Z_0 with respect to f for m-derived low-pass filter

The variation of attenuation with frequency is shown in Fig. 14.24(a). It is seen that the attenuation rises abruptly becomes infinity at f_∞ and then decreases. Thus, an m-derived filter gives a sharp cut-off. The decrease in attenuation for frequencies higher than f_∞ can be avoided by connecting an m-derived filter and constant K filter in cascade. Figure 14.24(b) shows the variation of β with respect to frequency. Figure 14.24(c) shows the variation of characteristic impedance with respect to frequency. The impedance matching can be achieved by using half-section terminations.

14.8.4 m-DERIVED HIGH-PASS FILTER

Figure 14.25 shows both m-derived high-pass T and π-section filters. The series resonance circuit in the shunt-arm of the T-section and the parallel resonant T circuit in the series arm of the π-section, produces infinite attenuation at the resonant frequency, which is the same for both T and π-networks.

The resonant frequency is given by

$$\omega_r^2 = \frac{1}{\frac{L}{m} \times \frac{4m}{1-m^2} C} = \frac{1-m^2}{4LC}$$

$$\Rightarrow \quad f_r = \frac{\sqrt{1-m^2}}{4\pi\sqrt{LC}} = f_\infty$$

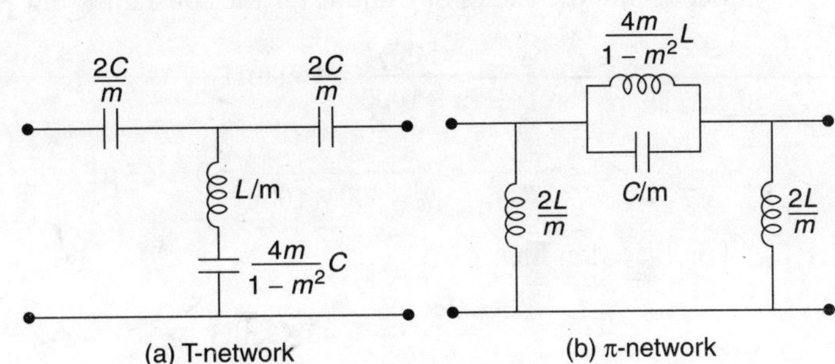

Fig. 14.25 m-derived high-pass T and π-filters

But for a prototype high-pass filter,

$$f_C = \frac{1}{4\pi\sqrt{LC}}$$

$$\therefore \quad f_\infty = \sqrt{1-m^2}\, f_C$$

$$\Rightarrow \quad m = \sqrt{1-\left(\frac{f_\infty}{f_C}\right)^2} \tag{14.81}$$

The variation of α in the stop-band and β in the pass-band can be obtained as in the case of low-pass filter. The characteristic impedance of both m-derived high-pass T-section and π-section filters are as given below:

$$Z_{0T} = R_0\sqrt{1-\left(\frac{f_C}{f}\right)^2}$$

$$Z_{0\pi} = \frac{R_0}{\sqrt{1-\left(\frac{f_C}{f}\right)^2}}$$

Figure 14.26 shows the variations of α, β and Z_0 with respect to frequency for an m-derived high-pass filter. The attenuation rises abruptly, becomes infinite at f_∞ and then decreases, thus giving a sharp cut-off. The use of m-derived and constant K high-pass filters in series gives a sharp cut-off and high attenuation in the entire stop-band. The half-section termination provides impedance matching.

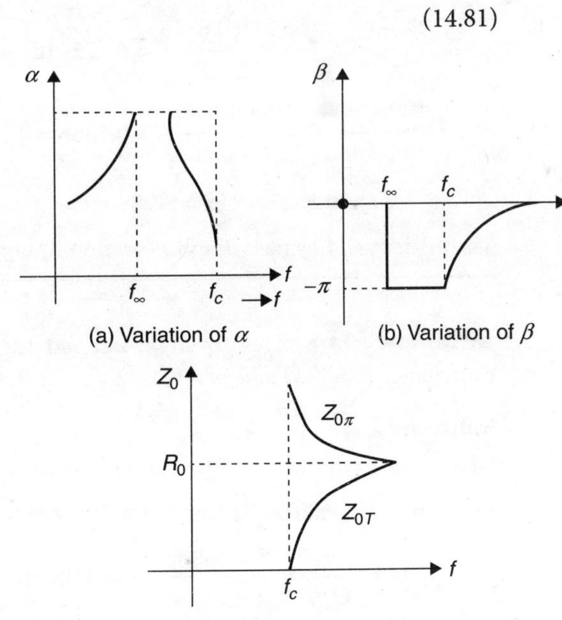

Fig. 14.26 Variations of α, β and Z_0 with respect to f

Problem 14.5 Design an m-derived low-pass filter having a cut-off frequency of 1 kHz, design impedance of 500 Ω and a resonant frequency of 1.2 kHz.

Solution:

Given that $R_0 = 500\ \Omega$, $f_C = 1000$ Hz, $f_\infty = 1200$ Hz

$$m = \sqrt{1-\left(\frac{f_C}{f_\infty}\right)^2} = \sqrt{1-\left(\frac{1000}{1200}\right)^2} = 0.5527$$

Let us find the values of L and C for the constant K low pass filter.

$$L = \frac{R_0}{\pi f_C} = \frac{500}{\pi \times 1000} = 159 \text{ mH}$$

$$C = \frac{1}{\pi R_0 f_C} = \frac{1}{\pi \times 500 \times 1000} = 0.6366\ \mu\text{F}$$

For T-section filter

$$\frac{mL}{2} = \frac{0.5527 \times 159}{2} = 43.93 \text{ mH}$$

$$mC = 0.5527 \times 0.6366 = 0.3517\ \mu\text{F}$$

$$\frac{1-m^2}{4m} L = \frac{1-0.5527^2}{4 \times 0.5527} \times 159 = 50 \text{ mH}$$

T-filter

For a π-section filter

$$\frac{mC}{2} = \frac{0.5527 \times 0.6366}{2} = 0.1759\ \mu\text{F}$$

$$\frac{1-m^2}{4m} C = \frac{1-0.5527^2}{4 \times 0.5527} \times 0.6366 = 0.2\ \mu\text{F}$$

$$mL = 0.5527 \times 159 = 87.88 \text{ mH}$$

π-filter

The m-derived low pass T and π-section filter are as shown in the figures.

Problem 14.6 Design an m-derived high-pass filler with a cut off frequency of 12 kHz, design impedance of 600 Ω and $m = 0.4$.

Solution:

Given that $f_c = 12$ kHz, $R_0 = 600\ \Omega$, $m = 0.4$

Let us find the values of L and C for the constant K high-pass filter.

$$L = \frac{R_0}{4\pi f_C} = \frac{600}{4\pi \times 12 \times 10^3} = 3.98 \text{ mH}$$

$$C = \frac{1}{4\pi R_0 f_C} = \frac{1}{4\pi \times 12 \times 1000 \times 600} = 11.05 \text{ nF}$$

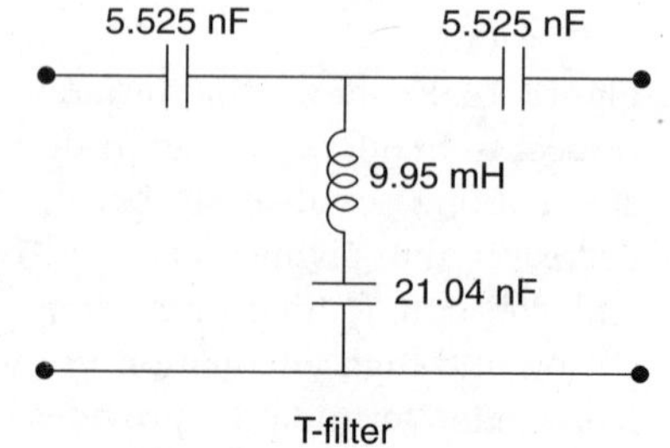

T-filter

For the T-section filter

$$\frac{2C}{m} = \frac{2\times 11.05}{0.4} = 5.525\ \mu\text{F}$$

$$\frac{L}{m} = \frac{3.98}{0.4} = 9.95\ \text{mH}$$

$$\frac{4m}{1-m^2}C = \frac{4\times 0.4}{1-.04}\times 11.05 = 21.04\ \text{nF}$$

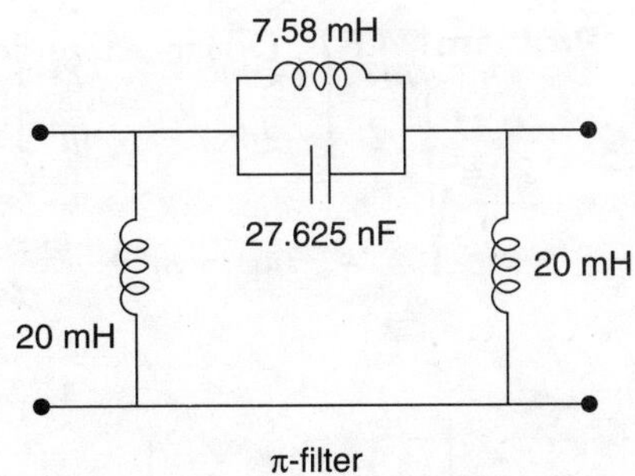

π-filter

For the π-section filter

$$\frac{2L}{m} = \frac{2\times 3.98}{0.4} = 20\ \text{mH}$$

$$\frac{4m}{1-m^2}L = \frac{4\times 0.4}{1-.04^2}\times 3.98 = 7.58\ \text{mH}$$

$$\frac{C}{m} = \frac{11.05}{0.4} = 27.625\ \text{nF}$$

The m-derived high-pass T and π-section filters are as shown above.

14.9 TERMINATING HALF OR *L*-SECTION

To improve the attenuation characteristic in the stop-band, a combination of the prototype and m-derived sections can be used. Any desired attenuation characteristic can be obtained by a suitable choice of prototype and a number of m-derived sections connected in cascade. Such a combination of filters is known as a composite filter.

However, the characteristic impedances still are not a constant over the entire pass-band. Hence terminating half-sections are used as impedance transformation networks. The half-section, sometimes called L-section, should be capable of changing its characteristics in such a way that the filter is approximately matched to the load at all frequencies in the pass-band.

Consider the π-section (Fig. 14.27) derived by rearranging the elements of a m-derived T-section [Fig. 14.27(a)]. The modified π-section [Fig. 14.27(b)] is split into two sections [Fig. 14.27(c)].

The image impedance of the left-half section at the terminal 1–1′ is given by

$$Z_{1i} = \sqrt{Z_{1OC}Z_{1SC}} \tag{14.82}$$

From Fig. 14.23(c),

$$Z_{1OC} = \frac{1-m^2}{2m}Z_1 + \frac{2Z_2}{m}$$

$$Z_{1SC} = \frac{\dfrac{mZ_1}{2}\left(\dfrac{1-m^2}{2m}Z_1 + \dfrac{2Z_2}{m}\right)}{\dfrac{mZ_1}{2} + \dfrac{1-m^2}{2m}Z_1 + \dfrac{2Z_2}{m}} = \frac{\dfrac{mZ_1}{2}\left(\dfrac{1-m^2}{2m}Z_1 + \dfrac{2Z_2}{m}\right)}{\dfrac{Z_1}{2m} + \dfrac{2Z_2}{m}}$$

$$Z_{1i} = \sqrt{\frac{\dfrac{mZ_1}{2}\left(\dfrac{1-m^2}{2m}Z_1 + \dfrac{2Z_2}{m}\right)}{\dfrac{Z_1}{2m}+\dfrac{2Z_2}{m}}} = \sqrt{\frac{\dfrac{4Z_2^2}{m^2}\left(1+(1-m^2)\dfrac{Z_1}{4Z_2}\right)^2\dfrac{mZ_1}{2}}{\dfrac{2Z_2}{m}\left(1+\dfrac{Z_1}{4Z_2}\right)}}$$

$$= \left[1+(1-m^2)\frac{Z_1}{4Z_2}\right]\sqrt{\frac{\dfrac{4Z_2^2}{m^2}\times\dfrac{mZ_1}{2}}{\dfrac{2Z_2}{m}\left(1+\dfrac{Z_1}{4Z_2}\right)}}$$

$$= \left[1+(1-m^2)\frac{Z_1}{4Z_2}\right]\sqrt{\frac{Z_1Z_2}{1+\dfrac{Z_1}{4Z_2}}} = \left[1+(1-m^2)\frac{Z_1}{4Z_2}\right]Z_{0\pi}$$

$$\therefore \quad Z_{1i} = \left[1+(1-m^2)\frac{Z_1}{4Z_2}\right]Z_{0\pi} \qquad (14.83)$$

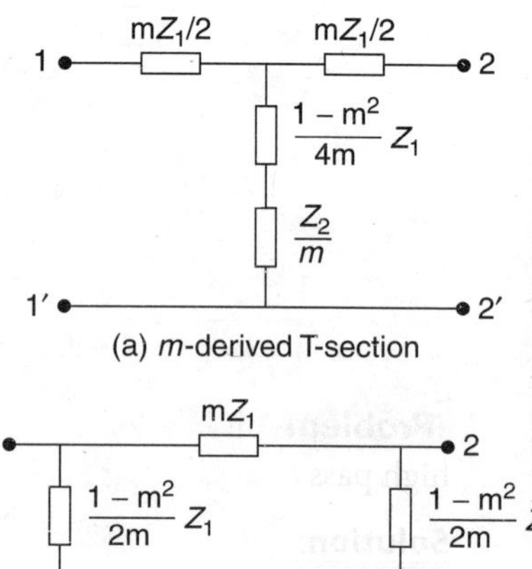

(a) *m*-derived T-section

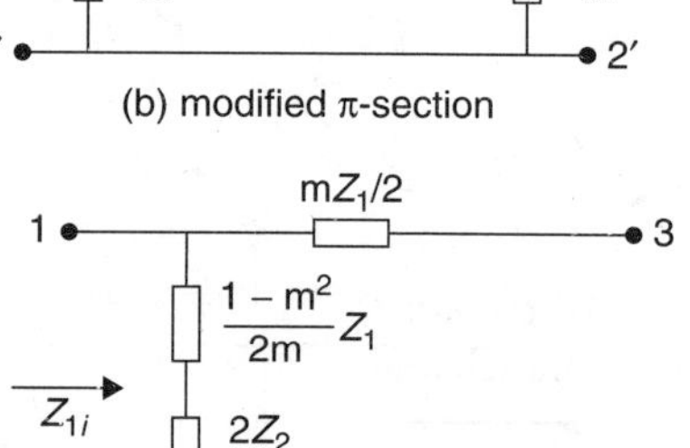

(b) modified π-section

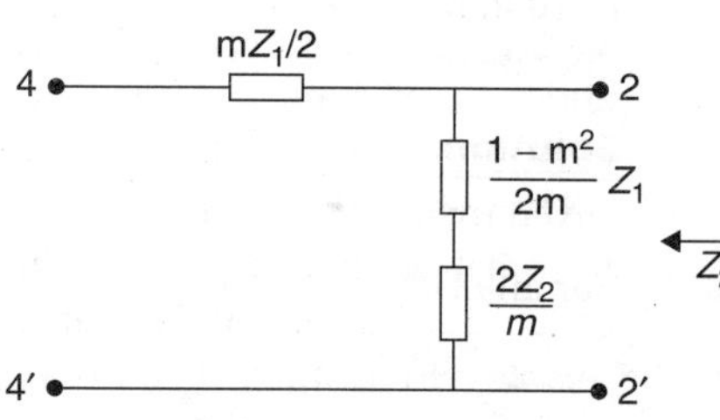

Fig. 14.27 *m*-derived *T*-section and modified π-section

Equation 14.83 shows that the image impedance at terminal 1–1′ of the half-section of the modified π-section is equal to $Z_{0\pi}$ multiplied by a factor $1+(1-m^2)\frac{Z_1}{4Z_2}$. Thus, it is possible to change this impedance by changing the value of m.

The image impedance of the left half-section at terminals 3–3′ in Fig. 14.27(c) is given by

$$Z_{3i} = \sqrt{Z_{3OC}Z_{3SC}} = \sqrt{\left(\frac{mZ_1}{2}+\frac{1-m^2}{2m}Z_1+\frac{2Z_2}{m}\right)\left(\frac{mZ_1}{2}\right)}$$

$$= \sqrt{\left(\frac{Z_1}{2m}+\frac{2Z_2}{m}\right)\frac{mZ_1}{2}} = \sqrt{\frac{2Z_2}{m}\left(1+\frac{Z_1}{4Z_2}\right)\frac{mZ_1}{2}}$$

$$= \sqrt{Z_1Z_2\left(1+\frac{Z_1}{2Z_2}\right)} = Z_{0T}$$

$$\Rightarrow \quad Z_{3i} = Z_{0T} \qquad (14.84)$$

Similarly the image impedance at terminals 4–4′ are the same. That is, Z_{0T} and the image impedance at terminals 2–2′ are the same (Eq. 14.83). Thus, a generator of impedance R_0 can be connected to the terminals 1–1′ of the half-section shown in Fig. 14.27(c) and a load of value R_0 can be connected to the terminals 2–2′ of the half-section shown in Fig.14.27(c), so that the load and generator are perfectly matched. Between the terminals 3–3′ and 4–4′ we may insert prototype and *m*-derived sections of the filter with design impedance R_0. The two *m*-derived half-sections are added at either end of any of filter to provide matching over the entire pass-band. These half-sections are known as terminating half-sections. An *m*-derived half-π-section can be obtained in a similar manner. The *m*-derived π-section is arranged as a *T*-section and split into two half sections and used at the two ends to get good matching characteristics. The *m*-derived half π-sections are shown in Fig. 14.28.

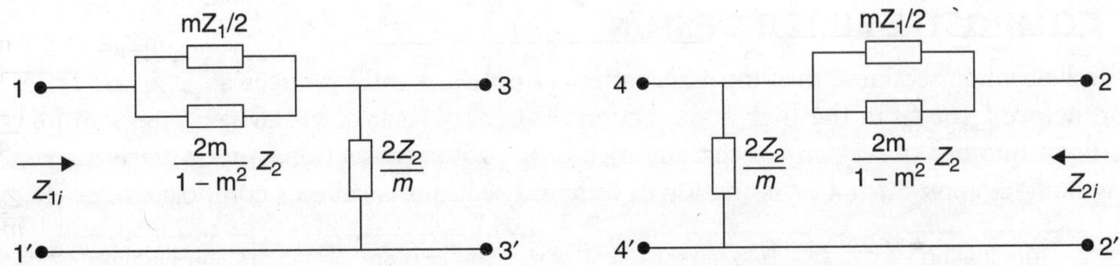

Fig. 14.28 Terminating half-sections to be used with π-section filter

Problem 14.7 Find the values of shunt and series elements of each half section of a constant K T-section high pass filter. The termination is 500 Ω and the filter is cut-off below 10 kHz.

Solution:

Given that $R_0 = 500\ \Omega,\ \ f_C = 10000$ Hz

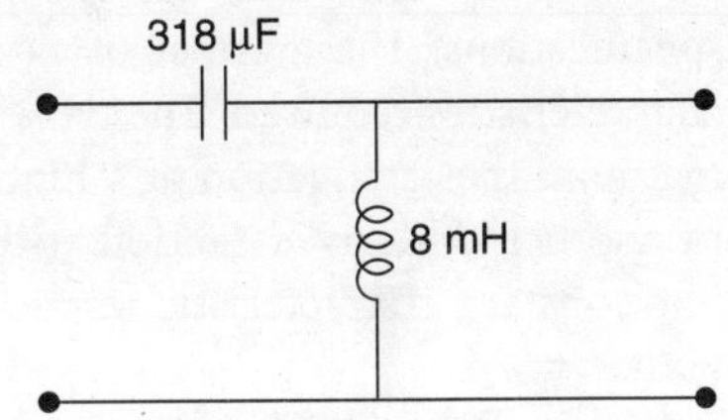

$$L = \frac{R_0}{4\pi f_C} = \frac{500}{4\pi \times 10000} = 4 \text{ mH}$$

$$C = \frac{1}{4\pi f_C R_0} = \frac{1}{4\pi \times 10000 \times 500} = 159\ \mu\text{F}$$

The half section of a constant K T-section high pass filter consists of a capacitor $2C = 318\ \mu$F in the series branch and an inductor $2L = 8$ mH in the shunt branch as shown.

Problem 14.8 A prototype high pass filter with $L = 4.77$ mH and $C = 0.0133\ \mu$F has a cut-off frequency of 10 kHz and design impedance of 600 Ω. Design a suitable terminating half section with m = 0.6 so as to operate with same cut-off frequency.

Solution:

Given that $R_0 = 600\ \Omega,\ \ f_c = 10000$ Hz, $\ L = 4.77$ mH, $\ C = 0.013\ 3\ \mu$F

For an m-derived T-section high-pass filter,

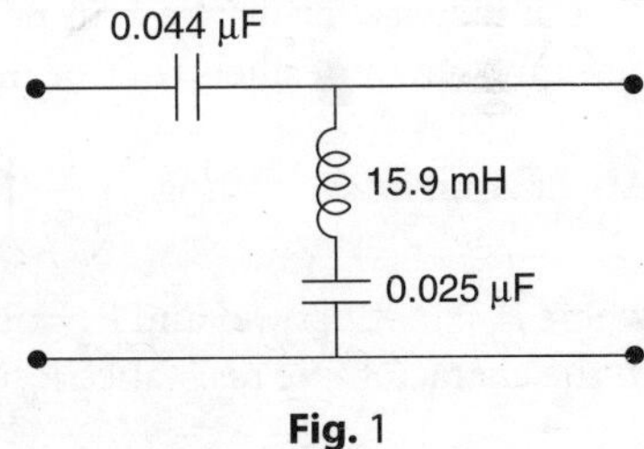

Fig. 1

$$\frac{2C}{m} = \frac{2 \times 0.0133}{0.6} = 0.044\ \mu\text{F}$$

$$\frac{L}{m} = \frac{4.77}{0.6} = 7.95 \text{ mH}$$

$$\frac{4m}{1-m^2} C = \frac{4 \times 0.6}{1-0.6^2} \times 0.0133 = 0.05\ \mu\text{F}$$

The m-derived T-half section high-pass filter is shown in Fig. 1.

For an m-derived π-section high-pass filter,

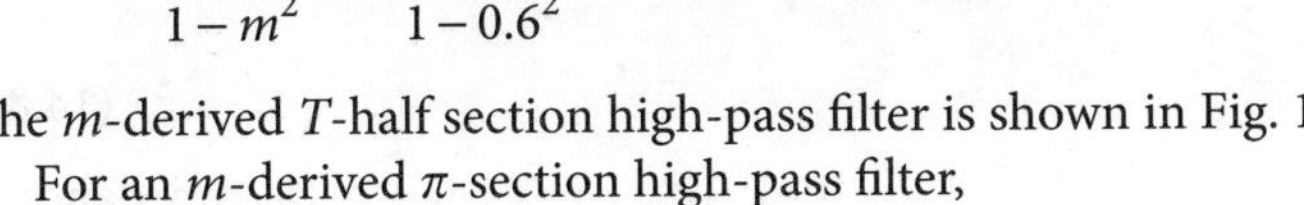

$$\frac{2L}{m} = \frac{2 \times 4.77}{0.6} = 15.9 \text{ mH}$$

$$\frac{4m}{1-m^2} L = \frac{4 \times 0.6}{1-0.6^2} \times 4.77 = 17.89 \text{ mH}$$

$$\frac{C}{m} = \frac{0.0133}{0.6} = 0.022\ \mu\text{F}$$

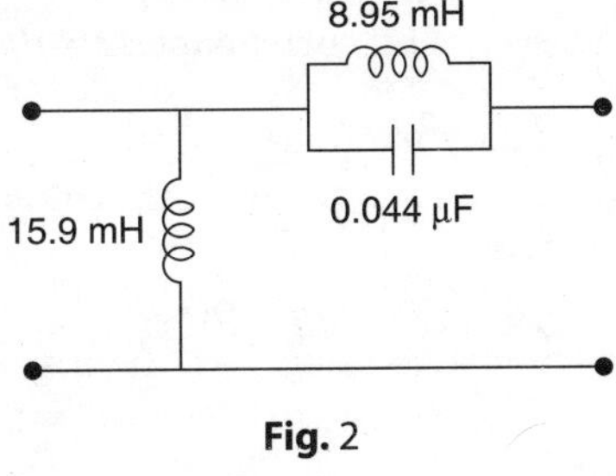

Fig. 2

The m-derived π-half section high-pass filter is shown in Fig. 2.

14.10 COMPOSITE FILTER DESIGN

In the m-derived filter sections, the stop-band attenuation drastically reduces after f_∞ (or f_r) in low-pass section and before f_∞(or f_r) in the high-pass section. This drawback of m-derived filter can be overcome by connecting a number of sections in cascade including prototype sections and m-derived sections with terminating half-sections. Such a combination of different sections is called a composite filter (Fig. 14.29).

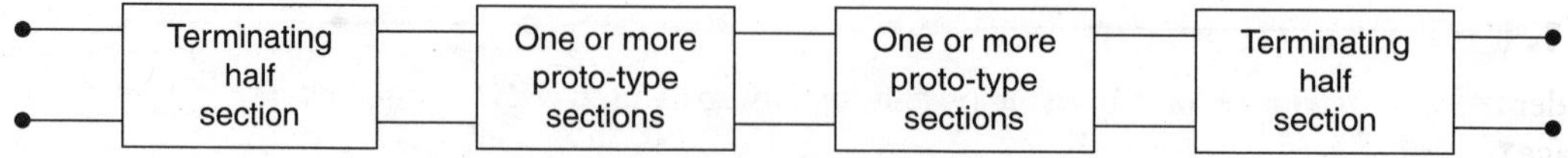

Fig. 14.29 Composite filter block-diagram

In the composite filter, the cut-off frequency and the design impedance are the two important design specifications. The number of various sections in the composite filter totally depends on the attenuation characteristics required. The typical value of m for attenuation at cut-off is $m = 0.3–0.35$. If it is required to maintain the attenuation at a high value in attenuation band, we must connect either a prototype section in another m-derived section with comparatively larger value of m to have proper impedance matching. For constant characteristic impedance through the pass-band, we must connect the terminating section with $m = 0.6$.

14.11 ATTENUATORS

An attenuator is a two-port resistive network and is used to reduce the signal level by a given amount. In a number of applications, it is necessary to introduce a specified loss between the source and a matched load. For this purpose attenuators may be used. Attenuators may be symmetrical or unsymmetrical, and can be either fixed or variable. Fixed attenuators are also known as a pad. Variable attenuators are used as volume controls in radio broadcasting sections. Attenuators are also used in laboratory to obtain small value of voltage or current for testing circuits.

The increase or decrease in power due to insertion or substitution of a new element in a network can be expressed in decibels (dB) or in nepers. Accordingly, the attenuation offered by a network in decibels is

$$\text{Attenuation in } dB = 10\log_{10}\left(\frac{P_1}{P_2}\right) \tag{14.85}$$

where P_1 = input power and P_2 = output power. For a properly matched network, both terminals are matched to the characteristic resistance R_0 of the attenuator.

$$\frac{P_1}{P_2} = \frac{I_1^2 R_0}{I_2^2 R_0} = \frac{I_1^2}{I_2^2} = \left(\frac{I_1}{I_2}\right)^2 \tag{14.86}$$

where I_1 = i/p current and I_2 = o/p current

or
$$\frac{P_1}{P_2} = \frac{V_1^2/R_0}{V_2^2/R_0} = \frac{V_1^2}{V_2^2} = \left(\frac{V_1}{V_2}\right)^2 \tag{14.87}$$

$$\text{Attenuation in } dB = 20\log_{10}\left(\frac{I_1}{I_2}\right) = 20\log_{10}\left(\frac{V_1}{V_2}\right) \tag{14.88}$$

If $\frac{V_1}{V_2} = \frac{I_1}{I_2} = N$ then $\frac{P_1}{P_2} = N^2$

Attenuation in dB = 20 $\log_{10} N$

$$\therefore \qquad N = \text{antilog}_{10}\left(\frac{dB}{20}\right) \tag{14.89}$$

Basically there are four types of attenuators T, π, lattice and bridged-T type. The basic design principles are discussed in the following sections.

14.11.1 *T*-Type Attenuator

Consider the symmetrical T-network (Fig. 14.30), terminated in its image or characteristic impedance R_0.

Applying KVL to loop (2)

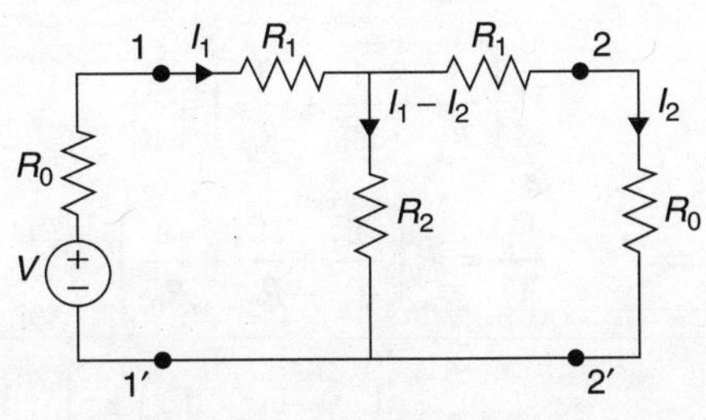

Fig. 14.30 Symmetrical T-type attenuator

$$I_2(R_1 + R_0) - (I_1 - I_2)R_2 = 0$$

$$I_2(R_1 + R_2 + R_0) - I_1R_2 = 0$$

$$\frac{I_1}{I_2} = \frac{R_1 + R_2 + R_0}{R_2}$$

$$N = \frac{R_1 + R_2 + R_0}{R_2} \tag{14.90}$$

The characteristic impedance of the attenuator is R_0 when it is terminated in a load of R_0.

$$R_0 = R_1 + \frac{R_2(R_1 + R_0)}{R_1 + R_2 + R_0} \tag{14.91}$$

From Eqs 14.90 and 14.91, we have

$$R_0 = R_1 + \frac{R_1 + R_0}{N}$$

$$R_0N = R_1N + R_1 + R_0$$

$$R_0(N - 1) = R_1(N + 1)$$

$$\Rightarrow \qquad R_1 = \frac{R_0(N-1)}{(N+1)} \tag{14.92}$$

From Eq. 14.90, we have

$$NR_2 = R_1 + R_2 + R_0$$

$$(N - 1)R_2 = R_1 + R_0$$

$$(N-1)R_2 = \frac{(N-1)}{(N+1)}R_0 + R_0 = \frac{R_0(N - 1 + N + 1)}{(N+1)}$$

$$\Rightarrow \qquad R_2 = \frac{2N}{N^2 - 1}R_0 \tag{14.93}$$

Equations 14.92 and 14.93 are the design equations for a symmetrical T-attenuator.

14.11.2 π-Type Attenuator

A symmetrical π-attenuator is shown in Fig. 14.31.

Applying KCL at node-2

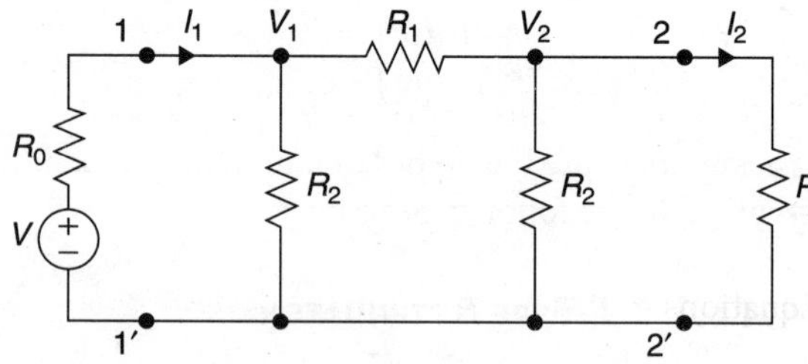

$$\frac{V_2 - V_1}{R_1} + \frac{V_2}{R_2} + I_2 = 0$$

$$\frac{V_2 - V_1}{R_1} + \frac{V_2}{R_2} + \frac{V_2}{R_0} = 0$$

$$V_2\left(\frac{1}{R_1} + \frac{1}{R_2} + \frac{1}{R_0}\right) = \frac{V_1}{R_1}$$

$$\Rightarrow \quad \frac{V_1}{V_2} = R_1\left(\frac{1}{R_1} + \frac{1}{R_2} + \frac{1}{R_0}\right)$$

$$\Rightarrow \quad N = R_1\left(\frac{1}{R_1} + \frac{1}{R_2} + \frac{1}{R_0}\right) \quad \left[\because \frac{V_1}{V_2} = \frac{I_1}{I_2} = N\right]$$

$$\Rightarrow \quad N = \frac{R_1R_2 + R_2R_0 + R_1R_0}{R_0R_2} \tag{14.94}$$

Fig. 14.31 Symmetrical π-attenuator

The characteristic impedance of the attenuator is R_0 when it is terminated in a load of R_0.

$$R_0 = \frac{R_2\left(R_1 + \dfrac{R_0R_2}{R_0 + R_2}\right)}{R_2 + R_1 + \dfrac{R_0R_2}{R_0 + R_2}} = \frac{R_2(R_1R_2 + R_2R_0 + R_1R_0)}{R_2(R_0 + R_2) + R_1R_2 + R_2R_0 + R_1R_0} \tag{14.95}$$

From Eqs 14.94 and 14.95, we have

$$R_0 = \frac{NR_0R_2^2}{R_2(R_0 + R_2) + NR_0R_2}$$

$$\Rightarrow \quad 1 = \frac{NR_2}{R_0 + R_2 + NR_0}$$

$$\Rightarrow \quad R_0(1 + N) + R_2 = NR_2$$

$$\Rightarrow \quad R_0(1 + N) = R_2(N - 1)$$

$$\Rightarrow \quad R_2 = \frac{R_0(1 + N)}{N - 1} \tag{14.96}$$

From Eq. 14.94, we have

$$NR_2R_0 - R_0R_2 = R_1(R_0 + R_2)$$

$$R_1 = \frac{R_0R_2(N - 1)}{R_0 + R_2}$$

$$= \frac{(N - 1) \times R_0^2 \dfrac{(N + 1)}{N - 1}}{R_0 + R_0\dfrac{(N + 1)}{N - 1}} \quad (\because \text{From Eq. 14.96})$$

$$= \frac{R_0(N^2-1)}{N-1+N+1}$$

$$\Rightarrow \qquad R_1 = \frac{R_0(N^2-1)}{2N} \tag{14.97}$$

Equations 14.96 and 14.97 are the design equations for a symmetrical π-attenuator.

14.11.3 Bridged-*T* Attenuator

Consider the symmetrical bridged-*T* attenuator (Fig. 14.32), terminated in its characteristic impedance R_0.

Let us first analyse the circuit to express the characteristic impedance (R_0) in terms of resistances R_1, R_2 and R_3. We know that for a symmetrical bridged-*T* attenuator,

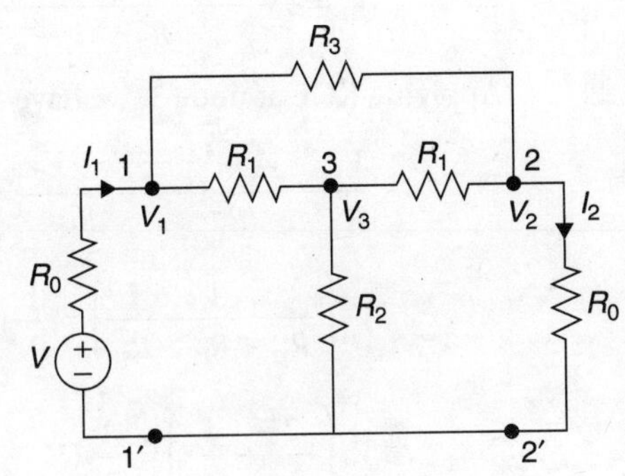

Fig. 14.32 Bridged-*T* attenuator

$$R_0 = \sqrt{R_{SC}R_{OC}}$$

From Fig. 14.32, the input resistance of terminals 1–1′ when terminals 2–2′ are short circuited is

$$R_{SC} = \frac{R_3\left(R_1 + \dfrac{R_1R_2}{R_1+R_2}\right)}{R_3 + R_1 + \dfrac{R_1R_2}{R_1+R_2}} = \frac{R_3(2R_1R_2+R_1^2)}{R_3R_1+R_3R_2+2R_1R_2+R_1^2}$$

Similarly, from Fig. 14.28, the input resistance at terminals 1–1′ when terminals 2–2′ is open circuited is

$$R_{OC} = R_2 + \frac{R_1(R_1+R_3)}{2R_1+R_3} = \frac{R_1R_3+R_2R_3+2R_1R_2+R_1^2}{2R_1+R_3}$$

$$R_0 = \sqrt{R_{SC}R_{OC}} = \sqrt{\frac{R_3(2R_1R_2+R_1^2)}{R_1R_3+R_2R_3+2R_1R_2+R_1^2} \times \frac{R_1R_3+R_2R_3+2R_1R_2+R_1^2}{2R_1+R_3}}$$

$$\Rightarrow \qquad R_0 = \sqrt{\frac{R_3(2R_1R_2+R_1^2)}{2R_1+R_3}} \tag{14.98}$$

Generally we take $R_1 = R_0$ and only R_2 and R_3 are made variable.

$$R_0 = \sqrt{\frac{R_3(2R_0R_2+R_0^2)}{2R_0+R_3}}$$

$$\Rightarrow \qquad R_0^2(2R_0+R_3) = 2R_0R_2R_3 + R_0^2R_3$$

$$\Rightarrow \qquad 2R_0^2 + R_0R_3 = 2R_2R_3 + R_0R_3$$

$$R_0 = \sqrt{R_2R_3} \tag{14.99}$$

Applying KCL at node 2, we have

$$\frac{V_2}{R_0} + \frac{V_2-V_3}{R_1} + \frac{V_2-V_1}{R_3} = 0$$

$$V_2\left(\frac{1}{R_0}+\frac{1}{R_1}+\frac{1}{R_3}\right)=\frac{V_3}{R_1}+\frac{V_1}{R_3}$$

$$V_2\left(\frac{1}{R_0}+\frac{1}{R_0}+\frac{1}{R_3}\right)=\frac{V_3}{R_0}+\frac{V_1}{R_3} \quad [\because R_1=R_0]$$

$$\Rightarrow \quad V_3=\frac{(2R_3+R_0)V_2-R_0V_1}{R_3} \tag{14.100}$$

Applying KCL at node 3, we have

$$\frac{V_3}{R_2}+\frac{V_3-V_1}{R_1}+\frac{V_3-V_2}{R_1}=0$$

$$V_3\left(\frac{1}{R_1}+\frac{1}{R_1}+\frac{1}{R_2}\right)=\frac{1}{R_1}(V_1+V_2)$$

$$V_3\left(\frac{2}{R_0}+\frac{1}{R_2}\right)=\frac{1}{R_0}(V_1+V_2)$$

$$V_3\left(\frac{2R_2+R_0}{R_0R_2}\right)=\frac{1}{R_0(V_1+V_2)}$$

$$V_3=\frac{R_2}{R_0+2R_2}(V_1+V_2) \tag{14.101}$$

From Eqs 14.100 and 14.101, we have

$$\frac{(2R_3+R_0)V_2-R_0V_1}{R_3}=\frac{R_2(V_1+V_2)}{R_0+2R_2}$$

$$\Rightarrow \quad (R_0+2R_2)(2R_3+R_0)V_2-R_0(R_0+2R_2)V_1=R_3R_2V_1+R_3R_2V_2$$

$$\Rightarrow \quad V_2(R_0^2+2R_0(R_2+R_3)+4R_2R_3-R_2R_3)=V_1(R_0^2+2R_2R_0+R_3R_2)$$

$$\Rightarrow \quad V_2(4R_0^2+2R_0(R_2+R_3))=V_1(2R_0^2+2R_2R_0) \qquad (\because R_2R_3=R_0^2)$$

$$\Rightarrow \quad V_2(2R_0+R_2+R_3)=V_1(R_2+R_0)$$

$$\Rightarrow \quad \frac{V_1}{V_2}=\frac{(R_2+R_0)+(R_3+R_0)}{R_0+R_2}$$

$$\Rightarrow \quad N=1+\frac{R_0+R_3}{R_0+R_2} \qquad \left(\because \frac{V_1}{V_2}=N\right)$$

$$\Rightarrow \quad N-1=\frac{R_0+R_3}{R_0+R_2} \tag{14.102}$$

From Eqs 14.99 and 14.102, we have

$$N-1=\frac{R_0+\dfrac{R_0^2}{R_2}}{R_0+R_2}$$

$$\Rightarrow \qquad N-1=\frac{R_0}{R_2}\left(\frac{R_2+R_0}{R_0+R_2}\right)$$

$$\Rightarrow \qquad R_2=\frac{R_0}{N-1} \tag{14.103}$$

From Eqs 14.99 and 14.102, we have

$$N-1=\frac{R_0+R_3}{R_0+R_2}=\frac{R_0+R_3}{R_0+\dfrac{R_0^2}{R_3}}=\frac{(R_0+R_3)R_3}{R_0(R_0+R_3)}$$

$$\Rightarrow \qquad R_3=(N-1)R_0 \tag{14.104}$$

Equations 14.103 and 14.104 are the design equations for a symmetrical bridged-T network.

The bridged-T attenuator is more economical and convenient to use as a variable attenuator because only two resistances have to be changed to change the attenuation without affecting R_0, whereas in T and π attenuators, three resistances have to be changed.

14.11.4 Lattice Attenuator

The symmetrical lattice attenuator is shown in Fig. 14.33(a). It is redrawn as a bridged network [Fig. 14.33(b)]. We know that the characteristic impedance of the symmetrical network is the geometric mean of the open circuit and short circuit impedances.

$$Z_0=R_0=\sqrt{Z_{SC}Z_{OC}}$$

In Fig. 14.33(b), we have

$$Z_{SC}=\frac{R_1R_2}{R_1+R_2}+\frac{R_1R_2}{R_1+R_2}=\frac{2R_1R_2}{R_1+R_2}$$

$$Z_{OC}=\frac{R_1+R_2}{2}$$

$$R_0=\sqrt{\frac{2R_1R_2}{R_1+R_2}\times\frac{R_1+R_2}{2}}=\sqrt{R_1R_2} \tag{14.105}$$

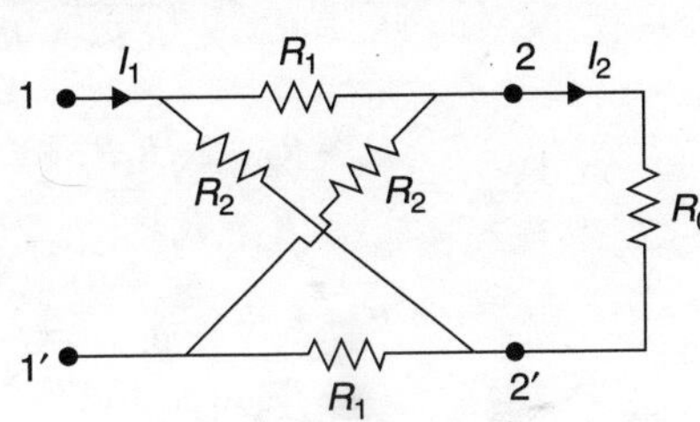

(a) Symmetrical lattice attenuator

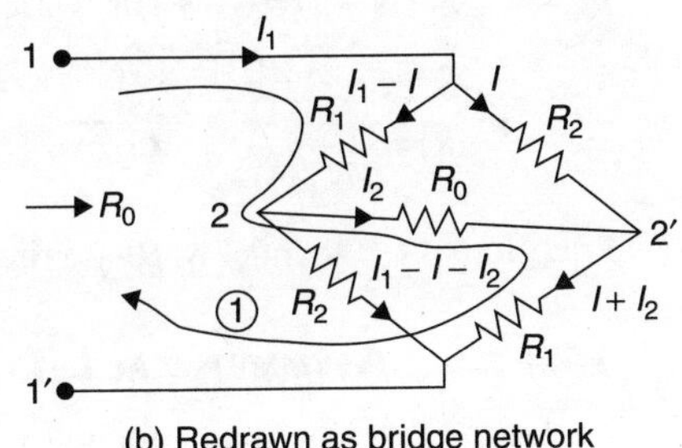

(b) Redrawn as bridge network

Fig. 14.33 Lattice attenuator

In Fig. 14.33(b), the input impedance at port 1–1′ is R_0 when the network is terminated in R_0 at 2–2′. Applying KVL to loop 1, we have

$$V_1=(I_1-I)R_1+I_2R_0+(I+I_2)R_1$$

$$I_1R_0=I_1R_1+I_2R_0+I_2R_1 \qquad [\because V_1=I_1R_0]$$

$$I_1(R_0-R_1)=I_2(R_0+R_1)$$

$$\Rightarrow \qquad \frac{I_1}{I_2}=\frac{R_0+R_1}{R_0-R_1} \tag{14.106}$$

But we know that $\dfrac{I_1}{I_2}=\dfrac{V_1}{V_2}=N=e^{\alpha}$

$$\Rightarrow \qquad N=\frac{R_0+R_1}{R_0-R_1} \tag{14.107}$$

Also, $$e^{\alpha} = \frac{1+\dfrac{R_1}{R_0}}{1-\dfrac{R_1}{R_0}} = \frac{1+\dfrac{R_1}{\sqrt{R_1R_2}}}{1-\dfrac{R_1}{\sqrt{R_1R_2}}} = \frac{1+\sqrt{\dfrac{R_1}{R_2}}}{1-\sqrt{\dfrac{R_1}{R_2}}}$$

$$\Rightarrow \quad \alpha = \log_e\left[\frac{1+\sqrt{\dfrac{R_1}{R_2}}}{1-\sqrt{\dfrac{R_1}{R_2}}}\right] = \text{Propagation constant} \tag{14.108}$$

From Eq. 14.107, we have $N = \dfrac{R_0+R_1}{R_0-R_1}$

$$NR_0 - NR_1 = R_0 + R_1$$

$$R_1 = \left(\frac{N-1}{N+1}\right)R_0 \tag{14.109}$$

From Eq. 14.107, we have

$$N = \frac{R_0+R_1}{R_0-R_1} = \frac{\sqrt{R_1R_2}+R_1}{\sqrt{R_1R_2}-R_1} = \frac{\sqrt{R_2}+\sqrt{R_1}}{\sqrt{R_2}-\sqrt{R_1}}$$

$$= \frac{R_1+R_2+2\sqrt{R_1R_2}}{R_2-R_1}$$

$$= \frac{R_1+R_2+2R_0}{R_2-R_1} \qquad (\because R_0 = \sqrt{R_1R_2})$$

$$\Rightarrow \quad R_2(N-1) = (N+1)R_1 + 2R_0 = (N+1)\frac{(N-1)}{(N+1)}R_1 + 2R_0 = (N+1)R_0$$

$$\Rightarrow \quad R_2 = \frac{(N+1)}{(N-1)}R_0 \tag{14.110}$$

Equations 14.109 and 14.110 are the design equations for a symmetrical lattice network.

14.11.5 Asymmetrical *L*-Type Attenuator

An *L*-type asymmetrical attenuator is as shown in Fig. 14.34. The attenuator is connected between a source with source resistance $R_S = R_0$ and a load resistance $R_L = R_0$.

From Fig. 14.34, we know that

$$V_2 = (I_1 - I_2)R_2$$

$$I_2R_L = (I_1 - I_2)R_2$$

$$I_1R_2 = I_2(R_2 + R_L)$$

$$\Rightarrow \quad \frac{I_1}{I_2} = \frac{R_2+R_0}{R_2} \qquad (\because R_L = R_0)$$

$$\Rightarrow \quad N = 1 + \frac{R_0}{R_2}$$

$$\Rightarrow \quad N - 1 = \frac{R_0}{R_2}$$

$$\Rightarrow \quad R_2 = \frac{1}{N-1} R_0 \qquad (14.111)$$

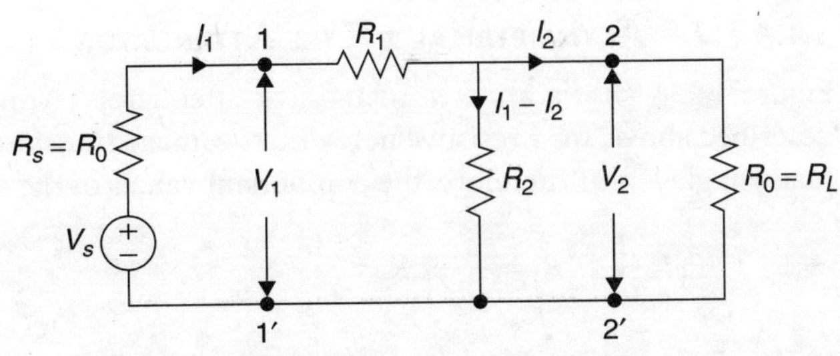

Fig. 14.34 *L*-type asymmetrical attenuator

The resistance of the network as viewed from 1–1′ into the network is

$$R_0 = R_1 + \frac{R_2 R_0}{R_2 + R_0}$$

$$R_2 R_0 + R_0^2 = R_1 R_2 + R_1 R_0 + R_2 R_0$$

$$R_1 = \frac{R_0^2}{R_2 + R_0} = \frac{R_0^2}{R_0 + \dfrac{R_0}{N-1}} = \frac{R_0 (N-1)}{N - 1 + 1}$$

$$\Rightarrow \quad R_1 = \frac{N-1}{N} R_0 \qquad (14.112)$$

Equations 14.111 and 14.112 are the design equations for the *L*-type asymmetrical attenuator.

14.11.6 Asymmetrical-*T* Type Attenuator

Figure 14.35 shows an asymmetrical-*T* attenuator which is terminated in its image impedances R_{i2} and widely used in communication circuits.

For such an attenuator, the image transfer constant θ is given by

$$N = e^{\theta} = \sqrt{\frac{P_1}{P_2}} = \sqrt{\frac{V_1 I_1}{V_2 I_2}}$$

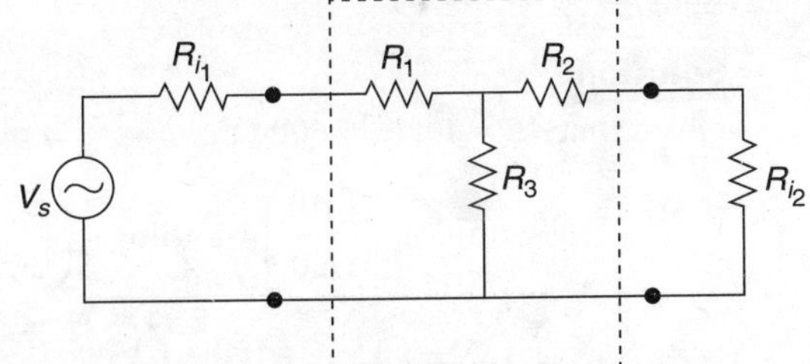

Fig. 14.35 *T*-type asymmetrical attenuator

The parameter θ can be represented as $\theta = \alpha + j\beta$, where α is the attenuation constant and β is the phase angle constant. Since the asymmetrical attenuator uses only resistors, V_1 and V_2 are in phase with I_1 and I_2 respectively so that $\beta = 0$ and $\theta = \alpha$ nepers.

The component values of an asymmetrical T-attenuator are given as follows:

$$R_1 = R_{i1} \cot h\alpha - \frac{\sqrt{R_{i1} \times R_{i2}}}{\sin h\alpha} \qquad (14.113)$$

$$R_2 = R_{i1} \cot h\alpha - \frac{\sqrt{R_{i1} \times R_{i2}}}{\sin h\alpha} \qquad (14.114)$$

$$R_3 = \frac{\sqrt{R_{i1} \times R_{i2}}}{\sin h\alpha} \qquad (14.115)$$

Equations 14.113, 14.114 and 14.115 are the design equations for the *T*-type asymmetrical attenuator.

14.11.7 Asymmetrical π-Type Attenuator

Figure 14.36 shows an asymmetrical π-attenuator terminated in its image impedance R_{i1} and R_{i2}. As described above, for a resistive network, the image transfer constant θ is purely real so that $\theta = \alpha$ nepers and phase angle $\beta = 0$. Therefore, the component values of the symmetrical π-attenuator are given as:

$$R_1 = \frac{1}{G_1},\quad R_2 = \frac{1}{G_2},\quad R_3 = \frac{1}{G_3}$$

$$R_{i1} = \frac{1}{G_{i1}},\quad R_{i2} = \frac{1}{G_{i2}}$$

$$G_1 = G_{i1}\cot h\alpha - \frac{\sqrt{G_{i1}\times G_{i2}}}{\sin h\alpha} \qquad (14.116)$$

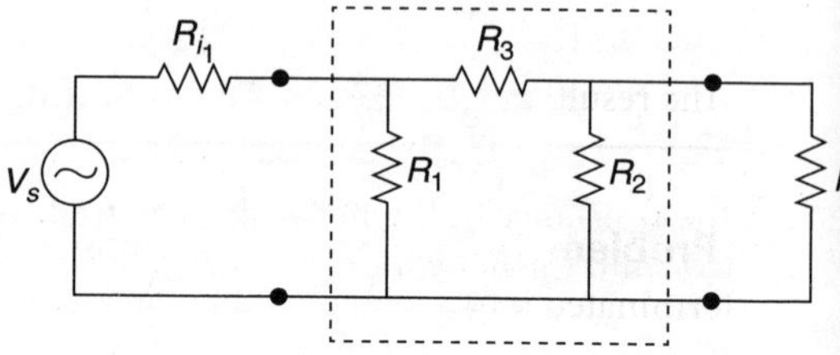

Fig. 14.36 π-type asymmetrical attenuator

$$G_2 = G_{i2}\cot h\alpha - \frac{\sqrt{G_{i1}\times G_{i2}}}{\sin h\alpha} \qquad (14.117)$$

$$G_3 = \frac{\sqrt{G_{i1}\times G_{i2}}}{\sin h\alpha} \qquad (14.118)$$

Hence, by knowing the image conductances G_{i1} and G_{i2} and the loss in nepers α, the asymmetrical π-attenuator can be designed.

Problem 14.9 Design a T-type attenuator to give an attenuation of 40 dB and to have a characteristic impedance of 600 Ω.

Solution:

Given that $dB = 40$, $R_0 = 600\ \Omega$

$$N = \text{antilog}_{10}\left(\frac{dB}{20}\right) = \text{antilog}_{10}\left(\frac{40}{20}\right) = 10^2 = 100$$

$$R_1 = \left(\frac{N-1}{N+1}\right)R_0 = \left(\frac{100-1}{100+1}\right)\times 600 = 588\ \Omega$$

$$R_2 = \frac{2N}{N^2-1}R_0 = \frac{2\times 100}{100^2-1}\times 600 = 12\ \Omega$$

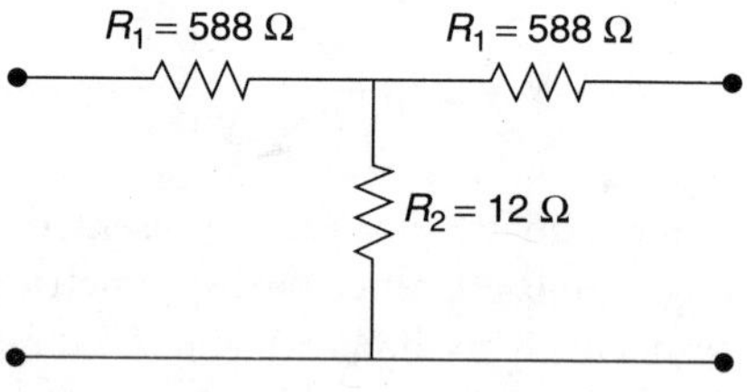

The resulting T-type attenuator is shown.

Problem 14.10 Design a π-type attenuator to give 20 dB attenuation and to have a characteristic impedance of 200 Ω.

Solution:

Given that $dB = 20$, $R_0 = 200\ \Omega$

$$N = \text{antilog}_{10}\left(\frac{dB}{20}\right) = \text{antilog}_{10}\left(\frac{20}{20}\right) = 10^1 = 10$$

$$R_1 = \frac{N^2 - 1}{2N} R_0 = \frac{10^2 - 1}{2 \times 10} \times 200 = 990\ \Omega$$

$$R_2 = \left(\frac{N+1}{N-1}\right) R_0 = \left(\frac{10+1}{10-1}\right) \times 200 = 244.44\ \Omega$$

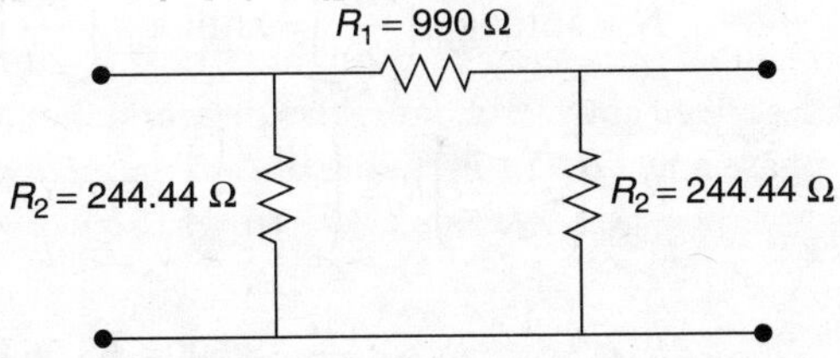

The resulting π-type attenuator is shown.

Problem 14.11 Design a symmetrical bridged-T attenuator with an attenuation of 40 dB and terminated into a load of 400 Ω.

Solution:

Given that $dB = 40$, $R_0 = 400\ \Omega$

$$N = \text{antilog}_{10}\left(\frac{dB}{20}\right) = \text{antilog}_{10}\left(\frac{40}{20}\right) = 10^2 = 100$$

$$R_1 = R_0 = 400\ \Omega$$

$$R_2 = \frac{R_0}{N-1} = \frac{400}{100-1} = 4.04\ \Omega$$

$$R_3 = (N-1)R_0 = (100-1) \times 400 = 39600\ \Omega$$

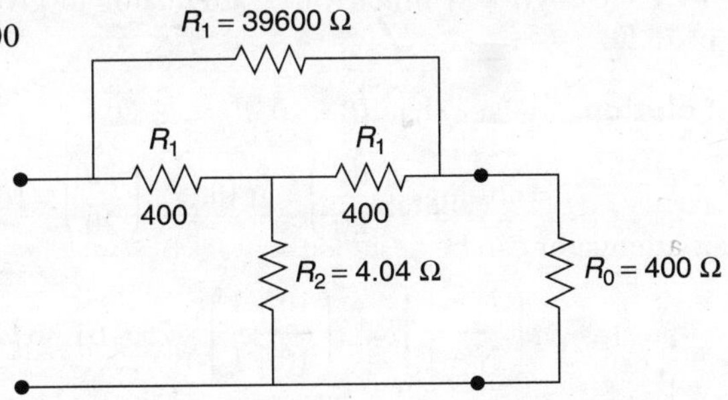

The symmetrical bridged-T attenuator is shown.

Problem 14.12 Design a symmetrical lattice attenuator to have a characteristic impedance of 900 Ω and attenuation of 30 dB.

Solution:

Given that dB = 30, $R_0 = 900\ \Omega$

$$N = \text{antilog}_{10}\left(\frac{dB}{20}\right) = \text{antilog}_{10}\left(\frac{30}{20}\right) = 10^{1.5} = 31.6$$

$$R_1 = \left(\frac{N-1}{N+1}\right) R_0 = \left(\frac{31.6-1}{31.6+1}\right) \times 900 = 844.78\ \Omega \approx 845\ \Omega$$

$$R_2 = \frac{N+1}{N-1} R_0 = \frac{31.6+1}{31.6-1} \times 900 = 959\ \Omega$$

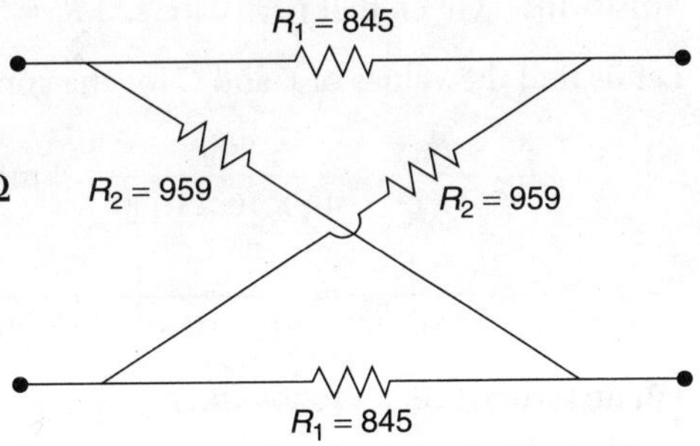

Symmetrical lattice attenuator is shown.

Problem 14.13 Design an *L*-type attenuator to operate into a load resistance of 500 Ω with an attenuation of 20 dB.

Solution:

Given that $dB = 20$, $R_0 = 500\ \Omega$

$$N = \text{antilog}_{10}\left(\frac{dB}{20}\right) = \text{antilog}_{10}\left(\frac{20}{20}\right) = 10^1 = 10$$

$$R_1 = \left(\frac{N-1}{N}\right)R_0 = \left(\frac{10-1}{10}\right) \times 500 = 450\ \Omega$$

$$R_2 = \frac{1}{N-1}R_0 = \frac{1}{10-1} \times 500 = 55.56\ \Omega$$

L-type attenuator is shown.

ADDITIONAL SOLVED PROBLEMS

14.1 Design a symmetrical *T*-attenuator to give 20 dB attenuation to have a characteristic impedance of 75 Ω.

Solution: Given that $dB = 20$, $R_0 = 75\ \Omega$

$$N = \text{antilog}_{10}\left(\frac{dB}{20}\right) = \text{antilog}_{10}\left(\frac{20}{20}\right) = 10^1 = 10$$

$$R_1 = \left(\frac{N-1}{N+1}\right)R_0 = \left(\frac{10-1}{10+1}\right) \times 75 = 61.36\ \Omega$$

$$R_2 = \frac{2N}{N^2-1}R_0 = \frac{2\times 10}{10^2-1} \times 75 = 15.15\ \Omega$$

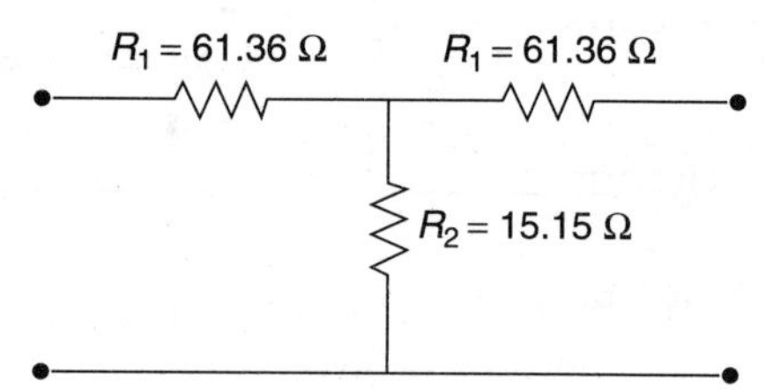

The resultant symmetrical *T*-attenuator is shown.

14.2 Design an *m*-derived HPF with a cut-off frequency of 10 kHz and design impedance of 500 Ω and $m = 0.4$.

Solution: Given that $f_c = 10$ kHz, $R_0 = 500\ \Omega$, $m = 0.4$

Let us find the values of *L* and *C* for the constant *K* high pass filter.

$$L = \frac{R_0}{4\pi f_C} = \frac{500}{4\pi \times 10 \times 1000} = 4\text{ mH}$$

$$C = \frac{1}{4\pi R_o f_C} = \frac{1}{4\pi \times 10 \times 1000 \times 500} = 15.9\text{ nF}$$

For an *m*-derived *T*-section filter,

$$\frac{2C}{m} = \frac{2\times 15.9}{0.4} = 79.5\text{ nF}$$

$$\frac{L}{m} = \frac{4}{0.4} = 10\text{ mH}$$

$$\frac{4m}{1-m^2}C = \frac{4\times 0.4}{1-0.4^2} \times 15.9 = 30.286\text{ nF}$$

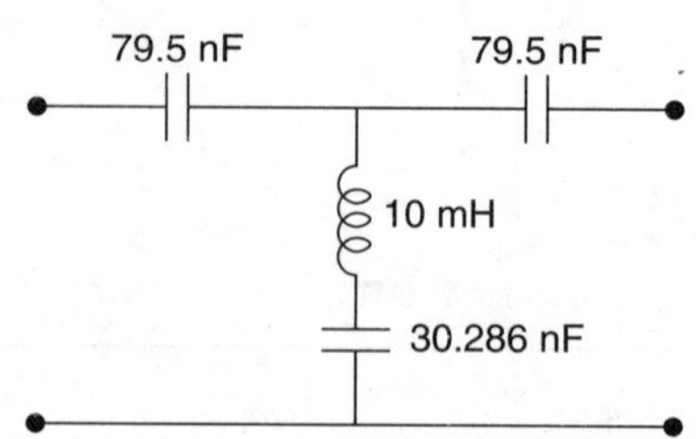

For an m-derived π-section filter

$$\frac{2L}{m} = \frac{2 \times 4}{0.4} = 20 \text{ mH}$$

$$\frac{4m}{1-m^2}L = \frac{4 \times 0.4}{1-0.4^2} \times 4 = 7.62 \text{ mH}$$

$$\frac{C}{m} = \frac{15.9}{0.4} = 39.75 \text{ nF}$$

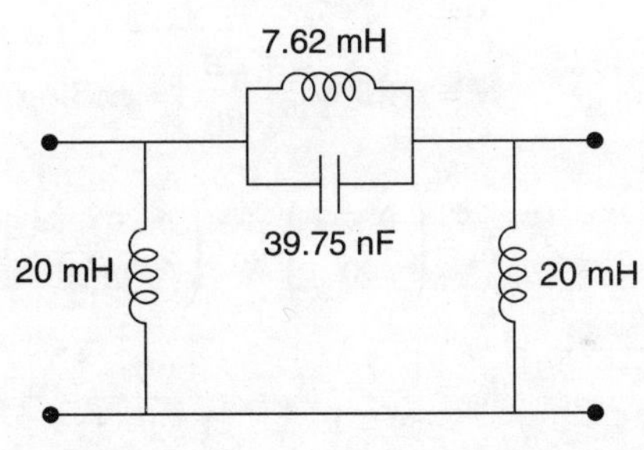

The m-derived high pass T and π section filter are shown.

14.3 Find the circuit parameters of a constant K band pass filter having a pass-band from 500 Hz to 10000 Hz and a characteristic resistance of 100 Ω.

Solution: Given that $f_1 = 500$ Hz, $f_2 = 10000$ Hz, $K = R_0 = 100\ \Omega$

Series arm inductance, $L_1 = \dfrac{R_0}{\pi(f_2 - f_1)} = \dfrac{100}{\pi(10000 - 500)} = 3.35 \text{ mH}$

Shunt arm-inductance, $L_2 = \dfrac{R_0(f_2 - f_1)}{4\pi f_1 f_2} = \dfrac{100 \times 9500}{4\pi \times 500 \times 10000} = 15.12 \text{ mH}$

Series arm capacitance, $C_1 = \dfrac{f_2 - f_1}{4\pi R_0 f_1 f_2} = \dfrac{10000 - 500}{4\pi \times 500 \times 10000} = 1.512\ \mu\text{F}$

Series arm capacitance, $C_2 = \dfrac{1}{\pi R_0(f_2 - f_1)} = \dfrac{1}{\pi \times 100 \times 9500} = 0.335\ \mu\text{F}$

Constant K T section band pass filter is shown below.

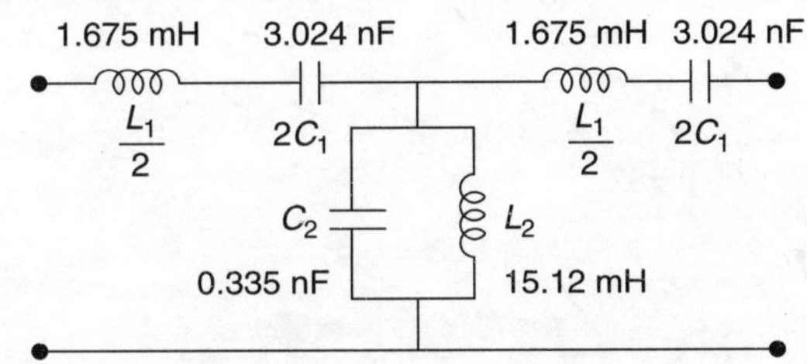

Constant K π-section band pass filter is shown below.

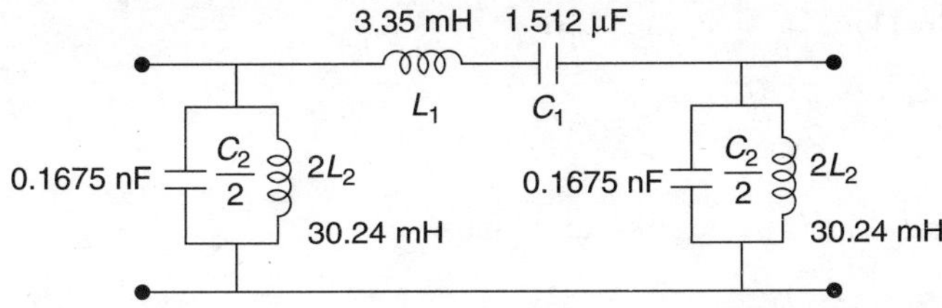

14.4 Design an asymmetrical L-attenuator to operate into a resistance of 300 Ω and to provide an attenuation of 30 dB.

Solution: Given that $dB = 30$, $R_0 = 300\ \Omega$

$$N = \text{antilog}_{10}\left(\frac{dB}{20}\right) = \text{antilog}_{10}\left(\frac{30}{20}\right) = 10^{1.5} = 31.62$$

$$R_1 = \left(\frac{N-1}{N}\right)R_0 = \left(\frac{31.62-1}{31.6}\right) \times 300 = 290.5\ \Omega$$

$$R_2 = \frac{1}{N-1}R_0 = \frac{300}{31.62-1} = 9.79\ \Omega$$

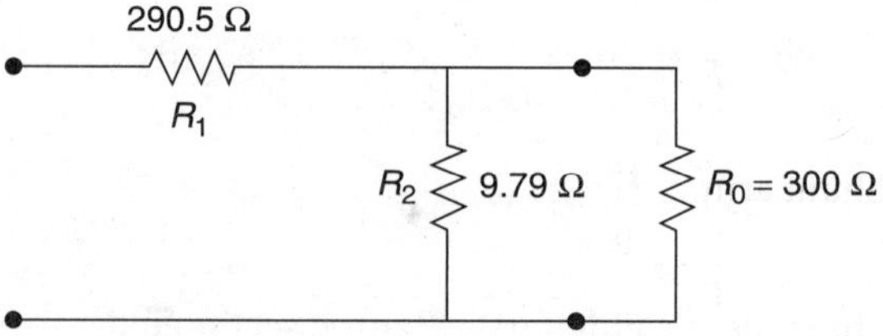

The desired configuration of the L-attenuator is shown.

14.5 An attenuator is composed of symmetrical T-section having series arm each of 175 Ω and a shunt arm of 350 Ω. Calculate the characteristic impedance of this network and attenuation per section.

Solution: Given that $R_1 = 175\ \Omega$, $R_2 = 350\ \Omega$

Series arm resistance $R_1 = \dfrac{R_0(N-1)}{(N+1)} = 175$ (1)

Shunt arm resistance $R_2 = \dfrac{2N}{N^2-1}R_0 = 350$ (2)

Dividing (1) by (2) $\Rightarrow \dfrac{(N-1)/(N+1)}{2N/N^2-1} = \dfrac{175}{350}$

$$\Rightarrow \quad \frac{(N-1)^2}{2N} = \frac{1}{2}$$

$$\Rightarrow \quad N^2 - 2N + 1 = N$$

$$\Rightarrow \quad N^2 - 3N + 1 = 0$$

$$N = \frac{3 \pm \sqrt{9-4}}{2} = 2.618\ (\text{or})\ 0.382$$

When $N = 2.618$, from Eq. (1)

$$R_0 = \frac{175(N+1)}{(N-1)} = \frac{175 \times 3.618}{3.618} = 391.3\ \Omega$$

When $N = 0.382$, from Eq. (1)

$$R_0 = \frac{175(N+1)}{(N-1)} = \frac{175 \times 1.382}{(0.382-1)} = -391.3\ \Omega$$

Characteristic impedance will not be negative and hence,

$$N = 2.618, \quad R_0 = 391.3\ \Omega$$

14.6 Design a symmetrical π-attenuator to have a characteristic impedance of 600 Ω with an attenuation of 40 dB.

Solution: Given that $R_0 = 600\ \Omega$, attenuation = 40 dB

$$N = \text{antilog}_{10}\left(\frac{dB}{20}\right) = \text{antilog}_{10}\left(\frac{40}{20}\right) = 10^2 = 100$$

For a π-type attenuator, the series arm impedance,

$$R_1 = \frac{R_0(N^2-1)}{2N} = \frac{600(100^2-1)}{2\times 100} = 30\ \text{k}\Omega$$

Shunt arm impedance,

$$R_2 = \frac{R_0(1+N)}{N-1} = \frac{600(100+1)}{100+1} = 612.12\ \Omega$$

The resultant π-type attenuator is shown.

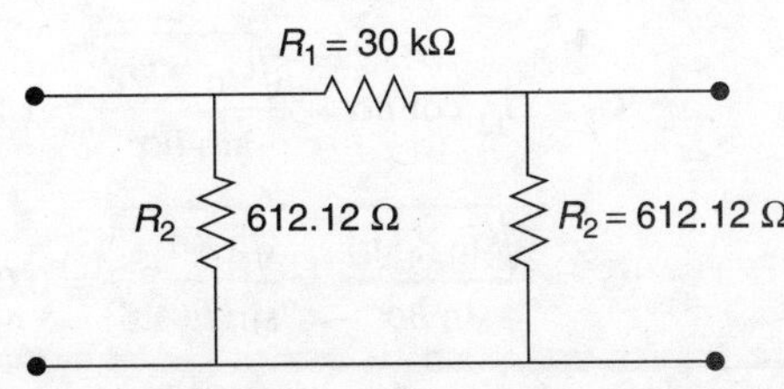

14.7 Design an asymmetrical T-attenuator to produce an attenuation of 20 dB and to work between a source impedance of 400 Ω and a load impedance of 900 Ω.

Solution: Given that

Source impedance $R_{i1} = 400\ \Omega$

Load impedance $R_{i2} = 900\ \Omega$

Attenuation, $\alpha = 20$ dB

$$\text{Attenuation in } dB = \frac{\text{attenuation in neper}}{0.115}$$

$\Rightarrow$ Attenuation, $A_i = 0.115 \times 20 = 2.3$ neper

$\Rightarrow$ $\theta = A_i = 2.3$ neper

$$\text{Circuit element, } R_1 = \frac{R_{i1}}{\tan h\theta} - \frac{\sqrt{R_{i1}\times R_{i2}}}{\sin h\theta} = \frac{400}{\tan h(2.3)} - \frac{\sqrt{400\times 900}}{\sin h(2.3)} = 286.7\ \Omega$$

$$\text{Circuit element, } R_2 = \frac{R_{i2}}{\tan h\theta} - \frac{\sqrt{R_{i1}\times R_{i2}}}{\sin h\theta} = \frac{900}{\tan h(2.3)} - \frac{\sqrt{400\times 900}}{\sin h(2.3)} = 769.9\ \Omega$$

$$\text{Circuit element, } R_3 = \frac{\sqrt{R_{i1}\times R_{i2}}}{\sin h\theta} = \frac{\sqrt{400\times 900}}{\sin h(2.3)} = 121.46\ \Omega$$

The circuit diagram for asymmetrical T-attenuator is shown.

14.8 Design an unbalanced asymmetrical π-attenuator with a loss of 40 dB to operate between the 200 Ω line and the 800 Ω line.

Solution: Given that

$$G_{i1} = \frac{1}{R_{i1}} = \frac{1}{200} = 5\ \text{m℧}$$

$$G_{i2} = \frac{1}{R_{i2}} = \frac{1}{800} = 1.25\ \text{m℧}$$

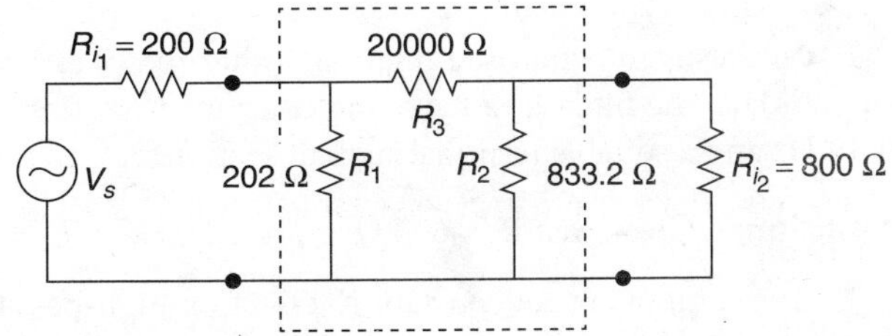

Attenuation $\alpha = 40$ dB $= 40 \times 0.115 = 4.6$ nepers

For an asymmetrical π-attenuator

$$G_1 = G_{i1} \cot h\alpha - \frac{\sqrt{G_{i1} \times G_{i2}}}{\sin h\alpha} = 5 \cot h(4.6) - \frac{\sqrt{5 \times 1.25}}{\sin h(4.6)} = 4.9 \text{ m℧}$$

$$G_2 = G_{i2} \cot h\alpha - \frac{\sqrt{G_{i1} \times G_{i2}}}{\sin h\alpha} = 1.25 \cot h(4.6) - \frac{\sqrt{5 \times 1.25}}{\sin h(4.6)} = 1.2 \text{ m℧}$$

$$G_3 = \frac{\sqrt{G_{i1} \times G_{i2}}}{\sin h\alpha} = \frac{\sqrt{5 \times 1.25}}{\sin h(4.6)} = 0.05 \text{ m℧}$$

Hence, $R_1 = \frac{1}{G_1} = 202\ \Omega,\quad R_2 = \frac{1}{G_2} = 883.2\ \Omega,\quad R_3 = \frac{1}{G_3} = 20000\ \Omega$

The asymmetrical π-attenuator is shown.

14.9 A low pass π-section filter consists of an inductance of 15 mH in the series arm and two capacitors of 0.4 pF in the shunt arms. Calculate the cut-off frequency, design impedance, attenuation at 6 kHz and phase shift at 1.5 kHz.

Solution: From the network, $L = 15$ mH, $C = 2 \times 0.4 = 0.8$ μF

(i) Cut-off frequency,

$$f_C = \frac{1}{\pi\sqrt{LC}} = \frac{1}{\pi\sqrt{15 \times 10^{-3} \times 0.8 \times 10^{-6}}} = 2905.75 \text{ Hz} = 2.905 \text{ kHz}$$

(ii) Design impedance,

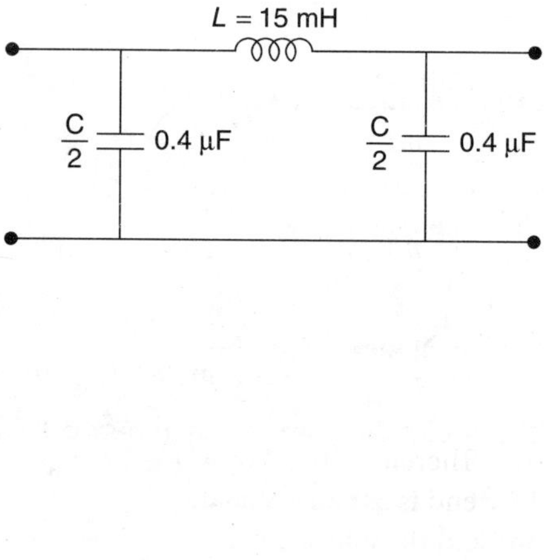

$$R_0 = \sqrt{\frac{L}{C}} = \sqrt{\frac{15 \times 10^{-3}}{0.8 \times 10^{-6}}} = 136.9\ \Omega$$

(iii) Attenuation at 6kHz,

$$\alpha = 2\cos h^{-1}\left(\frac{f}{f_C}\right) = 2\cos h^{-1}\left(\frac{6}{2905}\right) = 2.708 \text{ nepers}$$

(iv) Phase shift at 1.5kHz,

$$\beta = 2\sin h^{-1}\left(\frac{f}{f_C}\right) = 2\sin h^{-1}\left(\frac{1.5}{2905}\right) = 62.17°$$

14.10 Design a composite high pass filter to operate into a load of 600 Ω and have a cut-off frequency of 1.2 kHz. The filter is to have one constant K section, one m-derived section with infinite frequency of 1.1 kHz and a suitable terminating half section.

Solution: Given that $R_0 = 600\ \Omega,\quad f_c = 1.2$ kHz, $\quad f_\infty = 1.1$ kHz

(i) The components of constant K T-section high-pass filter are

$$L = \frac{R_0}{4\pi f_C} = \frac{600}{4\pi \times 1200} = 40 \text{ mH}$$

$$C = \frac{1}{4\pi R_o f_C} = \frac{1}{4\pi \times 1200 \times 600} = 0.11\,\mu\text{F}$$

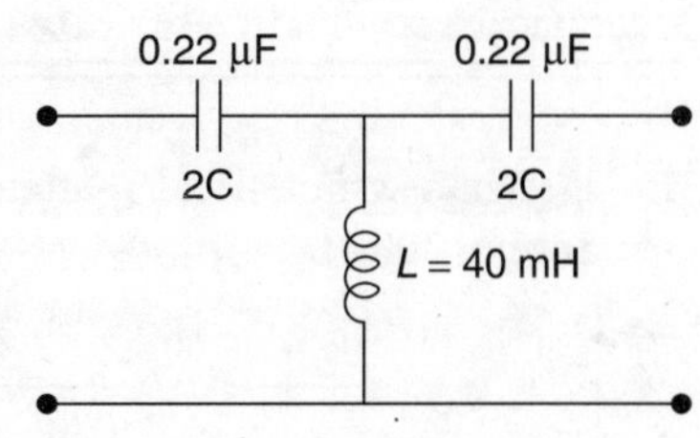

(ii) The components of the *m*-derived *T*-section high-pass filter are

$$m = \sqrt{1 - \left(\frac{f_\infty}{f_C}\right)^2} = \sqrt{1 - \left(\frac{1.1}{1.2}\right)^2} = 0.4$$

$$\frac{2C}{m} = \frac{2 \times 0.11}{0.4} = 0.55\,\mu\text{F}$$

$$\frac{L}{m} = \frac{40}{0.4} = 100 \text{ mH}$$

$$\frac{4m}{1-m^2}C = \frac{4 \times 0.4}{1-.04} \times 0.11 = 0.21\,\mu\text{F}$$

0.55 µF 0.55 µF

2C/m 2C/m

$\frac{L}{m}$ = 100 mH

$\frac{4\text{ m}}{1-\text{m}^2}$ C = 0.21 µF

(iii) The half-section *T* m-derived at each end will have element with $m = 0.6$.

Full section *T* with $m = 0.6$

$$mL = 0.6 \times 40 = 24 \text{ mH}$$

$$mC = 0.6 \times 0.11 = 0.66\,\mu\text{F}$$

$$\frac{1-m^2}{4m}L = \frac{1-0.6^2}{4 \times 0.6} \times 40 = 10.7 \text{ mH}$$

Half section values are

$$\frac{mL}{2} = \frac{24}{2} = 12 \text{ mH}$$

$$\frac{mC}{2} = \frac{0.0666}{2} = 0.0333\,\mu\text{F}$$

$$\frac{1-m^2}{2m}L = 10.7 \times 2 = 21.4 \text{ mH}$$

Therefore, the composite filter having one constant *K*, one m-derived and one half section *T* at each end is as shown below.

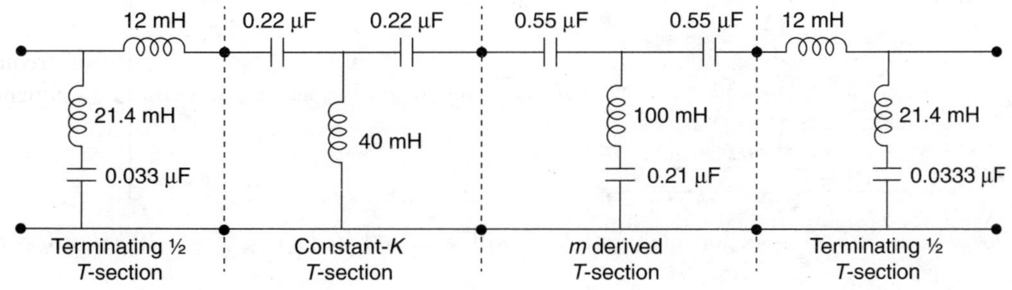

EXERCISE PROBLEMS

1. Design a symmetrical T-attenuator to give an attenuation of 20 dB and to have a characteristic impedance of 300 Ω.

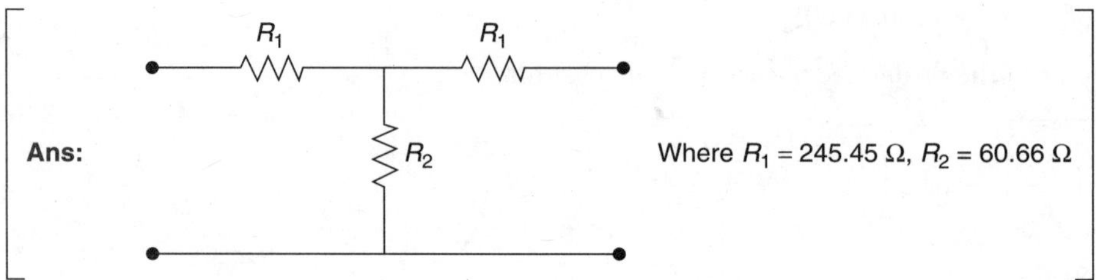

2. Design a symmetrical lattice attenuator to have an attenuation of 20 dB and characteristic impedance of 500 Ω.

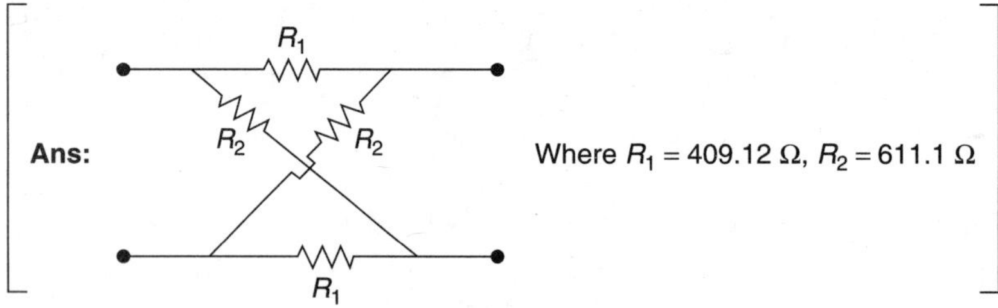

3. Design a symmetrical T-attenuator to produce an attenuation of 20 dB and to work between source impedance of 200 Ω and load impedance of 800 Ω. [**Ans:** $R_1 = 123.1\ \Omega$, $R_2 = 735.3\ \Omega$, $R_3 = 81\ \Omega$]

4. For an asymmetrical L-attenuator, operating between equal source and load impedances $R_1 = 396\ \Omega$, $R_2 = 4.04\ \Omega$. Calculate the value of image impedance or characteristic impedance R_i and magnitude of attenuation. [**Ans:** $R_i = R_0 = 400\ \Omega$, $N = 5.6$]

5. Design constant K, T and π-sections of the following filters having nominal characteristic impedance of $R_0 = 600\ \Omega$.
(a) LPF with a cut-off frequency of $f_c = 3$ kHz (b) HPF with a cut-off frequency of $f_c = 6$ kHz
[**Ans:** (a) $L = 63.68$ mH, $C = 0.1753\ \mu$F (b) $L = 7.962$ mH, $C = 0.0221\ \mu$F]

6. A prototype high-pass filter has a cut-off frequency of 8 kHz and a characteristic impedance of 600 Ω. Calculate the values of inductance and capacitance used in the filter. [**Ans:** $L = 5.97$ mH, $C = 0.0165$ pF]

7. Design an m-derived T-section low pass filter having a cut-off frequency $f_c = 2000$ Hz, design impedance $R_0 = 600\ \Omega$ and frequency of infinite attenuation $f_\infty = 2050$ Hz.

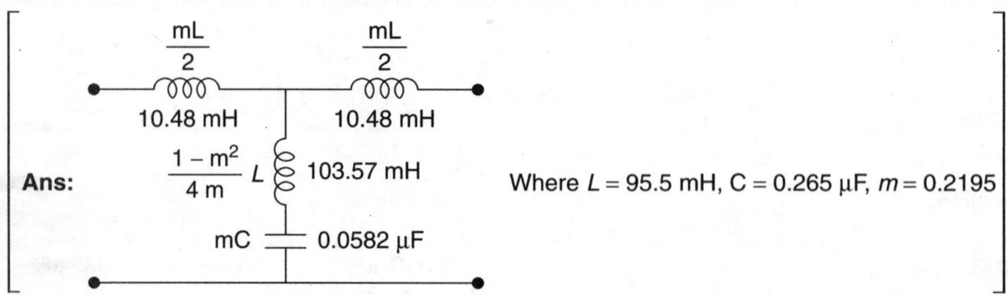

8. Design an m-derived π-section high pass filter with a cut-off frequency of $f_c = 10$ kHz, $R_0 = 600\ \Omega$, $f_\infty = 8$ kHz.

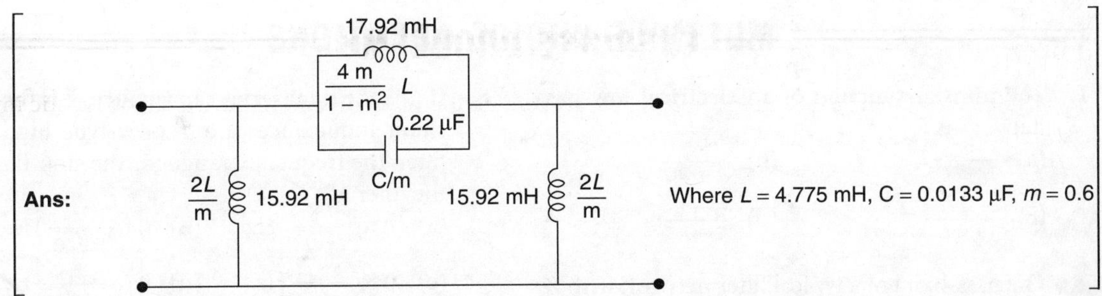

9. For a constant K T-section LPF as shown, calculate the numerical values of nominal characteristic impedance R_0 and the cut-off frequency f_c. [**Ans:** $R_0 = 2$ k Ω, $f_c = 7.96$ kHz]

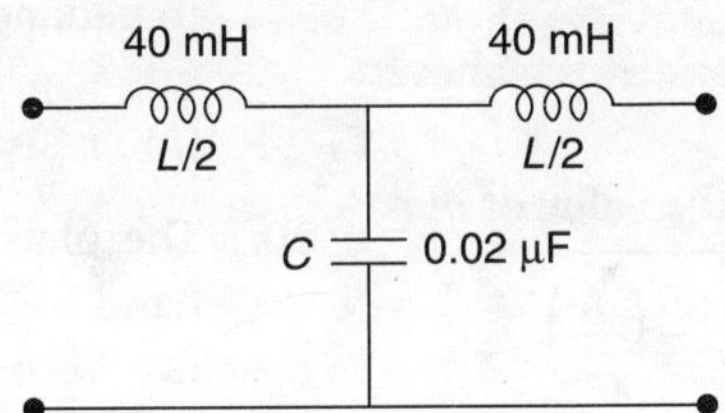

10. Find the component values of an asymmetrical π-attenuator to operate between 200 Ω and 500 Ω line. The attenuator provides a loss of 20 dB. [**Ans:** $R_1 = 224.1$ Ω, $R_2 = 713.8$ Ω, $R_3 = 1.56$ kΩ]

11. Design the following types of attenuators to provide an attenuation of 40 dB to work into a line of design impedance of 600 Ω.
(a) Symmetrical π-attenuator (b) Asymmetrical L-attenuator
[**Ans:** (a) $R_1 = 30$ kΩ, $R_2 = 612$ Ω (b) $R_1 = 594$ Ω, $R_2 = 6.1$ Ω]

12. Find the values of the attenuation per section and characteristic impedance of a symmetrical π-attenuator when the component values have been given as (a) series arm $R_1 = 20$ Ω, shunt arm (each) $R_2 = 400$ Ω, (b) series arm $R_1 = 100$ Ω, shunt arm (each) $R_2 = 300$ Ω? [**Ans:** (a) $N = 2.618$, $R_0 = 179$ Ω (b) $N = 2.215$, $R_0 = 113.4$ Ω]

REVIEW QUESTIONS

1. Define the following:
   (a) filter
   (b) pass-band and stop-band
   (c) cut-off frequency
   (d) low-pass and high-pass filters
   (e) neper
   (f) band elimination filter
   (g) propagation constant
   (h) attenuator
2. What will happen to the input signal when the transmission line is terminated by its characteristic impedance?
3. What is a prototype filter?
4. What is an m-derived filter?
5. What is a composite filter? Explain its design procedure.
6. List different types of attenuators. What are the uses of attenuators?
7. List the different types of filters.

MULTIPLE CHOICE QUESTIONS

1. The transfer function of an electrical low-pass network is
   (a) $\frac{sRC}{1+sRC}$ (b) $\frac{RC}{1+sRC}$
   (c) $\frac{s}{1+sRC}$ (d) $\frac{1}{1+sRC}$

2. The pass-band of a typical filter network with Z_1 and Z_2 as the series and shunt-arm impedances is characterised by
   (a) $-1<\frac{Z_1}{4Z_2}<0$ (b) $-1<\frac{Z_1}{4Z_2}<1$
   (c) $0<\frac{Z_1}{4Z_2}<1$ (d) none of the above

3. In an m-derived low-pass filter, the value of m is
   (a) $\sqrt{1-\left(\frac{f_\infty}{f_c}\right)^2}$ (b) $\sqrt{1-\left(\frac{f_c}{f_\infty}\right)^2}$
   (c) $\sqrt{1+\left(\frac{f_\infty}{f_c}\right)^2}$ (d) $\sqrt{1+\left(\frac{f_c}{f_\infty}\right)^2}$

4. For the lattice-type attenuator, the characteristics impedance R_0 is
   (a) $\frac{R_1+R_2}{2}$ (b) $\frac{2R_1R_2}{R_1+R_2}$
   (c) $\sqrt{R_1R_2}$ (d) $\sqrt{R_1+R_2}$

5. The attenuation of an attenuator is 20 dB. Its attenuation constant N is:
   (a) 1 (b) 2
   (c) 10 (d) 20

6. Tick the correct statement in the case of a filter.
   (a) Characteristic impedance is resistive in stop-band
   (b) Characteristic impedance is reactive in pass-band
   (c) Characteristic impedance is resistive in pass-band
   (d) None of the above

7. If L is the total series inductance and C the total shunt capacitance of a T or π-type low-pass filter, the pass-band frequency range of the filter is given as
   (a) 0 to $\frac{1}{2\pi\sqrt{LC}}$ Hz (b) 0 to $\frac{1}{\pi\sqrt{LC}}$ Hz
   (c) 0 to $\frac{2}{\pi\sqrt{LC}}$ Hz (d) 0 to $\frac{1}{4\pi\sqrt{LC}}$ Hz

8. If C is the total series capacitance, L is the total shunt inductance of a T or π-type high pass filter, the frequency range for the stop-band of the filter is
   (a) 0 to $\frac{1}{2\pi\sqrt{LC}}$ Hz (b) 0 to $\frac{1}{\pi\sqrt{LC}}$ Hz
   (c) 0 to $\frac{2}{\pi\sqrt{LC}}$ Hz (d) 0 to $\frac{1}{4\pi\sqrt{LC}}$ Hz

9. If f_1 and f_2 are the lower and upper cut-off frequencies of the band pass filter, the series impedance Z_1 is:
   (a) capacitive at f_1 (b) inductive at f_1
   (c) resistive at f_2 (d) none of the above

10. The phase constant β of a filter during stop-band is
    (a) zero radians (b) 2
    (c) π (d) 2π

11. If all the transmission zeros of a network are at infinity, it is a
    (a) low-pass filter
    (b) high-pass filter
    (c) band-pass filter
    (d) no criterion to decide the kind of filter

12. If all the transmission zeros of a network are at the origin, it is a
    (a) low-pass filter
    (b) high-pass filter
    (c) band-pass filter
    (d) no criterion to decide the kind of filter

13. If some of the transmission zeros of a network are at origin and other at infinity, it is a
    (a) low-pass filter
    (b) high-pass filter
    (c) band-pass filter
    (d) no criterion to decide the kind of filter

14. A high-pass filter circuit is basically
    (a) a differentiating circuit with a low time constant
    (b) a differentiating circuit with a large time constant
    (c) an integrating circuit with a low time constant
    (d) an integrating circuit with a large time constant

15. An ideal filter should have
    (a) zero attenuation in the pass-band
    (b) infinite attenuation in the pass-band
    (c) zero attenuation in the stop-band
    (d) infinite attenuation in the stop-band

16. Consider the following statement with respect to a constant K type band pass filter:
    (i) A band pass filter is obtained by the series connection of a low pass filter.
    (ii) It is obtained by the cascade connection of a low pass and a high pass filter.
    (iii) In this case the cut-off frequency of the low-pass filter is lower than that of the high-pass filter.

    Tick the correct statements.
    (a) 1 and 2 (b) 1 and 3
    (c) only 1 (d) 2 and 3

17. If L_1 and C_1 are the total series values and L_2 and C_2 the shunt values of a constant K type band pass filter; these are so chosen that the resonance frequency of the series arm and shunt arm are
    (a) such that series has higher frequency than the shunt
    (b) such that series has lower resonance frequency that the shunt arm
    (c) equal
    (d) not related

18. For the band pass filter, the normal characteristic impedance R_0 is given as:
    (a) $R_0 = \sqrt{\frac{L_1}{C_1}}$ (b) $R_0 = \sqrt{\frac{L_1}{C_2}}$
    (c) $R_0 = \sqrt{\frac{L_2}{C_2}}$ (d) (a) and (c)

19. If f_1 and f_2 are the lower and upper cut-off frequencies of a band pass filter (constant K) and f_0 the resonant frequency of the component of series arm of the filter, then
    (a) $f_0 = \frac{f_1 + f_2}{2}$ (b) $f_0 = \sqrt{f_1 f_2}$
    (c) $f_0 = \sqrt{2 f_1 f_2}$ (d) $f_0 = \sqrt{(f_1 f_2)/2}$

20. The frequency of resonance of the shunt arm of the m-derived filter is so chosen that, compared to the constant K type filter, it is:
    (a) slightly lower (b) slightly higher
    (c) equal (d) no restriction

Answers

1. d	**2.** a	**3.** b	**4.** c	**5.** c	**6.** c	**7.** b	**8.** d	**9.** a	**10.** c
11. a	**12.** b	**13.** c	**14.** a	**15.** a	**16.** c	**17.** c	**18.** b	**19.** b	**20.** b

15 Network Synthesis

Learning Outcomes

After reading this chapter, the reader will able to

- Define a Hurwitz polynomial and list its properties
- Outline the Hurwitz test on polynomials
- Define a positive real function and list its properties
- Outline the necessary and sufficient conditions for positive real function
- Illustrate the concept of network synthesis
- Synthesis of one-port networks using basic elements
- Synthesise *LC* driving point immittance function using Foster and Cauer forms
- Synthesise *RC* impedance/*RL* admittance function using Foster and Cauer forms
- Synthesise *RL* impedance/*RC* admittance function using Foster and Cauer forms

15.1 INTRODUCTION

In the study of electrical networks, broadly two topics are considered—network analysis and network synthesis. In general, any network consists of excitation, network function and response. In network analysis, network and excitation are given and the response has to be determined. However, in network synthesis, excitation and response are given, and the network has to be determined. Thus, in network synthesis we are concerned with the realisation of a network for a given excitation–response characteristic. In network analysis, there is a unique solution to the problem. But the synthesis problem is not unique, because we can find more than one network for the given excitation and response.

15.2 CAUSALITY AND STABILITY

To synthesise any network for the given excitation and response, we should know the network function, which is given by $F(s)=\frac{N(s)}{D(s)}$. The next step in the synthesis procedure is to determine whether the network function can be realised as a physical passive network or not. A network is realisable if it satisfies causality and stability conditions. Causality implies that a voltage cannot appear at any port before a current is applied or vice versa. In other words, the impulse response $f(t)=0$ for $t<0$.

For the network to be stable, the network function, $F(s)$ should satisfy the following conditions:

- it cannot have poles in the right half of the s-plane,
- it cannot have multiple poles on the $j\omega$ axis, and
- the degree of numerator polynomial cannot be more than unity when compared to the degree of the denominator polynomial.

15.3 HURWITZ POLYNOMIAL

A polynomial $P(s)$ is said to be Hurwitz, if it satisfies the following conditions.

- $P(s)$ is real, when s is real.
- The roots of $P(s)$ have real parts, which are to be zero or negative.

15.3.1 Properties of a Hurwitz Polynomial

If the polynomial $P(s)$ can be written as $P(s) = a_0 s^n + a_1 s^{n-1} + a_2 s^{n-2} + \cdots a_n$, then

- All the coefficients a_i must be positive.
- $P(s)$ must be real and positive for all s.
- If the polynomial $P(s)$ is either even or odd, the roots of the polynomial $P(s)$ should lie only on the $j\omega$ axis.
- If any complex roots are present, it should be on the left half of the s-plane and also simple and conjugate.
- $P(s)$ should not have any missing terms, unless the polynomial is completely even or completely odd.

15.3.2 Hurwitz Test on Polynomial

There are two testing methods:

(i) Continuous Fraction Expansion (CFE), and
(ii) Routh–Hurwitz (RH) criterion.

(i) Continuous Fraction Expansion (CFE): Let $P(s) = a_0 s^n + a_1 s^{n-1} + a_2 s^{n-2} + \cdots a_n$, where $a_n > 0$

(a) Divide $P(s)$ into two polynomials—even $E(s)$ and odd $O(s)$ polynomials.

$$P(s) = E(s) + O(s)$$

(b) The continued fraction expansion can be written as

$$Z(s) = \frac{E(s)}{O(s)} = K_1(s) + \cfrac{1}{K_2(s) + \cfrac{1}{K_3(s) + \cfrac{1}{K_4(s) + \vdots \atop \vdots \atop \cfrac{1}{K_n(s)}}}}$$

where $K_1(s)$, $K_2(s)\ldots K_n(s)$ are the coefficients of successive division and they should be positive, when the polynomial $P(s)$ is Hurwitz.

(c) If $P(s)$ is expressed as $W(s)\, P_1(s)$, then $P(s)$ is Hurwitz, if $W(s)$ and $P_1(s)$ are Hurwitz.

(d) If the ratio of polynomial $P(s)$ and its derivative $P(s)'$ gives a continued fraction expansion with all positive coefficients, then the polynomial $P(s)$ is Hurwitz

Note: If the order of $O(s)$ is higher than $E(s)$ then divide $O(s)$ by $E(s)$, otherwise divide $E(s)$ by $O(s)$.

Problem 15.1 Check whether the given polynomial $P(s) = s^4 + s^3 + 5s^2 + 3s + 4$ is Hurwitz or not.

Solution:

Given that $P(s) = s^4 + s^3 + 5s^2 + 3s + 4$

(i) Since all the coefficients of $P(s)$ are positive, $P(s)$ is real, for s real.
(ii) The even and odd parts of $P(s)$ are

$$E(s) = s^4 + 5s^2 + 4, \quad O(s) = s^3 + 3s$$

The continued fraction expansion $Z(s) = \frac{E(s)}{O(s)}$ is given by

$$s^3+3s)s^4+5s^2+4(s$$
$$\underline{s^4+3s^2}$$
$$2s^2+4)s^3+3s(\frac{1}{2}s$$
$$\underline{s^3+2s}$$
$$s)2s^2+4(2s$$
$$\underline{2s^2}$$
$$4)s\,(\frac{1}{4}s$$
$$\underline{s}$$
$$0$$

Since all the quotient terms are positive, $P(s)$ is Hurwitz.

Problem 15.2 Check whether the given polynomials are Hurwitz or not.

(i) $P(s) = s^5 + 2s^3 + 5s^2 + 10s + 20$ (ii) $P(s) = s^6 + s^5 - 3s^4 + 2s^3 + 5s^2 + 6s + 2$

Solution:

(i) $P(s) = s^5 + 2s^3 + 5s^2 + 10s + 20$
In the given polynomial, the s^4 term is missing and it is neither an even nor odd polynomial. So the given polynomial is not Hurwitz.

(ii) $P(s) = s^6 + s^5 - 3s^4 + 2s^3 + 5s^2 + 6s + 2$
In the given polynomial, the s^4 coefficient is negative, that is, –3, hence the given polynomial is not Hurwitz.

Problem 15.3 Check whether the polynomial $P(s) = s^4 + s^3 + 2s^2 + 3s + 2$ is Hurwitz or not.

Solution:

Given that $P(s) = s^4 + s^3 + 2s^2 + 3s + 2$

(i) Since all the coefficients of $P(s)$ are positive, $P(s)$ is real, for s real.
(ii) The even and odd parts of $P(s)$ are

$$E(s) = s^4 + 2s^2 + 2,\ O(s) = s^3 + 3s$$

The continued fraction expansion $Z(s) = \frac{E(s)}{O(s)}$ is given as

$$s^3+3s)s^4+2s^2+2(s$$
$$\underline{s^4+3s^2}$$
$$-s^2+2)s^3+3s(-s$$
$$\underline{s^3-2s}$$
$$5s)-s^2+2(-\frac{1}{5}s$$
$$\underline{-s^2}$$
$$2)5s\,(\frac{5}{2}s$$
$$\underline{5s}$$
$$0$$

Since two quotient terms are negative, $P(s)$ is not Hurwitz.

Problem 15.4 Check whether the polynomial $P(s) = s^5 + 3s^3 + 2s$ is Hurwitz or not.

Solution:

Given that $P(s) = s^5 + 3s^3 + 2s$

Since the given polynomial contains odd powers only, it is not possible to perform a continued fraction expansion.

$$P'(s) = \frac{dP(s)}{ds} = 5s^4 + 9s^2 + 2$$

Now, the continued fraction expansion $Z(s) = \frac{P(s)}{P'(s)}$ is given by

$$5s^4 + 9s^2 + 2)\ s^5 + 3s^3 + 2s\left(\frac{s}{5}\right.$$
$$s^5 + \frac{9}{5}s^3 + \frac{2}{5}s$$
$$\overline{\frac{6}{5}s^3 + \frac{8}{5}s)5s^4 + 9s^2 + 2\left(\frac{25}{6}s\right.}$$
$$5s^4 + \frac{20}{3}s^2$$
$$\overline{\frac{7}{3}s^2 + 2)\ \frac{6}{5}s^3 + \frac{8}{5}s\left(\frac{18}{35}s\right.}$$
$$\frac{6}{5}s^3 + \frac{36}{35}s$$
$$\overline{\frac{4}{7}s)\ \frac{7}{3}s^2 + 2\left(\frac{49}{12}s\right.}$$
$$\frac{7}{3}s^2$$
$$\overline{2)\frac{4}{7}s\left(\frac{2}{7}s\right.}$$
$$\frac{4}{7}s$$
$$\overline{0}$$

Since all the quotient terms are positive, $P(s)$ is Hurwitz.

Problem 15.5 Check whether the polynomial $P(s) = s^3 + 2s^2 + 3s + 6$ is Hurwitz or not.

Solution:

Given that $P(s) = s^3 + 2s^2 + 3s + 6$

(i) Since all the coefficients of $P(s)$ are positive, $P(s)$ is real, for s real.
(ii) The even and odd parts of $P(s)$ are

$$E(s) = 2s^2 + 6,\ O(s) = s^3 + 3s$$

The continued fraction expansion $Z(s) = \frac{O(s)}{E(s)}$. Since $O(s)$ has higher order than $E(s)$, it is given as

$$2s^2+6)s^3+3s\,(\frac{s}{2}$$
$$\underline{s^3+3s^2}$$
$$0$$

The division has terminated after one step, giving zero as the remainder, thus $E(s)$ and $O(s)$ have a common factor of $(s^3 + 3s)$. Thus,

$$P(s) = (s^3 + 3s)\left(1 + \frac{2}{s}\right) = W(s)\,P_1(s)$$

where, $P_1(s) = 1 + \frac{2}{s}$ is Hurwitz

$$W(s) = s^3 + 3s = s(s^2 + 3) = s(s + j\sqrt{3})(s - j\sqrt{3}) \text{ is Hurwitz.}$$

Since $W(s)$ and $P_1(s)$ are is Hurwitz, $P(s)$ is also Hurwitz.

Problem 15.6 Check whether the polynomial $P(s) = s^6 + 3s^5 + 8s^4 + 15s^3 + 17s^2 + 12s + 4$ is Hurwitz or not.

Solution:

Given that $P(s) = s^6 + 3s^5 + 8s^4 + 15s^3 + 17s^2 + 12s + 4$

(i) Since all the coefficients of $P(s)$ are positive, $P(s)$ is real, for s real.

(ii) The even and odd parts of $P(s)$ are

$$E(s) = s^6 + 8s^4 + 17s^2 + 4,\ O(s) = 3s^5 + 15s^3 + 12s$$

The continued fraction expansion $Z(s) = \frac{E(s)}{O(s)}$ is given as

$$3s^5 + 15s^3 + 12s)\ s^6 + 8s^4 + 17s^2 + 4\ (\frac{s}{3}$$
$$\underline{s^6 + 5s^4 + 4s^2}$$
$$3s^4 + 13s^2 + 4)\ 3s^5 + 15s^3 + 12s\ (s$$
$$\underline{3s^5 + 13s^3 + 4s}$$
$$2s^3 + 8s)\ 3s^4 + 13s^2 + 4\ (\frac{3}{2}s$$
$$\underline{3s^4 + 12s^2}$$
$$s^2 + 4)\ 2s^3 + 8s\ (2s$$
$$\underline{2s^3 + 8s}$$
$$0$$

The division has terminated after four steps, giving zero as remainder, thus $E(s)$ and $O(s)$ have a common factor of $(s^2 + 4)$. Thus

$$P(s) = s^6 + 3s^5 + 8s^4 + 15s^3 + 17s^2 + 12s + 4 = (s^2 + 4)(s^4 + 3s^3 + 4s^2 + 3s + 1) = W(s)\,P_1(s)$$

where, $P_1(s) = s^2 + 4 = (s + j2)(s - j2)$ is Hurwitz

$$W(s) = s^4 + 3s^3 + 4s^2 + 3s + 1$$

The even and odd parts of $W(s)$ are

$$E_1(s) = s^4 + 4s^2 + 1,\ O_1(s) = 3s^3 + 3s$$

The continued fraction expansion $Z_1(s) = \frac{E_1(s)}{O_1(s)}$ is given as

$$
\begin{array}{l}
3s^3 + 3s)s^4 + 4s^2 + 1(\frac{s}{3} \\
\underline{s^4 + s^2} \\
\qquad 3s^2 + 1)\ 3s^3 + 3s(s \\
\qquad\qquad \underline{3s^3 + s} \\
\qquad\qquad\quad 2s)3s^2 + 1(\frac{3}{2}s \\
\qquad\qquad\quad \underline{3s^2} \\
\qquad\qquad\qquad 1)\ 2s\ (2s \\
\qquad\qquad\qquad\quad \underline{2s} \\
\qquad\qquad\qquad\quad 0
\end{array}
$$

Since all the quotient terms are positive, $W(s)$ is Hurwitz.
Since $W(s)$ and $P_1(s)$ are Hurwitz, $P(s)$ is also Hurwitz.

Note: The number of partial quotients should be equal to the order of the polynomial.

(ii) **Routh–Hurwitz (RH) criterion:** A tabular method can be used to determine whether the given polynomial is Hurwitz or not. For an nth order polynomial, $P(s) = a_0s^n + a_1s^{n-1} + a_2s^{n-2} + \cdots a_n$, the Routh's table is given as

$$
\begin{array}{c|ccccc}
s^n & a_0 & a_2 & a_4 & a_6 & \cdots \\
s^{n-1} & a_1 & a_3 & a_5 & a_7 & \cdots \\
s^{n-2} & b_1 & b_2 & b_3 & b_4 & \\
s^{n-3} & c_1 & c_2 & c_3 & \cdots & \cdots \\
\vdots & \vdots & \vdots & \vdots & & \\
s^0 & a_n & & & &
\end{array}
$$

The coefficients for the first two rows are written directly from the given polynomial. From these two rows, the next rows can be obtained as follows:

$$b_1 = \frac{a_1a_2 - a_0a_3}{a_1},\quad b_2 = \frac{a_1a_4 - a_0a_5}{a_1},\quad b_3 = \frac{a_1a_6 - a_0a_7}{a_1} \cdots$$

From the second and third row, the fourth row can be determined as

$$c_1 = \frac{b_1a_3 - a_1b_2}{b_1},\quad c_2 = \frac{b_1a_5 - a_1b_3}{b_1} \cdots$$

This process has to be continued until the coefficient for s^0 is obtained, which will be a_n. From this array, whether the given polynomial is Hurwitz or not is decided.

In the Routh–Hurwitz table, if all the elements in the first column are positive (should have same sign) and there should not be any sign change, then the polynomial $P(s)$ is said to be Hurwitz.

Problem 15.7 Check whether the polynomial, $P(s) = s^4 + 5s^3 + 2s^2 + 3s + 2$ is Hurwitz or not. Use the Routh–Hurwitz criterion.

Solution:

Given that $P(s) = s^4 + 5s^3 + 2s^2 + 3s + 2$

The Routh's array or table is

s^4	1	2	2
s^3	5	3	0
s^2	1.4	2	0
s^1	−4.14	0	0
s^0	2		

There are two sign changes in the first column of Routh's table; hence the given polynomial is not Hurwitz.

Problem 15.8 Check whether the following polynomials are Hurwitz or not. Use Routh–Hurwitz criterion.

(i) $P(s) = s^4 + 21s^3 + 21s^2 + 36s + 20$
(ii) $P(s) = s^5 + 6s^4 + 3s^3 + 2s^2 + s + 1$

Solution:

(i) $P(s) = s^4 + 21s^3 + 21s^2 + 36s + 20$

The Routh's array is

s^4	1	21	20
s^3	21	36	0
s^2	19.28	20	0
s^1	14.22	0	
s^0	20		

There is no sign change in the first column of Routh's array; hence the given polynomial is Hurwitz.

(ii) $P(s) = s^5 + 6s^4 + 3s^3 + 2s^2 + s + 1$

The Routh's array is

s^5	1	3	1
s^4	6	2	0
s^3	2.67	1	0
s^2	−0.24	1	0
s^1	11.68	0	
s^0	1		

There are two sign changes in the first column of Routh's table; hence the given polynomial is not Hurwitz.

Problem 15.9 Check whether the polynomial $P(s) = s^6 + 2s^5 + 8s^4 + 12s^3 + 20s^2 + 16s + 16$ is Hurwitz or not. Use Routh–Hurwitz criterion.

Solution:

The Routh's array is

s^6	1	8	20	16
s^5	2	12	16	0
s^4	2	12	16	
s^3	0	0	0 ← Routh's test failed	
s^2				

To eliminate the above-mentioned difficulty, an equation is formed by using the coefficients of the array which is just above the row of zeroes. This equation is known as the auxiliary polynomial. Differentiate the auxiliary polynomial with respect to s, to get $\frac{dA(s)}{ds}$ and now replace the row of zeroes with coefficients of $\frac{dA(s)}{ds}$ and continue the construction of the array in the usual manner.

$$\therefore A(s) = 2s^4 + 12s^2 + 16$$

$$\frac{dA(s)}{ds} = 8s^3 + 24s$$

The above-mentioned Routh's array becomes

s^6	1	8	20	16
s^5	2	12	16	0
s^4	2	12	16	
s^3	8	24	0	
s^2	6	16		
s^1	2.67	0		
s^0	16			

There is no sign change in the first column of Routh's array; hence the given polynomial is Hurwitz.

15.4 POSITIVE REAL FUNCTION

It is used as the stability indicator of the response of a system subjected to excitation. A function $F(s) = \frac{N(s)}{D(s)}$ is positive real if the following conditions are satisfied.

- $F(s)$ is real when s is real.
- The real part of $F(s)$ is greater than or equal to zero when the real part of s is greater than or equal to zero. That is, R.P of $F(s) > 0$, for R.P of $s > 0$.

15.4.1 Properties of Positive Real Functions

- All the coefficients of $F(s)$ must be real and non-negative.
- Poles and zeroes of positive real functions cannot be present in the right half of the s-plane.
- Only simple poles with real and positive can be present on the $j\omega$ axis.
- If $F(s)$ is a positive real function, then $1/F(s)$ is also a positive real function.
- The highest and lowest powers of $N(s)$ and $D(s)$ differ by unity.
- The sum of the two positive real functions is also a positive real function, but the difference of the two positive real functions is not necessarily a positive real function.

15.4.2 Necessary and Sufficient Conditions for Positive Real Function

The necessary and sufficient conditions for a rational function $F(s)$ with real coefficients to be positive are listed.

(i) The function $F(s)$ cannot have any poles and zeros in the right half of the s-plane, that is, the numerator $N(s)$ and denominator $D(s)$ of $F(s)$ must be Hurwitz polynomials.

(ii) $F(s)$ must have simple poles on the $j\omega$ axis with real and positive residues.

(iii) If $F(s)=\frac{N(s)}{D(s)}=\frac{E_1(s)+O_1(s)}{E_2(s)+O_2(s)}$, $E_i(s)$ being the even parts and $O_i(s)$ being the odd parts, then for positive realness of $F(s)$, $E_1(j\omega)E_2(j\omega)-O_1(j\omega)O_2(j\omega)\geq 0$ for all ω such that $\text{Re}[F(j\omega)]\geq 0$ for all ω.

Testing of the above conditions

Condition (i) requires that the numerator and denominator roots of $F(s)$ must lie in the left half of the s-plane, that is, we must determine whether the numerator, $N(s)$ and denominator, $D(s)$ of $F(s)$ are Hurwitz. This can be tested through a continued fraction expansion of the odd to even parts or even to odd parts of the $N(s)$ and $D(s)$, in which quotients must be positive.

Condition (ii) can be tested by making a partial fraction expansion of $F(s)$ and checking whether the residues of the poles on the $j\omega$-axis are positive and real. Thus, if $F(s)$ has a pair of poles at $s = \pm jp$, a partial fraction expansion gives terms of the form $\frac{K_1}{s-jp}+\frac{K_1^*}{s+jp}$. Since residues of complex conjugate poles are themselves conjugate, $K_1=K_1^*$ and should be positive and real.

Condition (iii) requires that $\text{Re}[F(j\omega)]\geq 0$ for all ω. Now, to compute $F(j\omega)$ from $F(s)=\frac{N(s)}{D(s)}$, we first separate the even and odd parts of $N(s)$ and $D(s)$, that is,

$$F(s)=\frac{N(s)}{D(s)}=\frac{E_1(s)+O_1(s)}{E_2(s)+O_2(s)}=\frac{E_1+O_1}{E_2+O_2} \tag{15.1}$$

Now rationalising, we have

$$F(s)=\frac{E_1+O_1}{E_2+O_2}\times\frac{E_2-O_2}{E_2-O_2}=\frac{E_1E_2-O_1O_2}{E_2^2-O_2^2}+\frac{E_2O_1-E_1O_2}{E_2^2-O_2^2} \tag{15.2}$$

But the product of two even or odd functions is itself an even function, while the product of an even and an odd function is odd. So

$$\text{Even part of}\quad F(s)=Ev\,[F(s)]=\frac{E_1E_2-O_1O_2}{E_2^2-O_2^2} \tag{15.3}$$

$$\text{Odd part of}\quad F(s)=\text{Odd}\,[F(s)]=\frac{E_2O_1-E_1O_2}{E_2^2-O_2^2} \tag{15.4}$$

The substitution of $s=j\omega$ into an even polynomial gives the real part of $F(s)$ and the substitution of $s=j\omega$ into an odd polynomial gives the imaginary part of $F(s)$, that is,

$$\text{Re}[F(j\omega)]=Ev[F(s)]|_{s=j\omega} \tag{15.5}$$

$$j\text{Im}F(j\omega)]=\text{Odd}[F(s)]|_{s=j\omega} \tag{15.6}$$

Thus, to test the third condition for positive realness, we have to check $\text{Re}[F(j\omega)]\geq 0$ for all ω. The denominator of $\text{Re}[F(j\omega)]$ is always a positive quantity, because

$$[E_2(j\omega)]^2-[O_2(j\omega)]^2=E_2(\omega^2)-O_2(\omega^2)\geq 0 \tag{15.7}$$

Hence, the condition that $Ev[F(j\omega)]$ should be positive requires

$$A(\omega^2)=E_1(j\omega)E_2(j\omega)-O_1(j\omega)O_2(j\omega)\geq 0\quad\text{for all}\quad\omega\geq 0 \tag{15.8}$$

Problem 15.10 Determine whether the function, $F(s)=\frac{s+1}{s+2}$ is positive real or not.

Solution:

Given that, $F(s)=\frac{s+1}{s+2}$

Condition (1): The function has a pole at $s=-2$ and a zero at $s=-1$. Thus the poles and zeros are on the left half of the s-plane.

Condition (2): Since there is no pole on the $j\omega$-axis, the residue test is not required.

Condition (3):

$$\text{Re}[F(j\omega)]=\text{Re}\left[\frac{1+j\omega}{2+j\omega}\right]=\text{Re}\left[\frac{1+j\omega}{2+j\omega}\times\frac{2-j\omega}{2-j\omega}\right]$$

$$=\text{Re}\left[\frac{2+\omega^2+j\omega}{4+\omega^2}\right]=\frac{2+\omega^2}{4+\omega^2}$$

So, for all values ω, $\text{Re}[F(j\omega)]\geq 0$

Since all the three conditions are satisfied, the given function is positive real.

Problem 15.11 Determine whether the function, $F(s)=\frac{s^2+5s+4}{s^2+8s+12}$ is positive real or not.

Solution:

Given that $F(s)=\frac{s^2+5s+4}{s^2+8s+12}=\frac{(s+1)(s+4)}{(s+2)(s+6)}=\frac{N(s)}{D(s)}$

Condition (1): The function $F(s)$ has poles at $s=-2$ and $s=-6$ and zero at $s=-1$ and $s=-4$. Thus the poles and zeros are on the left half of the s-plane.

Condition (2): Since there is no pole on the $j\omega$-axis, the residue test is not required.

Condition (3):

Even part of $N(s)$, $E_1(s)=s^2+4$

Odd part of $N(s)$, $O_1(s)=5s$

Even part of $D(s)$, $E_2(s)=s^2+12$

Odd part of $D(s)$, $O_2(s)=8s$

$$A(\omega^2)=[E_1(s)E_2(s)-O_1(s)O_2(s)]_{s=j\omega}=[(s^2+4)(s^2+12)-40s^2]_{s=j\omega}$$

$$=[s^4-24s^2+48]_{s=j\omega}=\omega^4+24\omega^2+48$$

$\therefore$ $A(\omega^2)=\omega^4+2\omega^2+48\geq$ for all values of ω

Since all the three conditions are satisfied, the given function is positive real.

Problem 15.12 Determine whether the function, $F(s)=\frac{2s^3+2s^2+3s+2}{s^2+1}$ is positive real or not.

Solution:

Given that $F(s)=\dfrac{2s^3+2s^2+3s+2}{s^2+1}=\dfrac{2s^3+2s^2+3s+2}{(s+j1)(s-j1)}=\dfrac{N(s)}{D(s)}$

Condition (1): The function $F(s)$ has poles at $s=-j1$ and $s=j1$ and the numerator polynomial cannot be easily factorised; we will prove whether $N(s)$ is Hurwitz or not.

The even and odd parts of $N(s)$ are

$$E(s)=2s^2+2,\ O(s)=2s^3+3s$$

The continued fraction expansion $Z(s)=\frac{O(s)}{E(s)}$, is given as

$$\begin{array}{l}
2s^2+2)\,2s^3+3s\,(s \\
\qquad\quad \underline{2s^3+2s} \\
\qquad\qquad\quad s)\,2s^2+2\,(2s \\
\qquad\qquad\qquad \underline{2s^2} \\
\qquad\qquad\qquad\qquad 2)\,s\,(\frac{s}{2} \\
\qquad\qquad\qquad\qquad\quad \underline{s} \\
\qquad\qquad\qquad\qquad\quad 0
\end{array}$$

Since, all the quotient terms are positive, $N(s)$ is Hurwitz. This indicates that all the zeroes are in the left half of the s-plane. Thus all the poles and zeroes are in the left half of the s-plane.

Condition (2): Since the poles are on the $j\omega$-axis, we have to determine the residues. Here, the degree of denominator is less than that of the numerator, so division is first carried out, before partial expansion.

$$\begin{array}{l}
s^2+1)\,2s^3+2s^2+3s+2\,(2s+2 \\
\qquad\quad \underline{2s^3+2s\qquad\qquad} \\
\qquad\qquad\quad 2s^2+s+2 \\
\qquad\qquad\quad \underline{2s^2+2\quad} \\
\qquad\qquad\qquad\quad s
\end{array}$$

$$F(s)=\frac{2s^3+2s^2+3s+2}{s^2+1}=2s+2+\frac{s}{s^2+1}$$

Using partial fraction expansion, we have

$$F(s)=2s+2+\frac{s}{s^2+1}=2s+2+\frac{A}{s-j1}+\frac{B}{s+j1}$$

$$A=(s-j1)\times\left.\frac{s}{s^2+1}\right|_{s=j1}=(s-j1)\times\left.\frac{s}{(s+j1)(s-j1)}\right|_{s=j1}=\frac{j1}{j1+j1}=\frac{1}{2}$$

$$B=(s+j1)\times\left.\frac{s}{s^2+1}\right|_{s=-j1}=(s+j1)\times\left.\frac{s}{(s+j1)(s-j1)}\right|_{s=-j1}=\frac{-j1}{-j1-j1}=\frac{1}{2}$$

Thus, the residues are positive and real.

Condition (3):

Even part of $N(s), E_1(s) = 2s^2 + 2$

Odd part of $N(s), O_1(s) = 2s^3 + 3s$

Even part of $D(s), E_2(s) = s^2 + 1$

Odd part of $D(s), O_2(s) = 0$

$$A(\omega^2) = [E_1(s)E_2(s) - O_1(s)O_2(s)]_{s=j\omega} = [(2s^2+2)(s^2+1) - 0]_{s=j\omega}$$

$$= [2s^4 + 4s^2 + 2]_{s=j\omega} = 2\omega^4 - 4\omega^2 + 4$$

$\therefore$ $A(\omega^2) = 2\omega^4 - 4\omega^2 + 4 \geq$ for all values of ω

Since all the three conditions are satisfied, the given function is positive real.

Problem 15.13 Determine whether the function, $F(s) = \dfrac{s^3+5s^2+9s+3}{s^3+4s^2+7s+9}$ is positive real or not.

Solution:

Given that $F(s) = \dfrac{s^3+5s^2+9s+3}{s^3+4s^2+7s+9} = \dfrac{N(s)}{D(s)}$

Condition (1): The numerator and denominator polynomials cannot be easily factorised; we will prove whether $N(s)$ and $D(s)$ are Hurwitz or not.

The even and odd parts of $N(s)$ are

$$E(s) = 5s^2 + 3,\ O(s) = s^3 + 9s$$

The continued fraction expansion $Z(s) = \frac{O(s)}{E(s)}$, is given as

$$\begin{array}{l}
5s^2+3)\ s^3+9s\ (\tfrac{1}{5}s \\
\qquad\quad s^3+\tfrac{3}{5}s \\
\qquad\quad \overline{\tfrac{42}{5}s)\,5s^2+3\,(\tfrac{25}{42}s} \\
\qquad\qquad\quad 5s^2 \\
\qquad\qquad\quad \overline{3)\,\tfrac{42}{5}s\,(\tfrac{14}{5}s} \\
\qquad\qquad\qquad \tfrac{42}{5}s \\
\qquad\qquad\qquad \overline{0}
\end{array}$$

Since, all the quotient terms are positive, $N(s)$ is Hurwitz.

The even and odd parts of $D(s)$ are,

$$E(s) = 4s^2 + 9,\ O(s) = s^3 + 7s$$

The continued fraction expansion $Z(s) = \frac{O(s)}{E(s)}$, is given as

$$
\begin{array}{l}
4s^2+9)\ s^3+7s\ (\frac{1}{4}s \\
\qquad\quad s^3+\frac{9}{4}s \\
\qquad\quad\overline{\qquad\qquad} \\
\qquad\qquad \frac{19}{4}s)4s^2+9(\frac{16}{19}s \\
\qquad\qquad\qquad 4s^2 \\
\qquad\qquad\qquad\overline{\qquad\qquad} \\
\qquad\qquad\qquad\quad 9)\frac{19}{4}s\ (\frac{19}{36}s \\
\qquad\qquad\qquad\qquad \frac{19}{4}s \\
\qquad\qquad\qquad\qquad\overline{\quad\;} \\
\qquad\qquad\qquad\qquad\ 0
\end{array}
$$

Since, all the quotient terms are positive, $D(s)$ is Hurwitz. Thus all the poles and zeroes are in the left half of the s-plane.

Condition (2): Since there are no poles on the $j\omega$-axis, we need not consider this condition.
Condition (3):

Even part of $N(s)$, $E_1(s) = 5s^2 + 3$

Odd part of $N(s)$, $O_1(s) = s^3 + 9s$

Even part of $D(s)$, $E_2(s) = 4s^2 + 9$

Odd part of $D(s)$, $O_2(s) = s^3 + 7s$

$$A(\omega^2) = [E_1(s)E_2(s) - O_1(s)O_2(s)]_{s=j\omega} = [(5s^2+3)(4s^2+9) - (s^3+9s)(s^3+7s)]_{s=j\omega}$$

$$= [20s^4 + 57s^2 + 27 - s^6 - 16s^4 - 63s^2]_{s=j\omega} = [-s^6 + 4s^4 - 6s^2 + 27]_{s=j\omega}$$

$$= \omega^6 + 4\omega^4 + 6\omega^2 + 27$$

$\therefore$ $A(\omega^2) = \omega^6 + 4\omega^4 + 6\omega^2 + 27 \geq$ for all values of ω

Since all the three conditions are satisfied, the given function is positive real.

15.5 CONCEPT OF NETWORK SYNTHESIS

Synthesis is the art of finding the passive elements of the network from a given network function satisfying the given excitation and response relationships and to present them with proper connection by realising the basic rules.

The impedances and admittances of a passive network are positive real functions; hence addition of impedances or admittances of two passive networks also gives a positive real function. Thus $Z(s) = Z_1(s) + Z_2(s)$ is a positive real function, if $Z_1(s)$ and $Z_2(s)$ are positive real functions. Also $Y(s) = Y_1(s) + Y_2(s)$ is a positive real function, if $Y_1(s)$ and $Y_2(s)$ are positive real functions.

Network synthesis then refers to the operational procedure in which, for a given positive real function $Z(s)$ or $Y(s)$, it is required to select appropriate positive real functions of forms $Z_1(s)$ and $Z_2(s)$ or $Y_1(s)$ and $Y_2(s)$. Let us consider the circuit (Fig. 15.1), to illustrate the process of synthesis.

$$Z(s) = Z_1(s) + Z_2(s)$$

$$\Rightarrow \quad Z_2(s) = Z(s) - Z_1(s) \qquad (15.9)$$

Here $Z_1(s)$ is said to be removed from $Z(s)$, to form a new function $Z_2(s)$. Obviously if $Z_1(s)$ is removed from $Z(s)$, the poles and zeroes of $Z_1(s)$ would be removed from $Z(s)$. The different removal operations are explained below.

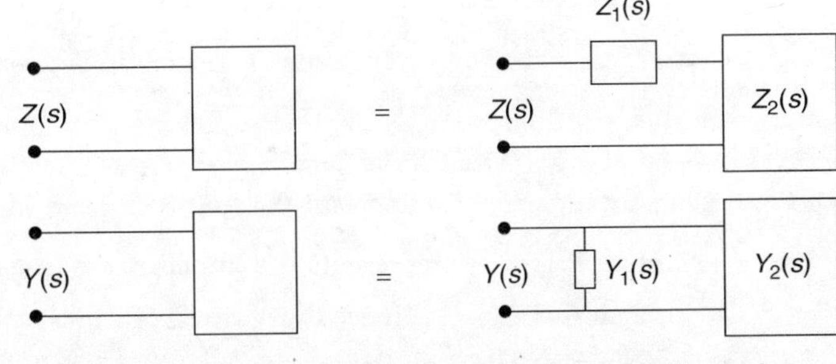

Fig. 15.1 Network interpretation of the removal of impedance and admittance

(i) **Removal of a pole at infinity:** Consider an impedance function $Z(s)$ having a pole at infinity; which means that the degree of the numerator polynomial is greater than the degree of the denominator polynomial by one.

$$Z(s)=\frac{a_{n+1}s^{n+1}+a_ns^n+\cdots+a_1s+a_0}{b_ns^n+b_{n-1}s^{n-1}+\cdots+b_1s+b_0} \tag{15.10}$$

Using long division, we have

$$Z(s)=Ks+\frac{c_ns^n+c_{n-1}s^{n-1}+\cdots+c_1s+c_0}{b_ns^n+b_{n-1}s^{n-1}+\cdots+b_1s+b_0} \tag{15.11}$$

where, $K=\dfrac{a_{n+1}}{b_n}$

Let $Z_1(s)=Ks$ and $Z_2(s)=\dfrac{c_ns^n+c_{n-1}s^{n-1}+\cdots+c_1s+c_0}{b_ns^n+b_{n-1}s^{n-1}+\cdots+b_1s+b_0}$, then

$$Z(s)=Z_1(s)+Z_2(s) \tag{15.12}$$

$$\Rightarrow \quad Z_2(s)=Z(s)-Z_1(s) \tag{15.13}$$

Fig. 15.2 Network interpretation of removal of a pole at infinity

Here $Z_1(s)=Ks$ represents the impedance of an inductor of value, $L=K=\dfrac{a_{n+1}}{b_n}$. Hence the removal of a pole at infinity corresponds to the removal of an inductor from the network [Fig. 15.2(a)]. If the given function is an admittance function, then $Y_1(s)=Ks$ represents the admittance of a capacitor of value, $C=K=\dfrac{a_{n+1}}{b_n}$. Hence the removal of a pole at infinity corresponds to the removal of a capacitor from the network [Fig. 15.2(b)].

(ii) **Removal of a pole at zero:** Consider an impedance function $Z(s)$ having a pole at zero; which means that the degree of the denominator polynomial is greater than the degree of the numerator polynomial by one.

$$Z(s)=\frac{a_ns^n+a_{n-1}s^{n-1}\cdots+a_1s+a_0}{b_ns^n+b_{n-1}s^{n-1}+\cdots+b_1s} \tag{15.14}$$

Using long division, we have

$$Z(s)=\frac{K}{s}+\frac{c_ns^{n-1}+\cdots+c_2s+c_1}{b_ns^{n-1}+\cdots+b_2s+b_1}=Z_1(s)+Z_2(s) \tag{15.15}$$

where, $K=\dfrac{a_0}{b_1}$

$$Z_1(s) = \frac{K}{s}$$

and $$Z_2(s) = \frac{c_n s^{n-1} + \cdots + c_2 s + c_1}{b_n s^{n-1} + \cdots + b_2 s + b_1}$$

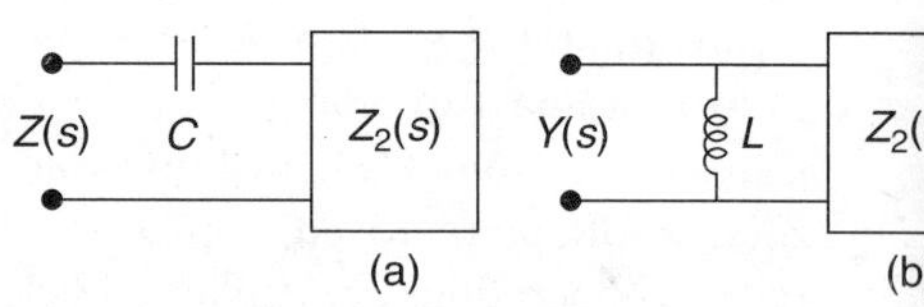

Fig. 15.3 Network interpretation of removal of a pole at zero

Here $Z_1(s) = \frac{K}{s}$ represents the impedance of a capacitor of value, $C = \frac{1}{K} = \frac{b_1}{a_0}$. Hence the removal of a pole at zero corresponds to the removal of a capacitor from the network [Fig. 15.3(a)]. If the given function is an admittance function, then $Y_1(s) = \frac{K}{s}$ represents the admittance of an inductor of value, $L = \frac{1}{K} = \frac{b_1}{a_0}$. Hence the removal of a pole at zero corresponds to the removal of an inductor from the network [Fig. 15.3(b)].

(iii) **Removal of conjugate imaginary poles:** If $Z(s)$ contains poles on the imaginary axis, say, a pole at $s = \pm j\omega_1$, then $Z(s)$ will have factors $(s + j\omega_1)(s - j\omega_1) = s^2 + \omega_1^2$ in the denominator polynomial, and may be written as

$$Z(s) = \frac{P(s)}{(s^2 + \omega_1^2)Q_1(s)} \tag{15.16}$$

Using partial fraction expansion, we have

$$Z(s) = \frac{K_1}{s - j\omega_1} + \frac{K_1^*}{s + j\omega_1} + Z_2(s) \tag{15.17}$$

The residues of $Z_1(s)$ at conjugate poles must themselves be conjugate and since $K_1$and K_1^* are residues at the imaginary poles of the positive real function, $Z(s)$, hence the residues must be real and positive.

That is, $K_1 = K_1^* = K$

Thus finally,

$$Z(s) = \frac{2Ks}{s^2 + \omega_1^2} + Z_2(s) = Z_1(s) + Z_2(s) \tag{15.18}$$

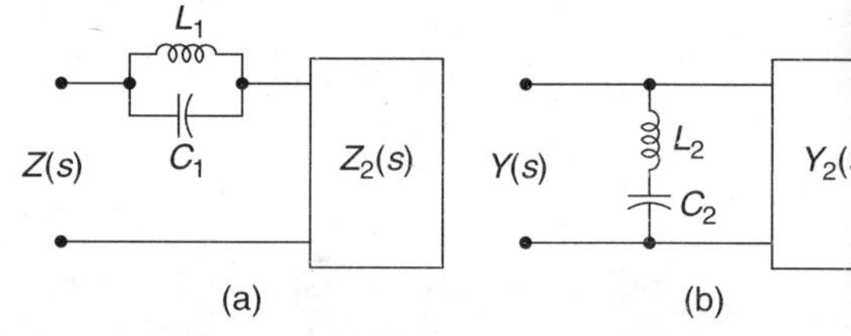

Fig. 15.4 Network interpretation of removal of a conjugate imaginary pole

where, $$Z_1(s) = \frac{2Ks}{s^2 + \omega_1^2} = \frac{1}{\frac{s}{2K} + \frac{\omega_1^2}{2Ks}} = \frac{1}{Y_a(s) + Y_b(s)} \tag{15.19}$$

Here, $Y_a(s) = \frac{s}{2K}$ is the admittance of a capacitor with a capacitance of $C = \frac{1}{2K}$. $Y_b(s) = \frac{\omega_1^2}{2Ks}$ is the admittance of an inductor with an inductance of $L = \frac{2K}{\omega_1^2}$. Obviously, these two elements are connected in parallel, that is, parallel LC combination, to form $Z_1(s)$ [Fig. 15.4(a)].

If the given function is an admittance function $Y(s)$, then

$$Y_1(s) = \frac{2Ks}{s^2 + \omega_1^2} = \frac{1}{\frac{s}{2K} + \frac{\omega_1^2}{2Ks}} = \frac{1}{Z_a(s) + Z_b(s)} \tag{15.20}$$

Here, $Z_a(s) = \frac{s}{2K}$ is the impedance of an inductor with an inductance of $L = \frac{1}{2K}$. $Z_b(s) = \frac{\omega_1^2}{2Ks}$ is the impedance of a capacitor with a capacitance of $C = \frac{2K}{\omega_1^2}$. Obviously, these two elements are connected in series, that is, series LC combination, to form $Y_1(s)$ [Fig. 15.4(b)].

(iv) **Removal of a constant:** If a real number K is subtracted from $Z(s)$ such that

$$Z_2(s) = Z(s) - K$$

$$Z(s) = K + Z_2(s) = Z_1(s) + Z_2(s)$$

then $Z_1(s) = K$ represents a resistance of value K. If the given function is an admittance function $Y(s)$, then removal of $Y_1(s) = K$ represents a conductance of value K. Thus, removal of a constant from the impedance function $Z(s)$ corresponds to the removal of a resistance, whereas removal of a constant from the admittance function $Y(s)$ corresponds to the removal of a conductance (Fig. 15.5).

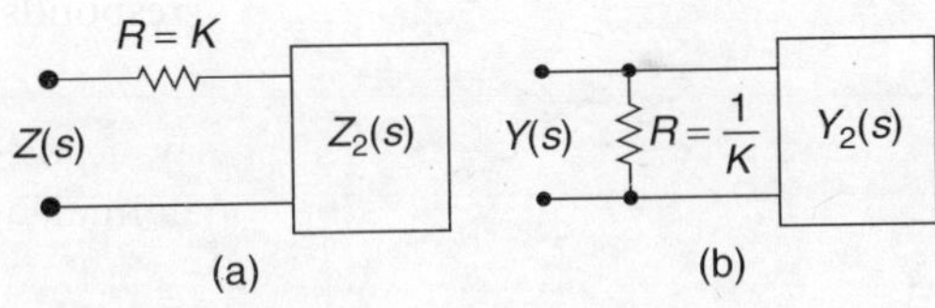

Fig. 15.5 Network interpretation of removal of a constant

Table 15.1 Removal of pole on the imaginary axis

S. no.	Location of pole	If pole of impedance (series element is)	If pole of admittance (parallel element is)
1	$s = \infty$	L	C
2	$s = 0$	C	L
3	$s = \pm j\omega_1$	LC parallel	LC series
4	$s = K$	R	G

Problem 15.14 Realise the network with an impedance function, $Z(s) = \dfrac{s^2 + 5s + 50}{s^2 + 10s}$.

Solution:

Given that $Z(s) = \dfrac{s^2 + 5s + 50}{s^2 + 10s}$

The given impedance function, $Z(s)$ has a pole at the origin ($s = 0$) which can be removed. The $Z(s)$ may be written as

$$Z(s) = \frac{s^2 + 5s + 50}{s^2 + 10s} = \frac{s^2}{s(s+10)} + \frac{5(s+10)}{s(s+10)} = \frac{5}{s} + \frac{s}{s+10} = Z_1(s) + Z_2(s)$$

where, $Z_1(s) = \dfrac{5}{s}$, can be realised as a capacitance of $\dfrac{1}{5}$ F in series with $Z_2(s)$ [Fig. 1(a)].

$$Z_2(s) = \frac{s}{s+10}$$

or $$Y_2(s) = \frac{s+10}{s} = 1 + \frac{10}{s} = Y_3(s) + Y_4(s)$$

Therefore, the admittance $Y_2(s)$ represents the parallel combination of $Y_3(s) = 1$ and $Y_4(s) = \frac{10}{s}$. Here $Y_3(s) = 1$ represents a conductance of 1 ℧ and $Y_4(s) = \frac{10}{s}$ represents an inductance of $\frac{1}{10}$ H. So $Z_2(s)$ represents a parallel circuit of conductance 1 ℧ (resistance 1 Ω) and an inductance of $\frac{1}{10}$ H [Fig. 1(b)]. The complete realisation of the network is shown in Fig. 1(c).

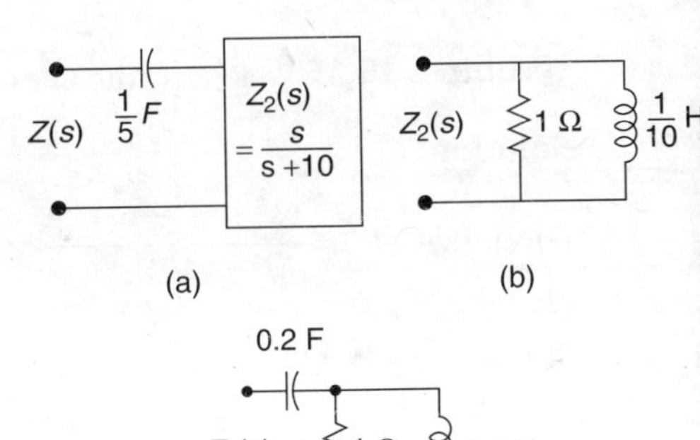

Fig. 1 Realisation of network for Problem 15.14

Problem 15.15 Realise the network with a driving point impedance function $Z(s)=\frac{s+2}{2s^2+5s}$.

Solution:

Given that $Z(s)=\dfrac{s+2}{2s^2+5s}$

The admittance function, $Y(s)=\dfrac{1}{Z(s)}=\dfrac{2s^2+5s}{s+2}$

From the admittance function $Y(s)$, it is clear that there is a pole at infinity. We can remove the pole at infinity using long division.

$$s+2)\,2s^2+5s\,(2s$$
$$\underline{2s^2+4s}$$
$$s$$

$$\therefore \qquad Y(s)=2s+\frac{s}{s+2}=Y_1(s)+Y_2(s)$$

where, $Y_1(s)=2s$, can be realised as a capacitance of $2F$ in parallel with $Y_2(s)$ [Fig. 1(a)].

$$Y_2(s)=\frac{s}{s+2}$$

$$Z_2(s)=\frac{s+2}{s}=1+\frac{2}{s}=Z_3(s)+Z_4(s)$$

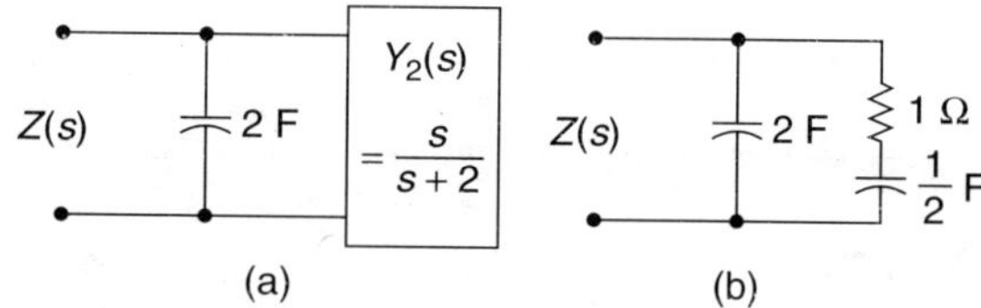

Fig. 2 Realisation of network for Problem 15.15

Therefore, the impedance $Z_2(s)$ represents the series combination of $Z_3(s)=1$ and $Z_4(s)=\frac{2}{s}$. Here $Z_3(s)=1$ represents a resistance of 1 Ω and $Z_4(s)=\frac{2}{s}$ represents a capacitance of $\frac{1}{2}$ F. This series combination is connected in parallel with a capacitance of 2 F [Fig. 2(b)].

Problem 15.16 Realise the network with a driving point impedance function of $Z(s)=\frac{6s^3+5s^2+6s+4}{2s(s^2+1)}$.

Solution:

Given that $Z(s)=\dfrac{6s^3+5s^2+6s+4}{2s(s^2+1)}$

Using long division,

$$2s^3+2s)\,6s^3+5s^2+6s+4\,(3$$
$$\underline{6s^3+6s}$$
$$5s^2+4$$

$$\therefore \qquad Z(s)=\frac{6s^3+5s^2+6s+4}{2s(s^2+1)}=3+\frac{5s^2+4}{2s^3+2s}=Z_1(s)+Z_2(s)$$

where, $Z_1(s)=3$ represents the impedance of a resistance of value 3 Ω.

$$Z_2(s) = \frac{5s^2+4}{2s^3+2s} \quad \text{and} \quad Y_2(s) = \frac{2s^3+2s}{5s^2+4}$$

Using long division again,

$$5s^2+4)\ 2s^3+2s\ (\frac{2}{5}s$$
$$2s^3+\frac{8}{5}s$$
$$\frac{2}{5}s$$

$$\therefore \quad Y_2(s) = \frac{2s^3+2s}{5s^2+4} = \frac{2}{5}s + \frac{\frac{2}{5}s}{5s^2+4} = Y_3(s) + Y_4(s)$$

where, $Y_3(s) = \frac{2}{5}s$ represents the admittance of a capacitance of value $\frac{2}{5}$ F.

$$Y_4(s) = \frac{\frac{2}{5}s}{5s^2+4}$$

and $\quad Z_4(s) = \dfrac{5s^2+4}{\frac{2}{5}s} = \dfrac{25s^2+20}{2s} = \dfrac{25}{2}s + \dfrac{10}{s} = Z_5(s) + Z_6(s)$

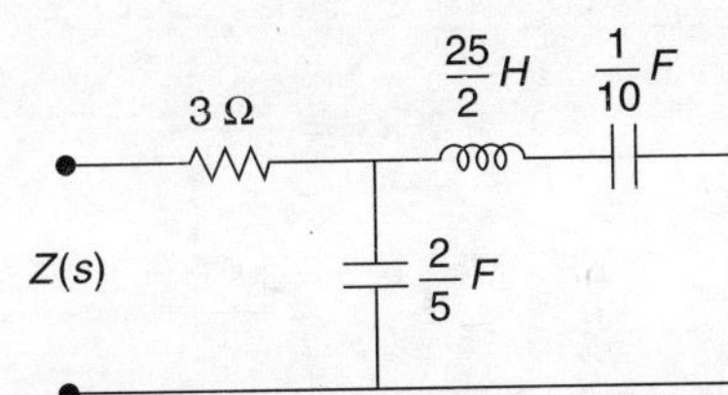

Fig. 3 Realisation of network for Problem 15.16

where, $Z_5(s) = \frac{25}{2}s$ represents the impedance of an inductance of value $\frac{25}{2}$ H and $Z_6(s) = \frac{10}{s}$ represents the impedance of a capacitance of value $\frac{1}{10}$ F. The impedances are connected in the series branches and the admittances are connected in the parallel branches. The complete realisation of the network is shown in Fig. 3.

Problem 15.17 Realise the network with a driving point impedance function of $Z(s) = \dfrac{s^4+10s^2+7}{s(s^2+2)}$.

Solution:

Given that $Z(s) = \dfrac{s^4+10s^2+7}{s(s^2+2)} = \dfrac{s^4+10s^2+7}{s^3+2s}$

Using long division,

$$s^3+2s)s^4+10s^2+7\ (s$$
$$s^4+2s^2$$
$$8s^2+7$$

$$\therefore \quad Z(s) = \frac{s^4+10s^2+7}{s^3+2s} = s + \frac{8s^2+7}{s^3+2s} = Z_1(s) + Z_2(s)$$

where, $Z_1(s) = s$, represents the impedance of an inductance of value 1 H and $Z_2(s) = \dfrac{8s^2+7}{s^3+2s} \Rightarrow Y_2(s) = \dfrac{s^3+2s}{8s^2+7}$.

Using long division again,

$$
\begin{array}{r|l}
8s^2+7) \; s^3+2s & (\frac{1}{8}s \\
\;\; s^3+\frac{7}{8}s & \\
\hline
\frac{9}{8}s &
\end{array}
$$

$$\therefore \quad Y_2(s)=\frac{s^3+2s}{8s^2+7}=\frac{1}{8}s+\frac{\frac{9}{8}s}{8s^2+7}=Y_3(s)+Y_4(s)$$

where, $Y_3(s)=\frac{1}{8}s$, represents the admittance of a capacitance of value $\frac{1}{8}$ F.

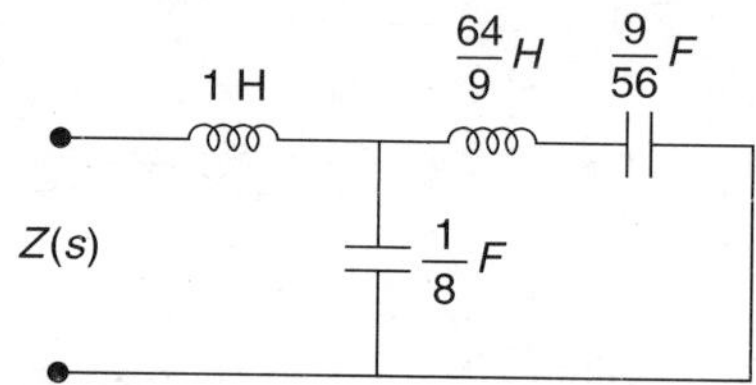

Fig. 4 Realisation of network for Problem 15.17

$$Y_4(s)=\frac{\frac{9}{8}s}{8s^2+7}$$

and $$Z_4(s)=\frac{8s^2+7}{\frac{9}{8}s}=\frac{64s^2+56}{9s}=\frac{64}{9}s+\frac{56}{9s}=Z_5(s)+Z_6(s)$$

where, $Z_5(s)=\frac{64}{9}s$, represents the impedance of an inductance of value $\frac{64}{9}$ H and $Z_6(s)=\frac{56}{9s}$ represents the impedance of a capacitance of value $\frac{9}{56}$ F. The impedances are connected in the series branches and the admittances are connected in the parallel branches. The complete realisation of the network is shown in Fig. 4.

15.6 SYNTHESIS OF ONE-PORT NETWORKS USING BASIC ELEMENTS

The network synthesis for a given one-port network can be done with two kinds of elements. Since we have three basic circuit elements *R*, *L* and *C*, the networks to be synthesised are either *LC*, *RL* or *RC* networks. There are a number of methods available for synthesising (or realising) a one-port network. The most important methods are listed below:

- Foster-I or Foster series form,
- Foster-II or Foster parallel form,
- Cauer-I form, and
- Cauer-II form.

The Foster-I and Foster-II forms are obtained by partial fraction expansion of *Z*(*s*) or *Y*(*s*) respectively, whereas the Cauer-I and Cauer-II forms are obtained by continued fraction expansion of the immittance function by arranging both the numerator and denominator in descending and ascending order respectively. The general diagrammatic representation of the above four forms are shown in Fig. 15.6.

The two Foster forms involve a sequential removal of the poles of an immittance function by first putting it into a partial fraction expansion form. If the pole is at the origin or at infinity, the order of the function is reduced by unity. If it is at $s=\pm j\omega_i$ the order of the function is reduced by two. The two Cauer canonical forms involve the removal of poles exclusively at the origin or at infinity. Note that the zeroes of the immittance function are not involved in the construction of one-port networks.

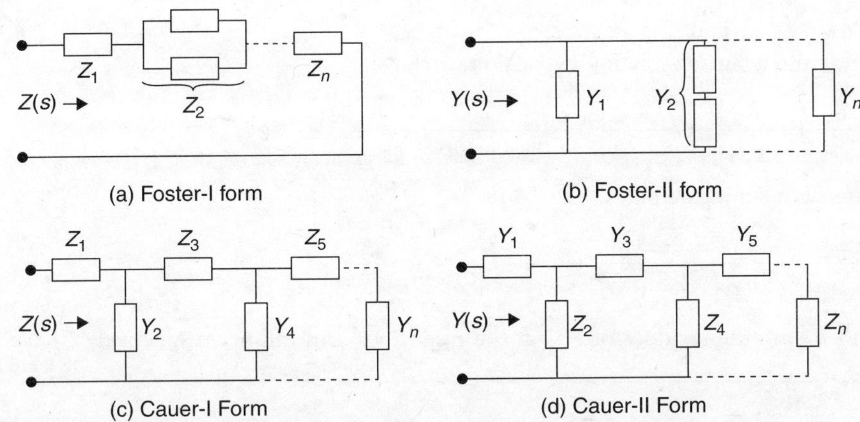

Fig. 15.6 General representation networks using different forms

Table 15.2 Important network synthesis methods

	Foster-I form	Foster-II form	Cauer-I form	Cauer-II form
Partial fraction expansion of impedance function	Applicable			
Partial fraction expansion of admittance function		Applicable		
Continued fraction expansion about the point at infinity			Applicable	
Continued fraction expansion about the origin				Applicable

15.7 SYNTHESIS OF *LC* DRIVING POINT IMMITTANCE FUNCTION

15.7.1 PROPERTIES OF *LC* IMMITTANCE FUNCTION

The various properties of *LC* immittance function are listed below:

- $Z_{LC}(s)$ or $Y_{LC}(s)$ is the ratio of even to odd or odd to even polynomials.
- The poles and zeroes are simple and lie on the $j\omega$-axis (including origin).
- There must be either a pole or a zero at the origin and at infinity.
- The poles and zeroes interlace (or alternate) on the $j\omega$-axis.
- The highest powers of the numerator and denominator polynomials must be differ by one; the lowest powers also differ by one.
- The residues at the poles are real and positive.

15.7.2 FOSTER REALISATION OF *LC* IMMITTANCE FUNCTION

A positive real immittance function $F(s)$ of a *LC* network, being a ratio of either even to odd or odd to even polynomials, can be synthesised by Foster form. In Foster synthesis, there are two types of networks for the realisation of one-port reactive networks. The first one is a series combination of parallel *LC* networks while the other is the parallel combination of series *LC* networks. The *LC* immittance function $F(s)$ can be written in a general form as

$$F(s) = \frac{K(s^2+\omega_1^2)(s^2+\omega_3^2)\ldots}{s(s^2+\omega_2^2)(s^2+\omega_4^2)\ldots} \tag{15.21}$$

where $0 \le \omega_1^2 < \omega_2^2 < \omega_3^2 \ldots$ and K is positive.

Expanding $F(s)$ into a partial-fraction expansion, we have

$$F(s) = \frac{K_0}{s} + \frac{K_2}{s + j\omega_2} + \frac{K_2}{s - j\omega_2} + \cdots + \frac{K_i}{s + j\omega_i} + \frac{K_i}{s - j\omega_i} + \cdots + K_\infty s \tag{15.22}$$

Combining terms with conjugate poles,

$$F(s) = \frac{K_0}{s} + \frac{2K_2 s}{s^2 + \omega_2^2} + \frac{2K_4 s}{s^2 + \omega_4^2} + \cdots + \frac{2K_i s}{s^2 + \omega_i^2} + \cdots + K_\infty s \tag{15.23}$$

where K_0, K_i and K_∞ are the residues of $F(s)$ at the origin, $j\omega_i$ and infinity respectively. These residues are given by,

$$K_0 = sF(s)\big|_{s=0}$$

$$K_i = \left.\frac{(s^2 + \omega_i^2)F(s)}{2s}\right|_{s^2 = -\omega_i^2}$$

$$K_\infty = \left.\frac{F(s)}{s}\right|_{s \to \infty}$$

(i) Foster-I form: If $F(s)$ represents an impedance function, it gives a series connection of impedances.

$$F(s) = Z(s) = \frac{K_0}{s} + \frac{2K_2 s}{s^2 + \omega_2^2} + \cdots + \frac{2K_i s}{s^2 + \omega_i^2} + \cdots + K_\infty s = Z_1(s) + Z_2(s) + \cdots + Z_i(s) + \cdots + Z_n(s) \tag{15.24}$$

The first term, $Z_1(s) = \frac{K_0}{s}$ represents the impedance of a capacitor of $\frac{1}{K_0}$ F.

The last term, $Z_n(s) = K_\infty s$ represents the impedance of an inductor of K_∞ H.

The remaining terms, that is, $Z_i(s) = \frac{2K_i s}{s^2 + \omega_i^2}$ represent an impedance of a parallel combination of capacitor C_i and inductor L_i.

$$\therefore \quad Z_i(s) = \frac{2K_i s}{s^2 + \omega_i^2} \tag{15.25}$$

For parallel combination of L_i and C_i, we have

$$Z_i(s) = \frac{L_i s \times \frac{1}{C_i s}}{L_i s + \frac{1}{C_i s}} = \frac{L_i s}{L_i C_i s^2 + 1} = \frac{\left(\frac{1}{C_i}\right)s}{s^2 + \frac{1}{L_i C_i}} \tag{15.26}$$

Comparing Eqs 15.25 and 15.26, we have

$$C_i = \frac{1}{2K_i} \quad \text{and} \quad L_i = \frac{2K_i}{\omega_i^2} \tag{15.27}$$

The network corresponding to Foster-I form is shown in Fig. 15.7(a). If $Z(s)$ has no pole at the origin, then capacitor C_0 is not present in the network. Similarly, if there is no pole at infinity, inductor L_∞ is not present in the network.

(ii) Foster-II form: If $F(s)$ represents an admittance function; it gives the parallel combination of admittances.

$$F(s) = Y(s) = \frac{K_0}{s} + \frac{2K_2 s}{s^2 + \omega_2^2} + \cdots + \frac{2K_i s}{s^2 + \omega_i^2} + \cdots + K_\infty s = Y_1(s) + Y_2(s) + \cdots + Y_i(s) + \cdots + Y_n(s) \tag{15.28}$$

The first term $Y_1(s) = \frac{K_0}{s}$ represents an admittance of an inductor of $\frac{1}{K_0}$ H. The last term $Y_n(s) = K_\infty s$ represents the admittance of a capacitor of K_∞ F. The remaining terms, that is, $Y_i(s) = \frac{2K_i s}{s^2 + \omega_i^2}$ represent an admittance of a series combination of inductor L_i and a capacitor C_i.

$$\therefore \quad Y_i(s) = \frac{2K_i s}{s^2 + \omega_i^2} \tag{15.29}$$

For a series combination of L_i and C_i, we have

$$Y_i(s) = \frac{1}{L_i s + \dfrac{1}{C_i s}} = \frac{C_i s}{1 + s^2 L_i C_i} = \frac{\left(\dfrac{1}{L_i}\right) s}{s^2 + \dfrac{1}{L_i C_i}} \tag{15.30}$$

Comparing Eqs 15.29 and 15.30, we have

$$L_i = \frac{1}{2K_i} \quad \text{and} \quad C_i = \frac{2K_i}{\omega_i^2} \tag{15.31}$$

The network corresponding to the Foster-II is shown in Fig. 15.7(b). If $Y(s)$ has no pole at the origin then inductor L_0 is not present. Similarly, if there is no pole at infinity, capacitor C_∞ is not present.

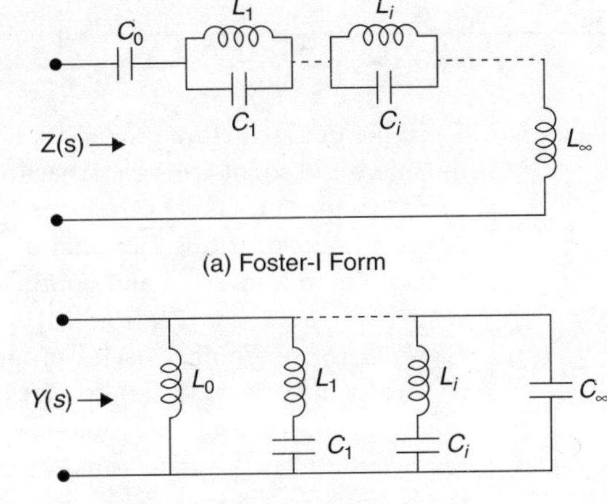

Fig. 15.7 Foster realisation of *LC* immittance function

15.7.3 Cauer Realisation of *LC* Immittance Function

The two Cauer canonical forms involve the removal of poles exclusively at the origin or at infinity. The basic form of the Cauer realisation being a ladder type network, the driving point impedance of this network may be represented in the form of continued fraction as

$$Z(s) = Z_1(s) + \cfrac{1}{Y_2(s) + \cfrac{1}{Z_3(s) + \cfrac{1}{Y_4(s) + \cdots}}} \tag{15.32}$$

(i) **Cauer-I form:** An useful property of an impedance or an admittance function is that it has either a pole or zero at $s = j\infty$. An immittance function has a pole at infinity if the degree of the numerator polynomial is one higher than the degree of the denominator polynomial. If $Z(s)$ or $Y(s)$ have no poles at infinity, their reciprocals do. The ladder network due to Cauer is obtained by a repeated removal of poles at infinity. If such a pole is removed from an impedance function, there is now a zero. However, the admittance function obtained by inverting $Z(s)$ now has a pole, which can be extracted again. This process is repeated until the degree of the polynomial is reduced to zero.

Consider an impedance function $Z(s)$ with a pole at infinity. By removing the pole at infinity, we have

$$Z_2(s) = Z(s) - sL_1$$

Now, $Z_2(s)$ has a zero at $s = \infty$. If we invert $Z_2(s)$, $Y_2(s)$ will have a pole at $s = \infty$. By removing this pole,

$$Y_3(s) = Y_2(s) - sC_2$$

Now $Y_3(s)$ has a zero at $s = \infty$, which we can invert and remove. This process is continued until the remainder is zero. Each time we remove a pole, we remove an inductor or a capacitor depending on whether the function is impedance or admittance. The impedance function $Z(s)$ can be written as a continued fraction expansion as given below:

$$Z(s) = L_1 s + \cfrac{1}{C_2 s + \cfrac{1}{L_3 s + \cfrac{1}{C_4 s + \cdots}}} \tag{15.33}$$

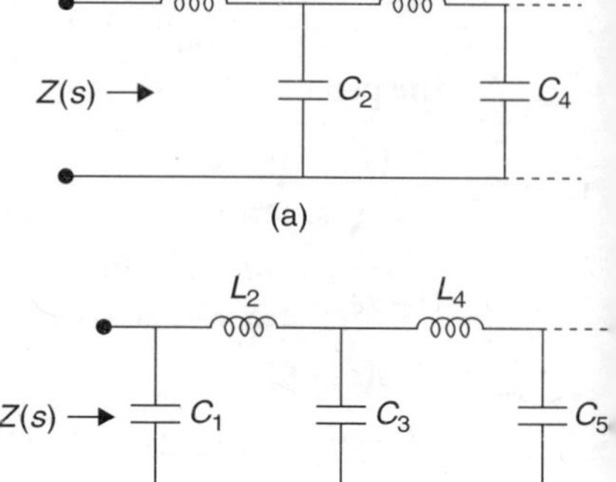

Fig. 15.8 Cauer-I realisation of LC immittance function

Thus, the final structure is a ladder network whose series arms are inductors and shunt arms are capacitors [Fig. 15.8(a)].

If the impedance function has zero at infinity, that is, if the degree of the numerator is less than that of its denominator by unity, the function is first inverted and continued fraction expansion proceeds as usual. In this case, the first element is a capacitor [Fig. 15.8(b)].

(ii) **Cauer-II form:** Another useful property of an LC immittance function is that it has always a pole or zero at the origin. If $Z(s)$ or $Y(s)$ has no pole there, its reciprocal does. The second Cauer ladder synthesis of an immittance function consists of the successive extraction of such poles. If a pole is removed at the origin there is now a zero there. However, inverting the function introduces a new pole there, which may once more be extracted.

In this method continued fraction expansion of $Z(s)$ is carried out in terms of poles at the origin by removal of the pole at the origin; inverting the resultant function to create a pole at the origin which is removed and this process is continued until the remainder is zero. To do this, we arrange both the numerator and denominator polynomials in ascending order and divide the lowest power of the denominator into the lowest power of the numerator. Then we invert the remainder and divide again. The impedance $Z(s)$ can be written as a continued fraction expansion as given below:

$$Z(s) = \frac{1}{C_1 s} + \cfrac{1}{\cfrac{1}{L_2 s} + \cfrac{1}{\cfrac{1}{C_3 s} + \cfrac{1}{\cfrac{1}{L_4 s} + \cdots}}} \tag{15.34}$$

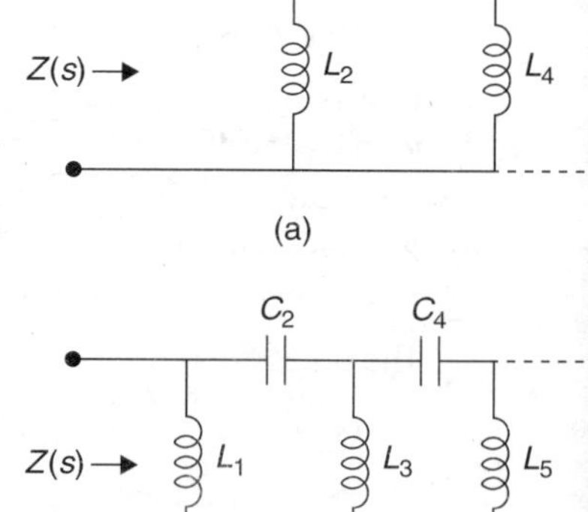

Fig. 15.9 Cauer-II realisation of LC immittance function

Thus, the final structure is a ladder network whose first element is a series capacitor and the second element is a shunt inductor [Fig. 15.9(a)].

If the impedance function has zero at the origin, then the first element is a shunt inductor and the second element is a series capacitor [Fig. 15.9(b)].

Problem 15.18 State whether the following functions are LC networks or not.

(i) $Z(s) = \dfrac{2s(s^2+9)}{(s^2+1)(s^2+4)}$ (ii) $Z(s) = \dfrac{5(s^2+1)(s^2+9)}{s(s^2+2)}$ (iii) $Z(s) = \dfrac{K(s^2+1)(s^2+9)}{(s^2+2)(s^2+10)}$

Solution:

(i) $Z(s)=\dfrac{2s(s^2+9)}{(s^2+1)(s^2+4)}$

The poles are given by

$$(s^2+1)(s^2+4)=0$$

$$s=\pm j1, \quad s=\pm j2$$

The zeros are given by

$$s(s^2+9)=0$$

$$s=0, \quad s=\pm j3$$

From the pole–zero plot in the s-plane (Fig. 1), it is clear that the poles and zeros are simple, lie on the $j\omega$-axis and do not interlace on the $j\omega$-axis. Thus, the function $Z(s)$ is not an LC impedance function.

(ii) $Z(s)=\dfrac{5(s^2+1)(s^2+9)}{s(s^2+2)}$

The poles are given by

$$s(s^2+2)=0$$

$$s=0, \quad s=\pm j\sqrt{2}$$

The zeros are given by

$$(s^2+1)(s^2+9)=0$$

$$s=\pm j1, \quad s=\pm j3$$

From the pole–zero plot in the s-plane (Fig. 2), it is clear that the poles and zeros are simple, lie on the $j\omega$-axis and interlace on the $j\omega$-axis. Thus, the function $Z(s)$ is an LC impedance function.

(iii) $Z(s)=\dfrac{K(s^2+1)(s^2+9)}{(s^2+2)(s^2+10)}$

The poles are given by

$$(s^2+2)(s^2+10)=0$$

$$s=\pm j\sqrt{10}, \quad s=\pm j\sqrt{2}$$

The zeros are given by

$$(s^2+1)(s^2+9)=0$$

$$s=\pm j1, \quad s=\pm j3$$

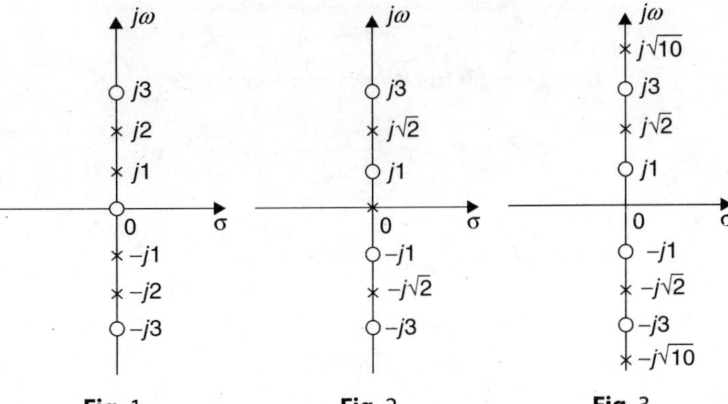

Fig. 1 **Fig.** 2 **Fig.** 3

From the pole–zero plot in the s-plane (Fig. 3), it is clear that the poles and zeros are simple, lie on the $j\omega$-axis and do not interlace on the $j\omega$-axis. Thus, the function $Z(s)$ is not an LC impedance function.

Problem 15.19 Realise the Foster and Cauer forms of an *LC* impedance function,

$$Z(s)=\frac{2(s^2+1)(s^2+9)}{s(s^2+4)}$$

Solution:

Given that $Z(s)=\dfrac{2(s^2+1)(s^2+9)}{s(s^2+4)}$

The poles are given by

$$s(s^2+4)=0$$

$$s=0,\quad s=\pm j2$$

The zeros are given by

$$(s^2+1)(s^2+9)=0$$

$$s=\pm j1,\quad s=\pm j3$$

Fig. 1

From the pole–zero plot in the *s*-plane (Fig. 1), it is clear that the poles and zeros are simple, lie on the $j\omega$-axis and interlace on the $j\omega$-axis. Thus, the function $Z(s)$ is an LC impedance function.

(i) **Foster-I realisation:** The Foster-I form is obtained using partial fraction expansion of the impedance function $Z(s)$. Here the degree of the numerator is greater than that of the denominator, so division is first carried out.

$$Z(s)=\frac{2(s^2+1)(s^2+9)}{s(s^2+4)}=\frac{2s^4+20s^2+18}{s^3+4s}$$

$$\begin{array}{r l}
s^3+4s)\ 2s^4+20s^2+18 & (2s\\
\underline{2s^4+8s^2\quad\ } & \\
12s^2+18 &
\end{array}$$

$$\therefore\quad Z(s)=\frac{2s^4+20s^2+18}{s^3+4s}=2s+\frac{12s^2+18}{s^3+4s}$$

Using partial fraction expansion, we have

$$Z(s)=2s+\frac{12s^2+18}{s^3+4s}=2s+\frac{K_0}{s}+\frac{K_1}{s+j2}+\frac{K_1^*}{s-j2}=2s+\frac{K_0}{s}+\frac{2sK_1}{s^2+2^2}$$

$$\text{where, } K_0=sZ(s)\Big|_{s=0}=s\times\frac{2(s^2+1)(s^2+9)}{s(s^2+4)}\Bigg|_{s=0}=\frac{18}{4}=\frac{9}{2}$$

$$K_1=\frac{(s^2+\omega_1^2)Z(s)}{2s}\Bigg|_{s^2=-\omega_1^2}=\frac{(s^2+2^2)}{2s}\times\frac{2(s^2+1)(s^2+9)}{s(s^2+4)}\Bigg|_{s^2=-4}=\frac{(-4+1)(-4+9)}{-4}=\frac{15}{4}$$

$$\therefore\quad Z(s)=2s+\frac{12s^2+18}{s^3+4s}=2s+\frac{\frac{9}{2}}{s}+\frac{\frac{15s}{2}}{s^2+2^2}$$

The first term represents the impedance of an inductor of 2 H. The second term represents the impedance of capacitor of $\frac{2}{9}$ F . The third term represents the impedance of a parallel LC circuit. So, for a parallel LC network,

$$Z_{LC}(s)=\frac{\left(\frac{1}{C}\right)s}{s^2+\frac{1}{LC}}$$

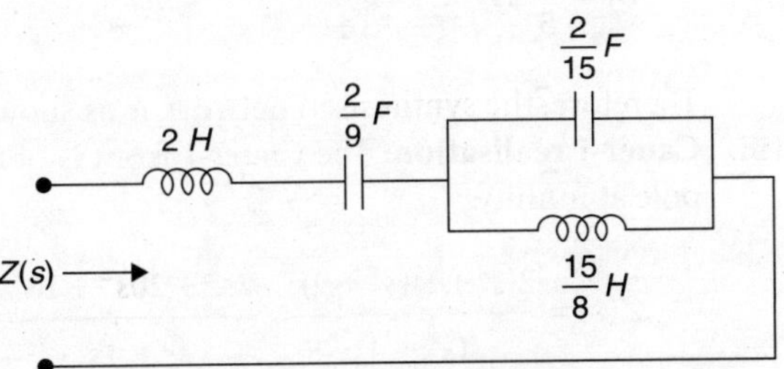

Fig. 2 Foster-I realisation

On direct comparison, we have

$$\frac{1}{C}=\frac{15}{2} \Rightarrow C=\frac{2}{15}\text{ F}$$

$$\frac{1}{LC}=4 \Rightarrow L=\frac{1}{4C}=\frac{15}{8}\text{ H}$$

Therefore, the synthesised network is as shown in Fig. 2.

(ii) **Foster-II realisation:** The Foster-II form is obtained using partial fraction expansion of the admittance function $Y(s)$.

$$Y(s)=\frac{s(s^2+4)}{2(s^2+1)(s^2+9)}$$

Using partial fraction expansion, we have

$$Y(s)=\frac{s(s^2+4)}{2(s^2+1)(s^2+9)}=\frac{K_1}{s+j1}+\frac{K_1^*}{s-j1}+\frac{K_2}{s+j3}+\frac{K_2^*}{s-j3}=\frac{2K_1s}{s^2+1}+\frac{2K_2s}{s^2+9}$$

$$\text{where, } K_1=\left.\frac{(s^2+\omega_1^2)Y(s)}{2s}\right|_{s^2=-\omega_1^2}=\left.\frac{(s^2+1)}{2s}\times\frac{s(s^2+4)}{2(s^2+1)(s^2+9)}\right|_{s^2=-1}=\frac{(-1+4)}{4(-1+9)}=\frac{3}{32}$$

$$K_2=\left.\frac{(s^2+\omega_2^2)Y(s)}{2s}\right|_{s^2=-\omega_2^2}=\left.\frac{(s^2+9)}{2s}\times\frac{s(s^2+4)}{2(s^2+1)(s^2+9)}\right|_{s^2=-9}=\frac{(-9+4)}{4(-9+1)}=\frac{5}{32}$$

$$\therefore \quad Y(s)=\frac{2K_1s}{s^2+1}+\frac{2K_2s}{s^2+9}=\frac{\frac{3}{16}s}{s^2+1}+\frac{\frac{5}{16}s}{s^2+9}$$

These two terms represent the admittance of a series LC network. So, for a series LC network,

$$Y_{LC}(s)=\frac{\left(\frac{1}{L}\right)s}{s^2+\frac{1}{LC}}$$

On direct comparison, we have

$$\frac{1}{L_1}=\frac{3}{16} \Rightarrow L_1=\frac{16}{3}\text{ H}$$

$$\frac{1}{L_1C_1}=1 \Rightarrow C_1=\frac{1}{L_1}=\frac{3}{16}\text{ F}$$

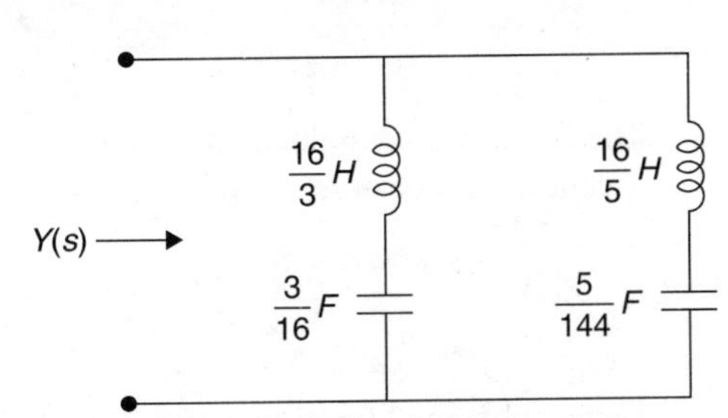

Fig. 3 Forster-II realisation

Similarly, we have

$$L_2 = \frac{16}{5}\text{ H},\ C_2 = \frac{5}{144}\text{ F}$$

Therefore, the synthesised network is as shown in Fig. 3.

(iii) **Cauer-I realisation:** The Cauer-I from is obtained using the continued fraction expansion about the pole at infinity.

$$Z(s) = \frac{2(s^2+1)(s^2+9)}{s(s^2+4)} = \frac{2s^4+20s^2+18}{s^3+4s}$$

Here the degree of the numerator is greater than that of the denominator by one, so it indicates a pole at infinity. Using continued fraction expansion, we have

$$\begin{array}{l}
s^3+4s)\ 2s^4+20s^2+18\,(2s \leftrightarrow Z_1 \\
\quad\ 2s^4+8s^2 \\
\hline
\qquad 12s^2+18)\ s^3+4s\,(\frac{1}{12}s \leftrightarrow Y_2 \\
\qquad\qquad s^3+\frac{3}{2}s \\
\hline
\qquad\qquad \frac{5}{2}s)\,12s^2+18\,(\frac{24}{5}s \leftrightarrow Z_3 \\
\qquad\qquad\quad 12s^2 \\
\hline
\qquad\qquad\quad 18)\ \frac{5}{2}s\,(\frac{5}{36}s \leftrightarrow Y_4 \\
\qquad\qquad\qquad \frac{5}{2}s \\
\hline
\qquad\qquad\qquad 0
\end{array}$$

The network elements are $L_1 = 2\text{ H},\ C_1 = \frac{1}{12}\text{ F},\ L_2 = \frac{24}{5}\text{ H}, C_2 = \frac{5}{36}\text{ F}$

The impedances are connected in the series branches, whereas the admittances are connected in the parallel branches in a Cauer or Ladder realisation. Therefore, the synthesised network is as shown in Fig. 4.

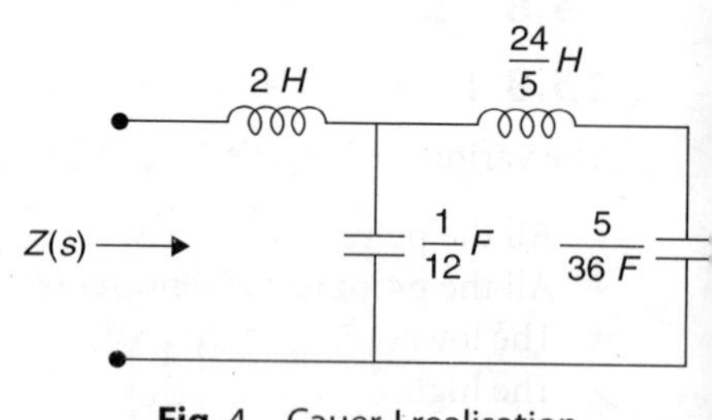

Fig. 4 Cauer-I realisation

(iv) **Cauer-II realisation:** The Cauer-II from is obtained using continued fraction expansion about the pole at the origin.

$$Z(s) = \frac{2(s^2+1)(s^2+9)}{s(s^2+4)} = \frac{2s^4+20s^2+18}{s^3+4s}$$

The function has pole at the origin. Arranging the numerator and denominator polynomials in the ascending order of s,

$$Z(s) = \frac{18+20s^2+2s^4}{4s+s^3}$$

Using continued fraction expansion, we have

$$
\begin{array}{l}
4s+s^3)\ 18+20s^2+2s^4\ (\frac{9}{2s}\leftrightarrow Z_1\\
\quad 18+\frac{9}{2}s^3\\
\hline
\quad \frac{31}{2}s^2+2s^4)\ 4s+s^3(\frac{8}{31s}\leftrightarrow Y_2\\
\qquad 4s+\frac{16}{31}s^3\\
\hline
\qquad \frac{15}{31}s^3)\ \frac{31}{2}s^2+2s^4\ (\frac{961}{30s}\leftrightarrow Z_3\\
\qquad\quad \frac{31}{2}s^3\\
\hline
\qquad\quad 2s^4)\ \frac{15}{31}s^3\ (\frac{15}{62s}\leftrightarrow Y_4\\
\qquad\qquad \frac{15}{31}s^3\\
\hline
\qquad\qquad 0
\end{array}
$$

The network elements are $C_1=\frac{2}{9}$ F, $L_1=\frac{31}{8}$ H, $C_2=\frac{30}{961}$ F, $L_2=\frac{62}{15}$ H

The impedances are connected in the series branches, whereas the admittances are connected in the parallel branches in a Cauer or Ladder realisation. Therefore, the synthesised network is as shown in Fig. 5.

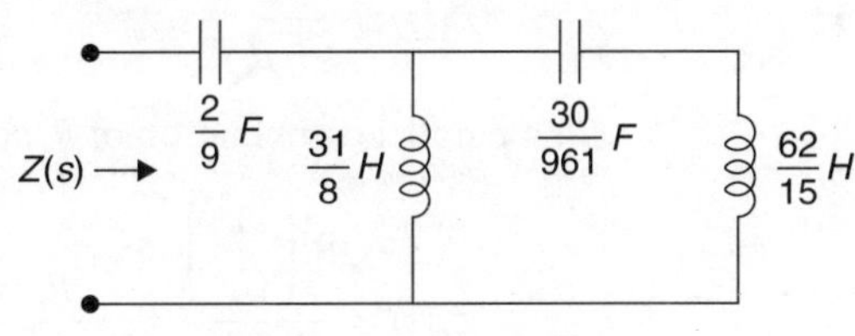

Fig. 5 Cauer-II realisation

Note: If the given function is impedance, then the first quotient must necessarily be impedance and if the given function is admittance, then the first quotient must necessarily be admittance.

15.8 SYNTHESIS OF *RC* IMPEDANCE/*RL* ADMITTANCE FUNCTION

15.8.1 Properties of *RC* Impedance/*RL* Admittance Function

The various properties of *RC* impedance/*RL* admittance function are listed below:

- All the poles and zeroes are simple and are located on the negative real axis of the *s*-plane.
- All the poles and zeroes interlace (or alternate) along the negative real axis.
- The lowest critical frequency nearest to the origin is a pole.
- The highest critical frequency farthest to the origin is a zero.
  - (i) The residues of the poles of $Z_{RC}(s)$ or $Y_{RL}(s)$ must be real and positive.
  - (ii) The residues of the poles of $Y_{RC}(s)$ or $Z_{RL}(s)$ are real and negative, however, the residues of the poles of $\frac{Y_{RC}(s)}{s}$ or $\frac{Z_{RL}(s)}{s}$ must be real and positive.
- The slope $\frac{d}{d\sigma}[Z_{RC}]$ is negative (or) the slope $\frac{d}{d\sigma}[Z_{RL}]$ is positive.
- $Z_{RC}(\infty)<Z_{RC}(0)$ (or) $Z_{RL}(\infty)<Z_{RL}(0)$.

15.8.2 Realisation of *RC* Impedance or *RL* Admittance Function

RC immittance functions can also be realised in four different ways—two Foster forms and two Cauer forms.

The impedance function of RC network is given by,

$$Z(s)=K\frac{(s+\alpha_1)(s+\alpha_2)\ldots}{s(s+\beta_1)(s+\beta_2)\ldots} \tag{15.35}$$

(i) **Foster-I realisation:** The Foster-I form is obtained by partial fraction expansion of $Z(s)$.

$$Z(s)=\frac{K_0}{s}+\frac{K_1}{s+\beta_1}+\frac{K_2}{s+\beta_2}+\cdots+\frac{K_i}{s+\beta_i}+\cdots+K_\infty \tag{15.36}$$

where K_0, K_1, K_2 and K_∞ are the residues of $Z(s)$; which are given by

$$K_0=sZ(s)|_{s=0}$$

$$K_i=(s+\beta_i)Z(s)\Big|_{s=-\beta_i}$$

$$K_\infty=\frac{Z(s)}{s}\bigg|_{s\to\infty}$$

In Eq. 15.36, the first term $\frac{K_0}{s}$ represents an impedance of a capacitor of $\frac{1}{K_0}$ F, the last term K_∞ represents an impedance of a resistor of K_∞ ohms and the remaining terms, that is, $\frac{K_i}{s+\beta_i}$ represent the impedance of a parallel combination of a resistor R_i and a capacitor C_i.

$$\therefore \qquad Z_i(s)=\frac{K_i}{s+\beta_i} \tag{15.37}$$

For a parallel combination of R_i and C_i, we have

$$Z_i(s)=\frac{R_i\left(\frac{1}{C_is}\right)}{R_i+\frac{1}{C_is}}=\frac{R_i}{1+R_iC_is}=\frac{\frac{1}{C_i}}{s+\frac{1}{R_iC_i}} \tag{15.38}$$

Comparing Eqs 15.37 and 15.38, we have

$$R_i=\frac{K_i}{\beta_i} \quad \text{and} \quad C_i=\frac{1}{K_i}$$

The network corresponding to the Foster-I form is shown in Fig. 15.10(a).

(ii) **Foster-II realisation** The Foster-II form is obtained by the partial fraction expansion of $Y(s)$. Since $Y(s)=\frac{1}{Z(s)}$ has negative residue at its pole, the Foster-II form is obtained by expanding $\frac{Y(s)}{s}$.

$$\frac{Y(s)}{s}=\frac{K_0}{s}+\frac{K_1}{s+\beta_1}+\frac{K_2}{s+\beta_2}+\cdots+\frac{K_i}{s+\beta_i}+\cdots+K_\infty \tag{15.39}$$

$$Y(s)=K_0+\frac{sK_1}{s+\beta_1}+\frac{sK_2}{s+\beta_2}+\cdots+\frac{sK_i}{s+\beta_i}+\cdots+sK_\infty \tag{15.40}$$

In Eq. 15.40, the first term K_0 represents the conductance of a resistor of $\frac{1}{K_0}$ ohms, the last term $K_\infty s$ represents the admittance of a capacitor of K_∞ F and the remaining terms, that is, $\frac{K_is}{s+\beta_i}$ represent the admittance of a series combination of a resistor R_i and a capacitor C_i.

$$\therefore \qquad Y_i(s)=\frac{K_is}{s+\beta_i} \tag{15.41}$$

For a series combination of R_i and C_i, we have

$$Y_i(s) = \frac{1}{R_i + \dfrac{1}{C_i s}} = \frac{C_i s}{1 + R_i C_i s} = \frac{\dfrac{1}{R_i} s}{s + \dfrac{1}{R_i C_i}} \qquad (15.42)$$

Comparing Eqs 15.41 and 15.42, we have

$$R_i = \frac{1}{K_i}\,\Omega \text{ and } C_i = \frac{K_i}{\beta_i}\,\text{F}$$

The network corresponding to the Foster-II form is shown in Fig. 15.10(b).

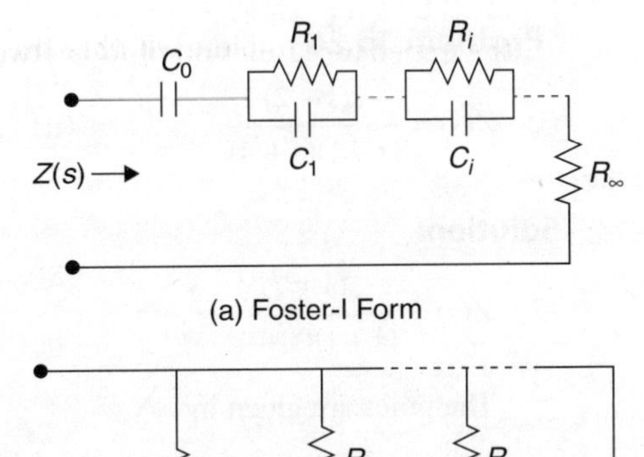

Fig. 15.10 Foster realisation of *RC* immittance function

(iii) **Cauer-I realisation** The Cauer-I form is obtained by removal of the pole from the impedance function $Z(s)$ at $s = \infty$. This is the same as a continued fraction expansion of the impedance function about infinity. The impedance $Z(s)$ can be written as a continued fraction expansion.

$$Z(s) = R_1 + \cfrac{1}{C_2 s + \cfrac{1}{R_3 + \cfrac{1}{C_4 s + \cdots}}} \qquad (15.43)$$

Thus, the final structure is a ladder network whose series arms are resistors and shunt arms are capacitors [Fig. 15.11(a)]. In the network, if $Z(s)$ has a zero at $s = \infty$, the first element is the capacitor C_1. If $Z(s)$ is a constant at $s = \infty$, the first element is R_1. If $Z(s)$ has a pole at $s = 0$, the last element is C_n. If $Z(s)$ is a constant at $s = 0$, the last element is R_n.

(iv) **Cauer-II realisation** The Cauer-II form is obtained by removal of the pole from the impedance function at the origin. This is the same as a continued fraction expansion of an impedance function about the origin.

If the given impedance function has a pole at the origin, it is removed as a capacitor C_1. The reciprocal of the remainder function has a minimum value at $s = 0$ which is removed as a constant of resistor R_2. If the original impedance has no pole at the origin, then the first capacitor is absent and the process is repeated with the removal of the constant corresponding to the resistor R_2. The impedance $Z(s)$ can be written as a continued fraction expansion as

$$Z(s) = \frac{1}{C_1 s} + \cfrac{1}{\cfrac{1}{R_2} + \cfrac{1}{\cfrac{1}{C_3 s} + \cfrac{1}{\cfrac{1}{R_4} + \cdots}}} \qquad (15.44)$$

Thus, the final structure is ladder networks whose series arms are capacitors and shunt arms resistors [Fig. 15.11(b)]. In the network, if $Z(s)$ has a pole at $s = 0$, the first element is C_1. If $Z(s)$ is a constant at $s = 0$, the first element is R_1. If $Z(s)$ has a zero at $s = \infty$, the last element is C_n. If $Z(s)$ is constant at $s = \infty$, the last element is R_n.

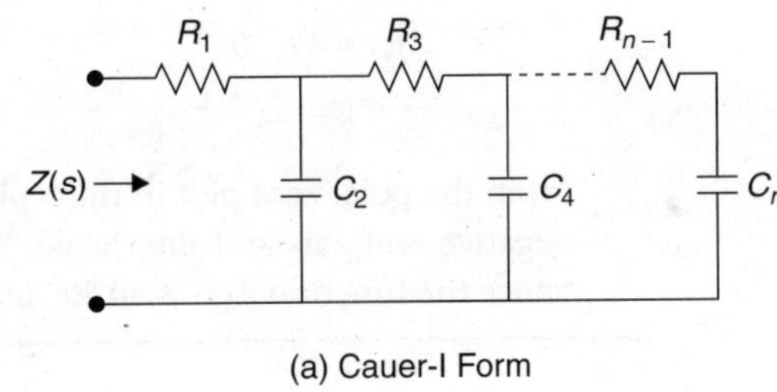

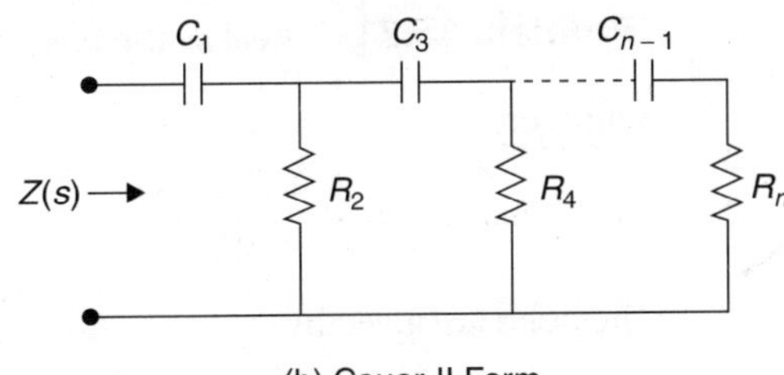

Fig. 15.11 Cauer realisation of *RC* immittance function

Problem 15.20 State whether the following functions are *RC* networks or not.

(i) $Z(s)=\dfrac{s(s+2)}{(s+1)(s+4)}$ (ii) $Z(s)=\dfrac{4(s+2)(s+4)}{s(s+3)}$

Solution:

(i) $Z(s)=\dfrac{s(s+2)}{(s+1)(s+4)}$

The poles are given by

$$(s+1)(s+4)=0$$

$$s=-1, \quad s=-4$$

The zeros are given by

$$s(s+2)=0$$

$$s=0, \quad s=-2$$

From the pole–zero plot in the *s*-plane (Fig. 1), it is clear that the poles and zeros are simple, lie on the negative real axis and interlaced. But, the lowest critical frequency nearest to the origin is zero, not a pole, hence the function *Z*(*s*) is not an *RC* impedance function.

(ii) $Z(s)=\dfrac{4(s+2)(s+4)}{s(s+3)}$

The poles are given by

$$s(s+3)=0$$

$$s=0, \quad s=-3$$

The zeros are given by

$$(s+2)(s+4)=0$$

$$s=-2, \quad s=-4$$

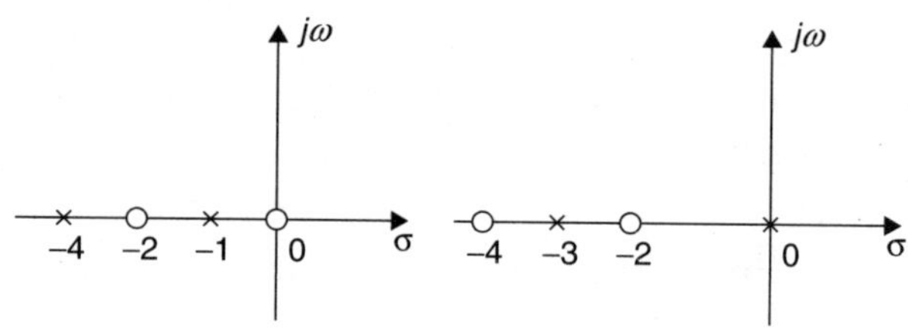

Fig. 1 **Fig.** 2

From the pole–zero plot in the *s*-plane (Fig. 2), it is clear that the poles and zeros are simple, lie on the negative real axis and interlaced. The lowest critical frequency nearest to the origin is the pole, and hence the function *Z*(*s*) is an *RC* impedance function.

Problem 15.21 Realise the Foster and Cauer forms of the *RC* impedance function, $Z(s)=\dfrac{(s+1)(s+4)}{s(s+2)(s+5)}$.

Solution:

Given that $Z(s)=\dfrac{(s+1)(s+4)}{s(s+2)(s+5)}$

The poles are given by

$$s(s+2)(s+5)=0$$

$$s=0, \quad s=-2, \quad s=-5$$

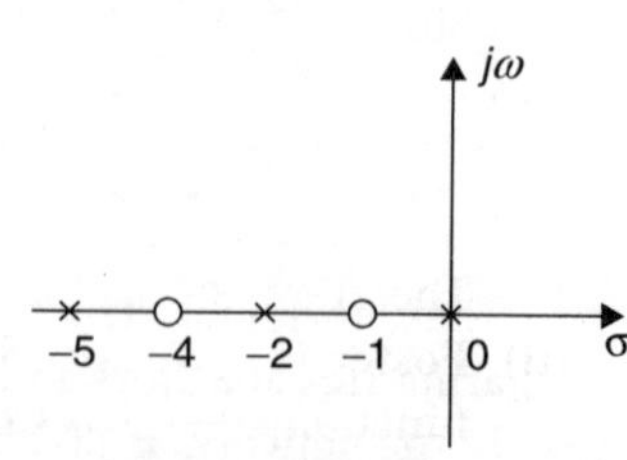

Fig. 1

The zeros are given by

$$(s+1)(s+4)=0$$

$$s=-1, \quad s=-4$$

From the pole–zero plot in the s-plane (Fig. 1), it is clear that the poles and zeros are simple, lie on the negative real axis and interlaced; the function $Z(s)$ is an RC impedance function.

(i) **Foster-I realisation** The Foster-I form is obtained using partial fraction expansion of the impedance function $Z(s)$. Using partial fraction expansion, we have

$$Z(s)=\frac{(s+1)(s+4)}{s(s+2)(s+5)}=\frac{K_0}{s}+\frac{K_1}{s+2}+\frac{K_2}{s+5}$$

$$\text{where, } K_0=sZ(s)\Big|_{s=0}=s\times\frac{(s+1)(s+4)}{s(s+2)(s+5)}\Bigg|_{s=0}=\frac{1\times 4}{2\times 5}=\frac{2}{5}$$

$$K_1=(s+\beta_1)Z(s)\Big|_{s=-\beta_1}=(s+2)\times\frac{(s+1)(s+4)}{s(s+2)(s+5)}\Bigg|_{s=-2}=\frac{(-2+1)(-2+4)}{-2(-2+5)}=\frac{1}{3}$$

$$K_2=(s+\beta_2)Z(s)\Big|_{s=-\beta_2}=(s+5)\times\frac{(s+1)(s+4)}{s(s+2)(s+5)}\Bigg|_{s=-5}=\frac{(-5+1)(-5+4)}{-5(-5+2)}=\frac{4}{15}$$

$$\therefore \quad Z(s)=\frac{\frac{2}{5}}{s}+\frac{\frac{1}{3}}{s+2}+\frac{\frac{4}{15}}{s+5}$$

The first term represents an impedance of a capacitor of $\frac{5}{2}$ F. The second and third terms represent the impedance of an RC parallel circuit. So, for a parallel RC network,

$$Z_{RC}(s)=\frac{\frac{1}{C}}{s+\frac{1}{RC}}$$

On direct comparison, we have

$$C_1=3\text{ F}$$

$$\frac{1}{R_1C_1}=2 \Rightarrow R_1=\frac{1}{2C_1}=\frac{1}{6}\,\Omega$$

Similarly, we have

$$C_2=\frac{15}{4}\text{ F}, \quad R_2=\frac{4}{75}\,\Omega$$

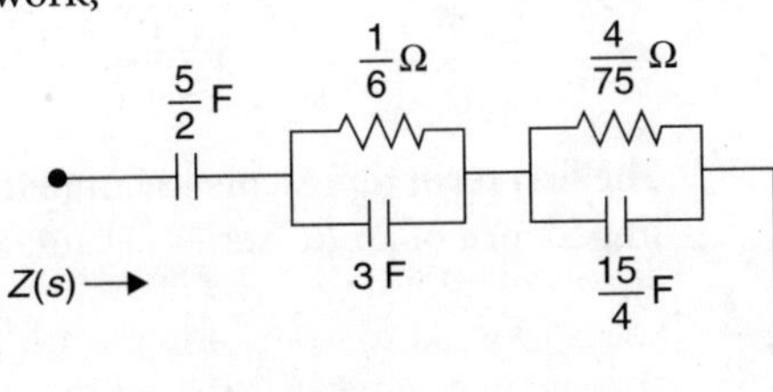

Fig. 2 Foster-I realisation

Therefore, the synthesised network is as shown in Fig. 2.

(ii) **Foster-II realisation** The Foster-II form is obtained using partial fraction expansion of the admittance function $\frac{Y(s)}{s}$. Here the degree of the numerator is equal to the degree of the denominator, so division is first carried out.

$$Y(s)=\frac{s(s+2)(s+5)}{(s+1)(s+4)}$$

$$\frac{Y(s)}{s}=\frac{(s+2)(s+5)}{(s+1)(s+4)}=\frac{s^2+7s+10}{s^2+5s+4}$$

$$s^2+5s+4)\ s^2+7s+10\ (1$$
$$\underline{s^2+5s+4}$$
$$2s+6$$

$$\therefore \quad \frac{Y(s)}{s}=\frac{(s+2)(s+5)}{(s+1)(s+4)}=1+\frac{2s+6}{(s+1)(s+4)}$$

Using partial fraction expansion, we have

$$\frac{Y(s)}{s}=\frac{(s+2)(s+5)}{(s+1)(s+4)}=1+\frac{K_1}{s+1}+\frac{K_2}{s+4}$$

$$K_1=(s+\beta_1)\frac{Y(s)}{s}\bigg|_{s=-\beta_1}=(s+1)\times\frac{(s+2)(s+5)}{(s+1)(s+4)}\bigg|_{s=-1}=\frac{(-1+2)(-1+5)}{(-1+4)}=\frac{4}{3}$$

$$K_2=(s+\beta_2)\frac{Y(s)}{s}\bigg|_{s=-\beta_2}=(s+4)\times\frac{(s+2)(s+5)}{(s+1)(s+4)}\bigg|_{s=-4}=\frac{(-4+2)(-4+5)}{(-4+1)}=\frac{2}{3}$$

$$\frac{Y(s)}{s}=\frac{(s+2)(s+5)}{(s+1)(s+4)}=1+\frac{\frac{4}{3}}{s+1}+\frac{\frac{2}{3}}{s+4}$$

$$\Rightarrow \quad Y(s)=s+\frac{\frac{4}{3}s}{s+1}+\frac{\frac{2}{3}s}{s+4}$$

The first term represents the impedance of a capacitor of 1 F. The second and third terms represent the impedance of an RC series circuit. So, for a series RC network,

$$Y_{RC}(s)=\frac{\frac{1}{R}s}{s+\frac{1}{RC}}$$

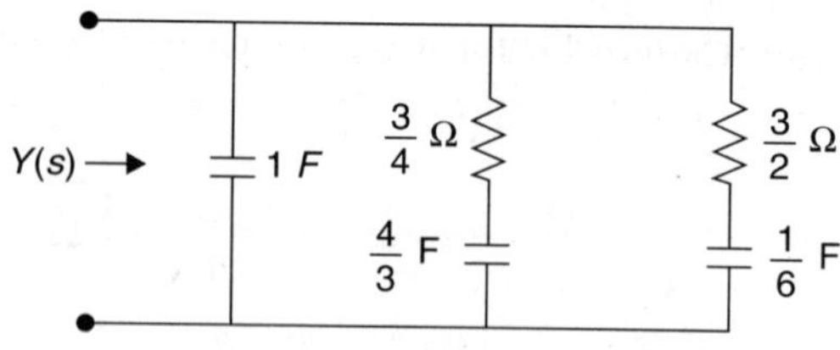

Fig. 3 Foster-II realisation

On direct comparison, we have

$$\frac{1}{R_1}=\frac{4}{3} \Rightarrow R_1=\frac{3}{4}\,\Omega$$

$$\frac{1}{R_1C_1}=1 \Rightarrow C_1=\frac{1}{R_1}=\frac{4}{3}\,\text{F}$$

Similarly, we have

$$R_2 = \frac{3}{2}\,\Omega, \quad C_2 = \frac{1}{6}\,\text{F}$$

Therefore, the synthesised network is as shown in Fig. 3.

(iii) **Cauer-I realisation** The Cauer-I form is obtained using continued fraction expansion about the pole at infinity.

$$Z(s) = \frac{(s+1)(s+4)}{s(s+2)(s+5)} = \frac{s^2+5s+4}{s^3+7s^2+10s}$$

$$\Rightarrow \quad Y(s) = \frac{s^3+7s^2+10s}{s^2+5s+4}$$

Using continued fraction expansion, we have

$$
\begin{array}{l}
s^2+5s+4)\; s^3+7s^2+10s\,(s \leftrightarrow Y_1 \\
\qquad\qquad\quad \underline{s^3+5s^2+4s} \\
\qquad\qquad\qquad 2s^2+6s)\; s^2+5s+4\,(\tfrac{1}{2} \leftrightarrow Z_2 \\
\qquad\qquad\qquad\qquad\qquad \underline{s^2+3s} \\
\qquad\qquad\qquad\qquad\qquad 2s+4)\; 2s^2+6s\,(s \leftrightarrow Y_3 \\
\qquad\qquad\qquad\qquad\qquad\qquad \underline{2s^2+4s} \\
\qquad\qquad\qquad\qquad\qquad\qquad\quad 2s)\; 2s+4\,(1 \leftrightarrow Z_4 \\
\qquad\qquad\qquad\qquad\qquad\qquad\qquad\quad \underline{2s} \\
\qquad\qquad\qquad\qquad\qquad\qquad\qquad\qquad 4)\; 2s\,(\tfrac{1}{2}s \leftrightarrow Y_5 \\
\qquad\qquad\qquad\qquad\qquad\qquad\qquad\qquad\quad \underline{2s} \\
\qquad\qquad\qquad\qquad\qquad\qquad\qquad\qquad\qquad 0
\end{array}
$$

The network elements are $C_1 = 1\,\text{F}, \; R_1 = \frac{1}{2}\,\Omega, \; C_2 = 1\,\text{F}, \; R_2 = 1\,\Omega, \; C_3 = \frac{1}{2}\,\text{F}$

The impedances are connected in the series branches, whereas the admittances are connected in the parallel branches in a Cauer or Ladder realisation. Therefore, the synthesised network is as shown in Fig. 4.

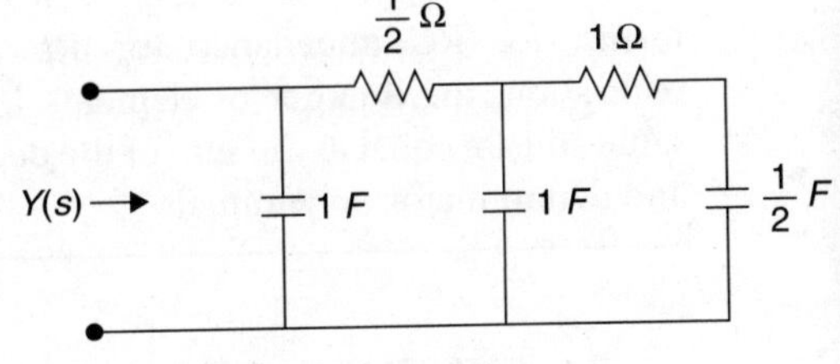

Fig. 4 Cauer-I realisation

(iv) **Cauer-II realisation** The Cauer-II form is obtained using the continued fraction expansion about the pole at origin.

$$Z(s) = \frac{s^2+5s+4}{s^3+7s^2+10s}$$

The function has a pole at the origin. Arranging the numerator and denominator polynomials in ascending order of s as follows:

$$Z(s) = \frac{4+5s+s^2}{10s+7s^2+s^3}$$

Using continued fraction expansion, we have

$$
\begin{array}{l}
10s+7s^2+s^3)\;4+5s+s^2\;\left(\dfrac{4}{10s}=\dfrac{2}{5s}\leftrightarrow Z_1\right.\\
\qquad\qquad\quad \underline{4+\dfrac{14}{5}s+\dfrac{2}{5}s^2}\\
\qquad\qquad\quad \dfrac{11}{5}s+\dfrac{3}{5}s^2)\;10s+7s^2+s^3\left(\dfrac{50}{11}\leftrightarrow Y_2\right.\\
\qquad\qquad\qquad\qquad\quad \underline{10s+\dfrac{30}{11}s^2}\\
\qquad\qquad\qquad\qquad\quad \dfrac{47}{11}s^2+s^3)\;\dfrac{11}{5}s+\dfrac{3}{5}s^2\left(\dfrac{11}{47}\cdot\dfrac{11}{5s}=\dfrac{121}{235s}\leftrightarrow Z_3\right.\\
\qquad\qquad\qquad\qquad\qquad\qquad\quad \underline{\dfrac{11}{5}s+\dfrac{121}{235}s^2}\\
\qquad\qquad\qquad\qquad\qquad\qquad\quad \dfrac{20}{235}s^2)\;\dfrac{47}{11}s^2+s^3\left(\dfrac{235}{20}\cdot\dfrac{47}{11}=\dfrac{2209}{44}\leftrightarrow Y_4\right.\\
\qquad\qquad\qquad\qquad\qquad\qquad\qquad\qquad \underline{\dfrac{47}{11}s^2}\\
\qquad\qquad\qquad\qquad\qquad\qquad\qquad\qquad s^3)\;\dfrac{20}{235}s^2\left(\dfrac{20}{235s}=\dfrac{4}{47s}\leftrightarrow Z_5\right.\\
\qquad\qquad\qquad\qquad\qquad\qquad\qquad\qquad\qquad \underline{\dfrac{20}{235}s^2}\\
\qquad\qquad\qquad\qquad\qquad\qquad\qquad\qquad\qquad 0
\end{array}
$$

The network elements are $C_1=\dfrac{5}{2}$ F, $R_1=\dfrac{11}{50}\,\Omega$, $C_2=\dfrac{235}{121}$ F, $R_2=\dfrac{44}{2209}\,\Omega$, $C_3=\dfrac{47}{4}$ F

The impedances are connected in the series branches, whereas the admittances are connected in the parallel branches in a Cauer or Ladder realisation. Therefore, the synthesised network is as shown in Fig. 5.

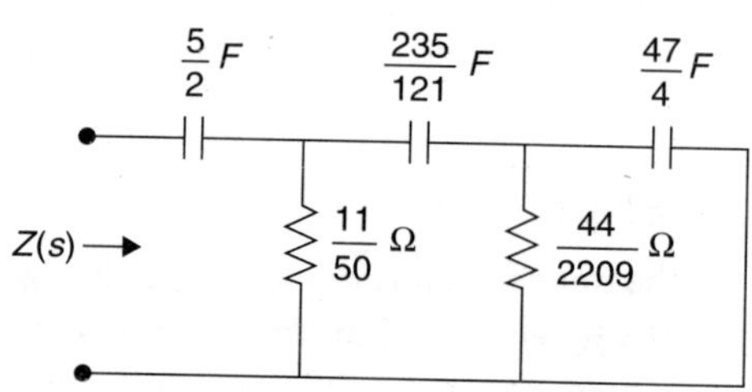

Fig. 5 Cauer-II realisation

Note: In all the four forms, that is, two Foster and two Cauer forms, for *RC* impedance (or *RL* admittance) function realisation, the number of elements in the network are the same and are equal to the sum of the degrees of the numerator and denominator polynomials.

15.9 SYNTHESIS OF *RL* IMPEDANCE/*RC* ADMITTANCE FUNCTION

15.9.1 Properties of *RL* Impedance/*RC* Admittance Function

The various properties of *RL* impedance/*RC* admittance function are listed below:

- All the poles and zeros are simple and located on the negative real axis of the *s*-plane.
- All the poles and zeros interlace (or alternate) along the negative real axis.
- The lowest critical frequency nearest to the origin is a zero.
- The highest critical frequency farthest to the origin is a pole.
  - (i) The residues of the poles of $Z_{RL}(s)$ or $Y_{RC}(s)$ are real and negative, however, the residues of the poles of $\dfrac{Z_{RL}(s)}{s}$ or $\dfrac{Y_{RC}(s)}{s}$ must be real and positive.
  - (ii) The residues of the poles of $Y_{RL}(s)$ or $Z_{RC}(s)$ must be real and positive.

- The slope $\frac{d}{d\sigma}[Z_{RL}]$ is positive (or) the slope $\frac{d}{d\sigma}[Z_{RC}]$ is negative.
- $Z_{RL}(\infty) > Z_{RL}(0)$ (or) $Z_{RC}(\infty) < Z_{RC}(0)$

15.9.2 Realisation of *RL* Impedance or *RC* Admittance Function

RL impedance or *RC* admittance function can also be realised in four different ways—two Foster forms and two Cauer forms. The impedance function of an *RL* network is given by,

$$Z(s) = K\frac{s(s+\alpha_1)(s+\alpha_2)\ldots}{(s+\beta_1)(s+\beta_2)\ldots} \quad (15.45)$$

(i) **Foster-I realisation** The Foster-I form is obtained by the partial fraction expansion of $Z(s)$. Since $Z(s)$ has a negative residue at its pole, the Foster-I form is obtained by expanding $\frac{Z(s)}{s}$ into partial fractions.

$$\frac{Z(s)}{s} = \frac{K_0}{s} + \frac{K_1}{s+\beta_1} + \frac{K_2}{s+\beta_2} + \cdots + \frac{K_i}{s+\beta_i} + \cdots + K_\infty \quad (15.46)$$

$$Z(s) = K_0 + \frac{sK_1}{s+\beta_1} + \frac{sK_2}{s+\beta_2} + \cdots + \frac{sK_i}{s+\beta_i} + \cdots + sK_\infty \quad (15.47)$$

where K_0, K_1, K_2 and K_∞ are the residues of $\frac{Z(s)}{s}$; which are given by

$$K_0 = s\frac{Z(s)}{s}\bigg|_{s=0}$$

$$K_i = (s+\beta_i)\frac{Z(s)}{s}\bigg|_{s=-\beta_i}$$

$$K_\infty = \frac{Z(s)}{s}\bigg|_{s\to\infty}$$

In Eq. 15.47, the first term K_0 represents the impedance of a resistor of $K_0\ \Omega$, the last term $K_\infty s$ represents the impedance of an inductor of K_∞ H and the remaining terms, that is, $\frac{K_i s}{s+\beta_i}$ represent the impedance of a parallel combination of a resistor R_i and an inductor L_i.

$$\therefore \quad Z_i(s) = \frac{K_i s}{s+\beta_i} \quad (15.48)$$

For a parallel combination of R_i and L_i, we have

$$Z_i(s) = \frac{sR_iL_i}{R_i + sL_i} = \frac{R_i s}{s + \dfrac{R_i}{L_i}} \quad (15.49)$$

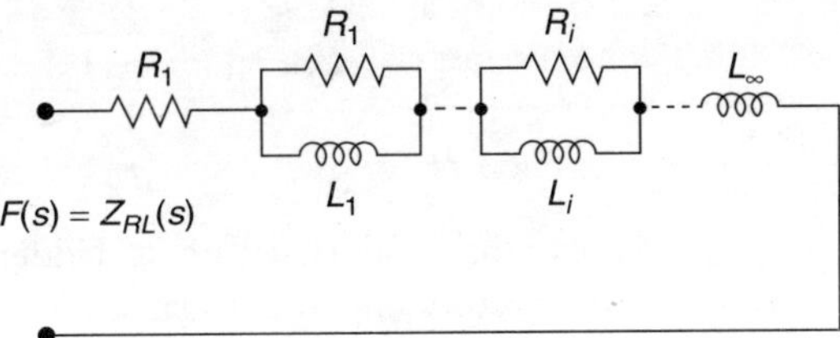

Fig. 15.12(a) Foster-I realisation of *RL* network

Comparing Eqs 15.48 and 15.49, we have $R_i = K_i\ \Omega$ and $L_i = \frac{K_i}{\beta_i}$ H.

The network corresponding to the Foster-I form is shown in Fig. 15.12(a).

(ii) **Foster-II realisation** The Foster-II form is obtained by the partial fraction expansion of $Y(s)$.

$$Y(s) = \frac{K_0}{s} + \frac{K_1}{s+\beta_1} + \frac{K_2}{s+\beta_2} + \cdots + \frac{K_i}{s+\beta_i} + \cdots + K_\infty \quad (15.50)$$

In Eq. 15.50, the first term K_0 represents the impedance of an inductor of $\frac{1}{K_0}$ H, the last term K_∞ represents the impedance of a resistor of K_∞ Ω and the remaining terms, that is, $\frac{K_i}{s+\beta_i}$ represent an admittance of a series combination of the resistor R_i and inductor L_i.

$$\therefore \quad Y_i(s) = \frac{K_i}{s+\beta_i} \tag{15.51}$$

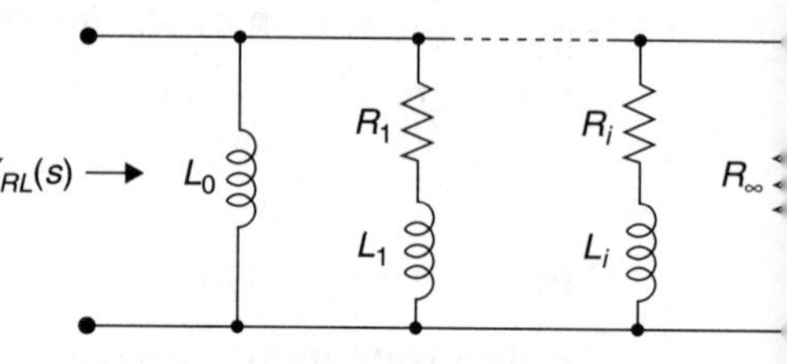

Fig. 15.12(b) Foster-II realisation of *RL* network

For a series combination of R_i and L_i, we have

$$Y_i(s) = \frac{1}{R_i + sL_i} = \frac{\frac{1}{L_i}}{s + \frac{R_i}{L_i}} \tag{15.52}$$

Comparing Eqs 15.51 and 15.52, we have $R_i = \frac{\beta_i}{K_i}$ and $L_i = \frac{1}{K_i}$.

The network corresponding to the Foster-II form is shown in Fig. 15.12(b).

(iii) Cauer-I realisation The Cauer-I form is obtained by the removal of the pole from the impedance function $Z(s)$ at $s = \infty$. This is the same as a continued fraction expansion of the impedance function about infinity. The impedance $Z(s)$ can be written as a continued fraction expansion.

$$Z(s) = sL_1 + \cfrac{1}{\cfrac{1}{R_2} + \cfrac{1}{sL_3 + \cfrac{1}{\cfrac{1}{R_4} + \cdots}}} \tag{15.53}$$

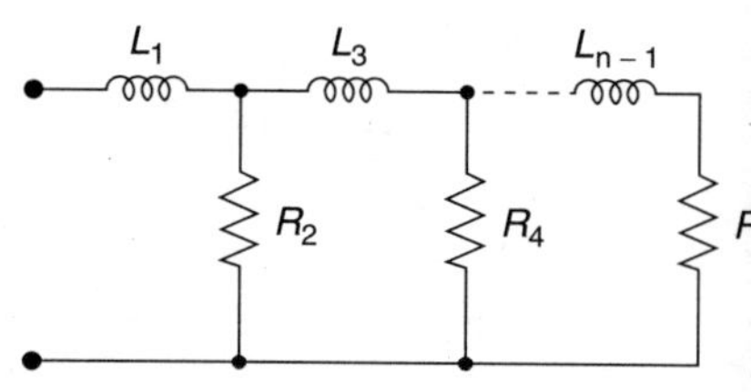

Fig. 15.13(a) Cauer-I realisation of *RL* network

Thus, the final structure is a ladder network whose series arms are inductors and shunt arms are resistors [Fig. 15.13(a)]. In the network, if $Z(s) \to \infty$ for $s \to \infty$ the first element is the inductor L_1 but if $Z(s)$ is a constant for $s \to \infty$, L_1 does not exist.

(iv) Cauer-II realisation The Cauer-II form is obtained by the removal of the pole from the impedance function at the origin. This is the same as a continued fraction expansion of an impedance function about the origin. The impedance $Z(s)$ can be written as a continued fraction expansion as

$$Z(s) = R_1 + \cfrac{1}{\cfrac{1}{sL_2} + \cfrac{1}{R_3 + \cfrac{1}{\cfrac{1}{sL_4} + \cdots}}} \tag{15.54}$$

Fig. 15.13(b) Cauer-II realisation of *RL* network

Thus, the final structure is ladder networks whose series arms are resistors and shunt arms are capacitors [Fig. 15.13(b)]. In the network, if $Z(s)$ has a constant value at $s \to \infty$, the first element is R_1. If $Z(s)$ has zero at $s = 0$, the last element is L_n. If $Z(s)$ is constant at $s = 0$, the last element is R_n.

Problem 15.22 State whether the following functions are *RL* networks or not.

(i) $Z(s) = \frac{10(s+1)(s+3)}{(s+2)(s+4)}$ (ii) $Z(s) = \frac{s(s+2)(s+7)}{(s+1)(s+5)}$

Solution:

(i) $Z(s)=\dfrac{10(s+1)(s+3)}{(s+2)(s+4)}$

The poles are given by

$$(s+2)(s+4)=0$$

$$s=-2, \quad s=-4$$

The zeroes are given by

$$(s+1)(s+3)=0$$

$$s=-1, \quad s=-3$$

From the pole–zero plot in the s-plane (Fig. 1), it is clear that the poles and zeros are simple, lie on the negative real axis and interlaced. The lowest critical frequency nearest to the origin is zero, and hence the function $Z(s)$ is an RL impedance function.

(ii) $Z(s)=\dfrac{s(s+2)(s+7)}{(s+1)(s+5)}$

The zeros are given by

$$s(s+2)(s+7)=0$$

$$s=0, \quad s=-2, \quad s=-7$$

The poles are given by

$$(s+1)(s+5)=0$$

$$s=-1, \quad s=-5$$

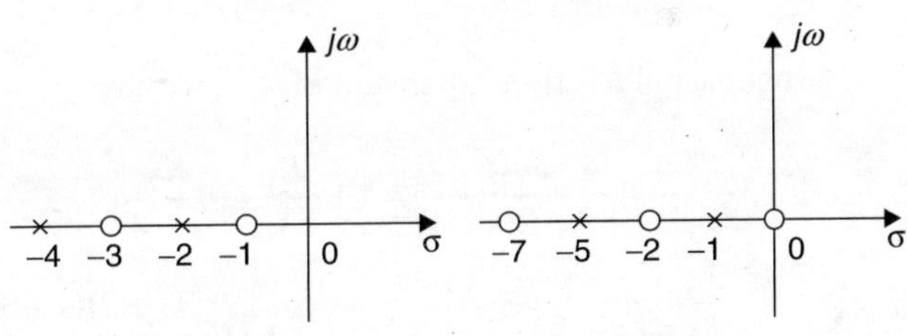

Fig. 1 **Fig.** 2

From the pole–zero plot in the s-plane (Fig. 2), it is clear that the poles and zeros are simple, lie on the negative real axis and interlaced. But, the lowest critical frequency nearest to the origin is a pole, not a zero; hence the function $Z(s)$ is not an RL impedance function.

Problem 15.23 Realise the Foster and Cauer forms of the LC impedance function $Z(s)=\frac{s(s+2)(s+5)}{(s+1)(s+4)}$.

Solution:

Given that $Z(s)=\dfrac{s(s+2)(s+5)}{(s+1)(s+4)}$

The zeroes are given by

$$s(s+2)(s+5)=0$$

$$s=0, \quad s=-2, \quad s=-5$$

The poles are given by

$$(s+1)(s+4)=0$$

$$s=-1, \quad s=-4$$

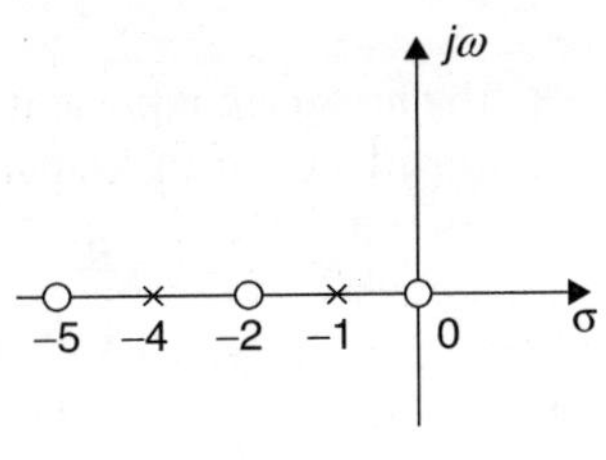

Fig. 1

From the pole–zero plot in the s-plane (Fig. 1), it is clear that the poles and zeros are simple, lie on the negative real axis and interlaced; the function $Z(s)$ is an RL impedance function.

(i) Foster-I realisation: The Foster-I form is obtained using partial fraction expansion of impedance function $\frac{Z(s)}{s}$.

$$Z(s)=\frac{s(s+2)(s+5)}{(s+1)(s+4)}$$

$$\frac{Z(s)}{s}=\frac{(s+2)(s+5)}{(s+1)(s+4)}=\frac{s^2+7s+10}{s^2+5s+4}$$

Since the degree of the numerator is equal to the degree of the denominator, division is first carried out.

$$s^2+5s+4)\; s^2+7s+10\; (1$$
$$\underline{s^2+5s+4}$$
$$2s+6$$

$$\therefore \quad \frac{Z(s)}{s}=\frac{(s+2)(s+5)}{(s+1)(s+4)}=1+\frac{2s+6}{(s+1)(s+4)}$$

Using partial fraction expansion of $\frac{Z(s)}{s}$, we have

$$\frac{Z(s)}{s}=\frac{(s+2)(s+5)}{(s+1)(s+4)}=1+\frac{K_1}{s+1}+\frac{K_2}{s+4}$$

$$K_1=(s+\beta_1)\frac{Z(s)}{s}\bigg|_{s=-\beta_1}=(s+1)\times\frac{(s+2)(s+5)}{(s+1)(s+4)}\bigg|_{s=-1}=\frac{(-1+2)(-1+5)}{(-1+4)}=\frac{4}{3}$$

$$K_2=(s+\beta_2)\frac{Z(s)}{s}\bigg|_{s=-\beta_2}=(s+4)\times\frac{(s+2)(s+5)}{(s+1)(s+4)}\bigg|_{s=-4}=\frac{(-4+2)(-4+5)}{(-4+1)}=\frac{2}{3}$$

$$\frac{Z(s)}{s}=\frac{(s+2)(s+5)}{(s+1)(s+4)}=1+\frac{\frac{4}{3}}{s+1}+\frac{\frac{2}{3}}{s+4}$$

$$\Rightarrow \quad Z(s)=s+\frac{\frac{4}{3}s}{s+1}+\frac{\frac{2}{3}s}{s+4}$$

The first term represents an impedance of an inductor of 1 H. The second and third terms represent an impedance of an RL parallel circuit. So, for a parallel RL network,

$$Z_{RL}(s)=\frac{Rs}{s+\frac{R}{L}}$$

On direct comparison, we have

$$R_1=\frac{4}{3}\,\Omega$$

$$\frac{R_1}{L_1}=1 \Rightarrow L_1=R_1=\frac{4}{3}\text{ H}$$

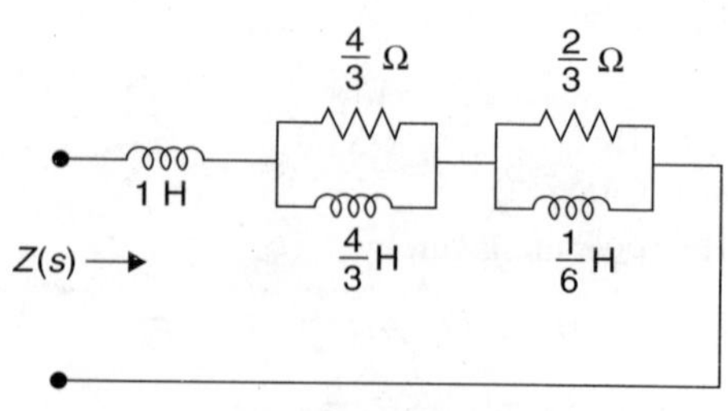

Fig. 2 Foster-I realisation

Similarly, we have

$$R_2 = \frac{2}{3}\,\Omega, \quad L_2 = \frac{1}{6}\,\text{H}$$

Therefore, the synthesised network is as shown in Fig. 2.

(ii) Foster-II realisation: The Foster-II form is obtained using partial fraction expansion of the admittance function $Y(s)$. Using partial fraction expansion, we have

$$Y(s) = \frac{(s+1)(s+4)}{s(s+2)(s+5)} = \frac{K_0}{s} + \frac{K_1}{s+2} + \frac{K_2}{s+5}$$

$$\text{where, } K_0 = sY(s)\big|_{s=0} = s \times \frac{(s+1)(s+4)}{s(s+2)(s+5)}\bigg|_{s=0} = \frac{1\times 4}{2\times 5} = \frac{2}{5}$$

$$K_1 = (s+\beta_1)Y(s)\big|_{s=-\beta_1} = (s+2)\times\frac{(s+1)(s+4)}{s(s+2)(s+5)}\bigg|_{s=-2} = \frac{(-2+1)(-2+4)}{-2(-2+5)} = \frac{1}{3}$$

$$K_2 = (s+\beta_2)Y(s)\big|_{s=-\beta_2} = (s+5)\times\frac{(s+1)(s+4)}{s(s+2)(s+5)}\bigg|_{s=-5} = \frac{(-5+1)(-5+4)}{-5(-5+2)} = \frac{4}{15}$$

$$\therefore \quad Y(s) = \frac{\frac{2}{5}}{s} + \frac{\frac{1}{3}}{s+2} + \frac{\frac{4}{15}}{s+15}$$

The first term represents an impedance of an inductor of $\frac{5}{2}$ H. The second and third terms represent an impedance of an RL series circuit. So, for a series RL network

$$Y_{RL}(s) = \frac{\frac{1}{L}}{s+\frac{R}{L}}$$

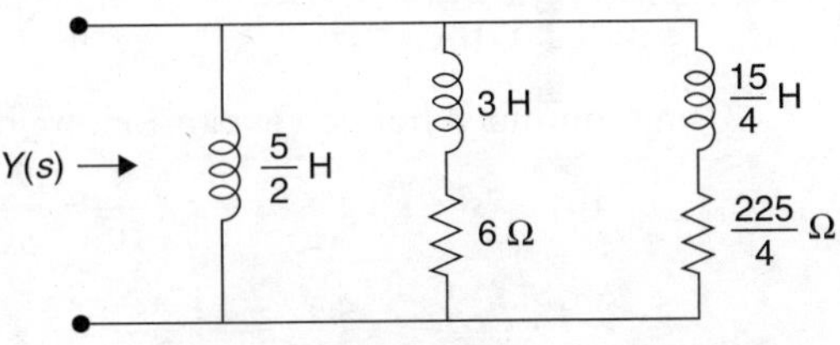

Fig. 3 Foster-II realisation

On direct comparison, we have

$$L_1 = 3\,\text{H}$$

$$\frac{R_1}{L_1} = 2 \Rightarrow R_1 = 2L_1 = 6\,\Omega$$

Similarly, we have

$$L_2 = \frac{15}{4}\,\text{H}, \quad R_2 = \frac{225}{4}\,\Omega$$

Therefore, the synthesised network is as shown in Fig. 3.

(iii) Cauer-I realisation: The Cauer-I from is obtained using continued fraction expansion of $Z(s)$ about the pole at infinity.

$$Z(s) = \frac{s(s+2)(s+5)}{(s+1)(s+4)} = \frac{s^3+7s^2+10s}{s^2+5s+4}$$

Using continued fraction expansion, we have

$$
\begin{array}{l}
s^2+5s+4)\ s^3+7s^2+10s\ (s \leftrightarrow Z_1 \\
\quad \underline{s^3+5s^2+4s} \\
\qquad 2s^2+6s)\ s^2+5s+4\ (\frac{1}{2} \leftrightarrow Y_2 \\
\qquad\quad \underline{s^2+3s} \\
\qquad\qquad 2s+4)\ 2s^2+6s\ (s \leftrightarrow Z_3 \\
\qquad\qquad\quad \underline{2s^2+4s} \\
\qquad\qquad\qquad 2s)\ 2s+4(1 \leftrightarrow Y_4 \\
\qquad\qquad\qquad\quad \underline{2s} \\
\qquad\qquad\qquad\qquad 4)\ 2s\ (\frac{1}{2}s \leftrightarrow Z_5 \\
\qquad\qquad\qquad\qquad\quad \underline{2s} \\
\qquad\qquad\qquad\qquad\quad 0
\end{array}
$$

The network elements are $L_1 = 1\,\text{H},\ R_1 = 2\,\Omega,\ L_2 = 1\,\text{H},\ R_2 = 1\,\Omega,\ L_3 = \frac{1}{2}\,\text{H}$

The impedances are connected in the series branches, whereas the admittances are connected in the parallel branches in a Cauer or Ladder realisation. Therefore, the synthesised network is as shown in Fig. 4.

(iv) Cauer-II realisation: The Cauer-II from is obtained using continued fraction expansion about the pole at the origin. Arranging the numerator and denominator polynomials in the ascending order of s,

$$Z(s) = \frac{s(s+2)(s+5)}{(s+1)(s+4)}$$

$$Z(s) = \frac{s^3+7s^2+10s}{s^2+5s+4} = \frac{10s+7s^2+s^3}{4+5s+s^2}$$

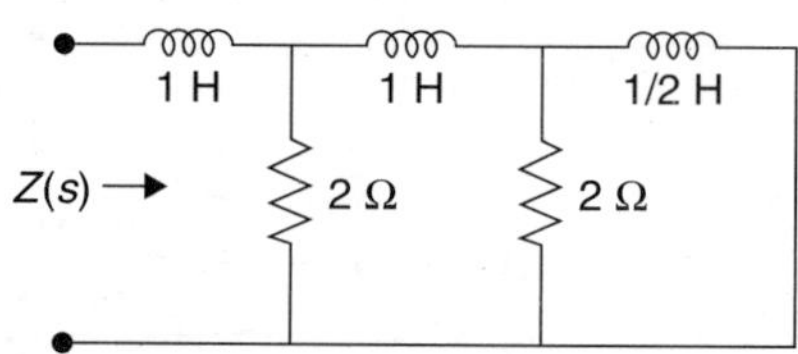

Fig. 4 Cauer-I realisation

The admittance function has a pole at the origin, so

$$Y(s) = \frac{4+5s+s^2}{10s+7s^2+s^3}$$

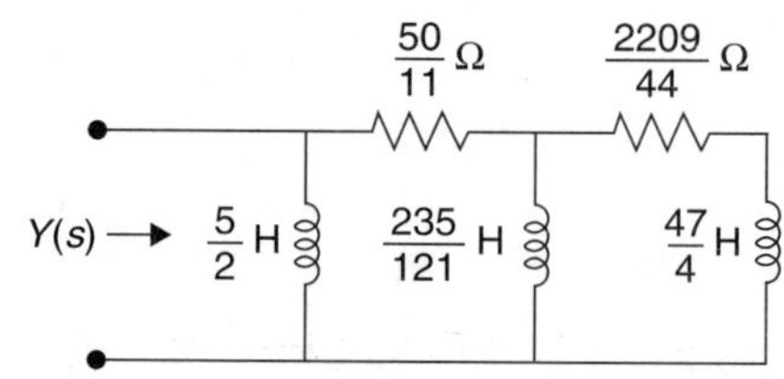

Fig. 5 Cauer-II realisation

Using continued fraction expansion, we have

$$
\begin{array}{l}
10s+7s^2+s^3)\ 4+5s+s^2\ (\frac{4}{10s} = \frac{2}{5s} \leftrightarrow Y_1 \\
\quad \underline{4+\frac{14}{5}s+\frac{2}{5}s^2} \\
\qquad \frac{11}{5}s+\frac{3}{5}s^2)\ 10s+7s^2+s^3(\frac{50}{11} \leftrightarrow Z_2 \\
\qquad\quad \underline{10s+\frac{30}{11}s^2} \\
\qquad\qquad \frac{47}{11}s^2+s^3)\ \frac{11}{5}s+\frac{3}{5}s^2\ (\frac{11}{47}\cdot\frac{11}{5s} = \frac{121}{235s} \leftrightarrow Y_3 \\
\qquad\qquad\quad \underline{\frac{11}{5}s+\frac{121}{235}s^2} \\
\qquad\qquad\qquad \frac{20}{235}s^2)\ \frac{47}{11}s^2+s^3\ (\frac{235}{20}\cdot\frac{47}{11} = \frac{2209}{44} \leftrightarrow Z_4 \\
\qquad\qquad\qquad\quad \underline{\frac{47}{11}s^2} \\
\qquad\qquad\qquad\qquad s^3)\ \frac{20}{235}s^2\ (\frac{20}{235s} = \frac{4}{47s} \leftrightarrow Y_5 \\
\qquad\qquad\qquad\qquad\quad \underline{\frac{20}{235}s^2} \\
\qquad\qquad\qquad\qquad\quad 0
\end{array}
$$

The network elements are $L_1 = \frac{5}{2}$ H, $R_1 = \frac{50}{11}$ Ω, $L_2 = \frac{2351}{121}$ H, $R_2 = \frac{2209}{44}$ Ω, $L_3 = \frac{47}{4}$ H

The impedances are connected in the series branches, whereas the admittances are connected in the parallel branches in a Cauer or Ladder realisation. Therefore, the synthesised network is as shown in Fig. 5.

ADDITIONAL SOLVED PROBLEMS

15.1 Check whether the polynomial $P(s) = s^4 + 3s^3 + 4s^2 + 3s + 1$ is Hurwitz or not.

Solution: Given that $P(s) = s^4 + 3s^3 + 4s^2 + 3s + 1$

(i) Since all the coefficients of $P(s)$ are positive, $P(s)$ is real for s real.
(ii) The even and odd parts of $P(s)$ are

$E(s) = s^4 + 4s^2 + 1$, $O(s) = 3s^3 + 3s$

The continued fraction expansion $Z(s) = \frac{E(s)}{O(s)}$ is given as

$$
\begin{array}{l}
3s^3 + 3s)\,s^4 + 4s^2 + 1\,(\frac{s}{3} \\
\qquad\quad \underline{s^4 + s^2} \\
\qquad\qquad 3s^2 + 1)\,3s^3 + 3s\,(s \\
\qquad\qquad\qquad\quad \underline{3s^3 + s} \\
\qquad\qquad\qquad\qquad 2s)\,3s^2 + 1\,(\frac{3}{2}s \\
\qquad\qquad\qquad\qquad\quad \underline{3s^2} \\
\qquad\qquad\qquad\qquad\qquad 1)\,2s\,(2s \\
\qquad\qquad\qquad\qquad\qquad\quad \underline{2s} \\
\qquad\qquad\qquad\qquad\qquad\quad 0
\end{array}
$$

Since all the quotient terms are positive, $P(s)$ is Hurwitz.

15.2 Check whether the given polynomials are Hurwitz or not.

(i) $P(s) = s^5 + 7s^4 + 15s^2 + 20s + 35$
(ii) $P(s) = s^6 + s^5 + 6s^4 - 3s^3 + 15s^2 + 18s + 20$

Solution: Given that

(i) $P(s) = s^5 + 7s^4 + 15s^2 + 20s + 35$

In the given polynomial, the s^3 term is missing and it is neither an even nor an odd polynomial. So the given polynomial is not Hurwitz.

(ii) $P(s) = s^6 + s^5 + 6s^4 - 3s^3 + 15s^2 + 18s + 20$

In the given polynomial, the s^3 coefficient is negative (−3), hence the given polynomial is not Hurwitz.

15.3 Check whether the polynomial $P(s) = s^4 + 10s^3 + 35s^2 + 50s + 24$ is Hurwitz or not. Use Routh–Hurwitz criterion.

Solution: Given that

$$P(s) = s^4 + 10s^3 + 35s^2 + 50s + 24$$

s^4	1	35	24
s^3	10	50	0
s^2	30	24	0
s^1	42	0	
s^0	24		

There is no sign change in the first column of Routh's array; hence the given polynomial is Hurwitz.

15.4 Check whether the polynomial $P(s) = s^5 + s^4 + 2s^3 + 2s^2 + 3s + 15$ is Hurwitz or not. Use Routh–Hurwitz criterion.

Solution: Given that

$$P(s) = s^5 + s^4 + 2s^3 + 2s^2 + 3s + 15$$

s^5	1	2	3	
s^4	1	2	15	
s^3	0	−12	0	⇐ Routh's test failed

Modify the original characteristic equation by replacing s by $1/z$. Apply the Routh's test on the modified equation in term of z. The number of z roots with positive real parts are the same as the number of s roots with positive real parts. So, replace s by $1/z$.

$$P(z) = \frac{1}{z^5} + \frac{1}{z^4} + \frac{2}{z^3} + \frac{2}{z^2} + \frac{3}{z} + 15 = 15z^5 + 3z^4 + 2z^3 + 2z^2 + z + 1$$

z^5	15	2	1
z^4	3	2	1
z^3	$\frac{6-30}{3} = -8$	$\frac{3-15}{3} = -4$	–
z^2	1/2	1	0
z^1	12	–	
z^0	1		

There are two sign changes in the first column of Routh's array; hence the given polynomial is not Hurwitz.

15.5 Find the range of values of k so that $P(s) = s(s^2 + s + 1)(s + 4) + k$ is Hurwitz. Use Routh–Hurwitz criterion.

Solution: Given that $P(s) = s(s^2 + s + 1)(s + 4) + k = s^4 + 5s^3 + 5s^2 + 4s + k$

s^4	1	5	k
s^3	5	4	0
s^2	4.2	k	0
s^1	$\frac{16.8-5k}{4.2}$	–	–
s^0	k		

For the given polynomial to be Hurwitz, there should not be any sign change in the first column.

Therefore, $k > 0$ and $16.8 - 5k > 0$

That is, $16.8 > 5k \Rightarrow 3.36 > k$

Therefore, the range of k is $0 < k < 3.36$

15.6 Check whether the polynomial $P(s) = s^6 + 3s^5 + 4s^4 + 6s^3 + 5s^2 + 3s + 2$ is Hurwitz or not. Use Routh–Hurwitz criterion.

Solution: Given that $P(s) = s^6 + 3s^5 + 4s^4 + 6s^3 + 5s^2 + 3s + 2$

s^6	1	4	5	2	
s^5	3	6	3	0	
s^4	2	4	2	0	
s^3	0	0	0	0	⇐ Row of all zeros

$$A(s) = 2s^4 + 4s^2 + 2 = 2(s^4 + 2s^2 + 1) = s^4 + 2s^2 + 1$$

$$\frac{dA(s)}{ds} = 4s^3 + 4s$$

s^4	2	4	2	0	
s^3	4	4	0	0	
s^2	2	2	0	0	
s^1	0	0	0	0	⇐ Row of all zeros

$$A'(s) = 2s^2 + 2$$

$$\frac{dA'(s)}{ds} = 4s$$

s^2	2	2	0	0
s^1	4	0	0	0
s^0	2			

There is no sign change in the first column of Routh's array; hence the given polynomial is Hurwitz.

15.7 Check whether the polynomial $P(s) = s^8 + 5s^6 + 2s^4 + 3s^2 + 1$ is Hurwitz or not. Use Routh–Hurwitz criterion.

Solution: Given that $P(s) = s^8 + 5s^6 + 2s^4 + 3s^2 + 1$

s^8	1	5	2	3	1	
s^7	0	0	0	0	0	⇐ Row of all zeros

$\therefore$ $A(s) = s^8 + 5s^6 + 2s^4 + 3s^2 + 1$

$$\frac{dA}{ds} = 8s^7 + 30s^5 + 8s^3 + 6s$$

s^8	1	5	2	3	1
s^7	8	30	8	6	0
s^6	1.25	1	2.25	1	0
s^5	23.6	−6.4	0.4	0	0
s^4	1.33	2.271	1	0	0
s^3	−46.6	−18.14	0	0	
s^2	1.75	1	0		
s^1	8.45	0			
s^0	1				

There are two sign changes in the first column of Routh's array; hence the given polynomial is not Hurwitz.

15.8 Determine whether the function, $F(s)=\frac{(s+1)(s+2)}{(s+3)(s+4)}$ is positive real or not.

Solution: Given that

$$F(s)=\frac{(s+1)(s+2)}{(s+3)(s+4)}=\frac{s^2+3s+2}{s^2+7s+12}=\frac{N(s)}{D(s)}$$

Condition (1): The function $F(s)$ has poles at $s=-3$ and $s=-4$ and zero at $s=-1$ and $s=-2$. Thus the poles and zeros are on the left half of the s-plane.

Condition (2): Since there is no pole on the $j\omega$-axis, the residue test is not required.

Condition (3):

Even part of $N(s)$, $E_1(s)=s^2+2$

Odd part of $N(s)$, $O_1(s)=3s$

Even part of $D(s)$, $E_2(s)=s^2+12$

Odd part of $D(s)$, $O_2(s)=7s$

$$A(\omega^2)=[E_1(s)E_2(s)-O_1(s)O_2(s)]_{s=j\omega}=[(s^2+2)(s^2+12)-21s^2]_{s=j\omega}$$

$$=[s^4-7s^2+24]_{s=j\omega}=\omega^4+7\omega^2+24$$

$\therefore$ $A(\omega^2)=\omega^4+7\omega^2+24\geq$ for all values of ω

Since all the three conditions are satisfied, the given function is positive real.

15.9 Determine whether the function, $F(s)=\frac{s^2+4}{s^3+3s^2+3s+1}$ is positive real or not.

Solution: Given that

$$F(s)=\frac{s^2+4}{s^3+3s^2+3s+1}=\frac{(s+j2)(s-j2)}{s^3+3s^2+3s+1}=\frac{N(s)}{D(s)}$$

Condition (1): The function $F(s)$ has zeroes at $s=-j2$ and $s=j2$ and the denominator polynomial cannot be easily factorised; we will prove whether $D(s)$ is Hurwitz or not. The even and odd parts of $D(s)$ are,

$$E(s)=3s^2+1,\ O(s)=s^3+3s$$

The continued fraction expansion $Z(s) = \frac{O(s)}{E(s)}$, is given as

$$3s^2 + 1)\ s^3 + 3s\ (\frac{1}{3}s$$
$$\underline{s^3 + \frac{1}{3}s}$$
$$\frac{8}{3}s)\ 3s^2 + 1\ (\frac{9}{8}s$$
$$\underline{3s^2}$$
$$1)\ \frac{8}{3}s\ (\frac{8}{3}s$$
$$\underline{\frac{8}{3}s}$$
$$0$$

Since all the quotient terms are positive, $D(s)$ is Hurwitz. This indicates that all the poles are in the left half of the s-plane. Thus all the poles and zeros are in the left half of the s-plane.

Condition (2): Since there are no poles on the $j\omega$-axis, we have to ignore this condition.

Condition (3):

Even part of $N(s)$, $E_1(s) = s^2 + 4$

Odd part of $N(s)$, $O_1(s) = 0$

Even part of $D(s)$, $E_2(s) = 3s^2 + 1$

Odd part of $D(s)$, $O_2(s) = s^3 + 3s$

$$A(\omega^2) = [E_1(s)E_2(s) - O_1(s)O_2(s)]_{s=j\omega} = [(s^2+4)(3s^2+1) - 0]_{s=j\omega}$$

$$= [3s^4 + 13s^2 + 4]_{s=j\omega} = 3\omega^4 - 13\omega^2 + 4$$

$\therefore$ $\quad A(\omega^2) = 3\omega^4 - 13\omega^2 + 4 \geq$ for some values of ω

Since the third condition is not satisfied, the given function is not positive real.

15.10 Realise the Foster forms of LC impedance function, $Z(s) = \frac{(s^2+1)(s^2+3)}{s(s^2+4)(s^2+2)}$.

Solution: Given that $Z(s) = \dfrac{(s^2+1)(s^2+3)}{s(s^2+4)(s^2+2)}$

The poles are given by

$$s(s^2+2)(s^2+4) = 0$$

$$s = 0, \quad s = \pm j\sqrt{2}, \quad s = \pm j2$$

The zeros are given by

$$(s^2+1)(s^2+3) = 0$$

$$s = \pm j1, \quad s = \pm j\sqrt{3}$$

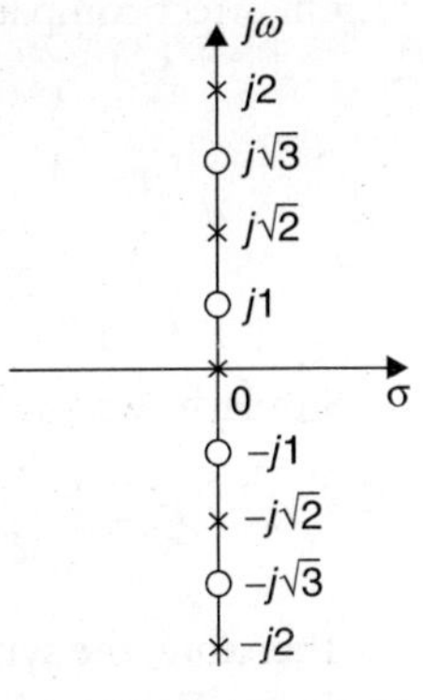

$j\omega$
$j2$
$j\sqrt{3}$
$j\sqrt{2}$
$j1$
0
σ
$-j1$
$-j\sqrt{2}$
$-j\sqrt{3}$
$-j2$

Fig. 1

From the pole–zero plot in the s-plane (Fig. 1), it is clear that the poles and zeros are simple, lie on the $j\omega$-axis and interlace on the $j\omega$-axis; the function $Z(s)$ is an LC impedance function.

(i) Foster-I form: The Foster-I form is obtained using partial fraction expansion of the impedance function $Z(s)$.

$$Z(s)=\frac{(s^2+1)(s^2+3)}{s(s^2+4)(s^2+2)}$$

Using partial fraction expansion, we have

$$Z(s)=\frac{(s^2+1)(s^2+3)}{s(s^2+4)(s^2+2)}=\frac{K_0}{s}+\frac{K_1}{s+j\sqrt{2}}+\frac{K_1^*}{s-j\sqrt{2}}+\frac{K_2}{s+j2}+\frac{K_2^*}{s-j2}=\frac{K_0}{s}+\frac{2sK_1}{s^2+2}+\frac{2sK_2}{s^2+4}$$

where, $K_0=sZ(s)\Big|_{s=0}=s\times\frac{(s^2+1)(s^2+3)}{s(s^2+4)(s^2+2)}\Bigg|_{s=0}=\frac{1\times3}{4\times2}=\frac{3}{8}$

$$K_1=\frac{(s^2+\omega_1^2)Z(s)}{2s}\Bigg|_{s^2=-\omega_1^2}=\frac{(s^2+2)}{2s}\times\frac{(s^2+1)(s^2+3)}{s(s^2+4)(s^2+2)}\Bigg|_{s^2=-2}=\frac{(-2+1)(-2+3)}{-2\times2\times2}=\frac{1}{8}$$

$$K_2=\frac{(s^2+\omega_2^2)Z(s)}{2s}\Bigg|_{s^2=-\omega_2^2}=\frac{(s^2+4)}{2s}\times\frac{(s^2+1)(s^2+3)}{s(s^2+4)(s^2+2)}\Bigg|_{s^2=-4}=\frac{(-4+1)(-4+3)}{2\times4\times2}=\frac{3}{16}$$

$$\therefore\quad Z(s)=\frac{(s^2+1)(s^2+3)}{s(s^2+4)(s^2+2)}=\frac{K_0}{s}+\frac{2sK_1}{s^2+2}+\frac{2sK_2}{s^2+4}=\frac{\frac{3}{8}}{s}+\frac{\frac{1}{4}s}{s^2+2}+\frac{\frac{3}{8}s}{s^2+4}$$

The first term represents the impedance of a capacitor of $\frac{8}{3}$ F. The second and third terms represent the impedance of a parallel LC circuit. So, for a parallel LC network,

$$Z_{LC}(s)=\frac{\left(\frac{1}{C}\right)s}{s^2+\frac{1}{LC}}$$

On direct comparison, we have

$$\frac{1}{C_1}=\frac{1}{4}\Rightarrow C_1=4\text{ F}$$

$$\frac{1}{L_1C_1}=2\Rightarrow L_1=\frac{1}{2C_1}=\frac{1}{8}\text{ H}$$

Similarly, we have

$$C_2=\frac{8}{3}\text{ F},\ L_2=\frac{3}{32}\text{ H}$$

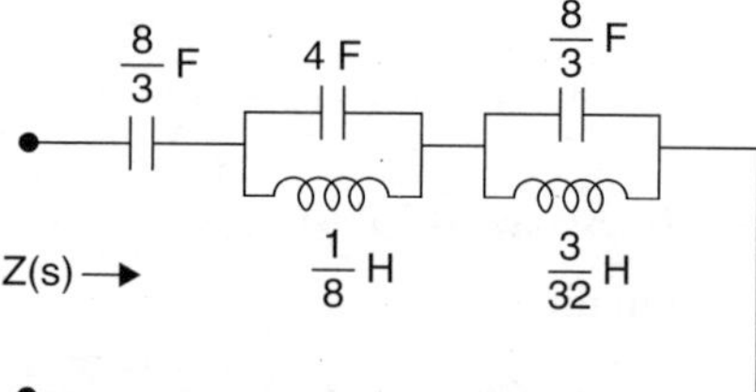

Fig. 2 Foster-I realisation

Therefore, the synthesised network is as shown in Fig. 2.

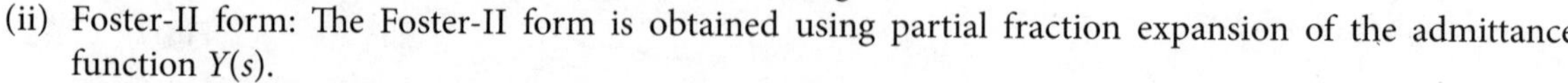

(ii) Foster-II form: The Foster-II form is obtained using partial fraction expansion of the admittance function $Y(s)$.

$$Y(s)=\frac{s(s^2+2)(s^2+4)}{(s^2+1)(s^2+3)}=\frac{s^5+6s^3+8s}{s^4+4s^2+3}$$

Here the degree of the numerator is greater than that of the denominator, so division is first carried out.

$$\begin{array}{r} s^4+4s^2+3\,)\ s^5+6s^3+8s\ (s \\ \underline{s^5+4s^3+3s} \\ 2s^3+5s \end{array}$$

$$\therefore\quad Y(s)=\frac{s^5+6s^3+8s}{s^4+4s^2+3}=s+\frac{2s^3+5s}{s^4+4s^2+3}$$

Using partial fraction expansion, we have

$$Y(s)=\frac{s(s^2+2)(s^2+4)}{(s^2+1)(s^2+3)}=s+\frac{K_1}{s+j1}+\frac{K_1^*}{s-j1}+\frac{K_2}{s+j\sqrt{3}}+\frac{K_2^*}{s-j\sqrt{3}}=s+\frac{2K_1s}{s^2+1}+\frac{2K_2s}{s^2+3}$$

$$\text{where, } K_1=\left.\frac{(s^2+\omega_1^2)Y(s)}{2s}\right|_{s^2=-\omega_1^2}=\left.\frac{(s^2+1)}{2s}\times\frac{s(s^2+2)(s^2+4)}{(s^2+1)(s^2+3)}\right|_{s^2=-1}=\frac{(-1+2)(-1+4)}{2(-1+3)}=\frac{3}{4}$$

$$K_2=\left.\frac{(s^2+\omega_2^2)Y(s)}{2s}\right|_{s^2=-\omega_2^2}=\left.\frac{(s^2+3)}{2s}\times\frac{s(s^2+2)(s^2+4)}{(s^2+1)(s^2+3)}\right|_{s^2=-3}=\frac{(-3+2)(-3+4)}{2(-3+1)}=\frac{1}{4}$$

$$\therefore\qquad Y(s)=s+\frac{2K_1s}{s^2+1}+\frac{2K_2s}{s^2+3}=s+\frac{\frac{3}{2}s}{s^2+1}+\frac{\frac{1}{2}s}{s^2+3}$$

The first term represents the admittance of a capacitor of 1 F and the remaining two terms represent the admittance of a series LC network. So, for a series LC network,

$$Y_{LC}(s)=\frac{\left(\frac{1}{L}\right)s}{s^2+\frac{1}{LC}}$$

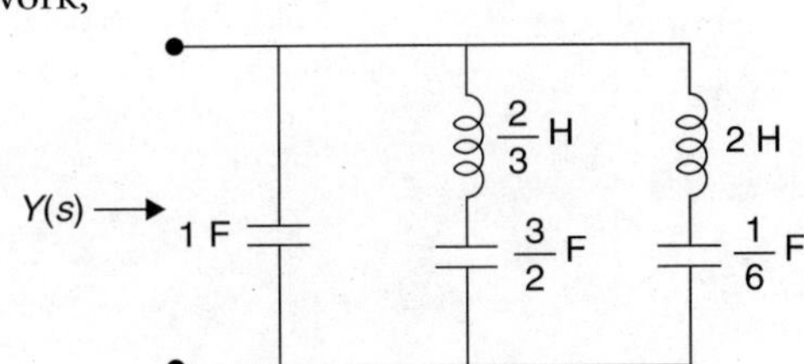

Fig. 3 Foster-II realisation

On direct comparison, we have

$$\frac{1}{L_1}=\frac{3}{2}\ \Rightarrow\ L_1=\frac{2}{3}\text{ H}$$

$$\frac{1}{L_1C_1}=1\ \Rightarrow\ C_1=\frac{1}{L_1}=\frac{3}{2}\text{ F}$$

Similarly, we have

$$L_2=2\text{ H},\quad C_2=\frac{1}{6}\text{ F}$$

Therefore, the synthesised network is as shown in Fig. 3.

15.11 Realise the Cauer forms of the LC impedance function, $Z(s)=\dfrac{s(s^2+3)(s^2+5)}{(s^2+2)(s^2+4)}$.

Solution: Given that $Z(s)=\dfrac{s(s^2+3)(s^2+5)}{(s^2+2)(s^2+4)}$

The zeros are given by

$$s(s^2+3)(s^2+5)=0$$

$$s=0,\quad s=\pm j\sqrt{3},\quad s=\pm j\sqrt{5}$$

The poles are given by

$$(s^2+2)(s^2+4)=0$$

$$s=\pm j\sqrt{2},\quad s=\pm j2$$

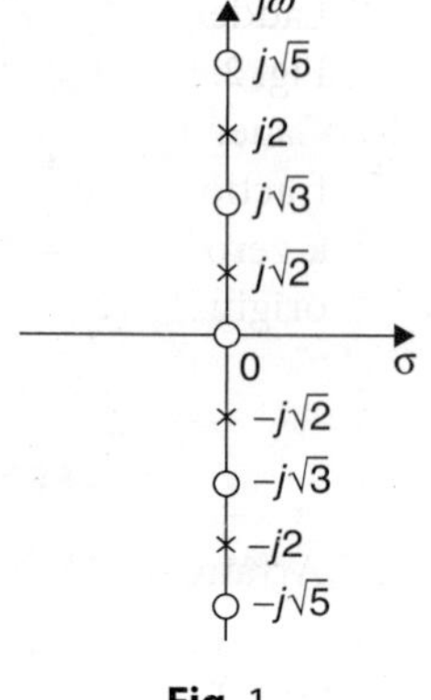

Fig. 1

From the pole–zero plot in the s-plane (Fig. 1), it is clear that the poles and zeros are simple, lie on the $j\omega$-axis and interlace on the $j\omega$-axis; the function $Z(s)$ is an LC impedance function.

(i) Cauer-I realisation: The Cauer-I form is obtained using continued fraction expansion about the pole at infinity.

$$Z(s)=\frac{s(s^2+3)(s^2+5)}{(s^2+2)(s^2+4)}=\frac{s^5+8s^3+15s}{s^4+6s^2+8}$$

Here the degree of the numerator is greater than that of the denominator by one, so it indicates a pole at infinity. Using continued fraction expansion, we have

$$s^4+6s^2+8)\,s^5+8s^3+15s\,(s \leftrightarrow Z_1$$
$$\underline{s^5+6s^3+8s}$$
$$2s^3+7s)\,s^4+6s^2+8\,(\tfrac{1}{2}s \leftrightarrow Y_2$$
$$\underline{s^4+\tfrac{7}{2}s^2}$$
$$\tfrac{5}{2}s^2+8)\,2s^3+7s\,(\tfrac{4}{5}s \leftrightarrow Z_3$$
$$\underline{2s^3+\tfrac{32}{5}s}$$
$$\tfrac{3}{5}s)\,\tfrac{5}{2}s^2+8\,(\tfrac{25}{6}s \leftrightarrow Y_4$$
$$\underline{\tfrac{5}{2}s^2}$$
$$8)\,\tfrac{3}{5}s\,(\tfrac{3}{40}s \leftrightarrow Z_5$$
$$\underline{\tfrac{3}{5}s}$$
$$0$$

The network elements are $L_1=1\,\text{H},\ C_1=\dfrac{1}{2}\,\text{F},\ L_2=\dfrac{4}{5}\,\text{H},\ C_2=\dfrac{25}{6}\,\text{F},\ L_3=\dfrac{3}{40}\,\text{H}$

The impedances are connected in the series branches, whereas the admittances are connected in the parallel branches in a Cauer or Ladder realisation. Therefore, the synthesised network is as shown in Fig. 2.

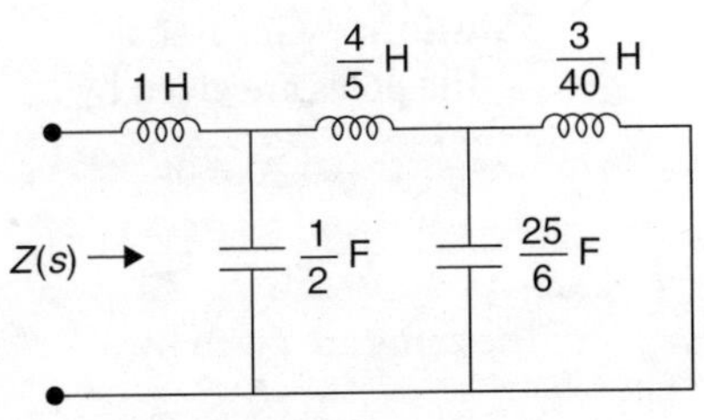

Fig. 2 Cauer-I realisation

(ii) Cauer-II realisation: The Cauer-II form is obtained using continued fraction expansion about the pole at the origin. The given function has a zero at the origin. The admittance function $Y(s)$ has a pole at the origin. Hence, continued fraction of $Y(s)$ is carried out.

$$Y(s)=\frac{(s^2+2)(s^2+4)}{s(s^2+3)(s^2+5)}=\frac{s^4+6s^2+8}{s^5+8s^3+15s}$$

Arranging the numerator and denominator polynomials in the ascending order of s:

$$Y(s)=\frac{8+6s^2+s^4}{15s+8s^3+s^5}$$

Using continued fraction expansion, we have

$$15s+8s^3+s^5)\;8+6s^2+s^4\;(\frac{8}{15s}\leftrightarrow Y_1$$

$$8+\frac{64}{15}s^2+\frac{8}{15}s^4$$

$$\frac{26}{15}s^2+\frac{7}{15}s^4)\;15s+8s^3+s^5(\frac{225}{26s}\leftrightarrow Z_2$$

$$15s+\frac{105}{26}s^3$$

$$\frac{103}{26}s^3+s^5)\;\frac{26}{15}s^2+\frac{7}{15}s^4(\frac{676}{1545s}\leftrightarrow Y_3$$

$$\frac{26}{15}s^2+\frac{676}{1545}s^4$$

$$\frac{3}{103}s^4)\;\frac{103}{26}s^3+s^5\;(\frac{103^2}{78s}\leftrightarrow Z_4$$

$$\frac{103}{26}s^3$$

$$s^5)\;\frac{3}{103}s^4\;(\frac{3}{103s}\leftrightarrow Y_5$$

$$\frac{3}{103}s^4$$

$$0$$

Fig. 3 Cauer-II realisation

The network elements are $L_1=\frac{15}{8}$ H, $C_1=\frac{26}{225}$ F, $L_2=\frac{1545}{676}$ H, $C_2=\frac{78}{103^2}$ F, $L_3=\frac{3}{103}$ H

The impedances are connected in the series branches, whereas the admittances are connected in the parallel branches in a Cauer or Ladder realisation. Therefore, the synthesised network is as shown in Fig. 3.

15.12 Realise the Foster forms of the RC impedance function, $Z(s)=\frac{(s+2)(s+4)}{s(s+3)}$.

Solution: Given that

The poles are given by

$$s(s+3)=0$$

$$s=0, \quad s=-3$$

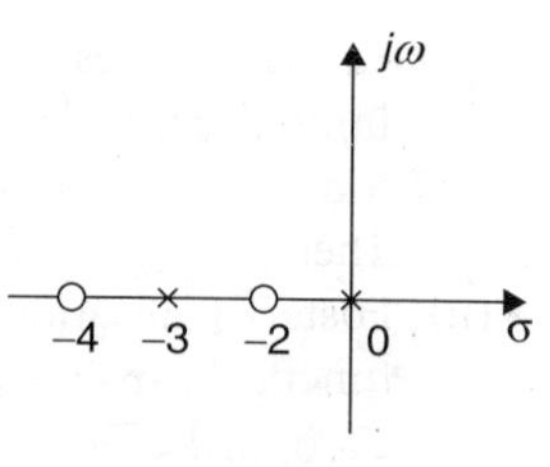

Fig. 1

The zeros are given by

$$(s+2)(s+4)=0$$

$$s=-2, \quad s=-4$$

From the pole–zero plot in the *s*-plane (Fig. 1), it is clear that the poles and zeros are simple, lie on the negative real axis and interlaced; the function $Z(s)$ is an *RC* impedance function.

(i) Foster-I realisation: The Foster-I form is obtained using the partial fraction expansion of the impedance function $Z(s)$. Here the degree of the numerator is equal to the degree of the denominator, so division is first carried out.

$$Z(s)=\frac{(s+2)(s+4)}{s(s+3)}=\frac{s^2+6s+8}{s^2+3s}$$

$s^2+3s)\ s^2+6s+8\ (1$

$\underline{s^2+3s+4}$

$3s+4$

Fig. 2 Foster-I realisation

Using partial fraction expansion, we have

$$Z(s)=\frac{(s+2)(s+4)}{s(s+3)}=1+\frac{3s+4}{s(s+3)}=1+\frac{K_0}{s}+\frac{K_1}{s+3}$$

where, $K_0=sZ(s)\Big|_{s=0}=s\times\frac{(s+2)(s+4)}{s(s+3)}\Bigg|_{s=0}=\frac{2\times 4}{3}=\frac{8}{3}$

$$K_1=(s+\beta_1)Z(s)\Big|_{s=-\beta_1}=(s+3)\times\frac{(s+2)(s+4)}{s(s+3)}\Bigg|_{s=-3}=\frac{(-3+2)(-3+4)}{-3}=\frac{1}{3}$$

$$\therefore\quad Z(s)=1+\frac{\frac{8}{3}}{s}+\frac{\frac{1}{3}}{s+3}$$

The first term represents an impedance of a resistor of 1 Ω, the second term represents an impedance of a capacitor of $\frac{3}{8}$ F and the third term represent an impedance of an *RC* parallel circuit. So, for a parallel *RC* network,

$$Z_{RC}(s)=\frac{\frac{1}{C}}{s+\frac{1}{RC}}$$

On direct comparison, we have

$$C=3\text{ F}$$

$$\frac{1}{RC} = 3 \Rightarrow R = \frac{1}{3C} = \frac{1}{9}\,\Omega$$

Therefore, the synthesised network is as shown in Fig. 2.

(ii) Foster-II realisation: The Foster-II form is obtained using the partial fraction expansion of admittance function $\frac{Y(s)}{s}$.

$$Y(s) = \frac{1}{Z(s)} = \frac{s(s+3)}{(s+2)(s+4)}$$

$$\frac{Y(s)}{s} = \frac{s+3}{(s+2)(s+4)}$$

Using partial fraction expansion, we have

$$\frac{Y(s)}{s} = \frac{s+3}{(s+2)(s+4)} = \frac{K_1}{s+2} + \frac{K_2}{s+4}$$

$$K_1 = (s+\beta_1)\frac{Y(s)}{s}\bigg|_{s=-\beta_1} = (s+2) \times \frac{(s+3)}{(s+2)(s+4)}\bigg|_{s=-2} = \frac{(-2+3)}{(-2+4)} = \frac{1}{2}$$

$$K_2 = (s+\beta_2)\frac{Y(s)}{s}\bigg|_{s=-\beta_2} = (s+4) \times \frac{(s+3)}{(s+2)(s+4)}\bigg|_{s=-4} = \frac{(-4+3)}{(-4+2)} = \frac{1}{2}$$

$$\frac{Y(s)}{s} = \frac{s+3}{(s+1)(s+4)} = \frac{\frac{1}{2}}{s+1} + \frac{\frac{1}{2}}{s+4}$$

$$\Rightarrow Y(s) = \frac{\frac{1}{2}s}{s+2} + \frac{\frac{1}{2}s}{s+4}$$

The above two terms represent the admittance of an *RC* series circuit. So, for a series *RC* network,

$$Y_{RC}(s) = \frac{\frac{1}{R}s}{s + \frac{1}{RC}}$$

On direct comparison, we have

$$\frac{1}{R_1} = \frac{1}{2} \Rightarrow R_1 = 2\,\Omega$$

$$\frac{1}{R_1C_1} = 2 \Rightarrow C_1 = \frac{1}{2R_1} = \frac{1}{4}\,\text{F}$$

Similarly, we have

$$R_2 = 2\,\Omega,\ C_2 = \frac{1}{8}\,\text{F}$$

Therefore, the synthesised network is as shown in Fig. 3.

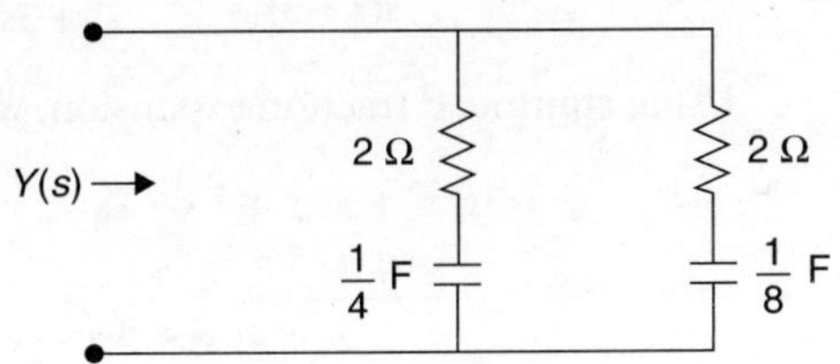

Fig. 3 Foster-II realisation

15.13 The RC driving point impedance of a network is $Z(s)=K\frac{(s+1)(s+4)}{s(s+3)}$. Realise the impedance function using the Cauer forms given $Z(-2)=1$.

Solution: Given that $Z(s)=K\frac{(s+1)(s+4)}{s(s+3)}$, $Z(-2)=1$

Putting $s=-2$ in $Z(s)$, we have

$$Z(-2)=K\frac{(-2+1)(-2+4)}{-2(-2+3)}=1$$

$$\Rightarrow \qquad K=1$$

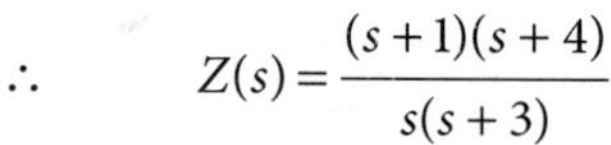

$$\therefore \qquad Z(s)=\frac{(s+1)(s+4)}{s(s+3)}$$

$j\omega$

$-4 \quad -3 \quad -1 \quad 0 \quad \sigma$

Fig. 1

The poles are given by

$$s(s+3)=0$$

$$s=0, \quad s=-3$$

The zeros are given by

$$(s+1)(s+4)=0$$

$$s=-1, \quad s=-4$$

From the pole–zero plot in the s-plane (Fig. 1), it is clear that the poles and zeros are simple, lie on the negative real axis and interlaced; the function $Z(s)$ is an RC impedance function.

(i) Cauer-I realisation: The Cauer-I form is obtained using continued fraction expansion about the pole at infinity.

$$Z(s)=\frac{(s+1)(s+4)}{s(s+3)}=\frac{s^2+5s+4}{s^2+3s}$$

Using continued fraction expansion, we have

$$s^2+3s)\ s^2+5s+4\ (1 \leftrightarrow Z_1$$
$$\underline{s^2+3s}$$
$$2s+4)\ s^2+3s\ (\tfrac{1}{2}s \leftrightarrow Y_2$$
$$\underline{s^2+2s}$$
$$s)\ 2s+4\ (2 \leftrightarrow Z_3$$
$$\underline{2s}$$
$$4)\ s\ (\tfrac{1}{4}s \leftrightarrow Y_4$$
$$\underline{s}$$
$$0$$

$\therefore$ The network elements are $R_1=1\,\Omega$, $C_1=\frac{1}{2}$ F, $R_2=2\,\Omega$, $C_2=\frac{1}{4}$ F

The impedances are connected in the series branches, whereas the admittances are connected in the parallel branches in a Cauer or Ladder realisation. Therefore, the synthesised network is as shown in Fig. 4.

(ii) Cauer-II realisation: The Cauer-II form is obtained using continued fraction expansion about the pole at the origin.

$$Z(s)=\frac{(s+1)(s+4)}{s(s+3)}=\frac{s^2+5s+4}{s^2+3s}$$

The function has pole at the origin. Arranging the numerator and denominator polynomials in the ascending order of s:

$$Z(s)=\frac{4+5s+s^2}{3s+s^2}$$

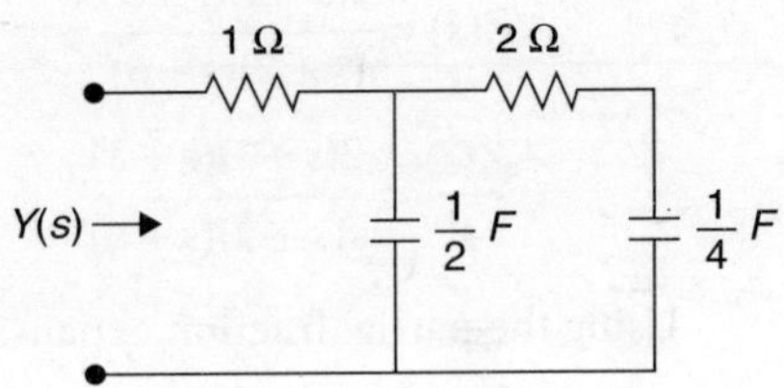

Fig. 4 Cauer-I realisation

Using continued fraction expansion, we have

$$3s+s^2)\ 4+5s+s^2\ (\frac{4}{3s}\leftrightarrow Z_1$$
$$\underline{4+\frac{4}{3}s}$$
$$\frac{11}{3}s+s^2)\ 3s+s^2(\frac{9}{11}\leftrightarrow Y_2$$
$$\underline{3s+\frac{9}{11}s^2}$$
$$\frac{2}{11}s^2)\ \frac{11}{3}s+s^2\ (\frac{121}{6s}\leftrightarrow Z_3$$
$$\underline{\frac{11}{3}s}$$
$$s^2)\ \frac{2}{11}s^2\ (\frac{2}{11}\leftrightarrow Y_4$$
$$\underline{\frac{2}{11}s^2}$$
$$0$$

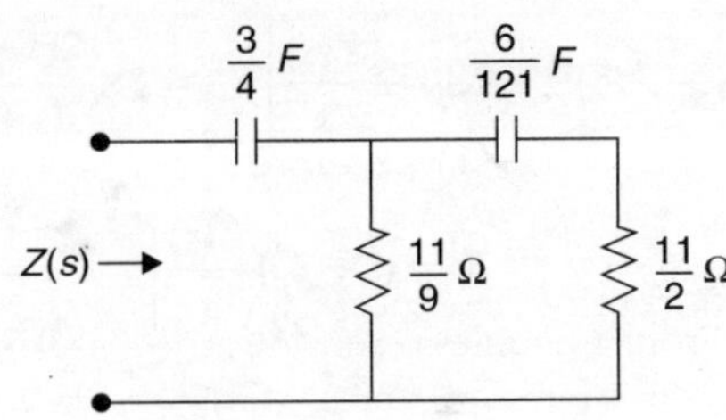

Fig. 5 Cauer-II realisation

$\therefore$ The network elements are $C_1=\frac{3}{4}$ F, $R_1=\frac{11}{9}\,\Omega$, $C_2=\frac{6}{121}$ F, $R_2=\frac{11}{2}\,\Omega$

The impedances are connected in the series branches, whereas the admittances are connected in the parallel branches in a Cauer or Ladder realisation. Therefore, the synthesised network is as shown in Fig. 5.

15.14 Realise the Foster forms of the RL impedance function, $Z(s)=\frac{2(s+1)(s+3)}{(s+2)(s+6)}$.

Solution: Given that $Z(s)=\dfrac{2(s+1)(s+3)}{(s+2)(s+6)}$

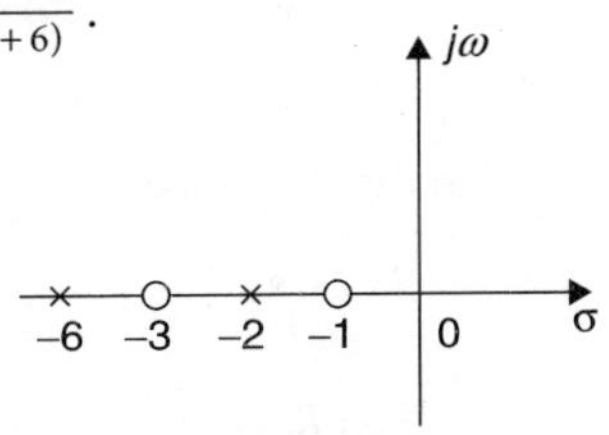

Fig. 1

The poles are given by

$$(s+2)(s+6)=0$$

$$s=-2,\quad s=-6$$

The zeros are given by

$$(s+1)(s+3)=0$$

$$s=-1, \quad s=-3$$

From the pole–zero plot in the *s*-plane (Fig. 1), it is clear that the poles and zeros are simple, lie on the negative real axis and interlaced; the function $Z(s)$ is an *RL* impedance function.

(i) Foster-I realisation: The Foster-I form is obtained using the partial fraction expansion of the impedance function $\frac{Z(s)}{s}$.

$$Z(s)=\frac{2(s+1)(s+3)}{(s+2)(s+6)}$$

$$\frac{Z(s)}{s}=\frac{2(s+1)(s+3)}{s(s+2)(s+6)}$$

Using the partial fraction expansion of $\frac{Z(s)}{s}$, we have

$$\frac{Z(s)}{s}=\frac{2(s+1)(s+3)}{s(s+2)(s+6)}=\frac{K_0}{s}+\frac{K_1}{s+2}+\frac{K_2}{s+6}$$

$$K_0=s\frac{Z(s)}{s}\bigg|_{s=0}=s\times\frac{2(s+1)(s+3)}{s(s+2)(s+6)}\bigg|_{s=0}=\frac{2(1)(3)}{(2)(6)}=\frac{1}{2}$$

$$K_1=(s+\beta_1)\frac{Z(s)}{s}\bigg|_{s=-\beta_1}=(s+2)\times\frac{2(s+1)(s+3)}{s(s+2)(s+6)}\bigg|_{s=-2}=\frac{2(-2+1)(-2+3)}{-2(-2+6)}=\frac{1}{4}$$

$$K_2=(s+\beta_2)\frac{Z(s)}{s}\bigg|_{s=-\beta_2}=(s+6)\times\frac{2(s+1)(s+3)}{s(s+2)(s+6)}\bigg|_{s=-6}=\frac{2(-6+1)(-6+3)}{-6(-6+2)}=\frac{5}{4}$$

$$\frac{Z(s)}{s}=\frac{2(s+1)(s+3)}{s(s+2)(s+6)}=\frac{\frac{1}{2}}{s}+\frac{\frac{1}{4}}{s+2}+\frac{\frac{5}{4}}{s+6}$$

$$\Rightarrow Z(s)=\frac{1}{2}+\frac{\frac{1}{4}s}{s+2}+\frac{\frac{5}{4}s}{s+6}$$

The first term represents the impedance of a resistor of $\frac{1}{2}\,\Omega$. The second and third terms represent the impedance of an *RL* parallel circuit. So, for a parallel *RL* network,

$$Z_{RL}(s)=\frac{Rs}{s+\frac{R}{L}}$$

On direct comparison, we have

$$R_1=\frac{1}{4}\,\Omega$$

$$\frac{R_1}{L_1}=2 \Rightarrow L_1=\frac{R_1}{2}=\frac{1}{8}\,\text{H}$$

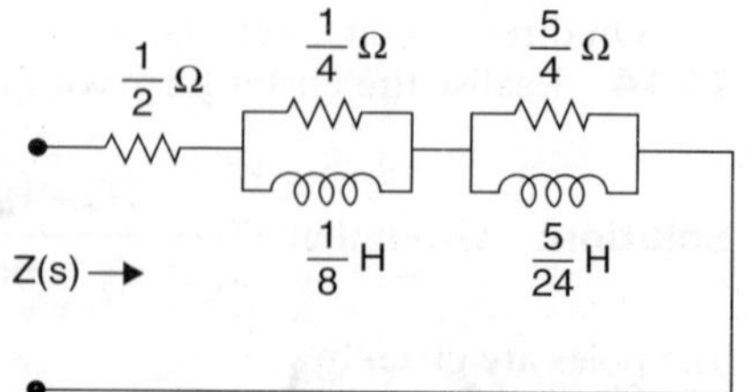

Fig. 2 Foster-I realisation

Similarly, we have

$$R_2 = \frac{5}{4}\,\Omega, \quad L_2 = \frac{5}{24}\,\text{H}$$

Therefore, the synthesised network is as shown in Fig. 2.

(ii) Foster-II realisation: The Foster-II form is obtained using the partial fraction expansion of the admittance function $Y(s)$. Since the degree of the numerator is equal to the degree of the denominator, division is first carried out.

$$Y(s) = \frac{(s+2)(s+6)}{2(s+1)(s+3)} = \frac{s^2+8s+12}{2s^2+8s+6}$$

$$\begin{array}{r} 2s^2+8s+6)\; s^2+8s+12\; (\frac{1}{2} \\ s^2+4s+3 \\ \hline 4s+9 \end{array}$$

$$\therefore \quad Y(s) = \frac{s^2+8s+12}{2s^2+8s+6} = \frac{1}{2} + \frac{4s+9}{2(s+1)(s+3)}$$

Using partial fraction expansion, we have

$$Y(s) = \frac{(s+2)(s+6)}{2(s+1)(s+3)} = \frac{1}{2} + \frac{4s+9}{2(s+1)(s+3)} = \frac{1}{2} + \frac{K_1}{s+1} + \frac{K_2}{s+3}$$

where, $K_1 = (s+\beta_1)Y(s)\big|_{s=-\beta_1} = (s+1)\times \left.\frac{(s+2)(s+6)}{2(s+1)(s+3)}\right|_{s=-1} = \frac{(-1+2)(-1+6)}{2(-1+3)} = \frac{5}{4}$

$$K_2 = (s+\beta_2)Z(s)\big|_{s=-\beta_2} = (s+3)\times \left.\frac{(s+2)(s+6)}{2(s+1)(s+3)}\right|_{s=-3} = \frac{(-3+2)(-3+6)}{2(-3+1)} = \frac{3}{4}$$

$$\therefore \quad Y(s) = \frac{1}{2} + \frac{\frac{5}{4}}{s+1} + \frac{\frac{3}{4}}{s+3}$$

The first term represents the admittance of a resistor of 2 Ω. The second and third terms represent the admittance of an RL series circuit. So, for a series RL network,

$$Y_{RL}(s) = \frac{\frac{1}{L}}{s+\frac{R}{L}}$$

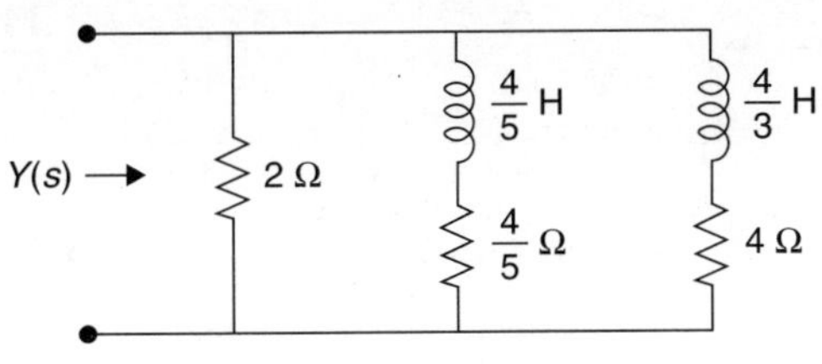

Fig. 3 Foster-II realisation

On direct comparison, we have

$$L_1 = \frac{4}{5}\,\text{H}$$

$$\frac{R_1}{L_1} = 1 \Rightarrow R_1 = L_1 = \frac{4}{5}\,\Omega$$

Similarly, we have

$$L_2 = \frac{4}{3}\,\text{H}, \quad R_2 = 4\,\Omega$$

Therefore, the synthesised network is as shown in Fig. 3.

15.15 Realise the Foster forms of the *RL* impedance function, $Z(s)=\frac{2(s+1)(s+4)}{(s+2)(s+6)}$.

Solution: Given that $Z(s)=\frac{2(s+1)(s+4)}{(s+2)(s+6)}$

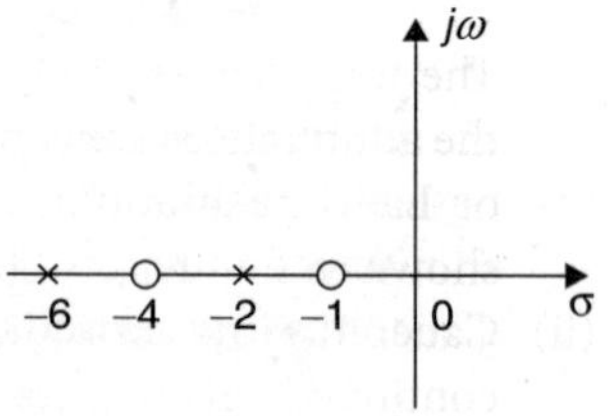

Fig. 1

The poles are given by

$$(s+2)(s+6)=0$$

$$s=-2,\quad s=-6$$

The zeros are given by

$$(s+1)(s+4)=0$$

$$s=-1,\quad s=-4$$

From the pole–zero plot in the *s*-plane (Fig. 1), it is clear that the poles and zeros are simple, lie on the negative real axis and interlaced; the function $Z(s)$ is an *RL* impedance function.

(i) Cauer-I realisation: The Cauer-I form is obtained using the continued fraction expansion of $Z(s)$ about the pole at infinity.

$$Z(s)=\frac{2(s+1)(s+4)}{(s+2)(s+6)}=\frac{2s^2+10s+8}{s^2+8s+12}$$

Using the continued fraction expansion, we have

$$s^2+8s+12)\ 2s^2+10s+8\ (2 \leftrightarrow Z_1$$

$$\underline{2s^2+16s+24}$$

$$-6s-16$$

Since a negative term results, continued fraction expansion of $Y(s)$ is carried out.

$$\therefore \qquad Y(s)=\frac{1}{Z(s)}=\frac{s^2+8s+12}{2s^2+10s+8}$$

$$2s^2+10s+8)\ s^2+8s+12\left(\frac{1}{2} \leftrightarrow Y_1\right.$$

$$\underline{s^2+5s+4}$$

$$3s+8)\ 2s^2+10s+8\ \left(\frac{2}{3}s \leftrightarrow Z_2\right.$$

$$\underline{2s^2+\frac{16}{3}s}$$

$$\frac{14}{3}s+8)\ 3s+8\ \left(\frac{9}{14} \leftrightarrow Y_3\right.$$

$$\underline{3s+\frac{36}{7}}$$

$$\frac{20}{7})\ \frac{14}{3}s+8\ \left(\frac{7}{20}\cdot\frac{14}{3}s=\frac{49}{30}s \leftrightarrow Z_4\right.$$

$$\underline{\frac{14}{3}s}$$

$$8)\ \frac{20}{7}\ \left(\frac{1}{8}\cdot\frac{20}{7}=\frac{5}{14} \leftrightarrow Y_5\right.$$

$$\underline{\frac{20}{7}}$$

$$0$$

$\therefore$ The network elements are $R_1 = 2\,\Omega,\ L_1 = \frac{2}{3}\,\text{H},\ R_2 = \frac{14}{9}\,\Omega,\ L_2 = \frac{49}{30}\,\text{H},\ R_3 = \frac{14}{5}\,\Omega$

The impedances are connected in the series branches, whereas the admittances are connected in the parallel branches in a Cauer or Ladder realisation. Therefore, the synthesised network is as shown in Fig. 1.

Fig. 1 Cauer-I realisation

(ii) Cauer-II realisation: The Cauer-II form is obtained using the continued fraction expansion about the pole at the origin. Arranging the numerator and denominator polynomials in the ascending order of s as follows:

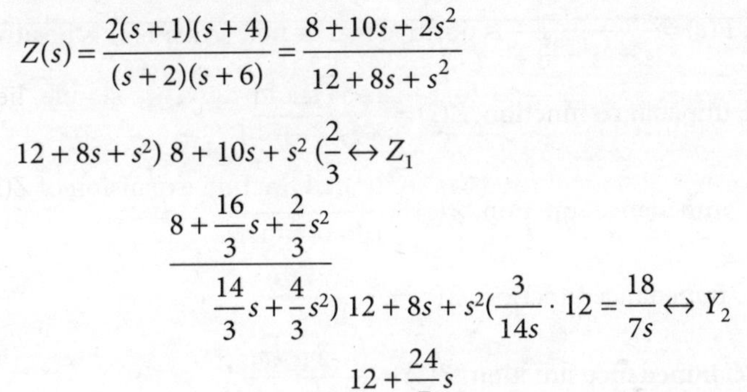

$$Z(s) = \frac{2(s+1)(s+4)}{(s+2)(s+6)} = \frac{8+10s+2s^2}{12+8s+s^2}$$

$$12 + 8s + s^2)\ 8 + 10s + s^2\ (\frac{2}{3} \leftrightarrow Z_1$$
$$8 + \frac{16}{3}s + \frac{2}{3}s^2$$
$$\frac{14}{3}s + \frac{4}{3}s^2)\ 12 + 8s + s^2 (\frac{3}{14s} \cdot 12 = \frac{18}{7s} \leftrightarrow Y_2$$
$$12 + \frac{24}{7}s$$
$$\frac{32}{7}s + s^2)\ \frac{14}{3}s + \frac{4}{3}s^2 (\frac{7}{32} \cdot \frac{14}{3} = \frac{49}{48} \leftrightarrow Z_3$$
$$\frac{14}{3}s + \frac{49}{48}s^2$$
$$\frac{5}{16}s^2)\ \frac{32}{7}s + s^2\ (\frac{16}{5} \cdot \frac{32}{7s} = \frac{512}{35s} \leftrightarrow Y_4$$
$$\frac{32}{7}s$$
$$s^2)\ \frac{5}{16}s^2\ (\frac{5}{16} \leftrightarrow Z_5$$
$$\frac{5}{16}s^2$$
$$0$$

Fig. 2 Cauer-II realisation

$\therefore$ The network elements are $R_1 = \frac{2}{3}\,\Omega,\ L_1 = \frac{7}{18}\,\text{H},\ R_2 = \frac{49}{48}\,\Omega,\ L_2 = \frac{35}{512}\,\text{H},\ R_3 = \frac{5}{16}\,\Omega$

The impedances are connected in the series branches, whereas the admittances are connected in the parallel branches in a Cauer or Ladder realisation. Therefore, the synthesised network is as shown in Fig. 2.

EXERCISE PROBLEMS

1. Check whether the following polynomials are Hurwitz or not.
   (a) $P(s) = s^5 + 5s^3 + 11s^2 + 25s + 6$
   (b) $P(s) = s^5 + 2s^4 + 5s^3 + 10s^2 + 9s + 18$

(c) $P(s) = s^3 + s^2 + s + 1$ (d) $P(s) = s^4 + s^2 + s + 1$
(e) $P(s) = s^7 + s^5 + s^3 + s$
[**Ans:** (a) Not Hurwitz (b) Hurwitz (c) Hurwitz (d) Not Hurwitz (e) Not Hurwitz]

2. Determine the range of k so that the polynomial $P(s) = s^3 + 3s^2 + 2s + k$ is Hurwitz. [**Ans:** $0 < k < 6$]
3. Check whether the polynomial, $P(s) = s^5 + 3s^3 + 2s$ is Hurwitz or not. [**Ans:** Hurwitz]
4. Determine whether the function, $F(s) = \dfrac{(s+4)(s+2)}{(s+3)(s+1)}$ is positive real or not. [**Ans:** $F(s)$ is positive real]
5. Determine whether the function, $F(s) = \dfrac{s^2+10s+4}{s+2}$ is positive real or not. [**Ans:** $F(s)$ is positive real]
6. Determine whether the function, $F(s) = \dfrac{2s^2+2s+1}{s^3+2s^2+s+2}$ is positive real or not. [**Ans:** F(s) is positive real]
7. Realise the Cauer forms of the *LC* impedance function, $Z(s) = \dfrac{10s^4+12s^2+1}{2s(s^2+1)}$.
8. Realise the Foster forms of the *LC* impedance function, $Z(s) = \dfrac{4s(s^2+4)}{(s^2+1)(s^2+16)}$.
9. Realise the Foster forms of the *RC* impedance function, $Z(s) = \dfrac{(s+1)(s+3)}{s(s+2)}$.
10. Realise the Cauers forms of the *RC* impedance function, $Z(s) = \dfrac{(s+2)(s+6)}{2(s+1)(s+3)}$.
11. Realise the Cauer-I form of the *RC* impedance function, $Z(s) = \dfrac{(s+4)}{(s+2)(s+6)}$.
12. Realise the Foster-II form of the *RC* impedance function, $Z(s) = \dfrac{2(s+2)(s+4)}{(s+1)(s+3)}$.
13. Realise the Cauer-I form of the *RL* impedance function, $Z(s) = \dfrac{(s+1)(s+3)}{(s+2)(s+4)}$.
14. Realise the Cauer-II form of the *RL* impedance function, $Z(s) = \dfrac{2(s+1)(s+4)}{(s+2)(s+6)}$.
15. Realise the Fosters forms of the *RL* impedance function, $Z(s) = \dfrac{s(s+2)(s+4)}{(s+1)(s+3)}$.

REVIEW QUESTIONS

1. Define a Hurwitz polynomial and write its properties.
2. List the conditions for stability of a network.
3. State the Routh–Hurwitz criterion.
4. Define a positive real function.
5. List the necessary conditions to be satisfied by a function to be positive real.
6. List the properties of a positive real function.
7. List the basic forms of synthesising.
8. List the properties of *LC* immattance functions.
9. List the properties of *RC* impedance or *RL* admittance functions.
10. List the properties of *RL* impedance or *RC* admittance functions.
11. Explain the procedure to obtain Foster's-I form.

12. Explain the procedure to obtain Foster's-II form.
13. Explain the procedure to obtain Cauer's-I form.
14. Explain the procedure to obtain Cauer's-II form.
15. Two functions $F_1(s)$ and $F_2(s)$ are Hurwitz. State with reasons whether the following functions are Hurwitz or not.
(a) $F_1(s)+F_2(s)$ (b) $F_1(s)-F_2(s)$ (c) $F_1(s)/F_2(s)$ (d) $F_1(s)\times F_2(s)$

MULTIPLE CHOICE QUESTIONS

1. For a network function, if $F(s)$ has to be Hurwitz,
(a) $F(s)$ must have poles in the right half of the s-plane
(b) $F(s)$ must have zeroes in the right half of the s-plane
(c) $F(s)$ cannot have multiple poles
(d) $F(s)$ cannot have multiple poles and poles in the right half of s-plane

2. Continued fraction expansion of a ratio of odd to even parts of Hurwitz polynomial yields
(a) all real positive quotients
(b) alternative positive and negative quotients
(c) must have abrupt termination
(d) none of the above

3. $s^4+s^3+2s^2+3s+2$ is not a Hurwitz polynomial because, it
(a) does not have a negative term
(b) yields negative coefficients in continued fraction expansion of odd to even terms
(c) cannot be factorised
(d) has multiple common factors

4. The function, $F(s)=\dfrac{5s(s^2+8)}{(s^2+1)(s^2+4)}$ is not a driving point impedance function because
(a) it is not an even to odd ratio function
(b) poles and zeroes are not simple
(c) poles and zeroes don't interlace on the $j\omega$-axis
(d) there is no zero or pole at infinity

5. A function is said to be positive real if and only if
(a) $F(\sigma)$ is real
(b) the real part of $F(s)$ is ≥ 0 when the real part of s is ≥ 0
(c) $F(s)$ is real when s is real
(d) all of the above

6. For a positive real function $F(s)$,
(a) $\frac{1}{F(s)}$ is also a positive real function
(b) $\frac{1}{F(s)}$ is not positive real
(c) $\frac{1}{[F(s)]^2}$ is positive real
(d) $[F(s)]^2$ is positive real

7. The function, $F(s)=\dfrac{(s+1)}{(s^2+2)}$ is not positive real because
(a) the numerator does not have the s^2 term
(b) in the denominator, the s term is missing
(c) in the denominator, the coefficient of the s term is less than the numerator constant term '1'
(d) the numerator degree is less than the denominator degree.

8. The function, $F(s)=\dfrac{3s^2+5}{s(s^2+1)}$ is not positive real because
(a) the s term is missing in the numerator
(b) the partial fraction expansion yields negative coefficients
(c) the residue of the pole $=\pm 1j$ is negative
(d) all of the above

9. The first critical frequency nearest to the origin of the complex frequency plane for an RL driving point impedance function will be a
(a) zero in the left-half plane
(b) zero in the right-half plane
(c) pole in the left-half plane
(d) pole in the right-half plane

10. The driving point impedance $Z(s)=\dfrac{s+3}{s+4}$ behaves as a
(a) resistance of 0.75 Ω at low frequencies
(b) resistance of 1 Ω at high frequencies
(c) both (a) and (b)
(d) none of the above

11. If an RC driving point impedance function has zeros at $s = -2$ and $s = -5$, then the admissible poles for the functions would be
(a) $s = 0, s = -6$ (b) $s = -1, s = -3$
(c) $s = 0, s = -1$ (d) $s = -3, s = -4$

12. The poles and zeros of a driving point function of a network are simple and interlace on the negative real axis with a pole closest to the origin. It can be realised by
(a) LC network
(b) RC driving point impedance
(c) RC driving point admittance
(d) RL network

13. If $F_1(s)$ and $F_2(s)$ are two positive real functions then the function which is always positive real, is
(a) $F_1(s)F_2(s)$ (b) $\frac{F_1(s)}{F_2(s)}$
(c) $\frac{F_1(s)F_2(s)}{F_1(s)+F_2(s)}$ (d) $F_1(s) - F_2(s)$

14. A network whose impedance function $Z(s) = \frac{4(s^2+1)(s^2+9)}{s(s^2+4)}$ is synthesised. It consists of n LC tank circuits in series with an inductance and/or capacitance. The value of n is
(a) zero (b) 1
(c) 2 (d) 3

15. The network function, $F(s) = \frac{(s+1)(s+3)}{s(s+2)}$ represents an
(a) RC impedance
(b) RC admittance
(c) RC impedance and RL admittance
(d) RL admittance

16. The realisation of impedance function $Z(s) = \frac{4(s^2+1)(s^2+9)}{s(s^2+4)}$ requires a minimum of
(a) 4 inductors and 4 capacitors
(b) 3 inductors and 3 capacitors
(c) 1 inductor, 1 capacitor and 1 resistor
(d) 2 inductors and 2 capacitors

17. A transient current in a network is, $i(t) = 2e^{-t} - e^{-5t} \geq 0$. The pole–zero configuration of $I(s)$ is
(a) poles are 1,5 and zero is 9
(b) poles are 1,–5 and zero is 9
(c) poles are 2,–1 and zeros are 1, –5
(d) poles are 2,–1 and zeros are 1, 5

18. The driving point impedance of an RC network is $Z(s) = \frac{2s^2+7s+3}{s^2+3s+1}$. Its canonical realisation will be
(a) 6 elements (b) 5 elements
(c) 4 elements (d) 3 elements

19. The network function, $F(s) = \frac{(s+2)}{(s+3)(s+1)}$ represents an ________ function
(a) RC impedance
(b) RL impedance
(c) RC impedance and RL admittance
(d) RC admittance and RL impedance

20. The method used to decompose $Z(s)$
(a) Removal of a pole at infinity
(b) Removal of a pole at zero
(c) Removal of conjugate imaginary poles
(d) all of the above

21. If $Z(s)$ has a pole at infinity ($s = \infty$) then $n - m =$
(a) zero (b) 1
(c) 2 (d) 3

22. Removal of pole at ∞ corresponds to the removal of a ________ from the network.
(a) resistor (b) inductor
(c) capacitor (d) all of the above

23. If the pole is at $s = \infty$, the impedance (series element) is
(a) resistor (b) inductor
(c) capacitor (d) all of the above

24. If the pole is at $s = \infty$, the admittance (shunt element) is
(a) resistor (b) inductor
(c) capacitor (d) all of the above

25. If the pole is at $s = \infty$, the impedance (series element) is
(a) resistor (b) inductor
(c) capacitor (d) all of the above

26. If the pole at $s = \infty$, the admittance (parallel element) is
(a) resistor (b) inductor
(c) capacitor (d) all of the above

27. If the pole is at $s = \pm j\omega$, the series element is
(a) LC in parallel (b) LC in series
(c) RC in parallel (d) RC in series

28. If the pole at $s = \pm j\omega$, the parallel element is
(a) LC in parallel (b) LC in series
(c) RC in parallel (d) RC in series

29. A polynomial $P(s)$ is said to be Hurwitz if
(a) the roots of $P(s)$ have non-zero real parts
(b) the roots are real for all 's', real or complex
(c) P(s) is real when 's' is real roots of $P(s)$ have real parts zero or negative
(d) $s = \pm j\omega_i$ when ω_i is real

30. The first and the last critical frequencies of a driving point impedance function of a passive network having two kinds of elements are a pole and a zero respectively. The above property will be satisfied by
(a) RC network only
(b) RL network only
(c) RC as well as RL network
(d) LC network only

31. The impedance function, $Z(s) = \frac{(s+2)(s+3)}{s(s+1)}$ can be synthesised as
(a) LC network (b) RC network
(c) RL network (d) RLC network

32. The partial fraction expansion for the impedance function, $Z(s) = \frac{5s^2+s+5}{s^2+1}$ is
(a) $5 + \frac{s}{s^2+1}$ (b) $5 + \frac{1}{s^2+1}$
(c) $1 + \frac{5}{s^2+1}$ (d) $5 + \frac{1+s}{s^2+1}$

Answers

1. d	**2.** a	**3.** b	**4.** c	**5.** d	**6.** a	**7.** b	**8.** b	**9.** a	**10.** c
11. b	**12.** b	**13.** c	**14.** b	**15.** c	**16.** d	**17.** b	**18.** b	**19.** a	**20.** d
21. b	**22.** b	**23.** b	**24.** c	**25.** c	**26.** b	**27.** a	**28.** b	**29.** c	**30.** a
31. c	**32.** a								

Bibliography

1. Abhijit Chakrabarti, *Circuit Theory (analysis and synthesis)*, 6th Ed., Dhanpat Rai & Co., 2014.
2. Akhilesh J Nimje and Kothari D P, *Electrical Circuit Analysis and Synthesis*, 1st Ed., New Age International, 2017.
3. Allan H Robbins and Wilhelm Miller, *Circuit Analysis: Theory and Practice*, 5th Ed., Cengage Learning, 2012.
4. Sudhakar A and Shyammohan S Palli, *Circuits and Networks: Analysis and Synthesis*, 5th Ed., Mc-Graw Hill, 2017.
5. Behrouz Peikari, *Fundamentals of Network Analysis and Synthesis*, 1st Ed., Jaico Publishers, 2006.
6. Gupta B R, *Network Analysis and Synthesis*, 3rd Ed., S Chand Publications, 2009.
7. Charles K Alexander, Mathew N O Sadiku, *Fundamentals of Electric Circuits*, 5th Ed., Tata McGraw-Hill, 2013.
8. Wadwha C L, *Network Analysis and Synthesis: (Including Linear System Analysis)*, 3rd Ed., Anshan Publishers, 2009
9. Wadwha C L, *Electrical Circuit Analysis: Including Passive Network Synthesis*, 2nd Ed., New Age International, 2006.
10. Debashisha Jena, *Basic Electrical Engineering*, 1st Ed., Wiley, 2012.
11. Kothari D P and Nagrath I J, *Theory and Problems of Basic Electrical Engineering*, 4th Ed., PHI, 2013.
12. Franklin F Kuo, *Network Analysis and Synthesis*, 2nd Ed., Wiley, 2006.
13. Gopal Bhise G, Prem Chadha R and Durgesh Kulshreshtha C, *Engineering Network Analysis & Filter Design*, 3rd Ed., Umesh Publication, 2011.
14. Isaak Mayergoyz W Lawson, *Basic Electric Circuit Theory*, 1st Ed., Academic Press, 2012.
15. Alice Mary K and Ramana P, *Electrical Circuit Analysis*, 1st Ed., Reem Publications Private Ltd, 2009.
16. Keith Brown, *Hughes Electrical and Electronic Technology*, 10th Ed., Pearson, 2011.
17. Mahmood Nahvi and Joselph Edminister, *Electric Circuits*, 5th Ed., McGraw Hill, 2010.
18. Van Valkenburg M E, *Network Analysis*, 3rd Ed., Prentice Hall of India, 2015.
19. Sukhija M S and Nagsarkar T K, *Circuits and Networks: Analysis, Design, and Synthesis*, 2nd Ed., Oxford University Press, 2016.
20. Sharma N K, *Network Analysis and Synthesis*, 1st Ed., Khanna Publishers, 2013.
21. Pradeep Kumar, *Fundamental of Network Analysis and Synthesis*, 1st Ed., Khanna Publishers, 2014.
22. Ravish R Singh, *Network Analysis and Synthesis*, 1st Ed., McGraw-Hill, 2013.
23. Ghosh S P and Chakraborty A, *Network Analysis and Synthesis*, 2nd Ed., McGraw Hill, 2009.
24. Paranjoth S R, *Electric Circuit Analysis*, 4th Ed., New Age International, 2011.
25. Sivanagaraju S, Kishor G and Srinivasa Rao C, *Electrical Circuit Analysis*, 1st Ed., Cengage Learning, 2009.
26. Hayt W H, Kimmerly J E and Durbin S M, *Engineering Circuit Analysis*, 7th Ed., Tata McGraw-Hill Publishers, 2013.

Index

V

Z